ICCA
CONGRESS SERIES NO. 22

INTERNATIONAL ARBITRATION CONGRESS
HONG KONG, 5-8 MAY 2024

Wolters Kluwer

INTERNATIONAL COUNCIL FOR COMMERCIAL ARBITRATION

International Arbitration: A Human Endeavour

GENERAL EDITORS:
CHIANN BAO & AUDLEY SHEPPARD KC

with the assistance of the
Permanent Court of Arbitration
Peace Palace, The Hague

Published by:
Kluwer Law International B.V.
PO Box 316
2400 AH Alphen aan den Rijn
The Netherlands
E-mail: lrs-sales@wolterskluwer.com
Website: www.wolterskluwer.com/en/solutions/kluwerlawinternational

Sold and distributed by:
Wolters Kluwer Legal & Regulatory U.S.
920 Links Avenue
Landisville, PA 17538
United States of America
E-mail: customer.service@wolterskluwer.com

Printed on acid-free paper.

ISBN 978-94-035-3209-7

e-Book: ISBN 978-94-035-3219-6
web-PDF: ISBN 978-94-035-3229-5

Preface

We chose 'International Arbitration: A Human Endeavour' as the theme of the XXVII ICCA Congress in order to examine the importance of people in the arbitration process and to reflect on how that might change. The theme was both a statement and a question.

That theme was especially apposite in Hong Kong, a city that epitomises human enterprise, international commerce and the meeting of East and West cultural traditions.

We wanted to recognise some of the notable influencers that have shaped international arbitration as we practise it today. Dr Bryant Garth, the co-author of the landmark sociological study on the development of international arbitration, 'Dealing in Virtue', was the keynote speaker on the first day. We also acknowledged Dr Pieter Sanders, the uber-visionary, by showing an interview of him talking about his trip to New York and his 'Dutch proposal' that became the 1958 Convention. Later in the Congress, we honoured Dr Albert Jan van den Berg, who has done so much to promote international arbitration and support ICCA.

The first day focused on 'The Arbitrator': what it means to be an arbitral decision-maker. The sub-topics included: is judging and arbitrating the same; what extraneous factors most influence arbitrators; is there an ideal personality type for an arbitrator; what is expected of an arbitrator by users; and to what extent does it matter to have a person rather than a machine decide disputes? The answer to that last question was enlightening: a number of people thought that presenting their client's case to a human decision-maker was essential to the feeling that justice had been done. And that experience, intuition and wisdom were invaluable, albeit sometimes fallible, qualities.

We also considered how people make decisions and the influences of: biases (in the sense of a person's background), with an explanation of what happens in the brain when we make decisions; sociology and education; and culture, localisation and regionalism.

Informing about the New York Convention is a key aspect of ICCA's mission. At the Congress, we launched the 2nd Edition of ICCA's Guide to the Interpretation of the

Convention, in English and also a translation into Chinese. Consistent with the overall theme, we also examined the consistency of decisions by human judges and their consideration of societal factors in the application of public policy.

The second day focused on 'The Advocate': what makes an effective advocate; what does the science of the human brain tell us about how persuasion works; and what tools or innovations can advocates draw upon? We also explored how procedure can impact the conduct of different participants in the dispute resolution process. And how much does the language used in an arbitration shape the process and influence the outcomes (this was a recurring question).

When humans are involved, inevitably, issues of behaviour arise. We looked at inter-personal conduct and ethics with a panel discussing ICCA's recent Guidelines on Standards of Practice in International Arbitration as they relate to our roles as advocates, arbitrators, experts, witnesses, and administrators, taking into account differing cultural perspectives and legal traditions. Arbitration is almost always confrontational, and we explored (inspired by the concept of 'doughnut economics'): the pressures on advocates (including junior lawyers in the team); the tension of cross-examination; how to optimise expert witness engagement; and practical psychology tips to help survive and thrive in adversarial environments.

ICCA's mission includes encouraging conciliation. We had a panel that described current initiatives tackling climate change and its impact on communities, practical experiences of designing rules for state-to-state and multi-stakeholder conflicts, and dispute resolution innovation addressing societal inequalities.

On the third day, we turned to 'International Arbitration: An AI Endeavour' and asked the question whether the incremental adoption of artificial intelligence across society, including in the delivery of justice, might shape assumptions not only of what is permissible but of how arbitration should be conducted. AI will impact advocacy and decision-making, access and transparency, and the skill sets needed by participants. Panellists discussed the impact this will have on the legitimacy of international arbitration.

Professor Richard Susskind, a global expert on AI's impact on the legal profession and author of *Tomorrow's Lawyers*, gave the closing keynote. His optimistic and cautionary outlook was that clients will still want the star-gladiators to represent them in important disputes, before the best human arbitrators.

We are very pleased that the theme, and the sub-topics, resonated with so many people. The history of arbitration and the impact of influencers, the human arbitrator, the human advocate, inter-personal conduct, and the challenges and opportunities of AI are of universal interest.

The Congress confirmed that international arbitration undoubtedly remains, at present, a human endeavour.

We are extremely grateful to ICCA for the opportunity to curate a Congress on a subject which we are both hugely invested in: what does it mean to dispense arbitral justice.

We are also grateful to the three hundred people who submitted expressions of interest asking to speak, we are sorry that we had to be selective, and to the Programme Committee for their assistance in framing the programme.

Mostly, we are grateful to all the speakers for their time and insights, many of which are included in this book.

Chiann Bao and Audley Sheppard KC
Programme Co-Chairs

XXVII ICCA CONGRESS

12-15 April 2026

Madrid

'International Arbitration: Local, Global or Both?'

For programme and registration information:

https://icca2026.es/

www.arbitration-icca.org

For the Young ICCA Event:

www.youngicca.org

Table of Contents

Welcome from the Co-chairs

Audley Sheppard KC

We are the Programme Co-Chairs for this Congress.

When we started discussing possible themes, Chiann and I soon realised that we were both very interested in the human dimension of what we do and that an ICCA Congress spanning 2½ days provided an opportunity to explore the topic in some depth, with insights from experienced arbitration practitioners, judges and social scientists from around the world.

Chiann Bao

It also struck us as an appropriate theme for Hong Kong, a city that epitomises human enterprise, and a place where the cultures of the East and West meet. So, we set about planning a programme that would explore what does it mean to be a human decision-maker and how is a human decision-maker influenced by personal advocacy? How are procedures and decisions influenced by the culture, language, and education of the participants?

No one can be unaware of the influence of technology and artificial intelligence on what we do, and what we will do in the future. Will it, and should it be allowed to, dispense with the human element?

Audley Sheppard KC

That led us to more profound questions on what does it mean to dispense arbitral justice? Are humans an essential element in order for international arbitration to be trusted and have legitimacy? How important is human experience, intuition and wisdom?

So, the theme, 'International Arbitration: A Human Endeavour' is both a statement and a question.

Chiann Bao

But there are other aspects of the human element of international arbitration that will be explored during the Congress, from the individual to the global.

For example, these days we are much more aware of the confronting effect that our working environment can have on us as individuals, especially a stressful, adversarial one. We will hear about 'doughnut economics' – the thesis that an economy's purpose is to promote human prosperity and personal welfare.

On the macro scale, can arbitration and effective dispute resolution, such as conciliation, help address challenges affecting the global community, such as climate change?

Everything comes at a cost, and that will also be addressed.

But one cannot explore the human dimension of international arbitration without reflecting on the visionaries and influencers who have had an impact on us individually and made international arbitration what it is today.

Audley Sheppard KC

My first experience of ICCA was reading articles in the 1987 ICCA Congress Series. The theme of that Congress was 'Comparative International Arbitration: Practice and Public Policy'. It contained a number of seminal articles, such as that by Professor Pierre Lalive on 'Transnational (or Truly International) Public Policy', which I have gone back to time and time again with respect to various projects I have worked on in relation to public policy.

Chiann Bao

And my first experience of ICCA was as Secretary-General of HKIAC in 2010 in Brazil. In 2011, at ICCA's 50th anniversary event in Geneva (where Hong Kong made its first pitch for the ICCA Congress), Professor Lalive was interviewed by Professor Tercier, and he explained that ICCA was founded by practitioners aiming to discuss serious problems in international arbitration. He said that the goal was to create a bridge, an intellectual bridge, an exchange of experience between people of different nationalities and different cultures. That vision resonates with me personally, and it is an ideal that I hope for all aspects of international arbitration.

Audley Sheppard KC

The arc of this Congress is to start with a reflection on what international arbitration was like 30 years ago, and who were the visionaries and influencers, particularly in Europe at that time. There are then a number of sessions to address the human dimension of international arbitration today across the world. Finally, we conclude on Wednesday with a crystal ball of what international arbitration might be like in the future.

To kick things off, we are very pleased to have as our Keynote speaker Professor Bryant Garth.

Professor Garth is very well known in the arbitration world as one of the co-authors of *Dealing in Virtue*, published in 1996, which was a ground-breaking study into the sociology of international arbitration.

Professor Garth two years ago wrote a postscript published in the Cambridge Companion of International Arbitration and that Cambridge Companion was edited by

Professor Chin Lim, of the Chinese University of Hong Kong. We have invited Professor Lim to comment after Professor Garth.

But before giving the stage to Professor Garth, we would like to show you a clip of an interview with, perhaps, international arbitration's greatest visionary and influencer, and who was instrumental in establishing ICCA: Pieter Sanders.[1]

I am sure you will agree with me what a wonderful human intervention that was by Pieter Sanders, one of the greatest influencers in international arbitration.

With that, we invite Professor Garth to the stage.

Chiann Bao and Audley Sheppard KC
Programme Co-Chairs

1. An Interview with Prof. Pieter Sanders | ICCA https://www.arbitration-icca.org/icca-geneva-2011-video-sanders-interview.

PANEL 1

Opening Keynote Address

Keynote Address: Unveiling the Human Dimensions of International Arbitration: Dealing in Virtue Then and Now[*]

* Please watch the address on ICCA's website on: https://www.arbitration-icca.org/icca-2024-hong-kong-opening-session.

CHAPTER 1

'Unveiling the Human Dimension of International Arbitration' Comment on Bryant Garth's Keynote Speech

Prof. Chin Leng Lim[*]

Opening Session, ICCA, Hong Kong, 6 May 2024

Professor Garth, I think they in this crowd aren't like us, but everyone, as someone said, has at least a friend who has read your book. Having said that, we don't usually see you at conferences like today's. So let me please put Dealing In Virtue in some context. You have written not about what we do daily, but about us. We and this industry are your subjects, your interest, your fascination, and that fascination is as Audley Sheppard and Chiann Bao just said with the humans.

Let me recall what I had read some years ago, well to be honest many, many years ago. We were made to read Bryant Garth before our arbitration course. Three points stand out in my memory and let me try and recollect. You have, just now, taken us into the past, and although I know you have a lot to say about the future, let me also try to bring us to the present.

First, you said the Grand Old Men were gone. That is not unique. One thinks of the death of amateurism elsewhere from football to motor racing. You then explained the rise of a new generation, a new generation of law firm-based technocrati, and the reader is entertained by the image of law firm partners wearing tweed jackets, smoking pipes, giving lectures, just like the professors whom they saw sitting on a lucrative business. It does capture what we do now with the talks, with the journals, with the conferences, with the books.

* Chin Leng Lim is the Choh-Ming Li Professor of Law at the Chinese University of Hong Kong, a titular member of the Institut de droit international, visiting professor at King's College London, an honorary senior fellow of the British Institute of International and Comparative Law and an editor of the I.C.L.Q. He practises from Keating Chambers, London and is currently also a member of the ICC/UNIDROIT Working Group on International Investment Contracts.

But, just now, you mentioned a difficult subject, the subject of new entrants. This is complex; I don't think I'm allowed to say controversial. We know here how much institutions like the HKIAC have done. In the case of the HKIAC, it has done a remarkable job widening the talent pool in many different ways: by geographical origin, by gender, by the nationalities represented, by increasing the participation of those infrequently appointed.

But I would like to ask if, after the grand old men and the technocrati who succeeded them, will there be a new generation? I am not asking who they will be, but what they will be. Will there be a new kind of arbitrator?

With high-value disputes between Chinese and Indian parties, similar disputes with Eurasian, Middle-Eastern or African parties, all going maybe in search of newer seats. It was Chiann Bao I think who said to me only a few days ago, does the seat then follow the dispute? Will then new names emerge in new places? And, will these new names be very different from us?

We already look different. The days are no more when one might say – and I think you just said – if you don't know everyone in here, then this isn't a real conference. How does one know everyone here? These are great people but less homogenous than at a Taylor Swift concert. While just outside there are events organised by other bodies, by arbitral institutions here in China, and these I suspect are not just caravans that follow a Roman army.

So how much have we already changed? Whatever the answer, we have changed. I don't want to make it sound like a domestic dispute – 'you haven't changed, yes I have', and so on.

Second you devoted attention to the late twentieth-century dilemmas of the English way of arbitration.

In Asia, people are driven, today, by seat thinking. They aren't English. In Asian Legal Revivals (at p. 212), you said '[t]he corporate bar', if I can quote, 'is ... in the mold of the traditional Hong Kong compradors ... who saw their mission as facilitating trade and commerce while ... enriching themselves'.

Some of us would be concerned if people looked at us like that, as compradors. How should I put it? I would say instead that you described a tension between developing the seat and maintaining deference to national authority against being cosmopolitan, which is our true nature. But today, that is no longer a story as you once told it about London versus Paris.

Today, the story is about the legal fictions, or delocalisation fantasies, playing on all our minds, but they play now across a larger global map.

Which then brings me to what I want to say finally, which has to do with national authority and nations. It brings me to my *third and final point*.

In 2021, in the Cambridge Companion to International Arbitration, which you kindly wrote for, you came back to something you had said almost thirty years ago with Yves Dezalay, and I quote again if I may: 'we suggested that the relative absence of the State from the world of the ICC and international commercial arbitration could change. The stakes are high enough and State battles could resurface'.

Some people in this hall will think that this just has to do with investment arbitration; they might say 'just isolate that part, separate all that from commercial disputes, and we don't think international commercial arbitration should be troubled by it'. We don't see a panel on investment arbitration at this ICCA Conference in the next three days.

Personally, I don't think ISDS cannot be reformed. Many have spent too much time on UNCITRAL WGIII, as well as more recently at least three people in this room have been travelling back and forth for the meetings of the UNIDROIT/ICC Working Group on investment contracts.

However, the criticisms and allegations now go beyond investment disputes. Allegations about quantum experts exaggerating claims and tribunals not being pious gatekeepers and handing down inflated awards. We see something else in disputes not involving investments but yet involving States. We see governmental arbitration conferences dedicated to criticising particular adverse awards. These are then supported by people familiar to us, by an academic caste, a new version of the grand old men of the past; and there it is, the ghost of arbitration's past.

So in sum, there is first a change amongst us; second this is occurring I think in a wider, broader world of international arbitration; in which, third, States and their legal advisers, and their professors, feel they need to participate.

This morning as I look around, the technocrats rule privately still. I see not just brimming confidence. Not just vast optimism. But a large auditorium filled with the people of a long, successful, golden age of international arbitration.

What I also see are idealists who know that it is important to have people who will settle international disputes, who will spend their time to do that, and this is what they do.

That is who we are.

Thank you.

PANEL 2

Plenary: The Arbitrator

This paper explores the meaning and responsibilities of being an arbitrator entrusted to dispense arbitral justice. It asks whether judging and arbitrating are truly the same, and how the role of the arbitrator has evolved over time. Have arbitrators become technocrats? What extraneous factors most influence arbitrators? Is there an ideal personality type for an arbitrator? What is expected of an arbitrator by users? To what extent does it matter to have a person rather than a machine decide disputes?

CHAPTER 2

Rethinking the Role of Arbitrators in Dispensing Justice

Aisha Abdallah & Natalia Mouzoula[*]

TABLE OF CONTENTS

I INTRODUCTION

In the realm of dispute resolution, commercial arbitration has emerged as an increasingly popular alternative to traditional court litigation. As international arbitration gains momentum on the international stage, questions arise regarding the concept of justice within the arbitral process, particularly considering the diverse cultural and multijurisdictional perspectives at play and the limited scrutiny. This chapter delves into the role of arbitrators in dispensing justice, discussing the challenges related to both the procedural aspects within an arbitration and the substantive dispensation of justice.

This examination begins by analysing the roles of arbitrators and judges, highlighting the fundamental distinctions between arbitration and litigation. Unlike judges in litigation, arbitrators hold unique positions with distinct appointment processes, conflict rules, and mechanisms for accountability. Additionally, the chapter

* Aisha Abdallah is a Partner at ALN Kenya | Anjarwalla & Khanna where she heads the regional Dispute Resolution Department based at the Nairobi Head Office; Natalia Mouzoula is a Principal Associate at ALN UAE | Anjarwalla, Collins & Haidermota and a member of the Dispute Resolution department.

will scrutinize court intervention in international arbitration, highlighting its role in upholding the integrity and enforceability of the arbitral process.

Moreover, the chapter will address potential obstacles to achieving justice in international arbitration, focusing on the delicate balance between efficiency and substantive justice. While arbitration prioritizes efficiency, concerns arise regarding the legitimacy of arbitral decisions and the potential compromise of substantive justice. Through analysis of national court decisions in various jurisdictions, this chapter aims to shed light on the tension between efficiency and justice in arbitration proceedings.

In light of potential obstacles to achieving justice, arbitrators should be adaptable and responsive to the needs and dynamics of each case. This can be achieved by considering hybrid approaches that blend elements of both adversarial and inquisitorial methods to achieve a fair and efficient resolution. This means that the choice between an adversarial and inquisitorial approach in arbitration depends on various factors, including the nature, type, and complexity of the dispute. In addition, it is recommended that, contrary to judges, arbitrators should adopt a more international approach, disconnected from the legal background or style of each individual arbitrator.

II KEY DISTINCTIONS BETWEEN ARBITRATORS AND JUDGES

1 Appointment Methods

Arbitrators, typically chosen from active professionals, are selected by parties who seek expertise in the subject matter of their case. Party-nominated arbitrators, especially, are chosen for their presumed sensitivity or sympathy towards a party's position. Parties often have the chance to meet or converse with potential arbitrators to ensure these qualities. This differs sharply from judicial decision-makers. Judges are usually isolated from the professional community by rules that prohibit professional affiliations and must recuse themselves from any case they are connected to, regardless of party consent.[1]

Another difference between judges and arbitrators relates to their respective qualifications. Judges are required to possess certain professional qualifications and legal training, while arbitrators are not formally required to have any minimum qualifications and, in certain cases, are not even required to possess any legal training.

Further, the arbitrators' appointment process may raise concerns about impartiality and potential conflicts of interest. While arbitrators are expected to adhere to ethical standards and disclose any conflicts, the absence of strict appointment protocols can leave room for unconscious bias to influence their decisions. In contrast, the formal structure of judicial appointments and oversight mechanisms help mitigate these risks to a certain extent.

1. Catherine A. Rogers, Regulating International Arbitrators: A Functional Approach to Developing Standards of Conduct, 41 Stan. J. Int'l L. 53 (2005).

2 Standards of Justice

While there is no universal code of conduct for arbitrators, it has been suggested that arbitrators are not bound by the same standard of justice as judges whose discipline and general conduct are often subjected to a strict code of conduct and disciplinary procedures laid down by law. For example, the Singapore Court of Appeal (*SGCA*) in *CVV and others v. CWB*. The SGCA upheld the Singapore International Commercial Court decision not to overturn an arbitral award, stating that arbitrators are not bound by the same standards as court judges when providing reasoned decisions.[2] The SGCA stressed the importance of thorough court reasoning, citing principles of open justice and the possibility of appellate review. This stands in contrast to arbitration proceedings, which are confidential and do not undergo the same level of scrutiny as judicial proceedings.[3]

Against this background, the SGCA's decision highlighted the distinctions between the standard of justice meted out by arbitrators and judges relating to the following aspects:

(a) *Legal authority*: Judges derive their power and remuneration from the state, while arbitrators derive their power and authority from private contracts, arbitral rules, and the law of the seat of arbitration and receive payment from the parties in exchange for professional services. Arbitration is a creature of contract. Consequently, an arbitrator's authority to hear and decide disputes is derived from and limited by the arbitration agreement.[4] The contractual nature of arbitration distinguishes it from litigation.[5]

(b) *Procedural differences*: Judges conduct their cases publicly, and their decisions are often publicly available. Conversely, arbitration proceedings and awards are often kept confidential, known only to the arbitral tribunal and the involved parties. Further, judges are bound by stringent rules of evidence and are called to ensure not only procedural justice but also substantive justice. Arbitrators, however, are masters of procedure and can therefore offer more flexibility in procedural matters, such as the admission of evidence and the conduct of hearings.

(c) *Security of tenure*: Arbitrators are appointed by parties and may be incentivized to adopt a certain stance to promote future appointments. This may be especially the case for inexperienced arbitrators seeking to make their name in what may be a crowded market. Conversely, judges are protected by security of tenure. Their remuneration is independent of parties' views on the outcome of decisions, and it is difficult to remove them from their positions once appointed.

---

2. *CVV and others v. CWB* [2023] SGCA(I) 9.
3. *Ibid.*, paras 33-34.
4. Cindy G. Buys, The Arbitrators' Duty to Respect the Parties' Choice of Law in Commercial Arbitration, 79(1) St. John's L. Rev. 69 (Winter 2005).
5. *Ibid.*

(d) *Appellate review*: Arbitral awards are subject to judicial scrutiny in very limited cases, usually based on party consent. Challenges to an arbitral award are therefore the exceptions and not the norm. In contrast, judicial decisions are usually the subject of at least one automatic right of review and/or appeal on facts and on law.[6]

Other distinctions between judges and arbitrators include the following:

(a) *Latitude in decision-making*: Judges are bound by the doctrine of stare decisis and are consequently bound by precedents set by higher-ranking courts. They will also be mindful that their decisions may have far-reaching effects on third parties and the overall rule of law. In contrast, arbitrators are not bound by precedent, nor do they create it. They only need to be concerned about the immediate dispute and parties before them, and not necessarily about wider considerations such as public policy.
(b) *Inherent jurisdiction*: Judges have inherent jurisdiction to effect justice and apply equitable principles. However, the jurisdiction of the arbitrator is strictly prescribed by the arbitral clause in the contract. It is unclear what steps, if any, an arbitrator should take when they face a concern about fairness or equity.
(c) *Coercive powers*: Judges have wider powers to enforce their decisions and control the conduct of parties and counsel, for example, via contempt of court orders. These are backed by state machinery. Arbitrators have no such powers and must rely on the backing of institutions. However, this is not available under ad hoc arbitrations. This means the potential for abuse is wider under arbitration.
(d) *Level of intervention*: The level of judges' and arbitrators' intervention differs depending on the rules and culture of different jurisdictions. Civil law judges and arbitrators are more likely to adopt an inquisitorial approach and descend into the arena of the dispute. However, common law practitioners and judges will leave the parties and their counsel to argue among themselves as part of the adversarial system.

All these differences could arguably result in a different standard of justice applied in arbitration proceedings.

In the case of *Commonwealth Coatings Corp. v. Cont'l Cas. Co.*, the US Supreme Court underscored the importance of safeguarding the impartiality of arbitrators, suggesting that their integrity should be held to even higher standards than that of judges.[7] Conversely, in a purported concurrence on the merits within the same case, Justice Byron White advocated for a different standard, asserting that arbitrators should not be bound by the same strict standards of judicial decorum as judges; as

6. Susan D. Franck, The Liability of International Arbitrators: A Comparative Analysis and Proposal for Qualified Immunity, 20(1) NYLS J. Int'l & Comp. L. (2000) Article 2.
7. *Commonwealth Coatings Corp. v. Cont'l Cas. Co.*, 393 U.S. 145, 148-149 (1968) 149-150.

individuals, arbitrators are immersed in the practicalities of the marketplace and should therefore not be expected to adhere rigidly to judicial norms.[8]

The above comparisons between arbitrators and judges may support the perception that arbitrators possess lower ethical standards than judges. Notably, arbitration lacks substantive appeal, which increases the severity of potential ethical violations. It is therefore more appropriate to view an arbitrator's ethical responsibilities as distinct yet comparable to those of judges – specifically tailored to the unique nature of their role.[9]

3 Accountability/Disciplinary Mechanisms for Arbitrators Versus Judges

The accountability mechanisms for arbitrators differ from those for judges. Arbitrators can be subjected to various liability claims based on their specific responsibilities, while the breach of an arbitrator's duty can be based on either contract or tort.[10]

Regarding contractual liability, arbitrators' liability should be based on the terms of their appointment agreement with the parties – although the precise nature of the contract between the parties and arbitrators is not yet settled. One perspective suggests that an arbitrator's authority and duties stem from the arbitration agreement of the parties, suggesting that by accepting the appointment, the arbitrator effectively becomes a third party to the original arbitration agreement between the parties.[11]

Arbitrators could potentially face liability due to their professional duty to execute their responsibilities competently.[12] There are two types of inappropriate behaviour by arbitrators. First, affirmative misconduct and failure to act, encompassing a range of behaviour, which includes but is not limited to unjustified withdrawal from arbitration proceedings, fraud, corruption, deliberate wrongdoing or inaction, and instances where arbitrators fail to meet their obligations regarding disclosing conflicts of interest and delivering awards.[13] Second, arbitrators may be subject to sanctions and disciplinary actions from both arbitral institutions and their professional associations.[14]

In contrast, judges are typically immune from judicial acts performed in the exercise of their judicial functions according to the judicial immunity principle. Judicial immunity is a legal doctrine that protects judges from personal liability for acts performed within their judicial capacity. Judicial immunity is rooted in the principle of

8. *Ibid.*
9. *Ibid.*
10. Susan D. Franck, The Liability of International Arbitrators: A Comparative Analysis and Proposal for Qualified Immunity, 20(1) NYLS J. Int'l & Comp. L. 4 (2000) Article 2.
11. *Ibid.*, pp. 5-6 (citing, among others, *Norjalv v. Hyundai* [1991] 1 Lloyd's Rep).
12. *Ibid.*, p. 10.
13. *Ibid.*, p. 11.
14. Andrew T. Guzman, Arbitrator Liability: Reconciling Arbitration and Mandatory Rules, Duke Law Journal (2000), pp. 1279-1334; Dolores Bentolila, *Arbitrators as Lawmakers*, International Arbitration Law Library (2017), pp. 51-80.

preserving judicial independence.[15] While the extent of judicial immunity can vary between civil law and common law countries, the underlying principle remains similar.

There have been ongoing deliberations about the extension of judicial immunity to arbitrators, which often hinges on the degree to which an arbitrator's duties mirror those of a judge. Especially in common law systems, courts seem inclined to grant immunity to arbitrators when they function in a quasi-judicial role.[16]

At an international level, there is a lack of international harmonization regarding the scope of liability for international arbitrators. Indicatively, the United Nations Commission on International Trade Law ('*UNCITRAL Model Law*') and the Convention on the Recognition and Enforcement of Foreign Arbitral Awards of 1958 (the '*NYC*') are completely silent regarding the immunity of arbitrators.

Under one approach known as the 'legal status approach', arbitrators are deemed to enjoy the same judicial immunity as judges and are therefore not liable for judicial acts. Consequently, under this approach, arbitrators cannot be sanctioned on account of their decision – although they may still be held accountable for personal misconduct during the arbitration process, instances of fraud, gross negligence, and clear attempts to undermine justice.[17] The legal status approach is followed by most arbitral institutions. For example:

- Articles 20 and 21(a) of the International Centre for Settlement of Investment Disputes (*ICSID*) Convention grant arbitrators immunity from legal process for acts performed in their role unless waived by the Centre.
- Similarly, the London Court of International Arbitration Rules (*LCIA*), 2020 include a limitation of liability clause in Article 31, which provides that no arbitrator shall be liable to any party for any act or omission in connection with any arbitration conducted under the auspices of the LCIA, save: (i) where the arbitrator can be liable for 'conscious or deliberate wrongdoing' and (ii) to the extent that any part of this provision is prohibited by the applicable law.
- The International Chamber of Commerce (*ICC*), 2021 similarly includes a limitation of liability clause in Article 41, which provides for a qualified immunity to arbitrators 'except to the extent such limitation of liability is prohibited by applicable law'.
- The Singapore International Arbitration Centre (*SIAC*), 2016 provides for a comparable exclusion of liability in Article 38, as do the Hong Kong International Arbitration Centre Rules (*HKIAC*), 2018 in Article 46.

15. *See, e.g.*, *Stump v. Sparkman* 435 U.S. 349, 355 (1978) (quoting *Bradley v. Fisher*, 80 U.S. 335, 347 (1871)), where it was held that judicial immunity is 'a general principle of the highest importance to the administration of justice', and that liability would destroy the judges' independence.
16. *Sutcliffe v. Thackrah* [1974] App. Cas. 727, 735; *Austern v. Chicago Bd. Options Exch.*, 898 F.2d 882, 884 (2 d Cir. 1990); William W. Park, Text and Context in International Dispute Resolution, 15 B.U. Int'l L.J. 191, 194, 206-207 (1997).
17. *Ibid.*

In contrast, the 'contractual approach' views arbitrators as service providers engaged by the parties to resolve disputes and receive compensation accordingly. As a result, if an arbitrator violates the terms of their contract, they should be held accountable for any wrongful actions leading to damages for the parties engaged in arbitration.[18]

The legal basis for arbitrators' liability and the subsequent penalties will be primarily determined by the governing law of the contract and the arbitration's seat. Commonly recognized grounds for arbitrator liability include lack of impartiality, unavailability, unjustified resignation, lack of disclosure, and inefficient conduct. Additional grounds may involve corruption, fraud, forgery, breach of confidentiality, and misconduct.

In view of the distinctions between judges and arbitrators, and especially the limited scope of review for arbitral awards, caution should be exercised about extending immunity to arbitrators. In fact, while arbitrators perform a function similar to judges in adjudicating disputes, they do so in a private, contractual context rather than within the public justice system.

III COURT INTERVENTION IN INTERNATIONAL ARBITRATION

Although arbitration is, by its nature, a process operating outside of national courts, court intervention in the context of arbitration proceedings has the potential of preventing and remedying injustices or abuses – by either the parties or the arbitral tribunal – that might occur at the outset of the arbitration or during the proceedings.[19] Consequently, states are entitled to exercise a degree of control over the arbitral process, ensuring compliance with a minimum standard of justice.[20]

In terms of the procedural involvement of courts during the arbitral process, their role can be delineated into three distinct phases:

- *Commencement of arbitration*: At the initiation of arbitration proceedings, courts may provide assistance, facilitating the process.[21]
- *Arbitration process*: Throughout the arbitration process, courts may exercise supervision and intervention, alongside assisting as necessary – e.g., in the form of interlocutory orders.
- *Post-award stage*: Following the issuance of an award, parties will need to seek court intervention. For instance, the losing party might challenge the award. Conversely, the winning party may request court assistance in enforcing the award.

18. Murray L. Smith, Contractual Obligations Owed by and to Arbitrators: Model Terms of Appointment, 8(1) Arbitration International 17-40 (Oxford University Press, 1992) https://doi.org/10.1093/arbitration/8.1.17 (accessed 16 August 2025).
19. Manuel A. Ǵmez, 'Article 5: Extent of Court Intervention' *in* Ilias Bantekas et al., 'UNCITRAL Model Law on International Commercial Arbitration' (Cambridge University Press 2020).
20. *Ibid.*, para. 1-138.
21. *See, e.g.*, Article 27 of the Model Law, which provides the court the power to assist the tribunal in taking evidence.

Article 5 of the UNCITRAL Model Law, which provides that 'no court shall intervene except where so provided in this Law', embodies the premise that the effectiveness of arbitral process relies – at least in part – on the coercive authority of state courts.[22] Further, Article 16(1) of the Model Law embodies the competence-competence principle, which promotes the inherent power of the arbitration panel to rule on its own jurisdiction. However, the arbitral tribunal's competence to rule on its own jurisdiction is subject to court oversight. For example, courts may be asked to determine whether an arbitration agreement exists or is valid when one party challenges it (e.g., during a stay of proceedings request). Even after the tribunal has issued its decision, courts can review the tribunal's ruling on jurisdiction if a party applies to set it aside or resists enforcement of the award.

Similar to the Model Law, the NYC involves court intervention to a significant extent.[23] Under the current provisions of the NYC, courts retain the authority to scrutinize arbitral awards and consider grounds for refusal as outlined in Article V. Therefore, the NYC provides a framework for recognising and enforcing arbitral awards while relying on national courts to oversee and intervene as necessary.

In short, arbitration relies on the support of courts as an essential component of its functioning. This support is crucial not only to guarantee the fairness of the arbitration process but also to prevent any breaches of natural justice.

IV POTENTIAL OBSTACLES TO ACHIEVING JUSTICE IN INTERNATIONAL ARBITRATION

As previously noted, the primary purpose of court intervention in the arbitral process is to ensure that parties have access to a fair and reliable mechanism for resolving their disputes. Where there has been a breach of the rules of natural justice, an arbitral award may be set aside under the law governing the arbitration, or its recognition and enforcement may be refused in the jurisdiction where enforcement is sought. This chapter examines the balance between efficiency and substantive justice by analysing national court rulings in different jurisdictions. It considers whether prioritizing efficiency could potentially undermine the legitimacy of arbitration and includes examples of significant challenges encountered in accessing justice within the realm of international arbitration as compared with litigation.

1 *P&ID v. Nigeria*

In a landmark decision dated 21 October 2023, the Commercial Court in London set aside a USD 11 billion award against Nigeria, holding that the award was obtained

22. Manuel A. Ǵmez, 'Article 5: Extent of Court Intervention' *in* Ilias Bantekas et al., 'UNCITRAL Model Law on International Commercial Arbitration' (2020 Cambridge University Press).
23. Convention on the Recognition and Enforcement of Foreign Arbitral Awards (New York, 1958).

through fraudulent evidence, corrupt payments, and improper retention of leaked documents.[24]

The dispute stemmed from a contractual agreement between P&ID and Nigeria's Ministry of Petroleum for the construction of a gas-processing plant in Calabar, Nigeria. However, the plant was never constructed. P&ID initiated arbitration proceedings in 2012, alleging that Nigeria failed to provide necessary infrastructure and wet gas as per the contract terms. The arbitration was seated in London, as specified in the contract.

In its final award in 2017, the tribunal, by majority, ordered Nigeria to pay USD 6.6 billion in compensation for two decades of lost gas contracts, with an interest rate of 7%. The award has since accrued to over USD 11 billion, which Nigeria claims constitutes one-third of its 2023 annual budget.[25]

Nigeria's initial attempt to challenge the liability award was dismissed by the Commercial Court in 2016 because it was filed late and had 'no merit'.[26] However, after securing discovery orders from the courts in the Cayman Islands, New York and Cyprus, Nigeria obtained an extension to bring a new set aside action against the awards in 2020. This extension was granted based on the argument that there was a strong prima facie case indicating that the award had been procured by corruption, perjury and dishonest conduct.

In its ruling dated 23 October 2023, the Court found compelling evidence that P&ID had bribed Grace Taiga, a former legal director at the Ministry of Petroleum Resources, to secure the contract. Additionally, P&ID had continued making payments to Taiga during the arbitration process. Consequently, the Court held that there was 'no hesitation in concluding that Nigeria suffered substantial injustice' as a result of the P&ID's actions.[27] The Court further noted that P&ID had obtained the award through 'the most severe abuses of the arbitral process'.[28] Based on these findings, the Court upheld Nigeria's challenge under section 68 of the English Arbitration Act 1996. Notably, the Court characterized the case as exceptionally uncommon, noting that it 'touches the reputation of arbitration as a dispute resolution process'.[29] According to the Court, although the tribunal 'did what it did with what it had', the arbitration had been a 'shell that got nowhere near the truth'.[30]

On 21 December 2023, a London judge refused permission to appeal his earlier ruling that a USD 11 billion award against Nigeria was obtained by fraud.[31]

24. *Process and Industrial Developments Ltd. v. The Ministry of Petroleum Resources of the Federal Republic of Nigeria* [2023] EWHC 2638 (Comm), 21 December 2023.
25. Susannah Moody, 'The Most Severe Abuses of the Arbitral Process': UK Court Overturns Mega-Award on Grounds of Fraud, GAR 23 October 2023.
26. *Process and Industrial Developments Ltd. v. The Ministry of Petroleum Resources of the Federal Republic of Nigeria*, Order and Reasons of the High Court of Justice of England and Wales, 10 February 2016, para. 3.
27. *Ibid.*, para. 511.
28. *Ibid.*, para. 516.
29. *Ibid.*, para. 14.
30. *Ibid.*, para. 580.
31. *Process and Industrial Developments Ltd. v. The Ministry of Petroleum Resources of the Federal Republic of Nigeria*, Ruling on Leave to Appeal of the High Court of Justice of England and Wales [2023] EWHC 3320, 21 December 2023.

2 *CBS v. CBP*

The Singapore Court of Appeal in *CBS v. CBP* upheld the High Court's decision, which set aside an arbitral award due to a 'material breach of natural justice'.[32]

The dispute revolved around non-payment by CBP, an Indian company, for coal purchased from a seller who assigned the debt to CBS, a Singaporean bank. The dispute involved a disagreement over the interpretation of SCMA Rule 28.1 regarding the conduct of hearings. The arbitration was seated in Singapore and referred to the Singapore Chamber of Maritime Arbitration (*SCMA*).

Article 28.1 of the SCMA Rules provides that '[u]nless the parties have agreed on a documents-only arbitration or that no hearing should be held, the Tribunal <u>shall</u> hold a hearing for the presentation of evidence by witnesses, including expert witnesses, <u>or</u> for oral submissions'.[33]

The bank opted for a documents-only arbitration, while the seller requested a hearing for oral witness evidence without providing written witness statements. The arbitrator decided to hold a hearing for oral submissions only, denying the seller's request for witness testimony. Ultimately, the buyer did not attend the hearing, and the bank's claim was allowed in full, including on the basis that the arbitrator rejected the buyer's case regarding an alleged oral agreement.

The buyer then applied successfully to the High Court for the award to be set aside on the ground that the arbitrator's decision to deny its right to call witnesses represented a breach of natural justice. The matter was eventually brought before the Court of Appeal, which emphasized that tribunals cannot arbitrarily limit oral witness evidence under their case management power, as this may violate natural justice principles. The Court ruled that Article 28.1 of the SCMA Rules does not grant tribunals the authority to choose the type of hearing, and in the absence of an agreement, a hearing must be held for both oral evidence and submissions. On this basis, the Court found that the arbitrator's decision constituted a breach of natural justice, leading to the setting aside of the arbitral award.

3 *Betamax v. STC*

On 14 June 2021, the Privy Council of the United Kingdom (the '*Privy Council*') handed down judgment in *Betamax Ltd* (*Betamax*) *v. State Trading Corporation* (Mauritius) (*STC*).[34] The decision of the Privy Council provides important guidance on the setting aside of arbitral awards on grounds of public policy in circumstances where the underlying contract is alleged to be illegal.

The dispute revolved around a fifteen-year Contract of Affreightment (*COA*) signed in 2009 between Betamax and STC for transporting petroleum products from India to Mauritius. The contract was governed by Mauritian law and included

32. *CBS v. CBP* [2021] SGCA 4, Civil Appeal No. 30 of 2020, para. 71.
33. Emphasis added.
34. *Betamax Ltd. v. State Trading Corporation*, SIAC Case No. ARB084/15/KJ, Judgment of the Judicial Committee of the Privy Council [2021] UKPC 14, 14 June 2021.

arbitration provisions. In 2008, a procurement regime was implemented in Mauritius, which was subsequently amended in 2009. In 2015, a new government took office and announced plans to terminate the COA due to perceived irregularities in the contract allocation process. In response, STC notified Betamax of its inability to continue using its services under the COA, leading Betamax to terminate the contract in April 2015, citing default provisions.

Betamax then filed a notice of arbitration under the COA. The proceedings were seated in Mauritius. In the final award in 2017, the tribunal held that Betamax had rightfully terminated the COA due to STC's clear intention not to perform. Additionally, the tribunal found that the COA was exempted from the relevant provisions of the Public Procurement Act (*PPA*) and the Public Procurement Regulations (*PPR*); thus deeming it legal and enforceable.[35]

STC sought to set aside the award in August 2017 under section 39(2) of the Mauritius International Arbitration Act (*IAA*), citing conflicts with public policy. In particular, the Court held that the PPA prescribed 'fundamental legal principles, the breach of which would [...] be injurious to public good and conflict with principles which are fundamental to the national economic and legal values of Mauritius'.[36] The illegality found by the Court was therefore sufficient to justify setting aside the award.

The case then proceeded to the Privy Council in January 2021, which addressed three key issues:

- First, whether the Mauritian Supreme Court had the authority to review the tribunal's decision regarding the legality of the COA under the PPA and PPR. The Privy Council found that the Supreme Court erred in reviewing this decision, emphasizing the 'limited supervisory role which requires the court to respect the finality of the award' under the IAA.[37]
- Second, the Privy Council confirmed the arbitrator's decision that the COA was exempt from the PPA and PPR, thus not illegal under those provisions. This conclusion was based on the interpretation of relevant Mauritian legislation.
- Third, the Privy Council did not address the issue of whether the award conflicted with public policy, as it deemed the first issue conclusive.

The Privy Council's decision underscores the principle of limited court intervention in arbitration matters and the finality of arbitral awards, unless there are clear grounds such as fraud or a breach of natural justice. However, the principle of minimum court intervention comes with a risk that arbitrators may act with less accountability, leading to decisions that are biased, arbitrary, or lacking in thoroughness.

35. *Betamax Ltd. v. State Trading Corporation*, SIAC Case No. ARB084/15/KJ, Final Award (No. 059 of 2017), 5 June 2017.
36. *Betamax Ltd. v. State Trading Corporation*, SIAC Case No. ARB084/15/KJ, Judgment of the Supreme Court of Mauritius, 31 May 2019, para. 163.
37. *Betamax Ltd. v. State Trading Corporation*, SIAC Case No. ARB084/15/KJ, Judgment of the Judicial Committee of the Privy Council [2021] UKPC 14, 14 June 2021, para. 49.

V THE EVOLVING ROLE OF ARBITRATORS TOWARDS AN 'INQUISITORIAL' APPROACH

In light of the challenges in achieving both procedural fairness and substantive justice, understanding the shifting dynamics of the arbitrator's role becomes paramount. While the pursuit of justice intertwines with the complexities of dispute resolution, the evolving role of arbitrators stands as a pivotal force. Traditionally, arbitrators have functioned within the framework of party autonomy, allowing the parties involved to dictate the course of proceedings according to their preferences. However, as arbitration evolves, there is a growing recognition of the need for arbitrators to adopt a more proactive stance in ensuring fairness and justice throughout the arbitral process.

One of the key areas where this evolution manifests is in the consideration of adversarial versus inquisitorial approaches to arbitration. In adversarial proceedings, the arbitrator assumes a relatively passive role, allowing the parties to drive the process by presenting their evidence and arguments independently.[38] This approach prioritizes party autonomy and procedural flexibility, often leading to a more efficient process, especially in cases where parties are well prepared. However, it carries the risk of delays and inefficiencies if parties engage in tactics to prolong proceedings and may result in unequal treatment if one party is more resourceful or experienced than the other.

Conversely, in an inquisitorial approach, the arbitrator takes on a more active role, intervening to ensure a comprehensive understanding of the case, particularly in complex matters.[39] By actively seeking out and assessing evidence, the arbitrator aims to level the playing field between parties and facilitate the resolution of disputes involving uncooperative or unprepared parties. Yet, this approach presents its own challenges, such as the risk of bias if the arbitrator's enquiries are perceived as favouring one party, or the requirement for a skilled arbitrator to balance the investigative role with maintaining impartiality.

The distinction between these two approaches holds significance, particularly in criminal proceedings, but its relevance in civil proceedings remains debatable.[40] Civil proceedings often hinge on arguments set forth by the parties, lending themselves more towards adversarial methods.

In arbitration, the background of the arbitrator should not necessarily dictate the approach adopted in arbitration. Instead, a more international approach should be adopted, which should not be influenced by the legal background or style of each arbitrator. Arbitrators may also consider hybrid approaches that combine elements of both adversarial and inquisitorial methods to achieve a fair and efficient resolution.

In 2019, the International Bar Association (*IBA*) published a Report on 'When arbitration ceases to be adversarial and becomes inquisitorial: the plight of arbitrators

38. Mino Han, 'When Arbitration Ceases to Be Adversarial and Becomes Inquisitorial: The Plight of Arbitrators Seeking to Reconcile Due Process', International Bar Association, 23 September 2019.
39. *Ibid.*
40. *Ibid.*

seeking to reconcile due process',[41] which shed light on the evolving role of arbitrators. Panellists shared anecdotes and insights, emphasizing the importance of maintaining party equality and due process while navigating complex disputes. Experience shows that legal practitioners from diverse backgrounds may exhibit varying degrees of interventionism, irrespective of their legal upbringing.[42]

An essential consideration in defining the authority of arbitrators revolves around the complexity of corruption-related matters. These issues often overlap between civil and criminal law and raise questions of public interest that extend beyond the limits of party autonomy.[43] Examples like the *World Duty Free v. Kenya* case, which was discussed above, highlight the importance of adopting an approach close to the inquisitorial model, especially in cases with public policy implications.

In contrast, in the *P&ID v. Nigeria* case, the tribunal failed to take proactive steps despite indications of bribery. As discussed above, this resulted in an award deemed lacking in substantive justice, as remarked by the English Commercial Court.

VI CONCLUSION

The examination of the role of arbitrators in dispensing justice underscores the intricate dynamics at play within the realm of international arbitration. As arbitration continues to gain prominence globally, the pursuit of justice within this framework remains an ongoing and essential endeavour. Arbitrators, as central figures in administering justice within the arbitration process, navigate a complex landscape influenced by cultural nuances, procedural intricacies, and ethical considerations.

Key distinctions between arbitrators and judges, as well as between arbitration and litigation, highlight the unique challenges and considerations inherent in the arbitral process. From the appointment of arbitrators to the standards of justice applied and mechanisms for accountability, it becomes evident that while arbitration offers flexibility and efficiency, it also presents risks and potential obstacles to achieving substantive justice. For this reason, the evolving role of arbitrators as guardians of fairness and equity remains paramount.

Court intervention in international arbitration serves as a crucial safeguard against potential abuses and injustices, upholding the integrity and enforceability of arbitral awards. Yet, the balance between efficiency and substantive justice remains a delicate one, as evidenced by recent court rulings addressing breaches of natural justice and irregularities in arbitral awards. Case studies such as *Nigeria v. P&ID* and *World Duty-Free Company v. Republic of Kenya* shed light on these discussions, emphasizing the arbitrators' duty to ensure a level playing field and intervene when necessary.

Exploring the potential for arbitrators to adopt a proactive stance in intricate disputes, while balancing procedural fairness with substantive justice, underscores the dynamic nature of their responsibilities. Traditionally, arbitrators have operated within

41. *Ibid.*
42. *Ibid.*
43. Diogo Pereira, 'Can You Enforce an Agreement Involving Bribery? From World Duty Free v. Kenya to Vantage Deep Water Co. v. Petrobras Am., Inc.', Kluwer Arbitration Blog, 7 July 2019.

the framework of party autonomy, allowing the parties involved to shape proceedings according to their preferences. However, as arbitration evolves, there is a growing recognition of the need for arbitrators to adopt a more proactive stance in ensuring fairness and justice throughout the process. The debate surrounding the adversarial versus inquisitorial approach in arbitration further emphasizes the need for arbitrators to navigate complex cultural, procedural, and jurisdictional factors to tailor their approach to each case. Adapting hybrid methods that blend elements of both approaches may offer a pathway to achieving a fair and efficient resolution.

Advancing justice in international arbitration could be achieved through the adoption of a universal code of conduct for arbitrators that encompasses key principles addressing arbitrator accountability, procedural fairness, and the equilibrium between efficiency and substantive justice, for example, through the adoption of a more inquisitorial approach by arbitrators. This code should further prioritize transparency, holding arbitrators accountable for their decisions and conduct, thereby bolstering trust in the arbitration process. Additionally, adherence to ethical standards must be paramount, ensuring integrity and fairness in every arbitration proceeding. Such a universal code could ultimately foster an arbitration system that reliably delivers justice on a global scale.

CHAPTER 3

Arbitral Foresight: The Arbitrator's Untapped Superpower

Christopher M. Campbell[*]

TABLE OF CONTENTS

I INTRODUCTION

There are several scenes in the Joel Silver-directed movies *Sherlock Holmes* and *Sherlock Holmes: Game of Shadows*, whereby Sherlock Holmes (portrayed by Robert Downey Jr.) uses the information and/or clues before him to foresee how a scuffle or a particular scene will play out. The screen fades to a dreamy-like sequence, and the scene plays out in slow motion with how Holmes imagines the events will unfold. Once that sequence concludes, the scene then plays out in real-time, often exactly as Holmes foresaw, but not always.

There is a moment at the end of an arbitral proceeding where the parties and arbitrators alike look back and wonder "what could have been," and where were the missed moments or pieces of information that could have brought these two sides to resolution sooner. They were likely there, but for whatever reason they were missed.

* Christopher ("Chris") M. Campbell is a Florence, IT based Senior Counsel—Litigation at Baker Hughes. He is an active figure in the international disputes community and host of the podcast, Tales of the Tribunal, where he discusses topics related to international law and interviews people from across the field. Chris regularly writes and speaks on topics related to technology, energy, oil & gas and DEI. He is a graduate of the Darla Moore School of Business and the Joseph F. Rice School of Law at the University of South Carolina (Formerly South Carolina School of Law).

From the parties' perspective, had they known that the tribunal would have ruled a certain way on a given issue earlier in the proceedings, perhaps there could have been an opportunity for resolution. If clients and counsel had the opportunity to peer into the mind of the tribunal at a pivotal moment in the case, perhaps they could have cracked the case; it would "be elementary, my dear reader." But alas, no such opportunity materializes, and both sides will instead spend months if not years and likely millions of dollars in fielding their cases.

But what if the parties, already at the mercy of the tribunal, bestowed a further power to the tribunal? Not one that materially changes arbitral process or limits the power for the parties to make their case, but instead gave tribunals the powers to pull back the veil of secrecy and to let the parties see a glimpse of their future in this case if the matter were to be decided right then and there. Some national legal systems already include a version of this ability, and other authors have written of similar versions of this procedural mechanism and described it as "arbitrator facilitation." With some strategic and practical adjustments to these sources of inspiration and as a means of ascribing the enhanced role this notion purports to give tribunals, this chapter coins the term Arbitral Foresight ("Foresight") for consideration for the broader arbitration community.

Foresight is the ability of tribunals to give preliminary perspectives on the issues in dispute before them, on an anonymous basis, and with party consent. This is a neatly distilled tribunal superpower and one that could greatly assist arbitrators and therefore the parties in resolving their claims without the need of continuing through standard arbitral proceedings.

From the beginning of the proceedings, arbitrators are imbued with a special trust, positioned by the parties as the arbiters of their fate in these proceedings. With that great power comes great responsibility.[1] The point is not to prejudge the case or to deprive any party of the opportunity to make their case, instead the goal is to give the parties foresight so that they can make informed decisions at the earliest point possible.

II THE PROBLEM: THE FINANCIAL AND TEMPORAL COSTS

Before delving into defining and explaining the virtues of Foresight, it is important to understand the problems that lead to this proposed solution. Indeed, there are three fundamental factors: (i) the cost of arbitral proceedings, (ii) the amount of time required to complete the arbitral process and (iii) understanding why clients go to arbitration in the first place.

1 Financial Costs

From the moment a matter fails to resolve itself in pre-dispute negotiations until the final award is rendered, the financial costs being to accrue. Whether that be theoretical

1. Stan Lee, The Amazing Spider-Man & Amazing Fantasy No. 15, 245 (1962), quoting, Convention Nationale, Collection Générale des Décrets Rendus par la Convention Nationale 72 (Chez Baudouin, Imprimeur de la Convention Nationale, Paris, 1793).

costs like opportunity or sunk costs, or the costs immediately realized with the processing of each invoice from the tribunal, the hired experts or external counsel.

The costs in international commercial arbitrations can vary widely. Industry reports advise that the low-end of such costs can be greater than USD 1 million but can also reach atmospheres of USD 10 million + .[2] A survey from the Chartered Institute of Arbitrators reported that both these costs tend to be between USD 1.6 million and USD 1.8 million, with nearly 74% of those costs being accrued in legal fees.[3] Therefore, in order to meaningfully control the overall costs of arbitral proceedings, one must endeavor to limit the primary cost drivers in the process, in this case, legal fees.

Framed another way, if we can shorten the length of the proceedings, then this presumably would also lessen the amount of legal support required and ultimately succeed in limiting costs.

2 Temporal Investment

Here, the old adage rings true "time is money,"[4] and for every moment a company's staff members are supporting dispute resolution, instead of their primary business function, this is time they are now providing substantive value to the company and thus subtracting from profit-inducing activities. Even in matters that are largely outsourced to external counsel, there are still likely to be hundreds of hours of non-productive time incurred that bear little chance of being recoverable but are costs realized, nonetheless.

Additionally, when one considers the average length of an arbitration from beginning to end, it is on average between fifteen and twenty-two months.[5] This is the time where both the previously mentioned internal resources are occupied and where parties to the proceedings are hostage to the time that it takes to resolve the dispute. In an era where companies are living quarter to quarter, a victory on the merits of the proceedings drawn out over the course of 1.5-2 years may simply be untenable. As the financial battles for a client are raging, the reinforcements of a favorable arbitral award may arrive after the commercial battles are already long concluded.

All of these are reasons why even the most fervent of clients will often look for off-ramps before the full development of the case, an opportunity to cut their losses or count their gains while still being able to frame the exercise as a positive.

2. Allocation of Costs, Jus Mundi, January 2, 2024. https://jusmundi.com/en/document/publication/en-allocation-of-costs (accessed March 1, 2024).
3. Chartered Institute of Arbitrators, CIArb Costs of International Arbitration Survey 11 (2011), https://shorturl.at/bgBN4 (accessed February 20, 2024).
4. Franklin B., "Advice to a Young Tradesman," in George Fisher (ed.), The American Instructor: or Young Man's Best Companion (1748).
5. For more information, *see* following article which quotes the ICC, ICDR, HKIAC, LCIA and SIAC statistics: "What is the Median Length of an International Arbitration?," MoloLamken LLP, https://www.mololamken.com/knowledge-what-is-the-median-length-of-an (accessed March 11, 2024).

3 Client Motivation

What exactly is it that client's look for when utilizing arbitration (or really any dispute resolution mechanism)? For many clients or in-house counsel, their wants can be summarized as follows:

(i) *Predictability*. Commercial operations need reasonable and reliable predictability in their dispute resolution process. They need to understand how their arguments will be weighted and judged as well as by whom and how. This allows commercial leaders to evaluate whether a dispute should be pursued vigorously or whether the business should push for a commercial resolution. Obviously, a tool in the arbitral process that would allow insight into where the tribunal's mindset is in specific moments and where it may be heading would be invaluable intel that would undoubtedly open up further paths to resolution.

(ii) *Cost Efficiency*. As mentioned above, while cost alone may not be determinative when evaluating a dispute, it is certainly a factor in balancing pragmatism in fighting a dispute. Indeed, when compared side-by-side whether it makes sense to settle or fight a dispute, the costs must not be so burdensome so as to dissuade the party from engaging.
In modern arbitration practice, once the submissions begin, it is somewhat rare for the parties to continue meaningful negotiations. This means that the process is likely to run the full course of the procedure and incur the full legal costs.
A technique that could provide for clear pictures of cost and exposure while providing earlier exits from the dispute would be attractive to many clients.

(iii) *Time savings*. Finally, as also mentioned and briefly summarized here, time is of the essence with disputes—i.e., non-profit producing activities—the more quickly they can be resolved, the better.

III THE CONCEPT OF ARBITRAL FORESIGHT

1 Overview of Arbitral Foresight

Foresight is a proposed ability activated in the midst of the proceedings that allows arbitrators to provide an anonymous and preliminary perspective on the issues before the tribunal, contingent upon the consent of the parties involved in the arbitration. The essence of this concept is to afford arbitrators a mechanism through which they can facilitate a quicker, more cost-effective resolution of disputes.

As with all arbitral mechanisms, Foresight should only be implemented with party consent either expressly or by codification in the various institutional arbitration rules.

If there is consent to apply this ability, when would be the ideal time? The better question is, at what point would the parties most benefit from the insights of such

Foresight? Indeed, there is not a fixed time where the ability could be activated, and instead the parties could apply to the tribunal to ask for their perspective at any time during the proceedings. That said, there are likely two points in time that make for attractive options:

- *Prior to Document Production*. At this point in the proceedings, the parties will have had an opportunity to place both their arguments and the evidence that they intend to rely upon before the tribunal. The tribunal will have had an idea to understand those arguments, and candidly, likely already formed some opinion about the matters before them. Although there can be significant cost in getting to this point, that cost is likely still only a fraction of what will be incurred in the next steps of the proceedings through document production and the hearing. By enacting Foresight, the counsel would have a sobering look at their case, how it is landing with the tribunal and importantly, if they need to express a more grounded reality to their client.

  However, perhaps there is information yet to be provided, hidden among the informational mines of document production. It may be premature to ask for even preliminary conclusions based on the submissions before the tribunal. If this is the case, the parties can ask for the tribunal's positions *after* document production.
- *Immediately Following Document Production*. Document production can cost each party hundreds of thousands of dollars in a commercial arbitration. So deciding to wait until after document production to trigger Arbitral Foresight ensures that a certain amount of cost (and time) will be incurred in the arbitral process. However, and admittedly, as a US litigator, the author appreciates that document production in the arbitral context (and its rued cousin Discovery) can often reveal case-changing information that will turn the perspective of a case on its head.

  Once document production is complete, the tribunal will have the vast majority of the submissions that the party will make. Rather than immediately going into post-document production submissions, the parties could be given the benefit of knowing where the case would land were it to end that day. Again, another opportunity for an off-ramp in the case before incurring the next major cost drivers of preparing for the final hearing, the hearing itself and then post-hearing submissions.

It is important to emphasize that Foresight *does not* render a decision that is binding upon the parties, nor should it be viewed as prejudicial such that a party could rely on favorable preliminary perspective, but rather it invites the parties into the current of the tribunals at a given moment in time of the case. The matter is not prejudged; it is considered with the then-known facts and arguments before the tribunal.

2 Comparative Example

Under standard arbitration procedures, parties coordinate with each other as well as the tribunal to fashion a timeline and procedure to bring the matter through the arbitration process. Unfortunately, once the matter progresses to arbitration, neither side is usually willing to amend its position without significant developments during the case, or unforeseen external factors.

Generally described, the phases of an arbitration consist of:[6]-[7]

(i) Phase 1—Beginning and Positioning of the case;
(ii) Phase 2—Initial Argumentation and Presentation of Evidence;
(iii) Phase 3—Document Production and Maturation of the Case;
(iv) Phase 4—Hearing Preparation; and
(v) Phase 5—The Hearing and Post-Hearing Submissions.

Within the framework of these phases, it is not uncommon for the parties to agree for there to be a "Settlement Window"[8] woven in among the planned issues outlined in the procedural order. Such a period can be as little as two to five weeks but is ultimately intended to give the parties an opportunity to reconsider their case before advancing to the next phase of the proceedings.

Table 3.1 contemplates a dispute valued at around USD 10 million, complex enough to warrant at least one expert, and with potential counterclaims from the respondent. Obviously, there is a wide-spectrum of variance that could occur in the below procedural framework; however, what is important are the opportunities to employ Foresight, and where those opportunities fall in terms of driving costs throughout the proceedings. These are the cost estimates for *one* party in this hypothetical dispute.

Table 3.1 Mock Arbitral Timetable

Phase	*Time Passage*	*Actions*	*Cost*
Phase 1: Beginning & Positioning of the Case	16 weeks	Request for Arbitration/Answer & Counterclaims/ Reply to Answer	USD 435,000
Phase 2: Initial Argumentation and Presentation of Evidence	28 weeks	Case Management Conferences/ Statement of Claim/ Statement of Defense/	USD 605,000

6. International Chamber of Commerce (ICC), "Arbitration Procedure," https://iccwbo.org/dispute-resolution/dispute-resolution-services/arbitration/rules-procedure/arbitration-procedure/ (accessed March 11, 2024).
7. American Arbitration Association (AAA) (2024) "Stages of the Arbitration Process."
8. Edna Sussman, The Mediation Window: An Arbitration Process Measure to Facilitate Settlement, 13(1) NYSBA New York Dispute Resolution Lawyer (Spring 2020).

Phase	*Time Passage*	*Actions*	*Cost*
Opportunity for Arbitral Foresight[9]	5 weeks	Application for Arbitral Foresight/Tribunal issues its preliminary perspective/Settlement Window	
Phase 3: Document Production and Maturation of Case	12 weeks	Parties exchange document production requests/Parties present objections/Tribunal rules on objections and orders production/Parties produce/Parties consider documents and evaluate next steps	USD 570,000
Opportunity for Arbitral Foresight	5 weeks	Application for Arbitral Foresight/Tribunal issues its prospective opinion/Settlement Window	
Phase 4: Hearing Preparation	33 weeks	Statement of Reply/Statement of Rejoinder and Reply/Statement of Rejoinder to Counterclaim/Expert Meetings/Final Hearing Preparations/The Hearing	USD 460,000
Opportunity for Arbitral Foresight	5 weeks	Application for Arbitral Foresight/Tribunal issues its prospective opinion/Settlement Window	
Phase 5: Hearing and Post-Hearing	1 week	The Hearing/ Final Submissions by the Parties	USD 550,000
TOTAL:			USD 2,595,000

What we *see* in Table 3.1 is that there are three general opportunities for the tribunal to provide its critical perspective that could assist the parties in resolving the case, immediately before or after Phase 3 (Document Production) and before Phase 5 (Hearing). Doing so *before* document production would represent a savings of 60% of the estimated cost figures, and even doing so before the hearing would save the parties a final 21% of their costs. These savings scale to the size of dispute, and even the most hardline believers in their positions would be hard pressed to ignore these savings.

3 Form of the Preliminary Perspectives

The tribunal would be free to provide their views in whatever written form that they wish, so long as the critical elements of anonymity for each arbitrator are respected, all

9. Note that the parties would be free to apply for Arbitral Foresight at whatever time they deemed appropriate; the author's suggestion is that the discretion of whether to grant such an application would be assistive to the parties at the time of the request—plainly, the idea is not that there be three required periods for application of Arbitral Foresight.

of the issues are addressed, and that they make clear that the views of the tribunal are preliminary in nature and non-binding.

For reference in imagining what such a schedule could look like, the below is an example of the relevant language and a prototype schedule:

Campbell's Preliminary Perspective Schedule

The tribunal hereby issues these preliminary perspectives ("Perspectives") pursuant to the application from [Claimant/Respondent/Both] and does so for the express purpose of assisting the parties in any potential discussions regarding the resolution of this matter. The perspectives contained herein are non-binding and without prejudice to the submissions previously made or to be made in these proceedings. The parties have agreed that provision of these Perspectives shall not be used as grounds to challenge or otherwise impede enforcement of the award.

Table 3.2 Campbell's Preliminary Perspective Schedule

	Arbitrator #1	*Arbitrator #2*	*Arbitrator #3*
Issue #1: [Description of issue]			
Issue #2: [Description of issue]			
Issue #3: [Description of issue]			
Additional Comments to the Parties at the current stage of the proceedings			

IV ARBITRAL FORESIGHT IN PRACTICE

1 Party Consent

As dynamic as Foresight could be, it is absolutely fruitless if the parties do not consent to apply such a mechanism *before* the dispute arises, either expressly through their contractual terms, arbitrator's inclusion in their Terms of References and Procedural Orders and/or finally implementation into institutional arbitral rules and guidelines themselves. Let us turn to each briefly in-kind.

2 Contractual Language & Institutional Model Clauses

Many model clauses from arbitral institutions have the same or similar elements, so for the purpose of focusing on the addition to such a clause, this chapter uses an ICC model clause as an example:

> [Language]. Once the tribunal has been constituted, and at any time prior to the issuance of the final award of the tribunal, either party may request that the tribunal issue an advisory preliminary perspective ("Perspective") that indicates how the tribunal would rule on the matters then before it, were no further submissions by the parties to be made. The tribunal, in its sole discretion, may provide such an Opinion so long as the Opinion is anonymized as to the identity of each member of the tribunal. Said Opinion is non-binding and may not be relied upon should the dispute continue after the Opinion is provided. The parties agree that the tribunal's provision of the Opinion shall not be grounds of any attempt to set aside, annul, or otherwise undermine the award.[10]

With a clause like the one above, the parties could directly opt in to the usage of Foresight, in what is probably the most immediate way to observe the utility of the mechanism. However, in order for the technique to gain wider application and therefore assist parties in mitigating financial and temporal investment in the process, persuading arbitral institutions to implement said rules would add meaningful authority. There need not be a fundamental overhaul or rewrite of the entire rule-set; instead, Foresight can be written into the powers of arbitrators appointed under such rules.

3 Arbitral Practice & Counsel Recommendation

Aside from express agreement in the parties' contractual terms, a more immediate step would be usage of Arbitral Foresight by counsel and arbitrators.

For counsel, the benefits of such a tool are obvious. Clients are already displeased about having to use a formalized legal process in the first place. Having external counsel recommend a procedure that could substantially decrease the amount of cost and time required to resolve a dispute would instill further trust in the client-attorney relationship as counsel would be recommending a process that might reduce their potential fees, but for the sake of pursuing resolution as efficiently as possible. Furthermore, even if the matter does not settle after an application for Foresight, counsel would gain valuable insight from the tribunal about the effectiveness of their arguments to the tribunal. This would in turn allow counsel to advise their clients in a more informed manner and make a decision about the strategy in the case.

As for arbitrators, the value in Foresight comes down to how the role of the arbitrator is perceived. Is an arbitrator meant to be passive, merely calling balls and strikes when it comes to the issues placed before them? Or is there a rightful expectation that arbitrators should be actively assisting the parties in coming to a resolution? Are they private judges or equitable peacemakers? These questions are

10. Draft language from the author that could be incorporated into the ICC Rules.

important in understanding the initial assumptions in the untapped power of a regime like Foresight.

Much like the incentives to counsel, arbitrators would benefit from this ability by helping parties have an ever sobering look at how their case is being perceived, exposing the porosity of the arguments that the clients assumed would hold water at the beginning of the proceedings. Effectively implemented, the parties, even the unsuccessful ones, would be thankful to the tribunal for saving them the increased time, resources and financial cost of a lengthy proceeding when, in actuality, there were key issues that were clear to the tribunal early in the process.

4 Party Disagreement

There may be times, for various reasons, when one party may not want to consent to an application for Arbitral Foresight. Is it problematic for the tribunal to provide its preliminary perspectives over the objection of the resistant party?

No.

Throughout the course of every arbitral proceeding, tribunals will make decisions that one or both parties may not agree with; that is a fundamental power imbued upon the tribunal to make decisions that the tribunal believes will most readily bring the parties to resolution.[11]-[12] Providing (pre-agreed) insight to the tribunal's preliminary perspectives bears little difference to other hallmarks of the arbitral process such as: (i) timetables, (ii) scope of evidentiary submissions, (iii) sequence of the proceedings, (iv) virtual versus in-persons hearings, (v) inclusion of settlement windows, (vi) teaching sessions for expert witnesses and other similar decisions. Foresight would merely be another tool for the parties to use to assist in resolving the dispute.

5 Challenges to Arbitral Foresight

When explaining the virtues of Foresight, listeners seldom disagree with the goal of finding more cost and time-efficient means of resolving disputes. Instead, there tends to be concerns related to: (i) biasing the tribunal and/or (ii) ensuring that each party has had an opportunity to fully present its case *before* an award is rendered.

Broadly stated, these issues trend toward concern related to the due process afforded to the parties in the proceedings. The theoretical issue is that an award rendered after a tribunal implemented Foresight (which would have been requested by at least one party) could be undermined (set aside or not enforced) if the non-prevailing party wanted to attack the award These concerns are not merely "Due Process

11. J. Allsop, Authority of the Arbitrator, 30 Arb. Int'l 639 (2014), https://doi.org/10.1093/arbitration/30.4.639 (accessed August 16, 2025).
12. Julian Critchlow, 'The Authority of Arbitrators to Make Rules' Arbitration: The International Journal of Arbitration, Mediation and Dispute Management 68(4), 369-388 (2002).

Paranoia" and do deserve consideration;[13] however, these hesitancies can be dealt with in a manner that mitigates lingering skepticism.

6 Set Aside and Enforcement

The 1958 New York Convention for the Recognition and Enforcement of Foreign Arbitral Awards ("New York Convention")[14] sets out the authority for contracting States, of which there are 172, to set aside arbitral awards on a particular and narrow set of grounds.[15] The New York Convention is widely viewed to act as a substantial guiding source for due process requirements. The UNCITRAL International Commercial Arbitration Model Law ("Model Law")[16] provides the basis for arbitration legislation in more than 85 States in 118 jurisdictions, also dealing with arbitral procedures. Validity and enforceability of the arbitration award under the New York Convention and the Model Law can be considered in regard to Foresight.

The New York Convention at Article V(1)(b) references insufficient notice related to the appointment of an arbitrator, but also if enforcement may be refused if a party was "otherwise unable to present his case" as a means for setting side an award. While there is no uniform approach to interpreting and applying this provision, one summary from the English courts is instructive:

> If the tribunal is procedurally entitled to conduct its own investigations into the facts in an inquisitorial system, the effect of this provision would be to avoid enforcement if the award is based on facts derived from such investigations where the enforcee was not given a reasonable opportunity to present its case in relation to the results of the investigations.[17]

However, the New York Convention's position via Article V(1)(b) has generally been construed narrowly by national courts, in light of the New York Convention's goal of encouraging timely and efficient enforcement of awards.[18]

The Model Law at Article 18 simply states that "[t]he parties shall be treated with equality and each party shall be given a full opportunity of presenting his case." Article 34(2) references a standard of "minimum requirements" of due process not being met; indeed Article 34 is understood to be exclusive, and its annulment grounds are viewed

13. Oldenstam R., "Due Process Paranoia or Prudence?," in Axel Calissendorff and Patrik Schöldstrom (eds.), Stockholm Arbitration Yearbook 2019, at 121 (Kluwer Law International 2019).
14. Convention on the Recognition and Enforcement of Foreign Arbitral Awards (New York, June 10, 1958), 330 U.N.T.S. 3.
15. *Id.*
16. United Nations Commission on International Trade Law, UNCITRAL Model Law on International Commercial Arbitration, U.N. Doc. A/40/17, Annex I (1985).
17. *Minmetals Germany GmbH v. Ferco Steel Ltd*, [1999] 1 All E.R. (Comm) 315 (Q.B.) (Eng.).
18. Bermann G., "Recognition and Enforcement of Foreign Arbitral Awards: The Interpretation and Application of the New York Convention by National Courts," in George Bermann (ed.), Recognition and Enforcement of Foreign Arbitral Awards, vol. 23 (Springer 2017) and J. Arbisman, A. Genest and E. Giakoumakis, "Due Process and Procedural Irregularities," in The Guide to Challenging and Enforcing Arbitration Awards, 3rd ed., GAR, https://globalarbitrationreview.com/guide/the-guide-challenging-and-enforcing-arbitration-awards/3rd-edition/article/due-process-and-procedural-irregularities#footnote-030 (accessed March 11, 2024).

as permissive, not mandatory, allowing a court to annul an award if the Article 34(2) ground is met, but not requiring it to do so.[19] Article 36 on enforcement of arbitration awards mirrors Article V(1)(b) of the New York Convention.

7 Biasing the Tribunal

An arbitrator has a duty to remain neutral throughout the duration of the proceedings.[20]-[21] Critics of Foresight might disagree with an arbitrator, let alone an entire tribunal, expressing their views on any issue prior to receipt of all submissions from a party on an issue. However, this critique can be addressed with several responses.

Would be critics suggest that Foresight might amount to "prejudgment" of the issues in dispute. Most likely every member of the dispute community, and rightfully so, would be against prejudgment of disputes in arbitration such that an arbitrator came to a *final* conclusion before all of the submissions were made. Indeed, such:

> Prejudgment would seem to impede the very heart of the arbitral process, which presumes a quasi-judicial function of deciding legal claims after weighing evidence and argument. The lack of independence may create an imperfect arbitration, but prejudgment renders the process a sham formality, an unnecessary social cost.[22]

Foresight, however, is not prejudgment; rather, it is both non-binding and provisional by nature. This is plain by revisiting the principles espoused in describing the technique.

First, as a mechanism that the parties have mutually agreed to implement, they have empowered the tribunal with the ability to provide such insights and cannot therefore complain later if the tribunal decides to exercise such authority.

Second, the critique assumes that arbitrators do not maintain any position on the issues before them until all of the evidence has been submitted, the hearing held, and the final award being written. For a diligent arbitrator, this is certainly not the case; in fact, it is more likely that the tribunal's positions are constantly evolving throughout the proceedings. Does that point undercut Foresight? No, because Foresight would provide a single snapshot in time that is informed by the submissions made by the parties thus far. Therefore, Foresight would incentivize counsel to provide their most compelling arguments and evidence *earlier* in the process so that if an application for Foresight is received, then their client will be cast in a more favorable light. Naturally then, both parties would understand where they are currently placed before the

19. Gary B. Born, International Arbitration: Law and Practice 183-184 (3rd ed., Kluwer Law International 2021).
20. 6(1) BCDR International Arbitration Review 93-106 (2019), https://doi.org/10.54648/bcdr2021006 (accessed August 16, 2025).
21. R. Feehily, Neutrality, Independence and Impartiality in International Commercial Arbitration: A Fine Balance in the Quest for Arbitral Justice, 7 J. Int'l & Comp. Arb. 1 (February 2019).
22. W.W. Park, Arbitrator Integrity: The Transient and the Permanent, 46 San Diego L. Rev. 3 (2009).

tribunal and the things that they would be best served in addressing should the matter continue, and whether the case should continue at all.

As a final note as to arbitrator bias, as things currently stand in international arbitration, the tribunal already does have their opinions on certain matters before they issue the award. They may well discuss these issues among themselves throughout the proceedings and may cultivate their opinions on certain issues. These informal perspectives are not prejudicial merely for existing and do not magically amount to bias merely because the parties become aware of the tribunal's *preliminary* perspective. To the contrary, the entire process is enhanced by transparency because the parties are able to peer into the future to see how the case might go for them and what they can do to adjust their fates.

8 Opportunity to Fully Present Their Case

By its operation, Foresight does not prevent any party from fully pleading its case. If the parties do not resolve their dispute, then the process will follow its usual course to the issuance of an award. As referenced in the previous section, prejudgment is already a basis for disqualifying an arbitrator. If an arbitrator were to already have an immovable position on any point, regardless of what the parties submit to them, that person would be unfit to serve as an arbitrator and would be a jeopardy to the award.

Foresight embodies just the opposite notion. It says with clarity to the parties: *this is a preliminary perspective at a singular point in time and could be subject to change.* Whatever decisions a party makes after such insight would be solely their own in how they want to plead their case. Furthermore, they may well be more able to effectively present their case, understanding how the tribunal is responding to the pleadings thus far.

V CONCLUSION

1 Already Existing Forms of Arbitral Foresight

In addition to further imagining the role of the arbitrator in arbitral proceedings, the coining of the term "Arbitral Foresight" is the evolutionary manifestation of similar discussions about similar attributes from other voices in the field.

One example is in the 2018 Prague Rules at Article 2.4,[23] which provide that the arbitral tribunal:

> may at the case management conference or at any later stage of the arbitration, if it deems it appropriate, indicate to the parties:
>
> ...
>
> e. its preliminary views on:

23. Rules on the Efficient Conduct of Proceedings in International Arbitration (Prague Rules), December 14, 2018.

i. the allocation of the burden of proof between the parties;
ii. the relief sought;
iii. the disputed issues; and
iv. the weight and relevance of evidence submitted by the parties.

Expressing such preliminary perspectives shall not by itself be considered as evidence of the arbitral tribunal's lack of independence or impartiality, and cannot constitute grounds for disqualification.

Notably, the primary distinction between the Prague Rules' expression of arbitrator facilitation and Foresight is the party triggering the tribunal to provide its preliminary perspectives. By placing that duty with one or both parties, even if one party objects, there is little room to suggest that the tribunal is acting outside of its mandate.

The rules from the Centre for Effective Dispute Resolution ("CEDR") at Article 5 also provide a framework for arbitrator facilitation which tracks many of the tenants described herein.[24]

Further still, some national legal regimes already empower judges to provide preliminary perspectives of the submissions before them, for example, the German "Güteverhandlung" process,[25] or the Swiss "Referentenaudienz."[26] In each of those examples, not only do the judges provide their opinions before the final submissions before the parties but the litigants also welcome these perspectives as they give a weighted push for the parties down the path of settlement rather than protracted legal proceedings. Even in common law jurisdictions, there has been a trend toward judges using pre-trial conferences to actively resolve disputes. In these instances, national courts in the United States[27] and in the United Kingdom[28] are encouraged to actively manage their cases.

2 Summary

In the television gameshow *Deal or No Deal*, contestants try their hand at selecting cases, attempting to find the one that has USD 1 million. After every few selections, they get a call from the mysterious "Banker" who attempts to get them to stop playing in exchange for his offer. The Banker's offer is never binding, and the contestant could play to their benefit, and sometimes to their detriment. The point is that at each milestone in the game, they were given off-ramps to end it. Arbitration in its current iteration is stuck in the quagmire of often being too slow and too expensive for what clients want.

24. Centre for Effective Dispute Resolution, Arbitration Rules (2021), https://www.cedr.com/alternative-dispute-resolution-processes/arbitration/rules/ (accessed August 16, 2025).
25. J.H. Langbein, "The German Advantage in Civil Procedure," 52 U. Chi. L. Rev. 823 (1985).
26. A. Kozmenko and L. Grosel, "Settlement Facilitation by the Arbitral Tribunal: A Swiss Perspective," Arbitration.ru (February 1, 2021), https://journal.arbitration.ru/analytics/settlement-facilitation-by-the-arbitral-tribunal-a-swiss-perspective/ (accessed August 16, 2025).
27. Pursuant to 18 C.F.R. § 385.603 (2024).
28. Hogan Loveels, Alternative Dispute Resolution in England and Wales (October 2017).

Foresight is a solution. It is a response to the ever-increasing chorus of demands for a more efficient world of dispute resolution. No client is pleased to be in arbitration, and while it is understood that commercial disputes are part of the cost of doing business, most clients are ever searching for ways to resolve disputes and cut cost and time.

It is appreciated that there are legitimate concerns as to jeopardizing the award with prejudgment or the infection of arbitrator bias. However, these are already sins that if an arbitrator is prone to, they would be likely to commit regardless of the attributes of Foresight. In addition, due process is not harmed by Foresight. This superpower of Foresight is something that goes to the heart of why tribunals are constituted in the first place, to assist the parties in resolving their dispute.

CHAPTER 4

The Arbitrator and the Human Factor

Elliott Geisinger[*]

TABLE OF CONTENTS

> Socrates: Writing, Phaedrus, has this strange quality, and is very like painting; for the creatures of painting stand like living beings, but if one asks them a question, they preserve a solemn silence. And so it is with written words; you might think they spoke as if they had intelligence, but if you question them, wishing to know about their sayings, they always say only one and the same thing. And every word, when once it is written, is bandied about, alike among those who understand and those who have no interest in it, and it knows not to whom to speak or not to speak; when ill-treated or unjustly reviled it always needs its father to help it; for it has no power to protect or help itself.[1]

I INTRODUCTION

Last summer, having submitted his expression of interest to be a speaker at this ICCA Congress, the author stumbled upon this quote by Plato (yes, the author's recreational

* Elliott Geisinger is partner at Schellenberg Wittmer Ltd, where he heads the international arbitration practice. He has been practising international arbitration since 1994. This pre-conference paper expands (considerably) on the author's Swiss Arbitration Association (ASA) President's Message, *It's the People Stupid*, 36 ASA Bulletin 4/2018 (December), pp. 815-817. The reader having an occasional sense of *déjà vu* will, it is hoped, be forgiving.

1. Plato, *Phaedrus*, from Plato in Twelve Volumes, Vol. 9 translated by Harold N. Fowler. Cambridge, MA, Harvard University Press; London, William Heinemann Ltd. 1925, p. 275.

reading includes materials referring to ancient Greek philosophers). It leapt off the page, for it encapsulates in the author's view one of the very core aspects of this panel's topic; and the author made a promise to himself that, if he were to have the honour of being selected, he would begin his chapter and his speech with a somewhat misleading pseudo-demonstration of a level of culture that your servant does not possess.

What, the reader may wonder, is the connection between the human factor in arbitral justice and an imaginary dialogue between Socrates and an ancient Athenian aristocrat?[2] The answer lies in the apparent sterility, the muteness of the written text, which, without its parent, is helpless (and presumably unhelpful) if questioned. By extrapolation, one could say the same of justice: it could all be in writing, dehumanised, dematerialised into the ethernet, but rendered helpless (and very likely unhelpful) if questioned. Just like the written text, justice needs its parent, the dispenser of justice, to have a full meaning; and the dispenser of justice needs the parents of the materials before it truly to understand the matter. It is submitted that arbitral justice is no exception.

This chapter will put forward this proposition from two perspectives. First, it will address the human factor seen from the arbitrator's perspective, and examine how arbitrators need the help of the actual human beings before them, be it the parties, witnesses or expert witnesses, to have a true (or, at least, the truest possible) picture of the case (section II below). Second, it will take the opposite perspective, that of the parties, and examine which human qualities of arbitrators are expected for the process to be true 'justice' (section III below).

II THE HUMAN FACTOR SEEN FROM THE ARBITRATOR'S PERSPECTIVE

Arbitration can, of course, be a process in which human contact[3] between the arbitral tribunal on the one hand and parties, their witnesses and experts on the other hand may be limited (one thinks of documents-only procedures, known to several institutional rules, especially in the context of expedited proceedings),[4] or even inexistent (as will generally be the case in online arbitration).[5] If and when (more likely when than if) AI-driven justice truly develops, human interaction in the process will be even more limited. Where the parties have agreed to such procedures, this choice should be respected and adhered to; this chapter does not suggest otherwise. What is less

2. Apart from the fact that Phaedrus had his own brush with justice – Athenian justice – that forced him to flee his native city-state after an indictment for profanation of the Eleusinian Mysteries.
3. For avoidance of any doubt, while the author believes firmly that in-person contact (as opposed to contact via video link) is by far more conducive to actual understanding, the author is not submitting that this contact *must* take place in person. The relative merits of in-person and remote meetings and examination are a different topic, which will not be addressed here.
4. *See*, for instance: Article 42.2(e) of the 2018 HKIAC Administered Arbitration Rules; Article 5.2(c) of the SIAC Arbitration Rules 2016; Article 42.2(d) of the 2021 Swiss Rules of International Arbitration; Article 3(5) of Appendix VI, Expedited Procedure Rules, to the 2021 ICC Rules of Arbitration.
5. *See*, for instance, Article 13 of the ICANN Rules for Uniform Domain Name Dispute Resolution Policy (UDRP).

straightforward is the question of whether parties that agree in advance to such procedures fully weigh what they are foregoing. And this balance-of-pros-and-cons issue becomes even more acute where there is no such advance agreement, but where a curtailment of direct human contact is envisaged after the proceedings have commenced. This section aims to describe the content of one of the bowls in the scales: the human factor, seen from the arbitrator's perspective.

1 The Human Factor and the Arbitrators' Understanding of the Case

The proposition that the author is offering up to critical scrutiny and debate is the following: arbitrators do not have a full picture of the case before them – and therefore truly to dispense justice – without having the benefit of the human factor. In this context, what is meant by the 'human factor'?

First, it is submitted that the arbitrator must have taken the time to actually see and hear the parties *personally*.[6] Of course, this proposition has a clear weakness: it is necessarily subjective, because what is seen to be necessary for a proper understanding of the case will inevitably vary from one individual arbitrator to another.

That said, all disputes arise from human behaviour. Even disputes between corporations or disputes involving states stem from: (i) decisions taken by human beings and (ii) how other human beings reacted to these decisions. Human decision-making is a field of vast philosophical and scientific research; the same applies to the study of human responses to the decisions of others. There is neither time nor space to address these matters here.[7] Suffice it to state that, without direct contact with the makers and addressees of human decisions, one is lacking information which might or might not be useful. Referring to Socrates' remark that writing is akin to painting, the same could be said of parties' submissions. By this, the author is not referring to the factual narrative and legal developments, which are drafted by the parties' counsel, but to the *fundamental message* that the parties' submissions intend to convey.

This is particularly true in the context of international arbitration, where parties frequently hail from very different cultural backgrounds, with different approaches to freedom of decision and communication. The papers of other speakers cover this aspect in detail. Suffice it here to mention a few examples.

For instance, in several civil-law jurisdictions, intentional breach of contract renders unenforceable contractual limitations or exclusions of liability.[8] A party may decide to breach a contract deliberately if it believes that it is in its economic interest to do so. However, what may seem like a deliberate decision based on a cold-blooded assessment of economic interest in certain societies may, in other societies, be the only choice left to save face when confronted by behaviour that is deemed to be provocative. Likewise, in certain cultures, the perpetuation of a mutually beneficial relationship (generally commercial, but sometimes simply personal) is more important than the language of a contract. A party that insists too bluntly on the letter of the contract may

6. The disclaimer made in (n 3) is repeated here.
7. In any event, the author would be woefully unqualified even to attempt to do so.
8. *See*, for instance, Article 100(1) of the Swiss Code of Obligations.

thus be acting, in the eyes of the other party, in an incomprehensible or even inappropriate or offensive manner without knowing it, and be seen by the other party as being the one that is in breach. In other words, the paradigm for deliberate breach may be a variable depending on the parties' respective cultural environments. Whether this will ultimately be legally relevant is another matter. The point being made here is that an arbitral tribunal that does not even attempt to explore and understand this type of issue runs the risk of being at best culturally insensitive, at worst of failing to discharge a key part of its duties as an *international* arbitral tribunal.

There is more: the quote from *Phaedrus* made at the start of this chapter applies most obviously to documentary evidence.

Of course, it does not apply to *all* documentary evidence. A test report on commissioning, signed jointly by the parties, attesting that an air-conditioning and ventilation system actually does deliver an air-renewal rate in excess of the contractually stipulated minimum requirements may be just a painting, but rarely will there be a need to question what it means.[9]

However, rare are the arbitrations in which the reasons for decisions or omissions or statements made in writing are *not* crucial to the case. In fact, while counsel are generally trained never to ask witnesses *why* they wrote this or that, this question is routinely put to witnesses by arbitrators – so routinely, in fact, that the question *must* be of interest for the tribunal. Similarly, arbitrators frequently discern (or believe to discern) discrepancies or even contradictions between documents authored by the same person. And just as frequently, a direct human discussion with the authors and/or the addressees of these apparently contradictory documents either dispels what was a misunderstanding by the arbitrator or highlights a true contradiction.

To put it differently, while contemporaneous documentary evidence is unquestionably one of the most reliable forms of evidence for arbitrators – perhaps even *the* most reliable one[10] – it needs to be approached with caution. Arbitrators need to be aware of their own limitations, and while they may be generally intelligent creatures (or believe themselves to be), they will invariably need guidance in order to understand the documentary record properly. The author submits that human contacts with those who were involved in originating and in digesting the written record is the only way of obtaining this necessary guidance.

Finally, arbitrators having a complete understanding of the subject matter of expert evidence based simply on their study, no matter how thorough, of the expert materials on record are rare creatures indeed. One of the roles of expert witnesses is to enlighten the arbitral tribunal. Enlightenment without any direct contact between the dispenser and the beneficiary seems, to the author, to be an oxymoron.

9. The author's very first experience with construction arbitration concerned, *inter alia*, a matter where a test report on these very issues actually did *not* mean what was written in it. The example was thus not chosen innocently.
10. This observation regrettably carries with it a certain degree of cultural bias, since in many cultures the conservation of documents 'for the record' does not have the importance it has in Western societies.

All of these remarks can be summarised in one observation: arbitrators need to be modest and to acknowledge the limits of their own abilities, and turning to the parties for guidance is a key tool for doing this.

2 The Human Factor and the Arbitrators' Weighing of the Evidence

Apart from understanding what the case is about, what brought about the dispute, what the messages are that the parties are conveying to the tribunal and what the evidence means, arbitral tribunals will, of course, at the end of the day, need to weigh the evidence and reach their findings. In this context, *credibility* is paramount.

Of course, one will always find examples of cases where credibility is not difficult to gauge (negatively): factual assertions in a first round of submissions that are completely contradicted by documents obtained in subsequent document disclosure; legal submissions replete with references to authorities that say the opposite of what they are argued to say; selective quotes from the documentary evidence or from legal authorities that are crude to the point of childishness; witnesses who, in their written witness statements, make assertions that are completely at odds with the contemporaneous evidence; etc. Parties that resort to these means invariably torpedo their own case, so that direct assistance from the 'parents' of the written text will do little, if anything, to salvage these parties' credibility in the eyes of arbitrators.

However – and very happily – this remains the exception and, far more often than not, the assessment of credibility *does* require a direct contact between the arbitrators on the one hand and, on the other hand, the parties, the witnesses and the expert witnesses (especially the witnesses and the experts). This point is so obvious that the author will not dwell on it.

What should be just as obvious but is sometimes (and perhaps too frequently) overlooked is that, when assessing credibility, arbitrators must never forget that they are dealing with human beings, who have their own 'cultural DNA', and that this 'cultural DNA' may be very different from that of the arbitrators. Thus, arbitrators must make the additional effort of understanding that a '*no*' does not come as easily in certain cultures as in others; that silence may mean opprobrium to some while it may mean acquiescence to others; that any given style of examination (not only cross-examination but also tribunal questions) may be offensive to some and make an otherwise forthcoming witness uncooperative; that 'answering the question' can mean different things in different cultures; etc. This means that there is a considerable overlap between the effort needed to understand the case, the evidence, the technical issues described above, and the effort needed properly to assess credibility. And this effort consists in making *human* contact, in seeking to understand what is truly going on in the hearing room, before jumping to any conclusions – especially conclusions that may be rooted in a cultural bias held by the arbitrator.

3 Conclusion on the Human Factor Seen from the Arbitrator's Perspective

Flexibility is in the nature of arbitration; and this well-worn platitude means, in this context, that arbitrators may well decide, in a given individual case, that there is no need for any direct human contact with the parties, their witnesses or their experts. And in any given individual case, that may well be entirely justified.

However, the author submits that any such decision must, at a minimum, be weighed carefully against the gains that arbitrators may achieve by having a direct human contact with the parties. It is all very well to be 'efficient', if 'efficiency' means being as cost- and time-'efficient' as possible. 'Efficiency' is, after all, another fundamental selling point of arbitration. However, the temptation to be (or appear to be) 'efficient' must not lead to sacrifices in quality to which the parties have *not* agreed, or not agreed in full realisation of what they were potentially doing. Indeed, what use is a cost- and time-'efficient' process if its 'efficiency' is achieved at the cost of a true understanding of the case?

There is hardly an arbitration practitioner on this planet who will not recall a case in which a discussion with the parties, their witnesses and/or their experts shed light, sometimes considerably or even decisively so, on what the dispute was about and how it arose, on the actual meaning of the documentary record, on the intricacies covered by expert evidence and, last but far from least, on weight and credibility of the evidence (in particular the testimonial and expert evidence) before the tribunal.[11] Of course, this will not be true for every case, but can one really renounce this possibility in advance? Turning again to philosophy (and being acutely aware of the difference in magnitude of the stakes involved), the issue here resembles Pascal's wager: can arbitrators afford not to believe in the gains they might achieve by having at least one direct contact with the parties, the witnesses and the experts? The author submits that the answer to this question is, '*No*'.

III THE HUMAN FACTOR SEEN FROM THE PARTIES' PERSPECTIVE

Taking now the reverse perspective, that of the parties, it is submitted that the 'human factor' is essential not only for the soundness and integrity of the proceedings in each individual case, but also for the future of arbitration itself. The author will illustrate this proposition by considering first the arbitral tribunal *in toto* (which should be understood as referring also to sole arbitrators) and then the specific case of the party-appointed co-arbitrator.

11. For a fascinating – frequently captivating – collection of examples and analyses of these benefits, *see* Ehle and Baizeau (eds), *Stories from the Hearing Room: Experience from Arbitral Practice. Essays in Honour of Michael E. Schneider*, Kluwer 2014.

1 The Human Factor and the Arbitral Tribunal *in Toto*

It is submitted here that the very first task to which an arbitral tribunal must apply itself is to create an atmosphere of *trust*. After all, the very reason why the parties are before a tribunal or a sole arbitrator is that they *chose* to be there; and being able to choose arbitrators in whom the parties can place their trust remains one of the main reasons why parties arbitrate in the first place.[12] This is a fundamental difference between arbitrators and judges, as the latter's position flows from the law and owes nothing to the parties' choice.

The philosophical question whether trust is earned or given (or neither) is currently the subject of much debate. The author submits that, for arbitral tribunals, it is *both*.

Trust is of course *given* by virtue of the parties' choice of the arbitrators – for otherwise their choice would have alighted on someone else. This form of trust is abstract: it may be based on prior experience with an arbitrator, on recommendation by someone having first-hand prior experience, on perusal of peer reviews, on reputation alone or on a combination of these factors. It is 'abstract' because arbitrators who are chosen are vested with a party's (or all parties') trust without having yet taken any action by which that trust could have been earned for the individual case at hand.

This initial 'abstract' trust constitutes a sort 'capital' of trust that arbitrators must continue to earn and even nurture as the case proceeds.

The first step in this trust-earning process should be the very first case management conference. It is highly recommended that parties participate in this first case management conference for a number of excellent reasons; the fostering and nurturing of concrete trust is perhaps one of the less frequently mentioned ones. And yet it should be obvious that, unless the proceedings involve early hearings (e.g., on urgent interim measures), the first case management conference is generally the *only* opportunity for the parties to have any direct human contact with the arbitral tribunal before either a second case management conference that takes place after the initial exchanges of written submissions or, worse, before a hearing on jurisdiction and/or on the merits.

This direct human contact as a trust-building and trust-earning exercise at a first case management conference will, of course, consist in the arbitral tribunal demonstrating its professionalism, its mastery of the (by definition limited) case file in its possession and its willingness to adapt the proceedings to come to the specific needs of the individual case. That, however, is the starting point, a strict minimum. What is just as important, especially in a multi-cultural dispute, is for the arbitral tribunal to demonstrate *human* skills. These human skills include cultural sensitivity, a point that cannot be overemphasised. This can consist in little things, but little things can go a long way. For example, the author recalls Turkish clients who were impressed by the fact that the chairperson opened the case management conference by greeting the parties in their own respective languages (neither of which was the language of the

12. *See*, for instance, Queen Mary University of London, *Future of International Energy Arbitration Survey Report*, published 20 January 2023, question 30 and pp. 30-31.

arbitration), even if the pronunciation was perfectible. Another example of trust-fostering was where the arbitral tribunal was aware of the fact that academic titles were of great importance in the home country of certain party representatives and went out of its way to address them using their titles. At the opposite end of the spectrum, the author recalls with dismay a case management conference attended by his Muslim clients, at which the sole arbitrator's office had the incongruous idea of organising a buffet consisting mainly of pork. To quote a well-known (if difficult to attribute) phrase, trust is easier to lose than to earn, and this occurrence regrettably had precisely that effect, for it conveyed an impression of adverse cultural bias.

Trust-earning (or trust-fostering) in the further course of the proceedings, after the first case management conference, could be the subject of a book. This chapter will therefore address only two selected aspects.

The first aspect is that the arbitral tribunal must demonstrate its willingness and ability to make the extra effort outlined in the first part of this chapter (which will not be repeated here), to establish a true human contact and to be aware of cultural differences or particularities. This is an ongoing effort that all arbitrators must make at all times. It is particularly important at hearings, which, as mentioned above, are the best opportunity for human contact. However, it should also be the norm for written communications. To take an obvious example, arbitrators can squander considerable trust capital by setting deadlines falling on Fridays for Muslim parties, or more generally, that fall during holidays (especially religious holidays) in the country where the party concerned is based (the same applies to legal teams). It does not appear to be asking too much from arbitrators that they avoid this kind of cultural tone-deafness. By contrast, arbitrators who prove at all times that they are keenly aware of such issues effectively nurture the human trust placed in them.

The second aspect selected here is an indispensable degree of polite firmness. At the start of the process, the arbitral tribunal and the parties agree on a set of rules on the conduct of the proceedings – and where there is no agreement, the tribunal lays down those rules. Once adopted, these rules must be adhered to. Of course, there are many situations in which a certain degree of procedural flexibility is justified or even diplomatically astute.[13] However, there are few things that are more disconcerting, even poisonous, from the parties' perspective than arbitral tribunals that do not uphold their own rules. Where a party acts in disregard of the rules of the game and thereby threatens to derail the process, the party that *does* play by the book invariably loses faith in the tribunal, and ultimately in the entire process. To put it differently, in order to maintain and nurture trust, arbitrators must at all costs avoid treating the process like a popularity contest. A firm hand, clad in a velvet glove, is always a trusted hand.

2 The Human Factor and the Party-Appointed Co-Arbitrator

Of course, everything that has just been said about the arbitral tribunal *in toto* (and, by implication, about the sole arbitrator) applies in full to party-appointed co-arbitrators.

13. The author outlined a few of these issues in another ASA President's Message, *No Solomon Please, We're Arbitrators*, 34 ASA Bulletin 4/2016 (December), pp. 825-831, at pp. 830-831.

However, the party-appointed co-arbitrator is the only member of the tribunal that a party nominates or appoints *alone*. The author submits that this circumstance creates a heightened level of trust into which the human factor necessarily flows. Like it or not, in the eyes of the nominating party, the party-appointed co-arbitrator is vested with a higher degree of trust than any other member of the tribunal. It is submitted that this enhanced level of trust carries with it heightened responsibilities for the party-appointed co-arbitrator.

For avoidance of any doubt, the author is not implying in any way that the co-arbitrator nominated or appointed by a party is or should act as that party's representative, let alone advocate, within the tribunal. That is anathema – in addition to being egregiously stupid. The heightened responsibilities referred to here are much subtler, and most importantly of all, they are all entirely within the boundaries of any arbitrator's obligations of independence and impartiality.

Coming back to the need for awareness of cultural sensitivity described in the first part of this chapter, a co-arbitrator is often selected precisely *because* they have an understanding of the culture of the nominating party. This may result in the nomination of a co-arbitrator having the same nationality or religion or ethnic background as the nominating party, but also more simply of a co-arbitrator who, for whatever reason, is familiar with the nominating party's culture. This means, it is submitted, that this co-arbitrator has a duty to ensure that the other arbitrators have a proper understanding of the nominating party's background. This can extend to a broad spectrum of issues: understanding the party's approach to the case; understanding how certain written positions come about (especially with regard to social or corporate hierarchy issues); understanding the demeanour of a party representative or a witness on the stand; etc.[14]

Very importantly, it is submitted that this duty of the party-appointed co-arbitrator extends to ensuring that no decision of the arbitral tribunal could convey, rightly or wrongly, an impression of cultural bias because of a culturally *gauche* formulation. This remark applies to procedural orders, which if drafted in a culturally tone-deaf manner can provoke resentment that could otherwise easily be avoided. It applies *a fortiori* to awards, which must eschew language that could be perceived, rightly or wrongly, as offensive.[15] In this regard, it is submitted that the party-appointed co-arbitrator should serve as a form of 'editor' to ensure that none of this occurs.[16]

However, the party-appointed co-arbitrator and the party having nominated that arbitrator must also be aware of the fact that the *other* party or parties and the other

14. Of course, if a party-appointed sole arbitrator believes that the tribunal is remiss on any of these points vis-à-vis *any* party, including the opponent of the party having nominated that co-arbitrator, that co-arbitrator has a duty to draw the arbitral tribunal's attention to this circumstance. However, this is a duty owed generally to the arbitral process; it does not flow from the relationship of trust between an arbitrator and the nominating party.
15. To take an example from the author's experience, it suffices for an award to state that the pace of a subcontractor's progress was insufficient or more simply that the subcontractor's works were delayed without the subcontractor having provided any justification. It is not necessary to write that the subcontractor in question was '*progressing its works at a snail's pace*'.
16. The remark made at (n 13) applies also in this context.

members of the arbitral tribunal are equally aware of this heightened level of trust between an arbitrator and the party having nominated or appointed that arbitrator. This, it is submitted, entails a duty of that arbitrator to avoid creating any appearance of bias in favour of the nominating party. As a general proposition, this seems both unobjectionable and banal. However, the practical implications can be subtle.

This is best illustrated by a personal experience of the author (who, despite appearances to the contrary, has little affection for war stories). The author was nominated in ICC proceedings by a respondent that was resisting payment claims on the basis of allegations of corruption. There were several troubling documents in the contemporaneous documentary evidence. In preparation of the hearing, the author had prepared no less than sixteen pages of questions on these documents for the claimant's witnesses (who had authored them), but did not expect to need to ask them as he anticipated that counsel for the respondent would do so in cross-examination. In the event and much to the author's surprise, none of these questions were asked. This led to an awkward situation: the tribunal could hardly leave these questions unasked – the arbitrators would arguably have been taking a legal risk of their own if they had sat passively like three see-no-evil, hear-no-evil, speak-no-evil monkeys. However, had the author simply gone ahead and put these questions to the claimant's witnesses at the end of cross-examination, he would certainly have created an impression of bias – the questions were not in favour of the claimant – thereby potentially compromising the integrity of the proceedings. The issue was resolved very simply: the presiding arbitrator reviewed the sixteen pages of questions and put to the witnesses those questions he saw fit.

Of course, the decision of the author not to put his questions and, instead, to consult with the other members of the tribunal in order to find a better solution was dictated by a general sense of duty towards the integrity of the arbitral process. However, it was also driven by a sense of duty towards the nominating party not to do anything that might appear to be crossing a red line, as this would have potentially damaged the trust placed in him by that party.

IV CONCLUSION

Very much can be written about arbitrators and the 'human factor'. This chapter only scratches the surface.

That said, especially with the development of artificial intelligence, there are few current subjects of greater importance than the deeply *human* nature of international arbitration. An understanding of what this means, from the point of view of arbitrators and that of parties, and an intelligent use of that understanding are essential for the health of arbitration today. Perhaps most of all, they will determine the future of international arbitration as a means of achieving truly *human* justice. It is hoped that this chapter, and more importantly the discussions to take place at the 2024 ICCA Congress in Hong Kong, will provide further food for thought and shine a guiding light for all.

CHAPTER 5

'The Arbitrator': Re-establishing Trust in a Changing Arbitration Landscape

João Ilhão Moreira[*]

TABLE OF CONTENTS

I INTRODUCTION

The ongoing debate surrounding the role of artificial intelligence (AI) in dispute resolution raises fundamental questions about the future of human involvement in arbitration. With AI's promise of creating a fully rational system capable of producing increasingly complex answers, there is speculation that human judges and arbitrators may eventually become obsolete. This speculation has prompted a deeper examination of whether the law is solely a product of rational decision-making or if it embodies unique human qualities beyond the reach of AI.

These questions, however, are not entirely new. Throughout the nineteenth and twentieth centuries, legal scholars and practitioners have grappled with ensuring that the administration of justice is not merely a product of the subjective whims of

* João Ilhão Moreira is an Associate Professor of Civil Procedure Law at the Faculty of Law of the University of Macau, Associate Director of the Center for Studies on Jurisprudence and Legislation of China and Portuguese-Speaking Countries.

decision-makers but is grounded in principles of fairness, impartiality, and procedural integrity. At the same time, the influence of human nature on legal decisions has been ever more understood as inevitable, with the idea of fully rational legal decisions being increasingly described as fiction. This historical discourse has laid the groundwork for contemporary discussions on the interplay between AI and human elements in legal decision-making.

AI will likely change how arbitrators and practitioners approach dispute resolution and legal work. Therefore, the rise of AI and its potential applications in dispute resolution invite revisiting the place of human arbitrators within the arbitration system, prompting a closer examination of the unique qualities and responsibilities of human arbitrators in upholding the legitimacy of the arbitral system. For the time being, and likely for the foreseeable future, arbitration will remain dependent on humans, and therefore, recentring our understanding of how human nature influences the nature of decisions and proceedings is paramount.

Against this background, the recent ICCA Hong Kong Congress, titled 'International Arbitration: A Human Endeavour', was a most welcome addition to the discourse on the human-centric nature of arbitration. As a whole, it celebrated the critical human elements underpinning the arbitral process' legitimacy and effectiveness, revisiting these ideas using both doctrinal and socio-legal lenses. This approach aligns with a longstanding jurisprudential tradition that seeks to make the application of the law more rational and transparent by considering the vast number of elements rather than solely relying on the perceived objectivity of the law.

Within the Congress, the panel discussion on 'The Arbitrator' at the ICCA Hong Kong Congress Plenary provided invaluable insights into the challenges and opportunities arbitrators face in this evolving landscape. Moderated by Chiann Bao, the panel session 'The Arbitrator' featured esteemed figures in international arbitration, such as Justice Mimmie Chan, Neil Kaplan CBE KC SBS, and VK Rajah. Commentators included Aisha Abdallah, Partner at ALN Kenya Anjarwalla & Khanna (Nairobi Head Office), Christopher M. Campbell, Senior Litigation Counsel for Baker Hughes, and Elliott Geisinger, Head of Schellenberg Wittmer's International Arbitration Group.

The panel discussion delved deeply into the core issues surrounding the role of arbitrators in international arbitration. In a thoughtful and wide-ranging dialogue, the panellists revisited several crucial topics that shape the arbitration process. This included examining arbitrators' responsibility in upholding procedural fairness, the dynamics behind the appointment of arbitrators, and how the competitive arbitration market can influence arbitrator behaviour. By exploring these different facets, a unifying theme emerged – the paramount importance of trust. The panellists emphasised that arbitrators must work to cultivate and project an essential aura of trustworthiness, as this is a fundamental expectation that parties have of the arbitral proceedings.

By exploring the central role of trust in the arbitral process, the panellists illuminated how arbitrators can cultivate and maintain the legitimacy of arbitration through their conduct, decision-making, and engagement with the parties. This analysis offers a timely contribution to the ongoing discourse on the future of international arbitration, underscoring the enduring importance of the human element in dispute resolution.

II BUILDING TRUST THROUGH PROCEDURAL FAIRNESS

A core tenet highlighted by the panellists was the critical role of procedural fairness in cultivating trust between the arbitrator and the parties. Chiann Bao kicked off the discussion by underscoring that trust is the inherent feeling that validates the system's legitimacy. Indeed, ultimately, any dispute resolution mechanism is only valuable if parties and society at large generally accept the validity of its decisions and agree to be bound by its outcomes. VK Rajah, however, elucidated the fundamental distinctions between the judicial system and arbitration. The judicial system is inherently perceived as legitimate, with the parties regarding the judge as having the 'backing of the state'. Conversely, arbitrators must 'actively' earn the trust of the parties themselves, particularly when at least two arbitrators are not appointed by one of the parties.

Current literature suggests that arbitrators' urge to render decisions that fully accord with principles of due process largely reflects the gradual 'judicialisation' of arbitration.[1] This is to say that the increasing pressure on arbitrators to respect all procedural rights of parties fully has transformed arbitral proceedings closer to judicial proceedings. However, arbitrators still differ fundamentally from judges,[2] thus making it more challenging for arbitrators to build trust with the parties compared to how judges do. Hence, conducting a functional analysis of the adjudicative features of the two systems is crucial to offer better insights into how arbitrators could appropriately establish trust with the parties involved.[3]

One significant difference between judges and arbitrators is the administration of the process.[4] Judges adhere to rigid rules of civil procedure and evidence, whereas, subject to party agreement, arbitrators have larger discretion to determine the applicable procedures. Regarding the flexibility in articulating the procedures, Neil Kaplan stressed the importance of procedural fairness, highlighting that, unlike judges who operate within established court rules, arbitrators often begin with a 'virtual clean slate' when designing the arbitral process. This presents both a challenge and an

1. Catherine A Rogers, 'Regulating International Arbitrators: A Functional Approach to Developing Standards of Conduct' (2004) 41 Stanford Journal of International Law 67; Charles N Brower and Richard B Lillich, *International Arbitration in the 21st Century: Toward 'Judicialization' and Conformity?* (Brill | Nijhoff 2023) https://brill.com/view/title/13935 (accessed 16 August 2025); Alan S Rau and Edward F Sherman, 'Tradition and Innovation in International Arbitration Procedure' (1995) 30 Texas International Law Journal 89, 95; 'The New Dispute Settlers (Half) Truths and Consequences', *The Globalization of International Law* (1st ed., Routledge 2017) 405, 411-415.
2. *See* Susan Franck, 'The Liability of International Arbitrators: A Comparative Analysis and Proposal for Qualified Immunity' (2000) 20 New York Law School Journal of International and Comparative Law 1, 23-24; Susan Franck, 'The Role of International Arbitrators' (2006) 12 ILSA Journal of International & Comparative Law 499, 507.
3. Franck, 'The Role of International Arbitrators' (n 2) 508.
4. *Ibid.*, 512. *See also* Carlos G Garcia, 'All the Other Dirty Little Secrets: Investment Treaties, Latin America, and the Necessary Evil of Investor-State Arbitration' (2004) 16 Florida Journal of International Law 301, 301, 322-323.

opportunity for arbitrators to establish trust. Kaplan emphasised the importance of the initial meeting with the parties, where the arbitrator can demonstrate their commitment to fairness and willingness to provide a transparent procedure. He argued that maintaining this approach throughout the arbitration, especially when dealing with complex or controversial issues, is crucial to ensure that even a losing party feels the process is fair and that the arbitrator can be trusted. Rajah suggested that while procedural sensitivity is essential for arbitrators to build trust with the parties, it must be balanced with the responsibility to maintain the integrity of the process. When dealing with parties who may not be acting in good faith, arbitrators should not excessively 'mollycoddle' the party acting in bad faith at the expense of the party arbitrating properly. Rajah sees this as a delicate balance where trust, legitimacy, and respect are interconnected.

While the previous discussion suggested that arbitrators have to 'actively' earn trust themselves, Elliott Geisinger added a key point. Geisinger noted that trust is initially given but needs to be continuously maintained in the context of the relationship between parties and arbitrators. Geisinger used the analogy of a flower that requires daily watering to highlight the importance of the arbitral tribunal in guiding the parties and the significance of establishing a set of rules at the beginning of the arbitration. He emphasised the detrimental effects of a party disregarding the rules, as it undermines the tribunal's authority and creates a sense of unfairness for the party that follows the rules. Geisinger also explained that parties would feel more assured when tribunals consistently enforce their rules, which is crucial for building trust.

III TRUST IN APPOINTMENTS AND RE-APPOINTMENTS: BALANCING NEUTRALITY AND CAREER DEVELOPMENT

The panel also discussed the delicate balance that arbitrators must strike between maintaining neutrality, taking a more proactive role in shaping the proceedings and the pressures arising from an increasingly competitive arbitration market. As mentioned by Justice Mimmie Chan, judges are not 'candidates of choice' and need not be concerned about future appointment prospects that might influence their decision. However, this is not the case for arbitrators.

In the arbitrator marketplace, professional credibility and word-of-mouth recommendations significantly affect the appointment and re-appointment of arbitrators.[5] For those 'repeat-players', reputation and credibility as a fair, independent, and reasoned decision-maker are vital. Parties are likely to be unwilling to appoint an arbitrator who is liable to be challenged, cannot fully consider the facts and laws at

5. Jack Coe, 'Toward a Complementary Use of Conciliation In Investor-State Disputes: A Preliminary Sketch' (2005) 12 University of California Davis Journal of International Law and Policy; *see* Andrew T Guzman, 'Arbitrator Liability: Reconciling Arbitration and Mandatory Rules' (2000) 49 Duke Law Journal 1279, 1303-1306 https://doi.org/10.2307/1373012 (accessed 16 August 2025); Carole Silver, 'Models of Quality for Third Parties in Alternative Dispute Resolution' 12 Ohio State Journal on Dispute Resolution 37, 82-85.

issue, and may be incapable of rendering an enforceable award.[6] Conversely, newcomers or 'one-shot-arbitrators' who may not be aware of these market mechanisms present a much greater challenge. There may be 'toxic' arbitrators who leak confidential tribunal deliberations to parties, and such disclosures may put a party, who may be dissatisfied with the application of the law to the facts, in a position to disrupt proceedings or challenge the award.[7]

Kaplan, who has been both a judge and an arbitrator, noted that the concern with being appointed versus not appointed tends to fade with time, especially for more experienced practitioners. However, he acknowledged that this consideration could be more significant for newer arbitrators, where the issue of being a 'candidate of choice' may be more relevant. Indeed, an over-concern with re-appointments can sometimes cause arbitrators to forget the importance of that initial perception of neutrality, particularly for those new to the field.

One potential solution to address the abovementioned concerns around arbitrator conduct is to leverage market-based incentives related to compensation.[8] Legislators can, for instance, explore regulatory approaches to reinforce this delicate balance. For example, laws can further detail rules on liability, namely to prevent arbitrators from receiving any remuneration if they have been removed from a case due to improper conduct.[9] This type of targeted regulation could create a solid financial disincentive for arbitrators to stray from the principles of neutrality and fairness. By linking compensation directly to an arbitrator's adherence to ethical standards, the market-based system could encourage self-regulation and heighten the sense of professional responsibility among members of the arbitration community. Such measures could further bolster trust between the arbitrators and the parties involved in the dispute resolution process. Ultimately, preserving the perception and reality of impartiality is crucial for the legitimacy and effectiveness of the arbitration framework.

IV THE IMPORTANCE OF ARBITRATOR DIVERSITY AND REPRESENTATION

Another key focus of the panel was the role of diversity in international arbitration. Rajah acknowledged that the field was historically dominated by Anglo-Saxon 'Western' arbitrators and lawyers but noted that this has started to change with the increased gender diversity on arbitral tribunals. Demographic analysis of the composition of arbitral tribunals supports this idea. In 1985, in North America, 91.5% of all arbitrators were male and 96.5% were white.[10] In recent years, gender diversity has gradually

6. Franck, 'The Role of International Arbitrators' (n 2) 517.
7. *See also Czech Republic v. CME Czech Republic B.V.*, 42 I.L.M. 919 (Svea Ct. App. 2003) (Swed.).
8. Franck, 'The Role of International Arbitrators' (n 2) 517. *See also* João Ilhão Moreira, 'The Insider/Outsider Divide and the Ethics of Commercial Arbitrators.' (2022) 19 Manchester Journal of International Economic Law 132.
9. Franck, 'The Liability of International Arbitrators: A Comparative Analysis and Proposal for Qualified Immunity' (n 2) 36-38.
10. *See* Nicole Buonocore, 'Resurrecting a Dead Horse: Arbitrator Certification as a Means to Achieve Diversity' (1999) 76 University of Detroit Mercy Law Review 483.

improved across arbitral tribunals. In the five years from 2015 to 2021, the proportion of women appointed as arbitrators almost doubled, from 12.6% to 26.1%.[11] This growth is largely due to the concerted efforts of arbitration institutions, which proactively nominate women practitioners in up to 54% of appointments for which they are responsible.[12] However, there are still significant challenges in increasing the representation of women at the tribunal level, where the parties or co-arbitrators make nominations. In these cases, female nominees are selected significantly less than half the time.[13]

However, a key point emerging from the discussion was the need to recognise that a truly diverse and inclusive arbitration community involves promoting all forms of diversity – including geographic, cultural, ethnic, religious, sexual orientation, and disability. The 2021 International Arbitration Survey reported that more than half of respondents agree that progress has been made in terms of gender diversity on arbitral tribunals over the past three years. However, less than a third of respondents believe there has been progress regarding geographic, age, culture, and ethnic diversity.[14] To address this limitation, Rajah expressed the urgent need for more progress in achieving geographic diversity among arbitrators and building a genuinely diverse and inclusive international arbitration community for both arbitrators and users.

The panel highlighted how the international arbitration community has overlooked the fact that a lack of diversity in arbitral tribunals could potentially impact the quality of arbitral awards.[15] 'Groupthink', a phenomenon proposed by Professor Irving Janis, shows that teams of homogenous decision-makers are particularly prone to making ineffective collective decisions. This is because similarities among decision-makers often lead to higher levels of social cohesion and produce pressures to conform to the majority view.[16] Justice Mimmie Chan's emphasis on the significance of considering cultural and contextual factors, particularly when evaluating evidence and credibility, suggests that diversity is indeed necessary to ensure fairness and accuracy in decision-making.

Naturally, ensuring the diversity of panels also allows the arbitral community to better understand and incorporate different legal cultures and sensitivities into arbitral proceedings. As Justice Mimmie Chan noted, failure to provide thorough documentation, for example, may be attributed to cultural norms rather than bad faith. Also, the fact that some parties may not aggressively pursue an adversarial stance should not be

11. Report of the International Council for Commercial Arbitration's (ICCA) Cross-Institutional Task Force on Gender Diversity in Arbitral Appointments and Proceedings, 2022 Update 6.
12. SCC Statistics 2022; The LCIA Court appointed women in 45% of its appointments in 2022.
13. According to data published by the institutions, in 2022, the LCIA recorded the highest rate of women arbitrator nominations by the parties, at 19%. Looking at co-arbitrator nominations, the SCC had the highest rate of women nominees in 2022, at 30%. The ICDR reported 28% diverse appointments but doesn't provide further information regarding that figure.
14. 2021 International Arbitration Survey: Adapting arbitration to a changing world 4.
15. Nathalie Allen, Leonor Díaz Córdova and Natalie Hall, '"If Everyone Is Thinking Alike, Then No One Is Thinking": The Importance of Cognitive Diversity in Arbitral Tribunals to Enhance the Quality of Arbitral Decision Making' (2021) Journal of International Arbitration 601.
16. *See generally* Paul't Hart, 'Irving L. Janis' Victims of Groupthink' (1991) 12 Political Psychology 247 https://doi.org/10.2307/3791464 (accessed 16 August 2025).

confused with that party having a weaker legal case. This is particularly relevant when dealing with cases involving parties who may be more inclined to avoid direct disagreement due to cultural influences. Recognising and accommodating these cultural differences is crucial in deciding cases and assessing the credibility of evidence and testimony.

In light of these considerations, a genuinely diverse tribunal is needed to acknowledge cultural differences and encourage all parties to feel comfortable sharing their perspectives. This diversity can help foster an inclusive and culturally sensitive environment where arbitrators are equipped to navigate the nuances of cross-cultural disputes effectively. Therefore, promoting diversity in arbitration is far more than just a concern for fairness; it is the key to improving the quality, legitimacy, and relevancy of the arbitral process and arbitral award. Increased cognitive diversity helps reduce the risk of biased decision-making and enhance the quality of awards; more cognitively diverse arbitral tribunals are necessary to preserve international arbitration's continued legitimacy and success.

V ADJUDICATOR BIAS INFLUENCING DECISION-MAKING

Another key focus of the panel discussion centred on the potential influence of arbitrator bias on the decision-making process. The integrity and legitimacy of international arbitration are largely dependent not only on the perceived integrity of arbitrators but also on the quality of their decisions – that is, the general notion that arbitrators are able to fully comprehend the facts of the case, evaluate the evidence, and apply the law free from the distorting effect of biases.

As highlighted by Rajah, drawing on Donald Rumsfeld's famous distinction between 'known unknowns' and 'unknown unknowns', an individual's personal experiences and surrounding environment can significantly impact their decision-making. However, it has proven challenging to definitively determine how one's experiences contribute to the formation of biases. Nonetheless, a growing body of literature has shed light on the various biases that can affect adjudicative decision-making. In this regard, research on judicial biases has linked judges' backgrounds, political preferences, cultural cognition, and group identity to judicial outcomes.[17] Other potential influences could be part of the human condition, including anchoring, hindsight bias, egocentric bias, framing, and representativeness bias.[18] In fact, judges and arbitrators have a subconscious need to reduce complex decisions to 'coherent mental models'.[19] Research has shown that decision-makers unconsciously transform how decisions are mentally represented, reducing a complex decision to a seemingly straightforward choice between a compelling and a weak alternative. As a result,

17. Catherine A Rogers, 'Reconceptualizing the Party-Appointed Arbitrator and the Meaning of Impartiality' 64 Harvard International Law Journal 160.
18. *Ibid.*, 161.
19. *See* Dan Simon, 'A Third View of the Black Box: Cognitive Coherence in Legal Decision Making' (2004) 71 The University of Chicago Law Review 511, 513.

cognitive biases affect not only adjudicators' conclusions but also their reasoning and fact-finding.[20]

As Kaplan acknowledged, it is unrealistic for individuals to assert that they are devoid of hidden biases due to their inherent nature as human beings. Justice Mimmie Chan reinforced that the 'human element' is unavoidable in judicial decision-making processes. Drawing from her experience as a judge, she, however, emphasised that judges must be able to exercise their discretion and consider various factors instead of simply producing a formulaic output. Exercising discretion involves a human touch – it is not just about counting which side has more favourable points. Judges must carefully consider all the different factors and assign appropriate significance before using their judgment.

This nuanced understanding of how human nature influences decision-making is crucial because deciding a case is more than just applying a set of rules formulaically. While the innate limitations of the human mind may introduce problems to how decisions are reached, human qualities are also a key aspect of what makes a good decision-maker. Elliott Geisinger echoed this, reinforcing the need for arbitrators to recognise the 'human factor' in arbitration. In arbitration, the parties are not just making legal arguments but are fundamentally seeking to have their experiences validated and recognised. It is the responsibility of arbitrators to conduct themselves in a way that is attentive to this human element beyond just the legal issues and solutions presented.

VI SCRUTINY ANXIETY IN SHAPING DECISION-MAKING APPROACH

The panellists also explored the influence of potential scrutiny from higher courts, which can lead first-instance decision-makers to consider their actions through the lens of a possible reversal, potentially shaping their approach to rendering judgments. Rajah argued that first-instance decision-makers often experience a form of 'scrutiny anxiety' – a concern that higher appellate courts may critically examine and view their decisions differently. He reflected that when he served as an appellate judge, it was common for first-instance judges to anonymise facts and seek his input, likely driven by this anxiety that their decision may ultimately be overturned. Rajah saw this anxiety as a natural human tendency, not necessarily a negative trait, as it could make judges more cognisant that their own perception may not always align with how others view the 'appropriate' decision.

Building on this point, Neil Kaplan noted that there is typically less scrutiny and anxiety when acting as an arbitrator since arbitral decisions are subject to very limited avenues of appeal in most jurisdictions. This suggests that the reduced threat of appellate review may allow arbitrators to approach decision-making with greater

20. *See* Elizabeth Thornburg, 'Unconscious Judging' (2019) 76 Washington and Lee Law Review 1567; *see also* Nancy Pennington N and Reid Hastie, 'A Cognitive Theory of Juror Decision Making: The Story Model' (1991) 13 Cardozo Law Review 519, 525.

confidence and autonomy, unencumbered by the potential for their rulings to be closely scrutinised and second-guessed by higher courts.

While arbitrators and judges are subject to different review processes, both processes provide an opportunity to evaluate their conduct.[21] Judges' determinations are typically judicially reviewable for substantive and procedural errors.[22] In contrast, while some jurisdictions do permit a limited evaluation of the legal merits of a tribunal's award, arbitral awards are generally subject to much more limited judicial review. Still, like judges, arbitrators prefer not to have their awards annulled, set aside or denied enforcement and exhibit great care to retain their reputation in the market.[23] Again, the equilibria between the market and the human nature of arbitrators provide fertile ground for trust in proceedings to emerge.

VII CONCLUSION

The role of arbitrators is undergoing a significant transformation in the dynamic and ever-evolving world of international arbitration. As the legal and geopolitical landscape shifts, arbitrators are being called upon to navigate an increasingly complex and interconnected global environment, where the demands for trust, cultural awareness, and adaptability have become paramount.

As stressed by Chris Campbell, the impact of arbitration awards can be significant, not only affecting the parties involved but also potentially leading to job losses, major operational changes, and significant financial implications for the businesses concerned. This heightens the responsibility placed on arbitrators to ensure their decisions are well informed and impartial, and serve the principles of cost-effectiveness, timeliness, and predictability that clients demand.

The emphasis on trust throughout the panel reflects the changing expectations of parties involved in international disputes, who seek dispute resolution mechanisms that deliver efficient and predictable outcomes and engender a sense of legitimacy and fairness. As Aisha Abdallah aptly observed, justice in arbitration transcends mere efficiency and timeliness. True justice, she argued, should serve the broader community, be sustainable, and benefit all stakeholders, not just those immediately involved in the current dispute. This perspective aligns with the growing recognition that arbitration systems must adapt to accommodate an increasingly globalised world's diverse needs and concerns. As new regions become more integrated into the international trade and investment ecosystem, the arbitration framework must evolve to meet

21. Franck, 'The Role of International Arbitrators' (n 2) 511. *See also* João Ilhão Moreira, The Regulation of International Commercial Arbitration: Arbitrators' Duties and the Emerging Arbitral Market (Hart Publishing 2024) 148.
22. Arthur D Hellman, 'Error Correction, Lawmaking, and the Supreme Court's Exercise of Discretionary Review' (1983) 44 University of Pittsburgh Law Review 795, 796; Robertson DW, 'Allocating Authority Among Institutional Decision Makers in Louisiana State-Court Negligence and Strict Liability Cases' (1997) 57 Louisiana Law Review 1079, 1082.
23. *See* João Ilhão Moreira, 'Arbitration Vis-à-Vis Other Professions: A Sociology of Professions Account of International Commercial Arbitrators' (2022) 49 Journal of Law and Society 48, 69 https://doi.org/10.1111/jols.12348 (accessed 16 August 2025).

their unique requirements and perspectives. This sentiment emphasises the need for the system to be more inclusive and responsive to the needs of a broader range of participants beyond the traditional user base.

This reinforces the idea that sustainability and long-term relevance should be the guiding principles of the future of arbitration. To achieve this, the arbitration framework must actively attract and retain new users from diverse backgrounds, fostering a sense of ownership and investment in the system. By serving the needs of a much broader constituency, the arbitration process can become more durable, adaptable, and, ultimately, better equipped to fulfil its primary objective of facilitating international trade and investment.

Furthermore, arbitrators must cultivate trust, cultural awareness, and adaptability to achieve 'true justice' and fairness in their rulings. Looking ahead, the panel's discussions underscore the need for the arbitration community to continually reflect on and refine its practices in order to uphold the integrity and credibility of this crucial dispute resolution mechanism. As the field navigates the challenges posed by shifting societal expectations, technological disruptions, and evolving ethical considerations, a steadfast commitment to the core principles of trust, neutrality, and impartiality will be paramount in ensuring international arbitration's long-term viability and success.

PANEL 3

Decision-Making and Biases

The panel explores the intricacies of decision-making in international arbitration. Is decision-making a science or art? Do arbitrators approach decision-making differently from judges? Should arbitrators adhere strictly to the traditional judicial doctrine of impartiality, or is a more nuanced perspective warranted? Is nationality still a relevant barometer for independence and impartiality? How profound is the impact of an arbitrator's personal background on rulings? How do values influence decision-making? The speakers endeavour to shed light on the various dynamics shaping arbitrators' decisions and influencing case outcomes.

CHAPTER 6

Cultivating a Culture of Cultural Diversity in Arbitration: Interplay Between Cultural Diversity and Arbitral Decision-Making Through the Lens of Key Players in the Arbitration*

*Sheila Ahuja & Curtis Fung***

TABLE OF CONTENTS

I INTRODUCTION

As arbitration practitioners, we preach the efficacy of arbitration in resolving transnational disputes, placing reliance on and confidence in its fundamental virtues of party

* This chapter was originally prepared for the ICCA Congress 2024 panel discussion on Decision-Making and Biases on 6 May 2024 and was updated as of that day, unless otherwise specified.

** Sheila Ahuja KC is a partner in Allen Overy Shearman Sterling's Global International Arbitration Group with oversight of the Singapore and Hong Kong arbitration practices. She is also joint chair of the firm's India Group. She is an adjunct associate professor at the National University of Singapore. She regularly sits as an arbitrator, and, more recently, as presiding arbitrator. She appears as an advocate in both commercial arbitrations and investor-State arbitrations, as well as arbitration-related court matters. Curtis Fung is an associate in the International Arbitration team of Allen Overy Shearman Sterling.

autonomy, procedural flexibility and wide enforceability. However, to be a truly international mechanism capable of serving the interests of all potential users worldwide, the arbitration community must also aspire to accommodate and serve the varied needs of its diverse user base.

Is the operative part of our arbitration community, as it presently stands, diverse enough to achieve this goal? There has been a rising awareness on diversity in the recent years, although this has most prominently featured in the area of gender diversity, while the progress for promoting other equally important forms of diversity is not as promising.[1] Cultural diversity, in particular, could be a crucial building block towards cementing arbitration as a truly international dispute resolution mechanism.

Drawing on our multi-cultural backgrounds and cross-jurisdictional practices, this chapter explores the interaction between decision-making in arbitration and cultural diversity, a concept capable of encapsulating multiple facets, including cultural background and exposure, geographical/national identity, ethnicity, language, to name a few. The object of our chapter is to argue that promoting cultural diversity in the arbitration process should not merely be a 'slogan' or an ethical aspiration. Rather, cultural diversity has an intrinsic and existential value in and of itself. Developing a culture of cultural diversity in international arbitration could enhance the quality, efficiency and credibility of the international arbitration system.

In the following sections, we explore the importance and value of cultural diversity through the lens of the key players in the arbitral process – starting from the perspective of the arbitrators and how cultural diversity at the decision-makers' level improves the arbitration process (*section II*), and then from the perspective of the advocates and the assistance they can offer to facilitate decision-making (*section III*) and finally, from the perspective of the users of the international arbitration system on how their perception should shape the development in this field (*section IV*).

II THROUGH THE LENS OF THE DECISION-MAKERS: HOW WOULD CULTURAL DIVERSITY IMPROVE THE ARBITRATORS' DECISION-MAKING

1 Introduction

At its core, arbitration, like all other forms of dispute resolution mechanisms, calls for adjudicators to decide contested issues based on facts and legal principles. Adjudicating transnational disputes inevitably entails decision-making in the context of distinctive factual issues arising from different socio-economic backgrounds and the application of the law of different legal traditions. Having an arbitrator on the panel who

1. *See*, for example, Queen Mary University of London & White & Case, '2021 International Arbitration Survey: Adapting Arbitration to a Changing World' https://arbitration.qmul.ac.uk/media/arbitration/docs/LON0320037-QMUL-International-Arbitration-Survey-2021_19_WEB.pdf accessed 18 April 2024 (*QMUL 2021 Survey*), p. 15, which noted that more than half of respondents agree that progress has been made in terms of gender diversity on arbitral tribunals over the past three years, but only less than a third of respondents believe that there has been progress in respect of geographical, age, cultural and, particularly, ethnic diversity.

appreciates the socio-economic and cultural context of the relevant jurisdiction(s) to which the dispute relates could rather directly increase the effective facilitation of the conduct of the arbitration proceedings.

This section explores the issue of cultural diversity through the lens of the arbitrators. It starts with a brief summary of the recent trend of cultural diversity in the appointment of tribunal members, followed by an evaluation of why cultural diversity of tribunal members would enhance the effectiveness and efficiency of the arbitral proceedings, and concludes with suggestions on how to promote cultural diversity in the appointment of tribunal members.

2 Cultural Diversity in the Appointment of Tribunal Members: Recent Trends

In contrast with the promising initiatives in recent years promoting gender diversity in arbitration,[2] it is clear that more can be done to improve the cultural diversity in the appointment of arbitrators.

Recent surveys suggest that the composition of tribunals remained predominantly Western European or North American. For example, using the 2014 ICCA Congress attendees as an approximation of the demographics of arbitrators, an article published by Franck and her co-authors reported that the 'median international arbitrator' was 'male, fifty-three years of age, with some training from a common law jurisdiction, and from a developed state'.[3] Data from ICSID arbitrations between 1972 and 2015 also revealed that the tribunals predominantly comprised Anglo-European arbitrators – in 45% of the cases, the entire tribunal were composed of all Anglo-European arbitrators, and in 84% of the cases, two or more of the tribunal members were Anglo-European, or the sole arbitrator was Anglo-European.[4]

That said, the above statistics are now almost a decade old, and it appears that some progress has been made in recent years. We are seeing a more diverse range of arbitrators being appointed and an increase in the appointment of local arbitrators by leading regional arbitration centres, even if a larger proportion of the appointments continue to be from Western countries. In 2020, the ICC confirmed or appointed arbitrators from 92 jurisdictions, of which 52.3% were from Northern and Western Europe and 13.3% were from North America.[5] The HKIAC's case statistics in 2023 reveal that among the top three nationalities of arbitrators designated by the parties or

2. Including the various initiatives by, among others, ArbitralWomen and the ICCA cross-institutional task force on gender diversity in arbitral appointments and proceedings.
3. Susan D. Franck et al., 'Diversity Challenge: Exploring the "Invisible College" of International Arbitration' (2015) 53 Colum. J. Transnat'l L. 429, 466.
4. C. Dolinar-Hikawa, 'Beyond the Pale: A Proposal to Promote Ethnic Diversity Among International Arbitrators' (2015) 12(4) TDM 3.
5. International Chamber of Commerce, 'Dispute Resolution 2020 Statistics' https://iccwbo.org/news-publications/arbitration-adr-rules-and-tools/icc-dispute-resolution-statistics-2020/ accessed 18 April 2024, p. 14.

co-arbitrators or appointed by the HKIAC (apart from dual nationals),[6] Hong Kong takes the top spot (27.6% for party/co-arbitrator-appointed arbitrators and 29.7% for HKIAC appointed arbitrators), followed by the United Kingdom (12.8%/16.1%) and Australia (8%/15.1%).[7] The SIAC in 2022 appointed arbitrators from thirty-six jurisdictions, the top five of which are Singapore (33%), the United Kingdom (27%), Australia (6.5%), the United States (6.2%) and India (4.1%).

It seems the arbitration community is well aware of the progress that needs to be made in the area of cultural diversity. In a 2019 survey, 80% of the respondents from the arbitration community opined that 'tribunals contained too many white arbitrators', and 64% considered that 'there were too many arbitrators from Western Europe or North America'.[8] Interestingly, however, only 26% of the respondents considered 'ethnical/national identity' as very important or important criterion for selecting an arbitrator.[9]

The skewed statistics in arbitrator appointments do not necessarily mean the arbitration community is consciously biased in favour of or against arbitrators of certain nationalities or ethnicities. One must bear in mind that the constitution of the tribunal is one of the most important strategic decisions for the parties in the proceedings as it has a direct correlation with and impact on the procedure as well as the outcome of a case. For example, when parties and their counsel select their arbitrator candidates for high-stake disputes, they would naturally adopt a risk-adverse approach and will likely default to someone who is well respected in the field with a proven track record, and may also rely on their (and their colleagues') prior experience and word-of-mouth in making the final judgment call.

In a field where the most experienced and well-respected practitioners often hail from the leading jurisdictions (at least at this stage), even if there is no conscious aversion against appointing or nominating practitioners from other parts of the world, the reality is that the parties would likely end up with a narrower pool of candidates than they should have been looking at and the cycle will likely continuously repeat itself in such a pattern of circumstances.

This pattern is rather undesirable, particularly in circumstances where there is an acknowledgement that selecting an arbitrator with the right qualifications and expertise to adjudicate parties' disputes should necessarily take into account the cultural background of the arbitrator candidates. And this must be right – we will explain why so.

6. Dual nationals comprise 21.4% of the arbitrators designated by parties or co-arbitrators and 16.9% of the arbitrators appointed by HKIAC.
7. HKIAC, '2023 Statistics' https://www.hkiac.org/about-us/statistics accessed 18 April 2024.
8. Berwin Leighton Paisner, 'International Arbitration Survey: Diversity on Arbitral Tribunals' https://www.bclplaw.com/a/web/147241/BLP-International-Arbitration-Survey-2016.pdf accessed 18 April 2024 (*BLP International Arbitration Survey*), p. 8.
9. *Ibid.*

3 Cultural Diversity and the Effectiveness and Efficiency of Arbitral Proceedings

Cultural diversity is not a mere slogan or aspirational concept, or worst still, some sort of tick-the-box exercise to demonstrate one's commitment to D&I (diversity and inclusion) initiatives. We should all start acknowledging the intrinsic value of cultural diversity, which bears direct correlation to a higher quality of arbitral decision-making. A culturally diverse tribunal is likely a more efficient and effective one for various reasons.

First, promoting cultural diversity naturally results in the expansion of the pool of arbitrators available for appointment.

Once one looks beyond the usual suspects, it becomes clear that there are plenty of home players from the local jurisdictions who are equally qualified to assist and are up for grabs. Borrowing economic terminologies, greater 'competition' in the arbitration 'market' generally leads to greater vibrancy, creating a bigger pie and improving the quality of services. In more concrete terms, one practical benefit of a broadened base of arbitrators is a more even distribution of caseloads among arbitrators. We have no doubt come across situations where delays in proceedings are caused by the arbitrators' packed schedules and overwhelming simultaneous caseloads. Tapping into a larger talent pool of arbitrators from different jurisdictions could alleviate (although unlikely eliminate) the issues arising from repeated appointments and overlapping engagements of the more popular and presently sought-after arbitrators (such as conflicts of interest and scheduling issues). It also provides an opportunity for other arbitrators from different backgrounds to establish themselves in the field, albeit at the initial stages, this will involve the appointing party taking a risk on arbitrators who do not have an established background or reputation. Importantly, it allows arbitrators to dedicate more time on average to their cases, which ought to have the impact of facilitating the efficient conduct of arbitration proceedings, though one could argue this of course depends on whether the arbitrator in question is, subjectively, procedurally efficient (but this is an assumption we will make, giving the average arbitrator the benefit of the doubt).

Second, having a culturally diverse tribunal would improve the quality of deliberation and the decision-making process of tribunals.

Arbitrators from different cultural backgrounds and different legal traditions offer their unique perspectives on the case. There are always two sides of the coin - while some may have concerns that the divergence in views and approach may result in greater risk of clashes, prolonged deliberation and thus inefficiency and potentially divergent outcomes, there is still great merit in the cross-pollination of ideas and there is a real need for constructive debate in reaching what might be seen as the right outcome for the case.

The views of arbitrators are no doubt influenced by their colleagues,[10] especially those in the same tribunal. The quality of deliberation between the arbitrators is

10. There are empirical studies which demonstrate that the views of judicial decision-makers are unlikely to be independent to those of his or her colleagues or those of the professional

therefore crucial to the quality of their decision, and in many ways, the more divergent their background, the more likely they will bring different views to the deliberation room. Ultimately, it cannot be disputed that we would want to avoid the pitfall of confirmation bias – putting a group of decision-makers sharing similar characteristics together risks creating an echo chamber. As research indicates, groups of like-minded people tend to act in a uniform manner, follow the actions of those who speak or act first, are prone to polarised opinions even after discussion and focus on shared information rather than novel ways of thinking.[11] One may legitimately argue that the risk of a panel of professional arbitrators falling foul of such bias is relatively low, but the difficulty with bias is that it could operate unconsciously (as practitioners well versed with challenge procedure are no doubt familiar) or subconsciously. Having a diverse tribunal with different perspectives can mitigate this risk.

Promoting the cultural diversity of a tribunal at the individual case level also has a broader effect on the institution of international arbitration as an entire mechanism. The risk of extremely divergent decisions rendered by different tribunals is likely lower if each decision involves the participation and effective deliberation of a diverse group of arbitrators.

Another advantage of having a culturally diverse tribunal adjudicating international disputes is that the arbitrator(s) closer to the culture or jurisdiction to which the dispute relates can serve the role as a 'cultural intermediary and translator'.[12] It is not uncommon for arbitrators from Europe or North America to be appointed to adjudicate disputes in the Asia-Pacific region, and in that scenario, one can expect there to be a gap in cultural understanding (in either direction). In fact, even the Asia-Pacific region itself is home to various jurisdictions with their own distinctive business norms and legal cultures. These cultural differences often underpin and intertwine with the factual issues and sometimes even legal principles upon which the tribunals need to make determinations.

In investor-state disputes, the tribunal members are chosen based on (among other things) their expertise in international law, but they may be called upon to consider and decide local law issues in order to determine whether the State is, for example, in breach of its obligations under the investment treaty. A common law lawyer by training may be asked to determine civil law issues, or vice versa. The approach taken by common law and civil law on certain issues, both on substantive points of law and on procedural issues, may be vastly different. For example, civil

---

community – *see* Sergio Puig, 'Social Capital in the Arbitration Market' (2014) 25(2) EJIL 387, 401 https://doi.org/10.1093/ejil/chu045 accessed 16 August 2025, citing studies relating to US judicial culture.

11. M. Winkler and M. Schinazi, 'Chapter 24: Diversity and Inclusiveness in International Arbitration' in Michael Reisman and Nigel Blackaby (eds), *Arbitration Beyond Borders: Essays in Memory of Guillermo Aguilar Álvarez* (Kluwer Law International 2023) 469-490, 484, citing Cass R. Sunstein & Reid Hastie, *Wiser: Getting Beyond Groupthink to Make Groups Smarter* (Harvard Business Review Press 2015) pp. 23-24.
12. Wong Partnership LLP, 'Cultural Considerations in Advocacy, East Meets West' in Global Arbitration Review, *The Guide to Advocacy* (6th ed.), citing Ilhyung Lee, 'Practice and Predicament: The Nationality of the International Arbitrator (With Survey Results)' (2007) 31 Fordham Int'l LJ 603, 604.

law-trained arbitrators are more likely to grasp concepts from a civil law system faster (even if that is not the law of his or her home jurisdiction) and can serve as an intermediary for their common law-trained co-arbitrators in the interactions with experts and counsel.

Even in commercial arbitration where arbitrators are selected for (among other things) their expertise in the governing law, tribunal members from the jurisdiction closely connected to the underlying transaction of the dispute are likely to have a better understanding of the social and economic framework, business norms and cultural niceties of that jurisdiction, which may be relevant as providing the context in which the tribunal assesses the factual evidence of the case. A tribunal member with the relevant cultural background can act as the 'cultural translator' of these subtleties for his or her co-arbitrators.

One caveat is that when deciding whether to choose an arbitrator from their home jurisdiction, parties and their legal advisers may have to weigh the benefits of having such a 'cultural intermediary' against the perceived risk of any challenge based on the arbitrator's independence or impartiality arising from choosing an arbitrator from their home jurisdiction; and this is *a fortiori* a concern in investor-state arbitrations. Nonetheless, it is difficult to conceive a successful challenge based solely on the arbitrator's nationality without any further circumstances suggesting a lack of independence or impartiality. Parties should also be conscious of any limitation imposed on the nationalities of arbitrators by arbitration agreements and institutional rules.[13]

Third, a culturally diverse tribunal would, in all likelihood, possess a broader range of cumulative language ability. While translation and interpretation have become an inherent part of the conduct and procedure of international arbitration proceedings, it has time and cost implications. There is always a risk of mistranslation and misinterpretation too, and some disputes come down to the very question of which translation is accurate. Multilingual arbitrators who are professionally fluent in the language spoken by the witness can greatly enhance the accuracy of the information received by the tribunal and improve efficiency. An arbitrator (and advocate) with the relevant linguistics skills can enhance the efficiency of the proceedings by assisting a witness where, for example, the response to a line of questioning is straying off topic, and to make clarificatory queries at the appropriate junctures. In one case where a bilingual advocate cross-examined a witness with the assistance of interpreters, a member of the tribunal invited the advocate to identify interpretation errors in real time. The advocate was able to correct certain inaccuracies in translation immediately and ensure the questions and answers were accurately reflected. This is a far better use

13. For instance, Rule 13 of the ICSID Arbitrator Rules 2022 provides that 'the majority of the arbitrators on a Tribunal shall be nationals of States other than the State party to the dispute and the State whose national is a party to the dispute' and that '[a] party may not appoint an arbitrator who is a national of the State party to the dispute or the State whose national is a party to the dispute', unless the parties agreed. Under Article 11.2 of the HKIAC Rules 2018, the general rule is that 'where the parties to an arbitration ... are of different nationalities, a sole or presiding arbitrator shall not have the same nationality as any party unless specifically agreed otherwise by all parties'.

of everyone's time than to raise challenges based on transcripts and recordings after the hearing was closed (which often leads to *ex post facto* debates and disagreements).

Fourth, a culturally diverse tribunal would likely be more sensitive to cultural issues specific to the relevant culture of the party and/or their counsel, and can avoid the pitfalls of stereotyping and cultural bias.

Specifically to the point of counsel, a tribunal consisting of both common law and civil law-trained lawyers would be more receptive and understanding of different advocacy styles. A common law-trained arbitrator can help his or her civil law-trained colleagues understand the approach and tone taken during cross-examination (a process which may not be prominent in an inquisitorial system in civil law jurisdictions), including, e.g., why counsel asks leading questions during cross-examinations.[14] Likewise, reliance on a party's approach if dictated by a particular evidence statute can be understood and explained to the tribunal by an arbitrator familiar with that culture and legal system.

An important feature of cultural understanding prevails in the topic of witness evidence. A tribunal that can understand the verbal and non-verbal cues of the witnesses would be in a much better position to accurately assess the witnesses' credibility and demeanour. For example, an Indian arbitrator may not been as fazed as his or her co-arbitrators by Indian witnesses responding with a 'yes' before actually answering the question in the negative[15] or with the 'Indian nod'; Russian or Ukrainian businesspeople often view themselves as 'the creators, and therefore saviours of their own business' and may be very defensive when acting as witnesses on behalf of their businesses.[16] Witnesses from cultures that value one's 'face' may refuse to back down and retract from their previous statements. Junior employees may not be willing to expressly disagree with someone of a higher rank in an organisation with a hierarchical culture.[17] A skilful advocate would no doubt be able to exploit these issues to their advantage. However, it is also crucial for tribunals to appreciate that these cultural subtleties may explain why certain witnesses behave in certain manners, even though they may differ from what the arbitrators' perception of how someone from their own culture would have reacted. A culturally diverse tribunal would be more sensitive to these issues and would be collectively less prone to being skewed by their preconception.

For these reasons, having the right degree of cultural sensitivity and familiarity in the tribunal is crucial to the effective and efficient conduct of the arbitration proceedings. It is not to say that we should always confine our choice of arbitrators, e.g., Asia-Pacific disputes, to practitioners born and raised in the region and disregard

14. *See*, for example, R. Doak Bishop and Edward G. Kehoe, *The Art of Advocacy in International Arbitration* (2nd ed., Juris Publishing 2010) Chapter 2, p. 42 – the author noted an example in which a German Arbitrator prevents counsel from asking leading questions at cross-examination.
15. R. Doak Bishop and Edward G. Kehoe, *The Art of Advocacy in International Arbitration* (2nd ed., Juris Publishing 2010), p. 578.
16. KIAP Attorneys at Law, 'Cultural Considerations in Advocacy: Russia and Eastern Europe', in Global Arbitration Review, *The Guide to Advocacy* (6th ed.), citing Noah Rubins KC.
17. Wong Partnership (n 12).

qualified practitioners who may originate from other jurisdictions. Someone from a culture would undoubtedly have some edge in understanding the subtleties of that culture. At the same time, the international nature of the arbitration practice means that the members of the community, like ourselves and a large number of our colleagues, often find a second or third home (or even more) in other jurisdiction(s) as he or she develops his or her professional career. They could be equally well placed to understand the market and the culture of the jurisdiction(s) in which they have built their career. One should avoid taking a narrow view of 'cultural diversity' which would defeat the very purpose of promoting it, i.e., to diversify rather than localise international arbitration practice. We must be cautious of how we promote cultural diversity in arbitration and tribunal appointment.

4 Promoting Cultural Diversity in Tribunal Appointment

Arbitral institutions, which often have the power to appoint arbitrators in specific circumstances, play a significant role in building the momentum for greater recognition of cultural diversity in the arbitration community. Leading institutions publish diversity statistics in their annual reports to raise awareness for the issue. They are also making encouraging efforts in this field. For example, the HKIAC recently proposed to add a specific article on diversity, encouraging parties and co-arbitrators to 'take into account considerations of diversity when designating arbitrators' and stipulating that 'HKIAC shall take into account considerations of diversity together with all other relevant considerations' in exercising its authority to appoint arbitrators.[18]

The call for changes in rules and the adoption of diversity policies by arbitral institutions reflects the community's sentiment. According to the 2021 White & Case and Queen Mary University of London Survey (*QMUL 2021 Survey*), 'appointing authorities and institutions adopting an express policy of suggesting and appointing diverse candidates as arbitrators' was the most chosen initiative which the respondents considered to be the most effective in encouraging greater diversity in terms of arbitral appointments,[19] and 'commitment to a more diverse pool of arbitrators' is the second choice for adaptations that would make other arbitral rules or institutions more attractive.[20]

One issue on which the community needs to reflect is whether arbitral institutions should take more affirmative action, such as imposing mandatory requirements or prescribed quotas, to more actively promote cultural diversity. This must be carefully weighed against two factors: (i) the risk of disregarding an existing pool of practitioners who may be well qualified for the job but may not satisfy the diversity

18. HKIAC, 'Proposed amendments to the HKIAC Rules 2018' https://www.hkiac.org/sites/default/files/ck_filebrowser/2024%20HKIAC%20Rules%20-%20Public%20Consultation%20Draft_tracked.pdf accessed 18 April 2024. Update: The HKIAC Rules 2024, which came into force on 1 June 2024, incorporate the diversity provisions in Article 9A.
19. QMUL 2021 Survey (n 1) pp. 11-12.
20. *Ibid.*, p. 17.

requirements (*see* above), and (ii) the implications of such an approach on the fundamental arbitral cornerstone of party autonomy.

Indeed, a better approach may be to allow the function of cultural diversity to take root organically in the wider arbitral community. The composition of arbitral tribunals largely remains driven by lawyers and co-arbitrators. It is important that they appreciate the benefit of appointing a culturally diverse tribunal as outlined above and understand that appointing a culturally diverse tribunal would in many cases align with the clients' interest. The goal is to encourage these groups to actively consider the cultural background of the arbitrator when considering the candidates for appointment. Growing cultural diversity organically as an intrinsic part of the arbitration culture would leave a more lasting and powerful impact than individual institutions imposing compulsory requirements through rules or even guidelines.

III THROUGH THE LENS OF THE ADVOCATES: IF COUNSEL MAY BE OF ASSISTANCE

International arbitration is at the end of the day a fusion of practices from different legal traditions. Lawyers from different jurisdictions shape its development through their diverse practices. As the international arbitration community and its decision-making body both grow more culturally diverse, advocates must adapt their advocacy style to cater to their audience.

After all, advocacy is the art of persuasion. Just as how the old adage of 'know your enemy' serves as a guiding principle in the art of war, knowing your tribunal and your witness is equally important for the art of persuasion. The advocate must determine the messages that he or she needs to convey and the means to do so effectively. What amounts to effective persuasion varies with the target audience. The advocacy style of an advocate should therefore be adapted in each case to cater for the preferences and backgrounds of the individuals with whom an advocate is interacting. Among other things, an advocate must be deft at navigating through cultural and linguistic differences and providing the assistance the decision-makers would expect. There are a few pointers pertaining to cultural and linguistic subtleties which advocates should be aware.

First, linguistic differences may hinder effective communication, even with the assistance of translators. Even if the common denominator language of many proceedings may be English, and even if witness statements are often drafted by lawyers in the language of the arbitration, it does not mean all participants can comprehend or speak English at the same level as native speakers. With non-English speaking witnesses, using simple and clear language is key. Convoluted and complicated sentence structuring increases the risk of mistranslation and misunderstanding, which results in a waste of time due to irrelevant responses and rephrasing questions.

Second, adopt the right style and tone for your target (witnesses) and audience (tribunal). There is no one-size-fits-all approach in a matter which is very much driven by the advocate's personality and their professional training and likely also their personal upbringing. That said, an outstanding oral advocate in one legal tradition might fall flat before a tribunal comprised of individuals from a different tradition who prize other characteristics in advocacy. What may be a highly effective cross-examination of key witnesses in one legal system may not have the same impact in another. The benefit of having a culturally diverse arbitration scene is the flexibility to adopt any style that fits the situation. A skilful advocate should be versatile enough to adjust their advocacy style to suit their audience – there are always judgment calls to be made for each case, from the broader direction of how aggressive one wants to be, down to the minute details of how much information one should put in the presentation slides, if at all.

Third, advocates should also be culturally sensitive. Advocates should avoid getting on the bad side of the witness (and the tribunal) by touching on cultural taboos or sensitive topics unless there is clear utility in doing so in the particular circumstances of the case. It is always a fine line to walk between being firm with a witness and being too harsh. Avoid going too hard on witnesses of advanced age unless you want the tribunal's sympathy to work against you. Always refrain from making inappropriate jokes and comments – some rules are culture neutral!

IV THROUGH THE LENS OF THE USERS OF INTERNATIONAL ARBITRATION: UNDERSTANDING THEIR EXPECTATIONS

When evaluating the interplay between cultural diversity and decision-making in arbitration, apart from focusing on what the arbitrators and the advocates should do, the perception and expectations of the users and the potential users of the arbitral process are also important. After all, justice must be done and be seen to be done. The users' perception of cultural diversity in international arbitration informs their expectations of how the international arbitration community is addressing the issue of cultural diversity and affects their view of the legitimacy of arbitration as a means of dispute resolution.

As highlighted in section II above, a recent survey collected the views of the key players of the arbitration community (including the users of arbitration)[21] and highlighted that they are alive to the issue of a lack of cultural diversity in arbitration. This echoes the findings of the user-centric SIDRA International Dispute Resolution Survey 2022 (*SIDRA 2022 Survey*).[22] The SIDRA 2022 Survey revealed that while a vast majority of users indicated that language (91%) and cultural familiarity (78%) are important factors influencing their choice of arbitrator, their level of satisfaction with their chosen arbitrators on these aspects is not as high (74% for language and 69% for

21. BLP International Arbitration Survey (n 8) p. 5. The survey's respondents include arbitrators, corporate counsel, external lawyers, users of arbitration and those working at arbitral institutions.
22. Singapore Management University, 'Singapore International Dispute Resolution Academy (SIDRA) International Dispute Resolution Survey: 2022 Final Report' https://sidra.smu.edu.sg/sites/sidra.smu.edu.sg/files/survey-2022/22_0068%20SMU%20SIDRA%20Survey%20Report%202022_FA4(C).pdf accessed 18 April 2024 (the *SIDRA 2022 Survey*), p. 1, noting that all respondents are users of arbitration (either client users or external counsels).

cultural familiarity).[23] At the same time, more than half of the respondents considered diversity to be important or absolutely crucial in their selection of an arbitrator.[24]

This apparent mismatch between user expectation and reality should raise an alarm. A question we should ask ourselves is why the users are concerned about cultural diversity in arbitration. This may be the result of the perceived effect of cultural diversity on improving the decision-making process in arbitration. It is understandable that the parties may feel more comfortable if the arbitrators (or at least some of them) come from the same cultural background or speak the same language as they did or are familiar with the types of issues faced by that party in the particular dispute in question. One noteworthy observation from the respondents of the QMUL 2021 Survey is that where an arbitral panel is composed entirely of arbitrators who have no relationship with or understanding of a specific country or culture central to a dispute, the parties may feel that the arbitrators might fail to fully appreciate cultural differences and (perhaps subconsciously) favour parties from areas or cultures with which the arbitrators are more familiar.[25] This is unlikely to be representative of what happens in fact in most cases, given the importance and pride with which we as an international community value our professionalism and diligence. Nonetheless, the perceived risk of bias is a real issue that the arbitration community needs to address in order to deliver a satisfactory user experience – no one wants to spend money litigating a dispute if they think they are playing on an unlevel playing field. One of the fundamental advantages of international arbitration after all is the neutral ground that it supposedly brings.

Ultimately, the legitimacy of arbitration as a dispute resolution mechanism for commercial or investment disputes depends on whether it is reflective of the needs of the constituency it serves.[26] Meeting users' expectations on cultural diversity (and indeed other forms of diversity) is critical to maintaining their satisfaction, trust and confidence in the system.

Another way in which arbitrators and counsel may contribute to enhance user's experience is to proactively resolve cultural and linguistic issues and barriers. For example, as discussed above, bilingual or multilingual arbitrators or counsel who can directly communicate with lay witnesses in their mother tongue can no doubt ease their mind and could minimise the risk of important points being literally lost in translation. A well-drafted, focused witness statement and proper witness preparation can mitigate the risk that the witnesses may fail to convey his or her messages during oral testimony, calm the witnesses' nerves and improve his or her performance at the oral hearing – although counsel must take care not to intervene in a heavy handed manner to deprive the witness evidence of its authenticity and not to overstep the boundary of the legal and professional codes binding on them.

23. *Ibid.*, p. 21.
24. *Ibid.*, p. 24.
25. QMUL 2021 Survey (n 1) p. 17.
26. Winkler and Schinazi (n 11) 485.

V CONCLUSION

In international arbitration, a system which at its core is designed to resolve cross-border disputes, the undesirable effect of cultural differences and language barriers cannot be completely eliminated. It can nevertheless be mitigated. Ultimately, cultural diversity improves the quality of decision-making and legitimacy of the arbitration system, and embracing and giving effect to cultural diversity in the arbitral process undoubtedly improves – rather than worsens – the arbitral process and likely even the ultimate outcome. Key players in the community, including arbitrators, advocates, arbitral institutions, are well advised to focus on cultivating a culture of cultural diversity and aim to establish arbitration as a truly international dispute resolution mechanism for everyone.

CHAPTER 7

Trust, Partiality, and the Rationalist Delusion in Investor-State Dispute Settlement

Prof. Stavros Brekoulakis & Anna Howard[*]

TABLE OF CONTENTS

I INTRODUCTION

For more than three decades now, the dispute resolution system of Investor-State Dispute Settlement (ISDS) has continued to attract controversy. The drafters of the 1965 Washington Convention on the Settlement of Investment Disputes between States and Nationals of Other States had noble intentions. By setting up the International Centre for the Settlement of Investor-State Disputes (ICSID), they wanted to create an 'apolitical'[1] alternative system to the national courts and 'gunboat

* Stavros Brekoulakis, Michael and Laura Hwang Professor in International Arbitration at the National University of Singapore; Anna Howard, Guest Lecturer at the University College London and Research Fellow at Singapore International Dispute Resolution Academy, Singapore Management University.

We dedicate this chapter to our collaborator, colleague and friend, Dr Daniel Behn. His passion, integrity and boundless curiosity shaped this work and will remain with us. He had so much more to contribute. We would like to thank Professor Kate Malleson and Professor Rachel Cahill-O'Callaghan, members of the project team, for their comments and support.

1. Charles N Brower and Sadie Blanchard, 'What's in a Meme: The Truth about Investor-State Arbitration – Why It Need Not, and Must Not, Be Repossessed by States' (2014) 52(3) Columbia Journal of Transnational Law 689, 696.

diplomacy' previously used for disputes between foreign investors and states.[2] More than half a century later, few commentators believe that the system is sustainable, at least in its current form. Criticism of ISDS has been wide-ranging. But one accusation stands out, namely that ISDS lacks impartiality and is often perceived as being structurally and systemically biased in favour of investors and against States.[3]

In response to ISDS' accusation, stakeholders have been looking at two different reform options. The first is a root and branch proposal to *replace* ISDS with a court-based system of adjudication. This approach is supported by a number of states and aims at eliminating elements of the procedural design of ISDS, notably the method of party appointment of arbitrators, which are perceived as the underlying structural cause of ISDS' lack of impartiality.

The second response to criticisms of the current system focuses on proposals to *reform* ISDS by aiming to strengthen the formal standards of arbitrators' conduct as a means of enhancing their impartiality. Notably, the Code of Conduct for Arbitrators in International Investment Dispute Resolution promulgated by the Secretariats of the International Centre for Settlement of Investment Disputes (ICSID) and UNCITRAL includes the far-reaching disclosure requirement on arbitrators[4] to 'disclose any circumstances likely to give rise to justifiable doubts as to his or her independence or impartiality'.[5]

However, absent from the debate and reform proposals is the fundamental question of what is being assessed in the first place. What is the idea of impartiality against which ISDS is assessed. Both of these options above (and the general debate on ISDS) are based on the assumption that the fact that parties appoint and pay ISDS arbitrators accounts for a structurally biased system of adjudication, where party-appointed arbitrators tend to favour the party who appointed them. But the idea that arbitrators tend to be biased because they are appointed and paid by parties is based on an idea of impartiality which has been transposed directly from a judicial doctrine which applies to national courts.[6]

Drawing on the findings of our large-scale empirical project,[7] this chapter questions the applicability of the judicial doctrine of impartiality which currently

2. Catherine A Rogers, 'The Politics of International Investment Arbitrators' (2013) 12 Santa Clara Journal of International Law 223, 226.
3. *See*, for example: Gus Van Harten, 'Arbitrator Behaviour in Asymmetrical Adjudication (Part Two): An Examination of Hypotheses of Bias In Investment Treaty Arbitration' (2016) 53 Osgoode Hall Law Journal 540; Thomas Shultz and Cedric Dupont, 'Investment Arbitration: Promoting the Rule of Law or Over-Empowering Investors? A Quantitative Empirical Study' (2014) 25(4) The European Journal of International Law 1147 https://doi.org/10.1093/ejil/chu075 (accessed 16 August 2025).
4. This disclosure requirement also applies to those who have been contacted regarding potential appointment as an arbitrator and have not yet been appointed. *See* Article A11(1) (Disclosure Obligations) and Article A1(d) (Definitions).
5. Article A11(1) (Disclosure Obligation), Code of Conduct for Arbitrators in International Investment Dispute Resolution. *See also*, Article A3 (Independence and Impartiality). The Code was adopted by UN Member states at UNCITRAL's 56th session in July 2023.
6. Rogers has identified 'the empty rhetoric of impartiality' in international arbitration. Catherine A Rogers, *Ethics in International Arbitration* (Oxford University Press 2014) 311.
7. The project conducted ninety-six interviews with key actors in the ISDS system. The interviewees included: highly experienced ISDS arbitrators and more recent entrants to the field, sharing

applies to ISDS on the grounds that trust in arbitrators is constructed on a fundamentally different basis from that of trust in judges.[8] As the findings of the project suggest, trust in ISDS is founded on the method of party appointment and has a dual function. First, it means that the parties *trust* that their party-appointed arbitrator holds certain predispositions which are important for the party's case. Second, it means that a party-appointed arbitrator is *trusted* to perform a role which of itself gives rise to predispositions to the appointing party's case. Specifically, the nature of the role of a party-appointed arbitrator places (in the words of the interviewees who participated in the project) a particular 'mandate', 'duty' or 'job' on a party-appointed arbitrator to ensure that the party's case is fully considered and properly understood which of itself gives rise to certain predispositions. Overall, trust in the appointment of ISDS arbitrators entails that party-appointed arbitrators are chosen for, and perform a role which results in, certain predispositions. Importantly, the findings of our project show that the choice of a predisposed arbitrator by parties and the predispositions which arise from the performance of the party-appointed arbitrator's specific role are, to a certain degree, considered compatible with the understanding of impartiality which applies in ISDS.

In sum, the chapter explains how trust in ISDS is constructed by parties to ISDS and how the foundation of that trust entails a different understanding of impartiality than that which applies in judicial adjudication. In particular, the understanding of impartiality in ISDS is compatible with a degree of predisposition by party-appointed arbitrators to the position of the appointing parties. This compatible degree of predisposition typically comes from a combination of the parties' careful choice of an arbitrator who holds legal views favouring the parties' case and the specific role of a party-appointed arbitrator to ensure that the appointing party's case is properly considered and understood in the deliberation room.

II THE CURRENT DOCTRINE OF IMPARTIALITY IN ISDS

It is generally accepted that the legal doctrine of impartiality in ISDS stems from the doctrine used in international arbitration. No specific doctrine has been developed for ISDS despite the distinct nature of ISDS disputes and the public policy interest these disputes typically implicate. This doctrine is structured around a set of legal rules and jurisprudentially developed tests of bias. Almost all national laws lay down the arbitrators' duty to act impartially as between the parties and disclose potential

---

between them over 1,300 ISDS arbitral appointments; senior representatives of institutions which administer ISDS arbitrations; and senior barristers and lawyers from international law firms who regularly serve as counsel in ISDS arbitrations. Ethical approval was obtained before approaching potential participants. The interviews were conducted from April 2018 to January 2022.

8. This chapter is an abridged version of two recently published articles which present the findings of our empirical project in more detail: 'Contextual Impartiality: A New Approach to Assessing Impartiality in Investor State Dispute Settlement' ICSID Review – Foreign Investment Law Journal, 39(1) (2024), 74-101; 'Impartiality and the Construction of Trust in Investor-State Dispute Settlement' ICSID Review – Foreign Investment Law Journal, 38(3) (2023) 644-669.

conflicts of interest.[9] Where circumstances give rise to *justifiable doubts* as to an arbitrator's impartiality, a party has the right to apply to a national court to remove an arbitrator.

While no single set of standards of impartiality of arbitrators exists across different jurisdictions, most national courts frame the legal test of arbitrators' bias in terms of *appearance of bias* rather than actual bias. The appearance of bias test is applied in ISDS too for arbitrations conducted, for example, under either the UNCITRAL Arbitration Rules or the ICSID Convention.[10]

It is striking to note that the doctrine of impartiality applied in ISDS and, more generally, international arbitration is, in turn, the judicially developed doctrine which has been adopted wholesale and unquestioningly from domestic and international courts. As was confirmed by the UK Supreme Court's decision in *Halliburton v. Chubb*,[11] the test which courts in England and Wales apply to remove an arbitrator in an international arbitration is the domestic *Porter v. Magill* common law test.[12] While the UK Supreme Court has recognised the differences in nature and circumstances between judicial and arbitral decision-making, it has stated that:[13]

> The objective test of the fair-minded and informed observer applies equally to judges and all arbitrators. There is no difference between the test in [English Arbitration law for arbitrators] which speaks of the existence of circumstances 'that give rise to justifiable doubts as to [the arbitrator's] impartiality' and the common law test [for English judges].

This transplantation of the judicial doctrine of impartiality into international arbitration and ISDS is predicated on an *absolutist* approach to impartiality, which is manifested in three different ways. First, it portrays a universal conception of impartiality which applies across differing methods of legal adjudication. The assumption that there exists only one version of impartiality that permeates legal adjudication has become something of a *grundnorm* for international lawyers. Indeed, under the ICSID and UNCITRAL Codes of Conduct for Arbitrators and Judges in International Investment Dispute Resolution, the same duty of impartiality applies to arbitrators, members of international ad hoc annulment or appeal committees, and judges on a court-based system of investment adjudication.[14] The judicial doctrine of impartiality has come to

9. E.g., English Arbitration Act 1996, section 33; *see also* institutional rules, e.g., UNCITRAL Arbitration Rules 2012, Article 11 and ICC Rules of Arbitration 2021, Article 11.
10. *See* Article 12 of the UNCITRAL Arbitration Rules provides that any 'arbitrator may be challenged if circumstances exist that give rise to justifiable doubts as to the arbitrator's impartiality or independence.' For arbitrations conducted under the ICSID framework, despite the language of Articles 14(1) and 57 of ICSID Convention, which suggests a higher threshold of disqualification of a 'manifest lack' of impartiality, ICSID tribunals have applied tests similar to the 'justifiable doubts' standard under the UNCITRAL Arbitration Rules.
11. *Halliburton v. Chubb* [2020] UKSC 48 [52] and [55].
12. *Porter v. Magill* [2001] UKHL 67.
13. *Halliburton* (n 11) [55].
14. ICSID and UNCITRAL Code of Conduct for Arbitrators in International Investment Dispute Resolution (adopted in July 2023) Article 1(c) and Article 3, and ICSID and UNCITRAL Draft Code of Conduct for Judges in International Investment Dispute Resolution (May 2023), Article 1(a) and Article 3.

reflect 'a transnational consensus' which applies universally across international arbitral tribunals and international courts.[15]

Second, and relatedly, the judicial doctrine of absolute impartiality suggests a *singular duty* of impartiality that applies irrespective of the role and function of an arbitrator. In this context, every arbitrator is subject to the same legal standards of impartiality, irrespective of the nature of their role, i.e., whether they act as party-appointed, sole or presiding arbitrators. The conception of impartiality as being a singular duty which applies irrespective of context has been confirmed by national courts on a number of occasions, including by the Swiss Tribunal Federal which held that 'the independence and impartiality required of the members of the arbitral tribunal applies equally to the arbitrators appointed by the party as to the president of the arbitral tribunal'.[16] Interestingly, however, the Swiss Tribunal Federal added, '[i]n stating this principle, the Federal Tribunal is certainly aware that an absolute independence of all the arbitrators constitutes an ideal which only rarely corresponds to reality'.

Third, the judicial doctrine of absolute impartiality entails a *binary conception* of impartiality with adjudicators being either entirely impartial or biased. Any form of partiality, even in the form of implicit bias, including subconscious and cognitive bias, is neither acknowledged nor accepted by the judicial doctrine of impartiality.[17] The English Court of Appeal in *Halliburton* stated that 'the risk of unconscious bias [...] does not affect the relevant legal test for apparent bias [...]. It provides an example of how bias may act, or appear to act, on the mind, but it is not part of the test for whether there is bias'.[18] While the Court of Appeal accepted that the risk of unconscious bias 'is a relevant risk for the fair-minded and informed observer to take into account', it offered no guidance as to what in practice that means for the legal test of impartiality.[19]

No attention appears to have been given as to whether this universal, singular and binary approach transposed from the judicial doctrine of impartiality is suitable for ISDS which was created as an alternative to the courts with a differing procedural design including, most notably, the disputants' ability to appoint the members of the arbitral panel on an ad hoc basis. As the interviewees' insights reveal, parties appoint arbitrators whom they trust to fulfil the role of the party-appointed arbitrator, which is to ensure that the party's case is fully heard and understood in its context. Accordingly, parties appoint arbitrators who have the attributes which enable parties to entrust them

15. *See also* the decision of the European Court of Human Rights in *Micallef v. Malta* App No. 17056/06 (ECtHR, 15 October 2009) para. 93 referring to 'legitimate doubt in respect of [the tribunal's] impartiality'.
16. Swiss Tribunal Federal 4A_234/2010 of 29 October 2010. The same approach has also been adopted by the English Court of Appeal in *Halliburton* which held that 'a party-appointed arbitrator in English law is expected to come up to precisely the same high standards of fairness and impartiality as the person chairing the tribunal'. *Halliburton* (n 11) at [63].
17. On the influence of implicit and subconscious bias on judicial decision-making, *see* Rachel Cahill-O'Callaghan, *Values in the Supreme Court: Decisions, Division and Diversity* (Hart 2020) 50-53.
18. *Halliburton* (n 11) [41].
19. *See also Locabail v. Bayfield Properties* [2000] QB 451, 471-472: 'the law does not countenance the questioning of a judge about extraneous influences affecting his mind'.

with the execution of this role. Both the *attributes* for which arbitrators are chosen and the *very nature* of the role with which they are entrusted have important implications for our understanding of impartiality in ISDS.

1 The Construction of the Value of Trust in ISDS

> 'Arb 37:[20] it [arbitration] is based on a system where you trust one person and you take the risk with that person, that's it.'
>
> 'Arb 89: how do you get a party to trust somebody sufficiently to appoint them? And that's what it's all about.'

Throughout the empirical project, the parties' ability to appoint on an ad hoc basis arbitrators *whom they trust* was identified as a fundamental value of international arbitration. Indeed, the party-appointment system is regarded as a cornerstone of the legitimacy of international arbitration and leads to trust in the arbitration process as a whole and trust in the outcome of the arbitration:[21]

> Arb 81: if one is opting out of the judicial system, [...] then the opportunity to have the option to be involved in the selection of the decision-making body, is fundamentally important to a sense of participation and ownership in and, therefore, trust in that decision-making body.

But what exactly does this trust mean? At a fundamental level, trust means that you appoint someone whom you can trust to ensure that the process will be fair, and that the parties will have a fair opportunity to present their case. In other words, it means trust in the fairness of the process:

> Arb 83: the reasonable expectation of parties in appointing a party-appointed arbitrator is that it will help increase the chances of their case getting a fair hearing before the tribunal, by having a party-appointed arbitrator in place. [...] A fair hearing [where] all parties have a full opportunity to be heard.

However, in ISDS, the expectation of trust goes beyond fair hearing. It crucially means that you trust that the arbitrator you appoint *will understand the substance of your case in its proper context.* Given the unique, political and national sensitivities surrounding ISDS disputes, the context of a party in this kind of disputes is important. In that sense, trust in the context of ISDS is the party's confidence that its

---

20. Almost all interviewees who participated in the project had experience in acting as both counsel and arbitrator. In the paper, an interviewee who is predominantly acting as arbitrator is identified as 'Arb', whereas an interviewee who is predominantly acting as counsel is identified as 'Coun'.
21. Brower and Rosenbery identify 'a close nexus between the perceived legitimacy of international arbitration and the parties' appointment of the arbitrators', adding that such legitimacy then leads to respect for the arbitral award, whether favourable or not. Charles N. Brower and Charles B. Rosenberg, 'The Death of the Two-Headed Nightingale: Why the Paulsson-Van Den Berg Presumption that Party-Appointed Arbitrators are Untrustworthy is Wrongheaded' (2013) 29(1) Arbitration International 7, 19 https://doi.org/10.1093/arbitration/29.1.7 (accessed 16 August 2025).

party-appointed arbitrator has the requisite attributes and qualities to ensure that the party's specific perspectives are carefully considered by the arbitral tribunal.

Interviewees identified three qualities that an ISDS arbitrator must have to properly understand the party's case in their right context: first, and perhaps the most important, is that the arbitrator must share similar perspectives with the party who appointed them: these perspectives can be legal or non-legal:

> Arb 81: but they are also looking for, I think, an understanding of their perspective. So if it is *an investor,* an understanding of *commercial investment, risk and protections*.
>
> If it is *a state,* a perspective of *how a state functions, how democratic process works, if it is, indeed, a democracy, and how laws are made and how people are protected within the state.*
>
> So I don't want to use the word ideology because I don't think that is the right word. I think the right word is *perspective.* If one has never worked with a state or for a state, there is a lot *of state law making process,* state governance process that you don't really appreciate. So I think it is that perspective.

Thus, it matters for ISDS disputants to appoint arbitrators with whom they share certain perspectives because it provides confidence that their positions will be properly engaged with in the decision-making process:

> 'Arb 46: Well, I think that the thing that's critical when you appoint an arbitrator is, of course you the arbitrator has to be impartial and independent but they need to be able to make sure that your party's position is properly heard and vetted within the tribunal. If I'm representing a state, I want my arbitrator to fully understand my position on FET in a given case and make sure that my position is heard, debated and argued within the tribunal or in their deliberation.
>
> Whatever the decision comes to, at least I'm satisfied, or I know that my party's position is being heard. The same thing if I'm representing an investor, I want to make sure that my arbitrator understands the commercial and financial stakes of what has happened and will be able to communicate that effectively within the tribunal and their deliberations.
>
> *At least from a counsel's perspective, that's what's key, that you want to at least have people who that if they have these positions, that the* ***strong views that they may have on certain issues get properly debated within the tribunal and then ultimately, the deliberations lead to whatever the result is***' (emphasis added).

In addition to the broad state-private investor categorisation of parties in ISDS disputes, parties also hail from a wide variety of countries. Accordingly, and in particular for state parties, parties value the ability to appoint an arbitrator who has cultural familiarity with the disputant's home state:

> Coun 100: for state parties in particular, it's *extremely important for them to have a role in nominating an arbitrator*. You know, given the example of an African state [...] most state advocates will feel passionately about having an arbitrator, let's say, with African heritage who they will feel confident with and who can understand where they're coming from [...] So, you want your arbitrator to bring various different things to the table, and you want to be able to select an arbitrator with those particular traits, and yes, that is one of the benefits of arbitration, isn't it?

The second key attribute of trust in a party-appointed arbitrator is *expertise*. In the context of ISDS arbitrator appointments, expertise includes technical specialisation and familiarity with industry norms and practices, as articulated by the following interviewees:

> 'Arb 54: – There is certainly an argument that, if you're having a dispute about the Deep Sea Horizon or the Deepwater Horizon, you want somebody who knows something about oil and gas law, and norms in the oil and gas industry, and knows about oil and gas contracts.
>
> *So in that respect- And if you really think your whole dispute hinges on the interpretation of Clause 85 in your contract, that trade usage is going to matter, then you know that you really want an* ***arbitrator that knows about trade usage***' (emphasis added).

In ISDS disputes, which are now considered an autonomous field of international law, expertise includes specialised legal knowledge in public international law, in particular. Expertise in public international law is an important element of trust in the party-appointed arbitrator's understanding of the state's perspectives and interests in an ISDS dispute:

> 'Coun 71: And that's when I thought we need completely different expertise. We don't need the arbitration gurus, **we need public international law specialists** in these cases. And that's when I started to appoint a different type of lawyer to these cases. You know, again, some, in my view, did a better job than others, others did a very, very good job. But I was clear that we needed a very different specialty, a very specialised area of law, and it is not private, commercial or transactional, as I thought it was' (emphasis added).

Relevant perspectives and expertise alone are insufficient for a party to fully trust their appointed arbitrator. Indeed, the third, and final, key attribute associated with trust is *professionalism*, and in particular a hard-working approach to conducting their duties as arbitrators. This attribute assures parties that their dispute will be dealt with in a thorough manner and that the party-appointed arbitrator will devote the requisite time and attention to actively engage with the typically large and complex file of an ISDS case in order to bring the parties' particular perspectives into play. Several interviewees emphasised this important element of trust:

> Coun 33: In terms of trust, though, it's trust to do two things, one is that they will do the work. [...] That they will actually review, particularly in a complex case, or a case that just involves, frankly, wading through a lot of crap, that they will actually get to the detail and understand the basis of your arguments. They may not agree with them, but at least they'll look at them and understand them ...
>
> And, you know, given that that trust is innate in every single appointment, the critical thing for me is a comfort that they will actually do the job.

III THE IMPLICATIONS OF TRUST FOR IMPARTIALITY IN ISDS

As explained above, trust in the appointment of ISDS arbitrators means the party's confidence that its party-appointed arbitrator has the requisite perspectives, expertise and professionalism to ensure that the party's specific perspectives are carefully considered by the arbitral tribunal. What are the implications of the value of trust for the idea of impartiality in ISDS?

The findings of the project show that trust in the appointment of arbitrators affects understandings of impartiality in ISDS in two ways: First, it means that the parties trust that the *specific perspectives* of their party-appointed arbitrator will lead to *a degree of predisposition that would favour* the position of that party:

> Arb 14: The first item for me is to draw a list of people whose decisions might go to some extent in the direction of the legal issues or in the direction of how we want the legal issues in the case *to be decided in favour of the client*. That is our first criterion.

An overwhelming number of interviewees indicated that this sort of predisposition amounts to some form of bias:[22]

> 'Arb 49: Yes, and, of course, *this does definitely go to your bias* in the broadest sense of the term. I think that you do look for a predisposition, if you're a claimant's counsel, that someone is not going to be too statist.'
>
> ***
>
> 'Arb 27: That's one of the things you [look at] when putting up the tribunal. That, I think, is – or should be – one of the values of arbitration: that you have people who understand what the dispute is about. That brings with it some element of bias.'
>
> ***
>
> 'Arb 94: what I am focusing on, is that it's not a question of being honest or dishonest, it's a question of being rather involved in certain areas rather than in others, more knowledgeable in one area rather than another. That may lead to what we *perceive as bias*.'

Further, those serving as arbitrators acknowledge the effectiveness of the thorough selection process in appointing an arbitrator with favourable predispositions. As an arbitrator puts it:

> Arb 10: I am struck by the fact that although I do not believe *I am partisan* in any way, every time I have dissented, it has been in *favour of the party who appointed me*. I think about that a lot and it tells me at a minimum, the notion that counsel and parties are trying to *choose party appointed arbitrators who are philosophically predisposed towards their conception of the case*. Must be working to some extent, because I find myself saying, 'Here's how I think about the law. Here's how I think about facts.' Then I'm outvoted 2-to-1, it may be that my dissent consists of one sentence.

The second way in which trust implicates the duty of impartiality in ISDS is that a party-appointed arbitrator is entrusted to perform a role which of itself gives rise to

22. Due to word constraints, only a few quotes are included here.

predispositions to the appointing party's case. As the interviewees described, the nature of the role of a party-appointed arbitrator, in and of itself, places (in the words of the interviewees) a particular 'mandate', 'duty' or 'job' on the arbitrator towards the party who appointed them:

> 'Arb 49: He does *have a job [said one interviewee who clearly thinks that arbitrators are only male]*. Any arbitrator does have a job to make sure that the party that appointed them is able to get their case out. I mean, that's a fundamental role that they have [...] they need to make sure that all the arguments are well vetted [...]. You rely on the other party appointed to do that for the people that appointed them.'
>
> 'Arb 18: It's the *duty* of the co-arbitrator to see to it that the standpoint of the party that appointed him is duly considered, the same way the other party's standpoint is duly considered.'

While interviewees were careful to distinguish this 'duty' from 'partiality', their insights clearly suggest that the role and position of a party-appointed arbitrator carry with it a degree of predisposition towards the appointing party's case:

> 'Arb 22: [T] he duty of the party-appointed arbitrator is to put the position, to make the tribunal understand the position of the party who appointed him or her. That is more and more in the **borderline of leading for the party**' (emphasis added).
>
> 'Arb 18: The reality is different. Even the most neutral co-arbitrator will always see to it that the party that appointed him will be treated fairly and **may advance arguments of that party**. As long as he or she is not biased and one sided, then that's alright. It's not realistic to think that party appointment has no effect whatsoever on the reasoning, the behaviour of an arbitrator' (emphasis added).
>
> 'Arb 92: As an arbitrator, so I now practise mostly as an arbitrator. As an arbitrator, I certainly have mixed feelings about it. I feel that I have served with arbitrators that I have felt are biased, and I think that that bias comes from the fact that they are party appointed. So there is, in my mind, **a linkage between party appointment and a sort of conscious or subconscious bias**. So it may not be deliberate per se, but there is this underlying bias that I sense' (emphasis added).

Looking back to the judicial doctrine of impartiality, it is obvious that the understandings of impartiality in ISDS do not readily reconcile with the absolute nature of the judicial doctrine of impartiality in national courts.

An absolute doctrine of impartiality makes good sense for judiciaries. Indeed, the doctrine of impartiality in the judiciary has public law and constitutional law origins. It developed as a constitutional theory in the eighteenth century to ensure that the judiciary remains entirely separate and impartial from the executive. The constitutional theory of separation of powers which holds a central position in liberal democracies rests on an effective and meaningful doctrine of judicial review. In this constitutional context, judges must be strictly detached from the disputing parties. Exhibiting any form of intuitive bias or taking account of the perspectives of certain parties is considered incompatible with the role of the judiciary.

However, while an absolute doctrine of impartiality has worked well both as a matter of practice and as the moral foundation for national judiciaries, the different historical origins and design of arbitration call into question the suitability of that doctrine for the specific context of ISDS.

Indeed, arbitration evolved as a private theory of adjudication (not a constitutional one); it came about as a distinct system of justice which is alternative to judiciaries and sits outside the constitutional triangle of legislature, judiciary and executive. Historically, arbitrators never had a judicial function; rather, they were treated by law as *agents* of the two disputing parties with a mandate of finding a solution to the dispute. As showed in earlier work, Court decisions in England from the nineteenth century demonstrate that the courts classified arbitration agreements as agency contracts under which arbitrators had fiduciary, not judicial, powers.[23] The ad hoc party-appointment system in arbitration is the corollary of the historical treatment of arbitrators as agents whom parties appointed because they trusted them and placed upon them fiduciary duties to resolve their case. While arbitration as a justice system has evolved all these years, the fundamental idea of a party-appointed arbitrator as a trusted decision-maker (who has a certain duty towards the party who appointed them) remains.

Indeed, the findings show that today arbitrators are alive to the fiduciary trust they assume when they accept the appointment by a party and that they respond to that trust, as identified, for example, by the following interviewees:

> Arb 09: You have to recognise that you're fulfilling a *special function* that you've been entrusted [by the parties who appointed you]. It's important to honour their trust in you and not exceed their trust in you. I do think there's an extra level of care [towards the party who appointed you].

In that sense, the trust in arbitrators is constructed differently from the trust in judiciaries. When two parties decide to submit their dispute in national courts, they cannot choose the perspectives, expertise and experience of the judge who will be assigned to decide their dispute. Rather, they choose to resolve their dispute in a national court because they trust the court system of that jurisdiction as a whole. In other words, it is *trust in the judicial system* which leads to trust in the individual judges.

By contrast, parties in ISDS trust certain individuals because of particular attributes these individuals have. It is *trust in the individual arbitrators* which leads to trust in the ISDS system as a whole. ISDS is not an integrated system of dispute resolution as national judiciaries are where all judges are chosen, and often trained, by a central appointing authority. The process and outcome of an ISDS arbitration are as good and trustworthy as the specific arbitrators who constitute the panel:

> Arb 90: I mean, the entire arbitration is all about appointment of arbitrators – in other words, parties – can actually choose who is going to be the decision-maker. And I think this is what really makes arbitration different from litigation, for instance.
>
> So, yes, it is essential to arbitration, and it is very important to keep it that way, in my view. Because that really enhances the trust in the system and confidence in the system.

23. Stavros Brekoulakis, 'The Policy Favouring Arbitration under English Law' (2019) 39 Oxford Journal of Legal Studies 124, 144.

This fundamental difference in the construction of trust between ISDS and judiciaries entails a different understanding of impartiality. While any degree of known or active predispositions in national courts would lead to disqualification of judges, this form of predisposition is considered compatible with the idea of impartiality which exists in the context of ISDS.

> 'Arb 50: You have to accept party appointed arbitrations; the party appointed arbitrator has an inclination towards. That's why also I don't mind it, I do not mind it. I think it's normal.'
>
> ***
>
> 'Arb 49: Yes, and, of course, this does definitely go to your bias in the broadest sense of the term. To me, that's a fine example of legitimate predilections. That doesn't mean that they're going to decide any case in any particular way necessarily. But to me, that's a completely legitimate bias if you want to use the term, obviously. The term is too strong; "predilection" is better.'

It should be pointed out that the different understanding of impartiality in ISDS does not suggest that the practice of ISDS is unprincipled or ethically compromised. Indeed, the system of ISDS is heavily regulated in terms of ethical laws and rules, and despite the criticism, examples of unprincipled behaviour on the part of arbitrators are very rare. Rather, under this more nuanced understanding of impartiality, the reason that certain forms of predisposition are considered legitimate is because of the idea of trust in the unique role of party-appointed arbitrators which has always been a foundational value for arbitration. Parties trust that the arbitrator they select has certain perspectives and experiences which entail a form of bias and also that the arbitrator will perform the role in a manner which of itself gives rise to a form of bias:

> 'Arb 66: It doesn't mean that they are not impartial, [and] it doesn't mean the system is any less legitimate in terms of impartiality.'
>
> 'Arb 50: It's a different understanding of [impartiality]. Whilst in international arbitration we've increasingly fallen for the idea these people are judges and therefore must be impartial. I think it's a misunderstanding of what international arbitration is, of what arbitration is at all. The parties want to keep a finger in the pie and that's also necessary for its credibility. It's a credibility issue. If it's taken away from the parties, they don't feel any kind of connection with it and I think they don't like it.'

IV CONCLUSION

Drawing on original empirical findings, this chapter has identified how parties' trust is constructed in the context of ISDS and has challenged the applicability of the judicial doctrine of impartiality to ISDS. The chapter further shows that trust in party-appointed arbitrators leads to some forms of predispositions or partiality in ISDS which is generally accepted in ISDS as part of our understanding of impartiality.

Our work therefore calls for a new assessment of impartiality in ISDS which is more nuanced and which can better correspond to the foundational value of trust in ISDS. In this nuanced approach, certain forms of partiality can be compatible.

Importantly, within this new assessment of impartiality, special concerns, intuitions, even strong emotions and passions, need to be recognised as a form of acceptable partiality in ISDS and indeed in legal decision-making.

This is not the case currently in law where the test of impartiality is exclusively informed by the idea of this 'third party observer who is entirely dispassionate and rational'. It seems that legal thinking is still under the ideological grip of a long line of Western thought from Plato and Aristotle[24] to Immanuel Kant and Jeremy Bentham, suggesting that rationality is the pure form of reason, including legal reason. The idea here is that passions and intuitions make human reason unfit to judge what is good or evil. But to insist that legal decision-making is carried out as a neutral, emotionless, dispassionate and impartial exercise flies in the face of insights reached in psychology, moral philosophy, anthropology and neurobiology which have demonstrated that human cognition works in concert with emotions and partialities to shape our perceptions and decisions. Even by law's well-known insularity and unwillingness to learn from other disciplines, this absolute demarcation between reason and emotion, decision-making and partiality is unsustainable.[25] Faith in pure reason is nothing more than a rationalist delusion. The legal doctrine of impartiality in law, and certainly in ISDS, has been operating under this rationalist delusion requiring all arbitrators irrespective of their role, background and perspectives to answer to the same unattainable standards of impartiality and be free of any form of partiality. This reconciles neither with the nuances of human nature nor with the practical understandings of impartiality in ISDS. The findings of the project show that a contextual approach, which allows legal and moral space for some forms of partiality, is not only possible but also desirable.

This call for a nuanced and contextualised approach to impartiality is likely to be met with apprehension. While absolutes provide an alluring certainty and simplicity, nuance suggests uncertainty and complexity. To allay such apprehension, there are a number of issues which this new approach to impartiality will need to address.

First, while certain forms of predisposition, as identified in this article, are compatible with the unique understanding of impartiality in ISDS, this does not suggest that other types of predisposition or partiality would also be compatible. The call for a new approach to impartiality is certainly not a call for a right to be partial, and there must be clear limitations to the forms of predisposition which are permissible under this approach. Therefore, an important issue to be addressed is whether a principled line can be drawn between forms of permissible and impermissible forms of predisposition.

Second, this chapter has demonstrated that a nuanced and contextualised understanding of impartiality in ISDS is more empirically accurate than the absolutist approach of the judicial doctrine of impartiality. Building upon these empirical insights, a further issue to explore is whether there is a theoretical basis for a

24. Aristotle Politics, III. XI 'ἄνευ ὀρέξεως νοῦς ὁ νόμος ἐστίν' ('law is reason without desire').
25. Susan Bandes, *The Passions of Law* (NYU 1999).

contextualised approach to impartiality and whether theory can assist in identifying the parameters of this approach.

Third, empirical resonance and theoretical foundations may not be sufficient to allay concerns about this proposed new approach to impartiality in ISDS. It is therefore important to consider the potential practical advantages of this approach, weighed against any potential disadvantages. In other words, what might this approach contribute to the ISDS field?

All of these issues are considered in detail in another work of ours which proposes the idea of contextual impartiality.[26] Under this more nuanced approach to impartiality, the question is not whether an arbitrator can meet universal standards of impartiality irrespective of the context within which the arbitrator operates. Rather, the question is what standards of impartiality should *reasonably be expected* from that arbitrator, given the specific characteristics of the context in which that arbitrator is operating.

26. *See* 'Impartiality and the Construction of Trust in Investor-State Dispute Settlement' ICSID Review – Foreign Investment Law Journal, 38(3) (2023) 644-669.

CHAPTER 8

The Science of Decision-Making: Improving Decision Quality

*Rachel Cahill-O'Callaghan**

TABLE OF CONTENTS

I INTRODUCTION

The science of decision-making spans a range of disciplines including neurophysiology, neuroimaging, computational modelling, psychiatry, psychology, neuropsychology, economics and more recently neuroeconomics. Each discipline, which draws on distinct approaches and methods, seeks to understand the underlying processes that are required for effective decision-making and identify the factors that influence these processes. While the majority of the early neurophysiological and neuroimaging experimental studies were carried out on the animal brain, recent advances in functional magnetic resonance (fMRI) have provided the mechanism to trace the dynamics of unfolding decision-making processes. Advances in electroencephalography and magnetoencephalography also allow researchers to map the neural time

* Rachel is a professor at Cardiff School of Law and Politics and holds PhDs in Science and Law. She works at the interface of law and psychology exploring the factors that influence judicial decision-making. Her work on judicial decision-making in the Supreme Court has won several prizes and her monograph *Values in the Supreme Court: Decisions, Division and Diversity* (Hart 2020) was shortlisted for the Birks prize for outstanding scholarship. Cahill-OCallaghanR@cardiff.ac.uk.

course of decision-making with millisecond precision.[1] These experiments are necessarily reductive, exploring the influence of a small number of simplified parameters. The data are extended with mathematical models of decision-making which start to link the functional areas of the brain with choice behaviour.[2] The addition of computational modelling and psychological studies provide a deeper understanding of the complexity of the psychological processes that underpin simple decision-making. It is important to recognise, from the outset, that arbitrators are not making binary decisions with simple parameters.

When we consider arbitration decisions, the process is typically viewed through the outcome and characterised as a choice between outcomes. But arbitration decision-making is not a single decision; it is a systematic (and sometimes less systematic) complex process of a series of choices.[3] Each determination shapes the choice architecture for the decisions that follow. Some of these decisions are quick, simple, and routine. Others have an element of uncertainty. Both have the potential to mediate bias. Bias in a legal context is typically conceptualised as negative bias, bias directed against those who are marginalised in society or traditionally disadvantaged. In the context of arbitration, academic debates of bias are concerned with bias towards parties or positions.[4] These are important and worthy of discussion and debate, but this chapter is concerned with bias in a psychological context. In this context, bias is a predisposition to a particular choice. It is not unacceptable; it is a normal and inevitable aspect of decision-making. In effective decision-making, bias is moderated and modified by reasoning. However, if acceptable bias is resistant to or not exposed to

1. Harris, A. and Hutcheson, C.A. (2022). Temporal Dynamics of Decision Making: A Synthesis of Computations and Neurophysiological Approaches. *Wiley Interdisciplinary Review of Cognitive Science* 13(3) 1586.
2. For example, Farrar, D.C. et al.(2018). Functional Brain Networks Involved in Decision-Making under Certain and Uncertain Conditions. *Neuroradiology*, 60, 61-69 https://doi.org/10.1007/s00234-017-1949-1 (accessed 16 August 2025); Forstmann, B.U., Ratcliff, R. and Wagenmakers, E.J. (2016). Sequential Sampling Models in Cognitive Neuroscience: Advantages, Applications, and Extensions. *Annual Review of Psychology*, 67, 641-666 https://doi.org/10.1146/annurev-psych-122414-033645 (accessed 16 August 2025); Turner, B.M., Van Maanen, L. and Forstmann, B.U. (2015). Informing Cognitive Abstractions Through Neuroimaging: The Neural Drift Diffusion Model. *Psychological Review*, 122(2), 312 https://doi.org/10.1037/a0038894 (accessed 16 August 2025); Basten, U. et al. (2010). How the Brain Integrates Costs and Benefits During Decision Making. *Proceedings of the National Academy of Sciences*, 107(50), 21767-21772 https://doi.org/10.1073/pnas.0908104107 (accessed 16 August 2025).
3. Howard and Seth demonstrate that even the simplest decision such as 'buying a car' is a process and a systematic series of choices. Howard, J. A. and Sheth, J.N. (1969). The Theory of Buyer Behaviour. *New York*, 63, 145.
4. *See* for example, Donaubauer, J., Neumayer, E. and Nunnenkamp, P. (2018). Winning or Losing in Investor-to-State Dispute Resolution: The Role of Arbitrator Bias and Experience. *Review of International Economics*, 26(4), 892-916 https://doi.org/10.1111/roie.12347 (accessed 16 August 2025); Puig, S. and Strezhnev, A. (2017). Affiliation Bias in Arbitration: An Experimental Approach. *The Journal of Legal Studies*, 46(2), 371-398 https://doi.org/10.1086/694416 (accessed 16 August 2025); Brekoulakis, S. (2013). Systemic Bias and the Institution of International Arbitration: A New Approach to Arbitral Decision-Making. *Journal of International Dispute Settlement*, 4(3), 553-583 https://doi.org/10.1093/jnlids/idt016 (accessed 16 August 2025); Luttrell, S. (2009). *Bias Challenges in International Commercial Arbitration: The Need for a 'Real Danger' Test*, Vol. 20, Kluwer Law International BV.

moderation, it could potentially predetermine the decision and thus become unacceptable. As such, if we understand the processes and factors that influence decision-making, we can use that knowledge to create structures to improve decision quality and limit the influences that could potentially predetermine our decisions.

II BRAIN PHYSIOLOGY AND DECISION-MAKING

Early studies of brain function identified a relationship between the prefrontal cortex and executive decision-making, with human patients who had damage to the prefrontal cortex exhibiting poor judgment, planning and decision-making.[5] This association with reasoning and the prefrontal cortex was confirmed by fMRI studies which map the brain's decision-making circuitry. Using simple choices, the studies extended the location of decision-making to several different areas of the brain, including the dorsolateral prefrontal cortex (memory and cognitive control), the right insula (associated with risk-reward behaviour), and the anterior cingulate cortex (error processing).[6] Decision-making is not limited to the reasoning and executive decision-making areas of the brain. The limbic system (including the amygdala, basal ganglia, and cerebellum) is also involved. Even in the simplest of decisions, the limbic system – the system associated with motivation, emotion, and memory – is activated.[7] While distinct areas of the brain, these do not operate independently, and the complex system of networking transmits signals rapidly from one area of the brain to another in less than 300 ms. It takes one-fifth of a second for a signal from the right side of the brain to move to the left side, and a simple decision can be made in less than a second.[8] When the decision-making moves from a simple decision with a clear and certain outcome to a decision with a level of uncertainty, the level of activation of all systems increases.[9]

5. *See*, for example, Mesulam, M-Marsel (2002). The Human Frontal Lobes: Transcending the Default Mode Through Contingent Encoding. *Principles of Frontal Lobe Function*, 54, 8-30. Stuss, Fuster, J. (2015). *The Prefrontal Cortex*. Academic Press; Goldman-Rakic, P.S. (1987). Development of Cortical Circuitry and Cognitive Function. *Child Development*, 601-662; Donald T. Stuss and David Frank Benson(1986). *The Frontal Lobes*. Raven Press, New York.
6. For example, Liu, T. and Pleskac, T.J. (2011). Neural Correlates of Evidence Accumulation in a Perceptual Decision Task. *Journal of Neurophysiology*, 106(5), 2383-2398 https://doi.org/10.1152/jn.00413.2011 (accessed 16 August 2025); Ho, S.S. et al. (2012). Neurocircuits Underlying Cognition–Emotion Interaction in a Social Decision-Making Context. *NeuroImage*, 63(2), 843-857 https://doi.org/10.1016/j.neuroimage.2012.07.017 (accessed 16 August 2025).
7. Please note that the limbic system singular is used here for simplicity. There is an argument that the limbic system consists of several distinct systems, *see* Rolls, E.T. (2015). Limbic Systems for Emotion and for Memory, but No Single Limbic System. *Cortex*, 62, 119-157 https://doi.org/10.1016/j.cortex.2013.12.005 (accessed 16 August 2025).
8. This speed is related to the drift diffusion model (DDM) which only applies to simply binary decisions and not the complex reasoning associated with judgment. For a review of the DDM, *see* Myers, C., Iterian, A. and Moustafa, A.A. (2022) A Practical Introduction to Using the Drift Diffusion Model of Decision-Making in Cognitive Psychology, Neurosciences and Health Sciences. *Frontiers of Psychology*, 13, 1039172 https://doi.org/10.3389/fpsyg.2022.1039172 (accessed 16 August 2025).
9. Gloy, K., Herrmann, M. and Fehr, T. (2020). Decision Making Under Uncertainty in a Quasi-Realistic Binary Decision Task–An fMRI Study. *Brain and Cognition*, 140, 105549 https://doi.org/10.1016/j.bandc.2020.105549 (accessed 16 August 2025).

The activation process is even more complex when we move from individual to group decision-making and where negotiation and trade interactions are uncertain.[10]

III DECISION-MAKING AND COGNITIVE PSYCHOLOGY

Cognitive psychology moves from the physiology of the brain to the processes of activation to action in decision-making. The two systems model (system 1 and system 2) of judgment and decision-making was brought to popular attention by Daniel Kahneman and Amos Tversky.[11] Both systems are a collection of processes which are distinguished by their speed and controllability. System 1 is intuitive, occurs spontaneously and does not require a high level of cognition. It is in this stage of the process that prior beliefs and heuristics (mental shortcuts) are generally thought to have the most influence. System 2 is slow, data-rich, deliberative, high-level reasoning which requires effort, concentration, and the execution of rules. This is the form of reasoning often described as 'logic', traditionally associated with legal decision-making. While some suggest that there are distinct areas of brain stimulation associated with each system, it is generally agreed that the processes do not work in isolation.[12] System 1 provides the instinctive initial response to the choice context, and this response is moderated by the system 2 deliberative reasoning. The systems are integrated and mutually supportive and continuously interact throughout the decision-making process. While little is known about the processes of arbitration decision-making, modern theories of judicial decision-making suggest that judges rely on both intuition and reasoning to reach a decision. Judges initially have a gut reaction, a system 1 response, as to what is 'right' or 'fair' in reaction to the stimulus of the case and legal arguments. The instinct can be affirmed, overruled, or adjusted by 'logic', system 2 reasoning. This theory is supported by the work of several authors who posit that even expert decision-makers initially make intuitive judgments (system 1) which they might or might not override with deliberation (system 2).[13] Indeed, Kahneman and Frederick

10. The studies demonstrate the complex cognitive and emotional processes which interact, activating areas of the brain including the anterior insula, ventral striatum and lateral orbitofrontal cortex – parts of the brain which are known to act in emotional self-regulation and reward processing related to subjective emotion and motivation and brain processes related to evaluation of incentives. Hollmann, M. et al. (2011). Predicting Decisions in Human Social Interactions Using Real-Time fMRI and Pattern Classification. *PLoS One*, 6(10), e25304 https://doi.org/10.1371/journal.pone.0025304 (accessed 16 August 2025).
11. Tversky, A. and Kahneman D. (1988). Rational Choice and the Framing of Decisions. *Decision Making: Descriptive, Normative, and Prescriptive Interactions* 167-192; Kahneman, D. and Tversky, A. (1984). Choices, Values, and Frames. *American Psychologist*, 39(4), 341 https://doi.org/10.1037//0003-066x.39.4.341 (accessed 16 August 2025); Kahneman, D. and Tversky A. (1982). The Psychology of Preferences. *Scientific American*, 246(1), 160-173 https://doi.org/10.1038/scientificamerican0182-160 (accessed 16 August 2025).
12. *See* for example De Neys, W. and Goel, V. (2011). Heuristics and Biases in the Brain: Dual Neural Pathways for Decision Making. *Neuroscience of Decision Making*, 125-141. Psychology Press; Sanfey, A.G. and Chang, L.J. (2008). Multiple Systems in Decision Making. *Annals of the New York Academy of Sciences*, 1128(1), 53-62 https://doi.org/10.1196/annals.1399.007 (accessed 16 August 2025).
13. Frederick, P.D. et al. (2017). The Influence of Disease Severity of Preceding Clinical Cases on Pathologists' Medical Decision Making. *Medical Decision Making*, 37(1), 91-100 https://doi.or

suggest that the intuitive judgment is expressed overtly only if it is endorsed by system 2 as 'system 1 quickly proposes intuitive answers to judgement problems as they arise, and system 2 monitors the quality of these proposals which it may endorse, correct or override'.[14]

There are a number of aspects of the system 1 response which act as initial biases in the decision-making processes, many are mediated through heuristics. Parsimony, minimising energy expenditure, is a guiding principle of the physiology of the brain. As such, the brain uses mental shortcuts as tools to reach decisions. These mental shortcuts are detailed elsewhere, but for completeness, it is important to highlight some of those heuristics that have been identified as a facet of experimental judicial decision-making.[15] In 2001, Guthrie, Rachlinski and Wistrich identified that judges were as susceptible to certain heuristics as lay decision-makers.[16]

Although better than lay decision-makers at limiting the effect of the anchoring heuristic, and framing heuristic, judges are equally susceptible to representative, hindsight, and egocentric heuristics. Both the representative and hindsight heuristics are engaged in a decision on probability or likelihood of an event. The representative heuristic bases the judgment on the extent to which the evidence is representative of the category. This subjective heuristic is based on the decision-maker's prior knowledge and the conception of chance. The hindsight heuristic is the subjective shortcut which often leads to an overestimation of prediction of the past, and an overestimation of another's ability to predict an outcome of an action or decision. This is a result of the decision–makers' reflections on a known outcome. The final heuristic is that of egocentric bias. Like the other tools of decision-making, this heuristic is an estimate of probability, but rather than the probability of an event occurring, this centres on the probability of decision-maker error. As with lay decision-makers, judges are as susceptible to overestimating their own ability. In part, this is because of a lack of an accurate comparator.

Although subjective, heuristics are sensible estimation procedures; they are not irrational and engage highly sophisticated mental processes, including feature matching and memory retrieval. Heuristics offer an effective starting point in the

g/10.1177/0272989x16638326 (accessed 16 August 2025); Nakhaeizadeh, S., Dror, I.E. and Morgan, R.M. (2015). The Emergence of Cognitive Bias in Forensic Science and Criminal Investigations. *British Journal of American Legal Studies*, 4, 527; Kahneman, D. and Klein, G. (2009). Conditions for Intuitive Expertise: A Failure to Disagree. *American Psychologist*, 64(6), 515 https://doi.org/10.1037/a0016755 (accessed 16 August 2025).

14. Kahneman, D. and Frederick S. (2002) 'Representativeness Revisited: Attribute Substitution in Intuitive Judgement' in T. Gilovich, D. Griffin and D. Kahneman (eds) *Heuristics of Intuitive Judgment: Extensions and Applications*, New York: Cambridge University Press, p. 51.
15. For a review of heuristics, *see* Gigerenzer, G. and Gaissmaier, W. (2011). Heuristic Decision Making. *Annual Review of Psychology*, 62, 451-482 https://doi.org/10.1146/annurev-psych-12 0709-145346 (accessed 16 August 2025).
16. *See* Guthrie, C., Rachlinski, J.J. and Wistrich A.J. (2001). Inside the Judicial Mind. *Cornell Law Review*, 86(4), 777. It is important to note that this study took place on judicial training day. While a very different context to the courtroom, the authors argue that even in the highly constrained context of judicial decision-making, heuristics will play a role. Arbitration decisions are not reached under the time constraints of many judicial decisions, but several studies demonstrate that in complex decisions with a level of uncertainty heuristics play a role.

decision-making process which can be moderated by system 2 reasoning facilitated by information, time, openness, and an opportunity to challenge the instinctive response. These studies do not suggest poor judicial decision-making, rather they highlight the subjective nature of decision-making and the humanity of the expert decision-maker.

1 Influence of Values on Decision-Making

Many of the heuristics are mental shortcuts, quick estimates, mediated by system 1 processes. Values are also mediated by heuristics but do not serve as a mental shortcut. In contrast, values serve as a filter through which a decision-maker evaluates the choice. Values are a central facet of individual identity.[17] Over the last three decades, there has been an increasing body of psychological research that investigates the content and structure of values and how an individual's personal value priorities shape decision-making.[18] Values in this context are defined as:

> [E]nduring beliefs that a specific mode of conduct is personally or socially preferable to an opposite or converse mode of conduct or end state of existence.[19]

This definition highlights one of the key characteristics of personal values, which is that values are tools of evaluation. They serve as the lens through which we view the world and the foundation for the evaluative decision of what is positive or desirable. The work of Schwartz suggests while value terms are numerous and granular, all conserved trans-situational abstract values can be encompassed into overarching motivations which are driven by three requirements: first, the needs of individuals as biological organisms; second, the requirements of coordinated social interaction; and finally the requirements for the smooth functioning and survival of stable groups.[20]

17. Values underpin our personality, ideology, moral positioning, *see*, for example, Anglim J. et al. (2017). HEXACO Personality and Schwartz's Personal Values: A Facet Level of Analysis. *Journal of Research in Personality* 23-31 https://doi.org/10.1016/j.jrp.2017.04.002 (accessed 16 August 2025).
18. *See*, for example, Rokeach, M. (1973). *The Nature of Human Values*, Free Press; Feather, N.T. (1995). Values, Valences and Choice: The Influence of Values on the Perceived Attractiveness and Choice Alternatives. *Journal of Personality and Social Psychology*, 68, 1135; Maio, G.R. and Olson, J.M. (1998) Values as Truisms: Evidence and Implications. *Journal of Personality and Social Psychology*, 74, 294 https://doi.org/10.1037//0022-3514.74.2.294 (accessed 16 August 2025); Sagiv, L. and Schwartz, S.H. (2000). Value Priorities and Subjective Well-Being: Direct Relations and Congruity Effects. *European Journal of Social Psychology*, 30, 177 https://doi.org/10.1002/(sici)1099-0992(200003/04)30:2 < 177::aid-ejsp982 > 3.0.co;2-z (accessed 16 August 2025); Bardi, A. and Schwartz, S.H. (2003). Values and Behaviour: Strength and Structure of Relations. *Personality and Social Psychology Bulletin*, 29, 1207 https://doi.org/10.1177/0146167203254602 (accessed 16 August 2025); Bernard, M.M., Maio, G.R. and Olson, J.M. (2003). The Vulnerability of Values to Attack: Inoculation of Values and Value-Relevant Attitudes. *Personality and Social Psychology Bulletin*, 29, 63 https://doi.org/10.1177/0146167202238372 (accessed 16 August 2025); Maio, G.R. et al. (2009). Changing, Priming, and Acting on Values: Effects via Motivational Relations in a Circular Model. *Journal of Personality and Social Psychology*, 97(4), 699 https://doi.org/10.1037/a0016420 (accessed 16 August 2025).
19. Rokeach, M. (1973). *The Nature of Human Values*. New York, NY, Free Press.
20. Schwartz, S.H. (1994). Are There Universal Aspects in the Structure and Content of Human Values? *Journal of Social Issues*, 50, 19, 21 https://doi.org/10.1111/j.1540-4560.1994.tb01196.x (accessed 16 August 2025).

These motivations can be further divided into those that have an internal (impact on the individual) or external (impact on wider society) focus. Schwartz has provided a model of the overarching motivations which organises the values based on the motivational goal (Table 8.1). Individual decision-makers may affirm all values, but in reaching a decision between one or more values, a value or values will be prioritised, and it is this value hierarchy which is central to decision-making. In an unconstrained choice, the decision-maker will make a decision that aligns with the values that are situated higher up their personal value hierarchy.[21] This unique feature distinguishes values from other constructs of self (such as attitudes and traits).

Table 8.1 Replicated and Adapted Table of 19 Values Defined by Motivation from Schwartz et al (2012)[22]

Value	*Conceptual Definitions in Terms of Motivational Goals*
Focus on self	
Self-Direction	**Autonomy**
- Thought	Freedom to develop one's own ideas and abilities.
- Action	Freedom to determine one's own actions.
Stimulation	Individual excitement, change, novelty.
Hedonism	Pleasure, gratification.
Focus on self in society (close relationships (social, work, professional))	
Benevolence	
- Dependability	Being a reliable and trustworthy member of the 'ingroup'
- Caring	Devotion to welfare of the 'ingroup'
Face	Maintaining public image and associated power and security
Achievement	Success based on social standards
Humility	Recognising one's insignificance in the wider world
Security	
- Personal	Safety of one's environment, family, close community
Conformity	
- Rules	Compliance with rules, law and formal obligations
- Interpersonal	Avoiding disrupting relationships
Focus on wider society	
Security	
- Societal	Safety and stability of wider society

21. Feather, N.T. (1995). Values, Valences and Choice: The Influence of Values on the Perceived Attractiveness and Choice Alternatives. *Journal of Personality and Social Psychology*, 68, 1135 https://doi.org/10.1037//0022-3514.68.6.1135 (accessed 16 August 2025); Bardi, A. and Schwartz, S.H. (2003). Values and Behaviour: Strength and Structure of Relations. *Personality and Social Psychology Bulletin*, 29, 1207 https://doi.org/10.1177/0146167203254602 (accessed 16 August 2025).
22. Schwartz, S.H. et al. (2012). Refining the Theory of Basic Individual Values. *Journal of Personality and Social Psychology*, 103(4), 663 https://doi.org/10.1037/a0029393 (accessed 16 August 2025).

Value	*Conceptual Definitions in Terms of Motivational Goals*
Tradition	Maintaining and preserving traditions
Universalism	
- Concern	Commitment to equality, justice and protection of all people
- Nature	Preservation of the natural environment
- Tolerance	Acceptance of those who are different
Power	
- Dominance	Power through control over others
- Resources	Power through control of material and resources

This value prioritisation is observed in the judgments of cases which divided the UK Supreme Court. In these most difficult cases, the decisions remain anchored in individual value priorities.[23] Indeed, Justices will reach decisions which align with a consistent set of values across a series of cases which divide judicial opinion.[24] This is not unexpected, or incorrect, it is an inevitable facet of decision-making when the evidence is complex and the outcome uncertain (two legally valid outcomes). Values are activated through the amygdala,[25] which is activated in the system 1 response, as such values are activated immediately and provide an anchor and a filter for system 2 reasoning. Values thus orientate mechanisms of decision-making towards value priorities and subsequently guide information processing and judgment in system 2 processes. Once engaged, values are infused with positive or negative feeling.[26] The intensity of feeling is related to the importance of the value to the individual, with increased emotional intensity associated with a violation of an important value. Values are mediated through the affect response.

The affect response operates when you have an immediate positive or negative reaction to some idea, proposal, person, or argument. In social cognition theory, this is commonly known as the 'gut reaction' and sets up an initial orientation, positive or negative, in the decision-maker towards the object.[27] The response occurs rapidly and automatically, typically without conscious thought. While some decisions elicit strong emotions, the affect response in decision-making is a constant 'faint whisper of

23. Cahill-O'Callaghan, R. (2020) *Values in the Supreme Court: Decisions, Division and Diversity*, Hart Publishing, UK.
24. Cahill-O'Callaghan, R. (2015). Winner of the SLS Annual Conference Best Paper Prize 2014: Reframing the Judicial Diversity Debate: Personal Values and Tacit Diversity. *Legal Studies*, 35(1), 1-29 https://doi.org/10.1111/lest.12074 (accessed 16 August 2025).
25. Chuang, Y.S., Su, Y.S. and Goh, J.O.S. (2020). Neural Responses Reveal Associations Between Personal Values and Value-Based Decisions. *Social Cognitive and Affective Neuroscience*, 15(12), 1299-1309.
26. Maio, G.R. (2010). 'Mental Representations of Social Values.' in Mark P. Zanna (ed.), *Advances in Experimental Social Psychology*. Academic Press, Vol. 42, pp. 1-43. Tamir, M. et al. (2016). Desired Emotions Across Cultures: A Value-Based Account. *Journal of Personality and Social Psychology*, 111(1), 67 https://doi.org/10.1037/pspp0000072 (accessed 16 August 2025).
27. Grabenhorst, F., Rolls, E.T. and Parris, B.A. (2008). From Affective Value to Decision-Making in the Prefrontal Cortex. *European Journal of Neuroscience*, 28(9), 1930-1939 https://doi.org/10.1111/j.1460-9568.2008.06489.x (accessed 16 August 2025); Persson, E. et al. (2018). Affective Response Predicts Risky Choice for Fast, But Not Slow, Decisions. *Journal of Neuroscience, Psychology, and Economics*, 11(4), 213.

emotion', but it is perhaps the animation of the activated value (s) with emotion which makes decisions which do not align with an individual's values most difficult.[28]

2 System 1 Instinctive Responses: A Filter for System 2 Reasoning

System 1 and system 2 processes are active concurrently. The automatic and controlled cognitive operations compete for the control of the explicit or overt response. This process between reasoning and the affect heuristic was aptly characterised by Finucane and others as 'the dance between affect and reason'.[29] Both are involved when the stakes are high and the issue is uncertain. Indeed, several studies of the processes of system 2 reasoning suggest that the priorities identified in the instinctive response shape the slow deliberative processes of system 2 reasoning.[30]

The starting point of decision-making is evidence accumulation.[31] Even at this stage of the process, priority is attributed to the evidence that aligns with the instinctive position, gathering more information that aligns with the initial preference.[32] Recent research also suggests that more attention is paid to the evidence that aligns with initial preferences, which can enhance the weighting of options and attributes in evidence accumulation.[33] Evaluation of the options depends on the accumulation of evidence from multiple sources, and the arbitration decision requires the review and evaluation of a significant number of interdependent items of evidence, prior to evaluating the available alternatives.[34] The process of evaluation is also anchored in the instinctive

28. Baron, J. and Spranca, M. (1997). Protected Values. *Organizational Behavior and Human Decision Processes*, 70(1), 1-16 https://doi.org/10.1006/obhd.1997.2690 (accessed 16 August 2025).
29. Finucane, M. L., Peters, E. and Slovic, P. (2003). 'Judgment and Decision Making: The Dance of Affect and Reason.' in S.L. Schneider and J. Shanteau (eds), *Emerging Perspectives on Judgment and Decision Research*, pp. 327-364
30. For a review, *see* Hallsson, B., Siebner, H. and Hume R. (2018). Fairness, Fast and Slow: A Review of the Dual Process of Fairness. *Neuroscience and Biobehavioural Reviews*, 89, 49-60.
31. Studies suggest that evidence accumulation (gradual build up) in the brain actually occurs within the lateral intraparietal (LIP) and motor cortices. *See*, for example, Wong, K.F. et al. (2007). Neural Circuit Dynamics Underlying Accumulation of Time-Varying Evidence During Perceptual Decision Making. *Frontiers in Computational Neuroscience*, 1, 115 https://doi.org/10.3389/neuro.10.006.2007 (accessed 16 August 2025); Ploran, E.J. et al. (2007). Evidence Accumulation and the Moment of Recognition: Dissociating Perceptual Recognition Processes Using fMRI. *Journal of Neuroscience*, 27(44), 11912-11924 https://doi.org/10.1523/jneurosci.3522-07.2007 (accessed 16 August 2025).
32. Krajbich, I. et al. (2012). The Attentional Drift-Diffusion Model Extends to Simple Purchasing Decisions. *Frontiers in Psychology*, 3, 23998 https://doi.org/10.3389/fpsyg.2012.00193 (accessed 16 August 2025); Wang, S. et al. (2012). The Role of Risk Aversion in Non-conscious Decision Making. *Frontiers in Psychology*, 3, 14557 https://doi.org/10.3389/fpsyg.2012.00050 (accessed 16 August 2025).
33. Teoh, Y.Y. et al. (2020). Attentional Priorities Drive Effects of Time Pressure on Altruistic Choice. *Nature Communications*, 11(1), 3534.
34. Parés-Pujolràs, E. et al. (2021). Evidence Accumulation under Uncertainty-A Neural Marker of Emerging Choice and Urgency. *Neuroimage*, 232, 117863 https://doi.org/10.1016/j.neuroimage.2021.117863 (accessed 16 August 2025); Schustack, M.W. and Sternberg, R.J. (1981). Evaluation of Evidence in Causal Inference. *Journal of Experimental Psychology: General*, 110(1), 101-120 https://doi.org/10.1037//0096-3445.110.1.101 (accessed 16 August 2025).

response, where the confirmation bias may result in selective overweighting of choice-consistent evidence.[35]

While there is little consensus on the processes of evaluation of evidence in complex uncertain decision, all models highlight the centrality of the subjective initial responses of the decision-maker.[36] This initial response - grounded in working memory, experience, expertise, knowledge and values - shapes every stage of the decision-making process.[37]

Arbitrators, albeit expert decision-makers, are not immune to these influences and the normal predispositions of a human decision-maker. If these influences are not challenged and disrupted, indeed if the decision-maker is not open to persuasion, then the initial instinctive influences may serve to predetermine the final decision and thus become unacceptable bias. So, what does the science of decision-making mean for arbitrators?

3 Science and Arbitration: Improving Decision Quality

> We believe that most judges attempt to 'reach their decisions utilising facts, evidence, and highly constrained legal criteria, while putting aside biases, attitudes, emotions and other individuating factors.'[38]

Guthrie, Rachlinski, and Wistrich, quoting Nugent, set the context in which judges and arbitrators make decisions, and there is no suggestion in this chapter that judges or arbitrators are making consciously unacceptable bias decisions. This chapter recognises that all human decision-makers have limited cognitive capacity and are constrained by contextual factors (including time and resources). As such, decision-making must be efficient. Many of the instinctive quick decisions are correct, indeed the ability to make accurate quick judgments is a hallmark of expertise, but if these instinctive judgments are not moderated by system 2 processes, there is a potential that

35. Cahill, L. and McGaugh, J.L. (1995). A Novel Demonstration of Enhanced Memory Associated with Emotional Arousal. *Consciousness and Cognition*, 4(4), 410-421 https://doi.org/10.1006/ccog.1995.1048 (accessed 16 August 2025); Talluri B.C. et al. (2018). Confirmation Bias Through Overweighting of Choice Consistent Evidence. *Current Biology* 28(19), 3128-3135.
36. The theoretical frameworks include bayesian models (a sequence of multiplicative products of a prior opinion); poisson process stochastic models (an accumulation of evidence until a critical weight is achieved and fixed); sequential weighting models (cumulative); and information integration models (each piece of evidence is weighted separately, and decision is based on the average). Vorms, M. and Lagnado, D. (2019). 'Coherence and Credibility in the Story-Model of Jurors' Decision-Making: Does Mental Simulation Really Drive the Evaluation of the Evidence?'. In *Model-Based Reasoning in Science and Technology, Technology: Inferential Models for Logic, Language, Cognition and Computation.* Springer International Publishing, pp. 103-119.
    This is increasingly under scrutiny in the context of the digital environment, *see*, for example, Topcu, Y.I., et al. (eds) (2021). *Multiple Criteria Decision Making: Beyond the Information Age*, Springer Nature.
37. Phelps, E.A. and Sharot, T. (2008). How (and Why) Emotion Enhances the Subjective Sense of Recollection. *Current Directions in Psychological Science*, 17(2), 147 https://doi.org/10.1111/j.1467-8721.2008.00565.x (accessed 16 August 2025).
38. Guthrie, C., Rachlinski, J.J. and Wistrich, A.J. (2007). Blinking on the Bench: How Judges Decide Cases. *Cornell Law Review*, 93, 1.

the initial instinctive position may serve to narrow the frame of the decision-making process and thus serve as an unacceptable bias and lead to errors.[39]

Several factors improve decision quality and reasoning, including time (system 2 processes require time), information (within the constraints of cognitive overload, additional evidence and data improve reasoning), structured decision-making (structured and process-driven decision-making improves decision quality) and justification of reasoning (the process of writing encourages reflection). But as the science suggests in complex decisions with no clear outcome, the instinctive response will anchor the initial decision, how the information is processed and the system 2 deliberation. It is, therefore, essential that the instinctive response is disrupted. For those arbitrators making decisions alone, it is difficult to challenge the instinctive response. Indeed, while individuals may recognise biased reasoning in others, there is little evidence that they can identify their own biases, despite education.[40] One disruption approach has had some traction; the 'consider the opposite' strategy requires the decision-maker to consider that their instinctive judgments may be wrong and revisit their decision from the opposite position. This strategy has been demonstrated to be effective, albeit time-consuming.[41]

Panel decision-making, in theory, has an inbuilt mechanism of challenge. Research on panel decision-making demonstrates that the expression of disagreement and dissent on panels improves decision quality, increases discussion intensity, creativity, and divergent thought and limits bias.[42] In this context, disagreement challenges existing norms and assumptions and encourages the majority to scrutinise their decision-making. It can disrupt, reshape, and reframe the dominant positions. The party appointed system should encourage challenge and divergent thought if all positions are equally heard and considered. However, despite the many structures to support discussion, even in the UK Supreme Court, some judges are quieter than others.[43]

39. Girgerenzer, G. and Gaissmaier, W. (2011) Heuristic Decision Making. *Annual Review of Psychology*, 62, 451 https://doi.org/10.1146/annurev-psych-120709-145346 (accessed 16 August 2025).
40. Pronin, E., Lin, D.Y. and Ross, L. (2002). The Bias Blind Spot: Perceptions of Bias in Self Versus Others. *Personality and Social Psychology Bulletin*, *28*(3), 369 https://doi.org/10.1177/0146167202286008 (accessed 16 August 2025); Risen, J.L. (2016). Believing What We Do Not Believe: Acquiescence to Superstitious Beliefs and Other Powerful Intuitions. *Psychological Review*, 123(2), 182 https://doi.org/10.1037/rev0000017 (accessed 16 August 2025); Scopelliti, I. et al. (2015). Bias Blind Spot: Structure, Measurement, and Consequences. *Management Science*, 61(10), 2468 https://doi.org/10.1287/mnsc.2014.2096 (accessed 16 August 2025).
41. Arkes, H.R. et al. (1988). Eliminating the Hindsight Bias. *Journal of Applied Psychology*, 73(2), 305; Mussweiler, T., Strack, F. and Pfeiffer, T. (2000). Overcoming the Inevitable Anchoring Effect: Considering the Opposite Compensates for Selective Accessibility. *Personality and Social Psychology Bulletin*, 26(9), 1142 https://doi.org/10.1177/01461672002611010 (accessed 16 August 2025).
42. Schulz-Hardt, S. et al. (2006). Group Decision Making in Hidden Profile Situations. *Journal of Personality and Social Psychology*, 91 (6), 1080-1093. De Drue, C., Karsen, K.W. and West, M.A. (2001). Minority Dissent and Team Innovation: Importance of Participation in Decision Making. *Journal of Applied Psychology*, 86, 1191 https://doi.org/10.1037//0021-9010.86.6.1191 (accessed 16 August 2025).
43. I use quieter here as a reflection of the external voice of the Justice heard through the delivery of judgments. Several studies demonstrate that many new arrivals to the Supreme Court bench

There is also a deference to expertise evident in the UK Supreme Court, which encourages consensus around the expert. While expertise is important as a source of knowledge, the deference to the expert can serve to perpetuate bias rather than challenge it. Indeed, this deference to expertise can underpin a psychological phenomenon known as groupthink and may result in a position or line of reasoning dominating. This form of groupthink is most evident when there is a small group of decision-makers, making an important and complex decision and the outcome is undetermined. The type of decisions being made by a panel of arbitrators.

Finally, challenge and different perspectives are only effective if the position provokes critical engagement.[44] Engagement in this context is not simply acknowledgement of the different view, but a discussion of the foundation of the disagreement and those who engage must also be open to persuasion away from their instinctive position.

IV CONCLUSION

This chapter explores the scientific foundations of decision-making and systems of activation, conduction and processing that result in the final outcome. Examination of the complexity and speed of decision-making highlights the many possible factors that predispose human decision-making and the very limited control the individual decision-maker has on the process. This knowledge allows us to consider the structures and processes that ensure that normal predispositions do not predetermine the outcome and become unacceptable bias.

---

are unlikely to deliver judgments in the early months of their arrival. Hagle, T.M. (1993) Freshman Effects' for Supreme Court Justices. *American Journal of Political Science,* 37, 1142 https://doi.org/10.2307/2111547 (accessed 16 August 2025). Cahill-O'Callaghan, R. (2020), *Values in the Supreme Court: Decisions, Division and Diversity,* Hart Publishing, UK.

44. Dooley, R.S. and Fryxell, G.E. (1999). Attaining Decision Quality and Commitment from Dissent: The Moderating Effects of Loyalty and Competence in Strategic Decision-Making Teams. *Academy of Management Journal,* 42(4), 389 https://doi.org/10.2307/257010 (accessed 16 August 2025).

CHAPTER 9

The Right to Impartiality

Dr Henry Forbes Smith KC[*]

TABLE OF CONTENTS

I INTRODUCTION

Impartiality is a constitutional right. Everybody is entitled to have their rights and obligations determined impartially by an independent judge, and to be heard in that determination. In this chapter, I consider the right to impartial determination, and how it relates to the rights to an independent judge, to be heard, and to a reasoned decision. I suggest that although those are procedural rights, concerned with choice of judge and with method of decision, the right to impartial determination is a substantive right, concerned with the object of decision: the determination which is impartial between the parties, in favouring no party over another. I suggest that choice of judge is not choice of object of decision, so that the right to an impartial determination is not removed because a non-independent judge is chosen to decide. And I suggest that judges are not impartial because they are independent and should explain why their decisions are impartial.

II THE RELEVANCE OF CHOICE OF TRIBUNAL TO THE OBJECT OF DECISION

Article 10 of the Universal Declaration of Human Rights declares that 'Everyone is entitled in full equality to a fair and public hearing by an independent and impartial

---

* LLB (Hons) (Otago); BCL (Oxon); PhD (Cantab); One Essex Court; admitted in New Zealand, New York and England and Wales.

tribunal, in the determination of his rights and obligations'.[1] This reflects the unwritten 'common law',[2] and ius commune, 'constitutional right'[3] which everybody has to have their rights or obligations ("cause") determined impartially by an independent judge, and to be heard in that determination. As an unwritten right which is constitutional, this right 'can only be curtailed by clear statutory enactment' of a competent legislator,[4] or by clear agreement of the person whose right it is. It is reflected in treaties, including Article 6(1) of the European Convention on Human Rights, Article 14(1) of the International Covenant on Civil and Political Rights, and Article 47 of the European Union's Charter of Fundamental Rights and Freedoms ("EU Charter").

The purpose of the right to an independent judge is to assure the right to impartial determination. When the cause of two or more persons or other bodies ("parties") is determined by one of those parties (a "party-judge"), 'a clear conflict of interest'[5] arises between their duty to decide impartially, so as not to favour one party over another, and their interest in deciding partially, so as to favour themselves. A similar conflict arises when a cause is determined by somebody who, although not a party, is interested in one party more than another, or in the cause being determined partially (an "interested judge"). To assure the right to impartial determination, everybody has the right to have their cause determined by somebody who is neither a party-judge nor an interested judge, so that, in judging the parties' cause, they do not judge their own cause, nor a cause in which they are interested (an "independent judge").

Choice of judge is not therefore choice of object of decision. Whomever is chosen to decide, the object of their decision is the same: the decision which is 'free from bias against any party',[6] in favouring no party over another. Although the judge may change,[7] the parties and the cause do not, and what is impartial in favouring no party over another does not either. Lord Denning therefore said that 'The result should be the same, no matter what tribunal resolves the case',[8] and Friedrich Carl von Savigny wrote that 'in cases of conflict of laws, the same legal relations (cases) have to expect the same decision, whether the judgment be pronounced in this state or in that'.[9]

Judges differ. Earl Loreburn said that 'Judges are like other people, and different judges look at facts differently'.[10] Justice Douglas noted that 'judges are not fungible; they cover the constitutional spectrum, and a particular judge's emphasis may make a world of difference'.[11] Not only do judges differ, but parties do too. As Lord Mance

1. Article 10 ends 'or of any criminal charge against him', which involves determining rights or obligations.
2. *Witham* [1998] QB 575909, 977D, Justice (later Lord Justice) Laws.
3. *Bremer Vulkan Schiffbau Corporation v. South India Shipping* [1981] AC 909, 977D, Lord Diplock; *Leech* [1994] QB 198, 210A, Lord Justice (later Lord) Steyn.
4. *UNISON* [2020] AC 869, §76, Lord Reed.
5. *Braganza v. BP Shipping Ltd* [2015] UKSC 17, §18, Baroness Hale.
6. *Attorney-General v. Times Newspapers* [1974] AC 273, 309B, Lord Diplock.
7. As where an arbitrator resigns, and is replaced by another, as in *Emirates Trading Agency* [2015] EWHC 1452, §8.
8. *Prestcold (Central) Ltd v. Minister of Labour* [1969] 1 WLR 89, 94H, Lord Denning.
9. Savigny, *System of Modern Roman Law*, 1849, vol. 8, section 5, §348, translated Guthrie, *A Treatise on Conflict of Laws*, T&T Clark, Law Publishers, Edinburgh, 1880, pp. 69-70.
10. *Lendrum v. Ayr Steam Shipping* [1915] AC 217, 223.
11. *Chandler v. Judicial Council* 398 US 74, 137 (1970).

observed, 'Individual members of the public ... have widely differing characteristics, experience, attitudes, and beliefs which could shape their answers on issues such as those before the court, without their being easily cast as unreasonable'.[12]

However, for judges to disagree, they have to ask themselves the same question. If they each ask a different question, so that they each have their own object of inquiry, any apparent conflict in their decisions is a false conflict. If every judge sought to decide partially, by asking themself, what reasonable decision most favoured themselves, no two judges would ask the same question or have the same object or rule of decision. Each judge would ask what reasonable decision most favours themself, a question necessarily differing for each judge.

When making a reasonable decision, the question is what the object of that reason is: what it is to be deployed for. The constitutional rule of common law is that, unless clearly otherwise enacted or agreed, causes are to be determined impartially, so as to favour no party over another. Everybody therefore has the right to have their cause determined by an 'unbiased and reasonable person',[13] dedicating their reason to the object of what is impartial between the parties, producing an 'unbiased and reasonable decision'.[14]

To ensure the right to impartial determination, enactments and agreements provide judges with the right to determine causes of parties on the demand of one of them ('jurisdiction'). Their jurisdiction sometimes is subject to a right or possibility of redetermination on appeal ("judges of redeterminable decision"), and other times is not ("judges of final decision"). The Earl of Selborne said that 'in the absence of special provisions as to how the person who is to decide is to proceed, the law will imply no more than that the substantial requirements of justice shall not be violated'.[15] Unless clearly otherwise enacted or agreed, a choice of even a judge of final decision is therefore only a choice of a decision which complies with the requirements of substantial justice (is 'substantially just').

A decision which is substantially just is sometimes described as a 'reasonable decision',[16] meaning a decision which a 'reasonable judge'[17] could properly make, whether or not other judges would make that decision if it was for them to decide. The range of such decisions forms a reasonable range of impartial decisions, each substantially just. Even the highest courts of final decision quash their own decisions when they fall outside this range.[18]

In order to make a substantially just decision, a judge of final decision must make the decision which they consider impartial between the parties, or, where they consider two or more decisions equally impartial, the one that they consider best for the parties (the "best impartial decision"). They cannot deliberately choose the decision from within the range of decisions which reasonable judges would make

12. *Abdroikov* [2007] 1 WLR 2679, §81.
13. US Supreme Court, Code of Conduct, Canon 3B§(2).
14. *Alconbury* [2003] 2 AC 295, §46, Lord Slynn.
15. *Spackman v. Plumstead Board of Works* (1885) 10 App Cas 229, 240.
16. *Lendrum v. Ayr Steam Shipping* [1915] AC 217, 222.
17. *Kwok v. Juan* [2022] UKPC 52, §40.
18. *Pinochet (No 2)* [2000] 1 AC 119.

which they consider favours one party over another, as if the choice of decision from within that range was their gift to make in favour of the party which pleased them more. Otherwise, the right to impartial decision would be merely a right to a reasonably impartial decision, rather than to what the judge considers the best impartial decision. That their decision may not be redetermined enhances their duty to make the best impartial decision they can.

III IS CHOICE OF A PARTY TO DECIDE CHOICE OF PARTIAL DECISION?

Since choice of judge is not choice of object of decision, choice of a party-judge is not choice of partial decision. Although enactments or agreements sometimes clearly depart from the right to an independent judge by providing a party-judge or interested judge with the right to decide, that is not itself a 'Waiver of the rule against bias'.[19]

This can be illustrated by three examples which Gaius called 'imperfectum' when agreed: 'when the vendor says to the purchaser: "You shall buy for what you choose to give, or what you think fair, or at your own estimate of its value"'.[20]

The first example, 'You shall buy for what you choose to give', clearly departs from the right to impartial determination by authorising the chosen judge of the price, the purchaser, deliberately to fix the price partially, so as to favour itself over the seller, and to choose the lowest purchase price consistent with sale rather than gift.[21]

The second example, 'You shall buy for ... what you think fair', is an agreement to buy for a price to be determined impartially by the purchaser. The promise to decide impartially is explicit: the Latin words are 'uantum aequum putaveris', with 'aequum' having been translated as 'fair', and Lord Justice Staughton referring to 'impartially, or fairly (I can see no significant difference)'.[22] The purchaser has agreed to determine the price so as, in their judgment, to favour neither themselves over the seller nor the seller over them.

The third example, 'You shall buy ... at your own estimate of its value', does not state the object of the valuation; it does not state, for example, 'at your own estimate of its value *to you*'. Since this chooses the judge without clearly departing from the object of the valuation, the right to impartial determination remains: the purchaser is to estimate the valuation impartially, so as to favour no party over another, rather than partially, so as to favour the purchaser over the seller or the seller over the purchase.

As another example, 'In November 1756, William Johnston, maltster of Aberdeen, and Provost Robertson, entered into a verbal agreement; whereby, the Provost sold his firm-bear of Pitmillan, for crop 1756, to Johnston, deliverable as soon as the

19. The title of Toy-Cronin, 'Waiver of the Rule Against Bias' (2000-2003) 9 Auckland University Law Review 850. Despite the title, the author considers waiver of the right to an independent judge, not waiver of the right to impartial determination.
20. D.18.1.35.1: 'Illut constat imperfectum esse negotium, cum emere volenti sic venditor dicit, "quanti velis, quantum aequum putaveris, quanti aestimaveris, habebis emptum"', translated Watson, *The Digest of Justinian*, University of Pennsylvania Press, 1985.
21. Birks, *The Roman Law of Obligations*, Oxford University Press, 2014, p. 69.
22. *Nestle v. National Westminster Bank plc* [1993] 1 WLR 1260, 1279A.

same could be got ready by the tenants, the price to be fixed by the seller'. The Provost claimed that this entitled him deliberately to fix the price above market so as to favour himself, while selling his crop at market price to others.[23] However, that agreement did not clearly waive the rule against bias. If the Provost wanted the right to fix the price so as to favour himself, he needed to contract clearly for that.

That choice of an interested judge is not the choice of an interested decision is illustrated by *Trowsdale*. Contractors agreed with a company that, at the company's initiative, the parties would 'submit and refer to the final sentence and decreet-arbitral of … Charles Jopp', the company's engineer on the project, who, it was agreed, could own shares or accept any office or situation in the company without that 'disqualify-[ing] him from acting as arbiter'.[24] The Lord President noted that 'it does not follow that any license is given to the arbiter to exercise his powers unfairly, or with bias'.[25]

Similarly, in *Jackson*, Mr Jackson and the Barry Railway Company agreed that Mr Jackson would construct a dock for the company and that 'any question or dispute arising between the company and the contractor' concerning the contract or the work 'shall be referred to the engineer, whose decision shall be conclusive and binding on both parties', defining 'the engineer' as 'J.W. Barry, Esq., or other … engineer for the time being appointed by the company'.[26] Mr Barry was an interested judge: he was the company's representative in the works, and prepared the contract, 'being responsible for its contents'.[27] The Court of Appeal of England considered that Mr Barry's duty was to decide impartially, so as to favour neither Mr Jackson over the company nor the company over Mr Jackson.[28]

That choice of a party to decide is not the choice of a partial decision is illustrated by *Braganza*. Mr Braganza and his employer, referred to as the company, agreed that if he died in its service, Mr Braganza's widow would be entitled to compensation unless 'in the opinion of the Company or its insurers, the death resulted from amongst other things, [Mr Braganza's] wilful act, default or misconduct'.[29] Mr Braganza disappeared in its service at sea. The company exercised its agreed right to determine, by its general manager, Mr Sullivan, whether Mr Braganza died from his own wilful act, so that no compensation was required. The Supreme Court of the United Kingdom considered that, to be determinative, Mr Sullivan's decision had to be reasonable, which, by a majority, the Court considered it was not. Since the agreement did not clearly entitle the company to opine so as to favour itself, the object of Mr Sullivan's decision was to decide impartially. Although there was no suggestion that he deliberately made whatever reasonable decision most favoured the company, had he done so, the entirety of the Supreme Court would have regarded his decision as ineffective for that reason.

23. *Steven v. Robertson* (1760) Mor 3158. The Provost made several arguments and the Court of Session gave no reasons for its decision in his favour. It is therefore unclear what the Court thought of this point.
24. *Trowsdale and Son v. Jopp and North British Railway Co* (1864) 2 M 1334, 1335.
25. *Trowsdale* (1865) 4 M 31, 34.
26. *Jackson v. Barry Railway Company* [1893] 1 Ch 238, 239.
27. *Jackson*, 239.
28. *Jackson*, Lord Justices Lindley (246), Bowen (248), and AL Smith (250).
29. *Braganza*, §1.

That choice of a party to decide is not choice of a partial decision is also illustrated by *Lehman*. The International Swaps and Derivatives Association ('ISDA')'s 2002 Master Agreement states that if one party becomes subject to an event of default, the other party may terminate the transaction, following which that other party will determine the value of the terminated transaction, using 'commercially reasonable procedures to produce a commercially reasonable result'.[30] Justice Robin Knowles stated that 'a number of results may be commercially reasonable. On the other hand, the fact that there is a range does not mean that the Determining Party can simply take the result that suits it best at one end of the range'.[31]

These principles raise the question of the correctness of a statement by Lord Kitchin delivering the judgment of the Court of Appeal of England and Wales in *Unwired Planet*. The European Telecommunications Standards Institute ("ETSI")'s intellectual property right ("IPR") policy includes a licensing undertaking to be given by owners of IPR which is essential for use of ETSI's standards ("essential IPR"). That is an undertaking by the owner 'that it is prepared to grant irrevocable licences on fair, reasonable and non-discriminatory ("FRAND") terms and conditions under such IPR'. When given by the owner, the undertaking (an "ETSI undertaking") is both an agreement with ETSI and an 'offer to the world in general',[32] or, at least, to many users of ETSI's standards ("offerees"), to grant them a licence on FRAND terms on their demand. The ETSI policy and undertaking do not state who is to determine the FRAND terms and conditions to which the offeree is entitled. Having noted that what may be FRAND between 'two parties' may differ from what may be FRAND between 'two other parties',[33] Lord Kitchin stated that:

> the tribunal will normally declare one set of terms as FRAND and that will be the set of terms the owner must offer to the prospective licensee. If, however, the outcome of the proceedings is that two different sets of terms are each found to be FRAND then in our judgment the [IPR] owner will satisfy its obligation ... if it offers either one of them. It will in that way be offering an irrevocable licence of its [essential IPR] on FRAND terms.[34]

Where two or more determinations are considered equally impartial between the parties, the right to impartial determination requires that tie be broken impartially, so as to favour neither party. Breaking the tie by allowing the owner to offer whatever FRAND licence it prefers, and therefore whatever FRAND licence it considers most favours itself, involves deciding partially, in its favour. That has to be clearly enacted or agreed. ETSI's policy and undertaking provide that they are governed by French law, and they do not clearly authorise partial determination. The right to impartial determination applies as part of French law under droit commune, and also under Article 47 of the EU Charter. It may be suggested that where a tribunal considers that two licences are FRAND, the tribunal should award the one that it considers the most FRAND, or if

30. ISDA Master Agreement, §6(a), 6(e)(i) and the definition of 'Close-out Amount'.
31. *Lehman Brothers Special Financing Inc v. National Power Corp* [2018] EWHC 487, §79.
32. *Carbolic Smoke Ball Company* [1893] 1 QB 256, 266.
33. *Unwired Planet International Ltd v. Huawei Technologies Co Ltd* [2018] EWCA Civ 2344, §121.
34. *Unwired*, §125.

it considers them equally FRAND, the one that it considers the best for both parties. That was the effect of the approach of Justice Birss at first instance.[35] The right to impartial determination is not displaced because it is difficult to decide.

IV THE RELEVANCE OF CHOICE OF TRIBUNAL TO THE METHOD OF DECISION

Gaius wrote that an agreement to purchase at the price which the purchaser thinks fair was considered 'imperfectum'. It has been suggested that the reason why Roman lawyers may have considered this is that 'the determination of an essential negotii had been left to one party and that thus the institutional check against the danger of gross and unreasonable contractual imbalance (namely negotiation about the price) had been removed'.[36] Agreements such as those in *Trowsdale*, *Jackson*, and *Braganza* have been criticised, both as agreements which contractors and employees have no choice but to agree[37] and as 'not a contract to arbitrate, but an agreement to capitulate'.[38] The International Bar Association considers that 'because no one is allowed to be their own judge, there cannot be identity between an arbitrator and a party', such that agreement to this 'shall be regarded as invalid'; the parties 'cannot waive the conflict of interest arising in such a situation' because 'acceptance of such a situation cannot cure the conflict'.[39] If that was correct, then Gaius' second and third examples would be 'nullum', not merely 'imperfectum',[40] and the agreement in *Braganza* would have been invalid, even though Mr Sullivan's decision would have been final had one further Justice of the Supreme Court considered it reasonable. In contrast, Lord Mansfield stated that 'a man may judge impartially even in his own cause'.[41] It may be thought that what may lawfully be done may lawfully be agreed to be done, and that invalidating agreements to decide impartially does not promote impartiality.

Nevertheless, agreements and undertakings to decide impartially need 'institutional checks'. When parties agree, not to negotiations in which 'Each party to the negotiations is entitled to pursue his (or her) own interest',[42] but that one of them will determine what is impartial between them, and thereby 'act as judges of the rights of others'[43] as well as their own rights, new 'institutional checks' replace negotiation to check imbalance.[44] In particular, unless clearly otherwise enacted or agreed, the institutional checks of the rights to be heard and to reasoned decision assure the right

35. *Unwired* [2017] EWHC 711, §164.
36. Zimmermann, *The Law of Obligations*, Oxford University Press, 1996, p. 254.
37. *Trowsdale* (1865) 4 M 31, 34, *Jackson*, 247, *Bristol Corporation v. John Aird & Co* [1913] AC 241, 257, Lord Moulton.
38. *Matter of Cross Brown Co* (1957) 167 NYS 2d 573, 576, Judge Valente.
39. International Bar Association, *Guidelines on Conflict of Interest in International Arbitration*, 2004, reissued 2014 and 2024, Explanation to General Standard 2(d), II.2.
40. Daube, "Certainty of price", Daube, edited, *Studies in the Roman Law of Sale*, Oxford, Clarendon Press, 1959, p. 21: '*imperfectum* in the province of sale is not equivalent to *nullum*'.
41. *Cowle* (1759) 2 Burr 834, 863, 97 ER 587, 604.
42. *Walford v. Miles* [1992] 2 AC 128, 138E, Lord Ackner.
43. *Frome United Breweries Co v. Bath Justices* [1926] AC 586, 590.
44. Du Plessis, 'The Unilateral Determination of Price in Roman Law' (2012) 18 Fundamina 15, 20.

to impartial determination. These rights are needed most before the judge of final decision, not in Royal Courts or Palaces of Justice discussing the reasonableness of that judge's decision. Since judges differ, in implementing these rights, choice of judge may to some extent be choice of method of decision, so that 'what that procedure is to be in detail must depend on the nature of the tribunal'.[45] But since choice of judge is not choice of object of decision, the chosen method of deciding 'shall not abridge, enlarge, or modify any substantive right',[46] and, in particular, the substantive right to impartial determination.

Once, the default tribunal was 'the nearest neighbours'. They were expected to 'have the best knowledge of the title in question', and to be 'indifferent',[47] restated as 'impartial'.[48] They were expected to use their knowledge of the parties and the cause to decide what was impartial between the parties, in favouring no party over another. That default tribunal then became what Lord Justice Bowen called 'a wholly different and far more agreeable kind of arbitrament before either some stranger or a jury of strangers'.[49]

When judges are strangers to the parties and the cause, their lack of knowledge of the parties and their cause brings its own conflict of interest. As strangers to the parties, they do not know what the parties' 'characteristics, experience, attitudes, and beliefs' are. In order to judge, they have to judge something. Rather than judge what they do not know, it is easier to judge the parties as if they were replicas of themselves, themselves in another body, themselves in another life, each having the 'characteristics, experience, attitudes, and beliefs' of the judge, as if the parties were replicas of one another as well as of the judge. When judges do that, they do, not 'justice between the parties who come before it',[50] but what would be justice between the parties if the parties were replicas of the judge: if the judge was in the collective position of the parties.

That judges inaccurately, by judging the parties as if they were the judge, when the parties differ from the judge, and from each other. It also judges partially: in judging what would be just if the judge was in the position of the parties, it judges as if the cause was, in a way, the cause of the judge. It produces decisions which favour both the party which is most like the judge, and the judge over the parties, by setting as the example of what people in the position of the parties should do what the judge would do in their position. That favours the judge precisely because it ignores the differences between the judge and the parties. It departs from the rule that choice of judge is not choice of object of decision because it ignores those differences, as well as differences between the judge and others. To presume that the parties should be like the judge is not how an 'unbiased ... person' decides. The effect is enhanced where judges ask what 'any reasonable state',[51] or 'any reasonable company',[52] would think or would

45. *Local Government Board v. Arlidge* [1915] AC 120, 132.
46. US Congress, Rules Enabling Act 1934, now 28 US Code §2072(a)-(b).
47. *Anonymous* (1478) Jenk 33, 33-34, 145 ER 24, 24-25.
48. *Anonymous* (1499) Jenk 97, 145 ER 69.
49. *Jackson*, 248.
50. *Scott v. Scott* [1913] AC 417, 444, Earl Loreburn.
51. *Dean v. Lord Advocate* [2016] SLT 1105, §95.

do, and answer by presuming that those are associations of people with the judge's 'characteristics, experience, attitudes, and beliefs'.

That this may be unconscious does not mean that it does not happen. In *Dallaglio*, Sir Thomas Bingham stated that 'The decision-maker should consciously shut out of his decision-making process any extraneous prejudice or predilection of which he is aware; but he cannot shut out an extraneous prejudice or predilection of which he is unaware'.[53] Judges become aware of the 'extraneous prejudice or predilection' of supposing that the parties are replicas of the judge, and therefore of each other, by becoming aware of how the parties differ from themselves, and therefore from one another. Adam Smith supposed that 'As we have no immediate experience of what other men feel, we can form no idea of the manner in which they are affected, but by conceiving what we ourselves should feel in the like situation'.[54] The difficulty of identifying how others differ from ourselves does not dispense with the duty to try, so as to determine their cause impartially.

When judges are parties, their duty is to set aside their interest in partial decision, and to decide impartially. When judges are neighbours who know the parties, they have acquired that knowledge naturally, through the imperfect process by which people get to know one another. Their process of deciding impartially involves ensuring that knowledge which they may have acquired partially becomes as impartial as it can, and expands to help them decide as impartially as they can. When judges are strangers to the parties and the cause, they begin not knowing what they judge, and their interest is in not changing that, since it will mean they treat the parties as replicas of themselves. Their process of deciding impartially involves acquiring the knowledge they need to decide as well as they can what favours no party over another. Although the object of the inquiry is the same in each case, the methods of decision diverge, reflecting the differing positions from which the judge began.

Despite this, independent judges often appear to presume that their independence assures their impartiality, allowing them to comply with their duty to make an 'unbiased and reasonable decision' by making whatever decision seems most reasonable to them. The Code of Conduct of the United States Supreme Court states that 'A Justice is presumed impartial.'[55] Many independent tribunals appear to make that same presumption.

The constitutional right to impartiality is to 'a tribunal which is free from bias against any party', not merely a tribunal which is presumed to be free from bias; to an impartial decision, not merely a decision which is presumed to be impartial. In *Sussex Justices*, Lord Chief Justice Hewart stated that 'it is not merely of some importance but is of fundamental importance that justice should not only be done, but should manifestly and undoubtedly be seen to be done'.[56] Not only must there be an 'appearance of justice',[57] but justice must be done. Each requires that the tribunal: (i)

---

52. *Kyla Shipping Co Ltd v. Freight Trading Ltd* [2022] EWHC 1625, §341.
53. *Dallaglio* [1994] 4 All ER 139, 161G.
54. Smith, *The Theory of Moral Sentiments*, 1.1.1.
55. US Supreme Court, Code of Conduct, Canon 3B§(1).
56. *R v. Sussex Justices* [1923] 1 KB 256, 259.
57. *Offutt v. United States* 348 US 11, 14 (1954), Justice Frankfurter.

must by reasoning conclude that its decision is impartial, rather than merely presumed impartial, unbiased, rather than merely presumed unbiased, and (ii) must appear to reach that conclusion, by providing reasons why its decision is impartial.

Tribunals should therefore provide reasons explaining why their decisions are not only reasonable, but also impartial. Since choice of judge is not choice of object of decision, the decision should be made from a perspective midway between the perspectives of the parties (the "mid-party perspective").[58] Judges should consider, and explain, the decision which the parties would have made had they determined their cause impartially for themselves. Lord Buckmaster said that 'I find myself quite unable to understand the distinction between an agreement to permit the price to be fixed by a third party and an agreement to permit the price to be fixed in the future by the two parties to the contract themselves. In principle it appears to me that they are one and the same thing'.[59] If the parties agree to fix the price impartially as joint party-judges, the two are 'one and the same thing' in that the object of the decision is the same: the decision which is impartial, in favouring no party over another. Considering an undertaking to grant a licence on FRAND terms, Lord Justice Arnold stated that 'FRAND terms are those that would be agreed by a willing licensor of a portfolio of SEPs and a willing licensee of that portfolio without discrimination'.[60] This involves disregarding the effect of 'compulsion or pressure, or ... some market distortion'[61] or the like, such as might cause one party's self-interest to prevail over the self-interest of another party; it therefore involves identifying the best impartial decision. When judges are 'experts in the field'[62] who have been chosen to decide because of their expertise, their role is to apply that expertise from the mid-party perspective, dedicating their expertise, as well as their reason, to the object of impartial decision.

This requires inviting the parties to be heard. Hearing from the parties, and reasoning what is impartial between them, helps the judge understand the 'characteristics, experience, attitudes, and beliefs' of each party, so as to decide what is impartial between them, in favouring no party over another. In *Spackman*, the interested judge of final decision, Mr Vulliamy, an architect, heard in person from the parties (including his employer) before deciding,[63] and in *Jackson*, Mr Barry rightly made it clear that he would as well. Yet in *Belchier*, the judge of final decision, Mr Harris, decided without informing the parties, and therefore without inviting them to be heard, and his decision was upheld, even though the agreement did not clearly dispense with the right to be heard.[64] In *Lloyd*, where an auditor was the judge of final decision, Lord Bridge accepted that if any party 'had asked to be heard orally and the auditor had refused,

58. Aristotle, *Nicomachean Ethics*, 5.4, 1132a21: 'they seek the judge as an intermediate'; translated *The Complete Works of Aristotle: Revised Oxford Translation*, edited Jonathan Barnes, Princeton University Press, 1984, vol. 2, p. 1786.
59. *May and Butcher, Ltd v. King* [1934] 2 KB 17, 20.
60. *Lenovo Group Limited v. Telefonaktiebolaget LM Ericsson* [2025] EWCA Civ 182, §21.
61. *InterDigital Technology Corp v. Lenovo Group* [2024] EWCA Civ 743, §41.
62. *Loper Bright Enterprises v. Raimondo* 603 US 369 (2024), p. 9 of Justice Kagan's opinion, citing *Chevron USA Inc v. Natural Resources Defense Council* 467 US 837, 865 (1984).
63. *Spackman* (1884) 13 QBD, 878, 879-880.
64. *Belchier v. Reynolds* (1754) 3 Keny 87, 87, 91, 96 ER 1318, 1318-1319.

there would have been clear ground for a complaint of unfairness',[65] but considered that it was reasonable for the auditor not to invite them to request an oral hearing if they wanted. If it would be unfair to deny a request for a hearing, it is unfair not to inform the parties of that right. To presume that there is nothing to be gained from hearing from the parties is to presume that they should not have the right to be heard.

When judges discuss people who differ from themselves, biases sometimes become apparent which they do not always themselves perceive. Although those biases are not always corrected by hearing from those people and providing reasons for decision, those protections often reduce or help avoid those biases, helping to assure the right of impartial determination. The *Sharington* tribunal said that 'men are for the greatest part more reasonable than women, and have more discretion to guide and manage things than women have, for to govern and direct is more suitable to the capacity of the male than of the female',[66] without explaining why, and, it appears, without inviting the wives of the men who were parties to be heard. Lord Chief Justice Willes considered that Christians are more truthful than non-Christians because, he considered, they fear greater sanction for perjury, without asking the non-Christian party and witnesses what they might say.[67] In *Cooper*, Lord Watson stated that 'There was no land law or tenure existing in [New South Wales] at the time of its annexation',[68] without explaining why, and without inviting those whose ancestors had been there for a long time to be heard. The *Catalina* tribunal said that 'The Italians are all liars in these cases and will say anything to suit their book. The same thing applies to the Portuguese. But the other side here are Norwegians, and in my experience the Norwegians generally are a truthful people. In this case I entirely accept the evidence of the [Norwegian] master of the *Norma*'.[69] He did not explain what experience he referred to, or why it could be extrapolated, nor did he allow the Portuguese present to comment.

When tribunals presume their impartiality from their own independence and provide no reasons explaining why they consider their decisions impartial, they are left secretly to judge their own cause, the cause of their own compliance with their duty of impartial decision, and they risk treating the parties as replicas of themselves. The more judges hear from the parties, the more they understand how the parties differ from themselves, and from each other. The more judges explain why they consider that their decisions are impartial, the more the impartiality of their decisions can be assessed and improved over time. To decide as an 'unbiased ... person', 'free from bias against any party', and thereby produce an 'unbiased and reasonable decision' which favours neither one party over another nor the tribunal over the parties, a tribunal cannot simply make whatever reasonable decision it considers best on the basis of its own 'characteristics, experience, attitudes, and beliefs'. Everybody has the right to

65. *Lloyd v. McMahon* [1987] AC 625, 706F.
66. *Sharington v. Strotton* (1564) 1 Plow 298, 305, 75 ER 454, 465.
67. *Omichund* (1744) 1 Willes 538, 550, 125 ER 1310, 1317, 1 Atk 21, 45, 26 ER 15, 31.
68. *Cooper v. Stuart* (1889) 14 App Cas 286, 292.
69. *Owners of Steamship Catalina* (1938) 61 Lloyds L Rep 360, 364.

impartiality, including the rights to be heard and to reasons explaining why determinations of their rights and obligations are not only reasonable but also impartial. An impartial decision is not whatever reasonable decision the tribunal considers best.

CHAPTER 10

The Human Experience and Interaction in Arbitration: Decision-Making and Bias

Dominique Hascher[*]

TABLE OF CONTENTS

I INTRODUCTION

Decision-making in the adversarial process environment that characterizes arbitration and litigation may be easily described externally: you look at the facts, you hear the arguments, you decide.

For all that, no one would expect an adjudicator with an empty mind. Background and biases affect decision-making because diverse and extensive bias are unavoidable in all Human societies. Even IA judicial or arbitral decision-making would not be immune from the cognitive biases of the algorithm designers.[1] My presentation will particularly focus on how the decision-making process should account for such cognitive and cultural biases. We should therefore assume for what follows the adjudicator's self-confidence that such cognitive or cultural biases will not influence one's own performance free of any extraneous factors to the parties' arguments, or favor or personal preference which otherwise would be a disqualifying element.

Cultural diversity has always been both a challenge and an asset for international dispute resolution. The major contribution in the field is that of the International

* Arbitrator, International Judge at the Supreme Court of Singapore, former judge at the Cour de cassation (France).
1. *See* Arbitration's Age of Enlightenment? ICCA Congress Series No. 21, Edinburgh 2022, Wolters Kluwer, 2023, pp. 683-707.

Chamber of Commerce which developed a know-how for bridging the gap between the differences in nationality, legal education, culture and language of all participants involved in an international arbitration process to achieve an acceptable result for the dispute.[2] This multicultural approach to international arbitration which makes way for diversity has been analyzed by Ms. Sheila Abuja and Curtis Fung as best serving the interests of the arbitration community worldwide, including users.

While a single-member tribunal has only one's conscience to consider, and Henry Smith will tell us later how you leave your inherited bias at the door, a monocultural and national panel is not free from diversity of opinions. Its members sometimes prone to profess to each have a better understanding of the applicable law to the dispute in which they were trained. Postures of superiority are also not unknown in judicial circles.[3] Open-mindedness and dialogue are inherent to any decision-making process. When they are lacking, it is at the detriment of the parties' right to legal certainty or to a decision.

A truly international panel raises more challenging questions. How are one's beliefs, cultural attitudes, professional practices, guiding principles for action and expectations in return, expressed? How do these interact with those of the other panel members?

II DECISION-MAKING AND DELIBERATIONS

Some codes of procedure or arbitration rules regulate the voting process of the panel, or provide for a casting vote of the chair, but the matter is largely left unorganized. Deliberations are pragmatically fixed for the particular case,[4] however, as Veeder noted, a rule of equal treatment and equal opportunity of the decision-makers to participate in the deliberations is to be drawn from the requirement of impartiality.[5]

Decision-making is much more than an addition of independent or individual votes. Dissenting or concurring opinions may be issued, but the judgment or award is generally a single leading decision based on common reasoning.[6] It can be reasonably inferred that a collective process decision involves a certain amount of compromise and negotiations which may only be explained through a number of interactions.

The mystery of the deliberation room might be better explained by considering that decision-making is a much wider concept than the restricted procedural meaning of deliberations, at least if conceived of as the discussions concerning the decision after

2. M. Schinazi, The Three Ages of International Commercial Arbitration, Cambridge University Press, 2022.
3. Apex courts which are large-size judicial bodies have internal mechanisms for preventing (or curing) divergences within their own case law. That different solutions may be reached by different panels assumes some recognition that different interpretations of the law are possible, which is an invitation to modesty and dialogue.
4. V.V. Veeder, Still More on Deliberations, on Arbitration, OUP, 2023, p. 366.
5. V.V. Veeder, Still More on Deliberations, on Arbitration, OUP, 2023, p. 366.
6. A judgment made of a collection of individual speeches, such as was the usage before the House of Lords in the United Kingdom, is rarely found in other judicial traditions or in arbitration.

completion of all written and oral exchanges. Otherwise expressed, deliberations should be considered as starting well before the discussions on the decision.[7]

When the panel members enter the deliberation room, their discussions often reflect the influence and positions adopted in the courtroom and before. When panel members assume an individual and active role in the debate with the parties, their questions or reactions are very likely to form the basis for the discussions *in camera*. A more passive member will face difficulties in raising issues before fellow members which have not been considered before and interacted with. There thus exists some emulation between panel members for influencing the decision-making process.

The nature of the proceedings and the degree of preparation and involvement of the panel members from the outset of the procedure have important consequences on the scope and shape of the discussions regarding the decision. As remarked by others, there exists no right to a judges' intellectual virginity which should be kept intact until the day the decision is made.[8] Knowing what's on the adjudicator's mind is important for the confidence of the parties in the decision-maker's impartiality.[9] This is of course distinct from expressing one's opinion on the merits of the dispute which might be regarded as affecting the outcome of the proceedings or impairing the fairness of the process with partiality. What do the panel members think when the hearing terminates? A passive role at the hearing and throughout the proceedings more generally cannot allow to infer any indication on what will be considered important for the discussions on the decision. Courts that follow such behavioral pattern, which is often dictated by the written nature of the procedure followed, chatter internally within members more than others, but that is no indication that the underlying reasoning will be laid out in the decision. Reasons are however the parties' guarantee. Anonymous benches who practice opacity in decision-making contribute little to the trust in justice. Parties' participation in decision-making should be valued, which somehow requires that the process should be apparent to them. This is without impairing the confidentiality of the substance of the deliberations, which is essentially for the protection of the freedom of expression of the panel members.[10]

It is also important for the other members of the adjudicatory panel, who will have to collegially decide together, to know what's on their colleagues' mind. Organizing the different stages of the deliberations becomes a much more difficult task when some panel members remain vague as to the contents of their minds and perspective on the parties' case.

Some emphasis should be laid on decision-making in the context of a collegial environment within which the collective mind of the panel will be expressed and reflected in its decisions.

Judges, who are members of permanent judicial bodies, do not need to recreate a collegial environment for each case. In common law systems, collegial work, in my

7. A. Reiner, ICC Schiedsgerichtsbarkeit: Ein Handbuch für den Praxis, Wien, Manz, 1989.
8. The former president of the Belgian Constitutional Court, P. Martens, La tyrannie de l'apparence, Rev. trim. Droits de l'Homme, 1996, p. 640.
9. G. Canivet, La convergence des systèmes juridiques par l'action du juge, Mélanges Blanc-Jouvan, Société de législation comparée, 2005, p. 11.
10. [2023] SGHC (1) 123, *CZT v. CZU*.

experience, does not actually begin until after the hearing. Until then, when the panel assembles, each judge has prepared individually. They may have briefly exchanged views before entering the courtroom. However, the individual dialogues which each of the panel judges has with the parties during the hearing will largely structure the deliberations of the decision. Whether the debate in the oral hearing has taken place before a cohesive judicial group is thus also likely to influence the decision-making process. In the latter case, it is likely that the individuality of the judge plays a far lesser role, and deliberations will be influenced by a hierarchical model according to each member's respective rank or seniority.

As compared with judicial bodies, any *ad hoc* international body, with a mission limited in time, must engage collegially, without always a prior working experience of its members with one another.[11] In arbitration, where the legitimacy of the members of the arbitral tribunal derives from the will of the parties expressed in the arbitration agreement, collegial work, which cements the arbitral tribunal, should begin at the earliest in order to build confidence of the participants in the process.

III THE DYNAMICS OF APPOINTMENT AND DECISION-MAKING

Approaching decision-making with how the dynamics of appointment affect the decision process is all the more sensible in a context where decision-making has an early start in the proceedings. The exercise of reciprocal influences and the preservation of the expression of diversity of minds of each of the tribunal's members considerably vary according to whether the panel members' nomination process is under the parties' control. This involves situations when the choice is determined by the parties, either directly or indirectly by the arbitral institution or by the arbitrators already appointed, to whom the choice is delegated by the parties. Beauty contests and interviews by parties before nomination should be regarded as improper, but even if prior contacts with the parties should be limited to information on the arbitrator's availability and qualifications to the exclusion of a discussion the merits or the procedural aspects of the case, it nonetheless remains that selection of an arbitrator cannot overlook the background and personal characteristics of the person considered for appointment.[12]

As a prominent English practitioner once reported, when seeking an arbitrator for appointment, he was looking at individuals with the maximum predisposition toward his client and the minimum appearance of bias.[13] We will hear from Professor Stavros Brekoulakis that this is also true for investor-State arbitration. Fadlallah aptly observed

11. See however relationships between an arbitrator and another arbitrator, IBA Guidelines on Conflicts of Interest in International Arbitration.
12. V.V. Veeder, L'indépendance et l'impartialité de l'arbitre dans l'arbitrage international, in L. Cadiet, Th. Clay and E. Jeuland, eds, Médiation et arbitrage, Litec, 2005, p. 219. IBA Guidelines on Conflicts of Interest in International Arbitration, Green List, Contacts between the arbitrator and one of the parties.
13. J.M.H. Hunter, Comments in The Arbitral Process and the Independence of Arbitrators, ICC Publication 472, ICC, 1991, p. 25. P. Bellet, Des arbitres neutres et non-neutres, Etudes Lalive, Helbing et Lichtenhahn, 1993, p. 399.

that a system whereby each of the parties chooses an arbitrator is hardly likely to result in a decision which is totally indifferent to the parties and their concern.[14] The origin of the appointment brings a personal color to the decision-maker's role which is likely to impact on the understanding and resolution of the parties' case.

Co-arbitrators appointed by the parties should be seen as fully participating in the conduct of the arbitration, and the chair should be mindful about associating with them in all decisions. It is beyond controversy today in international arbitration that party-appointed arbitrators are not party representatives. Nonetheless, they are close to the parties through their nomination process. A panel member's right to participate in the deliberations which was earlier alluded to also becomes the parties' right to collegiate participation in the deliberations. The presence of the party-appointed co-arbitrators secures the adversarial nature of the tribunal's discussions.[15] Bias or prejudice toward any person involved in the proceedings, including a fellow co-arbitrator, should be regarded as a breach of the equality of treatment between parties. It should also not be overlooked that unequal treatment of an arbitrator should be regarded as unequal treatment of the party who appointed that arbitrator.[16] Delayed or otherwise irregular participation always affects the substance of the deliberations. The disruption is even greater in arbitration where the influence of an arbitrator who advances the arguments of its appointing party is balanced by the influence of the others. As Ms. Sheila Ahuja reminds us, arbitrators often play the role of cultural intermediaries and translators. In a voluntary process such as arbitration, the parties' perception that the arbitrators effectively participated in the making of the decision greatly contributes to the legitimacy of the decision. The appointment mechanism has therefore repercussion on the perception of fair hearing in the arbitral context.

When the nominating process is isolated from the parties' influence (nomination by roster or equivalent) as it is for judges,[17] the approach to decision-making takes on other nuances. The individuality of the decision-makers is less important for the legitimacy of the decision in the parties' eyes. The discussions within the panel are no more organized to preserve the opportunity for members to ensure that their nominating party's position has been understood, examined and argued with the tribunal. The exchanges within the panel are not guided by the consideration that members appreciate the legal, cultural and business context of the dispute from the jurisdiction to which the parties that appointed them relate. Social, political, and economic assumptions of fact relevant to determining the contents of the law precisely play a major role in judging. Judges should reflect society, not represent it. As remarked, it is reasonable to expect that a judge will not be influenced by the weather of the day but would be sensitive to the climate of the era.[18]

14. I. Fadlallah, L'ordre public dans les sentences arbitrales, Collected Courses of The Hague Academy of International Law, 1994-V, vol. 249, p. 369.
15. V.V. Veeder, Still More on Deliberations, on Arbitration, OUP, 2023, p. 366; D. Hascher, Principes et pratique de procédure dans l'arbitrage commercial international, Collected Courses of The Hague Academy of International Law, Vol. 279, Martinus Nijhoff, 2000, p. 51.
16. V.V. Veeder, Still More on Deliberations, on Arbitration, OUP, 2023, p. 366.
17. or ICSID *ad hoc* committee members.
18. Paul Freund, cited by R. Ginsburg, 70 Years of EU Law, European Commission, 2023, p. 273.

An international bench reflects cultural diversity and backgrounds. Yet, the understanding of the law as well as other extra-legal factors by the different members mostly serves to enhance the quality of the judgment to a larger audience than the parties in dispute. Some nuances could be introduced regarding interstate international tribunals. Governments nominate nationals whom they regard particularly trustworthy to convey before such judicial fora the political and legal perspectives of the nominating State. This may not affect the outcome of a case in particular. It should be regarded as an element of influence in the law-making process and as advancing the State's understanding of the rule of law and justice. Here again, the dynamics of appointment are always present, although not in the forefront.

IV CONCLUSION

In closing, it may be said that different factors weigh on the decision-making process, which spans from the appointment of the panel to the deliberations stage. The individuality of the decision-maker, with all subconscious bias and cultural niceties, is an essential ingredient that cannot be overlooked. The nature of the appointment mechanism marks the watershed in decision-making. A nomination process under the parties' influence colors the expression of the diversity of the decision-makers' individualities. Collegiality, which is the setting within which such diversity should be organized and preserved, functions differently when decision-makers are close to the parties.

PANEL 4

Sociology and Education

The panel examines the organisation, structure, and change of participants and institutions in international arbitration, and the effect that education plays. Speakers address: the key sociological frameworks and associated empirical data; compare dispute resolution approaches in China, the 'west' and other systems; and explore why arbitration is less attractive in some jurisdictions. The panel also considers the impact of the proliferation of specialised degrees, the increased democratisation of access to arbitration know-how, and the challenge of training advocates and arbitrators whilst at the same time preserving cultural and legal differences.

CHAPTER 11

Sociology and Education: Introduction to the Panel

Prof. Julian DM Lew KC[*]

The title of this conference, 'Arbitration as a Human Endeavour', encapsulates the real nature of international arbitration, often forgotten or intentionally overlooked by legislators, judges and administrators, and at times even by arbitration institutions.

Arbitration as the preferred mechanism for settling all forms of international commercial, business, investment and other disputes is the choice of the parties in every case. This choice also manifests the parties' rejection of national courts as the main forum to resolve their disputes. In the absence of choice there can be no arbitration.

In fact, party autonomy occupies the fundamental place in all forms of international arbitration – both commercial and investment. The parties not only record the choice of arbitration in preference to national courts but also decide the form of arbitration, institutional or ad hoc; the seat or place of arbitration; the number of arbitrators, one or three; the law applicable to the substantive issue in dispute; and the procedure and timetable to be followed. This is of course subject to mandatory laws and international public policy at the place of arbitration with the intent that the final award will be enforceable if not voluntarily performed.

In this respect, party autonomy is the essential human determination behind the establishment and format of every arbitration.

* Professor Julian Lew KC is a well-known name in the field of international arbitration, having practised as an academic, counsel and arbitrator. He is now a full-time arbitrator in international commercial and investment disputes at Twenty Essex. Before 2005, he was a partner and for some years the head of the international arbitration practice group at a leading international law firm. Professor Lew was the founder and has been the head of the School of International Arbitration, Centre for Commercial Law Studies, Queen Mary University of London since its creation in 1985. He has written and lectured extensively on many different aspects of international arbitration.

ICCA has always sought to explore issues affecting or arising in international arbitration and to record the concerns of arbitration users and the need for international understandings and flexible regulations. ICCA conferences have often been the place where new practices and other instruments for application and assistance of international arbitration have been presented and debated.[1] For this conference, the ICCA organising committee entitled this session SOCIOLOGY AND EDUCATION to explore and help better understand the nature of arbitration and its various influences on development and efficiency.

This session, and the several presentations we will hear and the papers we will be able to read and contemplate, focuses on the nature of international arbitration, its purpose and controls. This in turn requires an understanding of not only the needs of the process itself but also the expectations and requirements of the arbitration users and the system.[2]

There is a fundamental question when considering the nature of arbitration, its structure and procedure selected by the parties: whose arbitration is it? Is party autonomy supreme? Or are parties limited by national laws, institutional rules, and guidelines, opt-in rules and specified best practices proposed by other organisations (including IBA, ICC Institute, ASA)?

Not that long ago, in some jurisdictions, and in some legal systems still today, arbitrations are considered a national procedure tied to the seat of arbitration chosen for its neutrality or fixed without intent. While the domestic laws of a country will generally regulate whether an arbitration can be held in its jurisdiction, and will regulate the circumstances where the national court can intervene to support an arbitration, e.g., by ordering documents in the possession of someone/entity within its jurisdiction, or to supervise and control the process by reviewing the jurisdiction of the tribunal, the determination made or the conduct of the tribunal.

In contrast, most arbitration laws are permissive allowing the parties to agree and specify not just the form and place of arbitration but also the procedural arrangements and timetable. The parties select the arbitrators directly or through a system they choose and can limit the issues to be determined by arbitration. There are today only limited restrictions on matters which can be determined by arbitration.

This is because in international arbitrations, the parties, the disputants or arbitrants and their counsel, the subject matter or purpose of the contract come from different places, legal systems, and from different cultural, political, religious and language systems – all of which affect the participants' expectations and approach.

Other major influencers affecting international arbitration are the institutions offering their services, their rules or other rules to administer the arbitration, and managing the funding of the arbitration. The past few years have witnessed an

1. The first ICCA conference I attended was in January 1975 in New Delhi. A major issue for discussion was the new draft UNCITRAL Arbitration Rules. Those Rules are now widely used and have influenced on the provisions of other international arbitration rules.
2. For this reason we commend those who put together this excellent and thought provoking session which will assist our understanding of the arbitration and our choices of form and procedures.

enormous increase in new arbitration institutions in many countries where there was no acceptable arbitral institution.

There have been many efforts to unify law and procedure to improve the effectiveness of international arbitration. Without reviewing the history of all developments, two specific instruments provide the bedrock of international arbitration: the *New York Convention of the Recognition and Enforcement of Foreign Arbitral Awards* (currently ratified in 172 States) and the UNCITRAL Model Law on International Commercial Arbitration (now adopted in ninety-three jurisdictions).

At first glance, these two international instruments have little or nothing to do with each other: the one seeks to provide international regulation for the enforcement of arbitration awards in countries other than where the award was made; the other provides and recommends a standard form for domestic arbitration law to help harmonise national arbitration laws and approaches. You will hear more how they enhance the effectiveness of international arbitration.

I will leave you to draw your own conclusions as to what extent our known arbitration systems are limited, narrow-minded, biased, and perhaps need to be developed.

I am privileged to moderate this panel of five distinguished scholars and practitioners from different cultural and legal backgrounds, and with various experiences in different systems. They will each speak for about ten-twelve minutes which may allow for a limited discussion or questions. I commend their full papers to you. For sure, you will find them interesting, informative, educational and perhaps even surprising.

CHAPTER 12

Why Arbitration Fails?: Understanding the Successes and Challenges of International Arbitration

Ginta Ahrel & Natalia Petrik[*,**]

TABLE OF CONTENTS

I INTRODUCTION

Arbitration has undergone a remarkable evolution, transitioning from an informal method for resolving commercial disputes to a sophisticated framework of rules and laws. Thanks to the efforts of UNCITRAL, the International Bar Association, and the International Council of Commercial Arbitration, an increasing number of countries are adhering to international best practices. Over ninety states have adopted or been influenced by the UNCITRAL Model Law on International Arbitration, aligning their legislation with international standards and fostering greater acceptance of arbitration

* Partner at Westerberg & Partners, Stockholm, Sweden; Member of the Board of the SCC Arbitration Institute; Member of the Board of the Swedish Arbitration Association; Former Member of the Board of the Swedish Women in Arbitration Network; Counsel at Westerberg & Partners, Stockholm, Sweden; Former Deputy Secretary General at SCC Arbitration Institute.

** Natalia Petrik is Counsel at Westerberg. She serves as a board member of the Finland Arbitration Institute, a member of the Advisory Board of the Stockholm International Hearing Center, and secretary of the executive committee of the Swedish Arbitration Association.

by the society. This trend is fundamental for international arbitration as it strengthens its legitimacy and trust on a global scale.

At the same time, the worldwide adoption and standardisation of arbitration laws do not inherently guarantee that arbitration functions effectively or gains widespread popularity. Some countries witness a flourishing arbitration landscape, while others face challenges in its adoption. Why is it so? Is there a link between economic and political well-being and success of arbitration? Which other factors incentivise or restrain arbitration?

In their book *Why Nations Fail: The Origins of Power, Prosperity, and Poverty*, Daron Acemoglu and James A. Robinson argue that nations' sustainable development requires the existence of inclusive institutions, which protect the interests of all members of the society, as opposed to extractive institutions that solely benefit privileged elites.[1] Inclusive economic institutions protect private property of all citizens, incentivising them to save, invest and advance, thus promoting entrepreneurship and sustainable economic growth.[2] It is, however, 'the political institutions that determine what economic institutions peoples live under' and 'whether politicians are agents of the citizens or are able to abuse the powers entrusted to them ...'.[3]

As discussed below, arbitration is influenced by a country's institutional strengths and weaknesses. Consequently, it should not be perceived solely as a mechanism that can function in any society. Certain basic prerequisites must be in place for the growth of arbitration to be feasible, such as, sustainable economy, supportive political environment, adequate legal framework and institutional infrastructure. Put simply, the factors defining inclusive or extractive political and economic institutions, as outlined by Acemoglu and Robinson, are relevant to the development of arbitration too.

Moreover, in the view of the author, the acceptance of arbitration does not invariably equate to its triumph. Although the fundamental premises for growth may be universal in all countries, the factors contributing to or retarding success are often country-specific. This explains why countries with similar legal, economic, and political systems may have different arbitration landscapes.

This chapter will explore the essential prerequisites defining the success of arbitration, its correlation with macro-economic and political trends, followed by a discussion of the role of legal framework. It will also offer an analysis of the country-specific factors advancing or retarding the development of arbitral venues with examples drawn from specific jurisdictions.

1. Daron Acemoglu and James A. Robinson, 'Why Nations Fail: The Origins of Power, Prosperity and Poverty', Profile Books Ltd, 2013.
2. *Ibid.*, p. 42.
3. *Ibid.*

II THE ESSENTIAL ROLE OF ECONOMY

1 The Impact of Global and Regional Economy

The popularity of arbitration varies considerably across the globe and depends on countries' longstanding capability to stimulate entrepreneurship, trade and investment. The prevalence of arbitration clauses and, consequently, the demand for arbitral services are therefore directly correlated with the frequency of commercial transactions and the scale of international commerce and investments within the country.

Most of the internationally renowned hubs for commercial arbitration, such as London, Paris, Stockholm, Geneva, New York ('the old seats'), are clustered in the wealthy countries with a deep-rooted tradition of trade. Until 1970s the European countries and the US collectively accounted for more than half of global exports. Today, these regions contribute approximately one-third of global trade and continue to score the highest GDP per capita rankings.[4]

According to the 2022 FTI Consulting Report on 'International Arbitration After the Pandemic', the pattern of international trade today is rebalancing towards developing economies, which account for the highest growth in export volume, 'from 32 percent of world exports in 2000 to a record high of 46 percent in 2020'.[5] This correlates with the quick growth of 'younger' arbitration seats, such as Singapore and Hong Kong, both known for their integration into the global trade and high GDP rankings.[6]

Another example of correlation between economic growth and the development of arbitral seats is the UAE. The Emirates rank high among the world's top twenty largest exporters and importers of commodities and since recently put considerable effort into the development of new and reform of existent arbitration centres.[7] Dubai, Abu-Dhabi and Riyadh actively promote their arbitration infrastructure, elevating local arbitral institutions to global standards by appointing high-profile arbitration experts to their governing bodies, recruiting international talent, and hosting prestigious events on a grand scale.

The sustainability of the younger seats, however, should be approached with caution, as they are situated within changing political and legal environments. We will revert to this.

Caseloads in established arbitration hubs typically mirror the growth of their respective nations and the global economy at large, displaying a gradual increase. For example, in 2000, the SCC Arbitration Institute (SCC) recorded 135 cases. The caseload

4. Worlddata.Info, 'The 50 Richest Countries in the World' https://www.worlddata.info/richest-countries.php (accessed 16 August 2025).
5. FTI Consulting Report 'International Arbitration after the Pandemic', published in March 2022, p. 6, https://www.fticonsulting.com/insights/reports/international-arbitration-after-pandemic (accessed 16 August 2025).
6. In 2022, Singapore held the second position in terms of GDP per capita in accordance with Worldometers.info, 5 March 2024.
7. Lloyds Bank, 'United Arab Emirates: Economic and Political Overview. Foreign trade figures of the United Arab Emirates', latest update: February 2024, https://www.lloydsbanktrade.com/en/market-potential/united-arab-emirates/trade-profile (accessed 16 August 2025).

surged to 197 cases in 2010 and to 213 cases in 2020.[8] The London Court of International Arbitration (LCIA) statistics increased from a total of 246 arbitrations in 2010 to 440 arbitrations in 2020.[9] Similarly, the International Court of Arbitration at the International Chamber of Commerce's (ICC) caseload progressed from 541 cases filed in 2000 to 793 cases in 2010 and 946 cases in 2020.[10] The Singapore International Arbitration Centre (SIAC) showed steeper growth with 58 cases in 2000, 198 cases in 2010 and 1080 cases in 2020.[11] The Hong Kong International Arbitration Centre (HKIAC) reported 291 arbitration cases in 2010 and 318 in 2020.[12]

The above-mentioned FTI Report indicates that 'international arbitration filings have grown steadily at more than 3% a year globally from 2010 to 2019 and increased 9.9% in 2020, with Asian arbitration centres – Singapore and Hong Kong most prominently – growing much more quickly than the more traditional centres in Europe and North America, mirroring the faster growth in cross-border economic activity in Asia'.[13]

The general trend of 'Easternisation' of the global economy and migration of cases to Asian seats has been also noted in the report of the UK All-Party Parliamentary Group for Alternative Dispute Resolution, which analysed the challenges of UK in keeping its position as a global disputes hub, arguing that 'the eastward shift of the world's economic and political centre of gravity is already impacting the size of the UK's lead over competitors in Hong Kong and Singapore' and that 'UK can learn much from Singapore's experience over recent decades.'[14]

Interestingly, the inverse dynamics of the global and regional economy, especially during periods of recession, have a more pronounced and immediate impact on the number of arbitrations at the arbitral seats. In 2022, amidst the post-pandemic recession and the onset of Russia's war against Ukraine, caseloads at institutions located in Europe had a significant drop, with the number of cases declining by 22 % in LCIA and 17 % in ICC.[15] Also, SIAC in Singapore had a similar dynamic with the number of cases decreasing by 24% in 2022.[16]

---

8. SCC statistics for 2008 and 2020, available at https://sccarbitrationinstitute.se/en/about-scc/scc-statistics/previous-years-statistics (accessed 16 August 2025).
9. LCIA annual report for 2010 and 2020, available at https://www.lcia.org/LCIA/reports.aspx (accessed 16 August 2025).
10. ICC statistical reports for 2000, 2010 and 2020, available at https://jusmundi.com/en (accessed 16 August 2025).
11. SIAC's annual report for 2010 and 2020, available at https://siac.org.sg/annual-reports (accessed 16 August 2025).
12. https://www.hkiac.org/about-us/statistics (accessed 16 August 2025).
13. FTI Consulting Report 'International Arbitration after the Pandemic', published in March 2022, p. 3.
14. The Chartered Institute of Arbitrators (CIArb), Report of the All-Party Parliamentary Group for Alternative Dispute Resolution 'Securing the UK's Position as a Global Disputes Hub: Best Practice Lessons Between Singapore and the UK', 2020, p. 2.
15. Dr Markus Altenkirch, Maria Barros Mota and Sebastian Rheinwald, 'Arbitration Statistics 2022: The Number of Arbitration Proceedings Continues to Drop' 2 October 2023, available at https://www.globalarbitrationnews.com/2023/10/02/arbitration-statistics-2022-the-number-of-arbitration-proceedings-continues-to-drop-but-the-amount-in-dispute-increases/ (accessed 16 August 2025).
16. SIAC's annual report for 2021 and 2022, available at https://siac.org.sg/annual-reports (accessed 16 August 2025).

Global and regional economy is just one of the fundamental prerequisites that define the success of an arbitral venue. Politics play a strategic role in shaping the arbitral landscape and can have more profound implications for arbitration compared to economic peaks or recessions.

III THE SIGNIFICANCE OF POLITICAL CONTEXT

The impact of politics on arbitration should not be underestimated, as political shifts often swiftly translate into policies, laws, and court judgments that change the legal landscape. Politics favouring arbitration are instrumental for its growth, but their effect is slow, often requiring decades for arbitral venues to establish their credibility and attract cases. Conversely, political upheavals that undermine economic institutions, judicial systems, and the rule of law can swiftly impede arbitration. Such disruptions lead to declines in caseloads, alterations in user behaviour, and the relocation of disputes to other jurisdictions.

1 Political Trends in the Twentieth Century

In the twentieth century, the political climate has largely favoured and advanced arbitration through conventions and legislative initiatives. In the aftermath of the Second World War, nations were particularly concerned with finding ways to coexist peacefully, to rebuild their economies and to resolve disputes through peaceful means. The International Chamber of Commerce's and UN initiatives to promote this aim resulted in the 1958 New York Convention on Recognition and Enforcement of Foreign Arbitral Award and the 1961 European Convention on International Commercial Arbitration. Similarly, the 1966 ICSID Convention was drafted under the auspices of the International Bank for Reconstruction and Development, creating a new specialised investor-state dispute resolution centre. In 1975, the Helsinki Conference on Security and Co-operation in Europe called 'to recommend, where appropriate, to organizations, enterprises and firms in their countries, "to include arbitration clauses in commercial contracts and industrial co-operation contracts, [...] and permit arbitration in a third country, taking into account existing intergovernmental and other agreements in this field."'[17]

Thousands of bilateral investment protection treaties and a number of multilateral agreements, such as GAFTA, NAFTA, and ECT, were entered into by nations, mandating the use of arbitration for resolution of disputes falling within their scope. All these developments stimulated advancement of knowledge and formation of best practices in the field. In other words, past century's international legal framework paved the way for growth and globalisation of arbitration. Certain political initiatives, as exemplified below by the case of Sweden, transformed domestic arbitration venues into internationally recognised hubs.

17. Conference on Security and Co-operation in Europe Final Act, Helsinki, 1975, section V, para. 5, p. 5.

Today, the political context is more nuanced. Singapore, for example, illustrates an ideal combination of strong economy, supportive political climate and proactive legislative and administrative measures taken by the state to facilitate the growth of the city as an international dispute resolution hub. At the same time, in other parts of the world, arbitration faces more challenges than ever before. States withdrawing from ECT changed policies towards investor-state arbitration in Europe, trade restrictions and sanctions imposed in response to Russia's invasion of Ukraine, to name a few.

2 The Case of Sweden and Norway

Norway and Sweden are both deeply entrenched in global trade, possess inclusive economies, share common history and culture. Norway's GDP and per capita exports and imports exceed those of Sweden. Yet Norway hosts fewer arbitrations and is less international as arbitral seat compared to Sweden.[18] Sweden gained a competitive advantage over its neighbour due to a unique combination of historical and political factors specific to the country.

Over the past century, Sweden maintained substantial trade with the USSR. To facilitate economic relations, in 1940, the countries entered into a trade agreement which contained, *inter alia*, an arbitration clause. The clause designated Stockholm as the seat for resolving disputes arising out of the Agreement. Moreover, in 1977, Stockholm gained further recognition when it was proposed by both the Soviet Chamber of Commerce and the American Arbitration Association as a venue for resolving disputes between Soviet and American parties. The main reason behind the USSR's endorsement of these political initiatives stemmed from Sweden's non-aligned stance in relation to NATO, coupled with the country's robust economic ties with the USSR. Thus, Stockholm became the primary destination for resolving disputes originating from the Soviet political block.

For similar reasons, the SCC was designated as an investor-state dispute resolution forum in the Energy Charter Treaty in the early 1990s, as well as in dozens of bilateral investment treaties.

The momentum accumulated by Stockholm during the Soviet era has defined its success as an international arbitration hub in the following decades. The SCC caseload steadily rose from an average of around 150 cases per year between 2000 and 2009 to an annual average of 187 cases between 2010 and 2020 and with a steady 50% share of international disputes.[19] However, the recent political developments such as Russia's invasion of Ukraine and the following economic sanctions, termination of intra-EU BITs, and countries' withdrawals from the ECT, can prompt a regionalisation of Sweden as an arbitral venue and a rebalancing of its caseload towards domestic and Nordic disputes.

18. A more detailed analysis of the arbitration landscape in Norway, inclusive the assessment of the caseload, might be found in the article of Knut Kaasen, 'International Arbitration in Norway', MarIus., 2019 (519), pp. 9-19.
19. SCC Arbitration Institute, statistical reports for 2008-2020, at https://sccarbitrationinstitute.se/en/about-scc/scc-statistics/previous-years-statistics (accessed 16 August 2025).

Sweden's example highlights that the impact of politics can be both powerful and volatile. Establishing sustainable dispute resolution venue requires a long-term strategy involving the country's own policymakers.

3 The Case of Hong Kong

Until recently, Hong Kong has been one of the most preferred seats for international arbitrations in Asia. International disputes accounted for approximately 80% of HKIAC's caseload in 2021–2022. Compared to 2010, where approximately 60% of cases were international, HKIAC's caseload has shown a positive trend towards the internationalisation of the venue.[20]

Hong Kong's emergence as an international arbitral hub stems from a number of factors: a robust economy, high rankings in the rule of law and judicial independence, as well as the prevalence of a common law system protected by the Hong Kong Basic Law.[21]

In 2020, the National Security Law was implemented in Hong Kong. Upon adoption of the Law, Hong Kong faced social protests, anti-government demonstrations and an exodus of foreign lawyers from the city.[22] In accordance with World Bank Governance Indicators, Hong Kong's percentile rank as a rule of law jurisdiction decreased from 93.8 in 2017 to 87.7 in 2022.[23] Similarly, the political stability rank decreased from 74.7 in 2017 to 66.5 in 2022.[24]

The implications of the new legislation for the rule of law and arbitration in Hong Kong are yet to be assessed. Several reports suggest that the new political situation in Hong Kong has undermined its reputation as an arbitral venue.[25] However, judging from the statistics published by HKIAC, the caseload has remained relatively stable over 2021-2023.[26]

4 Economic Sanctions Against Russia

The Russian aggression towards Ukraine, coupled with the imposition of extensive economic sanctions by the US, EU, and other global actors, has had profound

20. Hong Kong International Arbitration Center, statistical reports at https://www.hkiac.org/about-us/statistics (accessed 16 August 2025).
21. The Basic Law of the Hong Kong Special Administrative Region of the People's Republic of China, Article 8 https://www.elegislation.gov.hk/hk/A101 (accessed 16 August 2025).
22. James Pomfret et al., A Reuters Special Report, 'Lawyers Exit Hong Kong as They Face Campaign of Intimidation', filed on 29 December 2022. https://www.reuters.com/investigates/special-report/china-lawyers-crackdown-exodus/ (accessed 16 August 2025).
23. The World Bank, Worldwide Governance Indicators for Hong Kong https://www.worldbank.org/en/publication/worldwide-governance-indicators/interactive-data-access (accessed 16 August 2025).
24. *Ibid.*
25. Pak You and Echo Wong, 'Multinationals Turn Away from Hong Kong for Dispute Resolution', Nikkei Asia, 8 June 2023 https://asia.nikkei.com/Spotlight/Hong-Kong-security-law/Multinationals-turn-away-from-Hong-Kong-for-dispute-resolution (accessed 16 August 2025).
26. Hong Kong International Arbitration Center, statistical reports at https://www.hkiac.org/about-us/statistics (accessed 16 August 2025).

implications for international arbitration. The regulatory restrictions in, for instance, EU sanctions do not outright ban legal services linked to arbitrations. However, they introduce administrative hurdles and, most importantly, impose severe constraints on enforcing arbitral awards in arbitrations with designated entities, which impacts all parties to arbitration, whether sanctioned or not.[27]

The EU sanctions regime against Russia also displays diverging policies in relation to arbitral and court proceedings. While exemptions and derogations for litigation in courts are consistently included in the provisions dealing with court proceedings, e.g., enforcement of judgments and client-attorney privilege, arbitral proceedings are treated differently and less favourably.[28]

The EU legislator adopted a more restrictive approach to arbitration, leaving a great deal of uncertainty as to the scope of allowed legal services, reporting obligations and enforcement of arbitral awards in the context of sanctions. Therefore, while sanctions are not directly aimed at arbitration, they have a more profound adverse impact on arbitration compared to court proceedings.

IV THE ROLE OF LEGAL FRAMEWORK

Above, we explored political trends that have influenced the legal and economic environment of countries in general, consequently affecting the prospects for arbitration either positively or negatively.

Meanwhile, over the past decade, there have been instances where legislators have specifically targeted arbitration, implementing policies and legal frameworks that discourage its use or target operations of arbitral institutions. In some countries, arbitration has come under scrutiny, signalling a period of declining trust between the regulators and the business community, while in others there are signs of increasing trust.

1 Shifting Policy on ISDS in the European Union

The agreement among EU Member States to terminate intra-EU BITs, alongside the landmark *Achmea* judgment,[29] which considered arbitration clauses in intra-EU Bilateral Investment Treaties incompatible with EU law, represents a notable shift in policy from a supportive stance to a more critical view of arbitration in the EU. The *Achmea* and a later *Komstroy* ruling,[30] which took a similar position towards ECT-based

27. Council Regulation (EU) No. 269/2014 of 17 March 2014 concerning restrictive measures in respect of actions undermining or threatening the territorial integrity, sovereignty and independence of Ukraine, Article 5.1(b).
28. Kristin Campbell-Wilson and Natalia Petrik, Paving the Way for Justice: Arbitration and EU Sanctions Against Russia, Stockholm Arbitration Yearbook 2023, Christer Danielsson and Patrik Schöldström (eds), Kluwer Law International B.V., 2023, pp. 24-27.
29. Judgment of the European Union Court of Justice (Grand Chamber) of 6 March 2018 in case C-284/16.
30. Judgment of the European Union Court of Justice (Grand Chamber) of 2 September 2021 in case C-741/19.

intra-EU arbitrations, were the culmination of extensive and largely political debate regarding the suitability of investor-state arbitration as a mechanism for resolving disputes.

Although *Achmea* deals with intra-EU investment arbitration, it sparked discussions about its potential repercussions on commercial arbitration with state entities within the EU.[31] The concerns regarding the spillover effects of Achmea have proven to be justified with a ruling from the Hellenic Supreme Administrative Court,[32] which held, based on the *Achmea* judgment, that a commercial case related to a state concession may not be referred to arbitration. The judgment immediately fuelled the debate whether arbitration clauses in commercial contracts involving EU state-owned entities would stand court review in the light of the *Achmea* judgments.[33]

The EU's diverging approach to investor-state arbitration dissonates with policies and legal orders in other states, which continue to enforce the intra-EU ISDS awards.[34] In addition to the legal complexities involved, the EU's approach to investor-state arbitration raises questions about the legitimacy of both ISDS and commercial arbitration involving state entities. This stance may potentially impact the international legal order and incentivises investors to pursue arbitration and enforcement measures outside the EU.[35]

The economic consequences of dismantling the ISDS system within the EU are yet to be assessed, particularly given that the proposed substitute, the Multilateral Investment Court, is far from implementation.

2 The Cases of Hungary and the Latvia

In June 2023, Hungary introduced a new ground for setting aside arbitral awards. In particular, the amended Hungarian Arbitration Law enables courts to vacate an arbitral award if the arbitral tribunal 'has not assessed in its award – comprising the reasons for acknowledging or disregarding as evidence – the contents of the expert opinion made by the Expert Body for Performance Certification and submitted by any party on the merits'.[36]

The introduction of this new provision, which lacks analogy in the UNCITRAL Model Arbitration Law or within the New York Convention, requires Hungarian courts to apply it *ex officio*, akin to matters of public order. Although it seems to apply only within the scope of construction disputes, this novel provision has sparked legal

31. Alison Ross, 'Achmea: Where Do We Stand?', Conference Report on Global Arbitration Review, 2019.
32. Zepos & Yiannopoulos, Newsletter, dated 31 January 2023, referencing the Hellenic Supreme Administrative Court Decision No. 246/2022.
33. Volterra Fietta Client Alert: Recent decision of the Greek Supreme Administrative Court confirms businesses cannot rely on agreements to arbitrate disputes with EU Member States in the EU, 11 October 2023.
34. Nikos Lavranos, 'States Comply Less with Investment Treaty Arbitration Awards: Insights from a 2023 Report on Compliance', at Kluwer Arbitration Blog, 26 November 2023.
35. *Ibid.*
36. Hungarian Arbitration Act, section 47(2)(bc).

debates and has been viewed as departing from the established norms of the international legal framework.[37]

In contrast to Hungary, the Latvian Arbitration Law took a markedly different approach over a long time, as setting aside arbitral awards was not possible at all. This approach effectively denied parties any opportunity for recourse in challenging arbitral awards. The lacking regulation entailed a very low degree of state court control over the arbitration and resulted in the appearance of hundreds of 'pocket' arbitration institutions in Latvia.[38]

Currently, Latvia makes attempts to implement a reform of the arbitration legislation. The reform was prompted by a 2023 ruling of the Latvian Constitutional Court confirming that the existing control mechanism over arbitration in Latvia was incomplete and unconstitutional.[39] Moreover, the Constitutional Court noted that the legislator's failure to implement an effective mechanism for the control of arbitration proceedings for an extended period of time erodes public trust not only in arbitration but also in the state and the law itself.[40]

While Hungary and Latvia have contrasting legislation when it comes to challenge grounds, they both underscore a common premise: a legal framework that adheres to established international standards is indispensable for the efficiency and credibility of arbitration systems.

V ADVANCING ARBITRATION THROUGH EDUCATION

Our analysis would be incomplete if we were to only focus on the basic prerequisites. To gain a full understanding of what advances arbitration, it's essential to look beyond its basic setup and also examine other factors that facilitate its qualitative growth over time.

Arbitration, at its outset, was considered to be an honourable duty carried out on *pro bono* basis. In 1917, the first Arbitration Rules of the Stockholm Chamber of Commerce provided that 'an arbitrator does not have the right to charge a fee, only reimbursement for their expenses'. Serving as an arbitrator was a matter of honour, and the first Swedish arbitrators were not legal professionals.

Today, arbitration represents a complex legal niche, requiring lawyers to undergo specialised professional training. Until recently, such training was mainly acquired through on-the-job experience within law firms in countries where arbitration was used as an alternative dispute resolution method, or within local firms involved in international arbitration matters. Qualitative growth of arbitration requires, however,

37. Richard Schmidt, 'Storm in a Teacup: A New Ground for Annulling Hungarian Construction Arbitration Awards', at Kluwer Arbitration Blog, 22 September 2023.
38. Valts Nerets, 'What Has Changed in Six Years Since the Latvian Arbitration Law "Reform" and What Needs to Be Changed?', at Kluwer Arbitration Blog, 11 March 2021.
39. Decision of Latvian Constitutional Court, dated 23 February 23 2023 in case No. 2022-03-01.
40. Maija Tipaine and Toms Krumiņš, 'Latvian Constitutional Court: Absence of a Mechanism for Setting Aside of Arbitral Awards Violates the Rights to a Fair Trial', at Kluwer Arbitration Blog, 22 March 2023.

a more large-scale access to professional education at undergraduate and post-graduate levels.

Prestigious master programmes serve the purpose, opening career opportunities at both national and international levels and promoting arbitration among legal professionals. Thus, the Stockholm University International Commercial Arbitration Law programme has fostered a whole generation of attorneys from Baltic countries, now acting as arbitrators and lead counsel in arbitral proceedings seated outside their home countries.

Accessible education yields both quantitative and qualitative advantages. It not only enhances awareness about arbitration but also fosters qualitative improvements by expanding and diversifying the pool of arbitrators. Typically provided by branch organisations and arbitration associations, arbitrator trainings play a key role in this process. For instance, in 2006, the Swedish Arbitration Association introduced professional arbitrator training, serving as a knowledge hub for its participants while also fostering a more gender-balanced and youthful cadre of arbitrators for the SCC and other regional arbitral institutes. Thus, in 2006, the SAA arbitrator class comprised 11% female lawyers, a figure that surged to 43% by 2021. Similarly, in 2016 among the SCC-appointed arbitrators, 22.5% were female, while in 2023 the figure was as high as 55%.

Professional associations and accessible legal training tend to emerge in developed arbitral jurisdictions, establishing an advanced professional infrastructure that greatly benefits the further growth of arbitration. The existence of such infrastructure is, in itself, indicative of successful development.

VI CONCLUSIONS

Arbitration is a complex legal phenomenon. Its development is shaped by the institutional capacities and limitations of a nation and depends on a complex mix of factors. These can be characterised as essential prerequisites.

Essential prerequisites include basic elements necessary for arbitration to grow and function effectively. These consist of favourable pro-arbitration policies, a strong economic foundation, the rule of law, independent judiciary and legal frameworks that adhere to international standards. If one of these fundamentals fails, the arbitration will fail, too.

In countries, offering the essential prerequisites, arbitration and arbitral institutions emerge as autonomous catalysts for economic growth. They generate substantial added value and contribute to the rule of law.

By acknowledging this, governments and arbitration practitioners can better understand the dynamics and the perspective of arbitration within a given country and tailor their strategies accordingly.

CHAPTER 13

Arbitration Across Human Faculties and Human Societies: A Three-Dimensional Epistemological Analysis

Kun Fan[*]

TABLE OF CONTENTS

* Associate Professor, UNSW Law & Justice. Mediator, Arbitrator and Domain Name Panelist. This article arises from the research projects: "China's Belt and Road Initiative: A New Model of Economic Governance?," funded by the Australian Research Council (ARC), and "The Social and Psychological Underpinnings of Commercial Arbitration in Europe," funded by the Economic and Social Research Council (ESRC) and the University of Leicester. The author acknowledges and is grateful for the support of the ARC, ESRC and University of Leicester. The author thanks Professors Julian Lew, Xingzhong Yu, and Jonathan Bonnitcha for inspiring discussions and detailed comments on an earlier draft. The author also appreciates the feedback and questions from Professors Bing Shui, João Ilhão Moreira, Sara Migliorini, Rosalind Dixon, Christopher Michaelsen, Bronwen Morgan, and Nofar Sheffi, and all participants at the Sociology and Education Panel at the International Council for Commercial Arbitration (ICCA) Congress in Hong Kong on 6 May 2024, the Research Seminar at the University of Macau on 10 May 2024, and the Faculty Research Seminar at UNSW Law & Justice on 28 May 2024. The author is grateful for the helpful insights shared by all the interviewees over the years, including the 25 arbitration specialists working in China interviewed by Professor Gabrielle Kaufmann-Kohler and the author in 2007, the arbitrators who completed the survey distributed from 2011-12, the 29 Chinese judges from basic-level and intermediate courts in three different cities and three officials from the Supreme People's Court interviewed by author and Qingtao Xie in 2015, and the 85 participants involved in Belt and Road disputes interviewed in Beijing, Shanghai, Hong Kong, Singapore, London, and online by the author, Dr. Zhenyu Xiao and Xiaolei Han between December 2023 and August 2024. The author is also very grateful for the editing and reference assistance of Darius Dadgostar. Any omissions or errors are purely mine.

"ubi societas ibi jus, ubi jus ibi societas."

I INTRODUCTION

Discourse in the scholarly exploration of arbitration predominantly orbits around legal, procedural, and institutional dimensions. While the focus on codified rules and published decisions of arbitration is crucial,[1] it is equally important to study the sociological aspects of arbitration, as law is "made, interpreted, and implemented by humans, and humans are unavoidably affected by their social context."[2] In recent years, scholarship on the sociology of arbitration has evolved significantly, shaped by seminal works and ongoing empirical research.[3] One of the most influential sociological works on arbitration is the book *Dealing in Virtue* published in 1996 by Yves Dezalay and Bryant Garth, which examined how arbitrators gained their positions and earned the legitimacy to be selected in high-stakes disputes.[4] Using Pierre Bourdieu's concept of "symbolic capital," the authors described how the first generation of "Grand Old Men" (i.e., the leading figures of the European legal capitals, who typically had risen to the top of their domestic legal professions but had not specialized in arbitration)[5] were overtaken by the second generation of young "Technocrats" (i.e., arbitrators who typically spent their entire careers working in the field, in Anglo-American law firms)[6] in the 1980s and 1990s.

Scholars subsequently grounded new research on the arguments of Dezalay and Garth. In 2012, Thomas Schultz and Robert Kovacs revisited Dezalay and Garth's sociological study and argued that a third generation of arbitrators was emerging—the "managers of dispute resolution processes," who were highly skilled at managing proceedings, deliberations and the organization of tribunal work.[7] Based on a survey of ICSID appointments, Sergio Puig confirmed the narrative that the arbitration profession was dominated by a few, socially prominent actors ("Grand Old Men" and formidable women or "power-brokers"), based on different sources of "social capital," such as language or professional skills, nationality, background or diplomatic abilities, and

1. For instance, the ICCA's main publications are the Yearbook (court decisions), the Awards Series (arbitral awards), and the Handbook (domestic legal frameworks), *see* ICCA, "ICCA Publications" (2024) .
2. Joshua Karton, "International Arbitration as a Social Phenomenon: Using Sociological Theories and Methods in International Arbitration Practice," *ICCA Congress Series No. 22* (2024) Chapter 14.
3. For a comprehensive overview of sociological studies on arbitration, *see ibid*; Michael Waibel, "Sociology of Arbitrators" in Andrea K Bjorklund, Franco Ferrari, and Stefan Kröll (eds), *Cambridge Compendium of International Commercial and Investment Arbitration* (Cambridge University Press 2023).
4. Yves Dezalay and Bryant G Garth, *Dealing in Virtue: International Commercial Arbitration and the Construction of a Transnational Legal Order* (University of Chicago Press 1996).
5. *Ibid.*, 34.
6. *Ibid.*, 36.
7. Thomas Schultz and Robert Kovacs, "The Rise of a Third Generation of Arbitrators? Fifteen Years after Dezalay and Garth" (2012) 28 Arbitration International 161, 161-162 https://doi.org/10.1093/arbitration/28.2.161 (accessed August 16, 2025).

timely signaling of political preferences.[8] On a different account, using network analytics, Puig argued that the arbitration network was based on a combination of "timing, limited cognitive scope or heuristic biases, risk aversion, and a desire for predictable outcomes on the part of the parties making the appointments."[9] Emmanuel Gaillard identified social actors in the field to include essential actors (i.e., the parties and arbitrators), service providers (i.e., counsels, arbitral institutions, international organizations, expert witnesses, States, third-party funders) and value providers (i.e., States, international organizations, NGOs, arbitration clubs such as the ICCA, professional organizations). Examining the interactions between social actors, Gaillard observed the shifting landscape of international arbitration over the past forty years from a "solidaristic" model, where a close-knit group of arbitrators shared common values, to a "polarized" model in which a variety of actors shared different sets of values and beliefs.[10]

Others have provided alternative narratives on the development of international arbitration and the arbitration profession. Florian Grisel posited instead that international arbitration was constructed by a small group of actors—"Secant Marginals"—in the 1950s and 1970s, who were members of multiple social groups (national, ethnic, professional) and became skilled brokers at the intersection of systems. Grisel argued that the "Secant Marginals" succeeded in constructing a *cooperative* interface, rather than competition, between otherwise separate legal systems and professions, which formed a new transnational legal profession.[11] James Crawford, in his work, argued against the notion of an ideal type of arbitrator, with reference to investor-state arbitration in particular. He underscored that investor-state arbitration is a hybrid system, which blends elements from international commercial arbitration and public international law. This hybrid character, he argued, fosters an intermingling of professional groups, incorporating the procedural expertise from commercial arbitration and the substantive legal insights from public international law.[12]

The existing sociological work on arbitration provided important insights into the evolution of the arbitration field itself. A common theme from the different narratives is that international arbitrators are dominated by a small and homogenous group in terms of gender, national origin and educational background. The prominent figures who form the transnational legal profession tend to come from a particular tradition—legal societies based on the rule of law.

The inclination of framing arbitration within a predominately legalist paradigm comes as no surprise. From a historical perspective, the origin of arbitration as a private mode of dispute resolution is rooted in legal societies. The private and extrajudicial

8. Sergio Puig, "Social Capital in the Arbitration Market" (2014) 25 European Journal of International Law 387 https://doi.org/10.1093/ejil/chu045 (accessed August 16, 2025).
9. *Ibid.*, 424.
10. Emmanuel Gaillard, "Sociology of Arbitration" (2015) 31 Arbitration International 1 https://doi.org/10.1093/arbint/aiv021 (accessed August 16, 2025).
11. Florian Grisel, "Competition and Cooperation in International Commercial Arbitration: The Birth of a Transnational Legal Profession" (2017) 51 Law and Society Review 790 https://doi.org/10.1111/lasr.12295 (accessed August 16, 2025).
12. James Crawford, "The Ideal Arbitrator: Does One Size Fit All?" (2018) 32 American University International Law Review 1003.

nature of arbitration, and the principles of practicality and predictability, can be traced back to ancient civilizations, such as the Greeks and Romans, and further developed through the *lex mercatoria* during the medieval period in Europe.[13] An "arbitral chain" could be found that linked the eras of the West's arbitral past with its arbitral present.[14] The rationalist and legalist tradition in Western societies provides a philosophical foundation for arbitration to develop as a private method of dispute resolution, based on the application of shared, rational, and objectivized rules.

In contrast, traditional societies in the East, such as China, historically embraced different concepts of justice, which did not include the notion of private justice as understood in the West. There is no "arbitral link" between Chinese history and contemporary arbitration.[15] The concept of arbitration as understood today was transplanted into China during the late Qin Dynasty and early Republican period. Local authorities were strongly resistant to this transplanted institution and reluctant to recognize arbitration's adjudicatory function, which was historically reserved for the courts.[16] The transplantation of arbitration concepts, akin to those in the West, into China sparked a complex interplay between foreign legal concepts and deep-rooted local values. Adaptations were necessary to reconcile the newly introduced arbitration system with the Chinese moralist and relational tradition, illustrating a complex process of selection, resistance, reform, and integration in the transplantation process.[17]

Today, as international business is becoming more global and less nation-specific, international arbitration is developing toward a transnational institution for resolving cross-border disputes, which forms a "transnational legal order,"[18] or its own culture of "legal flamboyance."[19] However, the emergence of new market forces has injected fresh dynamics into the equation, prompting us to ponder a provocative thought posed by Bruno Oppetit in the *Théory de L'arbitrage*:

---

13. Dereck Roebuck, *Ancient Greek Arbitration* (Holo Books 2001); Dereck Roebuck and Bruno de Loynes de Fumichon, *Roman Arbitration* (Holo Books 2004); Derek Roebuck, "'Best to Reconcile': Mediation and Arbitration in the Ancient Greek World" (2000) 66 International Journal of Arbitration, Mediation and Dispute Management 275; Julie Velissaropoulos-Karakostas, "L'arbitrage dans la Grèce antique. Epoques archaïque et classique" [2000] Revue de l'arbitrage 9. For further discussion, *see* Kun Fan, *Arbitration in China: A Legal and Cultural Analysis* (Hart Publishing 2013) 1-9; Arthur J Gemmell, *Western and Chinese Arbitration: The Arbitral Chain* (University Press of America 2008).
14. Gemmell 2008 (n 13).
15. *Ibid.*
16. For detailed discussion of the transplantation of arbitration in China, *see* Kun Fan, "Glocalization of Arbitration: Transnational Standards Struggling with Local Norms" (2013) 18 Harvard Negotiation Law Review 175.
17. *See ibid.*
18. *See* Dezalay and Garth 1996 (n 4); Emmanuel Gaillard, "Transcending National Legal Orders for International Arbitration" in *International Arbitration: The Coming of a New Age?, ICCA Congress Series No. 17* (2012) 371; Emmanuel Gaillard, "The Arbitral Legal Order: Evolution and Recognition" in Thomas Schultz and Federico Ortino (eds), *The Oxford Handbook of International Arbitration* (Oxford University Press 2020); Thomas Schultz, "The Concept of Law in Transnational Arbitral Legal Orders and Some of Its Consequences" (2011) 2 Journal of International Dispute Settlement 59 https://doi.org/10.1093/jnlids/idq019 (accessed August 16, 2025).
19. Won L Kidane, *The Culture of International Arbitration* (Oxford University Press 2017) 285.

> Can we speak today of the universality of international commercial arbitration? Is it linked to a certain type of society, a particular legal tradition, a specific economic system? Was it forged by the developed world to serve its own interest? Does it only concern a limited number of conflicts and actors in international economic life? Is there only a dominant model, or in contrast, as many varieties as the diversities of legal traditions offer?[20]

If arbitration is not universal but a culturally contingent institution, then how do cultural, social, historical, and philosophical dimensions in diverse traditions influence the perceptions and practices of arbitration today? For hints to these questions, it is essential to recognize that norms or theoretical frameworks that are deeply rooted in one tradition—in this case, legal societies—may not be suitable to fully appreciate the intricacies of societies shaped by other traditions, such as those based on morality or religion. William Alford raises the challenges and limitations of using "grand theory"[21] to study foreign systems, especially those like China's, which are vastly different from Western traditions.[22] His concerns are that:

> our efforts at engaging in broad theoretical work may unwittingly lead us to believe that we are considering foreign legal cultures in universal or value-free terms when, in fact, we are examining them through conceptual frameworks that are products of our own values and traditions, and that are often applied merely to see what foreign societies have to tell us about ourselves.[23]

Some excellent work has been done to explore the intersection of culture, sociology, and dispute resolution practices beyond legal societies.[24] Building on others' work, this chapter aspires to present a novel lens on the sociological dimensions shaping the essence of law, the perception of justice, and dispute resolution mechanisms. The chapter uses Xingzhong Yu's theory of human faculties and human societies as a theoretical compass to guide us through the different traditions of mind, heart, and soul—law, morality, and religion—legal, moral, and religious societies.[25] Adopting this epistemological schema, the chapter navigates through the faculty of the mind in the legal tradition, manifested in rationality, and the faculty of heart in the moral tradition, manifested in human sentiments.[26] This chapter hopes to unveil the intricate ways in which different human faculties and societies shape the perceptions and practices of arbitration. The aim of this chapter is not to assess if a particular

---

20. Bruno Oppetit, *Théorie de l'arbitrage* (Presses Universitaires de France 1998) 110.
21. Quentin Skinner (ed.), *The Return of Grand Theory in the Human Sciences* (Cambridge University Press 1985).
22. William Alford, "On the Limits of 'Grand Theory' in Comparative Law" (1986) 61 Washington Law Review 945.
23. *Ibid.*, 946.
24. *See, e.g.*, Kidane 2017 (n 19); Joshua Karton, *The Culture of International Arbitration and the Evolution of Contract Law* (Oxford University Press 2013); Nathalie Najjar, *Arbitration and International Trade in the Arab Countries* (Brill Nijhoff 2018); John Miles, Tunde Fagbohunlu, and Kamal Rasiklal Shah, *Arbitration in Africa: A Review of Key Jurisdictions* (Sweet & Maxwell 2016); Maria Bhatti, *Islamic Law and International Commercial Arbitration* (Routledge 2020).
25. Xingzhong Yu, *Rule of Law and Civil Orders* (China Politics and Law University Press 2006).
26. This chapter only focuses on the legal and moral traditions. For a discussion of the religious tradition, *see* Nudrat Bayan Majeed, "Islamic Law and Arbitration in Pakistan: A Sociological Perspective," *ICCA Congress Series No. 22* (2024) Chapter 15.

tradition is normatively superior or inferior to another. Rather, the chapter seeks to underscore the significance of understanding these differences within the specific cultural contexts that have "given rise to them, shaped them, and been influenced by them."[27] It invites scholars and practitioners alike to re-evaluate not just *how* arbitration is practiced but more profoundly, *why* it is shaped in diverse and intricate ways, searching for deep-seated social and philosophical reasons underlying its diverse manifestations.

The rest of the chapter is organized as follows: section II introduces the three-dimensional cultural epistemology of human faculties and human societies. Section III analyzes how the legal tradition and the moral tradition influence the rationalist and the relational approaches of dispute resolution, respectively. Section IV illustrates the main manifestations of the different human faculties and societies in arbitration practices specifically. Section V concludes with reflections on the limitations of the study and proposals of avenues for future research.

II DIFFERENCES IN HUMAN FACULTIES AND HUMAN SOCIETIES

Xingzhong Yu uses the concept of "civil order" as a fundamental framework necessary for "harmonizing the relationships between man and man, man and oneself, man and society, and man and nature."[28] Civil order is crucial for regulating governance, compliance, rewards, and punishment within a society and underpins the "allocation of resources, commercial transactions, commodity production, social grouping, education, personal development, and individual beliefs."[29] Civil order is argued to be the most pivotal aspect among various binary oppositions such as order versus freedom, hierarchy versus equality, and cruelty versus humanity. Without civil order, values like freedom, equality, fairness, and justice would be submerged in the chaos of human desires.[30]

Under this framework, human societies can be broadly categorized into legal, moral, and religious civil orders, based on differences in conceptual categories, authority systems, institutional arrangements, and popular consciousness.[31] Legal civil order is centered around the rational aspects of humans (mind) and adopts a more permissive stance toward human desires. Individuals are encouraged to pursue their desires, which when externalized, manifest as rights. To ensure these rights, laws are deemed necessary, making the legal system the ultimate authority in this order. Moral civil order is rooted in the emotional aspect of humans (heart), which controls human desires, emphasizing self-cultivation and peaceful coexistence, with morality holding supreme authority. It is governed by moral principles accumulated over years and aims to maintain social stability by encapsulating individual ambitions, cultural creations, and other social activities within the scope of ethics and morality. Religious civil order

27. *See* Alford 1986 (n 22) 951.
28. Yu 2006 (n 25) 54.
29. *Ibid.*
30. *Ibid.*
31. Yu 2006 (n 25).

is anchored in the spiritual aspect of humans (spirit), under which the pursuit of freedom and fairness is entirely dependent on obedience to the divine. God is considered the ultimate authority, creator of conceptual categories, and designer of systems.[32] Yu believes that "frameworks in most societies can be understood within this classification with some being archetypical and others combining different elements of the three."[33]

In an attempt to provide a theory to trace the origin of law, morality and religion, Yu used the three-dimensional view of human faculties as an epistemological schema,[34] drawing on the philosophies about human faculties by scholars from different traditions, including Plato,[35] Aristotle,[36] Descartes,[37] Kant,[38] Hegel,[39] Habermas,[40] Hume,[41] Confucius,[42] Xunzi,[43] and Mencius.[44] Yu argued that societies and law, morality, and religion are the manifestations of *human faculties*, which can be understood as "the innate human capacities by which human beings discover, absorb, and improve spiritual value resources."[45] Human faculties have three dimensions: the mind, the heart and the soul. According to him, "mind produces rationality; heart produces sentiments and soul, faith, both belonging to the sphere of irrationality. The manifestations of these three faculties constitute law, morality and religion, and the legal, moral and religious societies."[46] Although the three human faculties of mind, heart, and soul may be present in all humans, there is a "difference of manifestation in terms of degree." The human faculties develop in three stages, namely: "(i) as instinctive manifestations of human faculties, (ii) as developed systems of knowledge, and (iii) as the predominant force in societies."[47]

---

32. *Ibid.*
33. Xingzhong Yu, "Human Faculties and Human Societies: A Three Dimensional Cultural Epistemology" in Zenon Bankowski (ed.), *Epistemology and Ontology: IVR-Symposium Lund 2003* (Franz Steiner Verlag Stuttgart 2005) 175.
34. *Ibid.*, 171-84.
35. *See* Plato, *The Republic of Plato* (Francis MacDonald Cornford ed. and tr, Oxford University Press 1961) Books IV (on the tripartite soul), V, and VI.
36. *See* Aristotle, *Nicomachean Ethics* (Sarah Broadie and Christopher Rowe eds, Oxford University Press 2002) Books I.9 (Is Happiness Acquired by Learning or Habituation, or Sent by God or by Chance?) and VI (on intellectual virtues and practical wisdom).
37. *See* René Descartes, *Meditations on First Philosophy: With Selections from the Objections and Replies* (John Cottingham ed and tr, Cambridge University Press 2013) 33-47, 137-49.
38. *See* Immanuel Kant, *Critique of Pure Reason* (Norman Kemp Smith tr, rev 2nd ed., Palgrave Macmillan 2007) 92-101.
39. *See* Georg Wilhelm Friedrich Hegel, *The Philosophy of Hegel* (Carl J Friedrich ed., Random House 1954).
40. *See* Jürgen Habermas, *Knowledge and Human Interest* (Jeremy J Shapiro tr, Beacon Press 1972) 301-17; Jürgen Habermas, "Discourse Ethics: Notes on a Program of Philosophical Justification" in Jürgen Habermas (ed.), *Moral Consciousness and Communicative Action* (MIT Press 1990).
41. *See* David Hume, *An Enquiry Concerning the Principles of Morals* (Open Court Publishing Company 1930) 125-36.
42. *See* Confucius, *The Analects* (DC Lau tr, Penguin Books 1979).
43. *See* Xunzi, *Hsün Tzu: Basic Writings* (Burton Watson tr, Columbia University Press 1963).
44. *See* Mencius, *Mencius* (DC Lau tr, Penguin Books 1970).
45. Yu 2005 (n 33) 174.
46. *Ibid.*, 174-77.
47. *Ibid.*, 176.

The faculty of mind manifests itself in reasonableness, formalism, utilitarianism, experience and the rule-following orientation, constituting rationality.[48] The developmental process of rationality and the emergence of legal societies can be summarized in the following three stages: first, as instinctual expressions of human cognitive abilities where reasoning and logic start to shape individual and communal actions, without a structured or predictable system; second, a conscious shift toward formalizing behaviors and actions through rules and procedures, transforming intuitive behaviors into a structured system of norms and interests. This stage, referred to as "rule rationalism," is marked by the conceptualization of behavioral norms and the regulation of social life, where law begins to emerge as a system of knowledge that can be explained and applied rationally; and third, when rule rationalism is turned into rule centrism, which places law, formalized by rules, in the predominant position in a society, where these rational structures and legal principles become the foundation of social order, governance, and the resolution of disputes, exemplifying a society governed by the rule of law. This is the stage of the legal society, or "rule of law."[49]

This progression from the faculty of mind to a legal society or legal civil order can be used to describe modern societies in Western Europe and North America, which are characterized by the rule of law. In legal civil orders, prevalent conceptual categories are centered on "rights" and "law," including the rule of law, democracy, freedom, rights, obligations, justice, rationality, property, individualism, contracts, and litigation. These concepts function as abstract principles, ideas, or values and can also be further delineated into specific rules, which focus on satisfaction of individual desires. The systems of authority are guided by the ideal of the rule of law and focus on legal texts and institutions. In legal societies, authoritative interpreters, authoritative institutions, and permanent authority figures arise from the same source—the judiciary. Authoritative documents occupy an exalted position in the authoritative system. Authoritative institutions are formalized legal institutions like courts. The judicial system is considered a fundamental institutional arrangement of legal societies, including specialized legislative bodies, the judiciary, law enforcement agencies, the legal profession, the defense system, the jury system, the evidence collection system, and the trial system. Public consciousness is based on the rule of law and individual rights. The contents and values of legal societies are spread through institutions and specific practical activities (public trials in courts, mass participation in political activities, individual participation in litigation).[50]

In contrast, the faculty of heart is manifested in human emotions, sentiments, temperaments, and feelings, which all exist in human relations. The standards by which to define the manifestations of the faculty of heart in human relations constitute morality.[51] The development from the faculty of heart into a moral society also occurs in three stages: first, as "instinctive interactions within human relationships driven by emotions, sentiments, and feelings," where reciprocity is naturally exhibited and yet to

48. *Ibid.*, 178.
49. *Ibid.*, 177-79.
50. Yu 2006 (n 25).
51. Yu 2005 (n 33) 179.

be institutionalized and conceptualized; second, morality develops into a system of knowledge that distinguishes and conceptualizes human relationships, associates specific emotions with them, and finally establishes moral standards; and third, morality becomes the dominant force in societies, leading to a moral society where morality guides social institutions and individual behavior, emphasizing ethics over procedures and values over utility. This is the stage of "rule of morality," "rule of virtue," or the moral society.[52] In moral societies or moral civil order, personal aspirations, collective activity, cultural creation and various types of social life must be in conformity with moral categories designed to nurture human beings in order to maintain a harmonious social order.[53]

Traditional Chinese society is an example of a moral society, characterized by the rule of virtue. In moral societies or moral civil order, dominant conceptual categories feature moral concepts such as *De* (ritual), *Ren* (benevolence), *Yi* (loyalty), *Li* (ritualism), *Zhi* (wisdom), *Xin* (sincerity), *He* (harmony), *Rang* (concession/yielding), and *Zhongyong* (the doctrine of middle way). The systems of authority are guided by the ideal of the rule of morality, with a focus on rituals, rather than texts and institutions. The bureaucratic system embodying the rule of morality constitutes the authoritative institution. The institutional arrangement is based on the relational networks to which an individual belongs. Public consciousness is based on the pursuit of harmony and avoidance of litigation.[54] This is reflected in popular Chinese proverbs: "to enter a court of law is to enter a tiger's mouth" and "avoid litigation, for once you resort to law there is nothing but trouble."

To be sure, there are significant divergences within societies, each with nuanced cultural distinctions. Civil orders are also not static; instead, they evolve with human behaviors and interactions. The three-dimensional model is a broad characterization, which highlights the dominating characteristics and differences in different types of societies. For instance, in legal societies, morality is also relevant in shaping behaviors, and relationships also play an important role in regulating social and economic activities. However, morality does not function as an explicit controlling force in legal societies. Morality in legal societies can be said to be in the second stage of development, in which conceptualization and systematization of these relationships and standards produce morality that, as a system of knowledge, has a potentially shaping implication on individuals.[55] What distinguishes different societies is which faculty becomes the dominant force in the society. With these caveats, this three-dimensional framework allows for a nuanced understanding of how different traditions shape perceptions of justice and dispute resolution processes beyond the narratives of the legal societies.

52. *Ibid.*
53. *Ibid.*, 180.
54. Yu 2006 (n 25).
55. Yu 2005 (n 33) 179.

III INFLUENCE OF THE THREE-DIMENSIONAL FRAMEWORK ON DISPUTE RESOLUTION TRADITIONS

The three-dimensional conceptual framework discussed in section II offers a panoramic view of societal structures, suggesting that the dominance of specific human faculties—the mind, heart, and soul—gives rise to distinct types of societies: legal, moral, and religious, respectively. Using this conceptual framework, this section will analyze how the faculty of mind and faculty of heart influence the respective dispute resolution traditions.

1 Rationalist Tradition

The faculty of mind aligns closely with William Twining's model of the "rationalist" tradition in Anglo-American adjudication.[56] The rationalist model of adjudication emphasizes a structured and evidence-based approach, aiming to accurately determine "the true past facts material to precisely specified allegations expressed in categories defined in advance by law,"[57] which prioritizes the vindication of individual rights. The rationalist model relies on the "careful and *rational* weighing of evidence which is both relevant and reliable presented … to supposedly competent and impartial decision makers with adequate safeguards against corruption and mistake and adequate provision for review and appeal."[58] Despite its Anglo-American roots, Twining points out that the "rationalist" concept is also compatible with the Continental inquisitorial system.[59]

This rationalist model embodies the essence of rationality in the faculty of mind—it is rooted in logical analysis, systematic procedures, and a preference for rules and standards that guide legal reasoning and decision-making. This tradition places a high value on procedural fairness, logical coherence, and the objective determination of facts, all of which are indicative of a legal society that prioritizes the mind's rational capabilities (manifested as reasonableness, formalism, utilitarian ethos, and a rule-following orientation) over the heart's sentiments or the soul's faith. With the conceptualization of justice focusing on principles of rationality, individual rights, and procedural fairness, the dispute resolution process is featured by heavy reliance on codified laws, formal procedures, and courts.

2 Relational Tradition

In contrast, Chinese society, traditional and present, was described by Xiaotong Fei as a "differential mode of association" (*chaxu geju*).[60] In these networks, *guanxi* (personal

56. William Twining, *Rethinking Evidence: Exploratory Essays* (Northwestern University Press 1994).
57. Richard D Friedman and J Frank Yates, "The Triangle of Culture, Inference, and Litigation System" (2003) 2 Law, Probability and Risk 137, 138 https://doi.org/10.1093/lpr/2.2.137 (accessed August 16, 2025).
58. Twining 1994 (n 56); Friedman and Yates 2003 (n 57) 138.
59. Friedman and Yates 2003 (n 57) 140.
60. Gary G Hamilton and Wang Zheng, *From the Soil: The Foundations of Chinese Society: A Translation of Fei Xiaotong's Xiangtu Zhongguo* (University of California Press 1992).

connections) plays a crucial role in determining the nature and dynamics of relationships. The differential mode of association allows for great flexibility in social interactions, as the nature of relationships can change depending on circumstances and the distance between individuals in the network. The expectations of a particular relationship rely heavily on context, including the history of interactions, the social status of the individuals involved, and the specific situation at hand.[61] In a relational structure deeply embedded in Chinese culture, the network of *guanxi* holds significant importance not only for social but also for economic activities. *Guanxi* enables collaboration beyond familial ties, allowing unrelated individuals and families to collaborate with each other.[62] In the Chinese perception, *guanxi* represents a form of "social capital," where relationships and networks can be leveraged for personal and business advantages. *Guanxi* shapes the way individuals interact and operate within Chinese society.

Unlike the rationalist approach, which seeks universal principles and rule-based justifications for behavior and decision-making, the Chinese approach to dispute resolution is characterized by a particularistic approach that takes into account the context and relationships involved. This attitude is evident in the tendency to provide compromise-based justifications for behavior, reflecting a more flexible approach to law and justice that is sensitive to the relationships involved rather than seeking a single, definitive resolution based on adversarial debate.[63] As Philip McConnaughay noted, "situational and circumstantial considerations prevail ... over contractual terms and expectations, conflict avoidance and negotiation or conciliation prevail ... over all-or-nothing adjudication."[64] Law is considered a flexible quantity and should consider particularistic situations, as opposed to trying to categorize every possible scenario into generalized legal categories. While relationships are also important in other traditions, such as in relational contracts in the legal tradition,[65] their significance in society differs. Relational contracts aim to foster collaboration and adaptability in complex business arrangements, which remain within the legal and formal framework of contract law. In contrast, *guanxi* emphasizes holistic relationships and implicit trust built over time and holds profound societal importance in Chinese culture, extending beyond business to shape personal, social, economic, and familial interactions.

Such a flexible and relational approach aligns closely with the faculty of heart and moral societies, which focus on emotions, human sentiments, and feelings. This moral orientation emphasizes the intricacies of relationships, focusing on understanding and navigating the complexities of various social interactions through moral cultivation

61. *Ibid.*
62. Fan 2013 (n 13).
63. Friedman and Yates 2003 (n 57).
64. Philip J McConnaughay, "Rethinking the Role of Law and Contracts in East-West Commercial Relations" (2001) 41 Virginia Journal of International Law 427, 443-44.
65. *See* Stewart Macaulay, "Non-contractual Relations in Business: A Preliminary Study" (1963) 28 American Sociological Review 55; Stewart Macaulay, "The Real and the Paper Deal: Empirical Pictures of Relationships, Complexity and the Urge for Transparent Simple Rules" (2003) 66 Modern Law Review 44 https://doi.org/10.1111/1468-2230.6601003 (accessed August 16, 2025); Catherine Mitchell, "Contracts and Contract Law: Challenging the Distinction Between the 'Real' and 'Paper' Deal" (2009) 29 Oxford Journal of Legal Studies 675 https://doi.org/10.1093/ojls/gqp023 (accessed August 16, 2025).

and personal achievement. In the context of dispute resolution, this moral framework prioritizes yielding and concessions, reflecting a societal preference for maintaining social harmony and repairing relationships rather than pursuing individual rights through adversarial legal proceedings. The emphasis on moral precepts and social harmony aligns with the Chinese dispute resolution style, which seeks to balance individual interests with broader societal goals, with a lesser inclination to make "accurate determination of the true past facts."[66] The Chinese approach to conflict resolution historically relied on social networks, emphasizing maintaining relationships and social order. Dispute resolution mechanisms were often informal, embedded within clan, village, or guild structures, and focused on reconciliation and compromise rather than formal adjudication.[67] The Chinese dispute resolution approach values harmony, relational ethics and moral integrity over legal formalism, procedural legitimacy and individual rights assertion.

IV MANIFESTATIONS OF THE DIFFERENT TRADITIONS IN CONTEMPORARY ARBITRATION

Such traditions are of course changing. With enhanced rights consciousness, Chinese parties are increasingly willing to initiate formal proceedings to protect their legal rights. However, these differing traditions still have profound implications in contemporary arbitration. They shape how arbitrators perceive their roles, how justice is conceptualized, how settlements are sought and achieved, and also influence the process and outcome of arbitration. This section will highlight the following four manifestations of different traditions in contemporary arbitration.

1 Perception of the Role of Arbitrator

In traditions dominated by the faculty of mind, such as those found in many Western legal systems, arbitration is fundamentally viewed through a lens of legalism and rationality. The arbitrator is perceived to be an impartial, neutral decision-maker who applies legal principles to render a binding decision. Arbitration is a private mechanism for dispute settlement based on consent of the parties, an alternative to national court but still an adjudicatory and formalized process focused on evidence, legal arguments, and past events.[68] This perspective aligns with a rationalist tradition in dispute resolution, where the primary focus is on the objective assessment of facts, adherence

66. Friedman and Yates 2003 (n 57).
67. *See* Fan 2013 (n 16); Bobby Wong, "Chinese law: Traditional Chinese Philosophy and Dispute" (2000) 30 Hong Kong Law Journal 304.
68. Such perception can be drawn from the definition of arbitration in authoritative work on arbitration by authors from common law and civil law traditions: *see, e.g.*, Emmanuel Gaillard and John Savage (eds), *Fouchard Gaillard Goldman on International Commercial Arbitration* (Kluwer Law International 1999) 9; Charles Jarrosson, *La* générale de droit et de jurisprudence (1987) 372; Nigel Blackaby et al. *Redfern and Hunter on International Arbitration* (6th ed., Oxford University Press 2009) 1; Julian DM Lew, Loukas A Mistelis, and Stefan M Kröll, *Comparative International Commercial Arbitration* (Kluwer Law International 2003) 3-4.

to legal norms, the application of universal rules to establish the truth of past events, and the vindication of individual rights. From this standpoint, the distinction between the role of an arbitrator and mediator is straightforward: the former is a decision-maker in an adjudicatory process, and the latter is a settlement facilitator in a non-adjudicatory process.[69]

Conversely, in traditions where the faculty of heart prevails, such as in traditional Chinese society, the role of the arbitrator extends beyond legal adjudication to encompass settlement facilitation. Historically, the so-called arbitration mechanism (*gongduan*) served more as an internal conflict resolution mechanism within traditional social organizations (i.e., families, clans, villages and guilds), rather than an independent, third-party adjudication based on party autonomy.[70] Even today, Chinese perceptions of the roles of an arbitrator and a mediator are still blurred. The Chinese Arbitration Law expressly authorizes arbitrators to act as mediators.[71] An arbitrator is often perceived as a problem-solver who will help the parties resolve their disputes by the most appropriate means, not limited to applying strict legal principles and rendering binding decisions. The arbitrator's role can also include assisting the parties in reaching a mutually agreeable solution or, failing that, allowing both parties to view the resolution as one to which each has freely agreed or one which will allow the parties to resume their relationship with as little loss of "face" as possible.[72] There is no unequivocal distinction between the role of the settlement facilitator and the decision-maker. My empirical research based on interviews and surveys with Chinese arbitrators shows that 88.9% of Chinese arbitrators consider it appropriate for them to facilitate settlement. In practice, most Chinese arbitrators will systematically ask the parties if they wish the tribunal to assist them in reaching an amicable settlement. Such a proposal is easily acceptable by Chinese parties.[73] It should also be noted that the Chinese model represents the most complete integration of mediation and arbitration (med–arb), where the arbitrator may become a mediator, then an arbitrator again at any stage of the proceedings. This differs from the way med–arb is conducted in other

69. It is recognized that there are divergences between different jurisdictions within the legal civil order. For instance, some empirical research shows great divergence in attitude and experience between German and American practitioners: *see*, Christian-Uhle, Lars Kirchhoff, and Gabriele Scherer, *Arbitration and Mediation in International Business* (2nd ed., Kluwer Law International 2006); Gabrielle Kaufmann-Kohler and Victor Bonnin, "Arbitrators as Conciliators: A Statistical Study of the Relation between an Role and Legal" (2007) 18 ICC International Court of Arbitration Bulletin 79. This traditional view has also evolved and is discussed in section IV(4).
70. *See* Fan 2013 (n 16).
71. *See* Article 51 of the Arbitration Law of the People's Republic of China (Chinese Arbitration Law), promulgated on 31 August 1994.
72. *See* M. Scott Donahey, "Seeking Harmony: Is the Asian of the in the West?" (1995) 50 Dispute Resolution, 74.
73. This observation is drawn from interviews conducted by the author and Gabrielle Kaufmann-Kohler with 25 arbitration specialists working in China during a field trip in 2007, and subsequent surveys by the author of more than one hundred Chinese arbitrators distributed between November 2011 and April 2012. Further details of empirical findings are discussed in Kun Fan, "An Empirical Study of Arbitrators Acting as Mediators in" (2014) 15 Cardozo Journal of Conflict Resolution 777; Gabrielle Kaufmann-Kohler and Kun Fan, "Integrating Mediation into Arbitration: Why It Works China?" (2008) 25 Journal of International Arbitration 479 https://doi.org/10.54648/joia2008035 (accessed August 16, 2025).

Asian countries such as Indonesia and Korea, where mediation is only attempted at the outset of arbitration proceedings.[74]

2 Settlement Considerations

In the legal civil order, although many disputes are resolved by some form of settlement before reaching formal adjudicatory processes,[75] this does not negate the fact that the dispute resolution system prioritizes truth-determination and rationality.[76] Settlement discussions are conducted "in the shadow of law,"[77] anticipating the probable outcome of litigation or the "BATNA" and "WATNA" if negotiations were to fail,[78] based on rational cost-benefit analyses. Even if the parties have not finally invoked their legal rights or have the factual findings officially made, those rights and the anticipated outcomes significantly influence the negotiation process and the eventual resolution of the disputes.[79]

In contrast, Chinese parties' decisions on settlement considerations and whether to initiate arbitration are guided by the moral precepts of tolerance (*ren*), concession/yielding (*rang*), and the doctrine of middle way (*zhongyong*). Empirical research conducted by the author and Xiao Zhenyu on the Belt and Road Initiative shows that *guanxi*, trust and long-term relationships are important considerations for Chinese enterprises in the choice of dispute resolution methods. When a problem arises, Chinese enterprises first approach someone they trust, such as their national managers, who are well connected with local parties, to lobby and try to assist the parties to reach a settlement. Only if this attempt fails, will Chinese enterprises consider engaging a third-party neutral, such as an arbitrator, to decide the issue. Interviewees also revealed that relationship damage and loss of face (*mianzi)* are important deterrence for the use of arbitration to resolve disputes,[80] reflecting a more holistic and relational-based way of thinking.

3 The Ideal of Justice

Unlike the ideal of justice in legal civil order, which springs from reason, rationality, and individual rights, the Chinese perception of justice evokes both reason and human

74. Donahey 1995 (n 72), 76.
75. For instance, the dispute pyramid model illustrates that only a small proportion of perceived injuries proceed to adjudication. *See* Richard E Miller and Austin Sarat, "Grievances, Claims, and Disputes: Assessing the Adversary" (1980) 15 Law and Society Review 525 https://doi.org/10.2307/3053502 (accessed August 16, 2025).
76. Friedman and Yates 2003 (n 57).
77. Robert H Mnookin and Lewis Kornhauser, "Bargaining in the Shadow of the Law: The Case of" (1979) 88 Yale Law Journal 950 https://doi.org/10.2307/795824 (accessed August 16, 2025).
78. *See* Roger Fisher, William Ury, and Bruce Patton, *Getting to Yes: Negotiating Agreement Giving In* (2nd ed., Penguin Books 1991).
79. Friedman and Yates 2003 (n 57) 142.
80. This observation is drawn from a series of interviews (some conducted by the author alone and others conducted together with Zhenyu Xiao) with a total of 72 participants involved in Belt and Road disputes in Beijing, Shanghai, Hong Kong, Singapore, London, and online between December 2023 and May 2024. The interviewees included lawyers, in-house counsel, arbitrators, delegates from arbitration institutions, academics and government officials.

sentiments. Rooted in the heart tradition, in the Chinese mind, a just decision must be *heli, heqing, hefa*—in accordance with reasonableness, human sentiments, and the law.[81] Law is only one element to be considered in the adjudicator's decision-making, together with the principle of fairness and reasonableness. Thus, in the Chinese tradition, there is a pronounced emphasis on equitable principles that take into account the broader context and relational dynamics of the parties involved.

The Chinese idea of equity is to be distinguished from the concept of "equity" in the common law system, which originated in the English Court of Chancery as a corrective mechanism to mitigate the sometimes harsh outcomes of the common law's rigid procedures.[82] Equity introduced principles aimed at achieving fairness when the strict application of common law would result in injustice. In essence, the common law concept of "equity" focuses on providing remedies for the limitations of the common law, ensuring fairness within a more individualistic, rights-based, and rational framework. In contrast, the Chinese reliance on equitable principles places a greater emphasis on human sentiments and the relational aspects of the idea of justice.

My empirical research based on interviews with Chinese judges reveals that non-rational factors, such as human sentiments, morality and empathy, have a meaningful impact on individual judicial behavior. The Chinese judges prioritize achieving subjective justice in particular cases over rigorously adhering to procedural fairness. They may turn to judicial mediation to obtain substantive justice if they believe that a strict application of the law could lead to unfair outcomes. Some judges may show a propensity to support the weaker party within the boundary of the law and their discretionary power, while others may actively search out evidence they believe will result in a more equitable outcome.[83]

Non-rational factors such as human sentiments also impact arbitral decision-making. The Chinese Arbitration Law expressly states that arbitration disputes shall be resolved in a fair and reasonable manner in compliance with the law.[84] A review of arbitral awards shows that, in the early years, arbitrators from CIETAC's predecessors "placed more emphasis on [the principle of] fairness than on the legal issues" in rendering their decisions. They were keen on "resolving disputes in a way that would result in each disputing party making a compromise" to restore the relationship.[85] With

81. Richard Fellows, Anita MM Liu, and Shuibo Zhang, "What Is Fair? Perceptions of Justice" (2011) 2 Journal of Quantity Surveying and Construction Business 20, 25
82. *See* John CP Goldberg, Henry E Smith, and PG Turner (eds), *Equity and Law: Fusion and Fission* (Cambridge University Press 2019) 31.
83. Such observations are drawn from the interviews conducted by the author and Qingtao Xie in 2015 with a total of twenty-nine Chinese judges from basic-level and intermediate courts, and three officials from the Supreme People's Court. The judges are from six courts in three different regions of China at different stages of economic developments. For details of the empirical findings, *see* Kun Fan, "Beyond Law and Politics: An Empirical Study of Judicial Mediation in China" (2023) 14 Journal of International Dispute Settlement 47 https://doi.org/10.1093/jnlids/idac027 (accessed August 16, 2025).
84. *See* Article 7 of the Chinese Arbitration Law (n 71).
85. Guiguo Wang, "The Unification of the Dispute Resolution System in China: Cultural, Economic and Legal" (1996) 13 Journal of International Arbitration 5, 30 https://doi.org/10.54648/joia1996011 (accessed August 16, 2025).

this human and relational approach, less attention may be paid to pertinent legal issues.

As arbitration in China has adapted toward transnational standards and become increasingly legalized, CIETAC arbitrators in recent years have tended to "base their conclusions on legal reasoning" and were "generally inclined to rely on the contractual rights and obligations of the disputing parties."[86] However, arbitrators' decision-making is still influenced by human sentiments. Jingzhou Tao noted that "by virtue of the principles of equity embodied in numerous fundamental Chinese statutes, arbitrators apply not merely the relevant provisions of Chinese law but also operate to a certain extent as *amiable compositeurs.*"[87] My empirical research demonstrates that Chinese arbitrators tend to adopt a more holistic thinking style compared to their Western counterparts. Many interviewed Chinese arbitrators consider that human sentiments and reasonableness are still relevant in their decision-making. They do not hesitate to refer to equitable principles to achieve substantive justice in specific cases.[88] It should be noted that Chinese arbitrators' reliance on equitable principles is not based on express authorization from the parties. This is different from the principle of *amiable compositeur* (sometimes referred to as ruling *ex aequo et bono* or "in equity") recognized in many jurisdictions, which allows arbitrators to render a decision solely based on equitable principles only if parties expressly grant such power by prior consent.[89]

4 Process and Outcome of Arbitration

How do the different human faculties and societies influence the process and outcome of arbitration? How are the differences in human faculties translated into rules of arbitration? To date, the prevailing rules in arbitration, such as the UNCITRAL Model Law on International Commercial Arbitration, New York Convention on the Recognition and Enforcement of Foreign Arbitral Awards, Convention on the Settlement of Investment Disputes between States and Nationals of Other States, are essentially driven by Western developed nations from a legal civil order and faculty of mind. Practices originating in common law jurisdictions, such as cross-examination and discovery, have been widely used in international arbitration.

As a result, parties from a different civil order are sometimes at a disadvantaged position in international arbitration processes. It has been observed that Chinese parties sometimes become the victim of their own generosity because they are reluctant to express their disagreements openly.[90] On evidence production, given that there is no discovery system in civil proceedings in China, it is quite common for a Chinese

86. *Ibid.*, 31.
87. Jingzhou Tao, *Arbitration Law and Practice in China* (3rd ed., Kluwer Law International 2012) 115-16.
88. This finding was drawn from a series of interviews conducted by the author and Gabrielle Kaufmann-Kohler in 2007: *see* (n 73).
89. *See,* Gaillard and Savage (eds) 1999 (n 68), 835-41.
90. *See* Henneke Brink, "Dispute Resolution in the Chinese Belt and Road Initiative: The Role of Mediation" [2021] Corporate Mediation Journal 45, 47 https://doi.org/10.5553/cmj/25424602

respondent to submit its defense and evidence at the hearing. Chinese parties and lawyers may take evidence ambush as a technique in arbitral proceedings.[91] However, such conduct may be viewed by counsel and arbitrators from common law jurisdictions as malicious surprise attacks of evidence. Furthermore, in the relational tradition, business is often conducted informally based on trust. Maintaining and presenting documentation may be considered secondary to the broader relational context of business dealings in China. As a result, many Chinese companies rarely keep documentary evidence in their business dealings, which may affect the quality of evidence presented in arbitral hearings.[92]

The dominance of arbitrators from legal civil orders can also lead to outcomes that may not align with the principles of the applicable law. For instance, in a PRC law-governed decades-long supply contract, after spending years on unsuccessful attempts to build necessary infrastructure, parties reached a deadlock and the buyer sought to withdraw from the contract. The majority of the tribunal, which was from common law jurisdictions, decided to enforce strict contractual terms, ruling for continued performance of the contract for the full remaining years. Notably, despite evidence that the seller had secured alternative performance from a third party, the tribunal rejected the buyer's request for the seller to produce evidence on the alternative performance, considering it to be irrelevant.[93]

This strict black letter law approach by the tribunal stands in contrast with the equitable and flexible approach traditionally favored by Chinese adjudicators. Although the Chinese Contract Law, which was in force at the time of arbitration, did not expressly give the breaching party the right to request termination of the contract,[94] Chinese courts have previously allowed the breaching party to terminate contracts, and in some cases, reduced the breaching party's liability for damages, by invoking some general principles, such as avoidance of waste of social resources, balance of interests between the parties, principles of fairness and equity, principles of good faith, principles of equality and voluntariness especially when cooperation fails, and protecting overall social interests.[95] These decisions emphasizes balancing considerations between the strict adherence to contracts and fairness and equitable principles, where continued performance is excessively burdensome or unjust to the breaching party.

This equitable approach was further demonstrated by the subsequent "Minutes of the Supreme People's Court Civil and Commercial Trial Work Conference" (Fa

---

2021005002004 (accessed August 16, 2025) (stating that openly criticizing, showing fury or pursuing personal gain is frowned upon and may result in "loss of face," which harms one's dignity). *See also* (n 80).

91. Fei Lu, "The Influence of Cultural Difference between the East and West on Dispute Resolution," *ICCA Congress Series No. 22* (2024) Chapter 20.
92. This observation is drawn from the 2023-24 interviews conducted with participants involved in the Belt and Road Initiative: *see* (n 80). *See also* Liang-Yi Yang, "The Cultural Influences on Maritime Arbitration" (2012) 23 Chinese Journal of Maritime Law 106, 108.
93. This case example was shared by a Chinese counsel on 6 May 2024 in Hong Kong and further discussed on 13 July 2024 online, on an anonymous basis.
94. *See* Article 110 of the Contract Law of China.
95. Chao Guo, "Legal Analysis and Judicial Rules of the Breaching Party's Right to Terminate Contracts" (2017) 2 Tianjin Law Journal, 95.

[2019] No. 254) (hereinafter "Minutes")[96] and the Civil Code of China (2021),[97] which introduced clearer guidelines for when a breaching party can request termination of a contract, addressing the inadequacies of Article 110 of the Contract Law to deal with contractual stalemates. The Civil Code, specifically Article 580, formalized conditions under which a breaching party could request for a termination of a contract due to legal or factual impossibility, excessively high performance costs, or failure of the creditor to request performance within a reasonable period. If, due to objective reasons, the breaching party finds it difficult to continue performance or adhering strictly to the contract terms would cause significant loss, these conditions would provide legal grounds for termination.

The above example underscores how arbitrators are still influenced by their own legal and culture background, consciously or unconsciously, even when applying a foreign law. It also highlights the importance to strive for diversity in the appointment of arbitrators and cultural competence of arbitrators.

That being said, the world is changing. Much of the growth of international commerce today is non-Western. According to the Global Trends 2030 report by the National Intelligence Council, by 2030, "Asia will have surpassed North America and Europe combined in terms of global power, based upon GDP, population size, military spending, and technological investment."[98] According to a report in *The Economist,*[99] more Chinese people live outside Mainland China than French people live in France. These "diasporan" nations that cross national boundaries operate largely according to relational principles, not the formalistic Western legal mechanisms.

We are beginning to see some shifts in arbitration. The arbitration community is taking strides to promote different forms of diversity, including racial, ethnic, cultural, generational, and gender diversity. For instance, the ICC International Court of Arbitration has recently introduced standard language in its model letters to parties and co-arbitrators, encouraging diversity when nominating arbitrators.[100] According to the latest ICC statistics, the 935 individual arbitrators confirmed or appointed in 2023 came

96. The Minutes were issued on 8 November 2019. Article 48 of the Minutes stipulates three conditions for the breaching party's request for termination, namely: (i) the breaching party must not have malicious intent; (ii) the breaching party has difficulty continuing performance or it would be clearly unfair to continue performance; and (iii) adhering strictly to the contract would violate the principle of good faith.
97. The Civil Code of China took effect on 1 January 2021.
98. National Intelligence Council, *Global Trends 2030: Alternative Worlds* (2012) "https://globaltrends2030.wordpress.com/wp-content/uploads/2012/11/global-trends-2030-november2012.pdf" accessed 18 June 2024.
99. "Weaving the World Together" *The Economist* (19 November 2011) "http://www.economist.com/node/21538700" accessed 18 June 2024.
100. *See* ICC, "Note to National Committees and Groups of the ICC on the Proposal of Arbitrators" (2022) para. 38: "For cases of lower complexity, Committees and Groups are encouraged to propose prospective arbitrators with experience in arbitration, but not necessarily as arbitrators (such as experience as counsel or as administrative secretary)"; and para. 40: "When proposing arbitrators, Committees and Groups are encouraged to consider diversity, broadly defined, including but not limited to racial, ethnic, cultural, generational, and gender diversity."

from 89 jurisdictions.[101] There is also an increasing diversity of users of international arbitration. In 2023 filings, parties came from 141 jurisdictions across Europe (40%), Asia and the Pacific (25%), Latin America (14%), North America (13%), and Africa (8%).[102]

With arbitrators, parties and counsel coming from diverse legal, cultural and other backgrounds coming together in a typical international arbitration, there will be greater cross-cultural fertilizations. We are beginning to see some influence from the faculty of heart toward a more consensual, and interest-based, process of dispute resolution. For instance, views on arbitrators' role in settlements have evolved in recent years. The change of the conventional view is considered to be "largely due to the influence of Asian cultures."[103] This shifting of mindset is supported by an International Mediation Institute Mixed Task Force report in 2021, which shows that a strong majority of respondents recognized that arbitrators have a part to play in facilitating settlement.[104] The change in attitude has also resulted in amendments of arbitration rules and guidelines. For instance, in the ICC 2021 Arbitration Rules, arbitrators are empowered to "encourage the parties to consider settlement,"[105] rather than simply "informing the parties that they are free to settle (their disputes)" as in previous versions.[106] The ICC Commission on Arbitration and ADR published a report on Facilitating Settlement in International Arbitration in 2023, which described techniques that are known to be effective in facilitating settlement in arbitration proceedings.[107]

V CONCLUDING REMARKS

This chapter introduces a novel lens by applying the three-dimensional theory of human faculties and societies to dissect the cultural and philosophical underpinnings of arbitration perceptions and practices. In summary, the Chinese tradition of heart and moral civil order focuses on morality and harmony, holistic reasoning, and a relational approach. This contrasts with the Western tradition of mind and legal civil order, which emphasizes individual rights, rational thinking, and a rationalist approach. This divergence shapes each society's ideal of justice, the role of law, perceptions of the role of arbitrators, and dispute resolution approaches.

101. *See* ICC, "ICC Releases Preliminary 2023 Arbitration and ADR Statistics" (10 June 2024) "https://iccwbo.org/news-publications/news/icc-releases-preliminary-2023-arbitration-and-adr-statistics" accessed 18 June 2024.
102. *Ibid.*
103. Donahey 1995 (n 72), 77.
104. Working Group 4 of the Mixed Mode Task Force, "Arbitrator Techniques and Their (Direct or Potential) Effect on Settlement" (16 November 2021), available at "https://imimediation.org/about/who-are-imi/mixed-mode-task-force" accessed August 16, 2024.
105. *See* Appendix IV of the ICC's 2021 Arbitration Rules.
106. *See, e.g.*, Appendix IV of the ICC's 2017 Arbitration Rules.
107. *See* ICC Commission on Arbitration and ADR, *Facilitating Settlement in International Arbitration* (2023) "https://iccwbo.org/wp-content/uploads/sites/3/2023/09/2023_Facilitating-Settlement-in-International-Arbitration-900-1.pdf" accessed 18 June 2024.

While the chapter attempts to adopt a more nuanced and inclusive theoretical framework to understand different traditions, there remains a risk of generalization. I acknowledge the inherent complexities and nuances within the broad categorizations, and the significant divergences between common law and civil law traditions, within common law and civil law traditions, and within a national legal system. Furthermore, given the globalized context within which arbitration operates, arbitration practices are no longer confined to rigid cultural demarcations. A certain degree of convergence of different cultures has emerged.[108]

I also acknowledge that the sociological analysis in this chapter is probabilistic as opposed to deterministic. There could be alternative explanations to the divergent perceptions and practices of arbitration. For instance, the elements of trust, good faith and reciprocity could also have rational choice explanations. However, even though sociological judgments are often indefinite and open to interpretation, they can still identify important characteristics that are directly relevant.[109] This chapter does not claim to provide comprehensive coverage or definitive conclusions on any of these fundamental questions, but only humbly hopes to enrich our understanding of arbitration as a complex socio-legal phenomenon and inspire future research.

Future scholarship on arbitration could benefit from blending insights from multiple disciplines, such as sociology, anthropology, psychology, philosophy, history, and economics, which can enrich the academic discourse. For instance, through the lens of human faculties and human societies, or engaging broadly with law and culture and anthropology of law literature, more empirical work can be done to further illustrate how the general different traditions influence international arbitration procedure, practice, and outcome.[110] Further work can be done to examine the impact of the soul-religious tradition on the development of arbitration in religious societies.[111] More research could involve delving deeper into how cultural norms, societal structures, and human interactions shape legal processes.[112] This could include ethnographic studies on the role of arbitration in indigenous and non-Western societies, evaluating the interactions between the cosmopolitan professional culture of arbitration and deeply rooted communal values.[113] Engaging with law and language discourse,[114] further studies could examine how the translation of legal terms and concepts affects understanding and outcomes in cross-cultural arbitration settings. This could extend to

108. *See,* Tom Ginsburg, "The Culture of (2003) 36 Vanderbilt Journal of Law 1335; Leon Trakman, Legal Traditions' and International Commercial" (2006) 17 American Review of International Arbitration 1.

109. Pierre Legrand, *Fragments on Law-as-Culture* (WEJ Tjeenk Willink 1999) 28-29.

110. The ongoing projects of "China's Belt and Road Initiative: A New Model of Economic Governance?" and "The Social and Psychological Underpinnings of Commercial Arbitration in Europe" are attempts to provide empirical evidence to address this question.

111. *See, e.g.,* Majeed 2024 (n 26), which conducts a sociological examination of Islamic law and arbitration in Pakistan.

112. *See, e.g.,* Karton 2013 (n 24).

113. *See, e.g.,* Kun Fan and Joanna Jemielniak, "Ethnographic Methods in the Study of Hybrid Processes in Arbitration: Chinese and Western" (2006) 27 European Business Law Review 555 https://doi.org/10.54648/eulr2016025 (accessed August 16, 2025).

114. *See, e.g.,* Ko Hasegawa, "Incorporating Foreign Legal Ideas through" in Andrew Halpin and Volker Roeben (eds), *Theorising the Global Legal Order* (Hart Publishing 2009).

analyzing how arbitrators and parties navigate linguistic challenges and the extent to which language shapes arbitration processes and decisions.[115] From the perspective of legal transplantation, further investigations can be taken into the challenges and implications of translating legal concepts across legal traditions. This could involve analyzing how legal terminologies, ideas, and practices are adapted or transformed when they cross cultural and jurisdictional boundaries, contributing to the discourse on legal hybridity and transnational law.[116]

Returning to the initial questions: Is international arbitration universalized, or is it tied to different human faculties and societies? I believe the answers lie in the latter. I argued a decade ago that the future of arbitration may continue to be a process of "glocalization," where global norms embrace local traditions.[117] I still believe that the persistent influence of deeply ingrained mind-heart-soul and law-morality-religion traditions will continue to shape arbitration today and tomorrow (Table 13.1).

Table 13.1 Comparison Between Legal Societies and Moral Societies in Terms of the Ideal of Justice, Role of Law and Dispute Resolution Process[118]

	West	*China*
Human faculties	Mind	Heart
Manifestations	Reasonableness, Utilitarianism, Formalism, Experience, Rule, Orientation	Temperaments, Emotions, Feelings
	Rationality	Sentiments
	Rules	Relations
	Law	Morality
Human societies	Legal society Society with the rule of law	Moral society Society with the rule of virtue
Differences between different human societies		
Conceptual categories	Centered on "rights" and "law" Rule of law, democracy, freedom, rights, obligations, justice, rationality, property, individualism, contracts, and litigation	Moral concepts *De* (ritual), *Ren* (benevolence), *Yi* (loyalty), *Li* (ritualism), *Zhi* (wisdom), *Xin* (sincerity), *He* (harmony), *Rang* (concession/yielding), and *Zhongyong* (the doctrine of middle way)

115. *See, e.g.*, Rainbow Willard, "Where Language, Identity, and Advocacy Meet Explicit and Implicit Codeswitching in International Arbitration Hearings," *ICCA Congress Series No. 22* (2024) Chapter 28.
116. *See, e.g.*, Fan 2013 (n 16).
117. *Ibid*; Fan 2013 (n 13); Kun Fan, "Glocalization of International Arbitration: Rethinking Tradition: Modernity and East-West Binaries Examples of China and" (2016) 11 University of Pennsylvania Asian Law Review 243.
118. Table created by author.

	West	*China*
Authority systems	Guided by the ideal of rule of law Focus on texts and institutions Legal authority	Focus on personal moral cultivation, rather than texts and institutions Means of governance is through persuasion, courtesy, harmony
Institutional arrangement	Judicial system is considered a fundamental institutional arrangement	Institutional arrangement is based on the relational networks to which an individual belongs
Popular consciousness	Rule of law and individual rights	Pursuit of harmony, avoidance of litigation
Influence on ideal of justice and dispute resolution		
Spirit and value of law	The pursuit of individual freedom and liberty Rights-oriented	The pursuit of social harmony and stability Interests-oriented
The role of law	Law as an abstract entity with truth-determining power The felt need to vindicate individual rights	Law as a flexible quantity as it should be personally applied Restore harmony, social stability
Dispute resolution model	Rationalist model	Relational model
The role of arbitrator	An unbiased decision-maker who renders a decision based on proven facts	Problem-solver to assist parties in resolving their disputes by the most appropriate means
Ideal of justice and role of equity	Universal rules or principles to govern behavior and justify beliefs Ruling *ex aequo et bono* or "in equity" is based on parties' express consent	Particularistic approaches that take into account the context and the nature of relationships involved *Heli, heqing, hefa* Arbitrators do not hesitate to apply equitable principles to achieve substantive justice
Considerations for settlement	Rational thinking on the probable outcome if negotiations fail	Relationship and face

CHAPTER 14

International Arbitration as a Social Phenomenon: Using Sociological Theories and Methods in International Arbitration Practice

Joshua Karton[*]

TABLE OF CONTENTS

I INTRODUCTION

All international arbitration lawyers are amateur sociologists. Each time counsel appoint a Swiss-trained lawyer to arbitrate because an emphasis on good faith will help their client; or a Chinese professor because they want someone who will push the parties to settle; or a London barrister because winning their case will turn on the tribunal enforcing the literal meaning of the words used in a contract – they are making a sociological judgment. That is, they are deciding based not (only) on the characteristics of the individual in consideration, but on the assumption that the norms and values said to be shared by members of a specific community will shape the conduct of every individual who is a member of that community. This kind of judgment lies at the core of sociological thinking.

The problem is that most such judgments are made without the rigour that would render them reliable. Arbitration practitioners tend to follow overgeneralized 'folk

* Independent arbitrator; Professor of Law and Associate Dean, Queen's University (Canada).

wisdom', which can lead them astray in individual cases, and to over-extrapolate from their experiences and those of their mentors, which may be unrepresentative. Practitioners tend to treat anecdotes as data and data as gospel truth.

This chapter will briefly describe what sociological research on law involves, and then move on to its main goal: describing and defending the utility of sociological theories and methods for arbitration practice. It will conclude with some implications of the sociology of international arbitration for education and training.

II INTRODUCING THE SOCIOLOGY OF LAW

Sociology of law is committed to the premise that law is a social institution, and cannot be adequately understood without an understanding of 'the social conditions within which legal ideas are formed and used, and which underpin their moral significance, determine their authority or legitimacy, inform the regulatory demands made of them, and provide the sources of their power to regulate and control'.[1] Put more simply, the socio-legal perspective is that 'law' cannot be conceived of separately from the social context within which legal rules and legal institutions operate. It is the legal instantiation of the simple proposition – perhaps the key axiom of sociology writ large – that 'individuals' behaviour and normative choices are significantly affected by social factors'.[2]

This proposition is unarguable in its most basic formulations. As even undergraduate law students with just one or two semesters' worth of education already know, the notion of 'the law' of any given jurisdiction cannot be reduced to 'binding rules of law' in that jurisdiction. As Legrand writes, the law of any given jurisdiction is 'much more than a compendium of rules and precepts. Accordingly, to assert that the study of French law consists in the study of French legislative texts and judicial decisions is plainly inadequate'.[3]

Like other social scientists, sociologists are concerned not just with identifying and describing social phenomena but also with developing and testing theories about human conduct, in order to explain and predict people's behaviour. Also like with other social sciences, much sociological research is deductive; the researcher begins with one of the prevailing sociological theories and applies it to the phenomena under consideration. The various theories not only describe these phenomena differently but also differ as to which phenomena ought to be the focus of social research.[4] By contrast, some sociological studies are inductive; they begin with a mass of data, from which a broad theory emerges through repeated comparisons between individual items within the data set. Such research is called 'grounded theory', since the theory is said

1. Roger Cotterrell, *Law's Community: Legal Theory in Sociological Perspective* (OUP 1997) 3.
2. Moshe Hirsch, 'The Sociology of International Law: Invitation to Study International Rules in Their Social Context' (2005) 55 U Toronto LJ 891, 893 https://doi.org/10.1353/tlj.2005.0033 (accessed August 16, 2025).
3. Pierre Legrand, *Fragments on Law-as-Culture* (WEJ Ejeenk Willink 1999) 5.
4. Moshe Hirsch, 'The Sociology of International Law: Invitation to Study International Rules in their Social Context' (2005) 55 U Toronto LJ 891, 898, 892-893 https://doi.org/10.1353/tlj.2005.0033 (accessed August 16, 2025) (citations omitted).

to be grounded in the data rather than being posited *a priori* and verified by the data, as in traditional sociological research.[5] Grounded theory is considered to be particularly appropriate for research into phenomena that have not yet been comprehensively described or for which no or few widely accepted theories have been advanced. Perhaps for this reason, it has become one of the core techniques of socio-legal research.[6]

Where sociology differs from other social sciences is in its unit of analysis. For psychology, the unit of analysis is the individual; for economics, it is the market; for political science, it is the polity; for sociology, it is the community.[7] What exactly defines a 'community' is a topic of enduring debate within the sociological literature, but often-cited indicia are shared values and norms, repeated mutual interactions, and a sense of shared identity.[8]

1 Varieties of Socio-Legal Research

Sociological analysis of law (also called 'sociology of/and law', 'socio-legal studies', or 'law and society') is a relatively new field, dating back only to roughly the 1960s.[9] In international law, it is even younger. Sociology of law is concerned with a set of questions at the intersection of society and law, ranging across those dealing with general jurisprudence (i.e., the implications of law's character as a social institution for the nature of law itself), with the social conditions that shape the formation and evolution of legal institutions, with the 'lived reality' of those interacting with the legal system, and with the sociological characteristics of legal professional communities. What ties these questions together is an understanding of law as a '*field of experience* shaped and structured by problems of government, social control, and social order'.[10] According to this view, legal doctrine has no existence independent of the community that shapes and recursively is shaped by it; legal doctrine is 'focused on, developed in,

5. The foundational text of grounded theory is Barney Glaser and Anselm Strauss, *The Discovery of Grounded Theory: Strategies for Qualitative Research* (Aldine 1967). The term is somewhat misleading since it refers to a method for generating theories of human interaction, not a kind of theory.
6. On the appropriateness of grounded theory for socio-legal research projects generally, *see* Opi Outhwaite et al., 'The Pursuit of Grounded Theory in Agricultural and Environmental Regulation: A Suggested Approach to Empirical Legal Study in Biosecurity' (2007) 29(4) L & Pol'y 493 https://doi.org/10.1111/j.1467-9930.2007.00264.x (accessed August 16, 2025).
7. Of course, these categories overlap. For example, the boundaries of a market may be coextensive with the borders of a political entity (e.g., 'the Brazilian market').
8. In this chapter, I use the term 'community' in a non-technical sense to describe the global population of practitioners involved in international arbitration practice.
9. As Hirsch observes, 'the sociological perspective was not included in the seven major methods of international legal scholarship that were presented in the 1999 Symposium on Methods in International Law published as a special issue of the American Journal of International Law'. Moshe Hirsch, 'The Sociology of International Law: Invitation to Study International Rules in Their Social Context' (2005) 55 U Toronto LJ 891, 898 https://doi.org/10.1353/tlj.2005.0033 (accessed August 16, 2025).
10. Roger Cotterrell, *Law's Community: Legal Theory in Sociological Perspective* (OUP 1997) 3 (emphasis in original).

and given its distinct characteristics' by social institutions, most prominently but not exclusively legislatures and courts.

In pronouncing (sometimes in laborious detail) on matters with which every member of a community has personal experience, the conclusions reached by sociological studies can sometimes seem obvious, the kind of thing that 'goes without saying' or 'everyone knows'.[11] Nevertheless, to the extent that empirical findings confirm the conventional wisdom, there is value in that confirmation, and more importantly, sometimes the conventional wisdom is wrong, and social science provides us with a means to escape its confines.

Methodologically, the sociological perspective is associated with empiricism. While sociological analysis of law has moral and theoretical implications, it is essentially an empirical discipline. As described by one of the founders of the field, Emile Durkheim, just as the natural sciences focus on facts about the natural world, sociology focuses on 'social facts', which Durkheim defined as 'every way of acting, fixed or not, capable of exercising on the individual an external constraint; or again, every way of acting which is general throughout a given society, while at the same time existing in its own right independent of its individual manifestations'.[12] Sociological research about law and legal institutions, whether it seeks to develop new theories of group behaviour or to test the robustness of existing theories, depends on quantitative and qualitative empirical research, employing methods such as surveys, interviews, statistical analysis of 'countable' legal phenomena like outcomes in litigation, and experiments under controlled conditions. Ultimately, sociology of law is concerned with the social realities of legal rules and institutions and the legal realities of social life.

Different socio-legal studies emphasize different aspects of our social life. Many such studies – including a majority of those that have been conducted on international arbitration – focus on the role of culture, which is used as a kind of shorthand for the cumulation of all social factors that influence behaviour within an identifiable group.[13]

For analytical purposes, social context is often broken down into individual social norms. The literature indicates that 'norms' have the same effects on specific behaviours as 'culture' does on behaviour generally: they both condition and are conditioned by the interactions between members of the community. To put it differently, social norms and cultures are micro-level and macro-level equivalents. In the legal context, the law and economics scholar Robert Cooter has identified three effects of social

11. Notably, the idea that something 'goes without saying' is inherent in the legal doctrine of trade usages, themselves an example of sociological influences – norms specific to an industry or region within the broader culture of a given business community. In this way, the law itself sometimes embeds social norms as rules of law without even the intermediate step of codifying them.
12. Quoted in Moshe Hirsch, 'The Sociology of International Law: Invitation to Study International Rules in Their Social Context' (2005) 55 U Toronto LJ 891, 898 https://doi.org/10.1353/tlj.2005.0033 (accessed August 16, 2025).
13. This theme within the sociological literature was largely pioneered by Geert Hofstede, who developed what evolved into a six-dimensional model for comparing national cultures, which he later applied to the professional cultures of organizations as well. *See, e.g.*, Geert Hofstede, *Culture's Consequences: Comparing Values, Behaviors, Institutions and Organizations Across Nations* (2nd ed., SAGE Publications 2001).

norms on law: expression, internalization, and deterrence. That is, norms express the customs and values of a given community, inculcate those customs and values into members of the community, and deter violations of the norms by sanctions.[14]

Social norms are obligations backed by social sanctions, which are 'punishments' meted out by fellow members of one's community, as when a dog-owner who does not clean up after their dog is shunned by their neighbours.[15] In practice, sanctions such as shunning are rarely imposed because they are unnecessary; members of the community will likely have internalized the norm, and thus feel that they ought to clean up after their dogs. Thus, for example, a party-appointed arbitrator who violates the neutrality norm by overtly advocating for the party that appointed them will not only lose credibility with the other two members of the tribunal but also harm their own prospects for future appointments as arbitrator.[16]

Not all socio-legal studies focus on culture. Structural accounts emphasize the role of, and relationships between, the institutions that give shape and structure to our social lives. Emmanuel Gaillard's brief but perceptive article, entitled simply 'Sociology of Arbitration', is an example. In it, Gaillard identifies the actors, institutions, and rituals – and the interactions between them – that make up the field of international arbitration practice.[17] Similarly, sociological studies could focus on what might be called the human structure of the field – the networks of relationships between practitioners – such as the relationships between counsel and arbitrators in the field of international arbitration.[18]

A third category of socio-legal studies focuses on shared priorities or precepts that demonstrate what is valued by a given community. A salient example of this type of sociological thinking is the French sociologist Pierre Bourdieu's concept of social interactions as competitions for 'symbolic capital' (also called social capital). This concept was a primary influence on *Dealing in Virtue*, the first significant sociological study of international arbitration.[19] Symbolic capital reflects 'recognized power' within

14. Robert D. Cooter, 'Three Effects of Social Norms on Law: Expression, Deterrence, and Internalization' (2000) 79 Oregon L R 1, 3.
15. *Ibid.*
16. An English arbitrator I interviewed described such overt partisanship as 'the kiss of death' for an arbitrator's professional reputation. Joshua Karton, *The Culture of International Arbitration and the Evolution of Contract Law* (OUP 2013) 55. *See also* Thomas H. Webster, 'Party Control in International Arbitration' (2003) 19(2) Arb Int'l 119, 129-130 https://doi.org/10.1093/arbitration/19.2.119 (accessed August 16, 2025).
17. Emmanuel Gaillard, 'Sociology of International Arbitration' (2015) 31 Arb Int'l 1 https://doi.org/10.1093/arbint/aiv021 (accessed August 16, 2025).
18. A key example is Sergio Puig, 'Social Capital in the Arbitration Market' (2014) 25 EJIL 387 https://doi.org/10.1093/ejil/chu045 (accessed August 16, 2025).
19. Yves Dezalay and Bryant G. Garth, *Dealing in Virtue International Commercial Arbitration and the Construction of a Transnational Legal Order* (U Chicago P 1998). A number of other socio-legal studies of international arbitration have explored the nature of symbolic capital in the field. *See, e.g.*, Karton (n 16); Puig (n 18); Florian Grisel, 'Competition and Cooperation in International Commercial Arbitration: The Birth of a Transnational Legal Profession' (2017) 51 L & Soc'y Rev 790 https://doi.org/10.1111/lasr.12295 (accessed August 16, 2025); Thomas Schultz and Robert Kovacs, 'The Rise of a Third Generation of Arbitrators?: 15 Years After Dezalay and Garth' (2012) 28(2) Arb Int'l 161 https://doi.org/10.1093/arbitration/28.2.161 (accessed August 16, 2025).

a social group, and the forms of symbolic capital that members of a field seek to amass are specific to the social norms of the group.[20] Leaders in a given field become leaders because of their stores of symbolic capital, while those seeking entrance to the field must conform to accepted norms and practice in order to amass symbolic capital of their own, thus reinforcing prevailing orthodoxies. Conformity to social norms helps one to accumulate symbolic capital, which, at least in the arbitration field, can be 'monetized' into literal capital through major client mandates and arbitral appointments.

As identified by Dezalay and Garth, symbolic capital in international arbitration includes attributes such as professorships, partnerships in multinational law firms, academic publications, invitations to speak at conferences, positions in the governing bodies of arbitral institutions or other transnational professional groups (like the IBA Arbitration Committee and ICC Commission on Arbitration and ADR), and facility with multiple languages.[21] One might observe that, in the years since Dezalay and Garth conducted their interviews for *Dealing in Virtue*, a practice as an independent arbitrator has come to represent greater symbolic capital than a law firm partnership.

2 Limitations of Socio-Legal Research

Like with the other social sciences, sociological insights share a range of limitations that can make them seem unsuited for use in a practical discipline like law. First, sociological insights are probabilistic, as opposed to deterministic. That is, sociological research can only tell you that members of a given community *tend* to share particular perspectives or subscribe to particular values, or that a given individual is *more likely* to act in a given way based on the characteristics of the community of which that individual is a member. Second, sociological determinations are indeterminate, in that they can amalgamate different activities and influences into a common bundle ('culture' or 'values'), and thereby can conflate different factors affecting behaviour or disguise the differences between them.[22] Third, sociology is 'impressionistic';[23] it is inherently incapable of indicating which variable in empirical research is 'the' decisive variable in shaping human behaviour.[24] For these reasons, no sociological researcher (except possibly in very tightly controlled experiments) can identify direct causal relationships between specific social norms and corresponding behaviours. Similarly, it can be impossible to distinguish cleanly between the effects of social context and the effects of other factors, from the threat of punishment to economic self-interest.

Given its inherent limitations – the subordination of legal doctrine to social context, the emphasis on empirical methods (many of them involving math), the sometimes abstruse theories, the probabilistic nature of sociological judgments – it is

20. Dezalay and Garth (n 19) 18, quoting Pierre Bourdieu and Loïc Wacquant 1991, 72.
21. *Ibid.*, 19.
22. Pierre Legrand, *Fragments on Law-as-Culture* (WEJ Ejeenk Willink 1999) 27, quoting EP Thompson, *Customs in Common* (Penguin 1991) 13.
23. Roger Cotterrell, *Law's Community: Legal Theory in Sociological Perspective* (OUP 1997) 21.
24. *Ibid.*, 14.

perhaps unsurprising that sociology of law has a highly 'academic' reputation. In particular, legal practitioners often recoil from the notion that they might make any use of sociology in their daily legal practice.[25]

Sometimes this is because practitioners maintain that they (and others in the profession) reach a particular conclusion in a legal case because the law dictates the outcome. But this is itself a kind of legal fiction. Sociology cannot be ignored because law is not self-executing: it is made, interpreted, and implemented by humans, and humans are unavoidably affected by their social context. Community norms shape behaviour in the same way human psychological characteristics do: reflexively. They 'make it unnecessary to think out afresh our reactions to situations. The situations become standardized. Their meaning and the appropriate way to act in relation to them become taken for granted'.[26]

However, social context cannot be ignored because it exerts a powerful force on human decision-making.[27] It shapes behaviour in the same way that psychology does: reflexively. Just because one cannot draw a cause/effect line from a cultural norm to a particular observed behaviour does not mean that the norm has no influence. Sociological influences are pre-cognitive; they operate prior to – and therefore frequently obviate – deliberate decision-making. Simply because sociological theories and methods cannot provide the kinds of deterministic explanations that the natural sciences offer, an impressionistic account of legal institutions that include the essential variable of social context is still more accurate than a concrete-seeming account that omits it.[28] So long as researchers are appropriately modest in drawing conclusions that are actually supported by their data (and thereby eschew a false determinism), the indeterminacy and impressionistic character of sociological judgments do not 'prevent the ascription of determinative efficacy and the articulation of various characteristics which can prove of direct relevance'.[29]

In the following section, I will describe and defend sociology as a practical science, one that every kind of stakeholder in international arbitration can use to practical effect. In doing so, I do not deny the value of other kinds of social science

25. US Chief Justice John Roberts famously displayed this attitude when he described the political science model proffered by the Respondents as 'sociological gobbledygook'. Transcript of Proceedings, *Gill v. Whitford* 40:14 (U.S. Supreme Court, 3 October 2017), available at https://www.supremecourt.gov/oral_arguments/argument_transcripts/2017/16-1161_mjn0.pdf (accessed August 16, 2025).
26. Roger Cotterrell, *The Sociology of Law: An Introduction* (Butterworths 1992) 146-147.
27. Social science studies repeatedly reaffirm the pervasive influence of social context, even when participants in studies cannot define that the nature of that influence. For example, when Flood conducted a series of interviews for a study of international law firm business, he discovered to his surprise that 'the concept of culture was continuously invoked as a means of explaining many things. I rarely raised the subject myself, but others found it inescapable'. John Flood, 'Megalawyering in the Global Order: The Cultural, Social and Economic Transformation of Global Legal Practice' (1996) 3(1/2) Int'l J Leg Prof 169, 175 https://doi.org/10.1080/09695958.1996.9960413 (accessed August 16, 2025).
28. C.f. Lawrence M. Friedman, 'The Concept of Legal Culture: A Reply' in David Nelken (ed.), *Comparing Legal Cultures* (Dartmouth 1997) 34.
29. Pierre Legrand, *Fragments on Law-as-Culture* (WEJ Ejeenk Willink 1999) 28-29, calling the indeterminacy of culture 'a handicap only for the positivist'.

findings. Economic analysis, in particular, has its fervent adherents in legal scholarship, and to the extent that arbitration is itself a business and is concerned with business matters, many of its characteristics can be explained by economic analysis of market forces.[30] Similarly, since arbitration practitioners are humans, and share basic psychological characteristics, psychology has enormous potential to help understand (and improve) arbitration.[31]

Nevertheless, I maintain that, if one had to choose just one set of social science methods to understand the operation of law and legal institutions, sociology would be the best choice. While economic analyses often disregard the impact of social forces, the reverse is less true – sociological analyses often account for the impact of economic forces. For example, Ogus argues that many of the characteristics of national legal cultures are explicable according to the economic value of networks.[32] As an example of legal culture developing from routine business practices, Trakman cites the informal practice of making deals over the phone, rather than relying on written contracts negotiated with the assistance of lawyers.[33] Indeed, cultural factors are no less cultural for the fact that they evolved from economically determined behaviours. Therefore, a sociological analysis will highlight many of the same factors as a purely economic analysis, but will also provide insights that cannot be expressed in economic models.

III SOCIOLOGY OF INTERNATIONAL ARBITRATION

Arbitration is a human endeavour, and sociology is how we can make sense of its humanity. Indeed, sociological insights are more valuable for international arbitration practitioners than for virtually any other area of legal practice. This is due in part to what I call the twin phenomena of 'too much law' and 'too little law'. For many issues that arise in international arbitrations, multiple laws could reasonably apply to them, so that a choice of law analysis is required at multiple steps in the arbitration process (often with the tribunal empowered to make a *voie directe*). In other areas, there is no applicable rule that dictates a single outcome, so the tribunal must rely on soft law instruments for guidance, identify (or even formulate) transnational rules, or simply

30. For some recent examples, *see, e.g.*, Zoe Phillips Williams, *The Political Economy of Investment Arbitration* (OUP 2022); Bruno Guandalini, *Economic Analysis of the Arbitrator's Function* (Kluwer 2020); Shen Wei, *Rethinking the New York Convention: A Law and Economics Approach* (Intersentia 2013).
31. *See* generally Tony Cole (ed.), *The Roles of Psychology in International Arbitration* (Kluwer 2017); Rebecca K. Helm et al., 'Are Arbitrators Human?' (2016) 13 J Empirical Leg Stud 666 https://doi.org/10.1111/jels.12129 (accessed August 16, 2025). A salient example of how psychology can be used to improve arbitral processes is the *ICC Arbitration and ADR Commission Report on the Accuracy of Fact Witness Memory in International Arbitration* (2020), available at https://iccwbo.org/news-publications/arbitration-adr-rules-and-tools/icc-arbitration-and-adr-commission-report-on-the-accuracy-of-fact-witness-memory-in-international-arbitration/ (accessed August 16, 2025). (Disclosure: the author was a member of this task force and made some small contributions to the report.)
32. Anthony Ogus 'The Economic Basis of Legal Culture: Networks and Monopolization' (2002) 22 Ox J Leg Stud 419 https://doi.org/10.1093/ojls/22.3.419 (accessed August 16, 2025).
33. Leon E. Trakman, '"Legal Traditions" and International Commercial Arbitration' (2006) 17 Am R Int'l Arb 1, 3.

decide on the best course of action in the particular circumstances of the case. At every stage, arbitration counsel have a range of legal rules for which they can advocate, and arbitrators have a range of doctrines they can invoke in order to reach what they see as just and commercially reasonable results.

For this reason, international arbitration is less bound by law than other forms of legal dispute resolution. Counsel and arbitrators have a wide scope to adapt the proceedings according to their own preferences and assumptions, far more than in litigation or even domestic arbitration. All of the non-legal factors that shape outcomes, which might be characterized collectively as the social context of international arbitration, do not remain in the background or at the margins, as they do in national court litigation, but are themselves directly determinative of procedures and outcomes.

1 Culture in Arbitration and Culture of Arbitration

It is therefore incumbent upon us to gain a better understanding of both culture *in* international arbitration and culture *of* international arbitration.[34] 'Culture in arbitration' is easier to explain. By it, I mean the influence of the various national cultures and legal traditions that mix together in the field as a whole and in any single international arbitration proceeding.[35]

By 'culture of arbitration', I mean the values, priorities, and perspectives that are shared across the field and that distinguish international arbitration from litigation in any national court system.[36] As Gaillard observes:

> There is no doubt that the international arbitration world possesses all the key features of a 'recognized area of institutional life' with a constellation of actors performing various roles and functions such as key suppliers, consumers, regulatory agents, and organizations, all of which share a 'common meaning system' and interact more frequently with one another than with other social agents.[37]

Culture develops from exactly this kind of repeated interaction among actors within a social group.[38] Over time, the norms that this process produces gain the force of tradition and habituate the members of the social group, forming a community with a common identity. Culture, in this context, can be described as the process by which

34. There are numerous definitions of 'culture' in the sociological literature. A standard definition is given by Cotterrell: 'the complex of beliefs, attitudes, cognitive ideas, values and modes of reasoning and perception typical of a particular society or social group'. Roger Cotterrell, *The Sociology of Law: An Introduction* (Butterworths 1992) 23 (citation omitted).
35. The leading book on the influences of disparate cultures on international arbitration practice is Won Kidane, *The Culture of International Arbitration* (OUP 2017). Numerous studies have been conducted on the influence of specific national cultures on international arbitration practice.
36. The pioneering text in this sub-field is Dezalay and Garth (n 19). A more recent, similarly comprehensive treatment is Karton (n 16).
37. Gaillard (n 17) 3 (citing W. Richard Scott, *Institutions and Organizations* (4th ed., SAGE Publications 2014)); Melissa Wooten and Andrew J. Hoffman, 'Organizational Fields: Past, Present and Future' in Royston Greenwood et al. (eds),*The SAGE Handbook of Organizational Institutionalism* (SAGE Publications 2008) 131.
38. Tom Ginsburg 'The Culture of Arbitration' (2003) 39 Vanderbilt J Transnat'l L 1335, 1337 (citation omitted).

the interactions between members of a community become self-reinforcing and determine the contours of future interactions. When these interactions reach a critical mass, the various norms of the culture create a harmonious whole that 'gives people a sense of who they are, of belonging, of how they should behave and what they should be doing'.[39] By understanding the culture of international arbitration and the individual norms that comprise it, counsel can better predict how arbitrators will make decisions, and arbitrators can better shape procedures to the needs and expectations of the parties. These themes will be explored in the following section.

2 The Utility of Socio-Legal Research for International Arbitration Practice

In international arbitration, sociological insights may be of practical utility to every kind of stakeholder.[40] For counsel, sociology emerges primarily as a tool for identifying the arbitrator(s) best suited to a particular case.[41] In cases such as *Jivraj v. Hashwani*[42] and *Carter et al v. Iconix Brand Group Inc.* (the 'Jay-Z case'),[43] the courts were confronted with parties who prioritized particular cultural attributes in their arbitrators (adherence to the Ismaili Muslim faith and an understanding of African-American hip-hop culture, respectively). But most such cultural judgments about potential arbitrators are more mundane, in the vein of appointing a British barrister on the basis that they are more likely to interpret a contract literally. As Licari points out, in the *Jivraj* case, the context was crucial. The parties were not seeking an arbitrator who could apply the governing (English) law: 'it is not only a question of resolving a conflict, but of restoring peace in the respect of the community ethos, of ensuring that the [...] arbitrator respects and protects the values of the litigants in a liberal society where traditional values have taken a back seat'.[44]

The difficulty is that, in many cases, such sociological judgments are based on overbroad generalizations, sometimes shading into pernicious stereotypes. Sociological research provides a key to better understanding the tendencies of arbitrators from

39. Philip R. Harris and Robert T. Moran, *Managing Cultural Differences* (3rd ed., Gulf Publishing 1991) 12.
40. I follow here the structure established in Giorgio Fabio Colombo, 'The Role of Culture in International Commercial Arbitration' (unpublished, on file with author), in which Colombo identifies three categories of influences of culture on international arbitration practice: on arbitral decision-making, on the applicable law, and on arbitral procedure.
41. *See, e.g.*, Francois-Xavier Licari, 'Beyond Legal Pluralism: Some Thoughts on Paideic Arbitration' in Horatia Muir Watt et al. (eds), *Global Private International Law: Adjudication without Frontiers* (Edward Elgar 2019) 182-190, exploring the cultural identity of arbitrators from the perspective of the parties' needs for culturally specific attitudes and expertise, utilizing the *Jivraj v. Hashwani* case as an example.
42. [2011] UKSC 40.
43. *Carter et al. v. Iconix Brand Grp., Inc.*, Index No. 655894/2018 (N.Y. Sup. Ct. 28 November 2018).
44. Licari at 186. *See also* Giorgio Fabio Colombo, 'Cultural Expertise and Commercial Arbitration' in Livia Holden (ed.), *Cultural Expertise, Law and Rights: A Comprehensive Guide* (Routledge 2023) 170, commenting that, in the *Jivraj* case, 'context was crucial'; the parties belonged to the same religious community, which has its own distinct legal institutions and systems of dispute resolution.

different cultural backgrounds. Some such studies focus on the legal cultures of a given jurisdiction,[45] or attempt to verify or falsify a particular (alleged) predilection of arbitrators from that jurisdiction.[46] Others are comparative, although these sometimes have an unfortunate tendency to lapse into overbroad 'West vs East' comparisons.[47]

Sociology can also inform advocacy by helping parties to pitch their arguments to fit their audience. All good lawyering requires empathy: the ability to see from the perspective of opposing counsel, or of the adjudicators, to predict how they will react to different gambits. But empathy too often relies on gut instinct, and when there is no shared set of cultural indicators, that gut instinct often leads us astray – witness the reams of social science studies showing that judges' assessment of witness credibility becomes dramatically less accurate across racial, cultural, and linguistic divides.[48] Sociological research provides counsel with a way to make empathy rigorous.[49]

For arbitrators, sociology provides a means of doing justice. Accurately assessing witness credibility and dealing even-handedly with differing styles of advocacy requires an understanding of different 'cultures in arbitration'. Identifying 'commercially reasonable conduct' requires understanding the relevant business culture. In turn, identifying a commercially reasonable outcome with parties from different states and backgrounds requires 'a subtle understanding of varying legal cultures and their likely impacts'.[50] A decision of whether to accept an appointment may depend not only on the arbitrator's sense of their legal expertise (e.g., familiarity with the governing law or a related law) but also whether they see themselves as equipped with the necessary cultural expertise to appreciate the parties' positions and expectations.

Perhaps most importantly, an understanding of the differences and overlaps between different cultures represented in international arbitration provides a means to design procedures for each individual arbitration that fit the particularities of the dispute and the assumptions and preferences of the parties as to what constitutes a fair procedure: matters like the scope of document discovery, the extent of an oral hearing (if any), and the appropriateness of efforts to press the parties to settle. Naturally, the parties' perspectives on these matters will depend on their positions in the specific

---

45. *See, e.g.*, Kun Fan, *Arbitration in China: A Legal and Cultural Analysis* (Bloomsbury Publishing 2013).
46. *See, e.g.*, Tony Cole, 'Commercial Arbitration in Japan: Contributions to the Debate on Japanese "Non-Litigiousness"' (2007) 40 NYU J Int'l L & Politics 29.
47. There is no need to name names here. Some books that avoid this unfortunate tendency include Kidane (n 35); Shahla Ali, *Resolving Disputes in the Asia Pacific: International Mediation and Arbitration in East Asia and the West* (Routledge 2010). I have the honour to be one of the researchers for *The Social and Psychological Underpinnings of Commercial Arbitration in Europe*, the largest-ever comparative study of arbitration practice and its social context across jurisdictions. *See* https://commercialarbitrationineurope.wordpress.com/ (accessed August 16, 2025).
48. *See, e.g.*, Lindholm Torun, 'Validity in Judgments of High- and Low-Accurate Witnesses of Own and Other Ethnic Groups' (2010) 13 LCP 107 https://doi.org/10.1348/135532506x152949 (accessed August 16, 2025) (dealing with eyewitness testimony).
49. *See* Michael Waibel, 'Sociology of Arbitrators' in Andrea K. Bjorklund, Franco Ferrari and Stefan Kröll (eds), *Cambridge Compendium of International Commercial and Investment Arbitration* (Cambridge UP 2021).
50. Joshua Karton, 'International Arbitration as Comparative Law in Action' (2020), 2 J. Disp. Resol. 293, 305.

dispute, but they are also contingent on expectations shaped by their respective legal cultures.

For the international arbitration system as a whole, sociology provides a vital tool to shape justice at the global level. As a community and as a field of practice, we cannot provide justice to all users of international arbitration without an appreciation of cultural diversity, because parties are entitled to a procedure – and to a tribunal – that reflects their perspectives. We may accept this instinctively when it comes to industry context – a construction arbitrator is effective in part because they understand both the technicalities and the business customs of the construction sector. But for some reason, as arbitration practitioners, we often forget or ignore this when it comes to cultural understanding.

Several decades of emphasis on harmonization, not just for judicial regulation of arbitration but also for arbitral procedures, have left many in the field with a sense that arbitration anywhere should be practised roughly as it is in London or Paris. But modern arbitration should not be one-size-fits-all, especially when that simply recapitulates patterns of colonial domination. Parties now seek – and within the party-driven international arbitration system are entitled to demand – a greater degree of appreciation of their culturally contingent priorities. To provide that culturally sensitive justice, the field must be diverse in its demographics and must practice diversity in its procedures.[51] In turn, to understand the kinds of diversity that are needed, we must internalize the sociological insight that what all parties want is justice, but how they define that justice differs, and differs in ways that are understandable and predictable through application of sociological theories and methods.

IV IMPLICATIONS FOR EDUCATION AND TRAINING

Pierre Lalive once said, 'In international arbitration, the conflict of cultures is even more important than the conflict of laws.'[52] The complex, multilayered social context within which international arbitrations take place is an integral feature of the international arbitration system, just as much as the complex, multilayered legal structure of the system.[53] Students should be educated in both. Embedding such cultural competencies (also called cultural intelligence or cultural expertise) into international arbitration education will require a reassessment of curricula, at least in the various specialist LLM programmes.[54] It will require that students be educated not just in the 'mainstream' ways of conducting arbitrations (which largely reflect the way arbitration is practised in the old colonial capitals) but also in the variety of perspectives and traditions that are woven together into the international arbitration tapestry.

51. Joshua Karton, 'Diversity in Four Dimensions', in Shahla F. Ali et al. (eds) *Diversity in International Arbitration: Why it Matters and How to Sustain it* (Elgar 2022) 12.
52. 'The Emerging Culture of International Arbitration', presentation at the Canadian Council on International Law 40th Annual Conference (Ottawa, ON, Canada, November 2011).
53. *See, e.g.*, Giorgio Fabio Colombo, 'Cultural Expertise and Commercial Arbitration' in Livia Holden (ed.), *Cultural Expertise, Law and Rights: A Comprehensive Guide* (Routledge 2023) 166 et seq.
54. To be fair, this shift that has already begun at some programmes.

Similarly, professional training programmes should include modules on cultural competence, meaning an ability to work effectively across a variety of culturally diverse situations. This includes not just awareness of different legal traditions – comparative law – but also a legal *comparativism*: budding international arbitration practitioners must be trained in 'the trick of mind of considering any given legal issue from multiple perspectives'.[55] That is, international arbitration practitioners should be explicitly trained away from the 'bag and baggage' of their national legal traditions and towards a kind of legal cosmopolitanism.[56] For example, I am one of the instructors for a leading Canadian professional training course, which leads to the ADR Institute of Canada's 'Qualified Arbitrator' designation; beginning with the 2023-2024 session, the instructors have included material on cultural competence in the core curriculum.

Such an educational and training programme would have the effect not only of increasing the cultural competence of existing practitioners but also of drawing to the field those from currently underrepresented backgrounds, who will come to see their particular cultural competences as niche skills to be cultivated rather than disfavoured backgrounds to be overcome.

V CONCLUSION

Over a century ago, the legal realists wrote of 'the need of a sociological jurisprudence'.[57] Sociology was then 'a young science, full of hopes and expectations', and as it aged, the realists' project lost momentum.[58] Today, at least in the transnational space where the bindingness of law recedes and culture fills the resulting gaps, we have come full circle. A 'sociological jurisprudence' of international arbitration would be a boon to both practice and principle. Sociological theories and methods may be employed not only to illuminate this legally and socially complex field of practice but also to inform the decision-making of practitioners, the rule-making of legislatures and institutions, and the education and training of the next generation.

55. Karton (n 50) 317.
56. The arbitration field could take inspiration from a more thoroughgoing effort to build cultural competencies in the legal profession: the EU-funded *Euro-Expert* project, which focuses primarily on training judges across Europe. https://culturalexpertise.net/ (accessed August 16, 2025).
57. Roscoe Pound, 'The Need of a Sociological Jurisprudence' (1907, October) 19 *The Green Bag* 607.
58. Jiří Přibáň, 'Review of *Sociological Jurisprudence: Juristic Thought and Social Inquiry* by Roger Cotterrell' (2018) 45(2) J Law & Soc 330.

CHAPTER 15

Islamic Law and Arbitration in Pakistan: A Sociological Perspective

Nudrat Bayan Majeed[*]

TABLE OF CONTENTS

I INTRODUCTION

1 Sociology of Education

Of the many intersections with international arbitration, perhaps one of the most informative is the intersection of sociology with law. Under the overarching theme of Sociology and Education, this chapter will look at the Sociology *of* Education vis-à-vis arbitration law in Pakistan. In doing so, it will posit three arguments: (i) Britain's colonization of Pakistan was a fatally damaging sociological experiment; (ii) the ensuing damage from this experiment altered an ancient legal and value system where norms and laws had evolved organically over centuries going back to the Indus Valley civilization/*Harappan* peoples and beyond; and (iii) with an informed understanding of the damage, the institution of international arbitration can contribute to restoring some balance through education and inclusivity.

* Four Golf Road Chambers, Lahore | Islamabad (www.fourgolfroad.pk); Drafter, Punjab Commercial Courts Bill 2021; Member, Committee of National Security Advisor on Bilateral Investment Treaties 2022; Bar-at-Law, England; Advocate, Pakistan. The author is grateful for the research assistance of Miss Shafaq Farooq, Mr Jahanzaib Maqbool and Mr Mashhood Shahzad. All errors remain the author's alone.

Sociological factors can bring variations in law which result in laws deviating from their original philosophy and impairing a natural progression. One such sociological factor is when laws are transposed inorganically from one legal tradition to another as was the case in Britain's colonization of Pakistan. *'Law is made for man, not man for law'* was applied by colonizers as *'Law is made for some men while all others are made for the law.'*

Law is a human behaviour shaped by our environment, by the conditions we are in and by the patterns of relationships between those involved in legal relations or disputes. Each society has its own norms of correct behaviour. Those norms are protected by codes of law. In Islamic law, the norm was identified by the Quran, at the same time, as inclusive i.e., a continuation of the norms practised by earlier prophets and exclusive, i.e., norms particular to Muhammad, the prophet of Islam:

> To each of you We have ordained a code of law and a way of life. Had God willed, He would have made you one community, but His will is to test you with what He has given you. So, vie with one another, only in doing good. To God you will all return when He will tell you of the truth behind your differences.[1]

Norms and codes in societies are what sociology defines as social control, i.e., the process of defining correct behaviour and responding to deviations from such behaviour. The mechanism for dealing with difference of opinions in defining societal norms and codes is what we know as conflict management or dispute resolution. Arbitration is one such legal method of conflict management. In Pakistan, the sociology of arbitration law has run a course not unlike a man-made river. Man-made rivers provide benefits of increased water supply, energy generation and transportation, but the damage done in the long-term, by altering a natural ecosystem,[2] is arguably greater than its benefits. In the same way, in Pakistan whose inhabitants inherited an ancient spiritual-legal heritage with sophisticated infrastructure going back to 5,000 BC, a violent blow was dealt by Britain's colonialization. An infrastructure that had, over time weaved into its fabric, the arrival of Hinduism, Buddhism, Islam and Christianity along with their respective laws was swiftly, and often times violently, replaced by norms and codes of English law; codes that were designed for 8 million inhabitants of a cold island at 55.78°N latitude occupying an area of around 130,000 sq. km in the North Sea were imposed on 200 million people at 37.1°N latitude occupying a land mass of over 4 million sq. km. A 5,000-year-old ecosystem was altered, destroying, among other things, the human condition in law.[3]

1. The Quran [5:48].
2. Numerous studies have shown adverse impact on fish birth, growth and migration, fragmentation of aquatic organisms, flooding from affected hydrology, increased water scarcity, among other things.
3. A difference of 20°N latitude can impact on working hours, cultural practices, economic activities, attitudes, and worldviews. *See* Marcela M. Mendes et al., Impact of High Latitude, Urban Living and Ethnicity on 25-Hydroxyvitamin D Status: A Need for Multidisciplinary Action?, 188 The Journal of Steroid Biochemistry and Molecular Biology (April 2019), pp. 95-102.

2 Sociology and International Arbitration

As a legal process, international arbitration encompasses a rich tapestry of human experience and interaction.[4] My first arbitration as a junior to the late, legendary Mr Johnny Veeder QC involved an Ecuadorian party and a Russian party, the former Spanish-speaking, the latter Russian-speaking. Neither side spoke English, yet all contract documents including the arbitration agreement were in English. This was not intuitively logical but unsurprising given that the *lingua franca* of international arbitration was English. Each day of the hearing was the opening of a new chapter in a political thriller. In the backdrop of the globalized village of the world, the tribunal waded through a mire of divergent linguistic and cultural perceptions. These kinds of circumstances play out daily in international arbitration proceedings around the world. Cultural factors, geopolitical/judicial challenges, semantics, heuristics, ethnic associations, civility, and ethics all impact the conduct and outcome of arbitration proceedings. Cultural differences influence the way parties communicate and perceive legal norms, e.g., what approach to adopt in choosing the correct conflict of laws to determine recognition of an arbitration agreement may be influenced by sociological factors. While technical and legal understanding of a dispute remains the foundation-stones of a dispute, the practice of international arbitration requires a cultural astuteness from all stakeholders for a smooth functioning of the arbitral process. The more culturally aware practitioners are the more productive is the collaboration with participants and the better it is for enforceability of an award. Fostering civility, identifying cognitive biases, and addressing ethical conduct are important indicators of the success of arbitration but are incomplete without an understanding of the sociological factors that shape modern arbitration laws in post-colonial states.

II COLONIALISM: THE MOST DAMAGING SOCIOLOGICAL EXPERIMENT IN HISTORY

> Scattered unevenly over a subcontinent the size of western Europe, divided by sectarian beliefs, dietary habits and often by language, most under Muslim but some, as in the empire of Vijayanagar or in the coastal towns of the south, under non-Muslim rule, medieval Muslims did not think or act as a nation.[5]

This sentiment expressed by P. Hardy and representative of the colonial approach was correct in its conclusion but flawed in its analysis. Medieval Muslims did not think or act as a nation precisely because diversity and *convivencia* were fundamental tenets of their constitution. There is no concept of a geographically delineated State in Islam. Its adherents are instructed to respect the ruler and rule of law in the lands they inhabit. This accounts for the very different rituals and practices in faith of Muslims from the

4. Kenneth S. Carlston, Theory of the Arbitration Process, 17 *Law and Contemporary Problems* (Fall 1952), pp. 631-651.
5. P. Hardy, *The Muslims of India*, Cambridge University Press, 1972, p. 1.

western-most reaches of Islam, i.e., Algeria to Muslims in southern Philippines, in its eastern-most reaches.[6]

At the beginning of the eighteenth century, Pakistan-Indian subcontinent's share of the world economy was 27%, larger than all of Europe put together. The Muslim Emperor Aurangzeb's treasury collected GBP 100 million in tax revenues alone. By the time the British left the Pakistan-Indian subcontinent, it had dropped to just over 3%. The reason was simple: India was governed for the benefit of Britain. Britain's rise for two hundred years was financed by its depredations in India.[7] The Subcontinent was the world's leading textile exporter/producer, ship-builder, steel manufacturer; industries that were destroyed deliberately to create a captive market by the British in the Subcontinent to unload their own goods.[8] Economically, Pakistan has had a more uphill battle compared to India after partition because along with all the plunder and systematic dismantling of law and culture that Britain's colonization left in its aftermath, Pakistan inherited an army disproportionately bigger than its population, and agricultural lands with hardly any industry. The British then dealt a final death-blow by the calculated division of the province of Punjab,[9] home to the headworks of major rivers supplying water to farmlands in Pakistan. An English barrister who had never, before, set foot on Subcontinental soil executed a boundary partition in a matter of two months.[10] In the process, the rivers of Pakistan and India, spanning a collective area of around four million square miles (the land size of China, Canada, or the United States), were also cut up. Pakistan had a mammoth task to build its agrarian economy on the inherited infrastructure of depleted, diverted waters and an alien law, understood, argued and implemented by lawyers in an alien language. It is unsurprising, then, that the agriculture sector's contribution to GDP at 53% at the time of Pakistan and India's partition in 1947 struggled to reach 23% in 2023. For Pakistan, colonialism has proven to be one of the most destructive sociological experiments in history.

III ARBITRATION LAW OF PAKISTAN

1 Current State of Law in Pakistan

When the British first came to the lands of Pakistan and India in 1600s, they found an active practice of collaborative/restorative dispute settlement on the ground which was very international given the multiplicity of ethnic origins, faiths, languages, and cultures of the disputants. The Silk Road had already been a well-trodden path for many millennia with the *panchayat* (local community resolution council) system for

6. *'O humanity! Indeed, We created you from a male and a female, and made you into peoples and tribes so that you may know each other and not despise each other.'* The Quran [49:13].
7. Shashi Tharoor, *An Era of Darkness*, Aleph Book Company, 2016, p. 4.
8. Shashi Tharoor, Debate of Britain's Colonial Legacy and the Impact on society Today (youtube-.com).
9. Punhab is a derivation of two words: *panch* (five) and *aab* (river) literally meaning the five rivers.
10. Ghazala Nawaz, The British Plan of the Partition of the Punjab in 1947, 34(2) *Pakistan Journal of History and Culture* (2013).

dispute resolution making an appearance soon after people became Hindu. Although the *Harappan* script has not yet been deciphered, archaeological excavations show the existence of a thriving business and market economy and, most interestingly, there were no courts and no army. This ancient legal ecology continued successfully through centuries of legal permutations of Hinduism, Buddhism and Islam because at the heart of each legal framework was a methodology for reconciliation and rehabilitation, not to force results by way of adversarial or inquisitorial approaches. This was as true of commercial relations as it was in other disciplines.

The British replaced the *panchayat* by introducing 'controlled local bodies' to safeguard their revenue interests. Courts were set up modelled on England's court system which signalled a systematic marginalization of the indigenous dispute settlement system.[11] People were divested of their right to practise, debate, and further develop their own laws. Arbitration law in Pakistan is now governed by an Anglo-US arbitration model with no connection, whatsoever, with the Hindu law base of the *panchayat* system or, indeed, Islamic law, despite the fact that Islamic law underpins all law in Pakistan as per its constitution.[12] Legal practice is further complicated by the fact that most lawyers will only learn the English language properly in law school, having been tutored in the national language of Urdu (itself a modern, artificial construct) or their regional languages. An added layer of complexity is that legal English with origins in Norman English and its lexemes from French and Latin[13] have no semblance to the spoken English which is learnt. The result is stunted jurisprudential analysis and on-ground enforcement and execution falling back on legal Urdu which has a heavy component of legal Persian and Arabic. The effect then is of an alien law, in an alien language, imposing an alien procedure on 240 million people, themselves adherents of 16 diverse ethnic groups with over 66 indigenous languages and 9 non-indigenous languages.

2 Pakistan Arbitration Act, 1940: Questions of Legitimacy

Domestic arbitration law in Pakistan which is codified by way of the Arbitration Act, 1940 is based on a nineteenth-century English statute of arbitration, and due to the above-mentioned factors is handicapped. Periodic surveys show an overwhelming majority of people desiring a more visible presence of Islamic law in the law. A distinction is drawn here with localized, informal arbitration and alternative dispute settlement practice which is actively practised in the country and the region.[14] The

11. In 1765, the *panchayat* institution was completely abolished by the East India Company in some main areas under its control, and it was substituted by the office of *patwari* – the record keeper of the village.
12. *'Islam shall be the State religion.'* Article 2 of the Constitution of Pakistan, 1973.
13. Mazhar-ul-Amin, Asim Mehmood, Zia Ahmad and Riaz Ahmad, Lexical Borrowing from Local Languages in Pakistan Legal English: A Corpus Based Study, 28(4) *Science International* (Lahore) (2016) pp. 647-652.
14. The author runs an active practice in effecting settlements of international disputes through informal commercial negotiations and mediations independently of court mandates. *See also* the 'Sialkot Study' which is a study of Pakistan's fastest growing economic city with a bustling trade

Arbitration Act, 1940s handicap is combined with additional obstacles in the form of adjournments, political turbulence, backlog of hundreds of thousands of cases in courts, and the courts' wide powers to intervene in arbitration proceedings. Domestic 'formal' arbitration is not as popular as its informal counterpart and raises questions of legitimacy.[15] For many, the fact that courts have roots in the British colonial system dilutes their legitimacy as upholders of justice as perceived by their users, leading to grassroots movements retaliating against the judicial system. However, lest all blame is put on the thief who walked through an open door and robbed the house, it is fair to identify the inhabitants who opened the door. Religion and law in Pakistan has been battered by its own believers. It has been hijacked by religious political parties to destabilize democracy;[16] it has been manipulated by the military to dictate on democracy;[17] and it has been sanitized by liberals as spirituality palatable to westernized sensibilities. The only social group that appears without an agenda to implement social norms of Islamic law are the youth. Interestingly, the country has never been as young as it is now, with over 40% of its population below the age of 20 years.

IV RESTORING THE BALANCE

1 User-Driven (Bottom-Up Reform)

Despite the very real challenges outlined above, the government and judiciary are alert to the issue of legitimacy and continue to explore ways to redress the balance. Notwithstanding the motivation behind its establishment, the Federal Shariat Court is supportive of arbitration laws (domestic and international).[18] The fact that it has not ruled to date on any provision of applicable arbitration statutes gives legal legitimacy

but not a single dispute in the courts of Sialkot on account of an informal, effective dispute settlement system. The case study is taught at Stanford University, USA by Professor Erik Jensen, 'What Is the Relationship of Law to Economic Development?' https://www.youtube.com/redirect?event=video_ (accessed 16 August 2025).

15. Studies show that questions of legitimacy are compounded by low levels of efficiency, prevalence of delays, inferior quality of legal training, corruption, and perceptions of the court system being a tool for the delay of justice, manipulated by rich and /or powerful interests in the society. https://panhandlepbs.org/wgbh/pages/frontline/afghanistan-pakistan/outlawed-in-pakistan/in-pakistan-a-delicate-balance-between-religious-and-secular-law/ (accessed 16 August 2025).
16. The *Shari Nizam-e-Adal* Regulation 2009 was promulgated by the Government in the province of KP in response to increasing civil disturbance on the absence of Islamic norms in law. Its objective is *'To provide for Nifaz-e-Nizam-e-Sharī'ah through Courts in the provincially Administered Tribal Areas for the North-West Frontier Province.'* The Regulation provides for appointment by court of a mediator (*musleh*) who performs a hybrid role of mediator and negotiator effecting negotiated compromise. Other laws were also made, e.g., the Local Government Ordinance 2001 which aims at the devolution of powers to the grassroots level by ensuring the participation of civil society representatives, in other words seeking to restore the *panchayat* system with modification.
17. The Federal Shariat Court was established which has no parallel in any other Muslims country. It has the sole task of ensuring that enacted laws do not violate Islamic principles.
18. The Federal Shariat Court was established on 26 May 1980 by President's Order No. 1 of 1980 as incorporated in Part VII of the Constitution of Pakistan, 1973 and has jurisdiction over the entire country. It is headed by the Chief Justice of Pakistan and comprises eight judges in total.

to the laws as well as fostering public perceptions of legitimacy.[19] In 2002, the Code of Civil Procedure, 1908, another law inherited by the British, was amended to provide for alternative dispute resolution mechanisms in civil cases and empower courts to refer disputes to arbitration, mediation, conciliation and any other form deemed appropriate.[20] In the spirit of speedy justice, commercial courts were also set up in various provinces.[21] The latest reform initiative is the Arbitration Bill which has been handed over to the Ministry of Law and Justice to be tabled as the new Arbitration Act. The government reform initiatives are assisted by the Supreme Court which has signalled a clear stance towards a *pro-enforcement bias* in the recognition and enforcement of foreign arbitral awards. In the 2024 judgment of *Taisei Corporation v. AMC Construction Company (Pvt.) Ltd.*, senior puisne judge, Mr Justice Mansoor Ali Shah ruled that:

> The role of courts in the context of international commercial arbitration has thus evolved to support and complement the arbitration process. Courts are no longer seen as competitors to arbitration but as essential partners in ensuring the effectiveness and integrity of the process. Their duty is to support, not supplant, the arbitral process.[22]

In elaborating on *pro-enforcement bias*, Mr Justice Shah said:

> This bias is critical in providing parties with the confidence that their decisions to arbitrate disputes will be supported by court around the world, thus enhancing the attractiveness of arbitration as a method of resolving international commercial disputes. This enforceability is crucial for the fluidity of international trade, providing businesses with the certainty and security needed to engage in cross-border transactions.[23]

2 Command-Driven (Top-Down Reform)

There is an increasing number of disillusioned communities in post-colonial states that are turning against the institution of international arbitration.[24] Cases like *Reko Diq* in

19. Efforts are now being made to expand the Research Wing of the Federal Shariat Court to provide guidelines and commentaries which could be used as supportive jurisprudence in commercial disputes including arbitration matters.
20. Section 89A was added to the Code of Civil Procedure, 1908 (CPC) in Pakistan through the Code of Civil Procedure (Amendment) Ordinance, 2002. It aims to promote the resolution of disputes through non-adversarial means and facilitate expeditious disposal of cases.
21. Punjab Commercial Courts Ordinance, 2021 was passed in April 2021 but lapsed in the absence of political will. Renewed efforts are now being made by the Board of Investment to table an enabling statute for commercial courts. In the meantime, commercial courts continue to operate in the province of Punjab by notification of the Lahore High Court.
22. *Taisei Corporation v. AMC Construction Company (Pvt.) Ltd.* para. 3, announced 28 February 2024 Islamabad, approved for reporting.
23. Among the many gray areas prevailing in the law of arbitration in Pakistan, Mr Justice Shah clarified once and for all that the controversial judgment in *Hitachi v. Rupali* [1998 SCMR 1618] can no longer be relied upon since it was based on the specific provision of a statutory law which has been replaced since 2011 by the enabling statute of the 1958 New York Convention, i.e., the Recognition and Enforcement (Arbitration Agreements and Foreign Arbitral Awards) Act, 2011.
24. ICSID is a case in point; an increasing number of countries have terminated their investment treaties and opted out of ICSID arbitrations, driven by factors among which is the perception that

Pakistan have raised questions in both the legal fraternity and civil society as to how a single, individual foreigner, the sole arbitrator, could issue an award of USD 11 billion on a government which has an annual national budget of USD 25 billion to distribute among 240 million people and is already crushed with circular debt from the IMF. The publication of the award led to social outrage along with lawyers criticizing the institution of international arbitration as a new Western attempt of colonization through trade laws. The Anglo-US model of arbitration is seen as antithetical and unethical to the culture and customs of Pakistan. International arbitration as an institution needs to exert its 'soft power' by being inclusive of diverse legal traditions, cultural norms, gender imbalances, languages, and qualifications of conflict managers.[25]

3 The Arabian Peninsula and Gulf Example

Dubai, Abu Dhabi, Riyadh, with their independent little commercial states, within the State, are an interesting case study on finding a middle ground to allow the Anglo-US model of arbitration to co-exist with Islamic norms and laws. In the Dubai International Financial Centre (DIFC), an arbitral award is first converted into a DIFC court judgment to align the award with the DIFC legal framework. The converted award, along with an Arabic legal translation, is then presented for execution in the Dubai courts by the DIFC court registrar acting as a 'conduit court' to facilitate enforcement.[26] The Dubai model has been adapted in Abu Dhabi as well as in Riyadh, Saudi Arabia.[27]

4 The Malaysian Example

In the Islamic world, the Asian International Arbitration Centre (AIAC) in Kuala Lumpur has initiated top-down reform. AIAC has arbitration rules providing a framework for resolving disputes arising from Shariah-governed contracts. The rules are structured on the familiar pattern of international arbitration rules and cover procedural matters like appointment of arbitrators, conduct of proceedings, language and seat, emergency arbitration, form of awards, costs, and deposits, etc. Where parties

---

the Anglo-US model does not provide a level-playing field and favours the foreign investor who is usually an Anglo-American multinational corporation investing in a country poor in effective legislation but rich in natural and human resources.

25. *'Soft power develops partly by governments and partly despite governments.'* https://www.youtube.com/watch?v=EiTrl0W1QrM (accessed 16 August 2025).
26. The DIFC court registrar has replaced the role of legal counsel and presents the converted award under the cover of a letter to the Chief Justice of the Court of First Instance, formally requesting enforcement.
27. The Abu Dhabi Global Market (ADGM) operates as a free zone with an independent legal and regulatory framework but its model of enforcement of arbitral awards is more along the lines of the English common law. The nascent Saudi Centre for Commercial Arbitration set up in 2014 offers services which were inspired by Shariah principles in harmony with international standards. Neom, the massive development project of Saudi Arabia by the side of the Gulf of Aqaba aiming to create an alternate route to the Suez Canal, is still in its design phase. It remains to be seen whether Islamic law or norms will have application in this mega-project, roughly the size of the country of Albania.

have not agreed to arbitrate under the main contract, the AIAC rules offer a model shariah arbitration clause which parties may adopt by way of a submission agreement.[28]

V CONCLUSION

1 Informed Inclusive Institutions

Arbitrators need to be 'international' not just in words but in action. In the 2023 Alexander Lecture of the Chartered Institute of Arbitrators, speaker Mr Toby T. Landau KC said:

> The time has come to return disputes to their actual socio-economic-political setting where the fiction of rule-based v policy-based objective of dispute resolution needs to be jettisoned and all interests / stakeholders / values need to be enfranchised.[29]

Such a move will help in pre-emptive positive action in response to inevitable criticisms of exclusion and imperialism through trade. With high stakes of international arbitration come related issues of political instability, civil and international armed conflict, and terrorism. Greater recognition and inclusion in international arbitration of localization and regionalism will help institutions become more informed and inclusive.[30] The *Reko Diq* case of Pakistan demonstrated, by default, the return of disputes to their socio-economic-political setting; the USD 11 billion award of damages has now been settled between the provincial government and the foreign investor. All claims and counterclaims have been withdrawn and work has resumed. In this new phase of socio-economic politics, the foreign investor has started an 'International Graduate Program' where the first nine graduates (all locals of the concerned province) have been selected for training by the foreign investor. These graduates will visit the assets of the foreign investor in its home state of Argentina and aim to return to their province to become future leaders to run the forty-year-long contract.

2 Restorative Justice

There are currently around twenty-seven armed conflicts in the world, with most of them taking place in countries that were colonized. In 2019, the late Moana Jackson, an international lawyer from New Zealand of Maori origin, said that in colonial countries there was a kind of social amnesia:

28. The Islamic law principles in the AIAC Rules provide a facility for referring a matter to a designated 'shariah council'; appointing a 'shariah expert'; penalties (*gharamah*) and compensation (*ta'widh*) due to late payment of financial obligations; and third-party funding.
29. https://www.youtube.com/watch?v=2ql6AlR6xec (accessed 16 August 2025).
30. For greater efforts towards localization and regionalism, *see* Carbonneau, T.E., Lex Mercatoria and Arbitration: A Discussion of the New Law Merchant, 58(5) William & Mary Law Review (2016) pp. 1817-1893, https://cadmus.eui.eu/bitstream/handle/1814/25204/2012_ELCIN_Vol 1.pdf (accessed 16 August 2025).

> A deliberate misremembering of history that obscured what colonization really was and is. It has replaced the harsh reality of racist violence and illegitimate usurpation of power with a feel-good rhetoric of Treaty-based good faith.[31]

For international arbitration to play a role in promoting peace through trade, legal approaches need to expand beyond the binary approaches of adversarial and inquisitorial and include restorative justice as was the norm in ancient societies such as Pakistan. Given that the theme of ICCA Hong Kong 2025 was 'The Human Condition in Law', it is apt to share an excerpt of a seventh-century CE letter written by the fourth Islamic caliph, Ali bin Abi Talib, to his newly appointed governor of Egypt. It is educative on the human condition in law, focussing on the restorative justice approach. In directing the governor on the selection of adjudicators, the Caliph said:

> For the settlement of disputes among people select an adjudicator from the people who is, by far, the best among them. One who is not vexed by disputes, one who cannot be intimidated, one who does not err too often. One who does not turn back from a correct position once it is found, one who is not self-centred or avaricious, one who will not decide before knowing all the facts. One who will weigh with care every attendant doubt. One who will not grow restive of the arguments of advocates and who will examine with patience every new disclosure of fact. One who will be strictly impartial in reaching a decision and pronounce a clear verdict after taking everything into full consideration. One who will not be misled by flattery nor be vain about the position. Such people are very few. Once you find them, pay them handsomely enough to let them live in comfort and in keeping with their position, enough to keep them above temptations. Give them a position so high that none can even dream of coveting it and so high that neither back-biting nor intrigue can touch them.[32]

Legal approaches should also take into account greater recognition and inclusion of localization and regionalism which will help institutions become more informed and inclusive. To conclude, a distinct sociological custom is shared which has long been a practice of senior advocates in Pakistan which is to end a legal argument with a couplet from a classical poet. The efforts at redressing the damage of colonization and reviving restorative justice approaches are best summed up by a verse of Allama Muhammad Iqbal – the poet-philosopher of Pakistan who said:

نہیں ہے نا امید اقبال اپنی کشتِ ویراں سے

ذرا نم ہو تو یہ مٹی بہت زرخیز ہے ساقی

Never is Iqbal despondent at the sight of his vast barren land,
 A few drops of moisture from your hand O water-bearer, and see life grows where desolation once spanned.

---

31. Mutu (Ngati Kahu, Te Rarawa and Ngati Whatua Nations), M. (2019), 'To Honour the Treaty, We Must First Settle Colonisation' (Moana Jackson 2015): The Long Road from Colonial Devastation to Balance, Peace, and Harmony, 49 *Journal of the Royal Society of New Zealand* (sup1), pp. 4-18 https://doi.org/10.1080/03036758.2019.1669670 (accessed 16 August 2025).
32. Ali ibn Abi Talib and Kattani, Sulayman (1989), 'Ruler and Society', In Nasr, Seyyed Hossein, Dabashi, Hamid and Nasr, Seyyed Vali Reza (eds), *Expectation of the Millennium: Shi'ism in History*. Translated by *Chittick*, William C. State University of New York Press, pp. 73-91, ISBN 978-0-88706-843-0.

CHAPTER 16

Competence Competence (Not Kompetenz Kompetenz): Study and Experience Alone Constitute the Equipment of an Arbitrator

*Jonathan Wood**

I have three daughters, now well grown up and well advanced in their careers. When they were teenagers, I gave them a book – the autobiography of Dame Margaret Anstee. Born in 1926, Margaret Anstee had a stellar career as a British diplomat, perhaps best noted as being the first female staff member to reach the rank of Undersecretary General of the United Nations in 1987.

Dame Margaret Anstee was born near where I live in the village of Writtle, Essex. Her father was a printer, her mother in domestic service, leaving school at 14 and 12, respectively, 'deeply determined to have only one child, and to ensure it the best education they could manage'. The village school mistress held the conviction 'that country children were not as intelligent as our town counterparts, and that those of us who had the misfortune to be female were even less so'.

Needless to say, in defiance of the school authorities, she got to Newham College, Cambridge, reading languages where she got a first. She joined the British Foreign Office in 1948 and was assigned to the South American department. It was FO policy

* Jonathan Wood FCIArb is President of the Chartered Institute of Arbitrators 2024, was Chair of the Board for five years and Trustee for eight years. He is Chair of International Arbitration at the firm of RPC, of London, Hong Kong, and Singapore. He is Chair of the Board of the London Chamber of Arbitration and Mediation (LCAM). He was Chair of IBA's International Sales Committee. He has over forty-five years of experience in international dispute resolution having started his career in criminal defence and human rights, diversifying into commercial law in relation to shipping, insurance, international trade and energy. He has a niche in art and cultural property law. Jonathan represented the UK Government's Export Credit Agency, ECGD (now UKEF) for thirty years. He has a track record in pro bono, teaching in Dar es Salaam and on the CIArb pathways courses. He was on the UK Government's pro bono panel for many years. He now sits mainly as an arbitrator (CIArb Journal 1922).

never to send a woman diplomat to Latin America, for fear she would succumb to the wiles of 'some passionate Latino'.

She joined the UN where she served in many overseas postings – Colombia, Uruguay, Argentina, Bolivia, Ethiopia, Morocco, and Chile. She was involved in peace-keeping missions as well as economic development.

Faced with the obstacles of her background, she was nonetheless highly successful, gifted with social skills and a sense of humour and a woman of high competence. She passed away in 2016.[1]

A hugely entertaining read, the title of her autobiography is *Never Learn to Type*. When asked by a fellow male colleague in the British FO of that time (or even now!) might she like to type up the minutes of the meeting they had both just attended, one can imagine her response, delivered somewhat archly! She had equipped herself with the ideal response. She was well able to rebuff confinement of her roles to those thought only suitable for women. My daughters, who have faced obstacles in their own careers, found the book both fascinating and inspirational.

Why relate this story? Aside from being a story of general interest of a remarkable woman, it is a tale of someone who is a model of social mobility, who achieved her position initially through education, but as her career developed, through experience. In her role as a diplomat, often engaged in resolving conflict at the highest level in an international and multicultural context, she deployed many of the skills that ADR neutrals call on to resolve disputes. I suggest many of us would profit from reading her book as part of our own ongoing education as ADR neutrals.

Let me now turn to the more specific and practical topic of education of ADR neutrals, and arbitrators in particular. Is study and experience sufficient to equip us as arbitrators? Many looking at themselves may think so. But how does this appear to users of arbitration services as a means of dispute resolution? How do they know or judge the competence of an individual arbitrator from an educational and experience standpoint?

I have often been asked: 'What do users want' out of an arbitrator? One can write a paper in itself on this topic.[2] My brief two-word response to this question is a 'Competent Neutral'.

We should all know what is meant broadly speaking by 'neutral' when it comes to this quality in an arbitrator. It is capable of definition, be it laid down in statute, case law, the Model Law, or institutional rules, in varying degrees of detail – someone who is impartial and independent, unbiased.

Competent or 'competence' is the more difficult quality to determine. How is 'competence' to be evaluated? Some might say the hallmark of competence is critical reasoning, objectivity, and sound judgment together with good communication skills and a sound knowledge of the process to achieve a fair outcome. How is that acquired?

Education through study of course provides the starting point. The global growth in tertiary education at universities in the study of not just international arbitration but

1. Obituary: The Guardian 1 September 2016.
2. *See* Christopher Vajda KC, 'What Makes a Good Arbitrator?' 89(3) Int'l J of Arb and Dispute Mgmt (2022).

also private and public international law, and the law relating to international trade, energy, construction, finance, technology and shipping, all of which may well end up as disputes before arbitral tribunals, has been remarkable.

The programme at Queen Mary University, London, to name but one, is perhaps the most well known, but it is by no means alone. There are courses in jurisdictions around the world competing to meet the demand of enquiring minds who are attracted to the subject. With the continued growth in globalisation and complexity in international business, together with a volatile geopolitical environment, giving rise to complex disputes involving different cultures and nationalities, this comes as little surprise.

The outcome from the universities and other educational institutions can be witnessed by the many mooting competitions that are now held. The Vis Moot, in its thirty-first year, and Vis Moot East, held here in Hong Kong, attracts international teams of students of the highest calibre from educational institutions globally. These are not the only mooting competitions. The competitions provide experience not just for the teams as counsel but also for experienced and the less-experienced and aspiring arbitrators, including former 'mootees'.

So academic study in an educational institution as a means of acquiring knowledge is now quite possibly the starting point for many who wish to engage in a career in arbitration, and in due course perhaps become arbitrators.

Beyond that, the availability of educational events and learning opportunities is now limitless. The use of technology and the internet supercharged the experience of virtual learning during the pandemic. My inbox is filled daily with invitations to conferences, seminars, webinars, arbitration events and weeks, and learned articles on every new development, aimed at improving my understanding in relation to the widest variety of issues relevant to international arbitration.

For many, and dare I say myself included, becoming an arbitrator is a second career. Many have practised as professionals of one sort or another, whether it be as lawyers, accountants, construction professionals, insurers, maritime professionals, commodity traders, financiers, and academics. For those of a certain age, taking time out of a busy career to devote to full-time study may not have been an option, compounded by the fact that years ago there was not the ready availability of courses at universities in any event. Knowledge and experience was acquired 'on the job', and to a degree, still is. If you were fortunate, your pupil master at the English Bar, or your principal, if you were a trainee solicitor, (or 'articled') might deal with international arbitration, and so you followed them and picked up the skills by a sort of osmosis. When I started out as an advocate in the criminal courts of the north of England, there was one book on the subject, *The Art of the Advocate* by Edward du Cann QC. The rest of my skills were achieved literally by trial and error, possibly at the expense of some unfortunate and luckless victim of the criminal court system.

But, I suggest, there are limitations to academic study and individualised learning alone. As this ICCA conference reminds us, International Arbitration is a Human Endeavour. To achieve competency, an understanding of human behaviour is necessary, both our own as neutrals and the many involved in the process – counsel, experts, witnesses, and our tribunal colleagues. And this is in the context of an international background, involving different laws of different jurisdictions, and different cultural approaches to dispute resolution.

So, the question is how best to achieve competence to fulfil properly the role of a neutral? To this end, I turn to my own organisation, the Chartered Institute of Arbitrators (CIArb).

A more comprehensive or holistic approach to education and training of neutrals on a worldwide basis is provided by CIArb. The Institute provides pathways to achieving a level of membership graded by post-nominal designation: Associate, Member, Fellow and Chartered. This in turn allows users to identify the level of competence of an individual who might be engaged in an adjudicative role as a neutral. The post-nominal designation is recognised worldwide and by a number of arbitral institutions as a condition or criterion for empanelment.

By way of background, CIArb was founded in 1915. It was granted its Royal Charter of the United Kingdom, in 1979.[3] It is a registered charity regulated by the UK Charity Commissioners. It set up its first Education Committee in 1929. It now has a worldwide membership of 19,000, with members in 152 jurisdictions, and forty-four branches globally, the most recent one, at the time of writing, having been launched at RIDW24 in the Kingdom of Saudi Arabia.

As a professional Chartered Institute, it offers a range of education and vocational training courses and qualifications – from introductory to advanced levels – in the various disciplines of dispute resolution, including arbitration, mediation, and construction adjudication. As part of its ongoing commitment to ensuring quality dispute resolution, it develops and publishes a variety of standards and guidelines based on the latest thinking from leading practitioners. It also runs a calendar of continuous professional development (CPD) events.

It has recently developed an integrated set of competence frameworks for ADR and the individual ADR disciplines of Arbitration, Adjudication and Mediation,[4] to be clearer on what arbitrators, mediators and adjudicators are offering users in terms of competence. This begins to bring the profession of ADR practitioner into line with practitioners in other professions such as law and medicine.

Many CIArb members spend at least some of their time as ADR practitioners in non-neutral roles. However, a significant number aspire to take on the role of a neutral, or are working in a context where the understanding of the neutral role from the inside when acting in the non-neutral role – as counsel or expert – is crucial.

The overarching competence framework identifies the core skill sets required by neutrals, complemented by discipline-specific frameworks, depending on the specific role, whether arbitrator, adjudicator or mediator. These frameworks are iterated out for the different CIArb membership levels (Associate, Member, Fellow or Chartered) through the specification of the minimum level of competence required for each

3. Nigel Watson, 'A History of the Chartered Institute of Arbitrators'.
4. Isabel Phillips, 'Ciarb ADR Competence Frameworks, Competence Statements, and Membership Levels' 88(4) Arbitration: Int'l J of Arb and Dispute Mgmt (2022): 675-709 https://doi.org/10.54648/amdm2022040 (accessed 16 August 2025).

membership level and corresponding sample indicators that could be used to demonstrate that an individual has the necessary level of competence. The competences within the framework articulate the different areas of knowledge, skill and attitude required in terms of 'minimum competence statements'. So, for example, a Fellow must demonstrate the knowledge, skills and attitudes required to run an arbitration independently and effectively, and that qualification may be relied upon as an indication that the neutral has a certain standard of competence.

In the context of a diverse membership of some 19,000 globally, considerable consultation throughout the institution was necessary to determine a common basis, including with Branch Chairs, the Education and Membership Committee, the Exam Board, the Board of Trustees, Faculty and Regional Pathway Leaders as well as individual members. Putting the competence framework into practice is a challenging undertaking.

One of the most contentious areas is how competence is demonstrated or 'proven'. Proxies in various forms are used as evidence of competence: university/professional qualification; reference /recommendation from a senior professional, the amount of professional experience expressed in years, the number of arbitrations attended in different capacities – counsel, neutral; feedback from other neutrals. These proxies are limited as proof of competence. And so, a combination of multiple proxies is usually necessary.

An important lesson from the consultation is that there needs to be some consensus and clarity as to what proxies are being used and their rationale. This will require further review as to the different pathways to membership in relation to how 'competence' is demonstrated – through both 'experience' and 'assessment' – to ensure workability, consistency and fairness across the membership levels and routes to membership.

It will demand patience and contribution from the CIArb membership across the world. It is anticipated to be an effective way of developing and sustaining common standards of professionalism and qualification which can be recognised by members, their clients and the public in general. And importantly, all membership levels are underpinned by members undertaking to abide by the 'CIArb Code of Professional and Ethical Conduct for Members'[5] to which each member signs up to annually, enforceable through the disciplinary process which is applicable worldwide, setting it apart from most other educational institutions.

In conclusion, perhaps we have not strayed away too far from the quote at the beginning that 'Study and experience alone constitute the equipment of an Arbitrator.' However, there is an important distinction between the neutral who avails himself or herself of the panoply of study opportunities widely available from the universities or the conferences, seminars, articles and webinars, and one who has a recognisable qualification, supported by a degree of regulatory oversight, which provides an objective measure of competence for the user.

5. https://www.ciarb.org/media/2x3a0n42/5-ciarb-code-of-professional-and-ethical-conduct-for-members.pdf (accessed 16 August 2025).

What I might have added some years ago is that, unlike Margaret Anstee's exhortation 'not learning to type', with email and Word, for a while, we all had to learn to type. With the advancement of technology in speech recognition software and the like, typing as a competency has now been taken out of our hands!

Panel 5

Judging the New York Convention

The panel discussed the interpretation and application of the New York Convention by courts and the role of judges and practitioners. The discussion included questions of consistency and uniformity, public policy reflecting societal interests and arbitrability issues in different jurisdictions, and the impact of local legal cultures. The speakers reflected on the visionaries and influencers who have shaped the NYC.

CHAPTER 17

Judging the New York Convention

Courtney Kemp & Paula Baldini Miranda da Cruz[*]

TABLE OF CONTENTS

'The New York Convention is nothing without judges' – Johnny Veeder

I INTRODUCTION

Since its adoption in 1958, the Convention on the Recognition and Enforcement of Foreign Arbitral Awards (the 'New York Convention' or 'Convention') has become a cornerstone of international arbitration. With over 170 state parties, it provides a uniform legal framework for the cross-border enforcement of arbitral awards. Its widespread success is often attributed to its simple and flexible drafting, which allows it to operate across a broad range of legal systems.

The Convention's real-world effect, however, is shaped not only by its text but equally by those who apply it: it is in the hands of national judiciaries that the Convention is interpreted, operationalised and ultimately brought to life. Judges play a key role in navigating the tensions between the pro-enforcement nature of the

* Courtney Kemp is a fellow at ICCA and Assistant Legal Counsel at the Permanent Court of Arbitration (PCA); Paula Baldini Miranda da Cruz is Deputy Executive Director (Publications) at ICCA and Legal Counsel at the PCA. The authors thank Adam Jankowski for his comments on this piece.

Convention and the reality of domestic frameworks. It is judges' interpretation and solutions for these tensions that determine the Convention's consistency, legitimacy and impact.

This report captures the insights shared during a panel discussion moderated by members of ICCA's Judiciary Committee, and featuring three judges who actively apply the Convention in their jurisdictions: Judge Fatima Faisal Hubail (Bahrain); Justice Judith Prakash (Singapore); and Judge Xi Xiangyang (China). The Panel was complemented by commentary from three legal practitioners with vast experience in the field – Lindsay Gastrell, Barton Legum and Guled Yusuf – who reflected on the judges' experiences and challenges and proposed frameworks for navigating the delicate process of applying the Convention.

What emerges is a rich discussion of how the judges see their own roles under the Convention. Their reflections show a shared commitment to principled interpretation, tempered by a sensitivity to domestic legal cultures and frameworks. After discussing the flexibility of the New York Convention and some of the practical elements shaping its varied interpretation across the globe (section II); they focused on in Article V(2)(b) of the Convention, a provision whose open-textured language demands judicial discretion and highlights the interpretive challenges posed by the Convention (section III). The Panel thus explored not only how divergences arise but also how it is possible to achieve greater coherence and harmonisation through dialogue, shared principles, and a structured approach to interpretation (section IV).

The Panel discussion ultimately shows that the Convention's success is not merely institutional or legal but also profoundly human. It depends on how judges see their task, weigh competing values and engage with both international practices and local realities.

II IMPLEMENTATION OF THE NEW YORK CONVENTION: VARIETY WITHIN UNITY

At first glance, the role of judges in applying international instruments such as the New York Convention may appear straightforward – a matter of implementing a single, universally accepted legal text. However, the reality is far more complex. Despite its seemingly uniform nature, the New York Convention operates within different domestic legal contexts. Each judge approaches it not only through the lens of the Convention itself but also through the specific procedural rules, interpretive traditions and legislative frameworks of their own legal system. As a result, what appears to be a single, coherent legal obligation becomes, in practice, a diverse and sometimes fragmented judicial endeavour.

The Convention's provisions are drafted in broad terms and must be aligned with each state's domestic legal framework to be applied effectively. This alignment involves not only completing the necessary formalities – such as publication in a state's official gazette – but also ensuring that the Convention's provisions are fully adapted and integrated into domestic law, which may otherwise conflict with the Convention's terms.[1] The way in which the Convention is implemented will shape how its terms are applied within a specific domestic legal system.

To the extent that the Convention allows it, states may, through legislative or judicial action, interpret or adapt the Convention's provisions to fit existing national laws and legal traditions. Conflicts between the Convention and domestic law are typically addressed through rules of hierarchy or precedence,[2] clarifications of applications in scope,[3] or through supplementary legislation that aligns national procedures with the Convention's requirements. The Convention itself already provides some solutions for some anticipated conflicts, namely:

(i) Precedence of the most favourable rule: Where the Convention and national law have differing rules addressing the same issue, the Convention will apply unless the national law (where recognition and enforcement is sought) is more favourable[4] – that is, if it facilitates or provides less onerous criteria for enforcement.[5]
(ii) Supplementation: National law may fill gaps in the Convention[6] such as by specifying the procedure for enforcement.[7]
(iii) Specific clarifications and accommodations for national law: The Convention provides for specific circumstances that may be governed by national law. This includes, for example, the possibility of states to make certain reservations (Article I of the Convention); and the public policy exception, which allows for states to refuse to recognise and enforce awards contrary to their public policy (Article V(2)(b) of the Convention).

These solutions are designed to integrate the Convention into national frameworks and ensure it operates in harmony with domestic laws and policies. However, this process inevitably leads to variations in how the Convention is applied across jurisdictions. Such differences are not only expected but also inherent in the way treaties are incorporated into domestic frameworks. Each state has its own approach to integration, which may lead to gaps in incorporation, or subtle shifts in meaning, particularly when technical terms are translated. Moreover, incorporation requires fitting the Convention into the logic and underlying principles of the national legal system, which can further shape how it is interpreted and applied in practice.

1. ICCA's Guide to the Interpretation of the 1958 New York Convention, 2nd ed. (2024) www.arbitration-icca.org/iccas-guide-interpretation-1958-new-york-convention accessed 13 May 2025 ('Judges' Guide') 31.
2. *Ibid.*, 28.
3. *Ibid.*, 28-29.
4. 1958 Convention on the Recognition and Enforcement of Foreign Arbitral Awards 330 UNTS 3 Convention, Article VII(1). *See also* Judges' Guide 28.
5. Convention, Article VII(1). *See also* Judges' Guide 28.
6. Convention, Article III provides that '[e]ach Contracting State shall recognize arbitral awards as binding and enforce them in accordance with the *rules of procedure of the territory where the award is relied upon* [...]' (own emphasis). *See also* Judges' Guide 28.
7. For example, time limits for filing a request for recognition and enforcement, the form of the request, the manner in which proceedings are conducted, remedies against a refusal to recognise and enforce, and the availability of the set-off defence or counterclaim against an award.

Judges Hubail, Prakash and Xiangyang reflected on how implementation processes have led to practical differences in the application of the Convention within their respective jurisdictions. Justice Prakash explained that Singapore requires treaties to be expressly incorporated into domestic law. In practice, this means that the Convention must be partially or fully translated into domestic legislation. Along with its accession to the Convention in 1986, Singapore also reviewed its arbitration laws. The International Arbitration Act of 1994 (revised in 2020), which applies to foreign awards from parties to the Convention,[8] incorporates both the Convention and the UNCITRAL Model Law as schedules. The grounds for refusal of enforcement contained in Article V of the Convention are also mirrored in section 31(2) and (4) of the International Arbitration Act. In addition to incorporating these grounds, the section 31(2) and (4) also clarify their scope of application, stipulating that a court may set aside an award if it finds that its making was induced by fraud or corruption,[9] or that a breach of natural justice occurred in the making of the award.[10]

The Singaporean model has the advantage that it completely integrates the most relevant provisions of the Convention into the domestic framework, making them more accessible to local practitioners, and subjecting them to the same principles of application and interpretation. Further, because the Convention is integrated as a schedule to national laws and without requiring any translation, its text and logic have been entirely preserved, allowing judges to ensure that its application in Singapore is consistent with its international interpretation.

Similarly, Bahrain, following the ratification of the New York Convention 1988,[11] has also incorporated several provisions of the Convention in its 2015 Arbitration Law. The 2015 Law adopts the UNCITRAL Model Law as the standard law applicable to the enforcement of international and domestic awards in Bahrain.[12] In doing so, Bahrain has effectively incorporated the Convention into its domestic framework, as the Model

8. Domestic awards and awards from foreign states that have not acceded to the Convention, however, fall under the Arbitration Act of 2001, which is silent on the grounds for refusal of enforcement.
9. Singapore International Arbitration Act 1994, section 24(a).
10. *Ibid.*, section 24(b).
11. Signed on 6 April 1988, incorporated by Legislative Decree No. 4 of 1988, in force from 17 March 1988. The Arabic UNCITRAL translation of the New York Convention was published in the Bahrain Official Gazette on 5 April 1995.
12. Bahrain Law No. 9 of 2015 on the Promulgation of the Law of Arbitration (the '2015 Arbitration Law'), Article 1(1) provides that:

> '[s]ubject to the provisions of international agreements in force in the Kingdom of Bahrain:
> 1. The provisions of the enclosed UNCITRAL Model Law on International Commercial Arbitration shall apply to any arbitration irrespective of the nature of the legal relationship around which the dispute, if the arbitration takes place in the Kingdom or abroad and the parties agreed to submit it to the provisions of the enclosed Law'.

Bahrain's accession to the Convention is also expressly noted in the recitals to the 2015 Arbitration Law.

Law was developed with the New York Convention in mind and is designed to be consistent with its principles.[13]

But not all legal systems require treaty provisions to be specifically transposed into domestic law. Although China's domestic laws contain concepts similar to those of the Convention, those similarities are not the result of transposing provisions from the Convention into domestic laws. In fact, the Chinese system does not require a reproduction of treaty provisions within domestic laws at all. Instead, a treaty retains its status as such and finds its application guided by the international principles of interpretation reflected in the Vienna Convention on the Law of Treaties.[14]

Judge Xiangyang also explained that, while the Convention is technically only applicable to arbitrations classified as 'international', similar provisions have been incorporated into laws applicable to domestic and foreign-related arbitrations. For example, the Convention's grounds for refusal of enforcement of awards are included in the list provided in Article 58 of China's Arbitration Law with respect to domestic and foreign-related arbitrations.[15] These overlaps result in greater consistency between the different frameworks that coexist in China, and show how the effects of the Convention extend beyond that of arbitrations classified as 'international'. Article 58 also clarifies instances where local interests may play a role, clarifying that enforcement may be refused where evidence was forged or withheld to affect the impartiality of the arbitrator,[16] or while arbitrating the case, the arbitrators committed embezzlement, accepted bribes, practised graft or made an award that perverted the law.[17]

This background shows the various landscapes within which domestic judges work when applying the New York Convention. As noted by Barton Legum, while one may expect international law 'to be the same no matter who is interpreting it or where they may be from',[18] there are in practice significant variations. In particular, the process by which the Convention is incorporated into a state's legal framework provides judges with a foundation for determining how it should be interpreted – whether its provisions should be interpreted through the lens of international or domestic legal principles, and whether domestic jurisprudence may influence its application. While the Convention's text – drafted in broad and open-ended terms – allows for such flexibility, it can also lead to divergent outcomes across jurisdictions. Here, judges have the power to mitigate or exacerbate these divergences through their roles as interpreters.

13. Aysha Mutaywea and Isra Alaradi et al., 'National Report for Bahrain (2021 Through 2023)' 56, in Lise Bosman (ed.), *ICCA International Handbook on Commercial Arbitration* (Kluwer 2023).
14. Lu Song, 'National Report for China (2020 Through 2024): Introduction' in Lise Bosman (ed.), *ICCA International Handbook on Commercial Arbitration* (Kluwer 2024).
15. The Arbitration Law effective from 1 September 1995, amended in 2009. Other grounds contained in the same provision include where evidence was forged or withheld to affect the impartiality of the arbitrator (Article 58(4)-(5)) or while arbitrating the case, the arbitrators committed embezzlement, accepted bribes, practised graft or made an award that perverted the law (Article 58(6)).
16. Arbitration Law 1994, Article 58(4)-(5).
17. *Ibid.*, Article 58(6).
18. Barton Legum ICCA 2024 Hong Kong Congress *Panel 5: Judging the New York Convention* 54:55-5:04, www.arbitration-icca.org/panel-5-judging-new-york-convention (accessed 13 May 2025).

III JUDGES AS INTERPRETERS: THE CONDUITS BETWEEN LOCAL AND INTERNATIONAL NORMS

The role of the judge is fundamental in harmonising (or fragmenting) the application of the Convention across the globe. She must interpret, discern and apply the Convention, essentially acting as a conduit between local and international norms. How she navigates interpretation is filtered through her and her jurisdiction's legal traditions and policy priorities. Judges Hubail, Prakash and Xiangyang shared their experiences in navigating this balancing exercise in the context of the so-called public policy exception contained in Article V(2)(b) of the Convention, which provides ample room for interpretation. The public policy exception under Article V(2)(b) allows for a signatory state to refuse the enforcement of an award if its recognition and enforcement would violate its public policy. The Convention and its associated documents provide little guidance as to how to interpret or apply this exception, leaving to judges the task of determining the scope of this exception while balancing domestic and international interests.

Justice Prakash provided a practical example of how judges manage this vagueness in a way that favours harmonisation. She noted that, although in Singapore the interpretation of the Convention is guided by domestic rather than international principles, judges remain very aware of the treaty origins of the domestic provisions. As such, they often consult foreign decisions and international commentaries to orient themselves while applying the Convention. This recourse to international practices is supported by Singapore law's tendency of favouring consistency of interpretation with international traditions. In other words, while the judiciary retains autonomy of interpretation and remains primarily guided by domestic law, there is a conscious effort to align with global jurisprudence to ensure coherence and predictability at an international level.

The main challenge faced by judges in Singapore during this exercise is to determine which trends to prioritise to achieve consistency. As Justice Prakash explains, while there is a general preference for aligning with international interpretations, judges only do so if they find those interpretations persuasive. Much like the use of precedent in common law systems, foreign judgments are not binding but carry persuasive authority. For example, when considering the recognition and enforcement of a foreign-seated arbitral award, a judge appointed in Singapore will usually refer to both international commentaries and to the legal principles of the jurisdiction where the award was rendered – that is, that jurisdiction's prevailing interpretation of the Convention. At the same time, Singaporean courts have occasionally applied international treaty interpretation principles, particularly in the case of enforcing ICSID decisions. This indicates that while consistency with international norms is an aspirational goal, outcomes can still vary. Such variations often arise because individual judges may be persuaded by different commentaries and precedents.

In this regard, Justice Prakash highlighted the public policy exception as a particularly challenging provision. She described it as the 'unruly horse' of enforcement. Each judge may have a different conception of public policy, which raises the risk of arbitrary and inconsistent decisions.[19] To mitigate these risks, Singapore's courts have adopted a narrow interpretation of the public policy exception. As Justice Prakash explains, enforcement will only be denied if it would 'shock the conscience,' be injurious to public good or violate Singapore's most fundamental notions of morality and justice.[20]

For example, an award that is tainted by fraud or corruption, or is illegal under the laws of a foreign jurisdiction, may be refused enforcement on public policy grounds. However, Singaporean courts draw a clear distinction between violations of Singaporean public policy and mere legal error. It is *not* contrary to Singapore's public policy for an arbitrator to misapply a foreign law, provided that the resulting award is not illegal under that foreign law. In such cases, the courts will not intervene merely because they disagree with the tribunal's legal reasoning. However, if the error violates Singapore's public policy – for instance, if an arbitral tribunal enforces a contract that is illegal under its governing law – Singaporean courts will step in. Even if such an agreement could be enforced under Singaporean law, the courts would refuse to uphold it if doing so would offend the principle that agreements illegal under their governing law should not be enforced.

In Bahrain, judges similarly look to international practices and principles when interpreting the New York Convention, but their decisions ultimately reflect a firm adherence to fundamental domestic legal principles. As explained by Judge Hubail, Bahraini courts do not refuse to recognise and enforce awards lightly. The New York Convention's application is still largely governed by the 2015 Arbitration Law, which provides the comprehensive framework for enforcement.[21] It is through the 2015 Arbitration Law and the domestic principles guiding it that the Convention is interpreted and applied in practice.

This domestic gloss is clearly seen in the application of the public policy exception. Bahraini judges are generally reluctant to refuse recognition or enforcement of arbitral awards solely on public policy grounds. Rather, refusal is reserved for instances where proceeding with enforcement would contravene *fundamental* principles of Bahrain's legal system (such as res judicata). While international public policy may also be invoked, it will be relevant to the extent that the underlying principle has been recognised as a fundamental element of Bahrain's domestic law.

Importantly, a mere contradiction with Bahraini law is not sufficient to trigger the public policy exception; the breach must reach the threshold of offending a fundamental principle. This illustrates a deliberate effort to balance domestic interests with international obligations, guided by the caveat that only violations of foundational legal principles could justify non-enforcement. This does not suggest that Bahraini decisions are in stark contrast to those of other jurisdictions. On the contrary, judges in Bahrain are mindful of the importance of upholding international standards and

19. Judge Prakash *Panel 5: Judging the New York Convention* 32:28.
20. The phrase 'most basic notions of morality and justice' historically has its origins in the American case of *Parsons & Whittemore v. RAKTA*, US Court of Appeals 2nd Circuit, para. 2.37.18.
21. Aysha Mutaywea 55.

principles when they align with or have been incorporated into Bahrain's own fundamental legal framework. This restrained approach supports Bahrain's broader commitment to international harmonisation and helps to avoid the issuance of outlier decisions.

In China, judges refer to foreign judgments and international principles when interpreting the New York Convention due to its status as a treaty under Chinese law. However, due to the traditional style of Chinese judicial writing, these sources are not always cited explicitly. As Judge Xiangyang explained, there is a congruence between international and domestic principles which creates a dynamic relationship where domestic legal understandings may subtly influence the interpretation of the Convention, with judges remaining cautious about allowing domestic perspectives to dominate. Conversely, understandings of the Convention may also shape interpretations of domestic principles. Thus, while there is a separation between international and domestic principles, they coexist in a mutually reinforcing and harmonious relationship. Nonetheless, Judge Xiangyang explained that selecting which foreign decisions to follow can be difficult.

In his opinion, the most important principle should be a pro-enforcement bias; judges should be oriented towards supporting enforcement as their 'north star'.[22] As he puts it, Chinese judges 'put support [for arbitration] before supervision',[23] reflecting the strong national policy favouring arbitration.

Regarding the public policy exception, while the Convention holds the status of international law, domestic law principles define the content of public policy. This shows how domestic law is employed to interpret and operationalise an international standard. The exception is interpreted narrowly, and enforcement will only be denied when an award offends fundamental principles of Chinese law, such as sovereignty, public security, good morals and public interest. Grounds such as corruption and fraud can justify refusal, but – as in Singapore – mere errors of law or incorrect application of foreign law do not rise to the level of a violation of public policy. Only severe transgressions that strike at the core of public policy can meet the threshold.

Ultimately, while the judicial approaches in Singapore, Bahrain and China reflect distinct legal traditions and frameworks, they converge around the common notion that the public policy exception must be applied sparingly and reserved for only the most serious of violations. The Panel commentators pointed to similar developments in other jurisdictions, where courts and legislatures have shaped the scope of the public policy exception to reflect national interests, yet still with a view to promoting enforcement. In Rwanda, for instance, the legislature has expressly provided that the enforcement of an arbitral award may be refused if it would conflict with 'public security'.[24] Although the term is undefined, it solidifies a national interest as a legitimate constraint on enforcement. It also reflects a broader trend where states integrate domestic concerns into the public policy ground, but generally refrain from invoking them too loosely.

22. Judge Xiangyang *Panel 5: Judging the New York Convention* 26:40.
23. Judge Xiangyang 04:53-05:12.
24. Law No. 5 of 2008 on Arbitration and Conciliation in Commercial Matters, Article 47(2)(b).

Yusuf highlights that elsewhere, courts have interpreted the exception to align with national interests, with direct effect on arbitral awards. For instance, in *Interfood Co v. RCMA*,[25] the Egyptian Court of Cassation reviewed an LCIA award granting 8% interest on the value of invoices and compound post-award interest of 4% from the due date until payment. The Egyptian Civil Code caps interest in commercial matters at 5%. Resultantly, the court held that enforcing the award as rendered would violate Egypt's public policy, and reduced the interest rate to conform with domestic limits. Another example cited by him is Russia, where a court has refused enforcement of an award on the grounds that doing so would harm 'economic welfare.' The court reasoned that enforcing the award would bankrupt the respondent and have a destabilising effect on the regional economy, using public policy as a safeguard against systemic economic disruption.[26]

Judges occupy the fundamental and challenging role of reconciling international obligations with domestic law: a complex and nuanced exercise that demands careful navigation between overlapping and at times conflicting legal norms. Nowhere is this more evident than in the interpretation of open-textured provisions of the New York Convention, such as the public policy exception, which invite judicial discretion and thus variation. This interpretative exercise is inherently influenced by the broader legal culture in which the judge operates as well as her personal sense as to which legal sources are most persuasive.

While national interests naturally feature in this process, they are balanced against coherence across jurisdictions. This harmony enhances legal certainty and, ultimately, access to justice. Some variation is expected and indeed inevitable, but not fatal to the system. As observed by Barton Legum, 'the question, however, is not whether there is perfect consistency, but whether the degree of inconsistent decisions is within the norm of a well-functioning system of administration of justice'.[27] If judges engage in transnational dialogue – implicit or explicit – they can collectively shape a more predictable and principled framework for balancing these competing considerations, furthering the Convention's aim of harmonised and reliable enforcement of arbitral awards.

IV HOW JUDGES NAVIGATE THE BALANCING EXERCISE: A PROPOSAL FOR A FRAMEWORK

So how can judges ensure that the interpretation of the New York Convention remains both harmonious across jurisdictions and compatible with domestic legal standards? Guled Yusuf suggested a two-part approach to reconciling domestic and international considerations, drawing on the Panel discussion. First, courts should identify an *irreducible core* of transnational public policy principles. Any violation of this core

25. *Interfood Co v. RCMA Asia Pte Ltd Singapore*, Egypt Court of Cassation, No. 282/89, 9 January 2020.
26. *United World v. Krasny Yakor*, Federal Arbitrazh Court of the Volgo-Vyatsky Region, Russian Federation, Case No. A43-10716/02-27-10, 17 February 2003.
27. Barton Legum *Panel 5: Judging the New York Convention* 55:55-56:08.

should always render an award unenforceable. Second, for public policy concerns that fall outside this core, domestic courts should be granted a *margin of appreciation*. In these cases, enforcement may only be refused following a structured, proportionate enquiry demonstrating that non-enforcement is necessary to protect legitimate national interests.

With respect to the first category, Yusuf argues that the irreducible core consists of substantive and procedural norms common to most legal systems. This body of law is often referred to as 'transnational public policy', or the public policy component of public international law.[28] Its procedural principles include impartiality of decision-makers, adherence to natural justice, the right to be heard, or equality in the appointment of the arbitrators. Substantive principles commonly referred to by courts include good faith, *pacta sunt servanda*, the prohibitions of abuse of rights, and prohibitions *contra bonos mores* conduct such as piracy, terrorism, genocide, slavery, smuggling, drug trafficking and child exploitation.[29]

Judges Hubail, Prakash and Xiangyang have each identified core principles that have informed their interpretation of the Convention, particularly in complex cases. According to Justice Prakash, an overarching interpretive principle is the need for consistency between domestic and foreign decisions. Judge Xiangyang emphasised the principle of pro-enforcement bias, encapsulated in Article III of the Convention. Judge Hubail in turn referred to the well-established principle of res judicata.

In continuation, Justice Prakash also referred to the principle of *limited judicial review*, noting that Singaporean courts do not re-examine the merits of an arbitral award – even where there may be factual or legal errors. While pro-enforcement bias encourages courts to support and facilitate arbitration, it must be balanced against other equally important principles, such as limited review and res judicata. Thus, the interpretive framework is shaped by a dynamic tension where some principles urge deference to arbitral outcomes, while others caution against unchecked enforcement.

Regarding the second category – the judicial margin of appreciation for public policy exceptions which fall outside the core – this may be interpreted as allowing judges some flexibility in applying the Convention when national and international obligations conflict. Specifically, this would allow judges to still deny recognition and enforcement when a national public policy concern is not clearly recognised at the international level. However, this approach presents significant risks, as it opens the door for individual judges to depart from Convention principles that have been expressly accepted upon accession. Excessive departures from the Convention could dilute its consistent application globally. That said, the Convention's text is broadly worded and provides safeguards against such departures. If judges choose to depart from prevailing trends and issue decisions that fall outside the most common practices, they should ensure that their rulings are grounded in the most fundamental principles.

Ultimately, some cases will continue to challenge the Convention's application and may lead to more refusals to recognise and enforce arbitral agreements and

28. Resolution of the ILA on Public Policy as a Bar to Enforcement of International Arbitral Awards, Arbitration International, vol. 19, No. 2, 1 June 2003, 251-252.
29. ILA Resolution 256.

awards. As discussed by the three judges in the Panel, differences in the processes of incorporation and the influence of the diverging legal cultures lead to variation in how the Convention is applied. Judge Hubail proposed that these variations may be reconciled through the fostering of greater transnational dialogue between judges. Such dialogue could help build greater consensus on two key points – first, the core set of minimum principles underpinning the Convention and, second, the circumstances under which departure from those principles might be justified.

This kind of judicial engagement is increasingly important in times of geopolitical shifts. As Guled Yusuf observed:[30]

> [a] relatively small number of states have served as target rich environments for enforcement – the likes of the US, England, France, or others – and therefore a limited number of individuals have had an outsized role in the interpretation of the New York Convention.
>
> That cast of individuals is due to expand.

With the world economy projected to double by 2050 and six of the world's seven largest economies in 2050 expected to be emerging markets,[31] recognition and enforcement proceedings are likely to become more common in a broader range of jurisdictions. As a result, the profile of judges interpreting the New York Convention will likely diversify, bringing with it the influence of new legal cultures and domestic peculiarities. This shift may bring more decisions, stretching and even redefining previously established concepts. Fortunately, the inherent flexibility of the Convention allows it to evolve alongside changing legal norms. While interpretation will remain a complex and context-dependent task, judicial dialogue offers the promise of greater clarity and harmony, especially around a core set of fundamental principles guiding recognition and enforcement.

V CONCLUSION

'The New York Convention is nothing without judges.'[32] Johnny Veeder's observation resonates powerfully through the reflections of Judges Hubail, Prakash and Xiangyang, each of whom has testified to how the Convention's continued relevance depends not only on its legal text but also on the individuals who interpret and apply it. For these judges, interpretation is not a passive function, but rather a careful balancing act that requires engaging with both international norms and domestic legal principles. The success of the Convention is inseparable from how judges see and carry out their role.

30. Guled Yusuf *Panel 5: Judging the New York Convention* 1:11:34-1:11:54.
31. Guled Yusuf 1:11:54-1:12:08. *See also* PWC Full Report *The World in 2050: The Long View* February 2017, www.pwc.com/gx/en/research-insights/economy/the-world-in-2050.html#downloads (accessed 13 May 2025).
32. Johnny Veeder ICCA Congress Singapore 2012 *Plenary Session D: Judicial Debate on the General Theme: State Courts and International Arbitration: The Future* www.arbitration-icca.org/ICCA-Singapore-2012-video-Plenary-Session-D (accessed 13 May 2025).

The Convention's flexibility has allowed for its broad adoption across jurisdictions but has also produced variations in its application. Whether through its incorporation is through a complete transposition into national law, as in Singapore; alignment via the Model Law, as in Bahrain; or direct treaty application, as in China, each legal system has shaped the Convention through its own lens. This interpretive work is especially visible in the handling of open-textured provisions such as the public policy exception. Rather than an open door to refusal, the judges on this Panel view this exception as a narrow safeguard that helps preserve domestic systems against the most fundamental breaches. At the same time, they have acknowledged that diverging legal cultures and the subjectivity inherent to legal discretion generate challenges in maintaining a harmonious and predictable system.

To reconcile these challenges, the judges and discussants on the Panel have voiced their support for a structured framework that rests, first, on a core set of international public policy principles, such as impartiality, natural justice, and good faith, while allowing for a reasoned margin of appreciation to protect fundamental principles of domestic law. They have also underscored the importance of a continuous judicial dialogue to promote mutual understanding, reduce fragmentation, and build a more harmonised interpretation and application of the Convention. This dialogue is ongoing and is expected to become more globalised. As recognition and enforcement proceedings expand into new and diverse jurisdictions, the interpretive influence of judges from emerging economies will grow, bringing new perspectives and new pressures to the Convention's application. The Convention's flexibility, combined with a shared commitment to principled interpretation, provides a resilient foundation for meeting these challenges.

Ultimately, it is through judges, their views, discretion, dialogue, and sense of duty, that the Convention is kept alive and evolving. Their work is not only legal but also profoundly human, and it is this human engagement that ensures that the New York Convention remains a living instrument, capable of adapting to a changing world while holding firm to its core purpose: reliable and harmonious enforcement of arbitral awards across borders.

PANEL 6

Culture, Localisation and Regionalism

Individuals fashion the culture of international arbitration, often in their own image. This session explores how the professional and personal background of participants in the system affects procedure, advocacy and outcomes, attitudes to foreign law and fact-finding. Are we seeing arbitration conducted in different ways in different parts of the world? Does the harmonisation of processes enhance understanding and effectiveness or mask misunderstanding? How can greater cultural sensitivity and competence be achieved?

CHAPTER 18

Global Harmonization of Arbitration and Respect of Cultural Differences. Comparative Law as Due Process?

Giorgio Fabio Colombo[*]

TABLE OF CONTENTS

I INTRODUCTION: CONTRADICTIONS IN THE WORLD OF ARBITRATION

This chapter needs to start with a disclaimer and spoiler alert: the author is a professor of comparative law professionally involved in international commercial arbitration, and the conclusions of this chapter are that we need more comparative law in arbitration. If this does not sound biased to you, I do not know what could.

This chapter continues research I started a few years ago, under the auspices of the "Decolonizing Arbitration" Unit funded by Nagoya University, and which led to a publication about the importance of diversity in arbitration.[1] It is also the product of a joint research project I am currently conducting together with Joshua Karton. I am

* J.D. equivalent (*Laurea in Giurisprudenza*), Bocconi University Milan; Ph.D. (LL.D.), University of Macerata. Full Professor of Law, Ca' Foscari University Venice. Former Director, Research Unit "Decolonizing Arbitration," Nagoya University. I am grateful to Evgeniya Goriatcheva, Joshua Karton, Sean McGinty, Luke Nottage, Bruno Savoie, and Dai Yokomizo for their comments on the draft and to Hosna Sheikhattar and Mansour Vesali Mahmoud for sharing their research with me.

1. Shahla F Ali et al. (eds.), *Diversity in International Arbitration: Why It Matters and How to Sustain It* (Edward Elgar Publishing 2022).

heavily indebted to Dr. Karton's work, especially with respect to the methodological approach.[2]

The general theme of ICCA 2024 is "arbitration as a human endeavor"; therefore, consistent with that, these short reflections will deal with the actors of the process, the individuals involved in solving disputes by arbitration and in particular the arbitrators.

Before entering the core of this chapter, however, it is necessary to acknowledge that arbitration is currently experiencing heavy criticism from both the legal community at large and the general public. Specifically, arbitration is accused by many (especially outside the restricted circle of scholars and professionals who are deeply involved in the study and practice of arbitral processes) of being yet another form of neo-colonialism. Rather than a neutral tool parties involved in legal disputes use to settle their differences, it is said to be an instrument used by sophisticated multinational companies to take advantage of less skilled parties in the Global South. While this criticism is mostly aimed at *investment* arbitration, *commercial* arbitration is not immune either.[3]

We are currently observing a tension between two opposite forces: on the one hand, the drive toward harmonization; on the other, the resistance to this phenomenon, framed as a form of opposition to legal colonialism. The arbitration community has long focused on a goal of procedural harmonization, with good reason: globally uniform procedures reduce transaction costs, alleviate legal risks, and help parties from different legal cultures to play by the same rules.[4] The widespread adoption of the UNCITRAL Model Law by developing and recently developed jurisdictions is a good example of a positive trend toward homogeneity.

However, the harmonization agenda can conflict with the human character of the arbitral endeavor. With harmonization has come the dominance of a certain procedural style:[5] these days, pretty much everyone arbitrates and pleads as if they were in London or New York or, less frequently, Paris. Harmonization has, in effect, required everyone to conform to a global mainstream that expresses Western ways of doing arbitration and prioritizes Western training and modes of argumentation. Critical legal studies are very good at pointing out the limits of this approach,[6] but the process of providing alternatives is still largely a work in progress. Moreover, local and "traditional" (whatever that means) forms of dispute resolution may reinforce undesirable

2. Joshua Karton, *The Culture of International Arbitration and the Evolution of Contract Law* (1st ed., Oxford University Press 2013); Joshua Karton, "International Arbitration as Comparative Law in Action" (2020) 2020 Journal of Dispute Resolution 293.
3. Maria Laura Marceddu and Pietro Ortolani, "What Is Wrong with Investment Arbitration? Evidence from a Set of Behavioural Experiments" (2020) 31 European Journal of International Law 405 https://doi.org/10.1093/ejil/chaa029 (accessed August 16, 2025).
4. Luke Nottage, "The Procedural Lex Mercatoria: The Past, Present and Future of International Commercial Arbitration (Sydney Law School Research Paper No. 06/51)."
5. Won Kidane, *The Culture of International Arbitration* (Oxford University Press 2017).
6. Mansour Vesali Mahmoud and Hosna Sheikhattar, "A Call for Rethinking International Arbitration: A TWAIL Perspective on Transnationality and Epistemic Community" (2023) Law and Critique https://doi.org/10.1007/s10978-023-09344-7 (accessed August 16, 2025).

intra-cultural practices (such as the dominance of local elites).[7] The fact that the strongest strain of critique to the harmonization agenda comes from the critical theory camp is a problem for us as well. For many people in arbitration, the often hyperbolic and misplaced nature of that critique only serves to reassure arbitration *aficionados* that such opposition can be easily dismissed. Harmonization has been missing so far, an informed, constructive critique from insiders.

To fully appreciate the three-dimensionality of the issue, we also need to address three other contradictions that affect the current study and practice of arbitration.

The first is the conflict between delocalization and the role of applicable law(s).[8] Arbitration has sometimes been defined as a semi-autonomous legal field (a definition borrowed from that used to define legal pluralism).[9] Advocates of the so-called delocalization of arbitration propose a vision under which such tools of dispute resolution should exist in a purely international (or transnational, or a-national) legal environment, where party autonomy rules almost unopposed and the influence of national legislation, if not entirely absent, is at least minimized. Yet we should not forget that arbitration only exists and functions because of the interaction of national laws and international instruments. The domestic legislation of each country still has a fundamental impact on arbitration, and the choice of the seat may radically affect the procedure. Also, commercial arbitration in particular always needs to engage in a productive dialogue with local judicial institutions. An award can only be enforced if a domestic court says so, and interim measures and the summoning of witnesses follow the same pattern. If arbitration is perceived to be "alien" to the local legal system, institutions may react with hostility, thereby jeopardizing the whole process. Scholars and practitioners may criticize decisions incorrectly applying public policy to refuse the enforcement of a foreign award, but unless we are able to engage with actors from different jurisdictions (including non-mainstream), we will not be able to create a productive dialogue.

Second, and partly related to the issue of applicable law, there is the contradiction between party autonomy on the one hand and mandatory rules of the forum on the other. There is often a deep misunderstanding about the extent and boundaries of these two juxtaposed issues. Flexibility and the possibility to tailor the proceedings in ways that the parties deem fit for their specific dispute are indeed some of the best features of arbitration. Yet we should not forget that in this regard party autonomy is not unlimited and needs to yield to mandatory requirements in the applicable law. We may find it bizarre that Ethiopian law requires the presence of two witnesses for the validity of an arbitration agreement,[10] as we may consider anachronistic that in Venezuela the

7. Marc Galanter and Jayanth K Krishnan, "'Bread for the Poor': Access to Justice and the Rights of the Needy in India" (2004) 55 Hastings Law Journal 789.
8. Adam Samuel and Karyl Nairn, "Boundless Arbitration: A Sentimental Voyage through the Delocalization Debate" (2023) 39 Arbitration International 268 https://doi.org/10.1093/arbint/aiad034 (accessed August 16, 2025).
9. John Griffiths, "What Is Legal Pluralism? " (1986) 18 The Journal of Legal Pluralism and Unofficial Law 1 https://doi.org/10.1080/07329113.1986.10756387 (accessed August 16, 2025).
10. Proclamation No. 1237-2021 Arbitration and Conciliation, Working Procedure, 1237–2021. Article 6.

first hearing of a proceeding must be held in person.[11] If these are mandatory requirements, however, we cannot simply brush them away in the name of party autonomy.

On the other hand, however, there is a tendency to overestimate the impact of general rules of civil procedure on arbitration proceedings. It is true that arbitration is governed by the procedural law of the seat, but that of course does not mean that in arbitration we must follow the same patterns or even the same evidentiary rules that we would apply in court (unless, of course, they are *also* mandatory in arbitration). While these observations may indeed sound obvious, even unnecessary, to those with even a cursory experience in arbitration, there is a misplaced tendency for lawyers to import *sic and simpliciter* their judicial practices into arbitral proceedings. Recently before an Italian court a party asked to set aside an arbitral award on the ground that the proceedings did not follow the same hearing pattern they would have taken in court. While the request was—correctly!—dismissed, it is telling that both the parties and the judge had to spend time and effort to deal with such an issue.

The last contradiction we need to explore is a direct consequence of those mentioned so far. On the one hand, cosmopolitan jurists push for the creation of a truly international arbitration praxis, while on the other, lawyers tend to show a resilient path dependency and apply their jurisdiction's rules and usages as the default option. Anybody engaged in international legal education is familiar with the challenges related to the fact that law, to a large extent, is still a domestic phenomenon and is taught and practiced by most jurists as such. One of the most notable consequences of this issue is that, most of the time, attorneys simply "carry over" their domestic training, mindset, and style to arbitration without understanding that what is the norm in their domestic legal environment may be different in international arbitration. Far from being just a question of posture (I am referring here to the famous definition of arbitration as "litigation while seated" offered by some common law practitioners), this may have direct legal consequences. As the arbitration community is aware, it is very difficult to find the correct alchemy between applicable laws, procedural styles, and the needs of international proceedings. Discovery (or disclosure) of documents is not *the* norm; it is *a* norm. Cross-examination is not *the* way; it is *a* way. While of course some practices have—for very good reasons—become the standard in arbitration, it is one thing to adopt them as a conscious, well-reasoned choice by the parties and the arbitral tribunal as the best option for their specific situation. It is however a completely different thing if these practices and styles are used a-critically, under the misconception that they are indeed the only possibility available.

How these contradictions may become issues of due process is fairly evident to any arbitration expert. The specific relevance and role of comparative law as due process and its contribution to solve these problems will be explained in the next paragraphs.

11. James Hosking, Jasmine Lahlou and Giacomo Rojas Elgueta (eds.), "Does the Right to a Physical Hearing Exist in International Arbitration?" in *ICCA Reports no. 10* (2022), p. 14.

II COMPARATIVE LAW AS A DUE PROCESS ISSUE

1 Addressing Comparative Bias in Arbitration

Imagine the following situation: party I from country A and party II from country B have an arbitration with a seat in country A. The arbitral tribunal is composed of a party-appointed arbitrator 1 national of A; a party-appointed arbitrator 2 national of B; and a chair 3 who is a national of country C but also happens to speak the language of country A. In a break during the hearing, 1 and 3 start chit-chatting in the language of A. Party II is furious and sees that as an appearance of bias.

Imagine the same situation, but in this case, A is a common law country and B is a civil law country, and during the break, arbitrator 1 and arbitrator 3 start discussing legal issues only using common law terminology (vested interest, estoppel, etc.). Would that be the same? Arguably, it would. Parties would be left with the impression that the arbitrators would favor a certain way of reasoning, certain legal categories, and perhaps even a specific approach to evidence. We must remember that it is not just the bias, but the *appearance* of bias which matters. These situations can affect a party's subjective perception of the members of the tribunal and their general confidence as to whether it is getting a fair trial.

Already in 1989, prominent commentators argued that "cultural neutrality" should have been a prerequisite, in addition to independence and impartiality, for any arbitrator willing to serve in an international environment.[12] Yet, and somehow unsurprisingly, the definition of culture and neutrality was confined to the divide between common law and civil law. Considering the current landscape, we need to broaden the scope of analysis and resort to comparative law to deal with the issue of multi-culturalism in international arbitration.

The importance of comparative law in arbitration has been recognized by generations of scholars. Already in the 1950s, the great French jurist René David understood that international arbitration is necessarily grounded in comparative law.[13] More recently, Emmanuel Gaillard also explored the issue,[14] and Joshua Karton in 2020 correctly defined international arbitration as "comparative law in action," concluding that "Comparative law reaches its greatest practical extent in the processes and decisions of international arbitral tribunals."[15] I fully agree with these remarks.

The very nature of arbitration requires familiarity with comparative law methodology. When the applicable law is the national law of one of the countries where either party is based, a common situation is that the tribunal will be composed of a sole arbitrator or will be chaired by a chairperson who should be at least knowledgeable with the applicable law, but often will not have received a formal training or

12. Giorgio Bernini, "Cultural Neutrality: A Prerequisite to Arbitration Justice" (1989) 10 Michigan Journal of International Law 39.
13. René David, "Arbitrage et Droit Comparé" (1959) 11 Revue Internationale de Droit Comparé 5 https://doi.org/10.3406/ridc.1959.12217 (accessed August 16, 2025).
14. Emmanuel Gaillard, "Comparative Law in International Arbitration" (2020) 1 Ius Comparatum 1.
15. Karton, "International Arbitration as Comparative Law in Action" (n 2).

qualification in that jurisdiction. Without a proper comparative law training, such arbitrator would be unable to correctly evaluate the situation.

Multilinguism and familiarity with several legal systems are ideal skills for a good arbitrator. I would also add openness to other (legal) cultures to the list.

My mentor Gabriele Crespi Reghizzi once wrote: "if language is the muscle of comparative law, then international commercial arbitration is a sport for comparative lawyers." He furthers elaborates:

> Both in the counsels' arguments [and] in the arbitrators' stances, their respective background appears. Their conceptual and linguistic culture, their different legal trainings, and procedural strategies surface, especially in the inevitable "compromise" which is the arbitration award. The influx of several factors, occasionally undefined or even undefinable—the "cryptotypes" as Rodolfo Sacco would call them—are blended together and sometime they are used as a corrective to the rigidity of national law(s).[16]

Indeed, the "rigidity of national laws" is a key issue. On the one hand, parties want their arbitrators to apply whichever law governs their specific dispute; on the other, however, we cannot forget the "international" nature of arbitration and the importance of *lex mercatoria* in transnational business operations.

Let us deal, therefore, with the role of comparative law in providing the most appropriate solution.

2 The Conundrum of Applicable Law: Comparative Law as the Answer

Should arbitrators apply the law in the same way as a national judge would? Let us take the example of "good faith"—the quintessential "legal irritant" as defined by Gunther Teubner.[17] "Good faith" is a radically different concept under US law, Japanese law, and the CISG. Suppose there is an arbitration seated in New York, with a contract governed by the CISG and, for issues not covered therein, by Japanese law. There is a question about good faith: how should arbitrators proceed with respect to it? If they apply "good faith" under the CISG that would produce a different outcome than if they apply Japanese law. And both the CISG and Japanese law are worlds apart from New York.

In this case, we have guidance in the CISG itself: Article 7 of the Convention reads that "In the interpretation of this Convention, regard is to be had to its international character and to the need to promote uniformity in its application and the observance of good faith in international trade." But this is more easily said than done. In fact, it is exactly one (judicial) case relating to the CISG that has demonstrated how radically different legal cultures may look at the same issue. The Belgian Court of Cassation did not hesitate to claim that hardship and the possibility for a court to adjust the contract

16. Gabriele Crespi Reghizzi, "L'Arbitrato e La Comparazione Giuridica," *Io Comparo, Tu Compari Egli Compara: Che Cosa, Come, Perché?* (Giuffré 2003).
17. Günther Teubner, "Legal Irritants: Good Faith in British Law or How Unifying Law Ends Up in New Differences" (1998) 61 Modern Law Review 11 https://doi.org/10.1111/1468-2230.00125 (accessed August 16, 2025).

are general principles in international law.[18] American scholars did not take it well, with some defining the decision "an aberration."[19]

Lawyers reflect about strategic "comparative law" choices all the time to appoint the more suitable arbitrator for their specific case. Irrespective of the applicable law, if evidence outside a contract may be detrimental to their client's position, they would push for the appointment of an arbitrator from the United States who will most likely take a "four-corners" approach. If such evidence favors their clients, they may want to appoint a Japanese arbitrator, as Japanese law is extremely open to the use of, *e.g.*, negotiation materials or even informal settlement proposals to interpret a contract. While, at least for the time being, arbitrators are humans and as such influenced by their own background, language, culture, and education, I have serious doubts about the correctness of this approach: arbitrators must possess the ability to break free of their legal background. As the arbitration community we shoulder the responsibility and privilege of creating "precedents" valuable for the entire business world. It is highly undesirable that two identical cases would be solved by radically different awards simply because of the background of the arbitrator.[20]

The solution to this problem is to embrace a comparative law approach that may put arbitrators in the position to evaluate the case from an external perspective rather than that provided by their own legal background. There is empirical evidence of this attitude, but it has also been observed that arbitrators tend to rely more on "transnational" or "international" sources rather than the underlying national legal system.[21] While this is not a problem in itself, there is the risk that this approach would replicate dynamics of legal dominance which are at the basis of the establishment of a certain rule or practice as the standard in international arbitration. It would be correct to reconstruct the (most likely) comparative effort that led to the creation of such rule and to evaluate its appropriateness for the specific context.

III COMPARATIVE LAW AS A WAY TO ACHIEVE DIVERSITY

As mentioned above, some common law-derived styles and procedural features have become the standard in international arbitration. The "Americanization" of arbitration has been commented on by very authoritative contributions, and this is not the place

18. Hof van Cassatie van België/Cour de cassation de Belgique, *Scafom International BV v. Lorraine Tubes S.A.S.*, C.07.0289.N (June 19, 2009).
19. Larry A DiMatteo, "Legal Tradition Bias in Interpreting the CISG: Hardship as Case in Point" in Francesca Benatti, Sergio García Long and Filippo Viglione (eds.), *The Transnational Sales Contract: 40 years influence of the CISG on national jurisdictions* (Wolters Kluwer 2022).
20. Maria Chiara Malaguti and Giacomo Rojas Elgueta, "Alcance y fuentes de las expectativas legítimas de los inversores en las sagas de energía renovable españolas e italianas" [2021] Arbitraje. Revista de arbitraje comercial y de inversiones 151 https://doi.org/10.31921/arbitrajeraci.n13.1a2285 (accessed August 16, 2025).
21. Luis Bergolla and Dorothée Goertz, "The Arbitrators' Use of Comparative Law Methodology: A Qualitative Assessment of Selected CAS, ICC, and ICSID Awards" (2020) 1 Ius Comparatum 360.

to reopen the debate.[22] Also, the arbitration community is well aware of the attempted response to this phenomenon: the best example of this backlash against US-style arbitration is embodied in the so-called Prague Rules. Again, this is not the venue to discuss their impact (which, *en passant*, is considered limited at best).[23] It is inevitable to note, however, that the dialogue happens almost exclusively within the boundaries of what the scholars of comparative law call the "Western legal tradition":[24] other legal systems are not considered possible options. This is largely justified for historical and factual reasons: after all, most countries in the world have a system which converges on either the civil law or common law tradition. And yet, this argument must now be critically assessed, considering the serious accusations of neo-colonialism being raised against international arbitration.[25]

The importance of providing culturally sensitive alternatives cannot be underestimated. Scholars who use a critical approach certainly are too often brushed away as if they were advocating the use of village assemblies to resolve complex transnational business disputes. This attitude prevents a constructive debate on the topic.

Some scholars suggest that we should rediscover arbitration *ex aequo et bono* as a solution to due process paranoia and as a tool to open the door to the application of different, more diverse approaches.[26] While I find this perspective intriguing, and while it is indeed necessary to be mindful that the option of *ex aequo et bono* is available and maybe welcomed in some cultural contexts,[27] I am reluctant to fully embrace it. Even setting aside for a moment the uncertainties that an equitable perspective entails, we have seen in the past how "Western" models have been used as synonymous to "natural" justice in legal disputes between the Global North and the Global South.[28]

As the arbitration community, we have other options to implement diversity in the technical process of dispute resolution. I will limit myself to two suggestions.

---

22. *Ex multis*, Eric Bergsten, "Americanization of International Arbitration" (2006) 18 Pace International Law Review 289 https://doi.org/10.58948/2331-3536.1081 (accessed August 16, 2025).
23. Anke Sessler and Max Stein, "The Prague Rules: Problem Detected, but Imperfectly Solved" (2019) 37 Alternatives to the High Cost of Litigation 67 https://doi.org/10.1002/alt.21786 (accessed August 16, 2025); Jung Won Jun, "A Critical Look at the Prague Rules: Rules on the Efficient Conduct of Proceedings in International Arbitration" (2019) 29 Journal of Arbitration Studies 53; Rekha Rangachari and Kabir Duggal, "Different but Similar?: Comparing the IBA Rules on the Taking of Evidence with the Prague Rules" (2021) 37 Arbitration International 631 https://doi.org/10.1093/arbint/aiab026 (accessed August 16, 2025).

    However, some arbitration institutions clearly took example from the Prague Rules to create specific sets of rules suitable for parties used to a civil law style. *See* the JCAA Interactive Arbitration Rules: https://www.jcaa.or.jp/en/common/pdf/arbitration/Interactive_Arbitration_Rules2021_en.pdf?211223 (accessed August 16, 2025).
24. Antonio V Gambaro, "Western Legal Tradition" in Peter Newman (ed.), *The New Palgrave Dictionary of Economics and the Law: Volume 1-3: A-Z* (Palgrave Macmillan UK 2002).
25. Kidane (n 5) 287; Vesali Mahmoud and Sheikhattar (n 6).
26. Nobumichi Teramura, *Ex Aequo et Bono as a Response to the "Over-Judicialisation" of International Commercial Arbitration* (Wolters Kluwer 2020).
27. Or even be the default option. *See, e.g.*, QICCA Arbitration Rules 2012, Article 2.2.
28. Amr Shalakany, "Arbitration and the Third World: A Plea for Reassessing Bias Under the Specter of Neoliberalism" (2000) 41 Harvard International Law Journal 419; Andrea Leiter, *Making the World Safe for Investment: The Protection of Foreign Property 1922-1959* (1st ed., Cambridge University Press 2023) 74-106.

One is the incorporation of cultural requirements into arbitration agreements. The road was definitively opened by the UK Supreme Court in the famous *Jivraj* case,[29] where the Court fully adopted the perspective suggested by the ICC in its written argument in the case:

> The raison d'être of arbitration is that it provides for final and binding dispute resolution by a tribunal with a procedure that is acceptable to all parties, in circumstances where other fora (in particular national courts) are deemed inappropriate (eg because neither party will submit to the courts or their counterpart; or because the available courts are considered insufficiently expert for the particular dispute, or insufficiently sensitive to the parties' positions, culture, or perspectives).[30]

We should therefore evaluate positively arbitration agreements which require arbitrators to possess certain cultural skills. Nobody would object to an agreement asking for a decision-maker with experience with construction contracts in the Middle East. Why should it be different if the requirement would instead ask for knowledge of family business practices in Hong Kong, or the religious conformity of penalty clauses with a specific Islamic school? As arbitrators are under the requirement to accept an appointment only if they possess the competence and preparation necessary to deal with the specific case, the explicit requirement for certain cultural knowledge would result in providing more chance of appointment to arbitrators coming from that specific background, or at least equipped with sufficient methodological (comparative law) tools to properly deal with the matter. For historical reasons, this is already the norm in several sectors, such as the trade of diamonds.[31] Nothing prevents the community from experimenting more in this direction. Arbitration is indeed, to borrow Licari's lexicon, "paideic."[32]

The other immediate suggestion is to create an appropriate training program for arbitrators. In most instances, those occasions showcase an arbitration specialist trained (also) in a common law jurisdiction teaching the American style of arbitration to an audience composed of jurists (mostly practicing attorneys, but often also judges or legislators) from a recently developed country. More rarely, civil lawyers are employed as instructors—even if most countries of the Global South belong to the civil law model.

I have personally been involved as an instructor in several capacity-building projects run by different institutions.[33] The assumption is that learners from developing

29. *Jivraj v. Hashwani* [2011] UKSC 40 (27 July 2011).
30. *Ibid.*
31. Ersoy Zirhlioglu, "The Diamond Industry and the Industry's Dispute Resolution Mechanism" (2013) 30 Arizona Journal of International and Comparative Law 447.
32. François-Xavier Licari, "Beyond Legal Pluralism: Some Thoughts on Paideic Arbitration" in Horatia Muir Watt et al. (eds.), *Global Private International Law: Adjudication without Frontiers* (Edward Elgar 2019).
33. For example, The Law and Justice Commission of Pakistan, Training in International Commercial Arbitration (2019); "Arbitration Workshop: Case Studies & Practice," Commercial Law Development Program, US Department of Commerce, Lao PDR (2023); Joint-Training Program, Supreme Court of Thailand-Nagoya University.

or recently developed countries should learn from instructors from advanced jurisdictions: the opposite is not considered an option. I believe it should be.

The theme of "cultural expertise" is increasingly more important in judicial practices, and it goes both ways.[34] Experts in the field have advised the judiciary in recently developed and transitional countries about, e.g., how to deal with female disputants in contexts where gender inequality is to a large extent inextricable from cultural practices, but they have also trained European judges on how to properly adjudicate family disputes when the court is unfamiliar with the cultural norms in the concerned family. The "cultural expertise" model requires close cooperation between jurists, anthropologists, linguists, and other experts from different social sciences, an interdisciplinary cooperation which, admittedly, makes lawyers uncomfortable. I dare to suggest that cultural sensitization could be an integral part of training programs based on exchange rather than on a unilateral relationship of teacher and learner.

This change in perspective could help alleviate the criticism about the fact that some, otherwise very laudable, initiatives, such as the New York Convention Roadshow, are perceived as providing a "one-size-fits-all" approach and to propagate a neo-colonial agenda. The implementation of cultural training for the trainers will help the image of a fruitful dialogue.

Then, why is comparative law so important in this construction? It is because of the familiarity of comparative jurists with both technical and cultural diversity in arbitration. Without attributing magical powers to comparative law, and mindful of the fact that even leading experts have relatively narrow areas of expertise, scholars and practitioners with a comparative background should know and appreciate the differences between estoppel and good faith; should know that *contract* in English and *contrat* in French are semantically the translation of the same word, but they refer to partly different underlying legal categories; should be aware of the fact that charging interests could be problematic under Islamic law; and should know that non-monetary penalties emphasizing the ethical duty to perform the country are not just embellishments, but in many legal cultures they have a deep significance.

Jurists with a comparative background are also better equipped to deal with perduring cultural stereotypes in law, for example, "legal Orientalism." It is often said that East Asian societies prefer harmonious, non-confrontational ways of dispute resolution. But is that really the case in arbitration? It is also extremely important not to conflate ethnicity or nationality with cultural belonging.

Finally, comparative lawyers normally possess a baggage of language skills that allow them to access sources written in a plurality of languages: this could help creating a *lex mercatoria* that does not only rely on materials in English (or French, or Spanish) but can include several legal traditions.

In a globalized arbitration world, it is very tempting to dismiss whatever happens outside the mainstream as a peculiarity: a background in comparative studies is of great help to appreciate the diversity of legal cultures.

---

34. Livia Holden (ed.), *Cultural Expertise, Law, and Rights: A Comprehensive Guide* (Routledge 2022).

IV CONCLUSION: EMBRACING PLURALISM IN INTERNATIONAL ARBITRATION

The age of the "grand old men" celebrated by "Dealing in Virtue" is long over,[35] and we are currently transitioning from the "pale, male, stale" situation to a genuine embracing of diversity.[36] In this regard, we observe some extremely significant steps toward gender diversity.[37] However, we should expand the notion of diversity to take into account also cultural, ethnical, geographical—perhaps even professional and socio-economic—diversity.[38]

One of the barriers to the enforcement of diversity in arbitration has traditionally been party autonomy. The idea is that parties should be free to appoint whoever they want as their arbitrators, and if they prefer systematically to choose old white men, so be it. However, it is time to reverse this perspective and consider diversity as an *expression* of party autonomy, or even a form of due process. The so-called *Jay-Z* case[39] has framed the problem as such: if a party can find in a list of arbitrators somebody they can relate to in terms of background, ethnicity, culture, etc., and the other party cannot, then it is legitimate to worry about due process and equal treatment of the parties.

In this regard, institutions are already working to provide a diverse list of arbitrators to the parties. Parties on their side may contribute greatly to fostering diversity by drafting arbitration agreements calling for further diversity. And we all should practice the sport of international commercial arbitration embracing a culturally sensitive, comparative mentality.

35. Yves Dezalay and Bryant G Garth, *Dealing in Virtue: International Commercial Arbitration and the Construction of a Transnational Legal Order* (University of Chicago Press 1996).
36. Erin Peters, "Pale, Male, and Stale: Addressing Diversity in Arbitration" (*ADR Research Institute of Canada*, February 22, 2018) https://adric.ca/adr-perspectives/pale-male-and-stale-addressing-diversity-in-arbitration/ (accessed August 16, 2025).
37. For example, the Equal Representation in Arbitration http://www.arbitrationpledge.com/ (accessed August 16, 2025).
38. Joshua Karton, "Diversity in Four Dimensions" in Shahla Ali et al. (eds.), *Diversity in International Arbitration* (Edward Elgar Publishing 2022).
39. *Carter et al v. Iconix Brand Group Inc et al*, New York State Supreme Court, New York County, No. 655894/2018.

Chapter 19

Cultural Incommensurability in International Arbitration: The Case of *Nigeria v. P&ID*

Prof. Won L. Kidane[*]

TABLE OF CONTENTS

I INTRODUCTION

Medical literature is full of studies on the effect of cultural miscommunication between doctors and patients. For example, a random online search of the term "cultural incommensurability" turns up a number of articles in the medical field, and one article published on the National Institute of Health (NIH) website contains the following conclusion: "Various forms of misunderstanding and culturally ignorant practices were found in the treatment of eight Japanese clients by these Western therapists. These ineffective and often harmful practices were unrecognized by the Western therapists."[1]

Not enough effort is made in the legal literature to understand the harmful effects of cultural incommensurability in international arbitration in which almost all players

---

* Professor of Law at the Villanova University School of Law. Partner at ALG, LLP (Washington). Author of The Culture of International Arbitration (OUP, 2017); Africa's International Investment Law Regimes (OUP, 2023), three more books, and more than forty law review articles and book chapters.

1. Yoriko Kozuki and Michael G Kennedy, *Cultural Incommensurability in Psychodynamic Psychotherapy in Western and Japanese Traditions* (2004) available at https://pubmed.ncbi.nlm.nih.gov/15098416/ (accessed August 16, 2025).

regularly come from different cultural backgrounds to resolve complex matters arising out of cross-border economic interactions.

Cultural miscommunication impacts our daily interactions in more profound ways than race, religion, and political opinion. And I would argue that they impact the outcome of serious arbitral proceedings in real and measurable ways.

I will use the recent *Nigeria v. P&ID* case to prove this proposition. This case is a supreme example of how things could go profusely wrong when there is a cultural mismatch between the tribunal and the case that it is supposed to decide. That is what I call cultural incommensurability.

II CASE BACKGROUND

The New York Times Magazine, in an article published on February 9, 2024 - descriptively titled: *How Two Irish Men Almost Took Nigeria for 11 Billion Dollars: A Mundane Contractual Provision Met with Rampant Corruption—Revealing a Serious Vulnerability in One of the Backbones of International Commerce*, says:

> Quinn and Cahill hadn't laid a single pipe for the gas-leaning facility, *but this fact was immaterial.* When the arbitration finished, the government of Nigeria had been thoroughly defeated. The decision was in P.&I.D.'s favor. The damages were $6.6 billion.[2]

Described in layman terms, the article helpfully states:

> And this is where the structure of the deal revealed its true asymmetry. The original contract said that Nigeria had to give P.&I.D. wet gas not for a year or two, but for 20 years. Nigeria had failed to do this. Even though P.&I.D. hadn't yet spent a penny on construction, *Nigerian law—like British law—held that the party who breached a contract had to make the other party whole by paying them the amount they would have made had the contract been fulfilled.* What this meant: When Nigeria paused on the wet gas, a legal wire was tripped. Nigeria owed P.&I.D. for

2. Jesse Barran, *How Two Irish Men Almost Took Nigeria for 11 Billion Dollars: A Mundane Contractual Provision Met with Rampant Corruption—Revealing a Serious Vulnerability in One of the Backbones of International Commerce* (February 9, 2024) available at https://www.nytimes.com/2024/02/09/magazine/nigeria-corruption-michael-quinn-brendan-cahill.html (accessed August 16, 2025).

   P.&I.D. had commissioned a report by a consulting firm, Berkeley Research Group, which laid out estimates of revenue and cash flow if the project had come to fruition. Financiers use something called a "discount rate" to calculate the value of future profits, taking into account all the risks that might be involved. The greater the risk of an investment, the higher the discount rate, and the lower the present-day value. Investments in Nigeria were considered risky because of political instability and corruption, so the standard discount rate at the time was more than 10%; the Berkeley report used 2.6%. On another page of the report, Berkeley predicted that oil—whose price historically correlates with that of natural-gas byproducts—would rise steadily, year after year, to USD 115 a barrel in 2024, but commodity prices fluctuate for all sorts of reasons, and today oil trades for USD 75 a barrel. One lawyer I interviewed, who has handled many investor-state arbitrations, called these calculations "simply primitive" (Berkeley Research Group declined to comment). Nigeria's lawyers tried weakly to whittle it all down, because Quinn and Cahill "had done nothing" yet expected "an income for 20 years," but it didn't persuade Hoffman. Was the contract violated? It was. If so, how much was owed? Hoffman came to a figure: USD 6.6 billion, with interest at 7%, or about a million dollars a day.

> two decades of hypothetical future profits from the sale of gas byproducts they had never processed, in a facility they had never built … .[3]

The New York Times Magazine story has more details than the facts as determined by the Tribunal but is fairly consistent with it. The two investors had extensive experience in Nigeria before they set up P&ID. The article describes it as:

> Quinn and Cahill founded a new company for this purpose and gave it a forgettable name, Process and Industrial Developments Ltd. The two worked out of an office in Abuja, Nigeria's capital. But P.&I.D.'s legal address was a P.O. box on Tortola, in the British Virgin Islands. This could shield the new entity from taxes and scrutiny, while also making it easier to raise capital on the international markets.[4]

The contract is described accurately in layman's terms as follows:

> The next step was to draw a proposal for the Ministry of Petroleum Resources, the department that oversees Nigeria's considerable fossil-fuel reserves. P.&I.D. would construct the $500 million facility. Nigeria would pipe in wet gas at no cost to the company. Then P.&I.D. would process it and pipe out the lean gas at no charge to the country. But in return, the company would retain the valuable byproducts of the gas-leaning process, like propane and butane, which it could sell at a profit. If Nigeria backed out at any point before the full 20-year term of the contract, it could be held liable for damages.[5]

And indeed:

> Days later, a man named Neil Hitchcock—P.&I.D.'s only full-time employee—wrote to Cahill, saying he needed $1.5 million to begin clearing the ground for the facility. But P.&I.D. did not have $1.5 million. The plan had been to raise capital for the project on the basis of the signed 20-year contract, then bring on engineers and laborers. This was how they'd always operated in Nigeria.[6]

These facts were not unknown to the Tribunal. The award of USD 6.6 billion to two businessmen who had no money to invest in the first place is not the reason for the Section 68 review and annulment; it was the fraudulent procurement of the contract in the first place. The arbitrators' decision to award that much money to people who had not invested any money was not even the essential part of the annulment decision although the Honorable Judge Knowles did not fail to mention the illogicity of the rigid adherence to old jurisprudence even when it made no sense.

---

3. *Id.*
4. Jesse Barran, *How Two Irish Men Almost Took Nigeria for 11 Billion Dollars: A Mundane Contractual Provision met with Rampant Corruption—Revealing a Serious Vulnerability in One of the Backbones of International Commerce* (February 9, 2024) available at https://www.nytimes.com/2024/02/09/magazine/nigeria-corruption-michael-quinn-brendan-cahill.html (accessed August 16, 2025).
5. *Id.*
6. *Id.*

III CULTURAL INCOMMENSURABILITY RELATIVE TO MATTERS OF SUBSTANCE

The most interesting question in this case is not the law, or facts or even the pervasive corruption: *what is most interesting is the question of why Lord Lenord Hoffman and Sir Anthony Evans, two of the most preeminent jurists of our time, jointly sanctioned a facially unreasonable and objectively implausible outcome?* I don't think the blind-folded goddess of adversarial justice would have congratulated this decision as a model of justice.[7]

So, why did they decide the way they did over the objection of the Nigerian-appointed Nigerian arbitrator Chief Bayo OJO? I argue that the result was a function of cultural incommensurability: the majority's misunderstanding of the essence of the Parties' agreement, and in particular, Nigeria's understanding of what it agreed to.

Consider the interesting cultural exchange during oral hearing between Nigeria's counsel, Nigerian-appointed arbitrator and the chair of the Tribunal, Lord Hoffman:

> (2) *If the Tribunal's conclusion on liability was correct, how did Nigeria come to agree a GSPA in such catastrophic terms?* The Tribunal's finding was that the Government's obligations under Article 6 (b) were not conditional upon P&ID having constructed the GPFs. How did Nigeria come to allow itself to agree obligations that were not conditional in that way, especially where, as the Tribunal itself said, reflecting a submission of Mr Shasore: "*Of course the Government could not actually deliver gas until there was a Site and, as we have said, until there was a plant to receive it.*"

Judge Knowles further observed: "*I admit that I do not find it easy to follow, even in the classic setting of one party having accepted as repudiatory the conduct of another, how the Tribunal identified the sequencing of obligations with the apparent confidence it did.*"[8]

The Contract selected Nigerian law as the law governing the contract, and Nigeria admitted during oral argument that the governing contract law rule comes from *Hardley v. Baxandel.*[9] The Tribunal applied the *Hadley v. Baxandel* rule. The essence of *Hadly v. Baxendale* (1854) is the following:

---

7. Adriano Prosperi, *Justice Blindfolded: The Historical Course of an Image* (2018). Translated by John Tedeschi and Anne C. Tedeschi. ("Justice: a system of laws and courts, a complicated institutional arrangement of men, of powers and of roles, a complex machine where rituals rich with tradition and rational, continually updated norms define crime and punishment—all of it summed up in the feminine image which holds a scale in one hand and a sword in the other. The sword is in itself a threat, but even the scale is worrying: one can be weighed there." p. 2.)
8. *Nigeria v. P&ID*, EWHC 2638, Judgment (2023), para. 313.
9. *Id.*, para. 359 ("Lord Hoffmann asked whether para. 18.1 of P&ID's written submissions "correctly set out the law." The paragraph read: "the Claimant is entitled to be placed, so far as money can do it, in the same position as he would have been in had the contract been performed." This sequence followed: "CHIEF AYORINDE: Yes, my Lord. Paragraph 18(1) states the law under the ambit of the locus classicus, the *Hadley v. Baxendale case*. However, my Lord, that case also says that it is ***what is in the contemplation of the parties.*** Therefore, my Lord, at the time of the breach—in *Hadley v. Baxendale* my Lord, and your Lordship has that in your Lordship's bosom, the facts and what happened in that case—THE CHAIRMAN: It must have been in the contemplation of the parties that if you didn't give them any gas, they wouldn't be able to make

> Contract damages are only recoverable for a loss from breach reasonably foreseeable or *actually foreseen* by the defendant. The Rule of Hadley v. Baxendale, 9 Ex. 341, 156 Eng. Rep. 145 (1854), is sometimes stated as two rules and sometimes as one. As two rules, they are: First, a plaintiff may only recover damages that are the natural result of the defendant's breach. Second, the plaintiff may only recover damages from *such losses as both parties might reasonably have expected at the time they entered the contract to have resulted later from a breach.* As a single rule, it is: *A plaintiff may only recover damages that were the natural consequence of the breach that the defendant should reasonably have expected to follow from it.*[10]

The key substantive question for the Hoffmann Tribunal was then what they thought that Nigeria should reasonably have expected. Whose standard should they apply?

IV CULTURAL INCOMMENSURABILITY RELATIVE TO MATTERS OF PROCEDURE

Judge Knowles expressly acknowledged: *"[y]et there was not a fair fight."* And the Tribunal took a very traditional approach. But was the Tribunal stuck with what parties did or did not appear to bring forward? Could and should the Tribunal have been more direct and interventionist?[11] Indeed, the Tribunal's "traditional approach" in both substance and process is the USD 11 billion dollar question. The Court's conclusion is frightening: *"But the fact is that the Arbitration was a shell that got nowhere near the truth."*[12]

But what should have the Tribunal done?

A relatively recent IBA Report captures a discussion by some of the leading authorities in the field about the role of the arbitrators:

> *Arbitration is a consensual process and once the rules of engagement are set in the arbitration agreement it is for the parties to participate in the manner they agreed.* To provide protections in the event of inattention or neglect from one party or the other would be to ignore this fundamental premise.[13]

Not infrequently is the cultural ignorance of the arbitrators perceived as inattention or negligence of the Parties' representatives or counsel. In this case, Judge Knowles found that the arbitral *"Awards were obtained by fraud and the Awards were*

---

any NGLs. CHIEF AYORINDE: Yes, my Lord. My Lord, at that point if we didn't give them any gas, they had nothing to receive the gas in order to make the profit in the billions. THE CHAIRMAN: That's correct")

10. Stephen Michael Sheppard, *Bouvier Law Dictionary Hadley v. Baxendale Rule, Hadley v. Baxendale Rule,* The Wolters Kluwer Bouvier Law Dictionary Desk Edition.
11. *Nigeria v. P&ID,* EWHC 2638, Judgment (2023), para. 588.
12. *Id.,* para. 580.
13. James Rogers is a partner at Jenner & Block, London, *A Case for the Arbitration Community to Reflect,* The Law Society Gazette, at last paragraph (October 27, 2023) available at https://www.lawgazette.co.uk/commentary-and-opinion/a-case-for-the-arbitration-community-to-reflect-on-nigeria-v-pandid/5117702.article?utm_source = gazette_newsletter&utm_medium = email&utm_campaign = Axiom + Ince& (accessed August 16, 2025).

the way in which they were procured was contrary to public policy."[14] Meaning that the arbitrators themselves were victims of fraud but they did not understand it. They kept themselves ignorant depending entirely on the Parties' submissions. That is a matter of legal culture.

V CONCLUSION

The Tribunal in the *Nigeria v. P&ID* case is thus a great example of the unquestioning fidelity to the common law and the adversarial judicial culture, which led to a clearly unreasonable result. The Tribunal was culturally incommensurate. The key message is thus in constituting tribunals all concerned must always consider the cultural suitability of the members of the tribunal in all cases involving culturally diverse parties.

14. *Nigeria v. P&ID*, EWHC 2638, Judgment (2023), para. 360.

CHAPTER 20

The Influence of Cultural Differences Between East and West on Dispute Resolution

Fei Lu[*]

TABLE OF CONTENTS

I INTRODUCTION

With the rapid development of the Belt and Road Initiative (BRI), trade and investment are boosted along the Belt and Road, which would lead to the increase of disputes unsurprisingly. As the legal environment along the Belt and Road is special and diversified, the related dispute settlement can be very complex. To deal with the complexity in the dispute resolution process, an important factor to be considered and addressed, *inter alia*, is the influence of cultural differences because cultural issues are the result of underlying differences related to the accumulation of deep-rooted beliefs and behaviors that a person is accustomed to, and a person's world view could have an

* Director of Business Development Division of China International and Economic Trade Arbitration Commission (CIETAC).

significant impact on the outcome of international arbitration.[1] If the party in the arbitration encounters unexpected cultural influence and especially when such influence drives an outcome that is unpopular with the party, dissatisfaction may be caused toward the procedure.[2] They may feel unfairly treated during the proceedings and have a bad experience of "subjective procedural justice."[3] Members of the same culture are usually able to reach a consensus on the connotation of procedural justice; in contrast, people who form their own inherent values in different cultural contexts inevitably have different understandings of subjective procedural justice in the same dispute resolution process. In the Belt and Road disputes, each of the parties, the members of arbitral tribunal, and the representatives of the parties involved in the procedure might come from different circles of cultures—some are uncrossed and some overlapped, making the dispute resolution process rather complex. Therefore, this chapter aims to explore the aspects that the cultural difference will have an obvious influence over the dispute resolution, to provide reference for and raise the awareness of the procedural participants in the proceedings. And as a person who has worked in a Chinese arbitration institution which deals with both domestic and international cases, the author will mainly focus on the unique feature of Eastern, especially Chinese, culture, and show how they influence the subjective evaluation of procedural justice in various aspects of cross-border dispute resolution procedures.

II CHARACTERISTICS OF EAST ASIA AND CHINESE LEGAL CULTURE

In fact, the concept of "East and West" is developed under the context of the binary opposition thinking pattern.[4] Since there has not yet been a consensus on the definition of "East and West" in consideration of its rich connotation, it is necessary to clarify that the West in this chapter refers to countries represented by U.S. and Europe, while the East is confined to East Asia.

It is undeniable that East Asian countries, represented by China, have been deeply influenced by East Asian law based on Confucian culture, especially the concept of harmonious law. After Western civilization was introduced in East Asia in modern times, Eastern and Western legal cultures went through sharp conflicts and then gradually began to integrate. Throughout its long history of development, the East

1. *See* Mary Howard, International Arbitration and Cross-Cultural Issues, in Stavros Brekoulakis (ed.), Arbitration: The International Journal of Arbitration, Mediation and Dispute Management, Kluwer Law International 2020, Vol. 86, No. 3, p. 332.
2. *See* Patrick Taylor, Shreya Aren, et al., Chapter 4: Harmonising Cultural Differences in International Arbitration: The Role of Parties' Reasonable Expectations and Counsel's Ethical Rules, in Axel Calissendorff and Patrik Schöldström (eds), Stockholm Arbitration Yearbook 2020, Kluwer Law International 2020, Vol. 2, p. 5.
3. *See* Liming Liu, A Jurisprudential Study of Subjective Procedural Justice, Doctor's Thesis of Nanjing Normal University, 2021, p. 16.
4. *See* Feng Zhang, Civilizations Learning from Each Other-Cultural Differences and the Unique Values of Eastern Cultures, Cultural Studies and Literary Theory, No. 2, 2023, p. 79.

Asian legal culture, has become a unique branch in the world's legal system with strong Confucian legal culture as the main feature.[5]

Despite that the legal traditions of East Asia have undergone different changes in different countries since modern times, the present regional laws in East Asia have certain similarities and convergences.[6] Those similarities or convergence in legal cultures includes the important role of customs and traditions, the inclination to value the community over individuals, the administrative system grown on autocracy, and the extensive participation of rural communities in the judicial activities, etc.[7] These commonalities make the legal and cultural systems of East Asia different from those of the Western countries. In traditional East Asian legal culture, the practice of "rule of virtue," or "prevent-litigation" is highly recommended and "no litigation" is the ideal. People regard no-litigation as a virtue, considering litigation to be shameful.[8] Compared with the Western legal culture, the Eastern legal culture emphasizes more on public interests and personal obligations, harmonious interpersonal relations, the comprehensive use of multiple dispute resolution mechanisms, and the stability and harmony of the social order. In China, for example, the culture of avoiding litigation has a long history, and when faced with a conflict, most people will hold the mentality that the less trouble the better, and take litigation as only a last resort.[9]

III ILLUSTRATION OF THE INFLUENCE OF EAST-WEST CULTURAL DIFFERENCES IN THE PROCESS OF DISPUTE RESOLUTION

1 Influence of Cultural Differences on Evidence Production

The conflict of evidence systems has been an area that is relatively controversial among countries. It is actually the game of legal cultures behind the scene. How to balance the conflicting legal cultures has undoubtedly become one of the key issues in handling evidence in international commercial arbitration.[10] The position of evidence in dispute resolution procedures is very important because it can reveal the background facts of the dispute. Unless there are special restrictions, the parties to the disputes, regardless of their cultural backgrounds, tend to use various techniques and skills of litigation to

5. *See* Yujun Feng, On the Ideal Prospect of Rule of Eastern Asia Common Law, Journal of HIT (Social Sciences Edition), Vol. 17, No. 1, January 2015, p. 27.
6. *See* Jinfan Zhang, Fresh Discussion of Chinese Legal Genealogy, Journal of Nanjing University (Philosophy, Humanities and Social Sciences) No. 1, 2017, p. 122.
7. *See* Pixiang Gong, The Logic Inherent in the Legal Culture of Traditional Eastern Societies-Theoretical Explorations in Marx's Later Years, Science of Law, No. 1, 1994, pp. 3-9.
8. *See* Shihao Hu, A "Chinese Solution" for a Pluralistic Dispute Resolution Mechanism, China Review of Administration of Justice, No. 3, 2017, p. 44.
9. *See* Zihan Feng, Study on the Localization and Internationalization of Chinese Commercial Arbitration under the Perspective of Cultural Differences-Taking the Arbitration Law as an Example, She Hui Ke Xue Dong Tai, No. 9, 2020, p. 85.
10. *See* Qifan Cui, Evidence in International Commercial Arbitration, Doctor's Thesis of East China University of Political Science and Law, p. 1.

gain an upper hand and advantages in the proceedings. This "competitive" model will naturally lead to certain malpractice such as surprise attacks of evidence.[11]

In response to this problem, the United Kingdom and the United States established the discovery system in civil proceedings in the 19th century to collect and fix evidence. Although there are arguments as to whether the U.S. judicial practice of discovery is applicable to international commercial arbitration,[12] in general, the legal culture of discovery of evidence is more familiar to lawyers and legal practitioners trained in the common-law system, who are, as a result, more inclined to responding to the discovery of evidence in international commercial arbitration. On the contrary, in East Asia, there is no such provision on the discovery of evidence in its legal culture for the time being, and it is rarely explicitly established by the laws of those countries. As a result, parties or lawyers from East Asian legal cultures may take evidence ambush as a technique in the dispute resolution proceedings. In the process of forming the procedural justice values, people believe that "compliance with the rules has its own value."[13] Nevertheless, for people trained under East Asian legal culture, there is no clear rule that they need to disclose evidence as what is taught in common-law systems. Therefore, on the issue of evidence production, the parties from different legal cultures cannot have empathy on the procedural justice. That is to say, when a Western attorney discovers that an East Asian attorney has conducted an evidentiary ambush, he or she may feel that such conduct is a violation of the rule.

Because of China's historical and cultural background, many commercial arbitrations conducted in China have serious "dependence" in terms of the evidence system—the establishment and application of the evidence system is to a large extent similar to the litigation evidence system and the court proceedings.[14] It is also rare that evidence rules are provided in the arbitration rules of international arbitration institutions until recently China International Economic and Trade Arbitration Commission (CIETAC) in its new CIETAC Arbitration Rules 2024 stipulates in Article 41 that the arbitral tribunal may decide to apply in whole or in part the CIETAC Guidelines on Evidence (Guidelines on Evidence) to hear the case. To expressly provide that certain evidence rules may be applied in the arbitration proceedings should be the first of its kind in China.[15] The CIETAC Guidelines on Evidence, effective as from January 1, 2024, explains in its Preamble that the guidelines are made "in accordance with the Arbitration Law of the People's Republic of China, the CIETAC Arbitration Rules,

11. *See* Xianhua Xia, Inspection and Enlightenment of Civil Evidence Discovery System in Anglo-American Law System, Journal of Hunan University of Technology (Social Science Edition), Vol. 24, No. 4, August 2019, p. 119.
12. *See* Shancong Song, Experiences and Insights from the Application of the United States Courts' Discovery Assistance Regime to International Commercial Arbitration, Commercial Arbitration & Mediation, No. 6, 2022, p. 32.
13. *See* Liming Liu, p. 23.
14. *See* Yuanzheng Hou, On the Perfection of the Evidence Presentation and Recognition System in Chinese Arbitration, Southwest University of Political Science and Law, LLM Specialized Dissertation, 2022, p. 12.
15. *See* Wei Zhang, Breakthrough in Change: Revising Arbitration Rules to Effectively Respond to the Needs of the Times: Interview with Wang Cheng, Deputy Chairman and Secretary General of CIETAC, Legal Daily, 26 September 2023: https://www.moj.gov.cn/pub/sfbgw/fzgz/fzgzgg flfwx/fzgzggflfw/202309/t20230926_486962.html, last visited date on April 14, 2024.

CIETAC's arbitration practice, and with appropriate reference to the IBA Rules on the Taking of Evidence in International Arbitration as well as those of the Chinese principles of evidence in civil litigation that are suitable for use in arbitration."[16] Article 5 of the Guidelines on Evidence provided a time period for the submission of evidence, and specially limited the deadline for submission and exchange of evidence such that it "shall in principle be completed before the Tribunal's oral hearing on the merits," which would in fact prevent the evidence ambush that is often seen in the arbitration proceedings in China.

Other than the different conception on evidence production between the East and West, it is also found in practice that some companies in East Asia seldom keep documentary evidence in their business dealings,[17] which may affect the adequacy and completeness of the evidence presented in the dispute resolution proceedings.

2 The Influence of Cultural Difference on Hearing Modes

The government-led authoritarianism is widely prevalent among China, Japan and South Korea.[18] Take China as an example, it has long been influenced by feudal rule and lacks the local arbitration system spontaneously formed by the business society. Arbitration was not transplanted to China until the late Qing Dynasty, and was established in accordance with the logic of government-led "top-down" mode.[19] Such historical background has led to a strong administrative color of arbitration in China, which is reflected in the hearing as the obvious imitation of court proceedings.[20] This has led to the fact that Chinese arbitrators tend to be more inquisitorial in the hearing, while it is known that adversarial and inquisitorial styles of hearings have their own focuses.[21]

In addition, the practice of combining arbitration and mediation is highly accepted in East Asian legal systems,[22] but is generally viewed as questionable in common-law jurisdictions. Such divergence is mainly caused by the Western concern that the switching identities between the mediator and the arbitrator in the med-arb process can lead to certain legal risks. Article 51 of the Arbitration Law of the People's

16. Guidelines on Evidence is accessible via official website of CIETAC: http://www.cietac.org.cn/index.php?m = Page&a = index&id = 68, last visited on April 14, 2024.
17. *See* Philip Yang, The Cultural Influences on Maritime Arbitration, Chinese Journal of Maritime Law, Vol. 23, No. 4, 2012, p. 108.
18. *See* Xiaohu Zhang, A Test of Law in Communalities in East Asia: The Past, Present and Future of the "Supranational Law," Studies in Foreign Legal History, No. 15, 2012, pp. 140-167.
19. *See* Yi Fang, A Study on the Return Path of Arbitration Institutions to Nongovernmental Nature, Min Jian Fa. Vol. 31, No. 1, 2023, p. 141.
20. *See* Yi Fang, p. 144.
21. *See* Patrick Taylor and Shreya Aren et al., pp. 43-64; *See also* Julian D.M. Lew and Simona Valkova, Chapter 1: Cultures and the Taking of Evidence, in Franco Ferrari and Friedrich Jakob Rosenfeld (eds), Handbook of Evidence in International Commercial Arbitration: Key Concepts and Issues, Kluwer Law International 2022, pp. 3-22.
22. *See* Yuhong Chai, International Civil Dispute Resolution Mechanisms in East Asia: A Combined Arbitration and Mediation Dispute Resolution System as a Medium, International and Comparative Law Review, 2021, pp. 227-233.

Republic of China is a clause with "Chinese characteristics," which combines mediation and arbitration, putting the mediation procedure before the arbitral award is made, and gives the mediation statement made by the arbitral tribunal the same legal effect as the arbitral award. These provisions are different from the international legal culture of arbitration, and there are no similar provisions in the UNCITRAL Model Law or in the arbitration rules of international arbitration institutions outside of China.

Practically, in many CIETAC arbitration cases, the arbitral tribunal will ask the opinion of both parties whether they are willing to have mediation during or at the end of the hearing. If the parties agree, the arbitral tribunal will act in the middle and make efforts to mediate for the two sides to reach a settlement. As the arbitral tribunal, after hearing the case, has a better understanding of what happened between the parties and knows clearly the concerns of each party, the chance that the mediation is successful is rather high. The consent award based on the parties' settlement agreement made by the tribunal, as is agreed and accepted by both parties, is easier to be performed or enforced. In this way, the peaceful resolution of the dispute once and for all is valued and favored by the Chinese can be achieved. Even if the mediation is unsuccessful, according to the CIETAC arbitration rules, the process of mediation is not recorded and statements made in the process cannot be invoked by the parties or the arbitral tribunal in any proceedings. Unless agreed by the parties, there is also no need to constitute a new arbitral tribunal to start the procedure all over after the unsuccessful mediation, which guarantees the efficiency of the procedure and the expectations of the parties are not affected.

3 Influence of Language Differences in International Arbitration

Language has a profound effect on legal thinking, and the law must rely on language, especially legal language to work well.[23] In international commercial arbitration, appropriate arbitration language further ensures the accuracy of the communication and presentation of the parties.[24] It has been observed that many Korean companies tend to begin their correspondence with the words "We wish your company prosperity," even in legally hostile relationships. For companies in other cultures, however, this may be perceived as ironic.[25]

In an arbitration case handled by the author, there was also an example of an unsuccessful cross-examination process conducted by the arbitration representative because of cultural difference and language barrier. This is a case from many years ago between a Chinese party and a French party. English was the language agreed in the

23. *See* Wuhan Zhang, Language and Law: Cognitive Transmutation from Instrumentalism to Ontology, Hebei Law, No. 7, 2010, p. 161.
24. *See* Yufan Wang, Study on Language Issues in International Arbitration, Human resources and social security of Heilongjiang, No. 141, 2021, p. 76.
25. *See* Alison Ross: Lost in translation?, in GAR, November 2010, also available via https://globalarbitrationreview.com/article/lost-in-translation, last visited on April 15, 2024.

arbitral clause. The Presiding Arbitrator was from the United States, and cross-examination procedure for the witnesses was arranged. The Chinese lawyer representing the Chinese party had to question the witness of the counterparty, a practice he was not familiar with nor trained on. As he did not speak English, he had to resort to an interpreter to translate his questions to the witnesses. The Chinese lawyer raised circuitous questions for the purpose of trapping the witness, but unfortunately the translator was confused by those expressions and missed a lot of important information in the process of translation. In the end, the meaning conveyed to the witness was far different from the original meaning, and of course, the answer would by no means meet the lawyer's expectation. In cross-examination, although the lawyer and the witness are talking about the same topic, their intentions and purposes are different, and the purpose drives the speaker to make choices about the form and focus of the discourse. This process is highly dynamic and cannot be separated from the meta-pragmatic awareness of both parties, and meta-language belongs to the realm of consciousness, which occurs prior to making linguistic choices,[26] and is an expression of the speaker's subconscious. If an unfamiliar language is used to express the original meaning, misunderstandings may occur.

Communication style can be divided into two main categories: low-context and high-context, and the differences between them are stark. In high-context cultures (particularly in Asia, and may also be found in some African cultures and in Latin America and Latin Europe), messages are conveyed by implication and require the listener to read between the lines of what is said to discern the speaker's true meaning, whereas in the low-context cultures (principally the United States, and other Anglo-Saxon cultures), the communication is expected to be literal and explicit.[27] In the above case, difference between the "low-context" and "high-context" communication styles also has an impact on the cross-examination of the witnesses. China, Japan and Korea are all high-context countries;[28] misunderstandings may happen when people in high-context cultures talk to people in low-context cultures in the West. For instance, between the East and the West, low-context texts convey information through literal meanings and rarely require cultural interventions from the translator,[29] whereas the East Asian cultures make the connotations conveyed by the East Asian speakers more culturally demanding for the translators. This also explains why the loss of information occurs when the translator translated the Chinese lawyer's circuitous questions.

The subjective procedural justice felt by the Chinese lawyers in the above case must have been reduced, because every participant in the process would want to have

26. *See* Yanzi MA and Lingling GE, Pragmatic Ambiguity and Functional Analysis of Cross-Examination, Journal of Nanhua University (Social Science Edition), Vol. 7, No. 5, 2006, pp. 92-95.
27. *See* Philippa Charles, Chapter IV: Science and Arbitration, The Hofstede Dimensions in International Arbitration: How Understanding National Characteristics Improves Arbitral Harmony, in Christian Klausegger and Peter Klein et al. (eds), Austrian Yearbook on International Arbitration 2020, Vol. 2020, pp. 489-491.
28. *See* Michael Leathes, Chapter 4: Culture, in Michael Leathes (ed.), Negotiation: Things Corporate Counsel Need to Know but Were Not Taught, Kluwer Law International 2017, pp. 67.
29. *See* Pengcheng Fan, Étude sur la Traduction sous l'Angle du Contexte Culture, Master's Thesis of Beijing Foreign Studies University, p. 12.

"meaningful participation," or more specifically, to "control the process," which of course does not mean to directly manipulate the process, but rather to indirectly control or influence the outcome after conveying "individualized information" that they consider important.[30] It is clear, however, that because of the distortion of language in the translation, the cross-examination did not give them a sense of control over the program and the resulting satisfaction of meaningful participation. Thus, differences in language, coupled with differences in culture, can have a significant impact on the cross-examination of witnesses in dispute resolution proceedings.

4 Impact of Different Modes of Thinking on Dispute Resolution

International arbitration frequently involves parties from different social cultures negotiating and agreeing on the terms of international arbitration. Generally speaking, westerners mainly believe in Christianity, advocate individual heroism, so in the negotiation process they tend to get straight to the point and put first what they are most interested in as an entry point, whereas they pay less attention to the non-focused issues including rigid rules and regulations; on the contrary, East Asians usually adopt holistic decision-making behavior, taking a holistic view of the negotiation process, strictly implementing each step of the whole negotiation process, and generally placing important negotiation goals in the last step. Due to the differences in negotiation styles and decision-making methods between the East and the West, their concerns do not concur; thus, the timing for reaching an agreement may be easily missed.[31] For example, there can be different understanding as to the action of signing a document. During his trip to Europe, the Chinese party signed a document which he regarded as only a step in the negotiation and proof that he had gone to Europe, whereas the European party regarded it as an act of agreeing to an invitation to offer.[32]

The interest of Eastern and Western parties in the dispute resolution proceedings is divided. Western parties may have a primary interest in compensation, whereas parties from East Asian cultures may just value relationship maintenance, with compensation being a secondary consideration.[33] For East Asian countries, including China, relationship is more a way of life and is therefore a way of business. In fact, relationship is a direct manifestation of high-context cultures.[34]

The arbitrator, as the decision-maker, is also inevitably influenced by the culture of the place he/she comes from. Arbitrators with different cultural backgrounds often make different judgments when they are faced with the same piece of evidence. For example, in an international arbitration case accepted by CIETAC, the parties disputed whether there existed fraudulent book-keeping by the Respondent for wedding banquets and group dinners. The claimant argued that this was forged information, as it

30. *See* Liming Liu, p. 52.
31. *See* Yan'an Si, Strategy Selection, Impact and Countermeasures in International Business Negotiations from the Perspective of Cultural Differences, Journal of Hubei University of Economics (Humanities and Social Sciences), Vol. 18, No. 2, p. 41.
32. *See* Philip Yang, p. 109.
33. *See* Harold Abramson, pp. 307-308.
34. *See* Michael Leathes, pp. 69.

contained many additional items to the set list of orders. The arbitral tribunal in this case consisted of two non-Chinese mainlanders (including the presiding arbitrator) and one Chinese mainland arbitrator. On this issue, the Presiding Arbitrator found that the large discrepancy between the list of orders and the actual spending incurred was indeed improper, and therefore supported the claimant's claim on this point, finding that the large amount of spending in excess of the set list of orders was not a normal situation.

The Chinese mainland arbitrator, on the contrary, believed that in wedding banquets or group dinner, the set menu might not satisfy the actual dietary needs of the guests, and it is normal in some Chinese wedding banquets or group dinners that the guests will order additional items with the consent of the host and thus make the real consumption exceeding the initial set list of orders. The Respondent may feel the findings of the Presiding Arbitrator on this issue dissatisfactory and even biased as it is out of different understanding by people with different cultural backgrounds. In international commercial arbitration, if a party gets a favorable result, his satisfaction toward the procedural justice is naturally high. However, if the result is not in his favor, and especially if there are different perceptions due to different cultural phenomenon, the subjective evaluation of procedural justice will be even lowered because he would think that he has not been treated "heart to heart" with empathy.

There are similar examples in international investment arbitration, when the cultural background of the arbitrator is different from that of the parties, resulting in different factual findings. For example, there exist divided perceptions as to the nature of private donations, i.e., whether private donations should be recognized as a bribe or a diplomatic courtesy.[35]

IV IMPACT OF CULTURAL DIFFERENCES ON DISPUTE RESOLUTION ALONG THE BELT AND ROAD

China's BRI starting from 2013 has gradually developed into the largest international cooperation platform.[36] The BRI covers 152 countries in different regions and countries.[37] In 2023, China's imports and exports with the Belt and Road countries amounted to RMB 19.47 trillion, a year-on-year increase of 2.8%, accounting for 46.6% of China's total foreign trade value.[38] With the gradual deepening of trade, the demand for cross-border commercial dispute resolution is also growing, and harmonizing the different legal cultures along the Belt and Road has become one of the biggest

35. *See* Hongwu Yin, p. 57.
36. *See* Haitao Du, Xiang Lee and Shanshan Luo, Overview of General Secretary Xi Jinping's Important Discussions on Building the Belt and Road Together, People's Daily, October 16, 2023: https://www.gov.cn/yaowen/liebiao/202310/content_6909316.htm, last visited on April 14, 2024.
37. *See* the official website of Belt and Road Portal: https://www.yidaiyilu.gov.cn/country, last visited on April 14, 2024.
38. *See* The Information Office of the State Council of People's Republic of China: https://www.gov.cn/lianbo/fabu/202401/content_6925700.htm, last visited on October 10, 2025.

challenges in cross-border dispute resolution. The BRI covers a wide range of geographic regions, including East Asia, South Asia and Central Asia, as well as three different legal systems, namely, common law, civil law and Islamic law, and there are huge social, cultural, racial and religious differences among the countries and regions.[39]

For instance, ASEAN countries have similar cultures as China. They are also influenced by traditional Confucian culture, with a high degree of centralization of decision-making power, while the Commonwealth of Independent States and Central and Eastern European countries along the Belt and Road are the opposite.[40] Central Asia has Turkic-Islamic culture, which is a kind of Islamic culture with Central Asian Turkic color,[41] and has long been influenced by Chinese traditional culture from the East before it was conquered by Arabs from the West.[42]

As a result, the conflict of cultures must be found easily in the dispute resolution procedures among the participants from different Belt and Road countries and regions. It is customary for an American lawyer to present a "draft award" to a Middle Eastern arbitrator prior to the commencement of the arbitration; however, it is highly likely that an arbitrator trained in a civil law system regards the American lawyer's behavior as completely strange or even inappropriate.[43] In Egypt, for instance, the award may be annulled for failure of the witness to observe the state rules on oaths.[44] The above-mentioned scenarios well illustrate the complicated conflict of legal cultures among regions along the Belt and Road. It is necessary to look into the cultural differences of those countries and regions, establish dispute resolution mechanisms suitable for them to increase the parties' evaluation of the procedural justice, so as to resolve the Belt and Road disputes effectively and properly.

In fact, there have been a series of measures taken to improve the dispute resolution mechanism along the Belt and Road by relevant Chinese organs, including measures to enhance understanding among countries and regions along the Belt and Road. For example, the Supreme People's Court of the People's Republic of China set up the First and Second International Commercial Courts in Shenzhen and Xi'an on the basis of the First and Sixth Circuit Courts, respectively, in June 2018, and incorporated a number of international commercial arbitration institutions and international commercial mediation institutions into the "one-stop" platform in November 2018, building up a diversified mechanism for international commercial disputes that effectively

39. *See* Weixia Gi, China's Belt and Road Development and A New International Commercial Arbitration Initiative in Asia, translated by Tang YI, Chinese Review of International Law, No. 1, 2020, p. 125.
40. *See* Jinglin Dang, A Study on the Influence of Cultural Differences on Trade Between China and "the Belt and Road" Countries, Doctor's Thesis of Northwest University 2020, p. 47.
41. *See* Chao Lee and Xianghong Zeng, Experimental Analysis of the Impact of Cultural Factors on Integration in Central Asia, Russian Studies, No. 2, Gen. No. 186, 2014, p. 32.
42. *See* Huiyue Ma and Yongqiang Lee, Mode of Transmission of Traditional Chinese Legal Culture in Central Asia, Journal of Lanzhou University (Social Science), Vol. 39, No. 3, p. 140.
43. *See* Hongwu Yin, Cultural Challenges and their Rule of Law Responses in the Practice of International Investment Arbitration Against Corruption, Journal of Social Science of Human Normal University, Vol. 51, No. 3, 2022, p. 58.
44. *See* Ibrahim Fadlallah, Arbitration Facing Conflicts of Culture, in William W. Park (ed.), Arbitration International, Oxford University Press, Vol. 25, No. 3, 2009, p. 317.

links litigation with mediation and arbitration.[45] The multiple choices of dispute resolution will be able to accommodate various legal cultures and traditions along the Belt and Road.

Arbitration institutions, such as CIETAC, have set up the CIETAC ASEAN Trial Center and the CIETAC Central Asia Trial Center, with an aim to promote regional cooperation and mutual understanding. In addition, CIETAC has also joined hands with more than forty major domestic and foreign arbitration institutions to launch the Beijing Joint Declaration of Arbitration Institutions of the Belt and Road. Further, in 2021, the Cooperation Mechanism of Beijing Joint Declaration of Arbitration Institutions of the Belt and Road was launched, which has already had fifty-five international and Chinese arbitration institutions participating, and forty of them have agreed on the cooperation on foreign law ascertainment.

These measures and initiatives mentioned above have actually provided more culturally inclusive options for Chinese and non-Chinese parties participating in the Belt and Road disputes. It is hoped that in addition to the efforts of courts and arbitration institutions, individual practitioners and all stakeholders of the disputes can also pay more attention to the influence of cultural differences when dealing with cross-border disputes along the Belt and Road, so as to guarantee a better subjective satisfaction of procedural justice of all parties.

V CONCLUSION

East Asian culture, represented by China, is deeply influenced by Confucianism, which puts it in sharp contrast to Western culture, valuing the "rule of virtue" and "no litigation." The differences between Eastern and Western legal cultures are reflected in the dispute resolution process in many aspects: in terms of evidence production, parties in Chinese legal cultures are prone to adopt the strategy of evidence ambush; in terms of the hearing mode, East Asian legal cultures generally accept the combination of arbitration and mediation, whereas Western legal cultures are skeptical of it; when the languages are different, the difference between "high-context" or "low-context" communication styles may affect the accuracy of the translation, and in turn affect the parties' effective participation in the proceeding; participants of the proceedings, including the arbitrators, who are from different cultures may have divided opinions toward the same fact, which may affect the outcome of the arbitration and lead to a dissatisfaction with the subjective procedural justice. As the Belt and Road Initiative progresses, the impact of cultural conflict on dispute resolution along the route will be a challenge, but with special attention being paid to the differences and measures taken to enhance mutual understanding and cooperation, it is hoped that the impact of the cultural conflict can be decreased, bringing the parties in the proceedings more satisfaction on subjective procedural justice.

45. *See* Xiaoli GAO, China's International Commercial Dispute Resolution Mechanism and Institution Building-The Supreme People's Court International Commercial Court as a Perspective, Chinese Rule of Law, No. 1, 2024, p. 99.

Chapter 21
How "Fast-Thinking" Through English Jargon Stifles Reform in International Arbitration

Ruth Teitelbaum[*]

TABLE OF CONTENTS

I INTRODUCTION

The power of linguistic and cultural influences to shape legal reality is laid bare in Anthea Roberts' book, *Is International Law International?*[1] Roberts exposes the dominance of Anglo-trained lawyers and common law concepts on the development of international law and demonstrates that international law is not international after all.

Roberts describes the capture of the international legal market by Anglo-trained lawyers as follows:

---

* Ruth Teitelbaum sits as an arbitrator and has her own law practice. She served as a reporter for the ASIL-ICCA Task Force on Issue Conflicts.

1. Anthea Roberts, *Is International Law International?* Oxford University Press (2017), 270-271. Roberts' work was the subject of a symposium at Boston University: https://www.bu.edu/bulawreview/bulronline/boston-university-law-review-online-symposia/online-symposium-anthea-roberts-is-international-law-international/ (accessed August 16, 2025).

> Globalization often produces distinct winners and losers. Just as America benefits from issuing the world's reserve currency, so the United States and the United Kingdom often enjoy the "exorbitant privilege" of issuing the world's "reserve law." This capture marginalizes civil law traditions, like the French and German systems.[2]

The acceptance of English as the "lingua franca" in international legal education, academic literature and the practice of international law results in a division between "what strikes some as an appeal to globalization and internationalization" and "others as a call to standardize legal thinking under an English speaking, common law model."[3]

As explained by Roberts, the disproportionate influence of English and common law concepts in the creation of international criminal courts in the 20th century means that international criminal justice is currently based on common law concepts. This is the case even though, as observed by Bohlander and Roberts, the majority of the world lives under a legal system grounded in civil law concepts. Roberts, citing Bohlander, observes that "[t]he cost of this near exclusiveness may seem low to international lawyers who are American, Australian, British, or Canadian because the concepts are familiar, but the 'cost to societal, historical and legal identity is high if you are none of these.'"[4]

The influence of English and common law concepts in the context of international tribunals has distorted what international law is and "how we use it."[5] International arbitration is a significant piece of the machinery of international legal disputes. Dezalay and Garth's 1996 book, *Dealing in Virtue*, which describes international arbitration as "off-shore justice" in "the service of merchants,"[6] reinforces Roberts' more recent conclusions about the dominance of Anglo culture and common law concepts on international law.

Delazay and Garth detail how Anglo-American law firms displaced the influence of Western Europe on institutions such as the Court of Arbitration of the International Chamber of Commerce (ICC) and imposed their language and their conception of international law practice.[7] Their dominance has had a disproportionate influence on the language used in defining the rules governing international arbitration.[8]

The following sections will explore how the influence of Anglo legal culture and language has impacted markets both inside the system of arbitration and outside capital markets. It will then address how the use of certain English jargon is having an impact on markets and ideas for reform of international arbitration.

2. Roberts (n 1) p. 271.
3. *Id.*, p. 268.
4. *Id.*, p. 270, quoting Michael Bohlander, *Language, Culture, Legal Traditions*, 12 J. Int'l. Crim. Just. 491 and Int at 491-492 (2014) https://doi.org/10.1093/jicj/mqu034 (accessed August 16, 2025).
5. Rosalyn Higgins, *Problems & Process: International Law and How We Use It*, Clarendon Press, Oxford (1994).
6. Yves Dezalay and Bryant G. Garth, *Dealing in Virtue: International Commercial Arbitration and the Construction of a Transnational Legal Order*, University of Chicago Press (1996), p. 8.
7. *Id.*, p. 48.
8. *Id.*

II INTERNATIONAL ARBITRATION'S IMPACT ON MARKETS

Dezalay and Garth note that international commercial arbitration is a "key institution in the structuring of international markets"[9] because what occurs in an international arbitration influences the "security of business investments and [...] the transaction costs of resolving transnational disputes."[10]

The market capitalization of a single public company can rise or fall to the tune of hundreds of millions and billions of dollars in the course of a single day due to the anticipation of an arbitration award to be issued, the issuance of an arbitration award or the enforcement and attachment of assets to pay for an award debt.[11] The failure to pay an arbitral award can disrupt the business of private commercial actors and interfere with a government's ability to export goods.[12]

In the context of international arbitration disputes involving sovereigns and their entities, the freezing or attaching of sovereign assets in domestic courts worldwide may result in sovereign default and the inability of governments to access capital. Creditors seeking to enforce an ICSID award debt owed by Ecuador have frozen Luxembourg bank accounts used by Ecuador to make coupon payments associated with Ecuador's sovereign bonds, for example.[13]

In addition to having an impact on commercial markets and sovereign debt, international arbitration creates its own market for services. There is a market for the selection of arbitrators and for arbitration counsel.[14] There is a market for arbitral institutions and for arbitral seats.

According to a global survey of general counsel and legal department heads, "when contracting parties came from different states and were relatively well-matched in terms of negotiating power, the law of each home state would be rejected in favor of a 'neutral' third option, the most frequent choices being English law (40 percent) and US law (22 percent), including New York law (17 percent)."[15]

In addition to the obvious costs to other countries which, due to their failure to capture arbitrations due to a perceived lack of neutrality, are the "losers" of the arbitral seat market, there are other costs to international arbitration caused by the dominance of Anglo influence and its language.

9. Dezalay and Garth (n 6) p. 7.
10. *Id.*
11. *See, e.g.,* Gabriel Friedman, "Gabriel Resources Investors Flee After Miner Loses $4.4-billion Arbitration Claim against Romania," March 14, 2024, https://financialpost.com/commodities/mining/gabriel-resources-investors-flee-miner-loses-arbitration (accessed August 16, 2025).
12. *See* Ruth Teitelbaum, *From Lena Goldfields to Crystallex: A Proposal for Collective Financing of Sovereign Award Debt,* 37(2) Arb. Int'l (June 2021) 549-576 https://doi.org/10.1093/arbint/aiab022 (accessed August 16, 2025).
13. *See* Cosmo Sanderson, "Perenco Secures Freeze on Ecuador Accounts in Luxembourg," August 1, 2022, available at https://globalarbitrationreview.com/article/perenco-secures-freeze-ecuador-accounts-in-luxembourg (accessed August 4, 2022).
14. Dezalay and Garth (n 6) p. 9.
15. Roberts (n 1) 271, footnote 325.

III THE INFLUENCE OF ENGLISH JARGON ON HOW WE THINK ABOUT ARBITRATION

The dominance of English, and Anglo-trained lawyers in arbitration, whether perceived as a way to create one common language in a globalized world, or as a form of imperialism that inevitably excludes and marginalizes other cultures,[16] inevitably standardizes how we think about international arbitration. The language we use for regulating and reforming arbitration impacts how parties experience arbitration and the perception of arbitration's legitimacy.

One aspect of the standardization of language through English is a tendency toward fast-thinking and shortcuts. According to Jan Paulsson, terms such as "carve-out" and "severability," unfortunate outgrowths of "fast thinking," may be logically wrong and dangerous for the development of international arbitration law.[17] He observes:

> It is that there are no shortcuts to resolving any issues in the law of arbitration that are worth thinking about. Thinking things through is hard work. There is no substitute for it. Yet substitutes are continually proposed. They get us into trouble.[18]

The English language is well suited for shortcuts and "fast-thinking," due to English's efficiency in grouping more than one noun together at once without the clumsiness of articles and prepositions.[19] We see that in the world of business, sports and tech, English terms are often adopted into foreign languages without any attempt at translation. As observed by the late, great Johnny Veeder, "[t]he success of international arbitration is due to surprisingly few wise and true individuals."[20] Given the fact that a relatively small pool of individuals define international arbitration's practice and culture,[21] international arbitration is fragile and can be harmed by linguistic shortcuts and fast-thinking, even when employed by well-meaning and wise individuals.

Some of these shortcuts are used, intentionally or unintentionally, to mask deeper policy challenges facing international arbitration. There are three shortcuts that are the subject of this chapter, two of which have also been the subject of specific reports by ICCA Joint Task Forces and all of which have been the subject of some

16. *Id.*, p. 268.
17. Jan Paulsson et al., *2013 Freshfields Arbitration Lecture*, 30 Arb. Int'l 615 (2014). "Thinking, Fast and Slow" is a 2011 best-selling book about cognitive biases by the late Nobel economics laureate Daniel Kahneman. Daniel Kahneman, *Thinking, Fast and Slow*, Farrar, Straus and Giroux (2011).
18. Paulsson (n 17).
19. Thinking, Fast and Slow is a 2011 best-selling book about cognitive biases by the late Nobel economics laureate Daniel Kahneman. Daniel Kahneman, *Thinking, Fast and Slow*, Farrar, Straus and Giroux (2011).
20. V.V. Veeder, "The Lena Goldfields Lecture," the inaugural lecture for the Arbitration Academy's Historic Arbitration series in honor of the late Berthold Goldman (July 2011). The lecture was given in July 2011 and organized by the late Emmanuel Gaillard. A video recording of the lecture is available at https://vimeo.com/28620082 (accessed May 13, 2021).
21. Dezalay and Garth (n 6) p. 8.

discussion at UNCITRAL: (i) "issue-conflict" (ii) "third-party funding" and (iii) "ISDS" or "investor-State arbitration." These shortcuts, and the way they are used to categorize international arbitration, are masking deeper policy issues and jeopardizing the future of international arbitration.

IV ENGLISH FAST-THINKING REGARDING ETHICS: "ISSUE CONFLICT" IN INTERNATIONAL ARBITRATION

The American Society of International Law and ICCA established a Task Force in 2013 to study and report on issue conflicts in investor-State arbitration. The Task Force was composed of a diverse group of leading experts in international arbitration from the USA, Europe, Asia and Latin America. One of the co-chairs of the Task Force is a native French speaker, the other a native English speaker. The Task Force sought public comments and conducted multiple public consultations over a two-and-a-half-year period. I served as one of the reporters for the Task Force.

As the ASIL-ICCA Final Report on Issue Conflict (Issue Conflict Report) indicates, a significant challenge at the outset was the very phrase that was the subject of the report: "issue conflict." The very first footnote of the report cites Jan Paulsson's "Metaphors, Maxims, and Other Mischief" warning against shortcuts and notes that "the terminology of 'issue conflict' is not ideal."[22]

The Report also notes that one significant problem with the term "issue conflict" is that it does not translate well into other languages. In French and Spanish, it wrongly translates as a "conflict of interest" and in other languages, it just does not translate at all. Therefore, for non-English speakers, the Anglicism "issue conflict" must be adopted in English in quotations, much like non-English speakers have adopted certain English words and expressions in business and technology.

However, it is one thing to use an English word in French to describe "le basketball," a word that is not ambiguous. It is another thing to use an English phrase to apply to a concept that does not have a clear meaning, not even in English. The fact that the ASIL-ICCA Final Report included no references to decisions or academic publications in languages other than English is a further indication that the discussion was captured by a term unique to English speakers and common law-trained lawyers.

While issue conflict appears to refer to a specific legal problem, like "issue estoppel," there is no consensus as to what the term "issue conflict" means. Moreover, there are dramatically different interpretations involving very distinct scenarios. For some, an issue conflict has to do with advocacy and the problem of "two-hatting," i.e., being an advocate on a legal or factual issue and then sitting as an arbitrator presented with that same issue. For others, "issue conflict" is a predisposition arising from a fixed point of view, including a point of view expressed in an academic study or speech. For others, previous experience as an arbitrator can also cause an "issue conflict," whether

22. Report of the ASIL-ICCA Joint Task Force on Issue Conflicts in Investor-State Arbitration, The ICCA Reports No. 3, March 17, 2016, available at https://cdn.arbitration-icca.org/s3fs-public/document/media_document/asil-icca_report_final_5_april_final_for_ridderprint.pdf (accessed August 16, 2025).

it be due to repeat appointment by a certain party or exposure to issues that are overlapping in multiple arbitrations.[23] That the concept of "issue conflict" remains ambiguous and unresolved is clear from ICSID's Background paper published in 2021[24] and the fact that no arbitration rules or codes of conduct have attempted to define "issue conflict."

In the meantime, a lot has been happening regarding the conduct of arbitrators during discussions of reform of international arbitration at UNCITRAL. The Code of Conduct for Arbitrators and Judges in Investor-State Arbitration has come up with a rule for preventing arbitrators from serving as advocates or experts in respect of disputes that are based on the same instrument of consent or similar parties. Article 4 of the Code of Conduct provides as follows:

> Article 4. Limit on multiple roles
>
> 1. Unless the disputing parties agree otherwise, an Arbitrator shall not act concurrently as a legal representative or an expert witness in any other proceeding involving:
>   (a) The same measure(s);
>   (b) The same or related party (parties); or
>   (c) The same provision(s) of the same instrument of consent.[25]

That concerns over "issue conflict" have become more narrowly focused around the dual role of practitioners and arbitrators[26] raises the question of whether it is not so

---

23. Code of Conduct—Background Papers, Issue Conflict, ICSID, February 2021, available at https://icsid.worldbank.org/sites/default/files/Background_Papers_Issue_Conflict_Final_2.26.2021.pdf (accessed August 16, 2025). The background paper was intended to assist the discussions of delegates to UNCITRAL concerning the Code of Conduct.
24. *Id.*
25. United Nations Commission on International Trade Law (UNCITRAL) Resolution adopted by the General Assembly on December 7, 2023 [on the report of the Sixth Committee (A/78/433, para. 13)] 78/105. Code of Conduct for Arbitrators in International Investment Dispute Resolution and Code of Conduct for Judges in International Investment Dispute Resolution with respective commentary of the United Nations Commission on International Trade Law Code of Conduct for Arbitrators in International Investment Dispute Resolution February 2024, available at https://uncitral.un.org/sites/uncitral.un.org/files/media-documents/uncitral/en/2318944_coc_arbitrators_e-book_eng.pdf (accessed August 16, 2025).
26. European Commission, Public Consultation on Modalities for Investment Protection and ISDS in TTIP, at 12-13 (March 27, 2014), available at http://trade.ec.europa.eu/doclib/docs/2014/march/tradoc_152280.pdf (accessed August 16, 2025) ("There is concern that arbitrators on ISDS tribunals do not act in an independent and impartial manner. Because the individuals in question may not only act as arbitrators, but also as lawyers for companies or governments, concerns have been expressed as to potential bias or conflict of interest") (emphases in original omitted); Cecelia Malström, "Commissioner of Trade, Opening Remarks: Discussion on Investment in TTIP" (March 18, 2015), available at http://trade.ec.europa.eu/doclib/docs/2015/march/tradoc_153258.pdf (accessed August 16, 2025) ("Many are concerned that the system creates conflicts of interest because arbitrators are also lawyers and might expect to get business from the investors in future"); *see also* UNCTAD, Reform of Investor-State Dispute Settlement: In Search of a Roadmap, IIA Issues Note No. 2, 4 (June 2013), available at http://unctad.org/en/PublicationsLibrary/webdiaepcb2013d4_en.pdf (accessed August 16, 2025) ("Particular concerns have arisen from a perceived tendency of each disputing party to appoint individuals sympathetic to their case. Arbitrators' interest in being re-appointed in future cases and their frequent 'changing of hats' (serving as arbitrators in some cases and counsel in others) amplify these concerns"); Nathalie Bernasconi-Osterwalder and Diana Rosert, "International Institute

much the conduct of arbitrators but rather the advocates—and the dominance of U.S. litigation culture on international arbitration—that is really at the heart of "issue conflict." According to Dezalay and Garth, "European 'jurists'—typically considered auxiliaries of a justice supposed to embody the general interest—were trained to maintain a distance from the claims of clients. The U.S. 'lawyer' in contrast, has no hesitation in demonstrating legal inventiveness and tactical aggressiveness. The cause of the client is defended by any available means."[27]

While the contours of "issue conflict" remain unsettled, and a narrow focus on multiple roles between advocacy and arbitration is regulated at UNCITRAL, a broader discussion of the role and professional responsibilities of arbitrators and advocates has not occurred. UNCITRAL's Code of Conduct for Investor-State Arbitration seems to favor academics over law firm practitioners as arbitrators, given that it says practically nothing about academic positions or articles giving rise to possible predisposition and bias.[28] But perhaps what is most surprising is that so little attention has been paid to the qualities, education and background that would make arbitrators suitable for the high stakes, complex, technical, politically charged arbitrations that are increasingly part and parcel of international arbitration, between private parties and between private and sovereign entities.

The international arbitration community, due to labels such as "issue conflict" and even "two-hatting" has been focused on the process of categorizing types of conflicts and ensuring greater transparency and disclosure. It has missed out on an opportunity to evaluate the markets that international arbitration has created and impacted. The dominance of aggressive, U.S.-style litigation has impacted international arbitration in terms of time, efficiency and cost. However, it may be said that the high-stakes nature of international arbitration disputes, combined with the uncertainty, time and cost of arbitration and the dearth of information on compliance with award payment has created the opportunity for large U.S. and Anglo law firms to enter this market and to maintain a dominant role.

What are the qualities that arbitrators should have to best handle these developments? Would international arbitration benefit from having more engineers and technical experts as arbitrators, or from including dispute panels devoted to certain aspects of disputes, such as damages? Would this make arbitrations more efficient? Looking back at the *Lena Goldfields* arbitration rendered almost a century ago, when

for Sustainable Development, Investment Treaty Arbitration: Opportunities to Reform Arbitral Rules and Processes," 13 (January 2014) ("One specific issue of concern relating to arbitrators' impartiality and independence lies in the fact that arbitrators sitting on treaty-based investor-state tribunals can simultaneously serve as counsel or expert in other such disputes (the 'dual-role' or 'multiple hat' issue")).

27. Delazay and Garth (n 6) p. 68.
28. United Nations Commission on International Trade Law (UNCITRAL) Resolution adopted by the General Assembly on December 7, 2023 [on the report of the Sixth Committee (A/78/433, para. 13)] 78/105. Code of Conduct for Arbitrators in International Investment Dispute Resolution and Code of Conduct for Judges in International Investment Dispute Resolution with respective commentary of the United Nations Commission on International Trade Law Code of Conduct for Arbitrators in International Investment Dispute Resolution February 2024, available at https://uncitral.un.org/sites/uncitral.un.org/files/media-documents/uncitral/en/2318944_coc_arbitrators_e-book_eng.pdf (accessed August 16, 2025).

was the last time a significant mining dispute between a company and sovereign was chaired by a professor of geology?[29] Is arbitration, as opposed to mediation or other methods of dispute settlement and prevention, the right tool for some of the complex and politically sensitive disputes entering the arbitration market?[30]

Instead of focusing the discussion on the deceptively narrow problem of "issue conflict," a broader discussion of the nature of arbitration and the qualities and skills of arbitrators to meet the complexities of modern international arbitration disputes might have been more useful. In particular, a broader discussion that invited comments in other languages, decisions and concepts from non-English speaking courts and non-English literature could have perhaps helped advance deeper policy discussion. Instead, the situation regarding arbitrators, their activities as lawyers or law professors and what might be considered an inappropriate predisposition remains uncertain.

In the meantime, discussions at UNCITRAL on the role of arbitrators are moving swiftly in the direction of doing away with the current system of party appointments and creating a permanent investment disputes court with judges. It is worth noting that the UNCITRAL Code of Conduct released in 2024 is to apply to both arbitrators and judges, in the event a permanent court for investment disputes is created.[31] To believe that calls for judges instead of arbitrators is limited to "investment arbitration" and does not affect "commercial arbitration" would be a miscalculation, to be discussed further below.

V ENGLISH FAST-THINKING ABOUT MONEY AND POLICY IN INTERNATIONAL ARBITRATION

"Third-party funding" is now a ubiquitous phrase in international arbitration disputes. Like "issue conflict," it is not easy to translate "third-party funder" into foreign languages. Like "issue conflict," "third-party funding" has been the subject of a joint task force and a report involving ICCA. The joint task force, between ICCA and Queen

29. The 1929 Lena Goldfields arbitration was chaired by Dr. Otto Stutzer of the Freiburg School of Mines, who rendered the award in German. *See* V.V. Veeder, "The Lena Goldfields lecture, which was the inaugural lecture for the Arbitration Academy's Historic Arbitration series in honour of the late Berthold Goldman" (July 2011). The lecture was given in July 2011 and organized by the late Emmanuel Gaillard. A video recording of the lecture is available at https://vimeo.com/28620082 (accessed May 13, 2021).
30. *See* Claudia Salomon, "Maslow's Hammer: An Over-Reliance on Familiar Tools," March 14, 2022, available at https://iccwbo.org/news-publications/uncategorized/maslows-hammer-an-over-reliance-on-familiar-tools/ (accessed August 16, 2025).
31. United Nations Commission on International Trade Law (UNCITRAL) Resolution adopted by the General Assembly on December 7, 2023 [on the report of the Sixth Committee (A/78/433, para. 13)] 78/105. Code of Conduct for Arbitrators in International Investment Dispute Resolution and Code of Conduct for Judges in International Investment Dispute Resolution with respective commentary of the United Nations Commission on International Trade Law Code of Conduct for Arbitrators in International Investment Dispute Resolution February 2024, available at https://uncitral.un.org/sites/uncitral.un.org/files/media-documents/uncitral/en/2318944_coc_arbitrators_e-book_eng.pdf (accessed August 16, 2025).

Mary University, was composed of renowned specialists in arbitration from different cultural and linguistic backgrounds.[32]

Despite the diversity in the composition of the Task Force, this Task Force was given a mandate defined by a vague and uniquely English phrase.[33] The term "third-party funding," and the way in which it is normally defined, comes directly from the definition of champerty under common law. According to Black's Law Dictionary, "[c]hamperty is the carrying on a suit in the name of another, but at one's own expense, with the view of receiving as compensation a certain share of the avails of the suit." Common law jurisdictions have moved away from upholding the defenses of champerty and maintenance in the context of litigation financing due to a shift in policy, namely, that finance for access to justice serves the public interest; therefore, unless the outside funding is purely for the purpose of vexation or harassment, it should be allowed.

The term "third-party funding" like "issue conflict" means different things to different actors. Like the issue conflict report, there is hardly any reference to a non-English decision or publication. The authors of the ICCA-Queen Mary Report, for example, observe that "the meaning and contours of the terms 'third-party funder' and 'third-party funding' can be ambiguous and, in some instances, contested."[34] For example, as to the question of whether insurance should be considered a form of "third-party funding" or not, Nieuwveld and Sahani conclude that "[i]nsurance is one of the most common forms of third-party funding."[35] Yet this is not necessarily so according to the ICCA-Queen Mary Report, which appears to draw a distinction in its analysis (and headings) between models of finance that the drafters of the report appear to suggest do *not* fall under the umbrella of "third-party funding" (referred to as "Other Dispute Funding Models")[36] and so-called classic non-recourse third-party funding.

Notwithstanding the lack of consensus or precision as to what exactly "third-party funding" means, the term has become an accepted expression in the international arbitration community, surfacing front and center in proposals to reform investor-state dispute settlement (ISDS), ethical guidelines, investment treaties, and arbitration

32. *See* International Council for Commercial Arbitration, *Report of the ICCA-Queen Mary Task Force on Third-Party Funding in International Arbitration*, ICCA Reports No. 4 (2018), https://www.arbitration-icca.org/publications/Third-Party-Funding-Report.html (accessed August 16, 2025) (hereinafter the "ICCA-Queen Mary Report").
33. Where "third-party funding" has been translated into other languages, its translation may be described as awkward at best. For French, *see, e.g.*, ICC France, *Guide pratique sur le financement de l'arbitrage par les tiers (third party funding)* (2014), http://icc-france.fr/docmail/Guide_pratique_financement_arbitrage_tiers.pdf (accessed September 7, 2018). *See also* ICSID's proposal to amend its rules, where it translates "third-party funding" as "financement par les tiers" in French and "financiamiento por terceros" in Spanish, https://icsid.worldbank.org/en/Documents/Amendments_Vol_Two.pdf (accessed August 16, 2025).
34. ICCA-Queen Mary Report, fn. 1.
35. Victoria Shannon and Lisa Bench Nieuwveld, *Introduction to Third-Party Funding in Third-Party Funding in International Arbitration*, Kluwer Law International p. 7.
36. The ICCA-Queen Mary Report, at 33, observes that "[a]lthough third-party funding has only relatively recently emerged as a distinct industry, it should be viewed in context as one of a number of the alternative ways of financing arbitrations."

rules.[37] Under ICSID's Rule 14, third-party funders are defined as "any non-party from which the party, directly or indirectly, has received funds for the pursuit or defense of the proceeding through a donation or grant, or in return for remuneration dependent on the outcome of the proceeding."

The goal of increasing references to "third-party funding" and its regulation appears to be disclosure and transparency, but transparency in and of itself fails to answer a number of questions. We know that arbitration has the effect of restructuring markets by virtue of settling business disputes through enforceable awards. But what do we think of the fact that international arbitration, due to the high costs of litigation, time and unpredictability of enforcement, has fueled a market for investors willing to gamble on cases and claimants willing to offload the cost of litigation for a smaller percentage of upside?

While uncertainty of time and high costs is one factor feeding the market for outside capital, there is one aspect of international arbitration involving sovereigns currently fueling the litigation finance market which is certain. A former hedge fund manager who successfully enforced awards against Argentina and who is now assisting creditors of India's unpaid investment treaty arbitration awards described India's move to withdraw from the international system of collecting airlines fees as confirming "the reality that deadbeat sovereigns that dishonour their treaty obligations and international judgments have nowhere to hide, and no choice but to withdraw from the civilized world of trade and commerce like other pariah states."[38]

Unlike the case of lawsuits against private commercial debtors, there is no international bankruptcy protection for governments, or "nowhere to hide." No mandatory stays of litigation and no court-mandated creditor haircuts. The only exception to this is where the United Nations has intervened to effectively immunize a State's commercial assets, such as it did in the case of Iraq in 2003 in order to help reconstruction. Hedge funds with billions under management discovered this investment opportunity in the 1990s with the Elliot Associates versus Peru case in the Second Circuit, which rejected Peru's champerty defense.[39]

---

37. For example, the Canada-European Union Comprehensive Economic and Trade Agreement (CETA), which is currently in force, contains a definition of third-party funding (Article 8.1); the European Union-Vietnam Investment Protection Agreement, as negotiated in August 2018, included both a definition of third-party funding (Article 3.28) and related disclosure requirements (Article 3.37), as did the European Union's proposal for investment protection and resolution of investment disputes under the Transatlantic Trade and Investment Partnership (TTIP) (respectively, Articles 1 and 8). For example, the Investment Arbitration Rules of the Singapore International Arbitration Centre (SIAC) empower the arbitration tribunal to order disclosure of the identity of a third-party funder and details of the third-party funding agreement (Article 24); the International Investment Arbitration Rules of the China International Economic and Trade Arbitration Commission (CIETAC) require disclosure of "the existence and nature of the third-party funding arrangement, and the name and address of the third-party funder" (Article 27).
38. Cosmo Sanderson, India Withdraws from Airline Payments System, Global Arbitration Review, May 16, 2022.
39. *Elliott Associates, L.P. v. The Republic of Peru and Banco de la Nación*, 12 F. Supp. 2d 328 (1998), *Elliott Assocs., L.P. v. Republic of Peru*, 176 F.R.D. 93 (S.D.N.Y.1997); *Elliott Associates, L.P. v. Republic of Peru*, 96 Civ. 7916, 1997 WL 436493 (S.D.N.Y. August 1, 1997); *Elliott Assocs., L.P. v. Republic of Peru*, 961 F. Supp. 83 (S.D.N.Y.1997); *Elliott Assocs., L.P. v. Republic of Peru*, 948

The convergence between sovereign debt litigation and the enforcement of unpaid arbitration awards is fueling, simultaneously, a market for investors and backlash against arbitration all at once, to the point where UNCITRAL is moving away from arbitration toward a permanent court for handling disputes between investors and sovereigns.

In sum, the phrase "third-party funding" is an empty shell of a phrase. The disclosure alone of this imprecise phenomenon of finance does nothing to address the policy concerns over fairness and access to capital arising in international arbitration disputes.

VI ENGLISH FAST-THINKING ON REFORM OF "INVESTOR-STATE ARBITRATION," A SHORTCUT THAT FALSELY CONNOTES A ONE-WAY STREET

Discussions of fairness in terms of States' access to capital have been stifled by the consequences of another shortcut in international arbitration, the phantom of the opera in this discussion, "investor-State arbitration" or "ISDS." "Investor-State arbitration," a phrase that is difficult to translate into other languages, has been created by English-speaking practitioners, arbitrators and institutions who have, willingly or unwillingly, perpetuated a false concept, one that ignores the friendly basis of mutual obligations under investment treaties between States. States that have entered into investment treaties have promised reciprocal protections to foreign investors of the other State in order to maintain peace with another State. An injury to a foreign investor is derivative of the injury to that investor's home State.

Due to the tendency, influenced by the dominance of U.S. and Anglo-trained lawyers, to "shoe-horn"[40] commercial litigation concepts into the dispute settlement under bilateral and multilateral investment treaties, the reciprocal basis of obligations

F. Supp. 1203 (S.D.N.Y.1996). Elliott purchased through give trades from January 31, 1996, to March 1, 1996, all right, title and interest, from Swiss Bank Corporation (SBC) and ING Bank, N.V. (ING), USD 20,682,699.04 in principal amount, together with all accrued and unpaid interest, of the working capital obligations of Banco de la Nación and Banco Popular del Peru under certain letter agreements. The letter agreements were guaranteed by Peru in a written Guaranty on May 31, 1983 (the "Guaranty"). The letter agreements and the Guaranty, both of which were governed by New York law, were considered valid outstanding obligations of Banco and Peru. The Letter Agreements and the Guaranty entitled Elliott Associates, the holder to, among other things, repayment of all principal, plus interest as provided in the Letter Agreements. The Letter Agreements and the Guaranty also entitled the holder to recover attorneys' fees, costs and disbursements incurred to enforce the Letter Agreements and the Guaranty. Of the total USD 20,682,699.04 in principal obligations Elliott acquired, Banco is the Obligor of USD 7,000,000 in principal. Banco Popular is the Obligor for the remaining USD 13,682,699.04 in principal. Peru, however, guaranteed to repay the entire amount. Banco and Peru did not pay any of the outstanding amounts due and owing under the Letter Agreements or the Guaranty. Banco and Peru were therefore in default of their obligations under those instruments. After extensive litigation and numerous attempts by Elliott to settle, the court awarded the hedge fund USD 58 million, including past due interest.

40. Toby Landau once warned at an annual meeting of the American Society of International Law that arbitrators must be wary of wearing a "commercial arbitration hat" when sitting as an arbitrator in investment arbitration claims under treaties. 109 Proceedings of the Annual

of investment treaties is being ignored. It is long-winded to describe arbitration based on mutual, reciprocal obligations between States which allows investors of a State to proceed with claims directly against the foreign State, without the need for diplomatic espousal of claims by the investor's home State. But the shortcut of the phrase "investor-State arbitration" has caused practitioners and arbitrators to forget the presence of the investor's home State altogether, and to portray this type of arbitration, falsely, as a one-way street, rather than as a as a shared privilege of both capital exporting countries and capital importing countries as part of their promise of reciprocity and friendly relations.[41]

The polarized environment of "ISDS" has reached a critical juncture, where States are increasingly unwilling or unable to pay awards,[42] their awards are being sold on a secondary market to a growing market of investors, and UNCITRAL is moving away from arbitration toward a permanent court. For those that tend to categorize these developments as unique to "ISDS" and believe that these developments will not affect the vitality of commercial arbitration, the decision of the UK High Court in *Federal Republic of Nigeria v. Process & Industrial Developments Ltd.* involving an ad hoc, commercial arbitration dispute, is a sobering read.[43] The decision does not provide any recipe for what to do and not to do in the context of document production in an

Meeting (American Society of International Law), Vol. 103 (March 25-28, 2009), Mapping the Future of Investment Treaty Arbitration, Remarks by Toby Landau, pp. 326-327.

41. Francisco Orrego Vicuña, "Arbitrating Investment Disputes," The Leading Arbitrators' Guide to International Arbitration, 2nd ed., Newman and Hill (ed.), pp. 709-710. The late Francisco Orrego Vicuña describes the arbitration of investment disputes as a "shared privilege" of both capital exporting countries and capital importing countries.

42. Emmanuel Gaillard and Ilija Mitrev Penusliski, *State Compliance with Investment Awards*, ICSID Review (2021), pp. 1-55. As observed by Gaillard and Penusliski, in their article, "The data examined indicates that the ICSID founders' prognosis that compliance with investment awards would be a non-issue—framed as it was in such sweeping terms—has not held true. Whereas the majority of States have complied with adverse awards (usually after seeking annulment), the instances of non-compliance or significantly delayed compliance are important. A significant proportion of the cases where States have been ordered to pay damages have required enforcement proceedings. Instances of home State's intervention—and inevitably re-politicization of the dispute—have resurged."

43. The *Federal Republic of Nigeria v. Process & Industrial Developments Limited* [2023] EWHC 2638 (Comm). The case concerned Nigeria's application under section 68 of the Arbitration Act 1996 challenging an arbitration award The award was overturned on the grounds that it was obtained by fraud. Much of the documentation uncovering bribery and corruption was obtained due to discovery orders in US courts. In the USA, on March 26, 2020 Nigeria applied to the US District Court for the Southern District of New York under §1782 of Title 28 of the United States Code to obtain discovery of bank accounts at ten different banks. Discovery orders were made on May 7, 2020. Documents disclosed pursuant to these orders showed the payments from Marshpearl and Kristholm to Mrs. Grace Taiga's daughter Vera of USD 4,969.50 on December 30, 2009 and USD 5,000 on January 31, 2012. In January 2021 On June 24, 2021 Orders were made in the Cayman Islands for disclosure of documents by various third parties including Arcadia Group Limited. On October 22, 2021 the District Court of Nicosia made an order for disclosure of documents against the Bank of Cyprus, and on January 13, 2022 an Order was made in the British Virgin Islands for disclosure against, among others, Nerine Trust Co (BVI) Ltd and Trident Trust Co (BVI) Ltd (the registered agents of P&ID). Between December 2021 and October 2022 Nigeria filed applications with the Commercial Court in London for further disclosure and related orders, and a notice to prove documents. Various orders were made by a number of judges of the Court. Of particular note was an order dated July 15, 2022 made by Jacobs J that P&ID and others provide disclosure of certain WhatsApp/SMS threads.

arbitration or how best to manage the misconduct of counsel. It requires us to reflect on the inherent fragility of the arbitration process and to wonder whether arbitration is really up for the task.

That bribery underlying a contract and irregular behavior between opposing counsel (including sharing opposing counsel's strategy and memos) during the arbitration was only found through Nigeria's discovery applications in New York courts is a black eye for international arbitration. That this dispute involved a sovereign-owned entity that would have owed billions in damages is a reminder that labels such as "ISDS" or "commercial arbitration" do not create strict boundaries around what disputes trigger the public interest, nor do they avoid the problem of sovereign indebtedness and dissatisfaction with the arbitration process.

At a time when the future of international arbitration is in jeopardy, the shortcuts and labels used to categorize and address policy concerns about international arbitration have fallen short. What is more urgently needed is: (i) solidarity between States through a mutual, intergovernmental solution for addressing sovereign indebtedness from arbitration awards and (ii) solutions to prevent arbitration disputes in the first place. As observed by Higgins:

> The role of law is to provide an operational system for securing values that we all desire—security, freedom, the provision of sufficient material goods. It is not, as is commonly supposed, only about resolving disputes. If a legal system works well, then disputes are in large part avoided.[44]

That disputes have resulted in the failure of international investment treaties to secure the values they purport to protect, such as friendship between States through foreign investment, has far-reaching consequences beyond the label "ISDS."

Regarding the arbitral process and the arbitration tribunal, the UK judge concluded in paras. 316-317:

> 316. If the Tribunal had known of bribes around the time of the GSPA [the contract underlying the dispute] the entire picture would have had a different complexion. And so too if the Tribunal had known that Nigeria was not, during the Arbitration process itself, enjoying confidentiality of advice within the legal professional privilege to which it was entitled.
>
> 317. Further the Tribunal did not know that Mr Michael Quinn's evidence was knowingly false in representing that "all the project finance was in place" and that (for the GSPA rather than Project Alpha in 2008) "90% of the engineering designs had been completed."

44. Rosalyn Higgins, Problems & Process, International Law and How We Use It, Clarendon Press, Oxford (1994), p. 1.

CHAPTER 22

The Invisible Hand of Culture: Cross-Cultural Dynamics and the International Arbitration Paradigm

Prof. Mohamed S. Abdel Wahab[*]

TABLE OF CONTENTS

I INTRODUCTION

International arbitration, being the business community's first choice for resolving cross-border disputes, is increasingly perceived as a complicated process involving an interplay of legal principles, procedural norms, factual controversies and cultural nuances. That said, arbitration practitioners do navigate their way through the factual matrix and the legal framework of the dispute they are destined to decide, but less attention is often given to cultural complexities that impact tribunal dynamics and inform the parties' factual, procedural and legal choices in arbitration cases. This is all

* Professor of International Arbitration, Private International Law and English Contract Law, Cairo University; Founding Partner and Head of International Arbitration, Construction and Energy Groups at Zulficar & Partners Law Firm (Egypt); Member of the Governing Board (ICCA); Chair of the ICC Governing Body for Dispute Resolution Services; President of the CIArb (2025); Dean of the Africa Arbitration Academy; Member of the Curatorium of the Hague Academy of International Law; Member of the Court, PCA (The Hague); Fellow of International Academy of Construction Lawyers; and Member of the Academic Council, Institute of Transitional Arbitration (ITA).

the more relevant as international arbitration often offers a platform where diverse cultures interact, collide and cross-pollinate. It is not uncommon to encounter cases where arbitrators come from diverse cultural backgrounds, parties are drawn from different jurisdictions and cultures, and their counsel teams are composed of culturally diverse individuals.[1]

By way of illustration, statistics show that institutions are increasingly making appointments from a more diverse pool of arbitrators with different nationalities and cultures.[2] For example, in ICC arbitrations, the 2024 statistics show that there were 1020 confirmed or appointed arbitrators that came from 91 jurisdictions.[3] With respect to the SIAC arbitrations, the 2024 statistics show that there were 202 arbitrators nominated and confirmed by the SIAC, and the SIAC made appointments from no less than 33 jurisdictions.[4] In the HKIAC, the 2024 Statistics demonstrate that it registered 503 cases with confirmed and appointed arbitrators coming from around 30 jurisdictions.[5] Similarly, the LCIA 2023 statistics show that the LCIA Court appointed around 430 arbitrators from 41 jurisdictions.[6] Moreover, the DIAC 2023 statistics demonstrate that the DIAC administered 323 arbitrations, with confirmed and appointed arbitrators coming from 29 jurisdictions.[7] Finally, the SCC 2024 statistics show that the SCC administered 204 cases with confirmed and appointed arbitrators coming from 26 jurisdictions.[8]

While this chapter is more concerned with cultural influences in international arbitration as opposed to influence in litigation, it should be noted litigation is also not immune to cultural influences. Even in local communities, there are sub-cultural differences (and consequently influences) that arise in national courts.[9] However,

---

1. Tejas Karia and Dr. Rishab Gupta, 'Cultural Considerations in Advocacy: India, Global Arbitration Review,' in Stephen Jagusch and Philippe Pinsolle (eds), *The Guide to Advocacy* (3rd ed. Global Arbitration Review 2018) 192; Dr. Mary Howard, 'International Arbitration and Cross-cultural Issues', in Stavros Brekoulakis (ed.), *Mediation and Dispute Management* (Arbitration: The International Journal of Arbitration, © Kluwer Law International; Kluwer Law International 2020, vol. 86, Issue 3) 338; Prof. Dr. Kaj Hober and Howard S, Sussman, *Cross-Examination in International Arbitration* (Oxford University Press 2014) 30.
2. Alvin Yeo SC and Chou Sean Yu, 'Cultural Considerations in Advocacy: East Meets West', in Stephen Jagusch and Philippe Pinsolle (eds), 183.
3. ICC, 'ICC Dispute Resolution Statistics: 2024', published on 24 June 2024, ICC News and Publications, available at https://iccwbo.org/news-publications/news/icc-dispute-resolution-statistics-2024/#top, accessed on 24 June 2025, 8.
4. SIAC, 'SIAC Annual Report 2024', published in 2025, SIAC Events, available at https://siac.org.sg/annual-reports accessed on 23 June 2025, 36.
5. HKIAC, '2024 Statistics', 2024, HKIAC's Website/About, available at https://www.hkiac.org/about-us/statistics, accessed on 23 June 2025.
6. LCIA, 'LCIA Annual Casework Report 2023', Published May 2024, LCIA Reports, available at https://www.lcia.org/media/download.aspx?MediaId=1032, accessed on 23 June 2025, 18.
7. DIAC, 'DIAC 2023 Annual Report', DIAC Annual Reports, available at https://www.diac.com/wp-content/uploads/2024/11/DIAC-Annual-Report-2023.pdf, accessed on 23 June 2025, 37.
8. SCC, 'Statistics 2024', SCC Statistics, 2024, available at https://sccarbitrationinstitute.se/en/statistics-2024/, accessed on 23 June 2025.
9. Dr. Mary Howard, 'International Arbitration and Cross-cultural Issues', in Stavros Brekoulakis (ed.), *Mediation and Dispute Management* (Arbitration: The International Journal of Arbitration, © Kluwer Law International; Kluwer Law International 2020, vol. 86, Issue 3) 336- 337; Prof. Dr. Yasuhei Taniguchi, 'Is There a Growing International Arbitration Culture? – An Observation from Asia', in Prof. Dr. Albert Jan van den Berg (ed.), *ICCA Congress Series No. 8 (Seoul 1996):*

unlike sub-cultural influences with a single community whether in litigation before national courts or even in domestic arbitration, cultures influences in international arbitration and in cross-border disputes often stem from a myriad of different cultural roots and involve an interplay between significantly different cultures.[10]

Such interaction between different actors from different cultures creates one main issue and develops one main product. First, the issue is how to deal with the affinity effect where a person is subconsciously more wedded and sensitive to his/her culture and less receptive to acts informed by cultural differences, especially that different cultures may respond differently to risk, management and even 'views on justice'.[11] Second, the product of this cultural interaction in international arbitration, beyond tension and friction, is the development of a 'third culture' that evolves from 'repeated interactions'[12] between players and actors who are carriers of these cultural codes.

Given the relative importance of culture in international arbitration as informing parties' choices, counsel conduct, arbitrators' perceptions and tribunal dynamics, and/or approaches to decision-making processes, scholars and practitioners have dedicated significant scholarship to the interplay between culture and law.[13] In a study dedicated to biases in international arbitration, it is argued that some tribunals may choose to focus exclusively on the 'written laws',[14] and deny the importance (or even the existence) of cultural manifestations and ramifications in an attempt to avoid bias and inappropriate predisposition. However, this may prove to be counterintuitive as explored at some length in this chapter. That said, it is has been suggested that decision-making goes through two thought processes: system 1 – 'an intuitive process' and system 2 – 'a deliberative process',[15] and this chapter aims at navigating through the cultural nuances and complexities to determine how best one can deal with cultural differences, explore how best to communicate and present his/her views with the aim of arriving at the most reasonable and fair outcome (in light of the submissions and

---

International Dispute Resolution: Towards an International Arbitration Culture (ICCA Congress Series, vol. 8, © Kluwer Law International; ICCA & Kluwer Law International 1998) 34.

10. Prof. Dr. Won Kidane, 'The Culture of Investment Arbitration: An African Perspective', in Meg Kinnear and Dr. Campbell McLachlan (eds), *ICSID Review: Foreign Investment Law Journal* (Oxford University Press 2019, vol. 34, Issue 2) 414.
11. Aisha Nadar, 'Construction Arbitration and Standard Forms of Contract in the Middle East: National Culture and Its Impact on Perception and Practice', in Prof. Nassib G. Ziadé (ed.), *BCDR International Arbitration Review* (© Kluwer Law International; Kluwer Law International 2017, vol. 4, Issue 1) 53 (emphasis added).
12. Prof. Dr. Joshua Karton, *The Culture of International Arbitration and the Evolution of Contract Law* (1st ed. Oxford University Press, 2013), 19 (emphasis added).
13. Dr. Mary Howard, 'International Arbitration and Cross-cultural Issues', in Stavros Brekoulakis (ed.), *Mediation and Dispute Management* (Arbitration: The International Journal of Arbitration, © Kluwer Law International; Kluwer Law International 2020, vol. 86, Issue 3) 336- 337.
14. Dr. Mary Howard, 'International Arbitration and Cross-cultural Issues', in Stavros Brekoulakis (ed.), *Mediation and Dispute Management* (Arbitration: The International Journal of Arbitration, © Kluwer Law International; Kluwer Law International 2020, vol. 86, Issue 3) 331 (emphasis added).
15. Edna Sussman, 'Biases and Heuristics in Arbitrator Decision-Making: Reflections on How to Counteract or Play to Them', in Tony Cole (ed.), *The Roles of Psychology in International Arbitrations* (Wolters Kluwer, 2017) 47.

evidence on record) while maintaining 'cultural openness' (as an ingredient of arbitral justice)[16] and controlling cultural inclinations throughout the deliberative thought process. Particularly, the author agrees with most of the literature on this topic that awareness of the cultural differences and acknowledgement of their influence is a first step to avoiding certain unwelcomed biases premised on distinct cultural considerations.[17]

This chapter tracks the critical role of culture in international arbitration throughout the various stages of arbitral proceedings, and challenges conventional misconceptions that may contaminate the decision-making process and lead to unconscious biases. That said, the chapter is structured as follows: *First*, the author will attempt to unveil and dispel certain common misconceptions about culture in the context of international arbitration. *Second*, the author will define culture and explore relevant cultural concepts. *Third*, the author will track and examine the manifestations of culture in different stages of the arbitration process, including case preparation, presentation, and determination. *Finally*, the role of the arbitrator in navigating cultural complexities will be examined before making some concluding observations. It is hoped that this structured analysis will afford practitioners a deeper appreciation of the cultural dynamics at play, enabling them to navigate the complexities of cross-cultural disputes with greater efficacy and better understanding.

II CULTURE IN INTERNATIONAL ARBITRATION BETWEEN PERCEPTIONS AND MISCONCEPTIONS

It is often said, with unverified attribution to Leo Tolstoy, that it is not ignorance that can lead to evil; it is misconceptions that lead to evil, and Goethe also said that nothing is more dangerous to a new truth than an old misconception.[18] This cannot be more relevant to the discussion over cultural influences in international arbitration.

In the specific context of culture, nothing is more dangerous than wrong perceptions and misconceptions. This is the greatest challenge in understanding the role of culture in international arbitration. Misconceptions hinder effective cross-cultural communication, collaboration and contaminate proceedings dynamics and decision-making. However, what is worse than having a misconception is believing

16. Dr. Horacio Grigera Naón, 'The Role of International Commercial Arbitration' (65 Arbitration 1999) 266 as cited by Aisha Nadar, 'Construction Arbitration and Standard Forms of Contract in the Middle East: National Culture and Its Impact on Perception and Practice', in Prof. Nassib G. Ziadé (ed.), *BCDR International Arbitration Review* (© Kluwer Law International; Kluwer Law International 2017, vol. 4, Issue 1) 71.
17. Dr. Mary Howard, 'International Arbitration and Cross-cultural Issues', in Stavros Brekoulakis (ed.), *Mediation and Dispute Management* (Arbitration: The International Journal of Arbitration, © Kluwer Law International; Kluwer Law International 2020, vol. 86, Issue 3) 337; Prof. Dr. Giorgio Bernini, 'Is There a Growing International Arbitration Culture?', in Prof. Dr. Albert Jan van den Berg (ed.), *ICCA Congress Series No. 8 (Seoul 1996): International Dispute Resolution: Towards an International Arbitration Culture* (ICCA Congress Series, vol. 8 (© Kluwer Law International; ICCA & Kluwer Law International 1998)) 42.
18. Johann Wolfgang von Goethe, *Maxims and Reflection*, Translated by Charles Stopp (Leipzig, 1833) Maxim 715.

that there are no misconceptions and then subconsciously acting upon a misconception. One should not be oblivious to the fact that bias could stealthily 'contaminate' the human mind.[19] Such contamination may be neutralised if one is conscious and aware of the common misconceptions or the pitfalls of the human intuitive mind. In the coming pages, the author will address five of the most common misconceptions about culture in the context of international arbitration.

1 Misconception 1: Culture & Individual Behaviour – Subjective Perceptions and Cultural Profiling

It is not uncommon to conflate the actions of a few with the values and culture of a nation or a group. For instance, many arbitrators may have sat as arbitrators in a case related to a certain region or a country with which they are not familiar, and, in light of that, they tend to benchmark conduct and cultural patterns in subsequent cases involving the same country or region in light of what they have seen in action in the first case. This is a common pitfall and a misconception that ignores simple facts such as: (a) what has been encountered in the first case may simply be a function of individual behaviour/conduct; (b) even within a region or a nation several cultural practices and patterns may exist and culture is not always homogenous; (c) cultural practices, patterns and values may change over time; and (d) one or few cases are not sufficient to judge or ascertain cultural practices, patterns and values.

More specifically, this misconception risks engaging in cultural profiling or cultural stereotyping, which can contaminate practitioners' perceptions and approaches to communication, advocacy, and decision-making. This is not exclusive to ethnic grouping and profiling; it can extend to professional stereotyping. For example, counsel in international arbitration, interacting with retired judges (who also sit as arbitrators) in certain jurisdictions may form a general view as to judges' approaches to arbitration, and may even conclude that judges appointed as arbitrators show less fidelity to parties' expectations and give less deference to parties' procedural choices, when compared to other arbitrators with no judicial background. This profiling carries a degree of bias and can be misunderstood and wrongly acted upon. Thus, one should appreciate that this could be an individual approach rather than a collective course of conduct by all judges. Accordingly, 'the relevant question must be not whether arbitrators decide differently from judges in the abstract, but how a particular arbitrator will rule compared to a particular judge'.[20]

As such, cultural and professional perceptions ought not to be made on individual encounters in limited professional contexts, and judgments ought not to be passed in a manner that informs future conduct based on one's own subjective views

19. Prof. Dr. Peter Ayton & Prof. Gevieve Helleringer, *Bias*, 'Vested Interests and Self-Deception in Judgment and Decision-Making: Challenges to Arbitrator Impartiality', in Tony Cole (ed.), *The Roles of Psychology in International Arbitrations* (Wolters Kluwer, 2017) 43.
20. Prof. Dr. Willian W. (Rusty) Park, 'Rules and Reliability: How Arbitrators Decide', in Tony Cole (ed.), *The Roles of Psychology in International Arbitrations* (Wolters Kluwer, 2017) 17.

and understanding of what may come across, perhaps wrongly, as cultural manifestations of human conduct. In brief, while individual behaviour can be influenced by cultural norms, practices, patterns and values, it is crucial to avoid general profiling and stereotyping that can create certain predispositions, which can contaminate the decision-making process. In other words, one needs to be conscious that not all, and even not the majority, of individual actions and choices are manifestations of cultural practices, patterns and values of a certain group of people.

2 Misconception 2: Cultural Linearism and Homogeneity

Another misconception relates to the tendency to think of culture in a given society as a linear and homogenous set of practices, patterns and values. Cultures are inherently dynamic and multifaceted, with regional sub-variations. Ignoring this complexity is a recipe for misunderstandings. For example, within one country or region in Africa, there exist several cultures and sub-cultures. To illustrate, within Egypt, several different cultural patterns, values and practices exist depending on the region, city, village and even class. The Bedouin culture, characterised by nomadic lifestyles and traditional desert practices, is prevalent in the Egyptian desert, and the Nubian culture, with its unique language, customs, and historical heritage is concentrated in the far southern part of the Nile Valley, and in urban centres and coastal cities, different cultural patterns and practices exist. Thus, cultures cannot be reduced to singular narratives. Encountering an Egyptian practitioner or arbitrator from one part of Egypt cannot inform one's knowledge of the totality of the Egyptian culture, and any such profiling ignores individual characteristics, and risks falling into the trap of cultural linearism. This is not just exclusive to Egypt, but equally applies across the board in Africa and in other distant localities.

In international arbitration, this misconceived linearism creates unconscious biases that impact communications and decision-making by judging witnesses, counsel and arbitrators based on isolated interactions with few practitioners from a given jurisdiction or locality.

3 Misconception 3: Cultures Are Hierarchical

The third misconception relates to certain tendencies to appreciate and judge actors in international arbitration based on unconscious cultural profiling in a hierarchical context. For example, some may perceive certain cultures to be more advanced than others and so deserve more appreciation. Apart from the immorality and disrespectful nature of this perception, the effect of this in international arbitration deserves careful reflection and perhaps structured surveys and studies. For example, it is a stern and unfortunate reality that some users, practitioners and arbitrators associate corrupt practices with certain cultures or jurisdictions more than others. This again contaminates the decision-making process, especially if the case involves corruption allegations, such that those who are not aware of their unconscious biases may be prepared to readily accept allegations depending on misinformed cultural hierarchies. Obviously, the facts and the governing law play critical and decisive roles in the decision-making process, but the risk of contaminating this process with misconceptions informed by subjective biases is not fictional and requires varying degrees of self-restraint and collective reflection within the arbitration community. Similarly, culture features prominently in the context of establishing trust and cooperation between arbitrators and counsel, or between counsel teams, or between arbitrators and witnesses and experts, etc. It is striking how sometimes one is more or less trusting of the other, depending on the interacting characters, the cultural affiliations of the engaged individuals and various perceptions of questionable cultural hierarchies.

Falling into the unwelcomed abyss of cultural hierarchies creates missed opportunities for cultural enrichment and risks undermining the need for 'open-mindedness', which is key for truly successful international arbitration players. Also, judging based on cultural hierarchies runs a clear risk of undermining the value of national laws in less-developed nations, which, in turn, leads to less readiness to uphold and apply these laws. This can also lead to a more condescending approach to judicial trends in these jurisdictions and cultures, despite the fact that the development of international commercial arbitration would not have been possible without the openness, assistance, endorsement and active support of national courts in various jurisdictions.[21]

Questionable perceptions of cultural hierarchies are also at odds with the notion of *glocalisation*, where global and international standards need to be adapted to local cultures and needs. Glocalisation is supposedly a safe space where both the global and the local cooperate to eventually create a 'third culture',[22] noting that the influence between international arbitration and national laws and cultures is not a one-way highway; it is rather a symbiotic relationship and a nexus of the different local and the global trends informing the trajectory of such influence.[23] After all, international arbitration players are indeed cosmopolitan, and have benefited from 'enculturation';[24]

21. Prof. Dr. Joshua Karton, *The Culture of International Arbitration and the Evolution of Contract Law* (1st ed. Oxford University Press, 2013) 123.
22. The concept of *glocalisation*, originating from the Japanese business model, emphasises thinking globally while maintaining local culture. Heather Voisey and Prof. Dr. Tim O'Riordan, 'Globalisation and Localization', in Voisey, H. and O'Riordan, Prof. Dr. Tim O'Riordan, *Globalism, Localism and Identity, Fresh Perspectives on the transition to Sustainability* (London: Earthscan, 2001) 25-42.
23. Prof. Dr. Mohamed S. Abdel Wahab, *Public Policy as a Fundamental Legal Conception Precluding the Application of Foreign Law in the Age of Globalisation* (Manchester School of Law, PHD Thesis 2004) 175.
24. This process of cultural acquisition is referred to as 'Enculturation', and it takes place over three levels: (1) the level of unconsciousness where our shaping by a particular set of social practices and values acclimatise us to how we comprehend self and the world; (2) the level of consciousness but beyond our control where human behaviour is founded on the reaction and compliance to the pressure exerted by the surrounding social forces. Under this level, some people are forced to comply with the some values adopted by other people at large in their society and which may differ from the former's own; (3) the cultural supermarket level where people are free to pick and choose the values and ideas they want. This is a level of both consciousness and control. This last level is further facilitated and unstoppable because of the forces of globalisation, which sustain an ever-increasing chain reaction of cultural interaction.

an infusion of various cultures at national and international levels. They come with their different cultural-baggage to work together and eventually develop a third culture where a set of autonomous 'professional norms'[25] materialise and are manifested through enculturation.

Thus, local cultures remain essential ingredients to the development of an all-inclusive 'third culture' in international arbitration. That third culture is the result of an interaction, cross-pollination and infusion of elements of national cultures and practices and international practices that transcend national borders. That said, both local professionals and international arbitration practitioners should not view the international arbitration community and the third culture it has spawned as closed and exclusive with a superiority complex over national cultures. Such a misconception often arises because international arbitrators often handle high-stakes disputes, leading parties to often select from a relatively limited pool of available arbitrators.[26]

The emergence of a new cosmopolitan third culture that co-exists alongside national cultures is a reality, and is informing international arbitration practices on all levels and is even impacting national practices, patterns, values and principles on procedural and substantive levels. Nonetheless, this does not entail total erosion or demise of local legal cultures, as there is always a margin of cultural preservation.[27]

4 Misconception 4: Culture and Law Are Synonymous

While there is an undeniable interplay between law and culture, there exists a misconception that legal norms and cultural practices are synonymous, and even if not synonymous, their evolutionary path is one and the same. Although there is indeed an overlap between law and culture, given that legal provisions and principles are genetic code carriers of certain cultural practices,[28] law is not always a follower of culture, and can sometimes lead and follow a separate path, especially when competing sub-cultures exist in a given jurisdiction. Law does not necessarily reflect the existing

Gordon Mathews, *Global Culture/Individual Identity, Searching for Home in the Cultural Supermarket* (Routledge, 2000) 12-16. Nevertheless, it is submitted that the cultural supermarket level may not be totally a level of consciousness and control because all three levels co-exist and occur simultaneously to a great extent. Thus, communicating and interacting with diverse people representing different cultural traditions and practices contribute to the shaping of the self and one's perception of the world, other individuals, and societies consciously or unconsciously. Accordingly, enculturation on the cultural supermarket level may not always be subject to awareness and control.

25. Prof. Dr. Joshua Karton, *The Culture of International Arbitration and the Evolution of Contract Law* (1st ed. Oxford University Press, 2013) 23.
26. Prof. Dr. Joshua Karton, *The Culture of International Arbitration and the Evolution of Contract Law* (1st ed. Oxford University Press, 2013) 61.
27. Prof. Dr. Mohamed S. Abdel Wahab, 'Cultural Globalisation and Public Policy: Exclusion of Foreign Law in the Global Village', in Michael Freeman (ed.), *Law and Sociology* (vol. 8, Oxford University Press, 2004) 375.
28. Prof. Dr. Lawrence M. Friedman, 'The Place of Legal Culture in the Sociology of Law', in Michael Freeman (ed.), *Law and Society* (vol. 8 2004) 185; Prof. Dr. Joshua Karton, *The Culture of International Arbitration and the Evolution of Contract Law* (1st ed. Oxford University Press, 2013) 20.

culture(s) of a given nation, but it can pave the way to an aspired cultural transformation.

In the specific context of international arbitration, jurisdictions may adopt established international norms that are reflective of the third culture of international arbitration such as the UNCITRAL Model Law on International Commercial Arbitration, the various guidelines and texts issued by organisations such as the ICCA, the IBA, the Ciarb, etc. Moreover, national and regional arbitral institutions are also subscribing to the best practices, norms and principles that apply in the context of international arbitration, without being constrained by local legal cultures and practices.

Thus, legal norms and practices may well advance at a different pace and in a different direction from cultural practices and patterns in a given society; especially, legal norms are visible, relatively tangible and easily discernible as opposed to cultural practices and patterns, which are mostly intangible.[29] However, these intangible cultural norms do have an undeniable impact on codified norms, hence the conundrum and the confusion.[30] As stated above, legal norms are genetic code carriers of cultural patterns and values, as laws do not exist in a vacuum and sometimes need to be fully understood in a cultural context, even if those legal norms deviate from existing cultural practices. All this plays a role in shaping and appreciating the conduct of parties, legal professionals, and arbitrators, and in ascertaining the interpretation and application of national law,[31] even if these laws refer to principle(s) that are common to a number of jurisdictions. On a substantive level, taking the principles of good faith and abuse of rights as examples, the difference in interpretation and understanding of the role and scope of these principles is not limited to a common-civil law dichotomy; it also exists within jurisdictions that belong to the same legal family, be it civil law, common law or Islamic *Sharī'ah* based.

5 Misconception 5: Culture and Inappropriate Bias

At the outset, it is worth noting that cultural inclinations and preferences do not automatically imply an inappropriate bias. However, parties, practitioners and arbitrators must be conscious and aware that any preferences and inclinations should not compromise their professional conduct and the international arbitration third culture. More specifically, for arbitrators, they must maintain their open-mindedness, integrity and impartiality and independence by not allowing those initial preferences or

29. Dr. Mary Howard, 'International Arbitration and Cross-cultural Issues', in Stavros Brekoulakis (ed.), *Mediation and Dispute Management* (Arbitration: The International Journal of Arbitration, © Kluwer Law International; Kluwer Law International 2020, vol. 86, Issue 3) 337.
30. Dr. Mary Howard, 'International Arbitration and Cross-cultural Issues', in Stavros Brekoulakis (ed.), *Mediation and Dispute Management* (Arbitration: The International Journal of Arbitration, © Kluwer Law International; Kluwer Law International 2020, vol. 86, Issue 3) 341.
31. Prof. Dr. Won Kidane, 'The Culture of Investment Arbitration: An African Perspective', in Meg Kinnear and Dr. Campbell McLachlan (eds), *ICSID Review: Foreign Investment Law Journal* (Oxford University Press 2019, vol. 34, Issue 2) 414.

inclinations to contaminate their procedural and substantive views or create inappropriate dispositions.

That said, in practice, it is worth mentioning that there are instances where the arbitrators' impartiality and independence may well have been beyond reproach, but cultural insensitivity did lead to tensions and misunderstandings,[32] which did mistakenly put the impartiality of the arbitrator into question. Conversely, there are instances where the arbitrators' cultural sensitivity and the care taken in understanding the parties' positions and communications have led to diffusing tension, achieving more cooperation and inducing more trust and efficiency into the process. Thus, international arbitrators should be culturally aware to avoid coming across as 'impartial but not neutral'.[33] However, one could argue that in certain circumstances, an arbitrator in a given case, who is readily dismissive of cultural differences and their impact, may unconsciously exhibit partiality towards parties from cultures with which they are familiar and indeed more receptive to, which is unwelcome and risky.

Having dealt with some misconceptions relating to culture and how this may impact and contaminate the decision-making process and lead to unconscious biases, the author shall now move to define culture and explore certain relevant cultural concepts referred to in the first part, and which will inform the discussion over the cultural manifestations during the various stages of arbitral proceedings.

III SETTING THE STAGE: CULTURE DECIPHERED

1 Definition

To address the influence of culture and the manifestations thereof in international arbitration, it is necessary to decipher culture and define same. Culture, as explored in anthropology, sociology, and law, encompasses a collective set of ideas and values shared by a group of people at a given time. It is a dynamic construct, evolving over time and influenced by various factors. That said, anthropologists have traditionally defined culture as 'the way of life of people'.[34] Less abstract and more precise definitions revolve around the idea that culture represents the set of practices, values, beliefs, customs acquired by individuals as members of a distinctive society, and those resulting from interaction between people, which have accumulated, assimilated and passed on to following generations.[35] Thus, each individual learns, interacts, and

32. Prof. Dr. Giorgio Bernini, 'Is There a Growing International Arbitration Culture?', in Prof. Dr. Albert Jan van den Berg (ed.), *ICCA Congress Series No. 8 (Seoul 1996): International Dispute Resolution: Towards an International Arbitration Culture* (ICCA Congress Series, vol. 8, © Kluwer Law International; ICCA & Kluwer Law International 1998) 43.
33. Prof. Dr. Giorgio Bernini, 'Is There a Growing International Arbitration Culture?', in Prof. Dr. Albert Jan van den Berg (ed.), *ICCA Congress Series No. 8 (Seoul 1996): International Dispute Resolution: Towards an International Arbitration Culture* (ICCA Congress Series, vol. 8, © Kluwer Law International; ICCA & Kluwer Law International 1998) 42.
34. Mathews (n 24) p. 1.
35. C. Kerr, J.T. Dunlop, F.H. Harbison, and C.A. Myers define it as 'that complex whole which includes knowledge, belief, art, law, morals, custom, and any other capabilities and habits acquired by man as a member of a society'. Clark Kerr et al., *Industrialism and the Industrial*

communicates with the society, and through such a process he is being culturally shaped. It is on that basis that practitioners and scholars have advanced several other definitions of culture, which the author sets out below:

(i) '([T]he collective programming of the mind distinguishing the members of one group or category of people from others).'[36]
(ii) '[S]hared knowledge and schemes created and used by a set of people for perceiving, interpreting, expressing, and responding to the social realities around them.'[37]
(iii) '[A] dynamic value system of learned elements, with assumptions, conventions, beliefs and rules permitting members of group to relate to each other and to the world, to communicate and to develop their creative potential.'[38]
(iv) '[T]hat complex whole which includes knowledge, belief, art, law, morals, custom, and any other capabilities and habits acquired by man as a member of a society';[39]
(v) It is 'both ideas and practices that have in common the function of providing meaning and identity for social actors and which combine cognitive, expressive, and evaluative elements';[40]
(vi) It is '[A] process by which the interactions between members of a community become self-reinforcing and determine the contours of future interactions [...] In sum, culture exists where members of a community share a set of norms that produce reflexive behaviour conditioned by tradition or community approbation.'[41]

Man (Penguin Books Ltd., 1973) 94; Wallerstein define it as 'the set of values or practices of some part smaller than some whole'. Immanuel Wallerstein, 'The National and the Universal: Can There Be Such a Thing as World Culture?' in A.D. King (ed.), *Culture, Globalisation and the World-System, Contemporary Conditions for the Representation of Identity* (University of Minnesota Press, 1997) 91; Holton refers to culture as 'both ideas and practices that have in common the function of providing meaning and identity for social actors and which combine cognitive, expressive, and evaluative elements'. Robert Holton, *Globalization and the Nation-State* (Macmillan Press Ltd., 1998) 162.

36. Prof. Dr. Geert Hofstede and Prof. Dr. Gert Jan Hofstede, *Cultures and Organizations: Software of the Mind* (2nd ed., McGraw-Hill 2005) 7 cited in Aisha Nadar, 'Construction Arbitration and Standard Forms of Contract in the Middle East: National Culture and Its Impact on Perception and Practice' in Prof. Nassib G. Ziadé (ed.), *BCDR International Arbitration Review* (© Kluwer Law International; Kluwer Law International 2017, vol. 4, Issue 1) 64.
37. Prof. Dr. John Paul Lederach, *Preparing for Peace: Conflict Transformation Across Cultures* (Syracuse University Press, 1995) 9 cited in Alvin Yeo SC and Chou Sean Yu, 'Cultural Considerations in Advocacy: East Meets West', in Stephen Jagusch and Philippe Pinsolle (eds), *The Guide to Advocacy* (3rd ed. Global Arbitration Review 2018) 184.
38. Prof. Dr. Alison Dundes Renteln, 'Clash of Civilizations? Cultural Differences in the Development and Interpretation of International Law', American Society of International Law Proceedings, *Cultural Bias in International Law* (1998) 233.
39. Dr. Clark Kerr et al., *Industrialism and the Industrial Man* (Harmondsworth, 1973) 94.
40. Prof. Dr. Robert Holton, *Globalization and the Nation-State* (Aldershot, 1998) 162.
41. Prof. Dr. Joshua Karton, *The Culture of International Arbitration and the Evolution of Contract Law* (1st ed. Oxford University Press 2013) 19.

It is submitted that all these definitions share a common understanding that culture represents a set of 'reflexive' practices,[42] values, beliefs, and customs acquired by individuals in a given society, and which have accumulated, assimilated, and passed on to following generations. Specifically, the *reflexive* element of culture is a key consideration for the purpose of this chapter. It is this reflexive effect of culture that describes the automatic influence that operates without consulting the deliberate and conscious process of the mind. Thus, having different cultural backgrounds without knowing how to embrace or deal with such differences may result in a subconscious friction between individuals, which could significantly affect the process and outcome of international arbitration. In psychology, this is called the 'affinity' effect, which is a special term used to describe factors such as culture, personal associations, and previous experiences affecting a decision maker.[43]

2 Elements of Culture

In light of the various definitions of culture, three basic elements of culture can be distilled: *symbols*, *heroes*, and *values*. Symbols represent the language, gestures, and visual expressions of a culture. Heroes embody the individuals who exemplify cultural ideals and aspirations. Values represent the shared beliefs and principles that guide behavioural patterns in a given culture. These constituting elements of culture feature prominently in international arbitration.

In terms of symbols, language, gestures and visual expressions are crucial when it comes to pleadings by counsel, witness testimony and tribunal reactions. More specifically, in terms of language, participants in an international arbitration generally tend to believe that linguistic competence is reflective of professional capabilities and that those who are less fluent in the working language of arbitration would be less impactful and convincing, especially that translation and interpretation may not fully convey the strength and the emotions that accompany the statements made. Translations and interpretation may not accurately capture the intended meaning of a non-native speaker.[44]

Moreover, the manner in which people of a certain culture communicate (e.g., facial expressions, body language, postures, hand gestures, etc.) can also be relevant in certain arbitration contexts. For example, when cross-examining witnesses, it may be

42. Dr. Rémy Gerbay, 'Chapter 36: "Literature Review? What Literature Review?!": The Influence of Legal Culture on Scholarship in International Arbitration', in Stavros Brekoulakis, Julian D.M. Lew et al. (eds), *The Evolution and Future of International Arbitration* (International Arbitration Law Library, vol. 37, © Kluwer Law International; Kluwer Law International 2016) 488.
43. Edna Sussman, 'Biases and Heuristics in Arbitrator Decision-Making: Reflections on How to Counteract or Play to Them', in Tony Cole (ed.), *The Roles of Psychology in International Arbitrations* (Wolters Kluwer, 2017) 65.
44. William K. Slate II, 'Luncheon Address The Impact of Culture on International Commercial Arbitration', in Albert Jan van den Berg (ed.), *ICCA Congress Series No. 12 (Beijing 2004): New Horizons in International Commercial Arbitration and Beyond* (ICCA Congress Series, vol. 12, © Kluwer Law International; ICCA & Kluwer Law International 2005) 13; Alvin Yeo SC and Chou Sean Yu, 'Cultural Considerations in Advocacy: East Meets West', in Stephen Jagusch and Philippe Pinsolle (eds), *The Guide to Advocacy* (3rd ed. Global Arbitration Review, 2018) 186.

useful to know that 'for South Asians, [...] a shake of the head by a witness may mean an affirmation of a point rather than a denial',[45] and that the OK sign is considered rude in Latin America,[46] and that some witnesses from shy cultures may find it difficult and rude to disagree with the cross-examiner, especially if the cross-examiner is older and more senior. Also, some cultures are accustomed to giving indirect and long answers as a way of courtesy such as Chinese speakers who 'tend to be less direct',[47] while others appreciate short and concise ones. Further, in negotiations, a Chinese party would not be willing to either show enthusiasm and would tend to force the other side to show their cards first, which is opposed to the American salesperson's approach in proactively conveying excitement to conclude the deal.[48]

However, one should be consciously aware not to stereotype and not fall into one of the misconceptions addressed above, because some individuals from the various cultures addressed above may exhibit different reactions and behavioural patterns that are distinct from their fellow compatriots belonging to the same cultural pool.

Being able to compare a person's own culture and the different cultures of others is a necessary step to establish effective communication and to overcome differences. Professor Geert Hofstede proposes six dimensions for this comparison, which give an indication of how a certain culture may react to certain actions. These are:[49]

(i) power distance, which measures the acceptance of inequality;
(ii) uncertainty avoidance, reflecting a culture's comfort level with ambiguity;
(iii) Individualism versus collectivism, prioritising individual or group needs;
(iv) Masculinity versus femininity, concerning gender roles and values;
(v) long-term orientation versus short-term orientation, focusing on future or past/present; and
(vi) indulgence versus restraint, related to the gratification of desires.

Some practitioners have argued that, in the context of construction disputes and arbitration, a comparative analysis of English and MENA cultures based on the first

45. Alvin Yeo SC and Chou Sean Yu, 'Cultural Considerations in Advocacy: East Meets West', in Stephen Jagusch and Philippe Pinsolle (eds), *The Guide to Advocacy* (3rd ed. Global Arbitration Review, 2018)186 (emphasis added).
46. Dr. Adhid Miri, 'Hands Clasped: From the ancient Sumerians to Modern-Day Chaldeans' (Chaldean News, 1 September 2022) available at https://www.chaldeannews.com/culture-and-history/2022/9/1/hands-clasped-from-the-ancient-sumerians-to-modern-day-chaldeans, accessed on 23 June 2025.
47. Emmanuel Jacomy, 'How to Cross-Examine Chinese speakers, the Guide to Advocacy', in Stephen Jagusch and Philippe Pinsolle (eds), *The Guide to Advocacy* (3rd ed. Global Arbitration Review, 2018) 186 (emphasis added). *See also* Guideline II.B and III.B of the ICCA Hong Kong 2024 (ICCA, ICCA Hong Kong 2024), 9 June 2024, available at https://arbitrationblog.kluwerarbitration.com/2024/06/09/embracing-the-human-in-arbitration-a-look-back-at-icca-hong-kong-2024/ accessed on 23 June 2025.
48. Prof. Dr. Lucian W. Pye, *The China Trade: Making the Deal, Harvard Business Review* (the Magazine 1986), available at https://hbr.org/1986/07/the-china-trade-making-the-deal accessed on 23 June 2025.
49. Aisha Nadar, 'Construction Arbitration and Standard Forms of Contract in the Middle East: National Culture and Its Impact on Perception and Practice', in Prof. Nassib G. Ziadé (ed.), *BCDR International Arbitration Review* (© Kluwer Law International; Kluwer Law International 2017, vol. 4, Issue 1) 64-65.

three of Professor Hofstede's cultural dimensions – where the most pronounced differences reside – reveals stark contrasts. English culture exhibits high individualism, low power distance, and low uncertainty avoidance. Conversely, MENA culture is characterised by collectivism, high power distance, and strong uncertainty avoidance. In this regard, English culture's low power distance and high individualism likely contributed to the development of contracts empowering engineers with decision-making authority. Conversely, MENA culture's hierarchical structure and preference for certainty may explain the prevalent recourse to arbitration, often bypassing engineer-led resolutions. On such basis, it has been argued that tribunals should consider these cultural factors when assessing the diligence of parties during pre-arbitration proceedings.[50]

3 Enculturation and Third Cultures

In the context of international arbitration, two culture-related concepts are particularly relevant, these are: 'enculturation' and 'third cultures'. Enculturation refers to the process of acquiring cultural patterns. Thus, each individual learns, interacts, and communicates with the society and through such a process he/she is being culturally shaped. This process of cultural acquisition is referred to as 'enculturation'.[51] Enculturation takes place over three levels:[52]

(i) The level of unconsciousness where our shaping by a particular set of social practices and values acclimatise us to how we comprehend self and the world.
(ii) The level of consciousness but beyond our control where human behaviour is founded on the reaction and compliance to the pressure exerted by the surrounding social forces. Under this level, some people are forced to comply with the same values adopted by the majority of people in their society and which may differ from the formers' own.
(iii) The cultural supermarket level where people are free to pick and choose the values and ideas they want. This is a level of both consciousness and control. This last level is further facilitated by the forces of globalisation, which sustain an ever-increasing chain reaction of cultural interaction.

A third culture is the product of the process of enculturation across various cultures. In other words, third cultures emerge because of the interaction between diverse players in specific contexts and environments. For example, international

50. Aisha Nadar, 'Construction Arbitration and Standard Forms of Contract in the Middle East: National Culture and Its Impact on Perception and Practice', in Prof. Nassib G. Ziadé (ed.), *BCDR International Arbitration Review* (© Kluwer Law International; Kluwer Law International 2017, vol. 4, Issue 1) 66-68.
51. Prof. Dr. Alison Dundes Renteln, 'Clash of Civilizations? Cultural Differences in the Development and Interpretation of International Law', American Society of International Law Proceedings, *Cultural Bias in International Law* (1998) 233.
52. Prof. Dr. Gordon Mathews, *Global Culture/Individual Identity, Searching for Home in the Cultural Supermarket* (London, 2000) 12-16.

organisations, such as the UN and the World Bank, have evolved to a point where professionals working therein have founded a unique set of established professional norms and shared practices that made them spawn their own third culture.

In the specific context of international arbitration, practitioners from different backgrounds come together to develop shared cultural practices that transcend their individual cultures,[53] hence the developed third culture of international arbitration. However, one should note that third cultures are not cultures in the strict sense of the word, but are standards of interpersonal behaviour, work-related norms, codes of reciprocity, styles of life, networks of communication, institutional arrangements, world views and new types of individual selves that are the outcome of interaction between people engaged in common dealings and enterprises.[54]

That said, on the macro level, due to the proliferation of international arbitral institutions and the increasing density of soft law, arbitration has become a ripe arena for cultural homogenisation[55] and consequently the emergence of an international arbitration third culture.[56] This third culture is manifested in the international arbitration community's guidelines and soft law instruments relating to codes of conduct, ethics, evidence, conflicts, and practice models that cover almost every aspect of the arbitral process. Examples include: the ICCA Guidelines on Standards of Practice in International Arbitration,[57] the IBA Guidelines on Party Representation in International Arbitration,[58] the IBA Rules on the Taking of Evidence in International Arbitration,[59] the IBA International Principles on Conduct for the Legal Profession,[60] the IBA's

53. Prof. Dr. Mohamed S. Abdel Wahab, 'Cultural Considerations in Advocacy: Arab World', in Stephen Jagusch and Philippe Pinsolle (eds), *The Guide to Advocacy* (3rd ed. Global Arbitration Review 2018) 214.
54. Prof. Dr. Updera Baxi, *Life of Law Amidst Globalisation* (Conference paper submitted in the 50th Anniversary Conference of the ALTA 1995), available https://ojs.ruc.dk/index.php/ocpa/article/view/3696/1875 accessed on 31 August 2024.
55. Tejas Karia and Dr. Rishab Gupta, 'Cultural Considerations in Advocacy: India', in Stephen Jagusch and Philippe Pinsolle (eds), *The Guide to Advocacy* (3rd ed. Global Arbitration Review 2018) 192.
56. Prof. Dr. Giorgio Bernini, 'Is There a Growing International Arbitration Culture?', in Prof. Dr. Albert Jan van den Berg (ed.), *ICCA Congress Series No. 8 (Seoul 1996): International Dispute Resolution: Towards an International Arbitration Culture* (ICCA Congress Series, vol. 8 © Kluwer Law International; ICCA & Kluwer Law International 1998) 44.
57. The ICCA Guidelines on Standards of Practice in International Arbitration, the ICCA Report No. 9, 2021, available at https://cdn.arbitration-icca.org/s3fs-public/document/media_document/ICCA_Reports_No_9_Guidelines_on_Standards_of_Practice_in_International_Arbitration.pdf, accessed on 23 June 2025.
58. The IBA Rules on the Taking of Evidence in International Arbitration, dated 23 May 2013, https://www.ibanet.org/MediaHandler?id=6F0C57D7-E7A0-43AF-B76E-714D9FE74D7F, accessed on 16 August 2025.
59. The IBA Rules on the Taking of Evidence in International Arbitration, dated 17 December 2020, https://www.ibanet.org/MediaHandler?id=def0807b-9fec-43ef-b624-f2cb2af7cf7b, accessed on 16 August 2025.
60. The IBA International Principles on Conduct for the Legal Profession dated 28 May 2011, https://www.icj.org/wp-content/uploads/2014/10/IBA_International_Principles_on_Conduct_for_the_legal_prof.pdf, accessed on 16 August 2025.

International Code of Ethics,[61] the IBA Guidelines on Conflicts of Interest in International Arbitration,[62] the Prague Inquisitorial Rules of Taking Evidence in International Arbitration,[63] the Rules on the Efficient Conduct of Proceedings in International Arbitration,[64] the UNCITRAL Model Arbitration law and Model Arbitration Rules, and the various Ciarb Guidelines on Interviewing Prospective Arbitrators, Jurisdictional Objections, Terms of Appointment, Security for Costs, Expert Witnesses, Witness Conferencing and the Use of AI in International Arbitration.[65]

This emergence of transnational guidelines and best practice instruments is a manifestation of a third culture in international arbitration. Professor Karton asserts that 'what arbitrators have in common will increasingly overshadow their desperate backgrounds and legal traditions. The elite transnational community that presides over the majority of international arbitrations may already share a common legal and professional culture'.[66]

On a more micro level, albeit not yet reflecting a full-fledged third culture with *reflexive* patterns, international arbitration practitioners have developed some standardised common norms, and have developed quasi-communities (epistemic communities).[67] For example, the ICCA Guidelines on Standards of Practice in International Arbitration reflect a common standard of professional conduct to be shared by all participants in international arbitration, where Guideline III.A provides that 'Arbitrators shall address all participants in an international arbitration in a courteous and impartial manner. Arbitrators shall not employ hostile, demeaning or humiliating terms in written or oral communications with participants in an international arbitration', and Guideline III.B provides that 'Arbitrators shall ensure that all participants in an international arbitration conduct themselves in a courteous and respectful manner throughout the proceedings.'[68] Also, Guideline II.B provides that 'Party representatives shall, at all times, act with respect and courtesy, and conduct themselves in a

61. The IBA International Code of Ethics adopted on 1956 (1988 ed.) https://www.ibanet.org/MediaHandler?id=DAD036E7-AF03-4BFC-806B-6A5CA4A0775A, accessed on 16 August 2025.
62. The IBA Guidelines on Conflicts of Interest in International Arbitration (2024), https://www.ibanet.org/document?id=Guidelines-on-Conflicts-of-Interest-in-International-Arbitration-2024#:~:text=Every%20arbitrator%20shall%20be%20impartial,proceedings%20have%20otherwise%20finally%20terminated, accessed on 16 August 2025.
63. The Inquisitorial Rules of Taking Evidence in International Arbitration (2018), https://praguerules.com/upload/iblock/a00/a00568c6787a8bc955f4fdfe93db5a10.pdf, accessed on 16 August 2025.
64. The Rules on the Efficient Conduct of Proceedings in International Arbitration (2018), https://praguerules.com/upload/medialibrary/9dc/9dc31ba7799e26473d92961d926948c9.pdf, accessed on 16 August 2025.
65. https://www.ciarb.org/resources/professional-practice-guidelines/international-arbitration/, accessed on 16 August 2025.
66. Prof. Dr. Joshua Karton, *The Culture of International Arbitration and the Evolution of Contract Law* (1st ed. Oxford University Press 2013), p. 21 (emphasis added).
67. Prof. Dr. Joshua Karton, *The Culture of International Arbitration and the Evolution of Contract Law* (1st ed. Oxford University Press 2013), p. 23.
68. The ICCA Guidelines on Standards of Practice in International Arbitration, the ICCA Report No. 9, 2021, available at https://cdn.arbitration-icca.org/s3fs-public/document/media_document/ICCA_Reports_No_9_Guidelines_on_Standards_of_Practice_in_International_Arbitration.pdf (emphasis added), accessed on 31 August 2024.

professional manner. Party representatives shall not act offensively or with disrespect towards any of the participants in an international arbitration.'[69]

These ongoing processes of cross-cultural integration and enculturation facilitated and accelerated by contemporary trends of globalisation have rendered the third culture of international arbitration in a continuous state of flux, where traditional and existing cultural patterns and practices are being transformed, **interpenetrated, and reshaped by internal and external trends of change. However, as any form of change involves resistance to that change, cultural transformation in the global age has necessarily generated regional and local pockets of resistance. This global-local paradox is inherently embedded in the cultural globalisation process, and continues to inform the development of the international arbitration paradigm, where the local, the regional and the international interact and cross-pollinate.**

IV CULTURAL MANIFESTATIONS IN INTERNATIONAL ARBITRATION

The impact of culture and its invisible hand are felt throughout the international arbitration process, and this section explores the effect of cultural differences and interaction at key stages of the international arbitration process, noting that cultural differences extend beyond the traditional civil-common law dichotomy. The key stages addressed below are: case preparation, case presentation and case determination.

1 Case Preparation

In terms of case preparation, this is a stage which is counsel-centric, and, as stated above, counsel may be drawn from diverse cultural backgrounds, and with varying shades of experience and expertise in international arbitration. Thus, counsel's approaches to communications, collaboration, client-handling, negotiations and professional conduct may vary considerably depending on personal, cultural and legal backgrounds. However, it has already been seen that international arbitration has spawned its own third culture, which includes guidelines on counsel conduct, ethics and obligations, such as the ICCA Guidelines on Standards of Practice in International Arbitration, which are already addressed above.

Thus, in international arbitration, there is a common expectation and common minimum professional standards that militate against engaging in guerrilla tactics, abusive conduct, excessive aggression that may adversely affect the client's interests and illicit conduct of all forms. That said, and taking into consideration that counsel's obligation towards clients is usually an obligation to exert reasonable efforts and exercise due care, it is not expected that counsel, irrespective of their cultural and

69. The ICCA Guidelines on Standards of Practice in International Arbitration, the ICCA Report No. 9, 2021, available at https://cdn.arbitration-icca.org/s3fs-public/document/media_document/ICCA_Reports_No_9_Guidelines_on_Standards_of_Practice_in_International_Arbitration.pdf (emphasis added), accessed on 31 August 2024.

professional background, will not adhere to these minimum standards of professional conduct when preparing for an arbitration case. However, this does not mean that there is always one golden standard that binds everyone and which all counsel must follow, because practices that may qualify as unacceptable, inappropriate, abusive and aggressive will vary based on personal, cultural and legal backgrounds and so there is a degree of flexibility and adaptability which is one of the main advantages of arbitration.[70] However, this flexibility requires arbitration practitioners, engaged in the early stages of dispute preparation, to understand and leverage the complexities and effects of cultural differences, whether when dealing with clients and/or opposing counsel and parties.

In the specific context of case preparation, there are some cultural manifestations that affect case preparation with varying degrees of visibility. For example, as to party representation, some cultures prefer to instruct qualified counsel from their own culture or at least counsel who is familiar with it. This is observed in the Chinese and some other Asian cultures. However, other cultures may not be concerned about counsel's cultural affinity, and may go with foreign counsel that has no cultural connection, but this will be most likely the case when the dispute is a cross-border international dispute involving foreign law(s) with which counsel is familiar or qualified in.

Moreover, invisible cultural considerations may be manifested during the case preparation stage, where counsel may have different approaches to case strategy. This is not only a function of experience, expertise, competence, and law, but is also affected by cultural considerations such as the type and formulation of the relief sought, reliance on documentary versus witness and expert evidence, and the approaches to the selection of arbitrators.

That said, practice and experience have shown that culture plays a role in the approach to gathering evidence, structuring legal arguments, and building relationships with opposing counsel. Cultural differences can even affect something as trivial as the length of the hearing day,[71] the assumptions and the 'argumentative moves'.[72] For instance, a culture that prioritises hierarchy may have different communication styles and expectations compared to a culture that values egalitarianism.

In the specific context of arbitrator selection, counsel preparing his/her case cannot disregard how relatable his/her line of arguments and pleadings would be for the tribunal. For that reason, it is often said that '[a] good lawyer knows the law, but

70. Dr. Torsten Lorcher, 'Cultural Considerations in Advocacy: Continental Europe', in Stephen Jagusch QC and Philippe Pinsolle (eds), *The Guide to Advocacy* (3rd ed. Global Arbitration Review 2018) 226; Prof. Dr. Kaj Hober and Howard S, Sussman, *Cross-Examination in International Arbitration* (Oxford University Press 2014) 30.

71. Tejas Karia and Dr. Rishab Gupta, 'Cultural Considerations in Advocacy: India', in Stephen Jagusch and Philippe Pinsolle (eds), *The Guide to Advocacy* (3rd ed. Global Arbitration Review 2018) 192, 197.

72. Dr. Rémy Gerbay, 'Chapter 36: "Literature Review? What Literature Review?!": The Influence of Legal Culture on Scholarship in International Arbitration', in Stavros Brekoulakis, Julian D.M. Lew et al. (eds), *The Evolution and Future of International Arbitration* (International Arbitration Law Library, vol. 37 © Kluwer Law International; Kluwer Law International 2016) 488-489 (emphasis added).

a great lawyer knows the judge'.[73] *Thus, it is commonly understood that the selection of arbitrators is the single most important decision when preparing for a case. If that decision is wrong, no amount of good lawyering can rectify and correct that mistake. That said, it is increasingly observed that parties and counsel spend considerable time pondering over the most suitable profile for an arbitrator and her/his identity. There is also an increasing tendency to select not only qualified and competent arbitrators who are familiar with the governing law, but also arbitrators who share a degree of cultural affinity or are not culturally insensitive. In today's divided, yet interconnected world, this cultural sensitivity in selecting arbitrators has even become central to disputes involving parties from jurisdictions that may be in conflict or experiencing tensions, whether political, economic, trade-related and/or legal.*

2 Case Presentation

In the specific context of case presentation, cultural considerations also play a role that increases and decreases depending on the nature of the dispute, the background of the parties, and the specific aspect of case presentation. Cultural differences are immediately discernible in advocacy and presentation styles (whether written or oral submissions), approaches to *document production, witness evidence,*[74] *expert evidence, cross-examination styles, etc.*

In relation to advocacy, the prevailing international arbitration 'third culture' mandates minimum standards of civility and professional conduct, as enshrined in the soft law instruments and guidelines referred to above, such as the ICCA Guidelines on Standards of Practice (2021) and the IBA Guidelines on Party Representation (2013). This minimum common denominator and universal standards that manifest the third culture and transcend cultural differences were best captured by the award of the arbitral tribunal in ICSID Case No. ARB/06/3 dated 6 May 2013 (*The Rompetrol Group NV v. Romania*), where the tribunal stated at paragraph 19: 'Counsel's duty is to present his Party's case, with the degree of dependence and partiality that the role implies, so long as he does so with diligence and with honesty, and in due compliance with the applicable rules of professional conduct and ethics.' However, cultural differences lurk in the details and the varying approaches to advocacy in case presentation.

At this stage of case presentation, diligent and competent counsel will have already acquainted themselves with most of the culture differences that may exist at

73. Alvin Yeo SC and Chou Sean Yu, 'Cultural Considerations in Advocacy: East Meets West', in Stephen Jagusch QC and Philippe Pinsolle (eds), *The Guide to Advocacy* (Global Arbitration Review 2018) 191 (emphasis added); Tejas Karia and Dr. Rishab Gupta, 'Cultural Considerations in Advocacy: India, Global Arbitration Review', in Stephen Jagusch and Philippe Pinsolle (eds), *The Guide to Advocacy* (3rd ed. Global Arbitration Review 2018) 197.

74. Some jurisdictions, based on cultural considerations of not equating arbitral tribunals with courts, do not permit the hearing of witnesses under oath or affirmation. This is the case of Egypt, for example, where Article 33(1) of Egyptian Arbitration Law No. 27 of 1994 provides that witnesses cannot be heard under oath. See also Dubai Court of Cassation, Challenge No. 96/JY2022, 2 June 2022. Challenge No. 1406/JY2023, 28 November 2023.

the preparation stage.[75] Again, in terms of advocacy styles, different cultures have different preferences for written and oral advocacy styles. For instance, some cultures may favour a direct and assertive approach, while others may prefer a more indirect and nuanced style. Additionally, the use of rhetorical devices, storytelling techniques, and nonverbal communication can vary across cultures. Furthermore, some cultures may be into exhaustive pleadings,[76] and others may dictate a more concise and less detailed pleading.

By way of illustration, and taking into consideration that there will always be individual differences even within the same culture, when presenting a case, for example, before an Indian arbitrator or a retired judge who is accustomed to court-style pleadings, counsel may start case presentation by focusing on the facts and then put more emphasis on the law at the final hearing.[77] However, if the case was before a French or Swiss arbitrator, counsel may better adopt memorial style submissions where he/she would plead the facts and the law, and set out his/her case fully from the beginning. Furthermore, if the case is pleaded before a traditional American arbitrator, counsel can expect that the arbitrator will not find aggressive cross-examination of witnesses and experts as offensive or inappropriate compared to English and other European arbitrators. Also, 'Indian arbitrators often dislike such conduct and will remind the advocate to be respectful and courteous to the witness.'[78]

Moreover, if the case is presented before a traditional civil law arbitrator from the MENA region, who may be more amenable to giving higher probative value to documentary over witness evidence, counsel may put more emphasis on documentary evidence. On the other hand, a common law arbitrator from Australia may tend to give more probative value to witness evidence when warranted. Further, a lawyer from Continental Europe may expect an arbitrator to take the lead in questioning the witness, whereas an American or English arbitrator may expect counsel to take the lead.[79] Even with respect to understanding the law, an English arbitrator may expect that parties are precluded from relying on post-contractual conduct in interpreting a contract, whereas an arbitrator based in New York (or in civil law countries) would expect the complete opposite.[80]

75. Edna Sussman, *Biases and Heuristics in Arbitrator Decision-Making: Reflections on How to Counteract or Play to Them*, in Tony Cole (ed.), *The Roles of Psychology in International Arbitrations* (Wolters Kluwer, 2017) 65.
76. Alvin Yeo SC and Chou Sean Yu, 'Cultural Considerations in Advocacy: East Meets West', in Stephen Jagusch QC and Philippe Pinsolle (eds), *The Guide to Advocacy* (3rd ed. Global Arbitration Review 2018) 189.
77. Tejas Karia and Dr. Rishab Gupta, 'Cultural Considerations in Advocacy: India', in Stephen Jagusch and Philippe Pinsolle (eds), *The Guide to Advocacy* (3rd ed. Global Arbitration Review 2018) 194.
78. Tejas Karia and Dr. Rishab Gupta, 'Cultural Considerations in Advocacy: India', in Stephen Jagusch and Philippe Pinsolle (eds), *The Guide to Advocacy* (3rd ed. Global Arbitration Review 2018) 192 (emphasis added).
79. Prof. Dr. Willian W. (Rusty) Park, '*Rules and Reliability: How Arbitrators Decide*', in Tony Cole (ed.), *The Roles of Psychology in International Arbitrations* (Wolters Kluwer, 2017) 10.
80. Prof. Dr. Willian W. (Rusty) Park, '*Rules and Reliability: How Arbitrators Decide*', in Tony Cole (ed.), *The Roles of Psychology in International Arbitrations* (Wolters Kluwer, 2017) 14.

In relation to production of document requests, this is again an area where a third culture of international arbitration exists through the IBA Rules on Taking of Evidence and the Redfern Schedule, which are widely used, irrespective of cultural differences. However, certain strong cultural inclinations have also led to the adoption of the Prague Rules in some civil law-based arbitrations. In any event, in relation to making and formulating document production requests, cultural differences still exist beyond the traditional civil-common law divide. Counsels' and arbitrators' experience, expertise and culture do play a role in how requests are formulated and considered.

With respect to witness evidence, this is a complex issue that involves multi-layered cultural influence. This influence is manifested in: (a) the preparation of witness testimonies, (b) arbitrators' assessment and perceptions of witness testimony, and (c) the behavioural patterns of witnesses during cross-examination. Given that issues (a) and (b) have already been touched upon above, it remains to address issue (c). In this respect, it should be noted that the behavioural patterns of witnesses of fact are a function of character, background, experience and culture. More specifically, in relation to culture, witnesses from certain cultures are generally more courteous, cooperative and shy than witnesses from other cultures. The impact of such behavioural patterns on the persuasiveness of witness testimony and the credibility of the witness cannot be overlooked. For instance, the over courteous attitude of a witness from a certain culture may come across as pretentious in the eyes of a culturally unaware arbitrator, and vice versa another witness' direct and confident answers may come across as a manifestation of over-confidence in the eyes of another culturally unaware arbitrator from a different background. As such, the testimonies of both witnesses from different cultures may leave negative impressions in the eyes of two different arbitrators from different cultural backgrounds. *Thus, it is important for counsel to be alive to these nuances and address the arbitral tribunal on them.*[81]

Finally, with respect to the pleading of the law governing the merits, counsels' and arbitrators' approaches may be informed by cultural considerations. For example, English counsel and arbitrators may be more familiar and culturally inclined to ascertain the content of the applicable law through expert evidence rather than submissions by counsel. Conversely, for Swiss and other civil law-cultured counsels and arbitrators, counsel submissions on the law would suffice. Also, when presenting a party's case, while Swiss and German counsel may generally devote a significant and separate part of the written submissions to legal issues and arguments, English and Indian counsel and arbitrators may be more focused on factual pleadings in written submissions.

Furthermore, cultural considerations also play a role in perceptions of *iura novit curia*.[82] Again, Swiss arbitrators and counsel may readily accept that arbitral tribunals can independently ascertain the content of the applicable law beyond the parties' legal pleadings, insofar as the tribunal has not surprised the parties or exceeded the parties'

81. Prof. Dr. Kaj Hober and Howard S, Sussman, *Cross-Examination in International Arbitration* (Oxford University Press 2014) 42.
82. For a detailed analysis and jurisdiction-specific considerations of *iura novit curia*, see Franco Ferrari and Giuditta Cordero-Moss, *Iura Novit Curia in International Arbitration* (Juris 2018).

relief, claims and defences. Conversely, English arbitrators would be less receptive to the idea of going beyond the parties' pleadings on law and the adversarial nature of the proceedings. However, the dividing line between these varying cultural and jurisdiction-specific approaches is blurring with the rise of the 'third culture' in international arbitration.

3 Case Determination

In the context of case determination, cultural considerations and differences are indeed manifested on both visible and invisible levels. These considerations and differences do impact the arbitrators' approaches to the assessment of evidence, communications and deliberations, reasoning and ultimately the decision-making process.

In terms of the assessment of evidence, it has already been stated above that different cultural backgrounds of arbitrators play a role in their perceptions of witness, expert and documentary evidence. By way of illustration, some scholars and practitioners have argued that arbitrators coming from civil law-based cultures will likely subconsciously give more weight to documentary evidence, whereas English and other common law-based cultures would be more receptive to giving greater weight to witness evidence,[83] and that is why more emphasis is usually placed on cross-examination in common law-based cultures to test the credibility of the evidence and the narrative advanced by the parties.[84] The same also applies to party-appointed and tribunal-appointed experts, where some arbitrators, motivated by some unconscious cultural inclinations, are less trusting of party-appointed experts and other arbitrators, from different cultures, will have no default inclinations and their views will be informed by the competence and the performance of the specific expert, whether party-appointed or not.

Moreover, the cultural background and inclinations of arbitrators do impact their view of contractual arrangements and whether the '*pacta*' (in *pacta sunt servanda*) is a dynamic concept that takes into account the parties' cultures and post-contractual conduct or not. This is of course subject to overriding legal considerations under the applicable law. Nevertheless, some scholars and practitioners have argued that in China, for example, the expectation is that a contract generally provides the principles or the framework for the parties' long-term or ongoing relationship. Thus, a Chinese cultured party would expect that the interpretation of the contract would be flexible and that the wording of the contract may be revisited from time to time. However, a western-cultured party (with differences among the various Western cultures) would actually expect the total opposite and would only be willing to revisit the wording of the

83. Dr. Torsten Lorcher, 'Cultural Considerations in Advocacy: Continental Europe', in Stephen Jagusch and Philippe Pinsolle (eds), *The Guide to Advocacy* (3rd ed. Global Arbitration Review 2018) 222.
84. Dr. Torsten Lorcher, 'Cultural Considerations in Advocacy: Continental Europe', in Stephen Jagusch and Philippe Pinsolle (eds), *The Guide to Advocacy* (3rd ed. Global Arbitration Review 2018) 223; Dr. Torsten Lorcher, 'Cultural Considerations in Advocacy: Continental Europe', in Stephen Jagusch and Philippe Pinsolle (eds), *The Guide to Advocacy* (3rd ed. Global Arbitration Review 2018).

contract in accordance with its express terms, in exceptional circumstances, or in case an agreement is struck between the parties to that effect.[85]

Despite all the above, it has also been observed that the rise of a third culture in international arbitration, through guidelines and soft law instruments, does operate to bridge cultural gaps and reduce differences in approaches which are informed by the visible and invisible hand of culture. By way of illustration, in respect of expert evidence, certain guidelines and protocols, such as the Ciarb Guideline on Party-appointed and Tribunal-appointed Experts (2015), expressly provide that experts owe the tribunal an overriding duty that prevails over the duties owed to their instructing party,[86] and the practice of international arbitration is now settled over the common use of party-appointed (more than tribunal-appointed) experts insofar as they are independent, qualified and competent, though tribunal-appointed experts are still used in some cases when the circumstances so warrant or necessity so requires.

In respect of communications, deliberations, reasoning and decision-making, some cultures prioritise consensus-building, while others value individual merit more, and so they are more amenable to confrontation during the decision-making process. Also, some cultures value direct and candid sharing of thoughts, which may come across for other cultures as being aggressive or insensitive to difference in opinion. Thus, a truly culturally aware arbitrator will endeavour to establish and build efficient, collegial and productive communication channels with other members of the arbitral tribunal. This is better for the overall decision-making process. That is why the ICCA Guidelines on Standards of Practice in International Arbitration provide that:[87] 'International arbitration brings together individuals from diverse cultures and backgrounds to resolve cross-border disputes. Cultural, linguistic, ethnic, religious, geographic, gender, disability, sexual orientation, and other forms of diversity are reflected in the practice of international arbitration. Diversity is recognized as an important factor in the maintenance of legitimacy of international arbitration as an accepted form of dispute resolution. The need to respect diversity is thus paramount in the cross-cultural environment that characterizes international arbitration.'

By and large, culture remains a dominant player in case preparation, presentation and determination, but the rise of an international arbitration third culture is helping to mitigate the sharp and stark differences in cultural manifestations.

---

85. William K. Slate II, 'Luncheon Address The Impact of Culture on International Commercial Arbitration', in Albert Jan van den Berg (ed.), *ICCA Congress Series No. 12 (Beijing 2004): New Horizons in International Commercial Arbitration and Beyond* (ICCA Congress Series, vol. 12 © Kluwer Law International; ICCA & Kluwer Law International 2005) 15.
86. Ciarb, Ciarb Guideline on Party-appointed and Tribunal-appointed Experts (2015) https://www.ciarb.org/media/zvijl3kx/7-party-appointed-and-tribunal-appointed-expert-witnesses-in-international-arbitration-2015.pdf, accessed on 23 June 2025.
87. ICCA, ICCA Reports No. 9 'Guidelines on Standards of Practice in International Arbitration' (The Hague, 2021), 3 https://cdn.arbitration-icca.org/s3fs-public/document/media_document/ICCA_Reports_No_9_Guidelines_on_Standards_of_Practice_in_International_Arbitration.pdf, accessed on 23 June 2025.

4 Post-Award Public Policy Review

Post-award review is also ripe ground for cultural manifestations through the emergency escape route of public policy, which is every jurisdiction's safety valve to guard against arbitral awards that offend against the public conscience and deep-rooted values of a given society. This safety valve, which acts as a defensive instrument that ensures the compatibility of awards with the prevailing deep-rooted cultural values and fundamental interests of a given society, is considered an indispensable device for every society and culture. It is an expression of the prevailing sacrosanct fundamental principles (whether social, cultural, economic, or political), intangible values, and social mores, which constitute the foundation of any organised society and which can never be sacrificed. It is also often perceived as a manifestation of the triumph of nationalism over internationalism; a triumph sometimes needed, in certain cases, to protect the fundamental socio-cultural principles of a given society.

In a world of intensified processes of interaction, convergence and divergence are likely to co-exist, and jurisdictions and cultures will certainly develop elements of commonality, yet differences will remain. Such differences reflect the existing cultural, legal, social and economic diversity between societies, which in turn are reflected in their principles of public policy.

Thus, public policy and its cultural manifestations that impact the setting aside arbitral awards and/or operate as a bar to the enforcement and recognition of foreign arbitral awards merit careful reflection. Case law is filled with examples from various jurisdictions and cultures where issues of public policy arise because of cultural clash, and so international arbitrators are usually concerned with ensuring that awards do not violate the public policy of the law governing the merits, the *lex loci arbitri* and/or the *lex loci executionis* to the extent possible, noting that national courts, in a post-award review, will indeed perform that role, and their assessment will be informed by sacrosanct values and principles. To illustrate the impact of culture and jurisdiction-specific trends, the current state of affairs, show that Saudi courts, for example, will not tolerate the awarding of interest and will thus decline to enforce arbitral awards ordering the payment of interest, as this offends against Saudi law and culture which are premised on the Saudi understanding of Islamic *Sharī'ah* principles. Conversely, in Egypt which is also a jurisdiction where Islamic *Sharī'ah* principles form the principal source of legislation, simple interest can be awarded by arbitral tribunals and this would not offend against public policy, unless it exceeds the 7% per annum threshold set in the Egyptian Civil Code and consistently upheld through the jurisprudence of the Egyptian Court of Cassation.[88] Moreover, cultural public policy has been the basis for setting aside an arbitral award by the Cairo Court of Appeal, as part of a judicial saga over the *Kharafi v. Libya* case, under the Unified Arab Investment Treaty (1980 as

88. Egyptian Court of Cassation, Challenge No. 12854, JY 85, 4 March 2024; Egyptian Court of Cassation, Challenge No. 282, JY 89, 9 January 2020; Egyptian Court of Cassation, Challenge No. 9619, JY 82, 19 June 2013

amended in 2013)[89] on the premise that the compensation awarded by the arbitral tribunal exceeded the limits of full reparation and operated as a penalty, which contravenes the fundamental philosophical and cultural role of compensation as a remedy for the sustained harm and prejudice.[90]

Nevertheless, it is undeniable that the scope of public policy has been affected by increasing trends of cultural, legal and economic interaction and the rise of an international arbitration third culture that opened the door to more tolerance and adoption of foreign practices, and eventually led to more tolerance on both conscious and subconscious levels. Thus, with an increased level of tolerance towards foreign practices, the frequency of operation of public policy declines, hence narrowing the scope of the concept,[91] and becoming more focused on its international dimension rather than its domestic applications. Most recently, on the specific issue of awarding interest in the MENA region, and, contrary to established jurisprudence in this regard, the Cairo Court of Appeal, being influenced by manifestations of this third culture, ruled that 'the issue of interest and its maximum limits no longer touches upon the rules of public policy [...] Looking at the fundamental changes that have occurred in living, economic, cultural, and political conditions, the issue of dealing with interest, its multiple fields and varying forms – even if it was prohibited or exceeding its limits [was prohibited] by mandatory rules – is a matter that does not constitute a violation of society's interests, its core values, or its rules that are considered pillars of its structure. Thus, there is no danger to the existence or the belief of any state from violating the rules regulating interest, whether by virtue of an agreement or the law. The rule of public policy actually reflects the horizons and scope of the development that society – every society – has achieved in one of its diverse areas of life'.[92] However, only time will tell whether the Egyptian Court of Cassation will reverse course and

89. This is the Unified Agreement for the Investment of Arab Capital in the Arab States, Economic Documents, No. 3 (Tunis: League of Arab States) adopted on 27 November 1980, and entered into force on 9 September 1981. Then, it was later amended on 22 January 2013, and entered into force on 24 April 2016, three months from the date of its ratification by five member States as per its Article 30. For further details regarding that Treaty and a comparison between it and the Organisation of Islamic Cooperation Agreement for Promotion, Protection and Guarantee of Investments Among Member States of the Organisation of the Islamic Conference signed on 5 June 1981, and entered into force on 25 February 1988, see Mohamed S. Abdel Wahab and Kabir Duggal, *The Resurgence of the Unified Arab Investment Agreement and the Organisation for Islamic Cooperation Investment Agreement: A Dawn of a New Chapter on Investment Protection?* (Brill, 2022).
90. *Mohamed Abdulmohsen Al-Kharafi & Sons Co. v. Libya and others*, Judgment of the Cairo Court of Appeal, 3 June 2020. For an overview of the Kharafi vs. Libya saga and the latest judgment by the Egyptian Court of Cassation judgment reversing the decision of the Cairo Court of Appeal, *see* Mohamed S. Abdel Wahab, *The State of Play of Arbitration in the MENA Region* (Ciarb, 2023) https://www.ciarb.org/news-listing/the-state-of-play-of-arbitration-in-the-mena-region/ accessed on 24 June 2025.
91. Prof. Dr. Mohamed S. Abdel Wahab, 'Cultural Globalisation and Public Policy: Exclusion of Foreign Law in the Global Village', in Michael Freeman (ed.), *Law and Sociology* (vol. 8, 2004) 361.
92. *Damietta International Ports Company S.A.E v. Damietta Port Authority*, ICC Case No. 21341/MCP/DDA/AYZ (C-21413/DDA), Judgment of the Cairo Court of Appeal, 9 December 2020.

exclude interest, in excess of the 7% per annum threshold, from the scope of the international public policy for Egypt, as should be the case.

In any event, as clarified above, there will remain an area reserved for protecting fundamental principles of public policy that will always be a source of cultural clash between diverse legal cultures and jurisdictions, but that area is continuously being re-defined and narrowed down by the cross-pollination between legal systems and the rise of a third culture in the international arbitration paradigm.

V A FINAL REMARK: *ARBITRATORS AND CROSS-CULTURAL DYNAMICS*

Culture in the context of international arbitration operates in mysterious ways that are sometimes visible and other times invisible, and the impact thereof is not always capable of being measured tangibly or with precision, but it is always felt. Thus, truly cultured international arbitrators come to proceedings with open minds, not empty minds. Arbitrators remain impartial and independent, and even party-appointed arbitrators are not expected to be partisan. The parties' expectations are that arbitrators would understand their positions and appreciate their cultural diversity and render justice on the basis of the factual matrix of the case, the parties' pleadings and the governing law, without contamination by prior cultural inclinations and misconceptions.

However, it would be too naïve to suggest that the arbitrators' thought and decision-making processes operate in a vacuum. There are certain biases on conscious and subconscious levels, but arbitrators should continue to probe and question those biases. The more aware an arbitrator becomes of his/her own cultural and unconscionable biases, the more effective he/she will be able to deal with them. Without such awareness, an arbitrator may not be willing to see through any other lens than his/her own personal perception of the world and the culture he/she is accustomed to and familiar with. That said, a prominent judge once advised that 'a conscientious judge will, as far as possible, make himself aware of his biases … and by that very self-knowledge nullify their effect'.[93]

The failure to acknowledge cultural differences may risk exporting a sense of 'exile and insecurity' among the different parties involved and the arbitrators.[94] While arbitrators are concerned with making determinations of the issues in dispute, it is sometimes necessary to understand the underlying cultural complexities, to establish effective and transparent communication channels with all parties and individuals involved, disambiguate the context and circumstances of the dispute, establish the relevant facts, and navigate smoothly through the issues to be determined.

93. US Court of Appeals for the Second Circuit – 138 F.2d 650 (2d Cir. 1943) 8 November 1943; Edna Sussman, 'Biases and Heuristics in Arbitrator Decision-Making: Reflections on How to Counteract or Play to Them,' in Tony Cole (ed.), *The Roles of Psychology in International Arbitrations* (Wolters Kluwer, 2017) 48 (emphasis added).

94. Prof/ Dr. Ignacio Gomez-Palacio, *International Commercial Arbitration: Two Cultures in a State of Courtship and Potential Marriage of Convenience* (The American Review of International Arbitration 2009) 248.

Cross-cultural dynamics and interactions occur at all stages of international arbitration proceedings, during case preparation, case presentation, and case determination. Even at the post-award stage, cultural considerations are clearly manifested through principles of public policy. From the perspective of international arbitrators, due consideration and implementation of certain measures and strategies may be needed to effectively manage cross-cultural dynamics.

First, arbitrators should be mindful of the various cultural misconceptions, including those addressed in this chapter, and they should not be culturally insensitive to the cultural backgrounds and divides among parties, counsel, witnesses and experts. *Second*, arbitrators should be mindful of their own cultural biases and aim to control those biases so as not to contaminate the decision-making process. *Third*, arbitrators should establish meaningful and appropriate channels of communication for the efficient and smooth management of the proceedings, and they should encourage parties to engage in open and respectful dialogue to bridge cultural divides and avoid misunderstandings. *Fourth*, in some highly contentious cases involving multi-layered cultural complexities, arbitrators, counsel and parties may benefit from instructing cultural experts or consultants to decipher cultural differences, unlock the proper frequency for effective communication, foster an environment of collegiality, and safeguard the parameters of civility and respect. This would induce trust and confidence in the arbitral process and in the arbitrators. *Finally*, arbitrators should be aware of the existing third culture in international arbitration and aim to work with the parties and counsel towards establishing workable protocols and procedures that are not only aligned with established best practices, but which also cater for cultural sensitivities and divides that may pose risks to the integrity and efficient conduct of the arbitral proceedings. By drawing on a variety of legal traditions and cultures but wedding themselves to none, truly international arbitrators can offer workable solutions tailored to the parties' needs.[95] Some scholars and practitioners have even warned that arbitrations may go 'profusely wrong when there is a cultural mismatch between the tribunal and the case that it is supposed to decide'.[96]

To seal the deal on the importance of being alive and tolerant to cultural manifestations in international arbitration where relevant and necessary, it is worth illustrating that an arbitrator in an ICC arbitration had to consider an issue of *Islamic Sharī'ah* law, and he conducted alternative analyses under both *Sharī'ah* law and the law governing the issue in question, which was the validity of the arbitration agreement. While the arbitrator's principle reasoning was that 'the Law of D Country

95. Alexander Baykitch and Edmund Bao, 'A Return to Innate Arbitration Culture: Implications from a Cost and Efficiency Perspective' in Prof. Dr. William W. Park (ed.), *Arbitration International* (© The Author(s); Oxford University Press 2019, vol. 35, Issue 1) 68. William K. Slate II, 'Luncheon Address The Impact of Culture on International Commercial Arbitration' in Prof. Dr. Albert Jan van den Berg (ed.), *ICCA Congress Series No. 12 (Beijing 2004): New Horizons in International Commercial Arbitration and Beyond* (ICCA Congress Series, vol. 12 © Kluwer Law International; ICCA & Kluwer Law International 2005), 12.

96. Valentina Faienza and Paula Baldini Miranda da Cruz, *Embracing the Human in Arbitration: A Look Back at ICCA Hong Kong 2024* (ICCA, ICCA Hong Kong 2024), 9 June 2024, available at https://arbitrationblog.kluwerarbitration.com/2024/06/09/embracing-the-human-in-arbitration-a-look-back-at-icca-hong-kong-2024/ accessed on 31 August 2024.

did not apply the principles of the Sha[rī'ah] to commercial cases such as this and hence accordingly upheld the validity of the arbitration agreement on that ground', he still presented an alternative analysis on the basis of *Sharī'ah* law, noting that the enforceability of the award may come before a national court that adheres to culturally distinct *Sharī'ah* principles. In his alternative analysis, the arbitrator made the following interesting remarks, exhibiting a degree of cultural sensitivity and awareness:

(i) He first acknowledged that 'if I were wrong in' excluding the *Sharī'ah* law, 'I would, nevertheless, have accepted the Claimants' arguments that, at Sharī'ah this arbitration agreement was enforceable.'[97]

(ii) Further, in his analysis, he went on stating that 'at Sharī'ah, contracting parties could agree terms "... to alter the balance of obligations..." and it would be somewhat surprising if that were not so. I would not, therefore, have held that, at Sharī'ah, this contract failed because it involved "two contracts in one"'.[98]

(iii) Finally, when making a point that may come across as culturally offensive (i.e., that the cultural contexts in which the *Sharī'ah* rule was made 'suggest an older, less developed' society), he quickly noted '(but not a worse)'.[99]

By and large, international arbitrators face a complex interplay of factual, legal, technical, and cultural challenges in international arbitration. While some believe that cultural differences are insignificant and irrelevant, others endorse and recognise their impact. Between sceptics and believers in the role of culture in international arbitration lies a path to the truth, that is: being totally oblivious to cultural nuances and differences can lead to misunderstandings, misinterpretations, inefficiencies and lack of trust and confidence, which undermines the legitimacy and success of international arbitration.

Thus, demonstrating reasonable appreciation of different cultural perspectives, without being wedded to specific cultural preferences, is crucial to unlocking the secrets of success. While arbitrators are indeed concerned with the factual, legal and technical aspects of a dispute when determining the same, understanding cultural divides and patterns that inform parties', counsel's, witnesses' and experts' conduct and behaviour can indeed assist in giving context to certain acts and omissions and facilitate realistic and fair decisions. The importance of this understanding has even been amplified to the extent that it has been suggested that establishing cultural hubs

97. *Parties Not Indicated*, Award, ICC Case No. 8677/FMS, 26 September 1997 (International Journal of Arab Arbitration; International Journal of Arab Arbitration, vol. 1, Issue 4 2009) 350-351 (emphasis added).
98. *Parties Not Indicated*, Award, ICC Case No. 8677/FMS, 26 September 1997 (International Journal of Arab Arbitration; International Journal of Arab Arbitration, vol. 1, Issue 4 2009) 350-351 (emphasis added).
99. *Parties Not Indicated*, Award, ICC Case No. 8677/FMS, 26 September 1997 (International Journal of Arab Arbitration; International Journal of Arab Arbitration, vol. 1, Issue 4 2009) 350-351 (emphasis added).

and providing access to independent cultural advisors can further support the effective navigation of cultural differences in international arbitration.[100]

While the author of the present chapter may not go as far as supporting the need to establish cultural hubs, given the continued development of a third culture in international arbitration, it remains important to emphasise that in an era where artificial intelligence is evolving from assisting human intelligence to substituting the same, the human arbitrator's edge lies not only in the ability to process and apply facts and laws, but also in the ability to exhibit social intelligence and sensitivity to cultural differences among other human players in the arbitral process, without contaminating the decision-making process by cultural misconceptions and/or specific inclinations and manifestations.

As the invisible hand of culture moves quietly through every phase of international arbitration, shaping perceptions, influencing conduct, and framing interpretations, it does not necessarily operate as a hindrance or source of conflict. When approached with awareness and discernment, this invisible hand can become a force to be harnessed and a tool to unlock the potential for more efficiency. By acknowledging and engaging with cultural undercurrents, international arbitrators can render determinations that are not only procedurally robust and evidentially grounded but also genuinely fair, anchored in objective standards and enriched by a deep sensitivity to the diverse realities that define our international arbitration paradigm.

100. Dr. Mary Howard, '*International Arbitration and Cross-cultural Issues*', in Stavros Brekoulakis (ed.), *Arbitration: The International Journal of Arbitration, Mediation and Dispute Management* (© Kluwer Law International; Kluwer Law International 2020, vol. 86, Issue 3) 343-345.

PANEL 7

Launch of the 2nd Edition of ICCA's Guide to the Interpretation of the 1958 New York Convention

with Prof Albert Jan van den Berg and Erica Stein

The launch of the second edition of ICCA's Guide to the Interpretation of the 1958 New York Convention ('Judges' Guide') was celebrated during the ICCA 2024 Congress in Hong Kong. With remarks presented by Erica Stein, the event also honoured the visionary work of Professor Albert Jan van den Berg, former Chair of the Judiciary Committee and a founding member of the project. A first copy of the Chinese-language edition was presented to Judge Xi Xiangyang of the Supreme People's Court of China.

The Judges' Guide was developed by the ICCA's Judiciary Committee as part of its Judicial Outreach Programme. It served as a key element of the Committee's efforts to harmonise the interpretation and application of the New York Convention across jurisdictions worldwide. No written contributions were submitted for this panel.

Panel 8

Plenary: The Advocate

What makes an effective advocate? Is there a universal ideal? What does the science of the human brain tell us about how persuasion works, and can advocates harness that science? Can advocacy in media, politics or other endeavours provide lessons? What tools or innovations can advocates draw upon? The panel considered how human qualities, including creativity and fallibility, can shape and inspire the advocate, and will provide pragmatic tips for stronger advocacy.

CHAPTER 23

Psychological Dynamics in International Arbitration Advocacy

Richard C. Waites & James E. Lawrence

I INTRODUCTION

One of the inherent strengths of the current system of international arbitration is the unique opportunity for advocates and students of advocacy from so many different cultures to learn from each other about ways to enhance the effectiveness of their arguments and presentations. Some approaches to effective advocacy that might at one time have been seen as radical have become routine as they were tested and found to be effective, while other approaches once thought to be expected and normal have been abandoned.

In addition to cross-cultural learning, we are all benefitted by the influences of disciplines other than law as we work to improve the effectiveness of our advocacy. For

* Richard C. Waites obtained his J.D. from the University of Houston Law Center and his doctorate in psychology from Walden University. James Lawrence is the Executive Director of the Blakely Advocacy Institute at the University of Houston Law Center. He is a mediator and arbitrator and consults internationally in Dispute Resolution (Trial, Arbitration, Mediation, Witness Preparation).

example, scientific research in the field of psychology has provided valuable information about how to improve communications and persuasion in arbitration and other types of legal decision-making, and thus, assist arbitration panels and individual arbitrators in better understanding the evidence and positions of the parties in an arbitration.

There is a substantial body of research and writing relating to the use of scientific methodology as applied in the context of both court trials and domestic arbitrations within the United States. For example, scientific methodologies have been used to study various aspects of lay jury and domestic arbitrator selection, lay juror and domestic arbitrator perceptions, the impact of using visual aids during the trial and arbitration process, and decision-making processes throughout court trial and domestic arbitration proceedings. The use of scientific methodology in preparing for court trials and domestic arbitrations in the United States is so widely accepted that the subject of such research has become popularized as exemplified by the success of the John Grisham novel and movie, *The Runaway Jury*.

Conversely, until now, there has been a dearth of research and writing related to the use of scientific methodology as applied to the study of advocacy and arbitrator decision-making in international arbitrations.

One of the premises of this chapter is that scientific methodology can and should be used in the international arbitration process for the purpose of improving the quality and effectiveness of advocacy. As shown in the context of the United States, all of the participants in the decision-making process—decision-maker, party, and advocate—are likely to benefit greatly from resulting improvement in communication. The same human qualities that are exemplified in the court and domestic arbitration process are also at play within the international arbitration context.

In this chapter, we will explore some principles and findings that we have discovered through the use of scientific research dedicated to a better understanding of the decision-making processes of arbitrators as well as other types of legal decision-making. In the process, we will also explore ways to make this information useful to every advocate for a party in international arbitration.

Science is a foundation for art. The more we understand the science of psychological dynamics, both of the self and of the group decision-making process, the more skilled we become in the art of advocacy.

II THE ARBITRATOR-ORIENTED APPROACH TO ADVOCACY

1 What Is Arbitrator-Oriented Advocacy?

When we ask an arbitration panel to accept our arguments and to decide a case in our favor, we are asking them to allow us into their world. It is like asking them to let us come into their homes. They must be the one to unlock and open the door from the inside.

Arbitrators, like all people, are complex. They use their logic and emotions in varying degrees to make decisions that will help them to experience pleasure and avoid pain. One way in which all legal decision-makers experience pleasure is to make decisions that make them feel good about themselves. This principle is absolutely true in persuading international arbitrators.

To motivate arbitrators to listen to us and to take action in our favor, we must understand their needs and what inspires them. Using the most correct and appropriate advocacy technique is not enough.

Persuading arbitrators involves meaningful two-way communication between the lawyer and the arbitrator(s) he or she wishes to convince. When it comes to interaction between lawyers and arbitrators, lawyers cannot dominate the fact finders and decision-makers. Lawyers can only inspire them and motivate them. The arbitrators choose for themselves how they will respond.

No matter who the arbitrators are in your cases, their individual perceptions and interpretations of the circumstances of the case are uniquely their own. For decades, interviews of arbitrators have revealed that each of them develops their own version of a case story by the end of the arbitration. Most of them have begun to form the story before the end of the opening statement.

It is not *our* power as advocates that results in a favorable decision. It is the power within the decision-maker that creates the magical experience and results in a decision.

As lawyers, we give homage to the power of the decision-maker. We honor and respect their power and should not try to upstage it. To the contrary, one of our goals is to empower fact finders by acknowledging their supreme authority.

2 The New Age of Advocacy and Arbitration

The world around us is changing. The practice of advocacy is changing. Historically, we have depended solely upon self-reliance and intuition in developing and presenting cases in arbitration as we were taught to do. We have relied solely upon advocacy skills that we learned from law professors, seminar speakers, mentors, and sometimes opposing advocates. We have developed our themes and case theories from ideas that sounded persuasive to us that we generated ourselves or that we borrowed from other sources.

However, despite our emphasis upon self-reliance, a revolution has occurred in how we develop and present cases to judges, juries, and arbitrators. This revolution began more than thirty years ago with the founding of the National Institute for Trial Advocacy (NITA) in the United States (www.nita.org), more recently with the founding of the Foundation for International Arbitration Advocacy (FIAA) in Switzerland (www.fiaa.com), as well as other teaching organizations that are dedicated to assisting lawyers in enhancing their trial and arbitration advocacy skills. NITA, FIAA, and these other groups believe that the ideals of our system of justice are furthered when attorneys work to develop their skills as advocates. The effect that these research and teaching organizations are having is profound.

One of the effects of the drive to become more successful as an advocate has been the need for more reliable and useful information about how our case presentations will be perceived by arbitrators.

Scientific decision-maker research is just one source of this information. There are many others.

As we learn more about how arbitrators make decisions, we discover new ways to apply this information to make every advocate's work more effective and more useful for the arbitration panel. By focusing case presentations on the needs of the arbitrators to better understand cases and their meaning, they can do a better job of making appropriate decisions. In the final analysis, then, the arbitration advocacy system itself is improved.

In this chapter, we spend a great deal of time looking at the results of scientific research and how to apply what we have learned. In the process, however, we may sometimes fail to acknowledge that advocacy is an art. It is one of the highest forms of art. It involves the use of oratory and expression that focuses on the meaning of life's circumstances.

Until now, we have spent years making sacrifices to learn this art. But now the basic learning is over. It is now time to use our skills and all of the resources we now have to create a masterpiece that is meaningful in the lives of our clients and the arbitrators as well.

3 How Do We Inspire Arbitrators to Decide in Our Favor?

Being the most competent lawyer in arbitration is not enough. It takes more than oratorical skills and arbitration savvy to convince arbitrators to enter a decision for our client. To win a case, the substance of our presentation must be compelling, meaningful, and inspiring.

Some of the most brilliant lawyers across the world tell us that they view themselves as messengers. They tell us that fact finders are more persuaded by the message and content of their arguments. They tell us many war stories about trials and arbitrations in which a less skilled advocate defeated them because the substance of the winning argument was more compelling.

Developing an effective arbitration strategy that will make an arbitration panel enthusiastic about deciding in our favor is dependent largely upon framing an argument in a way that is meaningful and motivational to them. The themes and case theory we rely upon must be in accordance with their attitudes about specific issues in the case, relevant life experiences, and other characteristics of the decision-maker which will influence their decision.

People do not make decisions in a vacuum. No arbitrator has ever made a decision without first taking into consideration their perceptions of the world around them and their previous life experiences.

4 The Secret to Motivating Arbitrators

The world of international arbitration advocacy is unique in many respects, but the fundamental dynamics of persuasion are the same everywhere. Because arbitration advocacy takes place within a legalistic environment laden with complicated rules and procedures, we sometimes forget that the people we try to persuade in arbitration are the same people who spend most of their time outside the arbitration.

Whether we want to admit it or not, arbitration advocacy is selling. It is the highest form of selling in the sense that we are selling ideas that will affect people's lives.

Why do people buy products or ideas? The answer is simple. They buy out of self-interest.

Benjamin Franklin, a famous author, diplomat and scientist from the United States, once said, "If you would persuade, you must appeal to interest rather than intellect."

The practice of persuading people in arbitration seems complex because of the hundreds of details that are present in every case and the fact that different arbitrators will view the case differently.

Nevertheless, the objective is to frame the issues and presentation of a case to address the needs of the arbitrators. They want to learn as much information as they can and they need to make a decision that makes them feel good about themselves.

In essence, therefore, they make important decisions the same way you do. Think about how you go about making decisions about family matters, law practice matters, and other personal matters. Do you make important decisions completely rationally and considering only the information that someone tells you is admissible? Probably not.

The more we are sensitive to the needs of arbitrators to form a story about what happened and why things happened the way they did, the better equipped we will be to develop themes and messages in the case which are meaningful and powerful to them. They need to know the important aspects of the case as clearly and simply as possible. Drenching them with unnecessary details makes their work more difficult and can dilute the possibility of presenting a cogent and persuasive argument.

Therefore, the secret to motivating arbitrators is to understand the subject of the arbitration from their perspective and to appeal to their self-interest in a world as they see it. Arbitrators, like all legal decision-makers, have strong senses of the importance or lack of importance of evidence and issues.

Likewise, they have a strong sense of how to fashion a solution that makes them feel comfortable and fits contentedly into their view of the world.

There is also another important aspect of presenting a case that all successful lawyers must understand. Arbitrators will make their decision in your case based on their own attitudes about specific issues in the case, their own life experiences, and their own set of life's influences.

III THE DYNAMIC OF AN EFFECTIVE ADVOCATE IN INTERNATIONAL ARBITRATION

Advocacy is persuasion, and psychology is the foundation for persuasion. Unfortunately, preparation for practicing law rarely includes instruction on the science and art of persuasion. Consider the amount of time devoted to communication theory and cognitive processing theory in legal education. Analytical reasoning is presumably developed through the legal education pedagogy, but the study of the psychology of the advocacy process is rare. The goal of this chapter is to provide information and insights relating to the science of persuasion that is rarely found in legal education, legal literature, and legal training.

The foundation for understanding the science of persuasion begins with the concept of internal roadmaps. A basic knowledge of internal roadmaps then provides a framework for discussing how the science of persuasion is applied in international arbitration.

1 The Internal Roadmap

Psychological roadmaps are the neural pathways along which the brain sends and receives information. The send/receive process operates primarily on two levels that we will refer to as *surface structure* and *deep structure*. *Surface structure* is what a person observes through the five senses: words, tonality, body language, visual images, and gestures. However, the information processed through the surface structure pathway is only factual data. The surface structure pathway does not give meaning or emotional value to the observation data. The meaning and emotional value to the observed data come from the *deep structure* pathway. A person's *deep structure*, on the other hand, contains that person's experiences, values, biases, prejudices, dreams, fears, and beliefs.

A simple illustration of the surface structure/deep structure dynamic is the "Ocean Word Test" as we refer to in teaching trial advocacy. The "Ocean Word Test" may be demonstrated by a comparison between a word's definition (i.e., surface structure) with the images that use of the word conjures up (i.e., deep structure).

The necessity of understanding the differential between a fact (as presented by the advocate) and the image(s) that the fact generates in one's mind of the arbitrator is what makes the surface structure/deep structure dynamic so critical in international arbitration advocacy. In the final analysis, then, the foundation for successful persuasion is understanding the significance of the arbitrator's internal roadmap.

The interplay between the individual advocate, the arbitration panel, and scientific methodology can be exemplified by the geometric shape of a triangle. In 1816, Dr. A. L. Crelle, a German mathematician, described a triangle, stating that "[i]t is indeed wonderful that so simple a figure as the triangle is so inexhaustible in properties."[1] Specifically, the simple figure of the triangle here is: Side (1) the dynamic of an effective advocate, Side (2) the decision-making processes of international arbitration panels, and Side (3) using scientific decision-maker research in arbitration advocacy. (*The triangle analysis has been used in the study of domestic lay jury and arbitration in the United States.*) Side 1 (the advocate) and Side 2 (the arbitration panel)

1. Crelle, A.L. "Einige Bemerkungen über die dreiseitige Pyramide," 1 *Sammlung mathematischer Aufsätze u. Bemerkungen* 105-132 (1821) as reported in Wells, D., *The Penguin Dictionary of Curious and Interesting Geometry* 21 (London, Penguin, 1991).

are both well-chronicled concepts in international arbitration. However, the international arbitration literature does not include discussions of the psychological dynamic of the effective advocate or of the arbitration panel. Also absent in the majority of literature regarding international arbitration is an analysis of how to connect the two concepts (the advocate and the arbitration panel) through scientific research and, thus, to complete the triangle. The triangle analogy, with the sides identified above, may be illustrated in the following sections—demonstration what Crelle reasoned to be "so inexhaustible in properties."[2]

Consider Figure 23.1.

Figure 23.1 Dynamics of a Single Human Interaction

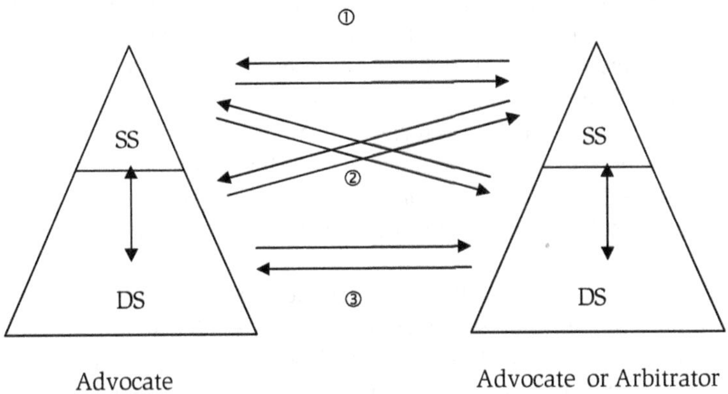

SS = Surface Structure

DS = Deep Structure

The figure illustrates the complexity of an interaction between an advocate or opposing counsel—with an arbitrator—in an arbitration hearing. Each set of arrows represents an element of the interaction.

a *Surface Structure to Surface Structure*

The "factual" exchange between the advocate or opposing counsel and the arbitrator includes information gained by the advocate through words, gestures, tone, body language, and other observations sent/received through the five senses.

2. *Id.*

b Surface Structure to Deep Structure

The exchange between a person's surface structure and another's deep structure is perhaps the most underutilized and unrecognized of the three exchanges shown in the diagram.

It is underutilized because the information sent/received in this exchange often reveals information about fears, biases, dreams, and prejudices that people often have difficulty acknowledging about themselves. For example, perhaps the opposing counsel is wearing an ill-fitting suit that is unduly wrinkled. Remember, however, that an ill-fitting, wrinkled suit observation (surface structure) only identifies that the opposing counsel is wearing an ill-fitting, wrinkled suit. It is the observer's deep structure that creates a meaning for that observation.

What does an ill-fitting, wrinkled suit mean? It *could* carry an infinite number of meanings because experience tells us that no two people have exactly the same life experiences and perceptions, and therefore, there is little chance that the deep structures of two different arbitrators, even though they may have similar backgrounds, will be alike. To one arbitrator, the meaning suggested by the images might reveal a negative bias or prejudice the observer has about individuals who wear ill-fitting, wrinkled suits. To another arbitrator, the meaning might be that the advocate is "down-to-earth," self-confident, and more credible than an advocate dressed quite fashionably.

The simple example of the "ill-fitting, wrinkled suit" is useful in understanding a much more important concept—that every detail of the evidence or of an argument has the potential to be interpreted differently by different arbitrators and to be applied differently by each arbitrator in interpreting the circumstances of a case and making an important decision.

Therefore, the need for thorough and objective study of likely arbitrator perceptions is of enormous importance.

One of the most curious aspects of this constant dynamic taking place during an arbitration proceeding is that most of the time neither arbitrators nor advocates recognize that this important underlying interpretive process is taking place. In those instances where an arbitrator or advocate recognizes that some underlying interpretation is taking place, the ability to accurately identify it and articulate it is missing. In science, for example, we recognize a phenomenon we call "fundamental attribution error" where we attribute an event or outcome wrongfully to one factor when, in truth the event or outcome was caused by something else entirely.

As a result of a lack of understanding of the existence or pervasiveness of underlying interpretations and misinterpretations, neither arbitrators nor advocates question the meaning their deep structure gives to a factual observation. Simply stated, observers make assumptions about their observations.

c Deep Structure to Deep Structure

If the exchange from surface structure to deep structure is mostly underutilized and unrecognized, then the exchanges between the deep structures of arbitrators and advocates are perhaps the most difficult to understand and deal with effectively.

The opportunity to persuade is dramatically increased when there is an exchange between the advocate's deep structure and the deep structure of the opposing counsel or arbitrator.

Because the deep structure holds the meaning for factual data, the advocate who understands how to create a deep structure exchange has an advantage. The difficulties in creating a deep structure exchange are: (1) individuals do not generally like to talk about their fears, biases, prejudices, goals, and dreams, (2) attorneys believe they only need the facts, and (3) it takes time and patience to develop the techniques necessary to create this exchange.

2 Effective Applications

A discussion of the science of persuasion is incomplete without exploring how the theory applies to the international arbitration hearing context. The applications are endless but, due to space limitations, the focus here will be limited to three of the most common applications: (a) the importance of narrative, (b) using scientific evidence, and (c) questioning witnesses.

a The Importance of Narrative

A narrative, for the purposes here, is the story of the case. The story of the case is often overlooked in the international arbitration context because advocates focus primarily on the factual data (surface structure) of the case. The use of an effective narrative, however, provides a context (deep structure) for the factual data. The context then creates an anchor point, or theme, for the advocate to use during the process of a hearing. It is important to note that a theme is *not* an emotional appeal but rather it is one way to create a deep structure to deep structure exchange.

For example, consider a shipping contract dispute between an Indian company and a Chinese company. The arbitration panel consists of arbitrators from Sweden, the United States, and France. The way for an advocate to reach the deep structure of every person involved in this process is either to select a universal theme, an anchor point that transcends culture, or to develop separate themes directed to each arbitrator, but that are complimentary to each other. A possible single theme in this case might be "doing what is right." While cultures differ in how "doing what is right" is applied, no culture is without a concept that mirrors this theme. An effective advocate would return to the "doing what is right" anchor point throughout the course of the hearing in order to continually remind the arbitral panel of the essence of the dispute.

Perhaps the most eloquent explanation of the role of narrative meaning (meaning in the context of a story) is reflected in the writings of Jerome Bruner, a famous educational and developmental psychologist, in his work *Acts of Meaning*.[3] In this work, Bruner explains that the central concept of human psychology is *meaning* and the processes and transactions involved in the construction of meaning. Bruner states that culture shapes human life and the human mind and gives meaning to the events and behaviors by creating an interpretive system. He states that our interpretations and perceptions are highly individualized in many ways, but that they are highly influenced by forces around us. He refers to this interpretive system as *folk psychology* or *common sense*. Bruner writes that this *folk psychology* is a system by which people organize their experience in, knowledge about, and transactions with the social world.

The vehicle with which people learn, organize and relay meaning and understanding is the *narrative* or *story* as Bruner recognizes. In his work, Bruner states that the function of *story* is to create an explanation, to give understanding, and to rationalize events, behaviors, and mental states of other people with whom an individual interacts. In this way, an individual and group can compare acceptable and normal cultural patterns with actions which deviate in matters of legitimacy, moral commitment, and values.

Another interesting and provocative writer on this subject was Joseph Campbell, the great social philosopher and cultural anthropologist. In his work, *The Power of Myth*,[4] Campbell explains his belief that the basic driving force for mankind is the search for *meaningful experience*. Throughout his lifetime he immersed himself in the cultural philosophies of human societies around the world and reached back into prehistoric times. Before his death in 1987, he stated in his last interviews and writings that he had reached the conclusion that it was not enough for man to discover the meaning of something intellectually in an objective way. He determined that it was more important for us to actually *experience* the meaning—to internalize it and feel its effects—a more subjective reaction.

The use of stories, myths, parables, and fables to proscribe acceptable behaviors and motivations is well documented in most every primitive and modern culture. Anthropologists who have studied dispute resolution in Western and non-Western societies have found clear and convincing evidence that laws or codes for conduct are represented and passed from generation to generation in the form of stories.

The conclusions of these authors are important to us in international arbitration in one significant respect—we must make the effort to develop and present a case presentation that offers real substantive meaning and experience for every arbitrator. Otherwise, we are simply going through the motions of advocacy and will wind up with a case presentation that offers neither meaning nor experience to which an arbitrator can identify and commit.

b Using Scientific Evidence

Scientific evidence may, at first glance, seem to be merely a factual (surface structure) element of a dispute. Indeed, from an intellectual point of view, scientific evidence

3. Bruner, *Acts of Meaning* (Cambridge, Massachusetts, Harvard University Press, 1990).
4. Campbell & Moyers, *The Power of Myth* (New York, Anchor Books, 1991).

includes data, findings, and perhaps discoveries that should be useful in helping the arbitration panel understand an important point(s). We also know from historical practice that in order to be considered useful, scientific findings must offer reliability which may be defined as the consistency of a measurement, or the degree to which an instrument measures the same way each time it is used under the same condition with the same subjects.

However, providing scientific evidence to support advocacy is much more than an intellectual exercise. To the arbitrator, scientific evidence must not only have scientific reliability and validity, but it must also have meaning in a much deeper sense that supports the overarching themes and narrative of the case. In this sense, the use of scientific evidence, including the way it is presented, creates a higher level of meaning and application for the data to support the advocacy points.

When an advocate uses scientific evidence, the reliability aspect of the evidence accesses the element of assurance in a person's deep structure. Assurance is important in the science of persuasion because it creates confidence that the conclusive outcome will be the same each time the data is processed.

Confidence in the conclusive outcome of scientific evidence establishes elements of trust and rapport—both of which are components of a deep structure to deep structure exchange.

In practice, therefore, a successful advocate will want to develop ways to persuade arbitrators that the scientific evidence supports the advocate's positions on central themes and narrative of the case.

Presentation and discussion of the detailed aspects of the actual scientific research questions, methodologies, research designs, and findings should be as brief, concise, and comprehensive as necessary, but without unnecessary discussion and detail. Only in this way can the advocate help the arbitrator to understand the important meaning that the scientific evidence has for the entire case.

We might look at the example of a communications technology issue in a patent dispute. The plaintiff might argue that the defendant was aware of the plaintiff's patented technology and specifically tried to design the defendant's technology in a way that would skirt the claims in the plaintiff's patent. Focusing on a possible defense strategy, the defendant could bring forth a stream of reputable scientists, all of whom might claim that the defendant's technology was unique and did not mirror the plaintiff's technology. The defendant could bombard the arbitrators with a steady stream of evidence focusing only on the scientific evidence for weeks, which in the end might overwhelm the plaintiff's expert witnesses and cause a pro-plaintiff decision, if the arbitrators were still interested in the case.

However, in the minds of the arbitrator in our example, the plaintiffs have actually brought a patent infringement dispute that is grounded in allegations of deception by the defendant, thus focusing on the defendant's character, which was not addressed in the steady stream of scientific evidence. Query whether it might be helpful for the defendant to address the deception allegation first and then go on to show with more concise proof that the defendant's technology is different from that of the plaintiff. The defendant might offer the actual inventor of its own technology to show the world-class trend-setting expertise of the defendant's inventor and the independent process by which the defendant's technology was developed. Furthermore, instead of offering a mind-numbing string of experts, to offer only 2-3 selected world-class experts to support the defendant's contentions with a casual mention of others who would concur.

Therefore, in the final analysis, it is best to squarely meet the core issue(s) from the arbitrators' perspective which usually involves issues that give meaning to the behavior of the parties in the evidence and give meaning to the dispute as a whole and how best to create a decision that gives meaning and significance to their decision.

c *Questioning Witnesses*

Asking questions is an essential skill for an attorney, regardless of whether the context is in an office setting, a trial setting, or an arbitration setting. However, many attorneys focus on the factual information (surface structure) because they do not know how to access information from a witness' deep structure that can effectively provide information to enlighten and persuade an arbitrator's deep structure.

Accessing information from one's deep structure requires discipline and willingness for the attorney to seek information rather than simply establishing power or control.

The most effective technique for accessing information from the deep structure of a witness, arbitrator or even another advocate is with *clean* questions. A *clean* question is one where the questioner refrains from including any personal bias, prejudice, or preconception in the question. Examples of clean questions are "what is important about ...," "tell me more about ...," and "what else is important about ... ." When a clean question is presented, it requires the answerer to reconsider an initial answer and give more information than in the initial answer. Each reconsideration pushes the answerer further into the deep structure, and so as the exchange continues, the questioner begins to learn more and more about the meaning (deep structure) of the factual information (surface structure).

No discussion about clean questions is complete without a brief explanation of the technique of "looping." Looping is taking a part of the answer and using it in the next question. The technique communicates that the questioner is listening and that what the answerer said is important. When the answerer feels that what has been said is heard and is important, the willingness to give more information increases significantly.

The following is an example of a Q&A where the technique of asking clean questions is combined with the technique of looping:

> Q: Why did your company include this clause in the contract?
> A: We wanted to know that we could count on receiving the widgets in a timely fashion.
> Q: What was important about your company receiving the widgets in a timely fashion? (an example of a clean question with looping)
> A: We had a deadline to meet and we couldn't meet the deadline if we didn't have the widgets.

Q: What was important about meeting your deadline? (an example of a clean question with looping)
A: If we didn't meet the deadline, we'd have to pay a penalty.
Q: What else is important about meeting the deadline? (an example of a clean question with looping)
A: This is our first contract with this company and we've worked hard to get their business. We'd like to do more business with them, and if it looks like we aren't dependable, then they may not want to sign additional contracts with us.

As this exchange demonstrates, using clean questions in combination with looping creates the rapport necessary for the questioner to get in-depth information from the answerer that is useful to address the needs of an arbitrator's deep structure.

IV THE DECISION-MAKING PROCESSES OF ARBITRATORS

1 Overview of the Communication/Persuasion Process

The persuasive process begins with basic communication as we have noted. Let's begin our discussion of the communication and persuasion process with an analysis of the communication process as it relates to persuasion and then examine the core principles involved in effective persuasion.

2 The Process of Communicating

a Basic Characteristics of Effective Communication

Because communication is inherently interactive, the communicator and the observer are both interdependent. In each of our communications with arbitration panels, we are dependent upon the arbitrators for response, whether spoken or unspoken. Otherwise, the interaction rapidly disappears.

Certainly, some conversation is *interactive* but not necessarily communicative. Quite often in arbitration, for example, people say things that are meaningless and intended only to fill the silence. Sometimes these meaningless interactions detract from the message to be communicated and sometimes they do not.

The best communicators, however, remain true to their message. They remain focused on the idea to be communicated. They work hard to make sure that all of their words, actions, and tools communicate *pure* messages without any distractions.

Regardless of the culture or setting, we think and communicate in symbols. A symbol is a sound, behavior, letter, or visual image that stands for something else. The most highly organized symbols we usually call *language*. A typical arbitration is filled with symbols, each of which will mean something special to one or more arbitrators. Therefore, we have to pay attention to the symbols we use and project so that the correct message is presented, and hopefully received.

b *Inner Selves and Communication*

Our internal states are both the beginning and the end of communication. The perceptions and mental state of the communicator are the source of the information to be communicated. Conversely, the perceptions and mental state of the listener form the end product of the communication.

One might argue that the things in our environment about which we are communicating are definite and that perceptions of the same object must be identical. After all, the sky is usually blue and trees are usually green. However, our memories and perceptual systems are highly selective about what they let in, and even more selective about the information that is stored in temporary or long-term memory. Each person perceives the sky or a tree in a very unique way. In this sense, our perceptions are not directly tied to specific events or objects, but are created by our individual perceptual systems.

c *Tools for Creating and Changing Perceptions*

There are actually many interesting tools that humans have created or used over the millennia to create, maintain, and change perceptions. These tools are derived from our understanding about our cognitive (thinking) processes and our affective (feeling) processes. We will look at three of these tools that are most useful in arbitration. They are language, schema and affect.

Language is a powerful communication tool in many respects. In a very basic way, it helps us to organize our thoughts and information in systematic ways. Language can be used in the form of words, concepts, or style of expression. Words convey meaning and concepts, and the same words can be spoken or displayed in many ways. Language is flexible and, in this sense, is a tool, not a constraint.

As children, we acquire language early on as symbols and concepts. It is not until later that we learn the spelling of the words and the rules of grammar. For this reason, in presenting a case in arbitration, it is more important to be concerned about the concepts and the connotations of our presentation, than the actual words used. Once the concepts are right, then the words will follow.

However, many times as lawyers we perceive language as a technical construct rather than a free flowing modem of communicating. We tend to be hyper-technical about our use of particular words that fit legal patterns rather than being focused on central concepts and messages that arbitrators will need to hear and see that positively affects their deep structure if we are to be persuasive.

As human beings, we tend to form preconceptions and expectations around our previous life experiences. Technically, psychologists refer to these preconceptions and expectations as schemas.

A schema is a group of concepts and perceptions and the systems we use to organize them. They are a type of mental shorthand. Schemas help us to quickly make sense of the things that are happening around us. For example, when we are following a car down the freeway and the car begins to swerve from a blown tire, we consult our schemas to try to understand what is happening and what, if anything, we need to do about it. Our brains tend to store information in an order that seeks to make sense or order out of life's events and to avoid disorder or inconsistencies.

When arbitrators are listening and observing your presentation, they are constantly testing and comparing the thoughts and messages in your presentation with their own life experiences in order to make sense out of the presentation. If there is an identical match between arbitrators' schemas and the messages in the presentation, they will readily accept the new information (matching schemas is an example of a deep structure to deep structure exchange). If the arbitrators' schemas are different from the messages or ideas in the presentation, they will generally feel uncomfortable with them and may even reject them. If the arbitrators have no schema with which to compare the ideas in the presentation, they will consider the attendant circumstances and how much they trust the presenter in order to form a new schema. Or they might reject the ideas in the presentation altogether.

Consider this example. If a lawyer tries to paint his corporate client as a company that makes decisions based upon their business interest in keeping customers happy, arbitrators will likely accept the message, assuming there is supportive evidence. This message will make sense to them, based on their own life experiences. On the other hand, if the lawyer tries to paint his corporate client as a company that makes decisions solely on the basis of humanitarian considerations, arbitrators will likely reject the message. Their experience tells them that this message is not true.

When there is a match between the arbitrators' schemas and the messages, the relationship between the arbitrators and the lawyer is enhanced. When arbitrators reject a message, however, the relationship between the arbitrators and the lawyer suffers.

One of the primary reasons for conducting pre-arbitration decision-maker research is to identify the schemas that arbitrators will use to process the case and reach a decision. We have learned through experience that when we try to guess the schemas that arbitrators will use, we are often wrong. Scientific mock arbitration panel research also helps us to identify which of the schemas arbitrators will use that will be dominant in reaching a decision.

Arbitrators, like the rest of us, often form schemas around subjects. Consider the example of banks.

With reference to banks, arbitrators expect to see a bank president, loan officers, tellers, vaults, cash drawers, expensive rugs, and elegant wood paneling. We expect banks to make loans to people, companies, and governments with good credit and to deny loans to those who have bad credit. We often expect bankers to be more interested in making money than benefiting society. Besides these perceptions, each of us has many other perceptions of banks and the people who work there. If an arbitration involves a bank or banking issues, these schemas will possibly come into play. The question, then, in pre-arbitration development of the case is to discover ahead of time how these schemas and representations will figure into arbitrators' thinking.

Schemas are formed primarily by perceptions and ideas that have been related to us by others. Socialization is perhaps the most powerful influence on how schemas (and stereotypes) are formed, maintained and changed. The significant people in our lives have a profound influence on how we view the world.

Arbitrators' perceptions are highly individualized. Even when the facts of a case are not disputed, each arbitrator will likely have a different version of the same schema to figure out what happened, why things happened as they did, and what the decision should be. Since arbitrators' schemas are preexisting, therefore, the objective for a lawyer is to set the stage with powerful messages that will cause an arbitrator to put these schemas into motion.

Interestingly, within the framework of our schematic structure often lies the key to changing attitudes or perceptions. Our value structure forms the backbone of our belief system and can often be of great use to a lawyer who wishes to change the perceptions that arbitrators might have at the outset of arbitration.

The last tool that we will discuss is affect. In contrast to our thinking processes, we share other experiences with arbitrators through our feelings. To demonstrate the differences, let's assume that you missed an important filing deadline. On the one hand, you know what happened factually from your cognitive processes. On the other hand, you are probably quite upset and perhaps even frightened about the possible consequences. These emotional reactions or emotional states we call affect.

In our example, the cognitive processes brought about the emotional state because we have learned through our experience to associate the two together. In other words, we have learned to link certain cognitive thoughts and perceptions to certain sets of emotions (which form our deep structure). The emotions only come as a result of our perception that a certain state of events or facts exists.

Now let's work on changing the perception and observe what happens. What would happen if the arbitration panel extended the deadline? The facts have now changed. Our perception of the state of the world has changed. And of course, our mental state changes from anxiety to calm.

Let's see what happens when we apply these principles to a particular case. This time let's consider a contract and fraud dispute between two businesses. One company is a Fortune 500 company that manufactures computer hardware and software. The company uses small companies to manufacture certain parts of their computer equipment. One such small company complains that the big company promised to order one million parts a year for ten years. It claims that in reliance on this promise, it borrowed and spent money to expand its plant size and machinery capacity. It also complains that the big company now orders only 200,000 parts per year. The big company replies by saying that the one million parts number was only a projection, not a promise. Furthermore, the big company says that it would order more parts when the economy in the industry improved and its customer demand increased.

What will arbitrators think? How will they feel about the big company? Will they mistrust the officers of the big company under the assumption that officers of big companies will tell a lie just to protect their jobs? Will they feel sorry for the small company because it had less power and control?

Will they believe that the drop in the number of parts ordered was due solely to the unexpected changes in the industry, and therefore, not a breach of contract or result of fraud?

To be sure, each new set of facts and circumstances in the case will prompt different cognitive and emotional responses from arbitrators based upon their attitudes, life experiences, personality traits, values, and demographic influences. The keys to success, therefore, lie in understanding the arbitration panel's attitudes, life experiences, and beliefs with respect to specific issues in the case. By understanding which attitudes, life experiences, and beliefs will dominate the arbitration panel's thinking, we have a better chance of developing a targeted presentation that will be persuasive. In addition, by understanding the breadth and depth of thinking or feeling about the issues that an arbitration panel will experience, we can shape the arguments and communication opportunities so that they coincide with arbitrators' schemas as well as their cognitive and affective processes. This important information about arbitrators is also one of the objectives of pre-arbitration decision-maker research.

The construction of a powerful argument is the product of systematic analysis and methodical development of messages and information that can be communicated effectively.

d Measuring Effectiveness of Communication

There are generally two ways to measure the effectiveness of communication. The first is to judge the quality of the communication by comparing the actual communication to its purpose. The second is to observe whether the recipient of the communication is motivated to behave in accordance with the purpose of the communication. The first measure is a more subjective measurement, while the second is more objective.

Regardless of how you judge effectiveness, the central question is *Does the communication have its desired effect?*

The reason this topic is so important for lawyers is that the effectiveness of advocacy is so often measured subjectively (i.e., whether the lawyer believes he or she did a good job in presenting the case), rather than the more objective standard. As a result, the communication efforts of the lawyer are often ineffective, even though the lawyer has communicated with great social skill.

3 The Importance of Listening and Making Arbitrators Want to Listen

Some people say that listening is an art. Perhaps that is true. Certainly, one of the best ways to understand another person is to listen to them. But the ability to listen is also a skill that can be enhanced with understanding and practice. Listening is an active behavior, not a passive one. Our success in listening to judges and arbitrators and getting them to listen to us can be markedly improved once we consider how the listening process works.

a How Listening Works

Listening in arbitration is critical to the process of communication and persuasion. Arbitrators must listen to understand the case. Lawyers must listen to arbitrators in order to understand arbitrators' perceptions and to measure how well the case is being presented and accepted. Lawyers must listen to them in order to pick up procedural cues.

However, as human beings, we do not listen to everything we hear and not everything we hear is important enough to seriously consider. Many things affect our listening ability. For example, we are sometimes accused by others of selective listening. Sometimes the selection process is deliberate and other times it is unconscious.

As attorneys, we have an obligation to train ourselves to listen carefully to arbitrators, witnesses, and other lawyers and to minimize the selectivity that we might be tempted to use outside the arbitration.

Arbitrators, on the other hand, do not have the same motivations. They feel quite free to listen when they want, or alternatively, not to listen, either consciously or unconsciously. Selective listening by judges, juries, and arbitrators is not the result of any disrespect to the presenter, but is a coping mechanism that legal decision-makers use to survive the decision-making process and make a decision based upon the most important evidence and ideas presented to them.

The average person's attention span is approximately ten-twelve minutes. Therefore, during a five-day arbitration, for example, any particular arbitrator would have "tuned in and out, then tuned in again" roughly two hundred times. Given the monumental amount of detail in most international arbitrations, the struggle of an arbitrator to remain focused on the important aspects of the case (in the perceptions of an arbitrator) is a mighty struggle indeed.

For the most part, arbitrators will listen to the things which coincide with their self-interest in knowing about the case and making a decision which makes them feel good about themselves. They will generally listen to a lawyer unless the lawyer has made them angry or created some other obstacle to acceptability.

Arbitrators, like most people, also listen selectively due to unconscious attitudes about the subject, the speaker, or some other element of the case. In addition, there are always competing stimuli in an arbitration.

By and large, however, the biggest obstacle to communication in the middle of arbitration is the striking difference between the presentation rate of information and the assimilation rate with which arbitrators absorb information. Most speakers talk at a rate of between 80 and 120 words per minute. However, arbitrators, like most people, can absorb words, images, and pieces of information at a much faster rate.

The difference in the presentation rate with which most arbitration teams present their cases and the assimilation rate at which arbitrators absorb it generally leads to some difficulties. Daydreaming, sleeping, and sometimes even frustration and anger are often the result of arbitration presentations, which are unnecessarily detailed and could be presented in more interesting and efficient ways.

b *Memory and Retention of Information*

Retaining information long enough to make a decision is an essential part of arbitration panel decision-making. Retention involves memory. To better understand how memory works, try this exercise. Answer the following questions using your memory:

(1) What is the name of the street you live on?
(2) What was your mother's maiden name?
(3) What major cities in the world are located on a coastline?

To be able to answer these questions, the answer must have been encoded, stored, and retrieved.

Memory refers to our ability to acquire, retain, and use information or knowledge.

Arbitrators retain information in several ways. Memories are stored in either short-term memory or long-term memory. Short-term memory is that part of our memory which is currently active and can change quickly when our focus of attention is shifted. We usually keep short-term information active in our minds for less than ninety seconds. For example, you might be trying to remember a telephone number when suddenly a friend asks you a question such as, "What time does the train arrive?" You may instantly forget the telephone number you were trying so hard to remember.

Long-term memory, on the other hand, is the repository of everything that we know. Generally, any piece of information that we hold onto in our brains for more than an hour is considered to be long term. Long-term memory is virtually limitless. However, memory can fool us. Sometimes we remember things differently than the way they actually were. On the other hand, sometimes we fail to remember things that we thought we knew very well.

In these ways, human memory is different from computer memory. Computers store information digitally in exactly the same form that was input. Computers do not create nuance or context without being instructed. Computers do not make judgments. Computers do not color memory with emotional responses. On the other hand, human memory does all these things.

Computers can generally recall every bit of data that was input even once. Human beings only store information in long-term memory that appears to be important or useful for future reference.

What is the benefit of short-term memory in arbitration? The most effective communicators are usually good at short-term listening. For example, during interactions with the arbitrators and during examination of witnesses, listening to the other person's responses is important in creating a productive flow of conversation.

In persuasion, we attempt to activate an arbitrator's long-term memory in a number of ways. The most typical ways involve association and repetition. The general idea is that if we can associate new information with information already stored in an arbitrator's long-term memory, storage of the new data will be facilitated. In addition, if new data is repeated long enough, it will usually be transferred to long-term storage.

The psychological messages that are the most persuasive and powerfully compelling in arbitration are those which are reflected already in an arbitrator's long-term reference memory. For this reason, some attorneys and trial scientists have mused that a case is decided before arbitrators ever come to the arbitration hearing.

4 How Persuasion Works: The Elements of a Persuasive Argument

Persuasion is communication that is intended to reinforce, shape, or change responses of the audience. In terms of arbitration persuasion, a lawyer or advocate is trying to reinforce, shape, or change attitudes and behavioral intentions (decision-making) of the arbitration panel and individual arbitrators. This idea implies that persuasion is more than just communicating objective facts and information as we noted in our discussion of surface structure and deep structure. If persuasion in arbitration simply consists of relating the facts of the case, we wouldn't need lawyers and arbitrators. We would simply type in the facts to a computer, and the computer would decide who wins the case.

Human beings are more complex, however. For the most part, persuasion takes place when a credible source of information presents an idea or attitude that differs from the ideas or attitudes already held by the audience in some way. The audience may have no preconceived ideas about the topic or may have different ideas or attitudes about the same topic. As a result of the presentation of a new or different idea, the audience will feel momentary tension that produces a kind of dissonance or incongruity.

Because of the discomfort that the audience feels, they are motivated to try to remove the dissonance by either accepting the new idea readily, or rejecting it, or reconciling it with previously held ideas and attitudes.

Realistically, most arbitrators will have preexisting attitudes and opinions about some or all of the topics that will arise in the arbitration. Nonetheless, there seems to be a great deal of extra space available for new ideas and attitudes for most arbitrators. As long as these new ideas or attitudes conveniently fit in with previously held ideas and attitudes, the job of persuasion is relatively simple. On the other hand, sometimes these new ideas or attitudes run head-on against an arbitrator's preexisting beliefs. In that case, the job of persuasion is more challenging. In other cases, the difficulty of the task falls somewhere in between, such as when new ideas or attitudes do not actually conflict with preexisting beliefs, but some adjustment is required. Indeed, where one set of beliefs is bad for your case, you should identify a different set of beliefs that provide a more helpful framework for your case. In other words, you will want to reframe the case and change the perspective.

Attitudes are visceral and implicit for most people. Clearly, the best option in the face of a pre-existing attitude is to try to find a way to reconcile it with the new idea that we want the audience (the arbitration panel) to accept. For example, if we want arbitrators to believe that our corporate client has a justifiable defense to the claimant's demands to punish the corporation, we would find it quite difficult to make an arbitrator believe that punishment is not justified in a case where a corporation has acted badly. On the other hand, if we state that we agree that punishment can be justified in the unusual instance where a corporation has acted badly, but that this particular corporation has demonstrated its contrition and punishment is not necessary, the persuasion process becomes easier.

5 The Elements of Persuasion

In order for us to be persuasive in arbitration, we must understand the elements that make up a persuasive communication. There are essentially four elements to a persuasive presentation: the communicator, the message, how the message is communicated, and the audience.

a The Communicator and Credibility

Credibility of the advocate and the advocate's message is important in persuasion. Credibility or the lack of it is the result of the arbitrator's observations of the quality and integrity of an advocate's character and behavior. Arbitrator perceptions of credibility are a threshold through which they all will pass before an arbitrator can ever seriously consider an advocate's arguments.

Source credibility (i.e., the credibility of the source of a piece of information) often diminishes over time, and the message may fade as the source of the message is forgotten or even dissociated from the message. Conversely, the effect of a message sometimes increases over time even though the messenger may not have had perceived credibility (no perceived expertise or trustworthiness). It may be, for example, that one of the advocates is obviously young or inexperienced, but has a powerful message, while the opposing advocate is obviously more experienced and steady in arbitration. In these instances, arbitrators will often tend to remember the message longer than the messenger. We sometimes refer to this as the *sleeper effect*.

In discussing expertise and persuasiveness, it is important to note the difference between similarity and credibility. Have you ever noticed that when people are buying things in the hardware store, they will rely upon other people who have experienced the same problem before they will trust the word of an expert? On the other hand, when discussing a more technical topic such as the composition of ozone, people tend to rely solely upon experts and will scoff at the opinion of a neighbor down the street.

After much research, we now understand that in some cases similarity is more important than credibility. If the topic relates to a subjective preference (i.e., personal choice), people tend to prefer the opinion of someone who shares their personal values, tastes, or way of life. But when making judgments about facts or objective reality, such as whether Madrid receives more rainfall than Rome, people prefer the opinion of someone with objective credibility.

Research in social psychology has supported the principle that only a credible speaker (someone hard to discount) can cause marked change in an arbitrator's thinking when advocating an idea that is greatly discrepant (different) from the preexisting attitude held by an arbitrator. It is also helpful to couple a difficult argument with other persuasive tools to help an arbitrator feel more comfortable considering an argument that seeks to cause an arbitrator to adjust his or her views.

One of the most important goals for an attorney at the outset of arbitration is to gain credibility as soon as possible. It is like building up the balance in a bank account before spending the money.

Experience tells us that no matter how strong an argument appears to be, there will come a time during the arbitration when an advocate will need the extra credibility to get over a difficult spot in the arbitration.

b *The Content of the Message*

When we talk about the content of a message, we are referring to the substantive information that is being transmitted as well as the style with which it is being conveyed. There are many lively debates in arbitration advocacy about a number of issues that relate to the content of our messages. Consider the following questions:

(1) Which is more persuasive—a carefully reasoned message or one that arouses emotion?
(2) Is it better to advocate an idea that is slightly different from an arbitrator's or to advocate an extreme point of view?
(3) Should a message express only one side of the argument, or should it try to refute the opposing view?

The answers to these questions are found in the great body of published and private scientific research available to us as arbitration advocates.

In the reason versus emotion debate, the correct answer comes from an understanding of the particular audience. If an arbitration panel is comprised of well-educated or analytical people, the rational appeal will usually obtain a better response than with less educated or less analytical people. Thoughtful and involved arbitrators are generally more responsive to reasoned arguments. Arbitrators who are not interested in the subject tend to make their decisions based upon their perceptions of the communicator and the message, as opposed to the logic of the argument.

The content of messages also becomes more persuasive if it is associated with good feelings. Likewise, happy (contented) people tend to make fast decisions and unhappy people tend to make decisions more slowly. Therefore, if you cannot make a strong case, it would be smart to put the arbitration panel in a good mood. It does not always work, but if both cases have equally powerful messages, the odds are better that you will win.

Conversely, some messages are very effective by invoking negative emotions. For example, fear and anger are strong motivators.

How do you handle a situation when you know in advance that some arbitrators will find one of your arguments hard to accept? Do you try to soft peddle the new idea or do you present it head-on in its most blunt form? We know that some new ideas or attitudes will produce discomfort, and sometimes discomfort causes people to change their opinions in response to the new idea. So, we might argue that a more direct and bold approach is preferable. On the other hand, sometimes a message that is uncomfortable causes the lawyer to lose credibility or interest of the arbitrator.

For example, there have been many instances where politicians and news reporters have taken positions different from a listener, and the listener then interpreted the speaker as biased, inaccurate, and untrustworthy. For the most part, therefore, people are most open to conclusions within their own range of acceptability. Greater disagreement between the new idea and the listener's preexisting attitude will produce less change in the arbitrator's attitude.

Research has indicated that arbitrators who are deeply involved in the subject of the arbitration will be able to accept only a narrow range of perceptions and attitudes. To these people, a moderately different message may seem radical, particularly if the message argues an opposing view to that of the arbitrator as opposed to an extreme version of the view the arbitrator already holds. Therefore, if you have gained credible authority and the arbitrator is only moderately involved in the issue, you should feel freer to advocate a more radical position.

One final thought about advocating a different view from an arbitrator. Most arbitration panels consist of people with widely ranging views on most topics. The smart advocate will construct an argument that will appeal to people from all these different perceptions. To be in a position to do that, it is most important to identify these widely ranging viewpoints using scientific arbitration panel research or other research techniques and to experiment with the combinations of messages that will form a stronger composite argument.

As for addressing the opponent's arguments, there is no one common-sense answer. There are times when we run the risk of weakening our own argument and confusing the audience. On the other hand, our message might seem more fair and perhaps even disarming if it recognizes and then refutes the opposition's arguments.

c *How the Message Is Conveyed*

Technically speaking, there are many methods with which to convey a point of evidence or argument. The primary considerations for determining which method(s) to use include: (1) whether the arbitrators will pay attention to the message embedded in the information communicated, (2) whether they will understand the information and the point to be made, (3) whether they will believe what they see and hear, and whether they will behave accordingly.

Perhaps one of the most frustrating aspects of communication and persuasion is that rarely does one medium of communication seem to be the most powerful. Let's consider, for example, the spoken word. Over the years we have heard, and perhaps delivered, stirring and powerful speeches and lectures. But try as we might, words are fleeting and memories fade. In addition, only approximately 30% of people rely primarily on the sense of hearing to learn new information. For most people, including arbitrators, however, the message in the speech is more powerful and lasting than the speech itself.

With respect to written words, we know from experience and research that arbitrators rely heavily on the words contained in written agreements and communications. However, in the scheme of things, arbitrators make their decisions based upon the overall messages that stimulate their belief systems. On the other hand, written words in evidence and demonstrative aids that convey messages are more powerful than written words that have no message, despite their being technically accurate. Therefore, a lawyer or advocate would be well advised to use words judiciously and to use words in visual aids that convey messages and mental pictures.

With respect to graphics and video presentations, research has indicated that the messages that are simple to understand are most persuasive when supported by some type of video presentation. Complex or difficult messages are more persuasive when written (they force the listener to think through the idea). Therefore, the level of difficulty of the message interacts with the medium to determine how persuasive the message is.

Regardless, it would be wise to use more than one medium to convey the most powerful messages in a case. There is a powerful anchoring effect that builds confidence in a message when they see and hear it repeated in different forms in different media.

d *The Audience: The Arbitration Panel*

Regardless of the audience, it is important to have an understanding of the decision-making and perceptive characteristics of members of the audience before developing or presenting a persuasive argument. The characteristics to consider generally fall into five categories: attitudes about specific issues in the case, life experience relevant to specific issues in the case, personality traits, general values/beliefs, and influential demographics.

Attitudes and life experiences relevant to specific issues in a case are often significantly or moderately related to decisions. Research by social psychologists has found that the relationships between the attitudes or life experiences and the attitudes about specific issues in a case that exist for an individual arbitrator are perhaps the most important characteristic to know about the arbitration panel before attempting to persuade them. One of the many advantages to performing scientific mock arbitration panel research in advance of arbitration is to identify the case-specific attitudes and life experiences that will shape the listening and mental processing of the likely arbitration panel in the case.

For the most part, general personality traits of arbitrators will not predict their responses to an argument. A particular trait may enhance the effectiveness of one argument or another or, alternatively, may work against it.

The characteristics most often used (although least reliable in predicting behavior) are demographics.

As a general subject, the demographics of arbitrators are not helpful in predicting how they will process the case or how they will vote. But a demographic characteristic can often raise a question or create a hypothesis in a particular case that can be helpful in forming a composite understanding of an arbitrator. Consider this example of an arbitrator's demographics. In a case that involves technical issues, such as patent, trade secrets, or toxic waste, an arbitrator who has a background in science may find it easier to comprehend the details and arguments, but may also have preexisting ideas that favor one side or the other of the argument.

There are certain hypotheses that can be formed by knowing a limited amount of information about the audience. However, until enough information is obtained which confirms or refutes the hypotheses, it is best to keep all options open.

6 Cultural Differences and Arbitrator Decision-Making

Although a great deal of attention is focused on the legal and procedural differences between the cultural customs, approaches, and styles of arbitrators and advocates from different countries and continents, perhaps the most frustrating issues for many participants are the differences in the methods of communication, meaning of communications, mental interpretations, and behavioral expectations that arise for arbitrators and advocates who come from different cultures.

It is beyond the scope or capacity of this chapter to fully explore the precise differences that exist between international arbitration participants from different parts of the world. However, we will discuss some of the thornier issues and recommend ways of preparing to effectively deal with them in a particular case.

To illustrate how the issue of cultural differences appears in the course of an arbitration, we note the observations of Pierre Lalive, a senior partner and founder of Lalive, a Swiss law firm in Geneva, and one of the world's leading specialists in international disputes. Professor Lalive has over fifty years of experience in international law and arbitration and has acted as arbitrator or counsel in several hundred international arbitration proceedings:

> "Cultural differences or even conflicts between such a counsel and the international arbitrator(s) are, as a result, numerous and sometimes costly, all the more so when the arbitrator also is lacking in international or comparative outlook. The task of counsel being to persuade the arbitration panel (i.e. the majority of its members, in particular its chairman), a rather elementary condition of success would seem to be for an attorney to understand the arbitrator's background and culture, both legal and non-legal."
>
> ...
>
> "I have stressed on other occasions the 'need to pay more attention to questions of communication between the arbitration panel and the representatives of the parties' and mentioned a few practical examples which, hopefully, could serve as a warning against the prevailing habit of so many lawyers of 'transposing,' sometimes most undiplomatically, national practices and forensic attitudes to the field of international arbitration."
>
> "I shall always remember my embarrassment when, many years ago, as I was acting as junior counsel to a distinguished New York attorney in an international arbitration in Europe, I was summoned by the chairman (a former law professor of mine), who bluntly asked me whether my New York colleague considered him and his fellow arbitrators as either stupid or untrustworthy, since

> he had pressed the tribunal to adopt his draft of a very detailed set of procedural rules, presumably hoping thereby both to protect himself and help the tribunal!"
>
> "In another case, a famous French arbitrator became increasingly irritated, over months of proceedings, by the practice of an English counsel of answering in detail every single letter or point of the other side, presumably on the assumption that, unless every point made was expressly refuted, even when marginal or irrelevant, it would be considered as conceded. Similarly, it appears that many experienced arbitrators, particularly Europeans, complain about the lack of 'synthetic spirit' or mere courage to select arguments or documents, of certain litigators, in particular American, an attitude which results in the arbitration panel being submerged by tons of (partly irrelevant) documents."
>
> ...
>
> "A last example, known amongst specialists of arbitration, may be taken from the manner in which arbitral proceedings are conducted: plaintiff's counsel was an English barrister, while defendant's counsel was a French avocat. Both of them, returning to their respective offices, were questioned about the proceedings and gave the same answer: 'Well, I was asked two questions by the chairman!' This identical answer conveyed in that case two completely different meanings. The Frenchman was surprised, if not shocked, that his well-structured 'plaidoirie' should have been interrupted at all, while the Englishman was dismayed to have received so little reaction or guidance in his presentation from the arbitrator!"[5]

The identification and objective analysis of the ways in which cultural differences manifest themselves in a particular arbitration are difficult and sometimes frustrating for most arbitrators and advocates at one time or another. However, there is a great deal that can be learned from science about how to deal successfully with the differences that arise from divergent languages, practices, interpretations of meaning, or some other culturally based aspect of mental processing and behavior.

From a psychological perspective, the study of the differences between cultures extends into two separate approaches. The first is a field we refer to as *cultural psychology* which is the study of the way cultural traditions and social practices regulate, express, and transform human behavior and mental processes within separate and distinct cultures, resulting in a focus on ethnic divergences in mind, self, and emotion.[6] *Cultural psychology* includes the study and impact of culture, tradition and social practices on members of any particular culture. The second is a more recently developed field we refer to as *cross-cultural psychology* in which psychologists generally use culture as a means of testing the universality of psychological processes across cultures while at the same time determining how local cultural practices shape psychological processes. For instance, a *cross-cultural psychologist* would focus on the aspects of social interaction that are universal across a variety of cultures, whereas a *cultural psychologist* would be interested in how the social practices of a particular set of cultures shape the development of cognitive processes of members of a culture in different ways.

To further our work in understanding and utilizing information helpful in successful international arbitration, we borrow information and study methods from both of these branches of psychology. The most important principle here that interna

5. Lalive, P., "Cultural Differences and International Arbitration," 9 *Euromoney* 13-15 (1995).
6. Shweder, *Thinking Through Cultures* (Harvard University Press, 1991) (at p. 72).

tional arbitration advocates can learn is that deeply held mental and behavioral differences between arbitration participants from different cultures does exist in a way that can be studied and understood scientifically. The awareness that is created from this principle should serve to remove the issue of cultural differences from a subjective analysis that fosters continued misunderstandings and to place it squarely on the examining table to allow for more objective analysis for use in any particular setting.

Once we accept that decision-making and successful persuasion can be studied using scientific methodologies, we can then utilize the tools that science offers us to study ways to enhance the effectiveness of advocacy in international arbitrations. By objectively studying the cultural differences that are likely to play a dynamic role in an arbitration, the knowledge gained through the use of a scientific approach is also likely to enhance the experience of arbitrators, advocates, and parties.

V PSYCHOLOGY AND THE DECISION-MAKING PROCESS OF THE ARBITRATION PANEL

Every day, professional men and women sit as arbitrators in international arbitrations. Each of them has a private story to tell about their successes and failures in life. Each of them has a family history that has helped make them who they are. Each of them has a unique life outside the arbitration that influences the way they will view the issues during arbitration.

This section will explore some of the things we know about the mental processing of arbitrators in arbitration and how it affects their behavior when deciding how a case should be resolved. We will discuss what *common sense* for arbitrators really is and how we can understand how it will be applied by a likely arbitration panel in a given case. We might even discover something about ourselves in the process.

1 An Overview of a Panel's Decision-Making Process

For many centuries, collective (small group) decision-making in both private and public affairs has been a hallmark of most societies. The conventional wisdom is that small groups of individuals who share a common purpose make better quality decisions than individuals acting alone. To better understand group decision-making in an arbitration setting, one must analyze the social structure and process within an arbitration panel as they affect each individual arbitrator and the arbitration panel as a whole.

The influences that will shape the way an arbitrator feels and thinks about a case begin long before arbitration. As a result, the decision-making process for an arbitrator in any particular case begins as soon as he or she enters the arbitration and begins making assessments of the people and the information that are presented.

Researchers who have studied the decision-making behavior of arbitrators have identified three levels of analysis. The first level refers to the decision-making behavior of individual arbitrators. The second refers to the social events that occur before and during the deliberation of the case. The third level of analysis is a review of the cognitive and affective experiences of individual arbitrators in the context of social interaction before and during deliberation (i.e., how the arbitration panel as a whole reaches a decision).

Understanding how an arbitration panel reaches its decision requires a review of each of these levels, so we should explore each one separately. The practical reason for doing so is that the most effective arbitration presentations should incorporate powerful themes that appeal to both individual arbitrators and the arbitration panel as a whole.

a *Arbitration Panel Decision-Making Model for Arbitrators*

Scientific research into arbitration panel decision-making and that of other legal decision-makers has concluded that there is a three-stage model which best describes the process a typical arbitrator goes through on his or her journey to making a decision. First, the individual arbitrator evaluates the facts, arguments, and technical evidence and constructs a mental summary in the form of a narrative story.

Second, the arbitrator comprehends the questions to be answered at the end of the arbitration concerning the legal decision alternatives that are available as decision categories. Third, the arbitrator attempts to find a match between his or her story of the case and a decision category in order to classify the story in the category it best fits. Upon completing this mental procedure, the arbitrators then interact with the rest of the arbitration panel to negotiate a solution that helps each arbitrator to reach the maximum goal of making a decision that gives meaning to their experience and helps them to feel good about themselves.

This general three-stage model for decision-making is referred to by social scientists as an *explanation-based model*. Within this mental structure, the arbitrator attempts to summarize the case by forming an explanation and creating a story of the case which is used in reasoning toward a decision.

This process begins as soon as the arbitrator begins learning about the case from direct and indirect cues in arbitration.

There are both cognitive (thoughtful and intellectual) and affective (emotional) processes which occur during this first stage of individual arbitrator decision-making. This formation of a summary of the evidence is the same process that occurs when each of us tries to make sense of the other events we encounter in everyday living. Beginning during the initial stages of the arbitration presentation, arbitrators assign meaning to the case by incorporating or overlaying on the actual case one or more reasonable explanations or narrative stories that explain the events that the lawyers and the witnesses have talked about. This search for meaning is perhaps the most profound explanation for why arbitrators decide cases as they do as we have already discussed.

A typical arbitrator concludes the initial stage of the decision-making process with a single dominant story in mind. In fact, researchers have determined that a sizable percentage of arbitrators and other legal decision-makers have established a clear leaning in the case by the end of the opening statement (prior to any exposure to witnesses or evidence). This would mean that for most arbitrators, the actual arbitration presentation is a process of filtering through the evidence to test their individual hypothesis about the case—to either confirm or to alter their original notion of what the case story really is.

As we have discussed, in the course of determining the narrative story of the case, each arbitrator will refer back to their life experiences, stereotypes, schemas, attitudes, and any other references in their minds that will help them to understand and find meaning within the particular facts and issues in the case. Arbitrators' cognitive structures (everything they know and how they reason) are fairly inflexible, and they will make every effort to fit their perceptions of the facts and circumstances of the case into the story they have formed.

b Direct Influence of Attitudes in Decision-Making By Arbitration Panels

Every arbitrator evaluates what transpires in arbitration on the basis of his or her life experiences, attitudes, and pre-dispositions. Arbitrators obviously do not come to the arbitration with blank minds. Their beliefs, values, attitudes, and morals are well entrenched, and everything that is heard and experienced will be filtered and colored by them.

Research in the field of cognitive psychology has indicated that attitudes take on a role of directing or guiding human behavior in one direction or another, as opposed to motivating particular behavior.

Therefore, attitudes may be considered to enter the picture predominantly at crucial decision junctures. There are literally thousands of published scientific studies designed to understand the formation, maintenance, and change of attitudes that are available to us as reference tools.

In the context of decision-making in arbitration, salient beliefs and attitudes will guide individual arbitrators and the entire arbitration panel to reach a decision which conforms to their beliefs and attitudes about the specific issues present in the case.

c How Arbitrator Attitudes and Beliefs Are Formed and Changed

Understanding the role of attitudes in arbitration panel decision-making requires an acknowledgement that individual arbitrators bring their life experiences (including ideas they have learned as well as their learned thinking processes) with them in their roles in arbitration. It is beyond the scope of our discussion to explore the myriad of earlier life experiences which arbitrators bring with them into the decision-making process. However, it is important to explore the role these experiences play in the decision-making process as well as the role that socially shared experience plays in arbitration decision-making process.

As we have seen, the results achieved by recent social science studies have clearly demonstrated that an arbitrator's cognitive life experiences have shaped the arbitrator's emotional processing, personality, persuadability, perceptions of causal attribution, perceptions of damages and reactions to attorneys and witnesses. It is equally clear that individual arbitrators and the arbitration panel as a whole are influenced by emotional or affective processing despite their inability to recognize and articulate it.

An arbitrator's appraisals of attitude objects (e.g., people, events, institutions, etc.) are likely to influence their subsequent emotional reactions to them. Conversely, an arbitrator's emotional reactions to an attitude object can yield information for us by inducing thoughts about it. In practical terms, it does not matter if the sequence is either: (a) emotion influences thoughts or, alternatively, (b) thoughts influence emotion; the result is the same: an attitude which influences the outcome of a decision is, as a rule, based on an arbitrator's emotional *and* intellectual experience.

Arbitrators' attitudes and beliefs are formed in response to information learned through personal experience, through information relayed by other people, and through personal observation. The formation of attitudes and beliefs is an arbitrator's way of understanding and experiencing the rest of the world around them. As a result, in order for us to understand how arbitrators perceive the issues, parties and facts of our case, we must make the effort to identify the likely attitudes and beliefs of arbitrators and understand how they were formed, why they have been maintained, and how they might be changed if necessary.

Attitudes are comprised of affect (emotions and instincts), cognition (perceptions, thoughts, and interpretations), and behavior (intention to act in accordance with the attitude). For example, consider an arbitrator's reaction in a trade secret case. An arbitrator may feel strongly that anyone who steals a secret and sells it to someone else is a bad person (feeling), that anything that a company keeps private is a secret (perception), and if given a chance to punish someone for stealing a secret, he would do so (behavioral intention). This same pattern can be adapted to any attitude about any subject.

In scientific mock arbitration panel research, we closely study these types of patterns in order to identify areas of weakness and strength of a particular issue in a case. We want to understand arbitrators' attitudes, the life experiences that are associated with them and the role they will play in arbitrator decision-making about the case. By studying attitudes, we learn a great deal about how to successfully deal with the attitudes that likely arbitrators will have. We will learn about the attitudes that may come into play that are beneficial to us as well as those that are not and how to disarm or change them.

This brings us to an interesting observation about attitudes: arbitrators will only apply those attitudes that are *salient*. Salient attitudes are those that are actually prompted to appear in arbitrators' minds by the case presentation as opposed to attitudes that we forecast should apply to the case, but which arbitrators do not find to be applicable. Every arbitrator, like every other person, has thousands of attitudes about something. The question is always, "Which ones will you encounter in this case?"

The only way to know which attitudes, beliefs, values, life experiences, and mental processes likely arbitrators will utilize to decide a particular case, is to conduct some kind of pre-arbitration research (whether scientifically conducted or not) to identify them, to understand them, and how to work with them to develop a powerful and persuasive case. There are many different methods to conduct such research that will be discussed in a separate chapter on scientific arbitration panel research.

For the most part, arbitrators form attitudes that are consistent with their view of the world around them and consistent with their other attitudes and beliefs. Arbitrators have many belief systems about almost every object, person, institution, life challenge, etc. that they have encountered in their lifetimes.

Lest one be frustrated by attitudes that at first appear to be insurmountable, there are a number of important characteristics of attitudes that are important for a lawyer or advocate to understand. While it is true that arbitrators are committed to their own perceptions, it is also true that there are a number of weaknesses in the attitude formation process that make many of them more susceptible to adaptability and change.

The first is that there is a value hierarchy that most people have in their overall belief system that often allows one attitude to be trumped by another, more important, attitude. Let's imagine a case against a major financial news publisher which involves allegations that the newspaper wrongfully published a critical expose of an investment brokerage company. The company alleges that the article was based upon false or misleading information, and, as a result, that the company had to close its doors due to the adverse effects of the article on its reputation. At arbitration, the claimant argues that the author of the article and the publisher had bad motives that interfered with objectivity. The claimant argues that the publisher knew the kind of effect that critical articles could have on such a company. It argues that because of the loss of the company, one hundred innocent employees lost their jobs at a company they loved working for.

In defense, the publisher states that it had no ill intent and that if the information was false, the fault lay with the sources of information, not the publishing company. The publisher also infers that the reason for the failure of the company was poor management.

Even the most experienced lawyers and advocacy consultants cannot always accurately predict which of the attitudes and belief systems of a likely arbitration panel will be activated in a particular case without conducting empirical arbitration panel research before arbitration. However, once the attitudes and perceptions of an arbitration panel are activated, they will most surely influence the arbitration panel's decision in the case.

2 Individual and Group Decision-Making in Arbitration

At the heart of the decisions reached by an arbitration panel are decisions which are made by individuals which make up the group. In this context, it is important to understand the cognitive and affective factors which affect the decisions of each individual as well as the entire arbitration panel group.

a *Role of Individual Arbitrators in Panel Decision-Making*

It is difficult if not impossible for a single arbitrator to comprehend all of the facts, events, and nuances contained in an arbitration case presentation. No matter how intelligent or experienced an arbitrator is in making important decisions, every arbitrator, like every person, has limitations. For example, individual arbitrators engage in a variety of coping mechanisms which "filter" information and shape perceptions so as to create understanding and comfortable feelings and to minimize dissonance.

Individual arbitrators are also limited in their decision-making abilities by varying emotional reactions, differing assessments of attribution, varying intellectual capacities, varying abilities to recall, differences in cultural views and sensitivities, widely varying life experiences, and many other factors.

As a result, arbitrators construct different stories or assessments of cases even though every arbitrator was exposed to the same facts, evidence and arguments in the case. They construct their own version of the facts and motivations with respect to each of the arbitration participants. This process of applying an arbitrator's understanding of life and the creation of a narrative or story for the case being presented to them in arbitration is the driving force behind an individual arbitrator's decision about the case as we have stated. Once a narrative has become firmly visualized, arbitrators will rarely change their opinions about what happened, although they will occasionally change their minds about how the events in the case should be legally classified.

Ironically, the same limitations and characteristics of arbitrators which give meaning to individuality are also strengths with which the arbitration panel group as a whole can arrive at a fair and equitable decision. Differing insights and differing views of events and motivations provide the group with a more complete perspective, out of which better quality decisions can be made.

b *Group Influences on Individual Arbitrator Decision-Making*

There are a number of ways in which various processes within an arbitration panel influence another arbitrators' individual decision-making. For example, in the context of group decision-making, information is exchanged as a by-product of the social interaction which occurs within the group.

Knowledge may be acquired that might not have otherwise occurred to individuals without the interaction because of inexperience or lack of knowledge. It is in this critical point in the arbitration panel deliberation process, for example, that arbitrators with relevant life experience will generally speak up, and sometimes apply their own expertise in the subject matter of the arbitration.

It is human nature for arbitrators to talk to each other about the case during the arbitration and certainly during deliberations. But regardless of when the substantive interaction begins, each member of the group typically begins with a set of ideas about his or her own goals and the alternative choices.

The information exchanged by members of the group includes both cognitive and affective information (i.e., how each of the arbitrators thinks and feels about the issues in the case). The differences in the effects of each are interesting and profound. As a practical matter, it is difficult if not impossible to separate one's thinking about a set of circumstances from one's emotional reaction to them. However, in the process of sharing cognitive and affective information, the recipient of a shared idea will likely react differently than the originator, although the recipient may be motivated to act in complete concert with the originator. As a result, arbitrators will often (if not usually) arrive at the same conclusion, although their thoughts and feelings (rationale) about the case may be different.

Similarly, in the quest to comprehend and solve any dilemmas presented in a case, arbitrators almost always learn and understand the case more completely only after discussion within the panel. There are many reasons which form the basis for this principle. For example, the panel as a whole usually has a more complete database than any of its members for problem-solving. It is not likely that any individual member of the arbitration panel has acquired or has access to all of the pieces of information needed to solve the group's problem.

Because of the limitations that an individual arbitrator experiences in the formation of a story which explains the case, a narrative which at first appears to be complete to those of us on the arbitration team is often determined to be inadequate or inappropriate once expressed before the rest of the arbitration panel. The checks and balances offered by a multiple-person arbitration panel are intended to ensure what is often referred to as *justice*.

Finally, the interaction between members of a panel can provide motivation to arrive at a more complete and morally supportable decision than one individual arbitrator acting alone. Interpersonal energy among arbitrators, either positive or negative, tends to enliven and stimulate more complete and acceptable discussion and results.

c Comparing the Decisions of Arbitration Panels with Those of Lay Juries

As we have noted, there are virtually no known scientific studies of the decision-making behavior of arbitrators in international arbitration. However, there are some significant studies of domestic arbitrations in the United States which have been organized in the same fashion as most international arbitrations. One such study was conducted by Professor Donald Wittman of the Economics Department at the University of California at Santa Cruz, California in the United States.[7] By way of background, the State of California has provided for court-annexed arbitration in certain kinds of cases. This essentially means that before a case could be tried to a jury, it must be tried to an arbitration panel. The arbitration decision would not be binding.

7. Wittman, D., "Arbitration in the Shadow of a Jury Trial Comparing Arbitrator and Jury Verdicts," 58 *Dispute Resolution Journal* 59 (November 2003/January 2004).

Wittman's study looked into a number of questions, including "How do the decisions made by arbitrators compare to the decisions made by juries?" To answer this question, the researchers reviewed the decisions made by professional arbitrators and juries in 383 automobile accident cases that were tried in the State of California over a nine-year period. The results of the trials were published in a publication entitled *Jury Verdicts Weekly*. The researchers studied the average awards, the percentage of pro-plaintiff (pro-claimant) verdicts and possible explanations for any variances.

The results of this study are consistent with the studies of other researchers who have compared the decisions of arbitration panels and lay juries. They found that arbitrators ruled in favor of the plaintiff 98% of the time while juries ruled in favor of the plaintiff 73% of the time.[8] In addition, they found that the average arbitration verdict was USD 22,521, whereas the average jury verdict was only USD 19,227. In other words, arbitration verdicts were on the average 17% higher than jury verdicts.[9]

In statistical terms, the correlation between jury awards and arbitration awards in Professor Whitman's study was 74%. (This means that a jury award and an arbitration award would be the same 74% of the time.) The data from the study also indicates that 26% of the time, the arbitration award would be *higher or much higher* than a jury verdict.

The differences in the decisions between arbitrators and juries may be understood in a number of ways. Before relying on any hypothesis, however, a more in-depth review of the actual arbitrators' characteristics and their likely perceptions in the case would be advisable.

VI SCIENTIFIC RESEARCH AND MOCK ARBITRATIONS

Decades of scientific research in the fields of psychology, marketing, social science, and others have allowed us to develop scientific research designs and methods that are directly applicable to studying likely perceptions of arbitrators in an upcoming arbitration. The most useful scientific tool we have in preparing for an arbitration hearing is a mock arbitration panel study. A mock arbitration panel study is conducted in an arbitration hearing-style setting using mock arbitrators who have characteristics which match those of the actual arbitrators in a case. Such research studies are created and conducted in a laboratory setting as if the case were going to hearing the day of the study.

Recruiting mock arbitrators requires attention to detail. The recruiter will need to match the type of practice, academic background, demographics, general attitudes about the issues in the case, and as many other characteristics as possible after researching the backgrounds of the actual arbitrators.

Procedures for setting the agenda (which will mirror the actual anticipated proceedings) and for collecting and analyzing useful, accurate, and reliable data from the mock arbitrators should be instituted. The information gathering stage of the

8. *Id.*
9. *Id.*

research study will include each mock arbitrator's views in the case prior to the proceedings (based upon the written documents) and after the mock presentations for each of the opposing parties. The mock arbitrators will discuss the case using the anticipated actual format selected. The trial team and client can observe the discussions either by audio link or audio-visual link as preferred by the trial team and the mock arbitrators. Afterward, the research scientist will engage the mock arbitrators in a qualitative interview similar to that of a mock trial study, often followed by a live and frank discussion directly with the advocacy team.

In general, scientific mock arbitration research offers a unique opportunity to bring the arbitration process into the laboratory for study and analysis that can be used to improve the advocacy process.

Successful mock arbitration research takes into account the peculiarities of the arbitration process in a particular case, while at the same time providing a rigorously scientific process for objective study.

Thirty years of mock arbitration research has taught us that there are a number of special steps that must be taken to insure a smooth and productive process.

Because normally only three research arbitrators are used in such research, it will be hard to generalize their decision to the actual case unless you have conducted extremely conscientious sampling in choosing who the research arbitrators will be and strictly followed scientific protocols. If the mock arbitrators are an almost identical match to the real arbitrators and strict scientific study methods are used, the perceptions and decisions which the mock arbitrators reach in the mock arbitration study will be more likely to forecast the perceptions and decision of the actual arbitration panel.

The degree to which there are differences in characteristics may or may not indicate that there will be differences in the perceptions of the actual panel. Nonetheless, experience tells us that there is much inherent value in conducting the mock arbitration panel study. Many, if not most, of the perceptions of the mock arbitrators will be close enough to those of the actual arbitration panel that the data will be valuable in developing recommendations for themes, case story, and other aspects of the actual presentation.

VII CONCLUSION

In this chapter, we have devoted most of our discussion to creating an awareness of the psychological aspects of the complex decision-making processes that exist in all international arbitration. We have described the importance of arbitrator-oriented advocacy in the successful quest for a favorable decision. We have suggested principles and methods for every advocate to use in understanding the likely perceptions of arbitrators in a particular arbitration. It is our hope that the information here is useful in helping an advocate to create a powerful and positive persuasive experience for arbitrators and clients, and indeed, for the advocate.

PANEL 9

Procedures and Behaviours

The panel explores how procedure(s) can impact the behaviour and conduct of different participants in the dispute resolution process. Speakers provide a number of distinct vantage points, including procedures specific to certain types of dispute (e.g., sports arbitration and infrastructure proceedings) and particular legal cultures. The panel also addresses the importance of tailoring procedure(s) to take account of the human element in the adjudicative process.

CHAPTER 24

The Impact and Importance of Human Engagement in the Arbitral Process: A Focus on Sports Arbitration

Susan Ahern SC[*]

TABLE OF CONTENTS

I INTRODUCTION

The concept of arbitration in sport is not new. It has been applied on the pitch/court/track every day by 'arbitres' or, more commonly, referees, in order to ensure that the rules of the specific sport are adhered to by all participants. Operating within the rules of the sport is essential for fairness and is intrinsic to the fabric of sporting competition, where the concept of the level playing field is a foundation stone. Contests and disputes in sport go hand in hand, as the competitive spirit of athletes asserts itself.

Arbitration is an effective medium to resolve disputes and sports arbitration, while it shares a common heritage with commercial arbitration, is really the younger

---

* Susan Ahern SC, FCIArb, is a dual qualified barrister, international arbitrator and mediator. She is an arbitrator of the Court of Arbitration for Sport, an arbitrator of the European Commission Disputes Settlement Pool, a member of the ICSID Panel of Conciliators and member of the ICC Commission on Arbitration and ADR. She is Vice President of Arbitration Ireland and a member of the Arbitration & ADR Committee of the Bar of Ireland. Susan is an experienced corporate counsel in banking & financial services, media, entertainment and sport and was formerly General Counsel of World Rugby.

sibling. The concept of sports arbitration is relatively new if it is considered that the Court of Arbitration for Sport (CAS) was established only in 1984. Especially when compared to the position of sports federations which have been dealing with the implementation of their own rules, and managing disputes arising, since their creation. But sports arbitration has many interesting and distinguishing features which render it quite different to commercial arbitration, not least because human factors, namely, the presence of the athlete in the room and considerations regarding their right to earn a livelihood, are key elements in many sporting disputes.

This chapter considers new and evolving mechanisms that sports dispute bodies are introducing in order to address the increasingly complex scenarios that are arising for participants, including vulnerable witnesses, in the arbitration of sporting disputes. To provide appropriate context, this chapter will first consider the nature of sports arbitration and how it differs from commercial arbitration. Then it will consider the most significant feature of sports arbitration, i.e., its expedition, and give some pertinent examples from the perspective of sports arbitral bodies. Finally, the chapter will consider specific mechanisms that different bodies have introduced to facilitate and improve the experience of participants in the arbitral process and empowered arbitrators to be proactive in situations where human vulnerability is a live factor.

II THE NATURE OF SPORTS ARBITRATION

As sport has professionalized and grown in popularity, sports federations have had to grow and evolve commensurately. This has meant taking a professional approach to dealing with disputes, be that with appropriate internal disciplinary processes, and/or recourse to external dispute resolution processes such as arbitration and mediation available from specialized arbitral institutions. The key advantage of such processes in the sporting context is that they can ensure affordable access to justice for athletes, sporting associations, and sports federations when compared to litigation. Arbitration also promotes finality and universal enforcement under the New York Convention.[1] The scope and flexibility of arbitration means that it can deal not only with certain regulatory matters (e.g., anti-doping, anti-corruption, eligibility) but also with the growing number of commercial disputes arising in sport.

The increasing prominence of arbitration in sport is particularly important where the career of an athlete lies in the balance. Time is also of the essence in sport when careers are short and international tournaments arise on an annual, bi-annual or quadrennial basis. The expedited nature of the settlement of sports disputes, including through arbitration, is essential to enable the athlete to get back on the field of play or to enable the competition to progress. Because many sports professionals have limited resources arbitration also gives access to sports justice which litigation might render otherwise financially prohibitive.

1. United Nations Convention on the Recognition and Enforcement of Foreign Arbitral Awards (New York, 1958).

The range of disputes that can arise is vast, but the typical sports disputes encompass the following categories: eligibility, discipline (e.g., on-field foul play); misconduct; anti-doping; match manipulation; commercial; safeguarding;[2] and increasingly human rights. Jurisdiction to arbitrate is ordinarily contained within the rules of a sporting body, or as part of the terms of an agreement that participants sign in order to compete in a competition or within a collective bargaining agreement (e.g., in US professional sports). Many international federations (IFs) provide in their rules that disputes, or designated types of disputes, will be settled exclusively by way of arbitration, with many nominating a final appeal to an independent tribunal process, a national sports arbitral institution, and/or the Court of Arbitration for Sport (CAS).

Arbitration is the dominant dispute resolution procedure in the sphere of anti-doping. This position has emerged under the umbrella of the World Anti-Doping Agency which in 2003 published the first World Anti-Doping Code (WADA Code) The import of arbitration and the status of the CAS increased exponentially when the WADA Code mandated that all final appeals for international-level athletes or arising from international events should be to CAS as the final sports court.[3] In 2019, the CAS Anti-Doping Division was established to deal with anti-doping cases at first instance.

III SIGNIFICANT FEATURES OF SPORTS ARBITRATION

As arbitration becomes more common in sport, it is also apparent that it does not share many of the characteristics of commercial arbitration. Sports arbitration is often the mechanism used to uphold the integrity of sport and deal with sporting disputes, which invariably involve an athlete and their right to participate, rather than a corporation, and therefore the human engagement quotient is amplified exponentially. It is a unique field of arbitration. Understanding the differences enables a clearer view of how the arbitral process has already been tailored by sports to suit its unique characteristics and requirements. These imperatives can be broadly characterized as follows.

Consistent Sanctioning – Sports arbitration has an overriding objective to facilitate consistent decisions for like offences and, frequently, public sanctioning, in order to uphold the integrity of sport in the eyes of athletes and the fans. This is especially evident in anti-doping and anti-corruption rules. The WADA Code[4] sets out the minimum mandatory anti-doping tariffs, while most sports have standard tariffs for on-field related discipline or a list of sanctions that arbitrators can have regard to in the exercise of their discretion.

2. *See*, https://www.lawinsport.com/topics/item/safeguarding-proceedings-how-to-balance-the-rights-of-the-accused-with-treatment-of-the-abused (accessed 6 October 2025) and Procedural Rules of the National Safeguarding Panel of SRUK, in https://www.sportresolutions.com/assets/documents/D_2_-_2021_NSP_Procedural_Rules_1_1.pdf (accessed 6 October 2025).
3. Article 13 of the WADA Code, available at: https://www.wada-ama.org/sites/default/files/resources/files/2021_wada_code.pdf (accessed 6 October 2025).
4. Promulgated by the World Anti-Doping Agency originally in 2003, the 2021 edition is currently in force: https://www.wada-ama.org/sites/default/files/resources/files/2021_wada_code.pdf (accessed 6 October 2025).

Bespoke or closed list of arbitrators – Bespoke disciplinary and arbitral bodies are necessary in order to administer justice in the unique context of sport, often referred to as the 'specific nature of sport'.[5] Such bodies are efficient in terms of cost, time and expertise, driven by the utilization of a closed list of expert arbitrators.

Flexibility – The flexibility of procedures that arbitration affords in the sporting environment enables accommodations to be made to fit the uniqueness of the environment and the fact that an athlete is ordinarily central to the proceedings. In this regard, flexibility and adaptability are key features of a number of bespoke guidelines and practices which have developed within sports tribunals in recent years (examples of which are highlighted further below). Many of these have emerged from individual cases and out of the desire by national and international sports bodies, often prompted by athletes to amplify the safeguarding of athletes.

Public Awards – Sports arbitration awards are more often than not public in nature – not least where they involve major events like the Olympics. This is in contrast to the cornerstone principle of confidentiality that applies, unless waived, in commercial arbitration. In the interests of transparency and deterrence, anti-doping awards are published by default under Article 14.3 of the WADA Code. The World Athletics Disciplinary Tribunal,[6] the CAS and other sports and sports arbitral bodies publish many of their Awards. FIFA has a policy of publishing all non-confidential CAS awards which involve FIFA directly with so as to 'increase transparency and provide information on the various issues dealt with before the CAS',[7] and some may be published in an anonymized or a redacted version.[8]

A Body of Awards – A harmonized body of sports law jurisprudence has developed over the years, known as *lex sportiva,* upon which sports arbitration users can rely, that ensures the fundamental principles of fairness and proportionality are borne in mind by decision-makers. While not binding, they are of highly persuasive authority and promote greater transparency and consistency between decisions and awards in the sports world. At CAS, the procedural rules provide that, while CAS arbitrators are subject to a general duty of confidentiality, Article R59 of the CAS Code of Sports Related Arbitration (the 'CAS Code') requires that an appeal award will be made public unless both parties agree that it shall remain confidential.[9]

Public Hearings – While most sports disciplinary and CAS hearings are private, the influence of the European Convention on Human Rights (ECHR) is a factor that has to be taken into consideration and public hearings (under Article 6(1) ECHR) are ordinarily accommodated at the request of an athlete provided they would not, *inter alia,* prejudice the interests of justice (e.g., R57 CAS Code). In the case of *Mutu and*

5. Article 165(1) and (2) Treaty on the Functioning of the European Union (TFEU).
6. Article 5.8.2 Athletics Integrity Unit Reporting, Investigation and Prosecution Rules – Non-Doping Rules (14.0823).
7. *See* https://inside.fifa.com/legal/court-of-arbitration-for-sport/awards (accessed 16 August 2025).
8. Article 20 FIFA Rule Governing the Procedures of Player's Status Committee and the Dispute Resolution Chamber. *See* https://digitalhub.fifa.com/m/259f1778a076a66/original/letcztzqlfnph1tjdulx-pdf.pdf (accessed 16 August 2025).
9. *See*: https://www.tas-cas.org/fileadmin/user_upload/CAS_Code_2023__EN_.pdf (accessed 16 August 2025).

Pechstein v. Switzerland,[10] the European Court of Human Rights reiterated that the principles regarding the public nature of hearings were valid both for ordinary courts and professional disciplinary bodies.

Enforcement – Awards and disciplinary decisions, including interim orders (such as provisional suspension or transfer bans pending the outcome or proceedings) are activated via the relevant sports federation. As such, even those decisions which are not strictly arbitral awards are enforced under the top-down approach of IFs, many of whom incorporate recognition provisions within their statues and rules.[11]

Expedited Proceedings – Sporting cases are heard, and decisions rendered, frequently within a 24-hour period (e.g., ad hoc CAS Tribunals at Olympic Games and the on-field Disciplinary regime of Rugby World Cup). This is an essential component, in the interests of fairness, in a tournament or major event context which is of limited duration and finite jurisdiction. Unresolved disputes can impact on athletes' participation, team composition, broadcasting and media rights, and sponsorship deals. They can even cause games/events to be rescheduled. The time and financial costs and inevitable adverse publicity mean that dispute resolution in the sporting world needs to be very quick. It follows that the vast majority of sports disputes need to be resolved in a more truncated period, such as before the next scheduled participation in a match or competition.[12]

While expedited procedures exist in the rules of many arbitral institution (e.g., DIAC, HKIAC, ICC, LCIA, etc.), they are not constructed to deal with the time imperatives during a live sporting event. Given that arbitration is such a flexible, customizable mechanism when applied on an expedited basis in a sporting context, the procedures employed are truncated to mirror competition timescales that are measured often in hours, not days or weeks. Speed, therefore, is a paramount focus in sports arbitration and is embedded within the procedural rules of the sports / sports arbitral bodies.

Sports bodies, IFs and major sports event organizers have to plan for expedited sports arbitration and create the conditions and structure for its deployment within the exigencies of the event itself. The first of the two predominant approaches involves a sport (Rugby Union) which created its own ad hoc expedited process to deploy during its tournaments. The alternative approach is to outsource the disputes function to an experienced third party arbitral body such as the CAS ad hoc Division[13] or the ad hoc deployment of the International Panel of Sports Resolutions UK.[14]

10. Applications No. 40575/10 and No. 67474/10. ECHR 324(2018), 2 October 2018.
11. World Rugby Regulation 18.17 – Recognition of Decisions in Misconduct cases.
12. Susan Ahern and Arran Dowing Hussey, 'Getting the Most out of Expedited Sports Arbitration', The MENA Business Law Review 2021, Second quarter No. 02.
13. The Arbitration Rules applicable to the CAS ad hoc Division for Sport for the Olympic Games for the resolution by arbitration of disputes covered by Rule 61 of the Olympic Charter insofar as they arise during the Olympic Games or during a period of ten days preceding the Opening Ceremony of the Olympic Games can be found at: https://www.tas-cas.org/en/arbitration/ad-hoc-division.html (accessed 16 August 2025).
14. Which was, for example, appointed to deal with disputes during the Rugby League World Cup 2021 (England) – https://www.sportresolutions.com/services/panels-for-major-events (accessed 16 August 2025).

1 Internal Arbitration Processes: World Rugby Example

World Rugby has created its own independent court structure to manage the implementation of the World Rugby Regulations.[15] Regulation 20 deals with disciplinary and judicial matters and sets out the foundation structure supporting the appointment by the World Rugby Council of independent judicial personnel (who are legally qualified and/or have an intimate knowledge of the game) to the Judicial and Disciplinary Panel (the 'Panel'), together with their accompanying powers and functions.

The World Rugby Regulations are not an arbitration procedure but rather a disciplinary procedure which is sport-specific, incorporating established thresholds, standards and a sanctioning regime which has been devised by the game. Some rugby unions designated the process as an arbitration by virtue of their own national regulations and governing laws, e.g., England.[16]

The court operates within quick timelines during normal times (within a number of days), and within a super-expedited timeframe during a tournament like the Rugby World Cup, where an ad hoc court structure is employed, with Disciplinary Committees and Citing Commissioners[17] in attendance on-site to aid expedition. The timing of ad hoc disciplinary hearings followed a clear timetable; a Red Card (or two on-field yellow cards in the same match) resulted in a hearing within forty-eight hours; a citing for foul play resulted in a hearing within twenty-four hours of the notification of the citing. Following the evidential hearing, the decision is advised orally by the Committee to the athlete who then has the immediate opportunity to make submissions on sanction mitigation, if applicable. The Committee, following further deliberations in private on those submissions, conveys the outcome orally to the athlete. A full written decision is issued within twenty-four hours of the hearing and is published immediately. An appeal hearing is possible within forty-eight hours of the notification of the decision. During the Rugby World Cup 2023 in France, the Disciplinary Programme dealt with ten cases.[18]

a Specific Procedures World Rugby Adopted to Accommodate the Athletes

At an early juncture, some fifteen and more years ago, World Rugby adopted the use of technology to enable cases (including anti-doping and misconduct) to be dealt with on a remote basis using telecom and video technology. This became the prevalent

15. The World Rugby Regulations Relating to the Game can be found at: https://www.world.rugby/organisation/governance/regulations/reg-1 (accessed 16 August 2025).
16. The Rugby Football Union classifies its internal disciplinary procedures as arbitral, governed by the Arbitration Act 1996 (RFU Regulation 19.15.3).
17. Citing Commissioners are off-field referees who have the power to assess Foul Play in the Game and, where they believe an act warrants a red card, they can 'cite' or refer the player to a disciplinary hearing.
18. The cases can be accessed at: https://www.world.rugby/organisation/governance/discipline/decisions (accessed 16 August 2025).

approach in the SANZAAR[19] region competitions due to the complexity and cost of travel for teams who were travelling to other countries and continents following match fixtures.[20] During the Rugby World Cup 2023, a pro bono legal counsel was made available by Rugby World Cup Limited (at its cost) for athletes and teams who needed those services.

2 External Arbitration Processes: The CAS Ad Hoc Division

The best-known example is the deployment of the CAS Ad Hoc Division at the Summer and Winter Olympic Games. First created in 1996 for the Atlanta Olympic Games, it has also been deployed at Commonwealth Games, UEFA European Championships and FIFA World Cups. The scope of the jurisdiction of the Ad Hoc Division for the Olympic Games is founded in Rule 61 of the Olympic Charter to which all sports and athletes sign up. Any dispute within a defined period starting ten days prior to the commencement of the Olympic Games and throughout the games will fall under the remit of the CAS Ad Hoc Division.

The objective was to have a final determination within a twenty-four-hour timeframe of any disputes arising. While the Ad Hoc Division and each Panel carry on their duties at the site of an Olympic Games, the seat is in Lausanne, Switzerland. The ad hoc procedure has become so well established that it has been a fundamental part of the fabric of every edition of the Olympic Games since its introduction. One of the biggest developments has been the allocation to CAS of the IOC's jurisdiction to deal with anti-doping cases during the Games time. The CAS Anti-Doping Division (ADD) has been represented on-site since the 2016 Rio Olympics, but now in its capacity as a permanent division of the CAS at ordinary level.[21] The CAS Ad Hoc Division primarily deals with qualification and selection matters, along with doping appeals from decisions rendered by other bodies, including the CAS ADD. Appointed arbitrators operate from the CAS temporary office which frequently utilized the facilities of a national dispute resolution centre.[22]

19. The designated regional grouping of South Africa, New Zealand, Australia and Argentina Rugby Unions.
20. In that context, for on-field foul play, the procedure is that a standing committee reviews all red cards and citings and following a review, offers a sanction to the athlete who can accept the sanction, or reject it and choose to attend a hearing in person.
21. At the France 2024 Olympics, this structure, in operation for the fourth time since its inauguration at the Rio 2016 Olympic Games, will handle potential doping cases referred to it by the International Testing Agency (ITA) in accordance with the International Olympic Committee (IOC) Anti-doping Rules. CAS Bulletin 2021-02, p. 4.
22. The Japan International Dispute Resolution Centre in 2020. Given the COVID-19 pandemic, hearings of the CAS Ad Hoc Division were held remotely via video-conference, with the arbitrators located in the JIDRC, the athlete and their support personnel located in the Olympic Village and counsel for the athlete located in one or other of those locations. Fifteen ad hoc cases were conducted during the Tokyo Olympic Games.

a Specific Procedures Which Have Been Adopted to Accommodate the Athletes/Users

During the Olympic Games, expedited anti-doping sample testing (twenty-four-hour turnaround) is conducted and where there is an Adverse Analytical Finding, these are dealt with as alleged anti-doping rules violations by the athlete(s) and heard before the ADD. Cases are determined within twenty-four hours, with most cases being determined by Sole Arbitrators. The CAS ADD may impose provisional suspensions pending the conclusion of the procedure, and this was the predominant outcome during the Tokyo Olympic Games.

IV THE ATHLETES' JOURNEY

Athletes have prepared their whole lives to achieve their sporting dreams. To participate in a world championship, world cup or Olympics is the pinnacle of their sporting journey. In addition, their livelihood, their reputation and the hopes of a nation rest on every performance. So when an athlete comes before a disciplinary or arbitral tribunal, all of that is on the line. Sports arbitrations are personal, they are emotional (even when emotions are kept in check) and their outcomes change lives. Those outcomes are rarely confidential; they are usually played out in the public eye, where everyone has an opinion.

1 Structure of a Typical Sports Dispute Process

Sports disciplinary bodies and tribunals, whether they are disciplinary cases or pure arbitrations, have similar structure and features, and both produce decisions which are enforced by the IF on an international basis under the sport's regulations. Jurisdiction is established by the relevant contract and/or sports governing body's regulations which will determine the appropriate forum for disputes to be resolved. Ordinarily, first instance disciplinary decisions are handed down by a non-arbitral dispute resolution panel of the sport, with a right to appeal such decisions to an arbitral body either internally (i.e., an arbitral body set up by the sport's governing body), nationally (e.g., a national sports arbitration institution) or internationally (e.g., CAS).

Frequently, IF rules contain a general prohibition on stakeholders (members, players, officials, agents, etc.) taking their disputes to local courts, e.g., FIFA Articles 57-59 FIFA Statutes 2016 which mandate CAS as the final Court of Appeal.[23] World Athletics has an independent first instance Disciplinary Tribunal dealing with anti-doping and disciplinary and eligibility matters, the secretariat for which is Sports

23. 'Recourse to ordinary courts of law is prohibited unless specifically provided for in the FIFA regulations. Recourse to ordinary courts of law for all types of provisional measures is also prohibited.'

Resolutions UK.[24] Appeals are to CAS, as are disputes falling under Article 84 of the Constitution, to the exclusion of any other court or forum.[25] The resulting decisions of CAS on appeal may not be challenged in any other court save as set out in Chapter 12 of Switzerland's Federal Code on Private International Law.[26]

2 Growth of National Sports Arbitration Bodies

The past decade in particular has seen an exponential growth in the number of domestic and regional sports arbitral institutions emerging to deal with the specific needs of sporting bodies and athletes. They emerged as a counterpoint to a growing number of high-profile sports litigation cases in some territories (e.g., Ireland[27] and the UK) and as the complexity and scope of disputes expanded beyond the skills, resources and independence of the sporting bodies. Such independent institutions provide accessible and cost-effective arbitration and mediation services to their sporting stakeholders, including, in particular, the athletes. There are a number of well-established national sports arbitral bodies which have developed processes that aid the resolution of sports disputes and provide advisory services.

Sports Resolutions UK (SRUK) – in addition to it running the National Anti-Doping Panel, the National Safeguarding Panel, Arbitration and Mediation Panels, it also has a well-established International Panel which acts as the first instance or appeal body for international sports governing bodies (under their rules or the SRUK arbitration rules), and provides a service for Advisory Opinions[28] and Independent Investigation in sports.[29] A key service which is of direct benefit to athletes is access to the Pro-Bono Legal Advice & Representation Service[30] which makes experienced sports lawyers available to athletes and individuals of limited financial means before SRUK panels and other national governing body tribunals.

Asian International Arbitration Centre (AIAC) – has created a set of bespoke Asian Sports Arbitration Rules[31] which will be applied by the Asian Sports Tribunal for which AIAC is the appointing authority. A special Appendix to the Sports Rules applies

24. SRUK is a specialist body created by umbrella representative bodies of British sport created in response to the crippling costs of the anti-doping litigation incurred by British Athletics and the catastrophic consequences for athletes and national governing bodies.
25. World Athletics Constitution, Article 84.2 available at: https://worldathletics.org/about-iaaf/documents/book-of-rules (accessed 16 August 2025).
26. World Athletics Constitution, Article 84.6, *ibid.*
27. Sports Disputes Solutions Ireland (SDSI) – was formed in 2007 and is very well established as the final dispute resolution forum for Irish sports bodies, in particular for those that are recipients of government funding or that do not have their own independent dispute resolution structure. It has a mandate to promote sports dispute resolution services and enhance relationships with sporting bodies. It currently deals with all disputes excluding employment and anti-doping matters. *See*: http://sportdisputesolutions.ie/ (accessed 16 August 2025).
28. The Rules for an Advisory Opinion can be found at: https://www.sportresolutions.com/assets/documents/D_5_-_Rules_for_an_Advisory_Opinion.pdf (accessed 16 August 2025).
29. For example, Welsh Rugby Union (2023), Professional Footballer's Association (2020) and Lawn Tennis Association (2019).
30. Available at: https://www.sportresolutions.com/services/pro-bono-legal-advice (accessed 16 August 2025).
31. Launched on 6 October 2023: https://www.aiac.world/ (accessed 16 August 2025).

for 'Selection and/or Eligibility Disputes' whereby arbitrations conducted under this schedule are free of charge for parties and are conducted by a Special Panel (being a sole arbitrator) which will render a decision within forty-eight hours of the lodging of the Application for Arbitration. This aspect of the Rules is aimed at the primacy of *athlete protection and development*. The AIAC model is not limited to domestic athletes but also includes international athletes in the ASEAN region.[32]

The Pro-bono panel and Selection and Eligibility structure provided by these respective bodies demonstrate clearly an intention to put the athlete first and a desire to create equality between the parties, procedural fairness and adherence to the principle of natural justice for those athletes of limited financial means, without compromising the independence of the process.

3 Judicial Process Accommodations

The scope of disputes and issues faced by sports disciplinary bodies has expanded very significantly and become ever more complex, bringing with it challenges to procedures that were created before such complexities were contemplated. In sport, dealing with minors in the arbitration process arises particularly in the anti-doping sphere, where they naturally have to be treated differently from adults, a fact contemplated in the WADA Code.[33] There are also the livelihood considerations for athletes, and there is growing jurisprudence on human rights considerations affecting sport.[34]

But probably the area which has had the most impact on the disciplinary procedural processes in sport is the number of safeguarding cases across multiple sports. Affected sports have introduced guidelines to deal with participants at risk and vulnerable witnesses. For example, the Gymnastics Ethics Foundation Guidelines complement Article 18 of the FIG Code of Discipline[35] which provides for 'special measures' in 'exceptional circumstances' to support witnesses giving evidence during disciplinary proceedings.[36] Rule 10 of the rules of the SRUK National Safeguarding Panel incorporate specific steps to deal with vulnerable witnesses and states that 'The Tribunal shall have special regard to, and shall always take into account the risk of harm which giving evidence may do to [children/adults at risk] and how to minimise that harm … .'

32. M.S. Kummar and D.S. Abdul Rahman (AIAC), 'Stepping into a Niche: Exploring the World of International Sports Arbitration' Kluwer Arbitration Blog, 27 October 2020.
33. Article 14.3.7 excludes minors and protected persons from the mandatory public disclosure requirement under the Code.
34. Estelle de La Rochefoucauld and Matthieu Reeb, 'Sport and Human Rights. Overview from A CAS perspective' (as at 20 June 2022). Available at: https://www.tas-cas.org/fileadmin/user_upload/2022.06.20_Human_Rights_in_sport__20_June_2022_.pdf (accessed 16 August 2025).
35. Available at: https://www.gymnastics.sport/publicdir/rules/files/en_Code%20of%20Discipline%202021.pdf (accessed 16 August 2025).
36. On 16 November 2023 the Gymnastics Ethics Foundation in an effort to continue to strengthen the protection of whistleblowers and witness in the sport developed the guidelines on special measures for protecting vulnerable witnesses (defined) while also ensuring that due process rights of the parties are respected. The Guidelines serve as a tool for panels. They are available at: https://www.gymnasticsethicsfoundation.org/post/new-internal-guidelines-on-special-measures-for-protecting-vulnerable-witnesses (accessed 16 August 2025).

a CAS Actions to Protect Vulnerable People in CAS Arbitrations

While CAS already has multiple and robust procedural safeguards within the CAS Code[37] and emerging from its jurisprudence, experience from a number of cases[38] prompted a review of best practice to enable vulnerable witnesses /vulnerable people to deliver testimony. This led to the introduction in December 2023 of the Guidelines for the hearing of vulnerable witnesses and testifying parties in CAS Procedures (the 'Guidelines').[39] The Guidelines set out best practice recommendations for all CAS Divisions and reflect CAS' 'continuing commitment to protect the privacy, confidentiality, and physical and mental well-being of vulnerable witnesses appearing before CAS'.[40]

The Guidelines address where a witness giving testimony may be vulnerable and, in such cases, special procedural safeguards may be necessary to enable that vulnerable witness to deliver testimony in a safe manner, and to incentivize reluctant vulnerable witnesses to testify. Therefore, it is the assessment of whether a witness or testifying party is 'vulnerable' which is the starting point. A party should be considered as vulnerable if:

> testifying may risk (re)traumatizing the witness, present a threat to personal safety of the witness (and possibly others) or create significant risk to reputation or of retribution. Minors and witnesses with a mental disability will also generally qualify as vulnerable witnesses.

Pre-Hearing phase: CAS Panels are afforded wide discretion to tailor procedural safeguards to the vulnerability of the witness and are encouraged to be proactive in notifying parties and witnesses of the availability of procedural accommodations.[41] Parties should seek procedural accommodations ahead of the hearing or they may be instigated by the Panel at its discretion. Equally, the Panel may adjust the accommodations sought to those it considers are more appropriate. In all cases, the other party will be afforded the opportunity to respond and the case management conference should be used by Panels to address the practicalities of the protection measures envisaged.[42]

Hearing phase: CAS hearings involving vulnerable witnesses should generally be held in private, as permitted by Articles R43 (confidentiality) and R57 §2 (proceedings in camera) of the CAS Code and by Article 6 of the European Convention on Human

37. Available at: https://www.tas-cas.org/fileadmin/user_upload/CAS_Code_2023__EN_.pdf (accessed 16 August 2025).
38. Cases where elements of the procedures contained in the CAS Guidelines have been employed include: *Keramuddin v. FIFA* CAS 2019/A/6388, *Aghazada v. FIFA* CAS2019/A/6669, *Jean-Bart v. FIFA* 2020/A/7371. *See* further – Richard Bush, 'Yves Jean-Bart v FIFA: Observations from a Safeguarding Regulation Perspective' Law in Sport, 29 June 2023, available at: https://www.lawinsport.com/topics/item/yves-jean-bart-v-fifa-observations-from-a-safeguarding-regulation-perspective#references (accessed 16 August 2025).
39. Available at: https://www.tas-cas.org/fileadmin/user_upload/ICAS_Guidelines_on_Protection_of_Witnesses__FINAL_.pdf (accessed 16 August 2025).
40. Guideline 19.
41. Guideline 8.
42. Guideline 9.

Rights, which provides that the press and public may be excluded from all or part of the trial where the interests of 'juveniles or the protection of the private life of the parties so require, or to the extent strictly necessary in the opinion of the court in special circumstances where publicity would prejudice the interests of justice'.[43]

The power of CAS Panels to order particular measures is extensive, and there is an emphasis on the permissibility of measures which are appropriate to the circumstances of the case. Therefore, measures such as: (i) permitting a remote hearing or evidence to be given remotely; (ii) anonymous witness testimony; (iii) advance review by the Panel of proposed questions for cross-examination; (iv) exercising control over the manner of questioning to avoid (re)traumatizing alleged victims of abuse, particularly with respect to highly sensitive questions during cross-examination; and (v) permitting the CAS Panel rather than the adverse party to ask questions of the witness, are all tools to which it is envisaged Panels will have recourse as needed to accommodate vulnerable witnesses.[44]

The discretion afforded the CAS Panel is not exercised without regard to the right of each of the parties to a fair trial. While CAS Panels have on numerous past occasions permitted witnesses to appear anonymously,[45] the Guidelines make clear that a request for anonymous testimony carries with it the requirement of sufficient proof that 'disclosure of the witness's identity would create a serious potential threat to the personal safety of the witness (or their relative(s))'.[46] Where this threshold is met, there are then a series of responsibilities which fall upon the CAS Court Office in terms of ensuring the safety and non-identification of the witness giving the anonymous testimony including that: (i) the identity of the witness can be officially verified, (ii) that they are located in a safe place together with CAS counsel away from the attendees in the hearing room and (iii) that their face and voice cannot be recognized (by using face/voice distortion technology). Importantly, the departure of the witness from the hearing location should also ensure anonymity.[47]

Publication phase: There are also limits at the publication stage to protect the identity of vulnerable witnesses, through redaction of sensitive information, anonymization or non-publication. A party may make an 'Anonymization Request' and the CAS Court Office has the final authority to decide the outcome.

---

43. The Convention for the Protection of Human Rights and Fundamental Freedoms 1950 (as amended) is available at: https://www.echr.coe.int/documents/d/echr/Convention_ENG (accessed 16 August 2025).
44. Guideline 13.
45. *See* CAS 2009/A/1920 FK Pobeda, *Aleksandar Zabrcanec, Nikolce Zdraveski v. UEFA* and CAS 2019/A/6388 *Karim Keramuddin v. FIFA* – regarding the use of anonymous witness statements; and CAS 2011/A/2384, *UCI v. Alberto Contador Velasco & RFEC* and CAS 2011/A/2386 *WADA v. Alberto Contador Velasco & RFEC* – regarding the admissibility of the testimony of a protected witness.
46. Guideline 14.
47. Guideline 15.

b ICC Actions to Protect Vulnerable People

Another judicial aid of more general use beyond sport is the ICC Guide on Disability Inclusion in International Arbitration and ADR – October 2023 ('ICC D&I Guide')[48] produced following the work of the ICC Commission on Arbitration and ADR. The Guide is intended to place disability on the same plane as other areas protected by law, each of which is equally deserving of inclusion and 'allows practitioners to educate themselves about the meaning of disability and how it can intersect with the practice of arbitration'.[49]

Recommendations are aimed at different actors within the international arbitration sphere, and the accompanying toolkit resource is intended to be used to guide the implementation of the recommendations. Concretely, it intends to shift the burden from persons with disabilities to everyone in the arbitration / ADR process so that there is a collective conversation about how to advance disability inclusion.

The ICC D&I Guide has developed a definition of disability that is specifically attuned to the international arbitration context: 'Disability is any physical or mental condition that – without reasonable accommodation – significantly impairs a person's ability to participate in work related to an arbitration. Disability is an evolving concept that must be construed within the particular context of international arbitration.'[50] From this emerges the concept of 'reasonable accommodation' and how this should be raised, discussed and considered in the arbitral context.

A key recommendation which has a practical effect for arbitrators is ascertaining if there is a disability consideration that might exist in an arbitration involving any participant in the arbitration, including panel members. Arbitrators are encouraged to make this objective a default item on the agenda of the initial case management conference (CMC) and to specifically address it in Procedural Order No. 1 and to 'consider applying and using the toolkit particularly in circumstances where an accommodation request is contested ... '.[51]

Within the toolkit there are practical measures suggested.[52] The procedural guidance is pragmatic and encompasses a series of recommendations to panels and parties notably: making the reasonable accommodation request as the earliest practicable opportunity; balancing the interests of the party seeking accommodation and that of the other party that could be prejudiced if the accommodation is granted; assessment respecting the parties respective rights to be heard and dealt with fairly; the disability

48. Available at: https://iccwbo.org/wp-content/uploads/sites/3/2023/10/2023_ICC-Guide-on-Disability-Inclusion-in-International-Arbitration-and-ADR-902.pdf (accessed 16 August 2025).
49. Simon Maynard and Todd Weiler, ICC Commission on Arbitration and ADR Task Force co-chairs.
50. Section 2.2 details the inputs that lead to this definition.
51. Recommendation 1.1.
52. Such as: (a) inclusion in the agenda for the first CMC and/ or Procedural Order No. 1 (PO 1) to facilitate the disclosure of disabilities and the requesting of 'reasonable accommodation'; (b) guidance for arbitral tribunals asked to consider and determine requests for reasonable accommodation; and (c) a disability/inclusion awareness checklist ('mindfulness exercise') for use by participants in international arbitration and ADR to promote mindfulness about disability, diversity, and inclusion in daily practice.

is to be considered at all stages and for all participants in the arbitration, adopting a pragmatic approach.

Reasonable accommodation for a disability in international arbitration is to be encouraged. It includes any necessary or appropriate modification/adaption required in a particular case to guarantee participation on equal terms so long as it does not impose a disproportionate or undue burden.[53] There are specific further recommendations in the Guide also for arbitral institutions around collecting data from appointees, also aimed at international arbitration activities and events.[54]

V CONCLUSION

Having considered the demands of sport, the impact this has had on athletes and in particular the way the sports arbitration's key features have evolved, it is apparent that a new phase in that evolution has emerged. What we are witnessing now from the emergence of guidelines and rules in areas that support the participation of all persons within the disciplinary process is a heightened level of understanding. Focus is increasingly about inclusion and facilitation, not exclusion, balanced against the rights of the opposing party to due process. In the longer term, we can perhaps expect that more IFs and sporting bodies will introduce their own bespoke disciplinary guidelines catering for vulnerable witnesses, but drawing on the good groundwork which has been done by the CAS, gymnastics, national safeguarding panels and individual IFs and national governing bodies. Procedural accommodations for vulnerable witnesses should be a standing consideration for every panel – be it sport or otherwise – and it may lead to less trauma for the witness and enable the IFs to implement their rules more efficiently. Perhaps there will be further procedural reforms to bed in the various guidelines and make them mandatory procedural rules. But for now, the movement is in the right direction and needs support from within sport to spread far and wide.

53. *See, e.g.*, UN CRPD, Article 2 defines 'reasonable accommodation' as 'necessary and appropriate modification and adjustments not imposing a disproportionate or undue burden, where needed in a particular case, to ensure to persons with disabilities the enjoyment or exercise on an equal basis with others of all human rights and fundamental freedoms'.

54. Such as venue and communication touch point audits and the representation of persons with disabilities in other arbitral contexts (e.g., on panels, in moots and mediation competitions – Recommendation 1.1.(b) and (c)).

CHAPTER 25

Cultural Clashes in International Arbitration: Identifying Key Issues Affecting the Parties, and the Way Forward

Gourab Banerji[*]

TABLE OF CONTENTS

I INTRODUCTION

Not so long ago, international arbitration was looked down upon as being solely for the benefit of developed nations. While some of the skepticism flowed from the developing nations' lack of success, the distrust primarily related to the *process*, and not merely the *outcome*. Grievances included the perceived biases of the arbitrators, alien values of a foreign legal system, and the lack of empathy toward the cultural nuances of parties and their representatives from developing nations.

The run-up to the celebrations for the 60th anniversary of the ICC Court highlighted some of these schisms. One such instance which underlined the stark divide was the exchange between Judge Howard Holtzmann and Judge Kéba Mbaye on the notion of an "system of international justice," where Judge Mbaye is reported to have said that "arbitration is seldom freely agreed to by the developing countries

* Gourab is a Senior Advocate, who practices before the Indian Courts. He is an arbitrator and also regularly represents clients in international arbitrations (both commercial and investment treaty arbitrations). He has previously served the Government of India as Additional Solicitor General in the Indian Supreme Court, in which capacity he represented the Union of India in several international disputes. The author gratefully acknowledges the assistance of Ms. Raka Chatterjee and Mr. Rakesh Talukdar Advocates, the Supreme Court of India.

[...and] is often included in contracts of adhesion the signature of which is essential to the survival of these countries."[1]

When I started practice, most public sector undertakings from India (then perceived as a third-world country) were unsuccessful in disputes against large multinationals. I can attest to the fact that the disappointment was mostly with the system's perceived problems, and not so much the merits of the case or the outcome.

Today, while some of those misgivings have been resolved, others remain. Much has changed. Standardized procedures have helped in reducing arbitrariness, and there is increased flexibility in consideration of cross-cultural issues. Parties and their representatives have also become much more familiar with the arbitral process and its dynamics. Nevertheless, while some of the distrust of international arbitration by parties from the developing world has ebbed away with rapid globalization and greater integration, new frontiers of concern have opened up.

Some of these modern-day misgivings have been powerfully highlighted by Won L. Kidane in his book "*The Culture of International Arbitration*," where he argues that:[2]

> The inconvenient truth is that a privilege left behind by the world's power and economic hierarchy and the resulting concentration of most of the world's high-value arbitration cases of all types in Europe have created the illusion that there is a supranational autonomous arbitral order seated in Europe. Manifestations of power relations as they were, the theories that consider international arbitration anything other than merely a framework "like mist on eye glasses obscure fact."

Nevertheless, it cannot be disputed that acceptability of international arbitration is on the rise. One (non-conclusive) indicator of greater acceptability is the diversity in the appointment of arbitrators. The ICC Dispute Resolution Statistics, 2020 reflect the fact that arbitrators confirmed or appointed in 2020 came from ninety-two jurisdictions. This included first-time inclusion of arbitrators from Afghanistan and Barbados. While 52.3% of the arbitrators appointed had North and West European nationalities, 15.5% belonged to Latin America and Caribbean. A total of 7% of the arbitrators in 2020 belonged to South & East Asian and the Pacific nationalities, while 4.7% belonged to Central and West Asian nationalities. In contrast, only 1.2% of the appointments related to arbitrators with nationalities in Sub-Saharan Africa, and 1.1% to North Africa.[3]

Further, in 2020, ICC Arbitrations were seated in 113 different cities, spread over 65 countries, the highest number of jurisdictions till then. The top countries selected as places of arbitration included Switzerland, France, the United States, the United Kingdom and Brazil. The increasing diversity and reach highlighted above reflects the greater acceptability and legitimacy of the international arbitral process.

This is however far from the entire picture.

---

1. Fali Nariman, "East Meets West: Tradition, Globalization and Future of Arbitration," Arbitration International, vol. 20, No. 2 (2004), pp. 123-138, at p. 125.
2. Won L. Kidane, "The Culture of International Arbitration" (Oxford University Press, 2017).
3. "ICC Dispute Resolution Statistics: 2020—ICC—International Chamber of Commerce" (ICC—International Chamber of Commerce), https://iccwbo.org/news-publications/arbitration-adr-rules-and-tools/icc-dispute-resolution-statistics-2020/ accessed 6 March 2024.

In a 2021 International Arbitration Survey by the Queen Mary University of London and White and Case, less than a third of respondents believed that there had been progress in respect of geographic, age, cultural and, particularly, ethnic diversity. Interestingly, 56% of the respondents stated that a diverse tribunal had a "positive effect on their perception of the arbitrators' independence and impartiality."[4]

Indeed, the path to the global acceptability of international arbitration, cutting through cross-cultural divides, is neither a linear progression nor capable of a straightforward solution. It requires redressal at various levels. Sustained macro-level efforts leading to structural changes (reform in rules, greater diversity) are as relevant and important as efforts at the micro level (mannerisms while addressing an arbitral tribunal, tailoring arguments, pleadings and advocacy to suit the sensitivities of the tribunal).

II IDENTIFYING CULTURAL ISSUES IN ARBITRATION

One key caveat in identifying cultural issues is to avoid stereotyping. In many cases, stereotypes are a combination of inadequate information and cultural apathy, even though they may not be actuated by malice. In an age of overwhelming information, it can be tempting to attribute unfamiliar experiences to cultural differences. It is equally tempting to lump countries and regions as homogenous cultural entities, ignoring the diversity within those categories. Such cultural blind spots are often easy to miss, but may have significant repercussions. For instance, Tahbaz highlights the stereotype of an *Asian* culture, as opposed to *Western* culture, although Asia is a vast region with many different cultures and countries.[5] Indeed, even within India itself, cultural differences between regions can be stark.

To avoid such stereotypes, commentators have suggested that being alive to these differences should be a fundamental component in case preparation and presentation.[6] This may range from the obvious (tailoring one's pleadings and arguments to suit the sensitivities of the tribunal), to issues which may appear trivial at first glance without being so (awareness of local laws beyond the arbitral proceedings, logistics and dietary preferences etc.). Importantly, the burden of cultural awareness does not lie only on the arbitrators or counsel but also on the parties and other actors involved in the process.

4. 2021 International Arbitration Survey: Adapting Arbitration to a Changing World, Queen Mary University of London, https://arbitration.qmul.ac.uk/research/2021-international-arbitration-survey/ accessed 25 February 2024.
5. Christopher K. Tahbaz, "Cross-Cultural Perspectives on Effective Advocacy in International Arbitration: or, How to Avoid Losing in Translation," Asian Dispute Review (© Hong Kong International Arbitration Centre (HKIAC)); Hong Kong International Arbitration Centre (HKIAC) 2012, vol. 14 Issue 2) pp. 51-54.
6. Christopher K. Tahbaz, "Cross-Cultural Perspectives on Effective Advocacy in International Arbitration: or, How to Avoid Losing in Translation," Asian Dispute Review (© Hong Kong International Arbitration Centre (HKIAC)); Hong Kong International Arbitration Centre (HKIAC) 2012, vol. 14 Issue 2) pp. 51-54.

1 Identifying an Approach

One of the fundamental challenges in identifying cultural issues in arbitration is the amorphous definition of "*culture.*" This also reflects in the uncertainty in the definition of "legal culture."

One of the more widely cited definitions of "*culture*" was suggested by Kluckhohn, as one which "consists in patterned ways of thinking, feeling and reacting, acquired and transmitted mainly by symbols, constituting the distinctive achievements of human groups, including their embodiments in artifacts; the essential core of culture consists of traditional (i.e. historically derived and selected) ideas and especially their attached values."[7]

More recently, UNESCO has defined "*culture*" as "the set of distinctive spiritual, material, intellectual and emotional features of society or a social group, that encompasses, not only art and literature, but lifestyles, ways of living together, value systems, traditions and beliefs."[8] This definition has maintained its utility over the years and provides a useful reference in understanding cultural issues in arbitration.

What comprises "*legal culture*" has also been debated by scholars over the years. Lawrence Friedman famously defined "legal culture" as "attitudes, values and opinions held in society with regard to law, the legal system and its various parts."[9] The more common understanding of legal culture equates and conflates it with a legal system, such as the French or the German legal system, or the civil and common law systems.

A different understanding of legal culture has been propounded by Professor Tom Ginsburg, "as consisting of shared norms and expectations produced by legal actors." He suggests that "actors engaged in repeated interaction over time produce culture," and that "lawyers form an epistemic community, that is, a community of professionals with common training and expertise."[10] He refers to a "culture of arbitration," as the gradual convergence in norms, procedures and expectations of participants in the arbitral process. Borrowing from the work of various commentators, he identifies certain key areas of convergence, for instance, the dominant test for determining law governing arbitration proceedings, the arbitral tribunal determining its own jurisdiction, party autonomy and procedural fairness.[11]

That international arbitration comprises its own culture, distinct from the national cultures relatable to a court system, is uncontroversial, albeit with caveats and reservations. As Karton argues, "despite the variety of laws that apply to international arbitrations and the variety of backgrounds possessed by international arbitrators, a

7. A.L. Kroeber and C. Kluckhohn, "Culture: A Critical Review of Concepts and Definitions," Harvard University Peabody Museum of American Archeology and Ethnology Papers (1952).
8. UNESCO Universal Declaration on Cultural Diversity, 2001, Resolution adopted on 2 November 2001 in Paris, France, https://www.unesco.org/en/legal-affairs/unesco-universal-declaration-cultural-diversity accessed 25 February 2024.
9. Lawrence M. Friedman, "Law and Society: An Introduction" (Prentice Hall 1977).
10. Tom Ginsburg, "The Culture of Arbitration," Vanderbilt Law Review, vol. 36 (2021), p. 1335.
11. Ginsburg (n 10).

common legal culture knits together the members of this distinct international community." Karton's analysis is based on "the governance provided by international arbitration," which he argues, "emphasizes legal and cultural neutrality, flexible and efficient procedures, deference to party autonomy, and substantive rules founded in standards of commercial reasonableness."[12]

Considering the fact that there are wide variations in the scope and understanding of "culture" and "legal culture," necessarily, there would be different approaches to locate cultural issues in arbitration. One way is to identify them through the lens of the persons involved, another way would be to consider the process adopted. These approaches help in understanding key cultural issues in arbitration, and identify the interactions and responses of the Government and State actors, among others.

2 The Person-Centric Approach

The person-centric approach aims at identifying key cultural issues through the lens of the persons involved in the arbitration. This includes the parties, party representatives, arbitrators, counsel as well as other actors involved in the arbitral process.

Mary Howard has suggested a useful visual map of cultural interactions of parties in international arbitration, which is depicted below:[13]

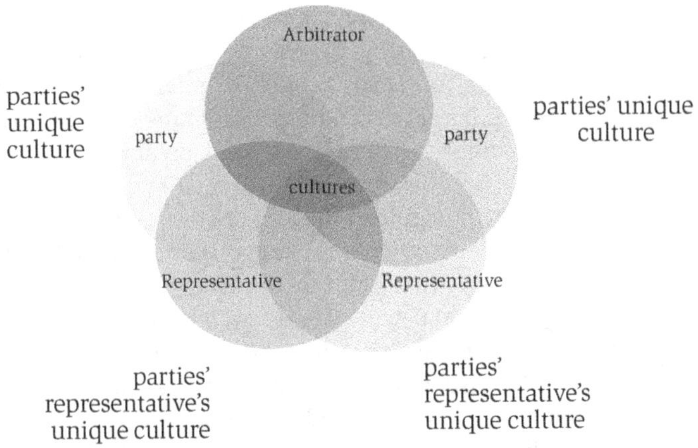

In this analysis, the key actors who may provide a useful lens to identify cultural issues in arbitration are the arbitrators, counsel, and the parties. However, in the present chapter, I refrain from focusing on the arbitrators in greater detail, as that is the subject matter of other articles.

12. Joshua Karton, "International Arbitration Culture and Global Governance," in Walter Mattli and Thomas Dietz (eds), "International Arbitration and Global Governance: Contending Theories and Evidence" (Oxford, 2014).
13. Mary Howard, "International Arbitration and Cross-cultural Issues," in Stavros Brekoulakis (ed.), "Arbitration: The International Journal of Arbitration, Mediation and Dispute Management" (© Kluwer Law International; Kluwer Law International 2020, vol. 86 Issue 3) pp. 331-346.

Counsel play a key role in locating and navigating cultural issues in arbitration proceedings. This is especially true when Government and quasi-government entities are involved. In the 2021 International Arbitration Survey conducted by QMUL and White and Case, the significance of the role of counsel was highlighted by about half the respondents in the process of selection of a diverse arbitral panel. The survey also found that in-house counsel played a crucial role in ensuring diversity through their choices and recommendations of arbitrators.[14]

Besides being involved in the choice of arbitral tribunals, counsel play a key role during the contract formation stage. Identifying potential cultural issues at the contract formation stage itself allows parties to better navigate them once disputes arise. For instance, in contracts involving informal interactions and transactions which may not be adequately documented, choice of governing law (laws permitting evidence of oral contract) and the arbitral tribunal (arbitrators who understand such transactions) are key. Similarly, considerations of seat, venue, mode of hearing (virtual versus physical), and applicable institutional rules ought to be negotiated, keeping these factors in mind.

However, as suggested by Edward T. Hall, "*culture*" is similar to an iceberg, as only around 10% of the of its constituents (external or surface culture, which includes easily observable behavior, traditions and customs) are visible. The majority of it (internal or deep culture, which includes attitudes, perceptions, assumptions, and values and thought patterns) is hidden below the surface, and not easily observable or discernable.

The role of counsel is to navigate through both the visible and the invisible. While the visible might be easy to address (attire, manner of address, communication), the invisible is equally key. Although this is easier said than done, adequate preparation and research are key, as these differences can be crucial to the outcome of the dispute itself. The perceptions and assumptions of the arbitrators on any aspect of the law, or assumptions about the conduct of the parties based on their own cultural experiences, will have a direct bearing on the outcome of the case. For instance, the determination of what constitutes "reasonable" or "rational" behavior is often crucial to the outcome of a case. This becomes even more important in contracts based on both formal and informal transactions, as the tribunal will have to weigh evidence beyond what is recorded in documents. It is thus incumbent upon the counsel to present the "*context*" of a dispute to the tribunal. Counsel must not only serve as a narrator of the case but also serve a translator of business, customs and practices.

Equally important is the role of party representatives, particularly when dealing with Government entities and State actors. In most Government organizations and entities, hierarchy plays a crucial role. Bureaucracy entrenches hierarchy, which is further reinforced by formal rules, roles and responsibilities, as also informal interactions and inter-personal communication. Further, issues of loyalty, particularly in Government organizations, may play a crucial role, particularly in certain developing

14. 2021 International Arbitration Survey: Adapting Arbitration to a Changing World, Queen Mary University of London, https://arbitration.qmul.ac.uk/research/2021-international-arbitration-survey/ accessed 25 February 2024.

nations. This is because, for Government officials, career progression is often dependent on the discretion of their superiors. Similarly, notwithstanding their designation, some cultures reinforce an age-based hierarchy. Senior persons, often occupying the same designation as a junior official, may have greater sway and authority. Being impolite and rude to persons significantly senior to oneself is perceived more unfavorably in some cultures than others.

Bernardo M. Cremades has identified four main points concerning communication between the tribunal and parties, viz.: "(a) the possible mediating or conciliating intervention of the arbitrators; (b) communication between the arbitral tribunal and parties on matters of evidence; (c) the influence of the arbitrator's cultural background in the decision-making process; and (d) the possible cultural friction which may arise in the collaboration between arbitrators and local state judges."[15]

Equally important, where parties and party representatives are concerned, are issues of business practices and business relationships, which vary depending upon the cultural background of the parties. Many cultures in Asia emphasize on an "informal dispute settlement processes," which tend to be more "consensual" rather than "confrontational."[16] In contrast, some cultures are more formal in their interactions, which is reflected in the written word. Correspondence, testimony and evidence must therefore be understood in the particular cultural context.

3 The Process-Centric Approach

While a person-centric approach is helpful, it does not capture in its entirety the impact of cultural issues in the arbitral process. One possible remedy to this limitation is to explore cultural interaction through the lens of the *process* adopted by parties. While tribunals have the flexibility to devise their own procedure, the reality is that litigation style procedures are common in many jurisdictions. As presciently argued by Pair, "while the substantive outcome in International Commercial Arbitration is not usually based on cultural expectation, procedure is."[17]

Some traditional dispute resolution systems, which are informal, have viewed international arbitrations with skepticism.[18] Further, differences in expected norms of confidentiality, procedures, and the influence of religion often result in differing procedures.

15. Bernardo M. Cremades, "Overcoming the Clash of Legal Cultures: The Role of Interactive Arbitration," Arbitration International, vol 14, No. 2 (LCIA, 1998).
16. Dr. AFM Maniruzzaman, "International Commercial Arbitration in the Asia Pacific: Asian Values, Culture and Context," International Business Lawyer, December 2002.
17. Lara M. Pair, "Cross-Cultural Arbitration: Do The Differences Between Cultures Still Influence International Commercial Arbitration Despite Harmonization?," ILSA Journal of International & Comparative Law, vol. 9, Issue 1 (2002), Article 2, https://nsuworks.nova.edu/ilsajournal/vol9/iss1/2 on 26 February 2024 accessed August 16, 2025, at p. 60.
18. Lara M. Pair, "Cross-Cultural Arbitration: Do The Differences Between Cultures Still Influence International Commercial Arbitration Despite Harmonization?," ILSA Journal of International & Comparative Law, vol. 9, Issue 1 (2002), Article 2, https://nsuworks.nova.edu/ilsajournal/vol9/iss1/2 accessed 26 February 2024.

Issues regarding the impact of culture on arbitral proceedings may arise at various stages of the proceedings. It may arise at the stage of pleadings—whether oral or in writing. It may arise during discovery and pre-hearing procedure. Finally, it may arise at the stage of evidence and treatment of witnesses and arguments before the tribunal.[19] Each of these stages is considered separately.

a *Oral and Written Advocacy*

In many jurisdictions based on the common law (including India), paper tends to be less persuasive than the spoken word. Similarly, while weighing evidence, greater credence is often given to live testimony and cross-examination. The increasing trend in international commercial arbitrations has been to provide greater importance to the written word. Article 24(1) of the UNCITRAL Model Law provides that "subject to any contrary agreement by the parties, the arbitral tribunal shall decide whether to hold oral hearings for presentation of evidence or for oral arguments, or whether the proceedings shall be conducted on the basis of documents and other materials." In cases where a tribunal proceeds purely on the basis of written pleadings, this gives rise to the potential for some friction. Losing parties, particularly from common law backgrounds, tend to raise natural justice grounds while assailing arbitral awards based solely on written pleadings.

Quite apart from the oral-written advocacy divide, the written word itself presents real cross-cultural issues. Tone, tenor and verbosity are often by-products of the legal culture one is trained in. Pleadings which might be the norm in some domestic legal systems may be perceived unfavorably by persons from other cultures and systems. For instance, allegations of fraud and dishonesty of the opponent features quite often in pleadings. While this is acceptable and the norm in certain jurisdictions, this can be quite off-putting to arbitrators with a European background, where the approach is very different and allegations of fraud and dishonesty are not lightly made.

b *Discovery and Pre-hearing Procedures*

Discovery and pre-hearing procedures vary vastly, depending on the institutional rules, agreement of the parties and the preferences of the arbitrators. Barkett and Paulsson have argued that IBA Rules on Taking of Evidence represent a compromise in traditions. Though common law lawyers rely on it, many civil law lawyers reject it.[20] While the IBA Rules have indeed brought about some uniformity, many parties do not refer to them as the uniform standard. While institutional arbitrations have rules which

19. This broadly follows the categorization suggested by Lara M. Pair, while discussing differences in Common Law and Civil Law legal cultures, in Lara M. Pair, "Cross-Cultural Arbitration: Do The Differences Between Cultures Still Influence International Commercial Arbitration Despite Harmonization?," ILSA Journal of International & Comparative Law, vol. 9, Issue 1 (2002), Article 2, https://nsuworks.nova.edu/ilsajournal/vol9/iss1/2 accessed 26 February 2024.
20. John M. Barkett and Jan Paulsson, "The Myth of Culture Clash in International Commercial Arbitration," FIU Law Review vol. 5 (2009), p. 1, https://doi.org/10.25148/lawrev.5.1.5 accessed August 16, 2025.

seek to deal with issues of production and discovery, ad hoc arbitrations continue to be plagued by uncertainty in the process.

The varying approach in the scope and width of discovery and document production can lead to severe differences in perception, particularly for Government entities. In many cases, Government entities are reluctant to share documents and files about decision-making processes. In some bureaucratic cultures, Government entities and representatives may not be used to extensive discovery processes. Such differences in perception can result in hesitation, if not resistance, in complying with broad and detailed discovery and production requests. Counsel, parties and their representatives need to be alive to these issues and not perceive resistance and recalcitrance.

c *Treatment of Witnesses and Final Arguments*

One area where cultural issues are particularly significant is the treatment of witnesses and procedures concerning the evidence obtained from them. In this context, the iceberg theory of culture is particularly relevant. While the visible aspects of culture may be easy to deal with, the invisible aspects are often at play while dealing with witness depositions and evidence. Not paying attention to the invisible can often lead to unintended and disastrous consequences.

There are, of course, more visible issues, which are easier to resolve. Witnesses not being comfortable in the language of proceedings, drawing up witness statements in verbose language, are some examples. Similarly, a witness whose evidence might appear concise to one arbitrator, may be perceived as curt and arrogant to another. Verbosity in one's reply to specific questions in cross-examination can similarly be perceived as evasive and non-committal, without the witnesses meaning to be so, given their particular cultural background.

It is important to ensure that witnesses who are likely to encounter cultural differences are adequately prepared prior to the proceedings. These sessions can help familiarize the witnesses with the cultural background not only of the arbitral tribunal but also counsel. Indeed, witnesses need to be alerted not only to cultural differences in general, but also need to be educated about the culture of international arbitration, which is a breed apart.

While arbitration is distinct from litigation, it remains a fundamentally adversarial process of dispute resolution. Both parties compete to prove their respective claims, or at least to disprove the other. Impeaching the reliability of documents and the credibility of witnesses becomes an important component in counsel's arsenal. This is often disconcerting to witnesses, who are not used to the cynicism of opposing counsel. Counsel who are familiar with the culture and processes of international arbitration often do not realize how esoteric the process is, when first encountered by witnesses and parties.

This is especially true of Government officials, who are often caught by surprise when cross-examined with some ferocity or aggression. In most Government settings, officials are used to deference and hierarchy, without much cross-questioning. This is particularly the case in highly bureaucratized cultures and elderly witnesses, who are also accorded deference due to their age. Such witnesses may perceive an aggressive cross-examiner with some suspicion, and even contempt. Attempts to question their decisions, particularly ones taken in good faith and exercising discretion, may elicit further hostility. It is possible that an East Asian arbitrator may not appreciate a zealous and aggressive cross-examination of an elderly Asian witness. Age-based courtesy is expected behavior for an advocate who wishes to command the respect of an Asian arbitrator.[21] Similarly, loosely threaded allegations of fraud or illegality may be viewed adversely if made against senior, elderly witnesses.

Most of these issues continue to be relevant while addressing final arguments before a tribunal. For instance, insinuations of fraud, dishonesty or suppression will have to be made with caution, depending on the composition of the tribunal. Further, counsel will have to carefully consider the extent of emphasis to be laid on oral arguments. Brevity and precision in final arguments, especially in cases with voluminous records, may be crucial, especially while addressing a tribunal used to such pleadings. Similarly, providing relatable examples and anecdotes, which appeal to the tribunal, may also prove to be helpful.

III THE WAY FORWARD: BEST PRACTICES

The cultural divide in international arbitration is a function of several factors, most of which are beyond the confines of dispute resolution itself. Primarily, they are a function of human diversity itself. A planet with over seven billion people, spanning many continents, and over 190 countries, is bound to witness diversity. Diversity, whether geographical, in shared and lived experiences in shared traditions and historical experiences, has given rise to attributes loosely described by scholars as "*culture*." The influence of decades of learning (both textually and through lived experiences) ingrains much of what we understand by "culture" in our subconscious. Thus, most of one's attitudes, biases, values and thought patterns (categorized by Edward Hall as invisible culture) do not manifest themselves in our conscious actions. To identify these cultural traits requires thought, awareness and research.

While research and preparation are key, one of the more crucial elements in bridging the cross-cultural divide is "empathy." Most procedures often leave it to the discretion of the "*rule-setters*" to accommodate cultural differences, if and when they arise. In most instances, accommodations are easy to make and come at little or no cost. These may include due deference to witnesses and parties, keeping scheduling and dietary preferences of participants in mind, and providing translations of pleadings and evidence to witnesses parties who are not well versed with the language or procedure of the arbitration. It has been suggested by some that lawyers must "be

21. Alvin Yo and Chou Sean Yu, "Cultural Considerations in Advocacy," Stephen Jagusch QC and Philippe Pinsolle (eds), *The Guide to Advocacy* (Global Arbitration Review, 2018).

aware of their own 'cultural baggage' and overcome communication challenges by understanding different cultural values."[22]

However, other issues are less amenable to a straightforward solution. As mentioned earlier, cultural schisms may present itself in unexpected ways: an innocuous application for discovery of documents, harsh but credible allegations of fraud (as reflected in the tone and tenor of the plea), aggressive cross-questioning of an elderly witness accused of impropriety, leading evidence of oral agreements often modifying terms of earlier written documents.

One way is to confront cultural issues at the earliest possible stage. As Tahbaz argues, "although it is common to consider the legal culture from which an arbitrator hails when considering whom to nominate, consideration of the business culture with which the arbitrator is familiar is also important."[23] Perhaps, institutional rules can attempt to bridge such divides by requiring pre-arbitral hearings exclusively to address these issues.

Informal sessions which permit interaction between counsel and witnesses, or even with the tribunal, beyond the adversarial setting of an arbitration may help bridge some divides. Flexibility in procedure and encouraging open communication will foster better results and allay apprehensions and misgivings.

All actors may benefit from providing a context of their cultural position, without reference to the dispute in question. Further, reasonable accommodations ought to be made by all actors to show respect to cultural differences, and even actively offered. In cases where the cultural context has a direct and substantial bearing on the outcome of the case, tribunals can explore appointing neutral "*cultural experts*." Arbitrators who come from different cultures and backgrounds also have a positive duty to empathize with the specific cultural context of the disputants.

Inculcating respect and empathy toward those culturally dissimilar is a constant process of learning (and unlearning). While preparation and research in the lead up to specific disputes (when such issues arise) is key, learning is a continuous process and takes place beyond the immediate confines of arbitral institutions. It is also important for national institutions to adopt "a transnational outlook, remembering always the true consensual nature of all international arbitration."[24]

22. Magdalene D'Silva, "A New Legal Ethics Education Paradigm: Culture and Values in International Arbitration" Legal Education Review, vol. 23 (2013), p. 83, https://doi.org/10.53300/001c.6270 accessed August 16, 2025.
23. Christopher K. Tahbaz, "Cross-Cultural Perspectives on Effective Advocacy in International Arbitration: or, How to Avoid Losing in Translation," Asian Dispute Review (Hong Kong International Arbitration Centre (HKIAC)); Hong Kong International Arbitration Centre (HKIAC) 2012, vol. 14 Issue 2) pp. 51-54.
24. Fali Nariman, "East Meets West: Tradition, Globalization and Future of Arbitration," Arbitration International, vol. 20, No. 2 (2004), pp. 123-138, at p. 137

IV CONCLUSION

The development of arbitration has been described by a commentator as "a hybrid blended and creolized process of glocalization."[25] Others suggest that "international commercial arbitration is conducted today with a broad consensus as to many important features."[26] Whatever be the true nature of international arbitration, "inasmuch as international arbitration proceedings transcend proceedings before national courts, its traditions should differentiate it from those national law traditions."[27]

Although a distinct "*culture*" of international arbitration is marked by increasing uniformity and standardization of rules and procedures, "yet there are problems rules do not solve."[28] Even if cultural issues in arbitration are reframed as an ethics issue, more fundamental issues of access and respect remain. Increasing globalization and democratization of information sources cast a burden on each of us to be culturally aware and sensitive to our immediate surroundings. "The age of globalization leaves no alternative to dialogue."[29] In other words, awareness is the only way out of two extremes on either end—cultural ignorance on one end and over-generalization and stereotyping on the other. It is a continuous process and requires consistent efforts by each member of the global arbitration community.

International arbitration has come a long way since the initial days of skepticism and suspicion. The only way forward is greater dialogue, empathy, and, most fundamentally, respect.

25. Kun Fan, "'Glocalization' of International Arbitration: Rethinking Tradition: Modernity and East-West Binaries through Examples of China and Japan," U Pa Asian L Rev, vol. 11 (2016) p. 243.
26. John M. Barkett and Jan Paulsson, "The Myth of Culture Clash in International Commercial Arbitration," FIU Law Review vol. 5 (2009), p. 1, https://doi.org/10.25148/lawrev.5.1.5 accessed August 16, 2025.
27. Trakman, Leon, "'Legal Traditions' and International Commercial Arbitration. American Review of International Arbitration" (Spring 2007, UNSW Law Research Paper No. 2007-29).
28. Lawrence W. Newman, "Pre-hearing Conferences: Cross Cultural Conflicts, Address at Seminar at Baker & MacKenzie New York (November 25, 1996)," World Arbitration and Mediation Review, vol. 8 (1997), pp. 82, 87.
29. Alexander, Chumakov, Culture in the Global World and Opportunities for Dialogue. Synthesis Philosophica, vol. 62 (2016), pp. 413-422 https://doi.org/10.21464/sp31214 accessed August 16, 2025.

CHAPTER 26

Understanding and Adjudicating Differences: Civil Law, Common Law, and Navigating International Arbitration

Kap-You (Kevin) Kim[*]

TABLE OF CONTENTS

I INTRODUCTION

When legal academics write about differences between various national legal systems, the prevailing view seems to be that each national legal system is so fundamentally different (a function of each nation's unique culture and historical development) that they can scarcely be *properly understood* by those without a well-developed understanding of that nation's legal history, culture, and language.

Prof. Fuglinszky and Somssich, when writing about this phenomenon, note that:

> Legal systems, the legislation of which is drafted and enacted in a language, which is less widely used and understood, suffer from isolation as they cannot be directly accessed by legal practitioners or scholars from other countries. Therefore, the various legal solutions of these legal systems can hardly be perceived as models and cannot easily be transplanted into other legal systems and, in the same way,

* Kap-You (Kevin) Kim is a founding Senior Partner at Peter & Kim. Kevin was assisted by Sameer Thakur and Célia Guignet, associates at Peter & Kim's Seoul office in the development of his remarks and this chapter.

their legal concepts can hardly if ever receive any international feedback or reflections.[1]

This position is not just a view held by academics but also the basis of how the practice of law is regulated across the world: most jurisdictions have strict licensing requirements, requiring years of study in law (conducted in the language in which law is practised in that jurisdiction) for an individual to be eligible to provide legal advice on issues arising from that legal system. There is an implicit understanding across jurisdictions, including those which may share a common historical source, that distinctions between various legal systems are significant and meaningful, and that proper understanding of the legal system requires long-term study conducted in the language of that specific legal system.[2]

As such, a lawyer that is not qualified in a particular jurisdiction *rarely* (if at all) engages professionally with questions of legal analysis arising from jurisdictions he or she is not qualified in.[3]

This general position is entirely inapplicable in international arbitration.

Not only do lawyers (who are not qualified in a particular jurisdiction), when acting as counsel (with or without the assistance of lawyers who are qualified in that jurisdiction), *regularly argue points of law arising from jurisdictions in which they are not qualified in*; arbitrators, who are very often, not qualified in the jurisdiction whose law is the governing law (or the *lex arbitri*) of the arbitration, *adjudicate questions of law arising from those jurisdictions* and issue enforceable decisions. In many cases, the above-mentioned legal analysis (and adjudication) is conducted entirely in a language (the language of the arbitration) that is different from the language in which the law is practised in the relevant jurisdiction.

Even if one were to take a step back from thinking about knowledge of specific jurisdictions and divide the world's diverse legal systems into two reductive but useful categories: common and civil law systems; one would still find that, while outside of international arbitration, civil law lawyers practice civil law, and common law lawyers practice common law; in international arbitration, common law lawyers often argue questions of civil law, and common law trained arbitrators often adjudicate questions of civil law (and vice versa) in English (or another third language, irrelevant to the governing law), when none of the underlying legal systems are originally practised in English.[4]

1. Á Fuglinszky and R Somssich, Language-Bound Terms: TermBound Languages – The Difficulties of Translating a National Civil Code into a Lingua Franca, *International Journal for the Semiotics of Law – Revue Internationale de Sémiotique Juridique*, 33(3):749-770, p. 749 (2020) https://doi.org/10.1007/s11196-020-09704-x (accessed 16 August 2025).
2. For example, Singaporean, Malaysian, Indian and Australian law are all technically derived from British law, but as of 2024, they depart widely from each other due to developments since these countries gained independence and established their own legal systems – understanding of one legal system does not automatically grant or create an expertise in others.
3. In fact, most (if not all) jurisdictions explicitly prohibit individuals who are not licensed to practise law in that jurisdiction to provide legal advice on questions arising from that jurisdiction.
4. For any analysis of this issue, it is important to consider that it is far more common for civil law practitioners to deal with, or have to educate common law arbitrators, when the governing law is civil law. The other situation, where two sets of common law lawyers are dealing with a civil law

The aim of this chapter is to evaluate and critique the process through which lawyers with different training, fundamentally different conceptions of legal concepts, who grew up with (and are informed by) unique cultural and linguistic archetypes translate and transpose different legal concepts, linguistic terms and 'meaning' to each other in international arbitration.[5]

II 'ACCURATE' TRANSLATION OF 'LEGAL CONCEPTS' IS OFTEN IMPOSSIBLE

1 The Expectation That 'Accurate' and 'Complete' Translation Between Concepts from Different Legal Systems Is Possible Is Unfounded

When thinking about differences in civil law and common law trained lawyers and their engagement with international arbitration, a lot of focus is directed towards procedural differences (expectation of discovery or not, for example).

A fundamental issue, which is often ignored, is that there are certain legal concepts (in both systems of law), which can never be accurately or completely translated into the lexicon used by the lawyers from the other legal system - even if they can be translated into English (or whatever language is the language of the arbitration).

This creates a difficulty: the very basis of international arbitration is that a lawyer arguing questions of say, Korean law, in English, to arbitrators who were trained in American or UK law (in English), is capable of accurately and completely explaining the relevant legal principles. Based on those arguments, the arbitrators are capable of not just understanding these discrete legal issues but conducting their own analysis to determine the correct position. The sub-heading above does not seek to imply that this process is impossible - if it were, my career (and those of many others) would simply not have been possible.

As such, I am not suggesting that it is impossible to *educate* a (common law trained) Tribunal or to equip them with the knowledge to determine the correct legal position (under Korean law, to continue the example above) - but simply that accurate and complete *translation* of Korean law concepts into English is often not possible. There is no doubt that it is possible to educate and inform a Tribunal as to what the position under Korean law is - it is not possible to always find a comparable word or translate it into a comparable common law concept.

Assuming 'accurate translation' is possible implies that a legal concept from one legal system can be directly translated or completely understood in the conceptual and

trained arbitrator, is far rarer (possibly because a significant number of civil law lawyers also receive training in common law jurisdictions, while the same cannot be said for common law lawyers).

5. In the absence of empirical data, much of the analysis in the chapter is sourced from my own experience as a civil law trained lawyer (who was first educated in law in a civil law system in Korean, but later received a legal education in a common law system in English in America) practising international arbitration for over thirty years.

linguistic frameworks provided by the other legal system and language. This is a largely uncontroversial position amongst academics who study legal translation:

(i) As an expert in legal translation, Prof. Mochny, articulates it: 'No literal interpretation of these terms would be comprehensive, as it is impossible to embrace all of the associated meanings, concepts and cultural heritage in a mere two words.'[6]

(ii) Prof. Fuglinszky and Somssich, express the dilemma as follows: 'The difficulty of translating a civil code of a country with civil law traditions into English lies in the challenge of expressing concepts of civil law in a language with a legal vocabulary that is intimately connected to common law,' noting that anyone who is seeking to translate concepts from one system into another must 'act beyond the role of a translator'.[7]

(iii) Prof. de Groot notes that: in legal translation, 'full equivalence can never be achieved between the concepts of different legal systems but only approximate equivalence'.[8]

My simple assertion, therefore, is that the commonly accepted wisdom that accurate translation is both possible and easily achieved is a major barrier to actual understanding of discrete legal issues by arbitrators and counsels who do not speak the language, and are not qualified to practise in that specific legal system. In fact, I am confident that if we actively encouraged consideration of the fact that accurate and complete translation of legal concepts across legal systems was difficult (if not impossible), it is likely that both counsel and arbitrators would be more circumspect when dealing with concepts that may seem familiar but are entirely alien.

The belief that accurate and complete translation is possible precludes arbitrators and counsel from actually attempting to understand the legal position in a legal system they do not understand; instead, looking for the 'equivalent' (or translation) in their legal system. While utilizing comparable concepts as a method of educating an arbitrator can be helpful, the belief that the comparable concept is *the same* causes fundamental 'misunderstandings'.[9]

---

6. D Mochny, Translating Law Texts Is Translating Culture, *The Translation Dictionary*, https://www.translationdirectory.com/article1064.htm (accessed on 12 March 2025).
7. Á Fuglinszky and R Somssich, Language-Bound Terms: TermBound Languages – The Difficulties of Translating a National Civil Code into a Lingua Franca, *International Journal for the Semiotics of Law – Revue Internationale de Sémiotique Juridique*, 33(3):749-770, p. 750 (2020) https://doi.org/10.1007/s11196-020-09704-x (accessed 16 August 2025). *See also*, R Alwazna, Testing the Precision of Legal Translation: The Case of Translating Islamic Legal Terms into English, *International Journal for the Semiotics of Law – Revue Internationale de Sémiotique Juridique*, 26(4):897-907 (2013) https://doi.org/10.1007/s11196-013-9331-z (accessed 16 August 2025).
8. G de Groot, Rechtsvergleichung als Kerntätigkeit bei der Übersetzung juristischer Terminologie, in H Ulrike (ed.), *Sprache und Recht* (De Gruyter, 2002), 228.
9. Á Fuglinszky and R Somssich, Language-Bound Terms: TermBound Languages – The Difficulties of Translating a National Civil Code into a Lingua Franca, *International Journal for the Semiotics of Law – Revue Internationale de Sémiotique Juridique*, 33(3):749-770, p. 754 (2020) https://doi.org/10.1007/s11196-020-09704-x (accessed 16 August 2025); *See*: 'Even basic concepts of the law which, according to their core function, are identical might show substantial differences. A contract to be formed in a common law country would always require consideration, while in civil

For instance, while the closest English translation for the Korean legal term 'Johap' is 'partnership'; despite some similarities between the two concepts, there are significant conceptual and legal differences between how a Johap is treated by Korean law, when compared to how a partnership is understood under common law jurisdictions.[10] However, if *Johap* is simply translated as *partnership*, then a common law trained lawyer, may understand (and apply) his/her knowledge of a 'partnership' under common law systems to a Johap under Korean law, resulting in a mistranslation.

This leads to a situation where concepts from one system are expressed in a particular manner in a different language, intending to convey the meaning as understood in that legal system. However, when they are understood from the conceptual framework of the other legal system, an imbalance or a mistranslation is created. For instance, in the case of the example above; common law trained arbitrators, when dealing with an arbitration governed by a civil law jurisdiction, in their analysis of the term/concept 'contract', presuppose a requirement for consideration – when none such requirement is necessary under the applicable legal system.

Unfortunately, we have many situations where common law arbitrators are *purportedly applying civil law*, but what they are *actually doing* is applying their understanding of civil law, which is informed not by civil law principles but their own common law training.[11] This is of course possible in the opposite direction as well – an arbitration governed by a common law jurisdiction but adjudicated by a civil law trained arbitrator is also prone to similar (and other unique) problems.

This is a situation without 'balance' that requires appropriate attention and adjustment from all stakeholders to avoid 'mistranslations'.[12]

2 The Possibilities for Mistranslation Significantly Increase When Cultural and Linguistic Differences Exist Alongside Differences in Legal Training

In terms of language, another common misconception that creates unreasonable expectations, in terms of the completeness and accuracy of 'translation' across different legal cultures, is the unfounded notion that concepts and words are as

law systems no such requirement appears. However, there would be no reason to translate a Vertrag in German law otherwise than contract, as the essential function of both concepts – that is to have a mutual and enforceable agreement between the parties – is the same.'

10. Jae-oh Jung, *Joint Venture* (Kyungin Publishing 2017), pp. 18-19; Exhibit YCS-011, I Hewitt and G Picot, Structuring the Joint Venture, in *Joint Ventures in English and German Law* (Hart Publishing 2000), pp. 13-16.
11. For further analysis, *see*, H Farahaty, Translating Lexical Legal Terms Between English and Arabic, *International Journal for the Semiotics of Law – Revue Internationale de Sémiotique Juridique* 29(2):473-493 (2016) https://doi.org/10.1007/s11196-016-9460-2 (accessed 16 August 2025).
12. To be clear, similar 'mistranslations' or 'misunderstandings' are also possible when dealing with two civil law or two common law jurisdictions, which may have once had similar (or identical) legal systems, which are now different as they developed differently. It is important then to not assume that certain concepts are the same simply because they once used to be – it is essential that one acts under the assumption that legal principles have developed differently across jurisdictions and attempts to understand fully, instead of looking for a comparable concept.

equally/easily translatable between different languages as they are amongst the European or Latin languages. Translating between German and French, or French and English, or Italian and English is fundamentally different from translating between English and Korean or Chinese and English.

This is specifically true when Chinese characters are being used, many of which are condensed; each character does not have an equivalent word in English but would probably require a sentence for even a rough translation to be done. In fact, as I have discussed above, I believe that there are concepts, and principles in civil law systems, that do not have a direct translation into a common law lexicon, and the same is true for 'words'.

What ends up happening is that you then use a word, which is most reasonable or nearest to the Korean or Chinese term. That term, say, illegality or wrongfulness, has connotations in English (and in common law) that do not apply to that word or concept in Korean or Chinese. However, since it has now been translated into that English word, common law trained lawyers, who do not speak the original language, may have two layers of misconceptions:

(i) First, they may impute the Korean concept to the connotations associated with that term in English to the Korean concept, even though it is not applicable.
(ii) Second, they may impute meaning from the common law concept, which that word in English represents, that has no relationship with the civil law concept.

To avoid this 'trap', we have begun, in our own practice, to specifically use the Korean or Chinese word, to explain the legal principle, instead of using an English translation. This acts, almost as a reminder, that while this Korean principle may have some relationship or share some meaning with the English word/common law phrase: it is not and should not be treated as the same.

III THE WAY AHEAD: UNDERSTANDING THROUGH EDUCATION INSTEAD OF TRANSLATION

1 Bridging Differences Through Focusing on 'Educating' Instead of 'Translating'

As I have argued above, it is not just that we struggle to find the right words when we deal with distinct concepts from different legal systems – it is that civil law and common law practitioners have distinct archetypes (if I were to employ Jungian concepts).

The same words, even when articulated in the exact same manner, evoke entirely distinct imagery and understanding in us; to reduce that to a linguistic or simplistic difference is to ignore the complexity that underlies the problem. The understanding of, for instance, what is procedural law and what is substantive law is fundamentally different across legal systems. In most civil law jurisdictions, post-award interest is a question of substantive law, while it is a procedural question under most common law jurisdictions. So, both parties, who may have civil law counsel, in a case with civil law jurisdiction as the governing law, may not end up making submissions on post-award interest, because they would expect the Tribunal to be aware that it is a question that it must decide. The natural reaction for common law trained arbitrators would be to provide pre-award interest, leaving post-award interest to be awarded by the court of enforcement.

However, a court in a civil law jurisdiction, if the award is being enforced there, would likely refuse to do so, since, under the applicable civil law system, that decision should have been made by the primary adjudicator (the Tribunal), as it is a question of substantive law under civil law.[13] This misunderstanding is of course solvable – it requires arbitrators and counsel to be alert to legal and cultural differences: to reject assumptions, and to strive for clarity even when the underlying concepts may seem 'obvious'.[14]

The larger point I am making is that we need to challenge the assumption or expectation of accurate and complete translation, at each level: in our written submissions, at the hearing and in the awards. We must seek to educate the Tribunal to treat a civil law principle as a civil law principle instead of looking for the closest common law equivalent (or vice versa). We must reject making looking for the closest equivalent principle the goal of our analysis and must accept that sometimes there are no equivalents – just the awareness of such a principle would significantly reduce instances of 'mistranslation'.

This requires that both counsel and arbitrators act in a more careful fashion; we must actively avoid the temptation to settle for/with 'familiar' concepts as the method of explanation.

In other words, we must avoid translation and focus on educating. Instead of suggesting to a Tribunal that a concept or a principle is more or less like this other concept in a legal system they understand, we must have the courage to tell the Tribunal that, yes, while this is a different and novel approach to the law when compared to your legal training, this is what the principle is – and this is how it works.

2 Bridging Differences Through Knowledge Sharing: A Database of 'Legal Expert' Reports

A simple rebuttal to many of my arguments so far would be to say that, yes, while counsel and arbitrators who are not qualified in a particular legal system (or do not

13. We see many cases like this when enforcing awards in front of Korean courts. It's also why, I guess, I ended up writing a book about post-award interest.
14. To illustrate this in non-legal terms, I would ask the reader to imagine an 'angel' or a 'dragon'. In both cases, if you are from what we generally call the 'western world,' you would have imagined entities with wings. Angels, in the western imagination have wings. So do dragons. However, if you are from the east, say, China, Korea or India – neither our angels nor dragons, as traditionally depicted, need wings to fly. So, in this case, while you and I are both using the same word – our understanding of the meaning of that word is fundamentally different – because of the cultural archetypes we grew up with. My argument in this chapter is that the same happens with legal concepts, which, in international arbitration, may have significantly more dramatic consequences than differences on whether wings are necessary for flight.

speak a particular language) often argue and adjudicate questions of law arising from that legal system; more often than not, they are aided by independent legal experts who provide testimony on what the law is, how it should be interpreted, and can reasonably be expected to clarify any linguistic or cultural issues that may arise. The fact that both sides in any case will have the opportunity to engage a legal expert will also preclude (or significantly minimize) the chances of a relevant issue (whether legal, cultural or linguistic) being ignored.

Based on this premise, it has been common for both sides to engage independent legal experts, who owe their duty to the Tribunal (and not the party that engages them) in international arbitrations over the last twenty odd years. This is also the approach that domestic courts across the world take, when they (due to conflict of laws, or some other situation) are asked to adjudicate a question of foreign law.

Unfortunately, despite the widespread use of legal expert reports, instances of 'mistranslation' are common. In my experience, experts, who are instructed by parties, can be prone to some of the same problems that I discussed above. The counsel teams wish for the expert report to articulate the legal position in a manner that is easily understood by the Tribunal (which is educated in a different legal system, and informed by different cultural and legal archetypes), and can sometimes be willing to sacrifice accuracy for 'equivalence'.[15]

At the same time, experts, often take positions that are 'technically' arguable, fortuitously aligning with the arguments being made by the party that engaged them; despite that position not being considered mainstream or reasonable in that jurisdiction. One of the reasons why experts in international arbitration may do so is explained by a fundamental difference between proceedings in front of domestic courts, and in international arbitration. Judgments of courts (and in many cases, the record of the proceeding itself) are made available to the public – allowing lawyers and clients to access it in perpetuity. Awards in international arbitration are generally confidential, and even in situations where awards become publicly available, the records of the proceedings (the transcript of the hearing, the parties' pleadings including the expert report and so on) are rarely, if ever, made available.

As such, my suggestion would be for legal expert reports to be made publicly available either via a database or a consultation group operating under the aegis of an arbitration institution. This would be helpful for two reasons:

(i) A welcome result of the existence of such a database would be a push for greater accountability: It would create a strong incentive structure for legal experts to *not take* positions on law in international arbitrations that they would be uncomfortable taking in academic conferences or published legal writing. Once their expert report is made public, it would be reviewed by their peers and other lawyers. Peer review in public would allow for spirited

15. Another proposal that recognizes and attempts to solve a similar problem is the suggestion that experts (whether legal or on any other subject) be appointed by Tribunals and not parties. The widespread adoption of Tribunal appointed legal experts would solve some(but not all) of these problems, but in a situation where, in most cases, experts are appointed by parties, it is important to consider solutions that provide for parties to appoint experts.

debate, while also acting as a method of quality control. People are unlikely to try and pass off unreasonable positions as mainstream or reasonable positions, when they are aware that their work will be publicly available.

(ii) In fact, this exercise could be seen as similar to the publication of an academic opinion to the extent that the Tribunal's or the parties' expert(s) agree to the publication of the report(s) with their names and credentials. This would effectively induce a virtuous circle – with more reports available comes greater knowledge of a particular legal system, which, in turn, results in greater accountability: an expert would hesitate to take a legal position that runs contrary to the consensus view amongst a majority of the lawyers in a particular jurisdiction without proper justification.

(iii) It would provide a database of sorts that can be utilized by arbitrators and counsel in subsequent cases – allowing lawyers from different jurisdictions to learn and avoid 'mistranslations' in their own practice. Anyone with access to the database would be able to review the expert reports available thereon and educate his or herself in a particular legal system and/or issue to determine the correct position to take in his or her practice.

To be clear, I am not calling for parties to unilaterally volunteer the entirety of their pleadings, or even parts of the legal expert report that deal with application of the law to the facts of that case to be made public. I understand that there would be significant confidentiality implications that could arise from that disclosure. However, there are sections in most, if not all, legal expert reports that simply articulate what the relevant legal principles are, and how they are understood in that legal system. Those parts of the expert report which do not deal with the facts can easily be made public (with party names redacted as necessary) without any significant complications arising from any applicable confidentiality obligations.

I can understand that practitioners may be reluctant at first to make public expert reports that have been utilized in cases. However, it has been the experience of the international arbitration community that greater transparency has led to better decision-making: be it the publication of decisions of institutional bodies like the SIAC and ICC Courts, to the publication of awards; all of which has been managed without any meaningful impact on parties' rights to confidentiality.

In any event, once *some* parties and law firms begin to declare that they intend to make public any expert reports they use, it would be difficult for the opposing party to also not agree to the proposal to make public the expert report of their expert, as their reluctance, may signal to the Tribunal that their expert is unwilling to publicly take the position that he/she is taking in the private, in front of the Tribunal. In the future, if this trend catches on, the number of expert reports that are available on a public database, may begin to act as a recognition of expertise, much like the number of academic publications does today.

A simple way to do this would be for an organization like ICCA to take the lead on the development of such a database – it would fit perfectly with ICCA's mission to promote international arbitration. All it would require is for a group of practitioners to agree on a protocol on redaction, some principles on when exactly the expert reports should be made public and so on. Some of these questions might be slightly complex and require some discussion, but are easily solvable.

CHAPTER 27

Efficiency in Arbitration Protects the Humans Involved in It

David W. Rivkin[*]

TABLE OF CONTENTS

Every choice made in the conduct of the arbitration must consider the impact on the humans involved in the process – all of them. If we do so, the result is a better process that actually serves the interests of the parties and that will help to preserve international arbitration, which we all know and love, from the takeover of the machines.

I INTRODUCTION

Arbitration is a human endeavour. I congratulate ICCA in choosing this theme while it is still the case. I am afraid that soon we will all be attending the AICCA (Artificial Intelligence Council on Commercial Arbitration) – that is, if the machines allow us to do so.

Every activity in an international arbitration – every decision we make as counsel, arbitrator or party – has an impact on the humans involved in the dispute. Long cases, late nights, midnight filing deadlines, Zooms across multiple time zones, submissions totalling hundreds (even thousands) of pages, all take a toll on everyone involved in the case: staff, associates, partners, witnesses, clients and arbitrators.

* David W. Rivkin is an independent arbitrator with Arbitration Chambers, based in New York, London, Hong Kong and Singapore; Co-Chair of the Hong Kong International Arbitration Centre.

For a moment, let's focus on the parties, who are of course the participants who matter the most. Having urged that any dispute be resolved by international arbitration, in-house counsel must explain to their internal clients why it takes months for a case even to get started, why once it has commenced the case is taking so long, why it is costing more than anticipated, and most of all, once the case is finally tried, why the Tribunal is taking so long to issue its award. This places an emotional toll on the in-house counsel, as their credibility and perhaps even their job are threatened by practices that too many outside counsel view as routine.

The challenge for all of us is how to accomplish what we need – a fair, efficient process that reaches a just result in an appropriate amount of time and at an appropriate cost given the value in dispute – while reducing the toll on all involved. My thesis is that every choice made in the conduct of the arbitration must consider the impact on the humans involved in the process – all of them. If we do so, the result is a better process that actually serves the interests of the parties and that will help to preserve international arbitration, which we all know and love, from the takeover of the machines.

II APPLICATION

Let's look at the choices to be made in any international arbitration. We can compare the decisions that human counsel and arbitrators, who are focused on the best interests of the humans involved in the process, should make with the decisions that a machine running the procedure would make.

1 Initial Pleadings

A machine would simply look at the information required by the pertinent rule and provide a bare-bones pleading.

Human counsel understand that the demand for arbitration or the answer is the first opportunity to persuade the decision-makers. A thorough, well-researched pleading can influence the Tribunal at the early stages of the case in making procedural decisions that are to the party's advantage, and it can assist them in determining the best and most appropriate procedures for that particular case.

2 Determining the Procedure of the Case; First CMC

Nearly two decades ago, I published an article advocating what I called the Town Elder Model. In the article, I urged arbitrators and counsel not simply to pull a standard PO#1 from the drawer and assume that the procedure for this case should be the same as for prior cases. Indeed, that is what the hypothetical machine arbitrator would do: simply pull a model from its database, plug in new party names, assign dates to the standard procedures and issue it. It is certainly not what a Town Elder, an arbitrator in ancient times, would have done.

Instead, what the Town Elder would have done, and we as their modern-day human descendants, should do, is gain a solid understanding of the issues in the case and what the parties truly need before determining which procedures are appropriate for that particular case.

The day is long past when arbitrators should issue a PO#1, then decide without a hearing any document request issues in a Redfern Schedule, and next interact with the parties only at the merits hearing. Parties need proactive arbitrators who work with them at each step of the arbitration, constantly considering what is best for the case and the parties. Doing so respects the humans involved in the process; a machine cannot do this. Human arbitrators can exercise this judgment. Let me give two examples: (a) Decision Tree Arbitration; and (b) Interim Conferences.

a *Decision Tree Arbitration*

For some cases, we have to move away from the standard process of two rounds of memorials and one or two rounds of discovery, followed by an all-encompassing merits hearing. Of course, we have long been used to bifurcating jurisdictional issues from merits issues where the evidence and issues are sufficiently separate, or bifurcating quantum issues until after liability has been determined.

In some cases, a decision on a threshold issue may lead to a different path in arbitration, one way or the other. Or a series of issues may be sufficiently separate that deciding them in sequence would be more efficient, with the decision on each influencing the next one.

This is consistent with the Town Elder approach, so in 2022, I published what I called the Town Elder Rules for a decision tree arbitration. These rules can be applied with any ad hoc or institutional rules. They are intended to provide a framework for such an alternate approach when it is appropriate for the case.

Arbitrators and parties cannot be afraid to try unusual approaches, such as a decision tree.

As counsel, I represented a political risk insurer in several arbitrations where the coverage issues were quite complex, but where we had a strong argument based on the language of the contract or on a smaller set of factual issues that, even if there were coverage, no compensation was due. In each case, we convinced the Tribunal to hear those arguments and factual issues first, without conceding liability. In each case, the Tribunal held a one-day factual hearing and determined that no compensation was due even if there was coverage. The result saved many months of work, a long liability hearing, and substantial fees on issues that would in the end have been irrelevant.

b *Interim Conferences*

In cases in which I am now sitting, I always suggest that, following the first substantive submissions, the Tribunal holds an interim conference with the parties in which we can give substantive comments that can help focus the next round of submissions. This can be done simultaneously with a hearing on any issues arising from the parties'

Redfern Schedules. Before the interim conference with the parties, the Tribunal confers on its reactions to the evidence and arguments so far.

The interim conference has multiple advantages.

First, it ensures that the Tribunal is reading the papers as they are submitted, rather than just prior to the merits hearing.

Second, it can save time and cost and human wear and tear in the parties' preparation for the next round. The parties can avoid submitting more evidence and argument on issues that the Tribunal feels have already been well briefed or will not be so important to the final decision-making. When we have done so, the parties have been grateful to be able to focus on their second round of submissions. Providing some substantive comments at this stage causes less wear and tear on the lawyers involved, reduces costs, and leads to better decision-making by the Tribunal.

Third, it can also lead to an interim decision on a key point of contractual interpretation. In one case, for example, the parties provided two critically different interpretations of the key contract provision. The meaning of the provision depended on interpretation of its language rather than on any factual issues. The Tribunal asked the parties if they would like us to decide the interpretation before the parties submitted their second round of submissions, and the parties readily agreed. Since the issue had already been briefed, we held a brief virtual argument and issued a decision providing the Tribunal's interpretation of the provision. As a result, the parties could focus their second round and the hearing on applying the facts to that interpretation.

Finally, the Tribunal's comments could lead the parties to renew or begin settlement conversations with the benefit of the Tribunal's thinking.

Arbitrators need not be afraid that offering these reactions can somehow lead to a challenge to an award. As an initial matter, the parties readily agree to it. In addition, the Tribunal can make clear that the comments are based on the evidence and arguments so far and that no final decision has been reached on any issue. And finally, as a study by the IBA Arbitration Committee has shown, fears of courts overturning awards on so-called due process concerns are vastly overblown.

3 What Else Can Arbitrators Do to Respect the Other Humans Involved in the Process?

The arbitrators should insist on party representatives at all procedural conferences. They can also impose appropriate page limits and, where appropriate, encourage settlement (without being involved in settlement discussions themselves). And most importantly, arbitrators should issue procedural decisions and the award PROMPTLY. The parties and their counsel have done their work, and now it is the Tribunal's obligation to fulfil its responsibility. This involves scheduling deliberations as soon as the hearing is scheduled – not waiting to do so at the hearing – so that they can be held while the impressions of the hearing are fresh. (We are humans, not machines with perfect memories.) And it requires the Chair to block out time immediately following the hearing to start drafting, not to wait until some break in one's other hearings.

Each of these possible actions simply reflects how we as human decision-makers can best protect the interests of the people who have hired us for this task. As in many other instances in life, we should place ourselves in others' shoes and think about how they would want us to behave.

By the same token, counsel need to think constantly about how best to assist the human decision-makers and how their actions may influence that decision-making. For now at least, counsel are not inputting all their evidence and arguments into a machine that will run some algorithm to decide the case. Arbitrators need persuasion.

So what can counsel best do to persuade? A few examples come to mind.

First, counsel should not overargue the facts or the law. Counsel must maintain credibility at all times because once it is lost, the algorithm in our brains tends to discount any subsequent statements.

Second, counsel should provide the Tribunal with well-organized, thorough submissions, but focus on the key evidence and arguments. Do counsel really expect the Tribunal to read 500 pages and then thousands more pages of witness statements and expert reports and understand every important detail? If one strong witness can make a point, then there is no need to have several more witnesses repeat the same testimony.

Third, counsel should make sure that experts are truly independent and present reports as independent experts whose goal is to assist the Tribunal. Expert reports that are advocacy submissions carry little weight.

Finally, counsel should organize their exhibits in the form that will be most useful to the Tribunal. A human reaction to hundreds of exhibits simply arranged chronologically is to ignore them and to wait until one is presented with those shown at hearing, but if the Tribunal is directed to a manageable number of key exhibits, they can carefully review and understand them before any hearing.

III CONCLUSION

Each of these choices reduces the physical and emotional toll on all the humans involved in the arbitration process. If that is not sufficient to convince you to undertake these steps, it is clear that each choice is also better advocacy. That is simply because arbitration is, and we hope remains, a human endeavour.

Panel 10

It's (Not) Just Semantics: The Hidden Power of Language

How much does the language used in an arbitration shape the process and influence the outcomes? Does the language of arbitration come with conscious and unconscious cultural norms and conventions attached or does each case leave space to develop its own speech community by adopting unique elements of culture and language from the relevant industry and various actors in the arbitration. When does (and should) meaning get attached to words and concepts used in a case? In bilingual arbitrations, are tribunals more open to a range of meaning being given to the words used? Does fluency help or hinder an advocate?

CHAPTER 28

Our Linguistic Currency Is Cosmopolitanism: Explicit and Implicit Code-Switching in International Arbitration

E. Rainbow Willard[*]

TABLE OF CONTENTS

I INTRODUCTION

Language is more than a sum of its parts. It is not just the words we use, but how we say them, our accents, our gestures, our tone and our facial expressions that convey meaning. The way we speak, the specific language we use, and how we use it are all important markers of our cultures and identities. Even without visual cues, the way we speak conveys important information about who we are: our gender, our race, our ethnicity, our nationality, our class, our educational background, and more. The same is true about how these messages are received. Every day, we make judgments about

* E. Rainbow Willard is the founder of Willard Arbitration, LLC, where she acts as independent arbitrator and counsel in international commercial and investment arbitrations. Over the course of fifteen years, she has acted in high stakes, cross-border disputes relating to energy, oil & gas, construction, and mining in a range of jurisdictions. Prior to becoming a lawyer, Rainbow received a Master of Arts and advanced to doctoral candidacy in Theoretical Linguistics at the University of California, Berkeley, with a focus in Linguistic Anthropology. She completed several years of linguistic anthropological fieldwork in the central highlands of Guatemala, where she assisted native linguists in the development of indigenous language resources. Rainbow is fluent in English, Spanish, and Kaqchikel Maya.

who people are based on how they speak, about how "intelligent" or "trustworthy" they may be, or how much like "us" they are—or, for that matter, how different. These judgments are often a result of ideas we have formed based on our own backgrounds, including our nationality, education level, class, race, and ethnicity.

Why does any of this matter to the international arbitration practitioner? Quite simply because language is the tool of our trade. As counsel, we use it every day to network, to pitch to clients, to advocate to tribunals—both orally and in writing. As arbitrators, we use language to ask questions, to read and listen to testimony and argument, to deliberate, and ultimately to form judgments and to draft those judgments into awards. Language is the way we communicate our judgments, but it also shapes the substance of the judgments themselves.

This was the topic addressed by the panel "It's Not Just Semantics, the Hidden Power of Language" at the 2024 ICCA Congress in Hong Kong. Moderated by May Tai, each panelist addressed a different topic relating to the power of language in our international arbitration practice. Samaa Haridi discussed how accents of advocates, experts, witnesses, and arbitrators may impact our views about them, and, in particular, how arbitrators may make unconscious value judgments about advocates based on their accents. Jern-Fei Ng KC discussed the power of gesture and how it can strengthen or weaken arguments and testimony. Lei Shi explained the results of a survey of bilingual Chinese-English arbitrators, including arbitrator preferences for different languages in bilingual arbitrations. I discussed how practitioners alternate between different "national" languages[1] in formal and informal international arbitration contexts.[2] All of these discussions highlighted the fact that how we speak, and how we listen, matters.

This chapter uses an analysis of code-switching, or alternating between languages, to illustrate that, despite the prevalence of English as a procedural and working language in international arbitration, participants carve out space for other languages, creating a complex, multilayered and multilingual space. *Section II* summarizes linguistic literature relating to the connections between language, culture, and identity and how code-switching may reveal information about all of these. *Section III* reviews the prevalence of English in international arbitration, and then analyzes publicly available hearing transcripts to identify instances of code-switching in English-language proceedings and explores the multiple functions that it serves. *Section IV* then analyzes how "implicit" code-switching occurs in the international arbitration context and the impacts it may have for participants. Finally, *section V* concludes that linguistic barriers to participation are often complex and multidimensional.

---

1. I occasionally use the term "national" language to clarify that I am referencing a specific language rather than discussing Language as a concept. However, specific languages are not static, hermetically sealed systems, and "national" languages do not have a one-to-one relationship with nation-states.
2. Code-switching is defined and explained in further detail in this chapter. I am indebted to my co-panelists for their comments on an earlier version of this chapter, as well as their remarks during the panel at the 2024 ICCA Congress. Any views expressed herein, however, and any mistakes I make, are my own. In addition, characterizations of my co-panelists comments during the 2024 ICCA Congress are my own.

II LANGUAGE, IDENTITY, AND CODE-SWITCHING

People often think of linguistics as the study of grammar. Linguistics, however, runs the gamut from the description of how we form sounds, to how grammatical rules work and change, to how language reflects and creates culture and identity.[3] In this chapter, I generally draw on linguistic anthropological literature to explain and analyze code-switching. The study of linguistics, and in particular the branches of that study such as sociolinguistics and anthropological linguistics, tells us that language use is inherently social. Speech provides us with information about the identities of speakers and how they relate to the world around them. Linguistic anthropology is not divorced from the study of grammar, however. Rather, linguistic anthropologists study how grammar can impact culture and social context, and how culture and social context can impact grammar. In the following sections, I briefly explore: (1) language as a social practice (section II.1), (2) the connection between language and identity (section II.2), and (3) what code-switching is and how it may provide information about the identity of a speaker and the social context in which they are speaking (section II.3).

1 Language as a Social Practice

Language is not simply a set of "formal rules" or a "conduit that merely conveys information without adding or changing anything of substance."[4] Rather, language is a social practice, and speakers are social actors who communicate information about themselves and their sociocultural context as they speak.[5] In a seminal work on linguistic anthropology, Alessandro Duranti explained the social nature of language in the following way:

> Words carry in them a myriad of possibilities for connecting us to other human beings, other situations, events, acts, beliefs, feelings. This is due to the ability that language has to describe the world as well as to its ability to connect us with its inhabitants, objects, places, and periods; each time reaffirming a socio-historical dimension of human action among others. The indexicality of language is thus part of the constitution of any act of speaking as an act of participation in a community of language users. We might come into a situation assuming a common language to later realize that it is through acts of speaking that such a language is constituted, challenged, and changed.[6]

3. This reflects my background as a theoretical linguist with an emphasis in linguistic anthropology (a.k.a. anthropological linguistics). For a detailed discussion of the history of the study of language, and the various branches of modern day linguistics, I recommend Linda R. Waugh, Monique Monville-Burston and John E. Joseph (eds.), *The Cambridge History of Linguistics* (Cambridge University Press 2023).
4. Laura M. Ahearn, *Living Language: An Introduction to Linguistic Anthropology* (John Wiley & Sons Ltd. 2021), at 8.
5. *See, e.g.*, Alessandro Duranti, *Linguistic Anthropology* (Cambridge University Press 1997), at 18.
6. Alessandro Duranti, *Linguistic Anthropology* (Cambridge University Press 1997), at 46.

Thus, language is "a set of socially embedded practices"[7] and "is not just a means through which we act upon the social world; the use of language is *itself* a form of social action."[8] Language use is dynamic; it "both presupposes and at the same time brings about ways of being in the world."[9] This means that we do not simply communicate social information when we speak, but our act of speaking often has the ability to create or change the social context in which we are operating. This then begs the question: when we use language in international arbitration, what contextual messages are we sending beyond the "plain meaning" of the words we say, and what kind of social context are we creating?

2 Language and Identity

Every time we speak, we send information to listeners about our identities, including, for example, our nationality, ethnicity, race, gender, class, and culture. But just as language use is dynamic, so too is identity:

> [I]dentity is a dynamic construct—a multifaceted assemblage of racial, ethnic, class, social, cultural, and gender properties, each also in a state of flux. We never belong to just one category, and at any given moment these identities emerge, disappear, mutate, and mix—either through our own intention, performance, or presentation of self, or as a reaction to those imposed upon us.[10]

Thus, it is only through the observation and analysis of real-time language use and discourse that we can learn about how language reflects our constantly changing, multifaceted identities. And, at the same time, the observation of language use also provides a window into how language itself may create, change, and challenge our identities in particular social contexts. This analysis is particularly interesting in the context of international arbitration, because as practitioners in an inherently international discipline, many of us have multilayered, multilingual, and multicultural identities.[11]

7. Laura M. Ahearn, *Living Language: An Introduction to Linguistic Anthropology* (John Wiley & Sons Ltd. 2021), at 1.
8. Laura M. Ahearn, *Living Language: An Introduction to Linguistic Anthropology* (John Wiley & Sons Ltd. 2021), at 8.
9. Alessandro Duranti, *Linguistic Anthropology* (Cambridge University Press 1997), at 1.
10. James Stanlaw, Nobuko Adachi, and Zdenek Salzmann, *Language, Culture, and Society: An Introduction to Linguistic Anthropology* (7th ed. Taylor & Francis, 2018), at 272.
11. Even in what we think of as monolingual, monocultural contexts, anthropologists and linguists have observed that heterogeneity—cultural and linguistic diversity—exist. For many linguists and philosophers, the idea of "linguistic homogeneity" is an "ideological construction, historically tied to the development of the European states and the efforts to establish a national identity through a national language to be called by one name: German, French, Russian, Italian." Alessandro Duranti, *Linguistic Anthropology* (Cambridge University Press 1997), at 75 (discussing the work of Mikhail Bakhtin, a Russian literary critic who developed the concept of heteroglossia). The idea of homogeneity bears very little relation to actual language use. Indeed, sociolinguistic research has demonstrated that "[e]very time we subject *a* language ... to systematic investigation, we discover that it displays a considerable variation across speakers and situations." *Id.* at 70.

3 Code-Switching as a Window to Social Context and Identity

The question then becomes how to identify key moments when speech signals information about the sociocultural context, gives us information about a speaker's identity, and shows us how identity may shift in the same conversation. For decades, code-switching has been a productive area of research in this area. Code-switching has a long history in the linguistic and linguistic anthropological literature, and as the study of it has developed, its definition has changed.[12] In essence, code-switching involves changing how we speak in a social interaction depending on who else is involved, the social context we're in, or both. Code-switching runs the gamut from alternating between speech registers (e.g., while in the office, a father may switch from "daddy" speak on a call with his children to "professional" speak as colleagues enter his office), to alternating between dialects of the same language, or alternating between entirely different "national" languages. Importantly, code-switching does not simply reflect the social situation in which we are speaking. As an aspect of language use, it also can create and change social context.

As international arbitration practitioners, we all have been in situations where code-switching occurs. At conferences and networking events, we often switch between different languages depending on the other participants in a particular conversation. At hearings, we may switch between the procedural language and other shared languages at different junctures, and we switch between speaking more informally during breaks and more formally during the proceedings. In bilingual hearings with simultaneous translation, the switching may occur across two separate tracks for each language. Each of these examples constitutes code-switching.

Code-switching can serve more than one purpose at a time, and speakers may not always be aware of all the information that code-switching communicates to listeners. Nor are listeners necessarily consciously aware of all the value judgments they are making as they process what they hear. Code-switching may be purely pragmatic—if a speaker of one language does not feel comfortable in the language of conversation, they may switch to another language in which they feel more comfortable. Even in purely pragmatic instances, however, the act of code-switching shares social and cultural information about the speaker as well as information about how the speaker perceives other conversation participants.

Code-switching also occurs in situations where the speaker is fully comfortable in each language. The speaker then may alternate for various reasons. For example, alternating languages can help to accommodate another conversation participant who appears to be struggling with the language of conversation. While a speaker "accommodates" another participant, the speaker may also be signaling some kind of solidarity or shared group membership with the other conversation participant (i.e., we

12. For a helpful survey of how code-switching research has developed over the past four decades, *see* Kira Hall and Chad Nilep, *Code-Switching, Identity, and Globalization*, in *The Handbook of Discourse Analysis* (John Wiley & Sons, Inc. 2015), 2nd ed., Deborah Tannen, Heidi E. Hamilton and Deborah Schiffrin, eds.

have a shared identity because we both speak Spanish, English, Italian, etc.). Code-switching can also signal information about the context: for example, in a Catholic mass, a priest may change to a more formal register as mass begins, and to a more informal register to make announcements during a break in worship.

In multilingual situations, code-switching may also be used to communicate "cosmopolitanism."[13] For example, one linguist studied the language alternation practices of a middle-class foreign language learners' club in Japan, called the "Hippo Family Club." Club members would draw from several languages in the same utterance to signal their "cosmopolitan citizenship."[14] Similarly, in studies of workplaces where people from different countries and linguistic backgrounds interact regularly with each other, some scholars have noted that language alternation can give rise to "recombinant identities," "a sense of simultaneous identification with multiple groups across transnational territories."[15] These studies are particularly useful in the context of international arbitration, which also is characterized by practitioners from different countries and linguistic backgrounds who work across transnational territories.

The choice to code-switch also provides information about how the speaker views other conversation participants. In one of the most well-known studies of code-switching, Bonnie Urciuoli, a linguistic anthropologist, observed that bilingual Puerto Ricans in New York chose to code-switch depending on the context and the perceived socioeconomic status of other participants in a conversation.[16] For example, Puerto Rican men alternated easily between Spanish and English when playing basketball with their English-speaking African-American neighbors of a similar social class (even when their African-American neighbors spoke no Spanish). However, little to no code-switching occurred in interactions between the same Puerto Ricans and white social workers (even when the social workers could speak Spanish). Thus, code-switching occurred when speakers felt they had some kind of shared identity with their interlocutors, even if they did not share the same language. At the same time, no code-switching occurred where speakers perceived "a stark difference in socioeconomic class, race, or ethnicity."[17] This example demonstrates how speakers can use code-switching to indicate solidarity with some and simultaneously distance themselves from others.

13. Kira Hall and Chad Nilep, *Code-Switching, Identity, and Globalization*, in *The Handbook of Discourse Analysis* (John Wiley & Sons, Inc. 2015), 2d ed., Deborah Tannen, Heidi E. Hamilton and Deborah Schiffrin, eds. The various registers, dialects, and languages that speakers may draw on in any given interaction are not hermetically sealed systems, but rather as all part of a unified linguistic repertoire that speakers use to express their multifaceted and dynamic identities.
14. Kira Hall and Chad Nilep, *Code-Switching, Identity, and Globalization*, in *The Handbook of Discourse Analysis* (John Wiley & Sons, Inc. 2015), 2d ed., Deborah Tannen, Heidi E. Hamilton and Deborah Schiffrin, eds.
15. Kira Hall and Chad Nilep, *Code-Switching, Identity, and Globalization*, in *The Handbook of Discourse Analysis* (John Wiley & Sons, Inc. 2015), 2d ed., Deborah Tannen, Heidi E. Hamilton and Deborah Schiffrin, eds.
16. Bonnie Urciuoli, *Exposing Prejudice: Puerto Rican Experiences of Language, Race, and Class* (Westview 1996).
17. Laura M. Ahearn, *Living Language: An Introduction to Linguistic Anthropology* (John Wiley & Sons Ltd. 2021), at 19-20 (discussing the work of Bonnie Urciuoli).

Much of the popular literature on code-switching has portrayed it negatively, focusing on the costs of code-switching. For example, studies have noted that black Americans often feel compelled to code-switch to be successful in professional contexts.[18] At the same time that these black professionals strive to speak more like their white colleagues, they may simultaneously be judged for doing so by their black American colleagues who choose not to code-switch. I certainly do not disagree with these observations, nor do I argue that there are no costs to code-switching in certain situations. However, the linguistic literature demonstrates that code-switching is not limited to situations where there is a real or perceived power differential between conversation participants. Everyone code-switches, and they do so for a range of reasons. The challenge, then, is to analyze when, how, and why code-switching occurs to determine what its effects may be.

In the following sections, I use code-switching observed in publicly available transcripts to analyze various exchanges in international arbitration.

III EXPLICIT CODE-SWITCHING IN INTERNATIONAL ARBITRATION HEARINGS

In this section, I use publicly available transcripts to demonstrate how international arbitration practitioners carve out space for additional languages in English-language proceedings or on English-language transcripts. Section III.1 summarizes the prevalence of English as a procedural language. Section III.2 identifies several instances of code-switching in publicly available hearing transcripts and analyzes what code-switching does in each instance.

1 The Prevalence of English as Procedural Language

Although arbitration is an international endeavor, English is the dominant procedural language both in commercial and investor-state proceedings. On the commercial side, not all institutions collect language-based data, but those that do demonstrate that English is often the dominant procedural language. For example, in 2023, 77% of ICC awards were rendered in English.[19] In 2024, 79.3% of HKIAC cases were conducted in English.[20] In 2023, ICSID conducted 58% of cases in English, 9% in Spanish, 4% in French, and 29% simultaneously in two languages, with simultaneous English-Spanish proceedings being the most frequent (eighty-nine cases).[21]

18. *See, e.g.*, Courtney L. McCluney et al., *The Costs of Code-Switching*, Harvard Business Review, November 15, 2019, available at https://hbr.org/2019/11/the-costs-of-codeswitching (last visited March 31, 2025).
19. ICC Dispute Resolution 2023 Statistics, available at https://iccwbo.org/wp-content/uploads/sites/3/2024/06/2023-Statistics_ICC_Dispute-Resolution_991.pdf (last visited March 31, 2025).
20. HKIAC 2024 Statistics, available at https://www.hkiac.org/about-us/statistics (last visited March 31, 2025).
21. International Centre for Settlement of Investment Disputes, 2023 Annual Report, at 33, available at https://icsid.worldbank.org/sites/default/files/publications/ICSID_AR2023_ENGLISH_web_spread.pdf (last visited March 31, 2025).

As arbitration practitioners, we often come to a dispute once a language already has been chosen. Indeed, leading arbitral institutions recommend that parties specify procedural language(s) in their arbitration agreements. For example, the LCIA and SIAC model clauses each include a sentence designating a language of arbitration.[22] The ICC notes that "it may be desirable for [the parties] to stipulate the place and language of the arbitration."[23] In the AAA-ICDR's ClauseBuilder tool, the institution notes that "[t]he language of the arbitral proceedings should be chosen with care. Among other issues, it will impact the need for translation and the pool of available arbitrators."[24] Party autonomy and consent are the cornerstones of international arbitration. In commercial proceedings, the source of arbitral tribunals' jurisdiction and how they exercise it is determined by the contents of the parties' arbitration agreement. If that agreement includes a choice of procedural language, it can only be altered by mutual party consent.

Commentators have noted that the dominance of English in international arbitration may unfairly privilege native English speakers and create barriers to entry for non-English speakers or non-native English speakers.[25] I do not necessarily disagree, nor do I seek to unpack here the global socioeconomic, cultural and linguistic forces that have gotten us to where we are. Rather, in this chapter I examine code-switching in both formal and informal international arbitration contexts. This code-switching analysis, along with our conversations during the ICCA panel, demonstrates that the situation is far more complicated. Even when English is chosen as the procedural language of the proceeding, this is rarely the whole story. There are multiple layers to a truly international proceeding that often reflect the linguistic identity of the various participants. The code-switching I analyze below suggests that it is not our ability to speak English that defines who we are as international arbitration practitioners, but rather, our multilingual, cosmopolitan identities.

22. *See* LCIA Model Clause, available at https://www.lcia.org/dispute_resolution_services/lcia_recommended_clauses.aspx (last visited March 31, 2025); SIAC Model Clause, available at https://siac.org.sg/siac-model-clause (last visited March 31, 2025).

23. *See* ICC Guidance on Arbitration Clauses, available at https://iccwbo.org/wp-content/uploads/sites/3/2016/11/Standard-ICC-Arbitration-Clause-in-ENGLISH.pdf (last visited March 31, 2025).

24. AAA ClauseBuilder, available at https://www.clausebuilder.org/umbraco/surface/options/items (last visited March 31, 2025).

25. *See, e.g.*, Kabir A.N. Duggal and Amanda J. Lee, *In Search of Civilization: Uncovering Overlooked Manifestations of Homogeneity in International Arbitration—Accent and Language*, Kluwer Arbitration Blog, January 16, 2023, available at https://arbitrationblog.kluwerarbitration.com/2023/01/16/in-search-of-civilization-uncovering-overlooked-manifestations-of-homogeneity-in-international-arbitration-accent-and-language/ (last visited March 31, 2025); Daniel Greineder, *Arbitrators Don't Speak Esperanto: The Difficulties and Dominance of English as a Procedural Language in Arbitration*, Kluwer Arbitration Blog, November 7, 2021, available at https://arbitrationblog.kluwerarbitration.com/2021/11/07/arbitrators-dont-speak-esperanto-the-difficulties-and-dominance-of-english-as-a-procedural-language-in-arbitration/ (last visited March 31, 2025).

2 Explicit Code-Switching in International Arbitration Hearings

In the following section, I use publicly available English-language transcripts from international arbitration hearings to identify instances of explicit code-switching, *e.g.*, when a speaker expressly switches from one language to another.[26] On the commercial arbitration side, I deliberately chose cases that involved at least one party from a non-English-language dominant jurisdiction, as I expected these would be more fertile ground for code-switching. On the investment side, many, if not all, of the transcripts chosen are the English transcripts from a bilingual proceeding, with simultaneous translation between Spanish and English.[27] In both instances, code-switching occurs, even when simultaneous translation would suggest that it is unnecessary for the English speaker to alternate between languages, because an interpreter simultaneously is doing the work of translation.

An analysis based solely on a transcript can, of course, only tell us so much. Each case has its own history, and each participant has their own dynamic, multifaceted identity that is not fully apparent in a transcript excerpt. The transcript will contain macro-contextual information, such as who is speaking and what language they are using. This information can be complemented by reviewing any publicly available documents, like awards or memorials, to determine the legal context. Based on our experience, we also can make educated guesses about the physical context—for example, how the hearing room was set up and where different participants sat. But a transcript does not give us micro-contextual information about the speakers and listeners, such as gesture, tone, or accent, which may simultaneously communicate information about age, class, culture, or education, among other aspects of identity, to others in the hearing room. Transcripts also do not tell us what is happening during breaks or offline chats at counsel table. As a result, code-switching observed in transcripts can give us interesting information about advocacy, context, and identity, but it will never give us the whole picture.

Code-switching can provide information relating to the context ("discourse-related code-switching") as well as giving information about the identities of the participant(s) ("participant-related code-switching").[28] The examples of code-switching I have identified tend to do both at the same time, although I have split them in the discussion below based on what appears to be the primary function. First, I examine instances where a speaker appears to be using code-switching primarily to provide information about context and subject matter (section III.2.a). Second, I

26. As discussed in section IV below, code-switching is not limited to alternations between different languages—people also can switch between different accents, different sets of gestures, and different registers.
27. In bilingual proceedings, code-switching is not always apparent in the transcript. For example, if a witness or advocate switches from one language to another to ask or answer a question, the transcript does not always reflect the switch because the speech is simultaneously interpreted and transcribed in both languages.
28. Laura M. Ahearn, *Living Language: An Introduction to Linguistic Anthropology* (John Wiley & Sons Ltd. 2021), at 149; citing Auer 1999 at 310.

examine instances where code-switching appears to be primarily participant-related—the code-switching provides information about the speaker's identity (section III.2.b).

a Discourse-Related Code-Switching in Arbitration Hearings

Many examples of code-switching at arbitration hearings appear at first glance to be primarily discourse-related. The alternation between languages contextualizes some aspect of the case. In the examples discussed in section III.2.a.i, code-switching signals "special," foreign, or non-translatable meaning. That is, the speaker appears to alternate between codes to signal that a term has a special meaning that belies expression in the procedural language. In the examples discussed in section III.2.a.ii, code-switching appears to be primarily "clarificatory," thereby signaling that the speaker is referring to a concept in the original language that has a natural translation in the language of procedure. However, it is important to note, as detailed further below, that in both instances: (1) the speaker's use of code-switching may be hotly contested by the opposing party, and (2) the language alternations communicate extra information about the speaker, whether intended to do so or not.

i Code-Switching to Signal Special Meaning

The following excerpt is taken from an AAA-ICDR arbitration between an Ecuadorian claimant and respondents from the United States and Israel.[29] The excerpt is from a hearing on a motion to dismiss for lack of arbitrability, which took place in English. The Israeli party, IDE, contended that it should be dismissed from the arbitration as it was a non-signatory to the contract at issue and a stranger to the relationship between the U.S. respondent, Indusys, and the Ecuadorian claimant, NIRSA. Counsel for the Ecuadorian Claimant makes the following argument to support the claimant's claims against *both* parties:

> So to say that they are a complete stranger to the relationship belies the contemporaneous documents and belies the reality. This relationship didn't begin yesterday. It didn't begin when the request for arbitration was filed. It began back in 1978 and it continued through 2014, 2016, 2018, 2019 and 2020.
>
> That is the relationship. And it is a relationship that IDE drove. It is a relationship that IDE managed. It is a relationship that IDE performed through its series of agents. And we will talk about some of those agents, the final one being Indusys.
>
> IDE updated the prior proposals. IDE introduced Indusys to NIRSA as its—*and I'm going to use a word in Spanish, "representante," representative, agent* ... And, in fact, with respect to all of the material terms concerning the contract in dispute, IDE, not Indusys, *the "representante" IDE had the final word. . .*—and here's a communication from November 27th, 2019 from NIRSA to IDE, not

29. *Negocios Industriales Real NISRA, S.A. v. I.D.E. Technologies, Ltd. and Industrial Systems, Inc.*, AAA-ICDR Case No. 01-20-0014-8047.

> Indusys, where they say—*they describe, NIRSA does, Indusys as the representative, "el representante," the agent of IDE.*[30]

The alternation between English and Spanish here is purposeful and multifunctional. It reminds the arbitrator of the original Spanish document at issue and the word "representante" used there. At the same time, it imbues the word "representante" with special meaning. Despite providing a translation with the first use of "representante," the claimant's counsel avoids using only the English translation in the following sentences. Rather, counsel repeatedly uses the Spanish word, "representante," signaling that there is something special about the word that defies translation. Indeed, the use of Spanish rather than English acts as a meta-signal of difference. The language change draws the listener's (and in particular, the arbitrator's) attention to the word and its asserted special meaning. Thus, the code-switching serves an overt advocacy purpose. It communicates that the legal relationship is something special, untranslatable, and important.

Notably, opposing counsel expressly rejects the suggestion that "representante" has a special meaning:

> The idea that counsel for IDE continues to press the point that they somehow are—*that the word agent, representative, "representante" in Spanish means something other than what it means,* well, I know that the Chair is fluent in Spanish, and I know that the Chair is fully aware of what the La Real Academia La Lengua Espanola is to help us define words in Spanish. And I'm sure when we look at the definition of "representante" there, the Tribunal will come to the same conclusion we have with respect to that issue.[31]

Instead of using the English translation, opposing counsel echoes the code-switching used by the claimant's counsel, repeatedly using the word "representante." Opposing counsel also *expressly* challenges the authoritativeness of the claimant's translation by pointing the arbitrator to a third-party definition of the word "representante."[32]

The code-switching also communicates information about the speakers and the arbitrator. In his presentation, the claimant's counsel's use of English and Spanish signals an aspect of his identity—he is someone who can alternate between English and Spanish. This alternation implicitly serves to indicate that the claimant's counsel understands the original Spanish words used in the contracts and therefore, he can serve as an authority on the meaning of "representante." Thus, the code-switching communicates linguistic expertise.

When opposing counsel begins to speak, he impliedly challenges the authoritative nature of the claimant's counsel's translation. Opposing counsel demonstrates that he, also, can switch from English to Spanish. Therefore, he also communicates his

30. *Negocios Industriales Real NISRA, S.A. v. I.D.E. Technologies, Ltd. and Industrial Systems, Inc.*, AAA-ICDR Case No. 01-20-0014-8047, Hearing transcript, July 22, 2021, pp. 27-28.
31. *Negocios Industriales Real NISRA, S.A. v. I.D.E. Technologies, Ltd. and Industrial Systems, Inc.*, AAA Case No. 01-20-0014-8047, Hearing transcript, July 22, 2021, p. 60, ll. 1-10.
32. Opposing counsel refers the arbitrator to the Real Academia de la Lengua Española.

linguistic expertise. Thus, the code-switching by each counsel becomes a metalinguistic argument regarding who has the authority to define the Spanish term.

In addition, the code-switching creates a special language for the case itself—a manner of speaking that is shared between case participants but would likely be opaque to outsiders. In this English-language case, suddenly the use of the Spanish word "representante" is an acceptable and understood way of referring to a particular concept, despite the ready availability of an English translation. In this regard, as international arbitration practitioners, we can all probably think of examples like this in our own cases, where we have used the name of something in another language throughout a case, rather than an easily available translation for it in the procedural language. Thus, our expectations about what a procedural language looks like change as our use of the procedural language in a specific case changes. In the words of Alessandro Duranti, "[w]e might come into a situation assuming a common language to later realize that it is through acts of speaking that such a language is constituted, challenged, and changed."[33]

Finally, code-switching in these instances may also be a tool to build rapport with the arbitrator, who, based on other entries in the same transcript, is also fluent in Spanish. Rapport may be built not simply through the use of Spanish, but by the development of a special case language, shared only by the case participants.

Thus, the code-switching is multifunctional: it serves an advocacy purpose, it communicates information about the speaker's identity, it creates a shared manner of speaking for a particular case, and it has the power to build rapport. At the same time that code-switching does all these things, it may well be exclusionary.[34] How many participants in the room can follow the fluid switching between English and Spanish?

ii Code-Switching as Clarification

Code-switching can also be used for what seems to be a near-opposite purpose. Rather than signaling "special" meaning, code-switching can be used to gloss over any translation issues. In the following examples, the speaker provides the Spanish and English versions for the same term, even though a simultaneous translator appears to be present in each hearing.

In an investment hearing involving claims relating to the Bolivian electricity sector, the original Spanish term for capacity prices from the Bolivian legislation is provided to clarify the English term:

> So much for Spot Prices. Let's turn to Capacity Prices or saying it in Spanish *precio básico por potencia*. These are payments made independently of whether the generation unit is called upon to dispatch. They ensure that generators have an incentive to maintain generation units to dispatch, even if they're not called upon

33. Alessandro Duranti, *Linguistic Anthropology* (Cambridge University Press 1997), at 46.
34. During the 2024 ICCA Congress, Samaa Haridi emphasized the power code-switching may have to exclude others.

> often enough to cover their costs. Capacity Payments are provided for in Article 49 E of the Electricity Law which is on Slide 30.[35]

Similarly, in the following excerpt from a hearing in an investment arbitration involving the Republic of Colombia, a key phrase is deftly mentioned in the original Spanish along with its English translation:

> This is a ten-year term which may be renewed once. Now, this morning we heard that there would be an explanation of the "may" but you didn't get any explanation on the renewal conditions or what is written, so we put here for the Tribunal. You have it here in Spanish at the top and in English at the bottom on the right side of this slide. *In Spanish, "el plazo podra ser prorrogado," may be renewed in English.* That is Article 4.[36]

In these examples, the link between the Spanish and English terms is treated as natural. In other words, the ease with which the translations are coupled together suggests that translation is a non-issue. This natural link is not just expressed by providing the clarificatory translation, but also by the speakers' facility in alternating between the two languages. There is also a marked *lack of emphasis* given to the translation, in contrast to the example above where the speaker emphasized the special meaning of the term "representante."[37]

But as discussed above, code-switching is multifunctional. While seeming simply to clarify a reference to the original Spanish, these speakers are also *translating* the meaning of the original term into a new language, a process that is not always without pitfalls. Thus, the speakers' ease of alternating between languages in itself signals that there is a relative ease in translating the concepts mentioned.

Unlike the above examples, where the translation was presented without further comment, the following excerpt in another case against the Republic of Colombia explicitly downplays the difference between the original Spanish and its English translation:

> Let's not get caught up in semantics. The reason we call it "Forced Collection Proceeding" is because the name of the phase in Spanish is "procedimiento de cobro coactivo."[38]

This express attempt to downplay a translation suggests that translation of this term was, in fact, a problem in this proceeding. Thus, the use of code-switching to clarify references can be deceiving, as it often obscures what are actually hotly contested translation issues. The following exchange demonstrates a situation where a witness attempts to de-link the "natural" connection between English and Spanish translations that the cross-examiner assumes:

35. *Guaracachi America Inc. and Rurelec PLC v. Plurinational State of Bolivia*, PCA Case No. 2011-17, Hearing on the Merits, April 2, 2013, p. 46, ll. 11-17.
36. *Security Services LLC v. Republic of Colombi*a, ICSID Case No. ARB 20/7, March 27, 2023, p. 110, ll. 10-20.
37. *See supra* section III.2.a.i.
38. *Amec Foster Wheeler USA Corporation, et al. v. Republic of Colombia*, Hearing on Provisional Measures, Nov. 4, 2021, p. 65, ll. 17-19 (ICSID).

> And in the next page you have a table explaining how that distribution of dividends will be done. Top line you have the net profit of the year. That's 23.9 million, to simplify.
>
> > Is that correct, sir?
> > A: Yes.
> > Q. And the—you will have to go down a few lines, the total dividends distributed were at 31.9 million; correct?
> > A: Well, *you were asking me a question in English, we declared the dividend, but we did not distribute because, in English, when we refer to it as "distribution," it's a payment. We did not make a payment. We declared the dividend, and that's what the junta de accionistas approved.*
> > Q. Yes. Well, you see where I have the problem, I thought we had agreed on the language. I'm reading from a Spanish document that says distribute. This is why I use that word.
> > So, we do agree, sir, that when I refer—and you could do whatever you want, but when I refer to distribution, I'm talking about what you call declaration?
> > A. But I do feel uncomfortable with the word "distribution" when you use it in English.
> > President Judice: *I think the witness was clear. You can see this, right or wrong, that when it is written "distribuido" does not mean to distribute but to declare.*
> > The Witness: Correct.
> > President Júdice: It's correct, not correct, is another issue.
> > The Witness: That's my understanding.
> > Mr. García Represa: We are not talking about payment of dividends. I haven't used the word "paid," so it should be rather clear, but . . .
> > President Júdice: But the Tribunal understood the point of the witness and yours. We understood.
> > Q. Going back to my question which you didn't answer yet, 2009 net profits were 23.89 million bolivianos; correct?
> > A. Correct
> > Q. *Dividends declared, according to your language, a distribuir in the Spanish version,* were 31.9 bolivianos; correct?[39]

Thus, in the above exchange, the arbitrator mediates a semantic debate between the witness and the cross-examiner relating to the meaning of the word "distribuir" in Spanish. At the same time that they negotiate meaning, all three participants in the exchange demonstrate some level of bilingualism—they speak English and Spanish and they switch fluidly between the two. This exchange suggests that there is at least one aspect of shared identity between arbitrator, counsel, and witness.

b *Participant-Related Switching*

As noted above, code-switching is almost always multifunctional. While section III.2.a analyzed examples of code-switching that seemed to have contextualization as their

39. *Guaracachi America Inc. and Rurelec PLC v. Plurinational State of Bolivia,* PCA Case No. 2011-17, Hearing on the Merits, April 3, 2013, pp. 342-343.

primary function, in this section I analyze an example of "participant-related switching," code-switching that seems primarily focused on some feature of the participant or participants in the hearing.

The following excerpt is from the same AAA-ICDR hearing discussed in section III.2.a above. Ecuadorian local counsel for the claimant addresses the arbitrator in Spanish, although the procedural language used in the hearing was English and no translator appears to have been present:

> The Arbitrator: Okay. Then I think we're done. And I thank you all for your time, for your concise arguments.
>
> And Mr. Noboa, do you have something to say?
>
> (Mr. Noboa addresses the arbitrator in Spanish.)
>
> The Arbitrator: Thank you, Mr. Noboa.
>
> And Mr. Parks and Mr. Solar, he was merely saying he wanted to formally introduce himself and thank us all for our work today and—but that obviously he is the lawyer for NIRSA in Ecuador, but that obviously Hogan Lovells is representing him. Not to represent myself as a translator, but I think under these circumstances, it's fine to communicate what he was communicating.
>
> Mr. Parks: Thank you.
>
> The Arbitrator: And the better Spanish speakers can correct me on that.
>
> So I would say, thank you, "Muchas gracias, Senior Noboa."[40]

The arbitrator accommodates the Spanish-speaking local counsel and then translates what has been said to English-speaking counsel for respondents. Without further context, it is difficult to theorize further about the cultural and procedural implications of this exchange, but it is certainly an interesting one. For example, it is unclear if the claimant's local counsel spoke in Spanish because he was unable to communicate in English, or for various other reasons. In other words, the transcript cannot tell us if local counsel's choice was pragmatic, strategic, or both. Importantly, the use of Spanish to directly address the arbitrator compels her to shift identities and roles, from arbitrator to translator, a shift that could be legally fraught in other situations.

c *Conclusion*

While many of the speakers in the excerpts reproduced above appear to be using code-switching as an advocacy tool, the code-switching has several other intended and/or perceived functions. As they code-switch, the speakers demonstrate knowledge, signal identity, and negotiate the meaning of key terms. They also communicate information about the context—they carve out space for a second language in the midst of an English-language proceeding or transcript.[41] In doing so, they signal that the hearing room is a complex, multilingual space.

40. *Negocios Industriales Real NISRA, S.A. v. I.D.E. Technologies, Ltd. and Industrial Systems, Inc.*, AAA Case No. 01-20-0014-8047, Hearing transcript, July 22, 2021, p. 63, ll. 6-23.

41. An interesting question is whether code-switching in some contexts may go too far and jeopardize the parties' choice of procedural language in the original arbitration agreement, thereby creating potential fuel for an argument to set aside an award.

IV OTHER INSTANCES OF CODE-SWITCHING IN INTERNATIONAL ARBITRATION

So far, I have focused on the explicit alternation between two languages that occurs in the hearing room. This type of code-switching appears to be a regular occurrence that, as discussed above, occurs for a wide range of reasons. It can be observed easily in transcripts, and is explicit and often commented on in real time as a hearing unfolds. However, other types of code-switching may also be occurring, but they are rarely observable in a transcript.

We often know a hearing is beginning in earnest when we hear an arbitrator say words like these:

> The President: Good morning everybody. We're resuming the hearing.[42]

These words signal to participants that it is time to operate and speak in a manner that we view to be "socially and culturally acceptable" for an international arbitration hearing.

First, when we hear these words, or similar ones, it is a signal that our register should change to a more formal one. While the international arbitration hearing register is less formal than court proceedings in many countries around the world, we still expect a certain level of formality. For example, we may be on a first-name basis with a member of the arbitral panel or with opposing counsel, but we would rarely use first names during a hearing.

Second, some of us are required to alternate to a new language when the hearing begins. For example, native speakers of Spanish or French must change to English in an English-language proceeding and vice versa.[43] Lei Xi's survey of bilingual arbitrators, summarized at the 2024 ICCA Congress, demonstrated that even in a bilingual proceeding, an arbitrator may find testimony and documentary evidence presented in one of the two procedural languages to be more authoritative. Preferences like these are rarely communicated to parties when the tribunal is constituted, which may leave parties guessing as they navigate a particular arbitrator's linguistic preferences throughout the proceeding.

Third, fearing conscious or unconscious biases of other hearing participants, some of us may consciously (or sometimes unconsciously) change or water down our

42. *Grupo Unidos por el Canal, S.A., Sacyr, S.A., Webuild, S.p.A. and Jan de Nul, N.V. v. Autoridad del Canal de Panamá (II)*, ICC Case No. 20910/ASM/JPA, Hearing transcript, January 22, 2019, p. 1.

43. Parties to arbitration regularly take into account the different languages involved and build a complex structure of bilingual counsel, arbitrators, interpreters, and document translations. The fact that this often complex structure seems "natural" to many of us as international arbitration practitioners is, perhaps, evidence that we have created our own micro-culture. This linguistic infrastructure would likely seem quite exotic to lawyers practicing in many national courts in the world, or, indeed, to professionals in other fields. In addition, within this linguistic infrastructure, we regularly make translation accommodations for witnesses and experts. These accommodations are not as common (or as practical) for arbitrators or counsel, and parties often feel constrained in their choice of arbitrators and counsel by the procedural language arbitration. The extent to which this limits party autonomy and choice is a topic for another day.

accents to make our speech (and by extension, our identity) more palatable to other participants.[44] At the 2024 ICCA Congress, Samaa Haridi discussed a UK study which concluded that barristers who spoke with "received pronunciation" rather than regional UK accents were viewed as more professional, intelligent, and confident.[45] An accent may well be a barrier to inclusion or success in international arbitration as well. Indeed, when a procedural language is chosen, most of us make assumptions, often seemingly unconsciously, about how that language should sound. We do not expect that the English speakers in an English-language, New York seated arbitration, will speak with the same accent as low-income residents of government housing in East New York. If French is the procedural language in a Paris-seated arbitration, we do not expect to hear the French of a Parisian banlieue in the hearing room. I do not mean to suggest that these assumptions are held by all, nor that they are correct. However, it is important that we are aware of our assumptions, whatever they may be, and that we question them.

Fourth, the gestures and body language we use are an important part of how we communicate, and they are often culturally determined. Jern-Fei Ng KC led a discussion of gesture and body language at the 2024 ICCA Congress that raised key questions about how gesture and body language may impact how we judge a witness or advocate. For example, lack of eye contact may communicate respect in some cultures; at the same time, it communicates a lack of trustworthiness in other cultures. International arbitration participants may well change how they move or gesture to accommodate the cultures and biases of others in the room.

Code-switching happens for several reasons in international arbitration, but it is important to remember that it may not always be done voluntarily. In addition, some people may not be able to code-switch, and some may choose not to do so. Thus, while code-switching may carve out space for a non-dominant language in the hearing room, our expectations about how language should look and sound also may create barriers that cannot be resolved by code-switching. Indeed, code-switching itself may exclude some people, thereby exacerbating linguistic barriers. This is true beyond the hearing room—in our offices and networking events, we often code-switch to chat with friends, former colleagues, and others. Who might we be excluding from the conversation as we do so?

This is not to say we should always operate in one language, but simply that we should be aware of how our linguistic choices impact others. In particular, are our assumptions implicitly or explicitly compelling others to switch languages, change accents, or modify body language to be able to operate successfully in an international

---

44. Some commentators have noted that the way we use language in international arbitration can be a source of potential discrimination. *See, e.g.*, Kabir A.N. Duggal and Amanda J. Lee, *In Search of Civilization—Uncovering Overlooked Manifestations of Homogeneity in International Arbitration: Accent and Language*, Kluwer Arbitration Blog, January 16, 2023 available at https://arbitrationblog.kluwerarbitration.com/2023/01/16/in-search-of-civilization-uncovering-overlooked-manifestations-of-homogeneity-in-international-arbitration-accent-and-language/ (last visited March 31, 2025).
45. Neil Rose, *Accent Bias Still Holding Back Regional Barristers, Research Finds*, January 30, 2023, available at https://www.legalfutures.co.uk/latest-news/accent-bias-still-holding-back-regional-barristers-research-finds (last visited March 31, 2025).

arbitration context? And do our cultural expectations about how language should look and sound create barriers to those who cannot code-switch, or those who choose not to do so?

V CONCLUSION

In this rapidly changing world, the prevalence of English as a procedural language may wane. If it does so, it will simply be replaced with another language, creating new and different linguistic barriers. No matter what language is chosen, however, barriers to entry will exist. As a group of practitioners, we are generally characterized by our multi-accented, multilingual way of speaking. Despite our diversity, we likely are all guilty of making assumptions—consciously or unconsciously—about the way others speak. We may view certain "national" languages as more complex or suited to professional situations. We may prefer certain dialects or accents—such as preferring UK "received pronunciation" over an American English accent. We may assume that speakers with certain accents are less intelligent. Or we may perceive speakers as less professional if they use what we deem to be incorrect grammatical forms.[46]

Even as the world changes, one key aspect of our practice is unlikely to do so—it will always be inherently international. This means there will always be multilingual, multicultural, and transnational facets to our practice. As a result, our very ability to code-switch fluidly between different languages and to create case-specific languages may itself create a barrier to entry or success. Only those who can make the switch will make the cut. We are not perforce selected as arbitrators, counsel, or experts simply for our ability to speak "English" or any other particular language. Rather, our ability to speak the right "version" of a language (a version that is spoken by highly educated classes) and our ability to alternate fluidly between languages, cultures, and legal systems seem to be a much more important factor. To a certain extent, as a community, our linguistic currency is cosmopolitanism. Thus, it is not necessarily by choosing a procedural language other than English that we will break down barriers to inclusion, but by questioning the assumptions we have about all languages and language speakers.

46. Speaking English or any language as a lingua franca may have an attenuating effect on some of these biases. "In cognitive terms, lingua franca speech orients to achieving mutual comprehension" with more of a focus on substance over form. Anna Mauranen, *Exploring ELF: Academic English Shaped by Non-native Speakers* (Cambridge University Press 2012), at 7. Most of us who practice in this field have the experience of practicing in a non-native language, or in a non-native dialect, so we are more willing to "forgive" what we perceive as grammatical errors when they are committed by non-native speakers, knowing that we too make the same errors when we operate in a non-native language.

PANEL 11

Inter-personal Conduct and Ethics

Civility in the practice of law is an essential aspect of maintaining the rule of law. How we conduct ourselves as participants in the process of international arbitration affects how the institution of international arbitration is perceived and its effectiveness. This panel discusses ICCA's Guidelines on Standards of Practice in International Arbitration as they relate to our roles as advocates, arbitrators, experts, witnesses, and administrators, taking into account differing cultural perspectives and legal traditions.

CHAPTER 29

Interpersonal Conduct in Arbitration Proceedings: The Role of the Arbitrator

Funke Adekoya SAN[*]

TABLE OF CONTENTS

I DEFINITION OF CIVILITY IN THE CONTEXT OF ARBITRATION PROCEEDINGS

The Merriam-Webster Dictionary defines civility as "an act or utterance that is a customary show of good manners."[1] Some authors have attempted to define the concept of civility within the general practice of law as "to treat others with courtesy and respect"[2] and "treating others including opposing counsel, parties, judges, court staff, colleagues, and co-workers with courtesy, dignity, and respect."[3] Civility in this

* Funke Adekoya SAN Arbitration Practice, Lagos Nigeria. I acknowledge and appreciate the assistance of my research assistant, Tobi Adesanmi in conducting research for this chapter.

1. "Civility." Merriam-Webster.com Thesaurus, Merriam-Webster, https://www.merriam-webster.com/thesaurus/civility (accessed April 15, 2025).
2. David Grenardo, A Lesson in Civility, 135 Geo. J. Legal Ethics 138 (2019).
3. Donald E. Campbell, Raise Your Right Hand and Swear to be Civil: Defining Civility as an Obligation of Professional Responsibility, 47 Gonz. L. Rev. 99. 141-42 (2012) cited in Grenardo (n 2).

context is also described as cooperation, restraint, and honesty.[4] The legal profession has attempted to capture the concept of "civility" as it relates to professional behavior through the rollout of various codes of professional conduct. Civility in the context of arbitration is no different from the meanings stated above but can be extrapolated as conduct between all the participants within arbitration proceedings that is professional, courteous, and respectful.

1 The Importance of Arbitrator Conduct in Ensuring a Fair and Efficient Process

Arbitration is fundamentally a party-driven process in which the arbitrators derive their powers from the arbitration agreement. Although the conduct of the arbitration is circumscribed by the substantive arbitration law which governs the dispute and the rules of procedure agreed upon by the parties,[5] the arbitrators otherwise have a wide laxity to manage the arbitration hearings in the absence of the agreement of the parties.[6] Parties therefore repose confidence in the character of their chosen arbitrator to conduct the arbitration proceedings in a way that reflects their intention in choosing arbitration as the dispute resolution mechanism. They expect that the proceedings will be conducted with sufficient speed and expertise, while parties are given a full opportunity of presenting their positions to the arbitrator for determination.[7] Consequently, the selection of arbitrators by the parties is of paramount importance, as these individuals are entrusted with resolving the dispute according to the terms outlined in the arbitration agreement.

As a result of the pivotal role which arbitrators play in a reference, their conduct throughout the proceedings must promote fairness and efficiency, particularly as these principles are agreed to be the underlying attributes of an acceptable arbitration proceeding. To promote fairness and efficiency, parties expect that the arbitrators will adhere to ethical principles such as impartiality, independence, disclosure of conflicts of interest, and proper case management.[8] To highlight the importance of these attributes, the rules of many arbitral institutions have codified the expectation of the

4. *Ibid.*
5. Julian M. Lew et al., Comparative International Commercial Arbitration, Kluwer Law International 2003, at pp. 413-417. *See also* Gary B. Born, International Commercial Arbitration (3rd ed.) Wolters Kluwer, at para. 15.02.
6. Lew et al. (n 5) at pp. 423-424. Born (n 5) at para. 19.03.
7. Irene Welser and Samuel Mimnagh, "Chapter II: The Arbitrator and the Arbitration Procedure, An Arbitrator's Imperative: How to Avoid Disappointing the Parties, Preventing Surprises and Enabling Efficient and Progressive Arbitral Proceedings," in Christian Klausegger et al. (eds), Austrian Yearbook on International Arbitration 2021, Austrian Yearbook on International Arbitration, vol. 2021 (Manz'sche Verlags- und Universitaötsbuchhandlung 2021) pp. 127-155, at p. 150 (accessed March 18, 2024).
8. Fabricio Fortese and Lotta Hemmi, Procedural Fairness and Efficiency in International Arbitration (May 29, 2015), 3(1) GroJIL at 112 (2015) https://doi.org/10.21827/5a86a89d8e651 and available at SSRN: https://ssrn.com/abstract=2611337 (accessed March 20, 2024).

parties that the arbitrator will conduct the arbitration proceedings in a diligent and expeditious manner that is fair to all parties involved.[9]

Therefore, the significance of arbitrator conduct in ensuring a fair and efficient process cannot be overstated. In fact, it has been said that the quality and success of an arbitration is as good as the quality of the arbitrators involved in it.[10] According to Professor Catherine Rogers, "arbitrator integrity is one of the cornerstones of legitimacy on which the international arbitration system was built."[11] What epitomizes a good arbitrator according to another legal scholar is that they must be someone "who imposes his ethical values and has full awareness that his reputation and his professional future will benefit by conducting himself according to these ethical values and subjecting himself to the demands of a particular case or a particular party."[12]

The manner in which the arbitrator manages the arbitration has a direct impact on the speed and efficiency with which it is conducted. Of utmost importance in ensuring the efficiency of the arbitration proceedings is that the process is not subjected to some of the idiosyncrasies associated with courtroom litigation. The procedures of many court systems permit parties to delay proceedings incessantly, file frivolous applications, and generally harass both witnesses and opposing counsel. In fact, such behavior has attracted recent attention as a form of "guerilla tactics" in arbitration.[13] Depending on the system of law involved, the judge as the dispute resolver may be averse to unduly restricting the litigation strategies employed by counsel on either side, for fear of being seen as "descending into the arena and give the impression of acting as advocate."[14] The behavior of judges in such circumstances has often focused on their personal interaction with one or both of the parties, with allegations of judicial unfairness being made.[15] However, while much attention has been devoted to arbitrator duties such as independence and impartiality, the regulation of interpersonal conduct in dispute resolution generally, not to talk of alternative dispute resolution mechanisms, has received comparatively less attention.

Research on the concept of civility within the litigation framework of thirty-two states in the United States identified ten major concepts in their Bar Codes of Ethics or Professional Responsibility: "(1) recognize the importance of keeping commitments

9. Article 5.4.1 of the LCIA Rules 2020—"whether the candidate is ready, willing and able to devote sufficient time, diligence and industry to ensure the expeditious and efficient conduct of the arbitration." Also Article 2 of Appendix III to the ICC Arbitration Rules 2021 titled "Arbitration Costs And Fees" states that "In setting the arbitrator's fees, the Court shall take into consideration the diligence and efficiency of the arbitrator, ..."
10. Datuk Rajoo, Importance of Arbitrator's Ethics and Integrity in ensuring Quality Arbitrations, 6(2) Contemp. Asia Arb. J. 329.
11. Catherine Rogers; Regulating international Arbitrators: A Functional Approach to Developing Standards of Conduct, 41 Stan. J. Int'l L. 53 (2005).
12. Datuk Rajoo; Importance of Arbitrator's Ethics and Integrity in Ensuring Quality Arbitrations, 6(2) Contemp. Asia Arb. J. 329.
13. Gunther J. Horvath and Stephan Wilske (eds), Guerrilla Tactics in International Arbitration, 7(2) New York Dispute Resolution Lawyer at 41 (2014).
14. *per Lord Parker CJ in R v. Hamilton* (unreported, June 9, 1969) cited by the Court of Appeal in *R v. Hulusi* (1973) 58 Cr. App. R 378, 382.
15. *See Michel v. The Queen* [2009] UKPC 41 at para. 1.

and of seeking agreement and accommodation with regard to scheduling and extensions; (2) be respectful and act in a courteous, cordial, and civil manner; (3) be prompt, punctual, and prepared; (4) maintain honesty and personal integrity; (5) communicate with opposing counsel; (6) avoid actions taken merely to delay or harass; (7) ensure proper conduct before the court; (8) act with dignity and cooperation in pre-trial proceedings; (9) act as a role model to the client and public and as a mentor to young lawyers; and (10) utilize the court system in an efficient and fair manner."[16]

Extrapolating from the above, the concept of civility in arbitration proceedings can be defined as encompassing professional, courteous, and respectful conduct toward all participants in the process. It involves cooperation, restraint, and honesty, aiming to foster an environment conducive to fair and effective dispute resolution.

II EMERGENCE OF GUIDELINES AND STANDARDS FOR ARBITRATOR BEHAVIOR

Within the context of international arbitration, the discussion of standards guiding the process has resulted in extensive efforts devoted to formalizing codes of acceptable ethical conduct. There are several notable sources of standards of professional guidelines and rules for arbitrators, some of which have been in existence since the late 1970s. However, most of these codes of ethics for arbitrators[17] focused on the conduct of the arbitration proceedings, referencing issues such as the appointment of arbitrators, requirements of impartiality and independence, the duty of disclosure, regulating communication with the parties, and a duty of diligence and fairness. Discussions of interpersonal behavior were generally passing references.[18] On a global basis, the International Bar Association first developed a set of guidelines in 1987—the Rules of Ethics for International Arbitrators, in relation to the obligations of arbitrators in international arbitration. However, the Rules did not address any issues of interpersonal conduct, either as between the arbitral tribunal and counsel or the tribunal members between themselves.

With respect to addressing the interpersonal conduct of arbitrators, the Code of Ethics for Arbitrators in Commercial Disputes [2003] was the first code published specifically for arbitrators which referred to issues of civility by the arbitrators and was published to provide "non-binding guidance for arbitrators and to be considered by the

16. Donald E. Campbell, Raise Your Hand and Swear to Be Civil: Defining Civility as an Obligation of Professional Responsibility, 47 Gonz. L. Rev. 99 at 109 (2011-2012).
17. For example, Korean Commercial Arbitration Board Code of Ethics for Arbitrators 2016, HKIAC Code of Ethical Conduct, SIAC Code of Ethics for an Arbitrator, Milan Chamber of National and International Code of Ethics for Arbitrators (2019), Spanish Arbitration Club Code of Best Practices in Arbitration (2019) and the CIARB Code of Professional and Ethical Conduct for Members.
18. In 2021 the ICC Note to Parties and Arbitral Tribunals on the Conduct of Arbitration under the ICC Rules of Arbitration (2021) paid a passing reference to the standards of interpersonal conduct during arbitration proceedings by stating that "arbitral tribunals, parties and representatives are expected to abide by the highest standards of integrity and honesty, to conduct themselves with honour, courtesy and professionalism, and to encourage all other participants in the arbitral proceedings to do the same."

AAA in making institutional decisions on challenges."[19] The Code is the result of a joint committee of the American Arbitration Association and a special committee of the American Bar Association and is a rare instance where the personal conduct of arbitrators was addressed in a Code of Ethics at a national level. Addressing the personal conduct of arbitrators, its Canon IV.A states that "An arbitrator should conduct the proceedings in an even-handed manner. The arbitrator should be patient and courteous to the parties, their representatives, and the witnesses and should encourage similar conduct by all participants" while Canon IV.G states that "Co-arbitrators should afford each other full opportunity to participate in all aspects of the proceedings." The Commentary does not however expatiate on what type of conduct would be considered a breach of these Canons.

In 2021, the Nairobi Centre for International Arbitration issued its Code of Conduct for Arbitrators. The Code applies to all arbitration proceedings in which disputes or claims are submitted to one or more arbitrators upon appointment by the Centre. The Code addresses the personal conduct of arbitrators appointed by the Centre as part of its "PRINCIPLE 2: Integrity and fairness of the dispute resolution process." Item number 4 of the Principle states that "An Arbitrator should be patient with and courteous to the parties, their lawyers and the participants, and should encourage similar conduct by all participants in the proceedings." Unfortunately although the Code references the type of personal conduct expected from the arbitrator and the expectation that the arbitrator would pass on the same expectation to participants in the arbitration proceedings in which they are acting, the Code neither gives further guidance as to how this can be attained nor does it provide any sanctions for non-compliance by arbitrators with this requirement.

III WHY HAVE INTERPERSONAL CODES OF CONDUCT EVEN BECOME NECESSARY?

Whilst previously the diversity of legal traditions in international arbitration could be labelled as common-law based versus civil law based, currently the focus on diversity in the international arbitration community is on the array of ethnically diverse backgrounds, regional traditions and cultures that make up the international nature of its constituents. The result of increasing diversity is the possibility of participants having different perspectives as to what constitutes ethical and moral norms. Where arbitrators come from ethnically diverse backgrounds, and are subject to different professional ethics rules or codes of conduct, what may be deemed as "acceptable" arbitrator conduct may vary from jurisdiction to jurisdiction, especially since unlike national court systems, it appears that except for the United States,[20] there are no set standards or rules relating to civility within the arbitration process at a national level. Behavior that one culture may deem to be arrogant and overbearing may be acceptable as a sign of "higher status" in another culture. A simple refusal to acknowledge the

19. Born (n 5) at p. 2847.
20. The Code of Ethics for Arbitrators in Commercial Disputes published in 2003 by the American Arbitration Association.

stretched hand of a female colleague would be termed rude by some, but accepted by others as in line with cultural, religious or societal norms. This absence of standards has created a situation in which "most attorneys rely on background assumptions based on their own national standards about what constitutes proper conduct."[21] As such, the evolution of codes which specifically address arbitrator interpersonal conduct is possibly a reaction to the increasing diversity reflected on arbitration panels as a result of the focus by the arbitration community on diversity and inclusion within arbitral tribunals.

Against this backdrop, the need for some sort of guidance for arbitrators as to what may be considered "best practices" in interpersonal conduct in international arbitration proceedings can be perceived as an attempt to "homogenise" what is increasingly targeted as a space that needs to become even more diverse. Furthermore, the general consensus is that failure to address the issues of interpersonal conduct within the arbitration framework will ultimately threaten the legitimacy of international arbitration.[22]

IV CURRENT GLOBAL EFFORTS AT REQUIRING CIVILITY BY ARBITRATORS

In 2021, ICCA faced the issue of interpersonal conduct head-on when it issued its Guidelines on Standards of Practice in International Arbitration—a document which focuses on interpersonal conduct in relation to arbitration proceedings. The Guidelines though not mandatory is to "encourage the use of same for the promotion of arbitration."[23] The Guidelines as it relates specifically to arbitrator conduct are considered in more detail below.

In 2024 ICSID announced on its website that "The Secretariats of the International Centre for Settlement of Investment Disputes (ICSID) and the United Nations Commission on International Trade Law (UNCITRAL) have collaborated on a Code of Conduct for Arbitrators in International Investment Disputes. The Code is intended to provide applicable principles and provisions addressing matters such as independence and impartiality, and the duty to conduct proceedings with integrity, fairness, efficiency and civility."[24] The Code deals with issues of independence and impartiality (Article 3) limit on multiple roles (Article 4), a duty of diligence (Article 5), integrity and competence (Article 6), ex parte communication (Article 7) and finally, confidentiality (Article 8). Article 6 of the Code titled " Integrity and Competence" focuses on the interpersonal conduct of all parties appearing before IID proceedings as an aspect of competency when it states that "An Arbitrator shall: (a) Conduct the IID proceeding competently and in accordance with high standards of integrity, fairness and civility."

21. C.A. Rogers, Ethics in International Arbitration, Oxford University Press 2014, at p. 99.
22. *Ibid.*, p. 132. *See also* Brower abd Schill, "Regulating Counsel Conduct Before International Arbitral Tribunals" cited at (n 21) in Rogers.
23. ICCA Guidelines on Standards of Practice in International Arbitration, The ICCA Reports No. 9, 2021, https://www.arbitration-icca.org/icca-reports-no-9-guidelines-standards-practice-international-arbitration (accessed March 5, 2024).
24. https://icsid.worldbank.org/resources/code-of-conduct (accessed April 7, 2024).

Paragraph 45 of the Commentary to the Code explains Article 6 by stating that "The term 'civility' means being polite and respectful when interacting with participants in the IID proceeding. It is also associated with the Arbitrator's demonstration of professionalism." This is the only reference to interpersonal conduct by arbitrators in the Code, indicating that the personal conduct of the arbitrator toward other participants in the proceedings is a reflection of their professionalism.

V THE ICCA GUIDELINES ON STANDARDS OF PRACTICE IN INTERNATIONAL ARBITRATION

In 2021, with the assistance of the Permanent Court of Arbitration, the International Council for Commercial Arbitration [ICCA] published a report containing Guidelines on Standards of Practice in International Arbitration.[25] The report states that "The Guidelines originated from a concern that there have been repeated examples in international arbitration practice of conduct that falls below minimum civility standards and that the arbitration community should take action in response to demonstrate our shared commitment to practice international arbitration in a fair and legitimate manner."[26]

"The purpose of the Guidelines for Civility in International Arbitration is to establish standards of practice and conduct for all participants in international arbitration. These guidelines aim to promote integrity, respect, and civility among participants, ensuring a fair and legitimate arbitration process. The guidelines emphasize the importance of professionalism, cooperation, and respect for diversity in the international arbitration community. They also address the need for efficiency, confidentiality, and disclosure of conflicts of interest. The guidelines serve as a reference for participants to adhere to and promote a culture of civility in international arbitration."[27]

The General Guidelines for All Participants deal with issues of "integrity, respect, and civility vis-à-vis other participants in the arbitral process," *diversity and cultural backgrounds represented, refrain from any form of discriminatory conduct and* "timely and cost effective" *attitudes*. In addition to this general guidance, the Guidelines provide specific guidance for arbitrators, party representatives and other participants in arbitral proceedings.

According to Guideline III of the Guidelines for Civility in International Arbitration, arbitrators have specific duties in addition to the general standards applicable to all participants. It focuses on three aspects/areas of the duty of arbitrators to participants in international arbitration to wit:

(a) Arbitrators shall address all participants in an international arbitration in a courteous and impartial manner. Arbitrators shall not employ hostile, demeaning or humiliating terms in written or oral communications with participants in an international arbitration.

25. ICCA Guidelines (n 23).
26. *Ibid.*, at p. 1.
27. *Ibid.*

(b) Arbitrators shall ensure that all participants in an international arbitration conduct themselves in a courteous and respectful manner throughout the proceedings.
(c) Arbitrators shall act efficiently.

Guideline III A

The Arbitral tribunal's duty to treat all participants courteously and impartially focuses on the interpersonal relationship between the arbitrator and all other participants in the proceedings. The report identifies "Participants" in international arbitration as the parties and their representatives, counsel, arbitrators, tribunal secretaries, personnel employed by arbitral institutions who act in a particular case, fact witnesses, experts (either tribunal-appointed or party-appointed), professionals, and all other persons participating in the arbitration proceedings in any capacity.

In complying with this guideline to act courteously and in an impartial manner, the ICCA report identifies the need for arbitrators to "act with empathy and be sensitive to other participants' unique backgrounds and/or attributes on their communications."

In arbitral proceedings, failure to comply with this guideline can play out in several scenarios, such as the following:

- Lack of sensitivity by an arbitrator where counsel for one of the parties has a language barrier and is unable to follow the proceedings at the pace of the arbitral tribunal and the arbitral tribunal shows its irritation either verbally or through correspondence.
- Where a participant has confidence issues or is dealing with nerves/anxiety/inability to express themselves succinctly and the arbitrator expresses impatience or lack of empathy.
- Where the arbitrator fails to recognize cultural differences which can act as a barrier to the tribunal communicating effectively with a participant or even within the tribunal. Examples of a complete disregard for such cultural differences and religious beliefs are failing to provide timings that acknowledge that a participant who is Muslim might need to pray at certain times during the proceedings, or the presiding arbitrator fixing tribunal discussions for a time when a Muslim member should be breaking their fast.
- A lack of equal treatment for participants throughout the process. Sometimes, the arbitrator may show undue deference to the distinguished status of one of the opposing counsel or one of the witnesses, in relation to the other counsel or witnesses. Also over-friendliness with a particular counsel or other participants or any appearance of hostility toward a particular counsel. The same standard must be accorded to all parties.
- Actions or statements that indicate prejudices such as unconscious bias with respect to race, gender or age.
- Frequent and unnecessary criticism of counsel's arguments.
- Showing impatience with aspects of witnesses' testimony.

- Uninterested conduct shown through body language, lack of attentiveness, and side comments/remarks made about witnesses or counsel during proceedings.

All of the above instances require a standard of decorum, self-control, and emotional intelligence on the part of the arbitral tribunal when relating to the parties.

The responsibility of being the decision-maker puts the arbitrator in control of the entire process from start to finish. The examples of personal behavior that they exhibit are likely to be noted and possibly emulated by the other participants.

Guideline III B

Arbitrators' duty is to ensure that all participants in an international arbitration conduct themselves courteously and respectfully throughout the proceedings.

Explanation to Guideline III.B: Arbitrators have the responsibility to maintain control over the proceedings and ensure that all participants behave in a courteous and respectful manner. This duty includes addressing any disrespectful conduct by participants and taking appropriate measures to demand its immediate termination. The goal is to foster a productive and fair proceeding by promoting respectful behavior among all participants.

For a participant acting as a counsel, there is an implied duty based on rules of professional conduct to act courteously toward each other. However, this can only be relevant where all counsel in the proceedings are bound by the same set of rules of professional conduct/practice within the same jurisdiction. From the moment a dispute arises between the parties and a party chooses to kick start an arbitration, tensions and in extreme cases- animosity builds up between the main parties and this slowly builds up from an intentional decision to agree on the choice of a sole arbitrator [where this is what the arbitration agreement dictates], to issues of discovery, dates for meetings and hearing, to the inability to agree on timelines for various parts of the proceedings, during the main hearing up until closing submissions are filed.

As the ICCA report identifies, it behoves the tribunal to exercise "control" and take the role of umpire assiduously in ensuring "respectful conduct from all participants" given the tensions that may have arisen between parties.

An arbitrator in exercising this duty can comply with this guideline by doing the following:

- At the outset of the proceedings, parties should be reminded of the need to be courteous and respectful in all their communications with each other[28]- emails, documents, and other correspondence. Where parties are unable to agree on issues relating to timelines, discoveries, etc., this should be brought to the attention of the tribunal and where it appears that a party is deliberately recalcitrant, the arbitrator should indicate that such "guerilla tactics" will not be tolerated.

28. Carissa Laughlin, Maintaining Civility in Arbitration, https://www.finra.org/sites/default/files/2023-01/neutral-corner-volume-4-2022-1231.pdf (accessed March 21, 2024).

- The tribunal must prevent any arguments by parties that may likely result in emotional outbursts by cautioning parties not to speak over each other and to speak in turns. Cross-examination of witnesses should not be permitted to descend into bullying and unnecessary aspersions of falsehood. Participants should be asked to address the tribunal directly and not other co-participants for any requests.
- In situations where tempers are inflamed during the proceedings, a tribunal can take the initiative by calling a short cool-off period/ mute period for participants to restore normalcy and an atmosphere of ease.

In relation to difficult, disruptive, and disrespectful participants, the tribunal should firmly address and criticize any unwarranted behavior and request a redress by the offending party. In adopting this approach, the same/equal standard must be adopted toward all participants. The tribunal must however ensure that such behavior does not taint its ability to decide the dispute fairly and devoid of sentiments.

Guideline III (c): Arbitrators Shall Act Efficiently

Explanation to Guideline III.C: Arbitrators have a duty to act efficiently in the arbitration process. This duty encompasses several aspects, including the following:

- Devoting sufficient time and attention to the arbitration, taking into account the nature and complexity of the dispute.
- Familiarizing themselves with the facts and arguments presented in a timely manner to understand the dispute and make suitable decisions.
- Making themselves available during scheduled oral hearings and preparing adequately for such hearings.
- Respecting the schedules of all relevant participants when scheduling hearings, meetings, or conferences.
- Enforcing the applicable procedural rules to ensure the efficient resolution of disputes.

The ICCA Guidelines underscore the need for an "efficient process" which is essential for upholding justice, and the role arbitrators play in making sure this happens. Since parties in arbitration have opted for and solely entrusted the resolution of their disputes to a tribunal, it is tantamount to an abuse of the power conferred on such a tribunal for it not to act efficiently. The failure of a tribunal to act efficiently goes to the root of the legitimacy of the arbitral process as a means of dispute resolution. The issue of the legitimacy of arbitration has become topical with issues such as—transparency, costs, inconsistent decisions, double hatting, incessant and needless challenge to awards, length of time, and inadequacies being the focal points.

VI CAN ARBITRATORS ENFORCE CIVILITY DURING THE PROCEEDINGS?

To prevent and deter unethical behavior by parties in arbitration, it has been proposed that tribunals should, at the beginning of proceedings, forewarn parties that effectiveness and good faith will be emphasized, and any conduct contrary to this will not be accepted.[29]

Other rules and guidelines which deal with uncivil behavior by participants in international arbitration include[30] the ABA/AAA Code of Ethics for Arbitrators in Commercial Disputes 2004 which states that "persons who act as arbitrators undertake serious responsibilities to the public as well as to parties whose responsibilities include important ethical obligations."[31] To ensure compliance with this guideline, an arbitrator can, upon acceptance of the appointment, strive to maintain a polite and official relationship with all participants even those with whom there already exists a previous relationship and refrain from discussing any aspects of the case. It goes without saying that meetings with participants even in matters outside of the reference should be discouraged until the conclusion of the proceedings. The IBA Rules on Party Representation in International Arbitration which were adopted on May 25, 2013, to *address issues of counsel conduct and party representation that are subject to or informed by diverse and potentially conflicting rules and norms*[32] also provides an opportunity for arbitrators to enforce a polite atmosphere during the proceedings. After laying down rules for party conduct, Guidelines 26-27 of the Rules provide for sanctions which an arbitrator can apply in cases of misconduct by a party representative [defined in the Rules as a breach of the Rules "or any other conduct that the Arbitral Tribunal determines to be contrary to the duties of a Party Representative"]. The Arbitrator can draw attention to the Code at the commencement of the proceedings, indicate their expectations as regards civil behavior between the parties other than as stated in the Rules and indicate their intention to sanction uncivil behavior.

VII LIMITATIONS IN ENSURING CIVILITY

Lack of effective sanctions—In a survey conducted by QMUL in 2015 on the evolution of international arbitration, 46% of Respondents identified as of the worst characteristics of arbitration—"the lack of effective sanctions during the arbitral process."[33]

29. Browne and Price, Saving Time and Money by Sanctioning Bad Behaviour, 15(4) Transnational Dispute Management, https://www.lw.com/admin/upload/SiteAttachments/tv15-4-article01.pdf (accessed March 21, 2024) at p. 11.
30. Code of Ethics for Arbitrators in Commercial Disputes, July 1, 2014, https://www.adr.org/sites/default/files/document_repository/Commercial_Code_of_Ethics_for_Arbitrators_2010_10_14.pdf (accessed March 6, 2024).
31. *Ibid.*, at p. 1(preamble).
32. IBA Guidelines on Party Representation in International Arbitration, May 25, 2013, https://www.ibanet.org/MediaHandler?id=6F0C57D7-E7A0-43AF-B76E-714D9FE74D7F (accessed March 25, 2024), at p. 1.
33. https://arbitration.qmul.ac.uk/media/arbitration/docs/2015_International_Arbitration_Survey.pdf (accessed March 26, 2024), at p. 7.

Incidentally, the latter was again selected as the second worst characteristic of international arbitration in 2018.[34] The 2018 survey further enunciated the necessity of broadening arbitrators' powers and for them to take bolder approaches during proceedings with cost sanctions being awarded for dilatory tactics by counsel.[35] Except to the extent that the arbitrator has the power to sanction parties under the IBA Rules where the actions of a party representative may derail the arbitration proceedings, there are no other sanctions for impolite and uncivil behavior in the various Codes of Ethics for Arbitrators.

Non-binding nature of the rules and guidelines—Nearly all of the codes or guidelines specifically state that they are not legally binding on parties.[36] They can become enforceable only via the contract of the parties [by incorporation into the parties' agreement] or if adopted by the tribunal with the consent of the parties as part of the procedure for the arbitration proceedings.

VIII BEST PRACTICES AND RECOMMENDATIONS

Civility in the arbitral process is important as it limits the grounds for challenges to awards and protects the objectives of arbitration as a fair, just, timely, confidential, and cost-effective process.[37] Civility also cements the confidence of users of the process as it is a clear sign of a level and equal playing field between the parties. This will in turn protect the independence, legitimacy, and effectiveness of international arbitration.[38] Politeness and equal respect of the parties and the co-arbitrators among themselves therefore play a crucial role in ensuring the integrity and success of the arbitration process. It is by demonstrating civility that arbitrators contribute to building trust, maintaining transparency, and ultimately delivering justice in dispute resolution.

Microaggression—behavior that can be considered impolite or abrasive by parties or a co-arbitrator from a different legal or ethnic background[39]— can only be changed if the arbitrator is aware of how this behavior is perceived. Diversity and inclusiveness training is one way in which arbitrators can discover if their interpersonal conduct produces a less-than-conducive atmosphere for the arbitration proceedings.

34. This option was selected by 45% of Respondents in the 2018 survey. *See* https://arbitration.qmul.ac.uk/media/arbitration/docs/2018-International-Arbitration-Survey---The-Evolution-of-International-Arbitration-(2).PDF (accessed March 26, 2024), at p. 8.
35. *Ibid.*, QMUL 2018 survey.
36. This is explicitly stated in the introductory parts of the prevalent rules and guidelines. *See* Guideline 1 of the IBA Guidelines on Party Representation in International Arbitration (n 32), the preamble of the AAA/ABA Code of Ethics for Arbitrators in Commercial Disputes (n 30), the preamble of the ICCA Guidelines (n 25).
37. Deborah Lockhart, Ethical Obligations in Arbitration, Australian International Disputes Centre, https://disputescentre.com.au/wp-content/uploads/2015/02/Ethical-obligations-in-arbitration.pdf (accessed March 21, 2024).
38. Rogers (n 21), at p. 138.
39. https://en.wikipedia.org/wiki/Microaggression (accessed April 4, 2024).

Where the arbitral tribunal is seen by the parties to be externally cohesive and respectful in their conduct toward each other, and then expecting similar conduct from the parties, the arbitrators contribute to the fair and effective administration of justice in international arbitration.

CHAPTER 30

Improving the Utility of Fact Witness Statements for Arbitral Tribunals: Tell It as It Is, Not How It Should Be

Brandon Bang[*]

TABLE OF CONTENTS

I INTRODUCTION

In every submission made in the arbitral process, the perennial question that vexes an advocate is this: *what is the tribunal's view of my client's case?* Effective persuasion in international arbitration is as much about presenting a compelling case as it is about 'understanding what arbitrators feel and know, what they believe, and then providing them with messages consistent with these predispositions'.[1]

In this sense, it is hard to take issue with the proposition enshrined in Guideline IV.B of the ICCA Guidelines on Standards of Practice in International Arbitration (the *ICCA Guideline*) – that '[e]xpert and fact witnesses shall assist the arbitral tribunal and follow its directions' (*Guideline IV.B*) – not least because assisting the tribunal should arguably be the goal of every party to the arbitration.

However, does Guideline IV.B potentially limit the party's freedom to present its case and design a procedure that it believes will maximize the chances of winning? In

* Partner (Senior Foreign Attorney), Shin & Kim LLC, Seoul, Korea.

1. Donald E. Vinson and Klaus Reichert, *Arbitration: The Art & Science of Persuasion* (Oxford University Press 2022), p. 8.

this chapter, I explore the limits of one of the principles underlying the guideline, namely, that tribunals have an overriding authority to dictate the procedure, which may in turn, predetermine the type of evidence they prefer, based on their preconceived notion of what they believe to be 'good' evidence.

I propose to undertake two broad lines of inquiry, focusing on fact witness evidence. *First*, what counts as 'good' evidence? I tackle this question by reference to the English court reforms that have been adopted to improve the effectiveness of fact witness statements for English court proceedings (*section II*). *Second*, what tools and procedures can be adopted to produce more 'good' evidence in arbitral proceedings? Here, I explore whether certain English court reforms could be applied in international arbitration (section III). Then I conclude (section IV).

II WHAT IS AT THE CORE OF 'GOOD' FACT WITNESS EVIDENCE?

1 Adapting English Court Reforms on Fact Witness Statements to International Arbitration

Witness statements take centre stage in almost every arbitration proceeding. Evidence of fact produced by the parties enable the tribunal to perform its fact-finding function.[2] In modern international arbitration, witnesses are produced not merely to prove disputed facts. Rather, witnesses are deployed for a variety of purposes - to tell a party's story on a more personal level, to explain the context of documents exchanged in a business transaction, to appeal to the tribunal's sense of fairness, or sometimes simply because the other party has produced a witness.

However, there is growing frustration that fact witness statements are not being deployed in a manner that is helpful for the tribunal.[3] The root cause appears to be that counsel, rather than witnesses, often take ownership of the entire drafting process. This is sometimes inevitable in high-stakes litigation, which demands perfectionism and complete control. The control of witnesses and what they produce is merely one facet of this process. Thus, while we complain, we have become numb to the experience: 100-page witness statements supported by 100 documentary exhibits, prose plucked out of legal submissions (with a change of pronouns to the first-person), and parlance more fitting for counsel's chambers than for canteens at a construction site.

There have been many calls for reform. Nearly 25 years ago, the late V. V. Veeder QC in his seminal 2001 Goff Lecture observed 'an increasing tendency for a factual witness statement to take the form of special pleading prepared substantially by lawyers, ... [which] diminishes the statement's probative value and increases the need

2. Nigel Blackaby et al., *Redfern and Hunter on International Arbitration* (© Kluwer Law International, 7th edn, Oxford University Press 2023,), para. 6.124.
3. Julian Bickmann, *Fact-Finding in International Arbitration: The Emergence of a Transnational Lex Evidentiae* (© Kluwer Law International, Kluwer Law International 2022), para. 3.66.

for oral cross-examination'.[4] The same observation was made almost a decade later by Toby Landau KC in his 2010 Kaplan Lecture, that counsel-led drafting process results in statements that 'are often detailed and lengthy documents, which are costly to produce'.[5]

More recently, Professor Doug Jones has similarly observed that modern witness statements are over-lawyered.[6] He has been a proponent of a procedure that draws inspiration from the reforms introduced in the Business and Property Courts of England and Wales in 2021 (Civil Procedure Rules 1998 (U.K.), Practice Direction 57AC),[7] which is essentially for a return of witness statements to their original and, arguably, purest form as 'a short and curt recitation of a factual witness' memory of the events'[8] in the spirit of the now largely defunct practice in the common law courts where evidence-in-chief was taken orally.

Professor Jones proposes that procedural orders should reflect the following principles in relation to fact witness statements:

(i) subject to providing background context, the witness statement must only contain matters relevant to the issues in dispute of which the witness has personal knowledge;
(ii) the witness statement must not contain any supposition, speculation, conjecture, or commentary on another person's knowledge;
(iii) the witness statement must not contain any argument;
(iv) there should not be a recitation of the documentary record, or quotations from contemporaneous documents;
(v) witnesses should only refer to documents which they had received or were aware of before the dispute arose, and only if it is necessary to refer to the document; and
(vi) the witness statement should identify where documents have been used to refresh the witness's memory (whether those documents have been referred to or not in the witness statement).[9]

The basic aim for the proposal is to produce a witness statement that is shorter, based on what the witness can recall from what he or she has 'seen, heard, touched, or otherwise perceived'.[10] In essence, the witness should convey his or her side of the

4. V.V. Veeder QC, 'The Lawyer's Duty to Arbitrate in Good Faith' (The 2001 Goff Lecture) in Sam Wordsworth KC and Marie Veeder (eds), *On Arbitration: V.V. Veeder QC, Selected Writings and Contributions to the Development of Law* (Oxford University Press 2023), p. 215.
5. Toby Landau KC, *Tainted Memories: Exposing the Fallacy of Witness Evidence in International Arbitration* (The Kaplan Lecture, The Hong Kong Club 17 November 2010,), p. 5.
6. Doug Jones and Robert Turnbull, 'Witness Statements and Memorials: Reforms to Serve Parties, Arbitrators, and Arbitrations', *Journal of the American College of Construction Lawyers*, Vol. 18, No. 1, 2024, p. 65.
7. The Working Group cites to the same problem as the main driver for reform, which is especially 'endemic in the litigation of well-funded, document-heavy, business disputes': *see* Implementation Report of the Witness Evidence Working Group, 'Factual Evidence in Trials Before the Business & Property Courts', July 2020, para. 10.
8. Doug Jones and Robert Turnbull, 'Memorials and Witness Statements: The Need for Reform', *Arbitration: The International Journal of Arbitration, Mediation and Dispute Management*, Vol. 88, No. 3, 2022, p. 339 https://doi.org/10.54648/amdm2022024 (accessed 16 August 2025).
9. Jones and Turnbull (n 6) p. 70.
10. *Ibid.*, p. 66.

story in his or her own words, which cannot be obtained from the documents; where one needs to refer to documents, these can be incorporated in a memorial-style submission rather than cited (or recited) in the witness statements.[11]

Will such an approach help to improve the effectiveness of fact witness statements? This question is addressed below.

a *Can We Trust Our Own Memory?*

Who dislikes shorter witness statements? Especially ones without exhibits? Yet the belief that humans are a reliable conduit of their own experiences needs to be challenged. Human memory is fallible and recent scientific studies back this up.

The ICC Commission established a Task Force to look into the science behind the fallibility of human memory and evaluate the effect of memory on the value of witness evidence. In 2020, the Task Force issued a report (the *ICC Report*),[12] which draws attention to findings showing that even the memory of an honest witness is imperfect and malleable, and thus, subject to alteration or contamination by distorting influences as soon as it is formed.

What is concerning is that these external influences – referred to in the report as 'post event information' – come from interactions that are perfectly innocent and commonplace in a modern corporate environment we take for granted, such as '[t]alking to co-witnesses after an event, viewing media reports, or retelling an experience to friends or officials'.[13]

In particular, the ICC Report cites several studies that found, among other things, that certain wording, such as qualifying descriptors in questions, can materially influence the answers. For example, in one study, participants responding to the question 'Do you get headaches *frequently*?' tended to report an average of 2.2 headaches per week, whereas the question 'Do you get headaches *occasionally*?' generated reports of far lower average of only 0.7 headaches per week.[14] Lesson for arbitration? Interviews conducted by in-house or external counsel can have a profound impact on how witnesses recall their memory in preparing witness statements.

In another study, co-participants, who each viewed slightly different versions of the same film and consequently discussed the conflicting details they had noted, would often report details they had not seen on the memory test. The risk of such 'misinformation effect' is high in international arbitration, where disputes involve multiple persons with knowledge of the relevant events, many of whom work in teams, interact with each other as co-workers and are often interviewed together as potential witnesses by counsel.[15]

11. *Ibid.*, pp. 68-69.
12. ICC Commission Report, The Accuracy of Fact Witness Memory in International Arbitration: Current Issues and Possible Solutions (2020), para. 1.33.
13. *Ibid.*, para. 2.4.
14. *Ibid.*, para. 2.11.
15. *Ibid.*, para. 2.17. The "misinformation effect" refers to "a phenomenon where typically misleading information which participants are exposed to after an event interferes with or impairs their original memory of that event": *Ibid.*, para. 2.13.

What do the studies identified by the Task Force tell us, as counsel and arbitrators, about the reliability of witnesses' recollection?

First, whilst we can take pride in the fact that the modern system of international arbitration has evolved to a (relatively) predictable way of resolving cross-border disputes through standardized procedures, as Toby Landau KC noted in his Kaplan Lecture in 2010, we need to acknowledge that the preparation and presentation of witness evidence has received little scrutiny and 'developed without any regard for what is a very substantial body of scientific research on the operation of human memory'.[16]

Second, when witness statements rely heavily on witnesses' recollection, great care is needed to minimize distortion of their original memory. Professor Jones' sixth principle – that the witness should identify where documents have been used to refresh his or her memory – aims to reduce this risk by making transparent the process in which the witness' account has been incorporated into a witness statement. This appears to be an attempt to discourage the practice of showing witnesses swathes of documents, of which they have no first-hand or contemporaneous knowledge. The intended outcome is to limit the areas in which factual witness evidence is required and encourage the use of documents alone to support a factual narrative where possible.

These same concerns about voluminous documentary record have given rise to one of the more drastic requirements in the recently introduced Practice Direction 57AC (*PD 57AC*) in English court procedures, namely, that a witness statement submitted in English courts must identify *by list* any documents the witness has referred to, or been referred to, for the purpose of providing his or her witness statement.[17] The Witness Evidence Working Group[18] observed that because human memory can be 'complex, fragile and malleable', the process of treating the witness' recollection must be approached with caution, which the document-listing requirement is intended to address.[19] The question of whether the same requirement should be applied in international arbitration is discussed in *section 2* below.

Third, the fallibility of witnesses' recollection does not mean that documentary evidence is always more reliable than witness evidence. Text in a document can be misleading or ambiguous.[20] For example, minutes of meetings may simply reflect the author's subjective perception of events, which other participants in the meeting were unable to review.[21] In these circumstances, the tribunal may benefit from hearing directly from the witness to explain his or her account of the surrounding context to the document in question.

With this in mind, I now take a more critical look at whether the recent English court reforms would in fact be effective in removing the vices of modern witness

16. Landau (n 5) p. 2.
17. PD 57AC, para. 3.2.
18. A group comprising judges, barristers and solicitors working in the Business and Property Courts of England and Wales and a nominee representing lay client users, that had worked on the development of PD 57AC.
19. Implementation Report of the Witness Evidence Working Group (n 7) para. 43.
20. ICC Report (n 12) para. 4.16.
21. *Ibid.*, para. 6.13.

statements, or whether a more nuanced approach is required for international arbitration.

2 Are the English Court Reforms Appropriate for International Arbitration?

The starting point for analysis is Professor Jones' six principles, which were inspired by the English court reforms in PD 57AC and which he has already put into practice in arbitration cases. I consider each in turn.

a *First Principle: Subject to Providing Background Context, the Witness Statement Must Only Contain Matters Relevant to the Issues in Dispute of Which the Witness Has Personal Knowledge*

This principle should garner little to no objection. There is however a nuanced point that is worth noting.

Witnesses come with differing degrees of personal knowledge of relevant events. This may be due to the witness' role within a company or on a project at the time. For example, a project director who assumes an overall managerial role over a project may not have personal knowledge of the particular defect that was discovered on the ground, but would have become aware of it through the reporting line within the project management team. In a complex construction dispute where it is an important element of the claim to establish that the counterparty's breaches were the result of poor management of the project, it may be helpful for the tribunal to understand how the project was managed from a project director's perspective.

In that context, the project director should be able to give evidence on events even if he or she does not have direct knowledge of the same. Such evidence is often critical in understanding how complex projects were performed, especially if the project has been in delay for many years, and a bird's-eye view of the dispute (from a project director's perspective) can help the tribunal to connect the dots between the more specific evidence from other witnesses (who were closer to the claim events). Neither the case nor any particular claim may turn on such evidence, but parties should be entitled to adduce such evidence if they believe doing so would enhance the tribunal's understanding of the claim.

b *Second Principle: The Witness Statement Must Not Contain Any Supposition, Speculation, Conjecture, or Commentary on Another Person's Knowledge*

This principle could be understood as a bar to providing one's views or opinions, which generally falls within the province of expert witnesses. This principle should be applicable in almost all cases, but more so where the dispute has aged through the passage of time and is not well documented, as was the case in the recent case of *The*

Federal Republic of Nigeria v. Process & Industrial Developments Limited.[22] There, Knowles J noted that he found cross-examination that invited the witnesses' 'views', as opposed to 'their recollection or claimed recollection' of lesser evidentiary value.[23]

There are however cases in the margins where commenting on another person's knowledge may be helpful, if not necessary, to establish the full picture of a particular story. For instance, in cases where there is a debate as to what was discussed and the meaning of certain statements made at a meeting, there is no reason why one witness should be prevented from commenting on whether he or she believes the other witness' account of the discussion is true. One can imagine a situation where an opposing party's witness, given his or her seniority, was known by all personnel involved to have no direct experience of the matters discussed at a meeting (which discussion is subsequently memorialized in a document). Here, a party should be entitled to produce a witness to comment on the opposing party's witness' knowledge, even if the witness did not participate at the meeting, if he or she is aware that the opposing party's witness lacks direct knowledge of the relevant events and is therefore not in a position to provide a direct account of the discussions that took place at the meeting.

The above example illustrates that documents are not *inherently* more probative evidence: it depends on the way in which the document was produced. Indeed, the commonly accepted belief that documentary evidence is superior than oral witness evidence is being shaken by the rapidly changing definition of what a document actually is. Modern business is increasingly, if not predominantly, conducted through social messaging applications where the risk of equivocation is much higher than in e-mails or letters, as message-driven communication rely heavily on idiosyncratic language or private lexicon developed by the parties involved – in other words, what one sees in an exchange of messages may be mere fragments of the larger unspoken mapping of understandings and concepts, where parties were able to say things to mend working relationships in the interest of the project without the fear of contractual repercussions. To have such statements weaponized as documentary evidence against the author of the statements is to disregard the reality of what the parties had intended at the time. In these situations, witness evidence that can at least explain the context of the messages, such as what the counterparty's witness' knowledge was at the time, is critical to determining whether the messages are in fact reliable evidence for the proposition they are produced to support.

The alternative would be for counsel to explain how the messages should be interpreted, which may risk counsel giving evidence from the bar.

22. *The Federal Republic of Nigeria v. Process & Industrial Developments Limited* [2023] EWHC 2638 (Comm). The case is well known and its facts are not repeated here, but the court's task was to determine whether the award subject to a setting aside challenge (worth around USD 11 billion) was obtained by fraud or was against public policy under section 68(2)(g) of the Arbitration Act 1996.
23. *Ibid.*, para. 19 (though it must be said that Knowles J made this remark with "no lack of respect" to the "rigorous" examination conducted by counsel given how challenging of a task it was in that case).

c Third Principle: The Witness Statement Must Not Contain Any Arguments

It is important to be more precise about what an 'argument' is. It is trite that any legal and factual conclusions to be drawn from the evidence fall within the domain of counsel.

However, there may be situations where 'argumentative' evidence may be needed, if not expected. For example, where the attack is personal and goes to issues of dishonesty, it is far more credible for the witness, rather than counsel, to respond directly in the witness' own words that may be argumentative in substance, structure and tone.

d Fourth Principle: There Should Not Be a Recitation of the Documentary Record, or Quotations from Contemporaneous Documents

As with the first and second principle, this principle should be applied flexibly. Impractical outcomes may result otherwise.

As a general matter, court proceedings for complex and large disputes can stretch out for weeks or even months. Arbitration hearings are considerably shorter. Long oral openings that take several days or more are not uncommon in common law-style litigation, but they are rare in arbitration, even for the most complex disputes. Thus, there is less time for counsel to take the tribunal through important documents in oral openings, which often means witness statements must bear the burden of incorporating documents so that key documents can be put to the tribunal during witness examinations. Tribunals willing to sit longer hours to go through the documents in openings and closings may be one solution, but generally there should be flexibility in how documents should be deployed in witness statements.

e Fifth Principle: Witnesses Should Only Refer to Documents Which They Had Received or Were Aware of Before the Dispute Arose, and Only If It Is Necessary to Refer to the Document

Every counsel should ensure that witnesses strive to comply with this principle. Witnesses trying to 'own' documents of which they have no contemporaneous authorship or knowledge is a serious vice that reduces the effectiveness of witness statements. It enlarges the scope for cross-examination and wastes precious hearing time.

f *Sixth Principle: The Witness Statement Should Identify Where Documents Have Been Used to Refresh the Witness' Memory (Whether Those Documents Have Been Referred to or Not in the Witness Statement)*

As discussed above, this principle closely resembles one of the more controversial requirements introduced in PD 57AC. The requirement was only introduced by a majority and not a full consensus. It is therefore worth recounting the reasons for and against the requirement to see whether the requirement can be applied to international arbitration.

The core argument in favour of the listing requirement is that it would enhance transparency of the process of how witness statements have been prepared. It is desirable for the court to know up front if the witnesses have been subjected to an unreliable means to provide their recollections that end up in their witness statements. For example, witnesses may be shown documents they did not see when the relevant event occurred, and this would amount to leading the witness that can influence what is ultimately presented as their testimony; it is important that the court is made aware that this has or may have occurred.[24]

The main view against the listing requirement is that it will not achieve its intended effect because there is a possibility of adverse inferences being drawn if it is known through a list that witnesses have been shown large numbers of documents. The main concern is that there will be a chilling effect: witnesses may not be shown relevant documents at all during preparation of their statements to avoid documents from being listed, and such an internal culling exercise will eventually add to overall costs.[25] There is also a practical concern: in certain cases where the witness is also a client or the witness has 'lived with' the dispute for many years, it will be substantially difficult to identify the relevant documents.[26]

In my view, if witness statements are to become shorter and more focused, greater transparency of the documents that the witness has been referred to by counsel during preparations is desirable. I put forward four reasons.

First, given the fallibility of human recollection, it is essential that tribunals are aware of the process through which the witness has given input that has become their testimony in the arbitration.

Second, the listing requirement can promote more effective cross-examinations. First, the list can be used by counsel to discipline the witness if the witness seeks to provide commentary on documents it has neither referred to nor seen. Second, and arguably, the real purpose of cross-examination is not to test whether the witness has recalled an event correctly (in which case counsel can do no better than elicit the response that 'that is how I remember it', which is not helpful for the tribunal) but to 'subject the documentary record to critical scrutiny and to gauge the personality,

24. Implementation Report of the Witness Evidence Working Group (n 7) paras 42-44.
25. *Ibid.*, paras 48-50.
26. *Ibid.*, para. 53.

motivations and working practices of a witness'.[27] This must be right, because, as the Witness Evidence Working Group recognized, 'the important parts of a factual witness's testimony will be those parts that are not covered, or are incompletely covered, by the documentary evidence, together with any parts that appear to conflict with the documentary evidence'.[28]

Third, the list can help to discipline counsel in hearings. In particular, counsel in either cross-examination or redirect examination would give second thought to asking questions on documents that the witness is not familiar with. The problem, in my view, is more acute during redirect examination, where a well-battered witness after cross-examination would be inclined to self-correct what he or she has said, often through counsel who would also be eager to swarm the record with supposedly helpful documents that the witness has not seen.

Lastly, the concern that the listing requirement would be impracticable appears overblown. To the extent that documents are already referred to in a witness statement, there would be limited additional work involved in producing a list of documents that were used to refresh the witness' memory. This is because identifying the documents to elicit evidence from a witness is already part of the preparation process. In cases where the witness is also the client, the difficulty in identifying the relevant documents due to (for example) the client's direct involvement in engaging counsel is all the more reason why the process of listing the relevant documents should be managed carefully, irrespective of costs, because the client-witness' close familiarity with the dispute and the documents may pose a substantial risk on the value of the witness' testimony.[29]

In practice, the courts have applied the requirement in a measured and reasonable manner. In *Mansion Place*, O'Farrell J clarified that paragraph 3.2 of PD 57AC 'does not require the witness statement to list every document which the witness has looked at during the proceedings'.[30] In that case, the fact that there was no indication that documents not referred to have been used to refresh the witnesses' memories was immaterial because the key exchange in question was a telephone conversation, which could be tested during cross-examination. In another case, *Primavera Associates*, HHJ Paul Matthews stressed that the requirement does not apply indiscriminately, but only in relation to 'important disputed matters of fact'.[31]

III A PROPOSAL TO ASSIST WITH THE PROMOTION OF RELIABLE FACT WITNESS STATEMENTS

In this section, I set out a proposal that tribunals can adopt to improve the probative value of fact witness statements, inspired in part by the English court reforms, certain

27. *See Gestmin v. Credit Suisse* [2013] EWHC 3560 (Comm), para. 22, where Mr Justice Leggatt (as he then was) aptly observed that "[a]bove all, it is important to avoid the fallacy of supposing that, because a witness has confidence in his or her recollection and is honest, evidence based on that recollection provides any reliable guide to the truth".
28. Implementation Report of the Witness Evidence Working Group (n 7) para. 47.
29. *Ibid.*, para. 54.
30. *Mansion Place Limited v. Fox Industrial Services Limited* [2021] EWHC 2747 (TCC), para. 59.
31. *Primavera Associates Ltd v. Hertsmere Borough Council* [2022] EWHC 1240 (Ch), para. 61.

of which had already been voiced (many years back) by eminent authorities in international arbitration.

1 Certification by Legal Representatives

One of the new requirements introduced in the English court reforms is that a witness must provide a 'confirmation of compliance' in terms set out in paragraph 4.1 of PD 57AC, which are as follows:

> I understand that the purpose of this witness statement is to set out matters of fact of which I have personal knowledge. I understand that it is not my function to argue the case, either generally or on particular points, or to take the court through the documents in the case.
>
> This witness statement sets out only my personal knowledge and recollection, in my own words.
>
> On points that I understand to be important in the case, I have stated honestly (a) how well I recall matters and (b) whether my memory has been refreshed by considering documents, if so how and when.
>
> I have not been asked or encouraged by anyone to include in this statement anything that is not my own account, to the best of my ability and recollection, of events I witnessed or matters of which I have personal knowledge.

Notably, the second paragraph is a departure from paragraph 18.1 of PD 32, which requires the witness statement to be in the witness' own words 'if practicable'.[32]

In addition to certification of compliance by the witness, the legal representative is required, under paragraph 4.3 of PD 57AC, to endorse the witness statement with a certificate of compliance, certifying that:

1. I am the relevant legal representative within the meaning of Practice Direction 57AC.
2. I am satisfied that the purpose and proper content of trial witness statements, and proper practice in relation to their preparation, including the witness confirmation required by paragraph 4.1 of Practice Direction 57AC, have been discussed with and explained to [name of witness].
3. I believe this trial witness statement complies with Practice Direction 57AC and paragraphs 18.1 and 18.2 of Practice Direction 32, and that it has been prepared in accordance with the Statement of Best Practice contained in the Appendix to Practice Direction 57AC.

Notably, a legal representative is required to confirm that the witness statement has been prepared through a proper *procedure* (i.e., being satisfied that 'the purpose and proper content... have been discussed with and explained to ...'), which presupposes that the legal representative will not play a substantial role in the *drafting* of the witness statement.

Are there any impediments to applying a similar requirement to fact witness statements in international arbitration? There have been calls, made as far as back in 2001 by the late V.V. Veeder QC, for legal representatives to provide a declaration

32. Practice Direction 32, para. 18.1.

'giving his or her name and professional qualification, and giving information about how, when and where the statement was prepared, including a statement of time spent by witness and representative respectively'.[33] Perhaps requiring the *witness* to certify that the witness statement is in his or her own words is a step too far, in the sense that in many cases, witnesses genuinely require assistance from counsel to prepare a statement that is logical, accurate and relevant, especially if the witness does not speak the language of the arbitration, which is common in cross-border disputes. However, there does not appear to be any good reason why legal representatives cannot explain the process of procuring the witness statement, because that is in fact the reality[34] and should therefore be subject to a requirement of transparency.

2 What Should Be the Subject of Certification by Legal Representatives?

It should be uncontroversial that the overriding objective is to ensure that the witness statement is as closest to the witness' own words as possible.[35] It should also be accepted that this objective can be achieved with or without counsel's assistance in the drafting process; but more often than not, there is good reason for counsel to guide the witness to produce the evidence that will assist the tribunal by, for instance, identifying the key issues and the order in which to address them (such as chronologically or by themes).

Then what are some of the procedural matters that could be the subject of certification by counsel? The following list draws inspiration from the ICC Report and is far from exhaustive, but is presented to facilitate a further discussion.

First, certification that adequate guidance was provided to the first interviewer of the witness (which would typically be in-house counsel), in line with the six principles outlined above. In particular, counsel should inform the first interviewers that:[36]

(a) the process of recollecting witnesses' memory should take place as early as possible after the experience of the relevant event. There is a firm body of scientific study that shows that the period of time that has elapsed between an experience and its recollection is one of the primary factors influencing the durability of human memory.[37] Thus, if recollection occurs long after the event, there is a higher risk of error in the memory being recalled. To be clear, however, we should avoid over-regulation by requiring counsel to disclose the precise duration between the experience and its recollection;
(b) leading questions should be avoided. Only neutral and open-ended questions should be put to the witness;

33. Veeder (n 4) pp. 223-224.
34. Report of the Witness Evidence Working Group, "Factual Evidence in Trials Before the Business & Property Courts", July 2019, para. 44(v).
35. Jane Jenkins, *International Construction Arbitration*, Arbitration in Context Series, vol. 1 (© Kluwer Law International, 3rd edn, Kluwer Law International 2021), p. 311.
36. ICC Report (n 12) para. 5.5.
37. Landau (n 5) p. 16.

(c) only contemporaneous documents the witness has authored or has personal knowledge of should be used as an aide-mémoire to facilitate the recollection process. But the witness must be instructed to recount their memory before providing them with documents. This is necessary to establish recollections that exist independently of the documents and those that rely on documents;
(d) interviews should be conducted individually, rather than as a group, as the latter can cause memory contamination;
(e) witness should be instructed to not discuss the matter amongst co-witnesses or colleagues involved in the dispute;
(f) the persons needed to conduct the interview should be limited to those who can most effectively elicit an honest response from the witness. For example, persons who have ulterior motives in obtaining a particular narrative because they themselves are personally vested in the dispute should not conduct the interview.

Second, certification that the legal representatives themselves have complied with the six principles. More specifically:[38]

(a) If counsel is the first responder who would interview the witness in question, counsel should be in a position to confirm that he or she has taken the steps that the first interviewer was expected to take (see above).
(b) If counsel is not the first interviewer, counsel should establish with the witness how much prior discussion and contact the witness has had with the first interviewer and other witnesses or personnel. This is necessary to establish whether the witness has potentially adopted a party-line prior to interviewing with counsel. Counsel should conduct a fresh interview, in whole or in part, if necessary.
(c) If counsel were to take a substantial role in the drafting process, counsel should avoid producing multiple drafts of fact witness statements and certify that he or she has exerted best efforts to achieve this goal. This is not only recommended in the Appendix to Practice Direction 57AC,[39] but also based on scientific findings that multiple drafts have proven to have an undue effect on memory.[40] The risk is especially acute if statements are drafted by a 'committee' (of co-witnesses and counsel, for example).
(d) If coordination is required amongst multiple witnesses, counsel should confirm that it has taken measures necessary to ensure that each witness' memory is not co-mingled, which can cause memory corruption. For example, one should avoid each witness reading the drafts of other witnesses and ensure each witness statement is prepared independently.[41]

38. ICC Report (n 12) paras 5.6-5.28.
39. Appendix to Practice Direction 57AC, para. 3.8.
40. ICC Report (n 12) para. 5.26.
41. *Ibid.*, para. 5.27.

IV CONCLUSIONS

It is trite that tribunals should be assisted by the parties and the evidence they present through a procedure that tribunals believe will produce the best evidence for arriving at the right result. But party autonomy, a defining feature that distinguishes arbitration from litigation, must inform discussions about the procedures the tribunal prefers to adopt. As noted in the explanation to Guideline IV.B, the duties of expert and fact witnesses to assist the tribunal and comply with its directions are to be 'collaborative' – witnesses should have a clear understanding of their roles and the purpose of their evidence early in the arbitration in order to perform their duties effectively.

We must be cautious not to adopt an entrenched view of a hierarchy of valuable evidence and instead, appreciate that witness evidence can be effective even if they are not produced to recall one's memory. Specifically, a fact witness statement may nevertheless be useful to set the scene of the dispute, explain the context to important documents, tell one's story at a more emotional or personal level, and provide technical explanations based on one's experience, education, and knowledge.[42]

However, the fact that there is no one-size-fits-all solution does not mean that lines in the sand cannot be drawn. There is (or should be) common ground on what every fact witness statement should contain and the procedures and tools that can be adopted by tribunals to promote probative witness evidence. As part of our obligation to assist the tribunal, when preparing fact witness statements, we should rid ourselves of our advocative tendencies and be more like a documentary photographer who strives for authenticity and clarity – to tell it as it is, not how it should be.

42. *Ibid.*, paras 4.13-4.26.

CHAPTER 31

The Attack of the Clones: On the Road Towards a Unified Culture in International Arbitration?

Nicolás Gálvez Solís[*]

TABLE OF CONTENTS

I INTRODUCTION

In 1996, the International Council for Commercial Arbitration held its 8th Congress in Seoul, South Korea, titled 'International Dispute Resolution: Towards an International Arbitration Culture'. Since then, much has changed regarding both international arbitration and culture.

The last three decades have completely revolutionized the way we interact with each other. Technology, social media, content consumption and the immediate availability of information have irreversibly transformed the structure of our societies.

* *International Court of Arbitration of the International Chamber of Commerce.* Nicolás is a Guatemalan lawyer with a master's degree in transnational arbitration and dispute settlement from the University of Sciences Po in Paris, France. He has worked in the field of international arbitration for different law firms in both Guatemala and Paris. He currently acts as Counsel for the Secretariat of the International Court of Arbitration of the International Chamber of Commerce.

Cultures, and their differences, have gained immense importance, and international arbitration has not been spared. How we perceive each other's actions in terms of civility has not only changed but also increased in relevance.

Although some international arbitration practitioners are not yet attuned to the harsh reality that they need to adapt to other cultures, culture has been, and will remain, one of the most important considerations in international arbitration.

Almost thirty years ago, the late Pierre Lalive made a statement that perfectly reflects the importance of culture in international arbitration:

> If I had to sum up, in a few words, the most significant lesson I learned in several decades of practical experience as counsel or arbitrator, my choice would unhesitatingly fall on the extreme importance of the so-called 'cultural dimension'; together with one of its main consequences: i.e. the necessity of a 'comparative' approach and of a really international outlook.[1]

Professor Lalive's statement is as true today as it was thirty years ago and justifies taking a new look at how culture and international arbitration intertwine. This chapter then attempts to provide deeper insight into the effects that culture might have in arbitration and more specifically, on how the individuals participating in these proceedings behave towards each other. It will also examine whether international arbitration is heading towards a shared and uniform culture which could override most of the consequences brought about by this plurality of cultures, and if that is the case, whether this is for better or worse.

However, this chapter is far from an attempt at providing a concrete answer to these questions or a definitive prediction on the future of the relationship between culture and international arbitration. Rather, it is a series of observations, anecdotes, and opinions on how we behave when a Request for Arbitration lands in our inbox.

II CULTURAL DIFFERENCES IN INTERNATIONAL ARBITRATION: CONTINUED GROWTH AND THE NEED TO ADAPT

By virtue of its very nature, international arbitration attracts individuals from all over the world, as parties, counsel, experts, witnesses, arbitrators, or any other role commonly found in these proceedings. And as global trade continues to increase, contractual relationships bring together even more individuals with very diverse cultural backgrounds.

According to the statistics of the International Court of Arbitration of the International Chamber of Commerce (the '*ICC*'), the number of nationalities of parties participating in ICC arbitration continues to increase and in 2020 reached a record number with 145 nationalities among the parties in arbitration proceedings conducted under the ICC Rules of Arbitration. Likewise, the nationalities of arbitrators in ICC arbitration increased from 76 in 2012 to 92 in 2022.

1. Ian Meredith and Hendrick Puschmann, 'Notes on the Cultural Dimension of International Commercial Arbitration', SAR, vol. 5 issue 1, March 2016, p. 32.

The continued expansion of international arbitration only adds to the importance of understanding the way our own culture may affect how we act and communicate when engaged in one of these proceedings. As its growth continues, and in order to retain its legitimacy, international arbitration is called to adapt to the effect that this convergence of cultures undoubtedly has in the world of dispute resolution.

This need to adapt is precisely one of the driving reasons behind the creation of the ICCA Guidelines on Standards of Practice in International Arbitration (the '*ICCA Guidelines*'). The relationship between civility and culture is in constant evolution and which deserves continuous study by international arbitration practitioners. As the ICCA Guidelines accurately point out, civility in the practice of law is an essential attribute of maintaining the rule of law, and civility in such a diverse context cannot be analysed but from a cultural perspective.

The task force behind the drafting of the ICCA Guidelines decided to highlight the current lack of instruments reflecting the convergence of settings, cultures, and situations which co-exist in international arbitration. In fact, to address this void, the ICCA Guidelines have even gone so far as to include a specific guideline related to cultural differences, which provides that 'all participants shall respect all forms of diversity and cultural backgrounds represented in the international arbitration community and refrain from any form of discriminatory conduct'.

The ICCA Guidelines not only recognize the fact that international arbitration is comprised of a wide array of different cultures, but also, the fact that culture has the power to impact the proceedings in many ways, including our perception of the minimum standards of civility.

Arbitration practitioners have long realized that the junction of different cultural backgrounds in arbitration proceedings has practical implications. However, the extent of their actual importance has been debated.

Some authors consider that the role that culture plays in international arbitration is minor. They argue that international arbitration is 'culturally neutral', and they classify most cultural driven conflicts as legal or simply considering them procedural issue.[2] Nevertheless, even if it were true that most disagreements arising out of cultural differences are procedural and thus can be resolved by the applicable provisions, culture might have other implications on arbitration proceedings.

On the contrary, beyond the borders of international arbitration, it is generally understood that culture affects the way we interact with each other, our perception of right and wrong, the decisions we make and our approach to dispute resolution, among others.[3]

In fact, research shows that one's culture will most likely affect the way in which that person perceives a situation or reacts to certain stimulus. However, it is debated whether a closed environment, which presents a uniformity of practice, can to some

2. *Ibid.*, p. 31.
3. Anne Katrin Neyer and Anne Wil Harzing, 'The Impact of Culture on Interactions: Five Lessons Learned from the European Commission', European Management Journal, vol. 26, 2008, pp. 325-334.

degree, overrule the importance placed upon cultural differences.[4] Whether international arbitration could be considered as a closed environment due to the ever growing uniformity of its practices remains to be seen.

As the popularity of international arbitration as an alternative method for dispute resolution continues to grow, it also continues to attract an ever increasing number of cultures. In order then to properly understand the effect that this confluence of cultures may have, it is necessary to adapt the way we think and analyse culture in international arbitration.

III THE SIGNIFICANCE OF CULTURE IN INTERNATIONAL ARBITRATION: BEYOND LEGAL TRADITIONS

To properly understand how our culture affects the way we behave in international arbitration, it is first necessary to determine what can be considered as culture, which is easier said than done.

Throughout history, several different meanings have been attributed to the term 'culture'. Notably, scholars have indicated that 'culture' is one of the two or three most complex terms in the English language.[5]

Initial notions of culture used to refer to the knowledge of subject matters that are commonly regarded as intellectual, such as the arts or literature, i.e., a definition more akin to literacy than culture. This initial concept of the term was limited by the fact that, what could be regarded as worthy of being called culture was defined by certain minority groups, thus making culture the property of a few.[6] However, during the past century, the concept of culture has deviated from this Eurocentric definition and is now understood in a broader manner.[7]

Today, and for the purposes of this chapter, culture can be defined as the coming together of beliefs, knowledge, language, art, morals, law, and custom, acquired by forming part of a society.[8] All of these elements as a whole define our perception and ultimately determine the way in which we interact with others and the decisions we make.

One of the most interesting elements of this definition is that, by recognizing that these elements are acquired by forming part of a society, it can be concluded that most cultural elements will be determined by the region in which an individual lives, seeing as societies have traditionally been anchored to a geographical location.

Nevertheless, it is also worth mentioning that the continuous development of technology will no doubt call this conclusion into question sooner rather than later. The proliferation of online interactions over the last two decades have radically changed the way in which we socialize and has facilitated the existence of societies that manage to exist separately from a specific geographical location. It is therefore possible

4. *Ibid.*
5. Kevin Avruch, 'Culture and Conflict Resolution', US Institute of Peace Press, 1998, pp. 6.
6. *Ibid.*, p. 8.
7. *Ibid.*
8. *Ibid.*, p. 6.

that culture will be equally affected by our involvement in online societies in the upcoming decades.

In the short term, however, geography is still paramount when determining the elements that will have an impact on an individual's culture. Recent research demonstrates that nationality continues to strongly influence an individual's opinion and actions. For example, in 2020, researchers from the Massachusetts Institute of Technology and the University of British Columbia published a study which examined how individuals from different cultural backgrounds behave when confronted with complex decisions.[9]

The study is based on the Footbridge variation of the Trolley Dilemma, a thought experiment involving specific ethical dilemmas in which a person must choose between harming a group of people or a single individual. In 1976, the American philosopher Judith J. Thomson wrote a paper called 'Killing, Letting Die, and the Trolley Problem', in which she introduced a second version of the Trolley Problem (the 'Footbridge variation'):[10]

> George is on a footbridge over the trolley tracks. He knows trolleys, and can see that the one approaching the bridge is out of control. On the track back of the bridge there are five people; the banks are so steep that they will not be able to get off the track in time. George knows that the only way to stop an out-of-control trolley is to drop a very heavy weight into its path. But the only available, sufficiently heavy weight, is a man, also watching the trolley from the footbridge. George can shove the man onto the track in the path of the trolley, killing the man; or he can refrain from doing this, letting the five die.

The 2020 study, demonstrated that, when presented with the Footbridge variation of the Trolley Dilemma, individuals from Eastern Asian cultures (such as China and Japan) showed a stronger rejection to the sacrifice of a single individual for the sake of the greater good in comparison with people from Western cultures (such as the United States). These results indicate that when presented with a complex situation, culture (understood as influenced by nationality) is determinative to the decision that will be taken.

However, the effect that culture has on our actions extends beyond the decisions we take when faced with moral dilemmas. While international arbitration practitioners may not be asked to choose whether to sacrifice one person for the survival of five, arbitrators are still tasked with making decisions that in some cases can affect the entire population of a country, and counsel are made to interact with individuals whose sole intention is to prove them wrong. Experts and witnesses are also subjected to severe scrutiny by trained interrogation professionals wishing to pick apart every sentence they voice.

---

9. Edmond Awad et al., 'Universals and Variations in Moral Decisions Made in 42 Countries by 70,000 Participants', Princeton University, Princeton, NJ, 21 January 2020, available at: https://www.pnas.org/doi/full/10.1073/pnas.1911517117 (accessed 16 August 2025).
10. Panahi Omid, 'Could There Be a Solution to the Trolley Problem?', Philosophy Now, 2016, available at: https://philosophynow.org/issues/116/Could_There_Be_A_Solution_To_The_Trolley_Problem (accessed 16 August 2025).

The kind of high-stress, high-stakes environment present in these proceedings is the perfect trigger for culturally driven behaviour that extends beyond decision-making into smaller and seemingly less noticeable actions. When exposed to stressful situations, such as the ones encountered in dispute resolution, individuals tend to opt for more habitual responses rather than goal-directed choices, are less likely to adjust their initial judgment and rely more on gut feelings or social conditioning.[11]

This research demonstrates that cultural responses and considerations extend beyond simple decision-making. Recently, ICC, Jus Connect and McCann Worldgroup conducted a comprehensive study into the influence cultural factors will have on the success of business relationships between parties from diverse cultural backgrounds. The conclusions of the study are based on more than 1,700 quantitative interviews across nine countries and 20,000 data points.

The study finds that emotional and cultural elements spanning across the entirety of the business relationship, including dispute resolution, have a seven-fold effect on the success of the relationship when compared to other elements, such as logic-driven behaviour.

Therefore, even though some arbitration practitioners may consider that culture has a limited impact on international arbitration, scientific research and empirical data demonstrate that culture is simply present in everything we do.

As discussed below, cultural driven misunderstandings may be less likely to occur when the two individuals who are interacting are aware of their cultural differences. Nevertheless, normally, high-stress situations will drive individuals to resort to more cultural or instinctual responses.

Culture then can be understood to be a crucial elements that will affect the entirety of the arbitration proceedings, from the way counsel interact with each other to the decisions taken by the arbitral tribunal and by extension, the outcome of the case. This is not a foreign idea to arbitration practitioners. However, as mentioned above, most of the research and analysis has focused on the difference between legal cultures.

While it is certainly important, an analysis on the relationship between international arbitration and culture that focuses solely on legal traditions is severely limited.

Fundamentally, culture is at the very core of our behaviour, and as such, will influence all our interactions and our perception of others, including whether they are civil or not.

IV PRACTICAL IMPLICATIONS OF CULTURE IN INTERNATIONAL ARBITRATION

Given the importance culture has in how we conduct ourselves, one could argue that cultural driven interactions and their effects on civility would be easily identifiable. But

11. Rongjun Yu, 'Stress Potentiates Decision Biases: A Stress Induced Deliberation-to-Intuition (SIDI) Model' Neurobiol Stress, vol. 3, 12 February 2016, pp. 83-95 doi: 10.1016/j.ynstr.2015.12.006. PMID: 27981181; PMCID: PMC5146206, available at: https://www.ncbi.nlm.nih.gov/pmc/articles/PMC5146206/ (accessed 16 August 2025).

that is not always the case. While some cultural differences and their effects are quite obvious, others are much more subtle and require a certain degree of assumption. In conducting this exercise, it must be stressed that one should be very careful about attributing causality to seemingly cultural driven interactions.

With this observation in mind, I describe below situations which I have come across, or which have been experienced by colleagues and relayed to me. I consider that in the examples below, cultural differences may have played a part in how the situation developed, with the caveat that my knowledge on some of these cultures is limited.

One of the situations in which the cultural differences were easily observed involved a dispute between a Central Asian and a European party. In this case, during the in-person hearing, representatives of the Central Asian party brought gifts for the members of the arbitral tribunal. The arbitrators were initially taken aback by this, however, counsel for that party intervened and explained that, in their country, this was common practice. Indeed, gift-giving in Central Asia is a very complex subject and forms an integral part of their culture, which clearly motivated said party's actions.

While presenting gifts to the arbitral tribunal would appear completely normal in certain Central Asian cultures, and even required as a show of respect and goodwill, it is perceived in a completely different manner in other regions. Latin America poses a great point of comparison in this respect. In Latin America, actions such as this would not be perceived to be appropriate, not because Latin Americans are less welcoming or respectful, but because of its long term struggle with corruption, which is at times, present in local adjudicators. Latin Americans, without a proper understanding of Central Asian culture, would most likely misinterpret this gesture as an attempt to gain the favour of the arbitral tribunal.

Another interesting situation showcasing the different type of interactions between the parties and the arbitrators comes from a case in which all parties, their counsel, and the arbitrator came from countries located in South Asia. After having been appointed, the sole arbitrator refused to be the one who initiated contact with the parties. When the institution administering the case urged him to set up a case management conference, the sole arbitrator openly expressed that 'chasing' the parties and setting up the conference would be 'demeaning' and therefore 'he would not do it'. He then doubled down on his position by stating that he would not perform undignified tasks such as sending emails or arranging meetings.

After the institution administering the proceedings contacted him one last time to remind him of his duties as arbitrator, the sole arbitrator responded, in a manner which would probably not be considered civil by most, that 'no matter what they said' he would not 'demean his position', and that the parties should come to his office in person for the case to progress.

There are three interesting elements in this example, first, the sole arbitrator, the parties and their counsel all came from a region in which social roles are very well defined and where hierarchy considerations still pervade everyday lives. Second, the sole arbitrator was a retired judge, which probably reinforced the idea of the difference in standing between him and the parties. This may also provide insight as to why, menial tasks, such as sending emails or contacting the parties, could have appeared to be 'demeaning'. Finally, the sole arbitrator did not have any experience in international arbitration and was therefore unaware of usual practice or expected behaviour in these situations.

More often than not, cultural elements that result in interactions below the minimum civility standards can be attributed to ignorance, either of culture or of practice. In this case, it is clear that the sole arbitrator was not aware of his obligations or of the usual practice in international arbitration regarding communication with the parties. Moreover, the sole arbitrator did not recognize the difference in nature between the judicial and the arbitral functions, instead he addressed the situation in a way which he perceived to be culturally appropriate in his own jurisdiction.

Another, less evident example of cultural differences which can affect the perception of civility, presents itself in interactions between individuals that speak the same language, but that come from different regions or countries. This is the case between individuals that come from most Latin American countries and Spanish nationals.

It is well known that Latin American countries have each developed their own different ways of speaking Spanish. The terms, accents, and verb conjugations used in Mexico differ completely from those used in Argentina, and those used in Argentina differ from the ones used in Ecuador, and so on. The difference however is even greater between Latin American countries and Spain.

In Spain, the use of imperative sentences is standard when asking someone to do something, which denotes a more direct and no-nonsense approach. In Latin America on the other hand, people often communicate using interrogative sentences when in need of something from someone and avoid using imperative sentences in favour of a more nuanced approach.

For example, when in the process of drafting the Terms of Reference, a Spanish party may ask the other party to 'Send the draft Terms of Reference with your edits, please', while a Latin American would instead say 'Would you kindly provide the draft Terms of Reference with your edits?' In such a case, the no-nonsense approach by the Spanish party might take the Latin American party by surprise and even generate a certain degree of discomfort or rejection to this kind of language denoting an order or a command.

This is precisely what happened in a case between a Mexican party and a Spanish party. Throughout the proceedings, the Spanish party drafted its emails in a more straightforward manner, to which the Mexican party was not accustomed. Ultimately, the Mexican party drew the arbitral tribunal's attention to the alleged lack of cordiality from its counterpart. Even though no practical consequences derived from this, it is worth noting that a party felt the need to raise this point.

This case perfectly exemplifies the differences between high-context and low-context cultures. Low-context cultures are based on direct and unembellished use of language, with little reliance on paralinguistic cues. Conversely, high-context cultures are drawn towards an indirect and nuanced use of language.[12] The approach to

12. Kevin Avruch, 'Cross-Cultural Conflict', George Mason University, 2022, p. 11.

language taken by the Spanish party in this case was based on its low-context culture, leading to straightforward communication. The Latin American party on the other hand, was used to a high-context approach, where the precise way in which something is said, is sometimes just as important as what is actually said.

In this respect, parties coming from the United States present an interesting mix of a low-context culture and what could normally be a highly litigious approach to conflict. In several instances, this resulted in actions which other high-context cultures with a less litigious approach to international arbitration could consider as falling below the minimum standard of civility.

Also interesting are the interactions that have developed between parties from the United States and the institutions administering the arbitration. In several cases, parties from the United States with little experience in international arbitration have engaged in adversarial conduct towards the institution administering the arbitration. This conduct can be characterized by a very direct, low-context, approach to communication. This is another situation in which, lack of knowledge of international arbitration, can lead a party to resort to culturally comfortable conduct. The lack of understanding regarding the role the institution plays, and the way in which the parties are expected to interact with it, can potentially result in dissonance as to the level of civility that is expected.

As explained above, these are merely examples in which culture might have influenced the actions of the parties. However, it is clear that culturally based disagreements regarding civility appear to be avoidable through the understanding of the different cultures with whom we interact.

It is important to question whether we will reach a point where, either through the understanding of different cultures, or the influence of other factors, cultural differences will be less impactful.

V WILL CULTURE CEASE TO MATTER IN INTERNATIONAL ARBITRATION?

The simple answer to this question is no, or at least, not any time soon.

However, there are two factors that might push international arbitration in that direction. The first one is a phenomenon that I like to call the 'Attack of the Clones'.

Today, international arbitration is taught as a separate, stand-alone, subject in many universities across the globe. The rise in popularity of international arbitration as a subject has resulted in the propagation of an international arbitration culture which ensues a uniformity of practice in both the way the proceedings are conducted and the way we behave while participating in them. Said arbitration culture has, no doubt, trickled down from senior arbitration practitioners who have developed the culture of international arbitration in the last decades and have cultivated certain standards and expectations of conduct.

This means that most students wishing to specialize in international arbitration will receive the same courses, recounting the same practical cases (including issues such as behaviour and civility) taught mostly by the same professors, and will finally end up working in the same cities, for the same law firms.

These young lawyers will then often apply for the same positions and, on paper, are almost indistinguishable from each other, not unlike the well-known clones in the Star Wars films. Following in the step of George Lucas' clone legions, the current landscape of international arbitration perpetuates the existence of a closed environment which calls for uniformity of practice and requires parties, counsel, arbitrators and other participants to adapt to a specific model of conduct and civility.

Another factor pushing towards the existence of a uniform arbitral culture is technology. The immediate availability of information, and the rate at which we consume digital content results in greater and continuous exposure to different cultures through digital means. As demonstrated by the examples above, the likelihood of cultural driven misunderstandings increases when one or both parties ignores the cultural elements driving the other's actions.

If we consider that most of the misunderstandings or actions below the minimum standard of civility arise from lack of knowledge, we can conclude that greater knowledge of different cultures will reduce the instances in which these differences impact the way we act.

As a side note, it is interesting to note that technology is also affecting our cultural composition by facilitating the existence of online societies, detached of any physical location. Ethnography now considers that, by constructing their own cultures, online communities are capable of affecting notions of self and the way in which we relate to others in both a personal and a professional environment.[13] Therefore, the way we think of culture in international arbitration, mainly linked to the idea of nationality, is also likely to change in the future.

The real question is therefore not whether culture will cease to matter, but rather whether our personal culture will be replaced by arbitral culture.

To a certain degree, that is already the case.

However, as indicated above, uniform arbitral culture is not going to completely eclipse the importance of our personal culture any time soon. There are two main reasons for this.

The first reason is international arbitration's call for diversity.

Until the first decade of the 21st century, international arbitration practitioners were mostly white, Western European, men. However, over the past fifteen or so years, international arbitration practitioners alongside international arbitration institutions, such as the ICC, have made a tremendous effort to increase diversity in international arbitration. The call for diversity and inclusion comprises, but has not been limited to, cultural, racial, ethnic, generational, disability and gender diversity. This new influx of cultures has highlighted our differences, in a positive way, and has increased the importance of understanding each other's cultures and our own cultural bias.

13. Robert V. Kozinets, Pierre-Yann Dolbec and Amanda Earley, 'Netnographic Analysis: Understanding Culture Through Social Media Data', 2014, in Uwe Flick, ed. Sage Handbook of Qualitative Data Analysis, Sage, pp. 262-275.

The second reason why uniform arbitral culture will not override personal culture is the fact that a uniform arbitral culture is not, in and of itself, detrimental to international arbitration. Being conscious of our differences and striving for common understanding has been a part of international arbitration since its inception. So long as arbitral culture continues to recognize the importance of personal culture, both can, and should, co-exist.

A uniform arbitral culture brings certainty to the table, provides a minimum standard of civility, and contributed to effective communication within the proceedings, reducing the risk of cultural driven misunderstandings. On the other hand, the personal culture of the parties, the arbitrators and other participants adds in depth to effectiveness of international arbitration as a dispute resolution mechanism. Knowledge of cultural nuances might help the arbitrators uncover the true meaning behind the actions of the parties and understand the way they interact with each other, be it contractual relationships or civility.

International arbitration is, first and foremost, a mechanism for the resolution of disputes, and as a tool, it must adapt to the requirements of its users, rather than the opposite. International arbitration should then be a catalyst for the convergence and understanding of different cultures and should serve as a reminder to everyone that they will most likely experience cultural differences with their counterparts, arbitrators, or counsel.

Personal culture and arbitral culture could then be considered as convergent parallel lines that continue to approach each other, without ever actually merging into one.

VI CONCLUSION

The traditional approach to cultural analysis on international arbitration may be relevant, but it is shortsighted. Culture affects international arbitration far beyond the traditional discussion on the differences between the civil law and common law legal traditions. This proves even more true as international arbitration continues to expand and attract individuals from all over the world.

Culturally influenced misunderstandings in issues such as civility are driven by other elements of our culture, such as language, religion, cordiality, and our general approach to communication. Notably, disagreements on civility are usually accompanied by a lack of knowledge of either arbitral practice or the other party's culture. In that respect, technology, by way of exposure to different cultures, is increasing our understanding and reducing the risk of a misunderstanding.

A uniform arbitral culture may also reduce the frequency of situations in which parties' behaviour may fall below the minimum standard of civility. However, a uniform arbitral culture won't displace the importance of personal culture any time soon. The call for diversity in international arbitration provides A New Hope, and once again increases the relevance of distinct cultures converging in international arbitration.

Twenty-eight years ago, at the 8th ICCA Congress in Seoul, Ahmed S. El-Kosheri endeavoured to analyse the relationship between arbitral culture and Arab-Islamic juridical culture. One of his conclusions at the time, which continues to echo, and perfectly exemplifies the sentiments of this chapter, was:

> We should not be striving for uniformity, but rather flexibility.[14]

14. Ahmed Sadek El-Kosheri, 'Is There a Growing International Arbitration Culture in the Arab-Islamic Juridical Culture?', 1996, in Albert Jan van den Berg, ed. International Dispute Resolution: Towards an International Arbitration Culture, ICCA Congress Series, No. 8 (Kluwer Law International; ICCA & Kluwer Law International 1998), pp. 47-48.

CHAPTER 32

ICCA Guidelines: Their Relevance to an Arbitrator's Duty to Investigate Suspicious Circumstances and Standards of Factual Witness Preparation

Matthew Gearing KC[*]

TABLE OF CONTENTS

I ICCA GUIDELINES: CONTEXT AND BACKGROUND

The ICCA Guidelines on Standards of Practice in International Arbitration (*ICCA Guidelines*) represented the culmination of the work of the ICCA Task Force on Standards of Practice in International Arbitration. The Guidelines set out the minimum standards of civility that extend to all participants in the arbitration process: the arbitrator, the party representatives, the witnesses as well as the parties themselves. The Guidelines, while not a binding set of rules, nonetheless reflect basic principles of civility shared across different legal cultures. This chapter focuses on three aspects set out in the Guidelines: guidelines for the arbitrators, guidelines for the party representatives vis-à-vis the witnesses, and guidelines for the witnesses.

At the heart of the ICCA Guidelines is the objective of preserving the integrity of the arbitral process. While arbitration usually creates a sphere of confidentiality

* Arbitration lawyer and former Chairperson of HKIAC. He is a Hong Kong solicitor-advocate, a member of the HKIAC, SIAC, and KLRCA arbitrator panels, and was previously a partner at a magic circle law firm.

favoured by commercial parties, the countervailing concerns of lack of transparency, lack of public oversight over the process could undermine the legitimacy of the system. Deliberate ethical breaches by arbitrators and party representatives obviously represent clear red lines not to be crossed. But more problematic is the grey zone – what if arbitrators fail to spot the red flags in the underlying transactions, and unwittingly aid corruption and bribery? What if party representatives prepare witnesses in a way that may be deemed acceptable in their home jurisdictions but constitute unacceptable witness coaching to the counterparties? The differences in legal culture and background of the parties, coupled with the lack of a consistent standard, continue to persist. This chapter attempts to explore the boundaries of appropriate lines in the sand for arbitrators and party representatives, and suggests how the Guidelines can be helpful in establishing the minimum standard of integrity in order to enhance the legitimacy of the arbitral process.

II ARBITRATOR ETHICS: THE DUTY TO INVESTIGATE CORRUPTION?

1 Whether Such a Duty Exists

Arbitrators should obviously be cognizant that the arbitral process can be abused to enforce an award pursuant to a contract procured through or tainted by corruption. There is little doubt that corruption contravenes international public policy.[1] It is widely accepted that an arbitral award that enforces a contract procured through corruption may be set aside based on the New York Convention.[2] However, whether arbitrators have a duty to investigate allegations of corruption sua sponte, i.e., of their own motion, where it is not otherwise argued, is far less clear. While there is no express mention of corruption in the Guidelines, it is axiomatic that a corrupt contract or a corrupt process directly contravenes the integrity of the process. Thus, the general duty of integrity (Guideline I.A) can be clearly deployed to justify an enquiry into potential corruption, or even into circumstances that just 'don't' look right'.

If an allegation of corruption was raised in parties' pleadings or raised in the course of the arbitral process, the argument that the tribunal needs to decide the issue is strong, in light of the tribunal's duty to consider and resolve public policy issues presented by parties.[3] In *Worley v. Ecuador*,[4] the tribunal found that the Worley entity had engaged in illegal conduct at the inception of its investment, and throughout the performance of the contracts. In particular, the tribunal found that Worley offered undue advantages to Petroecuador officials throughout the life of the contracts –

1. ICC Case No. 1110 (1963), cited in Case No. 5622/88 of Jean-Jacques Arnaldez et al., ICC Arbitral Awards III 220, 233-234 (1997).
2. *See, e.g.*, section 24 of the Singapore International Arbitration Act, US Federation Arbitration Act sections 10(a)(1) and (2), Chinese Arbitration Law, Article 58(6).
3. Gary B Born, Chapter 19: Choice of Substantive Law in International Arbitration, in International Commercial Arbitration 2706, 2915 (3rd ed. 2021).
4. *Worley International Services Inc. v. Republic of Ecuador*, PCA Case No. 2019-15, Final Award (22 December 2023)

including a USD 22,000 trip for four officials and two of their spouses to watch the Formula 1 grand prix in Austin, Texas. Such benefits granted to the Petroecuador officials had no legitimate business purpose, and had the ultimate effect of securing for Worley six complementary agreements for the Esmeraldas refinery without a public procurement process in 'blatant disregard' of Ecuadorean law. The tribunal was able to make such strong findings uncovering the underlying bribery because this allegation was in fact pleaded.

However, where there is no assistance from counsel, and the fraud or bribery allegation is not part of a party's case, the tribunal's duty to investigate fraud and corruption is less clear cut. That was in fact the case in *Nigeria v. Process & Industrial Developments Limited*,[5] an arbitral award granting the claimant Process & Industrial Developments Limited (P&ID) against the Federal Republic of Nigeria more than USD 11 billion based on the alleged failure to perform a 'Gas Supply and Processing Agreement for Accelerated Gas Development' (GSPA). The GSPA was entered into in 2010, and P&ID was awarded the right to process billions of dollars of natural gas despite the lack of any track record in the oil and gas industry. The duration of the contract was for twenty years. P&ID commenced arbitration against Nigeria, relying on the arbitration clause in the GSPA in the third year, alleging that Nigeria had failed to supply specified quantities of 'wet' gas to P&ID's Gas Processing Facilities pursuant to its obligations under the GSPA.

The arbitral tribunal found in favour of the claimant and awarded the claimant USD 6.6 billion plus 7% interest (as a result of the interest, the amount due increased to USD 11 billion). Before the setting aside of the award in the English Commercial Court in 2019, the change of government in Nigeria led to an investigation of the GSPA, where it was found that the legal director of the Nigerian Ministry of Petroleum Resources had received bribes from P&ID before and after entering into the GSPA. Armed with these findings, Nigeria sought to set aside the award in the English Commercial Court. Nigeria raised a host of arguments concerning bribery and corruption by P&ID before, at and after the time parties entered into the GSPA, and allegations that its own lawyers during the arbitration were corrupted by P&ID. Although Knowles J did not accept the entirety of Nigeria's case on corruption by P&ID, he found that the awards (comprising the liability award and the final award on damages) in favour of P&ID were obtained by fraud and procured in a manner contrary to public policy, and set them aside on that basis.

The fact remains that none of these corruption allegations were raised before the tribunal by Nigeria. In fact, the lack of proper representation on the part of Nigeria and the serious procedural irregularities that resulted were acknowledged in the judgment by Knowles J. The Judge found that the underlying GSPA had been procured by bribery and corruption, and the entire arbitration process, had been tainted by corruption by P&ID. P&ID had in its possession more than forty of Nigeria's internal legal documents, many of them privileged, which allowed P&ID to monitor the advice Nigeria had received in the course of the arbitration and related settlement discussions. There was

5. [2023] EWHC 2638.

no reasonable explanation for how P&ID came to possess such documents.[6] Although Knowles J did not go as far as to accept that there was corruption of Nigeria's lead counsel in the arbitration, he did state that 'legal representatives did not do their work to the standard needed, [...] experts failed to do their work, and [...] politicians and civil servants failed to ensure that Nigeria as a state participated properly in the Arbitration'.[7] There were many 'inexcusable delays and failures to engage' on the part of Nigeria. During the quantum phase of the arbitration, Nigeria's expert witness did not appear to have been shown the expert evidence presented by P&ID,[8] nor did its counsel address the issues raised by P&ID's experts. Nigeria was frequently allowed multiple opportunities to deal with P&ID's submissions and evidence, but did not do so.[9]

Besides the unsatisfactory way in which Nigeria's case was presented in the arbitration, the question remains as to what the arbitrators should have done. Knowles J's remarks were equally pointed. Knowles J did not consider that 'the Tribunal did all that it could to find out more about the points, by questions of Nigeria's legal representatives'.[10] Knowles J highlighted a few circumstances that should have warranted further intervention from the tribunal: (a) the briefness of the 20-page GSPA which was striking given the context of a multi-billion dollar long term project of national significance; (b) why Nigeria would have agreed to such 'catastrophic terms' if the tribunal's findings on liability were correct; (c) the vast sums of public money involved against Nigeria's struggling to meet deadlines, bringing forward factual and expert evidence in the conduct of the case.[11]

While Knowles J clearly found the arbitrators' approach wanting, there are contrary views in the arbitration community that arbitrators are not under a duty to decide corruption-related issues unless they are express requested to do so.[12] This is in line with the view that arbitrators are contracted to perform services in the interest of the parties and to decide the issues as put by the parties, not as they might be put. Arbitrators are remunerated by parties, and not bound by precedents, nor have any broader duty to contribute to the development of the law.[13] Further, if an arbitrator chooses to intervene and investigate corruption, where parties have not pleaded such issues, challenges may arise in particular in respect of an appearance of bias. Others question whether arbitrators, especially those sitting on their own, are equipped to

6. *See ibid.*, at [453].
7. *Ibid.*, at [587].
8. *Ibid.*, at [398].
9. *Ibid.*, at [337]-[352], [398].
10. *Ibid.*, at [399].
11. *Ibid.*, at [314].
12. Case No. 7047 of 1994, 21 Y.B. Comm. Arb. 79, 93 ¶ 54 (ICC Int'l Ct. Arb.) (The tribunal held that 'The word "bribery" is clear and unmistakable. If the defendant does not use it in his presentation of facts an Arbitral Tribunal does not have to investigate. It is exclusively the parties' presentation of facts that decides in what direction the arbitral tribunal has to investigate').
13. 'Chapter 5: An Obligation or Discretionary Power to *Sua Sponte* Investigate?', in Emmanuel O. Igbokwe (ed.), Dealing with Bribery and Corruption in International Commercial Arbitration: To Probe or Not to Probe, International Arbitration Law Library, vol. 65 (© Kluwer Law International; Kluwer Law International 2022), p. 204.

investigate corruption to the same level as a national public authority, especially where allegations of corruption do not form part of the parties' cases.

Nigeria v. P&ID is an exceptional case, but it sheds light on the issue of corruption and how arbitrations behind closed doors may be used as an improper vehicle for advantage.[14] Especially where a State is involved in the arbitration and public interests are at stake, the narrow contractual theory of the arbitrator's role no longer holds true. The Singapore International Commercial Court in *Lao Holdings NV v. Government of the Lao People's Democratic Republic* similarly affirmed, citing numerous investment arbitral awards, that investment arbitral tribunals, like 'national courts ... have a pro-active role and cannot simply ignore evidence of corruption'.[15] Hence, this duty arises not only where the arbitral tribunal has to deal with allegations of corruption in the dispute between the parties but also where the evidence in the case indicates *possible* corruption. Moreover, regardless of whether it is arbitration or litigation, illegality of a contract is often part of the overriding mandatory rules, and the failure to plead such issues cannot cure the illegality. There is also recognition that arbitrators perform judicial functions and are accorded quasi-judicial status, such as in the form of relevant immunities.[16] In many systems, their independence and impartiality are considered by reference to the same standards as judges.[17] Such status brings with it accompanying responsibilities, including that arbitrators should remain vigilant about any red flags present in the transactions. There is no dearth of guidelines to help arbitrators identify potentially suspicious transactions that call for an explanation, and there are practical steps for the tribunal to consider taking to discharge such a duty to investigate sua sponte.

2 Practical Steps for the Tribunal

Several guidelines are designed to help arbitrators to identify red flags in the arbitral process, as the Corruption Toolkit for Arbitrators,[18] the Guide to the U.S. Foreign Corrupt Practices Act setting out the common red flags associated with third parties,

14. There are also cases where the arbitration agreement and the resulting arbitration and award are a fiction, designed to give effect to a fraud. *See Contax Partners Inc BVI v. Kuwait Finance House (KFH-Kuwait) & Ors* [2024] EWHC 436 (Comm). Such cases are beyond the scope of this chapter.
15. *Lao Holdings NV v. Government of the Lao People's Democratic Republic and another matter* [2021] SGHC(I) 10 at [153].
16. *See, e.g., Song Lihua v. Lee Chee Hon* [2023] HKCFI 1954, where the Hong Kong Court of First Instance considered that arbitrators enjoy the same immunity available to judges in respect of their decision-making, such that they may not be compelled to give evidence. *See also* sections 3-4, English Arbitration Bill 2023, extending immunities enjoyed by arbitrators: https://bills.parliament.uk/publications/53038/documents/4022#sec_3 (accessed 16 August 2025).
17. The real danger of bias test, as set out by Lord Goff in *R v. Gough* [1993] AC 64, applies to judges and arbitrators in the English legal system (and elsewhere; *see* for example, *Grieve (T/As BG Grieve Builder) v. Gould* [2022] WASC 413; Western Australia Supreme Court).
18. Basel Institute on Governance Corruption and Money Laundering in International Arbitration – A Toolkit for Arbitrators.

such as third-party 'consulting agreements' with vaguely described services.[19] Other examples include over-payment of commission fees to an agent that are manifestly disproportionate to the value of his service, or other circumstances that give rise to a reasonable suspicion that the contract has been tainted by corrupt acts. Academics have further proposed the specific investigative steps the arbitrators could take under the relevant institutional rules, such as calling on the parties to provide for evidence, drawing adverse inference where the party in possession of the relevant evidence and fails to satisfy the burden of proof and requesting assistance from the court of a State.[20]

The duty to investigate is especially important where one side is disproportionately underrepresented. It is arguably open to a tribunal to take on a more interventionist role in examining the witnesses, in a manner that does not affect the appearance of its impartiality. In *Zhongshan v. Nigeria*, the Respondent state, facing a damages claim of over USD 1 billion, did not produce an expert witness during the quantum phase. The tribunal therefore made further enquiries in relation to the methodology and underlying assumptions adopted by the claimant's quantum expert, and arrived at a damages figure that was only a fraction of that contended for by the claimant.[21]

Tribunals should therefore remain vigilant as to red flags present in the arbitration, and take appropriate steps where there is prima facie evidence of corruption, or even something that 'does not quite like right'. Practical steps such as adopting a more interventionist approach in examination of the witness do not necessarily jeopardize the impartiality of the tribunal. On the contrary, there is not a body of precedent to show that tribunals are at real risk of a successful challenge where they have investigated claims of corruption on their own motion. The duty to investigate does not equate to the duty to ensure that there is no corruption – it is beyond the arbitrator's power to ensure such an outcome, similar to the arbitrator's duty of best efforts to render an enforceable award. Further, the duty to investigate prima facie suspicions of corruption should be deemed to be part of the arbitrator's duty to render an enforceable award.[22] In this regard, ensuring the integrity of the arbitral process is repeatedly emphasized in the ICCA Guidelines. Guideline I.A of the ICCA Guidelines makes clear that all participants shall act with integrity, respect, and civility vis-à-vis other participants in the arbitral process. Guideline I.F specifically requires parties to disclose conflicts of interests and/or facts or circumstances that may call into question the integrity of the arbitration process. The explanatory notes to these principles highlight the need to adhere to 'basic standards of integrity, honesty and candor'[23] to facilitate the administration of justice. The Guidelines therefore acknowledge the role of the

19. A Resource Guide to the US Foreign Corruption Practices Act, Criminal Division of the US Department of Justice, the Enforcement Division of the U.S. Securities and Exchange Commission (2012) at p. 22.
20. 'Chapter 6: Investigating Bribery and Corruption in Practice', in Emmanuel O. Igbokwe (ed.), Dealing with Bribery and Corruption in International Commercial Arbitration: To Probe or Not to Probe, International Arbitration Law Library, vol. 65 (© Kluwer Law International; Kluwer Law International 2022) pp. 251-290
21. *Zhongshan Fucheng Industrial investment Co Ltd v. the Federal Republic of Nigeria* (Case 1:22-cv-00170), Final Award, 26 March 2021.
22. ICCA Reports, pp. 8, 9,
23. *See* Explanation to Guideline I.A, ICCA Reports.

arbitrator as a person performing a judicial task, rather than a mere contracting party beholden to the parties.

III PARTY REPRESENTATIVE AND WITNESS PREPARATION: THE CLASH OF CULTURES?

Party representatives also have a key role in ensuring the integrity of the arbitration process. Guideline II.D specifically provides that '[p]arty representatives shall not engage, without legitimate reasons, in activities intended to obstruct, delay, or disrupt the arbitration process or to jeopardize the finality of any award'. This precludes conduct that jeopardizes the integrity of the arbitral proceeding, encompassing all aspects of the arbitration proceedings from the constitution of the tribunal, to dealings with witnesses and experts and the conduct of the hearing.[24] Some examples of unacceptable conduct are set out in the ICCA Guidelines, such as unreasonably delaying the production of evidence requested by arbitrators, challenging the jurisdiction of arbitral tribunal, or filing claims, defences or challenges without any good faith or serious basis.

The prohibition against obstructive conduct may also encompass interference with the honest and complete evidence of the witness. Guideline I.A has set out the broad rule of integrity which applies to all participants of the process. There is a corresponding duty on the part of the witnesses to 'speak the truth concerning the facts that are within their knowledge and to offer opinions that reflect their sincere belief', as emphasized in the explanation to Guideline IV.A that both the expert and fact witnesses 'shall be honest in their testimony before an arbitral tribunal.' The role of the expert and fact witnesses, as provided by Guideline IV.B, is to assist the tribunal. They are therefore duty-bound to follow the arbitral tribunal's instructions, despite any indication received to the contrary from any other participant, including counsel or parties.[25] These guidelines would be infringed if a fact witness was being used as a vehicle to give partial, incomplete, misleading or at worse incorrect evidence, which would not assist the tribunal. This is an area where international arbitration highlights the different legal cultures surrounding witness preparation. Witness preparation includes both the preparation of the witness statement and any preparation carried out by solicitors or counsel, or indeed others, for witnesses before their oral testimony. What is considered obstructive witness coaching to some may be considered as legitimate witness preparation for others, depending on the legal background and the relevant ethical rules to which the lawyer is subject. Traditionally, civil law jurisdictions generally impose a stricter prohibition against any form of witness preparation, and the judge usually takes on an inquisitorial role in leading the evidence.[26] However,

24. ICCA Reports, p. 8.
25. *See* Explanation to Guideline IV.B, ICCA Reports.
26. It is noted that witness preparation is uncommon in German courts. It is not technically illegal as the German Professional Guidelines which used to contain a prohibition on witness preparation had been abolished in 1987. *See*: Christian Wolf, 'The Limits of Witness Preparation in German Court and Arbitration Proceedings' (November 2016) Corporate and commercial

even among common law countries, the degree to which witness preparation is allowed varies drastically.

1 Different Ethical Rules for Different Counsel

Even in common law jurisdictions, the various ethical rules against witness coaching vary. At the risk of generalizing, the United Kingdom, Australia and Singapore fall on the more conservative end of the spectrum, whereas the United States is generally more permissive. In preparing the witness statement, a UK counsel would be prohibited from drafting any witness statement or affidavit that contains any statement of fact other than the evidence which one reasonably believes the witness would give if the witness were giving evidence orally.[27] The Western Australia Bar Association's Best Practice Guide regarding the preparation of witness statements in civil cases suggested that lawyers should not explain to the witness the legal significant of particular evidence; neither should the witness be taken through a version of events and asked whether he agrees with the version.[28]

In both the UK and Australia, witness coaching is strictly prohibited.[29] Barristers are not to advise what answers the witness should give to questions that may be asked.[30] Similar provisions exist for solicitors.[31] While witness preparation itself is not improper, so long as it does not amount to witness coaching, the Court of Appeal of England and Wales cautioned against extensive witness preparation which may undermine the credibility of a witness, who may appear evasive because they had been trained to give evidence in a particular way.[32] The Court of Appeal of Western Australia, in the context of a criminal case where the defence alleged that the prosecution had improperly coached a witness, explained that it would be improper if the prosecutor had taken a course of actions which had the effect of suggesting to the witness the evidence to be given, such as by asking questions which are leading in substance, or by placing inappropriate emphasis upon aspects of the evidence to be given.[33] While solicitors or counsel are allowed to confer with the witness prior to giving evidence and help the witness refresh his or her memory, questioning of

disputes review https://www.nortonrosefulbright.com/en/knowledge/publications/fdf9e798/the-limits-of-witness-preparation-in-german-court-and-arbitration-proceedings (accessed 2 March 2024).

27. Rule C9.2(d) of the Bar Standards Board Handbook.
28. Western Australian Bar Association, Best Practice Guide 01/2009-2011 (as at December 2021), at Question 11.
29. In criminal cases, the English position goes even further to say that witness training is prohibited as well, *see R v. Momodou and another* (Practice Note) [2005] 1 WLR 3442 at [62]; It could also be contempt of court to try to persuade the witness to alter his or her evidence: Re B(JA) An Infant [1965] Ch. 1112.
30. Rule 69, *Legal Profession Uniform Conduct (Barristers) Rules 2015* (Australia); Rule 9, Bar Standards Board Handbook (UK)
31. Australian Solicitors' Conduct Rules 2015 – Rule 24 (Integrity of Evidence) (Australia); Article 2, Solicitors Regulation Authority Code of Conduct (UK)
32. *Ultraframe (UK) Ltd v. Fielding & Ors* | [2005] EWHC 1638, at [25].
33. *Majinski v. The State of Western Australia* [2013] WASCA 10 at [40]; *see also R v. Momodou* [2005] 2 All ER 571.

witnesses becomes 'impermissible coaching' when the witness' true recollection of events is supplanted by another version suggested by the interviewer or other party, 'whether by repetitive reading of a statement to the point where their testimony is mere regurgitation or by otherwise influencing the witness'.[34] In another civil case by the Court of Appeal of New South Wales, the court considered that the defendants' solicitor had engaged in improper witness coaching, as the solicitor had prepared an extensive document for the defendant outlining 'possible areas of questioning', including suggestions as to the appropriate responses which would be in line with the defence's case.[35]

Even though the UK and Australia position prohibits witness coaching, witness familiarization is still allowed. There are also witness training courses conducted by independent third-party organizations without knowledge of the underlying proceedings, which teach the witnesses the necessary techniques without contaminating the witness' own evidence. Such training may in fact benefit the proceedings by improving the quality of the evidence.

The Singapore court has similarly set out the guidance to witness preparation in *De La Sala v. Compañia De Navegación Palomar SA*.[36] First, witness preparation must not allow a solicitor or other persons to supplant or supplement the witness' own evidence. Second, the preparation should not be too lengthy or repetitive. Third, witness preparation should not be done in groups to prevent contamination of the witness' own evidence after hearing from other witnesses.[37] In that case, the fact that the solicitor reiterated certain questions to allow the witness in question to give the 'right answer' created the danger that the witness may be influenced to adopt certain 'favourable' answers as a result of the repetitive drilling. Although the court did not find that any of the solicitors were knowingly influencing the witness' evidence, the court accorded little weight to the witness' evidence given serious doubts about the independence of his testimony.[38] This instance shows that witness coaching can undermine one's own case, regardless of whether it results in ethical breaches that affect the solicitors or counsel in question.

In contrast, the United States adopts a more liberal approach to witness preparation. Mock cross-examination is regularly held. In fact, a failure to fully prepare the witness may be deemed as negligence.[39] The American Bar Association's Model Rules of Professional Conduct sets out the lawyer's obligation to provide competent representation with the requisite 'legal knowledge, skill, thoroughness and preparation reasonably necessary for the representation', but does not set out any explicit prescription against witness coaching. In fact, the preamble to the Model Rules stresses that in an adversarial system, where the opposing party is well represented, 'a lawyer can be a zealous advocate on behalf of a client and at the same time assume that justice is

34. *Majinski v. The State of Western Australia* [2013] WASCA 10 at [32].
35. *Day v. Perisher Blue Pty Ltd* [2005] NSWCA 110.
36. *De La Sala v. Compañia De Navegación Palomar SA* [2018] SGCA 16.
37. *Ibid.*, at [138]-[140].
38. *Ibid.*, at [142].
39. Robert Rifkind, 'Practices of the Horseshed', in Laurent Levy and Johnny Veeder (eds) Arbitration and Oral Evidence (2004) 55, at p. 55.

being done.'[40] This is not to say, however, that all forms of witness coaching would be allowed. In Formal Opinion 508, the American Bar Association Standing Committee on Ethics and Professional Responsibility acknowledged that impermissible witness coaching can be hard to delineate in light of the concurrent ethical duties to diligently and competently represent the client. But it would amount to unacceptable witness coaching if the lawyer encourages the witness to present fabricated evidence, programmes the witness' testimony, or compensates a lay witness for the substance of their testimony.[41]

2 Harmonization or Minimum Standards

Surveying domestic ethical rules shows that harmonization may neither be achievable nor desirable. The ICCA Guidelines, to this extent, set out the minimum standard that should apply to all participants of the arbitral process to ensure its integrity. Despite the ethical and cultural divide in various jurisdictions, the general practice in international arbitration is that witness interviews and preparation are permissible.[42] But where both the counsel and arbitrators anticipate that the discrepancies in counsel's different legal backgrounds could lead to differing approaches to witness preparation, such issues can be addressed in procedural orders early on.

In terms of the preparation of witness statements, lawyers are to be guided by the notion of good faith in ensuring that the witness statement should originate from the witness himself.[43] Ethical guidelines from the respective jurisdictions remain helpful. The recent UK Commercial Court Practice Direction highlights the purpose of a trial witness statement which is to provide an honest account of matters known personally to the witness. The trial witness should not seek to argue the case, nor take the court 'through the documents in the case or set out a narrative derived from the documents, those being matters for argument'.[44] Although such practice directions are not binding in arbitrations, arbitrators and counsel could benefit from using at least this practice direction as a guide designed to uphold the integrity of the process. The spirit of such guidelines ensures that the witness statement is not a mere conduit for parties' submission, and that the witness statement is in the witness' own words and in accordance with their recollection of the events.

40. Model Rules of Professional Conduct: Preamble & Scope at [8].
41. Formal Opinion 508, at p 5.
42. Park, The 2002 Freshfields Lecture: Arbitration's Protean Nature: The Value of Rules and the Risks of Discretion, Arbitration International 19 (2003), vol. 3, 279, 288 https://doi.org/10.1093/arbitration/19.3.279 (accessed 16 August 2025); *see also* von Segesser, Witness Preparation, ASA Bulletin 20 (2002), 222 https://doi.org/10.54648/5096671 (accessed 16 August 2025); Buöhler/Dorgan, Witness Testimony Pursuant to the 1999 IBA Rules of Evidence in International Commercial Arbitration: Novel or Tested Standards?, Journal of International Arbitration 17 (2000), vol. 1, 12 https://doi.org/10.54648/267907 (accessed 16 August 2025).
43. *See also*, Veeder Q.C., The 2001 Goff Lecture: The Lawyer's Duty to Arbitrate in Good Faith, Arbitration International (2002), vol. 18, 431, 445-447.
44. Practice Direction 57AC – Trial Witness Statements in the Business and Property Courts (UK), at [3.6].

As for witness preparation, witness coaching carried out to supplant the witness' own testimony, which again distorts the purpose of witness testimony, is not in line with the spirit of civility and integrity underlying the ICCA Guidelines. A well-prepared witness is necessary in an adversarial setting in which arbitrations are often conducted, and where tribunals rely on their testimony to establish the facts of the case. But the minimum standard should still be maintained insofar as such preparation does not unduly interfere with the testimony of the witness. Further, regardless of the legal culture and background of the counsel, an overly prepared witness may hamper rather than promote that party's case, as the witness' credibility would be in question. Where allegations of impermissible witness coaching are raised, arbitrators are similarly duty-bound to maintain the integrity of its own process. It has been argued that arbitral tribunal has the power and obligation to decide on the counsel's conduct where it concerns the integrity of the proceedings. Impermissible coaching that constitutes obstructive conduct can lead to cost consequences – which arbitral tribunals are able to consider as a part of their toolkit to address ethical breaches.[45]

IV CONCLUSION

Differing professional standards and ethical rules present a challenge in codifying uniform practice. Perhaps, there is no one-size-fits-all solution, but lines should be drawn to safeguard the integrity and legitimacy of the arbitration process, which has come under increasing scrutiny in recent years. The key point at the heart of the Guidelines is the twin aim of promoting the integrity and civility of the arbitral process. This chapter has focused on two key stakeholders – arbitrators and counsel. In addressing the issue of corruption, both counsel and arbitrators have to remain vigilant for the presence of red flags that raise suspicions as to the propriety of certain transactions or dispute resolution processes. In terms of the procedural steps, such as witness preparation, the minimum standard should be that the witness of fact must present their witness evidence truthfully and completely, not as an extension of the party or counsel. The preparation of the witness should be carried out with a view to improving the objective quality of evidence taking, so as to assist the tribunal, rather than with a view to directly advocating the presenting party's case.

45. Andrii Zharikov, 'Conflicts and Ethics in International Arbitration', in Stravros Brekoulakis (ed.), Arbitration: The International Journal of Arbitration, Mediation and Dispute Management, vol. 85 (2019), 36, at 37, at 45.

CHAPTER 33

Guideline II(D) of the ICCA Guidelines and the Regulation of 'Guerrilla Tactics'

Jonathan Lim[*]

TABLE OF CONTENTS

I INTRODUCTION

Debates regarding the regulation of counsel conduct in international arbitration proceedings tend to generate more heat than light. Much has been said about the absence of a set of universal standards that can be applied uniformly to international arbitration counsel, particularly when they hail from different legal traditions and may be subject to different professional conduct rules promulgated by national bar associations.[1] Some have argued that this leads to an inequality of arms and might encourage

* Jonathan Lim is partner at Wilmer Cutler Pickering Hale and Dorr LLP. The author is grateful to his colleague Xiaohan Cai for her assistance on this chapter; He would also like to thank the following former or current colleagues: Goel Damkani, Ilan Gafni, Izaak Weaver-Herrera, Sanjana Sharma, Amila Pivic, Sviatoslav Syvakivskyi, Ashika Jain, and Gilliam Collinsworth-Hamilton. All omissions or errors belong solely to the author.

1. IBA Task Force on Conduct of Counsel in Arbitration, '2010 Survey: Counsel in International Arbitration' (63% of practitioners surveyed believed they were subject to their home jurisdictions' rules, while 27% were uncertain and 10% had no opinion or did not believe they were subject to home jurisdiction rules); C. Benson, *Can Professional Ethics Wait?* (n 4) at p. 81 ('in any given arbitration, even counsel from the same jurisdictions may have diverging views on the extent to which their national ethical codes apply to international arbitration'); Gary Born, *International Commercial Arbitration* (2014), at 2877 ('counsel in international arbitrations are frequently uncertain what rules of professional responsibility apply to their conduct').

'guerrilla tactics'.[2] At the same time, proposals that purport to address precisely this problem by setting forth universal guidelines specifically for international arbitration – such as the IBA Guidelines on Party Representation – have provoked equally trenchant criticism. For example, commentators have pointed out that such guidelines provide little normative guidance and fail to dispel uncertainty over applicable standards, particularly as applicable mandatory norms are likely to still apply.[3] Indeed, some argue that such guidelines may be counter-productive and instead add fuel to frivolous challenges against counsel.[4]

Against this context, this chapter considers the extent to which Guideline II(D) of the ICCA Guidelines on Standards of Practice in International Arbitration (ICCA Guidelines) meaningfully contributes to discussions about regulation of counsel conduct in international arbitration. By their own terms, the ICCA Guidelines are not intended as mandatory rules. Instead, they contain guiding principles of civility in international arbitration based on a survey of professional standards, ethical rules, and civility standards – minimum standards of conduct that are arguably common to all legal traditions. They may be capable of application either upon agreement by the parties or insofar as arbitral tribunals refer to them for guidance in procedural orders. In every case, they do not apply in isolation, but in conjunction with other applicable laws and rules.

Guideline II(D) is specifically directed at egregious conduct designed to obstruct, delay, or disrupt the arbitration process or to jeopardize the finality of any award. As discussed below, such conduct is sometimes referred to as 'guerrilla tactics,' but that description is vague and can obscure what kinds of conduct are in fact prohibited and subject to sanction. Guideline II(D) helps provide a more precise definition, giving both counsel and arbitrators additional practical means to address categories of conduct that may not already be expressly prohibited by existing written rules. To illustrate how this might work in specific cases, three scenarios of potential application are discussed in

2. *See, e.g.*, Cyrus Benson, 'Can Professional Ethics Wait', available at https://www.gibsondunn.com/wp-content/uploads/documents/publications/Benson-CanProfessionalEthicsWait.pdf (accessed 31 October 2025), at p. 79 ('[the lack of clarity on what national professional rules apply in the arbitration process] might permit arbitration counsel to entertain the following conclusion: national professional rules do not apply and there are no international rules; hence, conduct of counsel and their clients is not regulated by any minimal ethical standards but rather by a Machiavellian cost-benefit analysis of what conduct can be "gotten away with without undue risk of discovery or sanction by the tribunal"').
3. Paragraph 1 of the General Guidelines for the Authorised Representatives of the Parties annexed to the LCIA 2020 Arbitration Rules notes that '[T]hese guidelines [shall not] derogate from any mandatory laws, rules of law, professional rules or codes of conduct if and to the extent that any are shown to apply to an authorised representative appearing in the arbitration.' For commentary, *see, e.g.*, C. Rogers, *Context and Institutional Structure in Attorney Regulation: Constructing an Enforcement Regime for International Arbitration*, 37 Stan. J. int'l L. 1 (2003), at 3 ('important questions remain: Who is going to undertake the task of developing the specific content of the needed rules, and how are they going to be made binding and enforceable on attorneys in international arbitration? There are no obvious answers. No supranational bar association exists').
4. *See, e.g.*, T. Landau QC and J. Weeramantry, *A Pause for Thought*, in A.J. van den Berg (ed.), *International Arbitration: The Coming of a New Age?*, 17 ICCA Congress Series (2013), 496.

further detail: frivolous applications or challenges, a party's failure to pay its share of deposits, and serious document production misconduct.

II ICCA GUIDELINE II(D) AND GUERRILLA TACTICS

'Guerrilla tactics' is an umbrella term[5] that is used to describe certain disruptive behaviour by counsel in international arbitration proceedings. However, it is not a well-defined term. For example, some commentators have referred to 'guerrilla tactics' as encompassing 'ethical violations', 'criminal acts', as well as 'ethically borderline practices'.[6] In covering both conduct that breaches written ethical rules and laws, as well as conduct that does not clearly amount to such a breach, the term 'guerrilla tactics' is arguably overbroad – too capacious a label to provide actual meaningful guidance for counsel and arbitrators in specific cases. The bare allegation that certain conduct amounts to 'guerrilla tactics' is unlikely to of itself result in any procedural or legal sanction, unless one can invoke another rule or law that has been breached and provides a basis for such sanctions.

Guideline II(D) of the ICCA Guidelines speaks to such conduct, but it contains a very precise definition. Specifically, Guideline II.D provides that:

> Party representatives shall not engage, without legitimate reasons, in activities intended to obstruct, delay, or disrupt the arbitration process or to jeopardize the finality of any award.[7]

Guideline II(D) draws from prior standards and guidelines, but it goes further in terms of the specificity with which it describes the conduct proscribed. For example, the 2013 IBA Guidelines on Party Representation in International Arbitration stated in the preamble that they were broadly 'inspired' by the 'the principle that party representatives ... should not engage in activities designed to produce unnecessary delay or expense'.[8] Apart from the preamble, those set of guidelines did not contain rules that specifically proscribed such behaviour, with the exception of Guideline 13, which is limited to requests to produce and objections to such requests made for an improper purpose, such as to 'harass or cause unnecessary delay'.[9]

There are essentially two elements to Guideline II(D): first, counsel must not engage in activities 'intended to obstruct, delay, or disrupt the arbitration process or to

5. The term is widely attributed to Singaporean arbitrator, Dr Michael Hwang, who first coined the term 'arbitration guerrilla'. Robert Pfeiffer and Stephan Wilske, 'Chapter 1, §1.01: An Etymological and Historical Overview' in Günther J. Horvath and Stephan Wilske (eds), *Guerrilla Tactics in International Arbitration, International Arbitration Law Library* (Kluwer Law International 2013).
6. J. William Rowley, 'Chapter 1, §1.04: Guerrilla Tactics and Developing Issues,' in Günther J. Horvath and Stephan Wilske (eds), *Guerrilla Tactics in International Arbitration*, International Arbitration Law Library, vol. 28 (© Kluwer Law International; Kluwer Law International 2013), p. 21.
7. 2021 ICCA Guidelines, Guideline II(D), p. 8.
8. 2013 IBA Guidelines on Party Representation in International Arbitration, Preamble.
9. 2013 IBA Guidelines on Party Representation in International Arbitration, Guideline 13.

jeopardize the finality of any award'; and second, counsel must not do so 'without legitimate reasons'.

The first element covers a broad range of activities that have the requisite intention - to obstruct, delay, or disrupt the process or otherwise jeopardize the award's finality. While the ICCA Guidelines list specific examples, including frivolous attempts to disqualify an arbitrator, or filing claims or challenges without any good faith or serious basis, the list is not meant to be exhaustive. The Explanation to Guideline II(D) makes clear that it is intended to cover a wider range of conduct and activities in 'all aspects of an arbitration proceeding', from constitution of the arbitral tribunal to the taking of evidence and conduct at the hearing.

The second element - that there must be no 'legitimate reason' for the conduct - narrows the scope of Guideline II(D). It is intended to distinguish between legitimate but zealous advocacy on the one hand, and conduct undertaken with the 'sole purpose' of obstruction or delay on the other. That line may not be easy to draw in practice; one counsel's zealous advocacy could be another's 'guerrilla tactic', and cultural and legal backgrounds may shape perceptions. Nonetheless, in many jurisdictions, counsel is subject to an overriding duty to their clients of zeal and diligence in advocacy, and Guideline II(D) is not intended to displace or modify such ethical obligations.[10] Whether conduct is undertaken 'without legitimate reasons' will therefore depend in each case on the facts and circumstances, as well as the applicable law governing the conduct in question and the procedure in the arbitration. However, as the Explanation to Guideline II(D) elaborates, this is directed at conduct undertaken with the 'sole purpose' of obstruction, unreasonable delay, or jeopardizing the finality of any award - which imposes a relatively high threshold for a breach of Guideline II(D).

III THREE PRACTICAL APPLICATIONS

To illustrate how Guideline II(D) might be applied in particular contexts, this chapter considers three scenarios of potential application.

1 Frivolous Applications and Challenges

The Explanation to Guideline II(D) refers to frivolous applications and challenges as examples of the type of conduct that might be proscribed by the guideline. Specifically, this includes 'attempts to disqualify an arbitrator without serious basis', 'challenging the jurisdiction of the arbitral tribunal without material grounds', and 'filing requests or post-award challenges without any good faith or serious basis'.[11] In general, 'frivolous' applications or challenges refer to those that are made with no knowledge or

10. *See, e.g.*, ABA Guidelines Rule 1.3 Diligence - Comment ('[1] A lawyer should pursue a matter on behalf of a client despite opposition, obstruction or personal inconvenience to the lawyer, and take whatever lawful and ethical measures are required to vindicate a client's cause or endeavor. A lawyer must also act with commitment and dedication to the interests of the client and with zeal in advocacy upon the client's behalf. [...]').
11. 2021 ICCA Guidelines, Explanation to Guideline II(D) 8.

expectation of success, and therefore further the improper collateral purpose of causing delays, unnecessary costs, or harassing the opposing party.[12] It may not be possible, of course, to prove the subjective state of mind of a party making an application or challenge, and therefore arbitral tribunals have found to be frivolous applications that fall below *de minimis* legal and factual standards.[13] In such cases, the requirements of Guideline II(D) are likely to be established where there is no 'legitimate reason' for the conduct.

It is easy to see how frivolous applications and challenges can delay, obstruct, or disrupt an arbitration. Take, for example, frivolous challenges to arbitrators. There are many accounts of such challenges, including, numerous consecutive challenges to the same arbitrator, challenges based on far-fetched reasoning, or challenges with suspicious timings that are likely tactically motivated.[14] Although the threshold for a challenge is high, and the statistics reflect a relatively low success rate of such challenges, even unsuccessful challenges can cause significant delay and disruption. There are, in fact, perverse incentives to bring such challenge, and unmeritorious challenges are often brought with the knowledge that they can exact a real cost on the arbitration and the other parties.

Statistics indicate that challenged arbitrators frequently resign before a challenge is resolved. According to the ICC, in 2020, ninety-two challenges were filed in forty-one cases, of which five were accepted.[15] Despite this low success rate, thirty-eight arbitrators resigned that year, although the ICC does not report whether the resignations came on the heels of a challenge.[16] Curiously, the ICC notes that in one case, 'one party filed 29 successive challenges, which were all rejected, against the president of the arbitral tribunal and all three members of the tribunal'.[17] If one ignores that outlier, then out of sixty-three challenges in 2020 reported by the ICC, five were accepted and in the same year thirty-eight resigned. Even if one assumes that only half of the resignations were in response to challenges, that amounts to an estimated 38% of challenges resulting in a change to the composition of the tribunal.

In fact, as Table 33.1 illustrates, according to the ICC, from 2016 to 2020, challenges were made to arbitrators in 287 cases, of which twenty-nine were accepted

12. *See, e.g.*, *GUPC v. ACP (II)* (Concrete Arbitration), Final Award (17 February 2021) (citing to party's misuse of procedure to cause extensive delays by bringing groundless challenges as relevant for costs determination).
13. *See, e.g.*, *MTS Technologies v. Drive* (AAA), Final Award (31 March 2010), para. 55 (finding arbitration to be 'groundless and frivolous ... [as party] failed even to articulate a viable legal cause of action'); *Wendella v. Blount Boats* (AAA), Final Award (5 July 2017) (claims held frivolous when 'not supported by credible material evidence').
14. Robert Pfeiffer and Stephan Wilske, 'Chapter 1, §1.03: The Emergence of the Guerrilla Tactics Phenomenon in International Arbitration' in Günther J. Horvath and Stephan Wilske (eds), *Guerrilla Tactics in International Arbitration* (Kluwer Law International 2013) 18. *See also* *Claimant X v. Respondent Y*, LCIA Case No. 132551, para. 75 ('The Division finds this challenge frivolous.').
15. ICC, 'Dispute Resolution 2020 Statistics' (ICC 2021) 13.
16. ICC, 'Dispute Resolution 2020 Statistics' (ICC 2021) 13.
17. ICC, 'Dispute Resolution 2020 Statistics' (ICC 2021) fn 13.

(10.1%), but there were 201 resignations over that same period.[18] The ICC statistics do not draw a link between the resignations and the challenge, but the number of resignations over the period is significant, amounting to 70% of the challenges filed.

Table 33.1

Year	*Challenges Filed*	*Accepted*	*Replacement (Resignation)*
2020	92 (41 cases)	5	43 (38 resigned, 3 deaths)[19]
2019	52	6	58 (50 resigned)[20]
2018	45	7	55 (50 resigned)[21]
2017	48	6	37 (29 resigned)[22]
2016	50	5	33 (34 resigned)[23]

That is consistent with statistics published by ICSID in 2014. Then Secretary-General Meg Kinnear reported that out of eighty-four challenges, four challenged arbitrators were disqualified and twenty-one arbitrators resigned, resulting in the composition of a tribunal changing in approximately 30% (twenty-five out of eighty-four) of cases.[24]

Other types of frivolous applications and challenges can also similarly cause obstruction or delay. Another example is when proceedings are bifurcated into a prior jurisdictional and admissibility phase, and jurisdictional issues that are already resolved in a prior decision are relitigated by the losing party at a later phase. There may also be a re-litigation of issues that should have been raised and resolved in the prior phase. The doctrines of res judicata and abuse of process can provide a substantive basis to resolve some of these issues; however, they do not resolve the increased complexity and, consequently, increased costs of the arbitration – often unnecessarily – that are borne by the other party or parties.

One possible sanction for such conduct is cost-shifting in a final award,[25] but that is often of limited effectiveness in redressing the kinds of frivolous applications and challenges that fall within Guideline II(D). The final award can come many months –

18. ICC, 'Dispute Resolution 2020 Statistics' (2021) 13; ICC, 'Dispute Resolution 2019 Statistics' (2020) 12; ICC, 'Dispute Resolution 2018 Statistics' (2019) 10; ICC, 'Dispute Resolution 2017 Statistics' in ICC Dispute Resolution Bulletin (2018, Issue 2) 57; ICC, 'Dispute Resolution 2016 Statistics' in ICC Dispute Resolution Bulletin (2017, Issue 2) 52.
19. ICC, 'Dispute Resolution 2020 Statistics' (ICC 2021) 13.
20. ICC, 'Dispute Resolution 2019 Statistics' (ICC 2020) 12.
21. ICC, 'Dispute Resolution 2018 Statistics' (ICC 2019) 10.
22. ICC, 'Dispute Resolution 2017 Statistics' in ICC Dispute Resolution Bulletin (2018, Issue 2) 57.
23. ICC, 'Dispute Resolution 2016 Statistics' in ICC Dispute Resolution Bulletin (2017, Issue 2) 52-53.
24. Meg Kinnear, 'Challenge of Arbitrators at ICSID: An Overview' ASIL Proceedings (2014) 412, 416 https://doi.org/10.5305/procannmeetasil.108.0412 (accessed 16 August 2025).
25. *See, e.g., ICC Commission Report: Decisions on costs in international arbitration* (2015) 23; *Claimant(s) v. Respondent(s)*, ICC Final Award No. 18223, paras 527, 529; *MWN Group, Inc. v. MAG USA, Inc.* (ICC), Final Award (12 June 2006), para. 54.

even years – later, when memories have dimmed, the impact of the conduct complained of has faded, and the sanction neither compensates the injured party nor deters the conduct in question. Furthermore, as a practical matter, it can also be difficult to isolate the costs associated with making or defending against a particular frivolous application or challenge.

In the author's submission, Guideline II(D) can provide a basis for tribunals to immediately address frivolous applications or challenges made with no expectation of success, whose sole purpose is to obstruct, delay, or disrupt the arbitration process. Where there is a breach of Guideline II(D), arbitral tribunals may consider an immediate costs order or award at the point when a frivolous application or challenge is disposed of.[26] Most arbitration rules – for example, Article 42(2) of the UNCITRAL Rules and Article 38(3) of the ICC rules – permit ordering costs prior to a final award. Doing so will have a real effect on party behaviour, and the sanctioned party will have a strong incentive to comply, given that the tribunal has yet to resolve the merits of the dispute.

2 Refusal to Pay Advance on Costs

The Explanation to Guideline II(D) notes that 'advising clients/parties to refuse to pay the advance on costs in order to delay the proceedings or obligate the counterparty to pay them' is another example of conduct which may delay, obstruct, or disrupt the arbitration proceedings in breach of that guideline.[27]

The advance on costs is a deposit paid by the parties to cover fees and expenses of the tribunal and the institution's administrative expenses. Arbitral rules generally provide that the consequence of the failure to pay advance on costs is the suspension or termination of the arbitration, or the deemed withdrawal of claims or counterclaims.[28] These more serious effects can generally be mitigated by other parties making substitute payments, as permitted under virtually all rules.[29]

However, even where there has been such mitigation, the refusal to pay an advance on costs may exact further costs on the party making substituted payment. There is, of course, the immediate financial cost of having to make the payment, as well as the opportunity cost of the lost cashflow, which can be very significant in drawn-out cases involving large sums in dispute. In some cases, a claimant will need to obtain financing to make the payment, and that may come with yet further costs, particularly

26. This is similar to what is referred to in English litigation proceedings as a 'forthwith' costs order. *See, e.g.*, 'Chapter 30: Detailed Assessment: Procedure' in Jason Rowley and Simon Middleton (eds), *Cook on Costs* (LexisNexis 2024) ('"Forthwith" orders').
27. 2021 ICCA Guidelines, Guideline II(D) 8.
28. 2021 ICC Rules, Article 37(6); 2020 LCIA Rules, Article 24(8); 2021 UNCITRAL Rules, Article 43(4); 2021 ICDR Rules, Article 39(5); 2016 SIAC Rules, Rule 34.6; 2012 PCA Rules, Article 43(4); 2023 SCC Rules, Article 51(5); 2021 Swiss Rules of International Arbitration, Article 41(4); 2024 HKIAC Rules, Article 41(4).
29. 2021 ICC Rules, Article 37(5); 2020 LCIA Rules, Article 24(6); 2021 UNCITRAL Rules, Article 43(4); 2021 ICDR Rules, Article 39(4); 2016 SIAC Rules, Rule 34.5; 2012 PCA Rules, Article 43(4); 2023 SCC Rules, Article 51(5); 2021 Swiss Rules of International Arbitration, Article 41(4); 2024 HKIAC Rules, Article 41(4).

in cases involving litigation financing. Depending on the sums involved, all this can cause prejudice to the party making the substitute payment that cannot be remedied by simple cost-shifting in a final award. Again, this creates perverse incentives that reward respondents that seek to wear down their opponents by refusing to pay their share of the deposits.

One remedy available to the affected party may be to request immediate reimbursement of the advance on costs paid on behalf of the other party.[30] Several arbitration rules expressly provide for immediate reimbursement in a partial award as of right, for example, the SIAC Rules[31] and the SCC Rules.[32] The LCIA Rules even provide that the substitute sums paid constitute a debt immediately due, with interest.[33] However, even absent such express provisions, there are compelling arguments that a failure to pay an advance of costs should be regarded as a breach of the parties' agreement to arbitrate in good faith and the obligation to desist from actions that may hamper the arbitration, and that is a sufficient basis for a partial award on costs.[34]

Guideline II(D) is useful for supplementing the analysis and legal basis for such a partial award. Given the obstructive effects of an intentional failure to make payment of an advance on costs, reimbursement should generally follow unless non-payment is based on a 'legitimate reason'. There can be several reasons for a party's refusal to pay their share of costs, for example, if the party has objected to the tribunal's jurisdiction or impartiality. However, unless the tribunal's lack of jurisdiction is manifest, these are not generally legitimate reasons to withhold advances on costs, particularly where respondents have raised the jurisdictional objections before the tribunal and requested the use of shared resources and tribunal time to resolve their objections. In addition, a respondent would suffer no prejudice from having to bear its equal share of the advance on costs, because costs can be reallocated in an award in the event that a respondent prevails on its jurisdictional objections.

Guideline II(D) is useful for supplementing the analysis and legal basis for a partial award on reimbursement. Given the obstructive effects of an intentional failure to make payment, reimbursement should generally follow unless non-payment is based on 'legitimate reasons.' Applying Guideline II(D), a wilful refusal to pay an advance on costs can result in immediate reimbursement to be ordered at the discretion

30. *See, e.g., UAB Garsu Pasaulis v. The Kyrgyz Republic*, PCA Case No. 2020-59, Procedural Order No. 2, Decision on the Claimant's Request for a Separate Award on Costs, 29 June 2021, paras 52-65; excerpted in Matthew Secomb, 'Awards and Orders Dealing with the Advance on Costs in ICC Arbitration: Theoretical Questions and Practical Problems' 14(1) ICC International Ct. of Arb. Bull (2003) 60. *See also* a similar discussion in Nadia Darwazeh and Simon Greenberg, 'No One's Credit Is As Good As Cash: Awards and Orders for the Payment of the ICC Advance on Costs' 31(5) Journal of International Arbitration (2014) 557 https://doi.org/10.54648/joia2014027 (accessed 16 August 2025).
31. 2016 SIAC Rules, Article 27.
32. 2023 SCC Rules, Article 51.
33. 2020 LCIA Rules, Article 24 (5); 2024 HKIAC Rules contain a similar provision – Article 41.4.
34. Neil Kaplan, 'Non-Payment of Advances on Costs: No Pay, Can Play?' in David D. Caron et al (eds), *Practising Virtue: Inside International Arbitration* (OUP 2015) 330; Gabrielle Kaufmann-Kohler and Antonio Rigozzi, *International Arbitration: Law and Practice in Switzerland* (OUP 2015), para. 3.33.

of the tribunal, with costs allocated in a final award to ensure there is no ultimate prejudice to either party.

3 Document Production

The Explanation to Guideline II(D) notes that '[d]ocument production is another area that is ripe for procedural abuse and offensive tactics'.[35] Examples include 'unreasonably delaying the production of evidence requested by arbitrators' or using the production phase to 'unreasonably delay the resolution of a dispute or to harass opposing counsel [or] parties'.[36]

The open-ended nature of document production requests, as well as the power exercised by a party over documents in its custody or control, creates opportunities for tactical abuse. For example, a requesting party can request production of numerous broad categories of documents that places a disproportionate burden on the producing party, or a producing party can produce a huge number of documents that are of little relevance or in a format that is difficult to read.[37] Other forms of misconduct include improper withholding of documents, improper redactions, and in some cases even deletion or spoliation of evidence.

Some existing rules and guidelines already regulate misconduct in document production. For example, the IBA Guidelines on Party Representation in International Arbitration provides that '[a] Party Representative should not make any Request to Produce or any objection to a Request to Produce, for an improper purpose, such as to harass or cause unnecessary delay'.[38] The IBA Guidelines also prohibit counsel from concealing documents or recommending concealing documents to their client.[39] Such conduct is also often in breach of the tribunal's procedural orders.

Such misconduct obviously disrupts and delays proceedings, and therefore a key issue under Guideline II(D) will be whether such conduct was intentional. For example, parties may withhold documents out of inadvertence or (more likely) out of an honestly - albeit wrongly - held view that privilege or commercial sensitivity provides grounds for withholding certain documents. A breach of Guideline II(D) will result if documents have been deliberately withheld without legitimate reasons.

In terms of remedies, cost-shifting or written warnings in a final award are arguably too little too late and do not adequately address deliberate misconduct without legitimate reason under Guideline II(D). In such cases, arbitral tribunals may consider remedies with more teeth to penalize and deter the misconduct. What remedies are appropriate may depend on how pervasive and egregious the misconduct is, as well as the degree of prejudice caused by the misconduct.[40]

35. 2021 ICCA Guidelines, Guideline II(D) 8.
36. 2021 ICCA Guidelines, Explanation to Guideline II(D).
37. 'Chapter 6: Document Production Strategies' in Reto Marghitola (ed.), *Document Production in International Arbitration* (Kluwer Law International 2015) 125-126.
38. 2013 IBA Guidelines on Party Representation in International Arbitration, Guideline 13.
39. 2013 IBA Guidelines on Party Representation in International Arbitration, Guideline 16.
40. *See, e.g., Cook v. MKCI and McGivney* (AAA), Final Award (1 August 2023) para. 52.

One such remedy is the drawing of adverse inferences. An arbitral tribunal's power to draw adverse inferences is not controversial; it is provided for, for example, in Article 9(6) of the IBA Rules on Taking of Evidence,[41] the Prague Rules,[42] and most national laws.[43] The applicable rules in each case will depend on what rules the arbitral tribunal decides to apply, and the content and extent of the adverse inference sought will depend on the circumstances of the case. Under Singapore law, an element of deliberate intention is required for the drawing of adverse inferences. Thus, in *Ivanishvili, Bidzina v. Credit Suisse*,[44] the Singapore Court declined to draw the adverse inference sought because it held that the failure to comply with disclosure obligations was not deliberate, but instead a result of 'the pressures and complexities of the preparation for and conduct of the trial'.[45] Similarly, under English law, if there has been deliberate withholding or destruction of evidence, the Court may draw adverse inferences against a party as well as treat a party's evidence as lacking any credibility.[46]

In extreme cases, where the deliberate destruction of evidence has occurred such that a fair trial cannot take place, dismissal of the claim may even be warranted under English law.[47] This is also the case in some US jurisdictions, where dismissal of a claim is one possible remedy for spoliation of evidence, especially where the spoliation is intentional and results in significant prejudice.[48]

41. 2020 IBA Rules on Taking of Evidence, Article 9(6).
42. 2018 Prague Rules on the Efficient Conduct of Proceedings in International Arbitration, Article 10.
43. Gary Born, *International Commercial Arbitration* (3rd ed, Kluwer Law International 2022) 2497.
44. *Ivanishvili, Bidzina and others v. Credit Suisse Trust Ltd* [2023] 5 SLR 59.
45. *Ivanishvili, Bidzina and others v. Credit Suisse Trust Ltd* [2023] 5 SLR 59, paras 584-585.
46. *Rebekah Vardy v. Coleen Rooney* [2022] EWHC 2017 (QB) paras 55-57, 69, 71.
47. *See, e.g., Arrow Nominees Inc v. Blackledge* [2001] BCC 591, para. 54 ('I adopt, as a general principle, the observations of Mr Justice Millett in *Logicrose Ltd v Southend United Football Club Limited (The Times, 5 March 1988)* that the object of the rules as to discovery is to secure the fair trial of the action in accordance with the due process of the Court; and that, accordingly, a party is not to be deprived of his right to a proper trial as a penalty for disobedience of those rules – even if such disobedience amounts to contempt for or defiance of the court – if that object is ultimately secured, by (for example) the late production of a document which has been withheld. But where a litigant's conduct puts the fairness of the trial in jeopardy, where it is such that any judgment in favour of the litigant would have to be regarded as unsafe, or where it amounts to such an abuse of the process of the court as to render further proceedings unsatisfactory and to prevent the court from doing justice, the court is entitled – indeed, I would hold bound – to refuse to allow that litigant to take further part in the proceedings and (where appropriate) to determine the proceedings against him').
48. *See Computer Assocs. Int'l, Inc. v. Am. Fundware, Inc.*, 133 F.R.D. 166, 170 (D. Colo. 1990) ('Destruction of evidence cannot be countenanced in a justice system whose goal is to find the truth through honest and orderly production of evidence under established discovery rules … nothing less than default judgment on the issue of liability will suffice to both punish this defendant and deter others similarly tempted'); *Grange Mut. Cas. Co. v. Mack*, 270 F. App'x 372, 378 (6th Cir. 2008) (affirming default judgment because '[o]ur civil legal system hinges on voluntary discovery. Discovery abusers must be sanctioned, because "[w]ithout adequate sanctions, the procedures for discovery would be ineffectual"'); *Leon v. IDX Systems Corp.*, 464 F.3d 951 (9th Cir. 2006) (finding that plaintiff's wilful spoliation of data on his employer-owned laptop supported sanction of dismissal).

IV CONCLUSION

The ICCA Guidelines elucidate minimum standards of conduct essential to the fair and efficient administration of proceedings, with special emphasis on civility. Guideline II(D) contains an important set of minimum standards that apply to the conduct of counsel in international arbitration proceedings. Guideline II(D) is narrowly circumscribed and requires both intention to delay or obstruct, as well as the absence of any legitimate reasons for the conduct, in order for a breach to be established. Where the conduct fits the sanction, Guideline II(D) can play an important role in addressing 'guerrilla tactics' that cross the line and provide both a basis for censure and sanction of such misconduct.

PANEL 12

Dispute Resolution and the Global Community

For centuries, universally agreed dispute resolution rules have been pivotal in resolving some of humanity's greatest issues. Building on historical examples, this panel discussed the challenges and successes of dispute resolution in achieving a more harmonious and prosperous global community. This panel describes current initiatives tackling climate change, practical experiences of designing rules for state-to-state and multi-stakeholder conflicts, and dispute resolution innovation addressing societal inequalities.

CHAPTER 34

Inter-State Conciliation as an Effective Means for Resolving Disputes Related to Climate Change

Catherine Amirfar[*]

TABLE OF CONTENTS

I INTRODUCTION

Conciliation commonly features as the default method of international dispute resolution in multilateral environmental agreements (*MEAs*). Indeed, at least eight major MEAs incorporate conciliation mechanisms in some form, including the United Nations Framework Convention on Climate Change (*UNFCCC*) and the agreements and protocols developed within its framework, including the Paris Agreement.[1] This is for good reason. While there is no set definition of conciliation under international norms, such

* Partner and Co-Chair, International Dispute Resolution Group, Debevoise & Plimpton LLP. The author would like to thank the significant contributions of her Debevoise colleagues Christel Tham, Rhianna Hoover, and Evelin Caro Gutierrez to this chapter.

1. *See, e.g.*, Malgosia Fitzmaurice, "The Potential of Inter-State Conciliation Within the Framework of Environmental Treaties" in Christian Tomuschat and Marcelo Kohen (eds.), *Flexibility in International Dispute Settlement: Conciliation Revisited* (2020), at 93 (noting other MEAs, including 1985 Vienna Convention for the Protection of the Ozone Layer, Article 11; 1992 Biological Diversity Convention, Article 27; 1992 OSPAR Convention, Article 32; 1994 Desertification Convention, Article 28; 1997 Convention on Non-Navigational Uses of International Watercourses, Article 33; 1998 Rotterdam Convention on the Prior Informed Consent (PIC) Procedure for Certain Hazardous Chemicals and Pesticides in International Trade, Article 20; 2001 Stockholm Convention on Persistent Organic Pollutants, Article 18).

proceedings tend to be flexible, party-driven, and non-binding—features that make conciliation particularly well suited to the resolution of multilateral environmental disputes. Indeed, there is real potential for conciliation to facilitate the effective implementation of MEAs, while maintaining the collaboration and cooperation among States necessary for pursuing global environmental efforts, including responding to climate change.

Yet, conciliation is both understudied in the literature and rarely used in practice.[2] To date, there has not been a single conciliation proceeding brought under an MEA. In an effort to draw attention to this underutilized tool in environmental disputes, this chapter makes the case that conciliation, including as compared to other more frequently used methods of dispute resolution such as arbitration, is particularly well suited to the effective and peaceful settlement of such disputes, especially under the UNFCCC and the Paris Agreement.

In *section II*, this chapter discusses the key features and benefits of conciliation, with reference to specific examples of previous conciliation proceedings. In *section III*, this chapter turns to the nature of disputes under the UNFCCC framework and how the features of conciliation might be harnessed to maximize the likelihood, effectiveness, and long-term benefits of resolutions to disputes related to climate change.

II WHAT IS CONCILIATION?

1 Features and Benefits of Conciliation

There is no standardized definition of "conciliation," nor a fixed procedure for conciliation proceedings.[3] What definitions exist tend to focus more on what conciliation is not, rather than on what it is; that is, conciliation is neither an exercise of diplomacy, such as negotiation, nor a means of binding dispute settlement, such as arbitration or litigation. As the United Nations Handbook on Peaceful Settlement of International Disputes describes, conciliation is:

> a peaceful settlement procedure which would, on the one hand, provide [the parties] with a better understanding of each other's case by undertaking objective investigation and evaluation of all aspects of the dispute and, on the other hand, provide them with an informal third-party machinery for the negotiation and non-judicial appraisal of each other's legal and other claims, including the opportunity for defining the terms for a solution susceptible of being accepted by them.[4]

2. Jean-Pierre Cot, "Conciliation," in A Peters (ed.), *Max Planck Encyclopedia of Public International Law* (OUP 2006) para. 12 https://opil.ouplaw.com/view/10.1093/law:epil/9780199231690/law-9780199231690-e20#law-9780199231690-e20-div2-1 (accessed August 16, 2025).
3. Linda C. Reif, Conciliation as a Mechanism for the Resolution of International Economic and Business Disputes, 14 Fordham Int'l L. J. 578, 584 (1991).
4. United Nations Office of Legal Affairs, Codification Division, Handbook on Peaceful Settlement of International Disputes, UN Doc. OLA/COD/2394 (1992), para. 140; *see also* Jean-Pierre Cot, "Conciliation," in A Peters (ed.), *Max Planck Encyclopedia of Public International Law* (OUP 2006), para. 3 https://opil.ouplaw.com/view/10.1093/law:epil/9780199231690/law-9780199231690-e20#law-9780199231690-e20-div2-1 (accessed August 16, 2025) (defining conciliation as "a

Whatever its form, foundational to conciliation is that it is a party-driven process powered by consent. Originating in a series of bilateral treaties concluded in the early twentieth century, conciliation "classically addresses inter-State disputes" where consent is vital.[5] Consent is also critical to the effectiveness of this procedure because the appointed third party must "enjoy[] the confidence of the parties to the dispute."[6] Thus, while conciliation involves the assistance of a third party, the disputing parties maintain significant discretion to define the scope, procedure, and results of the conciliation. This includes deciding the extent to which the conciliation remains confidential—a feature that takes on particular importance when sensitive inter-State negotiations are involved.

The mandate of third-party conciliators also varies and can run the gamut from involving determinations of both legal and fact issues to an exclusive fact-finding role to playing a purely diplomatic function.[7] But regardless of the precise contours of that mandate, the overarching role of conciliators is to assist the parties in finding an amicable settlement by whatever mechanism best serves that mandate.

Indeed, it is this flexibility, in terms of subject matter, procedure, and method of resolution, premised upon the foundation of party consent, and facilitated by a trusted and neutral third party, that makes conciliation such a potentially powerful method of resolution in certain contexts.

2 Advantages over Other Dispute Resolution Mechanisms

To determine how and why conciliation may be more effective and useful in a particular context, it is helpful to consider key differences between conciliation and other more commonly used dispute resolution mechanisms, namely arbitration and mediation.

a Conciliation Versus Arbitration

A key distinguishing feature between conciliation and arbitration is that arbitration typically involves an adversarial process under a standardized set of procedural rules

half-breed method for the settlement of disputes. It stands some way between diplomatic methods for the settlement of disputes such as negotiation, good offices, or mediation on the one hand, and arbitral or judicial settlement on the other").

5. United Nations Office of Legal Affairs, Codification Division, Handbook on Peaceful Settlement of International Disputes, UN Doc. OLA/COD/2394 (1992), para. 141.
6. Jean-Pierre Cot, *International Conciliation* (1968) 9.
7. *See, e.g.*, Linda C. Reif, Conciliation as a Mechanism for the Resolution of International Economic and Business Disputes, 14 Fordham Int'l L. J. 578, 583 (1991) ("[Conciliation] can be utilized in the settlement of disputes that involved 'non-arbitrable' or 'non-justiciable' issues and is generally not hindered by jurisdictional challenges. Conciliation is used, even where there are relevant sources of law that can be applied, because the disputants may wish to soften the impact of legal principles concerned by implementing a conciliatory approach that focuses on reaching an equitable solution. Conciliators are given the flexibility in the pursuit of a just result and, although certain laws and obligations cannot be disregarded, extant conciliation rules reflect this freedom.").

under which third-party arbitrator(s) are empowered to reach a decision that is binding on the parties to the dispute.

There are several implications to the differences between conciliation and arbitration. *First*, the binding nature of arbitral awards may be useful for disputing parties that have consented to have their legal rights conclusively determined and enforced. On the other hand, some disputes might benefit from a more flexible array of solutions, including those of a non-legal and non-judicial nature. *Second*, the adversarial nature of arbitration may be useful for narrowing the legal and factual issues in dispute and assisting the arbitral tribunal in reaching its determination, particularly where an amicable settlement seems unlikely. This, however, may have a detrimental impact to the long-term relationship between the disputing parties. This is especially the case when arbitrations result in significant monetary judgments or costs that may feel punitive as a result. *Third*, arbitrations often are characterized by more rigid procedural rules that are designed to ensure due process in an adversarial context. Applicable rules, such as the preclusion of ex parte conversations between one disputing party and the tribunal, prevent more informal and closed-door caucuses between the parties and decision-makers that could assist the parties in identifying an amicable resolution. *Fourth*, and relatedly, most arbitration proceedings are administered by an arbitration institution and conducted under set arbitration rules, often selected by the parties in the underlying contracts or treaties even before the dispute has arisen. This may be less desirable in cases where the disputing parties need to diverge from standard rules to suit the dispute at hand. *Finally*, arbitrations can be prolonged, and disputing parties sometimes do not have control over the extent to which they are publicized. This may be problematic particularly for politically sensitive disputes that parties require confidentially in order to facilitate a potential amicable resolution.

b Conciliation Versus Mediation

While mediation and conciliation are similarly non-adversarial and often spoken about interchangeably, there can be distinct differences between the two procedures. Mediation is described by the UN Office of Legal Affairs as "a method of peaceful settlement of an international dispute where a third party intervenes to reconcile the claims of the contending parties and to advance his [or her] own proposals aimed at a mutually acceptable compromise solution."[8] While mediations come in various forms, with differing levels of "intervention" by mediators, some consider mediation to be less structured than conciliation, where a mediator's mandate can be simply to facilitate discussions between the parties to assist them in reaching an agreement.[9] A conciliation commission, on the other hand, can be charged with a more active role in elucidating the questions in dispute with bespoke procedures reflecting a greater focus

8. United Nations Office of Legal Affairs, Codification Division, Handbook on Peaceful Settlement of International Disputes, UN Doc. OLA/COD/2394 (1992), para. 123.
9. *See, e.g.*, Linda C. Reif, The Use of Conciliation or Mediation for the Resolution of International Commercial Disputes, 45 Can. Bus. L.J. 20, 22 (2007).

on the relationship between the parties themselves in reaching an amicable resolution. As compared to mediation, therefore, conciliation allows parties to drive the conciliation process, while providing the conciliation commission sufficient authority to meaningfully contribute to the resolution of a dispute through procedures specifically tailored to the unique characteristics of a dispute.

3 Conciliation Case Studies

The benefits and features of conciliation, particularly for resolving inter-State disputes, are perhaps best exemplified by considering conciliation proceedings that have taken place to date. In particular, the conciliation between Timor-Leste and Australia and multiple conciliations under the International Convention on the Elimination of All Forms of Racial Discrimination (*ICERD*) are well known inter-State proceedings that highlight the importance of party consent, flexibility, and an adequate balancing of confidentiality and transparency interests to effectively assist disputing parties to reach an amicable resolution of their disputes.

a Timor Sea Conciliation

The 2016 conciliation between Timor-Leste and Australia (*Timor Sea Conciliation*) relating to their ongoing maritime boundaries dispute is considered one of the most successful conciliations to date. After a long-standing deadlock between the parties in trying to reach a resolution through negotiation, arbitration, and contentious proceedings before the International Court of Justice (*ICJ*),[10] the parties submitted their dispute to the compulsory conciliation procedure under the United Nations Convention on the Law of the Sea (*UNCLOS*), making it the first publicly known instance of conciliation under that treaty.[11] The parties, with the support of the Conciliation Commission, settled their dispute and reached an agreement as set out by the 2018 Treaty on the Timor Sea Maritime Boundary.[12]

The success of the Timor Sea Conciliation is perhaps best attributed to its key procedural features, which emphasized flexibility and party autonomy, and were conducive to meaningful cooperation between the parties. The Conciliation Commission, after seeking the views of the parties, drafted supplementary Rules of Procedure to govern the conciliation proceeding.[13] In doing so, the parties sought to "maintain a

10. *Timor Sea Conciliation (Timor-Leste v. Australia)*, Report and Recommendations of the Compulsory Conciliation Commission between Timor-Leste and Australia on the Timor Sea (May 9, 2018), paras. 45-46.
11. Dai Tamada, The Timor Sea Conciliation: The Unique Mechanism of Dispute Settlement, 31(1) EJIL 322 (February 2020) https://doi.org/10.1093/ejil/chaa025 (accessed August 16, 2025).
12. *Timor Sea Conciliation (Timor-Leste v. Australia)*, Report and Recommendations of the Compulsory Conciliation Commission between Timor-Leste and Australia on the Timor Sea (May 9, 2018), para. 284.
13. *Timor Sea Conciliation (Timor-Leste v. Australia)*, Rules of Procedure (August 22, 2016).

flexible and informal approach to enable the Commission to follow the path that it considered most likely to lead to an amicable settlement."[14]

The Commission's mandate was limited to "mak[ing] proposals to the parties with a view to reaching an amicable settlement,"[15] again emphasizing the parties' control over the proceeding and the Commission's role in assisting them in reaching a resolution. The Rules expressly empowered the Commission to "draw to the attention of the Parties any measure which the Commission considers might facilitate an amicable settlement of the dispute."[16] In addition, the Commission was empowered to engage with the parties separately through informal discussions, a flexible feature that the Commission deemed "essential to the process."[17]

The Rules of Procedure also allowed the parties to retain control over the disclosure of information, seeking to strike a balance between two competing interests: on the one hand, ensuring a frank discussion with the Commission without significant risk of public disclosure of information without the parties' consent, and on the other, being conscious of the impacts of marine boundaries delimitation on non-disputing parties.[18] In furtherance of this balancing exercise, the Rules made the existence of the conciliation public, while leaving the disclosure of other information related to the conciliation to the discretion of the Commission, in consultation with the disputing parties.[19] For example, the Commission, in consultation with the parties, could "designate any hearing, or any portion thereof, as a public hearing or meeting"[20] and decide "whether to make the Commission's Report or any portion thereof public."[21]

These features of the Timor Sea Conciliation focused on "a positive outcome" for the disputing parties that was "preferable to a resolution of the dispute consisting merely of identifying a 'winner.'"[22]

14. *Timor Sea Conciliation (Timor-Leste v. Australia)*, Report and Recommendations of the Compulsory Conciliation Commission between Timor-Leste and Australia on the Timor Sea (May 9, 2018), para. 57.
15. UNCLOS, Annex V on Conciliation, Article 6.
16. *Timor Sea Conciliation (Timor-Leste v. Australia)*, Rules of Procedure (August 22, 2016), Rule 18(3).
17. *Timor Sea Conciliation (Timor-Leste v. Australia)*, Report and Recommendations of the Compulsory Conciliation Commission between Timor-Leste and Australia on the Timor Sea (May 9, 2018), para. 58; *Timor Sea Conciliation (Timor-Leste v. Australia)*, Rules of Procedure (August 22, 2016), Rules 12 and 18(4).
18. *Timor Sea Conciliation (Timor-Leste v. Australia)*, Report and Recommendations of the Compulsory Conciliation Commission between Timor-Leste and Australia on the Timor Sea (May 9, 2018), para. 57.
19. *Timor Sea Conciliation (Timor-Leste v. Australia)*, Rules of Procedure (August 22, 2016), Rule 16.
20. *Timor Sea Conciliation (Timor-Leste v. Australia)*, Rules of Procedure (August 22, 2016), Rule 16(2).
21. *Timor Sea Conciliation (Timor-Leste v. Australia)*, Rules of Procedure (August 22, 2016), Rule 16(5).
22. *Timor Sea Conciliation (Timor-Leste v. Australia)*, Report and Recommendations of the Compulsory Conciliation Commission between Timor-Leste and Australia on the Timor Sea (May 9, 2018), para. 285.

b Conciliations under the International Convention on the Elimination of All Forms of Racial Discrimination (ICERD)

States have also resorted to conciliation to resolve disputes concerning alleged human rights violations. The ICERD was the first human rights treaty to adopt conciliation as a mechanism to resolve human rights disputes. After remaining dormant for fifty years, this mechanism was invoked in three inter-state communications in 2018: *Qatar v. Kingdom of Saudi Arabia* (2018), *Qatar v. United Arab Emirates* (2018), and *Palestine v. Israel* (2018).[23]

Article 11 of ICERD allows States Parties to bring any matters to the Committee on the Elimination of Racial Discrimination (*CERD Committee*) relating to compliance with the Convention provisions.[24] Once the State brings the matter to the CERD Committee's attention, the Committee must transmit the communication to the State concerned, which is obligated to respond to the matter and clarify any remedies taken.[25] If the matter is not "adjusted to the satisfaction of both parties ... within six months," either State can then refer the matter to the Committee again.[26] Article 12 of ICERD provides for the appointment of an ad hoc conciliation commission to assist the disputing parties in reaching an amicable resolution of disputes concerning their compliance with the Convention.[27] In accordance with Article 12, the members of the Commission are appointed with the unanimous consent of the parties to the dispute and the Commission's "good offices shall be made available to the States concerned with a view to an amicable solution of the matter on the basis of respect for [the] Convention."[28] In turn, Article 13 of ICERD requires the Commission to "prepare and submit to the Chairman of the Committee a report embodying its findings on all questions of fact relevant to the issue between the parties and containing such recommendations as it may think proper for the amicable solution of the dispute."[29] Once the report is communicated to the disputing states, the CERD Committee shares the report with other States Parties to the Convention.[30]

In March 2018, Qatar submitted two inter-state communications under Article 11, against the Kingdom of Saudi Arabia and the United Arab Emirates, respectively, alleging various violations under the ICERD. After the CERD Committee declared both communications admissible, the Chairman appointed two ad hoc commissions, which were mandated to "make their good offices available to the States concerned with a

23. Committee on the Elimination of Racial Discrimination, Inter-state communications, https://www.ohchr.org/en/treaty-bodies/cerd/inter-state-communications (accessed August 16, 2025) I and colleagues at Debevoise & Plimpton LLP served as counsel to Qatar in the *Qatar v. Kingdom of Saudi Arabia* and *Qatar v. United Arab Emirates* matters. The views expressed in this chapter are my own and are not attributable to Debevoise or its clients.
24. International Convention on the Elimination of All Forms of Racial Discrimination, Article 11.
25. International Convention on the Elimination of All Forms of Racial Discrimination, Article 11(1).
26. International Convention on the Elimination of All Forms of Racial Discrimination, Article 11(2).
27. International Convention on the Elimination of All Forms of Racial Discrimination, Article 12. The Chairman of the Committee appoints the conciliation Commission, but the parties must consent to such appointment.
28. International Convention on the Elimination of All Forms of Racial Discrimination, Article 11.
29. International Convention on the Elimination of All Forms of Racial Discrimination, Article 13(1).
30. International Convention on the Elimination of All Forms of Racial Discrimination, Article 13(3).

view of an amicable solution of the matter."[31] Both conciliations were suspended, and ultimately terminated, once the parties concluded the Al Ula Declaration on January 5, 2021.[32]

In April 2018, Palestine submitted a communication to the CERD Committee against Israel under Article 11, making it the third invocation of this procedure. The communication was held admissible, and an ad hoc Conciliation Commission was formed pursuant to Article 12 of the Convention. The Commission has held six in-person meetings since May 2022, to address administrative matters, information gathering, strategies of conciliation and the drafting of the Commission's report.[33] The conciliation proceedings remain pending.[34] The ad hoc Commission in the Palestine-Israel conciliation adopted its own Rules of Procedure. In line with the goal of conciliation, the Rules of Procedure limit the mandate of the Conciliation Commission to "mak[ing] available its good offices to the State concerned with a view to an amicable solution of the matter on the basis of respect for the Convention."[35] The Rules of Procedure also emphasize flexibility by allowing both formal and informal communications with the parties. For example, the Commission is permitted to meet or communicate with the disputing parties "orally or in writing" and "together or with each of them separately."[36] In addition, the Rules seek to promote frank discussions between the parties by requiring the Commission and the disputing parties to "keep confidential all matters relating to the conciliation proceedings."[37]

III CONCILIATION AS AN EFFECTIVE MEANS OF RESOLVING CLIMATE CHANGE DISPUTES

For most States Parties, non-binding conciliation will be the default method for resolving disputes concerning the interpretation or application of the UNFCCC and the Paris Agreement. Under these instruments, "[i]n the event of a dispute between any two or more Parties concerning the interpretation or application of the Convention, the Parties concerned shall seek a settlement of the dispute through *negotiation* or any

31. Committee on the Elimination of Racial Discrimination, Inter-state communications, https://www.ohchr.org/en/treaty-bodies/cerd/inter-state-communications (accessed August 16, 2025).
32. *Qatar v. UAE*—Decision on the termination of the proceedings (January 26, 2023); *Qatar v. KSA*—Decision on the termination of the proceedings (January 19, 2022).
33. Committee on the Elimination of Racial Discrimination, Inter-state communications, https://www.ohchr.org/en/treaty-bodies/cerd/inter-state-communications (accessed August 16, 2025).
34. The six in-person meetings took place on May 4-5, 2022, August 31-September 1, 2022, December 5-6, 2022, May 1-2, 2023, 1, 4, 5 and September 6, 2023, and December 11-12, 2023. Committee on the Elimination of Racial Discrimination, Inter-state communications, https://www.ohchr.org/en/treaty-bodies/cerd/inter-state-communications (accessed August 16, 2025).
35. Rules of Procedure of the ad hoc Conciliation Commission on the interstate communication submitted by the State of Palestine against Israel under Article 11 of the International Convention on the Elimination of All Forms of Racial Discrimination (April 25, 2022), Rule 2.
36. Rules of Procedure of the ad hoc Conciliation Commission on the interstate communication submitted by the State of Palestine against Israel under Article 11 of the International Convention on the Elimination of All Forms of Racial Discrimination (April 25, 2022), Rule 13(2).
37. Rules of Procedure of the ad hoc Conciliation Commission on the interstate communication submitted by the State of Palestine against Israel under Article 11 of the International Convention on the Elimination of All Forms of Racial Discrimination (April 25, 2022), Rule 6.

other peaceful means of their own choice."[38] If negotiations fail, parties may submit the dispute to either the ICJ or arbitration, so long as both parties have previously agreed to do so through a written declaration.[39] These methods are largely unavailable since only a handful of States Parties have agreed to them.[40] For parties that have not agreed to resolve disputes before the ICJ or through arbitration and have not settled their dispute by negotiation or another peaceful means within twelve months, their disputes "*shall* be submitted, at the request of any of the parties to the dispute, to conciliation."[41]

Pursuant to Article 14(6) of the UNFCCC and Article 24 of the Paris Agreement, if a dispute concerning the interpretation or application of one of these legal instruments is submitted to conciliation, then:

> A conciliation commission shall be created upon the request of one of the parties to the dispute. The commission shall be composed of an equal number of members appointed by each party concerned and a chairman chosen jointly by the members appointed by each party. The commission shall render a recommendatory award, which the parties shall consider in good faith.

Article 14(7) of the UNFCCC also provides that: "Additional procedures relating to conciliation shall be adopted by the Conference of the Parties, as soon as practicable, in an annex on conciliation." However, these contemplated "additional procedures" have yet to be adopted.

The adoption of such conciliation annex is crucial for the effective implementation of the dispute settlement provisions under the UNFCCC and the Paris Agreement as it would provide disputing states with a blueprint for the effective, equitable resolution of disputes. Disputes that may arise over the interpretation and application of the UNFCCC or Paris Agreement are varied, and can include, for example: disputes relating to nationally determined contributions (NDCs);[42] bilateral or plurilateral agreements on the cooperative implementation of States' NDCs, including the direct exchange of carbon credits and other units;[43] and the provision (or lack thereof) of financial resources[44] and technology transfers[45] by one State to another State or States to assist with the implementation of mitigation and adaptation actions.

The key features of conciliation make it particularly well suited for effective resolution of these and other climate change disputes. In particular, as set out in further

38. UNFCCC, Article 14(1).
39. UNFCCC, Article 14(2).
40. Only the Netherlands has accepted to submit disputes to both arbitration and the ICJ. Solomon Islands and Tuvalu agreed to submit disputes to arbitration. *See* UNFCCC Declaration by Parties—Netherlands, Tuvalu, Solomon Islands, https://unfccc.int/process-and-meetings/the-convention/status-of-ratification/declarations-by-parties (accessed August 16, 2025).
41. UNFCCC, Article 14(5).
42. Paris Agreement, Article 4(2).
43. Paris Agreement, Article 6(1) and 6(2).
44. Paris Agreement, Article 9.
45. Paris Agreement, Article 10.

detail below, conciliation offers the flexibility, subject-matter expertise, and opportunity for enhanced collaboration and cooperation necessary to effectively resolve climate change disputes.

1 Tailored Procedures and Recommendations

As detailed above, conciliation is inherently flexible and offers disputing parties the ability to tailor the procedure of their conciliation to reflect the specific characteristics of their dispute. Disputing parties' ability to determine the scope, procedure and results of the conciliation is particularly beneficial in the context of climate change disputes, which are unique for their particular complexity and the fact that the issues in dispute may have wide-ranging impacts, including on parties not directly involved in the dispute.

To account for these characteristics, parties to a climate change dispute may wish to adopt a procedure that: allows for multiple disputing parties as well as non-disputing parties to play a role; takes account of the particular complexities and urgency of disputes resolving climate-related issues, including by providing options for the involvement of subject-matter experts; allows for public access to information on climate change; and encourages open communications between disputing parties and the conciliators. The inherent flexibility of conciliation allows for tailored procedures that incorporate these different considerations, while also reflecting any variety of specific cultural, economic, developmental and other interests and preferences of the disputing parties. These procedural aspects will be discussed in further detail below.

In addition, disputing parties maintain ultimate discretion over the mandate of the conciliators and the end result of the conciliation. As noted above, conciliators generally issue an advisory, non-binding recommendation to disputing parties. Disputing parties can agree to conciliation procedures in respect of this recommendation, including: specific topics to be addressed by the conciliators; whether the recommendation will include conclusions of factual issues and other matters, in addition to the recommendations of the conciliators; the extent to which the recommendation will be made public; and any measures for implantation of the conciliators' recommendations.

2 Balancing Transparency and Confidentiality Interests

Because climate change is a global issue with wide-ranging impacts, public awareness, public participation, and public access to information are especially important in this context. At the same time, confidentiality is important to ensure that disputing parties are given the space for frank and open communications, which can be far more likely to result in the amicable resolution of the dispute. There are two main implications involved in balancing these key considerations.

First, the need for transparency can be accommodated by procedures that take into account the importance of giving an opportunity for non-disputing parties to participate in some fashion in the conciliation itself. For example, disputing parties may agree that conciliators can affirmatively seek the views or otherwise facilitate the written and/or oral submissions of third parties—such as impacted communities, NGOs, or technical organizations with expertise in climate change science—likely to be able to furnish relevant information about the issues in dispute.[46]

Second, conciliation allows for special processes to be designed to increase transparency and further the goals of public participation and access to information related to climate change, while maintaining confidentiality of the dispute in accordance with the disputing parties' interests. For example, disputing parties may agree to certain presumptions in respect of transparency—such as the existence of the dispute and agreed details being public—or otherwise empower the conciliators to determine which aspects of the dispute should be made public. Disputing parties can still maintain control over sensitive information, for example, by agreeing that the conciliators will seek their views before making any information about the dispute public, or by providing that certain information designated by a party as confidential will never be shared.

In this way, conciliation allows the disputing parties to balance the key goals of public access to climate change information that could have global relevance and confidentiality as required for the efficient resolution of disputes.

3 Complexity and Urgency

Climate change disputes are likely to involve complex facts, potentially spanning wide geographic areas as well as a lengthy period of time, and involving complex questions of attribution and causation. They may also require urgent resolution in order to prevent or mitigate serious environmental harms. Conciliation procedures can be adapted to account for this complexity and urgency.

For example, disputing parties may agree to a conciliation procedure that involves subject-matter experts in the dispute, either serving as conciliators or assisting conciliators with the collection and assessment of technical evidence. Experts may have relevant technical or legal expertise to assist conciliators with understanding complex issues in dispute and the information submitted by disputing parties. Experts could also participate in site visits or assist with the collection of evidence, depending on the particular needs of the parties and the circumstances of the dispute. Examples of provisions providing for the involvement of experts can be found in the Permanent Court of Arbitration's Optional Rules for the Conciliation of Disputes Relating to Natural Resources and/or the Environment and the United Nations Model Rules for the Conciliation of Disputes between States which provide, respectively, for the conciliators to "propose the appointment of one or more experts to report on specific issues, after having obtained the views of the parties" and "propose to the parties that they

46. *Cf.* Statute of the International Court of Justice, Article 66 ("The Registrar shall also, by means of a special and direct communication, notify any state entitled to appear before the Court or international organization considered by the Court, or, should it not be sitting, by the President, as likely to be able to furnish information on the question, that the Court will be prepared to receive, within a time-limit to be fixed by the President, written statements, or to hear, at a public sitting to be held for the purpose, oral statements relating to the question.")

jointly appoint expert advisers to assist it in the consideration of technical aspects of the dispute."[47]

In addition to being potentially very complex, climate change disputes may require urgent resolution in order to prevent or mitigate future climate impacts or other harms. In such cases, conciliation offers the flexibility needed for disputing parties to agree on expedited processes and procedures—including in respect of timelines for party submissions and the recommendations of the conciliators—as well as specific provisions intended to assist the parties in urgently reaching a resolution.

4 Enhanced Collaboration and Cooperation

Because the principal objective of conciliation is the amicable resolution of disputes, it provides opportunities for disputing parties to build trust, increase communication, strengthen their relationship, and de-escalate differences. This is particularly important in the context of climate change disputes, where issues relevant to climate change of course are not constrained by national borders. As a result, climate change disputes may involve multiple States as disputing parties at a level far beyond traditional disputes in contentious cases. Climate change impacts may also give rise to multiple disputes involving related or overlapping parties and issues. Indeed, climate change is a global crisis that requires cooperation and coordination among the global community of States in order to prevent or mitigate future climate impacts.

Conciliation is flexible enough to allow for bespoke procedures tailored to potentially multiple disputes and/or parties and to balance the differing interests and priorities of these parties in a non-adversarial context. Conciliation procedures can be designed to equally balance the needs and interests of all disputing parties, along with cultural, economic, and other goals, and to facilitate open and frank communications between the parties and conciliators. The very purpose of conciliation is to encourage information exchange with the aim of reaching a resolution that is acceptable to all parties. As detailed above, for example, disputing parties are able to determine the appropriate balance between transparency and confidentiality goals, can provide for ex parte communications with the conciliators, and can agree on the particular topics and issues subject to recommendations or conclusions by the conciliators. Particularly, in comparison to adversarial methods of dispute resolution, conciliation is therefore well suited to resolving disputes, like climate change disputes, that require collaboration and cooperation in order to reach a long-term solution.

47. Permanent Court of Arbitration, Optional Rules for the Conciliation of Disputes Relating to Natural Resources and/or the Environment, Article 7(4); United Nations Model Rules for the Conciliation of Disputes between States, Article 15. *See also* United Nations Model Rules for the Conciliation of Disputes between States, Article 14 ("In cases where the parties disagree on joint issues of fact, the [conciliation] commission may use all means at its disposal, such as the joint expert advisers mentioned in article 15, or consultation with experts, to ascertain the facts").

IV CONCLUSION

The international community has entered a new phase of urgent climate action, where calls for collective negotiation and cooperation are accompanied by an increasing need for effective dispute resolution mechanisms. Conciliation is a powerful, yet underutilized tool that has the potential to enhance the effective implementation of multilateral environmental agreements in ways no other dispute resolution mechanism can. Its undeniable and proven benefits make it especially suitable for the effective and peaceful settlement of environmental disputes under the UNFCCC framework, including the Paris Agreement. Conciliation not only affords disputing parties the flexibility to tailor the procedures to the specific characteristics and needs of their dispute but also creates the conditions for ensuring the sustained collaboration and cooperation necessary to effectively address climate change on a global scale.

CHAPTER 35

Small- and Medium-Sized Enterprises: The Engines of the Economy but the Overlooked Dispute Resolution Stakeholders

Dr Petra Butler[*]

TABLE OF CONTENTS

I INTRODUCTION

During the COVID pandemic when global supply chains were disrupted, it became apparent who and what was required for a well-functioning global economy, namely, inter alia, a well-functioning international logistic systems that trans-shipped supplies and final goods in an efficient, reliable and timely fashion through an integrated network of airlines, marine shipping, railway, trucking and transportation systems.[1] The role of small- and medium-sized enterprises (SMEs) as an integral part in the

---

* Executive Dean and Professor, University of Canterbury, Faculty of Law; Director, Institute of Small and Micro States; Senior Research Fellow, British Institute of International and Comparative Law. I would like to thank my colleague Associate Professor Matthew Barber and Judith Levine, chair of the ICCA Panel, for their valuable comments – any mistakes are solely mine.

1. *See* Hamid Etemad, 'Chapter 1: Introduction to Small and Medium Sized Enterprises and the COVID-19 Response', in Hamid Etemad (ed.), *Small and Medium Sized Enterprises and the COVID-19 Response* (Elgaronline, 2022) 3; Laura Maria Franciosi, 'The Effects of COVID-19 on

international logistic system and the global supply chain infrastructure became more apparent than ever before, and institutions and academics paid suddenly particular attention to SMEs. The capacity of SMEs to safeguard domestic supplies also came to the fore. SMEs morphed from a stepchild into a love child.[2]

Curiously, despite the attention SMEs have enjoyed since the pandemic, the lack of engagement with the contracting behaviour of SMEs has not changed. Supporting SMEs' spasmodic contracting[3] is vital for global supply chain health and the growth of domestic (emerging) economies. The uncertainty over how to manage their dispute resolution risk has been identified as a trade barrier for SMEs which prefer to self-hedge rather than taking the risk of trading cross-border.[4] Any cross-border dispute resolution mechanism offering access to commercial justice for SMEs and thereby supporting SME cross-border trade has to take account of the spasmodic nature of their contractual behaviour.[5] This chapter will set out how such a possible cross-border dispute resolution mechanism might look.

The chapter will briefly set out the importance of SMEs for the economy, then describe some of the SMEs' contractual behaviour, and lastly discuss a default cross-border business-to-business dispute resolution framework that is mindful of the described behaviour.

II THE PLACE OF SMES IN THE GLOBAL AND DOMESTIC ECONOMY

SMEs globally comprise 90% of all businesses; account for 40% of the GDP; employ more than 50% of the workforce; and constitute the primary means for creating the 600 million jobs required by the year 2030.[6] While informal SMEs contribute demonstrably to employment in emerging markets (especially for women), formal (exporting) SMEs

International Contracts: A Comparative Overview' (2020) 51 Victoria University of Wellington Law Review 413 https://doi.org/10.26686/vuwlr.v51i3.6610 (accessed 16 August 2025).

2. 'Commission seeks to boost competitiveness and resilience of SMEs', EU Focus 2023, 432 paras 16 & 17; Johnny Wood, *Europe's Small Businesses Proved Resilient to COVID-19 Pandemic Disruption: Here's What that Means for SMEs' World Economic Forum* (3 January 2023); Alexander Bartik et al., The Impact of COVID-19 on Small Business Outcomes and Expectations' (July 2020) 117(30) Proceedings of the National Academy of Sciences 17656 https://doi.org/10.1073/pnas.2006991117 (accessed 16 August 2025); Abhishek Mukherjee 'Stay Home, Save SMEs'? The Impact of a Unique Strict COVID-19 Lockdown on Small Businesses' (2023) 29 International Journal of Entrepreneurial Behavior & Research 1884 https://doi.org/10.1108/ijebr-02-2023-0099 (accessed 16 August 2025); Petra Butler, 'UNCITRAL and MSMEs: An Enduring and Successful Marriage' in Rishi Gulati et al. (eds), *The Elgar Companion to UNCITRAL* (Edgar Elgar, 2023) 377.
3. Petra Butler and Eldrede Kahiya, '"I Don't Think About It, I Try Not To": Spasmodic Contractual Governance by Some Exporters' in F. Benatti et al. (eds), *The Transnational Sales Contract: 40 Years Influence of the CISG on National Jurisdictions* (Wolters Kluwer, 2022) 37.
4. *See* Commonwealth Secretariat (authors Petra Butler and Dharshini Prasad), *A Study of International Commercial Arbitration in the Commonwealth* (London, 2020) Executive Summary.
5. 'Spasmodic' refers to unpredictable behaviour and irregular patterns.
6. World Bank, 'Small and Medium Enterprises (SMES)- Overview' https://www.worldbank.org/en/topic/smefinance (accessed 1 April 2024).

are critical to the economic success of developing nations.[7] Given the importance of SMEs' participation in global trade for the overall well-being of local economies, supranational organisations such as the International Finance Corporation[8] and the OECD,[9] and international business scholars[10] place considerable weight and time on studying exporting SMEs.[11] The UN's Sustainable Development Goals confirm an international commitment to encouraging the growth of SMEs.[12]

While the size of SMEs varies significantly between states,[13] many of their common features are universal. Their management is generally time poor, they lack

7. Murat Bayraktar and Nese Algan, 'The Importance of SMEs on World Economics' International Conference on Eurasian Economies 2019, 56, 56 available at https://www.avekon.org/papers/2265.pdf (accessed 1 April 2024); OECD, *OECD SME and Entrepreneurship Outlook 2019* (OECD, Paris, 2019) Chapter 1 available at https://www.oecd.org/industry/oecd-sme-and-entrepreneurship-outlook-2019-34907e9c-en.htm (accessed 1 April 2024).
8. *See* Peer Stein, Oya Ardic and Martin Hommes, *Closing the Credit Gap for Formal and Informal Micro, Small, and Medium Enterprises* (International Finance Corporation, Washington, DC, 2013) 7.
9. Stein et al. (n 8) 7.
10. Ilayda Ipek, 'Organizational Learning in Exporting: A Bibliometric Analysis and Critical Review of the Empirical Research' (2019) 3 International Business Review 28, 544-559 https://doi.org/10.1016/j.ibusrev.2018.11.010 (accessed 16 August 2025); Ilayda Ipek and Nilay Bıçakcıoğlu-Peynirci, 'Export Market Orientation: An Integrative Review and Directions for Future Research' (2020) 4 International Business Review 29.4, 101659 https://doi.org/10.1016/j.ibusrev.2019.101659 (accessed 16 August 2025); Leonidas C. Leonidou, Saeed Samiee, Bilge Aykol, and Michael A. Talias, 'Antecedents and Outcomes of Exporter–Importer Relationship Quality: Synthesis, Meta-Analysis, and Directions for Further Research' (2014) 22 Journal of International Marketing, 21-46 https://doi.org/10.1509/jim.13.0129 (accessed 16 August 2025); Min Li, Xinming He, and Carlos MP Sousa, 'A Review of the Empirical Research on Export Channel Selection Between 1979 and 2015' (2017) 26 International Business Review, 303-323 https://doi.org/10.1016/j.ibusrev.2016.09.001 (accessed 16 August 2025).
11. Leonidas C. Leonidou, Constantine S. Katsikeas, and Dafnis N. Coudounaris, 'Five Decades of Business Research into Exporting: A Bibliographic Analysis' (2010) 16 Journal of International Management 78-91 https://doi.org/10.1016/j.intman.2009.06.001 (accessed 16 August 2025); Bilge Aykol and Leonidas C. Leonidou. 'Exporter-Importer Business Relationships: Past Empirical Research and Future Directions' (2018) 27 International Business Review 1007-1021 https://doi.org/10.1016/j.ibusrev.2018.03.001 (accessed 16 August 2025); Preet S. Aulakh and F. Esra Gençtürk, 'Contract Formalization and Governance of Exporter–Importer Relationships' (2008) 45 Journal of Management Studies 457-479 https://doi.org/10.1111/j.1467-6486.2007.00746.x (accessed 16 August 2025); David A. Griffith and Yanhui Zhao, 'Contract Specificity, Contract Violation, and Relationship Performance in International Buyer–Supplier Relationships' (2015) 23 Journal of International Marketing 22-40 https://doi.org/10.1509/jim.14.0138 (accessed 16 August 2025); Leonidas C. Leonidou, Saeed Samiee, Bilge Aykol, and Michael A. Talias, 'Antecedents and Outcomes of Exporter–Importer Relationship Quality: Synthesis, Meta-Analysis, and Directions for Further Research' (2014) 22 Journal of international Marketing 21-46 https://doi.org/10.1509/jim.13.0129 (accessed 16 August 2025).
12. United Nations 'Sustainable Development Goals' https://www.un.org/sustainabledevelopment/economic-growth/ (accessed 2 April 2024).
13. In New Zealand an SME is an enterprise with less than 100 employees (MBIE, 'Small Businesses in 2022- Factsheet' (MBIE, 2022, accessed 5 April 2024)); in the EU with less than 250 and annual turnover not exceeding EUR 50 million (European Commission, 'The new SME definition') (European Commission, 2003, accessed 5 April 2024), in Japan with less than 300, and in the US with less than 500 (OECD – Centre For Entrepreneurship, SMEs and Local Development, Fostering SMEs' Participation in Global Markets: Final Report (4 July 2013) CFE/SME (2012)6/FINAL para. 72).

resources and the foresight to plan ahead,[14] and have few reserves for rainy days.[15] They prefer to conduct business through informal networks; i.e., they rely on a limited number of close inter-firm and interpersonal relationships.[16] Many businesses feel that they have 'limited experience' when it comes to cross-border contracting,[17] in particular in terms of the enforcement of their rights vis-à-vis their business partners,[18] and therefore refrain from taking part or continuing to take part in cross-border trade.

The domestic and cross-border activities of the SMEs can therefore be described as 'at odds': the importance of SMEs for the domestic and global economy generally does not correspond with their preparedness to participate in the cross-border economy. This dichotomy warrants a more detailed and explanatory discussion on the contractual behaviour of SMEs.

III THE CONTRACTUAL BEHAVIOUR OF SMES

Many assumptions and conclusions made about international dispute resolution do not specifically consider the unique situation of SMEs. This problem is compounded by the fact that many of the concerns and cases involving SMEs are invisible to usual legal research techniques. Disputes involving SMEs are frequently the very cases that do not make it to the court or arbitral tribunal. In many cases, they do not even make it to the lawyer's office. It seems that SMEs, considering their market share, are largely underrepresented in international dispute resolution. A rare exception is *Nelson Honey v. William Jacks Trading.*

The plaintiff, *Nelson Honey*, dispatched, after receiving an order from *William Jacks Trading* (the defendant), two consignments of honey worth NZD 206,000 to a warehouse in Auckland, New Zealand. *William Jacks Trading* proceeded to consign both shipments to Shanghai, China, but alleged that upon receipt at destination, it became apparent the honey was not of acceptable quality. *William Jacks Trading* rejected the honey and refused to pay for both consignments. *Nelson Honey* did not accept the rejection and sued for the cost of the consignments in the Nelson High Court.[19] *William Jacks Trading* counter-sued in the Singaporean High Court,[20] for the

14. Georgia Whelan, 'Evaluating the Proposed Bilateral Arbitration Treaty' (New Zealand Institute of Economic Research (NZIER), Wellington, 2016) 2.
15. Hamid Etemad, 'Chapter 1: Introduction to Small and Medium Sized Enterprises and the COVID-19 Response' in Hamid Etemad (ed.), *Small and Medium Sized Enterprises and the COVID-19 Response* (Elgaronline, 2022) 10.
16. Petra Butler and Hanneke van Oeveren, 'SMEs and International Commercial Dispute Resolution: Without Leading the Horse to Water, It Is Unlikely That It Will Drink' (2022) XXVI Hors Series 29, 40; Pooran Wynarczyk and Robert Watson, 'Firm Growth and Supply Chain Partnerships: An Empirical Analysis of UK SME Subcontractors' (2005) 24 Small Business Economics 39, 39 https://doi.org/10.1007/s11187-005-3095-0 (accessed 16 August 2025).
17. *See* Whelan (n 14) p. 2.
18. Petra Butler and Campbell Herbert, 'Access to Justice for Small and Medium Sized Enterprises: The Case for a Bilateral Arbitration Treaty,' (2014) 26 New Zealand Universities Law Review 186, 188.
19. *Nelson Honey & Marketing (NZ) Ltd v. William Jacks and Company (Singapore) Private Ltd* [2015] NZHC 1215 (*Nelson Honey*).
20. *William Jacks & Co (Singapore) Pte Ltd v. Nelson Honey & Marketing (NZ) Ltd* [2015] SGHCR 21.

storage and testing costs as well as the 'inconvenience and embarrassment' emanating from the impasse. Both the New Zealand and the Singaporean High Courts decided that they had jurisdiction to hear the case.[21]

The New Zealand High Court in its judgment highlighted that just about everything between the parties was open to debate: *who was the offeror and offeree in this transaction, was there a contract, where was the contract concluded, where/when did risk/responsibility transfer, did a New Zealand court even have jurisdiction*?[22] The reason for this was that the parties did not document their contract negotiation and its outcome. The lack of a written contract (especially as one single document) as in *Nelson Honey* is characteristic for the contractual behaviour of SMEs. The lack of a written contract containing all rights and obligations between the parties reflects what is important for SMEs when they contract and/or what obstacles they face when contracting cross-border.

In the last nine years, the author has conducted and/or has been involved in a number of qualitative and quantitative empirical studies regarding the contractual behaviour of SMEs.[23] The findings can be summarised as follows.[24]

1 No, We Do N't Have Formal Contracts

The majority of SMEs do not have formal written contractual arrangements with their overseas counterparts.[25] As one business owner stated:

> Lots of people don't have contracts, forget contracts, I mean it's a joke, it is silly, you don't have contracts at our level.

21. No judgment on the merits exists in either jurisdiction suggesting that the parties settled.
22. *See Nelson Honey* paras 22 et seq., paras 51 et seq.
23. Two studies in New Zealand (2015 & 2018) 45 interviews, Singapore (2018) 4 interviews, Spain (2018/2019) questionnaires to 100 SMEs – 46 questionnaires returned; UK (2018) 4 interviews, Austria (2019) 21 interviews, the quantitative study done as part of the Commonwealth study into international commercial arbitration in Commonwealth countries also included questions relating to contractual behaviour, in particular regarding cross-border dispute resolution (Commonwealth Secretariat (authors Petra Butler and Dharshini Prasad), *A Study of International Commercial Arbitration in the Commonwealth* (London, 2020)).
24. The findings are drawn from the following studies: Commonwealth Secretariat (authors Petra Butler and Dharshini Prasad), *A Study of International Commercial Arbitration in the Commonwealth* (London, 2020) (Commonwealth Study); Hanneke van Oeveren, *'It Hurts My Head to Think About It': SMEs and the Legal Framework for International Commercial Contracts*, LLM thesis (Victoria University Law Faculty, Wellington, 2016); Petra Butler and Georgia Whelan, 'Does the Dispute Resolution Regime in Europe Really Serve MSMEs?' in Ben Beaumont, Alexis Foucard and Fahira Brodlija (eds), *International Arbitration: Quo Vadis* (Wolters Kluwer, 2022) Chapter 6; Petra Butler and Christina Geissler, 'Contractual Realities of SMEs: Access to Commercial Justice,' in Christian Klausegger et al. (eds), *Austrian Yearbook of International Arbitration: 2021* (Manz, 2021) 466; Cayetana Santaolalla Montoya – research conducted in Spain in 2019, results on file with the author. The empirical research was based on the same catalogue of questions.
25. *See* Commonwealth Study (n 24) 3.3.2.

Contracting is done in a piecemeal fashion frequently through a mixture of emails, phone calls, and even WhatsApp or WeChat.[26] Order forms, export documentation, or bills of lading are often the most comprehensive single document of the contract.[27] However, the more complex the product, for example, if the product contains intellectual property rights or involves distribution agreements, the more likely it is that a single all-encompassing contract document exists. Whether there is a 'need' for a formal contract document might also depend on in which country the contractual partner is located.[28]

One recurring theme that might explain in many cases the lack of a written contract was the expressed mistrust of contractual documents. There was some reluctance to require contractual counterparts to sign legalistic-looking documents, perceived as using verbose clauses that contemplate everything that has the potential to go wrong with a particular transaction. The importance of maintaining a relationship between the parties is substituted for any contractual document.[29] As one SME owner emphasised:[30]

> Good relationships are important to me; I am not really interested in doing deals just for the sake of a deal ... I would much rather work on relationships than signing documents and working at a level of distrust.

Interesting is also the following quote which exemplifies how haphazard formal contracting can be:[31]

> Some we do, and some we don't ... It just depends on who we're dealing with – history and those sorts of things. When you've been paid upfront, it's not always as effectual, and it also depends on the specifications and things, which are involved in the transaction. Most of it there is a contract, but there are some people

26. Butler and van Oeveren (n 16) p. 39 fn 41. One arbitrator commented when reading a draft of this paper: 'I would also say that as an independent arbitrator, when I was starting out, I used to get appointed in more cases like this, and I think that experience is shared by others. So it's important for those setting out on careers as arbitrators to be appreciative of this kind of behaviour and expectations as they are likely to feature in many cases at outset of working as arbitrator.'
27. Butler and van Oeveren (n 16) p. 40 fn 42; Commonwealth Study (n 24) 3.3.2 – only 50% of respondents to the Commonwealth Secretariat study used order forms or ancillary documents whereas 90% of the Spanish respondents used them.
28. *See* Commonwealth Study (n 24) 3.3.2.
29. This is consistent with research undertaken by colleagues from business schools which has found that 'good faith' is a driver for business relationships: Monika Maria Möhring and John Finch, 'Contracts, Relationships and Innovation in Business-to-Business Exchanges' (2015) 30 Journal of Business & Industrial Marketing 405-413 https://doi.org/10.1108/jbim-12-2012-0249 (accessed 16 August 2025); Carolina Camén, Patrik Gottfridsson and Bo Rundh, 'Contracts as Cornerstones in Relationship Building' (2012) 4 International Journal of Quality and Service Sciences, 208-223 https://doi.org/10.1108/17566691211269549 (accessed 16 August 2025); Stewart Macaulay, 'Non-contractual Relations in Business: A Preliminary Study' (1963) 28 American Sociological Review 55-67 https://doi.org/10.2307/2090458 (accessed 16 August 2025). The research undertaken by the author has found some regional differences, e.g., Austrian SMEs did not place as much emphasis on relationships as their New Zealand, Singaporean, or Spanish counterparts did. More research needs to be done. In particular it would be of interest whether particular industries behave differently.
30. Butler and van Oeveren (n 16) p. 40 fn 45.
31. Butler and van Oeveren (n 16) p. 41.

> we've been dealing with for a long time where there's no actual contract as such, there's just an email back and forth what they want, and we sort it out from there.[32]

2 The Knowledge of Contractual Governance Is Limited

Among those that have used or contemplate using contracts, reading, and mastering specific details is beyond their abilities. Knowledge and resource gaps are a reverberating theme for SME exporters.[33] Not only are they unlikely to read and understand contract terminology, but they also do not expect their customers to do so either, as one business owner stated:[34]

> For a layman like myself, even reading a legal document is already something, you have a bit of an idea of what it says, but what it really means you don't really know.

Smaller businesses are often run by an individual or by a small group of people who are responsible for everything from day-to-day management, human resources, right through to the company's approach to international transactions. This means that decisions are also frequently made by a single decision-maker, who lacks time to extensively research and consider international issues. This is illustrated by the following legal analysis:[35]

> If someone comes to us to do business then I guess my gut feeling would be that whatever law we work in always applies. So if somebody rings me from the US and wants to buy something from me then I assume that they came to us so our law must apply. The moment we call them instead, then US law might apply.

These knowledge and resource limitations explain why, according to Bortolotti,[36] SMEs take risky short-cuts such as simply 'cutting and pasting' from other contracts, any terms and conditions they deem logical and reasonable or not do anything relying on '*that everything will alright.*'

32. Long standing contractual relationships without a contract are not uncommon, even for medium-sized sophisticated parties, *see*: *Bomac Laboratories Ltd v. Life Medicals*, HC Auckland CIV-2010-404-4654 (5 August 2011).
33. Eldrede T. Kahiya, 'Five Decades of Research on Export Barriers: Review and Future Directions' (2018) 27 International Business Review, 1172-1188 https://doi.org/10.1016/j.ibusrev.2018.04.008 (accessed 16 August 2025); Sarah Park, Joseph A. LiPuma and Christiane Prange, 'Venture Capitalist and Entrepreneur Knowledge of New Venture Internationalization: A Review of Knowledge Components' (2015) 33 International Small Business Journal 901-928 https://doi.org/10.1177/0266242614526609 (accessed 16 August 2025).
34. van Oeveren (n 24) p. 27.
35. Butler and van Oeveren (n 16) p. 42 fn 50.
36. Fabio Bortolotti, *Drafting and Negotiating International Commercial Contracts: A Practical Guide* (International Chamber of Commerce, 2013) Chapter 6.

3 Walking Away as a Way to Settle Disputes

There is a very strong sentiment among SMEs that disputes should not be resolved via contract-related vehicles such as litigation, arbitration, or mediation since this would signal a relationship breakdown. Even though there is general consensus that litigation is seen as the absolute last resort, it has to be noted at the same time that many SMEs have no understanding of dispute resolution and are not able to distinguish between (international) arbitration and mediation. One SME explained their attitude to the dispute resolution:[37]

> We have a unique product and we partner with people that see the value to their business. We say we don't offer them a machine, we offer them a way to make a margin and it is a win thing for them ... In the event that things go bad because of something they do wrong and if a dealer decides to take the machine back ... in the case that it would go sour we would walk away, there is no need for a legal remedy.

And sometimes a down-to-earth approach to dispute resolution prevails:[38]

> No ... because America, you know, don't kid yourself. The Americans are not going to sue me, I could poison and kill an American [with my product], and they wouldn't sue me because the lawyers would not make enough. They could take me to the cleaners, they could take my business, they could take my wife and children and sell them into slavery, and they still would not make enough to pay their fee.

It appears, upholding relational norms[39] and maintaining an exchange relationship are far more important imperatives than fairness in procedural justice.

37. Butler and Kahiya (n 3) p. 56.
38. van Oeveren (n 24) p. 49 fn 201.
39. Danny Pimentel Claro, Geoffrey Hagelaar and Onno Omta, 'The Determinants of Relational Governance and Performance: How to Manage Business Relationships?' (2003) 32 Industrial Marketing Management 703-716 https://doi.org/10.1016/j.indmarman.2003.06.010 (accessed 16 August 2025); Anthony S. Roath, Stewart R. Miller and S. Tamer Cavusgil, 'A Conceptual Framework of Relational Governance in Foreign Distributor Relationships' (2002) 11 International Business Review 1-16 https://doi.org/10.1016/s0969-5931(01)00044-0 (accessed 16 August 2025); Lorraine M. Uhlaner, Roberto H. Floren and Jurgen R. Geerlings, 'Owner Commitment and Relational Governance in the Privately-Held Firm: An Empirical Study' (2007) 29 Small Business Economics, 275-293 https://doi.org/10.1007/s11187-006-9009-y (accessed 16 August 2025); Akbar Zaheer and Natarjan Venkatraman, 'Relational Governance as an Interorganizational Strategy: An Empirical Test of the Role of Trust in Economic Exchange' (1995) 16 Strategic Management Journal, 373-392 https://doi.org/10.1002/smj.4250160504 (accessed 16 August 2025); Chun S. Zhang, Tamer Cavusgil, and Anthony S. Roath, 'Manufacturer Governance of Foreign Distributor Relationships: Do Relational Norms Enhance Competitiveness in the Export Market?' (2003) 34 Journal of International Business Studies, 550-566 https://doi.org/10.1057/palgrave.jibs.8400051 (accessed 16 August 2025).

4 We Face Barriers to the Adoption of Contractual Governance

The cost and (perceived) quality of professional legal assistance is a contributing factor to the low uptake of contractual governance. One SME clarified:[40]

> For us the amounts are just too small, if we are doing a deal worth 50,000 the profit margin might only be 10%, if we use a lawyer 'poof' half the profit is gone.

Getting legal assistance appears prohibitively expensive to SMEs even if they choose to draw up the contract and then get a lawyer to look it over or get legal services to prepare a contract from the beginning. In this regard, legal assistance represents a cost-based barrier. Asked how they would get started with contractual governance and the extent to which they would involve a lawyer, an SME explained:[41]

> I wouldn't have a clue where to start and I also probably would fear that if I went to my usual lawyer he wouldn't have a clue either ... .

The quote indicates that, even where affordability is a non-issue, the quality of the expertise presents a separate concern. Especially in rural and remote locations the availability of a lawyer well versed in cross-border contracting poses an additional barrier.

Limited knowledge and resources, barriers to contracting, and inability or unwillingness to utilise dispute resolution mechanisms speak to access to justice – a major challenge for SMEs in the global marketplace.[42]

5 We Compensate for Lack of Contractual Governance

The first four themes have highlighted the underutilisation of contractual modes by exporting SMEs, the lack of knowledge about contractual governance, barriers to contract formation, and misgivings about dispute resolution via litigation. To compensate for the absence of contractual governance, exporting SMEs exploit relational governance and proxy or microcontracts associated with the exchanges.

a The Role of Relational Governance

A reverberating theme among SMEs is the importance of relationships in their exchanges with foreign customers where contract documents are seen as a sign of distrust.[43]

An SME explained:

> we sent a machine to the UK ... . I had known the dealer for a long time and there was mutual trust but once I sent the machine it was effectively out of my hands, he

40. Butler and van Oeveren (n 16) p. 43.
41. van Oeveren (n 24) p. 30 fn 124.
42. Butler and Herbert (n 18) pp. 187 et seq.
43. *See* re the examples: Butler and Kahiya (n 3) p. 57.

> had it but I owned it. I had a ten minute discussion with my solicitor but he said it was a complicated thing so I said we will forget it and go with the handshake.

In the same vein, another SME detailed:

> at the moment the relationships are really personal and I deal personally with all these people, and when you're sitting across the table face-to-face you work it out. But if we get bigger and employ salespeople then we need more detail. As I own the business I can see the big picture, but for a salesperson that is much harder to do.

And a Singaporean SME details the establishment of a relationship:[44]

> We do the checks on buyers. We visit them at least once and know them well. [Or we know them through another company]. And then you can also check the market information, how are their payments and [for information about the customer].

Both interpersonal and interorganisational trust-based relationship dynamics are at play, and the size of international venture appears to accommodate relational governance. The findings from the studies this chapter is based on are consistent with past studies that stress the advantages of and preference for relational governance in buyer-seller exchanges.[45] The results also corroborate past research that underlines the importance of trust in relational governance.[46] A number of businesses mentioned they would consider contractual governance once the size of their international footprint increases.

b The Role of Microcontracts or Proxy Contracts

The absence of contractual governance does not completely expose SMEs to risk, moral hazard, or opportunism. Some businesses mentioned risks and disputes related to non-payment or collection on foreign sales as the typical hazards they worry about. For these businesses, risk can be mitigated without a formal contract.

As one SME explains:

> our credit terms are payment before delivery, so we would never ship without the payment being complete or at the very least a letter of credit. So, no I would not say

44. Butler and van Oeveren (n 16) p. 46.
45. For example, Min Ju and Gerald Yong Gao, 'Relational Governance and Control Mechanisms of Export Ventures: An Examination Across Relationship Length' (2017) 25 Journal of International Marketing, 72-87; Anthony S. Roath et al., 'A Conceptual Framework of Relational Governance in Foreign Distributor Relationships' (2002) 11 International Business Review, 1-16 https://doi.org/10.1016/s0969-5931(01)00044-0 (accessed 16 August 2025).
46. For example, Danny Pimentel Claro et al., 'The Determinants of Relational Governance and Performance: How to Manage Business Relationships?' (2003) 32 Industrial Marketing Management, 703-716 https://doi.org/10.1016/j.indmarman.2003.06.010 (accessed 16 August 2025); Chun S. Zhang et al., 'Manufacturer Governance of Foreign Distributor Relationships: Do Relational Norms Enhance Competitiveness in the Export Market?' (2003) 34 Journal of International Business Studies, 550-566 https://doi.org/10.1057/palgrave.jibs.8400051 (accessed 16 August 2025).

> they are more risky but maybe that is just because we have mitigated against the risks.

One SME said that it will consider shipping against a letter of credit, while another SME views cash on delivery as the standard approach:

> Well obviously you mitigate it, you approach it differently, but the risk would be that it is much harder, or at least I perceive it to be much harder to enforce any payment. We just don't go there, it is sort of accepted in international transactions that there is a lot more cash on delivery, pay before it leaves.

While from a risk management perspective insisting on prepayment is prudent, it may make the exchange far less attractive to a foreign buyer, who for various reasons may require credit terms (e.g., lack of working capital, inability to secure a letter of credit or foreign currency restrictions).

c *Summary*

From the interviews and the quantitative surveys undertaken, the absence of written, single-document contracts can be explained by the adequacy of the protections, rights, and obligations stipulated by the 'micro-written contracts' in international buyer-seller transactions. These include contracts with carriers (bills of lading, air waybills and road consignment notes), banks (letters of credits/bank drafts), and customs brokers (Incoterms and documentation). Often quotes, purchase orders and invoices were also viewed as proxies for formal single-document contracts. Thus, these micro or proxy contracts may be viewed as containing a sufficient measure of 'bindingness' or 'obligatoriness' to substitute formal contractual mechanisms.[47] The majority of (micro) contracts will not have any reference to dispute resolution and will leave the parties without a clear dispute resolution process.

6 The Concept of Spasmodic Contractual Governance

To summarise the findings, it is worthwhile to use a spasmodic contractual governance model (SCG). The defining features of the model are as follows:

- SCG is typified by minimal or non-existent use of written, single-document international sales contracts in the governance of buyer-seller exchanges.
- While there is regard for the importance and potential value-add of contractual governance, exporters opt to 'hedge their bets' on various microcontracts underpinning international sales transactions. These micro or proxy contracts encompass exchanges with banks, freight forwarders, third-party logistics provider and customs brokers.

47. *See* Yadong Luo, *Global Dimensions of Corporate Governance* (Wiley-Blackwell, 2007); Peter Vincent-Jones, 'Contractual Governance: Institutional and Organizational Analysis' (2000) 20 Oxford Journal of Legal Studies, 317-351.

- SCG also implies a focus on one contractual term – payment. In the absence of a contract, exporters guard against risk by stressing cash up front.
- There is also a strong reliance on relational norms which help SMEs manage cross-border exchanges without resorting to contractual enforcement and its remedies which are often viewed as cumbersome.

Figure 35.1 Spasmodic Contractual Governance of SMEs[48]

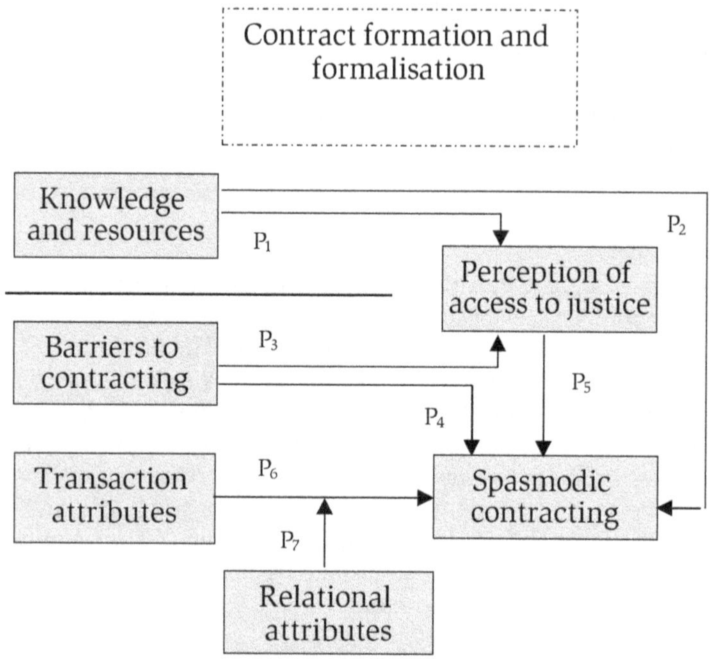

Given the spasmodic contracting of SMEs the next part will focus on how a cross-border business-to-business (B2B) commercial dispute resolution scheme supporting SMEs could look. The reason to focus on a supporting dispute resolution framework[49] lies in the empirical research findings: for over 50% of New Zealand, Spanish, and Austrian SMEs and 88% of Commonwealth Secretariat survey respondents, dispute resolution concerns were an issue when venturing into a foreign market – this corroborates the findings of the World Bank/IMF and European Commission studies.[50] Another way of looking at this phenomenon is that SMEs do not, or at least

48. *See* with more detailed explanation: Butler and Kahiya (n 3) p. 58.
49. The choice of law is of course also of utmost importance. The UN Convention on Contracts for the International Sale of Goods does provide a default framework: Petra Butler, '40 Years Convention on the International Sale of Goods (CISG): Even More Important Today than 40 Years Ago to Encourage Trade?' (2019) 118 ZVglRWiss 231-256.
50. *See* Commonwealth Study (n 24) 3.3.2; The World Bank & The International Finance Corporation (2012), 'Doing Business in a More Transparent World', available at: https://www.doingbusiness.org/content/dam/doingBusiness/media/Annual-Reports/English/DB12-FullReport.pdf

perceive not to, have access to commercial justice when venturing to trade cross-border.

IV AN SME SUPPORTING CROSS-BORDER COMMERCIAL DISPUTE RESOLUTION SCHEME

To summarise the situation SMEs find themselves in when contracting cross-border: The day-to-day demands of running an SME in which an owner/ manager has a diverse and an inordinate number of competing priorities imply time and money are better spent elsewhere (i.e., on value-adding activities instead of developing elaborate international sales contracts). The relatively high cost of hiring qualified legal expertise, if the SME has even access to such, and the opportunity cost of engaging in contract formation and formalisation curtails their ability to rely on bespoke single-document contracts. Also, the magnitude of the opportunity cost may discourage SMEs from exercising the required due diligence (e.g., taking the time to read a draft contract and understand its implications). Even easily and cheaply available sample contracts or dispute resolution clauses, which can be found on industry websites or in industry publications, do not reach SMEs.[51] The question, therefore, arises whether there is a better solution to safeguard SMEs from potential dispute disasters. How can access to commercial justice be achieved for SMEs?

The answer seems simple: access to commercial justice for SMEs lies in a default dispute resolution framework. A framework that takes account of the underlying characteristics of SME contracting, such as the high reliance on trust and good faith and the lack of resources. Thinking of the current default mechanism, (international) litigation, the answer is not that simple. International litigation, as the default mechanism, is contrary to what SMEs need from a default cross-border dispute resolution framework. The costs associated with resolving disputes in the international space, the possibility of parallel proceedings, difficulties with the enforcement of judgments against foreign trading partners, the concern that courts will be biased in favour of their own citizens, the time and expense associated with international litigation, and the unavoidable adversarial nature, even in civil law jurisdictions, of litigation do not resonate well with SMEs' spasmodic contracting.

A solution that would realise particular benefits for SMEs in regard to international dispute resolution would be a default mechanism that is based on the principles of international arbitration at its core while at the same time supporting mediated

(accessed 4 April 2024); European Commission (2011), 'European Contract Law in Business-to-Business Transactions', available at: https://ec.europa.eu/commfrontoffice/publicopinion/flash/fl_320_en.pdf (accessed 4 April 2024). It is acknowledged that the appropriate governing law of the contractual relationship is or can be of equal importance: *see* Petra Butler, '40 Years Convention on the International Sale of Goods (CISG): Even More Important Today than 40 Years Ago to Encourage Trade?' (2019) 118 ZVglRWiss 231-256.

51. *See* for example the International Chamber of Commerce (ICC) Model Contracts and Clauses https://iccwbo.org/resources-for-business/model-contracts-clauses/ (accessed 16 August 2025) and the International Trade Centre Model Contracts http://www.intracen.org/itc/exporters/model-contracts/ (accessed 6 April 2024).

solutions. Gary Born's Bi/Multilateral Arbitration Treaty regime (BAT) lays the foundation for such a solution.[52] Under Born's proposal, states would agree to substitute international litigation with international commercial arbitration as the default dispute resolution regime between commercial entities trading between those states. Such an agreement would be by way of a treaty. Of course, the treaty need not be bilateral – indeed, it would work best where many states were party to a single treaty, i.e., as a multilateral treaty. It does not need to operate as a standalone treaty – it could quite naturally fit into a preferential trade agreement or another multilateral treaty. The G20 Cross Thematic Group on SMEs, for example, emphasised that states ought to directly take into account the interests of SMEs when entering into trade agreements.[53] Importantly, there was significant support for a bespoke regional B2B cross-border commercial dispute resolution mechanism across all stakeholder groups surveyed as part of the Commonwealth Secretariat study into international arbitration in the Commonwealth:[54] the majority of the respondent Governments indicated a preference for such a mechanism, so did 94% of respondents to the university survey and the majority of respondents to the judges, arbitrator, and counsel surveys. There was also considerable support by Commonwealth arbitral institutions for such a mechanism.

The bespoke B2B cross-border commercial dispute resolution mechanism would be based on features of international arbitration. It would not simply substitute litigation with international arbitration but rather design a mechanism that harnesses the superior features of international arbitration and mediation. Parties would remain free to opt-out by selecting some other forum (by way of a forum selection or choice of court clause) or agreeing that the B2B default mechanism would not apply to disputes arising between those parties (in which case the ordinary rules of private international law would apply, and the dispute would fall to be resolved by the courts). The B2B default mechanism would set out the matters that can be subject to it. It would provide for the types of transactions that would fall within its scope, namely, B2B transactions of enterprises located in the contracting states.[55] States could decide whether they would design the mechanism only for disputes between SMEs (defining what constitutes an SME). And it would carve out those subject matters over which, for reasons of public policy, states wish to retain judicial oversight.[56] In addition, the B2B default mechanism would prescribe those factors ordinarily found in a full arbitration agreement: the rules according to which the proceeding is to be conducted, the number of

52. Gary Born, 'BITS, BATS and Buts: Reflections on International Dispute Resolution' file:///C:/Users/pbu37/AppData/Local/Temp/MicrosoftEdgeDownloads/f1b5fbdd-a996-4e3b-bb57-9f0c49596437/BITs-BATs-and-Buts.pdf (accessed 10 April 2024). Compare Ylli Dautaj, 'Fragmentation and Judicialization of International Commercial Arbitration: Expedited Arbitration and the "Arbitral Trial,"' (2021) 13 Arb Law Review 87, 92 who also identifies the particular problems SMEs face regarding dispute resolution but suggests expedited arbitration as the default mechanism.

53. B20 Cross-Thematic Group- Small and Medium Enterprises, 'Think Big for Small: Small and Medium Enterprises as Pillar for Future-oriented, Sustainable Growth' (G20, Policy Paper, 2017) 8.

54. Commonwealth Study (n 24) 4.7.2.

55. *See* Draft Model Bilateral Arbitration Treaty (Draft BAT), Article 1 'International Commercial Dispute'.

56. For example: competition and employment matters.

adjudicators, and the appointing mechanism. Importantly, the default mechanism would allow and encourage parties through a default procedure to find a solution themselves, paying tribute to trust and good faith as the core features of SME contracting. The mechanism could also include provisions as to the use of online dispute resolution to allow for cost and time savings.[57] Where a dispute was subject to the bespoke mechanism, the courts in both states would decline to find jurisdiction, would stay any proceedings, and would refer the dispute-to-dispute resolution under the bespoke mechanism, comparable with the current practice of national courts when faced with an arbitration agreement. Similarly, state courts would recognise and enforce the awards rendered in the course of the dispute resolution under the bespoke mechanism.

Default dispute resolution under a bespoke mechanism based on international arbitration and mediation could ease many of the concerns raised in regard to cross-border litigation generally. The mechanism would alleviate issues that are of particular concern to SMEs regarding their contractual relationship, such as trust, good faith, limited resources and capacity. In addition, a bespoke B2B commercial cross-border dispute resolution mechanism could level the playing field between larger and smaller businesses. In particular, a bespoke mechanism would be beneficial by:

(a) prescribing a dispute resolution mechanism, thus avoiding the costs associated with parties familiarising themselves with dispute resolution procedures in each of their trading partners states;
(b) prescribing a uniform procedure that sits independently from any national law. Proceedings that run according to a well-settled set of rules, which the parties can vary by agreement, and before an adjudicator that the parties played some role in selecting and who represents the parties' constituency will instil a greater sense of trust in the outcome;
(c) enabling counsel local to each party to represent that party throughout the dispute. This reduces the need for parties to brief multiple counsels, thereby substantially reducing the cost of resolution;
(d) allowing for the inclusion of negotiation and/or mediation of the dispute as a first step of the dispute resolution process. Given the general relational nature of SME contractual relationship, a non-adjudicative route will be central; and
(e) enabling being responsive to regional customs and circumstances.

As the bespoke mechanism would be the default, there would be no cost for SMEs in setting up a dispute resolution mechanism – neither for drafting a choice of forum

57. The use of technology by SMEs varies. A business relationship built on trust does not generally lends itself to an online format of dispute resolution. Digital literacy and the capacity to participate in online dispute resolution are further factors which might make online dispute resolution unpopular in certain parts of the world. *See*: Ashraf Mishrif and Asharul Khan, 'Technology Adoption as Survival Strategy for Small and Medium Enterprises During COVID-19,' (2023) 12 Journal of Innovation and Entrepreneurship 53 https://doi.org/10.1186/s13731-023-00317-9 (accessed 16 August 2025); *see also* Jo Stanley and Gerard Brisco, 'The ABC of Digital Business Ecosystems,' (2010) 15 Communications Law 12.

agreement nor as part of a bargain when attempting to include a favourable dispute resolution clause in an agreement. The default mechanism would reduce the risks of international transactions without increasing administrative costs at the time of contracting. In particular, a bespoke B2B cross-border dispute resolution mechanism would prevent parallel proceedings, allow for expert adjudicators and mediators, and provide for an easier means of enforcement of an award. A bespoke B2B dispute resolution framework has already a precedent when it comes to the applicable contract law in the form of the United Nations Convention on Contracts for the International Sale of Goods (CISG).[58]

V CONCLUSION

SMEs are the most prevalent and arguably the most important business form in all countries. There is a wide international consensus that governments and organisations need to enable SMEs to trade across borders. Empirical research indicates the lack of certainty of a dispute resolution process should a dispute arise or the SMEs' experience of cross-border dispute resolution to date contribute significantly to SMEs reluctance to trade cross-border. Empirical research further reveals that many SMEs neither have the practice nor the capacity of considering a dispute resolution mechanism that best suits their contractual circumstance or often do not consider dispute resolution at all when contracting. To foster cross-border trade of SMEs and thereby contributing to the supply chain resilience, it is important for states to consider how to support SMEs regarding their dispute resolution needs. Simplifying and solidifying access to international commercial justice for SMEs will allow SMEs to internationalise and take more risks internationally, thus allowing them to compete with larger companies more successfully. An increased representation of SMEs in international commercial dispute resolution would, in turn, encourage the further development of legal precedents, processes, and hard and soft laws that consider the unique needs of SMEs that are trading across borders.

Bilateral, multilateral, or regional trade agreements are an opportunity for states to agree on a bespoke B2B cross-border commercial default dispute resolution framework that will more adequately suit the needs of SMEs. One solution would be a default mechanism based on the rules of international arbitration and rooted in mediation.

58. Compare: Petra Butler, '40 Years Convention on the International Sale of Goods (CISG): Even More Important Today Than 40 Years Ago to Encourage Trade?' (2019) 188 ZVglRWiss 231.

CHAPTER 36

Novel Hybrid Mechanisms in Public International Law Dispute Resolution: Conciliation, Review Panels, and Expedited Grievance Mechanisms

Martin Doe[*]

TABLE OF CONTENTS

I INTRODUCTION

Public international law is reputed to be a conservative field steeped in, and often constrained by, history. Yet, the pace of innovation in public international law dispute resolution has quickened. Recent years have seen the emergence or re-emergence of various additional forms of dispute settlement, presaging an expanding universe of options to keep up with the ever-evolving needs of the modern international community.

Three recent examples are surveyed below. Their common thread is found in their hybrid forms and in the emphasis on expedited and non-contentious dispute resolution, with a view to rendering these mechanisms more efficient and effective. Their nature serves also to make them nimble enough to serve as part of the international legal and regulatory architecture, no longer confining public international

* Deputy Secretary-General and Principal Legal Counsel, Permanent Court of Arbitration.

law dispute resolution only to big questions of principle, looked upon with hindsight and regret at their non-observance by one party or another. And these novel mechanisms come not a moment too soon, given the fraught international landscape and the myriad challenges on the horizon.

II INTER-STATE CONCILIATION: THE *TIMOR SEA CONCILIATION*

On 11 April 2016, Timor-Leste took a leap into the void.[1] It commenced a compulsory conciliation against Australia. No one had commenced an inter-State conciliation under the *United Nations Convention on the Law of the Sea* (UNCLOS), or at all since the *Jan Mayen Conciliation* in 1981.[2] Yet, the oxymoronically-named 'compulsory conciliation' had certain redeeming qualities.

Timor-Leste had already brought two inter-State claims against Australia under the Timor Sea Treaty. The first concerned allegations that Australia had engaged in spying on the Timorese delegation during the negotiation of a resource-sharing arrangement concerning a large gas field in a disputed area of the Timor Sea.[3] The second arbitration concerned tax jurisdiction over the exploitation of other oil and gas resources in disputed areas of the Timor Sea.[4] Timor-Leste had also commenced yet another case against Australia before the International Court of Justice, claiming a violation of sovereign immunities and the privilege and confidentiality attaching to communications with its lawyers when, on the eve of the procedural meeting in the first of these inter-State arbitrations, the Australian Security and Intelligence Organisation (ASIO) raided the offices of one of Timor-Leste's legal advisers in Canberra.[5]

Each of these cases concerned a legitimate dispute in its own right. However, each of the existing cases dealt with accessory issues relating to a broader dispute. None would help Timor-Leste move more than a small step towards its ultimate goal of

1. A. Pereira, 'Perspective of Timor-Leste' in H.D. Phan, T. Davenport, R. Beckman (eds), *The Timor-Leste/Australia Conciliation: A Victory for UNCLOS and Peaceful Settlement of Disputes*, p. 197, https://doi.org/10.1142/9789811202711_0007 (accessed 16 August 2025) ('The decision to pursue compulsory conciliation was taken only after a period of deep consideration. This was an untried, untested UNCLOS dispute resolution mechanism and Timor-Leste did not want to volunteer as the "guinea pig"'); L. Reed, 'Conclusion' in H.D. Phan, T. Davenport, R. Beckman (eds), *The Timor-Leste/Australia Conciliation: A Victory for UNCLOS and Peaceful Settlement of Disputes*, p. 197 ('It is no exaggeration to say that when Timor-Leste invoked compulsory conciliation under Annex V of [UNCLOS], there was scepticism and even cynicism in the legal community about the prospects'). *See also Timor Sea Conciliation (Timor-Leste/Australia)*, PCA Case No. 2016-10, Report and Recommendations of the Conciliation Commission, 9 May 2018, para. 290 ('The Commission is cognizant that Timor-Leste initiated these proceedings as much due to the absence of other options as from a belief in the virtues of conciliation or in the likelihood of success.').
2. *Jan Mayen Conciliation (Iceland/Norway)*, Decision of June 1981, R.I.A.A. Vol. XXVII, p. 1.
3. *Arbitration under the Timor Sea Treaty (Timor-Leste v. Australia)*, PCA Case No. 2013-16. Publicly available details concerning the arbitration may be found at pca-cpa.org/en/cases/37/ .
4. *Arbitration under the Timor Sea Treaty (Timor-Leste v. Australia)*, PCA Case No. 2015-42. Publicly available details concerning the arbitration may be found at pca-cpa.org/en/cases/141/ .
5. *Questions relating to the Seizure and Detention of Certain Documents and Data (Timor-Leste v. Australia)*, International Court of Justice. Publicly available details concerning the case may be found at icj-cij.org/case/156 .

settling its permanent maritime boundary with Australia and achieving sovereignty over the natural resources found in the Timor Sea. A conciliation under Annex V of UNCLOS at least had maritime boundaries as its essential subject matter. In fact, the conciliation provided a platform to address all those other existing irritants in the same sweep. That is exactly what came to pass, as all three existing inter-State proceedings, along with a slew of other transitional and governance matters, were settled in the course of early confidence-building measures undertaken in the conciliation process.[6]

The conciliation also engaged certain helpful general principles and good faith obligations embodied in UNCLOS. The dispute resolution provisions of UNCLOS – the adoption of which was a major coup for multilateral dispute resolution – reflect a general obligation to resolve disputes arising under the Convention. While States are afforded broad autonomy in the choice of means for dispute settlement, they cannot opt out altogether, except in respect of pre-existing disputes and certain narrow categories of sensitive cases. Compulsory conciliation thus represented a bottom line that Australia was obliged to accept, notwithstanding any existing instruments purporting to provide otherwise.[7] And if compulsory conciliation failed, UNCLOS stipulated that Australia would be obliged to 'negotiate an agreement on the basis of [the conciliation commission's] report' and then 'shall, by mutual consent, submit the question to one of the [binding dispute resolution] procedures provided for in section 2 [of Part XV of UNCLOS]'.[8] Timor-Leste's principal grievance was Australia's unwillingness to negotiate permanent maritime boundaries during a fifty year 'moratorium' imposed by the resource-sharing agreements already in place. The legal framework of the conciliation helped to highlight the inconsistency of this state of affairs with the aforementioned principles embodied in UNCLOS, as eventually found by the Conciliation Commission in its Decision on Competence.[9]

The last redeeming quality of the compulsory conciliation was that it was quick. Annex V of UNCLOS prescribes that a conciliation commission shall render its report within twelve months of its constitution. As noted by the Conciliation Commission, this

6. *Timor Sea Conciliation (Timor-Leste/Australia)*, PCA Case No. 2016-10, Report and Recommendations of the Conciliation Commission, 9 May 2018, paras 95-96, 106. *See also ibid.*, Annex 12: Commission's Proposal on Confidence-Building Measures of 14 October 2016.
7. *Timor Sea Conciliation (Timor-Leste/Australia)*, PCA Case No. 2016-10, Decision on Competence, 19 September 2016, para. 66.
8. S. Jayakumar, 'Compulsory Dispute Settlement and Conciliation under UNCLOS' in H.D. Phan, T. Davenport, R. Beckman (eds), *The Timor-Leste/Australia Conciliation: A Victory for UNCLOS and Peaceful Settlement of Disputes*, p. 26, https://doi.org/10.1142/9789811202711_0001 (accessed 16 August 2025) ('The Commission Report did not address the question whether UNCLOS states parties are obliged to return to the compulsory dispute settlement procedures of Section of Part XV. Fortunately, in the *Timor-Leste/Australia Conciliation*, because Timor-Leste and Australia reached a successful agreement on their maritime boundary, the meaning of 'shall, by mutual consent' remains an open question').
9. *Timor Sea Conciliation (Timor-Leste/Australia)*, PCA Case No. 2016-10, Decision on Competence, 19 September 2016, para. 62 ('In the Commission's view, what CMATS is not – and what Article 281 requires – is an agreement "to seek settlement of the dispute by a peaceful means of [the Parties'] own choice." CMATS is an agreement *not* to seek settlement of the Parties' dispute over maritime boundaries for the duration of the moratorium').

time limit serves to 'ensure that a party is not compelled to continue endlessly a conciliation process that, in its view, has no hope of success'.[10]

The gamble on this untested procedure paid off. Although in a first phase of the proceedings, Australia initially resisted and objected to the competence of the Conciliation Commission, it ultimately accepted the Commission's decision dismissing those objections, and the successful implementation of the confidence-building measures mentioned above further encouraged it to take part in the process in earnest.[11] That engagement between the two States led to the *Comprehensive Package Agreement* of 30 August 2017, setting forth the agreed-upon elements for a full resolution of their dispute. Thus, beyond settling the various pending contentious proceedings, the conciliation was ultimately successful in resolving the two States' maritime boundary, transitional arrangements, and a special regime for joint development and resource-sharing in respect of the Great Sunrise gas fields in the Timor Sea. This agreement was then rendered into a comprehensive maritime boundary treaty regulating all these matters, signed at the United Nations in New York on 6 March 2018.

The simple fact that Timor-Leste and Australia managed to go from 'deeply entrenched' legal positions that 'had frustrated previous efforts to achieve a settlement through negotiation' to a comprehensive and fully implemented resolution of their dispute in less than two years makes the conciliation a precedent worthy of study.[12] The advantages of inter-State conciliation exhibited by the *Timor Sea Conciliation* have been invoked to justify the renewed interest in inter-State conciliation as a means of public international law dispute settlement.

In particular, the result of the conciliation on the maritime boundary was notable in that it drew a line that, while eminently justifiable on the basis of the legal principles in question, was unlike the outcome that might be expected from an arbitral tribunal or judicial decision. The new boundary gave different weight to the various relevant factors in different sectors. It provided contingent outcomes that accommodated expected future scenarios vis-à-vis Timor-Leste's further boundary negotiations with Indonesia. And it set forth transitional and governance arrangements likely beyond the remit of any arbitral or judicial body to pronounce. The flexibility of the conciliation process allowed the Commission not just to focus on the immediate elements of the

10. *Timor Sea Conciliation (Timor-Leste/Australia)*, PCA Case No. 2016-10, Decision on Competence, 19 September 2016, para. 107. *See also Timor Sea Conciliation (Timor-Leste/Australia)*, PCA Case No. 2016-10, Report and Recommendations of the Conciliation Commission, 9 May 2018, para. 68 ('the 12-month period set out in Annex V should be understood not as the timeframe in which a successful conciliation can likely be concluded, but rather as a safeguard to ensure that an unproductive conciliation is not unduly prolonged').
11. G. Quinlan, 'Perspective of Australia' in H.D. Phan, T. Davenport, R. Beckman (eds), *The Timor-Leste/Australia Conciliation: A Victory for UNCLOS and Peaceful Settlement of Disputes*, p. 185 ('Once competence had been determined, Australia decided to change tack. We had to put our previous misgivings about the way we had been brought to the process behind us'); L. Reed, 'Conclusion' in H.D. Phan, T. Davenport, R. Beckman (eds), *The Timor-Leste/Australia Conciliation: A Victory for UNCLOS and Peaceful Settlement of Disputes*, p. 201 ('Particularly noteworthy is Australia's full participation after losing its arguments against the Commission's competence').
12. *Timor Sea Conciliation (Timor-Leste/Australia)*, PCA Case No. 2016-10, Report and Recommendations of the Conciliation Commission, 9 May 2018, para. 285.

dispute but to comprehensively address all relevant issues necessary to enable reaching an amicable and durable settlement.[13]

Yet, it is precisely these characteristics of the outcome that draw to the fore a less evident but crucial ingredient for the success of the conciliation: the hybrid legal and facilitative character of the process stemming from conciliation's origins as a cross between good offices and commission of inquiry. Inter-State conciliation requires more active engagement by a conciliation commission than mediation or good offices alone, engaging to a certain degree with legal issues, even if their resolution is not strictly required in order to settle the dispute. The ability to move back and forth from evaluative to facilitative mediation, from legal assessment to identification and reconciliation of interests, defined the successful approach in the *Timor Sea Conciliation*.

This feature remains underappreciated as a key ingredient and distinguishing factor of inter-State conciliation among the spectrum of other means of public international law dispute resolution, and the value that it may add over simple interests-based mediation. Diplomacy already provides a well-oiled machine for interest-based negotiation, and even good offices. But the dignity of States may require that long-held legal positions be recognized and given weight in contemplated outcomes before the political will to find a compromise solution can emerge. In this sense, conciliation offers a truly neutral, independent, and disinterested third party uniquely placed to offer the 'careful mix of diplomatic and legal skills, backgrounds, and approaches [that need to] be deployed in varying combinations at different stages of the process' to reach a resolution of an otherwise intractable dispute.[14]

Perhaps because the legal aspects are second nature to those active in binding adjudicatory procedures, this genesis of inter-State conciliation was addressed only in passing in an early footnote in the Commission's Report:

> Historically, international mediation was generally carried out by another sovereign power. Thus, while focused on the achievement of an amicable settlement, mediation was generally characterized by the independent political authority (and, potentially, interest in the dispute) of the mediating power. International commissions of enquiry, in contrast, largely replicated the arbitration procedures of the 1899 Hague Convention for the Pacific Settlement of International Disputes, but were focused solely on the determination of disputed facts. In contrast to mediation, the hallmark of a commission of enquiry was the absence of any independent political authority or interest in the dispute and the commission's reliance instead on its expertise and judgment in considering the facts at hand. In practice, early commissions of enquiry, as in the *Dogger Bank Case*, were sometimes mandated to go beyond a strict presentation of facts and address the apportionment of responsibility between the parties, *de facto* engaging in conciliation. This combination of inquiry, combined with recommendations as to the amicable settlement of the

13. *Timor Sea Conciliation (Timor-Leste/Australia)*, PCA Case No. 2016-10, Report and Recommendations of the Conciliation Commission, 9 May 2018, para. 286 ('the Commission considers that a constructive outcome was enabled [...] by the possibility of managing the scope of the proceedings to encompass the elements necessary for a solution').
14. The Conciliation Commission noted this distinction as compared to the practice of inter-State mediation by high officials of third States. *Timor Sea Conciliation (Timor-Leste/Australia)*, PCA Case No. 2016-10, Report and Recommendations of the Conciliation Commission, 9 May 2018, para. 294.

dispute was then codified as conciliation in the many bilateral treaties on the resolution of international disputes concluded in the 1920s and 1930s.[15]

And perhaps because the facilitative, non-legal aspect of the proceedings presented the most novel challenge for seasoned international jurists, the Commission's account of the proceedings evinces trepidation with respect to engaging the two States on substantive matters of international law. However, between emphasizing the 'risk of entrenching positions' by inviting legal submissions and admonishing itself 'not to pronounce for its own sake on questions of international law', the Commission's Report did recognize that engagement on the law 'had the associated benefit of requiring the Parties to define their own positions in a more precise manner, especially where some of their own priorities may not yet have been reconciled within their respective governments and delegations', that the conciliation 'truly became productive at the point at which both Parties became convinced that the Commission's objective was not to push them to abandon long-held positions, but rather to understand and assist the Parties to identify a solution they had been unable to reach themselves', and most importantly that 'a conciliation commission should not encourage parties to reach an agreement that it considers to be inconsistent with the Convention or other provisions of international law'.[16]

Counterintuitive as it may be, it is the substantive legal engagement by highly-qualified independent and impartial jurists who could credibly render an arbitral award in binding dispute settlement proceedings that comprises an innovative element that aided in the success of the *Timor Sea Conciliation*. Embracing this evaluative-facilitative character of inter-State conciliation may yet help resurrect it from the annals of public international law.

III REVIEW PANELS: THE *SPRFMO REVIEW PANELS*

Signed in 2009 and entered into force in 2012, at a time when overfishing saw several species in the South Pacific in catastrophic decline, the *Convention on the Conservation and Management of High Seas Fishery Resources in the South Pacific Ocean* (SPRFMO Convention)[17] is one of the more recent international fisheries treaties concluded in the context of UNCLOS[18] and the 1995 Fish Stocks Agreement,[19] both of which envisage

15. *Timor Sea Conciliation (Timor-Leste/Australia)*, PCA Case No. 2016-10, Report and Recommendations of the Conciliation Commission, 9 May 2018, note 33.
16. *Timor Sea Conciliation (Timor-Leste/Australia)*, PCA Case No. 2016-10, Report and Recommendations of the Conciliation Commission, 9 May 2018, paras 69-70.
17. *Convention on the Conservation and Management of High Seas Fishery Resources in the South Pacific Ocean* (concluded 14 November 2009, entered into force 24 August 2012), 2899 UNTS 211, available at: https://www.sprfmo.int/assets/Basic-Documents/Convention-and-Final-Act/SPRFMO-Convention-2023-update-12May2023.pdf (accessed 16 August 2025).
18. *United Nations Convention on the Law of the Sea* (adopted 10 December 1982, entered into force 16 November 1994), 1833 UNTS 3, Article 118.
19. *Agreement for the Implementation of the Provisions of the United Nations Convention on the Law of the Sea of 10 December 1982 relating to the Conservation and Management of Straddling Fish Stocks and Highly Migratory Fish Stocks* (concluded 4 August 1995, entered into force 11 December 2001), 2167 UNTS 3, Article 8(1).

the establishment of regional fisheries management organizations (RFMOs) as a means of conserving and managing fisheries on the high seas. The Convention establishes the South Pacific RFMO (SPRFMO), which includes a Commission that is empowered to 'adopt conservation and management measures to achieve the objective of this Convention, including, as appropriate, conservation and management measures for particular fish stocks'.[20] Decisions by the Commission are taken by consensus, but in the event that this is not possible, then decisions are made by a 75% majority of the Members of the Commission.[21]

Most fisheries treaties establish negotiation and arbitration, either individually or in combination, as the means of dispute resolution, using traditional dispute settlement provisions as found in many other kinds of bilateral and multilateral treaties. Aside from a number of historic cases, there have been relatively few fisheries disputes brought to formal dispute resolution of any kind.[22] The SPRFMO Convention stands out, however, in the robustness of its dispute resolution framework.[23] Beyond formal dispute settlement procedures, the SPRFMO Convention establishes objection and review procedures in Article 17 and Annex II of the SPRFMO Convention, whereby any Member may present an objection to a decision on a question of substance adopted by the Commission within sixty days of the notification of the decision, on the grounds that the decision: (i) 'unjustifiably discriminates in form or in fact against the Member'; or (ii) 'is inconsistent with the provisions of the SPRFMO Convention or other relevant international law, as reflected in [UNCLOS] or the [Fish Stocks Agreement]'.[24]

Any SPRFMO Member that presents an objection must, at the same time, adopt 'alternative measures' that are 'equivalent in effect' to the decision to which it has objected.[25] A Review Panel of fisheries experts is then constituted to hear the objection, with one member appointed by the objecting State, one by the Chairperson of the SPRFMO Commission, and the chair of the panel appointed either by agreement or, where there is no agreement, the Secretary-General of the PCA.[26] Most significantly, the Review Panel must then hold a hearing within thirty days of its establishment and issue, within forty-five days of its establishment, its 'findings and recommendations on

20. SPRFMO Convention, Article 8(a).
21. SPRFMO Convention, Article 16.
22. For one relatively recent example, *see The Atlanto-Scandian Herring Arbitration (The Kingdom of Denmark in respect of the Faroe Islands v. The European Union)*, PCA Case No. 2013-30. Publicly available details concerning the arbitration may be found at pca-cpa.org/en/cases/25/ (accessed 16 August 2025).
23. R. Rayfuse, 'Settling Disputes in Regional Fisheries Management Organisations: Dealing with Objections' in *A Bridge over Troubled Waters: Dispute Resolution in the Law of International Watercourses and the Law of the Sea* (Helene Ruiz Fabri et al. (eds)) (Brill, 2020), p. 264, https://doi.org/10.1163/9789004434950_010 (accessed 16 August 2025) ('the SPRFMO Convention establishes by far the most comprehensive formal procedure for resolving disputes over objections').
24. SPRFMO Convention, Article 17(2)(c).
25. SPRFMO Convention, Article 17(2)(b)(ii).
26. SPRFMO Convention, Article 17(5)(a) and Annex II, Article 1.

whether the grounds specified for the objection presented by the [objecting Member(s)] are justified and whether the alternative measures adopted are equivalent in effect to the decision to which objection has been presented'.[27]

Depending on its 'findings and recommendations', the outcome of the Review Panel broadly falls into the following categories:

- if the Review Panel finds that the objection is *not justified* and the alternative measures proposed are not equivalent in effect, then the objecting SPRFMO Member can choose to abide by the original decision or institute formal dispute settlement proceedings under the SPRFMO Convention;[28]
- if the Review Panel finds that the decision *discriminates* against the objecting Member, and the alternative measures adopted by the objecting Member are *equivalent* in effect, then the alternative measures replace the original decision for that Member (noting that the Review Panel may also recommend modifications to the alternative measures that would render them equivalent in effect);[29]
- if the Review Panel finds that the decision *discriminates* against the objecting Member, but the alternative measures adopted by the objecting Member are *not equivalent* in effect, then the Review Panel will recommend other measures that are equivalent in effect, which the objecting Member may challenge by requesting an extraordinary meeting of the Commission or instituting dispute settlement proceedings;[30]
- if the Review Panel finds that the decision is inconsistent with the SPRFMO Convention or other relevant international law as reflected in UNCLOS or the Fish Stocks Agreement, then an extraordinary meeting of the Commission is convened within forty-five days to reconsider the decision.[31]

This procedure has already been used on three occasions. In a first case, Russia objected on the grounds of discrimination for not being allocated any allowable catch of *Trachurus murphyi* (Chilean jack mackerel), the main species of fish managed by the SPRFMO, claiming that its historical catch justified an allocation of 19,944 tonnes for 2013.[32] Russia proposed as an alternative measure that it be granted a 19,944 tonne catch limit in 2013, although it later qualified this proposal by stating that it would cease fishing when the total allowable catch of 360,000 tonnes had been reached.[33] The key issue in dispute was whether Russia could prove the historical catch on which it

27. SPRFMO Convention, Article 17(5)(e).
28. If the Review Panel finds that the alternative measures *are* equivalent in effect to the original decision, those alternative measures will replace the original decision, pending their confirmation at the next SPRFMO Commission meeting. SPRFMO Convention, Annex II, Article 10(i)-(j).
29. SPRFMO Convention, Annex II, Article 10(a)-(b).
30. SPRFMO Convention, Annex II, Article 10(c)-(e).
31. SPRFMO Convention, Annex II, Article 10(f)-(h).
32. *Review Panel established under the Convention on the Conservation and Management of High Seas Fishery Resources in the South Pacific Ocean*, PCA Case No. 2013-14, Findings and Recommendations (5 July 2013), para. 53 (quoting Russia's objection).
33. PCA Case No. 2013-14, Findings and Recommendations (5 July 2013), paras 53, 84-86.

based its current claim, all purportedly attributable to a single vessel, the *Lafayette*.[34] There were reasons to doubt this figure, including a news report suggesting the *Lafayette* was a processing rather than fishing vessel, a French inspection in January 2010 of the vessel which did not find any fishing equipment on board, inconsistent information in Russia's annual report to the SPRFMO for 2009, and information submitted by Peru showing that four of its vessels had transhipped 31,275 tonnes to the *Lafayette* in 2010.[35]

The Review Panel found that it did 'not have sufficient basis to determine the source of the portion of the *Lafayette's* reported catch that is not attributable to the Peruvian vessels'.[36] It therefore concluded that the failure to allocate any catch to Russia had resulted in unjustifiable discrimination against Russia.[37] However, it rejected Russia's alternative measure and instead recommended that Russia authorize its vessels to catch *Trachurus murphyi* in the Convention Area in 2013, but only after Russia concluded from data reported by the SPRFMO that it is likely the total catch in 2013 will not reach the 360,000 tonne total allowable catch, and until the SPRFMO reported that the total allowable catch had been reached.[38] Russia did not refer the matter to further dispute settlement and followed the Review Panel's recommendations.[39]

In a second case, Ecuador objected that the 1,377 tonne allocation it had received for 2018, despite repeated requests for a more-than-proportional increase, made it 'unfeasible and economically unsustainable' for Ecuador to operate even a single vessel. Ecuador claimed that this was discriminatory and inconsistent, given that: (i) Peru, South Korea, and Cuba had been granted more-than-proportional increases; (ii) decisions on catch limits going forward several years had been made at a SPRFMO Commission Meeting that Ecuador could not attend due to an earthquake; and (iii) basing catch allowances solely on historical catch data contravened norms protecting the special needs of developing coastal States under UNCLOS.[40] Ecuador therefore recommended an alternative measure of increasing its catch limit by an extra 5,123 tonnes, which would increase the total catch limit, but which was still below the 576,000 tonne limit recommended by the SPRFMO Scientific Committee.[41]

In response, the Review Panel held that relying exclusively on historical catch would indeed be inconsistent with the SPRFMO Convention, but that it was unconvinced that this was an accurate depiction of the SPRFMO Commission's decisions.[42] The Review Panel also held that there was no unjustifiable discrimination against

34. PCA Case No. 2013-14, Findings and Recommendations (5 July 2013), para. 34.
35. PCA Case No. 2013-14, Findings and Recommendations (5 July 2013), paras 27-40.
36. PCA Case No. 2013-14, Findings and Recommendations (5 July 2013), para. 91.
37. PCA Case No. 2013-14, Findings and Recommendations (5 July 2013), para. 100(a).
38. PCA Case No. 2013-14, Findings and Recommendations (5 July 2013), para. 100(c).
39. SPRFMO, 'Catch Data Submitted to the SPRFMO Secretariat' (undated), p. 7, available at: https://www.sprfmo.int/assets/Meetings/01-COMM/10th-Commission-2022-COMM10/information-papers/COMM10-Inf01-rev1-Data-Submitted-to-the-Secretariat.pdf (accessed 16 August 2025).
40. PCA Case No. 2018-13, Objection of Ecuador (28 March 2018), p. 7.
41. PCA Case No. 2018-13, Objection of Ecuador (28 March 2018), pp. 7-8.
42. PCA Case No. 2018-13, Findings and Recommendations (5 June 2018), paras 96-97.

Ecuador in either the process or the decisions being challenged.[43] The Review Panel then noted that the 'reserve' that Ecuador had sought to draw on in its proposed alternative measures was intended for areas under the national jurisdiction of Ecuador and Peru rather than the high seas, such that the alternative measures were not equivalent.[44] Notwithstanding these findings, the Review Panel discussed 'how Ecuador's aspirations in developing a future high seas fishery for *Trachurus murphyi* could be addressed',[45] and 'invite[d] the Commission to consider exploring the possibility of adjustments to the allocation transfer system that would address the sorts of difficulties experienced by Ecuador'.[46] Ecuador did not challenge the findings of the Review Panel and in fact cited the final part of the findings and recommendations approvingly in its submissions before the SPRFMO Commission in 2019.[47]

In the latest case in 2023, Russia objected to its catch allocation as part of a ten year quota arrangement from 2023-2033 devised by a working group of the SPRFMO Commission.[48] China then also objected to its share, but subsequently withdrew its objection.[49] In terms of inconsistency with the Convention, Russia argued that its quota had been twice reduced without taking into account historical catch data and other criteria set out in Article 21.[50] Russia proposed, as alternative measures a 35,452 tonne catch limit (i.e., a 20% increase on its 2022 allocation), which it submitted was consistent with the recommendations of the SPRFMO Scientific Committee.[51]

The Review Panel held that it had 'no reason to conclude that the Commission has acted outside of its wide margin of discretion',[52] and that, therefore, there had not been any inconsistency with the provisions of the SPRFMO Convention, UNCLOS, or Fish Stocks Agreement.[53] However, the Review Panel ultimately concluded that 'insufficient attention' was paid during the CMM 01-2023 process to 'ideas, factors, criteria, and proposals of interest to Russia and similarly situated Members', which was 'due in part to the relatively short duration of the negotiations, especially when compared to the relatively long [ten years] duration for which the allocation percentages will in principle remain unchanged, and that this hurried process culminating in the adoption of CMM 01-2023 by a divided vote resulted in unjustifiable procedural discrimination with respect to Russia's allocation interests'.[54] The Review Panel ultimately recommended a modification of Russia's alternative measures, reducing the

43. PCA Case No. 2018-13, Findings and Recommendations (5 June 2018), para. 108.
44. PCA Case No. 2018-13, Findings and Recommendations (5 June 2018), paras 116-118.
45. PCA Case No. 2018-13, Findings and Recommendations (5 June 2018), para. 122.
46. PCA Case No. 2018-13, Findings and Recommendations (5 June 2018), para. 127.
47. SPRFMO, 7th Annual Meeting of the Commission, 'Proposal by Ecuador to Amend CMM 01 on Jack Mackerel (EC)' (January 2019) p. 3, available at: https://www.sprfmo.int/assets/Meetings/01-COMM/7th-Commission-2019-COMM7/proposals/COMM7-Prop02-CMM-01-Trachurus-murphyi-EC-cv.pdf (accessed 16 August 2025).
48. PCA Case No. 2023-33, Findings and Recommendations (1 July 2023), para. 4.
49. PCA Case No. 2023-33, Findings and Recommendations (1 July 2023), paras 4, 16.
50. PCA Case No. 2023-33, Objection of Russia (10 April 2023) pp. 3-4.
51. PCA Case No. 2023-33, Objection of Russia (10 April 2023) p. 5.
52. PCA Case No. 2023-33, Findings and Recommendations (1 July 2023), para. 118.
53. PCA Case No. 2023-33, Findings and Recommendations (1 July 2023), para. 121.
54. PCA Case No. 2023-33, Findings and Recommendations (1 July 2023), para. 135.

increase on Russia's 2022 allocation from 20% to 15%, in line with the Scientific Committee's estimation of the overall sustainable increase in total allowable catch.[55]

The Review Panel also reflected on its duties being focused on 'problems and certain limited short-term responses', noting that 'longer term solutions' are entrusted to the Commission and commented that 'the further strengthening of the deliberative and negotiating processes would contribute to the effectiveness of the CMMs adopted in meeting the objectives of the Convention'.[56] It stated that 'Russia, jointly with other interested Commission Members, could advance the prospects of success in such an endeavour by indicating their willingness to find means in accordance with the Convention to enhance the fairness, transparency, and stability of allocations to Members whose flag vessels fish for *Trachurus murphyi*.'[57]

The simple fact that this procedure has thrice been able to resolve multiparty disputes involving several States and an international organization is already notable. The 'Solomonic' aspect of the panel decisions rendered has also been commended, allowing both the objecting and non-objecting Members room to compromise and move forward without need for further formal dispute settlement,[58] while at the same time 'assisting RFMOs to find ways to address more fundamental disagreements or differences of opinion which can give rise to these disputes in the first place'.[59]

Once again, the hybrid nature of the process enabled these positive outcomes. The Review Panels in each instance render a report of 'Findings and Recommendations'. The panel's findings act as a legal gateway that circumscribes the panel's mandate such that it does not veer wholly into equity and *amiable composition* that would usurp the SPRFMO Commission's mandate and discretion. The 'alternative measures' that an objecting Member is required to put forward also mean that it 'must identify not only the problem, but also a potential solution', which can then be further explored and refined by the Review Panel.[60] And the combined framework of such findings and recommendations allows for a process and a decision that remains non-binding on its own, but nevertheless transforms it into a binding dispute settlement through the absence of invocation of further procedures by the objecting Member(s).

55. PCA Case No. 2023-33, Findings and Recommendations (1 July 2023), para. 143.
56. PCA Case No. 2023-33, Findings and Recommendations (1 July 2023), para. 144.
57. PCA Case No. 2023-33, Findings and Recommendations (1 July 2023), para. 144.
58. P. Tzeng, 'Fisheries Review Panels: Lessons from Russia v. Commission and Ecuador v. Commission' *Chinese (Taiwan) Yearbook of International Law and Affairs* (2020) 37, p. 233, https://doi.org/10.1163/9789004443297_010 (accessed 16 August 2025) .
59. R. Rayfuse, 'Settling Disputes in Regional Fisheries Management Organisations: Dealing with Objections' in *A Bridge over Troubled Waters: Dispute Resolution in the Law of International Watercourses and the Law of the Sea* (Helene Ruiz Fabri et al. (eds)) (Brill, 2020), p. 269, https://doi.org/10.1163/9789004434950_010 (accessed 16 August 2025) .
60. P. Tzeng, 'Fisheries Review Panels: Lessons from Russia v. Commission and Ecuador v. Commission' *Chinese (Taiwan) Yearbook of International Law and Affairs* (2020) 37, pp. 228-229, https://doi.org/10.1163/9789004443297_010 (accessed 16 August 2025) .

The fast-track procedure stipulated by the SPRFMO Convention is even more remarkable.[61] In addition to requiring a hearing within thirty days, the Review Panel mechanism allows not only the objecting Member(s) and the representatives of the SPRFMO Commission but also cooperating non-contracting parties and all other members of the Commission to participate in the proceedings through oral and written submissions. Despite this high degree of procedural complexity – the conclusion of an inter-State proceeding involving multiple States and an intergovernmental organization within forty-five days being previously unheard of in international dispute settlement – the procedure has now been carried out successfully on three occasions. In fact, the speed of the process helps emphasize the less adversarial character of the procedure and the more active and inquisitorial role of the review panel, serving as an intermediate step prior to formal dispute settlement under the SPRFMO Convention.

Taken together, the nature and speed of the review panel procedure facilitate its integration into the broader regulatory structure of the SPRFMO Convention. The mechanism provides for an expeditious and flexible procedure to address real-time compliance with multilateral decisions against specific legal standards, while also affording the review panel latitude to make broader recommendations with respect to alternative measures, with a view to promoting adherence to said decisions and the overall objectives of the SPRFMO Convention. That is, the mechanism allows the review panel's decisions to plug into the Commission's iterative decision-making and SPRFMO Members' fishing activities as they occur.[62] Case in point, following the 2023 Review Panel decision, a new working group chaired by Vanuatu was convened during the following SPRFMO Commission session to consider the latest Findings and Recommendations and was able to achieve consensus on a new distribution of the increase in total allowable catch for both 2023 and beyond.[63]

IV BUSINESS AND HUMAN RIGHTS GRIEVANCE MECHANISM: THE *INTERNATIONAL LABOUR ARBITRATION AND CONCILIATION RULES*

On 24 April 2013, the Rana Plaza building collapsed, killing over one thousand people labouring in the garment industry in Dhaka, Bangladesh. Subsequent investigations

61. P. Tzeng, 'Fisheries Review Panels: Lessons from Russia v. Commission and Ecuador v. Commission' *Chinese (Taiwan) Yearbook of International Law and Affairs* (2020) 37, p. 228, https://doi.org/10.1163/9789004443297_010 (accessed 16 August 2025) .
62. A. Serdy, 'Implementing Article 28 of the UN Fish Stocks Agreement: The First Review of a Conservation Measure in the South Pacific Regional Fisheries Management Organisation' (2016) 47(1) *Ocean Development & International Law* p. 22, https://doi.org/10.1080/00908320.2016.1124482 (accessed 16 August 2025) .
63. SPRFMO, 'SPRFMO Commission: COMM 12: Report Annex 9a: Report of the Chairperson of the COMM12 Jack Mackerel Working Group' (2024), available at: https://www.sprfmo.int/assets/Meetings/01-COMM/12th-Commission-2024/Report-and-Annexes/Annex-9a-Report-from-the-Chairperson-of-the-2024-Jack-Mackerel-WG-COMM12.pdf (accessed 16 August 2025); SPRFMO, 'SPRFMO Commission: COMM 12: Report Annex 7a: CMM 01-2024' (2024), available at: https://www.sprfmo.int/assets/Meetings/01-COMM/12th-Commission-2024/Report-and-Annexes/Annex-7a-CMM-01-2024-Trachurus-murphyi.pdf (accessed 16 August 2025).

discovered that building and fire safety measures were deficient and responsible for the tragic and profound loss of human life. This disaster nevertheless galvanized the international community and the various players in the fast-fashion industry in Bangladesh to do better and prevent any similar catastrophe from recurring. The outcome of these efforts was the signature on 15 May 2013 of the Accord on Fire and Building Safety in Bangladesh (Bangladesh Accord), a legally binding agreement facilitated by the International Labour Organisation between global brands and retailers on the one side and trade unions on the other to establish fire and building safety standards for workers in the textile industry in Bangladesh. In a first, however, these standards were accompanied by binding and enforceable dispute resolution mechanisms. The Bangladesh Accord established a multi-tier dispute resolution mechanism ending with arbitration under the UNCITRAL Arbitration Rules.[64]

A short time thereafter, this mechanism was put to the test. In July and October of 2016, two arbitrations were commenced under the Bangladesh Accord, claiming that certain brands had failed to uphold the commitments made in the Accord.[65] These arbitrations provided the proof of concept for an arbitration backstop to voluntary human rights commitments, but they also exposed the particular nature of business and human rights disputes. For example, the tribunal grappled early on with the transparency regime that should be applicable to the case. The tribunal not only noted that there was a significant public interest involved in the dispute but also recognized that privacy and reputational considerations formed the heart of the bargain struck in the Bangladesh Accord:

> [There is] a genuine public interest in the Accord, including on the part of other stakeholders who would have a direct interest in its interpretation. [...] On the other hand, the Tribunal must take into account competing factors stemming from the language of the Accord and the practice under it, which point to an obligation to protect certain information about the participating brand companies.[66]

The tribunal ultimately decided 'to balance both sets of interests emphasized by the Parties by disclosing certain basic information about the existence and progress of the arbitration proceedings, while at the same time keeping confidential the identity of the Respondents'.[67] Yet, this apparent compromise solution was partially frustrated by the fact that the UNCITRAL Arbitration Rules constrained hearings to be held in private and any award to be published only with the consent of all parties, even if inconsistent with the principles just enunciated.[68] Had the tribunal reached the fact-finding phase of the case, they may have encountered further challenges there as well. However, on 17

64. In its first version, the arbitration provision referred to the UNCITRAL Model Law, which could have given rise to pathological consequences. Thankfully, the parties agreed that the provision should be taken as referring to the UNCITRAL Arbitration Rules instead.
65. PCA Cases No. 2016-36 and 2016-37. Publicly available details concerning these arbitrations may be found at pca-cpa.org/en/cases/152/ (accessed 16 August 2025).
66. *Bangladesh Accord Arbitrations*, PCA Cases No. 2016-36/37, Procedural Order No. 2, para. 94.
67. *Bangladesh Accord Arbitrations*, PCA Cases No. 2016-36/37, Press Release No. 1.
68. *Ibid.*, ('As the Parties have agreed to apply the 2010 UNCITRAL Arbitration Rules to the present proceedings, hearings are to be held in private and any award of the Tribunal can only be made public with the consent of the Parties'); UNCITRAL Arbitration Rules, Articles 28(3), 34(5).

July 2018, the Tribunal constituted in the two arbitrations issued termination orders following the settlement by the parties of both sets of claims, those settlements remaining entirely confidential as well.

The tension between the design of the UNCITRAL Arbitration Rules and the particular characteristics of arbitrations in the business and human rights field led to the creation of the *Hague Rules on Business and Human Rights Arbitration* (Hague Rules).[69] The UNCITRAL Arbitration Rules – originally created with commercial arbitration in mind, but aspiring to such flexibility that they had been successfully employed in investor-State and inter-State arbitration – worked well in the *Bangladesh Accord Arbitrations*. However, the human rights context exhibited particular features that still warranted specialized rules and guidance.[70] Likewise, the UN Guiding Principles already codified international standards to be met by human rights remedy mechanisms. The Hague Rules thus sought to marry the neutrality, expertise, flexibility, and enforceability hallmarks of international arbitration with the legitimacy, accessibility, equity, and other criteria stipulated by the UN Guiding Principles.[71]

The Hague Rules also included a nod towards expedited and facilitative mechanisms. Seeing as these elements were secondary to the core principles of the Hague Rules, however, they addressed each of them in a single additional article,[72] in a manner ironically reminiscent of the simplicity of the UNCITRAL Arbitration Rules as compared to the specialized provisions of the Hague Rules.

In the meantime, the Bangladesh Accord example developed and evolved, eventually into the International Accord for the textile industry and with an eventual view to expansion to other industries as well. At the same time, although reflection on the *Bangladesh Accord Arbitrations* remained very positive, aspirations grew for a more operational-level expedited form of dispute resolution, capable of swiftly addressing an individual claim. The *Bangladesh Accord Arbitrations* had addressed a number of broader questions and proven the value of arbitration in this context, but also entailed time and costs that would preclude claims that did not rise to the same level of systemic importance.[73]

---

69. *Hague Rules on Business and Human Rights Arbitration*, December 2019, available at: https://docs.pca-cpa.org/2019/12/The-Hague-Rules-on-Business-and-Human-Rights-Arbitration.pdf (accessed 16 August 2025).
70. *See International Labour Arbitration and Conciliation Rules*, 2 July 2021, Introduction ('The parties to the Bangladesh Accord, in moving forward to arbitrate two disputes in 2016-17 pursuant to their arbitration agreement, highlighted the challenges of labour arbitration under the UNCITRAL Arbitration Rules designed for commercial actors and disputes centered around pecuniary claims rather than worker rights and safety').
71. *See UN Guiding Principles on Business and Human Rights*, Principle 31.
72. *See* Hague Rules, December 2019, Articles 56-57.
73. *See* ILAC Rules, 2 July 2021, Introduction ('Global unions and non-profits acting on behalf of workers, including the most vulnerable workers in the global economy, cannot invest disproportionate funds into the costly systems of arbitration that govern international disputes between corporate actors. Nor can they afford the time required by such procedures: left unremedied, violations of international labour agreements threaten the economic security, rights, and even the lives of workers. MNCs bring their own concerns to dispute resolution under labour agreements, as proceedings often involve sensitive business information and can have reputational consequences. All parties to international labour agreements share an interest in resolving disputes efficiently, fairly, and effectively').

This provided the impetus for the development of the *International Labour Arbitration and Conciliation Rules* (ILAC Rules), developed in 2021 to incorporate 'best practices for speedy and efficient resolution of disputes arising under international labour agreements' into the Hague Rules model.[74] This rapid-response mechanism takes after some of the characteristics common to labour arbitration, notably a default timetable which foresees an early hearing at which the issues may be crystallized and refined, with written submissions to follow thereafter.[75] The ILAC Rules also feature an early administrative conference to be convened in parallel to the appointment of the arbitrator and which provide an explicit off-ramp towards conciliation proceedings (also to be administered and supported actively by the PCA).[76]

The ILAC Rules mechanism remains untested as of yet, but that test would seem to be imminent based on reports from the front lines. The 2021 version of the International Accord Agreement incorporated the ILAC Rules only as an option. The ILAC Rules themselves were only finalized in the midst of those negotiations. The most recent 2023 version of the International Accord Agreement, however, now provides that 'any arbitration shall be governed by the International Labor Arbitration and Conciliation Rules' instead of the UNCITRAL Arbitration Rules.

The ILAC rules also coincide with another major shift in the business and human rights landscape that augurs the use of these and other mechanisms. In 2024, the European Parliament and the Council of the European Union adopted *Directive 2024/1760 on Corporate Sustainability Due Diligence* (CSDDD). Representing a crystallization of the UN Guiding Principles into regional hard law, the CSDDD imposes due diligence obligations on companies meeting certain thresholds on the number of employees and turnover to prevent potential adverse impacts or to mitigate or bring to an end actual adverse impacts arising from their own operations, those of their subsidiaries, or their business partners when related to their chain of activities.[77] The CSDDD adopts a dual enforcement approach. On the one hand, it requires companies to establish grievance mechanisms through which persons or entities concerned with actual or potential adverse impacts can submit complaints, allowing for 'participation in collaborative complaints procedures and notification mechanisms, including those established jointly by companies, through industry associations, multi-stakeholder initiatives or global framework agreement'.[78] On the other, it introduces the possibility of civil liability, enabling legal proceedings against companies that fail to meet their obligations.[79]

74. ILAC Rules, 2 July 2021, Introduction, available at: https://docs.pca-cpa.org/2022/06/3dd0e0dd-2021-july-2-international_labour_arbitration__.pdf (accessed 16 August 2025).
75. ILAC Rules, 2 July 2021, Article 17(7) ('The hearing shall in principle take place within 30 days of the case management conference').
76. *See* ILAC Rules, 2 July 2021, Article 7.
77. *Directive (EU) 2024/1760 of the European Parliament and of the Council on Corporate Sustainability Due Diligence and Amending Directive (EU) 2019/1937 and Regulation (EU) 2023/2859*, 13 June 2024, Articles 7-12, available at: https://eur-lex.europa.eu/legal-content/EN/TXT/PDF/?uri=OJ:L_202401760 (accessed 16 August 2025).
78. CSDDD, Article 14.
79. CSDDD, Article 29.

While formally addressed to European companies and some non-EU companies,[80] its due diligence obligations extend across global value chains. This extraterritorial reach is likely to produce a Brussels Effect, accelerating the use of business and human rights grievance mechanisms and other means of dispute resolution across the globe. Efforts are already underway by the European Working Group for Responsible and Sustainable Supply Chains to translate the CSDDD's obligations into a set of model clauses.[81] The current iteration, known as the Zero Draft, outlines a tiered mechanism that begins with a dialogue-based resolution process involving an independent facilitator (an operational-level grievance mechanism) and escalates to arbitration or national courts if the grievance remains unresolved.[82] The Zero Draft expressly refers to the Hague Rules, the underlying model used to create the ILAC Rules, and an apt choice considering that they can accommodate multi-stakeholder participation.[83]

In the meantime, even as they await further implementation and operation, the ILAC Rules remain yet another example of using hybrid expedited dispute resolution at an operational level to support a broader system and policy objectives.

V CONCLUSION

The commercial dispute resolution community has seen a decided increase in interest for expedited and non-contentious dispute resolution options. Albeit in different configurations, States have shown an equal increase in appetite for diverse, ever speedier and more efficient alternatives in public international law as well. While the words of the 1899 Hague Convention still ring true – arbitration remains a 'most effective [and] equitable means of settling disputes that diplomacy has failed to settle' – its growing company and increasing number of flavours is to be welcomed. The tried-and-tested models of dispute resolution remain fit for purpose, but optimization and adaptation may be precisely what is needed to unlock their potential in novel contexts. Given the myriad conflicts plaguing the world today, States need as many tools in their arsenal as they can muster. One can only hope that agile mechanisms of the kind just explored might facilitate international cooperation and help the world adapt to the ever-evolving dynamics of global society.

80. CSDDD, Article 2.
81. Responsible Contracting Project, 'The European Model Clauses (EMCs)', available at: https://www.responsiblecontracting.org/emcs (accessed 16 August 2025). The European Working Group's final proposal might serve as a helpful resource for the European Commission to develop guidance on voluntary model contractual clauses under Article 18 of the CSDDD.
82. European Working Group, 'Zero Draft for Consultation: The European Model Clauses (EMCs) for Responsible and Sustainable Supply Chains' (July 2024), Articles 1.4, 5.1-5.2, available at: https://www.responsiblecontracting.org/_files/ugd/fcee10_538d4de3351d4b699cd1c47e81ba8f22.pdf (accessed 16 August 2025); European Working Group, 'Commentary to the Zero Draft for Consultation: The European Model Clauses (EMCs) for Responsible and Sustainable Supply Chains' (July 2024), p. 48, available at: https://www.responsiblecontracting.org/_files/ugd/fcee10_97c2e2a4323a4bf58cb20d1623cc2308.pdf (accessed 16 August 2025).
83. European Working Group, 'Zero Draft for Consultation: The European Model Clauses (EMCs) for Responsible and Sustainable Supply Chains' (July 2024), Article 5.2.

CHAPTER 37

Agreement on Climate Change, Trade and Sustainability (ACCTS)

Dyalá Jiménez Figueres[*]

TABLE OF CONTENTS

I INTRODUCTION

The Agreement on Climate Change, Trade and Sustainability (ACCTS) was launched in 2019 by a group of small trade-dependent States as an initiative to contribute to the reduction of climate change through trade. As declared by the countries that are spearheading this Agreement, negotiating an agreement on climate change, trade and sustainability has the potential to help bring together some of the interrelated elements of the climate change, trade and sustainable development agendas and demonstrate how they can be mutually reinforcing.

As of the date of this edition of the Congress, the Agreement is not yet finalized. It is being negotiated during a time when the world needs a comprehensive and robust agenda to deal with climate change.[1] Climate change is directly contributing to humanitarian emergencies from heatwaves, wildfires, floods, tropical storms and

* Dyalá Jiménez is a Costa Rican national and specializes in international arbitration. Dyalá is frequently appointed as arbitrator in institutional and ad hoc arbitrations, both in commercial and investor-State matters. She is a member of the panel of arbitrators for Costa Rica before ICSID, a member of the ICC International Court of Arbitration and a member of the ICCA Governing Board. She served as Minister of Foreign Trade of Costa Rica from 2018 to 2020. Dyalá works in Spanish, English, French and Portuguese. The author thanks Karima Sauma for her support in the preparation of this presentation.

1. Please note that the Agreement was later signed in November 2024.

hurricanes, and they are increasing in scale, frequency and intensity. The direct damage costs to health of climate change (excluding costs in health-determining sectors such as agriculture and water and sanitation) is estimated to be between USD 2-4 billion per year by 2030.[2]

The environmental challenges we face today must be addressed from all fronts. This is where the relationship between trade, climate change and sustainability comes into play. Trade can play a crucial role in the transition to a global low-carbon economy and a greener, more sustainable society.

As Dr. Ngozi Okonjo-Iweala, World Trade Organization (WTO) Director-General stated: "The well-being of people is dependent upon the well-being of our planet, and trade can play an important role here (...). By connecting people and markets, trade helps lower costs and disseminate new environmental technologies. Trade can make resource use more efficient, reducing the strain on our ecosystems. New trade rules can help our economies become greener, cleaner, more prosperous, and more inclusive."[3]

In addition, supply, transport and distribution chains infrastructure are likely to become more vulnerable to disruptions due to climate change. Furthermore, climate change is expected to decrease the productivity of all production factors, which will ultimately result in output losses and a decrease in the volume of global trade.[4]

Considering the above, it is urgent for countries to act now and implement aggressive strategies to mitigate these risks. Under the WTO, countries have undertaken a number of environment-related efforts,[5] and the ACCTS has the potential to take that progress and lead in a new direction.

There is not much publicly available information on the ACCTS, but this chapter aims to explain what is expected to come out of it, its importance, and the context in which it is being negotiated. The following section (section II) explains the aspects purported to be covered by the Agreement, while section III describes the Abu Dhabi Ministerial Declaration resulting from the 13th Ministerial Conference (MC13) held on 2 March 2024. Finally, section IV provides some conclusions.

II THE ACCTS

The ACCTS is an initiative launched initially by the governments of New Zealand, Costa Rica, Fiji, Iceland, Norway, and Switzerland. These are small, trade-dependent countries "who believe trade measures and disciplines can contribute to helping to address the urgent challenge we face for sustainable development in general and on

2. World Health Organization, "Climate Change." Available at: https://www.who.int/news-room/fact-sheets/detail/climate-change-and-health. Visited on April 3, 2024.
3. World Trade Organization, "Trade and Climate Change." Available at: https://www.wto.org/english/tratop_e/envir_e/climate_intro_e.htm. Visited on April 3, 2024.
4. OECD, "Trade and the Environment." Available at: https://www.oecd.org/trade/topics/trade-and-the-environment/. Visited on April 3, 2024.
5. *Ibid.*

climate change in particular."[6] These countries also have a lot in common regarding the alignment of trade policy issues.

Thus, the ACCTS focuses on trade-related issues that have the potential to address climate change, starting with the liberalization of tariffs on environmental goods and services, the definition of disciplines to eliminate harmful fossil fuel subsidies, and the development of high-integrity eco-labels.[7]

The ACCTS is a plurilateral agreement in the context of the WTO, which means that it is negotiated by a number of WTO Member States only.[8] Post-WTO Agreement plurilateral agreements were found as a solution to prevent the atomization of regional agreements and thus the disparity in liberalization of global trade while allowing states to make progress in the global agenda, especially concerning matters in areas such as (post-GATS) services, environment and labor. Usually, when plurilateral agreements are entered into, a threshold of a percentage of the relevant global market is required for its entry into force, since typical open plurilateral agreements become binding on non-signatories by virtue of the Most Favored Nation (MFN) rule. This threshold requirement is meant to prevent free riding and out of "justice and fairness."[9]

In the case of the ACCTS, from the limited information that has been gathered, the negotiating parties are mostly interested in finding a way contribute to climate action and presenting an ambitious solution for the intersecting agendas of environment and trade. They are discussing the way the specific commitments will be adopted by other WTO members, although it was initially fathomed as a typical open plurilateral agreement.[10] In any case, it will be open for more WTO members to join and/or assume similar obligations at a later stage.

This section will focus on the content of the ACCTS, covering the removal of tariffs on environmental goods and services (1), the elimination of harmful fossil fuel subsidies (2), guidelines to inform the development and implementation of voluntary eco-labelling programs (3), and the dispute settlement mechanism (4).

6. "Agreement on Climate Change, Trade and Sustainability (ACCTS) negotiations." New Zealand Foreign Affairs and Trade. Available at: https://www.mfat.govt.nz/en/trade/free-trade-agreements/trade-and-climate/agreement-on-climate-change-trade-and-sustainability-accts-negotiations/. Visited on April 3, 2024.
7. T. Voituruez and K. Cremers, "Is There a Case for the EU to Join the Agreement on Climate Change, Trade and Sustainability (ACCTS)?," IDDRI, 22 June 2023. Available at: https://www.iddri.org/en/publications-and-events/blog-post/there-case-eu-join-agreement-climate-change-trade-and. Visited on April 3, 2024.
8. It was actually at the 2005 ministerial conference in Hong Kong that plurilateral efforts were formally accepted as an option to proceed with the trade liberalization agenda that has been stagnated for more than twenty years. Rudolph Adlung and Hamid Mandouh, "Plurilateral Trade Agreements: An Escape Route for the WTO?" WTO Working Paper ERSD-2017-03, December 2016. Available at: chrome-extension://efaidnbmnnnibpcajpcglclefindmkaj/https://www.wto.org/english/res_e/reser_e/ersd201703_e.pdf. Visited on April 21, 2024.
9. *Ibid.*, pp. 5 and 10.
10. T. Voituruez and K. Cremers, "Is There a Case for the EU to Join the Agreement on Climate Change, Trade and Sustainability (ACCTS)?," IDDRI, June 22, 2023. Available at: https://www.iddri.org/en/publications-and-events/blog-post/there-case-eu-join-agreement-climate-change-trade-and. Visited on April 3, 2024.

1 Removal of Tariffs on Environmental Goods and New and Binding Commitments for Environmental Services

One of the key areas covered in the ACCTS relates to the liberalization of tariffs on environmental goods and services. The idea behind this is that the liberalization of environmental goods and services means that they will become less expensive in each of the ACCTS countries, which will hopefully accelerate access and uptake.

In order to understand why this is important, first we have to define "environmental goods and services." According to the United Nations, environmental goods and services are products manufactured or services rendered for the main purpose of:

(a) preventing or minimizing pollution, degradation or natural resources depletion;
(b) repairing damage to air, water, waste, noise, biodiversity and landscapes;
(c) reducing, eliminating, treating and managing pollution, degradation and natural resource depletion;
(d) carrying out other activities such as measurement and monitoring, control, research and development, education, training, information and communication related to environmental protection or resource management.[11]

Some examples of environmental goods are wind turbines, water treatment filters, and solar water heaters. As for environmental services, these include the cleaning of exhaust gases, noise and vibration abatement, remediation and clean-up of soil and water, nature and landscape protection, among others.

Economic growth resulting from trade expansion can have a negative effect on the environment by increasing pollution or degrading natural resources. However, increased trade can in turn, by supporting economic growth, development, and social welfare, contribute to a greater capacity to manage the environment more effectively. In addition, open markets can improve access to new technologies that make local production processes more efficient by diminishing the use of inputs such as energy, water, and other environmentally harmful substances.[12]

The liberalization of trade can also provide incentives to adopt more stringent environmental standards. As a country becomes more integrated within the world economy, its export sector becomes more exposed to environmental requirements imposed by the leading importers, and this trickles down the value chain.[13]

11. "Environmental Goods and Services," UNTERM Portal. Available at: https://archive.unescwa.org/environmental-goods-and-services#: ~ :text = Environmental%20goods%20and%20services%20are,eliminating%2C%20treating%20and%20managing%20pollution. Visited on April 3, 2024.
12. OECD, "Trade and the Environment." Available at: https://www.oecd.org/trade/topics/trade-and-the-environment/. Visited on April 3, 2024.
13. *Ibid.*

2 Disciplines to Eliminate Harmful Fossil Fuel Subsidies

The ACCTS also aims to eliminate fossil fuel subsidies, which "will help remove the perverse effects of these environmentally harmful and socially regressive subsidies."[14] Even though this subject has been addressed in other contexts, this is the first time that it has been discussed in an agreement of this nature.[15]

Fossil fuels are non-renewable sources of energy, and their production and use contribute significantly to climate change and pollution. The case for using trade rules to discipline fossil fuel subsidies is particularly compelling. Globally, fossil fuel subsidies were USD 7 trillion or 7.1% of GDP in 2022, reflecting a USD 2 trillion increase since 2020 due to government support from surging energy prices.[16] Subsidies make these greenhouse gas-emitting fuels cheaper to produce and buy, acting as an incentive to use and produce more. Just as trade rules are used in the WTO context to address industrial and agricultural subsidies, they have an important role to play here also.[17]

Subsidy reform is paramount to curb the current harmful effects of fossil fuels. "Raising fuel prices to their fully efficient levels reduces projected global fossil fuel CO2 emissions 43 percent below baseline levels in 2030—or 34 percent below 2019 emissions. This reduction is in line with the 25-50 percent reduction in global GHGs below 2019 levels needed by 2030 to be on track with containing global warming to the Paris goal of 1.5-2C."[18]

3 Guidelines to Inform the Development and Implementation of Voluntary Eco-Labelling Programs

The development of guidelines to inform the development and implementation of voluntary eco-labelling programs and associated mechanisms to encourage their

14. "Agreement on Climate Change, Trade and Sustainability (ACCTS) Negotiations." New Zealand Foreign Affairs and Trade. Available at: https://www.mfat.govt.nz/en/trade/free-trade-agreements/trade-and-climate/agreement-on-climate-change-trade-and-sustainability-accts-negotiations/. Visited on April 3, 2024.
15. Ministry of Foreign Trade of Costa Rica, "ACCTS." Available at: https://www.comex.go.cr/media/10075/21-08-19-presentacion-sesion-informativa-accts-agosto-2021.pdf. Visited on April 3, 2024.
16. International Monetary Fund, "Climate Change, Fossil Fuel Subsidies." Available at: https://www.imf.org/en/Topics/climate-change/energy-subsidies#: ~ :text = Underpricing%20for%20local%20air%20pollution,17%20percent)%2C%20and%20forgone%20consumption. Visited on April 3, 2024.
17. "Agreement on Climate Change, Trade and Sustainability (ACCTS) Negotiations." New Zealand Foreign Affairs and Trade. Available at: https://www.mfat.govt.nz/en/trade/free-trade-agreements/trade-and-climate/agreement-on-climate-change-trade-and-sustainability-accts-negotiations/. Visited on April 3, 2024.
18. International Monetary Fund, "Climate Change, Fossil Fuel Subsidies." Available at: https://www.imf.org/en/Topics/climate-change/energy-subsidies#: ~ :text = Underpricing%20for%20local%20air%20pollution,17%20percent)%2C%20and%20forgone%20consumption. Visited on April 3, 2024.

promotion and application will help support the development of high-integrity eco-labels that are transparent in their criteria and meaningful to consumers, and deliver their intended environmental objectives.[19]

The following topics have been discussed in relation to this subject:[20]

(a) The guidelines are based on international good practices.
(b) These will have a voluntary nature.
(c) The scope of application will include principles that apply to all types of eco-labelling.
(d) Institutional mechanisms to support the implementation of the guidelines and aid cooperation among countries.

4 Dispute Settlement Mechanism

We understand that the ACCTS will not include investor-State dispute settlement mechanism but rather a State-State dispute settlement mechanism foreseen in traditional trade agreements. As the ACCTS is an agreement that would result from a plurilateral negotiation, it will not refer to the dispute settlement mechanism under the WTO but rather to ad hoc arbitration.[21] This is an important aspect of any international agreement, especially one as novel as the ACCTS. One foreseeable aspect of potential conflict is the definition of the goods and services covered by the agreement, which could allegedly be already covered also by free-trade agreements. Another hypothetical area involves future developments in technology that may impact on the labelling obligations.

An argument can be made that for this reason precisely the State parties should stick to a familiar arbitration mechanism. On the other hand, a strong argument can also be made to support the idea that amicable mechanisms may prove helpful to allow for flexibility, speediness and voluntary enforcement, including also mechanisms involving professional experts, precisely due to the dynamic evolution of issues related to climate action. One idea could be for states to utilize something similar to the conciliation mechanism that is being developed for the Paris Agreement, in which ICCA is partaking, and which may involve services provided by the Permanent Court of Arbitration. Such a neutral and international center could prove to be the ideal go-to institution.

---

19. "Agreement on Climate Change, Trade and Sustainability (ACCTS) Negotiations." New Zealand Foreign Affairs and Trade. Available at: https://www.mfat.govt.nz/en/trade/free-trade-agreements/trade-and-climate/agreement-on-climate-change-trade-and-sustainability-accts-negotiations/. Visited on April 3, 2024.
20. Ministry of Foreign Trade of Costa Rica, "ACCTS." Available at: https://www.comex.go.cr/media/10075/21-08-19-presentacion-sesion-informativa-accts-agosto-2021.pdf. Visited on April 3, 2024.
21. This understanding comes directly from the author's tenure as Minister of Foreign Trade and informal confirmation from the Costa Rican government since there is not text publicly available to date.

III THE WTO AT MC 13

1 The Abu Dhabi Declaration

WTO members concluded the 13th Ministerial Conference in Abu Dhabi on 2 March 2024 with the adoption of the Abu Dhabi Ministerial Declaration. This Declaration recognizes the role that the multilateral trading system can play in contributing toward the achievement of the UN 2030 Agenda and its Sustainable Development Goals.[22] Interestingly, the Declaration does not mention climate change. Its reference to the environment was limited to the following paragraph: "we underscore the importance of trade and sustainable development in its three pillars—economic, social, and environmental."[23]

The Declaration emphasized the role and importance of services to the global economy as it generates more than two-thirds of global economic output and accounts for over half of all jobs.[24] It also recognized the contribution of women's economic empowerment and women's participation in trade to economic growth and sustainable development. Finally, it focused on developing and least-developed countries and their integration into the WTO agenda.

2 Dispute Settlement Reform

On dispute settlement reform, members adopted a Ministerial Decision recognizing the progress made with the view to having a fully and well-functioning dispute settlement system accessible to all members by 2024.[25] This Ministerial Decision expressly instructs officials "to accelerate discussions in an inclusive and transparent manner, build on the progress already made, and work on unresolved issues."[26] The pace of these discussions and whether they will be affected by the upcoming presidential election in the United States remains to be seen. Also, even if the discussions progress and the appellate body resumes, the backlog will have to be dealt with.

In the meantime, several WTO Member States, including Costa Rica, New Zealand and Norway, launched in 2020 the Multi-Party Interim Appeal Arbitration Arrangement that provides a temporary solution to the deadlock. This arrangement is

22. World Trade Organization, "MC13 Ends with Decisions on Dispute Reform, Development; Commitment to Continue Ongoing Talks." Available at: https://www.wto.org/english/news_e/news24_e/mc13_01mar24_e.htm. Visited on April 3, 2024.
23. Abu Dhabi Ministerial Declaration, adopted on March 2, 2024. Available at: https://docs.wto.org/dol2fe/Pages/SS/directdoc.aspx?filename=q:/WT/MIN24/DEC.pdf&Open=True. Visited on April 3, 2024.
24. World Trade Organization, "MC13 Ends with Decisions on dispute Reform, Development; Commitment to Continue Ongoing Talks." Available at: https://www.wto.org/english/news_e/news24_e/mc13_01mar24_e.htm. Visited on April 3, 2024.
25. Dispute Settlement Reform, Ministerial Decision. Adopted on March 2, 2024. Available at: https://docs.wto.org/dol2fe/Pages/SS/directdoc.aspx?filename=q:/WT/MIN24/37.pdf&Open=True. Visited on April 3, 2024.
26. *Ibid.*

evidence of the significance of dispute settlement mechanisms in the multilateral, multi-party international scenarios.

IV CONCLUSION

The ACCTS is an ambitious and groundbreaking Agreement. If adopted, it will send a powerful message on the direction that trade policies should be headed to curb climate change and promote sustainability.

However, we still do not have a final draft, and the final negotiated text is yet to be seen. Negotiations are set to be finalized in 2024. Certain challenges such as the attractiveness to join for non-signatories, the lobby from pressure groups with related interests, and the connected policies and frameworks needed to implement the Agreement's changes can all be obstacles for it to gain traction.

In addition, we wonder if the Agreement covers some pressing issues that contribute to carbon emissions, such as the international transportation of goods. Also, will the Agreement cover goods that are not themselves intended to reduce emissions but are produced with clean energy? There are still many important questions left unanswered.

It is too soon to tell if the Agreement will be successful; nonetheless, the ACCTS is a significant step in the right direction.

PANEL 13

Working in an Adversarial Environment

Inspired by the concept of doughnut economics, which prioritises balancing social needs and available resources, this panel explored how psychology and emotions intersect in adversarial settings, and how a greater understanding of the human condition may lead to more collaborative and sustainable approaches to dispute resolution. The speakers examined: emotions as catalysts for action; the pressures on advocates (including junior lawyers in the team); the tension of cross-examination; how to optimise expert witness engagement; and practical psychology tips to help practitioners survive and thrive in adversarial environments.

CHAPTER 38

Baking the Arbitration Doughnut: How Embracing Doughnut Economics Can Help Practitioners to Survive and Thrive in Adversarial Environments

Amanda J. Lee[*]

TABLE OF CONTENTS

I INTRODUCTION

When Pat Benatar reminded us that "Love is a Battlefield," it was not international arbitration she had in mind.[1] However, the practice of arbitration too often evokes the battlefield. Having plumbed the depths of the human condition during ICCA Congress 2024, it would be remiss of the arbitration community to fail to acknowledge that the practice of arbitration and the environment it creates are inherently adversarial.

---

* Amanda J. Lee FCIArb is an arbitrator trading as LML Arbitration, a consultant at Costigan King, a Visiting Lecturer at the University of Law, UK, and the Founder of ARBalance and Careers in Arbitration. The author thanks Kathryn Britten, Daniel Kalderimis, Yoko Maeda, Giacomo Rojas Elgueta and Emi Rowse Igusa, whose contributions at ICCA Congress 2024 inspired this chapter, Lise Bosman and Paula Baldini. ChatGPT (OpenAI, GPT-4) was used to assist with pre-writing research. All analysis, reasoning, and conclusions are the author's own.

1. Pat Benatar, "Love is a Battlefield" (*Genius*) https://genius.com/Pat-benatar-love-is-a-battlefield-lyrics accessed June 10, 2024.

Invoking notions of social Darwinism, international arbitration is rooted, in its unique way, in Herbert Spencer's notion of the "survival of the fittest."[2] In this context, "fitness" describes those who are "better designed for an immediate, local environment."[3] In a field typified by its adversarial nature, this leads us to the unavoidable conclusion that those who are best equipped to adapt to an adversarial environment will thrive as arbitration practitioners.

Competition is both "the lifeblood of industry" and a key feature of arbitration practice.[4] Aspiring arbitration practitioners are expected to compete for scholarships, academic accolades, internships and opportunities from the outset. Once established in practice, focus turns to advancing clients' interests and fighting their battles, running a gauntlet of guerilla tactics, legal budget and human resource limitations, punishing deadlines, and personal sacrifice.

The focus of more senior practitioners often shifts from competing for client mandates to seeking the approval of former adversaries in order to obtain arbitrator appointments. Such opportunities give practitioners the capacity to exert greater control over professional environments, as battlelines are drawn anew and former opponents now seek to persuade tribunal members of the veracity of their clients' positions. Adversity rears its head in new ways as practitioners strive to navigate tribunal dynamics and color within the lines established by applicable laws and rules.

As stakeholders in the arbitration ecosystem, arbitration practitioners must find ways to move beyond mere survival within the confines of their environment and the opportunities and resources available to them. Adaptation is necessary if the arbitration community is to thrive. However, striking a responsible balance between clients' needs, those of the organizations they represent, and their individual needs, and doing so within the scope of available resources, frequently puts practitioners in the shoes of aerialists performing high-wire acts without a net.

One of the ways in which arbitration practitioners can seek balance is to embrace and apply the principles of doughnut economics to international arbitration practice. Having introduced the topic (I), this chapter will: (II) explain the theory of doughnut economics; and (III) apply such theory to the practice of international arbitration, before concluding (IV).

II AN INTRODUCTION TO DOUGHNUT ECONOMICS

> You never change things by fighting the existing reality. To change something, build a new model that makes the existing model obsolete.

2. The term "survival of the fittest" was first used by Herbert Spencer in "Principles of Biology" (1864) and subsequently adopted by Charles Darwin in "The Variation of Animals and Plants Under Domestication" (1868).
3. Stephen Jay Gould, "This View of Life: Darwin's Untimely Burial" Natural History (1976) 85, 24-30, reproduced in Alex Rosenberg and Robert Arp (eds), Philosophy of Biology: An Anthology (John Wiley & Sons, May 2009) 99-102, 102.
4. Henry Ford, quoted in the Detroit News (July 30, 1941) https://www.thehenryford.org/collections-and-research/digital-resources/popular-topics/henry-ford-quotes/ accessed June 10, 2024.

Buckminster Fuller[5]

This section introduces the theory of doughnut economics and discusses its key tenets.

Doughnut economics is the brainchild of English economist Kate Raworth, a concept she first developed in 2012.[6] Raworth readily embraced the challenge set by Fuller above in her magnum opus, "Doughnut Economics: Seven Ways to Think Like a 21st-Century Economist," striving to sow the seeds of change by developing a new economic model better equipped to address the challenges of the twenty-first century.[7]

Raworth postulates that the greatest challenge humanity faces this century is finding a way to ensure that everyone's needs are met without exceeding available planetary resources. The "doughnut" provides a visible representation of sustainable development and the challenges to be overcome to achieve a brighter economic future. The concentric rings represent distinct boundaries: an ecological ceiling represented by the outer ring and a social foundation represented by the inner ring.

As illustrated below, the ecological ceiling encompasses available planetary resources. The negative consequences of exceeding the ceiling's limits include climate change, loss of biodiversity, air and chemical pollution, ocean acidification, land conversion and more. Likewise, the social foundation represents basic societal needs, both physical (e.g., food, water, energy, health, income, and housing) and social (e.g., social equity, gender equality, a political voice, peace and justice).[8] Such needs must be met using available planetary resources, providing the basis for a regenerative and distributive economy.

5. Buckminster Fuller, quoted in Kate Raworth, Doughnut Economics: Seven Ways to Think Like a 21st-Century Economist (1st Kindle ed., Cornerstone Digital 2017) 4.
6. Kate Raworth, "A Safe and Just Space for Humanity" (*Oxfam*, February 2012) https://www-cdn.oxfam.org/s3fs-public/file_attachments/dp-a-safe-and-just-space-for-humanity-130212-en_5.pdf accessed June 10, 2024.
7. Kate Raworth, Doughnut Economics: Seven Ways to Think Like a 21st Century Economist (1st Kindle ed., Cornerstone Digital 2017).
8. Doughnut Economics Action Lab, "About Doughnut Economics" (*Doughnut Economics*, Undated) https://doughnuteconomics.org/about-doughnut-economics accessed June 10, 2024.

Figure 38.1 The Doughnut of Social and Planetary Boundaries

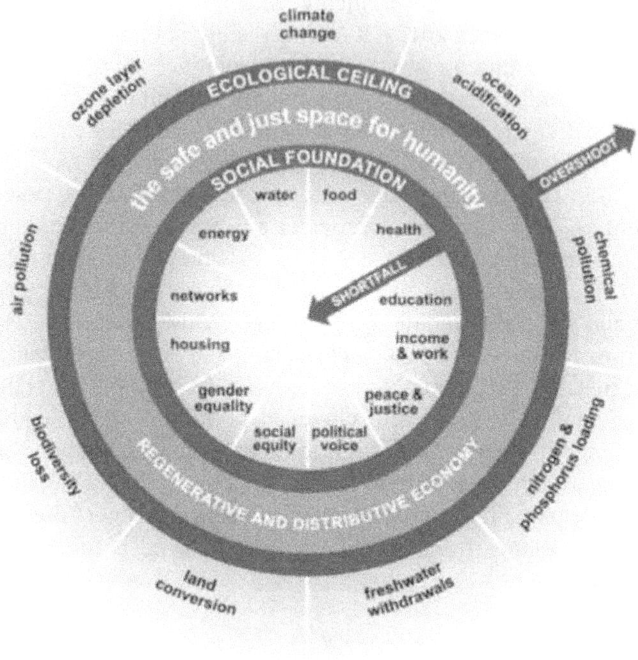

Kate Raworth and Christian Guthier. CC-BY-SA 4.0.[9]

The goal of the doughnut economist is to find ways to ensure society's needs are met without exceeding available resources. Within the concentric rings lies "the space in which we can meet the needs of all within the means of the planet."[10] To adopt the requisite mindset is accordingly to find the means to operate within the confines of the doughnut. Her goal is to reframe the paradigms that have historically dominated economic discourse (Figure 38.1).

To achieve such a mindset, Raworth identifies seven ways of thinking like a twenty-first century economist. In brief, she postulates that economists must: (a) change the goal; (b) see the big picture; (c) nurture human nature; (d) get savvy with systems; (e) design to distribute; (f) create to regenerate; and (g) be agnostic about growth. By changing the narrative, we permit ourselves to see things from a different, more balanced, and ultimately more sustainable perspective.

9. Kate Raworth, "Doughnut Economics: Seven Ways to Think Like a 21st-Century Economist" (London: Penguin Random House, 2017). Reproduced with attribution pursuant to the Creative Commons Attribution-ShareAlike 4.0 International License https://doughnuteconomics.org/principles-and-guidelines#license accessed June 10, 2024.
10. Kate Raworth, Doughnut Economics: Seven Ways to Think Like a 21st-Century Economist (1st Kindle ed., Cornerstone Digital 2017) 10.

To change the goal, Raworth advocates for a departure from the historical fixation on gross domestic product, an approach that prioritizes financial growth at the expense of the environment and the pursuit of economic equality. Instead, doughnut economics strives to bring humanity into the "safe and just space" within the concentric circles of the doughnut and learn to "thrive in balance."[11] Likewise, seeing the big picture encourages economists to visualize the economy in new and innovative ways, departing from the narrative depicted in the classic "Circular Flow" diagram.[12]

Raworth's encouragement to nurture human nature requires economists to depart from the model of the "rational economic man," who is traditionally depicted as "self-interested, isolated, calculating, fixed in taste, and dominant over nature."[13] Instead, economists must embrace the richer elements of human nature: "social, interdependent, approximating, fluid in values, and dependent upon the living world."[14] Such qualities promote sustainability and foster an awareness of the need to live within our means and without depleting our resources.

The dynamism of the economy is, Raworth postulates, better illustrated by "a simple pair of feedback loops" than classical supply and demand curves.[15] It is ever evolving and should be treated as such by savvy economic operators. Similarly, by challenging the notion that inequality is an "economic necessity" and recognizing it instead as a "design failure," economists open their minds to the development of economic systems that distribute not just income but wealth itself, particularly that rooted in control over assets of different types.[16]

Sustainability is at the heart of Raworth's sixth principle: create to regenerate. Contrary to traditional economic theory, it is unnecessary for the state of an environment to worsen before it improves. As Raworth notes, "ecological degradation is simply the result of degenerative industrial design."[17] By embracing regenerative design principles and seeking to develop a circular economy, humanity can return to its proper status as a caretaker and "full participant in Earth's cyclical processes of life."[18]

Most importantly, Raworth dares to advance an economic theory that focuses not on growth, but on creating a sustainable environment in which all may thrive. Doughnut economics rejects the notion of growth as the ultimate economic goal. Instead, emphasis is placed on the development of thriving economies, whether such economies lead to growth or not. This change of perspective invites humanity to reject its historical obsession with economic growth.[19]

Simply put, the goal of doughnut economics is sustainable development: a regenerative and distributive economic environment within which humanity can thrive, whether economic growth is a by-product or not.

11. *Ibid.*, at 27.
12. *Ibid.*, at 28.
13. *Ibid.*
14. *Ibid.*
15. *Ibid.*
16. *Ibid.*, at 28-29.
17. *Ibid.*, at 29.
18. *Ibid.*
19. *Ibid.*

III BAKING THE ARBITRATION DOUGHNUT

Savvy arbitration practitioners may draw inspiration from Raworth's teachings. The development of a sustainable arbitration ecosystem is a worthwhile goal, particularly mindful of the significant contribution arbitration makes to the global economy. By way of example, fees relating to arbitration practice are worth GBP 2.5 billion annually to the British economy alone.[20]

1 Applying New Ways of Thinking to Arbitration Practice

To determine the extent to which doughnut economic theory may be applied to the practice of international arbitration, it is appropriate to apply Raworth's seven ways of thinking to its practice.

a *Changing the Goal*

Parties often have multiple goals in mind when choosing to arbitrate. Whether the primary goal is to preserve party autonomy, protect confidentiality, select a neutral forum, promote efficiency, cost-effectiveness and expediency, or otherwise, the shadow cast by the adversarial nature of the field is unmistakable. Parties and their representatives are encouraged to see their opponents as adversaries, consistent with common law tradition.

Although the parameters and features of victory in arbitral proceedings differ, common goals include protecting the status quo, maximizing financial recovery, mitigating loss and holding commercial and investment counterparties to the terms of their agreements. Parties and their representatives are incentivized to win, whether by the promise of financial reward, market advantage, or a combination of both. Although success cannot always be measured in financial terms, recouping losses and reducing financial exposure remain core goals.

A significant cultural shift would be required to reorientate success in arbitration practice to reflect outcomes that prioritize fairness, equity and sustainability over financial compensation, but there are already signs, particularly in the investor-state dispute settlement (ISDS) arena, that arbitration's focus on profit must co-exist with "human" factors, such as the protection and promotion of environmental, social and governance (ESG) standards, and respect for human rights.

b *Seeing the Big Picture*

The global nature of international arbitration offers significant scope to see a bigger picture. The arbitration community is diverse, encompassing practitioners from

20. Ministry of Justice and Lord Bellamy KC, "Modernised Laws to Secure UK as World Leader in Dispute Resolution" *(UK Government*, November 22, 2024) https://www.gov.uk/government/news/modernised-laws-to-secure-uk-as-world-leader-in-dispute-resolution accessed June 24, 2024.

different professional backgrounds, legal and cultural traditions, geographical locations and more. Such diversity provides considerable scope for arbitration practice to incorporate and benefit from global perspectives.

The interaction between domestic courts and arbitral tribunals, and the extent to which jurisdictions are perceived as arbitration-friendly, has a significant impact on their use as seats for arbitral proceedings. Such perceptions have the potential to influence both international trade and international relations.

Likewise, it is vital that arbitration practitioners recognize the potential for arbitral awards, particularly those issued in ISDS proceedings in which jurisprudence plays a greater role, to have significant wider environmental, economic and social implications. United Nations (UN) Special Rapporteur on Human Rights and the Environment, David Boyd, highlighted the dangers of regulatory chill created by ISDS tribunals' decisions in a significant report to the UN.

Notably, Boyd categorized ISDS as "a major obstacle to the urgent actions needed to address the planetary environmental and human rights crises" and highlighted the rising number of ISDS cases taken by States to protect the environment from 2000 to 2021, perceived pro-investor bias, and inconsistent approaches adopted by tribunals to the calculation of damages in, for example, *Tethyan Copper v. Pakistan* and *Bear Creek v. Peru.*[21]

c Nurturing Human Nature

Despite the adversarial nature of the field, a strong sense of comradery and mutual respect pervades the global arbitration community. Collaborative attitudes are fostered by professional bodies with members based around the world such as the Chartered Institute of Arbitrators (Ciarb), the International Council for Commercial Arbitration (ICCA) and the International Bar Association (IBA).

Such bodies, together with domestic bar associations and young practitioner organizations, provide myriad opportunities for arbitration practitioners of all levels of seniority to serve on committees and contribute to soft law and thought leadership initiatives such as the IBA Guidelines on the Taking of Evidence in International Arbitration and the Ciarb's Practice Guidelines. The importance of fostering and nurturing professional relationships in international arbitration cannot be underestimated.

However, nurturing human nature goes beyond fostering positive working relationships with peers. The working practices adopted by many firms, including the emphasis placed on billable hours and poor time and resource management, may have a significant negative impact on the well-being of stakeholders in the arbitration ecosystem. The importance of protecting arbitration's human resources cannot be underestimated.

21. David R. Boyd, "Paying Polluters: The Catastrophic Consequences of Investor-State Dispute Settlement for Climate and Environment Action and Human Rights" (*United Nations*, July 13, 2023), 3-4, 11 https://documents.un.org/doc/undoc/gen/n23/205/29/pdf/n2320529.pdf?token=Rn38259N8AXUNd6u8n&fe=true accessed June 24, 2024.

d *Getting Savvy with Systems*

Arbitration practice is underpinned by a complex, interconnected web of treaties, legislation, arbitration rules, soft law, and practice guidelines. Practitioners must work within the confines of such ecosystem and recognize how it interacts with other important systems, such as international trade law, international investment law, human rights law, global sustainability standards and so on.

Only by properly understanding how this complicated web works can the arbitration community continue to develop practices and procedures to respond appropriately to new types of claims, technological developments, stakeholder demands, and difficulties presented by global challenges such as climate change and claims based on ESG objectives.

The ability of arbitration practitioners to adapt to changing circumstances was displayed to great effect during the Covid-19 pandemic. While practitioners sheltered responsibly in place, video conferencing replaced in-person hearings, webinars and online networking platforms allowed practitioners to continue to share ideas and connect globally despite being physically separated, and the wheels of dispute resolution continued to turn.

e *Designing to Distribute*

Despite its international scope, the ecosystem underpinning arbitration practice continues to be disproportionately focused on specific geographical locations and markets, with anecdotal evidence suggesting that those based outside major arbitral seats find it more difficult to practice arbitration, receive appointments to sit in international cases, or attract mandates to handle international proceedings.

Initiatives such as the Africa Arbitration Academy aim to highlight and educate the next generation of African arbitration specialists, while professional bodies such as the Ciarb pride themselves on offering courses of commensurate standard across the globe. However, surveys continue to highlight stalwarts such as London, Singapore, Hong Kong, Paris and Geneva as the leading arbitral seats.[22]

Likewise, the choice of arbitral seat is often sector-specific. London, for example, remains an important center for insurance arbitration due to its location, the presence of Lloyd's of London, the widespread application of English law to insurance contracts, the typical provision for London-seated arbitration in "Bermuda form" policies, the strength of English arbitration law, and the quality of its judiciary and arbitration practitioners.

Mindful of doughnut economics' focus on equality, work remains to ensure arbitration does not disproportionately favor those with greater bargaining power or access to greater resources. Several US and European authorities recognize that an

22. *See*, for example, Chart 2 on p. 6 of Queen Mary University of London and White & Case LLP, "International Arbitration Survey: Adapting Arbitration to a Changing World" (*Queen Mary University of London*, 2023). https://arbitration.qmul.ac.uk/media/arbitration/docs/LON0320037-QMUL-International-Arbitration-Survey-2021_19_WEB.pdf accessed June 24, 2024.

agreement to arbitrate may, unintentionally, deprive financially constrained parties of access to justice, including a 2024 decision by the Polish Supreme Court.[23]

f *Creating to Regenerate*

The concept of creating to regenerate has already found favor in arbitration practice. There has been widespread support for initiatives such as the Campaign for Greener Arbitrations, which was launched to "reduce the carbon footprint of international arbitration through behavioural change,"[24] with emphasis placed on using electronic correspondence and avoiding printing, considering videoconferencing instead of in-person hearings, avoiding unnecessary travel, and offsetting carbon emissions for arbitration-related travel.[25]

Stakeholders of all levels of seniority are increasingly expected to be sophisticated users of technology. Arbitral institutions offer online platforms for the filing of documentation, and videoconferencing software is widely used for hearings, particularly of a procedural nature.[26] Guidelines have been published by the Silicon Valley Arbitration and Mediation Center (SVAMC) to promote the responsible use of artificial intelligence.[27] Conferences have been held in the metaverse. In the not-too-distant future, witnesses will even be able to give evidence in holographic form.

Regeneration has been embraced in procedural practice. What remains is for the relief sought in arbitration proceedings to embrace the virtues of sustainability, regeneration and repair. This is particularly relevant in the ISDS space, where there is potential for tribunal decisions to foster community regeneration and support climate-conscious State conduct.

g *Being Agnostic about Growth*

Like economists, arbitration stakeholders have traditionally welcomed growth. Arbitral institutions celebrate growing annual caseloads and sums in dispute. By way of example, in 2023, the International Chamber of Commerce (ICC) celebrated the

23. The Polish Supreme Court held that although a party's "objective financial inability" to commence arbitration did not invalidate an arbitration agreement as a matter of Polish law, such agreement was unenforceable. *See* II CSKP 897/22.
24. Campaign for Greener Arbitrations, "Driving Sustainable Change in Arbitration" (*Campaign for Greener Arbitrations*, undated) https://www.greenerarbitrations.com accessed June 24, 2024.
25. Campaign for Greener Arbitration "The Green Pledge" (*Campaign for Greener Arbitrations*, undated) https://www.greenerarbitrations.com/sign-green-pledge accessed June 24, 2024.
26. By way of example, *see* SCC Arbitration Institute (SCC), "SCC Platform" (*SCC*, undated) https://sccarbitrationinstitute.se/en/case-management/scc-platform accessed June 24, 2024 and ICC, "Case Connect" (*ICC*, undated) https://iccwbo.org/news-publications/news/icc-launches-icc-case-connect-secure-online-case-management-made-easy/ accessed June 24, 2024.
27. The Silicon Valley Arbitration and Mediation Center's (SVAMC) Guidelines on the Use of Artificial Intelligence in Arbitration, published on April 30, 2024, provide a "principle-based framework for the use of artificial intelligence (AI) tools in arbitration at a time when such technologies are becoming increasingly powerful and popular." *See*: SVAMC, "Guidelines on the Use of Artificial Intelligence in Arbitration" (*SVAMC*, 1st ed. 2024) https://svamc.org/wp-content/uploads/SVAMC-AI-Guidelines-First-Edition.pdf accessed June 24, 2024.

third-best year in its history, registering 890 new arbitration cases, and aggregate and average amounts in dispute of USD 53 billion and USD 65 million, respectively.[28]

Law firms and expert witness practices embrace sizeable mandates. Global Arbitration Review (GAR) criteria for inclusion of firms in the GAR 30 include consideration of the number of hearings conducted with a value exceeding USD 10 million in a two-year period, sums at stake in such hearings, and hours billed during the same period.[29]

International arbitration represents big business. It is no longer perceived as a cheaper, more expeditious alternative to litigation. Legal fees, particularly in ISDS proceedings, are significant. Third-party funding often represents the only viable means for parties deprived of benefits due to the actions of counterparties to seek justice.

It is time to focus on the quality of arbitration outcomes for stakeholders, rather than the volume of cases handled. The quality, breadth and diversity of arbitrator panels is key to such outcomes. The application of project management principles, the use of properly resourced teams and closer collaboration with local co-counsel when appropriate all have a part to play. The emphasis on lean teams and billable hour maximization must end if stakeholders are to better invest in the long-term sustainability of arbitration practice.

2 Are Arbitration Practice and Doughnut Economics Compatible?

As demonstrated above, international arbitration has already embraced the building blocks of doughnut economics in a piecemeal fashion. Significant potential exists for arbitration to better contribute to the development of a more equitable and sustainable dispute resolution ecosystem. However, it is important to recognize the limited nature of the resources at our disposal.

Doughnut economics focuses on the responsible use and allocation of natural resources. The sustainable practice of international arbitration requires proper appreciation of a key human resource: the arbitration community. However, all resources are finite. Even human beings. Whether or not international arbitration can continue to thrive, and to do so in a sustainable way, ultimately depends on the extent to which stakeholders can work in balance with the adversarial environment it creates.[30]

28. ICC, "ICC Releases Preliminary 2023 Arbitration and ADR Statistics" (*ICC*, June 10, 2024) https://iccwbo.org/news-publications/news/icc-releases-preliminary-2023-arbitration-and-adr-statistics/#:~:text=In%202023%2C%20ICC%20registered%20a,of%20ICC%20as%20Appointing%20Authority accessed June 24, 2024.
29. Global Arbitration Review, "The GAR 30" (*Global Arbitration Review*, March 22, 2024) https://globalarbitrationreview.com/survey/gar-100/2024/article/the-gar-30-2024 accessed June 24, 2024.
30. For further discussion of the impact of adversarial environments on arbitration practice, *see*: Kathryn Britten and Grieg Taylor, "The Challenges of Working in an Adversarial Environment: The Expert Witness Perspective," Daniel Kalderimis, "A Journey of a Human Advocate: Reflections on the Philosophy of Advocacy (or, A Story of Demons and Dialogues)," Yoko Maeda and Bruno Savoie, "The Role of Culture in the Adversarial Process and How to Avoid Misunderstandings," Giacomo Rojas Elgueta, "Arbitration and Emotions: An Introduction" and

IV CONCLUSION

> Economics is the mother tongue of public policy, the language of public life, and the mindset that shapes society.
>
> Kate Raworth[31]

We ignore the role played by economics in the development of our field at our peril. We borrow the language of economics when we characterize users and service providers as stakeholders in the arbitral process. As with the global economy, the economics of arbitration practice are "both embedded within, and dependent upon, the living world."[32] Raworth recognizes that the "fundamental currency of life" is not money, but instead energy.[33] Only by learning to practice within our means can our field be truly sustainable.

As Butch Cassidy philosophically observed to the Sundance Kid while the duo contemplated the prospects of escaping from a rocky outcrop into the tempestuous water below, whether one can swim or not is ultimately irrelevant. It's the fall that stands to kill us. There is no point in fixating on the water. Instead, we must equip ourselves with the knowledge and skills required to preserve our energy, recognize difficult but potentially surmountable challenges and differentiate them from those that threaten our very survival and that of our field. If the tools to do so may be found in the principles of doughnut economics, so much the better.

Emi Rowse Igusa, "Practical Guidance on Working in and through an Adversarial Environment Using Counselling Concepts and Methods," in this book.

31. Kate Raworth, Doughnut Economics: Seven Ways to Think Like a 21st-Century Economist (1st Kindle ed., Cornerstone Digital 2017) 6.
32. Kate Raworth, "A New Compass for Economics" (*International Monetary Fund Finance & Development Magazine*, March 2024) https://www.imf.org/en/Publications/fandd/issues/2024/03/Point-of-view-a-new-compass-for-economics-Kate-Raworth accessed July 5, 2024.
33. *Ibid.*

CHAPTER 39

The Challenges of Working in an Adversarial Environment: The Expert Witness Perspective

Kathryn Britten FCA & Dr Jeremy Borys[*]

TABLE OF CONTENTS

I INTRODUCTION

The concept of an expert witness providing evidence of opinion in formal dispute resolution procedures has a long history. It dates back to at least the eighteenth century when, in 1782, Lord Mansfield stated '*in matters of science, the reasonings of men of science can only be answered by men of science*'.[1]

---

* Kathryn Britten is a chartered accountant and expert witness at AlixPartners, specialising in quantum, valuation, and accounting disputes. Dr Jeremy Borys is an organisational psychologist at AlixPartners, and is the firm's Chief Talent Officer, responsible for supporting the development of our leaders. The authors would also like to thank those anonymous expert witnesses who contributed their insights. Thanks also go to Greg Huitson-Little, and our colleagues at AlixPartners Greig Taylor, Zach Li, Oliver Rake and Rebecca Ruthven who helped to co-ordinate the content for this chapter.

1. *Folkes v. Chadd* [1782] 99 ER 589, 590.

Over the centuries, the role of an expert witness has evolved, particularly as legal cases, and the world, have become more technically complex. Decision-makers, arbitrators and judges often rely on an expert's opinion in dispute resolution, particularly where the expert's specialist knowledge, expertise and experience are beyond the court's or tribunal's own capabilities. This places a real burden of responsibility on the expert witness to present their specialist knowledge and experience in a way that assists the court or tribunal in making informed decisions.

There is growing recognition of the value that experts can bring throughout the entire dispute resolution process and, with that, growing pressure on expert witnesses throughout the process. Their involvement at an early stage can be crucial, with experts' reports and joint meeting processes often being instrumental in settlements. Therefore, those appointing expert witnesses should consider not only the experts' previous testifying experience alongside their technical expertise, but also their ability to withstand the various pressures and challenges that experts face throughout the entire adversarial process.

Hallmarks of a great expert witness are the capabilities to effectively manage stress as well as having constructive communication with the parties and the tribunal. Many experts find cross-examination before a judge or tribunal to be the most challenging and stressful part of their role. However, this is just one aspect of their involvement and usually only the final stage of their work.

In this chapter, we discuss the human and psychological experiences of experts participating in international arbitration, including the pressures and tensions that they typically face at different stages of the process, and how they address these challenges. All human beings have psychological needs. When these are met, we feel good and can perform at our best. For an expert witness, we identify three principal needs:

(i) clarity and control;
(ii) purpose and values; and
(iii) connection.

The pressures throughout the arbitration lifecycle can impact an expert's psychological needs, leading to stress: a feeling of emotional or physical tension. In this chapter, we examine the roots of stress for expert witnesses, driven by their deep psychological needs, and consider both healthy and unhealthy coping mechanisms.

It is important to note that stress is a natural reaction to challenges or demands. While short bursts of stress can be positive, prolonged stress can have physical and emotional consequences, such as burnout, anxiety, and distress. However, stress is not inherently negative. For many expert witnesses and other professionals, stress builds resilience – the ability to adapt and bounce back from adversity. Managed well, stress and resilience can lead to significant personal growth. This chapter concludes with practical observations and suggestions for managing stress, building resilience, and creating an environment where expert witnesses can perform optimally.

These insights are based on personal observations and anecdotes shared by expert witness colleagues, who remain anonymous and who we thank for their candid contributions. These experts, primarily from the quantum field, possess extensive sector and industry experience, with varying levels of testimony experience. Our analysis is enriched by AlixPartners' dataset of psychological insights from over 20,000 individuals in professional services, including nearly 3,000 profiles from investigations and dispute resolution fields.

The observations drawn from these materials are the result of the combined experience and expertise of the authors: an accounting and quantum expert witness and an organisational psychologist. Our discussion is divided based on the stages of the expert witness role in arbitration. We acknowledge that it is not strictly academic in nature; it is more narrative than study. This is intentional, as our aim is to raise awareness and to stimulate and provoke discussions about the human aspects of working as an expert witnesses.

II THE SELECTION STAGE

The first point of tension faced by an expert witness is to get their foot in the door. They must learn to communicate with potential clients – who are often unfamiliar with the expert's field of expertise – in a way that is quick, professional, authoritative, and easy to understand.

The initial communications are intense. When approached about a potential instruction, expert witnesses are typically required to put together detailed credentials documents, with relevant case studies and tailored CVs of the proposed expert and team, setting out their experience relevant to the potential engagement. Often, they are also required to include initial thoughts about how they will carry out their work and what it will cost. This must be done in a matter of days or even hours, and after receiving only a brief description of the dispute. The pressure is increased by the fact that the prospective expert knows that lawyers are often in touch with competitors and that any misunderstanding or miscommunication could cost them their appointment.

Experts only have this one chance and narrow timeframe to convey their technical skills and competence and, importantly, to convince the lawyers and the client that they will be good witnesses – capable of explaining complex ideas in a non-technical way, capable of persuading the tribunal; and easy to work with. Less experienced experts may face additional struggles at this stage, as they have limited references to include in their credentials. One of the experts we consulted, Expert #1, an experienced engineering expert with limited testifying experience, explained the challenge of establishing authority and expertise by observing:

> [o]nce I am in the room with the potential clients or on the shortlist, I often find there is a fair opportunity to demonstrate my expertise. However, getting in the room or on the shortlist can be a challenge.

Bias, conscious or unconscious, can be a particular challenge for female and early-career experts. They often report that they struggle to engage with the professional and personal networks that would allow them to get onto expert shortlists and that prospective clients do not appear to take them seriously. Expert #1 added:

> I still feel like many of the closed-door conversations that occur during the expert selection process disadvantage women and those of us who don't have many years of experience.

Bias, in its broadest sense, must be eliminated if parties are to have access to the widest possible pool of potential experts from which to select the best expert for the matter in hand.

III INSTRUCTIONS

Different points of pressure arise after the expert is selected and faces the full reality of the case itself. The first time the expert receives detailed information on the case is often at the instructions phase. Lawyers commonly provide a letter of instruction for the expert witness they choose to engage. This includes critical information that the expert will need to work on the case, such as the issues on which the expert is being asked to opine and any key factual assumptions they are to adopt. The letter of instruction usually includes details of the arbitration timetable, to the extent that it is known, including dates for serving individual reports, any joint reports, and the date of the hearing.

Problems arise at this stage if these details – whether it's the information disclosed with the instructions, the instructions themselves, or the timetable – have not been discussed with the expert in advance, or do not align with the expert's expectations. From a psychological perspective, we observe that the experts' need for clarity, control, logic and a plan is the paramount psychological need for those we spoke with. A diligent expert witness wants to be responsible, needs organisation and structure and is task-focused. People possessing these qualities will function optimally when they can establish clear objectives and well-defined expectations, a sense of the plan, and recognition for being an expert. In the absence of these elements, they start to micromanage, over-qualify, question their own competence and depersonalise situations.

Many of the problems faced by experts in the instructions phase are due to receiving ambiguous or conflicting instructions. Some experts have reported that they have later found themselves in situations where the opposing expert has been instructed to opine on issues that were (to varying extents) different to their own instructions.

When opposing parties' experts receive different instructions, it can lead to significant inefficiencies and increased costs. This misalignment not only detracts from the experts' duty to assist the tribunal but may also impede the decision-making process. Expert #2, a seasoned testifying expert specialised in disputes in the financial services sectors, stated that:

> [g]etting instructions might not sound too stressful but if you don't get this right, it has implications all the way through.

To ensure an effective process, lawyers must align, consider, and discuss instructions with experts.

Timetables can be another cause of extreme stress for expert witnesses. It is not uncommon for parties and their lawyers to agree these without consulting the expert witnesses. Unaware of the actual amount of time that the expert requires to complete their tasks, lawyers may end up agreeing with a timetable that is overly optimistic and stretches experts to the limits of what is humanly possible. Experts noted the personal impact of arduous timetables for arbitrations, citing adverse impacts on family life and their health. Expert #2 observed:

> [y]our life ceases to be your own. I find it difficult to get the things we need to keep life going. I have a very understanding family but it generally means that sleep, exercise and health generally suffer.

Although less common in arbitration, experts noted that when a simultaneous exchange of expert evidence is timetabled, there is often no time to pause and take stock between reports, depriving them of valuable time for reflection. Expert #3, a testifying expert and economic advisor with over twenty-five years of experience, described the 'relentlessness' of expert report deadlines and Expert #4, an experienced quantum expert with limited testifying experience, noted:

> no sooner have you signed your report, you are immediately reading the other expert's report.

Of course, experts understand that timetables provided at the instruction stage may be incomplete or subject to change. However, some arbitrations unexpectedly span years, making it particularly difficult to accommodate life events that can impact an expert's availability, such as planned personal events, unexpected family issues, or unforeseen health problems.

A key strategy to address the expert's need for clarity and control is to agree to a plan and stick to it, but this is not easy. Everyone involved in international arbitration understands that it is often difficult to anticipate how a matter will evolve. Having experts involved in the discussions about instructions and timetables before they are appointed and as they change over the course of the arbitration can help mitigate stress and ensure that timetables accommodate (to the extent to which they allow) valuable time for thoroughly considered opinions alongside a healthy quality of life.

IV AN EXPERT'S REPORT

Expert witnesses must provide clearly expressed independent opinions to assist the tribunal. Initially, this comes in the form of an expert report, which is the primary, and sometimes the only, direct evidence an expert witness delivers to the tribunal. As such, it is important that it presents the full depth of the expert's expertise. An expert's psychological need for clarity and control is also critical at the expert report stage.

The expert's report must be of high quality; this is the key document by which the expert's opinion will be judged. It is important that the reasoning and supporting analysis are robust. The report must also be independent; although an expert witness is (typically) engaged by one party, their duty is to the tribunal, and the report must be free from bias. Crucially the report must also fully address the instructions; if the report fails to completely address the question(s) posed, the tribunal will be unable to decide based on the expert's opinion.

As part of the drafting process, an expert and their team will undertake detailed reviews of documents, analyse information, and think deeply about the issues at hand. Opinions are formed, tested, challenged, and refined. Supporting evidence is marshalled and referenced. Assumptions are identified and agreed. Gaps are highlighted and sensitivities assessed.

Taking a psychological perspective, the preparation of an expert report involves several stress triggers. This stress often manifests itself in an expert's behaviour. It is crucial to recognise both the stress triggers and the indicators of stress so they can be addressed effectively.

Key triggers of stress for the expert include uncertainty and ambiguity, an overwhelming workload, lack of control, and a fear of inadequate preparation. The expert witness role can feel isolated with the expert experiencing a sense of vulnerability and a lack of connection. The absence of social activity and recreational activities can contribute to this isolation. These factors can create an emotional burden, causing the expert to feel underappreciated and to lose confidence.

For many of the experts we spoke with, their team commonly includes more junior, less experienced colleagues. The accuracy of the report depends on the quality of the team's analysis, and the expert must be able to rely on the accurate and precise work of their team.

Expert #5, a testifying expert with more than twenty years of experience in global financial markets and trading, explained:

> The report drafting process stands out as the most stressful phase, as it relies heavily on the support team's accuracy and involves the expert taking risks regarding the team's work accuracy, compounded by the fatigue and stress typically experienced by everyone involved as the deadline approaches.

The expert's observation demonstrates some of the stress triggers and underscores the risks involved. An expert may resist delegating, may become overly controlling, take on too much responsibility and sacrifice their wellbeing in response to stress.

The authors have also observed experts becoming frustrated, crusading, and pushing their views, portraying closed-mindedness, and becoming judgemental of others, spreading fear and doubt among the team. The management of personal stress levels is necessary to safeguard the well-being of the team and guarantee effective teamwork throughout the arbitration life cycle.

To assist with this, clear communication within the team, delineating each member's role and expectations, is key. As Expert #6, a testifying expert in economic consulting with more than thirty years of experience, stated, experts rely on:

> teamwork, preparation, professionalism, and common sense in our work; we prioritise effective communication of key report ideas with the team.

Effective communication is not only required within the expert team, but also with the legal team and clients. Meeting stringent submission deadlines was a major tension highlighted by experts: all accepted it as part of the process but were clear about the human toll that it could exact. This pressure can be exacerbated by the provision of new information or documentation by parties and their legal teams close to a reporting deadline. The need for the legal team to prepare the case submissions and make sure they align with the expert's findings can bring its own unique pressures on the expert too.

Expert #7, an expert with more than twenty years of experience in M&A transactions and restructuring, indicated that:

> [e]stablishing clear interim deadlines and maintaining regular communication with the lawyers is crucial for preventing surprises and ensuring a sense of progress throughout the process, rather than facing a single overwhelming deadline.

It is easy to underestimate the amount of work involved in finalising an expert witness report when all the drafting is complete. References and cross-references are added and checked; appendices and documents are collated, indexed, and attached. Checking and proof-reading are thoroughly carried out to ensure that no errors are missed. The incorporation of any late information and analysis can severely disrupt the quality control process, leading to excessive time pressure and extreme stress. In response, experts may come across as frustrated and judgemental.

Early and continual engagement between the legal team and the expert is valuable throughout the drafting process – both for the lawyers to understand and test what the expert is saying, and for the expert to avoid the risk of last-minute changes to their report.

It is not uncommon for an expert to be pressured to add to or remove parts of their report at a late stage. This pressure can include, for example, significant redlining that goes beyond editorial suggestions or requests for clarification.

Expert #6 also noted the stress that can arise from clients who lack understanding of the expert witness role:

> [C]lients who push for assertions unsupported by data poses occasional challenges, as does finalising expert reports when clients request last-minute changes, demanding meticulous revision under time constraints. Additionally, managing clients who rewrite sections without full comprehension of the discipline requires delicate addressing of factual inaccuracies and alignment with the expert's approach.

Expert #8, an experienced quantum expert with limited testifying experience, stated that:

> [i]t is crucial for the expert and the legal teams to work together in educating the client on the role of the expert. The client should also be made aware of the potential detrimental impact to the client's case of an expert adopting unsupported assumptions when being cross-examined during the hearing.

This issue can be amplified when experts are called upon to provide opinions based on little or insufficient information. Such a demand can jeopardise an expert's independence if they are put under pressure to adopt unsupported assumptions to fill in the gaps. Experts can lose confidence in the robustness of their expert opinion, as well as feel undervalued when their work undergoes significant revisions.

From a psychological perspective, there are three factors at play here:

- First, the typical expert likes to have the time and space to work things out.
- They have a need for logic, for clarity and for a plan.
- They want to solve the puzzle put before them in an efficient and effective way.

While the space to do so becomes constrained as the matter progresses, that is part of the normal course of proceedings, and experts are equipped to handle these adjustments. However, the introduction of new material or demands can compromise the expert's composition of the evidence and arguments – potentially to the point of causing discomfort or distress due to a lack of consistency and coherence in the logic flow. This second factor may push the expert into a more defensive position, which may manifest in the drafting and evidence. At the same time, experts have a strong drive to deliver. They understand the importance of the process and timelines in arbitration and of meeting expectations. They will find a way where possible, but that is not without risk for both the expert and the client's position.

For example, although experts can set out assumptions that they have applied in reaching their opinion, with a caveat due to the paucity of information available, this increases the risk of an opinion being derailed if a new piece of information emerges later in the proceedings. In the extreme, where legal teams and clients overstep and ask experts to opine based on insufficient information, this compromises the expert's independence and can create significant triggers of stress. Balancing client expectations with the need for impartial and credible analysis can be challenging, particularly when some lawyers and clients seek expert evidence that aligns closely with their objectives.

This ties to the third factor – experts have a psychological need to fulfil a purpose or mission and to adhere to a core set of principles. Experts, who must maintain the highest level of integrity, seek to stay consistent with their values and defend what is right versus wrong. This plays to the key strengths of an expert, who is dedicated, committed, persistent, loyal, value-driven and of strong conviction. However, there is a risk that a legal team or client overstepping their boundaries will compromise the integrity of the report. As a result, an expert can become judgemental, over-invested in defending conclusions, and stubborn and close-minded.

It is critical to ensure that the expert does not cross the line from independent to advocate, and that the client understands the importance of this. While experts bear primary responsibility for maintaining their independence, legal teams can help to alleviate stress by fostering an environment that respects and supports independence, facilitates clear communication and ensures the sharing of relevant information.

Awareness of the triggers of stress for the expert and recognition of any indicators of stress during this critical stage should put all of the individuals involved in the best position to manage the situation and ensure that the expert report fully addresses the instructions, is independent, and is of the highest quality.

V THE OPPOSING EXPERT'S REPORT

The submission of a completed report can evoke both relief and anxiety for an expert: relief that the job is completed, and anxiety about what's to come. An expert will rarely be the only expert in a matter. Usually, there is an opposite number, engaged by the other side. That opposing expert will also be providing expert evidence on (usually) the same question(s) for the arbitration.

While experts will be confident in their work product, there is a natural tendency to anticipate criticism. This is because, in addition to documentary evidence an expert must rely on well-developed assumptions and thoughtful prioritisation of the arguments, which can leave room for (mis)interpretation and exposure from the opposition. The opposing expert's report will frequently scrutinise and directly criticise the arguments underlying an expert's opinion. Although this is recognised as part of the job, it poses pressure, causing experts to dwell on any conceivable inadequacies in their work. An expert will always be thinking about the impact of these, as well as possible alternatives. The expert will also have in mind the tribunal's perspective, and how the tribunal may view anything the opposing expert might have to say about their report.

Expert #9, an expert with more than twenty-five years of experience in disputes and valuations, stated that:

> [r]eceiving the rebuttal or response to an expert report poses significant pressure, as it often critiques my expertise, pointing out perceived errors or inadequacies in my work.

An expert witness can never fully predict what will be in the opposing expert's report. In the extreme, a lack of certainty can be debilitating. In everyday life, uncertainty can cause people to display several behaviours, such as excessively seeking reassurance from others, micromanaging people, repeatedly checking things and procrastinating. But we should not expect to see this in experienced experts particularly often. Experts generally have confidence in their experience and opinions, and also in their ability to defend their positions and withstand pressures under examination. That means the uncertainty they feel can be short term and any negative behaviours displayed are much reduced.

The exchange of reports reveals the opposing expert's opinion, which experts often find to be substantially different from their own. When such differences occur, they are typically a result of differing instructions and/or factual assumptions presented to the experts, but differences in analysis, perspective or experience are also common.

Experts' reports may be exchanged simultaneously or sequentially. Each brings with it different pressures. When the exchange of reports is simultaneous, experts often find that the opposing expert's instructions, or the facts provided to them, are inconsistent with their own, making it difficult to identify the true differences of opinion to help the tribunal. The focus must then be on a joint statement process (if it is in the timetable), or on the cross-examination phase to resolve differences between experts.

In contrast, sequential exchange can involve strategic interactions between the experts. Sequential exchange may result in personal attacks by an expert aimed at discrediting the other expert, their work, or their expertise. The motives here may be complex. At one level, it may simply be a strategy of criticism: the attacking expert making points for the tribunal. But experienced experts may also use this as a way of asserting authority, holding other experts up to a particular standard, and testing the other experts' resolve and ability to withstand pressure. It may also be the precursor to expert meetings, and testing whether experts are willing to negotiate positions. In any event, the response must be careful, to ensure evidence remains focused on the tribunal's needs and to ensure the experts are not unduly influenced by their emotions. Experts quickly learn to deal with these sorts of personal attacks and to understand the strategies, and how to respond appropriately.

Receiving any opposing expert's report can trigger an immediate emotional response. Experts have described having to read an opposing expert's report several times before fully engaging with it particularly where the opposing expert is overcritical of the approach taken or the conclusions reached. This re-reading can help an expert witness come to terms with the contents of the opposing expert's report and accept that it is part of the process and not a personal attack. Nonetheless, experts should consider carefully how they phrase their differences of opinion. Maintaining professionalism throughout the process of serving as an expert witness is vital for an expert to preserve their reputation and earn respect from their clients, their peers and the tribunal.

We need to remember that when we are faced with uncertainty, it's easy to overestimate the likelihood of something bad happening – and underestimate our ability to cope if it does. But given that the likelihood of something really bad happening is low, even in this intense profession, it is necessary for an expert witness to live with that small chance and focus instead on the more likely outcomes.[2]

It is important that lawyers and their clients understand the pressures that an expert may suffer in anticipation and on receipt of the opposing expert's report. Although this is part of the process, there are ways that the parties and the legal team can help to reduce these pressures including accommodating sufficient time in the timetable for an expert to get familiar with the opposing expert's report before drafting a response or attending a joint meeting. Reframing the way in which the opposing expert's report is received and analysed may also be helpful. Helping the expert to depersonalise and decouple from their report may be a useful approach. Ultimately, it is a third party, the tribunal, reading the reports. The personal aspects between the experts – attacks, criticisms etc. – are much less relevant. Helping an expert to read the reports as the tribunal will read them will yield useful insight.

2. Lawrence Robinson and Melinda Smith, M.A., 'Dealing with Uncertainty' (helpguide.org, April 2020) <https://www.helpguide.org/articles/anxiety/dealing-with-uncertainty.htm> accessed 7 March 2024.

VI JOINT EXPERT MEETINGS

Tribunals may order experts for both parties to meet after the exchange of expert reports, to identify areas of agreement and/or disagreement to narrow and clarify their disagreements. In a meeting of experts, it is common for each expert witness to be supported by a member of their team who has assisted with the detailed analysis. Participation in joint expert meetings creates pressure for experts as it requires them to deploy different skills to those engaged when drafting their reports, and it is common for lawyers and their clients, who will normally not attend such meetings, to be concerned that they are losing some control.

Expert #8, an experienced quantum expert with limited testifying experience, stated:

> [t]his part can be a real unknown [...] preparation is key: working through what I want to say and the areas I want to cover first – with input from the legal team so they are happy with the direction I'm going – helps to establish the trust between us. But I will always go in with trepidation. I'm on my own. Will anything I say or write have unintended implications for the case at large?

Joint meetings can be stressful for everyone involved. This will normally be the experts' first face-to-face encounter with each other in the context of the arbitration. Therefore, the meeting has the potential to be either collaborative and constructive or adversarial and partisan.

Experts take many different approaches to the joint meetings. In some instances, experts may feel more inclined to defend their previous statements, not wishing to upset their client by appearing to concede any points. This can be compounded by the fact that neither expert feels a full sense of ownership over the output from the experts' joint meeting, the joint report. Meetings can be particularly difficult if the opposing expert uses this opportunity to be a 'hired gun' advocating for their client, or is reluctant to (or even refuses to) agree on points so as to reserve positions. This creates stress and particular pressure to ensure the meeting remains on track and that the output is a useful joint report, focusing on the real issues. Arbitration is inherently adversarial; however, it is counterproductive for expert witnesses to adopt adversarial or aggressive stances towards one another, especially during joint meetings. Productive engagement is essential for the process.

In the authors' experience, acknowledging each other's common humanity and treating the other expert with personal respect is essential for a successful joint meeting, and helps to ensure a meaningful outcome benefitting the tribunal. Expert #10, an experienced quantum and valuation expert with limited testifying experience, stated that:

> [m]aintaining professionalism is paramount for earning respect and preserving a positive reputation throughout each stage of the process. Despite its adversarial nature, it's essential to acknowledge the humanity of all involved and treat each individual with personal respect.

Such an approach is consistent with an expert's second-highest psychological need: to fulfil a purpose and adhere to a core set of principles.

There may also be elements of integrity and trust between experts: in the authors' experience, where experts trust one another to focus on the key points for the tribunal and not trade points of dispute, the resulting joint statement can be concise and effective. However, if there is any defensiveness among the experts, they may perceive closing down points in the joint statement as a concession. This creates a reluctance that can lead to lengthy joint statements that fail to serve their intended purpose thereby compromising the efficacy of the tribunal.

In the context of dealing with opposing expert witnesses, whether it be an opposing expert's report or in a joint expert meeting, it is important for experts to be able to lean on trusted colleagues to express their frustrations and to reinforce their core principles and values. It can also be helpful for an expert to reframe 'attacks' by the opposing expert – they are not a personal affront but are a normal part of a process. As hard as it may be, the expert has to focus on the issues and not the individual.

Lawyers can assist expert witnesses by communicating effectively before the joint meeting, including discussing the areas of expert evidence that are likely to be of key focus. Clients should also be made aware of the potential areas of disagreement and how these will be addressed and reminded of the expert's need to remain objective and unbiased. Ultimately, what works best is when clients and their lawyers trust the expert witness they have selected to handle the joint meeting in a professional manner, and when they demonstrate that trust. This recognition of their competence can do much to address an expert's need to have a sense of meaning and recognition of their values and beliefs. In turn, the expert remains balanced: they are able to think clearly, make decisions and conclude logically, without the distractions that layers of unhelpful pressures can bring.

VII THE HEARING

The hearing is the culmination of the arbitration process: a time when the expert's argument, analysis, and opinions are tested by opposing counsel in front of the tribunal. For an expert witness, the hearing normally involves presentation of their expert report, and cross-examination by the opposing party's counsel. It is no surprise that many of the experts we spoke with found this to be the highest-pressure stage of the arbitration process and numerous points of tension were identified.

The third-highest psychological need for experts is to connect emotionally and authentically with others and to minimise conflict. When we have harmony in our relationships, we feel good. Where there is conflict, we can make mistakes, hesitate to take decisions, and try to please others.

From a psychological perspective, in the context of a hearing, the expert's natural, social instincts – to build relationships and maintain a safe and supportive environment – are challenged. The whole process is intentionally designed to instigate constructive conflict, debate, and contradiction. When faced with this jarring reality and divisive interpersonal dynamic, experts and others need to have keen self-awareness of an expert's psychological needs and what happens when they are not met. It is important to appreciate their emotional side, even as they play the dispassionate expert role; to understand the pressures that the expert is experiencing and be aware of their frustrations.

One of the critical stress factors is an increased risk of error. On the stand, it is easier for the expert witness to make an error, incorrectly stating a fact or not being able to recall all the details to respond fully to a question upon cross-examination. Expert #11, a testifying expert with more than twenty years of experience in quantifying damages, stated that:

> [t]he worry of making a mistake looms large, leading to sleepless nights and pre-testimony anxiety.

This can be compounded when opposing legal teams take a personal and aggressive approach to cross-examination and can significantly impact the expert's confidence and performance. Expert #11 also recalled a specific incident:

> I nearly quit this work after one hearing where opposing counsel were so vile and aggressive during my day in the stand.

Aggressive cross-examination can also foster a perception that the expert is not impartial, potentially undermining their credibility. Expert #12, a highly experienced testifying economics and financial services expert, stated that:

> counsel may attempt to pressure an expert into taking positions that advocate for their engaging party, which would seriously damage an expert's credibility.

This leads to another serious pressure point, the potential for reputational damage. As Expert #3, a testifying expert and economic advisor with over twenty-five years of experience, identified, there is ***'large reputational capital at stake'*** in the cross-examination stage.

When being cross-examined, an expert is put on stage in front of law firms, opposing experts, the disputing parties, and the tribunal. Although the arbitral forum is less public than a courtroom, any underperformance by the expert might damage their professional reputation.

Another source of extreme stress for an expert witness at a hearing is uncertainty as to what they will be asked. As we have already observed, it is important for an expert to maintain control over the narrative of their report and the areas of focus. This helps them to address their need for purpose and mission and to uphold their core values. However, experts described a feeling of apprehension and trepidation during cross-examination because control of the narrative is effectively relinquished to opposing counsel. Expert #12 stated that:

> [t]here is constant uncertainty regarding the actions of the opposing party and what leeway the arbitration panel may grant them, contributing to heightened stress levels due to this unpredictability.

The hearing stage frequently imposes significant time demands, often requiring domestic or international travel for multiple weeks for all of those involved in the arbitral process. This can be detrimental for everyone's family and personal life while also creating pressure due to competing professional obligations. Expert witnesses, while potentially required for only part of the hearing, are no exception.

Notwithstanding this, and despite the hearing being the greatest stress trigger, experts generally agree that the hearing is the stage at which they can most thoroughly mitigate the stress. Many experts pointed out that preparation and having a firm grasp of all issues in the report are crucial. Expert #11 stated that the pressure ***'drives me to thoroughly prepare'***.

Experts also noted other ways to manage the stress, such as through training and coaching, physical exercise, breathing exercises and yoga.

VIII SUMMARY

An expert witness experiences extreme pressures at various stages of the arbitration process. Parties and their lawyers can support experts by providing them with information, support and the personal respect required for them to work diligently, with commitment and professionalism. For expert witnesses to effectively navigate and survive the adversarial nature of the international arbitration process, they need to ensure that their three highest-priority psychological needs are met at each stage of arbitration.

Each arbitration may span several years, from the pre-instruction stage through to the final hearing and ultimate payment. Expert witnesses are unsurprisingly kept at arm's length throughout much of the process. The resulting lack of communication can create a sense of isolation as well as unintended scheduling tensions: for example, if they are not promptly informed of timetable changes or breaks in the process while the parties attempt to settle the dispute.

Managing stress can feel like a second full-time job during arbitration. All of those involved are dealing with their own challenges while also anticipating and responding to the stress of others, and they do this by using coping mechanisms. Coping is defined as the thoughts and behaviours mobilised to manage internal and external stressful situations.[3] These can be healthy, such as seeking support, venting, physical recreation, relaxation or humour; or unhealthy, such as denial, isolation, self-blame, shutting out feelings, or compulsive risk-taking.

Everyone suffering stress will adopt coping mechanisms, taking actions to help them manage their psychological needs. As we have observed in the situations described, it is difficult for an expert witness to meet their top three psychological needs throughout the arbitration lifecycle: clarity, control, logic and a plan; purpose, mission and core principles; and connecting emotionally and authentically. These needs may

3. Susan Folkman and Judith Tedlie Moskowitz, 'Coping: Pitfalls and Promise' [2004] 55 Annual Review of Psychology, 745-74, https://doi.org/10.1146/annurev.psych.55.090902.141456.

even be deliberately denied. In terms of psychological health, expert witnesses can do several things to help meet their highest-priority needs.

To satisfy their paramount psychological need for clarity, control, logic and a plan, an expert can make their own plan and stick to it. They can find other ways to validate capabilities and expertise when competence is questioned. They can learn to accept the lack of control of their time during this temporary process and appreciate the order and structure in other aspects of their lives.

To address their second-highest psychological need, to fulfil a purpose or mission and to adhere to a core set of principles, an expert can lean on trusted colleagues for expressing their frustrations and to reinforce their values and beliefs. They can learn to reframe 'attacks' by the opposition and to see that there are multiple rights – not just a right and a wrong.

To meet their third-highest psychological need, to connect emotionally and authentically with others, an expert can take time for self-care, create moments of high-quality connection with key people in their life. They can learn to separate people from the role they are playing in the arbitration – they, too, are human. Ultimately, expert witnesses need to monitor and meet their own needs so they can stay balanced and fulfil their role of assisting the tribunal. At the same time, experts need to be aware of others' psychological needs and have the grace and professionalism to adapt to them.

The same applies to parties, lawyers and others involved in the arbitral process. They need to be aware of others' psychological needs as well as their own. If they are aware of the psychological needs of their expert witness, they can do a great deal to help the expert to do their best work by avoiding, or addressing, the triggers of stress throughout the arbitration process. The authors therefore provide the following practical suggestions for those engaging and working with expert witnesses throughout the arbitration lifecycle:

(i) At the ***selection*** stage, contact potential expert witnesses early and make clear what expertise is required before a prospective expert is invited to any pitch or beauty parade. Keep an open mind about previous experience, especially testifying experience, when selecting the right expert witness for the matter in hand. Maintain awareness of the potential experts' knowledge limitations when preliminary views are shared and when fee estimates are provided.

(ii) When providing ***instructions***, consult the chosen experts about how long they will need for relevant proposed steps in the arbitral process and discuss an expert's instructions and the arbitration timetable with the expert before finalising them. Take all necessary measures to ensure adherence to the agreed timetable and, where changes are unavoidable, ensure they are communicated promptly and discussed with the expert witness.

(iii) During the ***expert report*** writing stage, remain in regular communication and provide timely comments on drafts throughout the process. Take the time to explore and understand the expert's reasoning and opinions early and as they develop, and how the expert's work fits with the wider case. Avoid changing instructions or providing additional documents and information close to the deadline for an expert's report. Ensure that the client is clear about the expert's need to be, and be seen to be, independent.

(iv) When the ***opposing expert's report*** is served, accommodate time in the timetable for your appointed expert to get familiar with the report before drafting a response or attending a joint meeting. Recognise the pressures that an expert may suffer in anticipation and on receipt of the opposing expert's report.

(v) When ***joint expert meetings*** are required by the tribunal, it is important to communicate with the expert witness and the client before the joint meeting. Ultimately, trust the expert witness who has been selected to handle the joint meeting in a professional manner, and demonstrate that trust.

(vi) During ***the hearing***, understand the pressures that the expert is experiencing and be aware of their frustrations. Cross-examination is undoubtedly one of the loneliest times for an expert. Working with the expert's team to pick up points for re-examination, followed by a post-hearing debrief, can do much to re-establish stability.

Throughout the arbitration lifecycle treat expert witnesses as fellow human beings, acknowledging their need to be kept informed and to be involved on a regular basis. Understand the anxieties and stress experienced by experts throughout the arbitration lifecycle. Providing support and addressing and sharing concerns help to facilitate effective collaboration while preserving the expert's independence.

In preparing this chapter, we often asked ourselves, 'Why do we do this job?' 'Why do we put ourselves in the position of expert witness?' It can be a deeply distressing and lonely place, one where we are placed under immense challenge and pressure. That challenge goes to the heart of our professional expertise, judgement and opinion – years of training and experience placed on trial in a very public way. The risks are enormous.

We said at the start an expert witness has three primary psychological needs: (i) clarity and control, (ii) purpose and values, and (iii) connection. Perhaps, this can be simplified further: There is a fundamental need to find and share the right solutions. Many of us derive immense satisfaction from resolving issues and collaborating with others to address complex cases. Some might even consider this the most enjoyable aspect of our work. We take great pride in assisting the tribunal in reaching its decisions, and this is further enhanced when the tribunal acknowledges our contribution. The key question is: how do we manage the factors that detract from this core responsibility? While it is impossible to eliminate all stress and emotional challenges, by identifying their sources, we can work together to mitigate them and allow our true expertise to shine through.

CHAPTER 40

A Journey of a Human Advocate: Reflections on the Philosophy of Advocacy (or, A Story of Demons and Dialogues)

Daniel Kalderimis KC[*]

TABLE OF CONTENTS

I INTRODUCTION

This is not a chapter I would have thought of, let alone written, ten or fifteen years ago. It is about advocacy not as a matter of winning – or top tips for how to do so – but as a matter of a durable lifestyle. It is also not a chapter of (or only of) ideas. It is a chapter borne of experience, in my case of depression and disconnection. It describes what I learned about myself: as an advocate and as a human being, and how each sphere informs the other. It is hopefully of some use to some others in the profession. For those interested, I've written a book about my experience, which will be published later this year.[1]

Tell me if this is familiar. When you were growing up, you were smart. But you knew, somehow, that smarts were not enough. Because success turns on so many other variables, and we need to make our own luck. Undaunted, you work hard at high

* Barrister, Twenty Essex (Singapore / London), Thorndon Chambers (Wellington) and Richmond Chambers (Auckland).
1. D Kalderimis, *Zest: Climbing from Depression to Philosophy* (Ugly Hill Press, 2024).

school, sit many exams, and get good grades. Your undergraduate degree and law degree follow suit. You find you can absorb and marshal information quickly and argue well. You excel in mooting and can't wait for the chance to get into the real legal world. Your worst fear is not being able to achieve your full potential, which you can sense as a form of stored energy. You eagerly climb the ladder of advancement and achievement, which seems to stretch enticingly out before you.

You clerk for a judge and soon head overseas for a post-graduate degree and the first of your foreign bar qualifications. You join an international firm and focus on honing the craft of international arbitration, where excellence and attention to detail are taken for granted. You want to show that you can foot it with the best, anywhere. You attend conferences – like this one – and eventually achieve global rankings. You go from your first hearing – which produces an adrenaline high – to your first cross-examination, to your first lead advocate role, to dealing with ever-bigger cases. More adrenaline highs. You see yourself as engaged in a high-level contact sport in which, to win, you must seize every opportunity and mitigate every risk. You accordingly agonise over the first paragraph of closing submissions, chase down pinpoint citations to their true source, even correct punctuation on authorities' indexes.

You become a law firm partner. You lead growing teams on increasingly complex matters, and your rankings continue to rise. The cases keep coming, your reputation keeps growing, you get increasingly skilled in the craft of advocacy and the instinctive judgments it requires.

One day, you realise that the ladder you have been climbing has no end in sight. You are now one of those people you used to look at as having 'made it'. But you find that life does not work quite like that. You are not so different, really, than you were when you were starting out. To the contrary, you are the very product of your temperament and training – determined, ambitious, hyper-vigilant, perfectionistic. For all your achievements, you are really no further ahead. Because the ladder keeps going up and up, and you are still focused on the next rung. The reward for your hard work is more of it. Even when you are not at work, you are thinking about it, trying to crack the code of the next case.

II MY HYPER-PERFECT WORLD OF ADVOCACY

There is an exquisite torture to advocacy as a quest for perfection. In his 1962 Hamlyn lecture, Sir Robert Megarry explained that, in skilled hands, 'a shift of emphasis, a proper setting' and a 'small point that has laid hid in the mass of materials ... can be made to blaze with a terrible light'.[2] Advocates know this to be true, which means we are always searching, doubting, polishing. The job is all about taking and controlling risks, which, in my experience, have different shades for different kinds of cases. Cases where you are up against it and the margin for error is wafer-thin; to prevail, everything has to go your way. Cases when you ought to win, but there, the risk of mistakes is magnified. Finely balanced cases that depend ultimately on the gestalt the tribunal uses

2. R Megarry, *Lawyer and Litigant in England* (Stevens & Sons Ltd, 1962) at 19.

for key issues which, once formed, can be very hard to shift. There are cases turning on whether a fact witness will hold up under questioning, and cases that depend on whether an expert has the fortitude and dexterity to shade her opponent on key points. Few cases really turn on the law. But that does not guard against the risk of an arbitrator somehow thinking they should or do.

All of this pressure is experienced in a competitive, adversarial environment, which creates a unique frisson to trying to get everything right. An interviewee in a 2017 *New York Times* article captured the challenge of litigation well: 'Yes, there are other stressful professions ... Being a surgeon is stressful, for instance – but not in the same way. It would be like having another surgeon across the table from you trying to undo your operation.'[3]

For most of my career, I was inspired by the quest for perfection. I knew actual perfection was impossible. But the game was to get as close as humanly possible, and I loved playing the game. I saw advocacy as performance art – the intersection of a logic line with a story arc to craft the most satisfying narrative possible, cutting through the thicket of good and bad facts and helpful and less-helpful law. Sapna Jhangiani KC locates the territory well in her 'virtuous triangle of good advocacy': good judgment, sound case theory, thorough preparation. I didn't (and don't) mind the adversarial nature of the job. The relentless taskmaster was (and is) never my opponent, but what we might call the Platonic triangle of ideal advocacy, which is never quite within reach, no matter how much effort is expended. We can always judge more incisively, further polish our case theory and prepare better. Not to mention perform more fluently.

The idea of advocacy as a perennial search for the complete performance is nothing new. If we consult the standard text by David Ross KC, we learn that 'the best advocates are great artists'.[4] And that '[a]dvocacy is about winning cases. Nothing more and nothing less'.[5] And that '[t]he good advocate will treat every case like the most important ever. It will be prepared and conducted as if it is the last and the one on which the advocate's reputation hangs – as it does'.[6]

I believed all of these things. And to some extent still do. But when you say them out loud, you can see that they are not a recipe for living a full and happy life. Artistry sounds good, but not artifice – who wants their legacy to be that they had a knack for getting someone to believe just about anything? Winning sounds good. Except – to paraphrase Dr Seuss – when you don't, and sometimes you won't; bang-ups and hang-ups can happen to you.[7] Treating every case as mission-critical may serve as useful motivation, but any sensible advocate must know, at one and the same time, that no case is really *that* important when set against our loved ones, our values and the sheer joy of being alive.

3. E Zimmermann 'The Lawyer, The Addict', *The New York Times*, 15 July 2017, <https://www.nytimes.com/2017/07/15/business/lawyers-addiction-mental-health.html> (henceforth *NYT*) (accessed 16 August 2025).
4. D Ross KC, *Advocacy* (Cambridge University Press, 2007, 2nd ed.) (henceforth *Ross*) at xi.
5. Ross at 10.
6. Ross at 2.
7. Dr Seuss, *Oh, The Places You'll Go* (HarperCollins, 2011; originally published 1990).

You can lose a lot of yourself by striving – as I did – to turn yourself into a winning machine. David Pannick KC captured one reason why:[8]

> The advocate spends much of his working life as a cipher who is required to appear for anyone, pleading their case however reprehensible and hopeless, and professionally obliged not to give the court his opinions .... Occupying his professional life speaking on behalf of others, he may find that he has nothing to say for himself, no values which he holds dear, no firm opinions in opposition to which he is not appeared to perceive and to argue the competing contention.

If we accept that this doesn't sound ideal, where does that leave us? How do we truly fit the aspiration and human reality together?

III ACCEPTING THAT I AM A PERSON AND SO IS EVERYONE ELSE

Few of us naturally stumble into thinking too hard about these kinds of questions. They are, rather, the sort of questions that may come, one day, to find us.

Nothing of what is written above penetrated deeply into my consciousness until, in my early forties, I experienced bouts of depression, which caused me to reassess much about myself and my place in the world. I know I am not alone in this: repeated studies have found that approximately one quarter of lawyers suffer from depression.[9] As I explain in my book, the experience of depression is like living in a slate grey world, where even the idea of colour is hard to bring to mind, let alone see and experience. The shine that used naturally to attach to things I had sought after – success, money, recognition – fell away like the backdrop to a wooden stage set. It was not so much that everything seemed bad or sad. It just became hard to really see the purpose of it all. An advocate's success arises in a limited sphere (you can count on one hand the number of people who really understand the cases you argue and what made your argument excellent rather than merely good) and is ephemeral. How many of us can clearly remember the great advocates of previous generations?

I came to see that much of my striving wasn't justified because the things I sought had intrinsic value; it was itself a way of sustaining my belief that my endless striving was valuable in the first place. The thought process was circular. The ladder I was climbing was more like a rotating treadmill. It didn't exist out in the world, but in my own head, and I was always extending it higher. No matter what I did or got, or didn't do or didn't get, there would always be something else. The goalposts would always shift. I would never arrive. Because there was nowhere, really, to go.

Seeing this – living through it – helped me see also how stuck I was in my own head. That won't surprise anyone, because depression is the experience of being

8. D Pannick KC, *Advocates* (Oxford University Press, 1992) (henceforth *Pannick*) at 235.
9. *See* NYT, summarising a 1990 study finding that 28% of lawyers suffer depression and that, in a survey of more than 100 professions, lawyers are 3.6 times as likely to be depressed as people with other jobs; and also American Bar Association 'New Study on Lawyer Well-Being Reveals Serious Concerns for Legal Profession', 17 December 2017, https://www.americanbar.org/news/abanews/publications/youraba/2017/december-2017/secrecy-and-fear-of-stigma-among-the-barriers-to-lawyer-well-bei/ (accessed 16 August 2025), summarising a 2016 study of more than 13,000 practising lawyers finding, again, that 28% of lawyers suffer from depression.

trapped in our own heads, and trying to navigate the world through unproductive thoughts: cycling from hyper-vigilance to disillusionment to ruminating thought spirals to worry, anxiety and despair. I learned, as have many before me, that thoughts make better servants than masters.

But I learned also that I was not the only one. Being trapped by thought is not a symptom of 'sickness' that clears up by becoming 'well' again. It is a feature of the human condition, which is why we find ourselves intruding on our attempts to take a vacation. Moreover, our minds are unreliable mirrors of the world around us. What to us looks like a clear-sighted view of a place, person or situation looks very different from other vantage points. We know, on one level, that we each see the world through our constellations of ideas, feelings, wants and needs. We are, I think, less conscious of how effortlessly we contour our thinking to match those deeper impulses and desires. Most people's thoughts on most topics are moulded by their emotions and support their general station in life. Few can find sufficiently novel and penetrating thoughts to really challenge their deep instincts towards safety, comfort and self-interest.

I came to see that I am less rational than I used to believe I was. Much of what I thought and did reflected how I felt and what I wanted. This isn't only a problem for depressed people. We are just forced to see it more clearly. Looking inwards, I could see a lot of desires and aversions – actually an inexhaustible, continuous stream, such that, as soon as one is satisfied, another takes its place in the queue. Our thoughts often follow the path of this stream. Psychologist Jonathan Haidt explains the phenomenon through the metaphor of an elephant and rider. Our conscious will is the rider. But it rides an elephant of intuitions, judgments and feelings, conscious and unconscious.[10] This phenomenon has been identified (in different ways) by Darwin and Rousseau and is now studied by evolutionary psychologists and neuroscientists. Haidt's point is that the rider so often 'becomes a lawyer, fighting in the court of public opinion to persuade others of the elephant's point of view'.[11]

I needed to step off the treadmill somehow; to learn how to be happy here, now, without my little successes and failures being the measure of my life.

IV SHIFTING FOCUS FROM ACHIEVEMENT TO CONNECTION

The ancient Stoics and Buddhists each realised, in their own ways, that it is madness to keep trying to satisfy the endless appetites of our elephants. Because either you don't get the thing you want and you are unhappy. Or you do and it is not quite what you expected. Or it is but you now need to do more things to hang on to it. This is so even for one-off achievements, where unless you burnish and publicise, they lose their lustre and are forgotten. And so much of what we are trying to control we can't anyway. Pretending otherwise is the path to burnout and dissatisfaction.

10. J Haidt, *The Happiness Hypothesis* (Basic Books, 2006) (henceforth *Haidt*) at 4, 16 and 21.
11. Haidt at 21-22.

So, what is left? This really troubled me. What if nothing was left but mediocrity? This is the Sisyphean challenge posted by Camus.[12] Why bother hauling the rocks if they are just going to tumble back down again?

Here is what I found. I needed to look at things in a different way. The point of all of these activities wasn't to win them. There was no cosmic prize for being the best advocate or arbitrator or person or anything else. And the human prizes were ephemeral and not worth the dedication of a whole life. As Lao Zhu asked, which means more to you, you or your renown?[13] The traditional answer for an advocate is that reputation matters above all. But does it? What really mattered, in the end, was what was left over when I stopped seeing the world through the prism of my own cares, worries, achievements, likes and dislikes. There was a whole world out there, if I could just get out of my own way enough to see it.

In my book, I find myself agreeing with historian Theodore Zeldin:[14]

> I see humanity as a family that has hardly met. I see the meeting of people, bodies, thoughts, emotions or actions as the start of most change. Each link created by a meeting is a filament, which, if they were all visible, would make the world look as though it is covered with gossamer. Every individual is connected to others, loosely or closely, by a unique combination of filaments, which stretch across the frontiers of time and space. Every individual assembles past loyalties, present needs and visions of the future in a web of different contours .... It is in the power of everybody, with a little courage, to hold out a hand to someone different, to listen, to attempt to increase, even by a tiny amount, the quantity of kindness and humanity in the world. But it is careless to do so without remembering how previous efforts have failed, and how it has never been possible to predict for certain how another human being will behave. History, with its endless procession of passers-by, most of whose encounters have been missed opportunities, has so far been largely a chronicle of ability gone to waste. But next time two people meet, the result could be different. That is the origin of anxiety, but also of hope, and hope is the origin of humanity.

My pathway to Zeldin came partly through Stoic and Buddhist insights into our unceasing desires and the thoughts with which we clothe them. But particularly through the humanist philosophy of George Eliot, Iris Murdoch and Martha Nussbaum, which showed that what mattered was not merely techniques to be calmer, but an ethical underpinning behind the techniques. That underpinning is the perception that our humanity tends to get blocked, not by ill motives, but by ego, our evolutionary impulse to be right and to win, which inexorably separates us from others. It is often when we are most full of conviction that we are least able to see other people. Because our very ideas get in the way. So it is that good people can do terrible things, fortified by their own self-righteousness. A depressed person can see this because they know they are the protagonist in their own grim movie and feel the weight of their separation

12. A Camus, *The Myth of Sisyphus* (Tr. O'Brien, J) (Penguin Classics, 2000; originally published 1942) at 87-89.
13. L Zhu, *Tao Te Ching* (Tr. C Muller) (Barnes & Noble Classics, 2005), Ch. 44 ('Which is dearer, fame or your life?').
14. T Zeldin, *An Intimate History of Humanity* (Vintage Books Random House, 1998) at 465-466 and 471-472.

from the world. But to be human is to be the protagonist of the movie reel playing in our own heads. The risk for all of us is casting ourselves as the star, and reducing other everyone and everything else to supporting actors, scenery, and props.

What I needed to learn, and am still learning, are ways to experience the world without the mediating influence of my own – as Murdoch put it – 'fat relentless ego'.[15] As an advocate, a robust ego had always seemed like a good thing. Which was just as well, as I had one. I've since focused on learning to pay attention, not to be more efficient or effective, but to better appreciate the shared humanity – Zeldin's gossamer threads of connection – all around us.

V ANOTHER WAY TO THINK ABOUT ADVOCACY IN AN ADVERSARIAL SYSTEM

What does this mean for advocacy? I suggest that encourages us to ask some hard questions about our profession. These are old questions, which go back to the Ancient Greeks.

Plato thought advocacy was a ruse: mere sophistry, the sort of disreputable word-trickery that got Socrates killed. That is why 'in at least two of his dialogues, the Gorgias and the Phaedrus, he sets out his own fundamentally hostile approach to rhetoric'.[16] As Stewart explains: 'Plato had nothing but contempt for those who adopted the tricks of sophistic rhetoricians to make others believe they had learning which, in reality, they did not possess.'[17] Having no inherent connection with truth, rhetoric's equal use to any side of a controversy 'gave it the amoral utility of a knife, but with far greater potential for harm.'[18]

Aristotle was more sanguine, even writing a textbook on rhetoric. From him, we get the enduring acronym IAMDS: innovation, arrangement, memory, delivery, style.[19] This formula was perfected by the great Roman orators, Quintilian – who himself wrote an excellent textbook[20] – and especially Cicero – whose influence was such that it gave birth to a Renaissance tradition of 'Cicerolatry', in which an argument's value was assessed by reference to whether it could be derived from the great master himself.[21]

15. I Murdoch, *The Sovereignty of the Good* (Routledge Great Minds ebook edition, 2013; originally published 1970).
16. Aristotle, *The Art of Rhetoric* (Tr. and Int. by H Lawson-Tancred) (Penguin Classics, 2004) (henceforth *Aristotle*), Int. at 6. *See also* D Stewart, 'The Continuing Relevance of Plato's *Phaedrus*' (henceforth *Stewart*) in R Connors, L Ede & A Lunsford (eds), *Essays on Classical Rhetoric and Modern Discourse* (Southern Illinois University Press, 1984) (henceforth *Essays*) at 118, observing that 'harsh views on rhetoric' are found also in Plato's *Politics, Meno, Euthydemus, Apology* and *Republic.*
17. Stewart at 119.
18. O Brownstein, 'Aristotle and the Rhetorical Process' in W Fisher (ed.) *Rhetoric: A Tradition in Transition* (Michigan State Press, 1974) (henceforth *Brownstein*) at 19.
19. G Watt, 'The Art of Advocacy: Renaissance of Rhetoric in the Law School' (2018) 12(1) *Law and Humanities* 116 (henceforth *Watt*) at 134.
20. Quintilian, *Institutio Oratoria (The Orator's Education)* (Tr. D Russell) (Harvard University Press, 2001).
21. S Bakewell, *Humanly Possible: Seven Hundred Years of Humanist Freethinking, Enquiry and Hope* (Chatto & Windus, 2023) at 94-95.

When we read advocacy texts of our era, including those directed to international arbitration, we see the same essential advice repackaged, albeit with emphasis on procedural flexibility, technological savvy and cross-cultural variation.[22]

Aristotle's search was not, though, for effective techniques only, but for an ethical base from which to deploy them. We all know his formula: logos, pathos and ethos.[23] In Aristotle's view, character is central to the proper conduct of rhetoric. Aristotle's broader philosophical enquiry sought to unpick what might be called the paradox of advocacy: the better someone is, the more they demonstrate their powers to persuade, the less you should probably trust them. Because it is a fallacy to think that someone's pedigree or reputation means their side of a fee-paying case will invariably be the right one. This is a reason why Ancient Rome discouraged advocates (who were self-sufficient aristocrats) from collecting fees.[24] It is also why advocacy has developed as a regulated profession, in the tradition of ancient guilds. The implicit concern is that if reduced to a transaction, sophistry - success due merely to mastery of rhetorical techniques - beckons.

That is not to say advocacy is an unconfined search for truth, especially within an adversarial system premised on the decision-maker discerning facts and answers from the crucible of contestation.[25] Yet Aristotle was onto something. Good rhetoric, even if in service of only one side of the debate, is not mere performance: advertising, salesmanship or propaganda.[26]

This is where the concept of dialectic - or dialogue premised on a shared search for understanding - comes in. Plato tended to contrast rhetoric and dialectic.[27] Aristotle rightly saw them as counterparts.[28] The real problem with trying to persuade anyone of anything is that the image or concept in your mind cannot be directly transplanted onto another mind. That is why explaining one's position, even pellucidly, is often insufficient. People's words and ideas, their mental maps (including our own), hide us from each other. Pathos and ethos, used ethically, are not tricks, but devices to help connect differently constituted minds. Francis Bacon thus argued that ethical rhetoric consists of using the '*ornament of words*'[29] to overcome the gulfs between people and help foster genuine understanding. The aim should not be to capture but to communicate. In an adversarial contest, you are not really doing battle with your opponent. Your opponent is always confusion: the ways rival arguments obscure and confound the

22. *See, e.g.*, R D Bishop (ed.), *The Art of Advocacy in International Arbitration* (Juris Publishing, 2004) and D Cairns' insightful book review at 54 (2005) ICLQ 801 at 803. *See* too S Jagusch KC, P Pinsolle & T Foden (eds), *Global Arbitration Review: The Guide to Advocacy* (Law Business Research, 2017, 2nd ed.). *See also* A Whitfield KC, 'The Art of Persuasion: Tradition and Technique' (The Honourable Society of the Middle Temple, 2015).
23. Aristotle at 74 (§ 1356(a)).
24. Pliny the Younger, *Pliny: A Self Portrait in Letters* (Tr. B Radice) (The Folio Society, 1978) at 117.
25. Watt at 129.
26. D Bryant, 'Rhetoric: Its Functions and Its Scope' in *Essays* at 215.
27. *See, e.g.*, Stewart at 116-119.
28. Aristotle Article 66 (§ 1354(a)).
29. K Wallace, 'Bacon, Rhetoric and Ornament of Words' in *Essays* at 49-52. As Wallace asks rhetorically at 52, '[i]f something is ornamented or adorned, the implication is that there is something that is not adorned. What is it? There is something other than language which language reflects'.

process of effective communication with the tribunal. Even in uncontested matters, effective communication on complex matters of law, fact and justice is rarely straightforward.

The most thoughtful account I've read of all this is by James Boyd White, who set out to address the problem identified by philosophers Simone Weil and Elisabeth Anscombe.[30] Which is that our words and ideas can so easily and sweetly blind us to reality. We live surrounded by systems of meaning encoded so deep within our world that we do not see them. Weil's take on this was to describe an 'empire of force', our way of using speech to dominate others,[31] as a habit of mind.[32] Anscombe's approach was to use Wittgenstein's methods to try to penetrate through the ornament of words to get at the real matter or things or beings they describe.[33] Both Weil and Anscombe illustrated their point by considering common justifications for atrocities of war – too often means are disguised as ends through impersonal, detached, language.[34] This was something Orwell also saw clearly and which lives on well past 1984.

White's prescription is surprising and refreshing. Silence. This is so we can speak not from 'tags of remembered speech and gesture ... but from some deep place within the self – silent, below the words, a place where language can be the subject of conscious attention and where it can be remade'.[35] This kind of silence is a creative process, in which language is not automatic, but shaped or chosen:[36]

> And this silence is not simply empty space or time, an absence of words; it is a state or condition that must be attained, by work and art and discipline, and it must be used, and used well. It is a crucial part of what we mean by engagement of the whole mind.

Depression allowed me to see rote mental and language habits more clearly. These are weapons in an advocate's arsenal – we can use systems of meaning to dominate. But in doing so, we can find ourselves papering over the people and things we purport to describe. Murdoch's answer, 'unself', seems to me the appropriate ethical response. But what does this mean for the advocate? White says, and I agree, that we should strive to shift from mere exchanges of words to conversations between minds.[37] Not mesmerising with the tools of rhetoric. Not achieving perfection. But seeking genuine engagement and connection. We can use the tools of our craft to take on Zeldin's challenge, rather than make things worse.

30. J Boyd White, *Living Speech: Resisting the Empire of Force* (Princeton University Press, 2006) (henceforth *White*).
31. Or, as White puts it 'the ideology, the way of imagining the world and oneself and others within it': at 2.
32. *See* White at 1-4.
33. C Mac Cumhaill & R Wiseman, *Metaphysical Animals: How Four Women Brought Philosophy Back to Life* (Penguin Random House, 2022) (henceforth *Metaphysical Animals*) at 187-195.
34. White at 2 and *Metaphysical Animals* at 2 and 289-294.
35. White at 15.
36. *Ibid.*
37. White at 51-57.

There is an alternative account to White's view. This is that, while advocacy is really a performance, the best advocates affect their naturalness, trying to parley a winning attitude into a winning result. As Watt explains:[38]

> The rhetorical tradition can be refined into the following golden advice to the student advocate: a judge will be most persuaded by the advocate who engages in apparently unscripted conversation with the judge; presenting arguments to the judge in a sympathetic manner, listening attentively to the judge's observations and responding appropriately to the judge's questions.

We should be wary of this account. Recall the human problems we must confront: limited attention, short-term memory, rationality[39] and self-awareness (including limited awareness of one's limited rationality); cluttered mental maps; cognitive and emotional biases;[40] hidden wants and desires; and attraction to paths of least resistance. We can try, of course, to deal with this complex terrain by doubling down on preparation: trying, as it were, to 'work out' the arbitrator.[41] But we must be realistic. Humans are mysterious, even to themselves, and it is seldom possible to predict how they will respond to the intricacies of a new case.

The art of advocacy is not mastery of a bag of rhetorical tricks, effected through affected naturalness. True advocacy is the art of being able to leap mental maps. To be able to understand what language you need to translate a key insight into, and then be able to speak, even if haltingly, that language. We all know the difficulty of trying to penetrate through the web of someone else's memory fragments and suppositions towards a genuine meeting of minds. We all tend to use words to justify our conclusions rather than to form and convey them. And those conclusions are often led and hemmed in by other ideas and feelings we have, usually ones that sustain and support our wider world view – which itself is rarely created by each of us, but borrowed and inherited from others. The job is even harder in an adversarial environment, which can often generate more heat than light.

Watt says the 'golden word is "sympathetic". It literally means "with pathos"'.[42] By this, Watt means joining one's logic line to the best story arc. I suspect, though, that the essential quality is not sympathy but empathy. Sympathy is the attribute of a good story, crafted to appeal to the sensibilities of the decision-maker. Empathy is the quality of human engagement. Sympathy is feeling for another's predicament. Empathy is imaginatively standing in their shoes.

Depression teaches one to be suspicious of stories, which our minds produce incessantly. They are important. But, as *New Yorker* writer Parul Sehgal argues, they

38. Watt at 129.
39. Pannick at 228, referencing Quintilian's observation that even judges can get caught up in the torrent of emotions towards a natural landing point.
40. *See* Pannick at 232, citing *Rumpole* to the effect that irritable judges can suffer from bad cases of premature adjudication.
41. *See, e.g.*, E Sussmann, 'What Lurks in the Unconscious: Influences on Arbitrator Decision Making' 32(10) *Alternatives to the High Cost of Litigation* 152 at 154, https://doi.org/10.1002/alt.21551. *See also* Ross at 12.
42. Watt at 130.

also lull.[43] When we merely add story arcs to our logic lines, we are still absorbed in the task of persuading by performance. What if we took a step back? Rather than believe you can entirely work out an arbitrator, you can try to meet their humanity with your own. What you are trying to do is open the apertures to create the richest form of engagement. Logos and pathos both matter. But so too does ethos – not in the sense of a fine reputation, but in the sense of being a trusted guide to walk alongside a tribunal as they approach a difficult task.

In a world that has too much speech, where words can lose meaning, distort, and become ultimately reduced to pleas, claims and exhortations, advocates should always look for the real meaning under fine phrases and strive to connect divergent mental maps, notwithstanding the difficulties of doing so. Academically, this is advocacy as 'constitutive rhetoric'[44] or rhetoric as a method of inquiry.[45] In Platonic terms, it is a dialectic, building an ethical community of understanding. Practically, this is working out, really, what you are trying to say and being ready and willing to discuss the issue from all angles.

Of course we want to win. Yet we all know that we can win an argument, but somehow still lose the case. We tend, in those situations, to complain that the tribunal got it wrong. We could equally say that we failed, somehow, to quite connect. Trust can be earned by getting things right. But more often by taking one's own ego out of the picture to some degree. Striving can occlude listening. Some of the best advocacy I have observed was disarmingly unpolished, stumbling, inarticulate, part of a genuine conversation during which new mental territory was opened up and explored. As Leonard Cohen told us, the cracks are where the light gets in.[46]

VI MY ADVOCACY PRACTICE NOW

This does not mean I aim for imperfection and error in advocacy. Of course not. But I now have a new perspective. I used to aim for my logic line and story arc to intersect, and figured ethos meant being a straight shooter who was usually right. I now think that ethos is recognising that connection, not perfection, is the object. In an easy case, the difference is hard to spot. In a harder case, where the mire is more treacherous, you need to foster genuine curiosity and engagement. That is done by encouraging arbitrators and judges to twist and turn, and think, and feel, and test their assumptions. That is not always easy. Yet being willing to twist and turn, wonder, ponder and equivocate with a tribunal; sometimes these human expressions of empathy, presence of mind and imagination are what is really called for.[47]

At symposia like this, I've witnessed leading advocates explain how they rehearse their openings so many times they virtually perform themselves. But being too

43. P Sehgal, 'Tell No Tales' in *The New Yorker*, 10 & 17 July 2023 at 68-69.
44. J Crook, *Legal Advocacy in the Roman World* (Cornell University Press, 1995) at 26.
45. Bryant at 218.
46. From 'Anthem', on Leonard Cohen's 1992 *Album The Future*: 'Ring the bells that can still ring / Forget your perfect offering / There is a crack in everything / That's how the light gets in.'
47. Boyd White, 11.

slick is just another obstacle in the way of genuine connection. I think there is a better way to approach the craft. We should try to build rapport, ease, curiosity, to create a climate for real dialogue and communication. Rapport is not a dazzling performance where you educate the tribunal and vanquish the opposition through your own eloquence. It is a real and not (or not entirely) feigned sense of human connection. It is often built best by not being perfect, but by – as with a thoughtful answer to a puzzling question – evincing the essential quality of curiosity.

Much of the ancient advice about advocacy was written about '1-to-many' modes of address. Today, our advocacy style is more conversational.[48] This is especially true in arbitration, which, with its procedural informality and seated participants, is inherently '1-to-few', a natural setting for a dialogue. As with other conversations we have, it can be easier to convince if you stop trying so hard to be right, and just discuss, working through the kinks in your interlocutor's thoughts, as well as your own, creating a sense of ease in your direction of travel. We don't have conversations by being flawless. We listen, adjust and adapt.

I have found that life gets easier if I try to control less and connect more. Advocacy may not be so very different.

48. Pannick at 229.

CHAPTER 41

The Role of Culture in the Adversarial Process and How to Avoid Misunderstandings

Yoko Maeda & Bruno Savoie[*]

TABLE OF CONTENTS

I INTRODUCTION

International arbitration brings together parties, counsel and arbitrators from different cultures. Avoiding misunderstandings should be a priority for all involved, as a misperception by the arbitral tribunal could lead to an unfair result for one or both of the parties. Moreover, given the limited grounds for setting aside or refusing to enforce an arbitral award, there may be no recourse should a misunderstanding based on cultural differences play a role in the determination of an issue in an arbitration.

Culture is probably most often thought of by arbitration practitioners in terms of two broad categories: (1) legal cultures, i.e., legal traditions in each jurisdiction; and (2) other cultures, i.e., different cultural backgrounds based on geographical, ethnic, or national origins.

* **Yoko Maeda** Bachelor of Law, Tokyo University; LL.M., University of Pennsylvania Law School; Partner, City-Yuwa Partners (Tokyo, Japan). **Bruno Savoie** Hons. B.A., University of Toronto; J.D. and B.C.L., McGill University Faculty of Law; Foreign Attorney, City-Yuwa Partners (Tokyo, Japan).

The most typical examples of legal cultures are the common law and civil law traditions, as well as Sharia (Islamic) law. Differences between these legal systems or traditions affect the entire procedure of international arbitration, such as pleadings, document production, witness examination, etc. It should not be ignored that even within civil law/common law countries, legal practices sometimes significantly vary depending on the jurisdiction.

Such differences and conflicts in legal cultures have been well recognized and intensively discussed in international arbitration. In response, groups of practitioners—mainly though organizations such as the IBA and CIArb—have made an effort to develop a transnational, standardized procedure. The engine behind these soft law instruments is ensuring that parties, counsel and the arbitral tribunal can avoid misunderstanding based on legal cultural differences by recognizing the differences between different legal systems. While this work is ongoing, it is equally important to question the desirability of the standardization of arbitration, given that one of its differentiating factors from court litigation is its procedural flexibility.

The second type of culture (which will be referred to simply as "culture," as opposed to "legal culture") refers to different cultural backgrounds based on geographical, ethnical, or national origins. Unlike differences arising from the clash between legal cultures, not much attention has been paid to these other cultural differences, nor is it simple to develop a standardized, transnational solution in response to those cultural differences.

Section II of this chapter will discuss the influence of legal culture in international arbitration, while section III will discuss the influence of culture in international arbitration.

For clarity, all generalizations made in this chapter should be interpreted as mere hypotheses to facilitate our discussion. It is of crucial importance to understand and recognize that cultures are often—if not almost always—not a monolith. Moreover, this chapter does not purport to provide a comprehensive guide to the wide variety of cultural issues that can arise in an international arbitration, but rather merely hopes to contribute to an evolving understanding of the role of culture in arbitration and in the adversarial process.

II IMPACT OF LEGAL CULTURAL DIFFERENCES THROUGHOUT THE STAGES OF THE ADVERSARIAL PROCESS IN ARBITRATION

Without purporting to be exhaustive, this section II discusses the impact of legal cultures on various stages of the arbitral process. This chapter examines: (1) whether differences exist between legal traditions (i.e., civil law and common law), (2) what are the potential misunderstandings that may arise therefrom, and (3) whether there has been any response within the arbitration community to attempt to address these misunderstandings.

1 Document Production

Document disclosure or production refers to a process by which parties may request and obtain relevant documents from each other. Today, many arbitral proceedings include such a process. Document production is sometimes criticized as one of the reasons for the perceived increase in cost and delays in arbitration. In particular, this process is often mentioned as an example of the clash or convergence in arbitration between common law and civil law cultures.[1]

a Differences Between Legal Traditions

Civil law lawyers and their clients often do not have any expectation that discovery (of any significant scale, at least) will be available, and conversely, be required of them during arbitration. In contrast, common law lawyers and their clients often expect from their respective legal systems a strong guarantee that disclosure will be available and enforced by the courts, with the American court system being the prime example.

b Potential Misunderstandings

Because of the difference between the common law and civil law traditions in document production as described above, it can easily be the case that parties to an arbitration have different expectations regarding document production. Even if both parties accept that document production will be conducted to some extent, parties from different legal traditions may have a different understanding of the scope of documents that can be requested.

It can also be the case that counsel/parties who are not familiar with document production may not initially understand the outcome of non-compliance with a document production order, while counsel and parties from common law jurisdiction may naturally understand better the risks of refusing to comply with an order by the arbitral tribunal. Because of a lack of understanding of the outcome of non-compliance, one party may refuse or fail to seriously cooperate and undertake its obligations seriously in relation to the document production procedure, fail to disclose requested documents without any justifiable reason, and in turn that party may suffer from potentially disastrous consequences in the final award through damaging adverse inferences.

c Response from the International Arbitration Community

In light of this clash of legal cultures with regard to document production, the international arbitration community has attempted to bridge the gap and provide

1. *See* generally, Gordon Blanke, "Document Production in International Arbitration: From Civil and Common Law Dichotomy to Operational Synergies," 83(4) *The International Journal of Arbitration, Mediation and Dispute Management* (Kluwer Law International, 2017) p. 427.

guidelines that would level the playing field between common law and civil law lawyers.

The main response has been the release of the *IBA Rules on the Taking of Evidence in International Arbitration* (2010, revised in 2020) (the "*IBA Rules*"), which is one of the most widely used soft law instrument in commercial arbitration. In particular, Article 3(3) sets out the requirements for a request to produce documents, including the scope of the documents that can be requested (e.g., "*narrow and specific*" under Article 3(3)(a), etc.) and Article 9(6) sets out the outcome of a failure to produce requested documents.

The *Prague Rules on the Efficient Conduct of Proceedings in International Arbitration* (2018) (the "*Prague Rules*") were issued with considerable fanfare and were heralded as a civil law-oriented alternative to the IBA Rules that would help reduce costs and delays in arbitration, by allowing among others greater proactiveness and inquisitiveness by arbitral tribunals. However, the Prague Rules have not been widely used by the arbitration community despite much discussion at the time of their launch.

2 Witness Statements

One of the features of international arbitration is that witness evidence is usually given mainly by way of a written witness statement (akin to an affidavit in court litigation), rather than by an examination in chief (direct testimony), with the merits hearing being consumed by cross-examinations, and to some extent, opening presentations and expert presentations.

a Differences Between Legal Traditions

Counsel and arbitrators from different legal backgrounds may have divergent expectations with regard to the appropriate scope and purpose of witness statements. For example, common law lawyers may take for granted that witness statement would comprehensively set out evidence on most if not all issues, or otherwise comprise the entirety of a witness' knowledge or evidence. In contrast, some civil law lawyers trained in Asia might expect witness statements to serve the purpose of a summary, with more detailed evidence to be adduced orally at the hearing by the witness.

The issue of witness preparation brings to the fore the differences in ethical culture between different jurisdictions. The diverging obligations of counsels regulated in different jurisdictions with regard to witness preparation are often highlighted as one example of conflicting ethical rules in international arbitration. In particular, the commonly accepted practice of American lawyers is to perform extensive witness preparation, which is allowed under their applicable ethical rules. In contrast, English lawyers are prohibited by their professional conduct rules from "coaching" witnesses. For example, conducting a mock cross-examination is not ethically allowed for English lawyers.[2]

2. Sophie Nappert and Christopher Harris, "The English Approach to Cross-Examination in International Arbitration," in Lawrence W. Newman and Timothy G. Nelson (eds.), *Take the Witness: Cross-Examination in International Arbitration*, 2nd ed. (Juris: 2019).

b Potential Misunderstandings

Disputes often arise at the merits hearing when a witness gives evidence that is beyond the scope of their witness statement. In contrast to court litigation which has strict rules of evidence, arbitrators appear more lenient and tend to allow more evidence as admissible. This appears to be the result of the fear of limiting the parties' right to present their case, which is a potential ground for setting aside an arbitral award.

The different ethical requirements on witness preparation, an issue that is most likely to first arise through cross-examination at the hearing, it is likely to give rise not only to misunderstandings and dissatisfaction, but goes to the heart of the legitimacy of arbitration as a fair process, the result of which is worthy of enforcement worldwide.

c Response from the International Arbitration Community

With regard to witness statements, in order to avoid the foregoing issues, counsel should be well advised to seek directions in advance from the arbitral tribunal on their expectations for witness statements and the evidence of witnesses at the hearing.

With regard to witness preparation, one way to resolve the potentially unequal ethical playing field would be to attempt to agree on common standards between the parties in an arbitration, and/or to raise the issue and request directions by the arbitral tribunal, for example, in a procedural order or in terms of reference. Here, the more likely solution may be that both sides would be directed not to engage in witness coaching, as the English Bar Code of Conduct would not be otherwise overruled for an English lawyer.[3] Another response has been the issuance of the *IBA Guidelines on Party Representation in International Arbitration* (2013), although it is unclear to what extent these guidelines are incorporated into procedural orders by arbitral tribunals. Moreover, not all ethical issues are resolved by the guidelines, particularly to the extent that they conflict with mandatory requirements in a lawyer's own jurisdiction.

3 Pleadings (Written and Oral)

a Differences Between Legal Traditions

With regard to pleadings, it is difficult to make generalizations between common law and civil law, given the wide variety of jurisdictions with each legal tradition. By way of example, one difference might be that some American lawyers, perhaps due to the role of jury trials in that jurisdiction, tend to pay particular attention to the overall story of the claim even as a Respondent without counterclaims. In contrast, some English lawyers may be more likely to respond to a claim with denials and by noting the Claimant's burden of proof, rather than telling the Respondent's story in an equal amount of detail as the Claimant may have done.

3. *Id.*

Another example comes from Spanish-speaking Latin America, where it is reported that formalism plays an important role in court litigation, and that counsel tend to draft briefs that are long, detailed, and sometimes repetitive, in an attempt to avoid any of the claims being deemed waived.[4]

With regard to oral pleadings, it could be said that civil law jurisdictions put less emphasis on oral pleadings in comparison to common law jurisdictions, including in the civilian French-speaking African countries.[5]

Differences between adversarial versus inquisitorial legal systems can also be observed in arbitrators' involvement in oral pleadings. By way of example, it is reported that German arbitrators tend to be proactive and ask many questions, whereas an arbitrator from one of the Nordic countries may not ask any question during the hearing.[6]

Body language can also play a role during oral pleadings. For example, arbitration has been described as litigation while seated. Accordingly, it is reported by a well-known arbitrator that it is not uncommon for some American lawyers, who may or may not have limited experience with arbitration, to leave their seat at the counsel's table and make their arguments while standing, although he has never seen lawyers do so other than American lawyers.[7] One explanation may be that lawyers from other nationalities prefer not to stand up to create instead a more informal rapport with the tribunal rather than performing a formal speech.

b *Potential Misunderstandings*

The aim of pleadings being to persuade, there is a risk that an arbitral tribunal who is familiar with a particular style may not be persuaded easily if arguments are presented in an unexpected manner. For example, some counsel may be used to asking rhetorical questions in their pleadings, whereas some tribunals may not be used to such devices. Some counsel may file organized, comprehensive, and repetitive briefs that address every component of a claim in detail, but fail to convey a sense of the overall story and justice of the case.

c *Response from the International Arbitration Community*

The response to differences in legal culture in relation to pleadings appears to have been minimal. Beyond directing the parties to comply with page limits for certain types of pleadings, such as post-hearing briefs, arbitral tribunals appear to be reluctant to

4. Cecilia Azar, Santiago Cervantes and Ana Sofía Mosqueda, "Cultural Considerations in Advocacy: Spanish-Speaking Latin America" in GAR, *The Guide to Advocacy*, 6th ed. (Law Business Research Ltd., 2023).
5. Wesley Pydiamah, "Cultural Considerations in Advocacy: French-Speaking Africa" in GAR, *The Guide to Advocacy*, 6th ed. (Law Business Research Ltd., 2023).
6. Anna Grishchenkova, "Cultural Considerations in Advocacy: Russia and Eastern Europe" in GAR, *The Guide to Advocacy*, 6th ed. (Law Business Research Ltd., 2023).
7. Eric Schwartz, quoted in Amal Bouchenaki, "Cultural Considerations in Advocacy: United States," in GAR, *The Guide to Advocacy*, 6th ed. (Law Business Research Ltd., 2023).

limit a party's right to present its case as it sees fit. Nevertheless, both the prevalence of "memorial" style pleadings and the focus on written submissions rather than oral pleadings may be thought to be a movement toward standardization of the arbitral process.

4 Cross-Examination

a Differences Between Legal Traditions

Common law trained lawyers are more likely to be familiar and experienced with the art of cross-examination in comparison with civil law lawyers, leading to a number of potential pitfalls and misunderstandings. In some (but not all) civil law countries, the lawyers are accustomed to the judge, as opposed to the parties' counsel, taking the lead on the examination of witnesses.

The practice of employing barristers for the merits hearing is also one that differs between legal cultures. Common in the UK and Australia, it is, for example, relatively uncommon in many other countries, including Japan.

b Potential Misunderstandings

Civil law lawyers who are less familiar with cross-examination face many perils, including the risk of underestimating its importance, not only during the hearing but also in the steps leading to it. Perhaps the most common mistakes made by those who are not familiar with cross-examination include asking open-ended questions, asking questions to which one does not know the answer, or asking several questions at once.

Moreover, common law lawyers are more likely to have cross-examination in mind throughout the entire process of the arbitration, and ensure that witness statements are drafted in such a way that they cannot be effectively disproven through cross-examination.

Conversely, common law lawyers are not impervious to facing a reverse culture shock in arbitration. For example, English lawyers will be used to "putting the case" to the witness. Furthermore, common law lawyers who prepared a very aggressive cross-examination strategy may not have as much leeway from the arbitral tribunal as they would have in an American court because a common law lawyer's cross-examination of a witness is often perceived by civil law arbitrators as an advocate's efforts to trick and embarrass the witness.[8]

c Response from the International Arbitration Community

Regardless of the significant differences described above, it is common in international arbitration for cross-examination to be conducted by parties' counsel. Therefore, with

8. Robert H. Smit, "Cross-Examining Witnesses Before Civil Law Arbitrators," in Lawrence W. Newman and Timothy G. Nelson (eds.), *Take the Witness: Cross-Examination in International Arbitration*, 2nd ed. (Juris: 2019)

regard to civil law lawyers, training on cross-examination is likely to be beneficial to further their education on the topic. For their part, common law lawyers who are set in their cross-examination ways may need to adapt their methods when appearing in front of a civilian-trained arbitral tribunal.[9]

III IMPACT OF OTHER CULTURAL DIFFERENCES ON THE ADVERSARIAL PROCESS IN ARBITRATION

This section III addresses the impact of culture (i.e., non-legal culture) on the adversarial process in arbitration, by first discussing the impact of culture on arbitral tribunals' decision-making and the selection of arbitrators, before examining the effect of cultural patterns through five value patterns and two communication styles as lenses for this inquiry.

1 Impact of Culture on Tribunal's Decision-Making and Selection of Arbitrators

Where the arbitral tribunal and the parties have no or little cultural proximity, there is a greater risk of misunderstanding by the tribunal than if the tribunal members share the same culture with the parties. This is because the process of determining facts and the application of the facts to the law (and the interpretation thereof) is a deeply cultural exercise.[10]

One example that has been reported is that of a witness from the African region who saw orange saying during cross-examination that he saw "yellow." If the tribunal has clear evidence that what the witness actually saw was orange, tribunal members from other regions may suspect the credibility of the witness. However, the witness is in fact not lying, because in many African cultures, yellow represents a range of colors, including orange.[11] In Japan, a similar example is that the color green is sometimes described as blue. Accordingly, a green signal is called blue signal, green vegetables are blue vegetables, and green leaves are blue leaves in Japan.[12]

There is a concern that witnesses from different cultures may behave differently and give the wrong impression to arbitrators who are not familiar with their culture.

9. See generally, *Id.*; Sophie Nappert and Christopher Harris, "The English Approach to Cross-Examination in International Arbitration," in Lawrence W. Newman and Timothy G. Nelson (eds.), *Take the Witness: Cross-Examination in International Arbitration*, 2nd ed. (Juris: 2019).
10. Won Kidane, "Does Cultural Diversity Improve or Hinder the Quality of Arbitral Justice?" *Kluwer Arbitration Blog* (March 31, 2017) https://arbitrationblog.kluwerarbitration.com/2017/03/31/does-cultural-diversity-improve-or-hinder-the-quality-of-arbitral-justice/ (accessed August 16, 2025).
11. *Id.*
12. Differences in language rather than culture not being the focus of this chapter, we would nevertheless be remiss not to mention that differences in language itself can create a number of misunderstandings. *See* generally, James H. Carter, "The Perils of Cross-Examination in a Language Other than the Language of the Proceedings," in Lawrence W. Newman and Timothy G. Nelson (eds.), *Take the Witness: Cross-Examination in International Arbitration*, 2nd ed. (Juris: 2019).

Body language is another potential source of misunderstanding. One example in relation to South-Asian witnesses could be that a witness may shake their head laterally, which may appear to indicate "no" to a Western audience, whereas it is intended by the witness as an indication of agreement.[13]

Another source of potential misunderstanding is smiling. Smiling, especially during witness examination, can be interpreted in very different ways and sometimes cause misunderstanding, depending on the culture of the tribunal. Although numerous studies confirm that positive perceptions of smiling individuals seem to be universal, anecdotal evidence suggests that in some cultures the opposite may be true. In Russian culture, a famous proverb translates roughly as "Smiling with no reason is a sign of stupidity."[14]

In contrast, East Asian cultures view smiling differently. In Japan, smiling may be used *inter alia* to show respect or to suppress negative emotions in order to maintain social harmony. For example, one Japanese proverb says: "Smiling face, crying heart." Similarly, displays of anger may also be socially unacceptable and thus covered by a smile (and/or silence), with the Balinese people being one example of this behavior in Asia.[15]

Such cultural difference also becomes an issue when the tribunal tries to apply facts to law. For example, even if the tribunal is given exactly the same set of facts, whether the tribunal finds them to be force majeure or hardship can significantly change depending on the culture that the tribunal members are belonging to.

With regard to the selection of arbitrators, therefore, an extreme position would argue that arbitrators and judges would thus be "*unable to adequately conceptualize the thought and practice (and associated material artifacts) of the members of different cultures*"[16] or even that one "*will never understand Chinese people unless you understand Chinese language.*"[17]

2 Cultural Value Patterns and Their Impact

Cultural differences and their impact on the adversarial procedure can be more structurally understood by identifying and rating each culture using cultural value patterns, i.e., characteristic behaviors within certain national groups. Among various cultural value patterns, five value patterns and two communication styles are considered to be the most relevant to international dispute resolution.

13. Alvin Yeo SC, Chou Sean Yu and Frank Oh Sheng Loong, "Cultural Considerations in Advocacy: East Meets West" GAR, *The Guide to Advocacy*, 6th ed. (Law Business Research Ltd., 2023).
14. Kuba Krys et al., "Be careful where you smile: Culture shapes judgments of intelligence and honesty of smiling individuals," 40(2) *Journal of Nonverbal Behavior* (Springer, 2016), p. 103.
15. *See* generally, Robin Kurilla, "Everyday Life Theories of Emotions in Conflicts From Bali, the Spanish Basque Country, and the German Ruhr Area", 11 *Frontiers Psychology* (2020), Article 1339 (Frontiers Media S.A., 2020)
16. Anthony J. Connolly, *Cultural Difference on Trial: The Nature and Limits of Judicial Understanding* (Routledge: 2010) 167.
17. Niall Lawless, "Cultural Perspectives on China: Resolving Disputes Through Mediation," 4 *Transnational Disputes Management* (2008).

The five cultural value patterns are: (a) individualism/collectivism, (b) universalism/particularism, (c) power distance, (d) uncertainty avoidance, and (e) locus of control. The two communication styles are (f) low-context/high-context and (g) monochronic/polychronic time.

The categorization of the value patterns and communication patterns in this section is inspired by and buildings upon the framework set out in Julia Ann Gold's article titled "ADR through a Cultural Lens: How Cultural Values Shape Our Disputing Processes" (2005).[18]

a *Individualism/Collectivism*

Individualists believe that it is important to satisfy the needs of the individual before those of the group. For them, individual identity is more important than group identity, and individual rights are more important than group rights. On the other hand, in a collectivist culture, identity is tied to a primary group, usually the family. Members of a collectivist society believe that the survival of the group will ensure each member's survival because the success of the group benefits the individual.[19] The United States is ranked as an extremely individualistic country, while countries such as Guatemala, Ecuador, Egypt and Nepal are highly collectivist cultures.[20]

Counsel should be mindful that witnesses' behavior can vary depending on whether the witness is from an individualist/collectivist culture. For example, Japanese people tend to be extremely collectivist when it comes to the companies that they are working for, with the consequence that a Japanese witness would likely be willing to protect the interest of the company to which they belong, and will not wish to contradict their superiors/colleagues. Witnesses are often reluctant to disclose facts/evidence that can be detrimental to their employers, even when they are asked to do so by the employer's legal counsel. If the counsel and/or tribunal members are from an individualism culture, such behavior by a witness can easily be the cause of misunderstandings or the credibility of the witness can be damaged.

Such reluctance could disappear, for example, if a high-level officer or executive from the company gives clear and written instruction to the witness that they must tell the whole truth in the arbitration, and that doing so will benefit the company.

b *Universalism/Particularism*

The universalist perspective is to apply rules across the board. A universalist believes that what is right is right, regardless of the circumstances or who is involved. In contrast, particularists believe that circumstances should be taken into account, and

18. Julia Ann Gold, "ADR Through a Cultural Lens: How Cultural Values Shape Our Disputing Processes," 20205(2) *Journal of Dispute Resolution* [hereinafter "Gold, *Cultural Lens*"] p. 295.
19. *Id.*, p. 296.
20. Greet Hofstede, *Culture's Consequences: Comparing Values, Behaviors, Institutions and Organizations Across Nations*, 2nd ed. (Sage Publication, 2001) [hereinafter "Hopstede, *Consequences*"] at 215.

that what is right in one situation may not be right in another. Particularists accept that exceptions will always be made for certain people.[21] Switzerland and the U.S. are ranked as extremely universalism cultures, whereas Venezuela, Russia and Nepal are examples of very particularist countries.[22]

Arbitration is touted as offering among other things, more flexibility than court litigation, and in this way, may be thought of as embodying particularist values. A more extreme example of this flexibility is the concept of deciding *ex aequo et bono* or as *amiable compositeur*, with the clear intention not to be bound or limited by a uniform application of the law. The flexibility of arbitration being one of its strengths, this serves as a reminder to protect it in our search for solutions to the potential misunderstandings arising from cultural differences.

c *Power Distance*

Power distance refers to the extent to which less powerful members of a society "*expect and accept that power (e.g. wealth, prestige, access to education and other benefits that enhance power) is distributed unequally.*"[23]

In a low power distance culture, informality is encouraged, criticism of authorities is considered appropriate, and discussion and consultation are desirable. In a high-power distance society, people tend to accept inequalities in power and status as natural. Criticism or disagreement with those in authority by subordinates is viewed as undesirable. Subordinates are not encouraged to take initiative and are closely supervised. In a high-power distance society, obedience to and respect for elders is essential[24] .

Japan is one of the high-power distance cultures, and elders or superiors are supposed to be respected, among others at school and at work. For example, because of such high-power distance culture, employees in Japan will often not object to an idea expressed by their boss even if the employee suspects that the idea is wrong. Such behavior may be difficult for tribunal members from lower power distance societies to understand.

d *Uncertainty Avoidance*

Uncertainty avoidance is the degree of comfort with the unknown or unpredictable.[25] Uncertainty avoidance is described as "*the extent to which the members of a culture feel threatened by uncertain or unknown situations.*" This feeling can be expressed, among others, through "*nervous stress and a need for predictability: a need for written and*

21. Gold, *Cultural Lens*, p. 297.
22. Fons Trompenaars and Charles Hampden-Turner, *Riding the Waves of Culture: Understanding Diversity in Global Business*, 2nd ed. (McGrawHill, 1998) 8-11.
23. Geert Hofstede et al., *Cultures and Organizations: Software of the Mind* 5 (McGrawHill, 1997) at 28.
24. Gold, *Cultural Lens*, at 299.
25. Hostede, *Consequence*, at 145.

unwritten rules."[26] Singapore, Jamaica, Denmark and Sweden are countries with low uncertainty avoidance.

On the other hand, for people in high uncertainty avoidance cultures, ambiguity creates stress. Therefore, structure and predictability are important for them. Students will seek the "right answer" and teachers are expected to know the "right answer."[27] These cultures tend to be less accepting of differences because people believe that what is different may be dangerous. Greece, Portugal, Guatemala and Japan have a high uncertainty avoidance culture.[28]

Although many witnesses can be nervous in cross-examination, witnesses from high uncertainty avoidance cultures may become more nervous than witnesses from other cultures. Japanese witnesses tend to be willing to engage in multiple preparation sessions for witness examination, to be more comfortable. This mindset explains why they may even sometimes ask counsel to provide mock cross-examination questions and the "best" responses to all of those questions, so that they can be ready for all possible cross-examination questions, avoiding uncertainty.[29]

e *Locus of Control*

Locus of control is measured from internal to external and refers to the extent to which people believe that they control their fate.[30] A person with an internal locus of control will believe that they control their own destiny and that they are responsible for what happens to them. The United States, Uruguay, Israel and Norway exhibit an internal locus of control culture.[31]

In contrast, people with an external locus of control believe that some things in life are predetermined. Venezuela, China and Nepal are countries with a very external locus of control.[32]

If such differences in thinking are not recognized, witnesses from external locus of control cultures can be misunderstood by the tribunal members from internal locus of control cultures, who may form an impression that a witness is irresponsible and full of excuses.

f *Communication Pattern: Low Context or High Context*

Low and high context refer to how much of the meaning of a communication comes from the surrounding context, as opposed to the actual words exchanged. In a low-context culture, people tend to say exactly what they mean rather than to suggest

26. *Id.*, at 161.
27. *Id.*, at 169.
28. *Id.*, at 151.
29. The issue of witness preparation is addressed in section II of this chapter.
30. Julian B. Rotter, "Generalized Expectancies for Internal Versus External Control of Reinforcement," 80(1) *Psychological Monographs: General And Applied* (1966) https://doi.org/10.1037/h0092976 (accessed August 16, 2025).
31. Storti, *Foreigners*, at 82.
32. Trompenaars and Hampden-Turner, at 148.

or imply. The spoken word carries most of the meaning.[33] On the other hand, in high-context cultures, much of the meaning of a communication is already "programmed" into the receiver of the message. People are more likely to infer, suggest and imply than say things directly.[34] By way of example, Japan and China are very high-context societies, while the United States is a very low-context culture.[35]

One key source of misunderstanding arises from the difficulty for witnesses from high-context cultures in expressing themselves accurately in a low-context manner. Witnesses from high-context cultures sometimes avoid clear admissions/denials, or fail to adopt definitive terms and use vague expressions instead. Within the Asian context, a typical example may be that certain Asian witnesses may express their opinion or their version of the facts in a more nuanced or indirect manner, using words like "maybe," when they are in fact certain that a certain fact occurred, or avoiding answering with "yes" or "no." To an unfamiliar arbitral tribunal, this could be interpreted as a sign of doubt by the witness, when it is not the case.

It is the counsel's role, therefore, to avoid such misunderstanding by explaining the necessity of clear answers to the witness in advance. Even after such witness preparation, the witness may continue to testify in a nuanced, vague manner. In such case, the counsel would need to ask re-direct questions to clarify what the witness meant.

High/low context culture also influence evidence. In a high-context culture like Japan, there will often be no or very little supporting documentation for a decisive statement from one party to the other. For example, we can imagine a Japanese joint venture (JV) party terminating a JV contract based on the other party's misconduct over several years, having never complained to the JV partner expressly in writing, nor even orally, because the Japanese JV partner expected the other JV partner would notice the dissatisfaction of Japanese JV party even if they did not expressly convey such dissatisfaction.

g Communication Pattern: Monochronic or Polychronic

A monochronic culture perceives time as linear, quantifiable, and in limited supply. People believe that it is important to be timely, use time wisely and not waste it. Unforeseen events should not interfere with plans, and interruptions are seen as a nuisance. The United States is dominantly a very monochronic culture,[36] and so is Japan.

In a polychronic culture, time is perceived as limitless and not quantifiable. There is a sense that there is always more time. Time is adjusted to suit the needs of people. Schedules and deadlines get changed. Latin American, African, and Middle Eastern cultures all tend to be polychronic.[37]

33. Edward T. Hall, *Beyond Culture* (1989) 105-128.
34. *Id.*
35. Crag Storti, *Figuring Foreigners Out* (1999) at 5 [hereinafter "Storti, *Foreigners*"].
36. *Id.*, at 99.
37. *Id.*, pp. 298-299.

International commercial arbitrations, at least those conducted under major arbitration rules, tends to be monochronic. A timetable is set at an early stage, which sets forth all the deadlines for submissions from the beginning to the end of the arbitration procedure. Both parties are conscious about time, especially during witness examination, with both parties having an equal, limited amount of time.

If one party is monochronic and the other is polychronic, it could be a cause of frustration on one party and end up in some type of dispute. If tribunal members are from monochronic cultures, the tribunal would not understand why one party continuously failed to meet a contractual deadline. For example, even if such party had tried to comply with the contractual deadline, its supplier or logistics company, which are also polychronic, may have failed to comply with the deadline.

3 Summary

Two witnesses who had exactly the same experience can give very different testimonies if they are from different cultural backgrounds. This is because verbal/non-verbal expression can vary significantly across cultures, and different cultural value patterns and communication patterns influence the witnesses' way of thinking and behaving.

A simple solution to avoid misunderstanding is to appoint arbitrator(s) from the same culture as the parties/witnesses. However, that is not always possible, because parties/witnesses could be from multiple cultural backgrounds. Moreover, this could create an unequal playing field if a party/witness is from the same cultural background as the tribunal members while the other party/witness is not, because the party/witness from the same cultural background with the tribunal would likely be better understood.[38]

Better yet is to have a tribunal consisting of arbitrators from different cultural backgrounds, i.e., three tribunal members from three different cultures. Studies in the context of the jury system have found, for example, that "*research indicates that when jurors of different ethnic groups deliberate together, they are better able to overcome their individual biases.*"[39] Similarly, the United States Supreme Court stated in *Taylor v. Louisiana* 419 U.S. 522, 532 (1975) that "*[t]he broad representative character of the jury should be maintained, partly as assurance of a diffused impartiality.*"

IV CONCLUSION

Dealing with cultural issues involves dealing with "unknown unknowns." In other words, we often do not know what we do not know about different cultures, whether legal, geographical, ethnic, or otherwise.

38. Won Kidane, "Does Cultural Diversity Improve or Hinder The Quality of Arbitral Justice?" *Kluwer Arbitration Blog* (2017).
39. *Id.*, Jeffrey Abramson, *We, The Jury: The Jury System and the Ideal of Democracy* (Basic Books: 1994) 104, citing social science studies.

In international arbitration where the rules and commonly accepted practice can be both flexible or strict, written or unwritten, such cultural differences have the potential to create a minefield leading to unintended misunderstandings.

In seeking to reduce cultural misunderstandings, we should be wary of and question whether the uniformization of the arbitral process is the one-size-fits-all solution. One of the commonly cited benefits of arbitration is its inherent flexibility in comparison to court litigation. While uniformization provides more predictability to the arbitral process and reduces the potential number of cultural misunderstandings, individually and collectively raising our awareness of the diversity of cultures within international arbitration, and how to address it effectively, allows us not only to serve our clients better but also to maximize the flexibility inherent in the arbitral process.

Moreover, the risk of misunderstandings arising from cultural differences—more significantly, their potential impact—is greater in an adversarial setting than in the business world. In commercial contexts, parties from different cultural backgrounds are generally incentivized to understand each other's cultural norms and communication styles to reach a mutually beneficial outcome. In contrast, adversarial parties often lack such incentives; instead, they may interpret the other side's behavior strictly through the lens of their own cultural expectations or, in some cases, intentionally misrepresent it before the arbitral tribunal to gain an advantage.

Where feasible, it is highly beneficial for the arbitral tribunal to include members from diverse cultural backgrounds. Likewise, counsel should consider collaborating with co-counsel familiar with the relevant cultural context. Such measures can help ensure a more nuanced understanding of how certain facts or pieces of evidence might be perceived differently across cultures.

Crucially, unlike in commercial dealings, the adversarial process may not afford the tribunal sufficient opportunity to become well acquainted with the parties and their respective cultural backgrounds—particularly given the tribunal's role and the need to maintain strict neutrality. Therefore, it is essential for both arbitral tribunals and counsel to approach proceedings with cultural awareness, open-mindedness, and intellectual curiosity, and to take proactive steps to identify and understand relevant cultural differences.

CHAPTER 42
Arbitration and Emotions: An Introduction

Prof. Giacomo Rojas Elgueta[*]

TABLE OF CONTENTS

I ARBITRATION AND PSYCHOLOGY

> "Deep below consciousness are other forces, the likes and the dislikes, the predilections and the prejudices, the complex of instincts and emotions and habits and convictions, which make the man, whether he be litigant or judge."[1]

In the last decades, behavioral sciences, and in particular cognitive psychology, has shown that, to simplify the most complex decision-making processes (e.g., the calculation of probabilities), individuals resort to a series of mental shortcuts (so-called *heuristics*) and are victims of pre-comprehension mechanisms (so-called *biases*), which can lead to cognitive errors (e.g., a distorted perception, an inaccurate judgment or an illogical interpretation).[2]

---

* Co-Head of Arbitration at Chiomenti and Associate Professor of Private Law at Roma Tre University School of Law.
1. *See* Benjamin N. Cardozo, *The Nature of the Judicial Process* (Yale University Press 1921) p. 107.
2. For an overview of the evolution of (and the results reached by) behavioral sciences, *see* Richard Thaler, *Misbehaving: The Making of Behavioral Economics* (W.W. Norton & Company 2015). The expression "cognitive errors" encompasses errors that fall into two sub-categories: heuristics and biases. On the notion of "heuristic," *see* Chris Guthrie, "Misjudging," 7 Nev. L.J. (2007) p. 428 ("Psychologists have discovered that people do not make decisions based on a thorough accounting and rational calculation of all available information. Rather than behaving like fully rational actors, people use 'heuristics' or simple mental shortcuts to make decisions. These

Empirical studies conducted by behavioral sciences have shed light on the fact that human decisions are the result of a complex interplay between two cognitive systems: System 1 and System 2.[3]

The "fast thinking" of System 1[4] tends to dominate the cognitive processes of individuals who, unconsciously, prefer to rely on the simplest and most intuitive answers, often stemming from the mechanical repetition of a deliberative process refined through experience.[5]

On the other hand, System 2 identifies deductive cognitive processes, guided by "slow thinking" which, contrary to the "fast" one, relies on effort, motivation, attention and application of knowledge.[6]

If System 1 allows individuals to decide rapidly and without effort, most often reaching the correct outcome (an outcome consistent with the assumptions of "rational choice theory"),[7] problems arise every time System 1 determines sub-optimal cognitive processes from which stem choices and decisions that deviate from the assumption of perfect rationality.[8]

---

heuristics often lead to good decisions, but they can also create cognitive blinders that produce systematic errors in decision making"). *See also* Robert Coulson, "The Decisionmaking Process in Arbitration," 45 Arb. J. (1990) p. 38 ("'Heuristic' is not a commonly used term: it describes how the human mind uses learning from experience to shortcut the need for seemingly unnecessary calculations or data gathering. Heuristic systems are internalized strategies, adopted for reasons of operating efficiency, facilitating the ability to make complex decisions quickly, based upon a limited amount of data. Usually, such techniques result in reasonably accurate decisions, particularly when the decision maker is operating from a base of extensive practical experience"). On the notion of "bias" *see* Cass R. Sunstein, *Behavioral Law and Economics* (Cambridge University Press 2000) p. 135 (biases are "aversions that can lead [people] to inaccurate perceptions of facts"). *See also* Amos Tversky and Daniel Kahneman, "Judgment under Uncertainty: Heuristics and Biases," 185 Science (1974) pp. 1127 f.

3. Among others, *see* Chris Guthrie, Jeffrey J. Rachlinski and Andrew J. Wistrich, "Blinking on the Bench: How Judges Decide Cases," 93 Cornell L. Rev. (2007) pp. 7-9.
4. This expression is now widely used thanks to the renowned book of Daniel Kahneman, *Thinking Fast and Slow* (Farrar, Straus and Giroux 2011).
5. *See* Guthrie, Rachlinski and Wistrich, "Blinking on the Bench," (n 3), p. 9; Robin M. Hogarth, *Educating Intuition* (University of Chicago Press 2001) pp. 14 and 22.
6. *See* Shane Frederick, "Cognitive Reflection and Decision Making," 19 J. Econ. Perspect. (2005) p. 26 https://doi.org/10.1257/089533005775196732 (accessed August 16, 2025).
7. "Rational choice theory" is the dominant theoretical paradigm in microeconomics, which assumes that individuals choose the action that will maximize their benefits and minimize their costs. *See* Milton Friedman, *Essays in Positive Economics* (University of Chicago Press 1953) p. 15; Richard Posner, *Economic Analysis of Law*, 5th ed. (Aspen 1998) p. 3; Thomas S. Ulen, "Rational Choice Theory in Law and Economics" in Boudwijn Bockaert and Gerrit De Geest, eds., *Encyclopedia of Law and Economics* (Edward Elgar 1999). For a critique of the "rational choice theory" *see* Martha C. Nussbaum, "Flawed Foundations: The Philosophical Critique of (a Particular Type of) Economics," 64 U. Chi. L. Rev. (1997) p. 1197 https://doi.org/10.2307/1600214 (accessed August 16, 2025).
8. In behavioral studies, cognitive deviations from an idealized concept of perfect rationality are also referred to as "bounded rationality." The expression "bounded rationality" has been first used by Herbert A. Simon, "Rational Choice and the Structure of the Environment" in *Models of Man: Social and Rational* (Wiley 1957) pp. 270-271.

Empirical evidence has also shown that some cognitive errors are a systematic phenomenon, which is therefore observable, measurable and, what is most important, predictable.[9]

It is because of the studies conducted by behavioral sciences that today jurists (and among them judges, arbitrators and lawyers) acquired a more complete awareness of the fact that, after all, they are human beings and, like all other human beings, they are exposed to systematic cognitive errors, resulting from the automatic activation of System 1.[10]

In the last decade, the international arbitration community has looked at the interplay between psychology and arbitration with great interest, and there is now widespread awareness that arbitration proceedings are not immune to cognitive errors.[11]

---

9. *See* Dan Ariely, *Predictably Irrational: The Hidden Forces That Shape our Decisions* (HarperCollins 2008); Guthrie, "Misjudging," (n 2), p. 421; Stavros Brekoulakis, "Systemic Bias and the Institution of International Arbitration: A New Approach to Arbitral Decision-Making," 4 J. Int'l Disp. Settlement (2013) p. 564 https://doi.org/10.1093/jnlids/idt016 (accessed August 16, 2025) ("For scholars taking an empirical approach to judicial decision-making, bias is an observable and measurable phenomenon, despite its abstract and latent nature").
10. *See* Rebecca K. Helm, Andrew J. Wistrich and Jeffrey J. Rachlinski, "Are Arbitrators Human?," 13 J. Empirical Legal Stud. (2016) pp. 686 f. https://doi.org/10.1111/jels.12129 (accessed August 16, 2025) ("These results show that arbitrators are not superior to judges in terms of their ability to avoid common cognitive errors in judgment. The arbitrators relied heavily on intuition to answer the CRT questions, overwhelmingly committed the conjunction fallacy, expressed large framing effects, and failed to respond well to the confirmation bias problems. Although in objective terms the arbitrators performed poorly on some of the experiments reported in this article, it is important to keep that in perspective. Their performance was no worse than, and in fact fairly typical of, judges and lawyers who responded to identical or similar problems and tests. Therefore, the proper conclusion is not that arbitrators are poor decisionmakers as measured by our experiments, but that they share the same susceptibility to cognitive illusions and excessive reliance on intuition that plague other experienced and accomplished professionals, such as judges and lawyers"). A similar conclusion has been reached by Joseph M. Matthews, "Identifying and Overcoming Arbitrator Bias," 5 Transnat'l Disp. Mgmt. (2008) available at https://www.transnational-dispute-management.com/article.asp?key=1289 (accessed April 1, 2024) p. 1 ("Lawyers, judges and even internationally famous arbitrators carry their own biases with them as they take on the task of resolving disputes between people or institutions. While we may be more educated and have a broader range of experiences than a typical domestic judge and certainly are more worldly-wise than the jurors who are entrusted under the U.S. system of justice with enormous responsibilities for resolving disputes, international arbitrators nonetheless are also human beings").
11. *See* Matthews, "Identifying and Overcoming Arbitrator Bias," (n 10); Richard C. Waites and James E. Lawrence, "Psychological Dynamics in International Arbitration Advocacy" in Doak Bishop and Edward G. Kehoe, eds., *The Art of Advocacy in International Arbitration*, 2nd edn. (Juris Net 2010) p. 69; Giacomo Rojas Elgueta, "Understanding Discovery in International Commercial Arbitration Through Behavioral Law and Economics: A Journey Inside the Minds of Parties and Arbitrators," 16 Harv. Negot. L. Rev. (2011) p. 165; Philip K. Anthony and Les J. Weinstein, "The Social Science Edge in Arbitration and Mediation," 5 N.Y. Disp. Res. Law. (2012) p. 17; James Freda, "Heuristics and Arbitral Decision-Making: A Brief Discussion on How Arbitrators Make Decisions," 15 Asian Disp. Rev. (2013) p. 50; Edna Sussman, "Arbitrator Decision Making: Unconscious Psychological Influences and What You Can Do About Them," 24 Am. Rev. Int'l Arb. (2013) p. 487 https://doi.org/10.54648/rba2014020 (accessed August 16, 2025); Brekoulakis, "Systemic Bias," (n 9), p. 553; Kristina Klykova, "Bias in Arbitral Decision-Making: Rescuing the Mentschikoff Archives from a Half Century of Oblivion," 31 J. Int'l Arb. (2014) p. 289 https://doi.org/10.54648/joia2014012 (accessed August 16, 2025); Edna Sussman, "The Arbitrator Survey: Practices, Preferences and Changes on the Horizon," 26 Am. Rev.

If cognitive psychology is extremely helpful in understanding parties, counsel and arbitrators' decision-making processes, it only does so from a *negative perspective* (i.e., by highlighting how cognitive errors can impair individual's rationality).

On the other hand, notwithstanding the interferences between law and emotions have been extensively studied in the last two decades, and have the potential to bring into the discourse a *positive perspective*, international arbitration scholarship has thus far neglected to recognize emotions as another fundamental component of the human mind.[12]

II LAW AND EMOTIONS

1 Introduction: "Law and Emotions" as an Emerging Field

Following the publication of the volume "The Passions of Law" in 2000,[13] several scholars from various fields have turned their attention to the issues that lie at the intersection of emotions and law, investigating the role that various emotions play in different legal domains.[14]

Int'l Arb. (2015), p. 517; Helm, Wistrich and Rachlinski, "Are Arbitrators Human?," (n 10), p. 666; Tony Cole, ed., *The Roles of Psychology in International Arbitration* (Kluwer Law International 2017); Stefano Azzali, Umberto Morera and Giacomo Rojas Elgueta, eds., *Errori cognitivi e arbitrato* (il Mulino 2018); Ziya Akinci, Umut Tuğa and Şeref C. Arat, eds., *The Psychology of the Arbitration Hearing*, Istanbul Arbitration Centre (ISTAC) Publications—3 (On Iki Levha Yayıncılık 2020).

12. *See* Terry A. Maroney, "Emotional Regulation and Judicial Behavior," 99 Cal. L. Rev. (2011) p. 1492 ("First, it begins to fill an important gap in research on the psychology of judicial decision making. Though such research has grown in scale and importance in recent decades, the failure to address questions of judicial emotion is perhaps its most conspicuous omission"); Susan A. Bandes and Jeremy A. Blumenthal, "Emotion and the Law," Ann. Rev. of Law Soc. Science (2012) pp. 165 f. ("The emotions of judges have generally received scant attention, which is unsurprising in light of the tenacity of the belief that the jurist must rise above particular influences to dispense blind justice. Recently, however, the emotional dynamics of judicial decision making have attracted substantial attention, prompted in part by controversy over the role of empathy in judging (Bandes 2009a, Abrams 2010, West 2012). Scholarship has focused both on how judges deliberate (see, e.g., Posner 2008) and on how the emotional dynamics of judicial deliberation affect judges (see, e.g., Maroney 2011b, discussing how judges do and should regulate their emotions)").
13. *See* Susan A. Bandes ed., *The Passions of Law* (NYU Press 2000); Vesselin Popovski, "Emotion and International Law," in Yohan Ariffin, Jean-Marc Coicaud and Vesselin Popovski, eds., *Emotions in International Politics: Beyond Mainstream International Relations* (Cambridge University Press 2015) p. 186 ("Susan Bandes in her edited book The Passions of Law (2001) raises some profound questions: What role do emotions, ranging from disgust to compassion, play in the decision-making process of judges, lawyers, juries and clients? Which emotions can be linked to which legal contexts? How can one estimate the role of emotion in death sentencing, in hate crime legislation, in punitive damages or shaming penalties? Bandes destroys the myth that emotions have no place in law and argues that emotions are rampant in law, and that they are often central to positive decision-making"). For an account of "law and emotions" scholarship, *see* Kathryn Abrams and Hila Keren, "Who's Afraid of Law and the Emotions'," 94 Minnesota L. Rev. (2010) pp. 2003 ff.
14. *See* Terry A. Maroney, "Law and Emotion: A Proposed Taxonomy of an Emerging Field," 30 Law Hum. Behav. (2006) pp. 119 ff. https://doi.org/10.1007/s10979-006-9029-9 (accessed August 16, 2025).

Scholars interested in the interplay between law and emotions engaged in offering both a descriptive and a normative analysis.

From a descriptive perspective, similarly to cognitive psychology, studies on law and emotions reject the assumption that individuals are pure rational actors and, by challenging the traditional dichotomy between reason and emotions, they explore how emotions and cognition interact.[15]

From a normative perspective, the scope of this scholarship is to identify what role emotions should have "in the identification and implementation of legal norms and in the deliberative process for juries, judges, and other legal actors."[16]

Even if in its early stages, "law and emotions" is a fast-developing field, now considered one of the several postmodern legal movements that uses theories of other fields (such as theories of economics, sociology, philosophy, anthropology and literary criticism) to shed light on the legal phenomenon.[17]

2 Defining "Emotions"

Before delving deeper into the matter, it is worth attempting to provide a definition of "emotions" (drawn by "law and emotions" scholarship).

Emotions are processes mapped in (and distributed throughout) the body and the brain that help individuals to appraise and respond to stimuli.[18]

While "feelings" (e.g., happiness and sadness) are conscious experiences triggered by emotions, "emotions" are unconscious phenomena that:

> [I]nfluence the way we screen, categorize, and interpret information; influence our evaluations of the intentions or credibility of others; and help us decide what is important or valuable. Perhaps most important, they drive us to care about the outcome of our decision making and motivate us to take action, or refrain from taking action, on the situations we evaluate. In short, the current consensus across disciplines is that emotions are not, as folk knowledge would have it, occasional, intense, unpredictable moods that interfere with a steady state of rationality. They are dynamic processes that are integral to decision making.[19]

15. *See* Robin West, "Law's Emotions," 19 Rich. Pub. Int. L. Rev. (2015) p. 340 ("The emerging interdisciplinary field of 'Law and Emotions' brings together scholars from law, psychology, classics, economics, literature and philosophy all of whom have a defining interest in law's various relations to our emotions and to emotional life: they share a passion for law's passions. They also share the critical premise, or assumption, that most legal scholars of at least the last half century, with a few exceptions, have mistakenly accorded too great of a role to reason, rationality, and the cool calculations of self interest, and have accorded too small a role to emotion, to the creation, the imagining, the generation, the interpretation, and the reception of law"); Bandes and Blumenthal, "Emotion and the Law," (n 12), p. 162.
16. *Ibid.*
17. On the expanding eclecticism of legal studies *see* Gary Minda, *Postmodern Legal Movements: Law and Jurisprudence at Century's End* (NYU Press 1995). On "law and emotions" as a fast-developing field, not well known by legal practitioners and scholars, *see* Moa Bladini and Stina Bergman Blix, "The Judge under Pressure: Fostering Objectivity by Abandoning the Myth of Dispassion," in Dimitrios Giannoulopoulos and Yvonne Mcdermott, eds., *Judicial Independence under Threat* (Oxford University Press 2022) pp. 223 ff.
18. *See* Maroney, "Law and Emotion," (n 14), p. 124.
19. *See* Bandes and Blumenthal, "Emotion and the Law," (n 12), pp. 163 f.

As highlighted in the early twentieth century by the "legal realism" approach (in particular by Benjamin Cardozo, Jerome Frank and Karl Llewelyn), being judges humans, it is undeniable that judges' emotions ("informed by early life experiences of love, need, fear, and human connection")[20] play a role in legal reasoning and judicial deliberation.[21]

Being now uncontroversial that, similarly to heuristics and biases, emotions are an integral part of the decision-making process,[22] the next question is whether emotions play a negative or positive role.

III EMOTIONS AND (ARBITRAL) DECISION-MAKING

1 Emotions as a Departure from Rationality: The Traditional View

> "We're not robots to listen to evidence and don't have feelings. We have to recognize those feelings and put them aside."[23]

President Obama's statement that he would appoint to the Supreme Court of the United States a candidate with "empathy" and a "sense of compassion" led to a spirited confirmation hearing of Sonia Sotomayor, which prompted Sotomayor to defuse the tension by affirming that a judge must put feelings aside.[24]

The way Sotomayor confirmation hearing unfolded is not surprising given that the traditional cultural script for "good judging" revolves around the myth of a dispassionate judge.[25]

Notwithstanding legal realists acknowledged the presence of judicial emotions, the enduring conventional view is that judges (and, by analogy, arbitrators) shall push back emotions, grow a rhino skin, and put a poker face.[26]

---

20. *See* West, "Law's Emotions," (n 15), p. 341.
21. *See* Maroney, "Emotional Regulation," (n 12), p. 1489 and p. 1497 ("Judge Posner, too, has acknowledged judges' emotional labor, asserting that 'it would be misleading to say that good judges are less "emotional" than other people. It is just that they deploy a different suite of emotions in their work from what is appropriate both in personal life and in other vocational settings'"). *See* Benjamin N. Cardozo, "Jurisprudence, Lecture Before the Association of the Bar of the City of New York," in *Selected Writings of Benjamin Cardozo* (Fallon Publications 1947); Jerome Frank, *Law and the Modern Mind* (Brentano's Publishers 1930); Karl Llewelyn, "Some Realism about Realism: Responding to Dean Pound," 44 Harv. L. Rev. (1931) https://doi.org/10.2307/1332182 (accessed August 16, 2025).
22. *See* Terry A. Maroney, "The Persistent Cultural Script of Judicial Dispassion," 99 Calif. L. Rev. (2011), p. 654 ("This fundamental realist point is encapsulated in Arthur Corbin's then-heretical assertion that judge-made law 'grows up in the semi-darkness of ignorance and emotion,' rather than 'in the strong light of pure reason'").
23. *See* transcripts of Sonia Sotomayor confirmation hearing as associate justice of the Supreme Court of the United States available at https://epic.org/wp-content/uploads/privacy/sotomayor/sotomoyor_transcript.pdf (accessed April 1, 2024).
24. On the Sotomayor confirmation hearing *see* Maroney, "The Persistent Cultural Script," (n 22), pp. 636 ff.
25. *See* Bladini and Bergman Blix, "The Judge under Pressure," (n 17), pp. 223 ff.; Maroney, "The Persistent Cultural Script," (n 22), pp. 636 ff.
26. *See* Maroney, "Emotional Regulation," (n 12), p. 1536 ("The standard account of emotionless judging does not exist in a vacuum; rather, it flows from a specific set of beliefs about emotion

This is so if one considers that the ideal of an emotionless judge has been purported since the Enlightenment and that, in the Western legal tradition, emotions have been traditionally perceived in a negative way, as the opposite of reason and potential sources of subjective and partial beliefs and irrational decisions.[27]

In other words, emotions, not differently from heuristics and biases, are usually viewed as a departure from rationality, a departure that must be acknowledged, controlled, and corrected.

2 Overcoming the Reason Versus Emotion Dichotomy

> "So, emotions are not just mindless, they embody thoughts. Therefore, we cannot dismiss them from judicial reasoning and writing just by opposing them in an unreflective way to reasoning and thought."[28]

Differently from the "behavioral law and economics" approach, which main normative goal is to correct heuristics and biases in order to restore a rational decision-making process, "law and emotions" scholarship has challenged the traditional assumption that emotions only translate into a departure from rationality, bringing into the legal discourse a positive dimension of emotions.[29]

itself, beliefs that motivate those who hold them toward emotional suppression. The underlying beliefs-which long have animated legal theory-are that emotion is stubborn and irrational, the necessary enemy of objectivity and reason. That simplistic view has, in popular culture, been slightly eroded by the emotional-intelligence construct, and it has been largely abandoned in the sciences. However, in Western legal culture it remains firmly entrenched. The crude view of the target encourages a commensurately crude view of the manner in which it should be confronted: as with an enemy in battle, emotion must be pushed back or eradicated"). *See also* Moa and Bergman Blix, "The Judge under Pressure," (n 17), p. 228.

27. *See* Bandes and Blumenthal, "Emotion and the Law," (n 12), p. 162; Bladini and Bergman Blix, "The Judge under Pressure," (n 17), p. 226; Maroney, "Emotional Regulation," (n 12), p. 1488 ("Yet legal accounts long have perpetuated the conception of the emotionless judge. This author previously has explored the depth and persistence of this cultural script of judicial dispassion. The idea that a good judge is able to insulate her decision making from any emotional influence is deeply rooted in European Enlightenment notions of rationality and objectivity, to which emotion was thought to be opposed. Indeed, in 1651, Thomas Hobbes declared that the ideal judge is 'divested of all fear, anger, hatred, love, and compassion.' This notion became so entrenched that, two and a half centuries later, a leading continental theorist pronounced such judicial dispassion to be a 'fundamental tenet of Western jurisprudence.' In the United States at the time of the Founding, emotionless judging was seen as part and parcel of the democratic structure itself: necessary to the process of taming the self-interested passions of the public").
28. *See* Martha C. Nussbaum, "Emotions in the Language of Judging," 70 St. John's Law Rev. (1996) p. 25.
29. *See* Popovski, "Emotion and International Law," (n 13), p. 184 ("The role of emotions in law-making may vary—some may regard emotions as corrupting the legal judgement; others, in total contrast, may regard emotions as being essentially constitutive elements of legal judgements. Psychologists, engaging in empirical research on political and legal developments, may emphasize the latter approach. Conservative legal scholars may defend the former and advocate purely non-emotional justice with eyes bound, holding a sword in one hand and a scale in the other hand—as often portrayed"). Abrams and Keren, "Who's Afraid of Law and the Emotions'," (n 13), p. 2000 ("But for those who are prepared to understand emotion not simply as a departure from rationality, but as an affirmative mode of apprehension and response, the law

As shown by empirical studies, while in some context, emotions can impair the legal decision-making process, "emotions must also be understood as a fundament of the human predisposition to act, as the fuel of action."[30]

As a famous case study reported by the neurologist Antonio Damasio demonstrates, individuals are not able to make decisions if they are not in contact with their emotions. Following a brain surgery where a small tumor had been removed from the patient's cortex (near the frontal lobe of his brain), the patient, notwithstanding his IQ had remained the same, was incapable of making even simple decisions (taking several hours for tasks that should have taken few minutes). This was so because the patient felt nothing.[31]

Scholarship focusing on the interplay between emotions and judging has highlighted that there are subtle emotions, so-called background emotions (e.g., pride) that, instead of disrupting actions and decision-making processes (as it is the case, for example, when we feel angry or are too nervous), cooperate with and enhance them:[32]

> Background emotions are thus necessary to rational action: they inform, guide and support one's focus, help to distinguish important from less important details and do so in a quicker way than a cognitive evaluation would. Hence, background emotions typically operate in knowledge seeking processes and are relevant in a discussion on legal decision-making.[33]

Among background emotions, a certain set of emotions called "epistemic emotions" are strictly related to legal decision-making and are of relevance for both judges and arbitrators. Feelings of certainty or uncertainty, curiosity, and epistemic anxiety guide individuals' attention over what to inquire about and affect the way they deliberate.

An arbitrator that does not *feel* committed, interested, or have no curiosity or pride in his/her task (in other words, an arbitrator who lacks epistemic emotions) will deliver a poor decision, failing to keep an open mind throughout the course of the arbitration.[34]

---

and emotions perspective offers a way by which legal actors and institutions can both accommodate and influence crucial dimensions of human experience").

30. *See* Bladini and Bergman Blix, "The Judge under Pressure," (n 17), p. 226, where the authors cite empirical research within social psychology related to jurors' emotions and police officers' emotions (and how sad officers are more thorough than angry officers in carrying out investigative activity).
31. *See* Jonah Lehrer, *How We Decide* (Houghton Mifflin 2009) pp. 13 ff. ("When he chose where to eat lunch, Elliot carefully considered each restaurant's menu, seating plan, and lighting scheme, and then drove to each place to see how busy it was. But [...] Elliot still couldn't decide where to eat [...] [W]hy was Elliot suddenly incapable of making good decisions? [...] Elliot felt nothing [...] He had an emotional life of a mannequin"). On Damasio's case study *see also* Jennifer K. Robbennolt and Jean R. Sternlight, *Psychology for Lawyers* (American Bar Association 2012) p. 47; Bladini and Bergman Blix, "The Judge under Pressure," (n 17), p. 227.
32. *See* Robbennolt and Sternlight, *Psychology for Lawyers* (n 31), p. 46; Bladini and Bergman Blix, "The Judge under Pressure," (n 17), pp. 229 s.
33. *See* Bladini and Bergman Blix, "The Judge under Pressure," (n 17), p. 230.
34. Stina Bergman Blix and Alessandra Minissale, "(Dis)passionate Law Stories: The Emotional Processes of Encoding Narratives in Court," 49 J.L. & Soc. (2022) p. 5 https://doi.org/10.1111/jols.12355 (accessed August 16, 2025).

To put it briefly, if individuals (and among them, arbitrators) are disconnected from their emotional dimension, they lose their ability to deliver good judging.

IV PERSUASION AND EMOTIONS IN AN ADVERSARIAL ENVIRONMENT

1 Two Paths of Persuasion

Models on persuasion (in particular, the "Elaboration likelihood Model" and the "Heuristic-Systematic Model") explain that people process new information in two different ways: (i) through a central route, or systematically, and (ii) through a peripherical route, or heuristically.[35]

While the activation of the central route translates into focusing on the strength and quality of the arguments (i.e., on their content), the peripheral route gives relevance to peripheral cues (e.g., an honorific title; where an expert earned his or her degree; whether the counsel is a well-known figure in the arbitration community; etc.).[36]

Individuals use both the central and peripheral routes in processing the available information, but, according to their preferences, tend to activate one more than the other.[37]

Given that arbitrators are no different, it is essential for counsel to understand decision-making processes and be aware that different emotions can activate, alternatively, arbitrators' central or peripheral routes.

2 Ease and Relief Versus Irritation and Frustration

Bearing in mind that arbitrators, as any other individual, "are limited in the amount of cognitive effort they can allocate to processing new information,"[38] counsel should carefully balance the activation of arbitrators' central route with the use of peripheral cues.

As shown in the research project *Justemotions* conducted, under the auspices of the *European Research Council*, by the sociologist Stina Bergman Blix,[39] judges tend to focus (an activity related to the central route) only on a limited number of "relevant issues."

35. *See* Leslie Ellis, "Inside the Black Box: How Psychology Informs the Arbitration Hearing," in Akinci, Tuğa and Arat, eds., *The Psychology of the Arbitration Hearing* (n 11), pp. 36 f.
36. *See* Robbennolt and Sternlight, *Psychology for Lawyers* (n 31), pp. 116 f.
37. *Ibid. See also* Paolo Marzolini, "A Shortcut to the Arbitrators' Mind," in Akinci, Tuğa and Arat, eds., *The Psychology of the Arbitration Hearing* (n 11), p. 130 and note 43.
38. *See* Leslie Ellis, "Inside the Black Box: How Psychology Informs the Arbitration Hearing," in Akinci, Tuğa and Arat, eds., *The Psychology of the Arbitration Hearing* (n 11), p. 36
39. The research project *Justemotions* studies the emotive-cognitive components of assessments in criminal cases through comparative sociological research. *See* https://www.soc.uu.se/research/justemotions/ (accessed April 1, 2024).

Presenting to the decision-maker only the right amount of details creates a sense of ease and relief, while providing the "full story" with too many irrelevant details risks to irritate and frustrates him/her (which, in turn, translate in losing his/her focus and impairing the rational comprehension of the party's case).[40]

Eliciting the arbitrators' emotions such as relief (or, as mentioned above, pride) help channeling arbitrators' feelings of interest and curiosity toward the relevant matters of the counsel's narrative.

3 Empathy and Emotional Attunement

Empathy, intended here as "the same emotion one perceives the other to be feeling"[41] or "emotional attunement,"[42] also plays an important role in evaluating stories.

Counsel in arbitration should favor an empathic perspective taking by the arbitrators, meaning that the arbitrators should be put in the position to "feel" the party's perspective.[43]

Empirical research shows that emotional attunement of the decision-maker is more easily achieved using epistemic emotions, and, in particular, by eliciting emotions of doubt and certainty on the respective parties' stories.[44]

In other words, decision-makers are better positioned to process information and feel more certain about their decisions (e.g., whether a witness is credible or not) when, through empathic imagination, they have attuned with the story of the party (or of the witness):[45]

> In judging, empathy might be used as a tool to understand parties and witnesses, to assess someone's credibility or the defendant's criminal intent. Apart from that, empathy might also serve as a means and approach to legitimate the procedure by treating the victims, witnesses and other persons involved in an empathetic way during the trial. Empathy thus has two crucial functions in a legal decision-making perspective: the first in the knowledge-seeking process, and the second in the process of legitimation of the judiciary.[46]

40. *See* Bergman Blix and Minissale, "(Dis)passionate Law Stories," (n 34), pp. 12 f. ("In James' (and Judge Lydia's) understanding, emotions of ease and relief do not threaten rational adjudication but rather promote it. Judge Lydia is careful to stress that her ease does not come at the expense of the defendant (articulating this potential worry with a lowered voice); on the contrary, she believes that the demarcated and fragmented story helped the court to make a decision ('easier to grasp the case')").
41. *See* Maroney, "The Persistent Cultural Script," (n 22), p. 637.
42. *See* Bergman Blix and Minissale, "(Dis)passionate Law Stories," (n 34), p. 6.
43. *Ibid.*
44. *See* Natalia Ruiz-Junco, "Advancing the Sociology of Empathy: A Proposal," 40 Symbolic Interaction (2017) pp. 414 ff. https://doi.org/10.1002/symb.306 (accessed August 16, 2025); Alessandra Minissale, "Il percorso emotivo-cognitivo verso la decisione oggettiva," Riv. Trim. Dir. Proc. Civ. (2022) pp. 797 ff.
45. *See* Minissale, "Il percorso emotivo-cognitivo," (n 44), p. 801.
46. *See* Bladini and Bergman Blix, "The Judge under Pressure," (n 17), p. 232.

CHAPTER 43

Practical Guidance on Working in and Through an Adversarial Environment Using Counselling Concepts and Methods

*Emi Rowse (Igusa)**

TABLE OF CONTENTS

I INTRODUCTION

It is generally accepted that the international arbitration process can be fraught with challenges and stress. This leads to an adversarial environment for all involved, including the arbitrators, practitioners, parties and clients. The adversarial nature of arbitration proceedings can cause significant challenges, often escalating tensions and hindering constructive dialogue.

Legal arguments and evidence clearly play a crucial role in arbitration – however, at its core, arbitration should be a process of solving a disagreement between people by helping them agree to an acceptable solution. As such, the human elements –

* Emi Rowse (Igusa) is a partner in the Litigation and Arbitration team at Kudun and Partners in Thailand. Emi also holds a Master's in Counselling and offered mental health support to individuals across age groups as a counsellor between 2018 and 2022.

emotions, communication dynamics and psychological factors – also play an active role in influencing the outcome of an arbitration. This chapter will address these questions and show the positive interplay between psychology, counselling and the arbitral process.

In addition, a growing and concerning factor that arises as a result of working in an adversarial environment, particularly in the legal profession, is the lack of regard for the human condition and human fallibility. This has given rise to a generation of arbitration practitioners and counsel who are 'perfectionists' or experiencing 'imposter syndrome', which eventually leads to anxiety and burnout.

This chapter therefore also addresses the common issues faced by arbitration practitioners working in an adversarial environment, practical ways in which practitioners can overcome perfectionism and imposter syndrome and possible solutions for the arbitral community to create a healthier and more inclusive environment.

II FACTORS THAT CREATE AN ADVERSARIAL ENVIRONMENT IN INTERNATIONAL ARBITRATION

1 Dynamics of Conflict Escalation

Resorting to arbitration (or any dispute resolution mechanism) is often the last resort for parties. Most parties will not feel excited or joyful at the prospect of starting an arbitration, simply because it often signifies that a problem exists, there are conflicting interests or points of views, and it cannot be solved by negotiations.

According to Friedrich Glasl, there are nine stages of conflict escalation[1] and the deeper you go into the conflict, the less humane the methods become.[2] These nine stages are divided into three levels, and while parties are in the first level (tension, debate, actions instead of words), it is still possible for the parties to resolve a conflict without damage, and the conflict may result in a 'win-win' situation. However, in the second level (coalitions, loss of face and threat strategies), the conflict may still be resolved, but result in a 'win-lose' situation (where one party wins but the other party loses). In the third level (limited destruction, total annihilation and together into the abyss), both parties will find themselves in a 'lose-lose' situation.

In an arbitration, it is likely that most parties who commence an arbitration are at the cusp of level 1 and level 2. As the arbitration progresses, the parties descend deeper into level 2 and if the matter is not handled effectively, end up in level 3.

The arbitration process itself can also escalate conflict due to its adversarial nature. Arbitration proceedings can be very competitive, encouraging parties to present the strongest case and therefore undermine the other side's arguments. Tensions can also rise over disagreements on evidentiary issues, challenges to arbitrators, witness and/or expert credibility and interpretation of applicable laws.

1. Thomas Jordan, 'Glasl's Nine-Stage Model of Conflict Escalation' https://www.law.uh.edu/blakely/advocacy-survey/Conflict%20Escalation%20Glasl.pdf (accessed 16 August 2025).
2. https://dieprojektmanager.com/9-stages-of-conflict-escalation-according-to-friedrich-glasl/ (accessed 16 August 2025).

2 Emotional Triggers and Reactions

Conflict always involves many emotions. According to American psychologist Dr Robert Plutchik, there are eight primary emotions that are foundational to other emotions. The eight emotions are joy, sadness, acceptance, disgust, fear, anger, surprise and anticipation. In any given conflict, the primary emotions that may be prevalent include disgust, fear, anger and surprise.[3] During arbitration proceedings, we often see many of these primary emotions, as well as combinations of primary emotions identified as secondary dyads which include guilt (joy and fear) and despair (fear and sadness). One could say arbitration is an emotional rollercoaster, which can also contribute to an adversarial environment.

3 Stakes Involved for Parties, Counsel and Arbitrators

As arbitration tends to be the last resort for many parties, by the time a conflict reaches this stage, the stakes are high for the parties involved. The outcome of arbitration can have significant consequences, which may impact the parties' financial positions, their business operations, and it may even signify an end to business relationships. Therefore, this tension contributes to the adversarial environment of arbitration.

For counsel representing the parties, the pressure to bring about a successful outcome for their clients is significant. Their professional reputation is at stake, and winning a case means further work in the future.

Similarly, for arbitrators, the stakes are high as they have to render an enforceable award and maintain their reputation within the arbitration community to be nominated as arbitrator in future cases.

III PSYCHOLOGICAL IMPACT ON ARBITRATION PRACTITIONERS, TRIBUNAL AND WITNESSES

1 Stress, Anxiety and Pressure

Given the high stakes involved in arbitration proceedings, this field often leads to stress, anxiety and pressure for all stakeholders.

When supporting people with anxiety, counsellors will often refer to the concept of the 'circle of control'. There are three circles to consider: the Circle of Control, the Circle of Influence and the Circle of Concern. This first circle consists of things you can control, such as your thoughts, words, actions and behaviour, mindset and decisions. The second circle is your Circle of Influence, which includes factors you can influence, such as other people's feelings or actions and certain outcomes of your actions (e.g., whether you win a sports game or whether your business succeeds). Unlike your Circle of Control, the factors in your Circle of Influence are not directly controllable by you, but are affected or influenced by what you control. Finally, there is the Circle of

3. https://www.6seconds.org/2022/03/13/plutchik-wheel-emotions/ (accessed 16 August 2025).

Concern. In this circle, there are factors in our lives that we cannot really control, such as natural disasters, pandemics, news and the economy.[4]

Certain processes in arbitration proceedings enable the parties to have an element of control, such as the ability to choose their arbitrator(s), the seat and place of the arbitration and which arbitral institution will administer the arbitration. Party autonomy is a significant factor in international arbitration, and this enables the parties to bring matters within their circle of control, thereby helping them psychologically to gain confidence and security in the process.

However, there are still matters that are outside the parties' control and within the circle of concern which can cause significant stress. Examples include an arbitrator's unavailability or sickness, the political climate or regulatory changes at the seat of the arbitration.

For witnesses, there is a huge psychological impact, particularly for those who are not familiar with the arbitration process. Being a witness in arbitration proceedings can bring about uncertainty and unpredictability (both triggers for stress and anxiety). The witnesses may feel anxious during cross-examination, and in addition, there is enormous pressure to perform well to support a party's case.

Finally, for the tribunal, stress and anxiety can be triggered when there are challenges to their appointment, when their award is set aside or challenged by the parties, and from the pressure involved in rendering an enforceable award.

2 Cognitive Biases and Decision-Making in Arbitration

Cognitive biases are inevitable in human beings and have a huge impact on arbitration proceedings. They have an impact on arbitrators, whose cognitive biases will inform his/her decision-making, and on counsel, who may be led by his/her cognitive biases in making decisions on which evidence or witnesses to rely on that could have an impact on their strategy for the case. Even parties themselves will have cognitive biases which will guide their decisions on which arbitrator and counsel to appoint and which witnesses to rely on to support their position.

The cognitive biases that are often referred to in arbitration are: (a) confirmation bias; (b) anchoring bias; and (c) hindsight bias.

a Confirmation Bias

People may be subject to confirmation bias when they search for information that confirms their preexisting beliefs and disregard contradictory evidence. In the context of international arbitration, this is generally seen when arbitrators, counsel and parties selectively choose evidence or arguments that support their positions and do not pay enough attention to contradictory evidence or evidence that may weaken their position. This bias can therefore have the effect of narrowing the perspective of the

4. https://www.inhousecommunity.com/article/international-arbitration-and-the-circle-of-control/ (accessed 16 August 2025).

arbitrator/counsel/
parties, making them susceptible to a surprise challenge.

b *Anchoring Bias*

This bias happens when someone relies heavily on the first information with which they are provided and uses that as an anchor on which to base their subsequent decisions. For example, if an arbitrator or party is presented with a certain figure as the claim or settlement amount, that figure would be the reference point against which the arbitrator or party will consider other figures that are presented. This could clearly affect the outcome of the quantum of a claim or settlement negotiations.

c *Hindsight Bias*

At some level, hindsight bias is inevitable in arbitration proceedings as the arbitrators and counsel are required to always review evidence after the relevant event and with the benefit of hindsight. As Lucy Reed says: 'the inherent nature of the decision-making process means that hindsight bias can never be fully eliminated'.[5]

Therefore, even a brief exploration of a sample of biases shows how cognitive biases are rampant in arbitration as it involves decision-making, not only for arbitrators but also counsel when evaluating and presenting their cases. This psychological element can influence arbitrators and counsel in a significant way. The only way to deal with and address these biases is to first recognise they exist, acknowledge the impact they have on the adversarial nature of arbitration, and then find ways to tackle them.

3 Effects of Emotions in Arbitrations

A diverse range of emotions are prevalent in arbitration proceedings.

As mentioned above, the emotions triggered in conflict can contribute and lead to an adversarial environment. Furthermore, if emotions such as fear, anger and disappointment are not managed effectively during arbitration proceedings, this could have serious implications on the performance of a witness, counsel and arbitrator, which in turn can have an impact on the outcome of the case.

Emotions that are involved in negotiations can also have a direct impact on the effectiveness of such negotiations. For example, if the party enters into negotiations in fear or anger, the negotiations may end prematurely and/or lead to more distrust between the parties. Conversely, if the party feels hopeful or empathetic towards the other party, then it is likely that the negotiations will have a very different tone and outcome.

5. Lucy Reed, 'The Kaplan Lecture 2012 Arbitral Decision-Making: Art, Science or Sport?' https://cdn.arbitration-icca.org/s3fs-public/document/media_document/media113581569903770reed_tribunal_decision-making.pdf (accessed 16 August 2025).

As described by Kelly and Kaminskiene, 'simply put, the fundamental basis of negotiation and mediation practice is not merely the cognitive analysis of competing interests and the rational development of the most efficient outcome, but also the acknowledgment of the underlying emotional factors at play'.[6]

IV COUNSELLING CONCEPTS AND METHODS THAT CAN BE APPLIED

1 Emotional Intelligence in Arbitration

In light of the importance of emotions in contributing to the adversarial nature of arbitration as well as the potential outcome of the case, it is crucial for all stakeholders in arbitration to have emotional intelligence.

Emotional intelligence has been defined as 'the capacity for recognising our own feelings and those of others, for motivating ourselves, and for managing emotions well in ourselves and in our relationships'.[7] According to Bradberry and Greaves,[8] there are four core EQ skills that are needed to demonstrate emotional intelligence: (1) self-awareness; (2) self-management; (3) social awareness; and (4) relationship management.

Self-awareness is a critical concept in the counselling setting. In helping clients improve their mental well-being, counsellors will often ask questions that will help the client recognise the underlying issues that are troubling the client to improve his/her self-awareness. This is often the first step that a counselling client will need to take in order to start on their journey of recovery.

Similarly, in arbitration proceedings, it is essential for parties, counsel and arbitrators to be self-aware of their emotions, to be able to identify those emotions, and to understand how the emotions can impact their decision-making.

The second EQ skill is self-management, which is the ability to manage one's emotions once the need to do so has been identified and the individual has been made aware. It could be seen as a form of emotional regulation, or being able to exert control over one's emotional state. Emotional regulation is a common issue with children and adolescents, and if they are not taught to regulate their emotions at a young age, they will continue to fail to self-manage or self-regulate or regulate their emotions in unhealthy ways as adults (by use or abuse of alcohol or drugs, violence against others, self-harm and/or eating disorders).

Within the arbitration context, if a counsel, witness or arbitrator is unable to manage his/her emotions, such as anger or fear, this could lead to a disruption of the

6. Edward J. Kelly and Natalija Kaminskiene, 'Importance of Emotional Intelligence in Negotiation and Mediation', 2(1) International Comparative Jurisprudence (2016) 55-60 https://doi.org/10.1016/j.icj.2016.07.001 and https://www.sciencedirect.com/science/article/pii/S2351667416300130 (accessed 16 August 2025).
7. Daniel Bowling and David Hoffman, 'Bringing Peace into the Room: The Personal Qualities of the Mediator and Their Impact on the Mediation', 16(1) Negotiation Journal (2007) 5-28 https://doi.org/10.1111/j.1571-9979.2000.tb00199.x (accessed 16 August 2025).
8. Travis Bradberry and Jean Greaves, *Emotional Intelligence 2.0.* (TalentSmart, 2009).

proceedings, cause tension between those involved and may have a negative impact on the arbitration. On the other hand, if the stakeholders are able to regulate and manage their emotions during arbitration proceedings, this would generally lead to more effective and productive proceedings.

The third EQ skill is social awareness, which includes the ability to be aware of others' emotions and to be able to empathise with them. Empathy is a powerful tool to connect to people, which is often ignored or underestimated in the professional context. However, without empathy, arbitrators will not be able to understand the parties' true positions and may not be able to evaluate the evidence from an unbiased perspective. Similarly, counsel would not be able to understand their clients' position to enable them to represent their clients well or reach a successful settlement.

The final core EQ skill is relationship management. This appears to be the combination of the other core EQ skills to manage relationships with others. Kelly and Kaminskiene identify four skills of an emotionally intelligent mediator (which can apply equally to an arbitrator): 'the ability to identify one's own emotions and those of others; the ability to harness emotions and apply them to tasks such as thinking and problem solving; the ability to manage emotions, including the ability to regulate the negotiator's or mediator's own emotions, and the ability to effect the emotions of the others in the negotiation'.[9]

Possessing these four core EQ skills will enable the arbitrator/mediator/counsel/parties to understand not only the role of their own emotions in the arbitral process but also that of others, to try and achieve a successful outcome for all stakeholders.

2 Effective Communication Techniques

a The Four Horsemen and the Apocalypse and Their Antidotes

Dr John Gottman, an internationally renowned marriage counsellor, has identified four types of communication styles that are detrimental to relationship known as the 'Four Horsemen and the Apocalypse'. The Four Horsemen are: criticism, contempt, defensiveness and stonewalling.

Criticism refers to attacking or putting down a person's character, rather than complaining about a specific issue or type of behaviour. Contempt is where the other person is treated with disrespect, for example, mocked with sarcasm or ridicule, calling of names or usage of non-verbal cues such as eye-rolling. The third Horsemen is defensiveness, where someone responds to a criticism defensively by making excuses, blaming circumstances or other people. The final Horsemen is stonewalling, which is where the listener withdraws from the interaction and shuts down, ignores the other person and goes into denial.[10]

9. *See* (n 7), pp. 57-58.
10. Ellie Lisitsa, 'The Four Horsemen: Criticism, Contempt, Defensiveness, and Stonewalling' https://www.gottman.com/blog/the-four-horsemen-recognizing-criticism-contempt-defensiveness-and-stonewalling/ (accessed 16 August 2025).

For each of these negative communication styles, there are also antidotes.[11] Taking criticism first, the antidote is to have a gentle start-up using an 'I' statement that expresses one's feelings instead of attacking the other by using a 'you' statement. By focusing on one's feelings, it removes the focus on the other's fault and removes the blame element from the conversation.

The antidote for the second Horsemen, contempt, is to build a culture of appreciation and respect. This can be done by expressing appreciation and respect for the other person and focusing on their positive qualities as opposed to their negative ones.

For the third Horsemen (defensiveness), the antidote is to take responsibility. By taking responsibility, or even part of the responsibility, this could help diffuse a conflict as it moves the shift from blaming others to focusing on what one can do within its control to help the situation.

The antidote to the final Horsemen, stonewalling, is physiological self-soothing. By this, the arguing parties should take a physical break from each other to find ways to calm down (whether by drinking water, eating, reading, listening to music or anything else that may distract them) and then resume their conversations.

Whilst the concept of the Four Horsemen and the antidotes are primarily targeted at couples and personal relationships, the negative communication styles and strategies to overcome them are equally applicable in the arbitration setting, particularly when witnesses are giving evidence (as they may become defensive or resort to stonewalling), where counsel adopts guerilla tactics and in the absence of civility during the adversarial process. It is also highly relevant to understand the communication styles and antidotes in the context of negotiations, mediations and settlement talks, where it may be necessary to identify the communication style of the parties and find the antidotes to try and reduce tension to reach an amicable conclusion.

b *Active Listening and Empathetic Listening*

Active listening involves more than just removing your distractions and listening to the other person. According to Abrahams and Groysberg, it involves three aspects: cognitive, emotional and behavioural. To engage the cognitive aspect, one must pay attention to all the information, both explicit and implicit, that one receives from the other person. The emotional aspect involves staying calm and compassionate during the conversation, managing emotional reactions that may arise. Finally, the behavioural aspect involves communicating one's interest and understanding of what one heard.[12]

Some practical techniques for active listening include: being fully present, paying attention to non-verbal cues, keeping good eye contact, asking open-ended questions,

11. The Gottman Institute, 'The Four Horsemen: The Antidotes' https://www.gottman.com/blog/the-four-horsemen-the-antidotes/ (accessed 16 August 2025).
12. Robin Abrahams and Boris Groysberg, 'How to Become a Better Listener' (Harvard Business Review, 21 December 2021) https://hbr.org/2021/12/how-to-become-a-better-listener (accessed 16 August 2025).

reflecting what you hear, being patient and withholding judgment.[13] As noted by Kelly and Kaminskiene, 'listening is key to negotiation effectiveness. Too often in negotiation and mediation we "listen" to the words and fail to see the verbal language, the cultural context, the hidden meanings, the levels of emphasis of the various parties sometimes including even our own clients'.[14] Interestingly, they explain that the Chinese character for 'listen' includes the characters for ears, eyes, undivided attention, heart and you.[15] Therefore, active listening is key to ensuring that the speaker feels valued and properly heard, which in turn will enhance communication between every relationship in the arbitral process.

How is empathetic listening different from active listening? Empathetic listening is similar to active listening; however, the former puts a special emphasis on understanding the other's emotional experience and thereby builds a stronger relationship between the parties. It involves understanding the emotions and meaning behind what people are saying and not saying, which enables the speaker to feel truly heard and accepted.[16] In light of the emotions involved in arbitration and mediation, it would be wise to explore using empathetic listening in arbitration and mediation proceedings.

c *Assertive Communication*

Whilst listening actively or empathetically will certainly assist the speaker in feeling heard and valued, it is also important for those involved in the arbitral process to learn to speak effectively and in a way that reduces the stress often encountered in the adversarial process.

There are five communication styles that are often referred to: (1) aggressive; (2) passive; (3) passive-aggressive; (4) manipulative; and (5) assertive. The aggressive communicator speaks in an intimidating way, is hostile and argumentative, and uses aggressive body language such as hitting tables, showing their dissatisfaction overtly and intruding in people's personal spaces. The passive communicator is the opposite of an aggressive communicator, who is often quiet, fails to share their opinion and follows what other people are saying. The passive-aggressive communicator is someone who appears passive externally, but internally harbours anger which may manifest itself in back-stabbing, gossip and the use of patronising language. The manipulative communicator is one who tries to get his/her way through manipulation. Finally, the assertive communicator is the ideal communicator, as he/she will state his/her views clearly, without being aggressive or rude, actively listens to the others and will not allow their

13. Arlin Cunicic, '7 Active Listening Techniques for Better Communication' (Verwell Mind, 12 February 2024) https://www.verywellmind.com/what-is-active-listening-3024343#toc-7-active-listening-techniques (accessed 16 August 2025).
14. *See* (n 7) p. 59.
15. *Ibid.*
16. Kendra Cherry, 'How Empathetic Listening Can Build Deeper Connections in Your Life' (Verwell Mind, 20 February 2024) https://www.verywellmind.com/how-to-try-empathic-listening-8357721 (accessed 16 August 2025).

own emotions to control them.[17] They often use 'I' statements to communicate their feelings without making excuses and blaming others.

In arbitration, one often sees all of these communication styles: the aggressive counsel in cross-examination, the passive witness, the passive-aggressive or manipulative counterparty. The more assertive communication is encouraged in the process, the more likely the process will become less adversarial.

V TACKLING THE 'ADVERSITY' WITHIN: ADDRESSING PERFECTIONISM AND IMPOSTER SYNDROME FOR ARBITRATION PRACTITIONERS IN THE ADVERSARIAL PROCESS

1 What Is 'Perfectionism' and 'Imposter Syndrome'

The terms 'perfectionism' and 'imposter syndrome' are often used to describe legal practitioners. Given the competitiveness of the legal industry and constant pressure to perform at an excellent level all the time, it is not surprising that the industry is filled with perfectionists and those who experience imposter syndrome. The problem is exacerbated by the deluge of social media posts by colleagues and friends who frequently post about the latest deal they completed, event they spoke at or award they won.

According to a mental health survey conducted on the legal profession in the United States, about 71% of the 3,000 lawyers surveyed in 2023 said they had anxiety, and 38% said they had depression. More than half of the lawyers said they felt a sense of failure or self-doubt.[18]

Perfectionism is defined by psychologists as 'the tendency to demand of others or of oneself an extremely high or even flawless level of performance, in excess of what is required by the situation. It is associated with depression, anxiety, eating disorders, and other mental health problems'.[19]

In addition to the pressure of increasing billable hours, working in a highly competitive market, lack of sleep or quality time to spend with loved ones, there is also the significant challenge of stigma attached to seeking help. Lawyers often state that asking for work-life balance or going on holiday may hinder their chances of getting a job, staying in a job or getting a promotion. This drives people to continue to perform at a high level constantly without getting the rest or mental health support that they need.

---

17. Shefali Lohia, 'The 5 Communication Styles and How to Use Them Effectively' (The Predictive Index) https://www.predictiveindex.com/blog/the-5-communication-styles-and-how-to-use-them-effectively/ (accessed 16 August 2025).
18. Amanda Robert, 'Mental Health Initiatives Aren't Curbing Lawyer Stress and Anxiety, New Study Shows' ABA Journal (2023) https://www.abajournal.com/news/article/mental-health-initiatives-arent-curbing-lawyer-stress-and-anxiety-new-study-shows (accessed 16 August 2025).
19. American Psychological Association (2018) https://dictionary.apa.org/perfectionism (accessed 16 August 2025).

Imposter syndrome (also referred to as imposter phenomenon) is an equally prevalent problem for executives, particularly women. A KPMG poll and report found that 75% of female executives across industries have experienced imposter syndrome in their careers.[20] In the legal profession, 74% of lawyers and 83% of junior lawyers said they had experienced imposter syndrome in their careers.[21]

Imposter syndrome has been defined as 'a persistent inability to believe one's success is deserved or achieved by working hard and possessing distinct skills and capabilities, but by other means such as luck or being at the right place at the right time. It is often accompanied with feelings of self-doubt, fear or success of failure, or self-sabotage'.[22]

Both perfectionism and imposter syndrome cannot be ignored. They are both rooted in fear and hinder one's ability to try new things, challenge oneself, make decisions and reach one's full potential. When ignored or not managed well, they can also lead to mental disorders such as anxiety and depression.

2 Practical Methods to Support Arbitration Practitioners Experiencing Perfectionism and Imposter Syndrome

a Recognising and Sharing the Issue

The first step in overcoming perfectionism and imposter syndrome is to recognise the signs and acknowledge that there is an issue.

Perfectionists tend to have an 'all-or-nothing' mindset and may set unrealistic or achievable goals for themselves. They may be highly critical of themselves, and even when they achieve a goal, they will not take time to celebrate or find themselves picking on their mistakes. They also often only focus on results, and may often be weighed down by the fear of failure which can result in procrastination.[23]

Some common signs of imposter syndrome include thinking you got lucky with your promotion, you are not good enough to be assigned your position, a tendency to keep checking your work, believing that you must work harder than others for recognition, comparing yourself to others and believing they are better than you.[24]

20. Advancing the future of women in business – the 2020 KPMG Women's Leadership Summit Report (2020) https://info.kpmg.us/news-perspectives/people-culture/kpmg-study-finds-most-female-executives-experience-imposter-syndrome.html (accessed 16 August 2025).
21. Peter Ryding, 'Imposter Syndrome and How It Impacts Your Career Success' (May 2020) https://www.lawyer-monthly.com/2020/05/impostor-syndrome-and-how-it-impacts-your-career-success/ (accessed 16 August 2025).
22. *See* (n 21).
23. Elizabeth Scott, 'Perfectionism: 10 Signs of Perfectionist Traits' (Verywell Mind, February 2023) https://www.verywellmind.com/signs-you-may-be-a-perfectionist-3145233#toc-signs-of-perfectionism (accessed 16 August 2025).
24. Anita Gohil-Thorp, 'Breaking the Stigma: Understanding and Overcoming Imposter Syndrome in the Legal Profession' (LawCare) https://www.lawcare.org.uk/get-information/articles/breaking-the-stigma-understanding-and-overcoming-imposter-syndrome-in-the-legal-profession/? (accessed 16 August 2025).

Sharing the issue with trusted others can help reduce any misconceptions and can counter the feeling of isolation and stigma. When shared, the community should take concerns seriously and find practical ways to raise awareness and create a safe support network and environment for those experiencing these feelings.

b *Challenging Unrealistic Standards: Set SMART Goals*

As many people who experience perfectionism and imposter syndrome are high achievers and may set unrealistic standards for themselves, one way to overcome the issue is to examine the standards imposed and set more realistic goals.

One very effective way of setting a goal is to ensure it is a SMART goal – Specific, Measurable, Achievable, Relevant and Time-Bound. The specific criterion ensures that the goal is not too broad, simple, but with enough details to make it easy to understand what is trying to be achieved. Measurable usually involves a numerical element, to ensure the goal can be measured at different stages. Achievable ensures that the goal is realistic and the question of relevance of the goal is tied to the goal-makers' values, mission and resources. Finally, the goal maker should ensure that there is a timeframe within the goal to make sure it is achieved by a certain date.[25]

c *Developing a Growth Mindset*

According to Carol Dweck, a growth mindset is where 'people believe that their most basic abilities can be developed through dedication and hard work – brains and talent are just the starting point. This view creates a love of learning and a resilience that is essential for great accomplishment'.[26] This is to be compared with someone who has a fixed mindset, who believes that intelligence or talent are fixed traits. Therefore, someone with a growth mindset will see every challenge or mistake as a learning opportunity, and this will also build resilience.

As perfectionists and those experiencing imposter syndrome will often blame themselves for their mistakes or have a fear of failing and making mistakes, having a growth mindset would help them reframe their thinking regarding making mistakes and failures.

d *Challenging Negative Automatic Thoughts*

There is a relationship between our thoughts, feelings and actions and one therapeutic intervention that utilises this relationship is known as Cognitive Behavioural Therapy (CBT). CBT treatment includes helping the client recognise their negative automatic thoughts and distorted thinking patterns and helping them re-evaluate those thoughts

25. 'SMART Goals' https://www.mindtools.com/a4wo118/smart-goals (accessed 16 August 2025).
26. Renaissance 'What Is a Growth Mindset?' https://www.renaissance.com/edword/growth-mindset/#:~:text=Growth%20mindset%3A%20%E2%80%9CIn%20a%20growth,Dweck%2C%202015 (accessed 16 August 2025).

in light of reality. By changing the negative thoughts, this will have an impact on the client's feelings as well as his/her behaviour.[27]

In the case of perfectionists and imposter syndrome, they are constantly battling with thoughts such as 'I am not good enough', 'If I fail, people will think differently of me', 'I don't think I can do this', 'I am incompetent and people will find out'. Therefore, challenging such negative thoughts and reframing them in light of examples from reality would be an effective way to overcome perfectionism and imposter syndrome. There are case studies which demonstrate the efficacy of CBT for perfectionism[28] and imposter phenomenon.[29]

e Setting Boundaries

Boundaries in the psychological context mean 'a psychological demarcation that protects the integrity of an individual or group or that helps the person or group set realistic limits on participation in a relationship or activity'.[30]

Perfectionists are not very good at setting boundaries as their desire to produce high-quality work and please others usually outweigh the need to set clear boundaries on what is and not acceptable to them. For example, perfectionists may not be able to set boundaries with the amount of work they agree to take on and when they work (not being able to say 'no').

Setting boundaries can be empowering as it enables us to take back control over our time, relationships and well-being to make them more aligned with our values. Doing so enables us to feel more empowered and in control of our lives, which reinforces the benefits of focusing on what is within our circle of control. Some practical ways to set boundaries include determining your top priorities in work and life, identifying your hard and soft boundaries and putting them into practice.[31] In the work and business context, setting and communicating your boundaries may mean confronting people, which is where assertive communication skills would be helpful to avoid ruining relationships and causing resentment.[32] If you have communicated your boundaries and nothing changes, then it may be time to reconsider whether your work environment is a good fit for you.

---

27. 'Overview: Cognitive Behavioural Therapy (CBT)' https://www.nhs.uk/mental-health/talking-therapies-medicine-treatments/talking-therapies-and-counselling/cognitive-behavioural-therapy-cbt/overview/ (accessed 16 August 2025).
28. Alexander Rozental, 'Beyond Perfect? A Case Illustration of Working with Perfectionism Using Cognitive Behaviour Therapy' 76(11) Journal of Clinical Psychology (2020) pp. 2041-2054 https://doi.org/10.1002/jclp.23039 (accessed 16 August 2025).
29. Holly Hutchins and Jennifer Flores, 'Don't Believe Everything You Think: Applying Cognitive Processing Therapy Intervention to Disrupting Imposter Phenomenon' 33(4) New Horizons in Adult Education and Huma Resource Development (2021) pp. 33-47.
30. American Psychological Association (2018) https://dictionary.apa.org/boundary (accessed 16 August 2025).
31. Joe Sanok, 'A Guide to Setting Better Boundaries' (Harvard Business Review, April 2022) https://hbr.org/2022/04/a-guide-to-setting-better-boundaries (accessed 16 August 2025).
32. Dr Henry Cloud, 'Setting Boundaries at Work' (February 2022) https://www.boundariesbooks.com/blogs/boundaries-blog/setting-boundaries-at-work (accessed 16 August 2025).

f What Can the Arbitral Community Do?

Whilst perfectionism and imposter syndrome are often considered to be individualistic conditions, they cannot be ignored as an individual's problem. The environment and culture of the organisation or the arbitral community in general could contribute to, or exacerbate the problem. For example, through lack of appreciation of the individual, ignoring the signs of perfectionism and imposter syndrome, and prevalent biases and prejudices that are excused on the basis that 'this is the way it's always been done'.

What can the arbitral community and firms that engage arbitration practitioners do? The first step would be to educate and raise awareness of the problem within the community and organisations. There should be training and events to talk about what the signs are, how they can be managed or addressed, and to remove misconceptions surrounding them. Such training and education should aim to remove any stigma, biases or prejudices associated with perfectionism, imposter syndrome and/or any other mental health issues that many people face. Second, the community and organisations should implement policies to create a support network for those struggling (and ensure there are no adverse consequences as a result). Instead of shaming anyone who speaks up, they should be celebrated. Examples of a support network could include assigning mentors, regular check-ins from colleagues, and granting access to a mental health counsellor. Third, the leadership should intentionally take time to value and appreciate the individual's progress, and when mistakes are made, accept that we are all fallible and encourage the individual to learn from them and develop a growth mindset. Finally, the community and organisations should implement policies to encourage individuals to assess and prioritise their values and set boundaries. The leadership should have people in place to be role models for junior associates and foster an environment that promotes assertive communication and encourages people to set their boundaries.

VI CONCLUSION

Examining the dynamics of conflict escalation, emotional triggers and the stakes involved in an arbitration, it is unsurprising that arbitration creates and contributes to an adversarial environment. Understanding the breadth and depth of psychological impact an arbitration can have on the practitioners, tribunal and witnesses, including stress and anxiety relating to the process, cognitive biases in decision-making and effects of emotions in arbitrations, deepens our knowledge and awareness of the human element of arbitration. With this knowledge, it is imperative that the arbitration community and stakeholders shift their attention to how to effectively conduct and manage arbitrations, bearing the psychological impacts in mind and adopting counselling techniques in their interactions with others. This can be achieved through enhancing our emotional intelligence in arbitration (through self-awareness, self-management, social awareness and relationship management), understanding effective communication techniques in a conflict setting (bearing in mind the Four

Horsemen and the antidotes), learning active listening/empathetic listening and adopting assertive communication.

In addition to addressing the issues relating to working in an adversarial environment, it is important to focus on the internal adversity experienced by many legal practitioners, namely, perfectionism and imposter syndrome. There are some practical ways to overcome these challenges, such as speaking up, setting SMART goals, developing a growth mindset, challenging negative thoughts and setting boundaries. The arbitral community can also provide support by recognising the signs in those in their care, educating, providing training and creating a support network, showing appreciation and value, celebrating those who speak up assertively and encouraging people to develop a growth mindset and set boundaries.

Needless to say, arbitration involves conflicts, and some level of adversarial environment is inevitable. However, there are many practical ways we can reduce the stress and anxiety within the adversarial environment, at both the corporate and individual levels. It's time that we pay attention to the human and psychological elements of arbitration so that we don't merely survive but thrive in adversarial environments.

PANEL 14

Costs and Economics

Costs are an essential consideration in every arbitration. Commercial arbitrations are increasingly criticised for being too costly, with serious access to justice implications for all but the largest private and public entities. The panel discusses the costs incurred by the parties to an arbitration at various stages of the proceedings, security for costs applications, the barriers for impecunious parties, and the impact that third-party funding might have on these issues (and recent legislative developments).

Chapter 44

Access to Arbitral Justice and Costs in International Commercial Arbitration

Prof. Dr. Crina Baltag[*]

TABLE OF CONTENTS

I INTRODUCTION

Sixty-seven per cent of the respondents to the 2018 White & Case and Queen Mary University of London Survey have identified costs as the worst characteristic of international arbitration.[1] The finding is in line with the previous Surveys conducted by Queen Mary University of London.[2]

It is undoubtful that the issue of costs in international arbitration continues to remain a topic of discussion in the context of legitimacy of international arbitration.[3]

* Dr Crina Baltag is Associate Professor in International Arbitration and Dispute Resolution at Queen Mary University of London, arbitrator and legal expert, attorney-at-law, Managing Editor of Kluwer Arbitration Blog and on the editorial board of numerous publications in the field.

1. 2018 White & Case and Queen Mary University of London Survey: The Evolution of International Arbitration, 7-8, available at https://arbitration.qmul.ac.uk/research/2018/, last visited 15 March 2024.
2. Available at https://arbitration.qmul.ac.uk/research/, last visited 15 March 2024.
3. *See* as also identified by the UNCITRAL Working Group III on the Investor-State Dispute Settlement Reform.

However, the focus appears to be exclusively on the quantum of costs,[4] coupled with the procedural tools available to reduce costs and increase efficiency.[5]

This chapter points out that costs are primarily an issue of access to arbitral justice,[6] which, in turn, is directly linked to the legitimate expectations of the parties in and from the arbitral process. Ensured access to arbitral justice endorses the legitimacy of arbitration as a dispute resolution mechanism and, by way of consequence, the rule of law.

While the quantum of costs is an element to be addressed in the context of access to arbitral justice, several other concerns related to costs may impact such right. Of these, the recoverability of the costs of arbitration, and in particular of those other than the arbitrators' and institutions' fees. A proper insight into the matter of recoverability of costs necessarily includes an assessment of access to justice and reflects upon the principles of proportionality and/or compensatory role of costs of arbitration. Another such concern identified by the author, and which will be addressed in this chapter, refers to the procedural tools related to costs, and which may be restricting access to arbitral justice. From these procedural tools, security for costs against a party asserting a claim or a counterclaim appears to be the most intrusive one, with critical consequences on the party's fundamental right of access to justice. The chapter begins by discussing access to justice from costs' perspective, while taking into account the specific nature of the arbitration agreement, and then moving to addressing the security for costs measure from an access to justice perspective.

II EQUAL (AND FINANCIAL) ACCESS TO JUSTICE

When referring to the notion of 'justice', we tend to associate it with the idea of one's rights being recognized and enforced. In this sense, the notion of 'justice' is rather one of 'substantive justice', on the merits of what it is claimed. However, before even accessing substantive justice, one must have the right to 'formal justice' guaranteed, i.e., access to courts or to other means of recognizing and enforcing substantive rights. The legitimate expectations of the users are satisfied, and the rule of law is preserved if formal justice exists in any given society.

---

4. *See* the 2006 PwC and Queen Mary University of London Survey: Corporate Attitudes and Practices, 19, available at https://arbitration.qmul.ac.uk/media/arbitration/docs/IAstudy_2006.pdf, last visited 15 March 2024. Pursuant to the Survey, 65% of the respondents perceive international arbitration to be more expensive than transnational litigation. *See also*, Mohamed S. Abdel Wahab, *Costs in International Arbitration: Navigating Through the Devil's Sea*, in Jean Engelmayer Kalicki and Mohamed Abdel Raouf (eds), *ICCA Congress Series No. 20 (Sydney 2018): Evolution and Adaptation: The Future of International Arbitration* (ICCA & Kluwer Law International 2019), 466.
5. *See* 2021 White & Case and Queen Mary University of London Survey: Adapting Arbitration to a Changing World, 13, available at https://arbitration.qmul.ac.uk/media/arbitration/docs/LON0320037-QMUL-International-Arbitration-Survey-2021_19_WEB.pdf, last visited 15 March 2024.
6. *See* broadly on access to justice and arbitration, Leonardo V.P. de Oliveira and Sara Hourani (eds), *Access to Justice in Arbitration: Concept, Context and Practice* (Kluwer Law International 2020),

Paterson explains that the phrase 'access to justice' can be traced back to the nineteenth century; however, as a concept, it only came into frequent use in the 1970s.[7] Citing Roger Smith, Paterson explains that while the phrase 'access to justice' seems to be well accepted, it remains rather vague and 'denotes something which is clearly – like the rule of law – a good thing and impossible to argue you are against'.[8] Access to justice as a concept, while it may lack clarity,[9] undisputedly encompasses both formal and substantive justice, as indicated above. Cornford confirms that access to justice denotes the 'general subject of the extent to which citizens are able to gain access to the legal services necessary to protect and vindicate their legal rights'.[10]

However, access to justice, understood as the 'most basic "human right" – of a modern, egalitarian legal system',[11] should rather be properly framed as equal access to justice, since under the rule of law, 'each individual's case is worthy of equal consideration'.[12] This is confirmed by Article 8 of the Universal Declaration of Human Rights,[13] referring to everyone's 'right to an effective remedy by the competent national tribunals for acts violating the fundamental rights granted him by the constitution or by law'. Similarly, this is conveyed by Article 6(1) of the European Convention on Human Rights, proclaiming the right to a fair trial and which holds that 'everyone is entitled to a fair and public hearing within a reasonable time by an independent and impartial tribunal established by law'.[14]

And while the idea of justice is in stark contrast with the perception that something can be bought or sold,[15] costs are an essential element in the access to justice.[16] While institutions and adjudicators, as well as rules of procedure, may be efficiently designed by a State, access to them necessarily entails monetary expenditures. Certainly, any user will aim at securing a favourable result in the most efficient manner, by employing minimum costs and time.

That (equal) access to justice is intrinsically linked to the costs of formal justice was confirmed in the UK in the context of the civil litigation reform under Lord Woolf. The Final Report of Lord Woolf indicated that in order for the civil justice system to ensure access to justice, a review was needed into why it was too expensive, among

7. A. Paterson, *Lawyers and the Public Good: Democracy in Action?* (The Hamlyn Lectures) (Cambridge University Press, 2011), 60.
8. A. Paterson, *Lawyers and the Public Good: Democracy in Action?* (The Hamlyn Lectures) (Cambridge University Press, 2011), 60.
9. Tom Cornford, *The Meaning of Access to Justice*, 28.
10. Tom Cornford, *The Meaning of Access to Justice*, in Ellie Palmer et al. (eds), *Access to Justice: Beyond the Policies and Politics of Austerity* (Hart Publishing, 2018), 28.
11. Mauro Cappelletti and Bryant Garth (eds), *Access to Justice, Volume I: A World Survey* (Giuffrè Editore/Sijthoff/Noordhoff, 1978-1979), 7, cited in Tom Cornford, *The Meaning of Access to Justice*, 31.
12. Tom Cornford, *The Meaning of Access to Justice*, 29.
13. Available at https://www.un.org/sites/un2.un.org/files/2021/03/udhr.pdf, last visited 15 March 2024.
14. European Convention on Human Rights, Rome, 4 November 1950, UNTS vol. 213, 221.
15. Albert Weale, p. 51.
16. *See* Mauro Cappelletti and Bryant Garth, Access to Justice: The Newest Wave in the Worldwide Movement to Make Rights Effective, 27 Buffalo Law Review (1978), 181, 186-196, confirming that costs is one of the barriers to access to justice.

others.[17] Soon after the Lord Woolf Reforms, Lord Justice Jackson was entrusted with the Review of Civil Litigation Costs in the UK. The objective of the reform was '[t]o carry out an independent review of the rules and principles governing the costs of civil litigations and to make recommendations in order to promote access to justice at proportionate cost'.[18] In this context, Lord Justice Jackson effectively summarized the relevance of costs within the broader concept of access to justice:

> Access to justice entails that those with meritorious claims (whether or not ultimately successful) are able to bring those claims before the courts for judicial resolution or post-issue settlement, as the case may be. It also entails that those with meritorious defences (whether or not ultimately successful) are able to put those defences before the courts for judicial resolution or, alternatively, settlement based upon the merits of the case.
>
> Access to justice is only possible if both parties have adequate funding. If neither party has adequate funding, the litigation will not happen. If only one party has adequate funding, the litigation will be a walk over.
>
> Proportionate costs make access to justice practicable. Access to justice is only practicable if the costs of litigation are proportionate. If costs are disproportionate, then even a well-resourced party may hesitate before pursuing a valid claim or maintaining a valid defence. That party may simply drop a good claim or capitulate to a weak claim, as the case may be.[19]

---

17. The Woolf Reforms and the Civil Procedure Rules 1996, Chapter 7, 2-4 available at https://webarchive.nationalarchives.gov.uk/ukgwa/20060213223540/http://www.dca.gov.uk/civil/final/contents.htm, last visited 15 March 2024:

    2. Costs are a significant problem because:
       (a) litigation is so expensive that the majority of the public cannot afford it unless they receive financial assistance;
       (b) the costs incurred in the course of litigation are out of proportion to the issues involved; and
       (c) the costs are uncertain in amount so that the parties have difficulty in predicting what their ultimate liability might be if the action is lost.
    3. The adverse consequences which flow from the problems in relation to costs contaminate the whole civil justice system. Fear of costs deters some litigants from litigating when they would otherwise be entitled to do so and compels other litigants to settle their claims when they have no wish to do so. It enables the more powerful litigant to take unfair advantage of the weaker litigant. The scale of costs per case has an adverse effect on the scope of the legal aid system. It also adversely affects the reputation of our civil justice system abroad and may be making this country less attractive for overseas investment and as a forum for the settlement of commercial disputes. …
    4. Costs are also of great importance to my Inquiry because the ability of the court to make orders as to costs is the most significant and regularly used sanction available. The court's power to make appropriate orders as to costs can deter litigants from behaving improperly or unreasonably and encourages them to behave responsibly. Cost orders can also have a salutary effect on members of the legal profession.

    See also, Stephen Cragg, *Lord Woolf and JR*, 1(4) Judicial Review (1996), 236-239 https://doi.org/10.1080/10854681.1996.11426908, last visited 16 August 2025; Harry Woolf, *Civil Justice in the United Kingdom*, 45(4) The American Journal of Comparative Law (1997), 709-736 https://doi.org/10.2307/841013, last visited 16 August 2025.
18. Lord Justice Jackson, *Review of Civil Litigation Costs: Final Report*, December 2009, 2, available at https://www.judiciary.uk/wp-content/uploads/JCO/Documents/Reports/jackson-final-report-140110.pdf, last visited 15 March 2024.
19. Lord Justice Jackson, *Review of Civil Litigation Costs: Final Report*, paras 2.3-2.5, 41.

III ACCESS TO ARBITRAL JUSTICE AND THE ARBITRATION AGREEMENT

Having established that an important component of equal access to justice is the financial access to justice, mainly from the perspective of a formal justice, it is important to determine whether (equal) access to justice bears any significant variations in the specific context of international arbitration.[20] Is (financial) access to arbitral justice to be considered differently? Would the characteristics of arbitration compel distinct considerations when guarantees for access to justice are addressed?

Undoubtedly, the existence of an arbitration agreement, as the basis of the arbitral proceedings and of the arbitral tribunal's mandate, particularizes the analysis. While the flexibility of the arbitral proceedings and the parties' autonomy may be in stark contrast with the rigid court proceedings, due process is strictly enforced in arbitration, as well. Nonetheless, arbitration is the result of a binding arbitration agreement between the parties, which compels them to submit their dispute to arbitral justice and, therefore, seek substantive redress in this procedure only. Unless the arbitration agreement is 'null and void, inoperative or incapable of being performed',[21] parties to the arbitration agreement have made a valid exclusion of any other resolution mechanism, including court litigation. This may be coupled with the perception that international arbitration may be reserved to corporations, and the idea of a financial impossibility to proceed with the arbitral justice would be strange in such a business-to-business environment.[22] However, the absence of a system of legal aid,[23] or of an ex officio/court-appointed lawyer in international arbitration, places an onerous burden on the parties bound by an arbitration agreement,[24] but which find themselves in a

20. For a thorough discussion on the topic, *see* Leonardo V.P. de Oliveira, *To What Degree Should Access to Justice Be Secured in Arbitration*, in Leonardo V. P. de Oliveira and Sara Hourani (eds), *Access to Justice in Arbitration: Concept, Context and Practice* (Kluwer Law International 2020), 7-34.
21. United Nations Convention on the Recognition and Enforcement of Foreign Arbitral Awards (New York, 10 June 1958), United Nations, Treaty Series, vol. 330, 3, Article II.3.
22. The ICC Court of Arbitration recent statistics reveal that the disputes submitted to arbitration are usually of an average amount of USD 54 million, with the median approximately USD 6 million. *See* 2020 ICC Dispute Resolution Statistics, ICC, 2021. The 2020 Statistics report the following:

> Over 50% of the cases filed in 2020 and 50% of the pending cases at the end of 2020 had an amount in dispute between US$ 1 million and US$ 30 million. The average amount in dispute in cases filed during 2020 was US$ 54 million, with the median being close to US$ 6 million. The aggregate value of all pending disputes at the end of 2020 was US$ 258 billion, with an average value of US$ 145 million and a median value of US$ 10 million. With regard to lower-value disputes, 38% of cases registered involved an amount in dispute not exceeding US$ 3 million, the new threshold amount in dispute for the automatic application of the expedited procedure applicable to arbitration agreements concluded on or after 1 January 2021.

23. Although, generally in litigation legal aid is reserved only for natural persons. *See*, for example, Sweden Legal Aid Act (1996:1619), where monetary legal aid is reserved for natural persons, while legal advice up to two hours may be received by both natural persons and legal entities.
24. *See* Georg Von Segesser, *Inoperability of Arbitration Agreements due to Lack of Funds? Revisiting Legal Aid in International Arbitration*, Kluwer Arbitration Blog, 17 January 2015, available at

precarious financial situation or in an impossibility to honour the significant costs of an arbitration.

The validity of an arbitration agreement in the presence of an impecunious party has been addressed by courts, including in the context of access to justice. For instance, in *Uber Technologies Inc. v. Heller,*[25] the Canadian Supreme Court was faced with the question whether the arbitration agreement contained in the service agreement between an Uber driver and Uber, and which provided for an ICC Court of Arbitration agreement was valid or not. The Court noted that the filing fees of USD 14,500 reflected most of the claimant's annual income.[26] The Court, by applying the doctrine of unconscionability, found the arbitration agreement invalid since there was 'clearly inequality of bargaining power between Uber and Mr. Heller'.[27] In fact, the Court emphasized that there was 'a significant gulf in sophistication between Mr. Heller, a food delivery man in Toronto, and Uber, a large multinational corporation'.[28] Brown J's concurring opinion focused on the invalidity of an arbitration agreement, rather on its unconscionability. He approached this from the perspective of the agreement being contrary to public policy when financial requirements prevent a party from espousing its rights. Brown J concluded that this goes against 'the rule of law by denying access to justice', which 'is a precondition not only to a functioning democracy but also to a vibrant economy, in part because access to justice allows contracting parties to enforce their agreements'.[29] In *Pirelli c/ Licensing Projects,*[30] the court litigation related to an underlying ICC Court of Arbitration in which Licensing Projects, in liquidation, submitted a counterclaim against Pirelli, for which it failed to pay its advance on costs. Pursuant to the ICC Arbitration Rules, the ICC arbitral tribunal treated the counterclaim as withdrawn. The arbitral award was annulled by the Paris Court of Appeal on the ground that Licensing Projects was denied equal treatment and access to justice in violation of international public policy.[31] The French Court of Cassation reversed the decision of the Paris Court of Appeal, finding that while considering the counterclaims as withdrawn might qualify as denial of justice, this could only be sustained in cases in which counterclaims were indissociable from the main claims. In *Lola Fleurs v. Société*

http://arbitrationblog.kluwerarbitration.com/2015/01/17/inoperability-of-arbitration-agreements-due-to-lack-of-funds-revisiting-legal-aid-in-international-arbitration/, last visited 15 March 2024.

25. *Uber Technologies Inc., et al. v. David Heller,* 26 June 2020, 2020 SCC 16, available at https://decisions.scc-csc.ca/scc-csc/scc-csc/en/item/18406/index.do, last visited 15 March 2024.
26. *Uber Technologies Inc., et al. v. David Heller,* para. 2.
27. *Uber Technologies Inc., et al. v. David Heller,* para. 93.
28. *Uber Technologies Inc., et al. v. David Heller,* para. 2.
29. *Uber Technologies Inc., et al. v. David Heller,* para. 112.
30. *Pirelli c/ Licensing Projects,* Cour de cassation, Chambre civile 1, 28 March 2013, 11-27.770, available at https://www.legifrance.gouv.fr/juri/id/JURITEXT000027251564, last visited 15 March 2024.
31. Société Licensing Projects SL contre Société Pirelli and C Spa et al., Cour d'appel de Paris, Arrêt du 17 Novembre 2011, 30(2) ASA Bulletin, pp. 459-466.

Monceau Fleurs et Autres,[32] the Paris Court of Appeal held that 'the manifestly inapplicable character of the arbitration clause cannot be deduced from the alleged incapacity of LOLA FLEURS to face the cost of such a procedure because of its financial situation and the resulting denial of justice'. Similarly, before the English courts, the validity of the arbitration agreement in the context of costs of arbitration was resolved in favour of the agreement of the parties to arbitrate. For instance, in *El Nasharty v. J. Sainsbury Plc*, Justice Tomlinson considered that while a 'party who agrees to arbitrate is unlikely to have access to any form of public funding to assist him in defraying the cost of arbitration', 'the costs rules of the ICC pursue the legitimate aim of ensuring that arbitrators are properly remunerated and that the administrative expenses of the ICC are paid'.[33] Earlier, in *Paczy v. Haendler & Natermann*,[34] the English Court of Appeal held that a 'plaintiff cannot rely on his own inability to carry out his part of the arbitration agreement as a means of securing a release from the arbitration agreement' and that '[t]he arbitration agreement remains an agreement which is perfectly capable of being performed if the parties are themselves capable of performing it'.[35] The court stressed that in deciding so, it understands that 'legal aid unfortunately is not available in arbitration proceedings',[36] and that provisions of section 1(1) of the then 1975 English Arbitration Act are mandatory in obliging the courts to stay any court litigation in the presence of an arbitration agreement, unless they find the agreement to be null and void, inoperative or incapable of being performed, among others.[37]

An important takeaway from these cases reflects the general approach that courts favour the validity and performance of the arbitration agreement where concerns arise as to the impossibility of payments on advances on costs on claims and counterclaims. This may be a cause of concern, as impecunious parties would have no alternative to accessing justice, given the contractual commitment to arbitration. This was emphasized in *Paczy v. Haendler & Natermann*.

---

32. *SARL Lola Fleurs v. Société Monceau Fleurs et Autres*, Court of Appeal of Paris, N° 12/12953, 26 February 2013, available at https://icsid.worldbank.org/sites/default/files/parties_publications/C8394/Claimants%27%20documents/CL%20-%20Exhibits/CL-0388.pdf, last visited 15 March 2024.
33. *El Nasharty v. J. Sainsbury Plc* [2007] EWHC 2618 (Comm) (13 November 2007), para. 34, available at http://www.bailii.org/ew/cases/EWHC/Comm/2007/2618.html, last visited 15 March 2024
34. *Janos Paczy v. Haendler & Natermann GmbH*, Court of Appeal, 3 and 4 December 1980, Lloyd's Law Reports [1981] vol. 1, 302-308.
35. *Paczy v. Haendler & Natermann, 308.*
36. *Paczy v. Haendler & Natermann, 309.*
37. *Paczy v. Haendler & Natermann, 309.*
    Section 1(1) provided that:

    > If any party to an arbitration agreement to which this section applies, or any person claiming through or under him, commences any legal proceedings in any court against any other party to the agreement, or any person claiming through or under him, in respect of any matter agreed to be referred, any party to the proceedings may at any time after appearance, and before delivering any pleadings or taking any other steps in the proceedings, apply to the court to stay the proceedings; and the court, unless satisfied that the arbitration agreement is null and void, inoperative or incapable of being performed or that there is not in fact any dispute between the parties with regard to the matter agreed to be referred, shall make an order staying the proceedings.

Moreover, the absence of monetary legal aid in arbitration,[38] may prevent a party not only from commencing arbitration, but also from continuing arbitration where proceedings extend beyond the original procedural calendar, or when respondent refuses to pay its share of advances on costs and the impecunious claimant has to pay that share, or when respondent requests the arbitral tribunal to order the claimant to provide adequate security for adverse costs.[39]

IV SECURITY FOR COSTS AND ACCESS TO ARBITRAL JUSTICE

Access to arbitral justice may be restricted in the course of the arbitration proceedings by arbitral tribunals allowing parties to successfully employ certain procedural tools with impact on costs. Zuckerman recalls Lord Woolf's observation that the concern with costs hindering access to justice may be found in the way procedure is carried out, and, in particular, that 'the source of the problem is to be found in the proliferation of "adversarial tactics" which have resulted in the procedural tools "being subverted from their proper purpose"'.[40]

In the past years, several institutional arbitration rules have incorporated the specific regulation of the 'security for costs' measure for adverse costs in the event the claimant or the counterclaimant fails to succeed in the arbitration. Request for security for costs is usually brought against impecunious or insolvent claimants with or without third-party funding and typically ordered in the form of a bank guarantee or a deposit into an escrow account.

In arbitration proceedings in which the applicable arbitration rules do not provide for specific provisions for security for costs measures, as is, for example, the ICC Arbitration Rules,[41] parties have relied on the general provision on interim or provisional measures in requesting such measures.[42] However, this approach must be considered with caution. For example, until the 2017 version of the SCC Arbitration Rules in which a specific provision on security for costs has been incorporated, and despite the broad wording of the provision on interim measures allowing 'for wider

38. Third-party funding may be the closest one can come to a somewhat form of legal aid in arbitration. Arbitration institutions may also consider alternatives to the actual payment of such advances – *see* for example, Article 51(5) of the 2023 SCC Arbitration Rules providing that the SCC Board 'may decide that part of the advance on costs may be provided in the form of a bank guarantee or other form of security.'
39. Arguably, the discussion should also reflect, from the perspective of costs, the benefits of encouraging appropriate early dismissal requests to prevent unmeritorious claims from triggering the costs and time, burdening the responding party.
40. Interim Report to the Lord Chancellor on the civil justice system in England and Wales, 1995, cited in Adrian A.S. Zuckerman, *Reform in the Shadow of Lawyers' Interests*, in A.A.S. Zuckerman and Ross Cranston (eds), *Reform of Civil Procedure. Essays on 'Access to Justice'* (Oxford University Press, 1996), 61.
41. Similarly, in ICSID arbitrations before the enactment of the 2022 ICSID Arbitration Rules, specifically including a provision dedicated to security for costs.
42. *See* ICC awards considered in Samaa A.F. Haridi, *Security for Costs and Claim under the ICC Rules of Arbitration: Rare, but Possible – A Survey of 23 ICC Procedural Orders and Final Awards*, ICC Dispute Resolution Bulletin 2020 No. 2.

discretion of the arbitral tribunal with respect to ordering different types of interim measures',[43] arbitral tribunals were not empowered to grant security for costs.

Institutional rules generally highlight the exceptional character of the security for costs measures, while providing the arbitrators with a non-exhaustive list of elements which should be taken into account when ordering security for costs. For instance, Article 38 of the 2023 SCC Arbitration Rules provides that the *arbitral tribunal* 'may, in exceptional circumstances and at the request of a party, order any claimant or counterclaimant to provide security for costs', and, in doing so, it shall have regard to: '(i) the prospects of success of the claims, counterclaims and defences; (ii) the claimant's or counterclaimant's ability to comply with an adverse costs award and the availability of assets for enforcement of an adverse costs award; (iii) whether it is appropriate in all the circumstances of the case to order one party to provide security; and (iv) any other relevant circumstances'.[44] Similarly, Rule 53 of the ICSID Arbitration Rules provides that the arbitral tribunal, in granting security for costs, 'shall consider all relevant circumstances, including: (a) that party's ability to comply with an adverse decision on costs; (b) that party's willingness to comply with an adverse decision on costs; (c) the effect that providing security for costs may have on that party's ability to pursue its claim or counterclaim; and (d) the conduct of the parties'.[45] In contrast,

---

43. Johan Sidklev, *Security for Costs in the SCC Rules*, in Sherlin Tung et al. (eds), *Finances in International Arbitration: Liber Amicorum Patricia Shaughnessy* (Kluwer Law International 2019), 437-446, at 439.
44. *See* Article 38 of the SCC Arbitration Rules:

    (1) The Arbitral Tribunal may, in exceptional circumstances and at the request of a party, order any claimant or counterclaimant to provide security for costs in any manner the Arbitral Tribunal deems appropriate.
    (2) In determining whether to order security for costs, the Arbitral Tribunal shall have regard to:
        (i) the prospects of success of the claims, counterclaims and defences;
        (ii) the claimant's or counterclaimant's ability to comply with an adverse costs award and the availability of assets for enforcement of an adverse costs award;
        (iii) whether it is appropriate in all the circumstances of the case to order one party to provide security; and
        (iv) any other relevant circumstances.
    (3) If a party fails to comply with an order to provide security for costs, the Arbitral Tribunal may stay or terminate the proceedings in whole or in part.
    (4) Any decision to stay or to terminate the proceedings in whole or in part shall take the form of an order or an award.

45. Among others, Rule 53 provides that:

    (1) Upon request of a party, the Tribunal may order any party asserting a claim or counterclaim to provide security for costs.(1) ...
    (3) In determining whether to order a party to provide security for costs, the Tribunal shall consider all relevant circumstances, including:
        (a) that party's ability to comply with an adverse decision on costs;
        (b) that party's willingness to comply with an adverse decision on costs;
        (c) the effect that providing security for costs may have on that party's ability to pursue its claim or counterclaim; and
        (d) the conduct of the parties.
    (4) The Tribunal shall consider all evidence adduced in relation to the circumstances in paragraph (3), including the existence of third-party funding.
    (5) The Tribunal shall specify any relevant terms in an order to provide security for costs and shall fix a time limit for compliance with the order.

Article 25.2 of the 2020 LCIA Arbitration Rules leaves the decision on security for costs to the discretion of the arbitral tribunal, without providing guidance – except for ensuring that due process is followed – as to what considerations the tribunal should take into account when ordering the measure:[46]

> Increasingly, also by being regulated in separate provisions, as it is the case of Article 37 of the 2023 SCC Arbitration Rules, Article 25.2 of the 2020 LCIA Arbitration Rules, and of Rule 53 of the 2022 ICSID Arbitration Rules,[47] security for costs measure is recognized as being a distinct form of interim measures. This should be so given the exceptional character of the measure. Article 37 of the 2023 SCC Arbitration Rules refers to the possibility for an arbitral tribunal to order security for costs 'in exceptional circumstances', while Rule 53(3)(c) of the 2022 ICSID Arbitration Rules reflects this exceptional character in directing the arbitral tribunal to consider 'the effect that providing security for costs may have on that party's ability to pursue its claim or counterclaim'.

Such exceptional character of the security for costs measure stems from the fact that it not only adds an additional financial burden on the claimant but it also inherently restricts access to arbitral justice where the party against whom the measure was ordered is in the impossibility to post the security because of its impecuniosity or insolvency. Where the claimant fails to comply with the order of the arbitral tribunal, the arbitration proceedings are stayed or terminated. For instance, pursuant to Article 38(3) of the 2023 SCC Arbitration Rules and Article 25.2 of the 2020 LCIA Arbitration Rules, if a party fails to comply with an order to provide security for costs, the tribunal may stay or terminate the proceedings in whole or in part. Similarly, under Rule 53(6) of the 2022 ICSID Arbitration Rules, if a party fails to comply with an order to provide security for costs, the arbitral tribunal may suspend the proceedings and after ninety

---

> (6) If a party fails to comply with an order to provide security for costs, the Tribunal may suspend the proceeding. If the proceeding is suspended for more than 90 days, the Tribunal may, after consulting with the parties, order the discontinuance of the proceeding.

46. Article 25.2 of the 2020 LCIA Arbitration Rules reads as follows:

> The Arbitral Tribunal shall have the power upon the application of a party, after giving all other parties a reasonable opportunity to respond to such application, to order any claiming, counterclaiming or cross-claiming party to provide or procure security for Legal Costs and Arbitration Costs by way of deposit or bank guarantee or in any other manner and upon such terms as the Arbitral Tribunal considers appropriate in the circumstances. ... In the event that a claiming, counterclaiming or cross-claiming party does not comply with any order to provide security, the Arbitral Tribunal may stay that party's claims, counterclaims or cross-claims or dismiss them by an award.

47. *See also* section 38(3) of the 1996 English Arbitration Act, which provides that:

> The tribunal may order a claimant to provide security for the costs of the arbitration.
> This power shall not be exercised on the grounds that the claimant is –
>
> (a) an individual ordinarily resident outside the United Kingdom, or
> (b) a corporation or association incorporated or formed under the law of a country outside the United Kingdom, or whose central management or control is exercised outside the United Kingdom.

days and after consulting with the parties, the tribunal may order the discontinuance of the proceedings.

This exceptional nature of the security for costs measure is reflected in the statistics of the arbitration institutions. In a survey conducted in 2020, Haridi indicates that out of the twenty-three requests for security for costs under the ICC Arbitration Rules, only four were granted.[48] The same survey acknowledges that the low rate of approval of such request may also result from the fact that '[t]here is a strong presumption that by submitting to arbitration, the parties have undertaken to carry out any resulting award',[49] and circumstances must be, indeed, extraordinary to justify the measure. The SCC Practice Note on Security for Costs published in 2024 confirms the low rate of approval of security for costs, with only two applications granted out of the thirty-one submitted between 2017 and 2022.[50]

In addressing the impact of security for costs measure as a procedural tool affecting access to arbitral justice, Born notes that 'tribunals not infrequently conclude that the burden imposed by a security for costs order on a party may interfere unduly with its opportunity to be heard, particularly in instances where the party lacks the financial means to both post the required security, and fund presentation of its own case'.[51] Similarly, Gaillard and Savage explain that granting security for costs should remain an exceptional measure, because otherwise, '[a]ccess to arbitral justice would be systematically obstructed, which would be odd at a time when arbitration has become the normal means of resolving disputes in international commerce'.[52] The 2015 Guidelines of Chartered Institute of Arbitrators on Applications for Security for Costs cautiously take a similar approach in directing arbitral tribunals to 'balance the right of a party to pursue its claim against the right of an opposing party to recover the costs of a defense that defeats the claim'.[53] Furthermore, the Guidelines urge arbitral tribunals to take 'great care ... before making such an order to avoid any injustice, including, in particular, unjustly stopping genuine claims by impecunious parties'.[54]

This restrained attitude towards granting security for costs, considering the evident impact on access to arbitral justice, has also been acknowledged by arbitral

48. Samaa A.F. Haridi, *Security for Costs and Claim under the ICC Rules of Arbitration: Rare, but Possible – A Survey of 23 ICC Procedural Orders and Final Awards,* ICC Dispute Resolution Bulletin 2020 No. 2, 77.
49. Samaa A.F. Haridi, *Security for Costs and Claim under the ICC Rules of Arbitration: Rare, but Possible – A Survey of 23 ICC Procedural Orders and Final Awards,* ICC Dispute Resolution Bulletin 2020 No. 2, 77.
50. Jake Lowther and Gaurav Majumdar, *Security for Costs 2017-2022,* SCC Arbitration Institute, 2017-2022, https://sccarbitrationinstitute.se/wp-content/uploads/2025/01/practice-note-security-for-costs-2017_2022.pdf (accessed 3 October 2025).
51. Gary B. Born, *International Commercial Arbitration* (3rd ed., Kluwer Law International 2021), 2601-2758.
52. Emmanuel Gaillard and John Savage (eds), *Fouchard Gaillard Goldman on International Commercial Arbitration* (Kluwer Law International 1999), 655-708, 687.
53. 2015 Guidelines of Chartered Institute of Arbitrators on Applications for Security for Costs, Commentary on Article 1, para. (b), available at https://www.ciarb.org/media/epgj4eb2/5-security-for-costs-2015.pdf, last visited 15 March 2024.
54. 2015 Guidelines of Chartered Institute of Arbitrators on Applications for Security for Costs, Preamble para. 3.

tribunals. For example, in the ICC Case 15218, where the request for security for costs was made against an insolvent party, the arbitral tribunal emphasized that the request of such measure 'is first and foremost an issue about the conflict between the (insolvent) plaintiff's right to have access to arbitral justice on the one hand and the defendant's interest to have a reasonable chance of being able to enforce a future cost award issued in its favour on the other'.[55] As such, the tribunal concluded that a decision on an application for security for costs is a 'task of arbitral tribunals to balance these two conflicting interests against each other and about determining, on the basis of all relevant circumstances of the case, which of them shall prevail over the other'.[56] Similarly, in the ICC Case 12035, the arbitral tribunal came to the conclusion that the right of access to justice must prevail, unless the party against whom the measure is requested has put forward an unjustified or frivolous claim or has deliberately organized its insolvency or otherwise acted abusively.[57]

It is important to emphasize once more that security for costs measure restricts the access to arbitral justice during the arbitration proceedings, by placing an additional financial burden on the party bringing the claim or the counterclaim. In a holistic approach, this can be translated into Zuckerman's 'procedural tool subverted from its proper purpose', which can result in the impossibility of the claimant to access justice, in both its formal and substantive forms. Unless the exceptional character of the security for costs measure is upheld, the security for costs measure could be a dangerous tool in the hands of the parties taking advantage of the nature of arbitration, built upon the arbitration agreement, with the exclusion of any other procedural remedy. De facto, the claimant can have its access to justice restricted by the respondent successfully arguing on the necessity for a security for costs measure. By all means, arbitral tribunals have the responsibility of enforcing the arbitration agreement, which also triggers the obligation to observe the criteria indicated in the arbitration rules in allowing the exceptional measure of security for adverse costs in arbitration.

Article 38 of the SCC Arbitration Rules instructs arbitral tribunals to consider several factors in their decision on granting security for costs, and if exceptional circumstances warrant such a decision. As such, the arbitral tribunal shall have regard to: (i) the prospects of success of the claims, counterclaims and defences; (ii) the claimant's or counterclaimant's ability to comply with an adverse costs award and the availability of assets for enforcement of an adverse costs award; (iii) whether it is appropriate in all the circumstances of the case to order one party to provide security; and (iv) any other relevant circumstances. Evidently, the simple fact that the claimant is insolvent or bankrupt or it is demonstrated that it does not have sufficient assets

55. Procedural Order of July 2008 in ICC Case 15218 (Extract), Special Supplement 2014: Procedural Decisions in ICC Arbitration, ICC, paras 17, 79.
56. Procedural Order of July 2008 in ICC Case 15218 (Extract), Special Supplement 2014: Procedural Decisions in ICC Arbitration, ICC, paras 17, 79.
57. Procedural Order of 6 June 2003 in ICC Case 12035 (Extract), Special Supplement 2010: Decisions on ICC Arbitration Procedure: A Selection of Procedural Orders issued by Arbitral Tribunals acting under the ICC Rules of Arbitration (2003-2004), ICC, p. 10, paras 50-51.

is one of the factors in an entire suite of factors in assessing the need of a security for costs measure. By itself, the impecuniosity of a party is not sufficient to justify the existence of exceptional circumstances. Arbitral tribunals have emphasized the fact that lack of assets of the claimant is not sufficient to justify a security for costs measure which restricts access to justice. For instance, in *South American Silver v. Bolivia*, the arbitral tribunal pointed out that 'the general position of investment tribunals in cases deciding on security for costs is that the lack of assets, the impossibility to show available economic resources, or the existence of economic risk or difficulties that affect the finances of a company are not per se reasons or justifications sufficient to warrant security for costs'.[58] In the ICC Case 14355, the arbitral tribunal explained that 'there is no unanimous view as to whether financial difficulties of a claimant (with or without opening of insolvency proceedings) always justify the granting of security for costs'.[59] In the leading survey on the topic of security for costs, Haridi concludes that 'financial instability and risk alone are typically not enough to establish that the opposing party is unable or unwilling to pay a future award'.[60] Ragnwaldh et al., in the commentary to the 2017 SCC Arbitration Rules, confirm that 'a party lacks assets is not necessarily a sufficient reason for ordering a party to provide security. That other factors may need to be considered expressly follows from Article 38(2) [of the SCC Arbitration Rules]'.[61]

V CONCLUDING REMARKS

Costs of arbitration often appear in the binary setting of the legitimacy of arbitration versus efficiency of the arbitration process, which forces users to consider costs from the perspective of their quantum: how expensive arbitration is? However, this method does not reflect the real concerns with the barriers to access arbitral justice, and simply focuses on the economic value of arbitration proceedings in comparison with other dispute resolution processes. Any deviation from the fundamental right of access to justice may only be justified in exceptional circumstances. This is even more since the principle of *pacta sunt servanda* reinforces the obligation of the parties to arbitrate where an arbitration agreement is valid and capable of being performed, irrespective of their financial situation. While properly exercised, security for costs measures may be justified in truly exceptional circumstances,[62] where such measure is needed for

58. *South American Silver Limited v. The Plurinational State of Bolivia*, PCA Case No. 2013-15, Procedural Order No. 10 (Security for Costs) of 11 January 2016, para. 63.
59. Procedural Order of January 2007 in ICC Case 14355 (Extract), Special Supplement 2014: Procedural Decisions in ICC Arbitration, ICC.
60. Samaa A.F. Haridi, *Security for Costs and Claim under the ICC Rules of Arbitration: Rare, but Possible – A Survey of 23 ICC Procedural Orders and Final Awards*, ICC Dispute Resolution Bulletin 2020 No. 2, 77.
61. Jakob Ragnwaldh et al., *A Guide to the SCC Arbitration Rules* (Kluwer Law International 2019), 121.
62. *See* as an example, *Kazmin v. Latvia*, where the tribunal took into account, among others, the failure of the party against whom the measure was requested to pay its former legal representative, the national criminal investigations for tax evasion commenced against the same party, untraceable assets of the same party, unusual transactions performed by the same party etc. *See*,

protecting respondents from having to take the risks of a vexatious and unmeritorious claim, arbitral tribunal must exercise caution since this measure inherently restricts a party's access to justice, given the contractual obligation to comply with the arbitration agreement, with the exclusion of any other remedy.

Eugene Kazmin v. Republic of Latvia, ICSID Case No. ARB/17/5, Procedural Order No. 6 (Decision on the Respondent's Application for Security for Costs) of 13 April 2020, paras 31 et seq.

CHAPTER 45

Economic Vulnerability and Commercial Arbitration: The Issue of Costs

Rodrigo Garcia da Fonseca[*]

TABLE OF CONTENTS

I INTRODUCTION

In today's world of globalized business, commercial arbitration has evolved from being just one alternative means of dispute resolution to becoming the common and ordinary method of resolution for various kinds of contractual disputes.[1]

* Rodrigo Garcia da Fonseca is an attorney admitted to practice in Brazil, with more than thirty years of experience in domestic and international dispute resolution. Founding partner of Fonseca e Salles Lima Advogados Associados in Rio de Janeiro and President of the Center for Arbitration and Mediation of the Brazil-Canada Chamber of Commerce (CAM-CCBC) in São Paulo. rodrigo@fsla.com.br; rodrigo.fonseca@ccbc.org.br.

1. "International arbitration (...) is not really an 'alternative' dispute resolution mechanism because, as said, in the transnational realm it is so often the only realistic option." Jan Paulsson, "The Idea of Arbitration," Oxford University Press, Oxford, 1st ed., 2013, p. 176. It is usual and systematic to have arbitration in almost all sectors of international commerce—maritime commerce, commodities, construction, investments, distribution, franchising, agency, services in general, energy, and more recently in some new and different areas such as banking, pharmaceuticals and sports, for example. *See*: Jalal El Ahdab; Daniel Mainguy, "Droit de l'Arbitrage. Théorie et Practique", LexisNexis, Paris, 1st ed., 2021, p. 109. Therefore, one can say that arbitration has become a normal method, if not the normal method of resolving international disputes, given the trust of the parties and the will of the States that recognize and enforce arbitral agreements and

Commercial arbitration, unlike court litigation, is a private means of dispute resolution. State courts are funded by the taxpayers, through public budgets, and judges are public employees. Arbitral institutions, on the other hand, as a rule, regardless of whether they are non-profit or for-profit organizations, are privately funded, by their users, sponsors or private owners. Arbitrators are independent professionals that need to be paid by the parties to the cases in which they are appointed.

Although in most jurisdictions State courts also charge fees from the parties that file lawsuits, they usually have systems of legal aid in place, to allow parties that cannot afford the costs of a case to have access to justice. Legal aid varies from country to country, but it ranges from the exemption or reduction of the courts' fees to the availability of free counsel (either public attorneys or private attorneys funded by the State).[2]

There is no system of legal aid in the arbitration world. Parties to arbitrations have to pay the arbitrators, the fees of the institution (except in ad hoc cases) and bear all the costs of the dispute (attorneys, experts and other out-of-pocket expenses, such as travel, rental of space for hearings, court reporters, etc.). There is no way out of this reality. Most institutions have rules that will determine the withdrawal of the claims if the party does not advance its share of the arbitration costs.[3]

There is no doubt arbitration can function properly when all the parties involved are solvent and capable of bearing their costs. However, if one of the parties cannot pay its way through the arbitration process, a number of intriguing questions may arise.

Is there a problem of unfairness and lack of access to justice if a party cannot go to court because it is bound by an arbitration agreement, but at the same time it is unable to pay for the costs of the arbitration? Is this an issue that impacts fundamental human rights? On the other hand, if a party is allowed to go to court and benefit from state legal aid, even if it had entered into a valid arbitration agreement, would this violate the fundamental rights of the other party to go to arbitration?

This chapter will try to flag out some questions related to this conundrum and discuss some of the possible answers, from both economic and legal perspectives, in an attempt to strike a balance between the competing rights that are at stake in such situations.

---

arbitral awards. *See*: Emmanuel Gaillard, "The Contribution of French Legal Thought to International Arbitration" in "Revista de Arbitragem e Mediação," n. 61, April-June 2016, Revista dos Tribunais, São Paulo, p. 287.

2. In Brazil, for example, the Federal Union and the States employ public defenders who act as counsel to citizens who cannot afford private representation. There are also rules that allow for low income people to litigate without having to pay the courts' fees. In England and Wales, the legal aid program is funded by Parliament and largely administered by the Law Society. Although there are different systems, most countries offer some form of public funded legal aid.
3. For example: ICC, 2021 Arbitration Rules, Article 37(6); ICDR, 2021 Arbitration Rules, Article 39(3); SIAC 2016 Arbitration Rules, Article 34(6); CAM-CCBC 2022 Arbitration Rules, Article 35(4).

II PRESUMED VULNERABILITY

There are certain kinds of contracts in which the laws of most jurisdictions will presume some kind of vulnerability of one of the contracting parties. This is usually the case, for example, in consumer and employment contracts. The supplier of consumer goods or services and the employer are usually in a dominant position in the contractual relationship, and are able to impose most of the clauses and conditions of the agreement to the other party, the consumer or the employee. The same happens in the so-called contracts of adhesion.[4]

It is important to highlight that these are areas in which the law will presume that one of the parties is vulnerable. It is not necessary that a party be actually poor in order for the consumer or labor laws to apply. Even a millionaire is entitled to the protections of consumer laws when he/she is acting as a consumer.[5] It is true that in many instances the consumer, the employee or the adherent will be actually economically vulnerable vis-à-vis the other party, but this is not necessary for the special legal protections to apply. The existence of a dominant position in the contract is presumed by the law, and therefore it guarantees a priori certain rights to the contracting party it deems to be fragile.

As a matter of fact, consumers and employees, for example, usually do not have the necessary leverage to discuss arbitration clauses inserted in their contracts. Moreover, the costs of conducting an arbitration frequently inhibit the ability of these parties (usually individuals) to assert claims they might wish to pursue. By imposing arbitration clauses in their contracts, the suppliers of goods or services and the employers may actually be able to reduce their exposure to individual claims by consumers or employees.

In this context, the laws of many jurisdictions restrict the arbitrability of disputes arising out of such kinds of contracts.[6] Commercial arbitration is a creature of consent, and the imbalance of bargaining power between the contracting parties is deemed by law to affect the validity of the "consent" of the weak party to the arbitration agreement.

The issue of costs is also frequently considered as an impediment to the fairness of using arbitration to resolve disputes in these types of contracts. As mentioned above,

4. Contracts of adhesion are frequently also consumer contracts, but not necessarily so. Contracts of adhesion are characterized as form contracts, agreements in which all or almost all the clauses are predetermined and not subject to negotiation. One either adheres to the terms of the contract or there will be no contract at all.
5. It does not matter how wealthy a person is when he/she enters a supermarket, a department store or a pharmacy, for example; consumer laws will apply to any transaction made in those places.
6. It is considered by most to be necessary to have a special regime for arbitration involving parties that are presumed to be economically vulnerable, particularly consumers and employees. Arbitration cannot turn into "procedural oppression." Varying from jurisdiction to jurisdiction, the law will usually establish that the arbitration agreement is either null and void or unenforceable against the weak party (although the weak party may decide to abide by it once the dispute arises). *See*: Maximin De Fontmichel, "Le Faible et l'Arbitrage", Economica, Paris, 1st ed., 2013, p. 241.

the costs of an arbitration can be prohibitive to individuals, particularly in small claims (which are most of the claims a consumer or an employee would want to pursue).

However, certain jurisdictions, and the United States seems to be the most obvious example, have liberal policies toward arbitration of disputes arising from consumer and employment contracts. But even where such arbitrations are possible, institutions tend to enact special rules to attempt to preserve the fairness of the arbitration process and to ensure that it does not become a vehicle for the denial of justice to the consumers or employees.[7]

Class arbitration arose as a possible solution to minimize the costs of individual claims, bringing multiple similar small claims together in one single arbitration, thus making it viable that certain disputes are heard, which would otherwise not make economic sense. Institutions also enacted special rules for class arbitrations.[8] However, some companies started to insert class arbitration waivers in their standard agreements. The validity of such waivers went all the way to the Supreme Court in the United States, and were eventually found to be enforceable.[9]

The most recent new trend in this area is that of mass arbitrations. Numerous, sometimes thousands of individual claimants file simultaneously for arbitration against a single company. Institutions are beginning to look for ways to cope with this new type of arbitration.[10] Mass arbitrations are now apparently shifting huge costs to the side of

7. The AAA has enacted Consumer Arbitration Rules (www.adr.org/consumer (accessed August 16, 2025) latest version in force since 2014) and Labor Arbitration Rules, including Expedited Labor Arbitration Rules (www.adr.org/labor (accessed August 16, 2025)latest version in force since 2013), among other special rules. JAMS has a policy for minimum standards of procedural fairness in consumer arbitrations, effective since 2009 (www.jamsadr.com/consumer-minimum-standards/) (accessed August 16, 2025) and enacted Employment Arbitration Rules & Procedures https://www.jamsadr.com/rules-employment-arbitration/ (accessed August 16, 2025) latest version in force since 2021.
8. AAA Supplementary Rules for Class Arbitrations, effective 2003 (www.adr.org/ClassArbitration) (accessed August 16, 2025); JAMS Class Action Procedures, effective 2009 (www.jamsadr.com/rules-class-action-procedures) (accessed August 16, 2025). In the past few years Brazil has seen the emergence of class arbitrations in corporate disputes between minority shareholders and companies. There are still no local specific institutional or legal rules governing these class arbitrations. CAM-CCBC enacted special Corporate Arbitration Rules in 2023, but they do not deal with class arbitration.
9. Some of the recent decisions of the US Supreme Court in this area include *DirecTV v. Imburgia*, of 2015, on waiver of consumer class arbitration, and *Epic Systems Corp. v. Lewis*, of 2018, on waiver of labor class arbitrations. Moreover, *Lamps Plus Inc v. Varela*, of 2019, confirmed the principle already present in *Stolt-Nielsen SA et al v. AnimalFeeds International Corp*, of 2010—a class claim cannot be compelled in arbitration under the FAA if the arbitration agreement does not clearly provide for it.
10. The AAA enacted Mass Arbitration Supplementary Rules, the latest version in effect since January 2024 (www.adr.org/mass-arbitration) (accessed August 16, 2025), which include special fee schedules and procedures for consumer and employment mass arbitrations. The AAA considers that Mass Arbitration Rules may apply whenever there are 25 or more similar demands for arbitration with coordinated representation, or 100 similar demands if the matter is not related to consumer or employment/workplace disputes. JAMS also considers 25 coordinated filings as a threshold for determine the existence of a mass arbitration, but so far has chosen not to enact specific rules, *See* the JAMS policy regarding mass arbitration filings, of March 3, 2023: https://www.jamsadr.com/blog/2023/jams-policy-regarding-mass-arbitration-filings (accessed August 16, 2025).

companies in consumer cases, and potentially in labor ones as well.[11] Depending on how mass arbitrations evolve, companies may find themselves in an extremely burdensome situation, in which arbitration agreements that were crafted to limit the claims by consumers end up being very expensive to live by.

One may only wonder where consumer and labor arbitration will go from here, as this is an ever-changing landscape. In any event, it is undeniable that the issue of costs, fairness and access to justice will continue to set the tone of further discussions. An excessive liberal policy in favor of consumer and employment arbitrations has led to what many perceive as an abusive and unfair practice on the part of companies, to use the costs of arbitration as a means of effectively denying the individuals' rights of access to justice. Class and mass arbitrations have arisen as a way to fix this problem. As a matter of policy, it may be better to impose certain limits on arbitration agreements in these areas, as many jurisdictions do.

In any event, arbitrations involving parties that are presumed vulnerable by law show that institutions can do a lot in the way of levelling the playing field. By enacting specific rules and costs schedules for certain kinds of cases, institutions may be able to propose solutions that guarantee the fairness of the arbitration process and allow all parties to have access to justice. Expedited procedures,[12] rules governing small claims in arbitrations, online dispute resolution and AI-assisted dispute resolution are all different tools that can also be used in order to improve the arbitration environment and minimize the problem of costs that might otherwise jeopardize the use of arbitration in certain areas. To the extent that class and mass arbitrations are accepted by the applicable law, institutions may also have an important role in defining rules and costs that preserve the fairness and balance of the parties in the arbitration process.

III IMPECUNIOSITY

The issue of impecuniosity raises other questions. What happens if a party is perfectly sound economically when it enters into the arbitration agreement, but at the time the

11. Uber recently faced 31,000 arbitration demands from Uber Eats customers. A New York State Appeals court decided in 2022 that Uber had to pay USD 92 million in arbitration fees. *See*: Alisson Frankel, "Uber Loses Appeal to Block $92 million in Mass Arbitration Fees," in www.reuters.com/legal/litigation/uber-loses-appeal-block-92-million-mass-arbitration-fees-2022-04-18/ (accessed August 16, 2025). Samsung is facing 36,000 arbitration demands related to biometric privacy, and a Chicago judge ordered it to pay over USD 4 million in arbitration fees. Alisson Frankel, "Samsung Ordered to Pay Arbitration Fees for 36,000 Biometric Privacy Plaintiffs," in www.reuters.com/legal/transactional/column-samsung-ordered-pay-arbitration-fees-36000-biometric-privacy-plaintiffs-2023-09-14/ (accessed August 16, 2025).
12. Many institutions have enacted expedited arbitration rules, usually applicable for claims of less than a certain amount, establishing shorter deadlines for the rendering of the award, one single arbitrator instead of a three-member tribunal, simplified evidence rules and cheaper schedules of fees. For example: ICC, Appendix VI of the 2021 Arbitration Rules; ICDR 2021 International Expedited Procedures, Article E-1 to E-10; SIAC, Article 5 of the 2016 Arbitration Rules; CAM-CCBC, 2022 Arbitration Rules, Articles 36 and 37.

dispute arises, it is not capable of bearing the costs of the arbitration?[13] Does this impecuniosity, or the inability to pay for the costs of the arbitration, affect the validity or enforceability of the arbitration agreement?

First of all, one must define impecuniosity. It is not a simple definition. Is it equal to a de facto insolvency? Is it the inability to pay for the costs of arbitration without sacrificing one's basic personal needs? How strict or flexible should this definition be?[14] In practice, it is very difficult to have a strict pre-defined notion of impecuniosity that would encompass all possible scenarios. Impecuniosity is something that must be verified in a case-by-case analysis.

In some cases, parties to an arbitration agreement go to court alleging that they cannot fund the arbitration, and therefore should be allowed to proceed before the Judiciary, otherwise they would be denied access to justice, which is a fundamental right in most legal systems. The issue is complex and allows for various approaches.

In Brazil, the Superior Court of Justice decided that the alleged economic disparity of the parties is not a reason to disregard the arbitration agreement and that the competence-competence principle should prevail. The mere allegation of economic insufficiency and the excessive onerousity of the arbitration does not allow the Judiciary to entertain a lawsuit and disregard the effects of the arbitration agreement before a decision is rendered by the arbitrators on the matter.[15]

In Switzerland, the Federal Court refused a request to annul an arbitral award for violation of the right to access to justice due to the absence of a system similar to legal aid in the arbitration context. This was a case from the Court of Arbitration for Sport—CAS—involving a cyclist who faced disciplinary sanctions. The decision dismissed arguments of violation of public order and equality of the parties due to the financial difficulty of the appellant and the absence of any type of assistance similar to judicial aid.[16]

The Constitutional Court of Portugal decided in 2008 that procedural laws should be made more flexible to allow a party without resources to access the Judiciary despite having signed an arbitration agreement. In the decision, as the party could not afford the costs of arbitration, the Court understood that the litigant would be defenseless and that the right to legal protection and access to justice should prevail over the contractual and procedural rights regarding how the dispute should be resolved (via

13. Sometimes a party also alleges some kind of unconscionability in the agreement to arbitrate, as it was not fully aware of the costs involved in a potential arbitration (although it could have been aware, as institutional schedules of fees are public).
14. Impecuniosity has to do with the inability to pay for the costs of the arbitration, not with the unwillingness to pay. However, the analysis tends to be subjective and on a case-by-case basis. *See*: Marcel Carvalho Engholm Cardoso, "Impecunious Parties in International Commercial Arbitration", in "Arbitration International", 2020, Vol. 36, Oxford University Press, Oxford, pp. 123-124, https://doi.org/10.1093/arbint/aiaa002.
15. Decision of the 3rd Chamber of the Superior Court of Justice in Special Appeal n. 1.598.220-RN, rapporteur Justice Paulo de Tarso Sanseverino, Official Gazette of 1.7.2019, full opinion available at www.stj.jus.br (accessed August 16, 2025).
16. Georg von Segesser, "Inoperability of Arbitration Agreements Due to Lack of Funds? Revisiting Legal Aid in International Arbitration". January 17, 2015, available at: http://arbitrationblog.kluwerarbitration.com/2015/01/17/inoperability-of-arbitration-agreements-due-to-lack-of-funds-revisiting-legal-aid-in-international-arbitration/ (accessed August 16, 2025).

arbitration, according to the franchising agreement being discussed).[17] This was a case of an "interpretation in accordance with the Constitution," in which the procedural rules that refer parties to arbitration were not deemed unconstitutional, but only the interpretation according to which such an obligation to arbitrate would persist even in face of the party's inability to bear the costs of the arbitration process. In such a factual situation, access to the Judiciary should be permitted.

The decision was criticized by some practitioners and scholars, among other reasons, for being overly generic, and for opening a dangerous flank for reluctant parties to resort to the Judiciary, claiming the impossibility of paying arbitration costs and thereby frustrating the objectives of the freely agreed arbitration clause.[18] A later decision by the Supreme Court of Justice of Portugal took a slightly more flexible approach, stating that the allegation of an obstacle to justice can be made, but before the arbitral tribunal, respecting the competence-competence principle, by which the arbitral tribunal is the first to decide on its own jurisdiction, not the Judiciary.[19]

The Polish Supreme Court rendered a decision in January 2024 in which it stated that the objective inability of a party to bear the costs of an arbitration does not render the arbitration clause invalid under Polish law, but it may become unenforceable, and access to the state courts would be preserved.[20]

It would be difficult to generalize from these isolated cases that are selected from certain jurisdictions. The costs of arbitration as a potential obstacle to access to justice for those who cannot afford them will continue to be an important topic, mostly treated on a case-by-case basis. The outcome of each case depends heavily on the jurisdiction and on the governing law eventually applicable.

The line of reasoning adopted in the second Portuguese decision referred to above is well structured, but it seems not to resolve the central dilemma of these cases. If the party does not have the financial resources to initiate an arbitration, how can it ask the arbitral tribunal to be authorized to go to court? It is a chicken and egg

17. Decision of the 2nd section of the Constitutional Court of Portugal, Opinion n. 311/2008, Proceedings n. 753/07, Official Gazette of 1.8.2008, pp. 34401-34405. Full opinion available at: https://dre.pt/home/-/dre/2658981/details/maximized (accessed August 16, 2025).
18. For example: José Miguel Júdice, "Anotação ao Acórdão 311/08 do Tribunal Constitucional," in "Revista Internacional de Arbitragem e Conciliação da Associação Portuguesa de Arbitragem," Almedina, Coimbra, 2009, pp. 161-190.
19. Decision of the 6th section of the Supreme Court of Justice of Portugal, Proceedings n. 1212/14.5T8LSB.L1.S1, rapporteur Justice Min. Ana Paula Boularot, Official Gazette of 26.4.2016. Full opinion available at: https://dre.pt/pesquisa-avancada/-/asearch/90169275/details/maximized?emissor = Supremo + Tribunal + de + Justi%C3%A7a&perPage = 100&types = JURISPRUDENCIA&search = Pesquisar (accessed August 16, 2025) The 2008 case of the Constitutional Court was discussed at large. Of course the solution makes sense because Portuguese law embraces the competence-competence principle in arbitration. Other legislations, as the FAA in the United States, for example, allow state judges to decide on arbitrability issues and the jurisdiction of the arbitral tribunal regardless of whether the arbitrators have previously rendered a decision on these matters.
20. *See*: Marcin Menkes, Alicja Zielinska-Eisen and Maria Paschou, "Can the Inability to Bear Arbitration Costs Render the Arbitration Clause Unenforceable? According to the Polish Supreme Court, It Can." Kluwer Arbitration Blog, March 21, 2024. https://arbitrationblog.kluwerarbitration.com/2024/03/21/can-the-inability-to-bear-arbitration-costs-render-the-arbitration-clause-unenforceable-according-to-the-polish-supreme-court-it-can/ (accessed August 16, 2025).

problem—if the party cannot access the arbitral tribunal, how can it put before the arbitrators the issue of whether or not it can go to the judicial courts?[21]

Different from the situations of consumer or labor arbitrations, it is less clear what arbitration institutions could do to lower the barriers that impecunious parties face. Simply extending deadlines or offering special arrangements for payments is helpful, but it is clearly not enough. Imposing an additional financial obligation on the other party does not seem to be a fair or doable solution.[22] Also, frequently the major hurdle is the cost of competent counsel and experts, and apart from streamlining procedures and encouraging best practices, there is little institutions can do to reduce the costs of representation.[23] The cost of representation derives from the legal market and seems to be much more in the hands of the parties than of the institutions.

Third-party funding of arbitrations, for example, may be a way to enable access to arbitration for a party without resources. There is no doubt it can work as a facilitator of access to justice, or at least as a mitigator of the inequality between parties. However, it must be recognized that third-party funding does not solve the problem as a whole. Not everyone has access to such financing, and the funder may not be interested in a particular case. The market is limited and concentrated. The costs of financing can also be quite high, and it would not be fair to impose an obligation on the impecunious party to accept any and all conditions a funder might want to impose.[24] Third-party funding of arbitrations cannot be equated with mechanisms of legal aid such as public defenders or the waiver of courts' fees in terms of solving the problem of access to justice. Third-party funding may help and alleviate the problem of access to arbitral justice, but it does not solve it.

Often, the issue is not exactly the impossibility of the expenditure, but a matter of priority. A party, even in a difficult financial situation, might have the resources to pay

21. If a certain jurisdiction does not adopt the competence-competence principle, and some do not, then this problem should not arise. The party will be free to go to court to question the enforceability of the arbitration agreement.
22. Many institutions have rules that allow the case to continue even if a party has defaulted in the payment of its share of the costs, as long as the counterparty steps up and advances the outstanding amounts. This works as a solution when the defaulting party is the defendant, but not when it is the claimant (or counterclaimant). No one would find reasonable that a party would have to fund a claim of the other party against it. Even if such a rule existed, parties would simply not pay to be prosecuted, and there would not be anything the institution could do to resolve the situation. Moreover, the final allocation of costs in the arbitration award would not solve the problem. Even if the final award authorizes the recovery of the costs advanced, in many cases there will be no assets to guarantee such repayment, as the impecunious party was unable to pay those costs in the first place.
23. The 2015 ICC Commission Report on "Decisions on Costs in International Arbitration" showed that at least in ICC arbitrations, the institutional and arbitrators' costs amounted to only 17% of the overall costs of a case, the remaining 83% being comprised of the party's costs with lawyers' fees and expenses, and other expenses with witnesses, experts, etc. Full report available at: https://iccwbo.org/wp-content/uploads/sites/3/2015/12/Decisions-on-Costs-in-International-Arbitration.pdf (accessed August 16, 2025).
24. Maurício Pestilla Fabbri, "Inapplicability of the Arbitration Agreement Due to the Impecuniosity of the Party," in "Revista Brasileira de Arbitragem," Vol. 57, January-March 2018, Wolters Kluwer, Alphen aan den Rijn, p. 90, https://doi.org/10.54648/rba2018004. Thiago Dias Delfino Cabral, "Impecuniosidade e Arbitragem. Uma análise da ausência de recursos financeiros para a instauração do procedimento arbitral." 1st ed., Quartier Latin (ed.), São Paulo, 2019, p. 149.

for arbitration, and if successful, the expense could turn to profit. This is why the very definition of impecuniosity is so crucial. It must be carefully examined on a case-by-case basis whether there is truly an impediment to access to justice or rather some kind of difficulty or embarrassment, but that cannot be characterized as an unavoidable impossibility.

While it is true that everyone should have the opportunity to pursue their rights before a valid jurisdiction, impecuniosity should not serve as a free pass for the filing of any claims without costs, which could encourage unreasonable or baseless claims.

On the other hand, it is arguable that a party to an arbitration agreement has a fundamental right to have its disputes resolved by arbitration.[25] Facilitating access of the other party to State courts to preserve one's fundamental rights could also amount to a violation of fundamental rights of the other party. Can the right of access to justice trump the right to arbitrate? A situation of clash of opposing fundamental rights is not easily resolved, and usually treated through the pondering and weighing of the competing values and principles at stake.[26]

In the realm of commercial arbitration, where most disputes are of a business nature, the preservation of a strict enforceability of the arbitration agreement and the respect for the competence-competence principle (where applicable) seem to make sense. After all, it is the companies and the businesspeople themselves who freely agreed to the arbitration agreement. If they later on face difficulties in abiding by it, this is part of the business risks they decided to take, out of their own volition. It is arguable that access to justice is not denied. The parties freely chose arbitration to resolve specific disputes related to specific contracts, and they knew, or should have known, the costs involved and the risks that they might not be able to pay for them.

IV INSOLVENCY

Beyond factual impecuniosity, the applicability of insolvency laws may also affect the arbitrability of commercial disputes. While impecuniosity is a situation of fact, insolvency laws impose a specific legal regime on those affected by it. What happens

25. French law seems to recognize a fundamental right of access to an arbitrator ("*droit à l'arbitre*") if there is a valid arbitration agreement, based on the European Convention on Human Rights. *See*: Claire Debourg, "Les investisseurs et la prohibition de recourir à l'arbitrage à l'épreuve de procès équitable," in Jérémy Jorudan-Marques; Marie Nicolas-Gréciano (coord.), "Arbitrage et Procès Équitable", LGDJ, Paris, 2023, pp. 65-68. The French Constitutions of 1791 and 1795, and the Spanish Constitution of 1812, for example, recognized a fundamental right of citizens to submit their disputes to arbitration. But even if a Constitution does not mention the right to arbitration explicitly, it may be derived from other constitutional principles, such as the rights to privacy or of freedom of contract. *See*: Victor Ferreres Comella, "The Constitution of Arbitration," 1st ed., Cambridge University Press, Cambridge, 2021, p. 30.
26. Chief Justice Luis Roberto Barroso, of the Brazilian Supreme Court, cites examples of Brazilian case law and also precedents of the German Supreme Court to conclude that the situations which present a clash of fundamental rights have to be pondered in accordance with the principles of proportionality and reasonability, on a case-by-case basis, in order for the judge to find the most acceptable decision for each case. Luís Roberto Barroso, "Curso de Direito Constitucional Contemporâneo," 9th ed., Saraiva, São Paulo, 2020, pp. 315-323.

when one of the parties to the arbitration agreement becomes formally insolvent before or during the arbitration?

In general, the rules governing insolvency are considered to be of a nature of public order, and impose legal restrictions on those who become insolvent. A company in bankruptcy or judicial recovery or reorganization, whichever the applicable law is, becomes restricted in its capacity to dispose of its assets, in order to preserve the principle of the *par conditio creditorum*. Most jurisdictions have rules that concentrate all claims related to the bankrupt estate in a single "universal" bankruptcy court that oversees the collection of all assets and the payment of the debts. Does this "universal" court's jurisdiction trump the arbitration agreement?

Brazilian law clearly establishes that the validity and enforceability of the arbitration agreement is not affected by the supervening bankruptcy, liquidation or judicial reorganization of one of the parties.[27] If an arbitration has already started, it shall continue all the way to the award. If a dispute arises after the bankruptcy, it will still go to arbitration. Only the enforcement of the arbitral award may be subject to the restrictions of bankruptcy, recovery, or liquidation, and will be subject to the restrictions affecting other similar debts of the insolvent estate.

One interesting Brazilian case occurred in the context of the Judicial Recovery (Chapter 11) of Oi, a large Brazilian telecommunication company. At a certain point, during the processing of the Judicial Recovery, a dispute arose among the shareholders regarding a capital increase of the company. The company's by-laws provided for resolution through arbitration, but some shareholders alleged that the case should be decided by the bankruptcy court, due to the effects it could have on the economic situation of the company and the repercussions on the plans of the Judicial Recovery. The Superior Court of Justice decided that in spite of the Judicial Recovery, the arbitration clause of the by-laws remained intact and enforceable, and therefore, the decision belonged to the arbitral tribunal.[28] The court correctly applied the rule of Brazilian law that the judicial recovery should not affect the enforceability of the arbitration agreement.

Some national legislations, however, expressly deprive of legal effects any arbitration clauses signed prior to the declaration of bankruptcy of a party, usually on the basis of the loss of the party's capacity.[29] There are also jurisdictions where, in principle, there is no restriction on arbitrators deciding matters related to the estate and related to bankruptcy law, but depending on the circumstances of each specific case, the arbitration may be suspended or its decision set aside by the insolvency court.[30] In

27. *See* Article 6, §9, of Law 11.101 of 2005, as per Law 14.112, of 2020. The legal provision was enacted in line with the already previously prevailing case law of the Superior Court of Justice.
28. Decision of the 2nd section of the Superior Court of Justice in the Conflict of Competence n. 157.099-RJ, rapporteur Justice Nancy Andrighi, Official Gazette of 30.10.2018. Full opinion available at: www.stj.jus.br (accessed August 16, 2025).
29. For example, in the Netherlands and in Latvia, the arbitration agreement becomes ineffective when the party is declared bankrupt. Gary Born, "International Commercial Arbitration", Vol. I, Wolters Kluwer, Alphen aan den Rijn, 2009, pp. 754-755.
30. There is French case law in this sense: Phillipe Fouchard, Emmanuel Gaillard and Berthold Goldman, "International Commercial Arbitration," Kluwer Law International, The Hague, 1999, pp. 344-345. French Bankruptcy law does not nullify the arbitration agreement, but it limits the

other jurisdictions, there are no restrictions, and the bankrupt estate can sue and be sued in arbitration.[31]

Due to this discrepancy in various national laws, the issue can be much more complex in an international setting, in which there may be different competing laws applicable to the parties and to the dispute. The difficulty of the topic can be illustrated by the *Elektrim v. Vivendi* case, with a bankruptcy declared in Poland and arbitrations and judicial decisions in Switzerland and the United Kingdom.[32]

To cut a long story short, it suffices to say that the company Elektrim was declared bankrupt in Poland and was a party to several arbitrations involving companies of the Vivendi group, due to a joint venture and various deals they had previously entered into. Polish law defined that the declaration of bankruptcy led to the dismissal of any ongoing arbitrations, in favor of the jurisdiction of the Polish Bankruptcy Court. On the other hand, the regulation of the European Union defined that the effects of the bankruptcy on pending lawsuits (or arbitrations) should be considered in accordance with the law of the Member State where the lawsuit (or arbitration) was taking place.

In one case, under the rules of the LCIA, in England, the arbitral tribunal decided to proceed with the arbitration in accordance with English law. In another case, under the rules of the ICC, seated in Geneva, the arbitral tribunal decided to stay the arbitration based on Polish law.[33] In both cases, the judicial courts of the seats confirmed the arbitral decisions. In other words, the effects of the insolvency of the party were different in each arbitration, depending on the seat and the applicable *lex arbitri*.

This example shows that, in international cases, the practical results may depend on the interaction of a series of factors, including the laws applicable to the insolvency and to the arbitration (both in terms of substantive law and of the law governing the arbitration agreement), the seat and the location of any enforcement of a future award.

The potential transnational effects of bankruptcies, that are becoming more and more ordinary, add another layer of complication to international disputes involving

---

scope of arbitrable matters. When it comes to foreign bankruptcies, the French judge will apply the *lex concursus*, the foreign bankruptcy law applicable to the insolvent party and will also ensure that the award does not violate a number of rules and principles of procedural law, essentially of a procedural nature which are matters of public policy. Christophe Seraglini; Jérôme Ortscheidt, "Droit de l'arbitrage interne e international", Montchrestien, Paris, 2nd ed., 2019, pp. 631-634.

31. As is the case in Brazil, as mentioned above.
32. For a brief description of the case, *see*: Kubas Kos Galkowski, "Elektrim case era comes to an end", June 23, 2015, available at: https://www.lexology.com/library/detail.aspx?g=461ea330-c8dc-42ac-a196-45b5c843f69b (accessed August 16, 2025).
33. In a later case, Swiss courts took a different approach and did not recognize the effects of the bankruptcy of a Portuguese party in relation to an arbitration pending in Switzerland. *See*: Natalie Voser, "Insolvency and Arbitration: Swiss Supreme Court Revisits Its Vivendi vs. Elektrim Decision", December 5, 2012, available at: http://arbitrationblog.kluwerarbitration.com/2012/12/05/insolvency-and-arbitration-swiss-supreme-court-revisits-its-vivendi-vs-elektrim-decision/ (accessed August 16, 2025).

insolvent parties.[34] It is quite possible, or even likely, that other sagas like the *Elektrim v. Vivendi* case may occur more frequently in the future.

Some other issues also present challenges to arbitrations with bankrupt companies. The insolvent party may be unable to bear the costs of the arbitration.[35] This situation has already been discussed above, in light of the impecuniosity. To what extent the costs of the arbitration can constitute a barrier for the insolvent party to have access to justice? Is there something the law or institutional rules can do to minimize this problem? Unlike the de facto situation of impecuniosity, insolvency involves *de iure* restrictions on the legal capacity of a party, and therefore special institutional rules must take this into account.[36]

Finally, the bankruptcy or judicial recovery of a company involves interests of third parties (at least those of the various creditors); therefore, issues of joinder, intervention or consolidation may come up. Furthermore, the confidentiality of the arbitration may be a problem, as all the creditors have a similar right to know the assets and liabilities of the estate.[37]

V FINAL REMARKS

Arbitration involving parties that are economic vulnerable is tricky. The costs of the arbitration are one of the main problems that have to be tackled.

Access to justice is an essential fundamental right, historically recognized in most declarations of rights, starting from the period of the French and American Revolutions, and consolidated with the expansion of constitutionalism and democracy over the twentieth century. Although arbitration is an extrajudicial method of dispute resolution, it provides access to justice, through the parties' consensus to delegate the resolution of the dispute to private arbitrators. In contemporary society, access to justice is no longer thought of strictly as a State institution, but rather in terms of the

34. The UNCITRAL Model Law on Cross-Border Insolvency, of 1997, has already been adopted or inspired legislation enacted in fifty-nine countries (including sixty-two different jurisdictions) (https://uncitral.un.org/en/texts/insolvency/modellaw/cross-border_insolvency/status) (accessed August 16, 2025).
35. It may be quite complicated for a formally insolvent company to seek third-party funding for an arbitration, due to the many restrictions it may have according to the applicable law and also due to the risks the funder might not be willing to run if there is no legal certainty it will have preference on the recovery of the proceeds of a future award. The possibilities of financing of insolvent companies depends heavily on the applicable law and on the likelihood of their future economic recovery.
36. In Brazil, in arbitrations involving the public administration, the private party is obligated by law to advance all the costs of the institutions and the fees of the arbitrators, subject to the final allocation in the award. One could think of a similar rule in relation to insolvent companies, so that someone filing an arbitration against a bankrupt estate, for example, would have to advance all the costs and the fees of the arbitrators. It would not solve the problem of the cases in which the bankrupt party is the claimant, but it would reduce the burden in those in which it is the defendant.
37. Many of the matters raised here, and others, are treated in the IBA Toolkit on Insolvency and Arbitration. https://www.ibanet.org/MediaHandler?id=087B4D4A-B82E-4FAC-817F-64EE500 91D66 (accessed August 16, 2025).

facilitation to access to a fair legal order, which also includes extrajudicial methods of conflict prevention and resolution.

However, arbitration being a private means of dispute resolution, it must be privately funded. The costs of the institution, expenses of the proceedings and the arbitrators' fees can reach significant amounts. The costs of representation tend to be even higher.

Everyone who provides services in an arbitration, be it the staff of an institution, the arbitrators themselves, or the lawyers and experts, is worker in the private sector. Institutions are private entities. Everything in arbitration involves the provision of private services. Money is part of arbitration, and it helped creation of a market of private justice.[38] There is no free arbitration.

In this context, the costs of the arbitration should not work as a barrier to access to justice. On the other hand, the economic difficulties of one party should not work as a free pass to avoid an arbitration agreement that was freely and lawfully entered into. This could constitute a violation of the other party's fundamental right to arbitrate the dispute.

There is no easy solution to the dilemma, but the various stakeholders must step up to the challenge. The market can play an important role, through third-party funding or other financial mechanisms that enable parties to pay for the costs of arbitrations. Legislators may help clarifying and solving some of the shady legal issues, in domestic and international settings. Finally, arbitral institutions can do a lot in this area. Helping to reduce costs in general, and creating special rules (and in some instances special cost schedules) for situations involving parties that are economically vulnerable, and for legitimate claims that might otherwise not see the light of day, can be a big step toward building a more inclusive and fair arbitration world.

38. Thomas Clay, "Le marché de l'arbitrage," in Walid Ben Hamida Thomas Clay (coord.), "L'Argent dans l'Arbitrage," Lextenso ed., Paris, 2013, pp. 13-28.

CHAPTER 46

Costs and Access to Justice: An Institutional Perspective

Joanne Lau & Kelly Chan[*]

TABLE OF CONTENTS

I INTRODUCTION

Cost of arbitration has become a perennial issue, with many voicing concerns in recent years that international arbitration has become increasingly expensive. Costs of arbitration can pose access to justice barriers in the strictest sense if a party lacks the financial means to pursue its claims at all. Even if a party has some financial means, it may nevertheless see the cost of arbitration as being disproportionately high, as compared with the party's financial resources or the value that it expects to derive from

[*] Joanne Lau is the Secretary-General of the Hong Kong International Arbitration Centre. Kelly Chan is a recent graduate of the University of Oxford and the University of Hong Kong. The views expressed in this chapter are those of the authors and do not necessarily represent those of their organisations.

the arbitration proceedings. This is not conducive to access to justice as it deters some parties from using arbitration to resolve their disputes, and the legitimacy of arbitration is undermined if it is viewed as a process that is reserved for, or favours, those with deeper pockets.

For international arbitration to function and flourish as a system, and because of its inherent nature, there are necessarily costs associated with the process. In maximising access to justice in arbitration, the goal is not to eliminate costs but to ensure that the costs are reasonable, proportionate and controllable in the context of each case, and to have the tools to mitigate the effects of financial disparity between parties where appropriate.

This chapter will start with an overview of the meaning of access to justice in the context of international arbitration. Based on observations from an institutional perspective, we will then outline five areas where there can be more scope to address cost issues and examine the underlying access to justice considerations, including with respect to: (i) remuneration of tribunals; (ii) third-party funding and outcome-related fee structures; (iii) issues with payment of deposits; (iv) security of costs applications; and (v) underutilised case and cost management tools.

II ACCESS TO JUSTICE IN THE CONTEXT OF INTERNATIONAL ARBITRATION

On a macro level, the development and use of alternative dispute resolution, including arbitration, enhances overall access to justice. By providing another forum for parties to resolve their disputes, it lessens the burden faced by some judicial courts which are experiencing backlog and delays. It has been found that promotion and recourse to alternative dispute resolution is increasingly identified as a principal strategy in reducing access to justice barriers.[1]

Within the confines of international arbitration, the expression of access to justice is not identical to that in court litigation due to their different nature. Courts belong to the public justice system, whereas arbitration is a private dispute resolution mechanism. At its core, arbitration is a consensual process whereby a dispute is only resolved through arbitration because the parties voluntarily agree to submit their disputes to arbitration, whereas parties may find their disputes subject to the jurisdiction of the courts for reasons other than by choice. Unlike court litigation, where the procedures are generally more standardised and judges are assigned, parties in arbitration enjoy autonomy and flexibility, for example, over the choice of arbitrator(s), the arbitral institution, the procedure and rules to be adopted. Therefore, while there is strong rationale for the provision of state-sponsored financial assistance in appropriate cases in court litigation, there is less expectation and justification in arbitration for state-sponsored legal aid, legal representation and decision-makers owing to its private character.

1. 'International Access to Justice: Barriers and Solutions, Bingham Centre for the Rule of Law Report', 2014.

Because of the private, voluntary and consensual character of arbitration,[2] there is also a general understanding that parties to arbitration are expected to fund the process, subject to cost allocation at the end of the process. On occasions, parties, often on the respondent side, may seek to argue that they should not be required to put in funds for the arbitration because, for example, they consider the arbitration to have been wrongly brought against them. Tribunals usually have little sympathy for this type of position. Where parties have agreed to arbitration under the HKIAC rules, a tribunal remarked in one case that by this agreement, parties must be taken to have agreed to be liable for the relevant fees and costs for services to be rendered by the tribunal and the arbitral institution,[3] and they must be secured in advance from the parties.[4] Where parties have freely entered into a binding arbitration agreement, they should and probably did envisage that if a dispute were to arise, there would be expenses involved in resolving such a dispute, and that they would be required to shoulder such expense equally, pending determination on the merits and cost allocation by the tribunal.

Notwithstanding the general acceptance that costs are part and parcel of the arbitration process, the level of costs is nevertheless highly relevant to the concept of access to justice in arbitration. In Lord Woolf's Final Report on Access to Justice,[5] he identified the following principles in which the civil justice system should meet in order to ensure access to justice:

> The system should:
>
> (a) be *just* in the results it delivers;
> (b) be *fair* in the way it treats litigants;
> (c) offer appropriate procedures at a reasonable *cost*;
> (d) deal with cases with reasonable *speed*;
> (e) be *understandable* to those who use it;
> (f) be *responsive* to the needs of those who use it;
> (g) provide as much *certainty* as the nature of particular cases allows; and
> (h) be *effective*: adequately resourced and organised.

In ensuring that international arbitration remains a legitimate process, the above principles are equally applicable. Specifically on the issue of costs, parties to arbitration similarly expect the system to offer appropriate procedures at a reasonable cost. Parties' concern as to costs is evident from the results of the 2018 and 2021 Queen Mary Survey on International Arbitration, which noted 'time and cost are perennially acknowledged as the biggest concerns for arbitration users'.

---

2. It is beyond the ambit of this chapter to consider specific types of disputes where there are additional public interest considerations, for example, concerning consumer protection and employment matters. In Hong Kong, there are additional statutory safeguards to examine if such matters should be referred to arbitration, *see* section 15 of the Control of Exemption Clauses Ordinance (Cap. 71) and section 20(2) of the Arbitration Ordinance (Cap. 609).
3. HKIAC 2024 Administered Arbitration Rules, para. 2.8 of Schedule 1 and para. 2.4 of Schedules 2 and 3.
4. Article 41, HKIAC 2024 Administered Arbitration Rules ('2024 Rules').
5. Lord Woolf, 'Access to Justice: Final Report' (July 1996).

It is undeniable that there are market forces at play in the costs in arbitration, particularly when it comes to legal costs of the parties, which often account for the largest proportion of the parties' overall costs. There is market segmentation at play: the most well-regarded counsel may be in higher demand and may command a premium in rates, whereas in other segments, counsel may be prepared to charge low fees to attract more cases. There could also be differences between jurisdictions and legal markets. Although the more commonly expressed concern is that arbitration has become too costly, it would also be undesirable if parties choose counsel or arbitrators solely based on cost, which may encourage a 'race to the bottom'. For arbitration to flourish, there needs to be a deep and growing pool of high-calibre arbitration counsel and arbitrators, and their services need to be reasonably remunerated as well.

The goal is therefore for costs of arbitration to be reasonable, proportionate and controllable. This ensures that arbitration can continue as a viable alternative to litigation to enhance overall access to justice, and for parties to feel that they had effective access to justice via the arbitration process.

III DIFFERENT CATEGORIES OF COSTS OF THE ARBITRATION

What are the different categories of costs in international arbitration then? Article 34(1) of the HKIAC 2024 Administered Arbitration Rules (*2024 Rules*) sets out exhaustively the different categories of costs of the arbitration to be determined by the arbitral tribunal:

(a) the fees of the arbitral tribunal, as determined in accordance with Article 10;
(b) the reasonable travel and other expenses incurred by the arbitral tribunal;
(c) the reasonable costs of expert advice and of other assistance required by the arbitral tribunal, including fees and expenses of any tribunal secretary;
(d) the reasonable costs for legal representation and other assistance, including fees and expenses of any witnesses and experts, if such costs were claimed during the arbitration;
(e) the costs of the Emergency Relief proceedings referred to in paragraph 16 of Schedule 4; and
(f) the Registration Fee and Administrative Fees payable to HKIAC in accordance with Schedule 1, and any expenses payable to HKIAC.

In general terms, this includes fees and expenses of the tribunal (and tribunal secretary), legal counsel fees, expert fees, administrative fees of the arbitral institution, and incidental expenses such as the cost for hiring a hearing room and cost of interpretation and transcription services and the like.

Articles 34.3 and 34.4 of the 2024 Rules address cost allocation. Article 34.3 gives arbitral tribunals the discretion to make apportionment if it 'determines that apportionment is reasonable'. Article 34.4 gives tribunals the discretion to take into account any factors it considers relevant, both in determining the reasonableness of the costs of the arbitration and in determining whether and how to apportion the costs. One of the factors is the relative success of the parties, which is often taken into account by tribunals.

Cost allocation is intertwined with access to justice. The possibility for a claimant to recover a portion of its own costs in the event that it prevails in the arbitration may make the commencement of an arbitration more palatable to the claimant, such that it is more likely to bring a meritorious claim to arbitration. It does not fully remove access to justice barriers however, since depending on a claimant's financial resources, cost concerns can still present obstacles at the stage of deciding whether to commence or continue with a case, particularly if there is no certainty over the total amount of costs that would be required to see the arbitration through to its end and where the chances of success are unclear. Further, it could also be argued that the risk of having to also cover the other side's costs in addition to its own costs, if its claim is unsuccessful, may deter some claimants from pursuing their claims. This is not necessarily negative as cost shifting could reduce the chances of frivolous claims being brought and encourage early settlement. Nevertheless, what the above illustrates is that even if there is cost shifting at the end of arbitration, it is still in the interest of parties to keep costs reasonable throughout the process.

In the next few sections, the chapter seeks to outline the tools and strategies available to parties and tribunals in ameliorating the issues with costs.

IV STRATEGY 1: UPFRONT CHOICES AT THE DRAFTING STAGE WHICH INFLUENCE COSTS

The amount of costs in arbitration depends on many factors, some of which may not be fully ascertained at the stage of drafting the arbitration agreement. For example, the scale and complexity of the dispute often have an effect on how much costs, such as legal fees and arbitrator fees, parties end up incurring.[6]

There are, however, features in the arbitration clause which do influence the level of costs. While cost should certainly not be the only factor that parties take into account when designing their arbitration clause, there is scope for parties to pay more attention to those features. For example:

(1) On the number of arbitrators, whether to select a sole arbitrator or a three-member tribunal.
(2) Indicating the method in calculating tribunal's fees (*see* below).
(3) In some cases, parties agree upfront in their contract on adopting the expedited procedure.
(4) If there is a chance of related disputes under multiple contracts, preserving the possibility of having them heard in a single arbitration through ensuring compatibility of arbitration clauses.

Many of the above factors are self-explanatory, but the method in calculating tribunal's fees is worth examining, as the HKIAC is unique in giving parties a choice.

6. This is identified as one of the relevant factors under Article 34.4 of the HKIAC 2024 Administered Arbitration Rules in assessing the reasonableness of costs.

Arbitral institutions typically offer parties one of two methods to calculate the tribunal's fees, either: (i) on the basis of the amount in dispute, i.e., ad valorem; or (ii) by agreed hourly rates.[7] While most institutions offer an exclusive approach, HKIAC seeks to give parties the flexibility to suit their differing needs by offering both methods of calculation by Article 10.1 of the 2024 Rules. Should parties fail to agree upon a single method, the default approach of hourly rates will apply.

There are pros and cons to the two approaches. It has been argued that an hourly rate approach does not provide a strong incentive for arbitrators to run an arbitration efficiently. However, the benefit of an hourly rate approach is that it is often seen as providing the fairest remuneration to arbitrators based on the actual amount of work they have invested into the arbitration. Further, there are countervailing incentives for arbitrators to act efficiently, given they would want to maintain a good reputation to secure future appointments from parties and institutions. Conversely, for the ad valorem approach, it provides more certainty to parties as to the amount of arbitrator fees that would be payable, and for cases of lower value, this would likely result in lower costs for the parties as compared to the hourly rate. However, some have suggested that the ad valorem approach does not encourage care and thoroughness, since there is an upper limit to the fees that can be received by the arbitrator no matter the time that they put into the case. As rightly observed by Professor Waincymer,[8] 'from the perspective of economic incentives, any method of determining fees is problematic unless arbitrators retain high standards of ethical responsibility and ensure that they do all that is necessary and appropriate for a fair and efficient resolution of the dispute'.

By and large, HKIAC's experience, both with respect to cases where the hourly rate approach or where the ad valorem approach is adopted, has been that arbitrators do treat their responsibilities seriously and problems with tribunal fees are few and far between. It is recognised that when problems do arise, parties are often in a difficult position in that with an arbitration case still ongoing, parties are generally cautious not to unnecessarily irritate the tribunal and may turn to arbitration institutions for assistance.

In the case of hourly rates, HKIAC imposes a cap on the hourly rate,[9] thereby preventing arbitrators from proposing exorbitant rates. Otherwise, in line with its light-touch approach, HKIAC leaves it to the designating party and the co-arbitrator (or the designating parties and the sole or presiding arbitrator, as applicable) to agree on the applicable rate. As a further safeguard, paragraph 9.1, Schedule 2 of the 2024 Rules makes it clear that the remuneration for an arbitrator is restricted to 'work reasonably carried out in connection with the arbitration'. The requirement for work to be 'reasonably' carried out seeks to prevent abusive overcharging. Further, in case there

---

7. For the sake of completeness, there are other approaches – *see* CIETAC's policy, whereby it charges a composite 'arbitration fee' based on a fee schedule, which is inclusive of arbitrators' fees, and decides how much to pay to the arbitrator(s).
8. J. Waincymer, 'Procedure and Evidence in International Arbitration', Kluwer Law International 2012, 5.17.3.
9. Schedule 2, paras 9.3 to 9.5, 2024 Rules. As of the date of writing, the cap is set at HKD 6,500 per hour.

are exceptional cases which require HKIAC to intervene, the 2024 Rules introduced a new institutional power for HKIAC to review and adjust the arbitral tribunal's fees and expenses. Paragraph 5.1, Schedule 2 of the 2024 Rules provides that 'HKIAC may review an arbitral tribunal's fees and expenses. Following such review, and where HKIAC considers appropriate in the circumstances of the case, HKIAC may make adjustments to the arbitral tribunal's fees and expenses.' Based on past positive experience of tribunals, this power is anticipated to be used infrequently.

There is no universal answer as to whether an ad valorem or hourly rate approach is preferable, but given the flexibility under the HKIAC Rules, parties are encouraged to elect the method of remuneration in their arbitration clause. This is reflected in recent amendments to HKIAC's Model Clause, which includes the following sub-clause: 'The fees and expenses of the arbitral tribunal shall be determined on the basis of ... (Schedule 2 or Schedule 3) of these Rules.'

V STRATEGY 2: EXPLORE FUNDING OPTIONS IN ARBITRATION AT COMMENCEMENT OF ARBITRATION

Prior to the commencement of an arbitration, claimants are also encouraged to consider funding options. There are two major legislative reforms in Hong Kong in recent years in enhancing access to justice in arbitration: third-party funding and outcome-related fee structures. From HKIAC's observations, these funding tools are gaining traction but arguably remain underutilised.

1 Third-Party Funding

Even prior to the legislative reforms, Hong Kong courts have sought to carve out exceptions from common law offences of champerty and maintenance based on access to justice considerations.[10] As was recognised in the Hong Kong Court of Final Appeal judgment in *Unruh v. Seeberger*, 'an attack on an arrangement said to constitute maintenance or champerty could well result in a claim which is perfectly good in law being stifled where the plaintiff, deprived of the support of such an arrangement, is unable to pursue it. This is a powerful argument for such cases to be excluded from the ambit of maintenance and champerty'.

Access to justice considerations were central in the consultation process for allowing third-party funding in international arbitration in Hong Kong, which culminated in the Hong Kong Arbitration and Mediation Legislation (Third Party Funding) (Amendment) Ordinance 2017 in February 2019. Mirroring this position, HKIAC's Administered Arbitration Rules also supported parties' engagement of third-party funding, subject to disclosure requirements. More specifically, once the funding agreement is reached, the funded party must give written notice to denote the 'funding

10. *Unruh v. Seeberger*, FACV Nos 9 & 10 of 2006, [91]-[98]; *Berman v. SPF CDO I Ltd* [2011] 2 HKLRD 815, [25]

agreement and the identity of any third-party funder'.[11] In HKIAC's experience, it appears that third-party funding has gained traction in the past few years, with eighty-nine cases having disclosed third-party funding as of the end of 2024, but there is still scope to increase its usage.

Third-party funding cannot go unregulated as they can pose risks when third-party funders are commercial entities that are driven by commercial incentives to maximise their return. Three risks which are relevant to access to justice considerations are: (i) whether third-party funding would promote unnecessary arbitration proceedings; (ii) whether third-party funders would exert too much control over the arbitration proceedings; and (iii) whether unsophisticated funded parties would be subject to onerous terms (e.g., with the majority of the claim proceeds flowing to the funder).

Particularly with respect to point (iii), there has been renewed debate in some jurisdictions as to whether funded parties benefit from true access to justice if they are unable to retain most of the proceeds from the successful claim. There is no straightforward answer, particularly if the alternative could be that the third-party funder is then simply unable or unwilling to fund the arbitration. For the funded party, getting imperfect access may still be better than having no access. In the case of Hong Kong, one safeguard is that under the relevant Code of Practice for Third Party Funding of Arbitration, the third-party funder must take reasonable steps to ensure that the funded party is made aware of the right to seek independent legal advice on the funding agreement before entering into it.[12] There are concepts under common law, e.g., duress, unconscionability, undue influence, which provide grounds for avoidance of contract, but where a funding agreement is voluntarily entered into by a funded party, whether the share of proceeds as between a funded party and a funder is fair or not could be said to be the outcome of a contractual bargain.

2 Outcome-Related Fee Structures

Following the introduction of third-party funding, the Arbitration Ordinance and the Arbitration (Outcome Related Fee Structures for Arbitration) Rules (Cap. 609D) (ORFSA Rules) were passed to permit three types of outcome-related fee structures (ORFSAs) in Hong Kong, namely, conditional fee agreements (CFAs), damages-based agreements (DBAs), and hybrid damages-based agreements (Hybrid DBAs).

Under CFAs, lawyers will be paid a 'success fee' if the client enjoys a successful outcome in the arbitration, which is effectively an uplift on the lawyer's standard fees. CFAs commonly manifest in two forms: first, parties may agree to a 'no win, no fee' arrangement, where clients need not pay any legal fees unless they are victorious, though disbursements such as expert costs are typically carved out and made payable upfront. Alternatively, 'no win, low fee' arrangements may be entered into, whereby

11. Article 44.1 & 44.2, 2024 Rules. *See also* para. 2(i), Schedule 4; Articles 4.3(i), 5.1(g), 27.6(i), 27.7(f), & 44.3, 2024 Rules.
12. Code of Practice for Third Party Funding of Arbitration, para. 2.3(1).

legal fees are paid at a discounted fixed rate by default unless the arbitrating party succeeds in its claim, to which the success fee would be payable.

For DBAs, the client is only obliged to pay the lawyer if the client obtains a financial benefit in the arbitration award, and the payment would be calculated by reference to the financial benefit obtained by the client (a 'DBA Payment').

Finally, parties may further maximise the flexibility in funding outcomes via a hybrid DBA. Lawyers in this arrangement will be paid: (i) a DBA Payment if the client succeeds and obtains a financial benefit and (ii) an unconditional, typically discounted, sum in any event. This can likely lessen the working capital pressure and financial risks of law firms.

The introduction of outcome-related fee structures again has access to justice considerations, although safeguards are required to prevent abuses. For CFAs, to prevent parties from being charged grossly exorbitant fees and profit-minded lawyers from encouraging frivolous claims, the success fee payable to a lawyer is subject to a ceiling of 100% of the lawyer's benchmark fees to ensure that the success fee paid by the parties is within reasonable realms. As for DBAs, it is worth noting that they are not universally accepted (e.g., Singapore only legalised CFAs). In Hong Kong, by way of contrast, DBAs in international arbitration are permitted, but the DBA Payment to a lawyer is subject to a cap of 50% of the financial benefit. This ensures that parties can enjoy the fruits of arbitration without having their awards effectively depleted by the funding firm.

Since the introduction of ORFSA regime in December 2022, and as of the time of writing, HKIAC has recorded seventeen disclosures of outcome-related fee structures being adopted in arbitration. Roughly 41% were entered into prior to the commencement of arbitration, and 59% after commencement. It is still in its early days, but as with third-party funding, there is scope for further use by parties.

VI STRATEGY 3: IN-BUILT INSTITUTIONAL MECHANISMS IN DEALING WITH VEXATIONS ARISING FROM DEPOSITS FOR COSTS

Where one party to an arbitration lacks sufficient financial resources, the first sign of trouble often appears during the stage of payment of deposits, which is the advance on costs for payment of tribunal's fees and expenses and HKIAC's administrative fees.

In normal circumstances, the claimant and respondent bear the same burden in payment, whereby each shall deposit with HKIAC an equal amount that makes up the requisite deposit.[13] However, should any and all parties fail to pay the deposits in full to HKIAC within thirty days of receiving HKIAC's payment request, HKIAC shall inform the parties so that one or another of them may make the required outstanding payment.[14] Two scenarios are set out below to illustrate some observations as to how

13. Article 41.1, 2024 Rules.
14. Article 41.4, 2024 Rules.

the issue often plays out and the mechanisms available to the parties in mitigating the effects of the non-payment.

1 Scenario 1: Claimant Fails to Pay Its Share of the Deposits

Although this is less common, there are situations where a claimant, after commencing an arbitration, fails to pay the deposit to the arbitration. Where a claimant fails to do so, there is seldom any incentive for a respondent to pay on the claimant's behalf.

Under the HKIAC Rules, unless HKIAC determines otherwise, it shall transmit the case file to the tribunal as soon as it has been constituted, subject to the condition that any deposit requested by HKIAC has been paid.[15] Therefore, where neither party is willing to make the payment, the case could effectively be stalled. The 2024 Rules introduced an amendment to the effect that where the deposits remain unpaid, and where the arbitral tribunal is not yet constituted, HKIAC may also suspend or cease to administer the arbitration.[16] Where a tribunal has been constituted, the tribunal may order the suspension or termination of the arbitration.[17] Indeed, we have seen cases where the tribunal requests the transfer of the case file, solely to make an order for the termination of the arbitration due to the parties' persistent failure to pay the deposits.

On the one hand, terminating an arbitration due to a claimant's failure to put in funds may appear to be an impediment to access to justice, particularly if the failure is due to a claimant's impecuniosity. However, as elaborated in section II above, unlike court litigation, due to the private nature of arbitration, it must be accepted that there are costs associated with the process and to that extent, a claimant's right of access is circumscribed. The claimant's best bet in such circumstances may be to resort to funding options outlined above, such as third-party funding and/or ORFSA, which may assist a claimant who lacks financial resources to pursue a meritorious claim. HKIAC has no means to, and will not, investigate whether a non-paying claimant's failure to pay the deposits is due to its inability or unwillingness to do so. However, regardless of the reason, it could be unfair to a respondent to have an arbitration commenced against it indefinitely. A mechanism for the suspension or termination of the arbitration is therefore required.

2 Scenario 2: Respondent Fails to Pay Its Share of the Deposits

Unsurprisingly, it is more common that the party that fails to pay the deposit is the respondent. Unlike scenario 1, the claimant often has an incentive to pay for the non-paying respondent. What access to justice considerations are there?

In the case of an impecunious respondent, if a claimant is nevertheless interested in pursuing the claim, the fact that a respondent lacks financial resources is no impediment to the claimant's exercise of its right to have its claims heard. Provided that

15. Article 5.4, 2024 Rules.
16. Article 41.4(a), 2024 Rules.
17. Article 41.4(b), 2024 Rules.

the claimant can continue to fund the arbitration and pay for the respondent's share of the deposits, the arbitration can continue under the HKIAC Rules.[18] From the respondent's perspective, it can also be said that its failure to contribute towards the deposit of the arbitration does not deprive it of the ability to continue to participate in the proceedings and put forward its defences.

There are two possible forms of abuse arising from a respondent's non-payment of deposits. First, where a respondent continuously fails to contribute towards the deposits in the arbitration, the claimant is then required to shoulder the entire financial burden for the duration of the arbitration when based on the arbitration agreement, both parties should be jointly and severally liable for the costs, and ought to equally contribute towards the deposits.

Under Article 41.5 of the 2018 Administered Arbitration Rules and the 2024 Rules, parties may seek an award for reimbursement for deposit payments they have made on another's behalf.[19] Based on HKIAC's experience, these are regularly sought by claimants in the above scenario, and arbitral tribunals do not shy away from issuing such awards ordering reimbursement.

The second form of potential abuse is where a respondent baselessly puts forward an inflated counterclaim, potentially substantially larger than the claimant's claim, which would significantly increase the amount of total deposits payable by the parties. If the respondent refuses to pay its share of the deposit, and a claimant is unable to pay the full share of the deposit (much of which could be due to the size of the counterclaim), the case would be stalled. The respondent may not be genuinely interested in pursuing the counterclaim but would have successfully used its inflated counterclaim as a tactic to effectively block the claimant's access to justice in having its claim heard.

There are a couple of safeguards under the HKIAC Rules. First, if a respondent advances a counterclaim or cross-claim, HKIAC may request separate deposits under Article 41.2 of the 2024 Rules. Second, where deposits are not fully paid, tribunals have the option of continuing with the arbitration 'on such basis and in respect of such claim or counterclaim as the arbitral tribunal considers fit'.[20] This includes potentially continuing with the claim and not the counterclaim.

VII STRATEGY 4: SECURITY FOR COSTS APPLICATIONS

Turning the focus back to the case of an impecunious claimant. Assuming deposits are fully paid, a respondent may still be concerned that a claimant under financial pressure may have enough resources to fund the costs of its own claim, but not necessarily enough to satisfy an adverse cost order in the event that it loses. In ordinary circumstances, if a respondent is faced with an unmeritorious claim by a claimant, and the respondent ultimately succeeds in having the claimant's claim dismissed, it is likely

18. It is beyond the scope of this chapter to address situations where, subject to applicable law, there are moratoriums preventing commencement or continuation of arbitration proceedings.
19. Article 41.5, 2024 Rules.
20. Article 41.4(b), 2024 Rules.

that the respondent will be compensated for at least a portion of its legal costs. The same cannot be said when there is a risk that the claimant will not be able to honour any adverse costs award. It would mean that the respondent could be unnecessarily dragged into unmeritorious or frivolous arbitrations and expend money to defend itself, and potentially be left without the prospect of recovering its incurred costs. Claimants could be encouraged to pursue frivolous claims without any downsides while exposing respondents to financial liability. This is the rationale for security for costs applications. Typically, applications are made by respondents against impecunious claimants, although HKIAC has also seen applications made by claimants against impecunious counterclaiming respondents.

While a security for costs order is an important tool in protecting respondents, there are access to justice considerations in that it has the danger of impeding the claimant's access to justice by prematurely halting a genuine claim, before the merits of the claim can be fully examined.

Article 24 of the 2024 Rules provides a clear basis for arbitral tribunals to order security for costs.[21] Article 24 does not specify a test and many parties, when applying for security for costs, refer to other sources, including the Chartered Institute of Arbitrators' Practice Guideline on Applications for Security for Costs.

Based on our review of twenty-three recent security for costs applications, of which approximately 40% were successful, some observations could be made:[22]

(1) Most tribunals are unwilling to comment on the merits of the parties' claims, noting that it was premature to take a view on merits.
(2) For those which granted the applications, the claimant's inability to satisfy an adverse costs award often weighs heavily in the tribunal's consideration, albeit it is not the only factor (one tribunal described it as a necessary but insufficient factor).
(3) As to the evidence demonstrating a claimant's inability to satisfy an adverse costs award:
    - Where the claimant was under moratorium protection and had a third-party funding arrangement, a tribunal readily accepted that the claimant does not have assets to satisfy any adverse costs award.
    - Where a respondent was solely relying on the fact that the claimant is a foreign resident such that enforcement of any costs award would be difficult, a tribunal rejected such argument (consistent with the position under the Hong Kong Arbitration Ordinance (Cap. 609)).
    - In another case, a respondent relied on evidence demonstrating that the claimant was not in active trading and was not forthcoming about its overall assets.

21. For Hong Kong seated arbitrations, parties would often rely also on section 56(1) of the Hong Kong Arbitration Ordinance (Cap. 609), which similarly clarifies an arbitral tribunal's power in granting security for costs.
22. These examples are not binding, and each security for costs application must be assessed individually with reference to the specific circumstances of each case.

(4) A respondent's non-payment of its share of the deposits for costs of the arbitration was taken into account in some cases:
   - In one case, where a claimant had been in a position to fund the entire costs of the arbitration, including the respondent's share due to the respondent's own continued failure to pay, the tribunal viewed that as one of the many factors weighing against the respondent's assertion regarding the claimant's impecuniosity.
   - In another case, a tribunal considered that due to a respondent's non-payment of its own share of arbitration costs, it was not equitable for the respondent to seek a security for costs order against the claimant in such circumstances.

(5) Even if the tribunal is satisfied that a claimant was impecunious, the fact that the financial position of the claimant had been known to the respondent at the time of entering into the arbitration agreement is relevant too. In some cases, where a respondent sought to rely on the fact that the claimant is merely a special purpose vehicle or an asset-holding vehicle with no trading activities, a tribunal noted that it was an accepted business risk at the inception of the relationship and does not provide a ground for seeking security for costs.

(6) In some instances, the delay in making an application has resulted in the dismissal of an application which may otherwise have succeeded, as the passage of time suggests that the respondent was prepared to proceed with the arbitration without the protection of security of costs, and that the respondent should be taken to have assumed the risks of enforcement difficulties.

(7) Although argued by some parties, not all tribunals accepted the view that security for costs should only be granted in 'exceptional circumstances', but almost all expressed the view that it should be exercised carefully, noting concerns regarding impeding access to justice and stifling genuine claims.

(8) In some cases, although the tribunal granted the security for costs application, it exercised a broad-brush discretion to adjust the amount of security sought.

(9) In some cases, the claimant is funded by third-party funders, and despite the claimant's argument that the funder will cover an adverse costs award, tribunals reviewed the terms, including whether the funding agreement could be terminated early, to determine if other forms of security of costs are more appropriate.

VIII STRATEGY 5: PROPER CASE AND COST MANAGEMENT THROUGHOUT THE PROCEEDINGS

1 Case Management Tools

One of the most effective ways of reducing the cost of arbitration is through reducing the duration of arbitration. Arbitral tribunals are generally required to adopt procedures that 'avoid unnecessary delay or expense' while ensuring that parties are treated equally and are given a reasonable opportunity to present their cases,[23] and 'shall do everything necessary to ensure the fair and efficient conduct of the arbitration'.[24]

In addition to the use of technology, there are many case management tools which allow parties and tribunals to maximise procedural efficiency, including but not limited to: (i) early determination procedure;[25] (ii) expedited procedure;[26] and (iii) mechanisms to deal with multi-contract and multi-party scenarios, such as joinder of additional party,[27] consolidation of arbitrations,[28] and commencement of single arbitration under multiple contracts.[29]

In furtherance of greater time and cost-efficiency in arbitral proceedings, HKIAC has introduced a new Article 13.6 of the 2024 Rules, which clarifies (on a non-exhaustive basis) the range of case management powers available to a tribunal, including to: (i) determine preliminary issues that it considers could dispose of all or part of the case, (ii) bifurcate the proceedings, (iii) conduct the arbitration in sequential stages, and (iv) decide the stage of the arbitration at which any issue or issues shall be determined, or otherwise adopt procedures to decide the case efficiently.[30] One of the advantages of arbitration is the flexibility of its procedure; yet, many Procedural Orders No. 1 and procedural timetables are vastly similar. Tribunals and parties can put more conscious thought into the procedures that would best suit the circumstances of each case.

2 Capping of Recoverable Costs

HKIAC rules empower arbitral tribunals to set ceilings on the recoverable amount of parties' legal costs.

By Article 34.2 of the 2024 Rules, the arbitral tribunal, taking into account the circumstances of the case, may direct that the recoverable costs of legal representation and other assistance of the arbitration, or any part of the arbitration, shall be limited to a specified amount.

This provision allows a tribunal to set a cap on recoverability *prior to* the costs being incurred. This is similar to section 57 of the Hong Kong Arbitration Ordinance (Cap. 609), which drew reference from section 65 of the English Arbitration Act 1996. Section 57 of the Hong Kong Arbitration Ordinance provides:

> (1) Unless otherwise agreed by the parties, an arbitral tribunal may direct that the recoverable costs of arbitral proceedings before it are limited to a specified amount.
> (2) Subject to subsection (3), the arbitral tribunal may make or vary a direction either—

23. Article 13.1, 2024 Rules.
24. Article 13.5, 2024 Rules.
25. Article 43.1, the 2018 Administered Arbitration Rules ('2018 Rules') and 2024 Rules.
26. Article 42.1, 2024 Rules.
27. Article 27, 2018 Rules and 2024 Rules.
28. Article 28, 2018 Rules and 2024 Rules.
29. Article 29, 2018 Rules and 2024 Rules.
30. Article 13.6, 2024 Rules.

(a) on its own initiative; or
(b) on the application of any party.

(3) A direction may be made or varied at any stage of the arbitral proceedings but, for the limit of the recoverable costs to be taken into account, this must be done sufficiently in advance of—
(a) the incurring of the costs to which the direction or the variation relates; or
(b) the taking of the steps in the arbitral proceedings which may be affected by the direction or the variation.

Interestingly, the provision does not seek to cap the actual costs of the parties, but merely the amount to which they may recover. The rationale is likely to avoid interfering with parties' freedom as to how they wish to conduct preparation for their case. However, there is no doubt that a cap on recoverability would encourage more accurate cost budgeting and deter counsel and parties from incurring excessive costs given costs that exceed the cap may not be recoverable.

This cost management tool has great potential as it encourages parties' sensible budgeting through tribunals' proactive engagement with parties and counsel(s) to discuss costs.

IX CONCLUSION

Parties would naturally want the cost of arbitration to be as low as possible, but counsel, arbitrators, arbitration institutions and other service providers require reasonable remuneration for international arbitrations to continue to function and thrive. HKIAC has constantly refined its rules and practice notes to make arbitration more accessible and efficient. Given the private nature of arbitration, there would always be costs involved, but in an ideal world, the financial constraints of parties or parties' financial disparity should not pose access barriers to parties in having their disputes resolved fairly through arbitration.

To summarise the practical suggestions offered in this chapter in addressing cost issues:

- more conscious thought can be given to the design of the arbitration clause, including the upfront choice on the number of arbitrators and how arbitrators should be remunerated;
- there is potential for third-party funding and outcome-related fee structures to be utilised more;
- for a claimant, when faced with a respondent which fails to pay its share of the deposit, a claimant may be compelled to make the outstanding payment, but it is possible for the claimant to seek an award for reimbursement;
- for a respondent, when faced with an impecunious claimant, there may be basis to seek security for costs;
- Article 13(6) of the HKIAC 2024 Rules encourages tribunals to exercise their powers to adopt the most suitable case management tools to conduct cases efficiently; and

- a cap on parties' recoverable legal costs as provided for under Article 34.2 of the HKIAC 2024 Rules and section 57 of the Arbitration Ordinance can be very powerful, but would require early engagement by the tribunal and parties on costs and budgeting.

CHAPTER 47

The Impact of Costs on the Economics of Commercial Arbitration: A Funder's Perspective

Ruth Stackpool-Moore[*]

TABLE OF CONTENTS

As the name suggests, cases arising in the international commercial arbitration context typically have commerce and economics at their heart. Good claims are valuable assets and important sources of commercial revenue that should be prioritised, not least of all in a challenging economy. For prospective parties, decisions about the pursuit or defence of claims should be economic, focused on maximising revenue and optimising cash flow, with decision-making dependent on the outcome of a cost-benefit analysis of pursuing the contemplated course of action.

However, parties are not always rational nor are the economics always clear. Claimants naturally focus on the perceived strength of their claims and the anticipated

* Portfolio Manager – Global International Arbitration, Senior Investment Manager, Omni Bridgeway. The views and opinions expressed in this chapter are the author's own and are not to be construed as or imputed to Omni Bridgeway.

benefits: recovery of the headline value of a claim, without necessarily taking proper account of counsel's prospects of success analyses and often materially underestimating the significant risks attached to achieving the hoped-for outcome through arbitration which is a highly uncertain process. A failure to critically analyse anticipated costs, including the possibility of outright loss and attendant adverse cost consequences, can lead parties to make decisions that are not aligned with their economic interest, objectively assessed.

This chapter examines the key role funders play in assisting disputing parties properly assess and mitigate the economic impact of costs in the arbitral process. Putting aside the legal fees of the lawyers which should, in theory, be the subject of control by each party,[1] this chapter considers key costs fixed by third parties (institutions and arbitrators) including: advances on costs; orders for security for costs; the possibility of whether and how much of a party's costs (including funding costs) can be recovered on success and liability for adverse costs if a case is lost. In doing so it highlights the attendant social benefit of third-party funding and the access to justice it provides for impecunious parties who would be unable to meet those costs without assistance, while also explaining how sophisticated funders approach the economic analysis of an arbitral claim to arrive at a claim's risk-adjusted net present value, a key metric for parties and the funders which stand behind them to understand the true economic value of any claim.

I THE BASICS: WHAT IS THIRD-PARTY FUNDING?

At its simplest, third-party funding of arbitration involves a commercial funder agreeing to pay some or all of a party's costs to pursue or defend an arbitration claim. Those costs can include lawyer, expert, institution and tribunal fees. In return, if the claim or defence is successful, the funder is reimbursed the costs it has paid and receives a share of any sum recovered or liability defrayed (often referred to as the funder's fee or commission). If the award debtor refuses to pay, enforcement of the award will be required and select funders provide specialist services to assist with this process.

In contrast to traditional forms of finance, third-party funding is typically non-recourse. The funder only recovers its costs and receives a return on its investment if the case is successfully resolved. The funder assumes the risk of pursuing the claim. If the case is lost, or if no recovery is received, the funded party is not required to repay any of the funded costs of the claim and the funder receives nothing.

The financial terms on which a funder agrees to fund or defend a claim, as well as other rights and responsibilities of each of the parties, are set out in the funding agreement. Key terms include those relating to confidentiality and provision of documents to the funder; managing conflicts of interest and the parties' respective rights to terminate the agreement. Importantly for this discussion, in addition to

1. Discussion of the control parties can exert over the fees of counsel and the discipline third-party funders can bring to the budget and fee management process is an important but separate topic which is beyond the scope of this chapter.

specifying the amount of funding to be provided to meet the costs of the proceedings, the funding agreement should also specify the funder's liability for adverse costs, expressly stating the extent to which the funder agrees to provide any security for costs that are ordered; assume liability for any adverse costs (where applicable) and/or pay any insurance premium for an after-the-event (*ATE*) insurance policy. If these costs are to remain the responsibility of the funded party, the funding agreement should say so.

In return for paying the costs and assuming the risk of pursuing a claim, funders will be entitled to a prescribed fee or commission. Generally, the funder's fee will be a multiple of the funder's investment in the case or a percentage share of the recovery or, alternatively, the higher of these two options. The level of the fee will be negotiated and depend on a number of factors, including the size or quantum of the claim, the estimated budget to pursue the claim (including legal and expert fees, institution and tribunal fees and any ATE insurance premium) and the risks involved in the case.

As a rule of thumb, funders which have achieved longevity in the market typically seek to fund claims where the economics (as understood at the time of funding) permit the funded party to retain more than half of the anticipated award or resolution sum. For this reason, funders often require a minimum ratio between the likely resolution sum and costs of investment.[2] For example, many funders require a minimum ratio between the amount of funding and realistic claim value of 1:10.[3]

II MINIMISING OR ELIMINATING COSTS WITH THIRD-PARTY FUNDING

Greater regulatory openness in key arbitral jurisdictions and increasing market education, coupled with continuing economic uncertainty following the COVID-19 pandemic and the general expense of pursuing complex cross-border claims in a higher interest rate fiscal setting, have resulted in more parties than ever seeking some form of external finance.

This may be because parties lack the financial resources to pursue or defend their claims without assistance, or increasingly, it is because of an expanding recognition of third-party funding as a means of improving the economics of pursuing good claims: unlike normal lending, third-party funding is not recorded on a company's balance sheet, removing drag on its financials, and it is a vehicle to share or completely shift the financial risk allowing funded parties to pursue claims with no or minimal cash outflow, saving companies years of budgeted legal spending over the lifetime of a dispute, releasing that capital for investment in other parts of the business.

2. https://cdn.arbitration-icca.org/s3fs-public/document/media_document/Third-Party-Funding-Report%20.pdf (accessed 16 August 2025), April 2018 (International Council for Commercial Arbitration) (**ICCA-QMUL Report**), pp. 25-26.
3. *Ibid.*, p. 25.

At the same time, the funding industry has grown and funders are attracted to high-value international arbitration claims which enjoy the benefit of enforcement under international treaties.[4]

Supply and demand for third-party has therefore increased significantly in the last decade[5] and, as a result, third-party funding is now considered to be an established part of the international arbitration system.[6] Increasing prevalence of third-party funding means more and more parties' consideration of the economics of their cases will be influenced by their use of external finance.

III ACCESS TO JUSTICE AND OTHER BENEFITS OF FUNDING

In addition to its economic benefits, third-party funding provides considerable social benefits by giving parties that are unable to finance their own claims the opportunity to access justice. Strong access to justice in a society increases the likelihood that losses due to misconduct will be adequately compensated and that wrongdoing will be deterred. The desire to increase access to justice is one of the reasons that third-party funding of international arbitration has received strong support in many jurisdictions around the globe.[7]

Even where parties have some resources, third-party funding can also assist parties to 'level the playing field' in circumstances where a case would otherwise likely be won or lost on the basis of inequality of arms rather than the merits.

Cross-border commercial disputes can be highly complex and take years to resolve, especially where a counterparty is well resourced and its assets lie in more than one jurisdiction. Despite being conceived as a quicker and cheaper method of resolving such international commercial disputes, the unfortunate reality is that the costs of arbitration can be prohibitive, creating a significant barrier to parties' access to justice, particularly for impecunious claimants who do not have the required resources to bring their claims. Third-party funding is increasingly relied on as a means for parties to overcome the barrier to entry that the significant costs of arbitration can pose.

---

4. For example, under the New York Convention on the Recognition and Enforcement of Foreign Arbitral Awards of 1958.
5. This is supported by an increasing number of arbitral institutions and some national legislators introducing specific rules and laws relating to third-party funding of arbitration.
6. The latest data on arbitration finance from the annual Global Arbitration Review 100 survey shows there were an average of 196 funded arbitrations per year between 2019 and 2023, with 208 funded arbitrations in 2023, with the number of firms reporting funded arbitrations increasing from 54 in 2019 to 72 in 2023 https://www.pinsentmasons.com/out-law/analysis/developments-jurisdictions-third-party-funding-integral-international-arbitration?utm_source=PM+website&utm_medium=feed&utm_campaign=RSS+Outlaw (accessed 16 August 2025).
7. For example, in 2017, the Paris Bar Council adopted a resolution confirming that third-party funding is a positive development for access to justice in international arbitration and does not contravene French law Resolution adopted on 21 February 2017, by the Paris Bar Council (*Conseil de l'Ordre*). In the same year, both Hong Kong and Singapore passed legislation permitting third-party funding of international arbitration claims and related proceedings. In 2023, both Ireland and Nigeria followed suit.

IV EXAMINING THE ECONOMICS: A FUNDER'S DECISION TO INVEST[8]

Because of their unique perspective, viewing and valuing an arbitral dispute as an asset, of all non-parties to a dispute, a funder's assessment of the economics of a case aligns most closely with that of the parties. The analysis by a funder with a track record of generating consistent and high investment returns over multiple decades and economic cycles of the value of a dispute and the strategic insights it may bring for the pursuit of a case can be just as valuable as the capital provided by the funder it ultimately invests in the case.

A claim's economics lie at the heart of a funder's decision to invest in a case, along with an assessment of the legal merits or prospects of success and the likelihood of recoverability in the event of a positive outcome. In making their investment decision, funders will undertake extensive due diligence and thoroughly analyse these factors as well as other 'investment criteria', including consideration of the arbitral institution and composition of the tribunal (if appointed), the seat of the arbitration, the governing law and anticipated timing to resolution. Due diligence results are then used to inform a fair value assessment of expected return and risk metrics.

The value of a potential investment to a funder is not solely determined by the objective quantum of a claim (for single case funding) or claims (for a portfolio). This figure has to be balanced against the estimated costs required for their pursuit and considered in the specific context of the possible available outcomes, understood through a probabilistic scenario analysis. A funder will try to ensure that the estimated costs and risks of pursuing a claim or claims are not disproportionate to the likely recovery. It does this by calculating the net present value of the expected loss-adjusted and probability-weighted investment cash flows.

In order to make this assessment, a funder will require the lawyers to prepare a detailed budget that includes the estimated legal fees[9] and arbitration costs, including the arbitrator and institutional fees. The funder will also consider what portion of those arbitration costs its client will likely be required to bear[10] as well as expected cost recovery outcomes, including an estimated amount of adverse costs exposure (where applicable in accordance with the governing law and/or terms of the funding agreement) which may apply if the claims are lost. The budget and costs exposure is considered in the context of the anticipated duration of the case as well as likely

8. Commentary in this section reflects the market leading practice employed at Omni Bridgeway to value complex disputes (whether for or against a company) under which it leverages its multi-disciplinary platform and proprietary risk assessment and valuation techniques to arrive at a net present fair value of assets and/or liabilities, which its funded clients can then use to inform settlements, provisions, insurance discussions, strategy and more.
9. The funder may require a fee cap or fixed fee from the legal team and/or an agreement on the treatment of budget overruns, to provide certainty over this aspect of the estimated budget.
10. For example, when considering funding a claimant a funder will need to take into account the likelihood of the respondent paying its share of the institution and arbitrators fees, *see* discussion further below, or, if funding a respondent with significant counter claims, whether and to what extent separate deposits may be levied.

outcome scenarios, which are assigned probabilities based on legal opinions, statistical legal databases and leveraging internal and historical expertise.

Following this detailed assessment, estimated future cash flows associated with the claim(s) are discounted to their present value using an appropriate discount rate, taking into account the time value of money and the expected duration of the arbitration process.

Leveraging the sophisticated case assessment process employed by an experienced third-party funder like Omni Bridgeway, funded parties with an informed view of the risk-adjusted net present value of their claims are able to maximise the chances of achieving the claim's fair value and converting it to cash.

V GUIDANCE ON THE INTERPLAY BETWEEN COSTS AND FUNDING

In response to the increasing use and availability of third-party funding in arbitration, a number of sources of guidance have emerged to assist arbitration practice, including in relation to costs, where third-party funding is involved.

In 2013, a task force on third-party funding was convened by the International Council for Commercial Arbitration (*ICCA*) and Queen Mary University of London (*QMUL*) to address practical issues about third-party funding in the context of international arbitration processes, including cost issues. The ICAA-QMUL taskforce published its final report (*ICCA-QMUL Report*) in April 2018; Chapter 6 covers costs and security for costs.[11]

A number of arbitral institutions have imposed specific rules relating to third-party funding,[12] including in relation to certain aspects of the imposition and recovery of costs.[13] For this chapter, the author considered the rules of the ICC International Court of Arbitration (*ICC*), London Court of International Arbitration (*LCIA*), Singapore International Arbitration Centre (*SIAC*), Hong Kong International Arbitration Centre (*HKIAC*) and Australian Centre for International Commercial Arbitration (*ACICA*). Neither the ICC nor LCIA have published any specific rules relating to funding and costs. However, HKIAC, SIAC and ACICA have each introduced rules relating to costs in funded cases. Some arbitral institutions, including the ICC and SIAC, have covered issues relating to funding in practice or guidance notes.[14] The relevant rules and notes are discussed below.

Published awards and/or decisions of tribunals where available can also provide guidance on how costs issues in funded cases may be treated.

---

11. *Ibid*. The task force comprised a range of stakeholders including representatives from arbitral institutions, lawyers, academics and funders.
12. Primarily relating to conflicts of interest and disclosure, which are outside the scope of this chapter.
13. For example, allocation of costs and security for costs in funded cases.
14. The ICC Commission Report on Decisions on Costs in International Arbitration, 11 November 2016 provides guidance on the allocation of costs in ICC arbitrations and includes a section on funding costs and success fees or uplifts ay pp. 16-17. In 2017, the SIAC also issued a Practice Note PN-01/17 on Arbitrator Conduct in Cases Involving External Funding.

VI FUNDING AND ADVANCES ON COSTS

Costs payable at the commencement of proceedings usually include a fixed fee, the institution's administrative fee and a deposit on account for arbitrators' fees and expenses. The institution's administrative fee may be calculated with reference to the amount in dispute (aggregating the value of claims and counterclaims)[15] or may be charged at a fixed annual rate.[16] The LCIA is an exception and charges its administrative fees based on hourly rates for the time spent by its staff or the LCIA Court on the case. The institution will usually also fix an advance on costs (also called a deposit) at the commencement of proceedings or shortly thereafter.[17]

Generally, the party commencing the arbitration will pay the filing fee and both parties will be jointly liable to pay the advance on institution and arbitrator's fees in an amount fixed by the institution, calculated on the basis of the sum in dispute.[18] Payment of the institution and arbitrator's fees is generally shared equally between the parties; however, under some sets of rules, this allocation may be varied on application of a party or subject to the Court's power to determine otherwise in the case of the ICC.[19] Supplementary advances or deposits may also be requested during the arbitration if the amount in dispute increases or the institution determines additional funds are required on deposit.[20]

Any unused portion of the advances will be returned to the parties at the end of the proceedings[21] usually in the same proportion as their contributions. And whether and how much of the fees paid will be shifted to the other party will be determined under the tribunal's discretion to award costs at the end of the proceedings.[22]

If one party (usually the claimant) pays its share of the advance on costs and the other refuses to pay, the former will be invited to pay in lieu of the recalcitrant party, to enable the arbitration to proceed. If payment is not made, then most rules provide that the tribunal may order the suspension or termination of the arbitration.[23]

It is not uncommon for respondents to use non-payment of advances on costs as a tactic to try and prevent the claims against them from being pursued. Being required to pay the full amount of the advance on costs can be a serious additional economic burden for parties and in certain cases can serve to stifle a party's access to justice even before their claims have had a chance to get off the ground.

15. ICC, LCIA, SIAC and HKIAC. ACICA calculates its administrative fees based on a combination of factors, including the amount in dispute, the complexity of the case, and the number of arbitrators appointed.
16. ICSID.
17. *See* SIAC Rules 2016, Rule 34; HKIAC Rules 2018, Article 41; LCIA Rules 2020, Article 24; ICC Rules of Arbitration, Article 37; and ACICA Rules 2021, Rule 49.
18. SIAC Rules 2016, Rule 30.1; ACICA Rules 2016, Article 37; HKIAC Rules 2018, Article 41.1.
19. ICC Arbitration Rules 2021, Article 37(2); HKIAC Rules 2018, Article 41.3; SIAC Rules 2016, Rule 34.4; LCIA Rules 2020, Article 26.2.
20. LCIA Rules 202, Article 24.5; SIAC Rules 2016, Rule 34.2.
21. ICC Rules 2021, Article 38(7); LCIA Rules 2020, Article 24.10; SIAC Rules 2016, Rule 34.7; HKIAC Rules 2018, Article 41.7.
22. *See* section below dealing with recovery of costs.
23. ICC Rules 2021, Article 38(6); LCIA Rules 2020, Article 24.9; SIAC Rules 2016, Rule 34.6; HKIAC Rules 2018, Article 41.6.

In these cases, the claimant may have no option but to seek third-party funding in order to pay the advance and other costs of the arbitration.[24] As a funder's terms will usually involve a return based on the greater of a multiple of funded costs or percentage of the resolution sum, every additional dollar spent by a party increases the potential minimum return to the funder and many respondents will try to use this to its advantage, hoping to upset the economic balance of the case from the claimant's or the funder's perspective.

Where a party has paid the other party's share of the advance, the paying party may choose to wait until the end of the arbitration to try and recover the payment in the final award on costs or it can ask the tribunal to make a partial award in respect of the advance on costs.[25] If a partial award is made, the paying party can seek to recover that amount as a debt immediately due and payable by the defaulting party, together with any interest. A partial award could allow the paying party to regain leverage in the proceedings against the defaulting party. However, it may not be worth much if enforcement of that award is difficult - not all jurisdictions will recognise a partial interim award - and/or costly.

VII FUNDING AND SECURITY FOR COSTS

Arbitrators have broad discretion when it comes to ordering security for costs,[26] typically guided by the specific facts and circumstances of each case. Such orders will usually be made when financial concerns or party conduct suggest payment the costs of the arbitration, including potential adverse costs if they are unsuccessful in the proceedings, may be an issue.

The history of decisions on security for costs and third-party funding has been mixed.[27] In March 2013, a PCA tribunal dismissed a respondent's request for security for costs on the basis it had not shown a sufficient causal link between the mere existence of third-party funding and the claimants' inability to pay an eventual costs

24. *See Zbigniew Piotr Grot and others v. Republic of Moldova* ICSID Case No. ARB/16/8. In that case the respondent requested information about the existence and identity of a funder backing the claimants. The claimants confirmed that there was a funder and that its recourse to funding was the result of the respondent's failure to pay the advance on costs of the arbitration which were then paid by the claimants. The president of the ICSID tribunal commented that '*since Moldova has not contributed to the costs, it is perhaps not unreasonable for the Claimant to have looked elsewhere to top up funds*' (Transcript of hearing, 11 December 2017, [16]-[19]).
25. Arbitral rules generally do not explicitly address the concept of seeking a partial award specifically for the other party's share of deposits paid. However, some rules allow parties to request interim or partial awards which could extend to payment of costs. Whether such requests will be granted depends on the discretion of the tribunal and the specific circumstances of the case. *See* HKIAC Rules 2018, Article 36; SIAC Rules 2016, Rule 29; ICC Rules 2020, Article 28; LCIA Rules 2020, Article 26.
26. Many sets of institutional rules provide for the tribunal's power to order security for costs, but little by way of guidance as to how such power is to be exercised. *See* for example HKIAC Rules 2018, Article 24 which simply states '[t]he arbitral tribunal may make an order requiring a party to provide security for the costs of the arbitration'. *See also* SIAC Rules, Rules 30.1 and 27(j).
27. Source information typically comes from the investor-state arbitration context given the higher number of decisions available publicly.

award, regardless of whether the funder was liable for costs or not.[28] In August 2014, a majority award by an ICSID tribunal ordered a claimant to provide security for costs on the basis of the claimant's history of non-payment of costs awarded against it and the fact that the claimant had received third-party funding to bring its claim.[29] There the tribunal considered that the claimant's lack of financial resources and its receipt of third-party funding increased the risk that it would not comply with any adverse costs ordered against it. In June 2015, an ICSID tribunal rejected an application for security for costs on the grounds that third-party funding did not, of itself, constitute exceptional circumstances that would justify ordering security.[30] In April 2017, in a case where the claimant was bankrupt and was unlikely it could pay an eventual costs order, and the tribunal was not aware of any terms in the third-party funding agreement requiring the funder to meet any adverse costs award made against the claimant, an ICSID tribunal refused a request for security for costs and other provisional measures relating to disclosure of funding arrangements because there was an ATE insurance policy in an amount well above the amount sought by the respondent as security.[31]

These decisions pre-dated the release in April 2018 of the final report of the ICCA-QMUL task force on third-party funding.[32] The guiding principles relating to applications for security for costs set out in that report are clear: an application for security for costs should, in the first instance, be determined on the basis of the applicable test, without regard to the existence of any funding arrangement, and the terms of any funding arrangement, including an ATE insurance policy, *may* be relevant *if* relied upon to establish that the claimant (or counterclaimant) can meet any adverse costs award (including, in particular, the funder's termination rights).

In June 2018, a PCA tribunal ordered the claimants to provide security for costs on the basis that there were extraordinary circumstances because the claimants' third-party funding agreement expressly provided that the third-party funder would not cover an adverse costs order or the costs of defending an application for security for

28. *Guaracachi v. Bolivia,* UNCITRAL Permanent Court of Arbitration (**PCA**) Case No 2011-17 (Procedural Order No. 14) https://www.italaw.com/sites/default/files/case-documents/italaw1331.pdf (accessed 16 August 2025).
29. *RSM Production Corporation v. Saint Lucia* (ICSID Case No. ARB/12/10) https://www.italaw.com/sites/default/files/case-documents/italaw3318.pdf (accessed 16 August 2025).
30. *EuroGas Inc and Belmont Resources Inc v. Slovak Republic* (ICSID Case No. ARB/14/14) (Procedural Order No. 3) https://www.italaw.com/sites/default/files/case-documents/italaw6272_0.pdf (accessed 16 August 2025); *See also South American Silver Ltd v. Plurinational State of Bolivia* (PCA Case No. 2013-15) (Procedural Order No. 10).
31. *Eskosol SpA in liquidazione v. Italian* Republic (ICSID Case No. ARB/15/50) (12 April 2017) https://www.italaw.com/sites/default/files/case-documents/italaw8996.pdf (accessed 16 August 2025).
32. *Supra* (n 8). At the time the ICCA-QMUL Report was published, only a handful of arbitral institutions had addressed third-party funding directly. Therefore, the aim of the task force was for the principles and commentary in the report to assist parties, counsel and arbitrators, as well as to provide guidance for regulatory bodies and arbitral institutions that sought to address these issues.

costs.[33] In January 2020, an ICSID tribunal also found exceptional circumstances existed to justify ordering security for costs because the third-party funder had expressly stated that it did not accept liability for any adverse costs award.[34] The respondent argued that it had been unable to recover costs from funded claimants in several other cases and cited the *RSM Production Corporation v. Saint Lucia* case as to why security should be paid. The tribunal considered that the non-liability of the funder for an adverse costs award gave rise to a 'more extreme situation' and was therefore an exceptional circumstance. In May 2021, an ICSID tribunal dismissed an application for security for costs where the claimant was funded and the funding agreement contained a clause excluding payment of any adverse costs award.[35] The tribunal decided that, although it had the power to make an order for security for costs, the application did not satisfy the criteria required for making such an order.

Given the varying decisions that have been made, there is still considerable uncertainty for parties and funders as to whether and, if so, what form of security will be ordered by a tribunal. It would be helpful if more arbitral institutions provided rules and/or guidance to promote greater uniformity and consistency in this area.

VIII FUNDING AND ALLOCATION OF COSTS

The allocation of costs on conclusion of an arbitration is typically within the discretion of the arbitral tribunal, guided by the relevant institutional rules. These rules may provide that costs should follow the event, meaning that the unsuccessful party typically bears the costs of the arbitration, or that they be apportioned between the parties based on the circumstances of the case, including the parties' conduct during the arbitration.[36]

In accordance with Practice Note PN-01/17 on Arbitrator Conduct in Cases Involving External Funding (*2017 SIAC Practice Note*) issued in 2017,[37] tribunals empanelled in accordance with the SIAC Rules may take into account the existence of any third-party funder in apportioning the costs of the arbitration and the involvement of a funder in ordering in its award that all or a part of the legal or other costs of a party be paid by another party.[38]

33. *Manuel García Armas and others v. Bolivarian Republic of Venezuela,* PCA Case No. 2016-08 https://www.italaw.com/sites/default/files/case-documents/italaw9849_2.pdf (Spanish) (accessed 16 August 2025).
34. *Dr Dirk Herzig as Insolvency Administrator over the Assets of Unionmatex Industrieanlagen GmbH v. Turkmenistan* (ICSID Case No. ARB/18/35) https://www.italaw.com/sites/default/files/case-documents/italaw11243.pdf (accessed 16 August 2025).
35. *Hope Services LLC v. Republic of Cameroon* (ICSID Case No. ARB/20/2) http://icsidfiles.worldbank.org/icsid/ICSIDBLOBS/OnlineAwards/C8233/DS16392_En.pdf (French) (accessed 16 August 2025).
36. HKIAC Rules 2018, Article 34; SIAC Rules 2016, Rule 28.4; ICC Rules 2021, Article 38(4); LCIA Rules 2020, Article 28.4.
37. https://siac.org.sg/wp-content/uploads/2022/08/Practice-Note-for-Administered-Cases-%E2%80%93-On-Arbitrator-Conduct-in-Cases-Involving-External-Funding.pdf (accessed 16 August 2025).
38. *Ibid.*, at [10]-[11].

The guiding principles set out in the ICCA-QMUL Report regarding the allocation of costs are emphatic that recovery of costs should not be denied on the basis that a party seeking costs is funded by a third-party funder.[39] This reflects earlier decisions in investor-state arbitration cases.[40]

In the absence of an express power in applicable national legislation or procedural rules, a tribunal lacks jurisdiction to issue a costs order against a third-party funder.[41] In May 2023, the Delhi High Court set aside an order directing a third-party funder to provide security for the amount awarded under an arbitral award.[42] The court held that a third party is only bound by an award if it was a party to the arbitration proceedings. In its decision, the court said that third-party funding was essential for securing access to justice. It was also essential that funders have certainty about their potential exposure and cannot be imposed with liability to pay an award where they have not accepted that risk.

Given the confidential nature of international commercial arbitration and the publication of relatively few awards and decisions, the full extent to which commercial arbitral tribunals are taking into account any third-party funding arrangement in determining all or part of the costs of the arbitration is unclear. In the author's view, if the funded party is successful, then, as set out in the *RSM* and *Kardassopoulos* cases, there is no reason why the existence of funding should be taken into account in the apportionment of costs, except to the extent that the recovery of the funding costs themselves are being sought (*see* below). On a successful recovery, the funder will be reimbursed the costs it has expended on the arbitration. Therefore, denying a funded party a costs order against the unsuccessful party, solely because it was funded, would reduce the amount it receives from the recovery.

If a funded party is unsuccessful and it appears it is unable or unwilling to pay, the question will likely arise as to whether the funder can be ordered to pay any adverse costs directly. Where the funder has assumed liability for adverse costs, for example by submitting to the jurisdiction of the tribunal for the purposes of costs or has provided a costs undertaking to satisfy an order for security for costs, it will be directly liable for

39. *Supra* (n 8), p. 145.
40. In 2011, an ICSID ad hoc committee dismissed an argument that the successful party should not be awarded costs in respect of its legal fees on the basis that those legal fees had allegedly been met by an undisclosed third-party (*RSM Production Corporation v. Grenada* (ICSID Case No ARB/05/14) at [68]). The committee agreed with an earlier ICSID tribunal which stated that it knew '*of no principle why any ... third-party financing arrangement should be taken into consideration in determining the amount of recovery*' of the costs incurred in the arbitration (*Kardassopoulos and another v. Georgia* (ICSID Case Nos ARB/05/18 and ARB/07/15), Award of 3 March 2010 at [691]).
41. In 2011, an ICSID ad hoc committee dismissed an argument that the successful party should not be awarded costs in respect of its legal fees on the basis that those legal fees had allegedly been met by an undisclosed third-party (*RSM Production Corporation v. Grenada* (ICSID Case No ARB/05/14) at [68]). The committee agreed with an earlier ICSID tribunal which stated that it knew '*of no principle why any ... third-party financing arrangement should be taken into consideration in determining the amount of recovery*' of the costs incurred in the arbitration (*Kardassopoulos and another v. Georgia* (ICSID Case Nos ARB/05/18 and ARB/07/15), Award of 3 March 2010 at [691]).
42. *Tomorrow Sales Agency Private Ltd v. SBS Holdings, Inc and others* [FAO(OS)(COMM) 59 of 2023].

any adverse costs award. In circumstances where the funder has not assumed this liability and is not party to the proceedings, the tribunal lacks jurisdiction to make an order against the funder as it is not a party to the arbitration agreement. No known arbitral rules provide tribunals the power to issue a costs order against a third-party funder.

IX RECOVERY OF FUNDED COSTS

The ability of funded parties to recover funded costs has a substantial impact on the value of a claim. Passing the costs of funding on to an unsuccessful counterpart is obviously an attractive proposition for funded parties who will ultimately be entitled to retain a greater share of the damages awarded in the proceedings as a result. There are two advantages from a funder's perspective. Not only are the client and funder's interests even more closely aligned (with both the funder's and the client's returns coming solely from the counterpart rather than the funder's return comprising part of the damages awarded to the funded client), opposing parties must take the risk of having to meet funded costs into consideration when assessing their exposure in ongoing cases. Counterparts who appreciate a significant risk of having to meet funding costs in addition to potential damages can be expected to be more open to reasonable settlement, an outcome which is valuable not only because it creates value certainty for both the funder and funded client but also because it brings forward cash revenue from the claim.

Whether the costs of funding, including a third-party funder's fee, is recoverable as costs of the arbitration will depend on the definition of recoverable costs in the applicable national legislation and procedural rules.

A number of institutional rules use language which is sufficiently broad to allow the tribunal's discretion to apportion costs to extend to funding costs, by referencing the tribunal's authority to make orders in respect of a party's legal 'and other' costs.[43] In a Singapore-seated SIAC award rendered in 2020, the tribunal held that Rule 33 of the SIAC Rules 2013 which provides (in the same terms as the equivalent Rule 37 in the 2016 edition) that '*[t]he Tribunal shall have the authority to order in its award that all or a part of the legal or other costs of a party be paid by another party*' is '*extremely broad*' such that it '*provides the Tribunal with authority to award recovery of the Claimants' legal and other costs, including* [third-party funding] *Costs, as long as those costs are incurred in connection with the arbitration*'.[44] In 2021, in a Singapore-seated arbitration under the ICC Rules, a funded party was awarded its third-party funding costs on similar grounds.

43. For example, SIAC Rules 2016, Rule 37.
44. *Blair James Speers & Graham Paul Johnson v. Makemytrip Limited & Hotel Travel Limited* (SIAC Case No. ARB169/16/AB, Final Award dated 9 June 2020, at [159]), a case funded by Omni Bridgeway (*see* https://omnibridgeway.com/docs/default-source/investors/asx-announcements/103-b-fund-5---arbitration-award) (accessed 16 August 2025).

Under the HKIAC Arbitration Rules 2018, the arbitral tribunal is expressly permitted to take into account any third-party funding arrangement in determining all or part of the costs of the arbitration.[45]

In updated rules introduced by ACICA in April 2021, the recoverable costs of arbitration expressly include the costs of obtaining third-party funding. Rule 48(d) provides that the term 'costs of arbitration' includes '*the parties' legal and other costs, including, but not limited to, in-house costs, such as in-house counsel and other non-independent experts, and third-party funding costs, directly incurred by any party in conducting the arbitration, if such costs were claimed during the arbitration proceedings and only to the extent that the Arbitral Tribunal determines that such costs are reasonable*'.

In 2015, the ICC Commission on Arbitration and ADR published a report on costs decisions in international arbitration which provided guidance on recovery of funded costs, specifying that '*a tribunal only needs to satisfy itself that a cost was incurred specifically to pursue the arbitration, has been paid or is payable, and was reasonable*', going on to clarify that '*it is feasible that in certain circumstances the cost of capital, e.g. bank borrowing specifically for the costs of the arbitration or loss of use of the funds, may be recoverable*'.[46] The ICC Commission noted that the requirement that the cost be reasonable serves as an important check and balance in protecting against unfair or unequal treatment of the parties in respect of costs, or improper windfalls to third-party funders.[47] The latter was emphasised in the ICCA-QMUL Report which specified that recovery of funded costs should be subject to the test of reasonableness and be awarded only where details of the funding costs have been disclosed from the outset of or during the arbitration, so that the other party can assess its exposure.[48]

The recovery of third-party funding costs under certain conditions is also permitted under English law. In September 2016, in refusing to set aside a partial award in which funding costs had been awarded, the English Commercial Court confirmed that an arbitrator's general power to award costs does include the power to award the costs of third-party funding.[49] In the underlying English-seated ICC arbitration, the arbitrator had considered it reasonable and in the interests of justice to award indemnity costs, including almost GBP 2 million in funding costs, as a result of the respondent's '*reprehensible conduct going far beyond technical breaches of contract*' which had driven the claimant to commence arbitration; the claimant's impecuniosity and the relationship between that impecuniosity and the actions of the respondent. More recently, in 2021, the English Commercial Court upheld the decision of another ICC tribunal that had awarded the successful claimant its costs of funding.[50]

45. HKIAC Rules 2018, Article 34.4.
46. https://iccwbo.org/wp-content/uploads/sites/3/2015/12/Decisions-on-Costs-in-International-Arbitration.pdf (accessed 16 August 2025) at p. 17.
47. *Ibid.*
48. *Supra* (n 8) p. 145.
49. *Essar Oilfields Services Ltd v. Norscot Rig Management PVT Ltd* [2016] EWHC 2361 (Comm) https://www.bailii.org/ew/cases/EWHC/Comm/2016/2361.html (accessed 16 August 2025).
50. *Tenke Fungurume Mining S.A. v. Katanga Contracting Services S.A.S.* [2021] EWHC 3301 (Comm) https://www.bailii.org/ew/cases/EWHC/Comm/2021/3301.html (accessed 16 August 2025).

Following the decision in *Essar*, claims for the recovery of funding costs have become a more common and accepted feature of the arbitration landscape. Arbitral tribunals are increasingly more comfortable exercising their wide discretion to award third-party funding costs provided the funded party has shown those costs were reasonable. In that respect, there appears to have been a move away from the requirement articulated in *Essar* that reasonableness be determined with reference to the claimant's impecuniosity and the relationship between that impecuniosity and the actions of the respondent towards a broader approach. Post-*Essar* tribunals have accepted that it is '*entirely commercially reasonable*' even for a claimant of considerable means to turn to third-party funding.[51]

X THIRD-PARTY FUNDERS: ADDING VALUE BEYOND CAPITAL

Despite the intentions underpinning the creation of the system, the costs of engaging in international commercial arbitration are high, in many instances so high as to be prohibitive, impacting parties' access to justice. Understanding the nature and extent of costs faced, including in the form of advances on costs; orders for security for costs; the possibility of whether and how much of a party's costs (including funding costs) can be recovered on success and liability for adverse costs if a case is lost, is a necessary first step to facilitate decision-making based on the economic rationale for the pursuit or defence of any claim.

With greater regulatory openness in key arbitral jurisdictions and increasing market education, the demand for and use of third-party funding is increasing. Positive evolution of the legislative landscape and arbitral rules both supports and imbeds the growing role third-party funders play in the international commercial arbitration ecosystem. A number of uncertainties persist, particularly regarding the award of security for costs and the recovery of funding costs, but recent positive developments signal a shift towards a more certain and unified approach.

Third-party funding helps parties address the impact of costs on the economics of an arbitration in two key ways. First, the provision of capital by a third-party funder to meet the costs of an arbitration in circumstances where they would otherwise not be met is an obvious rebalancing of the economic equation. It provides a means for parties to overcome the barrier to entry that the significant costs of arbitration can pose, facilitating access to justice and allowing impecunious parties to rebalance the playing field. The viability of claims which could otherwise not be pursued due to lack of funds is then able to be assessed in a more holistic manner, which is the second key way in which third-party funding influences the impact costs have on the economics of an arbitration. By leveraging the rigorous and sophisticated case assessment process employed by an experienced third-party funder like Omni Bridgeway, funded parties can understand the risk-adjusted net present value of their dispute. The analysis by a funder with a track record of generating consistent and high investment returns over

51. *Blair James Speers & Graham Paul Johnson v. Makemytrip Limited & Hotel Travel Limited* (SIAC Case No. ARB169/16/AB, Final Award dated 9 June 2020, at [175]).

multiple decades and economic cycles of the value of a dispute and the strategic insights it may bring for the pursuit of a case can be just as valuable as the capital provided by the funder it ultimately invests in the case. Armed with this insight, parties, with the support of their funder, can better evaluate the impact estimated costs and risks of pursuing a claim will have on likely recovery and weigh up strategies to minimise or eliminate cost exposure while maximising the chances of achieving a claim's fair value and converting it to cash.

PANEL 15

Plenary: International Arbitration: An AI Endeavour

The panel explores how the incremental adoption of artificial intelligence across society, including in the delivery of justice, may shape assumptions not only of what is permissible but of how arbitration should be conducted. AI will impact advocacy and decision-making, access and transparency, and the skill sets needed by participants. Speakers also discuss the impact this will have on the legitimacy of international arbitration. Should we be optimistic or pessimistic?

CHAPTER 48

Generative AI and Arbitration Finance: Not Yet a Paradigm Shift

Christopher Bogart[*]

TABLE OF CONTENTS

I INTRODUCTION

There is no doubt that generative artificial intelligence (AI) is revolutionizing the world in which we live, as daily headlines attest since the introduction of ChatGPT in late 2022. And the legal industry is no exception. Indeed, according to a 2023 Goldman

* Christopher Bogart is Chief Executive Officer, a director and co-founder of Burford Capital—the world's largest legal finance provider, and also serves as a member of its Management and Commitments Committees. Under his leadership, Burford has become the largest global provider of legal finance and a force in the global legal market. He has been featured on sixty minutes, named by the Wall Street Journal as one of the world's most influential decision makers and as a top ten legal innovator by the Financial Times. He is also the only person to be ranked by Chambers in Band 1 in both the US and the UK in their inaugural litigation finance rankings. Before co-founding Burford, Mr. Bogart held numerous senior executive positions with Time Warner. As Executive Vice President & General Counsel of Time Warner Inc., he managed one of the largest legal functions in the world. He also served as Chief Executive Officer of Time Warner Cable Ventures and one of four senior executives operating Time Warner Cable, with USD 9 billion in revenue and 30,000 employees, and as Chief Executive Officer of Time Warner Entertainment Ventures.

Sachs report, generative AI has the potential to be particularly disruptive in the legal industry (44%), second only to the administrative sector (46%).[1]

Although AI has become a buzzword in recent times, it is not a new concept. As early as 1951, Alan Turing, the father of modern computer science, predicted that machines would be capable of answering questions in a way that would be indistinguishable from human responses: "At the end of the [20th] century it will be possible to program a machine to answer questions in such a way that it will be extremely difficult to guess whether the answers are being given by a man or by the machine."[2]

What is new, however, is *generative* AI, which is capable of generating meaningful text, image or other types of output that extrapolates beyond the data in the large language model (LLM) that was used for the relevant training. ChatGPT-4 is the prime example of how this form of AI can emulate human-like conversation and has sparked the popular imagination in illustrating the vast potential across many industries. It hit headlines for passing the "Turing test"[3] and scoring in the top 10% on the bar exam.[4] Despite these headlines, the integration of generative AI into decision-making processes raises important questions about the ongoing need for human supervision, both in the conduct of international arbitration by counsel and arbitrators, as well as in decisions taken by funders on whether or not to finance those proceedings. This is reflected in the theme of the 2024 ICCA conference in Hong Kong, "International Arbitration: A Human Endeavour."

This theme highlights the enduring significance of human involvement in arbitration, from its origins in the seventeenth century to the present. While AI systems possess remarkable capabilities that present significant efficiencies in international arbitration for counsel, human judgment, insight and oversight remain crucial even in AI-driven decision-making processes. There is likewise no doubt that generative AI has the potential to revolutionize the field of third-party funding or arbitration finance, but it is just as clear, as we explain below, that for the foreseeable future there will be no replacement for human judgment and insight in our industry.

It is very important to distinguish between "mere" AI and *generative* AI. Almost all use of AI in law today is not in fact generative AI. We already use AI tools in all sorts of ways, but those tools hardly ever extrapolate beyond their data sets. And because those tools grow more sophisticated and more pervasive every year, it is easy to blur the line between "mere" AI and generative AI, because "mere" AI is on its own a game-changer, improving the quality and efficiency of so many legal tasks, from document review to legal research to memorial and hearing preparation. However, the quantum leap—in both potential and risk—comes from generative AI.

1. Goldman Sachs, "The Potentially Large Effects of Artificial Intelligence on Economic Growth (Briggs/Kodnani)", March 26, 2023.
2. Alan Turing on a BBC Third Program broadcast, May 15, 1951.
3. Leif Weatherby, "ChatGPT Broke the Turing Test," Boston Globe, November 13, 2023.
4. Karen Sloan, "Bar Exam Score Shows AI Can Keep up with 'Human Lawyers,' Researchers Say," Reuters, March 15, 2023.

II AI IN THE FIELD OF ARBITRATION FOR COUNSEL

The use of AI tools in international arbitration is a topic of growing interest and debate among arbitration practitioners. One widely agreed-upon use case for all forms of AI is their ability to enhance efficiency in routine tasks. As noted by Lucy Reed in her 2022 ICCA paper, "AI already is and will increasingly be a useful tool for data and document-driven tasks in international arbitration, including: e-discovery document review and production, proofreading, translation, and legal research."[5] Indeed, a leading arbitration research tool, Jus Mundi, just released Jus AI Legal Assistant in February 2024, purporting to leverage large language models, including ChatGPT-4 and Jus Mundi's global case law database to assist legal research, analysis, and instantaneous translation.

It is therefore unsurprisingly widely acknowledged by practitioners that generative AI will enhance legal operations by making them more efficient, reducing the time lawyers spend on non-billable tasks and low-value, commoditized legal work. A 2023 arbitration survey by Bryan Cave Leighton Paisner revealed that 30% of arbitration experts had already used AI tools for document review and production, while another 30% had used AI tools for text formatting and editing.[6] A recent independent survey of chief financial officers and general counsel found that legal and finance leaders see various cost-saving benefits of technology in legal departments, particularly for automating routine legal tasks (72%) and improving document review efficiency (68%).[7] As a result, more than half of the respondents (53%) said that they plan to invest at least 3% of their total legal budget into data analytics and AI in the next year.[8]

Allocating routinized tasks to AI presents some clear benefits to parties. Most obviously, increased efficiency in handling these routinized tasks could have the effect of reducing arbitration costs, including costs of counsel, as well as tribunal costs, as arbitrators could automate the more procedural aspects of the role like drafting the more formulaic sections of an award, including a recitation of the procedural history and claims of each party.[9]

III THE LIMITATIONS OF AI FOR ARBITRATION FINANCE

1 AI Cannot Currently Predict Outcomes

At the ICCA conference in Edinburgh in September 2022, Lucy Reed and Maxi Scherer discussed two studies that suggested AI models could accurately predict legal decisions.

5. Lucy F. Reed, "Chapter 5: AI Versus IA: End of the Enlightenment?", ICCA Congress Series No. 21 (Edinburgh 2022): Arbitration's Age of Enlightenment?, ICCA Congress Series, vol. 21 (© Kluwer Law International; ICCA & Kluwer Law International 2023) pp. 65-76.
6. Bryan Cave Leighton Paisner, 2023 Annual Arbitration Survey: The Rise of Machine Learning.
7. Burford Capital, 2024 Litigation economics: CFOs and GCs weigh in on best practices in optimizing legal department value, February 20, 2024.
8. *Ibid.*
9. Freshfields, International arbitration in 2024: Key Trends, February 2024.

The first, a 2016 study, focused on decisions by the European Court of Human Rights. Using natural language processing and machine learning, researchers trained a computer model on a dataset of 584 decisions. The model was trained on a 10% subset of the dataset and was asked to predict the Court's decision (i.e., whether or not the Court found a violation) for the remaining 90%. The model achieved an overall accuracy of 79% in predicting the Court's decision.[10]

The second, a 2017 study of decisions by the US Supreme Court, examined more than 28,000 US Supreme Court case outcomes and 240,000 votes of individual justices from 1816 to 2015. The model claimed to predict individual justices' votes with 71.9% accuracy and the outcome of decisions with 70.2% accuracy.[11]

Based on this, Scherer suggested that "these studies disprove the assumption that AI models would not be able to predict legal decisions accurately,"[12] a position that Reed characterized as "the reasonable consensus position on the impact of AI."[13] To be sure, neither of these academic studies was testing generative AI, and the outcomes cannot be extrapolated easily. For instance, in the 2016 ECHR study, the focus was limited to a data set of 584 English-language court decisions (all structured in the same manner owing to court rules), involving only three articles of the Convention, and a binary classification task—whether or not a violation of the Convention occurred, nothing more. As you might imagine, the limited damages typically awarded in ECHR cases (not analyzed in the 2016 study) as well as the significant rate of non-compliance with ECHR decisions (also not considered in the 2016 study), render such cases of limited utility for funding purposes.[14]

And in the time since ICCA 2022, LLMs have entered the mainstream, and with that, generative AI has been the subject of rigorous and robust testing and experienced a significant advancement in capabilities and processing power. The results are less encouraging, and in some instances, disconcerting, although the passage of time will likely get us to the world postulated by Reed and Scherer—we are simply not there, or close to being there, yet.

In January 2023, Scotusblog conducted an anecdotal study of one particular LLM—ChatGPT—creating a list of 50 questions about the Supreme Court covering a range of topics from important rulings, procedure, history, doctrine, and the justices. ChatGPT answered just 21 of the 50 questions correctly, making a wide array of

10. Nikolaos Aletras et al., "Predicting Judicial Decision of the European Court of Human Rights: A Natural Language Processing Perspective", PeerJ Computer Science 2:e93 (2016) https://doi.org/10.7717/peerj-cs.93 (accessed August 16, 2025).
11. Daniel Katz, Michael Bommaritoii and Josh Blackman, "A General Approach for Predicting the Behavior of the Supreme Court of the United States", PloS One 12:4 (2017).
12. Maxi Scherer, "Chapter 39: Artificial Intelligence in Arbitral Decision-Making: The New Enlightenment?", ICCA Congress Series No. 21 (Edinburgh 2022): Arbitration's Age of Enlightenment?, ICCA Congress Series, Volume 21 (© Kluwer Law International; ICCA & Kluwer Law International 2023) pp. 683-694.
13. Lucy F. Reed, "Chapter 5: AI Versus IA: End of the Enlightenment?", ICCA Congress Series No. 21 (Edinburgh 2022): Arbitration's Age of Enlightenment?, ICCA Congress Series, Vol. 21 (© Kluwer Law International; ICCA & Kluwer Law International 2023) pp. 65-76.
14. Veronika Fikfak, "Changing State Behaviour: Damages Before the European Court of Human Rights" EJIL 29, 4 (2018) https://doi.org/10.1093/ejil/chy064 (accessed August 16, 2025).

mistakes, from misstating a particular factual detail to inaccurately describing the holding of one justice on a recent Supreme decision.[15]

A year later, in a more rigorous study conducted by Stanford RegLab and the Institute for Human-Centered AI, three popular LLMs (ChatGPT 3.5; PaLM 2 and Llama 2) were tested on a wide range of legal research tasks, from low to moderate to high complexity tasks. The results showed that legal hallucinations are both pervasive and concerning, with rates of hallucinations ranging from 69% to 88% in response to specific legal queries.[16]

What is particularly notable about the January 2024 study is that the LLMs performed worst on the very kinds of cases that funders are typically presented with by counsel or plaintiffs as potential funding opportunities, namely, cases at the trial court level. According to the study, "LLMs perform best on tasks at the SCOTUS level, worse on tasks at the USCOA level, and worst on tasks at the USDC level."[17] And when dealing with complex tasks—such as measuring the precedential relationship between two cases or answering questions about a court's ruling—most LLMs do no better than random guessing and hallucinate at least 75% of the time.[18] Equally concerning, LLMs exhibit a bias toward accepting legal premises not anchored in reality (contra-factual bias), as well as an unjustified certainty in responses (an inability to always "know what they know").[19]

2 Even if LLMs Could Accurately Predict Outcomes, Data for International Arbitrations Is Lacking

Even if AI could be relied upon to accurately predict outcomes in court litigation, AI faces additional hurdles when it comes to international arbitration, either commercial or treaty arbitration.

Unlike national court litigation, in which parties' submissions and court judgments are readily available, the same is not true for international arbitration. In international commercial arbitration, the majority of final awards remain confidential to the parties. The consequence of this is that there is no publicly available data upon which to base AI-led predictions. Further, international arbitrations typically involve a variety of different applicable laws, unlike national court decisions, and this comparative complexity increases the difficulty of making direct predictions on the basis of past outcomes. As Professor Scherer put it, "International arbitration cases are typically

15. James Romoser, "No, Ruth Bader Ginsburg Did not Dissent in Obergefell: And Other Things ChatGPT Gets Wrong about the Supreme Court," SCOTUSblog, January 26, 2023.
16. Matthew Dahl et al., "Large Legal Fictions: Profiling Legal Hallucinations in Large Language Models," Stanford University, January 2024.
17. *Ibid.*
18. *Ibid.*
19. *Ibid.*

complex, fact-specific and governed by different applicable law and hence non-repetitive, offering little data of value for predictive programming."[20]

In investor-state arbitration, although the majority of final awards are available, the underlying evidence and party submissions are typically not; the cases involve scores of different investment treaties, and hundreds of arbitrators as decision-makers. Again, this creates a significant obstacle to making predictions on the basis of what is publicly available, even for investment arbitration.

This is all why a data set of someone like Burford can be so valuable, because it contains a substantial quantity of non-public material which can be used to train a model.

In arbitration as in so many other fields, AI is only as helpful as the quality and size of the available data. And in law as in other fields, the consensus among those studying human-machine interaction is that the best outcomes come from a combination of both human and AI together. As the founder of a GPT-4-powered legal tool put it, "It's not true that lawyers cannot trust generative AI for legal practice. It's only true that they cannot trust generative AI alone—a crucial distinction."[21]

It's critical to recall that generative AI is not actually performing legal analysis. Rather, it is extrapolating conclusions based on performing statistical analysis of language.

It is thus no surprise to learn that those at the forefront of AI in arbitration finance also use a combination of machine learning, data insights and human legal expertise. At Burford, we invest heavily in data science and machine learning, and we now have a 92% track record for deploying into winning cases, and this rate of success derives from a history of successfully leveraging data, including proprietary data not elsewhere available, led by the human insights of our team of litigation and arbitration specialists. But AI output, including that of generative AI, is far away from making investment decisions on its own; rather, the output is an important component of a multi-faceted investment decision-making process.

3 The "Black Box" Problem

The black box problem refers to the challenge of identifying the specific factors that led to a particular outcome prediction from AI models. In the 2023 Bryan Cave survey, 90% of respondents rated understanding how AI tools make decisions as highly important, with a rating of seven or above out of ten.[22] This illustrates how important it is to not only understand the output of an LLM but also how it reached that decision.

However, AI models, including those used in the legal sector, often struggle to explain their results, raising concerns about transparency and accountability. Instead

20. Maxi Scherer, "Chapter 39: Artificial Intelligence in Arbitral Decision-Making: The New Enlightenment?," ICCA Congress Series No. 21 (Edinburgh 2022): Arbitration's Age of Enlightenment?, ICCA Congress Series, Vol. 21(© Kluwer Law International; ICCA & Kluwer Law International 2023) pp. 683-694.
21. Ryan McKeen, "What It Takes to Build an AI Legal Assistant Lawyers Can Rely On," Casetext, Thomson Reuters, May 12, 2023.
22. Bryan Cave Leighton Paisner, 2023 Annual Arbitration Survey: The Rise of Machine Learning.

of using deductive, causal reasoning, AI models calculate probabilities and make predictions based on complex probabilistic calculations. As a result, the outputs of AI models may lack intelligible reasoning. Providing a reasoned decision that outlines the premises on which it is based constitutes one of the fundamental features of legal decision-making.

In other fields where AI is already used for decision-making, the determination required is often binary with no need to articulate how the technology got to that decision. For example, in professional tennis tournaments, AI is used to determine whether serves are in or out, based on precise measurements to the millimeter. In this case, there is no discretion; the ball either hit the line or it didn't.

In contrast, legal determinations often involve gray areas that require the application of human judgment. According to Scherer, "Deductive, causal reasoning is replaced by an inverse approach because the machine learning program extracts the algorithm from the observable data. Rather than using logic, the AI model calculates probabilities, i.e., the likelihood for any given outcome."[23] A claim cannot be granted solely based on an 80% chance that the established facts constitute a violation of the contract. The AI approach to predicting outcomes, known as legal determinism, determines future outcomes by using probabilistic calculations based on past data—which can be inherently faulty.

The black box nature of AI models hinders the ability to understand and address any biases or errors in the decision-making process. If the data used to train the model contains human biases, the machine learning algorithm may perpetuate or even exaggerate those biases in its future predictions.

4 "Hallucinated" Cases and Bad Lawyering

Consistent with the January 2024 Stanford study, the legal industry has—so far—done a spectacularly poor job showcasing effective use of AI. Instead, as each week passes, more instances of bad lawyering with AI emerge. Broadly speaking, the cases have involved AI generating "hallucinated" cases that appear plausible but are fictitious and unchecked by counsel, and at least one instance of AI being used by counsel as an authority, a "cross check," for a fee application. The result: failed motions and applications, disciplinary proceedings, and in some cases, fines. And although these examples come mainly from courts, there is no reason to think international arbitrations are immune, but owing to confidentiality, such instances may not soon come to light, if at all.

In *Park v. Kim*, counsel admitted to citing a non-existent state court decision in a reply brief to the court, explaining that she relied on ChatGPT to identify precedent that might support her arguments but did not read or otherwise confirm the validity of the

23. Maxi Scherer, "Chapter 39: Artificial Intelligence in Arbitral Decision-Making: The New Enlightenment?", ICCA Congress Series No. 21 (Edinburgh 2022): Arbitration's Age of Enlightenment?, ICCA Congress Series, Vol. 21(© Kluwer Law International; ICCA & Kluwer Law International 2023) pp. 683-694.

non-existent decision she cited.[24] This January 2024 decision is no outlier, not for the New York courts, nor for courts around the world, as examples of conduct falling well below the basic obligations of counsel have proliferated since last year.

In the case of *Mata v. Avianca,* one of the first cases of its kind before the courts in June 2023, a US district court found that ChatGPT generated fictitious court decisions and quotations that were cited by counsel in a legal brief.[25] These invented cases were not found by anyone involved in the case and counsel unfortunately doubled down on the non-existent cases, continuing to stand by the fake opinions after judicial orders called their existence into question. Similarly in *People v. Zachariah C. Crabill,*[26] a Colorado lawyer cited case law found through ChatGPT without reading or verifying the citations, failing to promptly alert the court about the inexistent cases. In a November 2023 decision, the Colorado Supreme Court held that counsel violated Colorado Rules of Professional Conduct and imposed a ninety day suspension and a fine. And these instances are not just limited to US courts, and not just limited to counsel. In *Harber v. HMRC,*[27] a UK taxpayer appealed a tax decision to a First-tier tax tribunal (FTT) relying on nine AI-generated precedents that had been provided by "a friend in a solicitor's office." None were genuine FTT decisions, and in its December 2023 decision, the taxpayer's capital gains tax penalty was upheld.

And most recently, in a February 2024 decision, a US district court found a party's invocation of ChatGPT as support for a fee application "utterly and unusually unpersuasive."[28] In the words of that district court judge: "As the firm should have appreciated, treating ChatGPT's conclusions as a useful gauge of the reasonable billing rate for the work of a lawyer with a particular background carrying out a bespoke assignment for a client in a niche practice area was misbegotten at the jump."[29] In so doing, Judge Engelmayer took notice of the *Park* and *Mata* decisions in the Second Circuit as instances in which ChatGPT proved unable to distinguish between real and fictional case citations. What is more, Engelmayer pointed out that the firm in that case made no effort to identify the inputs on which ChatGPT relied, did not reveal if any of the inputs were similarly imaginary and as a result, advised the firm to excise references to ChatGPT from any future fee applications absent "a paradigm shift in the reliability of this tool."[30]

These examples reflect a feature of how AI works: ChatGPT generates realistic responses by making guesses about which fragments of text should follow other sequences, based on a statistical model that has ingested billions of examples of text pulled from all over the internet. As this quote from the Solicitor's Regulation Authority states: "All computers can make mistakes. AI language models such as ChatGPT, however, can be more prone to this. That is because they work by anticipating the text that should follow the input they are given, but do not have a concept of 'reality'. The

24. *Park v. Kim*, 91 F.4th 610, 615 (2d Cir. 2024).
25. *Mata v. Avianca*, No. 22 Civ. 1461 (S.D.N.Y. June 22, 2023).
26. *People v. Zachariah C. Crabill*, 23PDJ067, November 22, 2023.
27. *Harber v. HMRC* [2023] UKFTT 1007 (TC).
28. *J.G. v. New York City Department of Education*, No. 23 Civ. 959 (S.D.N.Y., February 22, 2024).
29. *Ibid.*
30. *Ibid.*

result is known as 'hallucination', where a system produces highly plausible but incorrect results."[31]

The stories of lawyers being deceived by AI highlight the importance of responsible use and do not reflect the inherent value of the technology itself. AI plainly requires expert human handling, and the increasing number of stories of bad lawyering say more about the counsel and very little, if anything, about the technology itself. And as observed recently by another court in February 2024 forced to wrestle with fictitious cases, "the blind acceptance of AI-generated content by attorneys undoubtedly will lead to other sanctions in the future, but a defense based on ignorance will be less credible, and likely less successful, as the dangers associated with the use of generative AI systems become more widely known."[32]

IV HOW AI CAN BE USEFUL IN ARBITRATION FINANCE

Although AI is currently far from ready to predict arbitration outcomes, it does already have many useful applications in the legal finance context.

1 Identifying Potential Claims

AI may assist legal finance providers in better identifying claims that ought to be brought and could benefit from funding. This could be either through the identification of filed cases that are good candidates for funding or the identification through publicly available documents of latent claims that should be filed.

To achieve this, legal finance providers can use heuristics and prompting techniques to identify lawyers and cases that align with their investment parameters. For example, Burford conducted a "skunkworks" project where we scraped the web to identify lawyers who have shown interest in funding opportunities through their prior involvement in contingency cases. These lawyers were then added to Burford's database.

By analyzing the data and patterns from lawyers' past work, legal finance providers can identify potential investment opportunities that align with their investment strategy. This approach could help parties effectively identify meritorious claims that have the potential to generate significant value for their businesses and which might otherwise be overlooked. Naturally, since generative AI is backward-looking, it can only serve as a supplementary tool in identifying claims, as it would be of limited utility for the latest developments and cases unfolding and filed in real time.

2 Streamlining Underwriting Decision-Making

Legal finance is typically provided on a non-recourse basis, meaning that providers only receive a return if the case being financed resolves successfully. Therefore,

31. Solicitor's Regulation Authority, Risk Outlook report: The use of artificial intelligence in the legal market, November 20, 2023.
32. *Smith v. Farwell*, No. 2282 Civ. 1197 (Mass. Sup. Ct. February 12, 2024).

funders must carefully assess the merits and viability of a case before providing funding, conducting a rigorous diligence process. This diligence process can take several weeks or months, as funders are understandably keen to ensure they have very carefully considered every aspect of an investment that will be entirely lost if the matter is unsuccessful.

Given this, one common criticism of the legal finance industry is that the diligence process is too slow. We certainly strive to seek ways to make the process more client-friendly (and note that the diligence process is often slowed by client delays in providing documents). AI could be at least a partial solution. Advanced technology, including algorithms, machine learning and AI, have the potential to enhance and speed up the underwriting diligence process, which would make the funding application process more efficient and client-friendly. For instance, generative AI could prove particularly useful in arbitrator selection, allowing claimants, counsel, as well as funders, to identify patterns in the decisions of particular arbitrators, and arbitrator track records.

However, despite advancements in legal technology, the underwriting process in litigation finance still necessarily involves complex assessments of risk and subjective variables, which requires specialized expertise and human judgment. While AI is currently most effective in early-stage issue-spotting and identifying elements of the underlying cause of action, it lacks the computational ability and experiential data set required to make investment decisions outright. Human expertise remains crucial in assessing the nuances of a case, understanding the significance of certain factors, and making informed investment decisions.

3 Improve Legal Finance Modeling Capabilities

Lack of widely available data on commercial disputes is a significant challenge in the legal field. Approximately, 90% of commercial disputes are settled and do not end up before a court or arbitral tribunal, resulting in confidential terms of resolution. Thus, building a predictive model for commercial disputes based solely on publicly available data would fail.

After fifteen years in business and having reviewed thousands of matters, Burford has built up a unique data set not available to others. This data, paired with our people and experience, enables us to effectively model the outcome or value of litigation or arbitration. We employ an internal model for each investment, using coded and tagged nodes to establish a comprehensive understanding of the matter.

The quality of AI models is heavily reliant on the quality of the data they are trained on. Parties (and the law firms that represent them) lack sufficient data and breadth of experience in-house to evaluate their litigation portfolios. As an assistant GC and director of litigation at a health insurance company put it, "We don't have a portfolio of cases from which we can create metrics for application to future matters. Many of these cases tend to be their own little unicorns."[33]

33. Burford Capital, 2022 Affirmative Recovery Programs Report, February 7, 2022.

Burford continues to close this data gap for our funded clients. We have built a significant proprietary data set since our inception in 2009, and we use this data alongside third-party data to undertake quantitative modeling using our own proprietary analytical tools. Clients receive the benefit of our robust data sets on high-stakes commercial disputes as well as our acumen and precision in modeling to help their companies better identify, prioritize and extract value from litigation and arbitration assets.

V THE POTENTIAL FOR AI IS VAST, BUT HUMAN SUPERVISION IS NEEDED

AI is poised to become an integral part of our future world, and arbitration is no exception to this transformative trend. Governments and arbitral bodies are racing to put rules and regulations around the safe use of AI: We are already seeing efforts to regulate AI being made in the EU (the final text of which, the EU AI Act, was approved on February 2, 2024)[34] and referred to in a 2023 White House Executive Order.[35]

I expect to soon see similar efforts by arbitral bodies and centers—the Silicon Valley Arbitration and Mediation Center has already submitted draft guidelines on the use of AI in arbitration.[36] Concerns about the limitations and issues raised by AI in international arbitration are valid, and the arbitration community needs to engage with them. However, we should resist the knee-jerk trend in international arbitration to codify or regulate everything new and avant-garde. Legal finance was once met with skepticism but is now ubiquitous in commercial disputes. As one GC of a multinational logistics company put it: "Fifteen years ago, if someone asked about funding litigation it sounded radical, but now it is mainstream."[37] Arguably, the same will eventually be said for the use of AI.

As the White House Executive Order says: "AI reflects the principles of the people who build it, the people who use it, and the data upon which it is built."[38] While AI holds the potential for both great promise and peril, ultimately human supervision is needed, and it is the quality of that supervision that will determine its usefulness.

Finally, it is the two most experienced jurisdictions that have been at the forefront of the litigation finance industry—the US and the UK—to which I now turn for salient observations on the use of generative AI. As Chief Justice Roberts remarked in his year-end report on the US Supreme Court, "Machines cannot fully replace key actors in court" but he also acknowledged that "judicial work—particularly at the trial level—will be significantly affected by AI."[39] And as the Master of the Rolls, the Right

34. Foo Yun Chee, "EU Lawmakers Ratify Political Deal on Artificial Intelligence Rules" Reuters, February 13, 2024.
35. White House Executive Order on the Safe, Secure, and Trustworthy Development and Use of Artificial Intelligence.
36. Silicon Valley Arbitration and Mediation Center, Guidelines on the use of artificial intelligence in arbitration, Draft of August 31, 2023.
37. Burford Capital, 2022 Affirmative Recovery Programs Report, February 7, 2022.
38. *Ibid.*
39. Chief Justice Roberts, 2023 Year-End Report on the Federal Judiciary.

Hon. Sir Geoffrey Vos observed in his speech to the Bar Council of England and Wales last year, "Will the use of AI to predict litigation outcomes materially reduce the work needed to be done by lawyers. I doubt it. Similar, if less sophisticated technically, has been in use for years."[40]

These same observations could be made about legal finance decisions for international arbitrations. While the industry is no doubt set to be profoundly changed and hopefully improved by AI, it is unlikely AI will ever replace a funder's investment committee. But provided that AI as a tool is integrated effectively, it has the potential not to replace us but to make us better at what we do.

40. Speech by the Master of the Rolls to the Bar Council of England and Wales, July 18, 2023.

CHAPTER 49

Thinking Outside the Black Box: Arbitration and Artificial Intelligence

Emily Hay[*]

TABLE OF CONTENTS

I INTRODUCTION

The advent of artificial intelligence (AI) offers challenges and opportunities to human endeavour. Almost no profession or sector is immune from these impacts, and international arbitration is no exception. AI forces us to reexamine what it means to be human, to be intelligent, and to do justice. These questions are being answered by technologists, by societies, by governments, by courts, and by legal professionals across the globe. We need to be a part of that debate in order to ensure that arbitration remains a method of dispute resolution that is legitimate, relevant to users, and upholds fairness.

Building on important contributions that are already being made in this volume and elsewhere,[1] in section II below, we examine the terminology around AI and recent

* Emily Hay is Managing Counsel at ArbBoutique. She acts as arbitrator and counsel in international arbitrations. She writes, speaks and teaches on arbitration matters related to technology, data protection, ESG and European law.

1. *See* other contributions in this volume, and, *inter alia*, Paul Cohen and Sophie Nappert, 'The March of the Robots' (*Global Arbitration Review*, 15 February 2017) https://globalarbitrationreview.com/article/the-march-of-the-robots (accessed 16 August 2025); Maxi Scherer, 'Artificial

developments in technology. To situate our discussion, in section III we will look at how AI is being, and will be, used in international arbitration and courts. Section IV explores the limitations and risks of AI in arbitration, and section V looks forward to some ways to address those limitations.

II AI: THE HUMAN BRAIN AS INSPIRATION

'AI' can be defined in various ways. Part of the difficulty in pinning down its meaning is that the 'artificiality' of AI is defined in opposition to 'human' intelligence. It was first conceived of by John McCarthy in 1955 as 'making a machine behave in ways that would be called intelligent if a human were so behaving'.[2] To focus on its technological functioning, for the purpose of this contribution, AI is taken to refer to automated pattern analysis and decision-making.[3] This contribution will not explore the functioning of AI, machine learning, and natural language processing in any detail, which is well addressed elsewhere.[4]

AI not only mimics human capacities, but is built with human biology as its inspiration and guiding premise: the 'neural network' structure of AI computing is a simulation of the neurons found in the human brain. The very concept of AI therefore raises questions about what it means to be human and the nature of intelligence. However, the anthropomorphism of ascribing 'intelligence' to technology may obscure its true nature, leading to confusion and misuse. A particular tool which uses AI may produce output that would require astounding intelligence on the part of a human, but have no resemblance to human thought patterns.[5] We have seen several examples already of lawyers using generative AI either as a research tool or for drafting submissions, while misunderstanding that its output is not 'intelligent' in the sense of a human lawyer, or even the familiar technology of a search engine, but produces text using a predictive and probabilistic algorithm.[6]

Intelligence and Legal Decision-Making: The Wide Open?' (2019) 36(5) *Journal of International Arbitration* 539, https://doi.org/10.54648/joia2019028 (accessed 16 August 2025); Mohamed S. Abdel Wahab, 'Chapter 28: Welcome to the Future: The AI Arbitrator: An Unwelcomed Reality or Science Fiction?' in Stavros Brekoulakis and Romesh Weeramantry et al. (eds), *Achieving the Arbitration Dream: Liber Amicorum for Professor Julian D.M. Lew KC* (Kluwer, 2023); Gizem Halis Kasap, 'Can Artificial Intelligence ("AI") Replace Human Arbitrators? Technological Concerns and Legal Implications' (2021) 2021(2) *Journal of Dispute Resolution* 209, https://doi.org/10.31235/osf.io/k4g8s (accessed 16 August 2025).

2. J. McCarthy et al., 'A Proposal for the Dartmouth Summer Research Project on Artificial Intelligence' (31 August 1955) https://www-formal.stanford.edu/jmc/history/dartmouth/dartmouth.html (accessed 10 April 2024).
3. Rachel E. Stern et al., 'Automating Fairness? Artificial Intelligence in the Chinese Courts' (2021) 59 *Columbia Journal of Transnational Law* 515, 517.
4. *See, e.g.*, Kasap (n 1) 211-215; Scherer (n 1) 542-546; Ray Worthy Campbell, 'Artificial Intelligence in the Courtroom: The Delivery of Justice in the Age of Machine Learning' (2020) 18 *Colorado Technology Law Journal* 323 https://dx.doi.org/10.2139/ssrn.4425791 (accessed 10 April 2024), 2-7; Damien Charlotin, 'Large Language Models and the Future of Law' (22 August 2023) https://dx.doi.org/10.2139/ssrn.4548258 (accessed 10 April 2024).
5. Scherer (n 1) 545.
6. Nate Raymond, 'Ex-Trump Fixer Michael Cohen Says AI Created Fake Cases in Court Filing' (*Reuters*, 30 December 2023) https://www.reuters.com/legal/ex-trump-fixer-michael-cohen-say

A similar observation was made by the District Court of The Hague, in deciding on the lawfulness of an automated system ('SyRI') used by the Dutch authorities to prevent and combat fraud in tax and social security. When considering the algorithmic nature of the system, the Court found that '[t]he term "self-learning" is confusing and misleading: an algorithm does not know and understand reality'.[7]

If the aim of AI is to assist humans to solve difficult problems, rather than to possess the same intelligence as a human, then 'complementary' or 'augmented' intelligence may be a better term than artificial intelligence.[8]

In March 2024, OpenAI and robotics firm Figure released a humanoid robot called 'Figure 01' which uses a 'visual language model'. It can have full conversations and make decisions based on external stimuli, simultaneously undertaking physical and mental tasks.[9] Also in March 2024, a study found that the rate at which algorithms for pre-training language models has improved since the advent of deep learning has halved approximately every eight months.[10] A month earlier, OpenAI announced research progress on an AI video generator 'Sora', which 'can create realistic and imaginative scenes from text instructions'.[11]

Various trackers exist to predict the timing of AGI, which is AI that would be as good or better than a human in any field.[12] As of March 2025, AI expert Alan D. Thompson estimates that we are 90% of the way to AGI.[13]

As technology develops, there may not even be such a clear division between 'human' and 'artificial' intelligence. In January 2024, Neuralink implanted its first chip in a human brain, followed by two additional individuals with implants by February 2025. Called 'Telepathy', it acts as a wireless interface between brain and computer,

---

s-ai-created-fake-cases-court-filing-2023-12-29/ (accessed 10 April 2024); Jason Proctor, 'B.C. Lawyer Reprimanded for Citing Fake Cases Invented by ChatGPT' (*CBC News*, 26 February 2024) https://www.cbc.ca/news/canada/british-columbia/lawyer-chatgpt-fake-precedent-1.7126393 (accessed 10 April 2024); Neil Rose, 'Litigant Unwittingly Put Fake Cases Generated by AI Before Tribunal' (*Legal Futures*, 7 December 2023) https://www.legalfutures.co.uk/latest-news/litigant-unwittingly-put-fake-cases-generated-by-ai-before-tribunal (accessed 10 April 2024).

7. *NCJM et al and FNV v. The State of the Netherlands*, District Court of The Hague, 6 March 2020, ECLI:NL:RBDHA:2020:865, available in English at https://uitspraken.rechtspraak.nl/details?id=ECLI:NL:RBDHA:2020:1878 (accessed 10 April 2024) (hereinafter '*SyRI* decision', District Court of The Hague), para. 6.46.
8. Felicity Bell et al., 'AI Decision-Making and the Courts: A Guide for Judges, Tribunal Members and Court Administrators', Australasian Institute of Judicial Administration (June 2022) https://aija.org.au/wp-content/uploads/woocommerce_uploads/2022/06/AI-DECISION-MAKING-AND-THE-COURTS_Report_V5-2022-06-20-1lzkls.pdf (accessed 10 April 2024), 8.
9. Figure, 'Figure Status Update: OpenAI Speech-to-Speech Reasoning' (13 March 2024) https://www.youtube.com/watch?v=Sq1QZB5baNw (accessed 10 April 2024); Aaron Drapkin, 'ChatGPT Has a Body Now: What Is Figure 01 and How Does It Work?' (*Tech.co*, 15 March 2024) https://tech.co/news/what-is-figure-01-chatgpt (accessed 10 April 2024).
10. Anson Ho et al., 'Algorithmic Progress in Language Models' (9 March 2024) https://doi.org/10.48550/arXiv.2403.05812 (accessed 10 April 2024), 1.
11. OpenAI, 'Creating Video from Text' https://openai.com/sora (accessed 10 April 2024).
12. *See, e.g.*, Metaculus, 'When Will the First Weakly General AI System Be Devised, Tested, and Publicly Announced?' https://www.metaculus.com/questions/3479/date-weakly-general-ai-is-publicly-known/ (accessed 10 April 2024); https://aicountdown.com/ (accessed 10 April 2024).
13. Alan D. Thompson, 'Alan's Conservative Countdown to AGI' (*LifeArchitect.ai*, March 2024) https://lifearchitect.ai/agi/ (accessed 6 March 2025).

allowing the individuals in question to operate their phones and computers with their thoughts alone.[14]

III AI IN IA AND THE COURTS

AI is increasingly being adopted by businesses across every sector to facilitate and optimise all kinds of tasks, including decision-making.[15] As the businesses that use arbitration become accustomed to AI-enabled services, they will naturally expect a dispute resolution mechanism that is enhanced by AI. In order to meet user expectations and maintain the competitiveness of arbitration, international arbitration must engage with AI.

As AI permeates business practices, it will also become the subject matter of increasing number of disputes. Familiarity with AI gives our profession valuable expertise in the handling of such disputes. This ties in with a key advantage of arbitration over court litigation, being the possibility to participate in the selection of a decision-maker with specific expertise in the subject matter of a dispute.

In dispute resolution, some AI tools are already available and are at various stages of integration into practice, such as systems powered by generative AI to assist in document review, analysis, drafting, research and summarising.[16] Other applications which either exist or are anticipated include prediction of case outcomes, databases of arbitrator information and selection tools, and providing live transcription and interpretation services. Predictive applications will be useful to reach settlement or to avoid disputes altogether, as well as being used in litigation funding decisions. AI can also assist in greater automation of administrative and procedural tasks by institutions, such as the filing of submissions, verification of party details, and case correspondence. AI will no doubt reduce the amount of time lawyers spend reviewing documents, summarising legal texts, and drafting documents. This holds great potential for digesting the ever-increasing size of arbitration case files, which can be made up of thousands of pages of documents.

While many people recognise the benefit that greater efficiency would bring to dispute resolution, the administration of justice without human intervention brings

14. Robert Hart, 'Elon Musk Teases First Neuralink Products after Company Implants First Brain Chip in Human' (*Forbes*, 30 January 2024) https://www.forbes.com/sites/roberthart/2024/01/30/elon-musk-teases-first-neuralink-products-after-company-implants-first-brain-chip-in-human/?sh=22ca556c2ac3 (accessed 10 April 2024); Neuralink, 'A Year of Telepathy' (*Neuralink*, 5 February 2025) https://neuralink.com/blog/a-year-of-telepathy/ (accessed 6 March 2025).
15. *See, e.g.*, in relation to 'Intelligent Decision Support Systems' (IDSS): Symanto, 'Unleashing the Power of AI Decision Support Systems: The Future of Business and Investment' (13 October 2022) https://www.symanto.com/blog/artificial-intelligence-decision-support-systems/ (accessed 10 April 2024).
16. *See, e.g.*, Deloitte's 'NavigAIte' https://www2.deloitte.com/us/en/pages/about-deloitte/articles/business-innovation-automated-document-review.html (accessed 10 April 2024); Jus Mundi's 'Jus AI Assistant': Jus Mundi Launches the First International Legal AI Assistant (13 February 2024) https://dailyjus.com/news/2024/02/jus-mundi-launches-the-first-international-legal-ai-assistant-en (accessed 10 April 2024); Ketrone, https://www.ketrone.io/ (accessed 6 March 2025); Lawdify https://www.lawdify.ai/ (accessed 6 March 2025); Casepal https://www.casepal.co/ (accessed 6 March 2025).

universal discomfort. Without human involvement, will the 'artificiality' of AI compromise the rule of law and fairness?

Of particular concern is the prospect of the 'robot' judge or arbitrator which would substitute human decision-making in the resolution of disputes. It is not as far-fetched as it may sound. In September 2023, an AI 'arbitration assistant' resolved the first dispute between two domestic companies at the Guangzhou Arbitration Commission. This tool can complete procedural tasks such as acceptance of cases, multilingual realtime translation, blockchain recognition of evidence, record-keeping, and inputting parties' positions.[17] In August 2019, Canadian electronic negotiation specialists ICan Systems used an AI tool 'Smartsettle ONE' in place of a human mediator to resolve a dispute before a court in England and Wales.[18]

In terms of the adoption of AI in decision-making, there are some differences between international arbitration and litigation. As governments experiment with the use of AI to achieve policy goals, deliver public services, and make legal and administrative decisions,[19] courts are already being asked to answer questions about the use of this technology for public purposes. Among other things, courts will have to consider whether administrative agencies have given sufficient reasons as required by administrative law when those agencies use AI tools.[20]

States are also committing public resources to the use of AI in courts, for the purposes of improving efficiency, predictability in the application of the law and consistency of decisions.[21] Courts have some natural advantages in this respect. Where arbitral decisions are confidential, a vast amount of court decisions are public, providing a rich data set that is lacking in arbitration. Court cases also outnumber the cases filed for arbitration in any jurisdiction. Many sub-sets of cases that come before courts follow a pattern, lacking the complexity of international arbitration which often involves different laws applicable to parties, their counsel, tribunal members, the arbitral proceedings, and the contract. Courts may also have greater incentive than arbitration to achieve consistency in decisions, which AI can assist with. Indeed, significant research and development is underway on using AI for judicial tasks based

17. Qiu Quanlin, 'AI Arbitration Used for Dispute in Guangzhou' (*China Daily*, 1 September 2023) https://global.chinadaily.com.cn/a/202309/01/WS64f13406a310d2dce4bb34ad.html (accessed 10 April 2024).
18. Kate Beioley, 'Robots and AI Threaten to Mediate Disputes Better Than Lawyers' (*Financial Times*, 14 August 2019), https://www.ft.com/content/187525d2-9e6e-11e9-9c06-a4640c9feebb (accessed 10 April 2024).
19. *See, e.g.*, Ombudsman of New South Wales, 'The New Machinery of Government: Using Machine Technology in Administrative Decision-Making' (29 November 2021) https://www.ombo.nsw.gov.au/__data/assets/pdf_file/0003/138207/The-new-machinery-of-government-special-report_Front-section.pdf (accessed 10 April 2024); The White House, 'Fact Sheet: President Biden Issues Executive Order on Safe, Secure, and Trustworthy Artificial Intelligence' (30 October 2023), stating that AI 'can expand agencies' capacity to regulate, govern, and disburse benefits, and it can cut costs and enhance the security of government systems'.
20. Ashley Deeks, 'The Judicial Demand for Explainable Artificial Intelligence' (2019) 119 *Columbia Law Review* 1829, 1839-1840.
21. European Commission for the Efficiency of Justice (CEPEJ), 'European Ethical Charter on the Use of Artificial Intelligence in Judicial Systems and Their Environment' (Council of Europe, February 2019) https://rm.coe.int/ethical-charter-en-for-publication-4-december-2018/16808f699c (accessed 10 April 2024) 5.

on public databases.[22] In the People's Republic of China, AI is being utilised by courts to give guidance to judges on similar factual and legal situations, in order to align decisions.[23] In Stuttgart, Germany, an AI tool called 'OLGA' was used to help categorise, search and organise a large backlog of cases.[24] A separate tool called 'FraUKe' was used in Frankfurt to reduce the time used to prepare judgments on air passenger rights which are repetitive and similar.[25] In Taiwan, an automated system for the generation of judgments is under consideration.[26] In some jurisdictions, courts will therefore receive significant exposure to AI.

Inevitably, international arbitration must therefore consider how to best use AI in order to keep pace with business practices, government adoption and usage by courts. In order to give further consideration to the question of the role of AI in international arbitration, we will next examine some of its limitations.

IV LIMITATIONS AND RISKS

AI tools have significant limitations which impact on how they can and should be used in legal proceedings. Tools which aid document review or otherwise optimise time-consuming tasks are less controversial. Of greater ethical and legal significance are tools used to draft legal submissions presented on behalf of counsel, tools used to create documents, images or videos submitted as evidence, outcome prediction, and decision-making support or substitution. These limitations have already been explored by others, sometimes in the context of judicial decision-making.[27] Understanding the

22. *See, e.g.*, Zhitao He et al., 'SimuCourt: Building Judicial Decision-Making Agents with Real-World Judgement Documents' (5 March 2024) https://doi.org/10.48550/arXiv.2403.02959 (accessed 10 April 2024) 4; Dovile Baryse and Roee Sarel, 'Algorithms in the Court: Does It Matter Which Part of the Judicial Decision-Making Is Automated' (2 September 2022) https://dx.doi.org/10.2139/ssrn.4208203 (accessed 10 April 2024).
23. Jinting Deng, 'Should the Common Law System be Intelligentized? A Case Study of China's Same Type Case Reference System' (16 October 2018) https://dx.doi.org/10.2139/ssrn.3267045 (accessed 10 April 2024).
24. Eckard Schindler, 'Judicial Systems Are Turning to AI to Help Manage Vast Quantities of Data and Expedite Case Resolution' (*IBM*, 8 January 2024) https://www.ibm.com/blog/judicial-systems-are-turning-to-ai-to-help-manage-its-vast-quantities-of-data-and-expedite-case-resolution/ (accessed 10 April 2024).
25. *Ibid.*
26. Winkler Partners, 'Taiwan Courts to Introduce AI-Assisted Judgment Drafting' (*Lexology*, 1 November 2023) https://www.lexology.com/library/detail.aspx?g=c864e6aa-3195-44ba-8019-28e073dca454 (accessed 10 April 2024).
27. *See, e.g.*, Scherer (n 1) 554-561; Kasap (n 1) 221-236; Orlando Federico Cabrera Colorado, 'The Future of International Arbitration in the Age of Artificial Intelligence' (2023) 40(3) *Journal of International Arbitration* 301; Christine Sim, 'Will Artificial Intelligence Take Over Arbitration' (2018) 14(1) *Asian International Arbitration Journal* 1; Rebecca Crootof, '"Cyborg Justice" and the Risk of Technological-Legal Lock-In' (2019) 119 *Columbia Law Review Forum* 233; Christoph Winter, 'The Challenges of Artificial Judicial Decision-Making for Liberal Democracy', LLP Working Paper No. 3-2021 in P. Bystranowski, P. Janik and M. Próchnicki (eds), *Judicial Decision-Making. Economic Analysis of Law in European Legal Scholarship* (Vol. 14, Springer, 2022); Willem H. Gravett, 'Judicial Decision-Making in the Age of Artificial Intelligence' in H. Sousa Antunes et al. (eds) *Multidisciplinary Perspectives on Artificial Intelligence and the Law* (2024), Law, Governance and Technology Series 58, https://doi.org/10.1007/978-3-031-41264-6_15 (accessed 10 April 2024).

limitations of AI is not about dismissing its use in international arbitration, but rather allows us to better address those limitations and design technology and ways of using it that are compatible with fairness and the rule of law.

Issues of concern in arbitration include the following:

- Lack of publicly available data in sufficient volume to provide accurate analysis and predictions: this is due to both the low number of arbitration cases, as well as the confidential nature of proceedings and many awards.
- Hallucinations by generative AI that can lead to legal errors.
- Lack of transparency about how AI algorithms produce their output ('black box' or 'explainability' problem).
- Bias in the training of an AI tool that may impact on the presentation of analysis or recommendations.
- Natural conservatism as tools will only produce output based on their training data, failing to evolve the law where necessary and appropriate in light of changing practices and values.
- Inability to appropriately weigh the relevance of differing legal authorities that factor into a given analysis.
- Compromising the personal mandate of an arbitrator.
- Automation bias, which is the propensity for humans to favour suggestions from automated decision-making systems and ignore contrary information.
- Uncertainty over compliance with existing legal frameworks, as well as new regulations applicable to AI, which may impact on the enforcement of arbitral awards.
- Inability to discern AI-produced evidence from non-AI-produced evidence, leading to authenticity issues.
- Inequality of arms arising from uneven access to technology.
- Failing to recreate the inherently human nature of legal reasoning and judgment.

Some of the limitations of AI have already been brought to light in court proceedings. Two well-known examples are the US decision of *State of Wisconsin v. Loomis* in relation to the automated system 'COMPAS', and the Dutch decision on the tool 'SyRI'. Both of these cases highlight some of the difficulties in explaining the output of AI and the consequences of using it to make decisions affecting individuals.[28]

COMPAS is a risk-need assessment tool, which includes a report predicting recidivism, based on a comparison of information about the individual to a similar data group.[29] Although not designed to determine the severity of a sentence or whether an offender is incarcerated, the high-risk score of Mr Loomis was referred to by the court

28. Adamantia Rachovitsa and Niclas Johan, 'The Human Rights Implications of the Use of AI in the Digital Welfare State: Lessons Learned from the Dutch *SyRI* Case' (2022) 22 *Human Rights Law Review* 1-15, 11, https://doi.org/10.1093/hrlr/ngac010 (accessed 16 August 2025).
29. *State of Wisconsin v. Eric L. Loomis* 881 N.W.2d 749 (2016) (hereinafter '*State v. Loomis*') paras 13-15.

along with other sentencing factors in ruling out probation.[30] The Supreme Court of Wisconsin rejected Mr Loomis' arguments based on alleged breach of due process arising out of the use of the tool, but held that sentencing courts using the tool must be provided with a caution about its limitations.[31] Commentary on this decision has raised issues about the potential bias of such systems, their opacity, and automation bias on the part of judges relying on such tools, even where accompanied by a caution message.[32]

The SyRI tool was used by the Dutch government to detect various forms of fraud, including social benefits, allowances and tax fraud. It generated risk reports that deemed a person worthy of investigation in relation to such fraud, based on record linkage among government files.[33] The District Court of The Hague ruled that its use breached the right to respect for private and family life, home and correspondence under Article 8 of the European Convention on Human Rights.[34] The Court found that the lack of explainability of SyRI prevented the administration from understanding the connections made by the AI tool, and therefore prevented the agency from properly justifying its actions and decisions.[35] The Hague District Court commented that 'it cannot verify the correctness of the State's position on what exactly SyRI is. After all, the State has not disclosed the risk model and the indicators that the risk model consists of or may consist of'.[36]

The risks and limitations of AI are not trivial, and some of them go to the very heart of fairness and the rule of law. Even so, AI is here, and total rejection is not an option. We therefore need to look closer at whether and how some of these limitations may be addressed.

V ADDRESSING AI

In this section, we explore some ways to address AI's shortcomings that may be relevant in the arbitration context, in particular for tools which may assist decision-making functions. Below we consider: (i) technological solutions; (ii) human solutions; and (iii) legal solutions.

While these issues will not disappear, probing reveals that not all of the challenges of working with AI are insurmountable.

---

30. *State v. Loomis* (n 29) paras 17, 19.
31. *State v. Loomis* (n 29) paras 66, 120.
32. Deeks (n 20) 1844-1845; Ignacio N. Cofone, 'AI and Judicial Decision-Making' in Florian Martin-Bariteau and Teresa Scassa, *Artificial Intelligence and the Law in Canada* (LexisNexis, 2021) 7.
33. *SyRI* decision, District Court of The Hague (n 7) paras 3.1, 3.2, 3.8.
34. *SyRI* decision, District Court of The Hague (n 7) para. 7.2.
35. *SyRI* decision, District Court of The Hague (n 7) para. 6.46.
36. *SyRI* decision, District Court of The Hague (n 7) para. 6.49.

1 Technological Solutions: Better AI

The most obvious way to address AI's unsuitability to certain tasks is with technological solutions to counter or improve upon its limitations. While current AI offerings became publicly visible very recently, these tools have been under development for decades.[37] Research and development for legal tools continues, acknowledging that present models may lead to unfairness and are often not fit for use in a legal context.[38] While some flaws may be inherent to the way that AI functions, the ability to overcome technological challenges should not be underestimated. In large language model (LLM) research, for example, progress is being made for legal-specific tools on issue-spotting, rule-recall, interpretation and rhetoric understanding.[39] Researchers are also working on LLMs which use smaller, curated data sets.[40] As reflected in the Ethical Charter on the Use of Artificial Intelligence in Judicial Systems and their environment prepared by CEPEJ (European Commission for the Efficiency of Justice), part of ensuring that technology preserves the values that we want to uphold is to pursue 'ethical-by-design' or 'human-rights-by-design' approaches.[41]

An important shortfall in AI is the 'black box' or explainability problem, which does not sit well with the practice of providing reasons for an arbitrator's decision. Reasons allow for the accountability of decision-makers and preserve the contestability of decisions.[42] They also allow a reviewing court to understand the basis of an arbitral award.

To address the explainability problem, 'explainable' AI or 'xAI' has received growing attention. As opposed to transparency about the functioning of an algorithm, which may not give real insight into the output of an AI tool, and may not be interpretable by non-experts, an explanation via xAI would provide 'human-interpretable information about the logic by which a decision-maker took a particular set of inputs and reached a particular conclusion', or permit 'a human observer to determine the extent to which a particular input was determinative or influential on the

37. Zhongxiang Sun et al, 'Logic Rules as Explanations for Legal Case Retrieval' (3 March 2024) https://doi.org/10.48550/arXiv.2403.01457 (accessed 10 April 2024); He et al., 'SimuCourt' (n 22).
38. Ruizhe Zhang et al, 'Evaluation Ethics of LLMs in Legal Domain'(17 March 2024) https://doi.org/10.48550/arXiv.2403.11152 (accessed 10 April 2024) 7; Christian A. Schiller, 'The Human Factor in Detecting Errors of Large Language Models: A Systematic Literature Review and Future Research Directions' (13 March 2024) https://arxiv.org/abs/2403.09743 (accessed 10 April 2024); Nishchal Prasad, Mohand Boughanem and Taoufiq Dkaki, 'Exploring Large Language Models and Hierarchical Frameworks for Classification of Large Unstructured Legal Documents' (11 March 2024) https://arxiv.org/abs/2403.06872 (accessed 10 April 2024); He et al., 'SimuCourt' (n 22); Pierre Colombo et al., 'SaulLM-7B: A Pioneering Large Language Model for Law' (7 March 2024) https://doi.org/10.48550/arXiv.2403.03883 (accessed 10 April 2024) 1.
39. Colombo et al. (n 38) 8.
40. John Nosta, 'The Rise of Small Data' (*Medium*, 6 May 2023) https://johnnosta.medium.com/the-rise-of-small-data-8e6546f57960 (accessed 10 April 2024).
41. CEPEJ, 'European Ethical Charter' (n 21) 8.
42. Scherer (n 1) 562; Kasap (n 1) 232; Susan Landau et al., 'Recommendations for Government Development and Use of Advanced Automated Systems to Make Decisions about Individuals' (4 March 2024) https://doi.org/10.48550/arXiv.2403.01649 (accessed 10 April 2024).

output'.[43] It can be debated whether xAI can be said to give 'reasons' for a decision or output, in the legal understanding of reasoning. It may rather reveal the 'probabilistic inferences' carried out by the AI.[44] xAI also poses challenges, as it currently may decrease the accuracy of an algorithm, reveal trade secrets, and is expensive.[45] This may entail balances and compromises to achieve the desired result.[46] That being said, research is being carried out into models which deliver 'logical faithful and interpretable explanations' for use in legal decision-making.[47] xAI may have the potential to unlock the black box of AI in a way that would improve its suitability for use in legal proceedings.

Bias is another real issue and has been observed in AI.[48] It can arise due to problems with the data set (e.g., that they are non-representative, not fit-for-purpose, not relevant, not accurate, or not generalisable); inappropriate objectives steering the design and deployment of AI; unfairness built into the model architecture; or lack of sufficient user training.[49] Each of these elements of an AI system can be managed in order to improve and ensure fairness in the way a tool operates.[50] For LLMs, another way to ameliorate bias is by 'fine-tuning' the model by 'reinforcement learning from human feedback' (RLHF), to tweak its responses. This is a delicate exercise, as it effectively combats bias by introducing other biases.[51] Being alert to the dangers of bias can help us to develop AI with the right data and design.

Benchmarking is another tool that can be used to evaluate the performance and output of AI tools, and therefore hold them accountable. Accountability is particularly important to address the issue of bias. One such tool is LawBench, which works by testing LLMs on: (i) legal knowledge memorisation; (ii) legal knowledge understanding of entities, events and relationships within legal text; and (iii) application of legal knowledge with reasoning steps to solve legal tasks.[52]

To address issues of authenticity of documents and media, efforts are underway to allow the origin of digital content to be traced, such as by the integration of visible

43. Finale Doshi-Velez et al., 'Accountability of AI under the Law: The Role of Explanation', Berkman Center Research Publication (3 November 2017) https://dx.doi.org/10.2139/ssrn.3064761 (accessed 10 April 2024) 4.
44. Scherer (n 1) 565-566. Kasap (n 1) 232; AbdelWahab (n 2) 313.
45. Deeks (n 20) 1834.
46. CEPEJ, 'European Ethical Charter'(n 21) 11.
47. Sun et al. (n 37) 1.
48. For example, Amazon's recruitment algorithm cited in Kasap (n 1) 225.
49. David Leslie et al., 'AI Fairness in Practice' (*The Alan Turing Institute*, 2023) https://arxiv.org/abs/2403.14636 (accessed 10 April 2024) 23.
50. *Ibid.*
51. Charlotin (n 4) 10.
52. Zhiwei Fei et al, 'LawBench: Benchmarking Legal Knowledge of Large Language Models' (28 September 2023) https://doi.org/10.48550/arXiv.2309.16289 (accessed 10 April 2024). *See* another benchmarking tool 'LegalBench-instruct' described in Colombo et al. (n 38).

and invisible (metadata) watermarks in AI-produced content.[53] However, current detection tools are far from robust.[54]

Clearly, not all technological issues are close to being solved. Case outcome prediction technology is insufficiently advanced for complex international disputes.[55] Accurate generalisation without 'overfitting' of results remains a challenge.[56] Other obstacles still appear very difficult to overcome, such as how to entrust an algorithm with the development of new law, and to decide disputes based on novel circumstances.

Legal reasoning is another conundrum. As reported by CEPEJ: 'The results achieved by AIs are in reality unrelated to the question of the legal conformity of a particular solution and cannot discriminate between legal and illegal arguments.'[57] The question of whether AI can engage in legal reasoning has been debated for decades.[58] In 1988, referring to the community of researchers who believe that applying AI in the legal realm is difficult but not impossible, Dr Edwina Rissland identified legal reasoning as requiring:

> (1) The ability to reason with cases and examples, particularly through analogy; (2) the ability to handle ill-defined, open-textured predicates; (3) the ability to handle exceptions; (4) the ability to handle fundamental conflicts between rules; (5) the ability to argue and justify in a case-based manner; and (6) the ability to handle change and nonmonotonicity [i.e., reasoning based on assumptions, incomplete or unknown facts, entailing the adjustment of prior conclusions].[59]

Breaking down the elements of legal reasoning serves to demonstrate that AI is not there yet. However, taking into account rapid technological developments, it is also possible to imagine tools which may be able to approximate such reasoning, for specific kinds of cases and with the right kind of data input. Research carried out on the ability of GPT-3 and GPT-4 to engage in 'zero shot' reasoning, i.e., reasoning about novel problems without direct training, showed the LLMs outperforming human

53. *See* 'Coalition for Content Provenance and Authenticity' https://c2pa.org/ (accessed 10 April 2024); Emilia David, 'OpenAI Is Adding New Watermarks to DALL-E 3' (*The Verge*, 7 February 2024) https://www.theverge.com/2024/2/6/24063954/ai-watermarks-dalle3-openai-content-credentials (accessed 10 April 2024).
54. Siddarth Srinivasan, 'Detecting AI Fingerprints: A Guide to Watermarking and Beyond' (*Brookings*, 4 January 2024) https://www.brookings.edu/articles/detecting-ai-fingerprints-a-guide-to-watermarking-and-beyond/ (accessed 10 April 2024).
55. Ilias Chalkidis et al., 'Neural Legal Judgment Prediction in English' (2019) *Proceedings of the 57th Annual Meeting of the Association for Computational Linguistics* 4317 https://aclanthology.org/P19-1424/ (accessed 16 August 2025); *see* Scherer (n 1) 547-550, Kasap (n 1) 217-219.
56. 'Overfitting' occurs when the AI's output 'fits' too closely to the training data and fails to generalise. *See* Kasap (n 1) 224.
57. CEPEJ, 'European Ethical Charter' (n 21) 37.
58. *See, e.g.*, Edwina L. Rissland (ed.), 'Special Issue on "AI and Legal Reasoning"' (1991) 34(6) *International Journal of Man-Machine Studies* 751-787 and (1991) 35(1) *International Journal of Man-Machine Studies* 1-118.
59. Edwina L. Rissland, 'Artificial Intelligence and Legal Reasoning: A Discussion of the Field & Gardner's Book' (1988) 9(3) *AI Magazine* 45, 48.

capabilities in most settings.[60] Analogical reasoning is therefore not a uniquely human skill.

The missing element in AI reasoning remains the 'human' one, of value judgments, discretion, deliberation, common sense and imagination.[61] On this basis, Sunstein opined in 2001 that AI cannot engage in true legal reasoning, which has an evaluative, value-driven character.[62] He pointed to the crucial step in analogical reasoning as being the identification of a principle that justifies an analogy (or distinction), rather than merely the identification of relevant similarities and differences.[63] There are good reasons to seek to preserve the human part of decision-making, while acknowledging the added value of the impressive abilities of AI.

The above technological solutions demonstrate that AI is not a 'take it or leave it' proposition: we are only at the outset of the AI endeavour, and we have not yet exhausted the technological options to render it more suitable to our purposes.

2 Human Solutions: Appropriate Use

Looking realistically at the current limitations of AI, the technology is by no means ready to autonomously dispense justice in the kinds of disputes presented to international arbitration. The 'robot arbitrator' is a real but still-distant prospect. Moreover, the role of an arbitrator (like that of a judge) goes beyond reaching and drafting a decision.[64] Unless and until the technology is reliable and trusted, the level of human supervision should reflect our comfort with AI making decisions that would impact on the legal rights of individuals, companies or governments. Appropriate use supports engaging with technology without compromising the integrity of arbitration proceedings.

In this context, it is helpful to recall that AI may be better conceived of as 'augmented intelligence', to assist humans to complete tasks better, or more efficiently. Rather than considering and rejecting the robot arbitrator as a blanket proposition, we may break down the tasks of the arbitrator to better determine how AI may assist. In general terms, the use of an AI tool should not compromise the mandate of an arbitrator to decide on the dispute, and should always be used under the instruction and supervision of the arbitrator. What does this mean in practice for the arbitrator's specific tasks?

Arbitrators already use technological tools, and often tribunal secretaries, to assist them in performing their mandate. AI tools that perform similar functions, always under supervision, will be more readily acceptable. This may include assistance with drafting procedural backgrounds and other non-substantive sections of orders and

60. Taylor Webb et al., 'Emergent Analogical Reasoning in Large Language Models' (3 August 2023) 1.
61. Kasap (n 1) 247; Crootof (n 27) 237-238.
62. Cass R. Sunstein, 'Of Artificial Intelligence and Legal Reasoning' (2001) 8 *University of Chicago Law School Roundtable* 29, 31.
63. *Ibid.*, 32.
64. Campbell (n 4) 19.

awards; taking notes of deliberations; and navigating and summarising case documents. What about a tool that draws up a list of issues to be decided by the tribunal based on the parties' submissions, with cross-references to the file? What about a tool that provides a provisional determination in a draft procedural order, for example, in relation to security for costs, interim measures, or document redactions? These may be some of the next layer of tasks to be considered.

Another aspect of appropriate use and supervision is training. We should all be educated on the principles of AI tools that will be used in our legal proceedings, and expertise in supervising them will be highly valuable. User understanding and control of AI are fundamental.[65]

3 Legal Solution: More Law

Governments, institutions and organisations around the world are putting in place 'guardrails' for the use of AI, in the form of guidelines,[66] policies,[67] regulations[68] and legislation.[69] Minimum standards, verification, and accountability frameworks are our current efforts to draw boundaries around the acceptable use of AI. While it can be difficult for the law to keep pace with technology, it remains an important way to improve the development and appropriate use of AI, as well as to support trust in its use.[70]

Regulations and guidance on the use of AI in decision-making emphasise transparency, predictability, reliability and understandability, as well as human oversight.[71]

The European Union (EU) has set out more comprehensive regulation of this area. Under the new EU AI Act AI approved by the European Parliament in March 2024, AI tools 'can support the decision-making power of judges or judicial independence, but should not replace it, as the final decision-making must remain a human-driven

65. CEPEJ, 'European Ethical Charter' (n 21) 7; UK Courts and Tribunals Judiciary, 'Artificial Intelligence (AI): Guidance for Judicial Office Holders' (12 December 2023) 3.
66. *See, e.g.*, UK Courts and Tribunals Judiciary, 'Artificial Intelligence (AI): Guidance for Judicial Office Holders' (n 65); Peter Homoki, 'Guide on the Use of Artificial Intelligence-Based Tools by Lawyers and Law Firms in the EU', Council of Bars and Law Societies of Europe (2022).
67. *See, e.g.*, 'The Bletchley Declaration by Countries Attending the AI Safety Summit, 1-2 November 2023' (1 November 2023) https://www.gov.uk/government/publications/ai-safety-summit-2023-the-bletchley-declaration/the-bletchley-declaration-by-countries-attending-the-ai-safety-summit-1-2-november-2023 (accessed 10 April 2024).
68. President of the United States of America, 'Executive Order on the Safe, Secure, and Trustworthy Development and Use of Artificial Intelligence' (30 October 2023) (hereinafter 'Biden Executive Order on AI').
69. Proposal for a Regulation of the European Parliament and of the Council laying down harmonised rules on artificial intelligence (Artificial Intelligence Act) and amending certain Union legislative acts (26 January 2024) 2021/0106(COD) (hereinafter 'EU AI Act').
70. Saleh Afroogh et al., 'Trust in AI: Progress, Challenges and Future Directions' (4 April 2024) https://doi.org/10.48550/arXiv.2403.14680 (accessed 10 April 2024) 24.
71. *See* United Nations General Assembly, 'Seizing the Opportunities of Safe, Secure and Trustworthy Artificial Intelligence Systems for Sustainable Development' A/78/L.49 (11 March 2024) para. 6(k); Biden Executive Order on AI (n 69), section 10.1(b)(iv).

activity and decision'.[72] The final draft of the Act classifies as high-risk certain AI systems, whether used by a judicial authority or in alternative dispute resolution, where they will assist 'in researching and interpreting facts and the law and in applying the law to a concrete set of facts'.[73] In a complex series of exceptions and exceptions-to-exceptions, AI systems are not considered high risk if they are 'intended to perform a narrow procedural task', 'intended to improve the result of a previously completed human activity', intended to detect patterns and not 'to replace or influence the previously completed human assessment, without proper human review', or 'intended to perform a preparatory task to an assessment' relevant for the purpose of one of the high-risk use cases.[74] However, those that profile natural persons are always considered high risk.[75] This legal framework is of direct relevance to arbitration, and systems falling under its scope will have to comply with a number of protective measures.

The use of AI will have other legal implications that remain to be clarified, which will provide legal certainty and ultimately support trust in its use. For example, whether AI is considered to have legal personality, and understood to act as an agent, may evolve as the technology develops.[76] At present, there is no general recognition of the legal personality of AI tools and creators and users typically remain the beneficiary of or responsible for the actions of AI.[77] Other questions arise around whether arbitrators must be natural persons and the validity of arbitration agreements entered into with AI.[78] It is also conceivable that public policy concerns may be raised if the use of AI is perceived to significantly impact on arbitral procedure or the outcome of a dispute.[79] The use of AI by arbitrators must also fulfil due process requirements.[80] The

72. EU AI Act (n 69).
73. EU AI Act (n 69) Article 6(2) and Annex III, para. 8(a); Press Releases, 'Artificial Intelligence Act: MEPs Adopt Landmark Law' (*European Parliament News*, 13 March 2024) https://www.europarl.europa.eu/news/en/press-room/20240308IPR19015/artificial-intelligence-act-meps-adopt-landmark-law#:~:text=On%20Wednesday%2C%20Parliament%20approved%20the,46%20against%20and%2049%20abstentions (accessed 10 April 2024).
74. EU AI Act (n 69) Article 6(2a)(a)-(d).
75. EU AI Act (n 69) Article 6(2a).
76. Daniel Seng and Tan Cheng Han SC, 'Artificial Intelligence and Agents', NUS Law Working Paper 2021/019 (October 2021) https://dx.doi.org/10.2139/ssrn.3935446 (accessed 10 April 2024).
77. British Colombia Civil Resolution Tribunal (Canada), *Moffatt v. Air* Canada, 2024 BCCRT 149 (in relation to Air Canada's liability for the actions of its chatbot); David Fixler, 'Can an AI System Be an Inventor? Full Court Says No' (*Corrs Chambers Westgarth*, 11 May 2022) https://www.corrs.com.au/insights/can-an-ai-system-be-an-inventor-full-court-says-no (accessed 10 April 2024) (in relation to decisions in Australia, the US, Europe and the UK rejecting arguments that AI can be an inventor); *cf.* Diogo Antunes, 'Artificial Intelligence as an Inventor: A Brief Exploration of South African Intellectual Property Law' (*Inventa*, 13 November 2023) https://inventa.com/en/news/article/921/artificial-intelligence-as-an-inventor-a-brief-exploration-of-south-african-intellectual-property-law#:~:text=Stephen%20Thaler%2C%20was%20acknowledged%20as,system%20being%20granted%20patent%20rights (accessed 10 April 2024) (in relation to South Africa's acceptance of AI as an inventor in the same set of cases).
78. Kasap (n 1) 238; Huan Ying (Irene) Ng and Valeria Benedetti del Rio, 'Chapter 8: When the Tribunal Is an Algorithm: Complexities of Enforcing Orders Determined by a Software under the New York Convention' in Katia Fach Gomez and Ana M. Lopez-Rodriguez (eds), *60 Years of the New York Convention: Key Issues and Future Challenges* (Kluwer, 2019) 121.
79. Guillermo Argerich, María Blanca Noodt Taquela and Juan Jorge, 'Could an Arbitral Award Rendered by AI Systems by Recognized or Enforced? Analysis from the Perspective of Public

question of whether the output of an AI tool will satisfy the requirement to give reasons in an arbitral award (where relevant) will likewise require further consideration[81] and will have overlapping relevance to other fields where AI will be used in decision-making, such as administrative law.

VI CONCLUSION

The development and use of AI is a human endeavour with cross-cutting relevance. It demands that we stay abreast of technological developments, efforts to regulate AI, and uses of it by governments, companies and courts. While the field of international arbitration has a vibrant niche of tech-enthusiasm, in practice it is typically conservative in the adoption of new technology that might be perceived to impact on the enforceability of an arbitral award. Taking due note of the need to adopt AI with care, it would be a mistake to allow caution to lapse into disengagement. Grappling with AI's limitations is crucial to shaping the future of international dispute resolution, both in terms of the legitimacy of international arbitration as a method of resolving disputes and preserving its fairness.

While legal reasoning and legal judgments cannot yet satisfactorily be replicated by AI, we may be surprised by what it will soon be able to achieve. In the author's view, AI may eventually be able to provide output that is consistent with value-driven decision-making and legal reasoning, with appropriate explanations. As technology develops, we must therefore continue to examine what uses of AI will optimise our ability to resolve disputes efficiently and fairly, while protecting the humanity and integrity of the process and outcome.

Policy' (*Kluwer Arbitration Blog*, 6 February 2020) https://arbitrationblog.kluwerarbitration.com/2020/02/06/could-an-arbitral-award-rendered-by-ai-systems-be-recognized-or-enforced-analysis-from-the-perspective-of-public-policy/ (accessed 10 April 2024).

80. *See*, in relation to procedural fairness in the judiciary, Bell et al. (n 8) 53-54.

81. *See*, *e.g.*, UNCITRAL Model Law 2006, Article 31(2). This requirement is not a universal one and can typically be waived. *See Cour d'appel du Québec*, *Smart Systems Technologies Inc. v. Domotique Secant Inc.* (11 March 2008), refusing recognition and enforcement of an award for failure to state reasons on the basis that it was required by the arbitration agreement and was not waived.

CHAPTER 50
Why Artificial Intelligence Cannot Deliver Justice

Rahim Moloo & Praharsh Johorey[*]

TABLE OF CONTENTS

I INTRODUCTION

> 'I had brains, and a heart also; so, having tried them both, I should much rather have a heart.'
>
> – Tin Woodman, *The Wonderful Wizard of Oz* (1900)

Humankind's exploration of their fundamental nature vis-à-vis machines began long ago. One early example is Frank L. Baum's iconic book, *The Wonderful Wizard of Oz*, written at the turn of the twentieth century. Through the character of Tin Woodman – a sentient being made of tin – the reader was invited to a then-novel existential pursuit: is Woodman, who communicates in human language and expresses emotions such as empathy and sensitivity, human? And if he isn't, does it matter?

In recent years, these questions have come to dominate scientific and popular inquiry. Across the world, governments, corporations and scientists are furiously engaged in developing artificial intelligence (*AI*), a set of sciences, theories and techniques that aim to imitate – and potentially exceed – the cognitive abilities of

* Rahim Moloo is a Partner and Co-Chair, and Praharsh Johorey is an Associate, of the International Arbitration Practice Group at Gibson, Dunn & Crutcher LLP.

human beings.[1] Over the course of the twentieth century, the rapid development of computer processing power meant that, by 1997, a computer program was able to recognize human speech, outwardly display human emotions and defeat Grandmaster Gary Kasparov at chess.[2] Now, in 2024, we have generative AI systems that are capable of producing entirely 'new' text and graphics that are facially indistinguishable from human output.[3]

The extraordinary capabilities of these systems have prompted the exploration of their use in legal practice. Recent surveys have noted that a significant majority of lawyers and law firms intend to integrate AI tools in executing numerous legal tasks.[4] Even courts have opened their doors to AI: in December 2023, the UK's Courts and Tribunals issued an 'AI Guidance for Judicial Office Holders' setting out several potentially useful tasks for AI, such as summarizing text and writing presentations.[5] In the same month, across the Atlantic ocean, the Chief Justice of the U.S. Supreme Court John Roberts also commended AI for its potential to re-shape legal research and increase access to key legal information.[6]

In this chapter, we critically examine AI's adoption in the legal practice and urge caution. In particular, we argue that while AI is undeniably efficient (and even effective) in processing data and generating human-like output in certain contexts, the method by which it does so is inherently incompatible with the dispensation of justice. In making this argument, we agree with Chief Justice Roberts that AI 'risks ... dehumanizing the law', which is a concern because 'legal determinations often involve gray areas that still require application of human judgment'.[7] This chapter sets out our argument in the following sections:

1. Council of Europe Portal, *History of Artificial Intelligence*, available at https://www.coe.int/en/web/artificial-intelligence/history-of-ai (accessed on 25 March 2024).
2. R. Anyoha, *The History of Artificial Intelligence*, Harvard Science in the News Blog, 28 August 2017, available at https://sitn.hms.harvard.edu/flash/2017/history-artificial-intelligence/ (accessed on 25 March 2024).
3. M. Heikkilä, *What's Next for AI in 2024*, MIT Technology Review, 4 January 2024, available at https://www.technologyreview.com/2024/01/04/1086046/whats-next-for-ai-in-2024/ (accessed on 25 March 2024).
4. Thomson Reuters Institute, *ChatGPT and Generative AI Within Law* Firms, Thomson Reuters, 2023, available at https://www.thomsonreuters.com/en-us/posts/wp-content/uploads/sites/20/2023/04/2023-Chat-GPT-Generative-AI-in-Law-Firms.pdf (accessed on 25 March 2024); Bryan Cave Leighton Paisner, *Annual Arbitration Survey: AI in IA*, 9 November 2023, p. 13, available at https://www.bclplaw.com/a/web/tUW2SW6fjHrpXVrA7AfWkS/102932-arbitration-survey-2023-report_v10.pdf (accessed on 25 March 2024).
5. UK Courts and Tribunals Judiciary, *AI Guidance for Judicial Office* Holders, 12 December 2023, available at https://www.judiciary.uk/wp-content/uploads/2023/12/AI-Judicial-Guidance.pdf (accessed on 25 March 2024).
6. J. Roberts, *2023 Year-End Report on the Federal Judiciary*, 31 December 2023, p. 5, available at https://www.supremecourt.gov/publicinfo/year-end/2023year-endreport.pdf (accessed on 25 March 2024).
7. J. Roberts, *2023 Year-End Report on the Federal Judiciary*, 31 December 2023, pp. 5-6, available at https://www.supremecourt.gov/publicinfo/year-end/2023year-endreport.pdf (accessed on 25 March 2024).

(b) *Section II* details how AI technology works and the means by which it processes data and produces output, and assesses the current and near-future state of 'legal tech';

Section III argues that achieving 'justice' is an inherently human endeavour, and that AI technology is definitionally unsuited to this endeavour in any given context;

Section IV takes stock of the advantages that AI does offer legal practitioners, and assesses when AI tools may be most gainfully employed by these practitioners during the life-cycle of a standard arbitration.

We then conclude.

II AI: DEFINITION AND DESIGN

'AI isn't magic. It's math.'

– AiAdvertising Prospectus, Description of Business (2022)

In a 1973 revision of his book *Profiles of the Future*, science fiction author Arthur C. Clarke pondered the nature of technology and discovery, distilling his observations into three principles (now canonically known as his 'Three Laws'). Of these, the most famous is his third: '[a]ny sufficiently advanced technology is indistinguishable from magic'.[8] Modern-day generative AI – capable of instantaneously creating seemingly infinite text, pictures and video – would seem to come closest to the technology Clarke envisioned.

But the framing of AI technology as magical (and therefore unexplainable) obscures more than it informs. AI tools are built by humans, and as these tools are integrated deeper into the legal profession, we must understand – to the extent we can – how the sausage is made. Doing so is crucial to revealing the limitations of AI tools, and accordingly, where – and to what extent – we should adopt them.

1 'Software 1.0'

Traditionally, software programs were developed by a human programmer setting out lines of instruction (or 'code') in a computer language for what it would like the program to do in response to specific inputs (or 'data'). This is commonly understood as 'Software 1.0'.[9] The number of lines of code written for a program (its 'architecture') depended on the complexity of tasks the program was intended to handle. The more complicated the task, the wider and more unpredictable the range of data the program

8. *Clarke's Three Laws*, New Scientist, available at https://www.newscientist.com/definition/clarkes-three-laws/ (accessed on 25 March 2024).
9. Andrej Karpathy, *Software 2.0*, Medium, 12 November 2017, available at https://karpathy.medium.com/software-2-0-a64152b37c35 (accessed on 25 March 2024).

would have to process, the more instructions the programmer would have to create for the program to respond to this data.

But the forays of software into the real world, where the range of input data is wider and therefore harder to predict, demonstrated the limitations of Software 1.0. Take, for example, a programmer trying to create software that can drive a car without human involvement. The range of data that the human programmer would have to account for in creating this code is near-infinite, including millions of possible permutations relating to weather scenarios, traffic laws, road conditions, dynamic traffic conditions and car performance.

2 'Software 2.0'

Enter AI and 'Software 2.0'. Fundamentally, this new age of software alters the role that humans play in the programming process by assigning the task of writing the relevant code to the program itself via a human-created 'neural network'.[10] Put simply, a neural network (so-called to mimic how the human brain receives, transmits and processes information) is a computer program that is designed to identify 'patterns' from vast amounts of data relevant to the program's function. Therefore, rather than a human explaining to a program what output should follow from a specific input, the network predicts this output based on pattern-recognition.[11]

The network identifies patterns by passing the data through a series of electronic 'nodes', each of which extracts certain information from that dataset. Once the information is passed through each node, the information is collated for the network to discern a pattern within that dataset. Once identified, this pattern then forms the program's code. In theory, the more data that is uploaded to the network (i.e., the more it is 'trained'), the more sophisticated its identification of the pattern in question, and the better its coding. In this way, the program can 'learn' from experience. This has opened the doors to the possibility that 'strong' AI tools will – soon – replicate, or even surpass, the cognitive abilities of human beings.[12]

3 A Mystery Box

But there is a fundamental difference between how AI and human beings 'learn': humans are capable of expressing themselves and explaining their learning, whereas an AI neural network can only express itself in numbers (i.e., a series of 0s and 1s) in a manner that cannot be interpreted by humans. This means that even the network's

10. *Ibid.*
11. SAS Help Center, *Neural Network Node*, available at https://documentation.sas.com/doc/en/emref/14.3/p0zbgj1tu3h1uhn1x6regixbdg7v.htm (accessed on 25 March 2024).
12. IBM, *What Is Strong* AI, available at https://www.ibm.com/topics/strong-ai (accessed on 25 March 2024).

human designers cannot explain what the network's identified pattern is and why it generated a certain output.[13]

Take, for example, OpenAI's now-well-known 'ChatGPT' tool. ChatGPT almost instantaneously generates text output in response to specific prompts. For example, when asked 'how would you describe how you work, in a single sentence?' it responds: 'I generate human-like text based on the input I receive, drawing upon a diverse range of pre-existing knowledge and patterns learned during training.'

But how did it generate this output? Essentially, ChatGPT is a highly sophisticated text predictor. ChatGPT's human programmers designed neural networks (in this context called 'Large Language Models' or '*LLMs*'), trained on millions of natural human-language texts to discern patterns in these texts. This pattern is then employed to predict/continue text in a reasonable way.[14] The process by which an LLM does so can be summarized as follows:

- For the purpose of training the LLM, each human-language 'token' (a unit of text, such as punctuation, words or part of words, such as 'ing') is assigned a numerical value.
- During training, the LLM reduces natural-language texts into tokens (and thus further into numbers) and calculates which tokens commonly appear with the others.
- Through a process called 'embedding', each token is clustered with other tokens that commonly appear with it – the pattern.
- In response to each new text input, the LLM identifies the embedding – i.e., the series of numbers – that represents it.
- The LLM then operates on this embedding to generate a probabilistic ranking of the tokens that will likely follow the inputted text.
- The LLM's output is dependent on how these ranked words are used (the program's 'temperature' parameter). For example, a temperature of '1' means that the highest-ranked word will be used each time, and '0' means that the highest-ranked word is no more likely to be used than any other word.

In summary, LLMs make predictions based on their assessment of the patterns in the natural-language text they were trained on. These patterns constitute millions of numerical digits and are inscrutable to human beings: As a prominent AI expert notes, 'when a lab invests in training a new LLM … they're buying a mystery box'.[15] Based on these inexplicable patterns, the LLM stitches together words to form sentences without

13. S. Zoldi, *Deep Dive: How to Make 'Black Box' Neural Networks Explainable*, 14 January 2019, available at https://www.fico.com/blogs/deep-dive-how-make-black-box-neural-networks-explainable (accessed on 25 March 2024).
14. S. Wolfram, *What Is ChatGPT Doing … and Why Does It Work*, 14 February 2023, available at https://writings.stephenwolfram.com/2023/02/what-is-chatgpt-doing-and-why-does-it-work/ (accessed on 25 March 2024).
15. S. Bowman, *Eight Things to Know about Large Language Models*, 2 April 2023, https://cims.nyu.edu/~sbowman/eightthings.pdf (accessed on 25 March 2024).

any conception of what these words mean.[16] It is no surprise, then, that LLM tools sometimes generate text as persuasive as it is wrong.[17]

4 The Current State of 'Legal Tech'

Yet, the legal industry is buzzing with the possibility that LLM and other AI tools could fundamentally re-shape the practice of law. In January 2024, Thomson Reuters, owner of the popular 'Westlaw' legal research service, promoted its generative AI offerings as providing 'faster answers to legal questions', 'legal drafting … within minutes', 'document automation … with a few clicks', and 'contract review ... in seconds'.[18] Similarly, LexisNexis – Westlaw's primary competitor in the U.S. – touts the 'efficiency' of its own range of AI products.[19] Several law firms are also piloting 'Harvey AI', an LLM tool built on ChatGPT's technology that purports to 'help[] legal teams find leverage in time-consuming tasks like legal research, due diligence and more'.[20] For example, Allen & Overy recently announced a 'ContractMatrix' tool it developed with Harvey, which it claims can 'write' standard legal contracts based on existing templates.[21] And in the international arbitration context, 'Jus Mundi' – a prominent database of arbitral records – announced its 'Jus AI' product in July 2023, which used OpenAI's GPT tool to summarize case documents.[22] It has recently expanded its AI offerings to include a 'Jus AI Assistant', which not only summarizes documents but can also extract information from cases, analyse them and determine whether their relevance to a user-specified legal issue or question.[23]

While these products offer clear benefits, these companies acknowledge the core deficiency of any AI technology. LexisNexis, for example, proclaims a desire to 'explain how our [AI] solutions work', but notes that, for now, it will continue to use '"closed

16. IBM, *What is Retrieval-Augmented Generation?*, 22 August 2023, available at https://research.ibm.com/blog/retrieval-augmented-generation-RAG (accessed on 25 March 2024).
17. I. Schwartz et al., *Black Box Warning: Large Language Models and the Future of Infectious Diseases Consultation*, Clinical Infectious Diseases, 2023, https://doi.org/10.1093/cid/ciad633 (accessed on 25 March 2024).
18. C. O' Leary, *Legal Technology's Authoritative Guide: List of Use Cases and Benefits*, Thomson Reuters, 19 December 2023, available at https://legal.thomsonreuters.com/blog/technology-in-law-is-the-new-norm/ (accessed on 25 March 2024).
19. Lexis +, *Experience a New Era in AI Legal Research* Tools, available at https://www.lexisnexis.com/en-us/products/lexis-plus.page (accessed on 25 March 2024).
20. P. Grady, *Partnering with Harvey: Putting LLMs to Work*, Sequoia, 26 April 2023, available at https://www.sequoiacap.com/article/partnering-with-harvey-putting-llms-to-work/ (accessed on 25 March 2024).
21. D. Yao, *Major Law Firm Debuts AI Tool That Writes Contracts*, AI Business, 27 December 2023, available at https://aibusiness.com/nlp/uk-law-firm-debuts-ai-tool-that-writes-contracts (accessed on 25 March 2024).
22. A. Ciraolo, *Jus AI: AI Powered Decision Summaries*, JusMundi, March 2024, https://help.jusmundi.com/en/articles/8062738-jus-ai-ai-powered-decision-summaries (accessed on 25 March 2024).
23. L. Chlapowski, *Discover Jus AI Assistant*, JusMundi, March 2024, available at https://help.jusmundi.com/en/articles/8926887-discover-jus-ai-assistant (accessed on 25 March 2024).

box" models'.[24] This is not surprising: an inherent feature of AI technology is that the process by which it determines its output (i.e., its neural network's pattern-recognition) is generally indecipherable by – and therefore unexplainable to – human beings. Ongoing efforts by these companies to reduce output errors by training LLMs on more refined/higher-quality data,[25] or making its output more personalized,[26] do not address this basic problem. AI offerings such as these thus 'may not reflect all recent legal developments, be accurate, comprehensive, or applicable to a particular matter or case'.[27]

But understanding the process of *how* an outcome is achieved – and thereby assessing its legitimacy – is inherent to the law, and therefore, to the legal practice. At bottom, the law is a means of attaining justice. A malleable concept in a complicated world, much of what is 'just' in a given context depends not only on what the law (or other legal instrument) explicitly says, but also: (i) what it means, and crucially, (ii) who decides what it means, and (iii) how they make this decision. As we explore below, an AI tool, no matter how sophisticated, is inherently incompatible with a modern-day understanding of how justice is – and should be – achieved. This is a particularly pressing issue given that judicial (and arbitral) authorities – society's gatekeepers of justice – are beginning to use AI tools themselves, including to help inform decisions about bail, parole and sentencing,[28] and, in some jurisdictions, draft judgments altogether.[29]

III JUSTICE: A HUMAN ENDEAVOUR

> It is not merely of some importance but is of fundamental importance that justice should not only be done, but should manifestly be seen to be done.
>
> – Lord Hewart, *Rex v. Sussex Justices* (1924)

24. Relx, *Responsible Artificial Intelligence Principles at RELX*, available at https://www.lexisnexis.com/pdf/relx-responsible-ai-principles.pdf (accessed on 25 March 2024).
25. C. Brooker, *Legal Industry Reaction to AI-Assisted Research on Westlaw Precision and the Thomson Reuters Generative AI Strategy*, Thomson Reuters, 20 November 2023, https://www.legalcurrent.com/legal-industry-reaction-to-ai-assisted-research-on-westlaw-precision-and-the-thomson-reuters-generative-ai-strategy/ (accessed on 25 March 2024). This is done through a process called 'Retrieval-augmented generation' which narrows the dataset that the LLM is applied to, thereby reducing the likelihood that its output will contain errors (or 'hallucinations'). IBM, *What Is Retrieval-Augmented Generation?*, 22 August 2023, available at https://research.ibm.com/blog/retrieval-augmented-generation-RAG (accessed on 25 March 2024).
26. OpenAI, *Memory and New Controls for ChatGPT*, 13 February 2024, available at https://openai.com/blog/memory-and-new-controls-for-chatgpt (accessed on 25 March 2024).
27. Jus Mundi, *User Terms*, §10, available at https://jusmundi.com/en/terms-of-use (accessed on 25 March 2024).
28. J. Baker et al., *AI for Judges: A Framework*, CSET Policy Brief, December 2021, p. 27, available at https://cset.georgetown.edu/publication/ai-for-judges/ (accessed on 25 March 2024).
29. Winkler Partners, *Taiwan Courts to Introduce AI-Assisted Judgment Drafting*, 1 November 2023, available at https://www.lexology.com/library/detail.aspx?g=c864e6aa-3195-44ba-8019-28e073dca454 (accessed on 25 March 2024).

Lord Hewart's aphorism neatly captures the dual facets of justice that law (and consequently all legal determinations) must generally endeavour to achieve: that the process and outcome of a legal determination be just. As we argue below, these determinations are imprecise and value-driven, making AI/LLM tools unsuited to making them.

1 The Language of Law

Law is the regulation of the life of a community expressed in language.[30] For the expression to be effective, the receivers – here the relevant community – must understand what has been expressed. In some instances, provisions are easily and objectively understood. Take, for example, the following provision of the U.S. Constitution: 'No Person shall be a Senator who shall not have attained to the Age of thirty Years ...',[31] which has an exact scope and applicability.

But such precise expressions are difficult, and even undesirable, in certain contexts. Chief among them, the dynamism and complexity of human behaviour means that a draftsman cannot specifically predict – and therefore legislate for – the entire range of behaviour implicated by a proposed law.[32] This requires the draftsman to use language that is deliberately broad, even vague, to give a general idea of what is sought to be accomplished without explicating how.[33] As John Marshall, a former U.S. Supreme Court Chief Justice remarked, this allows laws – in that context, the U.S. Constitution – to 'endure for ages to come, and consequently, to be adapted to the various crises of human affairs'.[34] Constitutional laws, which form the bedrock upon which other legal structures are built, are uniquely susceptible to such vagueness. A famous example is the First Amendment to the U.S. Constitution, which requires that: 'Congress shall make no law ... abridging the freedom of speech.'[35] The meaning of this provision – and its application in different contexts – has been contested now for over two centuries.

This deliberate vagueness is not the exclusive province of constitutional law, pervading legal instruments of every type, from standard commercial contracts to inter-State treaties. A commercial contract may require that the parties act in 'good faith' towards each other, avoid 'undue delay', and make 'best efforts' to resolve disputes. Similarly, contracts often employ 'hardship' clauses that may excuse a party's non-performance when events have rendered performance 'more onerous' than could

30. Stanford Encyclopedia of Philosophy, *Law and Language*, 21 December 2021, available at https://plato.stanford.edu/entries/law-language/#UseLangLaw (accessed on 25 March 2024).
31. Article 1, section 3, U.S. Constitution.
32. B. Coleman, *Are Clarity and Precision Compatible Aims in Legal Drafting?*, Singapore Journal of Legal Studies 376-408 (1998), pp. 390-391, available at https://www.jstor.org/stable/24867255?read-now=1&seq=15#page_scan_tab_contents (accessed on 25 March 2024).
33. G. Christie, *Vagueness and Legal Language*, 48 Minn. L. Rev. 885-911 (1964), pp. 889-890, https://scholarship.law.duke.edu/cgi/viewcontent.cgi?referer=&httpsredir=1&article=1207&context=faculty_scholarship, pp. 889-890 (accessed on 25 March 2024).
34. *McCulloch v. Maryland*, 17 U.S. 316, 407.
35. First Amendment, U.S. Constitution.

reasonably have been anticipated.[36] Legal instruments on evidentiary rules instruct parties to produce documents that are 'relevant to the case and material to its outcome'.[37] Under U.S. law, an interpreter of a sales contract without a price term must determine its 'reasonable' price.[38] Similarly, a bilateral-investment treaty between two States is likely to mandate that they each accord investments of the other State 'fair and equitable treatment', avoid 'unreasonable or discriminatory measures' and treatment that is 'not less favourable', than they accord their domestic investments or third States.[39]

2 The Meaning of Law

The crucial question, then, is what *these* provisions mean. But this jumps the gun: we must first assess *who* should answer this question, and whether AI tools can – or should – forge into this still-exclusively human domain.

a Who Decides?

All modern societies – without exception – accord the responsibility of legal decision-making to humans (and not, for example, the flip of a coin) because humans have a robust and deeply ingrained aversion to randomness and chance in decisions of importance.[40] We accept the role of a coin in deciding which team gets the ball first in American football, or which team gets to bat first in cricket – relatively inconsequential decisions – but not over whether a defendant can be pronounced guilty of a crime. Because laws pervade crucial aspects of a community life, a society of laws only tolerates legal decision-making that reduces the impact of randomness to the maximum extent possible, with each decision being the product of reason; a contemplative, deliberative and cognitive process. As Alexander Hamilton recognized over two centuries ago, the authority of a legal determiner rests solely on the adequacy of its 'judgment'.[41] And so, in a time where the capacity to reason has been the exclusive domain of human beings, it is natural that humans remain the sole judges of its laws.

Yet we now confront AI tools that, when probed to explain their answers to questions, will instantaneously be able to do so. But the tool is not *reasoning* or exercising 'judgment': it is *predicting* a text output based on an inexplicable assessment of an arbitrary (and likely incomplete)[42] collection of textually-expressed human

36. *See, e.g.*, the ICC Model Hardship Clause, https://iccwbo.org/wp-content/uploads/sites/3/2020/03/icc-forcemajeure-hardship-clauses-march2020.pdf (accessed on 25 March 2024).
37. IBA Rules on the Taking of Evidence in International Arbitration, Article 3(b).
38. U.C.C. §2-305(1).
39. *See, e.g.*, Agreement between the Government of the Republic of Mauritius and the Government of the Republic of India for the Promotion and Protection of Investments, Article 4.
40. G. Keren, *Decisions by Coin Toss: Inappropriate but Fair*, Judgment and Decision Making, Vol. 5, No. 2, pp. 83-101 (2010), p. 99, available at https://www.cambridge.org/core/services/aop-cambridge-core/content/view/D4884A0D0E6A569A2F85924CB9708AC8/S1930297500000942a.pdf/decisions-by-coin-toss-inappropriate-but-fair.pdf (accessed on 25 March 2024).
41. A. Hamilton, *Federalist* 78 (1788).
42. This is particularly true in the arbitration context, where a number of decisions and other relevant records – particularly those of procedural nature, or concerning a specific subject or

reasoning. In this way, an algorithmically driven predictor lacks the basic features of how humans reason – and therefore interpret laws – and that is why humans must remain the law's sole arbiters (at least for complex and important cases).

b *How?*

A law or legal instrument can be understood based on a number of its features, including its literal meaning, context and implied content. As a preliminary step, the interpreter must discern the theory of meaning they will ascribe to the text. Among others, the interpreter must toggle between the choice of a text's objective meaning (how a reasonable person would understand it) or subjective meaning (how its drafters understood it); the relevant time-period at which the meaning crystallized (as at the time of its adoption or when it is being interpreted); and the sources for deriving this meaning (dictionaries, common usage, negotiating history, etc.).[43] All of this is conditioned by the interpreter's understanding of a text's fundamental nature and what interpretive methodology would best serve its objectives.[44]

Resolving these complex questions – and the exercise of discretion more broadly – requires the interpreter to make value judgments on what 'justice' requires in that context. The interpreter's conception of justice, in turn, is premised on their individual context, including (possibly) their nationality, upbringing, education and legal training. Generally speaking, 'common law' jurisdictions – the USA, UK and Australia, for example – accord decisive binding authority to prior-decided cases ('precedents'), whereas civil law jurisdictions – prevalent across continental Europe – do not.[45] Interpretative methodologies also differ across legal systems: some accord more weight to the parties' contractual intent when interpreting a text than others.[46] And so, when reviewing the same legal language, changes in applicable law (among other things) necessitate the application of different values to the interpretive exercise.

forum (such as those before the Court of Arbitration for Sports) – are confidential and never made public. Indeed, confidentiality is one of arbitration's primary attractions, particularly in the commercial context. *See* Nigel Blackaby et al., *Redfern and Hunter on International Arbitration* (7th ed., Oxford University Press, 2023), §1.125. Accordingly, an arbitration-focused LLM tool (such as 'Jus AI') is unlikely to have been trained on anything close to an exhaustive database of relevant information.

43. W. Baude, *The Law of Interpretation*, 130 Harv. L. Rev. 1079 (2017), available at https://harvardlawreview.org/print/vol-130/the-law-of-interpretation/ (accessed on 25 March 2024).
44. K. Tobia, *Testing Ordinary Meaning*, 134 Harv. L. Rev. 726 (2020), available at https://harvardlawreview.org/print/vol-134/testing-ordinary-meaning/ (accessed on 25 March 2024). And this assessment is unique for each contract that is specifically negotiated between the parties to them, While prior-decided cases may generally indicate what a '*reasonable*' price would be for sales contracts or when performance may be said to be '*onerous*', this determination is conditioned by the parties in question and the manner in which they expressed their distinct aims, objectives and risk-allocations in the contract.
45. S. Lewis, *Precedent and the Rule of Law*, Oxford Journal of Legal Studies, Vol. 41, Issue 4, Winter 2021, pp. 873-898, available at https://academic.oup.com/ojls/article/41/4/873/6161245 (accessed on 25 March 2024).
46. W. Barnes, *The Objective Theory of Contracts*, 76 U. Cin. L. Rev. 1119 (2008), available at https://scholarship.law.tamu.edu/facscholar/302 (accessed on 25 March 2024).

And even *within* a given legal system or applicable law, the process of reviewing applicable law – and precedent in particular – is often an art rather than science, laden with discretion. The primary task of ascertaining what a given case says and stands for – its so-called concrete and binding 'ratio' – requires assessing what the prior interpreter said, meant to say, and whether it was strictly necessary for them to say it.[47] This assessment may differ from person to person and place to place, and is inherently dynamic – continuously developing with experience through time. The mere newness of cases is therefore not a conclusive indicator of their authority: for example, in December 2023, the Indian Supreme Court overturned – as grossly incorrect – its own decision on the implications of deficiently stamped arbitration agreements issued just five months prior.[48] Once this determination is made, it is expressed in language that could itself subtly evolve in meaning, a process of 'semantic change.'[49]

All of this makes possible law's development. The same text is capable of being interpreted differently in the service of justice both presently and over time, and a society may accord certain interpretations the authority of law today that it could wholly reject tomorrow. The evolution of non-discrimination and equality law in the United States – from the 'separate but equal' segregation doctrine found to be constitutional in *Plessy v. Ferguson* (1868), to the declaration that segregation was inherently unconstitutional in *Brown v. Board of Education* (1954) – exemplifies how the meaning of static legal text can fundamentally shift over time, often through incremental shifts reflected in the language of decisions, and even concurring opinions and dissents.[50]

AI tools are incapable of this kind of reasoning. They neither judge nor interpret text – they *predict* it. This prediction is based not on a value-system but on an inscrutable numerical representation/potabilization/ranking of written language, which is assumed to crystallize the entire range of complex human values at a particular point in time. As Chief Justice Roberts noted, you also cannot train an LLM model to do what every human being does on a daily basis: perceive and draw inferences from the conduct of others.[51] In this way, LLM tools – even the theoretical 'strong' variety – are inherently incapable of employing the value-based reasoning that we require of human decision-makers. And to the extent that an LLM model is making some value judgments, it is not transparent and does not necessarily accord with what values humans might apply in particular place and time. Alternatively, if certain

47. A. Goodhart, *Determining the Ratio Decidendi of a* Case, 40 Yale Law Journal 161 (1931), available at https://openyls.law.yale.edu/bitstream/handle/20.500.13051/12305/17_40YaleLJ 161_1930_1931_.pdf?sequence=2&isAllowed=y (accessed on 25 March 2024).
48. *See Re Interplay Between Arbitration Agreements under the Arbitration and Conciliation Act 1996 and the Indian Stamp Act 1899*, Curative Petition (C) No. 44 of 2023, 13 December 2023.
49. J. Williams, *Synaesthetic Adjectives: A Possible Law of Semantic Change*, Language, Vol. 52, No. 2 (June 1976), pp. 461-478, available at https://www.jstor.org/stable/412571 (accessed on 25 March 2024).
50. A. Amar, *Plessy v. Ferguson and the Anti-Canon*, 39 Pepp. L. Rev. 75 (2011-2012), https://core.ac.uk/download/pdf/72831765.pdf (accessed on 25 March 2024).
51. J. Roberts, *2023 Year-End Report on the Federal Judiciary*, 31 December 2023, p. 5, available at https://www.supremecourt.gov/publicinfo/year-end/2023year-endreport.pdf (accessed on 25 March 2024).

criteria are coded into a particular LLM model, it is the values of the programmer made at the time the code is written that are given priority – again without transparency or assessment as to whether that programmer's values (fixed at a particular point in time) are the lens through which we want all decisions to be made.

Ultimately, as imperfect as humans are, justice for humans is inherently something that only humans can assess in a particular place, time and context. And that assessment will evolve in a way that is unique to humans of a particular society. AI cannot pave the future of what a particular society deems as being just – only the people comprising that society can. Accordingly, we believe that, to be 'just', legal judgments can only be made by human beings engaging in the deliberative process necessary to reach a given decision.

IV A CAREFUL BALANCING: AI AND ARBITRATION

But that is not to say that AI tools have *no* role to play in the legal practice. AI's ability to generate human-like text at almost no cost – and quickly – can unquestionably aid human decision-making. And perhaps, in the future, society could consent to AI making certain decisions despite the design-limitations discussed above.

1 An Aid

AI's utility as an aid to human decision-making can take several forms at each stage of the life-cycle of an arbitration, beginning with drafting an arbitration agreement. The American Arbitration Association, for example, has built a 'ClauseBuilder' Tool that 'assist[s] individuals and organizations develop clear and effective arbitration and mediation agreements' by proposing – in response to various data inputs (such as the nature of dispute and number of proposed arbitrators) – a template clause that the parties can build off of.[52] Parties can then deploy systems like that developed by Litera (called 'Kira') to review the clause (against its database of existing agreements) to identify potential errors and omissions.[53]

Once the parties have adopted an arbitration agreement in a contract, and a contractual dispute has arisen, the parties can use AI to determine whether to invoke it. Predictive AI tools can (imperfectly) probabilize outcomes of existing disputes and help inform the decision on whether to commence arbitrations regarding them.[54] Unsurprisingly, the use of such technologies is widespread in the litigation funding context, where funding decisions are informed, in part, by a numerical likelihood of

52. American Arbitration Association, *Clause Builder Tool*, available at https://www.clausebuilder.org/umbraco/surface/options/items (accessed on 25 March 2024).
53. *Kira for Law Firms*, Kira, available at https://kirasystems.com/solutions/law-firms/ (accessed on 25 March 2024).
54. J. Burgess, *Using Artificial Intelligence (AI) in Litigation Funding*, Sentry Funding, 20 November 2023, available at https://sentryfunding.co.uk/insights/using-artificial-intelligence-ai-in-litigation-funding/#:~:text=Predictive%20analytics,-One%20of%20the&text=By%20analysing%20vast%20amounts%20of,invaluable%20insights%20to%20litigation%20funders (accessed on 25 March 2024).

success and ultimate recovery.[55] This predictive analysis can also inform a parties' assessment of its relative strengths and weaknesses should they attempt settlement negotiations prior to implementing the arbitration agreement.

Were these negotiations to fail and the arbitration agreement is invoked, AI can aid the parties' diligence of potential arbitrator nominees. Jus Mundi, for example, offers a 'Jus Connect Conflict Checker' tool that instantaneously identifies existing 'relationships' between potential arbitrator candidates, allowing the user to then assess the conflict – if any – this relationship raises.[56] In addition, it collates publicly available decisions issued by this candidate and other data on their cases, streamlining the ability to diligence their legal outlook, temperament and suitability for the proposed appointment.[57]

Once the tribunal is constituted and proceedings commence, AI tools are now commonly used by lawyers to supplement their legal research and strategy. As noted above, Westlaw and LexisNexis offer AI products that identify cases that correspond to certain search terms, summarize their conclusions, note their treatment by other judicial authorities and even assess their likely precedential value. And during an arbitration's document discovery phase, a human attorney can develop a protocol against which AI tools can quickly sift through and categorize thousands of documents submitted by a counterparty.[58] Generative AI tools can even draft natural-language justifications for these categorizations based on this protocol, a mundane and repetitive task that can save significant time and expenditure.[59]

2 Decision-Maker?

These undeniably useful AI products retain – and indeed boost – human decision-making over consequential aspects of the legal process. Yet, cost and efficiency imperatives may cause parties to choose to outsource decision-making to AI tools altogether. Indeed, AI tools now make some decisions of consequence: Amazon, for example, uses AI to decide whether a parties' return of a product bought on its website complied with its return policy.[60] AI-powered cameras across India now determine whether drivers violated numerous traffic laws.[61]

55. E. Siegel, *AI Helps Litigation Funders Mine Court Dockets for Legal Gold,* Bloomberg Law, 2 March 2024, available at https://news.bloomberglaw.com/business-and-practice/lawsuit-investors-use-ai-to-mine-cases-for-promising-returns (accessed on 25 March 2024).
56. Jus Mundi, *Conflict Checker,* available at https://jusconnect.com/en/conflict-checker (accessed on 25 March 2024).
57. Jus Mundi, *Jus Connect,* available at https://jusconnect.com/en/directory/arbitrators/all (accessed on 25 March 2024).
58. DISCO, *How to Use Generative AI for Document Review,* 31 January 2024, available at https://csdisco.com/blog/blog-generative-ai-for-document-review (accessed on 25 March 2024).
59. *Ibid.*
60. S. Kapner, *Amazon, Walmart Using AI to Decide on Economic Sense to Process a Return,* Fox Business, 10 January 2021, available at https://www.foxbusiness.com/retail/amazon-walmart-using-ai-to-decide-on-economic-sense-to-process-a-return-wsj (accessed on 25 March 2024).
61. A. Rajput, *AI-Powered Cameras to Detect 19 Different Traffic Violations on Delhi Roads,* Times of India, 10 January 2024, available at https://timesofindia.indiatimes.com/city/delhi/ai-to-use-numberplate-detect-19-different-violations-on-road/articleshow/106681437.cms (accessed on 25 March 2024).

But these use-cases of AI decision-making are limited to disputes that are capable of objective, non-discretionary, resolution – usually of relatively low value. An Amazon AI's 'determination' that a product return after six months falls outside its ninety-day return policy is an objective and universal one, where the application of the 'law' (the return policy) to the 'facts' (when the purchase and return were made) is non-discretionary. Similarly, assessing whether a driver crossed the specified speed limit, or was wearing a helmet when required to do so, ought to – but may not[62] – be clear and objective.

But a significant number of legal disputes – whether eventually submitted to arbitration or not – involve more complex human conduct, where what the law is, what the facts are, and how the facts relate to that law, are disputed. These cases involve discretion, exercising which, we posit, is an inherently human trait when those decisions concern human conduct in a particular time, place and context. Where parties consent to use AI tools to resolve their disputes, they must be cognizant of – and comfortable with – the definitional limitations of these tools.

V CONCLUSION

AI decisions are expedient, but not necessarily just. There might be a place and time to prefer expediency over justice – where getting it right most of the time is preferred to the time and resources required to achieve justice. But important and complex cases that can have a significant impact on the disputing parties, or society as a whole, should not be left to AI. Those cases require humans to make value judgments – that are based on a particular time, place, culture and state of human evolution – when applying the law to a particular set of facts.

Our position is not meant to suggest that human decision-making is without weaknesses or that human decision-making guarantees justice. To the contrary, history – continuing to the present day – is rife with examples of obviously unjust laws and legal decisions. And one can attribute these injustices to the same capacity to reason that, we argue, makes human beings uniquely placed to decide disputes. However, we believe that the *process* by which these outcomes are obtained – a deliberative one where human beings are forced to apply the law through a context-specific human value lens – are crucial to the ongoing development of the law for any given society and the eventual attainment of justice. We must preserve it.

62. U. Balakrishna, *In Bengaluru, AI traffic Cameras Fail Accuracy Test*, Deccan Herald, 11 March 2024, https://www.deccanherald.com/india/karnataka/bengaluru/in-bengaluru-ai-traffic-cameras-fail-accuracy-test-2930585 (accessed on 25 March 2024).

CHAPTER 51

Will AI Fundamentally Disrupt International Arbitration as a Practice and as a Profession for Young Lawyers?

Maxim Osadchiy[*]

TABLE OF CONTENTS

> 'I think we are seeing the most disruptive force in history here; we will have for the first time something that is smarter than the smartest human.'
>
> Elon Musk, businessman and investor, 2023

> 'AI will keep getting radically better at everything, and so far there seems no obvious upper limit on what's possible.'
>
> Mustafa Suleyman, *The Coming Wave*, 2023

I INTRODUCTION

Thousands of years of history have lulled many of us into the false sense of security that automation is something that happens to other people's jobs, never our own.[1] It is thus tempting to assume, against that historical background and our long-held belief that

* Teaching Associate, Queen Mary University of London. The views expressed herein are solely those of the author. Email: mosadchiy.cls@gmail.com.
1. John Burn-Murdoch, *Here's What We Know about Generative AI's Impact on White-Collar Work*, Financial Times (10 November 2023), https://www.ft.com/content/b2928076-5c52-43e9-8872-08fda2aa2fcf (accessed 16 August 2025).

arbitration is essentially a 'people business',[2] that the coming technological revolution will have limited impact on the practice of international arbitration. Indeed, while artificial intelligence (AI)[3] is expected to have a profound effect on just about every area of human activity,[4] many remain sceptical about its future in international arbitration.

The reality is that arbitration – long reliant on review and analysis of large swathes of unstructured data and prediction of case outcomes – is well suited for automation. AI will insert itself firmly into all core facets of arbitration practice, augmenting and potentially supplanting much arbitration work. Whether or not AI will one day become sentient and/or replace arbitrators as decision-makers can be debated. That it will transform the practice of international arbitration as we know it today and will have major implications for young lawyers cannot be seriously denied.

II AI WILL RADICALLY ALTER THE PRACTICE OF INTERNATIONAL ARBITRATION

1 AI and the Power of Automation

The AI's ability to cut through the morass of unstructured data and create new content means that the tasks that were once thought to require human judgment can now be completed by – or with the aid of – AI. Yuval Noah Harari, a celebrated historian and intellectual, reckons that 'any job that is basically data coming in, being analysed and data coming out' is potentially at risk of being replaced; 'this is the easiest job to automate by AI'.[5] Many professionals have already seen the automation of some of the more mundane aspects of their work – such as calculations, spreadsheets, and risk assessment[6] – across a range of industries, including in banking, insurance, transportation and healthcare.[7]

2. Susannah Moody, *Artificial Intelligence or Stupidity: The Future of Arbitration?*, Global Arb. Rev. (22 June 2023), https://globalarbitrationreview.com/article/artificial-intelligence-or-stupidity-the-future-of-arbitration (accessed 16 August 2025).
3. The term 'AI' typically refers to systems able to perform tasks normally requiring human intelligence. *See, e.g.*, Jeremy Barnett and Philip Treleaven, *Algorithmic Dispute Resolution: The Automation of Professional Dispute Resolution Using AI and Blockchain Technologies*, The Computer Journal, vol. 61, Issue 3 (March 2018), p. 402, https://doi.org/10.1093/comjnl/bxx103 (accessed 16 August 2025). This chapter uses this term broadly to refer to all modern types of AI tools.
4. McKinsey & Company, *The Economic Potential of Generative AI: The Next Productivity Frontier* (14 June 2023) ('Generative AI will have a significant impact across all industry sectors'), https://www.mckinsey.com/capabilities/mckinsey-digital/our-insights/the-economic-potential-of-generative-ai-the-next-productivity-frontier (accessed 16 August 2025).
5. Yuval Noah Harrari, *Piers Morgan vs Yuval Noah Harari on AI*, The Full Interview (October 2023), 5:58, https://www.youtube.com/watch?v=lEt6OJEArM8 (accessed 16 August 2025).
6. Benjamin Alarie, Anthony Niblett and Albert Yoon, *How Artificial Intelligence Will Affect the Practice of Law* (7 November 2017), p. 2, https://ssrn.com/abstract=3066816 or http://dx.doi.org/10.2139/ssrn.3066816 (accessed 16 August 2025).
7. Roger Parloff, *Why Deep Learning Is Already Changing Your Life* (Fortune, 28 September 2016), http://fortune.com/ai-artificial-intelligence-deep-machinelearning/ (accessed 16 August 2025).

The legal profession is no less amenable to automation. Goldman Sachs, a bank, estimates that 44% of legal tasks could be performed by AI, more than in *any* occupation surveyed except for clerical and administrative support (all industries average is 25%).[8] McKinsey & Company, a consultancy, in an earlier study estimated that 23% of lawyers' work can be completed by automated technology.[9]

The practice of arbitration may be particularly vulnerable. Much arbitration work involves reviewing and analysing large volumes of data in order to determine the best way to proceed, essentially predicting what would happen if a tribunal were to consider and decide the matter.[10] These are AI's core areas of excellence, and precisely the sort of things that AI has demonstrated it can do well. Although there are obstacles to the broader adoption of AI in international arbitration – in the form of AI's current technological limitations, lawyers' reluctance to innovate, and people's preference for human interaction – such obstacles are not insurmountable, as discussed further below.

The exact ways in which AI will transform the practice of international arbitration are difficult to predict. However, given the current pace of technological progress and AI's proven capabilities to date, it has the potential to transform the practice in at least three big ways: (i) it will change how we work and what we do (practice implications), (ii) it will change how many lawyers there are and where they work (market implications), and (iii) it will have implications for the system of international arbitration (systemic implications).

2 Implications for Arbitration Practice

AI will change the practice of arbitration as we know it, augmenting and potentially automating much arbitration work and inducing significant time and cost savings in all major aspects of the practice. Laborious and time-consuming tasks such as document review, conflict checks and legal research (among other areas) will be carried out by, or with assistance of, AI-powered tools,[11] allowing lawyers to focus on

8. Goldman Sachs et al., *The Potentially Large Effects of Artificial Intelligence on Economic Growth* (26 March 2023), p. 7, https://www.gspublishing.com/content/research/en/reports/2023/03/27/d64e052b-0f6e-45d7-967b-d7be35fabd16.html (accessed 16 August 2025).
9. The study was conducted before the advent of advanced large language models, like ChatGPT-3, in November 2022, which stunned even their creators with the strength and breadth of their capabilities.
10. Orlando Federico Cabrera Colorado, *The Future of International Arbitration in the Age of Artificial Intelligence*, Journal of International Arbitration, vol. 40, Issue 3 (2023) p. 313 https://doi.org/10.54648/joia2023014 (accessed 16 August 2025) ('The ability to make predictions is a central contribution to legal decision-making'). *See also* Benjamin Roe, *The Year Ahead: Innovation – A New Generation of Legal Analysis Tools Is Emerging*, Global Arb. News (21 January 2019) ('Predicting the outcome of a case is at the core of an experienced dispute lawyer's skill'), https://globalarbitrationnews.com/the-year-aheadinnovation-a-new-generation-of-legal-analysis-tools (accessed 16 August 2025).
11. John O. McGinnis and Russell G. Pearce, *The Great Disruption: How Machine Intelligence Will Transform the Role of Lawyers in the Delivery of Legal Services*, Fordham Law Review, vol. 82 (2014) p. 3041.

more intellectually stimulating work and reducing stress and anxiety often associated with these potentially mind-numbing tasks.[12]

An arbitrator conflict check, to take one example, used to be a tedious exercise requiring considerable time and review of multiple sources. It now takes only a fraction of time for 'Jus Mundi Conflict Checker', an AI-powered tool, to generate detailed insights into past and current relationships between arbitrators, counsel, parties and, more recently, experts.[13] Another example is Aiscension AI, a pre-trained document review tool designed to identify potential bribery and corruption risks. It can reportedly review half a million documents in as little as 90 hours – compared to estimated 8,500 hours required for a first-level human review. Finally, Jus Mundi recently launched 'Jus-AI', a new GPT-powered intelligence tool that offers 'rapid' relevance assessment and concise summaries of arbitral awards and national court judgments.[14] These are useful tools which can bring much-needed time and cost savings into the process.

With technology continuing to advance, AI will be applied more widely to complex tasks such as arbitrator selection, evidence gathering, and trial preparation. As to arbitrator selection, there is already a vast trove of data about arbitrators' profiles, work-connections and past decisions, including rates of recovery and details of arbitrators' procedural rulings, thanks to online platforms such as Arbitrator Intelligence and GAR Arbitrator Research Tool.[15] It won't be a massive leap to apply advanced AI tools to trawl through this data to identify a suitable arbitrator candidate based on a set of criteria developed by the parties (or an arbitral institution) for a particular case.[16] Designed properly, such tools could make the arbitrator selection process less susceptible to human bias,[17] although there is also a risk that they could in fact perpetuate it.[18]

12. Kate Apostolova and Mike Kung, *Don't Fear AI in IA*, Global Arb. Rev. (27 April 2018), p. 2, https://globalarbitrationreview.com/article/dont-fear-ai-in-ia (accessed 16 August 2025).
13. Luciana Collinet, *About the Conflict Checker* (November 2023), https://help.jusmundi.com/en/articles/4396122-about-the-conflict-checker (accessed 16 August 2025). Kluwer Arbitration Practice Plus, another research tool, also provides information about arbitrators' publications and awards.
14. Jus Mundi Introduces Jus-AI: A Game-Changing GPT-Powered AI Solution for the Arbitration Community (29 June 2023), https://dailyjus.com/news/2023/06/jus-mundi-introduces-jus-ai-a-game-changing-gpt-powered-ai-solution-for-the-arbitration-community (accessed 16 August 2025).
15. Arbitrator Intelligence also contains feedback on arbitrators from individual lawyers.
16. For a detailed discussion of AI as a tool for arbitrator selection and how it could work in practice, *see* Cabrera Colorado (n 10) pp. 328-330.
17. Allyson Reynolds and Paula Melendez, *AI Arbitrator Selection Tools and Diversity on Arbitral Panels*, IBA, Back to Arbitration Committee publication (undated), https://www.ibanet.org/article/97cb79fa-39e9-48c1-8cb0-45569e2e62af (accessed 16 August 2025). *See also* Global Arb. Rev. (author unspecified), *The March of the 'cobots'* (2 March 2021) (noting Loretta Malintoppi's observation that the use of AI to select arbitrators could increase diversity in international arbitration), https://globalarbitrationreview.com/article/the-march-of-the-cobots (accessed 16 August 2025).
18. Matthew Hutson, *Even Artificial Intelligence Can Acquire Biases Against Race and Gender* (Science, 13 April 2017), www.sciencemag.org/news/2017/04/even-artificial-intelligence-can-acquire-biases-against-race-and-gender (accessed 16 August 2025).

AI will also change the way in which parties gather, analyse and present evidence in international arbitration.[19] A sound evidentiary footing is integral to credible advocacy and robust decision-making. Yet the sheer volume of evidentiary record often pushes the boundaries of what is humanly possible, especially where one is forced to operate under significant time constraints. By preparing a summary of key evidentiary materials, identifying documents relevant to a particular issue, and alerting to potential inconsistencies in the record, AI could facilitate review of the arbitration file and help counsel advance work on legal arguments,[20] or allow arbitrators to deliver their decisions faster.[21] AI could also be deployed to identify and select the documents potentially relevant for and responsive to document production requests – potentially on the basis of prompts in the AI model (as opposed to search terms which take time to develop and often generate false hits)[22] – or to search for potential gaps and weaknesses in the evidentiary record.

As machines become increasingly capable and users more adept at using them, AI can be deployed in more ambitious contexts, such as outcome prediction and arbitral decision-making. Machine learning has the potential to predict case outcomes more accurately and objectively than lawyers.[23] Although existing empirical studies in this area are limited and narrow in scope, they suggest that machines are able to predict case outcomes with a very high degree of certainty.[24] Early application of these machines to predict case outcomes in real-life cases is promising too. For example, Blue J Legal, a Toronto-based start-up, applies machine learning to review the facts of the case and relevant precedents in the selected jurisdiction and can reportedly predict

19. Martin Magal, Alexander Calthrop and Katrina Limond, *Artificial Intelligence in Arbitration: Evidentiary Issues and Prospects*, Global Arb. Review (11 October 2023), p. 1, https://globalarbitrationreview.com/article/artificial-intelligence-in-arbitration-evidentiary-issues-and-prospects (accessed 16 August 2025).
20. AI-powered systems 'trained' by lawyers can search through voluminous litigation bundles and identify relevant documents more precisely than junior lawyers and paralegals. Richard Susskind, *Tomorrow's Lawyers: An Introduction to Your Future* (2nd ed., Oxford University Press 2017), p. 186.
21. Hanna Roos, *Arbitration Tech Toolbox: Let's Chat Some More about ChatGPT and Dispute Resolution* (8 April 2023) ('[AI] could speed up the judge or arbitrator's review of the evidentiary material and hence allow them to deliver their decisions faster'), https://arbitrationblog.kluwerarbitration.com/2023/04/08/arbitration-tech-toolbox-lets-chat-some-more-about-chatgpt-and-dispute-resolution/ (accessed 16 August 2025).
22. Magal, Calthrop and Limond (n 19) p. 2.
23. Harry Surden, *Machine Learning and Law*, Univ. of Wash. L. Rev., vol. 89 (2014), pp. 87, 102-110. *See also* Daniel Martin Katz, Michael Bommarito and Josh Blackman, *A General Approach for Predicting the Behavior of the Supreme Court of the United States*, PLoS ONE, vol. 12 (2017) p. e0174698 https://doi.org/10.1371/journal.pone.0174698 (accessed 16 August 2025).
24. Maxi Scherer, *Artificial Intelligence and Legal Decision-Making: The Wide Open?*, Journal of International Arbitration, vol. 36, Issue 5 (2019), pp. 4-6 https://doi.org/10.54648/joia2019028 (accessed 16 August 2025) (discussing two studies on the prediction of legal decision-making and certain limitations as to their general applicability).

litigation results in employment cases with 90% accuracy.[25] It bears note that machines, unlike humans, do not tire, nor need to take any time off.[26]

And while we may not see a robot arbitrator for a while,[27] or may not want to have one at all,[28] using AI to assist with certain aspects of arbitral decision-making is no longer science fiction. Earlier this year, ChatGPT was successfully deployed by a senior judge in Cartagena, Colombia, to help him reach a legal decision in a hearing concerning social benefits.[29] ChatGPT also exhibited credible abilities to resolve an array of legal issues in simple maritime disputes, including the ability to make reasoned determinations in a human-like fashion and consider facts and submissions.[30] Modria-.com, an online dispute resolution platform, uses algorithms to analyse case information and issue decisions in simple low-value disputes, without human oversight.[31] For less complex disputes, therefore, AI can play an increasingly important role in supporting arbitral decision-making.

All in all, it is difficult to think of any aspect of the arbitration practice that will remain unaffected by the coming wave of technological revolution. With the exception of top-notch oral advocacy, which is highly bespoke in nature and cannot be standardised,[32] AI will pervade all key facets of the arbitral process and will change the way we work, augmenting lawyers and ultimately supplanting some of their functions.

25. Lyle Moran, *Law Firm Teams up with Canadian Legal Tech Company on AI-Powered Case Prediction Tool* (25 August 2020), https://www.abajournal.com/web/article/law-firm-teams-up-with-canadian-legal-tech-company-on-ai-powered-case-prediction-tool (accessed 16 August 2025).
26. Alarie and Niblett and Yoon (n 6) p. 3.
27. Paul Cohen and Sophie Nappert, *The March of the Robots*, Global Arb. Rev. (15 February 2017), p. 14 ('[O]n the current trajectory, a computer would be able to serve as a fact-finder and arbitrator on its own within the next two decades: sifting through the applicable law more thoroughly, assessing the credibility of witness evidence more accurately, and deliberating a great deal more quickly than human arbitrators') (emphasis added). *See also* James Hope, Chapter 7, *Can a Robot Be an Arbitrator?*, in Axel Calissendorff and Patrik Schöldstrom (eds), Stockholm Arbitration Yearbook 2019, Stockholm Arbitration Yearbook Series, vol. 1, p. 117 ('If I may offer a personal observation, I find it difficult to imagine that robots will be allowed to sit as arbitrators any time soon, and probably not in my lifetime'). It should be noted that these predictions were made before the advent of advanced large language models such as ChatGPT-3. A timescale based on what AI has now proven it can do could look very different today.
28. Cohen and Nappert (n 27) p. 14 ('Given our predilection and preference for human interaction, parties may well decline the opportunity to have their dispute decided by a computer programme, even at the risk of having more fallible humans potentially decide it "wrongly"').
29. Arthur Piper, *ChatGPT and the Legal Profession* (23 March 2023), https://www.ibanet.org/ChatGPT-and-the-legal-profession (accessed 16 August 2025).
30. Kevin Chan, *A New Era of Maritime Arbitration: Ex Machina Determinations*, Journal of International Arbitration, vol. 40, Issue 5 (2023), pp. 521-550, https://doi.org/10.54648/joia2023022 (accessed 16 August 2025) (exploring the possibility and potential benefits of using large language models like ChatGPT as arbitrators in maritime disputes).
31. According to Colin Rule, Mondria.com has already helped resolve over 400 million disputes between consumers and sellers. James Melamed and Colin Rule, *Online Dispute Resolution Pioneer Colin Rule Named Mediate.com CEO* (13 June 2020), https://mediate.com/online-dispute-resolution-pioneer-colin-rule-named-mediate-com-ceo/ (accessed 16 August 2025).
32. Susskind (n 20) p. 65 ('Indeed, oral advocacy at its finest is probably the quintessential bespoke legal service').

3 Implications for Arbitration Market

In light of this rather alarming background and the likely magnitude of the upcoming change, it is reasonable to ask whether there would still be a need for junior lawyers in arbitration. Indeed, if machines are able to do what humans do more cheaply, wouldn't employers turn to computers instead?[33]

That would be too hasty a prediction to make. While there will ultimately be fewer jobs for young lawyers in conventional law firms,[34] AI will not eliminate the need for junior practitioners altogether.[35] *First*, machines will need to be supervised. In the short term at least, a lawyer will need 'to tell the machine what to look for, correct it when it inevitably makes mistakes and improve it through experience'.[36] The story of a personal injury lawyer in New York who used ChatGPT to help him prepare a court filing which turned out to be replete with non-existent cases is a cautionary tale.[37]

Second, some tasks cannot be performed by machines yet, well or at all. Machines cannot, for example, put up IKEA bookshelves – but nor can humans.[38] More seriously, AI cannot replace the human qualities that make lawyers valuable, such as critical thinking, empathy and, arguably, creativity (amongst others).[39] Fundamentally, client advice is a multifaceted product that often entails consideration of the broader factual matrix, understanding of the client's commercial objectives and a good grasp of strategy; it rarely is confined to a narrow legal issue – and nor can it be reduced to a single prompt. Even with seemingly routine tasks such as arbitrator selection, human factor is essential as one needs to ensure you get the right 'mix of people'.[40] Moreover, machines can make accurate predictions only where there is sufficient non-confidential

33. The Economist, *What Will Artificial Intelligence Mean for Your Pay?* (16 November 2023). *See also* The Economist, *Generative AI Could Radically Alter the Practice of Law* (6 June 2023), p. 2 ('If AI can do in 20 seconds a task that would have taken a dozen associates 50 hours each, then why would big firms continue hiring dozens of associates?') (citing Lawrence Lessig of Harvard Law School notes).
34. Susskind (n 20) p. 133 ('I predict that conventional lawyers will not be as prominent in society as today'). *See also* Mustafa Suleyman and Michael Bhaskar, *The Coming Wave* (2023), p. 11 ('First come more efficient ways of doing specific tasks, and then entire roles become redundant, and soon entire sectors require orders of magnitude fewer workers').
35. Andrew Perlman, *The Implications of ChatGPT for Legal Services and Society* (March/April 2023), https://clp.law.harvard.edu/knowledge-hub/magazine/issues/generative-ai-in-the-legal-profession/the-implications-of-chatgpt-for-legal-services-and-society/ (accessed 16 August 2025).
36. Apostolova and Kung (n 12) p. 1. Alarie and Niblett and Yoon (n 6) p. 12 ('A lawyer who uses artificial intelligence will still need to exercise her reasoned judgment to evaluate the accuracy of the purported facts, as well as the appropriateness of the technology in resolving the legal dispute').
37. Sara Merken, *New York Lawyers Sanctioned for Using Fake ChatGPT Cases in Legal Brief* (26 June 2023), Reuters, https://www.reuters.com/legal/new-york-lawyers-sanctioned-using-fake-chatgpt-cases-legal-brief-2023-06-22/ (accessed 16 August 2025).
38. The Economist, *Generative AI Generates Tricky Choices for Managers* (27 November 2023), p. 1.
39. Magal, Calthrop and Limond (n 19).
40. Paul Friedland, *Selecting the Party Appointed Arbitrator: Key Considerations* (1 April 2019) ('The appointee obviously should be capable of acting collegially with the other arbitrators'), https://www.whitecase.com/insight-alert/selecting-party-appointed-arbitrator-key-considerations (accessed 16 August 2025).

case data.[41] Where there is a novel legal issue for which no or little precedent is available, lawyers will remain superior to machines.[42]

Third, AI could create new roles and opportunities for junior lawyers. While AI will inevitably displace some arbitration professionals, it could open up the possibility of important new jobs for those who are sufficiently flexible to adapt to changing market conditions.[43] Beyond knowing how to maximise the quality of output from the machines (prompt engineering), mentioned above, there will be a need for algorithm development, machine training, and data interpretation specialists (among other new roles).[44] Moreover, since AI increasingly obviates the need for massive labour power emblematic of large law firms,[45] smaller firms can become more competitive and offer new and exciting opportunities to young professionals; also, ambitious law school graduates may find it easier to start a solo practice.[46]

As well as creating new opportunities, AI could have a positive impact on the quality of work that juniors do, and perhaps their job satisfaction as well. As technology removes laborious and time-consuming tasks from their diet, they can focus more readily on higher-level functions such as drafting submissions, legal analysis and preparing substantive portions of client advice. In addition, AI could improve training and capacity building opportunities by offering bespoke learning materials and alerting junior lawyers to new developments in their specific area(s) of practice. In time, AI could even provide bespoke mentorship guidance, monitoring publication and speaking opportunities and identifying potentially useful contacts within the arbitration community. In an area where time is in short supply and hardly a day passes without a new opportunity coming up, this could be a very helpful career-building tool.

4 Implications for Arbitration System

AI will also bring systemic implications to the practice of international arbitration. Those are harder to predict with precision, but they will be numerous, multipronged and likely significant. This discussion is beyond the scope of this chapter, but a few examples may be worth highlighting.

First, AI will likely make arbitration more accessible to a much wider pool of litigants and help ensure a level playing field. As more arbitration work becomes automated and as the costs of litigation decrease, there will be fewer barriers to

41. Scherer (n 24) pp. 555-557.
42. Cabrera Colorado (n 10) p. 317.
43. Susskind (n 20) p. 133. Information technology, for example, not only displaced some workers in the early 2000s but also directly led to the creation of new occupations like webpage designers, software developers, and digital marketing professionals, and indirectly increased labour demand in service industries such as healthcare, education, and food services. Goldman Sachs, *Global Macro Research Report, Top Mind, Generative AI: Hype, or Truly Transformative?* (5 July 2023), Issue 120, p. 14.
44. Cabrera Colorado (n 10) p. 302.
45. Alarie and Niblett and Yoon (n 6) p. 13, https://ssrn.com/abstract=3066816 or http://dx.doi.org/10.2139/ssrn.3066816 (accessed 16 August 2025).
46. The Economist, *Generative AI Could Radically Alter the Practice of Law* (n 33) p. 3.

bringing a claim and securing effective legal representation. Moreover, as the use of AI in arbitration becomes more prevalent, more companies will be able to benefit from enhanced research and arbitrator selection capabilities, as well as advanced trial preparation and advocacy aids – often expensive and difficult to operate. As such, the 'big firm advantage' will likely be reduced, although not altogether eliminated – top advocates and experienced arbitration partners will continue to be in high demand.

Second, AI could have implications for legitimacy of the process. Assuming that it becomes an important part of arbitral decision-making (as it one day might), it could over time fuel concerns over legitimacy of the process. Already, there are calls for greater transparency in arbitration,[47] especially in cases involving matters of public interest.[48] Inserting an algorithm that even its creators do not fully understand into the process that is already under some degree of criticism for lack of transparency in certain categories of cases[49] will do little to build confidence in the system.[50]

III CURRENT OBSTACLES TO THE WIDER ADOPTION OF AI ARE NOT INSURMOUNTABLE[51]

The potential of AI to transform the practice of international arbitration is sometimes challenged on the basis that there are significant technological limitations inherent in the use of AI. Machines have a tendency to make things up when they don't know the answer (or 'hallucinate'), and, furthermore, computer scientists do not fully understand how they work (the 'black box' problem).[52] AI's dependence on big data (still

47. *See, e.g.*, Ben Juratowitch, *Departing from Confidentiality in International Dispute Resolution*, Indian Journal of International Economic Law, vol. 12 (2020), p. 134; Constantine Partasides and Simon Maynard, *Raising the Curtain on English Arbitration*, Arbitration International, vol. 33, Issue 2 (June 2017), pp. 197-202 https://doi.org/10.1093/arbint/aix008 (accessed 16 August 2025).
48. *See, e.g.*, Stavros Brekoulakis and Margarett Devaney, *Public-Private Arbitration and the Public Interest under English Law*, The Modern Law Review, vol. 80, Issue 1 (2017), pp. 22-56 https://doi.org/10.1111/1468-2230.12241 (accessed 16 August 2025).
49. *Federal Republic of Nigeria v. Process & Industrial Developments Ltd* [2023] EWHC 2638 (Comm) (23 October 2023), para. 582 ('The facts and circumstances of this case, which are remarkable but very real, provide an opportunity to consider whether the arbitration process, which is of outstanding importance and value in the world, needs further attention where the value involved is so large and where a state is involved'). *See also* paras 589-591.
50. Questions could also be raised about the impact of AI on the development of commercial law and whether machine's current inability to give reasons could exacerbate concerns about depriving the common law of new important precedents. For background to this discussion, *see, e.g.*, Rt Hon the Lord Thomas of Cwmgiedd, *Commercial Dispute Resolution: Courts and Arbitration* (6 April 2017), The National Judges College, Beijing.
51. Other obstacles exist, such as a lack of the necessary regulatory framework and a risk that AI tools may perpetuate human biases in the underlying training data, but are not discussed in this chapter due to space limitations.
52. Guidelines on the Use of Artificial Intelligence in Arbitration, Silicon Valley Arbitration and Mediation Centre, draft of 31 August 2023, pp. 6-8, https://arbi-city.typeform.com/ai-guidelines?typeform-source=globalarbitrationreview.com (accessed 16 August 2025).

scarce in arbitration) and inability to reason in the way humans do are also cited as obstacles to its broader adoption in arbitration.[53]

These are significant constraints. However, AI's future should not be defined by its current technological limitations. First trains were slow, unwieldy and could not go very far.[54] Yet it would have been unwise to assess their potential based on these early attributes. Given the pace of AI's development over the last ten years – fivefold-tenfold increase in capabilities per year[55] – and a widely shared prediction that its 'mental power' will soon 'far exceed human intelligence',[56] it is likely that AI's existing technological limitations will soon be reduced, if not altogether eliminated.[57] Although the scarcity of data in arbitration will remain a constraint for some time, it is possible that as more arbitral awards become public and as AI becomes better at making accurate predictions with less data, this constraint will become less prominent.

The potential of AI to transform the practice of international arbitration can also be questioned on the basis that lawyers, a conservative bunch, can be reluctant to change.[58] Moreover, as much of technology is not customised for arbitration and lawyers are often too busy serving their clients, they may have little time for innovation.[59] Indeed, 'it is not easy to change a wheel on a moving car'.[60] So how does the arbitration community make this massive technological leap in the absence of innovation-inducing events like the COVID-19 pandemic? Market forces – is the short answer. As clients begin to see the value of AI-powered technology in their business operations, they will increasingly look to lawyers to deploy AI more widely in the provision of legal services. And as rival firms begin to do so in earnest, the market will

53. Cabrera Colorado (n 10) p. 335 ('Despite the precision of machines and their future development over time, in law, predictive machines still maintain a major problem today: they cannot reason. Instead, they simply analyse probabilities'). *See also* Maxi Scherer, *International Arbitration 3.0: How Artificial Intelligence Will Change Dispute Resolution*, Austrian Y.B. Int'l Arb. 503 (2019), pp. 511-512.
54. The first practical steam locomotive, launched in 1804, averaged less than 10 mph. First railway line, connecting Liverpool and Manchester, was only 35 miles (56 km) long.
55. Suleyman and Bhaskar (n 34) p. 66 ('Not long ago, language models struggled to produce coherent sentences. This is far, far beyond Moore's law or indeed any other technology trajectory I can think of').
56. Elon Mask, Rishi Sunak and Elon Musk, *Talk AI, Tech & the Future* (3 November 2023), 2:00, https://www.youtube.com/watch?v=R2meHtrO1n8 (accessed 16 August 2025). Geoffrey Hinton, a computer scientist, makes a similar prediction: 'I think in five years time it may well be able to reason better than [humans].' Geoffrey Hinton, *'Godfather of AI' Geoffrey Hinton: The 60 Minutes Interview* (9 October 2023), 10:20, https://www.youtube.com/watch?v=qrvK_KuIeJk (accessed 16 August 2025).
57. For example, the latest iteration of OpenAI's GPT model – GPT-4, released in March 2023, roughly one year after the GPT-3.5 model – is 40% more likely to produce accurate responses, and can now accept visual input (rather than just text). *See* OpenAI, GPT-4 Technical Report (27 March 2023), https://cdn.openai.com/papers/gpt-4.pdf (accessed 16 August 2025).
58. Roos (n 21). *See also* Susskind (n 20) p. 60 ('[T]here is still reluctance amongst mainstream partners in many firms to believe that they really need to change').
59. Dmitry Evseev, *Young EFILA in conversation with … Dmitri Evseev* (March 2023) ('We don't have the time to understand how newer technology can work for us to make things more efficient'), https://efilablog.org/2023/03/17/young-efila-in-conversation-with-dmitri-evseev/amp/ (accessed 16 August 2025).
60. Susskind (n 20) p. 59.

follow. Already, companies are making the use of technology a criterion when selecting counsel for litigation work.[61]

Finally, sceptics could argue that AI is unlikely to have a major impact on the practice because arbitration is essentially a 'people business'.[62] Since many aspects of arbitration work require the so-called people skills[63] and since people prefer human interaction to computer programmes,[64] machines are unlikely to play a dominant role in this area of human activity. It is true that some aspects of the process require human interaction.[65] However, that is not a reason to deny the benefits of automation to the rest of the practice.[66] Moreover, while it is natural to assume a predilection for human interaction – we are, after all, humans – one should be slow to extend that assumption to all arbitration users. Above all, users want a solution to their legal problems; if one can be provided by machines in a reliable and cost-effective manner; 'they will often happily forego human service'.[67]

IV CONCLUSION

Geoffrey Hinton is widely regarded as the godfather of AI. Reflecting on its future, he said: 'We are entering a period of great uncertainty where we are dealing with things we've never dealt with before. And normally the first time you deal with something totally novel you get it wrong.'[68] The broader adoption of AI in arbitration portends significant changes in all major aspects of our practice. With foresight, and better understanding of the trajectory and contours of the change that the chapter sought to outline, we can get it right. For, as one commentator remarked, better learn how to ride the technological wave before you get swept away by it.[69]

61. Apostolova and Kung (n 12) p. 3.
62. Moody (n 2).
63. Hope (n 27) p. 115 ('Many of [the tasks performed by arbitrators] require the so-called "people skills". They require human interaction, and the success of the arbitrator often depends on winning the parties' trust and demonstrating that their submissions are being heard and properly considered.').
64. Cohen and Nappert (n 27).
65. Think about hearing logistics, case management issues, meet and confer meetings, not to mention tribunal deliberations and many other aspects of arbitral decision-making.
66. As explained in section 2 above, much arbitration work is well-suited for automation.
67. Susskind (n 20) p. 190 ('People with legal problems want a solution that is trustworthy – if this can be delivered online in a way that fixes their problems reliably, they will often happily forego human service').
68. Hinton (n 56) 11:34.
69. *See also* Global Arb. Rev. (author unspecified), *The March of the 'cobots'* (2 March 2021), p. 4 (concluding remarks by Stefano Azzali, secretary general of the Milan Chamber of Arbitration), https://globalarbitrationreview.com/article/the-march-of-the-cobots (accessed 16 August 2025).

CHAPTER 52

The Use of AI in Dispensing Justice: A China Perspective

Winnie Tam SC[*]

TABLE OF CONTENTS

> "Let society and the technology co-evolve, and sort of step-by-step with a very tight feedback loop and course correction, build these systems that deliver tremendous value while meeting safety requirements."—Sam Altman, CEO of OpenAI at the 2024 World Economic Forum at Davos.
>
> "China believes technology must serve the common good of humanity, it must do good, and the same applies to AI."—Premier of the State Council of the PRC, at his Special Address at the 2024 World Economic Forum at Davos.

I INTRODUCTION

In the legal sector and in international arbitration in particular, the use of Artificial Intelligence (AI) has long been prevalent in a wide variety of mechanical tasks, mainly

* Winnie Tam is a Senior Counsel of the Hong Kong Bar and an Independent Arbitrator. As an IP specialist barrister she practices from Des Voeux Chambers in Hong Kong. She holds qualifications to practice in the Greater Bay Area of Mainland China, England and Wales, and Singapore.

in data processing. These include legal research, document analyses, management and organization, and case management by lawyers, courts and arbitral institutions. Further, technological developments in Big Data, Large Language Models and Generative AI have popularized the use of AI technology and sparked debates on the future of the legal profession.

The increasing use of legal technology on the legal profession is reflected in the optimistic outlook on investment return in legal tech businesses. Despite a notable decrease in legal technology investments and acquisitions in 2023 due to unstable economy worldwide, a major acquisition by an established legal database platform was recorded. There remains a high level of interest and an increasing appetite in the legal sector to use generative AI technology as productivity tools.

Within months of the release of GPT-4 in March 2023, leading legal tech firms like LexisNexis and Thomson Reuters started integrating Generative AI into their offerings. Additionally, many other legal technology companies released beta generative AI tools, further popularizing this technology. In fact, according to surveys released in January, nearly 27% of legal professionals reported using generative AI for work-related purposes, indicating a rapid adoption rate within the profession. The advent of ChatGPT based on LLMs, Generative AI has fueled further developments to meet the needs of legal services of the day.

Amidst calls for caution and regulation, both private and public sectors in technology and dispute resolution continue to explore and innovate at an astounding speed. In Mainland China, the progressive approach regarding the use of Generative AI technology in dispute resolution has been driven by various factors, not least the pressure felt by the courts in major cities to get through the enormous case load in a justice system that aims to provide access to the courts to resolve civil dispute at nearly no cost. Another driving factor is the proven ability of members of the general public to adapt to the use of digital technology in daily life.[1]

While the type of AI technology employed in various legal uses differs from one another, the aspirations are focused on Generative AI to assist in the decision-making process. Recent developments have shown Generative AI not only possessing the ability to provide answers through processing vast amounts of data to identify patterns, but reasoning capabilities that enable conclusions to be explained and reasoning traced.

In this chapter, the author aims to provide an overview of the use of types of AI technology in the courts and in commercial dispute resolution institutions in China and how it has impacted on the delivery of justice, with an outlook for future development in international arbitration.

1. Digital payment and the provision of public services via mobile digital communication devices, and the use of disruptive technology on the devices, have been widespread in China: https://www.scmp.com/economy/china-economy/article/3215592/how-mobile-phones-china-have-gone-status-symbol-disruptive-technology (accessed August 16, 2025).

II AN OVERVIEW OF THE DEVELOPMENT OF MODELS OF AI TECHNOLOGY FOR USE IN LEGAL DISPUTE RESOLUTION

To properly understand the potentials of how AI technology may impact upon legal dispute resolution, it is necessary for lawyers to have a basic understanding of how it does the work. It is not however the aim of this chapter to provide a technical briefing on the subject.

"Artificial intelligence" has been defined in the following terms: "the theory and development of computer systems able to perform tasks normally requiring human intelligence, such as visual perception, speech recognition, decision-making, and translation between languages."[2] Inherent in the definition of intelligence is "the ability to learn, understand and make judgments or have opinions that are based on reason."[3]

1 Early Rule-Based Models

Early attempts of computer scientists to build programs that mimic human intelligence by deciphering the human cognitive process and replicating it did not meet with much success. The process can be likened to teaching a language by stipulating a set of strict grammatical rules. These are called expert systems or rule-based programs dependent on logical inferences. In these systems, defined rules are carefully defined and laboriously coded into the program to form the knowledge base from which computation can be carried out. Where the tasks to be performed are complex or the rules difficult to exhaustively define, results are disappointing.[4]

2 Predictive Models

Next came models built on statistics and probabilities. In this model of AI, the ability of the algorithm to decide what the outcome should be is based on statistics and probability calculations, as opposed to any replication of the human cognitive process. An important characteristic of this model is that the larger the dataset, the higher the accuracy of the prediction.

A study back in the 2000s using a statistical model[5] suggested that forecasting of judicial outcomes was possible provided there is reliable data that is capable of being characterized into a replicable scheme.

---

2. The Oxford Dictionary of Phrase and Fables https://www.oxfordreference.com/display/10.1093/acref/9780198609810.001.0001/acref-9780198609810-e-423 (accessed April 8, 2024).
3. Cambridge Dictionary https://dictionary.cambridge.org/dictionary/english/intelligence (accessed April 8, 2024).
4. Alpaydin, *Machine Learning pp.50-52* cited in Scherer, M., *Artificial Intelligence and Legal Decision-Making: The Wide Open? Study on the Example of International Arbitration*, Queen Mary School of Law Legal Studies Research Paper No. 318/2019 (May 22, 2019).
5. Martin AD et al., *Competing Approaches to Predicting Supreme Court Decision Making*, Perspective on Politics, vol. 2:4, pp. 761-767 (2004) https://doi.org/10.1017/s1537592704040502 (accessed August 16, 2025).The accuracy rate of the legal professionals on individual justices' votes was shown to be higher.

3 Big Data and Generative AI

The advent of "Big Data" made possible by increased computing power and enhanced speed of processors led to the development of machine learning, a sub-category of AI. Instead of relying on programming rules and parameters to imitate the cognitive process, a large amount of data is fed to the algorithms to "train" its predictive ability. The algorithms process huge amounts of data to identify patterns and gain insight from them. This ability enabled a continuous process of self-improvement of the algorithm.[6]

As an example, in 2017, researchers developed another prediction model that aims to forecast the behavior of the U.S. Supreme Court. The researchers employed machine-learning techniques and leveraged historical data from nearly two centuries (1816-2015) to construct their prediction model. The model outperforms the baseline models in predicting both justice votes *and* case outcomes, achieving an accuracy of 70.2% at the case outcome level and 71.9% at the justice vote level.[7] At this stage of development, the prediction model was dealing with binary outcomes in appeals.

Generative AI represents a step-change in artificial intelligence. The term refers to AI systems capable of generating new content, such as text, video, voice or images, in response to human prompts. This distinguishes it from early AI capabilities that involved processing information. The Large Language Models (LLMs) underpinning the technology have likewise been trained on a vast amount of text data. Having an enhanced understanding of linguistic, creative and deductive patterns enables AI tools to produce new written works in a matter of seconds.[8]

Another study had been conducted on decisions of the European Court of Human Rights.[9] Researchers utilize natural language processing and machine-learning techniques to build predictive models that identify patterns that drive judicial decisions. The study again formulates binary classification tasks, where the input of the classifiers is the textual content extracted from a case, and the target output is the actual judgment regarding whether there has been a violation of an article of the European Convention of Human Rights. The models achieve a staggering accuracy of 79% on average in predicting the court's decisions.

Outside predictive analytics, the accuracy of Generative AI translation, summarization and drafting tools for general use, such as those made available by Google is a testament to the success of this model. Using an LLM known as GPT4, the Generative AI tool ChatGPT by Open AI generates natural language texts in answer to questions posed in natural language. It acquired 100 million users in just over two months of its launch in early 2023. Microsoft's answer to ChatGPT is Microsoft 365 Copilot, which

6. https://ai.engineering.columbia.edu/ai-vs-machine-learning/ (accessed August 16, 2025).
7. Katz DM, Bommarito MJ II and Blackman J, *A General Approach for Predicting the Behavior of the Supreme Court of the United States*, PLoS ONE, vol. 12:4, p. e0174698 (2017) https://doi.org/10.1371/journal.pone.0174698 (accessed August 16, 2025).
8. Microsoft, *Generative AI for Lawyers* (2024 March) https://www.microsoft.com/cms/api/am/binary/RW1dRAC (accessed August 16, 2025).
9. Aletras N et al., *Predicting Judicial Decisions of the European Court of Human Rights*, PeerJ Computer Science, vol. 2, Article e93 (2016) https://doi.org/10.7717/peerj-cs.93 (accessed August 16, 2025).

leverages LLMs with other Microsoft apps to capture natural language commands to automate production of content, analyze data and build presentations. While designed for general use, it is offered to the legal profession with special features to assure legal and regulatory compliance. It enables subscribers to limit access to materials by the service, protects client confidentiality and restricts third-party use in a closed environment.[10]

To legal service providers, the potentials of Generative AI models trained on professional or specialist data with text-generating abilities are seen at once to be attractive as it is devastating. It further fuels imagination on the future "robot lawyer" who will deliver thoroughly researched opinions to clients on demand, within seconds, and at a fraction of the costs of a good junior lawyer.

In the paper published in March 2024 by Microsoft on "Generative AI for Lawyers,"[11] the software developer admitted that "*generative AI systems and tools are only as good as the material they have been trained on, as well as their probability-based approaches. As such, legal practitioners must maintain a 'human in the loop' to review, edit, customise and quality-assure content.*"

As much as models of AI algorithms have heightened predictive capabilities, delivering effective outcomes or seemingly intelligent solutions in natural language, there remain serious limitations in their generative functions.

III LIMITATIONS

1 Scarcity of Data for Training

There are four Vs that computer scientists have identified as characteristics and challenges of Big Data: Volume, Variety, Velocity and Veracity.[12] First and foremost, AI algorithms based on machine learning and Big Data depend on a high-volume diet of sample data. A sufficient amount of non-confidential case data input is required to be effective. Limited data availability can hinder the accuracy and reliability of the predictions.[13]

LLMs built on general data as opposed to specific legal data is likely to yield more unreliable results. There already exist examples of LLMs trained on specialist legal data, e.g., Spellbook.[14] It remains to be seen whether the data is of a sufficient volume and sample size to yield meaningful output, for the models to gain traction.

For arbitration more so than for court proceedings, the issue of scarcity of data is more critical. Given the confidential nature of international commercial arbitration, only a very limited proportion awards, most notably ICSID awards are publicly

10. King & Wood Mallesons is one of such firms, according to the paper at (n 6).
11. *Supra* (n 6).
12. https://opensistemas.com/en/the-four-vs-of-big-data/ (accessed August 16, 2025).
13. Schere, M., *Artificial Intelligence and Legal Decision-Making: The Wide Open? Study on the Example of International Arbitration*, Queen Mary School of Law Legal Studies Research Paper No. 318/2019 (May 22, 2019).
14. Spellbook is an AI tool built on ChatGPT that helps draft contracts in Microsoft Word.

accessible. Some arbitral institutions have begun to publish selected, partially redacted, awards from time to time, on parties' consent.[15] This is a far cry from the volume of court judgments that can be made available for an AI model to perform statistical analysis and prediction.

Further, in the legal tech context, an effective Generative AI model will require a variety of data even for repetitive issues. If the issues in the sample data are complex, diverse or not repetitive, it will make the discerning of any hidden pattern more difficult, and will impact on the machine-learning process and hence the reliability of the outcome.[16]

2 Risk of Bias and Hallucinations

The ability of Generative AI tools to understand linguistic, creative and deductive patterns through training also means that it is prone to hallucination. Its ability to formulate its predictions in natural language imitating the style of legal text makes its output look credible, but not always accurate or true. It is known to hallucinate, making up baseless responses with well-written texts that sound convincing.[17]

As data-based computer models are only as good as the input data, any biased or corruption in the data diet for training the program will have negative consequences on the extracted model. There are justifiable concerns over risks that an AI model might extract patterns from the data and extrapolate them in a way that might lead to systemic mistakes. For instance, some studies have shown that the use of algorithms in criminal risk assessment in the U.S. may lead to racially biased outcomes.[18] It is unclear whether this racial bias in the computer program was based on existing human biases in the training data.

If similar technologies were relied on to assist decision-making in legal processes, it could dent confidence in rule of law and the judicial process unless the risk of the adverse impact of biased data material can be discovered and managed.

3 Opaqueness in Reasoning

The inherent difficulty in the propensity for Generative AI models to hallucinate underscores the need for a generated response to be explainable and verifiable by reference to its source. However, hidden patterns are detected and extrapolated by AI

15. E.g., the ICC Court of Arbitration, the SIAC and the HKIAC.
16. *See* Scherer (n 4).
17. *See* news reports of the infamous incident of a U.S. lawyer appearing before a Manhattan court having filed submissions after "consulting ChatGPT." The submissions were found to contain six legal citations that were fabricated and did not exist at all. He went on affidavit to say that he did "press" ChatGPT for confirmation that the cases cited were real, and it did: https://www.cbsnews.com/news/lawyer-chatgpt-court-filing-avianca/ (accessed August 16, 2025); https://www.theguardian.com/technology/2023/jun/23/two-us-lawyers-fined-submitting-fake-court-citations-chatgpt (accessed August 16, 2025).
18. Larson, J. et al., *How We Analyzed the COMPAS Recidivism Algorithm, ProPublica* (May 23, 2016), available at https://www.propublica.org/article/how-we-analyzed-the-compas-recidivism-algorithm (accessed August 16, 2025).

algorithms in the training process in ways that cannot be traced to explain the output or conclusion.

There is therefore a fundamental incompatibility between the unexplainable predictive functions performed by Generative AI and the object of providing a reasoned conclusion that outlines the premises on which it is based. An outcome based on probabilities lacks the legitimacy that is required of legal decision-making. It has been argued that it would in fact represent a departure from the common understanding that judicial reasoning is based on pre-determined rules, nor the result of logic and deduction.[19]

4 AI and Discretion in Decision-Making

An important element of judicial decision-making and in commercial dispute resolution is the exercise of discretion to ensure fairness, taking account of the unique facts and circumstances of individual cases. The exercise of discretion is widely recognized by eminent jurists to involve the individual judge's assessment of what is fair and just to do in the particular case. It often requires the judge to consider and balance factors involving wider and often shifting social, cultural and societal values.[20]

Unlike an AI judge, a human judge can be persuaded through reasoned legal argument. Arguably, until further technological development, AI cannot mimic general human cognition and intelligence to understand intents, emotions and implied assumptions as a seasoned judge or arbitrator may be trusted to do.[21]

IV THE CHINA PERSPECTIVE

In China, the policy objectives of fairness and efficiency that spearhead development of the use of AI in public justice provide guidance and incentive to similar developments in alternative dispute resolution, albeit in a smaller scale. Some arbitral institutions with a strong innovative spirit and technical support are forging ahead with groundbreaking uses of Generative AI in selected types of cases in an online environment.

1 AI in Court Proceedings

In Mainland China, the development of the use of technology, including AI, for the judicial process has been driven by the sheer need to manage the tens of millions of

19. Scherer (n 4).
20. For instance, the Right Hon Lord Justice Bingham, *The Discretion of the Judge*, The Denning Law Journal, vol. 5, p. 28 (1990) https://doi.org/10.5750/dlj.v5i1.191 (accessed August 16, 2025), where he postulates: "the judges exercise their discretion at the time of choosing a course of action, orders, penalties or remedies to determine the fact and ruling on the law."
21. Sharaban Tahura, U. et al., *The Use of Artificial Intelligence in Judicial Decision Making: The Example of China*, International Journal of Law, Ethics and Technology (February 28, 2023), https://typeset.io/papers/the-use-of-artificial-intelligence-in-judicial-1a7cc9j4 (accessed August 16, 2025).

cases filed each year. The mounting pressure on the judiciary and arbitral institutions to meet a high rate of timely resolution makes innovation a necessity.[22] In particular, the Chinese government has since the last decade adopted a policy framework of "smart courts" and "E-justice" set to be implemented between 2019-2023 as part of the 14th five-year plan set out in the Reform Outline of the People's Court.[23]

In a document dated 2017 setting the direction of development,[24] the Supreme People's Court targeted on increasing the use of Generative AI to assist in generating written judgments, to proofread, and provide prompting on legal terminology and applicable law through legal reasoning and deduction. The objective was to increase precision in professional knowledge, efficiency and uniformity in the administration of justice.

To deal with the large volume of e-commerce and Internet-related cases, three Internet Courts have been established in Hangzhou, Guangdong, and Beijing between 2017 to 2019, along with a number of Internet Tribunals in Chengdu, Suzhou and Changchun.[25] The Internet Courts operate on an online platform fully integrated with external business information.[26] Digital case filing and management aside, pre-trial meetings and hearings are over 90% virtual, and include judges powered by artificial intelligence, visually represented by an icon in black robes. Litigants can interact with virtual "judges" via text messaging on the smartphones through the internet court platform.

In December 2022, the Supreme People's Court of the People's Republic of China issued the Opinions on Regulating and Strengthening the Applications of Artificial Intelligence in the Judicial Fields.[27] The document set out the key principles for developing AI technologies for use in the justice system such as safety and legality, fairness and impartiality, and transparency and credibility. Importantly, China has adopted the principle that while AI will take on an increasingly important role in the

22. On March 7, 2024, the Supreme People's Court delivered a report by Chief Justice Zhang Jun at the annual meeting of the 14th Session of the China People's Political Consultative Committee on the main statistical figures of the People Courts in 2023. The filing of the number of new cases in 2023 was stated to be 45 million cases.
23. Zheng, G.G., *China's Grand Design of People's Smart Courts,* Asian Journal of Law and Society vol. 7, p. 567 (2020) https://doi.org/10.1017/als.2020.20 (accessed August 16, 2025).
24. The Supreme People's Court—Opinions Concerning Speeding Up the Establishment of Smart Courts (April, 17 2017) http://gongbao.court.gov.cn/Details/5dec527431cdc22b72163b49fc0284.html (accessed August 16, 2025).
25. Including intellectual property, e-commerce, financial disputes related to online conduct, loans acquired or performed online, domain name issues, property and civil rights cases involving the Internet, product liability arising from online purchases and certain administrative disputes.
26. In the White Paper on the Application of Internet Technology in Judicial Practice published by the Beijing Internet Court in 2019, it was reported that since the establishment of the Beijing Internet Court in 2018, the electronic litigation platform has received a total of 41.8 million visits, an average of 208,000 visits per day, and a cumulative number of registered users up to 18,941. It has dealt with 15,748 online payments, which amounted to RMB 9,863,812.55; it has delivered 68,575 electronic summons, of which 16,749 were judgment documents, representing a delivery rate of 96.05%. Court hearings have been definitely held online if the parties agree to do so. The rate of online court hearings reached 99.19% with a total of 5,942 online hearing. https://www.chinadaily.com.cn/specials/WhitePapertheApplicationofInternetTechnologyinJudicialPractice.pdf (accessed August 16, 2025).
27. http://fzzfyjy.cupl.edu.cn/info/1080/15639.htm (accessed August 16, 2025).

justice system, including in the judicial decision-making process, its role will remain supportive only and will be regulated with safeguards to ensure judicial fairness. "AI shall not make judicial decision substituting for the judge in any case," and judicial accountability will continue to fall squarely on the judicature, as stated in the Opinions.

The concept of smart courts can be expressed in the following four areas of work using the Internet and AI technologies: (1) "Smart Services" for access by the public to judicial services; (2) "Smart Management" for administering a fully integrated internet-based information to facilitate processing and research; (3) "Smart Judicial Process," meaning AI-assisted adjudication in guiding examination of evidence, drawing attention to applicable laws and similar precedents, and generating legal texts, and in examination of legal submissions: and (4) "Smart Execution"—an internet-based operation for execution of judgments (including auctioning of assets, posting related public notices, etc.).

Driven by national policy, China has achieved admirable success in the use of AI in judicial administration.[28] Quite apart from the use of AI to enhance access to justice and administrative efficiency by leaps and bounds, the policy has been driving the systematic construction of a large database of judicial decisions and documents that impact on the application and interpretation of Chinese law to complement existing databases for legal research. This is by far the most prominent feature of Generative AI assistance used by judges in public justice, namely, providing compatible case law for achieving more consistent adjudication nationwide. This is made possible by a highly digitized legal database including reasoned judgments of courts up and down the country, published laws, regulations and a plethora of written instruments having the effect of laws and on their interpretation.[29]

Academics and the legal profession both give recognition to AI in significantly improving access to justice, transparency, and in managing heavy caseloads to achieve judicial efficiency in Mainland China. There are however concerns expressed which reflect the limitations of the algorithms as identified in the previous section. Many expressed doubts on whether reliance on AI-generated judgments with uniformity of adjudication of similar cases as its aim would usurp judges as the ultimate administrators of justice. Other concerns expressed relate to privacy and data protection and judicial independence, and the categorization of legal issues for the purpose of machine learning.[30] Others doubt whether the same results can be applied and yield a "fair"

28. Shi, C., Sourdin, T. and Li, B., *The Smart Court: A New Pathway to Justice in China?*, International Journal For Court Administration, vol. 12, p. 4 (2021) https://doi.org/10.36745/ijca.367 and https://iacajournal.org/articles/10.36745/ijca.367 (accessed August 16, 2025). Xiaoling, D., *Huang Zijuan: Reasonable Use of AI to Enhance Impartiality and Efficiency*;代晓玲、黄子娟，*合理利用人工智能* http://society.people.com.cn/n1/2023/0722/c1008-40041296.html (accessed April 12, 2024).

29. Peng, S., *Enhancing "Similar Case, Similar Judicial Outcome" Through AI* 邵鹏，*人工智能助推类案同判* https://www.chinacourt.org/article/detail/2023/08/id/7465811.shtml (accessed April 12, 2024).

30. *Ibid.; 廖旋 智慧法院：人工智能介入司法的忧患与展望* Xuan, L., *The Intrusion of AI into Judicial Administration: Concerns and Outlook* http://www.chinalawlib.org.cn/LunwenShow.aspx?FID=20081224141110233122&CID=20160518155022540388&AID=20200509112335350847 (accessed March 11, 2024); 山西省朔州市朔城区人民法院网， *司法人工智能的实际应用与展望* https://szscfy.shanxify.gov.cn/article/detail/2023/02/id/7165682.shtml (accessed

adjudicative outcome using predictive analytics and constructing categorization links,[31] especially when the dataset may not be sufficiently comprehensive, up-to-date or of a consistently high quality, and the algorithms are not sufficiently developed to perform cognitive reasoning.[32] Regulatory measures are urgently called for.[33,34] Experts are unanimous in pointing out the inadequacy of AI in producing fair and just outcomes without any human understanding of diverse factors relevant to a case and achieving a balance and coordination of responsibilities, rights and interests in society.[35]

2 AI in Arbitrations

The 2022 Opinion[36] encourages the application of AI in alternative dispute resolution, including arbitration. Given the objectives are similar though the context is private commercial dispute resolution, the same principles apply.

In commercial dispute resolution, AI has been known to provide tools for case-filing assistance, search and appointment of arbitrators, case management, legal research, hearing arrangements (such as instantaneous transcripts or simultaneous foreign language interpretation) and mechanical tasks involving processing of neutral information, and to review draft awards on factual matters which are not controversial. Like in Internet Courts, the development and general use of the above functions are particularly advanced and user-friendly where online arbitrations are provided for.

A worthy example is a specific online arbitration platform of the Shenzhen Court of International Arbitration (SCIA). Nested within Shenzhen, the technological hub of Southern China, the SCIA's Online Arbitration Platform for Financial Disputes provides a fully digitalized experience where the use of Generative AI is evident. A claim for recovery of a debt arising from bank loans under standard-term contracts is made easy by submission to online arbitration based on the terms of the loan agreements. Information on non-payment is submitted. The claim may be disputed by the respondent on the facts or on the law if the respondent files its defense. Much of the rest of the process is left to the algorithms, as are the generating of correspondence between institution and parties, procedural orders, the selection of arbitrators, notices to the parties, translation on demand, as are transcripts of any hearing. The well-organized case file is accessible at any time to the parties and the tribunal.

March 11, 2024); 雷磊，司法人工智能能否实现司法公正？ Lei, L., *Can Judicial AI Achieve Judicial Fairness?*, http://www.socio-legal.sjtu.edu.cn/wxzy/info.aspx?itemid=4186 (accessed March 18, 2024).

31. *Ibid.*, Lei Lei 雷磊.
32. *Supra* (n 30).
33. Shuwen, L. and Mengkang, Z., *Regulating Use of AI to Maintain Judicial Impartiality* 李书文、杨孟康，*规范使用人工智能 主力维护司法公正* https://www.chinacourt.org/article/detail/2023/05/id/7309772.shtml 26 May 2023 (accessed April 11, 2024).
34. Yuechen, H., *The Limitations of AI in Judicial Decision-Making and Methods of Improvement*: 黄悦晨: 人工智能在司法裁判领域应用的局限性及其改进对策 https://doi.org/10.12677/OJLS.2023.113257 (accessed August 16, 2025).
35. *Ibid.*
36. *Supra* (n 27).

On this platform, Generative AI performs impressive supportive functions in assisting in award writing: even before the first hearing is convened, a draft award in the form of a template with sections left open for analysis and reasoning awaits the tribunal, accessible on the arbitrators' online platform. The procedural history automatically updates as more steps are taken. Relevant facts have all been set out, award-style, based on the claim and documentary evidence submitted. Terms of the arbitral agreement and provisions of the governing law are laid out as one would expect in any arbitral award. The claimed relief is included in the award template for the tribunal's consideration, to match the contract terms identified in it.

The above preparatory work proves to be much-welcomed assistance to the arbitrator. Precious time is saved in drafting the procedural and factual portions of the award from scratch, and human errors are minimized. It incentivizes the arbitrator to complete the award promptly after receipt of oral evidence, which involves simply stating the reasons for its findings one way or another, once the tribunal has deliberated on the evidence. In these cases, Generative AI performs the role of the super-efficient and reliable tribunal secretary, at no extra cost to the parties.

The maintenance of SCIA's online platform with Generative AI is carried out by a team of in-house engineers. Teams of counsel at the Secretariat supervise the proceeding of each case with the help of prompts generated by the system.

Some arbitral institutions offer AI-powered assistance to provide guidance at case filing.[37] As of the time of the writing of this chapter, it is confined to procedural guidance to members of the public and the profession, rather than for any analysis of the merits of a party's case. On the online arbitrators' platform of SCIA, the arbitrator accesses research tools from established databases for both Chinese law and arbitration law, functioning in the form of traditional legal search engines only.

It remains to be seen if Generative AI will be able to function as efficiently where the dispute is of a more complex nature that goes beyond the application of standard contract terms of a particular nature, with a narrow range of defenses and potential factual disputes. As referred to in section III above, where Big Data meets AI, the ability of an AI model to deliver accurate answers in text will very much depend on the amount of data that can be used to train it. As more and more arbitral institutions are making redacted awards available, the arbitration sector will be curious to see the enhancement of such capabilities in due course.

3 Legal Consultation by LLMs

Some interesting developments are worth mentioning as a possible precursor of AI tools that may be adapted for the analytical work in decision-making. One such platform on Chinese law and in the Chinese language is MetaLaw developed by a Shanghai tech company that emerged in November 2023.[38] The company offers an AI-powered legal research product that claims to integrate advanced deep semantic

37. These include SCIA and Guangzhou Arbitration Commission.
38. https://meta.law/ (accessed August 16, 2025).

understanding in case retrieval and analysis. The tool is notably different from other popular legal database search engines by accepting search prompts in the form of questions in natural language in place of keyword search, and delivering its output in the form of a legal opinion. The opinion explains its statement of the law, and supports it with citations of the relevant provisions of legislative or other sources of the law and court judgments, ranked according to the weight of authority they carry under the rules, practice and norms of the Chinese legal system. The legal materials cited are made available by hyperlinks, with the relevant parts highlighted in the context of the full document for easy reference.

The building of such a model would not have been possible without the systematic digitization and availability of a large enough body of official case law data within the Chinese justice system.[39] This may not be achievable in the short run, where the law in a jurisdiction is more fragmented (e.g., with states applying different laws) and where the availability of judgments or arbitral awards to form input data is more limited. Nevertheless, a model of this construct can be expected to continue to build its strength as a powerful cost- and time-saving research tool usable by trained lawyers and laymen alike.

According to the latest information provided by the operator of MetaLaw, in the pipeline is yet another exciting product by MetaLaw, one helpful even for the untrained lawyer. In this model scheduled to be published later this year, the Retrieval Enhancement Engine enhances the retrieval functions and collaborates with Generative AI to generate rich and diverse, yet more accurate, results. The Vector Search Engine powers the search for relevant information to form the context for the LLM to enable the latest information beyond the training cut-off to improve the quality of output without fine-tuning. This technique helps update information in real time and ensures the accuracy of search results. A particular feature of this interactive model is its Query-Expansion Method. It utilizes the LLM's ability to understand and expand on the user's original query by pushing relevant questions to the user to tease out relevant information, and to provide a contextual response that captures the user's intent.

The potential of a model with analytic capabilities combined with heightened skill in legal text generation will certainly provide inspiration for future AI-assisted judgment and award writing. Parties to arbitrations will likely support the use of technology by the tribunal to save time and cost where judgment-neutral tasks can be performed more efficiently. However, it is important for boundaries in the practice of using Generative AI to be set upon a wider consensus within the arbitration community and the users of arbitration service to ensure that the fairness and legitimacy of the process.

V OUTLOOK FOR THE FUTURE

At present, artificial intelligence technology is still in the early stage of development. The reasoning engine applied with LLMs to a specialist database is set to change the

39. MetaLaw has in its database 150 million authentic court judgments from PRC courts.

black-box characteristic of Generative AI that has made it unattractive as a potential tool in the core functions of dispute resolution.

Just as this chapter was in its final stages of preparation, closed-door discussions among major Mainland arbitral institutions are already underway on the possibility of utilizing a combination of LLMs and legal reasoning models to assist in predictive analyses to motivate mediation at an early stage.

The technology is predicted to become exponentially more powerful with the use of quantum computing. However, most of the limitations or drawbacks of Generative AI will remain, such as weakening judicial discretion, a weak judicial data foundation, algorithm secrecy, etc. There are policy decisions to be made and regulatory measures to be taken to give this line of development clearer direction such as a data sharing platform, optimizing algorithm technology, and cultivating compound talents.

Last but not least, it has been pointed out that the costliest part of constructing an AI platform is the computing power needed to train and maintain it. The higher the quality of the content that users think they get, the more time they need to invest in specialized training to achieve the desired effect.[40]

LLMs are not human, however eloquent, and reasoning engines, however smart, do not uphold human values. Generative AI output should remain supportive, not determinative of outcomes of disputes agreed to be arbitrated. This will require the arbitral community to work together on a set of living standards that will rise above rapid technological advance and to uphold the values of the rule of law while balancing the need for maximizing efficiency and minimizing costs in international dispute resolution.

40. Yingying, C., *Further Thoughts on the Use of Ai in International Arbitration* (November 27, 2023) 蔡莹莹：*菜摊人工智能的技术应用前景* It is estimated that GPT-3 costs about USD 1.4 million for one training session, and between USD 2 million and USD 12 million for some larger LLMs (large language models). Based on ChatGPT's average unique visitors of 13 million in January 2023, its corresponding chip demand is more than 30,000 NVIDIA A100 GPUs, with an initial investment cost of about USD 800 million and a daily electricity bill of about USD 50,000. https://www.jtn.com/CN/booksdetail.aspx?type = 06001&keyid = 0000000000000007535&PageUrl = majorbook&Lan = CN (accessed April 13, 2024).

Closing and Thank You from the Co-chairs

Chiann Bao

These past 2½ days of the Congress have explored the human endeavour of international arbitration.

We would like to wholeheartedly thank all of our wonderful speakers, who have given so much time thinking about challenging their assumptions and the status quo, and providing interesting and thought-provoking presentations. They have drafted chapters that will in due course be published in the Congress Series.

We hope you agree that we have achieved our goals for this Congress.

We have certainly explored what it means to be a human decision-maker, and we have educated ourselves on how decisions are made, chemically as well as electronically, and also with logic, experience, intuition and wisdom.

We have heard a lot about Systems 1 and Systems 2, which achieved wide recognition as a result of Daniel Kahneman's book *Thinking, Fast and Slow*. Audley and I invited Daniel Kahneman to this Congress. We quickly received a warm reply indicating that he had retired. Sadly, he passed from us recently.

We also explored advocacy and how we can appeal to the human decision-maker. We learned a lot about different cultures and languages, which was very appropriate in this great city of Hong Kong, and we looked at the issues facing SMEs and communities in micro-States. We looked within and considered our own well-being in this adversarial environment.

Audley Sheppard KC

The arc of the Congress has taken us from the Arbitrator, to the Advocate, to AI.

We also took the opportunity to reflect on some of the visionaries and influencers in international arbitration. We recalled with fondness Pieter Sanders and his massive contribution. We were reminded of the research written up in *Dealing in Virtue* by Bryan Garth and his co-author and we honoured Albert Jan van den Berg.

We have looked at 'International Arbitration: A Human Endeavour' from several angles. As to the more profound questions we asked at the beginning, what does it mean to dispense arbitral justice? Are humans an essential element in order for international arbitration to be trusted and to have legitimacy? We will leave that to you to consider and reach your own conclusions.

We expect those questions will be revisited regularly in the years ahead as AI advances. Even if AI can replace a lot of advocacy tasks and decision-making, it cannot replace the pleasure of meeting with friends and colleagues at conferences such as this, and we hope you have had a full opportunity to do that.

Chiann and I have very much enjoyed putting together this programme for you. Thank you to ICCA for that privilege.

We thank you for attending and for your interest in this topic, 'International Arbitration: A Human Endeavour'.

Chiann Bao and Audley Sheppard KC
Programme Co-Chair

ICCA Hong Kong Congress List of Participants*

Argentina

Olivetti, Emiliano
Court of Arbitration for Sport

Australia

Allman, Daniel
Norton Rose Fulbright

Allsop, James
Sydney Arbitration Chambers;
Atkin Chambers

Anthony, David
Corrs Chambers Westgarth

Artemenko, Mariia
Herbert Smith Freehills

Bambagiotti, Philip
3PB Chambers

Rix, Sir Bernard

Brimer, Elizabeth
County Court of Victoria

Buffard, Madeleine
Australian Centre for International
Commercial Arbitration

Carlstedt, Carolina
LCM

Carroll, Monique
Cite Legal

Chandler, Ashley
Michael Pryles Arbitration and Mediation

Chenoweth, Jeremy
Ashurst Australia

Clarkin, Marian
Victorian Bar

Colquhoun Sc, Charles
Tenth Floor Chambers, Sydney, Australia

Cucinotta, Domenico
King & Wood Mallesons

Davis, Simon
Francis Burt Chambers

Delaney, Jo
HFW

Dempsey, Mark
7 Wentworth Selborne

Di Pasquale, Andrew
Victorian Bar

Di Pasquale, Maree

* The List of Participants is based on the information provided by the participant upon registering for the Congress.

Einfeld, Alexandra
Oxfam

Fan, Kun
University of New South Wales

Feldman, Jo
Norton Rose Fulbright

Gao, Ruimin
King & Wood Mallesons

Hando, Amy
Victorian Bar

Highfield, Benjamin
HKA Global

Humphrey, Jonathan
HKA Global

Jeffries, Andrew
Jeffries Arbitration

Jenaway, David
Allen & Overy

Jorissen, Juliana
King & Wood Mallesons

Kaplan, Neil
ICCA Advisory Board Member
Arbitration Chambers

Rix, Lady Karen

Kay Hoyle SC, Jonathan
11 St James' Hall Chambers

Kayvani, Kourosh
HKA Global

Kennedy, Jesse
Eleven Wentworth Chambers

Kenny KC, Caroline
4-5 Grays Inn, London

Khan, Faraz
FTI Consulting

Kwan, Edwina
King & Wood Mallesons

Levine, Judith
Levine Arbitration

Lincoln, Bronwyn
Thomson Geer

Lincoln, Mark
SJA Construction Services

Lockhart, Deborah
Australian Disputes Centre

Longley, Nick
HFW

Mallett, Daisy
Arbitrator

Martinez, Lucy
Martinez Arbitration

Mcqueen, Mary Angela
Peter Mcqueen Pty Ltd.

Mcqueen, Peter
ArbDB Chambers

Morrison, James
Peter & Kim

Neelakandan, Shamila
HKA Global

Newbold, Beverley
Minterellison

Pache, Charlotte
Epiq

Petch, Karen
New Chambers

Quan-Sing, Jeremy
Allens

Quick, Georgia
Australian Centre for International
Commercial Arbitration

Roberts, Paul
Secretariat

Rudge, Nick
Allens

Sanghera, Kiran
Australian Centre for International Commercial Arbitration

Santos, Christian
Australian Centre for International Commercial Arbitration

Sheldon, Mark
7 Wentworth Selborne

Sophocles, Michael
Sophocles Lawyers

Suhadolnik, Nastasja
Corrs Chambers Westgarth

Taylor, Susanna
Litigation Capital Management

Thirgood, Russell
Arbitra International

Timpano, Mia
Deakin University

Tomkinson, Deborah
Australian Centre For International Commercial Arbitration

Valenzuela, Geraldine
HFW

Van Brakel, Mark
Allen & Overy

Williams, Erika
Independent Arbitrator

Witt, Jeremie
CMS Cameron Mckenna Nabarro Olswang

Austria

Goriatcheva, Evgeniya
Permanent Court of Arbitration

Joubin-Bret, Anna
UNCITRAL

Karollus-Bruner, Daniela
CMS Reich-Rohrwig Hainz Rechtsanwälte Gmbh

Pernt, Victoria
Schoenherr

Sabanogullari, Levent
Permanent Court of Arbitration

Stanisavljevic, Marina
Schönherr Rechtsanwälte Gmbh

Stefan, Florian
Vavrovsky Heine Marth Rechtsanwälte Gmbh

Todorovic, Djordje
Schönherr Rechtsanwälte Gmbh

Vavrovsky, Nikolaus
Vavrovsky Heine Marth Rechtsanwälte Gmbh

Bahamas

Nottage, Theominique
Government of the Bahamas

Bahrain

Ahmed, Salman
Bahrain Chamber for Dispute Resolution

Alonaisi, Ameena
Bahrain Economic Development Board

Hubail Mansoor, Fatima
Supreme Judicial Council of the Kingdom of Bahrain

Husain, Ahmed
Bahrain Chamber For Dispute Resolution

Matar, Mai
Supreme Judicial Council of the Kingdom of Bahrain

Paulsson, Jan
Honorary President and Advisory Board Member of ICCA
Court of Cassation of the Kingdom of Bahrain

Paulsson, Marike
Bahrain Economic Development Board

Bangladesh

Fu, Xiangyu
Beijing Arbitration Commission/Beijing International Arbitration Center

Belarus

Korochkin, Aleksei
Chamber of Arbitrators

Belgium

Bingham, Lisa
ICCA

Capiau, Heidi

De Meulemeester, Dirk
DMDB Law

Fremault, Edouard
Deminor Litigation Funding

Hanotiau, Bernard
ICCA Advisory Board Member
Hanotiau & Van Den Berg

Jan Van Den Berg, Albert
Honorary President and Advisory Board Member of ICCA
Hanotiau & Van Den Berg

Stein, Erica
Stein Arbitration

Bermuda

Elkinson, Jeffrey
Conyers

Brazil

Braghetta, Adriana
ICCA Advisory Board Member
CAM-CCBC

Coelho, Eleonora
Eleonora Coelho Advogados

Damiao Goncalves, Eduardo
ICCA Governing Board Member
Mattos Filho Advogados

Flavia Furtado, Ana
CAM-CCBC

Fonseca, Rodrigo
CAM-CCBC

Kobayashi, Patricia
CAM-CCBC

Lo, Chi Yeung
CAM-CCBC

Matteucci Gomes, Marcus Alexandre
Felsberg Advogados

Mejias, Lucas
Tozzini Freire Advogados

Nakagawa Baptista, Adriane
Nakagawa Baptista & Baptista

Pachikoski, Silvia
CAM-CCBC

Pereira, Cesar
Justen, Pereira, Oliveira & Talamini

Ribeiro, Alice Viana
Nakagawa Baptista & Baptista

Bulgaria

Kaymedzhieva, Evelina
Independent law practice

Canada

Badri, Kamlish
Investor-State Law Guide (ISLG)

Ferris, Craig
Lawson Lundell LLP

Karton, Joshua
Queen's University Faculty of Law

Oberoi, Tanya
McGill University

Weiler, Todd
Arbitra International

Chile

Conejero Roos, Cristián
Cuatrecasas

Jana, Andrés
ICCA Governing Board Member
Jana & Gil Dispute Resolution

China, People's Republic of

An, Shouzhi
Fujian Lawyers Association/Anjie Broad Law Firm

An, Xin
Shenzhen Court of International Arbitration

Ann Lord, Victoria
Harneys

Ao, Wanquan
Changsha Arbitration Committee

Bai, Lu
G&D Law Firm

Bai, Xianyue
Grandall Law LLP

Blackwell, Holly
King & Wood Mallesons

Cao, Lijun
Zhong Lun Law Firm

Che, Tian Chi
Guangzhou Lawyers Association (ADR)

Chen, fang
Guangzhou Lawyers Association (ADR)

Chen, Fuyong
Beijing Arbitration Commission/Beijing International Arbitration Center

Chen, Huajun
Hainan International Arbitration Court (HIAC)

Chen, Jianbin (James)
Guangzhou Lawyers Association

Chen, Jianling
University of International Business & Economics

Chen, Jingjing
Haiwen & Partners

Chen, Mingyuan
Hong Kong University

Chen, Oscar
Duan & Duan Law Firm

Chen, Shaokai
Dacheng Law Office Suzhou Branch

Chen, Xianglin
Han Kun Law Offices

Chen, Xiao Jing
Hainan Arbitration Association

Chen, Yanzhong
Xiamen Maritime Court

Chen, Youkun
Chongqing Bar Association

Chen, Zhou
Shenzhen Court of International Arbitration

Chu, Mengmeng
Xinhua News Agency

Dai, Wen
Zhong Lun Law Firm

Dong, Arthur
Junhe LLP

Dong, Chungang
Jingtian & Gongcheng

Dong, Shi
Goldengate Lawyers

Dong, Yin
Beijing Dacheng (Zhuhai) Law Office

Du, Nan
Zhong Lun (Qingdao) Law Firm

Fan, Wenjing
Shenzhen Court of International Arbitration

Fan, Xiu Ling
Guangdong Gain Law Firm

Fang, Chunhui
Jingtian & Gongcheng Law Firm

Fang, Fanjia
Fujian Xufeng Law Firm (Fujian Law Society)

Fei, Jia (Jessica)
King & Wood Mallesons

Fei, Siyi
Hunan Lawyer Association

Feng, Melissa
Beijing Gen Law Firm

Fu, Linyong
T&C Law Firm

Fu, Qiong Fen
Hainan Arbitration Association

Fu, Ying
Jingsh Canada Law Firm

Gao, Helen (Yumei)
Qilu (Qingdao) Law Firm

Gao, Jun
Zhong Lun Law Firm

Gao, Tereza
Arnold & Porter

Gao, Zhuang
Beijing Arbitration Commission / Beijing International Arbitration Center

Gon, Michelle
Han Kun Law Offices

Gu, Yanning
Nanjing Arbitration Commission

Guo, Jing
Shenzhen Court of International Arbitration

Guo, Zhen
The Universal Legal Corporation

Han, Gang
Shanghai International Arbitration Center

He, Huang
Chongqing Arbitration Commission

He, Leon
BRG

HE, Rongxin
Guangzhou Lawyers Association (ADR)

Ho, Shi King
Hong Kong Polytechnic University

Hu, Jeff
Hua Fa Shanghai

Hu, Ke
Jingtian & Gongcheng

Hu, Miaomaiao
Hefei Arbitration Committee

Hu, Zhen
Beijing Tiantai (Haikou)Law Firm

Hua, Xiulan
Beijing Tian Yuan Law Firm

Huang, Frank Fulong
Guantao Law Firm

Huang, Guoyong
Shenzhen Court of International Arbitration

Huang, Henry
Grandall Law Firm (Shanghai)

Huang, Hui
Huang & Huang Co. Law Firm

Huang, Qing Feng
Beijing Long'an Law Firm Guangzhou Substation

Huang, Wenchao
Hainan Arbitration Association

Huang, Yi
Hunan Lawyer Association

Huo, Wilson Wei
Zhong Lun Law Firm and China Forum of Financial and Investment Dispute Forum (CFFID)

Jia, Hongwei (David)
Cross-Border Dispute Resolution Committee of Guangdong Bar Association

Jiang, Lili
Beijing Arbitration Commission / Beijing International Arbitration Center

Jin, Bingyi
Shanghai Bar Association

Jin, Hong Xia
Tianjin Arbitration Commission

Jin, Liyu (Denning)
Jin Partners, PRC Lawyers

Jin, Xiao
Hunan Lawyers Association

Jing, He
Chongqing Arbitration Commission

Jing, Liu
Han Kun Law Offices

Li, Jack (Zhiqiang)
Jin Mao Partners

Li, Jing
Shanghai Allbright Law Offices

Li, Lianjie
Hainan International Arbitration Court (HIAC)

Li, Lu
Chengdu Bar Association

Li, Mi
BIAC

Li, Nan
Hunan Tiandiren Law Firm

Li, Ping
China University of Political Science and Law

Li, Qishi
Commerce & Finance Law Offices

Li, Shan
Guangzhou Arbitration Commission

Li, Tingwei
Shanghai International Arbitration Center

Li, Wen
Guantao Law Firm Tianjin Office

Li, Xiaoming
Han Kun Law Offices

Li, Yuan
Shanghai Co-Effort Law Firm

Li, Ziyan
Tsinghua University

Li, Zongyi
Shenzhen Court of International Arbitration

Liang, Keming
BRG

Liang, Qian
Chu Qian Law Firm

Lin, Haofu
Tenet &Partners

Lin, Luda
Chinese University of Hong Kong

Lin, Mujuan
Jincheng Tongda & Neal (JT&N)

Liu, Chenjing
Chengdu Bar Association

Liu, Dan
Grandall Law Firm (Dalian)

Liu, Dao Jun
Hainan Arbitration Association

Liu, Dingmin
Jincheng Tongda & Neal (JT&N)

Liu, Dong
Han Kun Law Offices

Liu, Erchan
Wisely Law Office

Liu, Guolin
Grandall Law Firm (Nanjing)

Liu, Jingtao(David)
Zhong Lun Law Firm

Liu, Long
Han Kun Law Offices

Liu, Prof.
Xiamen Maritime Affairs Court

Liu, Qingqing
Tianjin Lawyer's Association

Liu, Shihu
Ministry of Justice of the People's Republic of China

Liu, Xiaochun
Shenzhen Court of International Arbitration

Liu, Yang
East China University of Political Science and Law

Liu, Zhao
ENN Energy Holdings Limited

Liu, Zhihong
China International Economic and Trade Arbitration Commission(CIETAC)

Liu, Zihan
Jiangsu Nankunlun Law Firm

Loke, Rachel Joey Yuan Ting
Tsinghua University

Lu, Fei
China International Economic and Trade Arbitration Commission (CIETAC)

Lu, Xi
Kingbird Law Firm

Luo, Jianwen
Sun Yat-Sen University

Ma, Arthur
Dahui Lawyers

Ma, Han
Hui Zhong Law Firm

Ma, Hui Lian
Guangzhou Lawyers Association (ADR)

Ma, Yadong
China Zhenhua Oil Co., Ltd.

Ma, Yi
Shanghai International Arbitration Center

Mao, Huigang
Jin Mao Law Firm

Mei, Feng
Guangdong Kingbridge Law Firm

Meng, Tim
Goldengate Lawyers

Mi, Si
Shenzhen Court of International Arbitration

Mu, Fei
Hylands Law Firm

Mu, Vincent
Llinks Law Offices

Nicklin, Jon
Accuracy

Ning, Jie
Changsha Arbitration Committee

Niu, Tongxu
Tianjin Lawyers Association

Nu, Jian
Fazeming Law Firm

Pan, bing
Changsha Arbitration Committee

Peng, Diane
Fangda Partners

Qing, Yang
Chongqing Bar Association

Qingyou, Wang
All China Lawyers Association

Ramsden, Scott
HKA Global

Ronghua, Shen
SGLA Law Firm

Ruobing, Zhang
Chongqing Arbitration Commission

Shao, Wanquan
Shanghai Bar Association

Shen, Li
Grandall Law Firm (Shanghai)

Shen, Sibao
Shenzhen Court of International Arbitration

Shen, Vanessa
Singapore International Arbitration Centre (SIAC)

Shi, Bei
Jiangsu Shicheng Law Firm

Shi, Catherine
Dkl Qianhai Law Firm

Shi, Helen Hong
Fangda Partners

Shi, Lei
Clifford Chance

Shi, Ping
Huamao&Guigu Law Firm

Shi, Xin
Guangzhou Lawyers Association (ADR)

Shi, Yi Ran
Allbright Law Offices (Guangzhou)

Sun, Binbin
Zhonglun Law Firm, Shanghai Offices

Sun, Han Hui
Beijing Celue Law Firm (Guangzhou)

Sun, Huawei
Zhong Lun Law Firm

Sun, Jing Ze
Grandall Law Firm

Sun, Shu Yu
Tianjin Arbitration Commission

Sun, Vincent
Han Kun Law Offices

Sun, Wei
Zhong Lun Law Firm

Sun, Yindong
Tsinghua University

Tang, Minli
Allbright Law Offices

Tian, Claire
Goldengate Lawyers

Wang, Guiguo
Zhejiang University

Wang, Hao
Guangzhou Lawyers Association (ADR)

Wang, Heng
Beijing Global Law Office

Wang, Hui
Changsha Arbitration Committee

Wang, Jing
Chengdu Bar Association

Wang, Lin
Tsinghua University

Wang, Na (Renata)
Globe-Law Law Firm

Wang, Wei
Guangzhou Lawyers Association (ADR)

Wang, Weijun
Shanghai International Arbitration Center

Wang, Weisheng (Wilson)
Wang Jing & Gh Law Firm / Guangdong Bar Association

Wang, Xiujuan
Anjie Broad Law Firm

Wang, Yao
Hainan Arbitration Association

Wang, Yingmin
Beijing Hylands Law Firm

Ware, Anton
Arnold & Porter

Wei, Jun
Grandall Law Firm (Nanjing)

Wen, Qi
Chongqing Arbitration Commission

Wencan, Huang
Hainan Realiser Law Firm

Wenjie, Gao
Tian Yuan Law Firm

Wu, Jiji
Hui Zhong Law Firm

Wu, Ming
Beijing Dacheng Law Offices, LLP (Shanghai)

Xi, Xiangyang
China International Commercial Court

Xiangnan, Yin
Hunan Province Lawyer Association

Xiao, Jianli
Hunan Lawyers Association

Xie, Jiachao
Grandall Law Firm (Hangzhou)

Xu, Fang
Hefei Arbitration Committee

Xu, Jie
Beijing Jundu Law Firm

Xu, Jun
Guangdong Lawyer Association

Xu, Suosheng
Shanghai International Arbitration Center

Xu, Zhihe
Shanghai International Arbitration Center

Xue, Xu
Tian Yuan Law Firm

Yang, Chen
Jincheng Tongda & Neal (JT&N)

Yang, Ling
Hong Kong International Arbitration Centre (HKIAC)

Yang, Weidong
Shanghai Bar Association

Yang, Xiangbin
Ministry of Justice of the People's Republic of China

Yang, Xiangbing
Ministry of Justice of the People's Republic of China

Yang, Xiaojie
Beijing Deheng Law Firm Chengdu Office

Yang, Yuanqing
Beijing Huamao & Guigu Law Firm

Yanhong, Xiong
Chongqing Bar Association

Yao, Hongmin
Shanghai International Arbitration Center

Yao, Yu
Beijing Huamao & Guigu Law Firm

Ye, Weina
Herbert Smith Freehills Kewei (FTZ) Joint Operation Office

Ye, Yong
Tenet & Partners

Yi, Ran
Shenzhen Court of International Arbitration

Yin, Tong
Beijing Arbitration Commission / Beijing International Arbitration Center

Yu, David
Shanghai Arbitration Association

Yu, Jianlin
Xiamen Maritime Court

Yu, Wenqian
Zhongnan University Of Economics And Law

Yu, Zijin
Hong Kong International Arbitraiton Centre (HKIAC)

Yuan, Weiming (Nick)
Zhonglun W&D Law Firm

Yuan, Xinjie
Fangda Law Offices

Zeng, Ying
Han Kun Law Offices

Zhang, Binbin
Hainan International Arbitration Cour (HIAC)

Zhang, Chen Rong
Fujian Province Lawyers Association Arbitration Law Committee

Zhang, Cunyuan
Singapore International Arbitration Centre (SIAC)

Zhang, Haoliang
Beijing Arbitration Commission / Beijing International Arbitration Center

Zhang, Libo
China Zhenhua Oil Company Ltd.

Zhang, Lixia
Beijing Huamao & Guigu Law Firm

Zhang, Min Xuan
Tianjin Arbitration Commission

Zhang, Wei
Legal Daily

Zhang, Xiaoyu
China International Economic and Trade Arbitration Commission (CIETAC)

Zhang, Xu feng
Guangzhou Lawyers Association (ADR)

Zhang, Yulin
Beijing Linli Law Office

Zhang, Yunyan
Jincheng Tongda & Neal (JT&N)

Zhang, Zhen Hua
Guangdong Lianyue Law Firm

Zhang, Zhenan (Tony)
Effort Law Firm

Zhao, Baao
Han Kun Law Offices

Zhao, Charles
Gen Law Firm

Zhao, Fang
Hui Zhong Law Firm

Zhao, Han Gen
Guangzhou Lawyers Association (ADR)

Zhao, Jian
Zhong Lun Law Firm

Zhao, Ping
Jincheng Tongda & Neal (JT&N), Shanghai Office

Zhao, Xue
Beijing Dacheng Law Offices, LLP

Zhao, Yuxian
Han Kun Law Offices

Zheng, Jiawei
China News Service

Zheng, Patrick
Llinks Law Offices

Zhong, Cheng
Commerce & Finance Law Offices

Zhou, Jingmin
Grandway Law Offices

Zhou, Ruoyao
Tsinghua University

Zhou, Yi
Shenzhen Court of International Arbitration

Zhou, Zhaoxia
Hainan Arbitration Association

Zhu, Haicheng
Zhejiang Chession Law Firm

Zhu, Hongwen
Sunshine Law Firm

Zhu, Lin
Beijing Weiheng Law Firm

Zhu, Ziqi
Shenzhen Court of International Arbitration

Zou, John (Zhiqiang)
Beijing Dacheng Law Offices, LLP (Shanghai)

Zou, Rui
Shanghai International Arbitration Center

Zuo, Vera
Jincheng Tongda & Neal (JT&N)

Colombia

Benavides-Galvis, Claudia
Baker McKenzie

Costa Rica

Filloy Zerr, Marcela
BSK Legal

Jiménez Figueres, Dyalá
Vice-President of ICCA
DJ Arbitraje SRL

Czechia

Čáp, Michal
Rowan Legal

Olík, Miloš
Rowan Legal

Egypt

Allam, Lubna
ALC-Alieldean Weshahi & Partners

Ehab Mohamed Ahmed Negm, Mai
ALC - Alieldean Weshahi & Partners

Wahab, Mohamed Abdel
ICCA Governing Board Member
Zulficar & Partners Law Firm

Zaher, Abdalla
Cairo University / Baker Mckenzie

Ethiopia

Haile, Zewdineh B.
Addis Law Group LLP

Finland

Katajoki, Minna
Avance Attorneys Ltd

Lehtinen, Jussi
Dittmar & Indrenius

Lehto, Helen
Dittmar & Indrenius

France

Barrington, Louise
Vis East Moot Foundation

Bationo, Didier
Jean Moulin Lyon 3 University

Chinn, Christopher
Chinn Arbitration

Chu, Gisèle Stephens
Stephens Chu Dispute Resolution

Comair-Obeid, Nayla
ICCA Governing Board Member
Obeid & Partners

De Maistre, Jean-Remi
Jus Mundi

Dupeyron, Carine
Darrois Villey Maillot Brochier

Fry, Jason
Clifford Chance

Galvez Solis, Nicolas
International Chamber of Commerce
Greenberg, Céline
Franklin

Gurdova, Shirin
Young ICCA

Hascher, Dominique
ICCA Advisory Board Member
Supreme Court of France

Hennessee, Karl
ICCA Governing Board Member
Airbus

Huynh, Hanh
Jus Connect

Legum, Barton
Honlet Legum Arbitration

Mantilla-Serrano, Fernando
ICCA Governing Board Member
Latham & Watkins

Mourre, Alexis
MGC Arbitration

Penushliski, Ilija Mitrev
Three Crowns LLP

Schroeder, Catherine
Schroeder Arbitration

Stern, Brigitte
Université Paris 1 Panthéon Sorbonne

Stoyanov, Marie
Allen & Overy LLP

Thorp, Peter
Thorp Arbitration

Turner, Peter
39 Essex Chambers

Vagenheim, Alexandre
Jus Mundi

Virjee, Hafez
Delos Dispute Resolution

Zhang, Qidi
Linklaters Zhao Sheng

Ziadé, Roland
Linklaters Zhao Sheng

Germany

Baumann, Antje
Baumann Resolving Disputes

Bolthausen, Oliver
DWF

Bryant, Jennifer
Noerr

Cengiz, Hatice
Julius-Maximilians- Universität Würzburg

Haller, Heiko
Baker Mckenzie Rechtsanwaltsgesellschaft Mbh Von Rechtsanwalten Und Steuerberatern

Happ, Richard
Luther Rechtsanwaltsgesellschaft Mbh

Heppner, Heiko
Dentons Europe

Herzberg, Axel Benjamin
Bodenheimer

Hirth, René-Alexander
Buse Rae Stb Partg Mbb

Klingel, Katharina
Brödermann Jahn Ra Gmbh

Knott, Hermann
Kunz Lawyers

Krotten, Nicolas
Luther Rechtsanwaltsgesellschaft Mbh

Lada, Valeriia

Lörcher, Torsten
CMS Hasche Sigle

Maurer, Anton
Anton Maurer International Legal Services Ra Gmbh

Pickrahn, Guenter
Baker Mckenzie Rechtsanwaltsgesellschaft Mbh Von Rechtsanwaelten Und Steuerberatern

Pröstler, Tom
CMS

Ruckteschler, Dorothee
Dorothee Ruckteschler Dispute Resolution

Schill, Stephan
ICCA General Editor
University of Amsterdam

Stepanova, Ksenia
German Arbitration Institute (Dis E.V.)/ Humboldt University of Berlin

Wirth, Johanna
Hengeler Mueller

Ghana

Omenyo, Cephas
Alexander & Partner Ghana PRUC

Hong Kong SAR

Alder, Edward A.G.
Hong Kong Bar Association

Ali, Shahla
University of Hong Kong Faculty of Law

Allen, Mike
Secretariat

Ang, Desmond
Sidley Austin

B. Nasir, Amirali
The Law Society of Hong Kong

Bancroft, Colum
AlixPartners LLP

Barrett, Paul N
Hong Kong Bar Association

Bartlett, Jeremy
Hong Kong Bar Association

Beeley, Edward
HFW

Bertrand, Joris
Herbert Smith Freehills

Boyle, Edward
AlixPartners

Brandt, Keith
Dentons Hong Kong LLP

Branson, David
BW Arbintl Ltd

Brock, Denis
O'Melveny

Caldwell, Peter Scott
Independent Arbitrator

Chan, Ada
Department of Justice of Hong Kong SAR

Chan, C. M.
The Law Society of Hong Kong

Chan, Elizabeth
Tanner De Witt

Chan, Isaac C.K.
Hong Kong Bar Association

Chan, Jonathan
Des Voeux Chambers

Chan, Nick
Aalco Hong Kong Regional Arbitration Centre

Chan, Nicole
Hong Kong Bar Association

Chan, Rollin
Rollin & Co

Chan, Stephen
Charles Russell Speechlys LLP

Chapman, Simon
Herbert Smith Freehills

Chen, Fanghan
Hong Kong International Arbitration Centre (HKIAC)

Chen, Junsheng
China Legal Service (HK) Ltd

Chen, Xiongchao
Fangda Partners

Cheng, Krystal
Hong Kong International Arbitration Centre (HKIAC)

Cheng, Teresa
ICCA Advisory Board Member
Tony Neoh's Chambers

Cheung, Aria T.C.
Hong Kong Bar Association

Cheung, Horace
Department of Justice of Hong Kong SAR

Cheung, Michelle
Hong Kong International Arbitration Centre (HKIAC)

Cheung, Venus
Department of Justice of Hong Kong SAR

Chin, Andrew
Gallant

Chiu, Barbara
King & Wood Mallesons

Chong, Seung
Arbitrator

Choong, John
Freshfields Bruckhaus Deringer

Chow, Justin
Freshfields Bruckhaus Deringer

Chow, Peter
Acacia Arbitration Chambers

Chow, Val
Temple Chambers

Chu, Heidi
The Law Society of Hong Kong

Chui, Heidi
Stevenson, Wong & Co

Clark, Douglas
Tanner De Witt

Cock, John
On Q Consulting Limited

Crockett, Antony
Herbert Smith Freehills

D'Agostino, Justin
Herbert Smith Freehills

Dawes, Victor
Temple Chambers

Dimsey, Mariel
CMS

Fan, Alex Hoi Kit
Hainan International Arbitration Court (HIAC)

Fares, Nowak
Allen & Overy

Fearis, Thomas
BRG

Fei, Ning
ICCA Governing Board Member
Hui Zhong Law Firm

Ferguson, Donovan
King & Wood Mallesons

Fong, Shiu Man David
Hong Kong Bar Association

Fun Leung, Mei
Legislative Council of Hong Kong SAR

Gao, Lilian
Hong Kong International Arbitration Centre (HKIAC)

Geiser, Dominic
Latham & Watkins LLP

H.B. Suen, Matthew
Hong Kong Bar Association

Hanusch, Philipp
Baker Mckenzie

Haocheng Wang, Brad
China International Economic and Trade Arbitration Commission (CIETAC)

Heitzmann, Pierre
Jones Day

Hill, Timothy
Arbitra

Ho, Cyrus
Robertsons

Ho, Sabrina
Des Voeux Chambers

Ho, Wilfred
White & Case

Hong, Kevin
Norton Rose Fulbright Hong Kong

Howard, Karah
Pinsent Masons

Hu, Sicen
Hong Kong International Arbitration Centre (HKIAC)

Hu, Stella
Karas So LLP

Huang, Yashan
CMS Hasche Sigle, Hong Kong LLP

Huen Albert Wong, Kwai
The South China International Arbitration Center (HK)

Hughes, Gareth
Debevoise & Plimpton

Hui, John KC
Des Voeux Chambers

Hui, Sui-Hang
Sidley Austin

Humphrey, Kieran Victor Falconer
O'Melveny & Myers

Hung, Denise
Department of Justice of Hong Kong SAR

Hunter, Catriona
HFW

Jiang, Jane
Allen & Overy LLP, Shanghai Office

Jiang, Muhan
Hong Kong University

Jiang, Zixin
Des Voeux Chambers

Jin, Luna
China Business Law Journal, Law.Asia

Johnson, Ben
FTI Consulting

Joite, Max
CMS Hasche Sigle Hong Kong LLP

KK Yu, Christopher
The Law Society of Hong Kong

Kagalwala, Gautam
Law.Asia

Kat, Nigel
Hong Kong Bar Association

Kay, Paula
Harneys

Kee, Kevin
Karas So LLP

Khandrimaylo, Victoria
Hong Kong International Arbitration Centre (HKIAC)

Khemka, Sonali
Hong Kong Lawyer

Khong, Cheng-Yee
HKA Global Ltd

Kim, Dana
Herbert Smith Freehills

Knight, Sian
King & Wood Mallesons

Koo, Natalie
Berkeley Reserach Group (BRG)

Kuan Wong, Un
Thomson Reuters

Kwan, James
Hogan Lovells

Kwok, Charlotte
Hong Kong International Arbitration Centre (HKIAC)

Lai, Adrian
Des Voeux Chambers

Lai, Katy
Stevenson, Wong & Co

Lai, Stephen
Conventus Law

Lai, Xiangdong
Long An Law Firm

Lalwani, Paras
Bayfront Law (In Alliance With Nishimura & Asahi)

Lam, Catrina
Des Voeux Chambers

Lam, Gillian
Baker Mckenzie

Lam, Jade
Hong Kong International Arbitration Centre (HKIAC)

Lam, Paul
Department of Justice of Hong Kong SAR

Laracy, Damien
Hill Dickinson Hong Kong

Lau, Alanna
Deminor

Lau, Garry
University of Hong Kong

Lau, Gemma
Hong Kong International Arbitration Centre (HKIAC)

Lau, Jean
Dentons Hong Kong LLP

Lau, Joanne
Hong Kong International Arbitration Centre (HKIAC)

Lau, Martin
Des Voeux Chambers

Lee, Irene
Deminor

Lee, Johnson
Kroll (HK) Limited

Lee, Thomas
Rede Chambers

Leng Lim, Chin
Chinese University of Hong Kong/Keating Chambers

Lesser, Su
Arbitration Chambers

Leung, Elsie
South China International Arbitration Center (HK)

Leung, Leona
Department of Justice ofHong Kong SAR

Li, Chenzhang
Alixpartners LLP

Li, Jiankun
Han Kun Law Offices

Li, Lillian
Quinn Emanuel

Li, Miao
China Merchants Port Holdings Company Ltd

Li, Mingrui
China Legal Service (HK) Ltd

Li, Qi Ying
City University Hong Kong

Li, Valerie
DLA Piper / HK45

Li, Xiongfeng
South China International Arbitration Center (HK)

Li, Yun
China International Economic and Trade Arbitration Commission (CIETAC)

Li, Zhongfang
China Telecom Global

Lin, Jiaqi
Chartered Institute of Arbitrators

Ling, Chun Wai
Des Voeux Chambers

Liu, Edward
Haiwen & Partners LLP

Liu, Isabella
Des Voeux Chambers

Liu, Joe
Jliu Dispute Resolution Services Limited

Liu, Xin
Freshfields Bruckhaus Deringer

Lok, Frances
Des Voeux Chambers

Long, Dong
Hong Kong International Arbitraiton Centre (HKIAC)

Lum, Alvin
Ming Pao

Luxton, Nick
Gilt Chambers

Ma, Geoffrey
Temple Chambers

Ma, Johnny
Des Voeux Chambers

Malanczuk, Peter
South China International Arbitration Center (HK)

Mcalpine, Rory
Skadden, Arps, Slate, Meagher & Flom

Mcdonald, Damien
Prince's Chambers and Outer Temple Chambers

Mok, Murphy
Herbert Smith Freehills

Moser, Michael
ICCA Advisory Board Member
Twenty Essex

Mun, Catherine
Li & Partners

Munro, Susan
K&L Gates

Murphy, Peter
HFW

Neoh, Anthony
South China International Arbitration Center (HK)

Ng, Eric
Prince's Chambers

Ng, Eric Kar-Yan
Hong Kong Bar Association

Ng, Felicity Wing Yee
King & Wood Mallesons

Ng, Jern-Fei
Temple Chambers

Oh, Nicholas CM
Hong Kong Bar Association

Ooi, Zhao Rong
Ince & Co

Othman, Saniza
Family and Castle Limited

Pang, Nigel
Skadden, Arps, Slate, Meagher & Flom

Pang, Ronald
Pantheon Chambers

Park, Moses
Liberty Chambers

Perez, Byron
Hong Kong International Arbitration Centre (HKIAC)

Phillips, Byron
Hogan Lovells

Qiu, Calvin
Berkeley Research Group (BRG)

Qu, Yinsheng
Hong Kong International Arbitration Centre (HKIAC)

Rhie, John
Quinn Emanuel Urquhart & Sullivan, LLP

Rhoda, Robert
Dentons Hong Kong LLP

Rigden Green, Andrew
Stephenson Harwood

Rogers, Martin
Davis Polk & Wardwell

Rooney, Kim Margaret
Rede Chambers

Rooney, Kim
Hong Kong Bar Association

Sanger, Kathryn
Herbert Smith Freehills

Seah, Jessica
Law.Com

Seib, Gary Anthony
Baker & Mckenzie

Sellar, Ralph
Slaughter and May

Sercan Evcin, Kerim
Turkish Consulate General

Sethia, Kritika
Tanner De Witt

Sharma, Abeer
University of Hong Kong

Shaw, Marnie
Hong Kong International Arbitration Centre (HKIAC)

Shipchandler, Alefiyah
Hong Kong International Arbitration Centre (HKIAC)

Sim, Cameron
Debevoise & Plimpton

Sin, Alvin
O'Melveny

Sin, Jacob
eBRAM International Online Dispute Resolution Centre

So, Thomas Shiu Tsung
Grandall Zimmern Law Firm

So, Wing Winky
Rede Chambers

Starr, Paul
King & Wood Mallesons

Suen, Jenkin
Des Voeux Chambers

Sussex, Charles
Des Voeux Chambers

Ta, Pui-Ki Emmanuelle
eBRAM International Online Dispute Resolution Centre

Tai, May
Herbert Smith Freehills

Tam, Edwina
FTI Consulting

Tam, Winnie Wan Chi
Des Voeux Chambers

Tang, Alexander K.M
Hong Kong Bar Association

Tang, Hanjie
Herbert Smith Freehills

Tang, Helen
Department of Justice, Hong Kong SAR

Tang, Justin
Linklaters

Tang, Lydia
Berkeley Research Group (BRG)

Tavares, Clifford
Department of Justice of Hong Kong SAR

Taylor, Edward
A&O Shearman

Tee, Ren Xin Sylvia
Ashurst Hong Kong

Tennison, James
Skadden, Arps, Slate, Meagher & Flom

Teo, Benjamin
Debevoise & Plimpton

Teoh, Yi-Shun
Reynolds Porter Chamberlain

Thomson, Mary
Pacific Chambers HK, 36 Stone Ldn & S'Pore

Tillett, Emily
Burford Capital

To, Ka Hui Christopher
Hong Kong Bar Association

Tong, Roden M.L
The Law Society of Hong Kong

Tung, Sherlin
Withers

Ung, Monin
Mung Blockchain Law

Walsh, Thomas
Clifford Chance

Wan, Eugene
Department of Justice of Hong Kong SAR

Wang, Clark L
Hong Kong Bar Association

Wang, Chengjie
China International Economic and Trade Arbitration Commission (CIETAC)

Warburton, Kevin
HFW

Watson KC, Duncan
Quinn Emanuel Urquhart & Sullivan, LLP

Wei, Amy Wen
CMS Hasche Sigle, Hong Kong LLP

Wiegand, Nicolas
CMS Hasche Sigle, Hong Kong LLP

Wilks, Mark
Corrs Chambers Westgarth

Willems, Jane
BW Arbintl Ltd

Wong, Anson
Des Voeux Chambers

Wong, Becky
Berkeley Research Group (BRG)

Wong, Christie
Skadden, Arps, Slate, Meagher & Flom

Wong, Clara KP
Des Voeux Chambers

Wong, Echo
Nikkei Asia

Wong, Harold
South China International Arbitration Center (HK)

Wong, Isaac
Berkeley Research Group (BRG)

Wong, Jason PH
Hong Kong Bar Association

Wong, Louise
Hong Kong International Arbitration Centre (HKIAC)

Wong, Samuel Chat Chor
18LC

Wong, Terence
Loeb & Loeb LLP

Wong, Wai Kit
Twenty Essex (London and Singapore) / Denis Chang's Chambers (Hong Kong)

Wong, Wesley
Department of Justice

Wong, William
Des Voeux Chambers

Wong, Yuen Ching
Tsinghua University

Wu, Dennis
Sidley Austin

Wu, Xianshu
University of Hong Kong

Wyllie, Kate
Opus 2

Xi, Cindy
Exponent, Limited

Xu, Cherry
Des Voeux Chambers

Yan, Yueming
Chinese University of Hong Kong
Faculty of Law

Yang, Ernest
DLA Piper Hong Kong

Yang, Ing Loong
Independent Arbitratior

Yang, Xueyu
Hui Zhong Law Firm

Yating, Lin
University of Hong Kong

Ye, Alex
Withers

Yeo, Kee Chong
Herbert Smith Freehills

Yeoh, Friven
Sidley Austin

Yeon, Kai Yiu Thomas
Hong Kong Bar Association

Yeung, Joshua
Des Voeux Chambers

Yeung, Kwan Ho Rex
Fairbairn Catley Low & Kong

Yeung, Man Sing
Li & Partners

Yeung, Yu Kwan
RW Chambers

Yip, Richard HL
Hong Kong Bar Association

Yip, Wai Fung
Hong Kong Bar Association

Yonzon, Prakritee
University of Hong Kong

Yu, Chen
City University of Hong Kong

Yu, Jason
Des Voeux Chambers

Yu, Jiejin
Dignari Capital

Yu, Karis
Hong Kong International Arbitration
Centre (HKIAC)

Yuen, Kenix
Lewis Silkin

Yuen, Rimsky
Temple Chambers

Zamir, Noam
City University of Hong Kong

Zhang, Manvis
Hong Kong International Arbitration
Centre (HKIAC)
Zhang, Yan
Sidley Austin

Zhao, Charles
Asian Academy of International Law

Zhao, Zhenhua
China Legal Service (HK) Ltd

Zhi, Leo Wei
Hong Kong Bar Association

Zhong, Mariana
Hui Zhong Law Firm

Hungary

Berzeviczi, Attila
Arbitration Court Attached to the Hungarian Chamber of Commerce and Industry

Damjanovic, Gábor
Forgó, Damjanovic & Partners

Kovács, Bálint
University of Szeged

India

Banerji, Gourab
Self-employed

Barot, Rajendra
AZB & Partners

Bhargava, Ajay
Khaitan & Co

Bhat, Anirudh
Law Links

Bhat, Shripathi Ravindra
Supreme Court of India

Chandru, Ganesh
Dua Associates

Chaturvedi, Aseem
Khaitan & Co

Chaturvedi, Megha
HK Law Offices

Garg, Shashank
Chambers of Shashank Garg

Gaur, Ketan
Trilegal

Goel, Khushi
Maims

Jain, Nishtha
Chambers of Shashank Garg

Jain, Nitesh
Trilegal

Jalan, Aditya Vikram
AZB & Partners

Jha, Abhijnan
AZB & Partners

Kachwaha, Mamta

Kachwaha, Sumeet
Kachwaha & Partners

Kapoor, Sanjeev
Khaitan & Co

Khushu, Ankit
Kachwaha & Partners

Liddle, Swapna

Mody, Zia
ICCA Advisory Board Member
AZB & Partners

Mukerjee, Vishrov
Trilegal (Member)

Nair, Dheeraj
JSA Law

Pachnanda, Gaurav
Chambers of Gaurav Pachnanda Sa and Fountain Court Chambers, Fountain Court, Temple, London

Palli, Anant Vijay
India International Arbitration Centre

Parikh, Shaneen
ICCA Governing Board Member
Cyril Amarchand Mangaldas

Patil, Shalaka
Trilegal

Prakash, Ranjeet
Archeus Law

Rukhana, Karan
Chambers of Darius Khambata

Saxena, Adarsh
Cyril Amarchand Mangaldas

Shankhar, Rahul M
Chamber 28 - Advocates And Solicitors

Sharma, Siddharth
Siddharth Sharma Law Office

Singh, Kanika
KSR Chambers

Singh, Vijayendra Pratap
AZB & Partners

Veeraraghavan, Inbavijayan
Kove Global LLP

Indonesia

Adiyasa, Narendra
Widyawan & Partners in Association with Linklaters

Krisnawenda, N
Bani Arbitration Center

Roosdiono, Anangga W
Bani Arbitration Center

Roosdiono, Tuti
Bani Arbitration Center

Saskia, Madah
Bani Arbitration Center

Iraq

Wang, Dongwei
China Zhenhua Oil Company Limited

Yuan, Rui
China Zhenhua Oil Company Limited

Ireland

Ahern, Susan
The Bar of Ireland

Israel

Cohen, Eli
Gornitzky & Co

Lerner, Nuna
Gornitzky & Co

Italy

Cicogna, Michelangelo
De Berti Jacchia Franchini Forlani Studio Legale

De Stefano, Carlo
Roma Tre University Department of Law

Durante, Valentino
Casa&Associati

Durante, Valentino Durante
Casa&Associati

Ebau, Eleonora
University of Turin

Faienza, Valentina
ICCA

Landi, Niccolò
Arbitration Chambers

Mcilwrath, Michael
MDisputes

Rojas Elgueta, Giacomo
Chiomenti

Japan

Fabio Colombo, Giorgio
Nagoya University Graduate School of Law / Ca' Foscari University Venice

Inoue, Aoi
Anderson Mori & Tomotsune

Macarthur, David
Yulchon LLC

Maeda, Yoko
City-Y

Markert, Lars
Nishimura & Asahi

Nakahara, Chié
Nishimura & Asahi

Ohara, Yoshimi
ICCA Governing Board Member
Nagashima Ohno & Tsunematsu

Sugimoto, Kaori
Nagashima Ohno & Tsunematsu

Takatori, Yoshihiro
Kasumigaseki International Law Office, International Arbitration Chambers

Terceño, Joaquin
Freshfields Bruckhaus Deringer

Tezuka, Hiroyuki
Nishimura & Asahi

Kazakhstan

Kussaiyn, Asset
Kimep University

Kenya

Abdallah, Aisha
ICCA Governing Board Member
Anjarwalla & Khanna LLP

Ahmed, Leyla
TripleOKLaw, LLP

Godofa, Ibrahim
Bowmans

Kerubo Nyamweya, Deborah
Nyachoti & Partners Advocates

Kidunduhu, Noreen
Noreen & Co

Ohaga, Carolla
TripleOKLaw LLP

Ohaga, John
ICCA Governing Board Member
TripleOKLaw LLP

Okiro, Mercy
National Construction Authority

Korea, Republic of

Baek, Yun Jae
Yulchon LLC

Bang, Brandon
Shin & Kim LLC

Bang, John
Peter & Kim

Billiet, Braden
FTI Consulting

Chang, Seung Wha
Korean Commercial Arbitration Board International

Cho, Ara
Peter & Kim

Choe, Seyoung
Yulchon LLC

Chung, Hong-Sik (Justin)
Deputy Minister, Ministry of Justice of the Republic of Korea

Chung, Kyongwha
Covington & Burling LLP

Han, Mino
Peter & Kim

Han, Sanghoon
Lee & Ko

Jun, Somin
Jipyong LLC

Jung, Sunkyung
Peter & Kim

Kim, Beomsu
Baker McKenzie & KL Partners Joint Venture Law Firm

Kim, David
Baker McKenzie & KL Partners Joint Venture Law Firm

Kim, Jinhee
Jipyong LLC

Kim, Joongi
Yonsei Law School

Kim, Junu
BKL

Kim, Kap-You (Kevin)
ICCA Advisory Board Member
Peter & Kim

Kim, Sae Youn
Kim & Chang

Kim, Saemee
Lee & Ko

Kim, Steve
Korean Commercial Arbitration Board International

Kim, Woojae
Bae, Kim & Lee LLC

Kyung, Munjeong
Yoon & Yang LLC

Lee, Chul-Won
Kim & Chang

Lee, Hyungkeun
Kim & Chang

Lee, Junsang
Yoon & Yang

Lee, Yong Ik
Jipyong LLC

Ng, Elaine
UNCITRAL

Park, Eun Young
Park Arbitration Chambers

Park, Hyunah
Yulchon LLC

Park, Jaesung
Ministry of Justice of the Republic of Korea

Park, Ji Yoon (June)
Hong Kong International Arbitration Centre (HKIAC)

Park, Sion
The Korea Economic Daily

Shin, Hi-Taek
ICCA Governing Board Member
Twenty Essex

Shin, Yunsoo
Peter & Kim

Yoo, Eunkyung
Peter & Kim

Yun, Seok Chun
Peter & Kim

Lebanon

Obeid, Zeina
Obeid & Partners

Luxembourg

Laniez, Antoine
Nautadutilh Avocats Luxembourg Sarl

Macao

Esteves, Mariana Afonso
C&C Lawyers and Notaries

Ilhão Moreira, João
University of Macau

Migliorini, Sara
University of Macau

Malaysia

Abraham, Beatrice

Abraham, Cecil
ICCA Advisory Board Member
Cecil Abraham & Partners

Abraham, Sunil
Cecil Abraham & Partners

Amirudin, Aniz Ahmad
Cecil Abraham & Partners

Lim, Mary
Judiciary of Malaysia

Navaratnam, Nahendran
Navaratnam Chambers

Selvaratnam, Sitpah
Sitpah Selvaratnam Arbitration Chambers

Mauritius

Adamjee, Ali
Chambers of Sir Hamid Moollan KC

Griffiths, Jillian
Selfemployed

Namdarkhan, Mushtaq
BLC Robert & Associates

Mexico

Alvarez Roman, Edwin Nemesio
ENARLAW Arbitration

Becerril Vega, Sergio
Becerril Vega Abogados

Brown De Vejar, Kate
ICCA Governing Board Member
DLA Piper

Flores Rueda fCIArb, Cecilia
Floresrueda Abogados

Gonzalez De Cossio, Francisco
Gonzalez De Cossio Abogados

Moino, Elsie

Mosqueda Gutierrez, Ana Sofia
Galicia Lawyers

Von Wobeser, Claus
ICCA Governing Board Member
Von Wobeser Y Sierra

Montenegro

Bozovic, Vesko
VMB Law Firm

Nepal

Dongol, Nikhil
Reliance Corporate Advisors

Kumar Khatiwada, Ram
High Court Bar Association

Netherlands

Ambast, Ashwita
Permanent Court of Arbitration

Aragon Cardiel, Jose Luis
Permanent Court of Arbitration

Baldini Miranda Da Cruz, Paula
ICCA / Permanent Court of Arbitration

Bordaçahar, Julian
Permanent Court of Arbitration

Bosman, Lise
Executive Director of ICCA

Burns, Lucy
ICCA

Daly, Brooks
Brooks Daly Arbitration

De Vries, Gwen
Wolters Kluwer

Doe, Martin
Permanent Court of Arbitration

Eliëns, Marco
Lemstra Van Der Korst NV

Fleuren, Bart
Linklaters

Jankowski, Adam
ICCA / Permanent Court of Arbitration

Knottenbelt, Dirk
Houthoff

Korthals Altes, Bregje (Becky)
YSQUARE / Netherlands Arbitration Institute

Kuscher, Matthias
De Brauw Blackstone Westbroek

Leijten, Marnix
De Brauw Blackstone Westbroek

Meijer, Gerard
Linklaters

Payne, Stuart
The Hague & Partners Convention Bureau

Peters, Niek
Legaltree

Seok, Jinyoung
Permanent Court of Arbitration

Stouten, Thomas
Houthoff

Van Baren, Willem
Van Baren Arbitration

Van De Hel, Mirjam
Nauta Dutilh

Verschoor, Vincent
Wolters Kluwer

Wassenaar, Ingmar
Lemstra Van Der Korst NV

New Zealand

Butler, Petra
University of Canterbury

Foote KC, Simon
Bankside Chambers

Green, Catherine
New Zealand International Arbitraiton Centre (NZIAC)

Green, John
New Zealand International Arbitraiton Centre (NZIAC)

Kalderimis, Daniel
Twenty Essex

Kirk, Anna
Bankside Chambers

Kreider, David L
David L Kreider, International Arbitrator

Lindsay, Lauren
Bankside Chambers

Lindsay, Timothy
Lindsay Francis & Mangan

Smith, Nicole
Arbitrators' And Mediators' Institute of New Zealand

Swan, Nicola
Chapman Tripp

Walton, John
Bankside Chambers

Abdul, Abdullateef Olasubomi
Goldlex Legal

Nigeria

Adekoya, Funke
ICCA Advisory Board Member
Funke Adekoya SAN Arbitration Practice

Akeredolu, Abimbola
Banwo & Ighodalo

Aluko, Adebowale
Nigerian Bar

Chukwuemerie, Andrew
Okibe Lawhouse

Nweke-Eze, Stanley U
Templars

Ojo, Christopher
Bayo Ojo & Co

Ojo, Folasade
Court of Appeal of Nigeria

Oman

Al Azri, Moosa
Independent Arbitrator

Al Salmi, Mohammed
Oman Tourism Development Company

Ali, Ahmed
Hussain Al-Toubi Law Firm

Al-Toubi, Hussein Mohsin Salim Said
Hussain Al-Toubi Law Firm

Pakistan

Bayan Majeed, Nudrat
Four Golf Road Chambers

Lin, Qidi(Donnia)
International Centre for Appropriate Dispute Resolution and Prevention Pakistan

Majeed, Nudrat
Four Golf Road Chambers

Naqvi, Feisal
Bhandari Naqvi Riaz (BNR)

Piracha, Nudrat
International Centre for Appropriate Dispute Resolution and Prevention / Samdani Qureshi Aqlaal

Shaif, Hamid
Samdani Qureshi Aqlaal

Philippines

Amoroso, Dranyl Jared
Quisumbing Torres (Member Firm of Baker Mckenzie)

Galacio, Elmar
Cruz Marcelo & Tenefrancia Law Office

Lopez, Carlos Roberto
Sycip Salazar Hernandez and Gatmaitan

Lynn, Jacques
Cruz Marcelo & Tenefrancia

Magtibay Jr, Arleo Antonio
Philippine Dispute Resolution Center

Malaya, Joseph Anthony
Angara Abello Concepcion Regala & Cruz (ACCRALAW)

Nazareno, Jomini
Romulo Law

Nicandro, Rogelio
Romulo Mabanta Buenaventura Sayoc & De Los Angeles

Paz, Antonio Jose Gerardo
Angara Abello Concepcion Regala & Cruz (ACCRALAW)

Sanchez, Aaron Zibeon
Romulo Mabanta Buenaventura Sayoc & De Los Angeles

Tensuan, Jose Martin
Angara Abello Concepcion Regala & Cruz (ACCRALAW)

Poland

Jamka, Maciej
DWF

Portugal

Coimbra Trigo, Ana
PLMJ Law Firm

Romania

Vasile, Cosmin Cristian
Zamfirescu Racoti Vasile & Partners Attorneys at Law

Russian Federation

Drobyshevskaia, Margarita
Russian Arbitration Center

Grishchenkova, Anna
International Chamber of Commerce (ICC)

Grunis, Denis
Prosecutor General's Office of the Russian Federation

Kobesova, Alina
MGIMO

Korchuganova, Sofiia
Moscow State University

Kuptsov, Dmitry
ALRUD Law Firm

Kuritcyna, Kseniia
Higher School of Economics in Moscow

Lepa, Anastasiia
Petrol Chilikov

Mullina, Yulia
Russian Arbitration Center

Nikiforov, Ilya
EPAM Law Offices

Rachkov, Ilia
Moscow State Institute of International Relations (MGIMO)

Udovichenko, Kirill
MZS&Partners

Vinogradov, Mikhail
Prosecutor General's Office of the Russian Federation

Vyacheslavov, Feodor
Vlawyers Law Firm

Saudi Arabia

Albathli, Ghadah
Moj-Sa

Alhamad, Ali
Commercial Court of Saudi Arabia

Alshehri, Suad
Ministry of Justice of Saudi Arabia

Althuwaini, Khalid
Commercial Court of Saudi Arabia

Alzamel, Abdulaziz
Ministry of Justice of Saudi Arabia

Alzeer, Saleh
Ministry of Justice of Saudi Arabia

Serbia

Milosevic, Blagoje
Schoenherr Serbia - Moravčević Vojnović I Partneri In Cooperation With Schoenher

Singapore

Ahuja, Sheila
Allen & Overy

Ang, Tze Siong
Allen & Overy

Arora, Chaitanya
Secretariat

Artero, Christine
The Arbitration Chambers

Bailey, Christopher
Stephenson Harwood LLP

Ban, Jiun Ean
Maxwell Chambers

Bao, Chiann
ICCA Governing Board MemberBao Arbitration Services Pte Ltd

Bateson, David
39 Essex Chambers

Battisson, Andrew
Linklaters Singapore Pte Ltd

Bell, Gary F
National University of Singapore

Bhat, Rohit
Freshfields Bruckhaus Deringer

Bose, Raja
K&L Gates Straits Law LLC

Brabant, Peter
Charles Russell Speechlys LLP

Chan, Hock Keng
Wongpartnership LLP

Chan, Yong Wei
Freshfields Bruckhaus Deringer

Chew, Daryl
Three Crowns LLP

Chou, Sean Yu
Wongpartnership LLP

Chow, Karen
Bankside Chambers

Denton, Gavin
Arbitration Chambers

Dewan Sc, Nakul
Twenty Essex

Dhillon, Dinesh
Allen & Gledhill LLP

Di Giacomo Toledo, Túlio
Permanent Court of Arbitration

Dulac, Elodie
King & Spalding

Eliasson, Nils
King & Spalding (Singapore) LLP

Elliot, Simon
Three Crowns LLP

Ellis, Jonathan
Hka Global (Singapore) Pte Ltd

Foxton, Rachel
39 Essex Chambers

Furlong, Tomas
Herbert Smith Freehills LLP

Garg, Amit
Secretariat

Grief, David
David Grief International Consultancy

Grimmer, Sarah
Twenty Essex

Gu, Miao
Secretariat

Gunawan, Erick
Gunawan

Haylock, Amita
Mayer Brown

Henderson, Alastair
Herbert Smith Freehills LLP

Horrigan, Brenda
Brenda Horrigan Pte Ltd

Hughes, Benjamin
Fountain Court Chambers

Hwang, Laura
Linyi Investments Pte Ltd

Hwang, Michael
Honorary Vice President and Advisory Board Member of ICCA
Michael Hwang Chambers LLC

James, Rebecca
Linklaters

Jeremiah, Herman
Dentons Rodyk

Jhangiani, Sapna
Attorney-General's Chambers of Singapore

Jones, Katie-Beth
Opus 2

K Rajah, V
V K Rajah LLC

Kabra, Ashish
Nishith Desai Associates

Kanagasabai, Nira Sailakshmi
Mohanadass Partnership

Koh Sc, Swee Yen
WongPartnership LLP

Landau, Toby
ICCA Governing Board Member
Duxton Hill Chambers

Lau SC, Christopher
3 Verulam Buildings

Lee, Eddy
MDD Forensic Accountants

Lee, Amanda
King & Wood Mallesons LLP

Leong, Qianyu
Tan Kok Quan Partnership

Lim, Gloria May Ern
Singapore International Arbitration Chambers (SIAC)

Loong, Tse Chuan
Allen & Gledhill LLP

Mak, Yvonne
Withers Khattarwong LLP

Malintoppi, Loretta
ICCA Governing Board Member
39 Essex Chambers

Mangan, Mark
Dechert (Singapore) Pte Ltd

Marsman, Albert
De Brauw Blackstone Westbroek

Martin, Penny
Three Crowns LLP

Mathew, Oommen
Omni Law LLC

Milburn, Roger
Litigation Capital Management (LCM)

Minn, Naing Oo
Allen & Gledhill

Nash, Kevin
Singapore International Arbitration Centre (SIAC)

Ng, Benjamin
Relativity

Ng, Eddee
Tan Kok Quan Partnership

Ng, Kelvin
JS Held

Nicholson, James
FTI Consulting

O'Doherty, Seamus
Berkeley Research Group (BRG)

Pak, Quentin
Burford Capital

Palmer, Rob
Ashurst LLP

Pandjaitan, Jelita
Linklaters Singapore Pte Ltd

Panlilio, William
Litigation Capital Management (LCM)

Potter, Iain
JS Held

Prakash, JudithSupreme Court of Singapore

Pullen, Andrew
Fountain Court Chambers

Ragnwaldh, Jakob
Mannheimer Swartling

Rai, Mahesh
Drew & Napier LLC

Raneda, Julie
Schellenberg Wittmer

Ross, Donna
Donna Ross Dispute Resolution

Rubini Gopalan, Thara
American Arbitration Association-International Centre For Dispute Resolution (AAA-ICDR)

Secomb, Matthew William
White & Case

Siddiqui, Farooq
Exponent

Sinenian, Nareg
Exponent

Singh, Aditya
White & Case

Soh, James
Opus 2

Stackpool-Moore, Ruth
Omni Bridgeway Singapore

Strick, Stephen S
Strick Arbitration Chambers

Sucharitkul, Vanina
Rajah & Tann

Tan, Cheng-Han
National University of Singapore Faculty of Law

Tan, Chuan Thye
Rajah & Tann Singapore LLP

Tan, Karen
Maxwell Chambers

Tan, Karen
Supreme Court of Singapore

Tan, Samantha
Freshfields Bruckhaus Deringer

Tay, Yu-Jin
Mayer Brown

Teh, Lawrence
Global Co-Head of Dentons' International Arbitration Group

Teo, Paul
Mayer Brown Pk Wong & Nair Pte Ltd

Thio, Shen Yi
Tsmp Law Corporation

Toh, Shin Hao
Attorney-General's Chambers of Singapore

Weatherley, Michael
Ashurst LLP

Wegner, Kay-Jannes
Mayer Brown

Winkler, Claudia
The Negotiation Academy

Woodward, Joel
Berkeley Research Group (BRG)

Xavier, Francis
Rajah & Tann Singapore LLP

South Africa

Alp, Nick
Webber Wentzel

Barnes, Jonathan
Bowmans

Mkiva, Clement
Bowmans

Porter-Wright, Michelle
A&O Shearman

Raimanová, Lucia
A&O Shearman

Rebecca Mirembe, Ruth
University of Cape Town

Warmington, Erin
Webber Wentzel

Spain

Alonso Puig, José María
Centro International de Arbitraje de Madrid (CIAM)

Arias, David
Arias SLP

Baptista Serna, Krystle
Club Español e Iberoamericano del Arbitraje (CEIA) / KB Arbitration

De Luis Y Lorenzo, Jose Félix
Legal 21 Abogados

Gómez-Acebo, Alfonso
Cuatrecasas

Iglesia, Alfonso
Cuatrecasas

Lopez, Heidi
Uria Menendez Abogados SLP

Menendez, Maria Jose
Menendez Arias - Arbitration

Puertas Álvarez, Omar
Cuatrecasas

Roekaert, Jean Paul
B Cremades & Asociados

Saiz, Patricia
Saiz Arbitration

Sri Lanka

Azhar, Fathima Ajra Mohamed
Colombo Associates

Hettiarachchi, Christina
F J & G De Saram

Sweden

Ahrel, Ginta
Westerberg & Partners Advokatbyrå Ab

Baltag, Crina
Stockholm University

Berglind, Sebastian
Advokatfirman Vinge KB

Dahlberg, Silvia
Vinge

Dalin, Karl-Oscar
DLA Piper Sweden KB

Falconer, Caroline
SCC Arbitration Institute

Hope, James
Vinge

Johansson, David
DLA Piper Sweden KB

Lundblom, Fredrik
Vinge

Magnusson, Annette
Climate Change Counsel

Nadar, Aisha
Advokatfirman Runeland

Runeland, Per
Advokatfirman Runeland

Rylander, Robin
Mannheimer Swartling Advokatbyrå AB

Sandberg, David
Mannheimer Swartling Advokatbyrå AB

Switzerland

Baizeau, Domitille
ICCA Governing Board Member
Lalive SA

Bärtsch, Philippe
Schellenberg Wittmer

Boog, Christopher
Schellenberg Wittmer

Boras, Filip
Baker Mckenzie

Brown-Berset, Dominique
Brown&Page SA

Dasser, Felix
Homburger

Favre-Bulle, Xavier
Lenz & Staehelin

Frey, Harold
Lenz & Staehelin

Furner, Courtney
Lalive

Geisinger, Elliott
Schellenberg Wittmer/ The Swiss Arbitration Marketing Committee

Gottlieb, Benjamin
Schellenberg Wittmer

Habegger, Philipp
Habegger Arbitration

Johnson, Alexandra
Pestalozzi Attorneys at Law Ltd

Keller, Moritz
Clifford Chance Part MBB

Kozmenko, Anna
Curtis, Mallet-Prevost, Colt & Mosle Ltd

Lenggenhager, Fadri
Lenz & Staehelin

Mazuranic, Alexandre
BMG Avocats

Meier, Andrea
Walder Wyss Ltd

Peter, Wolfgang
Peter & Kim

Petti, Angelina
Von Segesser Law Offices

Pfiffner, Nadine
Rothorn Legal Ag

Potestà, Michele
Levy Kaufmann-Kohler

Radjai, Noradèle
Lalive

Rom, Robert
RLR Arbitration

Schneider, Michael E.
Lalive

Schramm, Dorothee
Swissarbitrator.Com

Stutzer, Hansjörg
Thouvenin

Tercier, Pierre
ICCA Advisory Board Member
Peter & Kim

Voser, Nathalie
Rothorn Legal Ag

Yasseen, Rabab
Mentha Avocats

Yasseen, Zainab

Ye, Xin
Lenz & Staehelin

Zenhaeusern, Urs
Baker Mckenzie

Taiwan

Hay, Emily
Hanotiau & Van Den Berg

Kuo, Houchih
Kuo & Kuo Attorneys-At-Law

Wu, Yeong-Chyan
Chinese Arbitration Association

Tanzania

Thomas, Lydia
Office of the Solicitor General of the United Republic of Tanzania

Thailand

Jaimsuwan, Suruswadee
Tilleke & Gibbins International Limited

Netngamsawang, Chokchai
Construction Lawyers Society

Respondek, Andreas
Respondek & Fan Ltd

Rix, James
Nishimura & Asahi

Rowse (Igusa), Emi
Kudun And Partners

Sutanont, Vorapong
Berkeley Research Group (BRG)

Turkey

Tokat, Ahmet
Istanbul University Faculty of Law

United Arab Emirates

Alsuwaidi, Mohammed
Alsuwaidi & Company LLC

Attalah, Abdelhak
Attalah Legal Consultancy

Campbell-Wilson, Kristin
Abu Dhabi International Arbitration Centre

Chadwick, Adrian
Hadef & Partners

Chen, Kate Yang
RAALC Law Firm

Dennehy, Hannah
ADGM

Emmerson, Alec
Adr Management Consultancies

Fitz-Alan, Linda
Abu Dhabi Global Markets

Hedberg, Christoffer Coello
Dubai International Arbitration Centre

Hoffmann, Anne K
Hoffmann Arbitration

Holloway, David
Al Tamimi & Co

Hussain, Mahmood
M&Co Legal

Kazim, Jehad
Dubai International Arbitration Centre

Khudairi, Lina
RAALC Law Firm

Mohamed, Ehab
RAALC Law Firm

Ragheb, Shourouk
Abu Dhabi Global Markets

Saoud, Ritta
Dubai International Arbitration Centre

Snider, Thomas
Charles Russell Speechlys

Snider, Tsion

Stephen, Robert
Dubai International Arbitration Centre

Tonkin, Michael
HKA Global

Zagonek, Julia
White & Case LLP

United Kingdom

Aglionby, Andrew
Aglionby ADR

Aliker, Phillip
Tanfield Chambers

Ansell, Rachel
4 Pump Court

Aswani, Ravi
36 Stone

Auchecorne, Taryn
Opus 2

Bagshaw, Duncan
Howard Kennedy LLP

Barnes, David
Atkin Chambers

Bauer, Cristen
The Chartered Institute of Arbitrators

Beechey, John
ICCA Governing Board Member
Arbitration Chambers

Blair, Sir William
3 Verulam Buildings

Brekoulakis, Stavros
ICCA Governing Board Member
3 Verulam Buildings / National University of Singapore

Britten, Kathryn
AlixPartners

Brumpton, Paul
White & Case LLP

Cahill-O'Callaghan, Rachel
Cardiff School of Law And Politics

Cannon, Andrew
Herbert Smith Freehills LLP

Carvalho, Carlos
Opus 2

Chai, Vivien
Belgravia Law

Cheng, Serena
Atkin Chambers

Cheyne, Calum
Zeiler Floyd Zadkovich

Child, Nick M.
Secretariat

Cholakov, Rumen
3 Verulam Buildings

Claypoole, Charles
Latham & Watkins

Clifford, Philip
Latham & Watkins

Coles, Nikki
Alvarez & Marsal Disputes and Investigations LLP

Corby, Kate
Baker & Mckenzie LLP

Daele, Karel
Taylor Wessing LLP

Davies, Edward
Innsworth Advisors

Davies KC, Kate
Skadden, Arps, Slate, Meagher & Flom(UK) LLP

De Verneuil Smith, Peter
3 Verulam Buildings

Deniger, Christiane
Burford Capital

Dixon, Catherine
The Chartered Institute of Arbitrators

Dymond, Tony
Debevoise & Plimpton LLP

Eken, Can
Durham Law School

Everson, Colin
Kroll

Forbes-Smith KC, Henry
One Essex Court

Frankish, Robert
Quadrant Chambers

Fu, Judy
3 Verulam Buildings

Gavaghan, Holly
Accuracy

Gearing KC, Matthew
Fountain Court / Temple Chambers

Giaretta, Benjamin
Fox Williams LLP

Gibbs, Stewart
4 Pump Court

Goh, Nelson
Sidley Austin

Harrison, Jamie
London Court of Internaitonal Arbitraiton (LCIA)

Hawes, Julian
International Arbitraiton Centre (IAC)

Heilbron, Hilary
Brick Court Chambers

Hodges KC, Paula
Herbert Smith Freehills LLP

Hodgson, Matthew
Allen & Overy LLP

Holiner, Drew
Monckton Chambers

Hollander De Groot, Yael
Wolters Kluwer

Honey, Damian
HFW

Hughes KC, Adrian
39 Essex Chambers

Indge, Richard
Ankura Consulting (Europe) Ltd

Jain, Maanas
Paul Hastings

Jain, Mrinal
Secretariat

Johnson, Jamey
FTI Consulting

Kapoor, Vivek
39 Essex Chambers

Kiddell, Richard
Charles Russell Speechlys LLP

Kleist, Paul
Cleary Gottlieb Steen & Hamilton LLP

Lady Goldsmith, Joy

Lamb, Sophie
Latham & Watkins LLP

Leaver, Peter
One Essex Court

Lee, Amanda
LML Arbitration and Costigan King

Lee, Krista
Keating Chambers

Lew, Julian
Twenty Essex

Li, Justin
Willkie Farr & Gallagher (UK) LLP

Lim, Jonathan
Wilmer Cutler Pickering Hale and Dorr LLP

Lloyd-Williams, Mark
Arbitration Chambers

Lord Goldsmith KC, Peter
Debevoise & Plimpton LLP

Macdonald, Ken
Brodies LLP

Mackenzie, Andrew
Scottish Arbitration Centre

Madden KC, Penny
Gibson, Dunn & Crutcher LLP

Malek KC, Ali
3 Verulam Buildings

Malone, Brandon
Scottish Arbitration Centre

Martin, Adrian
Ankura

Mcclintock, Oliver
Opus 2

Minaeva, Tatiana
RPC

Mizner, Andrew
CDR News

Molloy, Matthew
MCMS

Nathwani, Sheena
Wolters Kluwer

Neuberger, Edmund
Atkin Chambers

Osadchiy, Maxim
Debevoise & Plimpton LLP

Page, Richard
FTI Consulting

Park, Sang Joon
Mayer Brown

Partasides KC, Constantine
ICCA Governing Board Member
Three Crowns LLP

Passmore KC, John
Quadrant Chambers

Pe, Robert
Arbitration Chambers

Perry, Sebastian
Global Arbitration Review

Ramadoss, Arunn
Opus 2

Ramsey, Barbara
Ramsey, Vivian
Singapore International Commercial Court

Raymont, Mark
Pinsent Masons LLP

Rees-Murphy, Leo
Zeiler Floyd Zadkovich

Reeves, Catherine
Twenty Essex

Rogers, James
Jenner & Block

Rowe, Samantha
Debevoise & Plimpton LLP

Rushton, Matthew
Opus 2

Sabharwal KC, Dipen
White & Case LLP

Scherer, Maxi
ICCA Governing Board Member
Wilmer Cutler Pickering Hale and Dorr / Queen Mary University of London

Schwarz, Franz
Wilmer Cutler Pickering Hale and Dorr

Scott, Lindsay
39 Essex Chambers

Sheppard KC, Audley
President-Elect of ICCA
Clifford Chance LLP

Shrubsall, Will
Keating Chambers

Spalton, George
4 New Square

Speller, Duncan
Willkie Farr & Gallagher LLP

Stanic, Ana
E&A Law

Swallow, Richard
Slaughter and May

Thomson, James
Edinburgh University

Tirado, Joseph Manuel
Garrigues

Tsang, Karen
Zeiler Floyd Zadkovich

Uff, Alexander
Quadrant Chambers

Uyar, Gökçe
Debevoise & Plimpton LLP

Van Haersolte-Van Hof, Jacomijn
London Court of International Arbitration (LCIA)

Wade, Shai
RPC

Walker, David
Deminor Recovery Services (UK) Ltd

Weiniger, Matthew
Linklaters LLP

Wells, Benjamin
Belgravia Law

Willicombe, Natasha
Secretariat

Wong, Garreth
Paul Hastings (Europe) LLP

Wood, Jonathan
The Chartered Institute of Arbitrators

Wreford, Dominic
Interpath Advisory

Yan, Bing
Skadden Arps Slate Meagher & Flom LLP

Young, Briana
Three Crowns LLP

Yusuf, Guled
Allen & Overy LLP

Zitver, Arron
Twenty Essex

United States

Adams, Scott
Welch ADR

Aitelaj, Kamel
Milbank LLP

Alexandrov, Stanimir
President of ICCA
Stanimir A Alexandrov PLLC

Ali, Arif
Dechert LLP

Amirfar, Catherine
ICCA Governing Board Member
Debevoise & Plimpton

Andersen, Steven
American Arbitration Association-International Centre For Dispute Resolution (AAA-ICDR)

Baker, C. Mark
Norton Rose FulbrightUS LLP

Bédard, Julie
ICCA Governing Board Member
Skadden, Arps, Slate, Meagher & Flom LLP

Bejarano, Santiago
Latham & Watkins LLP

Benton, Gary
Gary Benton Arbitration

Bogart, Christopher
Burford Capital

Campbell, Christopher
Baker Hughes

Chakrabarti, Sharmistha
Skadden, Arps, Slate, Meagher & Flom LLP

Chan, Eva
Skadden, Arps, Slate, Meagher & Flom LLP

Chawla, Aastha
American Arbitration Association-International Centre For Dispute Resolution (AAA-ICDR)

Cohen, Paul
4-5 Gray's Inn Square Chambers

Cohen Smutny, Abby
Vice President of ICCA
White & Case LLP

Damamme, Claire-Naila

Donovan, Donald Francis
Honorary President and Advisory Board Member of ICCA
Arbitration Chambers

Flanagan, Mark
Wilmer Cutler Pickering Hale and Dorr LLP

Friedman, Ema Vidak
Vidak Arbitration

Friedman, Mark W.
Debevoise & Plimpton LLP

Gans, Kiera
DLA Piper LLP (US)

Garth, Bryant
University of California-Irvine

Gastrell, Lindsay
Arbitration Chambers

Gopalan, Surya
White & Case LLP

Greenwald, Brody
White & Case LLP

Hamilton, Jonathan
Paul Hastings LLP

Hao, Alex
JunHe LLP

Haridi, Samaa
ICCA Treasurer
King & Spalding LLP

Harpole, Sally
Independent Arbitrator & Mediator

Haworth Mccandless, Jennifer
Baker Botts LLP

Hosking, James
ICCA Governing Board Member
Chaffetz Lindsey LLP

Howes, Bradford Ted
Mayer Brown LLP

Kahn, Sherman
Maschoff Brennan

Kang, Christine Yi
Hughes Hubbard & Reed LLP

Kern, Jackson Shaw
ALG LLP

Kidane, Won
Addis Law Group LLP

Kim, Grant
Limnexus LLP

Kunsman, Isabel Santos
AlixPartners

Lamm, Carolyn
ICCA Advisory Board Member
White & Case LLP

Lawrence, James
University of Houston Law Center

Lee, Serena
JAMS

Litt, Gregory
Skadden, Arps, Slate, Meagher & Flom LLP

Llamzon, Aloysius
King & Spalding LLP

Mays, Tammy
New York State United Teachers

McCormack, Bridget
American Arbitration Association - International Centre For Dispute Resolution (AAA-ICDR)

Meade, Tyler
Presidio Adr, LLC

Miles, Craig
King & Spalding LLP

Moloo, Rahim
Gibson Dunn & Crutcher LLP

Mouscardy-Willis, Lisa
New York State United Teachers

Nelson, Timothy
Skadden, Arps, Slate, Meagher & Flom LLP

Neumann, Peter
Neumann PC

Nolan, Michael
Arbitration Chambers

Norton, Patrick M.
Arbitration Chambers

Pearsall, Patrick
Allen Overy LLP

Pierce, John
Latham & Watkins LLP

Prager, Dietmar
Debevoise & Plimpton LLP

Profaizer, Joseph
Paul Hastings LLP

Rivera Rios, Julio
Debevoise & Plimpton LLP

Rivkin, David
Arbitration Chambers

Robertson, Ann Ryan
Locke Lord LLP

Rossi, Francesco
American Arbitration Association – International Centre For Dispute Resolution (AAA-ICDR)

Saka, Onur
White & Case LLP

Schmidt, Lindsey
Gibson Dunn & Crutcher LLP

Schwartz, Steve
FTI Consulting

Skulnik, Steven
Practical Law - Thomson Reuters

Sloane, Elizabeth
Stephenson Harwood

Snodgrass, Liz
Three Crowns LLP

Tahbaz, Christopher
Debevoise & Plimpton LLP

Tang, Alexander
Stephenson Harwood

Teitelbaum, Ruth
Ruth Teitelbaum

Tuchmann, Eric
American Arbitration Association-International Centre For Dispute Resolution (AAA-ICDR)

Tumpovskiy, Anna
Falcon Technology Holdings, Inc

Utterback, Mary
King And Wood Mallesons

Welch, Dana
CalArb

Willard, Rainbow
Willard Arbitration, LLC

Yang, Isabel Yishu
ArbiLex

Uzbekistan

Tuychieva, Shakhzoda
Tashkent State University of Law

Vietnam

Bui, Hong
LNT & Partners

Hoang Thanh Le, Truong
ACSV Legal

Le, Net
Judicial Academy

Linh Ha, My
ADR Vietnam Chambers

Nguyen, Manh Dzung
ADR Vietnam Chambers

Nguyen, Ngoc Minh
Dzungsrt & Associates

Nguyen, Thi Thu Trang
Dzungsrt & Associates

Tran, Tam
Foreign Trade University & Southern Trade Arbitration Center

Virgin Islands, British

Greer, Shan
BVI International Arbitration Centre

Zambia

Banda, James
AMW And Company Legal Practitioners

Joseph Chitupila, Muleba
Gill & Seph Advocates

Rattray, Suzanne
Rankin Engineering Consultants

Other

Strick, Emilie

Strick, Stephen

Wenjie, Niu

INTERNATIONAL COUNCIL FOR COMMERCIAL ARBITRATION (ICCA)

Correspondence address:
ICCA Bureau
Peace Palace, Carnegieplein 2
Phone: + 31 70 302 2834
E-mail: bureau@arbitration-icca.org

LIST OF ICCA OFFICERS AND GOVERNING BOARD MEMBERS

OCTOBER 2025

OFFICERS

President

DR STANIMIR A. AlEXANDROV (Washington, DC, USA)

Dr Stanimir Alexandrov serves as an arbitrator in numerous cases administered by the International Centre for Settlement of Investment Disputes (ICSID), the International Chamber of Commerce (ICC), the London Court of International Arbitration (LCIA), and the Permanent Court of Arbitration (PCA), as well as ad hoc arbitrations under the UNCITRAL Rules. He has been appointed to the ICSID Panel of Arbitrators and is also a member of the panel of arbitrators of the Hong Kong International Arbitration Center (HKIAC), the Dubai International Arbitration Center (DIAC), the Chinese International Economic and Trade Arbitration Commission (CIETAC), and the Arbitration Center at the Institute of Modern Arbitration (Moscow).

President-Elect

MR AUDLEY WILLIAM SHEPPARD KC (London, United Kingdom)

Mr Audley Sheppard KC is an Arbitrator Member of Twenty Essex, London. He is a former partner of Clifford Chance LLP and co-head of the firm's international arbitration group. He has been Chair of the LCIA Board and a Vice-President of the LCIA Court, Member of the ICC Court, Co-Chair of the IBA Arbitration Committee, and Rapporteur of the ILA Arbitration Committee. He is also Chair of Sport Resolutions.

Vice-Presidents

MS DYALÁ JIMÉNEZ (San José, Costa Rica)

Dyalá Jiménez is a Costa Rican national and specialises in international arbitration. She is frequently appointed as an arbitrator in institutional and ad hoc arbitrations, in both commercial and investor-State disputes. She is a member of the ICSID panel of conciliators and arbitrators for Costa Rica and of the ICC International Court of Arbitration. She is a Fulbright Scholar and alumnus of Georgetown University Law Center, is author of numerous publications (visit www.djarbitraje.com) and has taught in several universities. Dyalá served as Minister of Foreign Trade of Costa Rica (2018-2020).

MS ABBY COHEN SMUTNY (Washington, DC, USA)

Abby Cohen Smutny is the Global Co-Head of White & Case's International Arbitration Practice. She is widely recognised as one of the leading international arbitration practitioners globally. Abby's leadership positions have included: ICCA Vice-President; Chair of the Institute of Transnational Arbitration (ITA); ASIL Vice-President and Counsellor; President of LCIA North American Users Council; AAA Advisory Board Member; IBA Arbitration Committee Vice Chair and Chair of IBA Investment Treaty Sub-Committee; co-Chair of the ICCA Task Force on Standards of Practice in International Arbitration; and Chair International Law Section of Washington DC Bar. Abby is a member of the SIAC Court of Arbitration and a member of the SCCA Board.

Treasurer

MS SAMAA A. HARIDI (New York, USA)

Samaa A. Haridi is a common and civil law-trained, trilingual partner at King & Spalding. Ms Haridi has significant experience representing clients in multi-jurisdictional international commercial and investment arbitration proceedings under the arbitration rules of all the major arbitral institutions. Ms Haridi also frequently sits as an arbitrator in international commercial and investment disputes. Ms Haridi is a member of the bars of New York, California, and England & Wales. She is fluent in French and Arabic and is also conversant in Spanish.

ICCA General Editor (Ex Officio)

PROF. DR STEPHAN W. SCHILL (Amsterdam, The Netherlands)

Stephan W. Schill is General Editor of ICCA Publications, the Yearbook Commercial Arbitration, and the ICCA Awards Series. He is Professor of International and Economic Law and Governance at the University of Amsterdam, specialising in international investment law and investor-State dispute settlement and its connections to general public international law, specialised international legal regimes, such as human rights or international environmental law, regional economic integration, as well as domestic administrative and constitutional law and international commercial arbitration. He is admitted as a Rechtsanwalt to the bar in Germany and as an Attorney-at-Law in the State of New York, is a Member of the ICSID Panel of Arbitrators, and regularly sits as arbitrator in investor-State proceedings under all major institutional and ad hoc rules. He is the General Editor of Schreuer's Commentary on the ICSID Convention (3rd ed., CUP 2022), has served as Editor-in-Chief of *The Journal of World Investment and Trade* (2014-2023) and has published widely on international investment law and investment arbitration.

Executive Director

MS LISE BOSMAN (The Hague, The Netherlands)

Lise Bosman is based at the Peace Palace in The Hague, as Executive Director of the International Council for Commercial Arbitration (ICCA) and Senior Legal Counsel at the Permanent Court of Arbitration (PCA). She is also appointed as Adjunct Professor at the University of Cape Town, South Africa, where she teaches the LLM course in Commercial Arbitration, and acts as PCA Counsellor to the Secretary General for South Africa. Lise is the General Editor and contributing author to *Arbitration in Africa: A Practitioner's Guide* (Kluwer Law International, Second Edition, September 2021) and the General Editor of the *ICCA International Handbook on Commercial Arbitration* (a seven-volume loose-leaf collection of arbitration-related legislation and commentary on over eighty-five jurisdictions; Kluwer Law International, published since 1984). She is a member of the Court of the AFSA and LACIAC arbitral institutes and a founding member of the Board of the African Arbitration Association. Her areas of specialisation are: international commercial arbitration law and practice; the practice and development of international arbitration in Africa; international investment law; investor-State arbitration; and State-State arbitration.

GOVERNING BOARD MEMBERS

MS AISHA ABDALLAH (Nairobi, Kenya)

Aisha Abdallah is a Partner at ALN Kenya | Anjarwalla & Khanna, where she heads the regional Dispute Resolution department based at the Nairobi Head Office. She is dual qualified as an Advocate of the High Court of Kenya and Solicitor of England and Wales. Aisha specialises in economic crime. She is passionate about the rule of law and the impact of quality legal training on raising professional standards. Aisha is a board member of the Kenya National Chamber of Commerce, Hong Kong International Arbitration Centre, LCIA Africa Users Council and Court of Arbitration for Sports. She is the officer for Africa at the IBA Asset Recovery Committee and a Law Society of Kenya representative. She is a director of the ALN Academy, the patron of ALN Kenya's Pro Bono Committee and a member of the governing council of the Kenya Pro Bono Institute.

PROF. DR MOHAMED SALAH ELDIN ABDEL WAHAB (Cairo, Egypt)

Mohamed Abdel Wahab is Professor of International Arbitration, Private International Law and English Contract Law, Cairo University; Founding Partner and Head of International Arbitration, Construction and Energy Groups at Zulficar & Partners Law Firm (Egypt); Member of the Governing Board (ICCA); and Dean of the Africa Arbitration Academy. He has served as 'Arbitrator', 'Legal Expert' and 'Counsel' in more than 255 cases, involving parties from Africa, Asia, Canada, Europe, the Middle East and the United States. He received the LAW Magazine 2017 Best Legal Practitioner Award, the 2018 ASA International Arbitration Advocacy Prize, the 2019 AYA Hall-of-Fame African Arbitrator Award, the 2020 and 2021 Client Choice International Award. He is listed in Who's Who Global Elite Thought Leaders: International Arbitration; selected among the Legal500 Africa Powerlist and the AYA's Africa's Top 30 Powerlist. He is the co-editor (with Prof. Maxi Scherer and Ms Niuscha Bassiri) of *International Arbitration and the COVID-19 Revolution* (2020); co-editor (with Prof. Ethan Katsh and Mr Daniel Rainey) of *Online Dispute Resolution: Theory and Practice* (2021).

MS CATHERINE M. AMIRFAR (New York, USA)

Catherine Amirfar is Co-Chair of the International Disputes Resolution and Public International Law Groups at Debevoise & Plimpton LLP and sits as a member of the Firm's Management Committee. She is the immediate Past President of the American Society of International Law (ASIL), the pre-eminent learned society in the United States dedicated to international law. With over twenty years of experience, Ms Amirfar is recognised as a top practitioner in international disputes globally. Her practice focuses on international commercial and treaty arbitration, international litigation and public international law. She regularly appears in US courts and before international courts and arbitration tribunals, including the International Court of Justice (ICJ). Ms Amirfar serves as a Member of the U.S. Department of State's Advisory Committee on International Law, the Council on Foreign Relations, the Advisory Committees of the American Law

Institute for the Restatement (Fourth) of Foreign Relations Law of the United States and for the Restatement of the U.S. Law of International Commercial Arbitration. She is a member of the Governing Board of the International Council for Commercial Arbitration (ICCA), the leading global organisation of international arbitrators and arbitration practitioners, and serves as Co-Chair of the ICCA-ASIL Task Force on Damages in International Arbitration. She is also a member of the Court of Arbitration of the Singapore International Arbitration Cen tre and the International Centre for Dispute Resolution of the American Arbitration Association. From 2014 to 2016, Ms Amirfar served as Counsellor on International Law to the Legal Adviser at the U.S. Department of State in the Obama Administration, for which she received the State Department's Superior Honour Award in recognition of her contributions to the Department.

MS DOMITILLE BAIZEAU (Geneva, Switzerland)

Domitille Baizeau is a partner at LALIVE, based in Geneva. She has been acting as counsel and arbitrator in arbitrations governed by civil law and common law and international law for nearly twenty-five years, with a focus on joint venture, M&A, shareholders, sales and investment disputes in the energy (oil & gas, renewables), mining, finance and pharmaceutical sectors. In 2018, she received the GAR ART award of the Best Prepared and Most Responsive Arbitrator. She has always been an active member of arbitral institutions and associations, most recently the ICC Court, the Swiss Arbitration Center, the HKIAC and the Mumbai Centre for International Arbitration. She has served as Managing Partner of LALIVE since 2015.

MS CHIANN BAO (Singapore)

Chiann Bao is a Chartered Arbitrator and CEDR-Accredited Mediator. Tri-qualified in New York, England and Wales and Hong Kong, she has been appointed in nearly one hundred ad hoc and institutional arbitrations totalling several USD billions in dispute. She is the Co-Chair of the IBA Arbitration Committee and has held institutional leadership positions, including as a vice-president of the ICC Court of Arbitration and as Secretary General of the HKIAC. Chiann has practised in international law firms in New York and Hong Kong. She is one of the most highly ranked arbitrators in publications such as Who's Who Legal Arbitration's Global Elite Thought Leaders and Chambers and Partners' Most in Demand arbitrators (globally and regionally). A regular speaker and lecturer, Chiann was awarded the GAR 'best lecture' for her Proskauer Rose lecture in 2022.

MS JULIE BÉDARD (New York, USA)

Julie Bédard is head of Skadden's International Litigation and Arbitration Group for the Americas. Fluent in French, Spanish and Portuguese, Ms Bédard practises in four languages in complex disputes and investigations. Trained in both civil and common law, she has a Doctorate in Conflict of Laws and represents clients in connection with litigation and arbitration proceedings throughout the world, raising disputes on governing law, jurisdiction, the enforcement of arbitration agreements, extraterritoriality and international judgment enforcement. Ms Bédard has repeatedly been recognised as a leading lawyer in a variety of legal publications, including *Chambers Global, Chambers USA, Chambers Latin America, Euromoney* and *Latinvex.*

MR JOHN BEECHEY (London, United Kingdom)

Mr John Beechey CBE, a past President of the ICC International Court of Arbitration, has served as chairman, party-appointed arbitrator, or sole arbitrator on more than one hundred international arbitral tribunals in both 'ad hoc' (including UNCITRAL) and institutional arbitrations under the Rules of all major arbitral institutions, including, *inter alia*, the EDF, ICC, ICDR/AAA, ICSID, LCIA, PCA, SIAC and Stockholm Chamber. He is the current Chairman of the Board of the BVI International Arbitration Centre. In June 2016, he was appointed CBE (Commander of the Order of the British Empire) for services to international arbitration.

MR PIERRE BIENVENU (Montréal, Canada)

Pierre Bienvenu is a disputes lawyer with more than thirty-five years' experience in international commercial arbitration, commercial litigation, and constitutional law and acted as counsel or served as arbitrator in international arbitrations involving disputes in energy, transportation, telecommunications, international distribution and joint ventures, mergers and acquisitions, construction, pharmaceuticals, and foreign investment. A former co-chair of the IBA's Arbitration Committee (2008-2009), he has served on the LCIA Court (2010-2015), of which he was a vice-president (2011-2015), the ICC International Court of Arbitration (2015-2021), and is currently a member of the Court of Arbitration of the Singapore International Arbitration Center (SIAC). He was appointed to ICSID's Panel of Arbitrators in 2021 and elected to ICCA's Governing Board in 2024.

PROF. STAVROS BREKOULAKIS (Singapore)

Stavros Brekoulakis is the Michael & Laura Hwang Professor in International Arbitration at the National University of Singapore and an arbitrator practising at 3 Verulam Buildings (Gray's Inn). He has been involved in international law and arbitration for more than twenty years and is widely recognised as a leading authority in the field. He is regularly listed in Who's Who Legal: Arbitration, Who's Who Legal: Construction and Who's Who Legal: Thought Leader, being included in the Legal 500 Arbitration Power List and ranked as a WWL Arbitration: Global Elite Thought Leader and one of the twenty-five most highly regarded arbitrators in the EMEA region. He has been shortlisted twice for the Global Arbitration Review Best Prepared and Most Responsive Arbitrator Award and received the 2020 GAR Award for Best Public Speech.

MRS KATE BROWN DE VEJAR (Mexico City, Mexico)

Kate Brown de Vejar is a Partner and Global Co-Chair of International Arbitration at DLA Piper, where she specialises in both international commercial and investor-State arbitration. An Australian and New York qualified attorney, resident in Mexico City for the past fifteen years, Kate is widely recognised for her experience and results handling complex, high-profile disputes, notably in the energy and infrastructure sectors. She is Senior Vice Chair of the IBA's Arbitration Committee, and is slated to take the helm of the committee in 2026. She is a Member of the LCIA Court and President of the LCIA's Latin American & Caribbean Users' Council, and also acts as Co-Chair of ICCA's Working Group on Arbitrator Liability. Kate is also on the Law 360 Editorial Board for International Arbitration (appointed in 2022). Outside of the arbitration world, Kate is the President of ANZMEX (the Australia, New Zealand, Mexico Business Council). From 2008 to 2017, she was a member of the Australian Delegation to the United Nations (UNCITRAL) Working Group on Arbitration and Conciliation. She is a graduate of Harvard Law School and the University of Queensland, and is fluent in English, French and Spanish.

MR CAVINDER BULL SC (Singapore)

Mr Cavinder Bull SC is Chief Executive Officer of Drew & Napier LLC. He is also Vice-President of the SIAC Court of Arbitration. He is called to the bars of Singapore, New York and England & Wales. He handles both investor-state cases and commercial cases as arbitrator or counsel. He has published work in the areas of international arbitration and contract law. Beyond arbitration, he has held a number of appointments, including being a member of the Securities Industries Council of Singapore and the Advisory Council to the Faculty of Law of the National University of Singapore.

PROF. DR NAYLA COMAIR-OBEID (Dubai, United Arab Emirates)

Prof. Dr Nayla Comair-Obeid is the Founding Partner of Obeid & Partners where she heads the firm's dispute resolution practice. She is also an associate member of 3VB Chambers in London and a Professor of International Arbitration. She has been actively involved in over 170 domestic and international commercial and investment arbitrations conducted in Arabic, French and English-language, whether ad hoc and/or institutional (ICSID, ICC, LCIA, DIAC, CRCICA, BCDR, DIFC-LCIA, UNCITRAL, etc.). Throughout her career, Professor Comair-Obeid has held and continues to hold pre-eminent positions. She has been elected the Vice Chair of the ICC Global (as of June 2022) and appointed the Chair of the Jury of the ICC Institute Prize (2023 edition). She sits, among others, as a member of the ICC Executive Board, former member of the LCIA Court, member of the CRCICA Board of Trustees, Companion of the CIArb, and member of the international commercial expert committee of China's Supreme People's Court. She has authored numerous publications, including the book *The Law of Business Contracts in the Middle East*, among others.

MR BABATUNDE FAGBOHUNLU (Lagos, Nigeria)

Mr Babatunde Fagbohunlu is a Partner and head of the Litigation, Arbitration and ADR Practice Group in Aluko & Oyebode. He regularly acts as counsel to Nigerian as well as foreign and multinational clients in ad hoc and institutional arbitrations, and has served as arbitrator in several cases, including arbitrations administered by the ICC and the LCIA. Mr Fagbohunlu has also served on the Federal Government of Nigeria's Committee on the Reform and Harmonization of Arbitration/ADR Laws. He co-authored the book *Arbitration in Africa: A Review of Key Jurisdictions* published by Sweet and Maxwell in 2016.

MR EDUARDO DAMIÃO GONÇALVES (São Paulo, Brazil)

Eduardo Damião Gonçalves is a partner with Mattos Filho and has more than thirty years of experience representing clients in complex domestic and international disputes submitted to arbitration and court litigation. He also frequently sits as arbitrator in international commercial and investment disputes. Eduardo was a VP of the International Court of Arbitration of the ICC from 2018 thru 2024. He was a founder and former president of the Brazilian Arbitration Committee (CBAr). Eduardo is also a co-founder and was a vice-president of the Latin American Arbitration Association (ALARB) and was Vice Chair of the IBA Arbitration Committee. Eduardo has PhD in International Law from the University of São Paulo and has a Master of Laws from the University of Paris II. Eduardo is fluent in Portuguese, English, French, Spanish and Italian.

MR NING FEI (Beijing, People's Republic of China)

Mr Ning Fei has been practising as counsel and arbitrator in the international commercial disputes arena for over thirty years. He is a co-founder and the managing partner of Hui Zhong Law Firm, the first and the leading international dispute resolution boutique based in China. During 2013-2019, he was a Council Member of HKIAC, and in 2024 he was newly appointed as the member of the Nomination Committee of HKIAC, both titles vested to persons from mainland China for the first time in history. He led the endeavour to amend SCIA's arbitration rules, the first of its kind that fully integrates with international standards. Mr Fei serves as a Governing Board Member of the International Council for Commercial Arbitration (ICCA).

DR JUAN FERNANDEZ-ARMESTO (Madrid, Spain)

Dr Juan Fernandez-Armesto is a professional arbitrator and specialises in commercial, investment and construction arbitration. He has extensive experience in both Spanish domestic arbitrations and international arbitrations administered by bodies such as the ICC, LCIA, VIAC, DIAC and ad hoc arbitrations under the UNCITRAL Rules. He has been President of the Spanish Securities and Exchange Commission (CNMV) (1996-2000), partner of Uría Menéndez (1983-1996) and Chaired Professor of Commercial Law (1988-2009).

MS JUDITH GILL KC (Singapore)

Ms Judith Gill is recognised as one of the leading practitioners in international arbitration. She was a partner in the global law firm Allen & Overy for more than twenty-five years and was Head of the International Arbitration Group for eleven years. She moved to Singapore in September 2015 and joined Twenty Essex Chambers in Singapore in May 2018. Since May 2022, she practises exclusively as an independent arbitrator and has extensive experience in matters involving construction, energy contracts, manufacturing, distributorship agreements and other commercial agreements. She is the immediate past President of the LCIA Court. She was the second female solicitor-advocate to be appointed KC in England.

MR KARL HENNESSEE (Blagnac, France)

Karl Hennessee, FRAeS, is SVP Litigation, Investigations & Regulatory Affairs at Airbus, where he leads the Group's global activities in these areas. Separately, he occasionally sits as an arbitrator and serves on the board of directors of companies and nonprofits. Until July 2019, he also served as Chairman of the Governing Body of the ICC Court of International Arbitration and is now a member of the HKIAC Council as well as its Proceedings Committee. He also serves on the Advisory Council for the School of International Arbitration at Queen Mary University of London.

MR JAMES HOSKING (New York, USA)

James Hosking has been practising in the international disputes arena for over twenty-five years. As co-founder of international dispute resolution boutique Chaffetz Lindsey, he leads the firm's international arbitration team. James' practice has seen him appear in over one hundred arbitrations as counsel, while he also sits as arbitrator in commercial and investor-state cases. He is an adjunct pro fessor at NYU School of Law, co-author of the leading Commentary on the ICDR International Rules, and a Fellow of the Arbitrators and Mediators Institute of New Zealand. James was previously a partner in a leading international firm and also practised in New Zealand.

MR ANDRÉS JANA (Santiago, Chile)

Mr Andrés Jana is a litigation and arbitration partner at the Chilean law firm of Bofill Mir & Alvarez Jana and a Professor at Universidad de Chile. He has wide experience in international disputes, as a lawyer, arbitrator and expert. These disputes involved international arbitration as well as international public law issues and have been carried out, among others, before the ICJ, ICSID, ICC, LCIA, AAA, and SCC. He is the Chilean delegate before UNCITRAL and has been elected to Chair the WGII work on Expedited Proceedings in International Arbitration. He is on the Chilean List of Arbitrators for ICSID, a former member of the LCIA, former Vice Chair of the IBA Arbitration Committee, and former Chair of the ITA Americas Initiative.

MS NDANGA KAMAU (Grenoble, France)

Ndanga Kamau is an independent arbitrator. She has considerable expertise and experience in disputes related to Africa and is proficient in issues related to compensation, damages, taxation, interest, and costs. Ndanga speaks, teaches, and writes on topics related to her areas of specialisation. She is a member of the ICCA Governing Board; council member of the ICC Institute of World Business Law; trustee and honorary senior fellow of BIICL; PRIME Finance expert in dispute resolution; and member of the advisory board of the UCT ADR Unit. Ndanga was Vice-President of the ICC Court from 2018 to 2024. She was called to the Bar of England and Wales by the Honourable Society of the Middle Temple.

MR TOBY LANDAU KC (Singapore)

Mr Toby Landau KC is a barrister, advocate and arbitrator practising as a sole practitioner in London and as a member of Duxton Hill Chambers (Singapore Group Practice) in Singapore. He specialises in international arbitration and has argued hundreds of major international commercial, investor-State and inter-state arbitrations, as well as ground-breaking cases in the courts of numerous jurisdictions. As an arbitrator, he has extensive experience under most of the world's leading ad hoc and institutional rules and is a member of various panels. He is on the Panel of Advisers to the Attorney-General of Singapore; Vice-President of the SIAC Court of Arbitration; and a draftsman of arbitration legislation in a number of jurisdictions.

MS LORETTA MALINTOPPI (Singapore)

Ms Loretta Malintoppi is dually qualified (Paris and Rome Bars) and has been registered to practise as a Foreign Lawyer in Singapore since 2012. She practised in the Paris office of Eversheds from 1991 until 2012 and thereafter in the Singapore office until 2016. Loretta joined 39 Essex Chambers in January 2017. She acts as counsel, advocate and arbitrator in international commercial and investment arbitration and has represented private companies, states and state entities in proceedings under a variety of arbitration rules, including ICSID, ICC, UNCITRAL, SIAC, LCIA and DIAC.

MS CAROLE MALINVAUD (Paris, France)

Carole Malinvaud is a partner at Gide Paris where she co-heads the interna tional arbitration activity of the firm and chairs the Gide Pro Bono endowment fund. Carole is a member of the Paris and New York Bars. Carole has recently been focusing on arbitrations relating to construction, energy and defence, as well as post-acquisition disputes. She also acts as arbitrator in several ICC and ICSID arbitrations. Carole is a lecturer at the University Paris II and at Sciences Po Paris. She was appointed Vice Chair of the ICC Court in 2021, is a member of the ICCA Governing Board and of the International Council of Arbitration for Sport (ICAS) and she chairs the Ordinary Division of the Court of Arbitration for Sport (CAS). Carole was designated by the French State to the Panel of ICSID arbitrators as of 2019.

MR FERNANDO MANTILLA-SERRANO (Paris, France)

Mr Fernando Mantilla-Serrano is a partner and co-chair of the International Arbitration Practice at Latham & Watkins. He has served as both lead counsel and arbitrator under the ICC, ICSID, LCIA, SCC, ICDR, IACAC, UNCITRAL and EDF arbitration rules. Mr Mantilla-Serrano is Fellow of the Chartered Institute of Arbitrators (FCIArb) and member of the International Law Association (ILA). He is also member of the Governing Board of the International Council for Commercial Arbitration (ICCA) and member of the Dispute Resolution Governing Body of the International Chamber of Commerce (ICC). Mr Mantilla-Serrano is admitted to the bars of Colombia, New York (USA), Paris (France) and Madrid (Spain).

MS SYLVIA NOURY KC (London, United Kingdom)

Ms Sylvia Noury is a partner at Freshfields Bruckhaus Deringer, where she heads the International Arbitration Group in London. Her practice focuses on high-stakes international commercial and treaty arbitration in high-risk jurisdictions. She is a Member of the Board of the Arbitration Institute of the Stockholm Chamber of Commerce (SCC); the Advisory Council of Africa Arbitration; the ITA Advisory Board; and a former Member of the Arbitration Committee and Nominations Sub-Committee of the ICC UK. She is the Founder and Co-Chair of the Equal Representation in Arbitration Pledge.

MR JOHN MORRIS OHAGA SC CARB (Nairobi, Kenya)

John Ohaga is the Managing Partner in the law firm of TripleOKlaw LLP. He holds an LLM in International Dispute Resolution from Queen Mary University of London. He is a Senior Counsel and a Chartered Arbitrator.

MS YOSHIMI OHARA (Tokyo, Japan)

Ms Yoshimi Ohara is a partner at Nagashima Ohno & Tsunematsu in Tokyo, Japan. She served as counsel in international arbitration under the rules of the ICC, ICSID, AAA/ICDR, SIAC and JCAA. She also served as co-arbitrator, sole arbitrator and chair arbitrator under the Rules of the ICC, SIAC, JCAA, KCAB, ICDR and UNCITRAL. She is a member of the Governing Board of the ICCA, a council member of HKIAC, a member of the Board of the Swiss Arbitration Association (ASA) and a member of the Executive Director of the Japan Association of Arbitrators (JAA). She is a former Vice-President of the London Court of International Arbitration (LCIA) and the ICC International Court of Arbitration (ICC) and is listed as a member of the ICSID panel of arbitrators. She is admitted to the Japanese Bar and the New York Bar and has an LLM from Harvard Law School.

MS SHANEEN PARIKH (Mumbai, India)

Shaneen is dually qualified (in India and England and Wales) and is the head of international arbitration at Cyril Amarchand Mangaldas. As counsel, Shaneen has over three decades of experience in dispute resolution and specialises in complex multi-forum, multi-jurisdictional commercial disputes with particular expertise in arbitration. She has experience in arbitrations under various institutional rules and international seats. She has also participated in some precedent-setting arbitrations (and litigations) in India, including the Supreme Court's ruling that two Indian parties can designate a foreign seat of arbitration. She also sits as an arbitrator in international arbitrations.

Shaneen is consistently ranked for her arbitration practice in leading directories, including as a 'Thought Leader' in arbitration by Who's Who Legal (now Lexology), in 2023, 2024 and 2025.

Shaneen is the Vice Chair to the ICC Commission on Arbitration and ADR, Member of the Council of the Mumbai International Arbitration Centre, Ambassador of the Asia Pacific Group of the IBA, and a former Member of the SIAC Court of Arbitration. She was also a member of an expert committee to draft institutional arbitration rules for an IFSC at the GIFT City, a special economic zone in Gujarat.

MR CONSTANTINE PARTASIDES KC (London, United Kingdom)

Mr Constantine Partasides KC has appeared as counsel on some of the largest commercial arbitrations of the last decade, many of which relate to the energy sector. He has been named as one of the 'top 20' individuals in the world of arbitration each year since 2011 in 'Who's Who' of Commercial Arbitration. He is a co-author of the fourth, fifth and sixth editions of the leading textbook on international arbitration, Redfern and Hunter on International Arbitration. He is a solicitor-advocate (Higher Courts Civil) and was appointed Queen's Counsel in 2014.

PROF. VLADIMIR PAVIC (Belgrade, Serbia)

Prof. Vladimir Pavic is an independent arbitration practitioner based in Belgrade, Serbia. He regularly sits as arbitrator and has also acted as counsel in a number of investment and commercial cases. His experience includes over sixty arbitrations, both ad hoc and institutional (under the ICC, LCIA, SCC, VIAC, DIS, RAC, UNCITRAL, ICSID, ICSID Additional Facility and Swiss rules), at various seats and under a broad range of applicable laws. He is currently a full-time Professor of law at the University of Belgrade, President of the Belgrade Arbitration Center, member of the International Advisory Board of VIAC, ICC and a national CLOUT correspondent for UNCITRAL.

PROF. DR MAXI SCHERER (London, United Kingdom)

Maxi Scherer has over twenty years of experience in international arbitration in both civil and common law systems. She is admitted to the bar in Paris (France) and as a solicitor in England and Wales. Maxi has represented clients and served as arbitrator or legal expert in more than 140 commercial and investor-State arbitrations. Her arbitrations regularly involve states, concern multi-billion amounts in dispute and are conducted in English, French and German. Regularly ranked by Who's Who Legal, The Legal 500 etc., as a leading arbitration practitioner, she has been identified among the top 20 'Global Elite Thought Leaders'. She has received the 2023 GAR Award for 'Best Prepared Arbitrator'.

PROF. HI-TAEK SHIN (Seoul, Republic of Korea)

Prof. Hi-Taek Shin is a professor (emeritus) at Seoul National University School of Law. He is an independent arbitrator at Twenty Essex Chambers (practice based in Seoul, Korea). He has taught the resolution of commercial and investment disputes arising from cross-border transactions. Prior to moving to academia, he was a partner of Kim & Chang, the leading Korean law firm. He regularly sits as an arbitrator in both international investment treaty arbitrations and international commercial arbitrations.

MR TOMASZ (TOM) SIKORA (Humble, United States)

Tom Sikora is Senior Counsel in the International Disputes Group of the ExxonMobil Law Department. He manages international investment and commercial arbitration for Exxon Mobil Corporation. Prior to joining ExxonMobil, he spent ten years at El Paso Corporation managing the company's international arbitration and complex litigation. Tom initially practised international arbitration of energy, construction and insurance disputes at Vinson & Elkins LLP in Houston, Texas. Tom graduated from Harvard with an A.B. in History and Literature and from the University of Virginia School of Law with a J.D.

DR CLAUS WERNER VON WOBESER (Mexico City, Mexico)

Claus von Wobeser is the Founding Partner of Von Wobeser y Sierra. He has acted in over two hundred international arbitration proceedings, and has served as Vice-President of the International Court of Arbitration of the ICC, Co-Chair of the IBA Arbitration Committee, President of the Arbitration Commission of ICC Mexico, Member of the Panel of Arbitrators of ICSID, Member of the London Court of International Arbitration, Member of the Board of Directors of the AAA, and as a Member of the ICC Court. In 1994, he founded and since teaches in the diploma course on arbitration co-organised by the Escuela Libre de Derecho and ICC México. Currently, he serves as President of ALARB and ICC Mexico. He studied law at Escuela Libre de Derecho in Mexico City and for a PhD at Université de Paris 2, Sorbonne.

Honorary Presidents

PROF. ALBERT JAN VAN DEN BERG (Brussels, Belgium)

Professor Albert Jan van den Berg is a partner at Hanotiau & van den Berg (Brussels, Belgium). He is Honorary President of ICCA, having served as President from 2014-2016. He is a Visiting Professor at Georgetown University Law Center, Tsinghua University School of Law and University of Miami School of Law; Emeritus Professor (Arbitration Chair) at Erasmus University, Rotterdam;

and member of the faculty of the University of Geneva Master in International Dispute Settlement Program. He is Honorary President of the Netherlands Arbitration Institute, and former Vice-President of the London Court of International Arbitration. Professor van den Berg has published extensively on international arbitration (*see* www.hvdb.com), in particular, the New York Convention of 1958 (*see* www.newyorkconvention.org).

MR DONALD FRANCIS DONOVAN (New York, USA)

Mr Donovan is Co-Head of the International Disputes Group at Debevoise & Plimpton LLP and teaches International Arbitration and International Investment Law and Arbitration at the New York University School of Law. He is also a visiting professor at the School of International Arbitration at Queen Mary University of London. He serves as a member of the US Secretary of State's Advisory Committee on International Law, a member of the Advisory Committees of the American Law Institute for the Restatement of US Foreign Relations Law and for the Restatement of the US Law of International Commercial Arbitration (ITA), and he has also served as an Alternate Member of the ICC International Court of Arbitration.

DR GEROLD HERRMANN (Vienna, Austria)

Dr Gerold Herrmann was President of ICCA from 2002 until 2010. Until his retirement in 2001, he worked for twenty-six years for UNCITRAL (United Nations Commission on International Trade Law), the last ten years thereof as its Director. His major achievement was the elaboration and promulgation of the UNCITRAL Model Law and the concomitant assistance in establishing or internationalising arbitration centres all over the world. Dr Herrmann is Honorary Professor of Vienna University, Honorary Vice-President of the LCIA Court and former President of the LCIA Court. In 2001, INSOL International presented to him the Scroll of Honour and the International Insolvency Institute honoured him in 2006 with the Outstanding Contributions Award.

PROF. DR GABRIELLE KAUFMANN-KOHLER (Geneva, Switzerland)

Prof. Dr Gabrielle Kaufmann-Kohler is a Founding Partner of Lévy Kaufmann-Kohler and has extensive experience as an international arbitrator in commercial and investment cases. She is also Professor Emerita at Geneva University and Visiting Professor at various universities, including NUS, Sciences Po Paris, Tsinghua and MIDS. She is Honorary President of ICCA, the Swiss Arbitration Association (ASA), as well as the founder and former director of the Geneva LLM in International Dispute Settlement (MIDS).

PROF. JAN PAULSSON (Manama, Bahrain)

Judge, Bahrain Court of Cassation (authorised to act in personal capacity in international arbitrations). Past positions: Partner successively in Coudert Frères, Freshfields Bruckhaus Deringer and Three Crowns; President, ICCA, LCIA & World Bank Administrative Tribunal; Vice-President, ICC Court of International

Arbitration; Member, SIAC Court of Arbitration; tenured professor at the University of Miami; Centennial Professor, London School of Economics. Law degrees: Yale, Paris.

MS LUCY REED (New York, USA)
Ms Lucy Reed, Past President of ICCA, currently is an independent arbitrator with Arbitration Chambers in New York. Lucy is a member of the Board of the Register for Damages Caused by the Aggression of the Russian Federation Against Ukraine. From 2016 to 2019, Lucy was the Director of the Centre for International Law and Professor of Practice at the National University of Singapore and, before her retirement in 2016, led the global international arbitration group of Freshfields Bruckhaus Deringer. Now the President of the SIAC Court, Lucy has served as a Vice-President of the ICC Court, Chair of the Institute for Transnational Arbitration, and President of the American Society of International Law.

Honorary Vice-Presidents

DR MICHAEL HWANG SC (Singapore)
Dr Michael Hwang SC currently practises as an Independent International Barrister and Expert Witness and (selectively) as Leading Counsel. He has served as Chief Justice of the Dubai International Financial Centre (DIFC) Courts, a Judicial Commissioner (Contract Judge for a fixed period) of the High Court of Singapore, a member of the Court of Cassation in the Kingdom of Bahrain, President of the Law Society of Singapore and Singapore's Non-Resident Ambassador to Switzerland and Argentina.

MS TINUADE OYEKUNLE (Lagos, Nigeria)
Mrs Tinuade Oyekunle is the managing partner and founder of Tinuade Oyekunle & Co (now known as Sonotina Chambers). She is a seasoned Chartered Arbitrator, handling complex national and international commercial arbitration disputes. She has been appointed in disputes under the auspices of the ICC, ICSID, and other arbitration institutions. She is a member of the Governing Council of the Lagos International Centre for Commercial Arbitration. Tinuade is an ardent participant in discussions dealing with issues relating to the development of ADR and enforcement of Awards. Mrs Tinuade Oyekunle, with her colleague Chief Bayo Ojo SAN, co-authored the *Handbook on Arbitration and ADR Practice in Nigeria*, published by LexisNexis in January 2019.

Honorary Secretary General

MR ANTONIO RICARDO PARRA (Easton, USA)
Mr Antonio R. Parra was Secretary General of ICCA from 2004 to 2010. He is a former Deputy Secretary General and Legal Adviser of ICSID.

Advisory Board Members

DR MOHAMED ABDEL RAOUF (Sheikh Zayed, Egypt)

Partner, ABDEL RAOUF LAW FIRM (Egypt); Associate Professor, Université Paris 1 Panthéon-Sorbonne; Vice Chairman of the Board of Trustees and Member of the Advisory Committee of the CRCICA; Alternate Member ICC Court; Chairman of the Egypt Branch of the Chartered Institute of Arbitrators (CIArb); Member of the Arbitration Committee of the Lagos Court of Arbitration (LCA); Member of the Board of Directors of the Saudi Center for Commercial Arbitration (SCCA); Arbitrator, Court of Arbitration for Sport (CAS); Conciliator, ICSID Panel of Conciliators; CEDR-Accredited Mediator; Director of the CRCICA (2012-2016); Member of the Board of the Arbitration Institute of the Stockholm Chamber of Commerce, SCC (2012-2017); Vice-President, the International Federation of Commercial Arbitration Institutions, IFCAI (2011-2015).

MR CECIL WILBERT MOHANARAJ ABRAHAM (Kuala Lumpur, Malaysia)

Cecil Abraham, Senior Partner of Cecil Abraham & Partners, is a Barrister and a Bencher of the Middle Temple. He is a Fellow of Queen Mary & Westfield College, the Chartered Institute of Arbitrators UK, Malaysian Institute of Arbitrators, Singapore Institute of Arbitrators and the Australian Centre for International Commercial Arbitration. He is a Chartered Arbitrator and is a member of various arbitral tribunals. Cecil has an extensive arbitration practice and appears as counsel in domestic and international arbitrations. Cecil is a Member of the ICSID panel.

MS FUNKE ADEKOYA SAN (Lagos, Nigeria)

Olufunke Adekoya is an independent arbitrator, having retired as Head of the Disputes Practice Group at AELEX, a Lagos, Nigeria-based law firm. She is regularly appointed as an arbitrator in commercial and investment-related disputes in the energy and construction sectors. She is a Fellow and Chartered Arbitrator of the Chartered Institute of Arbitrators and sits on the Court of the Singapore International Arbitration Centre. She is listed on the panel of arbitrators of the Kigali International Arbitration Centre, SIAC, ICSID and CIETAC, among others. She is also a member of the African Users Council of the London Court of International Arbitration and ArbitralWomen.

MR MAKHDOOM ALI KHAN (Karachi, Pakistan)

Mr Makhdoom Ali Khan is a Senior Advocate of the Supreme Court of Pakistan and a former Attorney-General for Pakistan. He has appeared in many important commercial cases before the High Courts and the Supreme Court. He also sits as an arbitrator in ad hoc and institutional domestic, international commercial and investment arbitrations. He was a member of the Court of the London Court of International Arbitration and is a member of the Board of AAA. He is a former

Member of the Board of DIAC. He is on the panel of arbitrators of SIAC and KLRCA and has been designated as an arbitrator on the ICSID panel.

MR DOAK BISHOP (Houston, USA)

Mr Doak Bishop is a partner in King & Spalding's Houston office and co-chairs the Firm's International Arbitration Practice Group. He has served as both an arbitrator and counsel under the auspices of ICSID, the ICC, LCIA, UNCITRAL, ICDR, AAA, IACAC, and CPR, as well as in ad hoc arbitrations. He has served as Chairman of the Institute of Transnational Arbitration, Advisor to the American Law Institute's Restatement of Law (3rd) of International Commercial Arbitration, a member of the Board of Directors of AAA, as a member of the Courts of the LCIA and of the Singapore International Arbitration Centre, as a member of the Executive Committee of ASIL, and others.

PROF. DR KARL-HEINZ BÖCKSTIEGEL (Frankenforst, Germany)

Prof. Dr Karl-Heinz Böckstiegel is an arbitrator, sole practitioner and member of Law Faculty of the University of Cologne as Professor Emeritus. He has practised as parties' counsel, as mediator, and as arbitrator and president of arbitration tribunal in many national and international arbitrations of the ICC, ICSID, NAFTA, AAA, SCC, UNCITRAL and others. He is a Past Patron of the Chartered Institute of Arbitrators; Honorary Chairman (Chairman 1996-2012), German Arbitration Institute (DIS); President, International Law Association (ILA) 2004-2006 and President, German Association for International Law 1993-2006. In view of his age, in 2018, he stopped accepting new arbitrator appointments, and by the end of 2019, he resigned from the remaining cases still pending at that time. In 2021, the Karl-Heinz Böckstiegel Foundation was created.

MS ADRIANA BRAGHETTA (São Paulo, Brazil)

President of the Câmara do Mercado (CAM B3), together with Francisco Satiro. Professor at FGV-Fundação Getúlio Vargas in São Paulo (arbitration and international contracts). Visiting Professor at Science-Po LLM in International Arbitration & Dispute Settlement (2024). PhD from USP – University of São Paulo; Founding partner at Adriana Braghetta Advogados. Member, ICCA Advisory Board (Governing Board from 2012 to 2023, Vice-President for three years); President, CBAr – 'Comitê Brasileiro de Arbitragem' (2009-2013); Vice-president (2005-2009) and co-founding member. Member: ILA International Arbitration Committee; ICC Latin-American Arbitration Commission; Former Member of different commissions in other institutions – CCBC, CIESP, AMCHAM-SP. P. Member of the editorial council of the CBAr journal.

PROF. DR NAEL GEORGES BUNNI (Dublin, Ireland)

Prof. Dr Nael G. Bunni is a Chartered Engineer, Chartered Arbitrator, Conciliator/ Mediator and Visiting Professor in Construction Law and Contract Administration, Trinity College Dublin. He is currently a member of the Commission on International Arbitration of ICC and is involved in many of its Standing Committees; Advisory Member to the Governing Board of the International Council for Commercial Arbitration, ICCA; and, since September 2009, a special advisor of FIDIC's Contracts Committee.

MS TERESA CHENG (Hong Kong SAR)

Ms Teresa Cheng is Senior Counsel of the Hong Kong SAR and served as founding Chairman of the Asian Academy of International Law. She was the Vice-President of ICCA, Deputy President for 2007 and President for 2008 of the Chartered Institute of Arbitrators and Vice-President, ICC Court of International Arbitration. She established the International Arbitration and Dispute Settlement Program at the Law School of Tsinghua University and served as Course Director and adjunct professor. She also sat as a Recorder in the Court of First Instance of the High Court and served as the Secretary for Justice of Hong Kong.

PROF. BERNARDO CREMADES (Madrid, Spain)

Bernardo M. Cremades is senior partner of the Spanish law firm, B. Cremades & Asociados, a Professor of Law and a member of the Spanish Royal Academy of Jurisprudence and Legislation. He is the leading Spanish international arbitration practitioner ('number one practitioner in Spain for commercial arbitration legal expertise' and 'one of the top names in the industry', Who's Who legal, July 2005). His international recognition includes Germany's distinguished Verdienstkreuz award and the French distinction of Chevalier de l'Ordre National du Mérite.

MR DUSHYANT DAVE (New Delhi, India)

Mr Dushyant Dave is a Senior Lawyer practising in the Supreme Court of India and the High Courts across the country. He joined the Bar in 1978 and practised in the Gujarat High Court till 1986 and then moved to Delhi. His practice over a span of more than four decades involves various branches of law, including civil laws, criminal laws and corporate laws. He has appeared in a large number of matters involving Constitutional and Public Law issues as well as issues including Fundamental Rights and Civil Liberties of citizens. He has defended many citizens and their causes pro bono. He actively participates in the field of International Com mercial Arbitration and has been on the Governing Board of the International Council of Commercial Arbitration (ICCA), American Arbitration Association (AAA) and London Court of International Arbitration (LCIA).

MR YVES DERAINS (Paris, France)

Mr Yves Derains is Partner of Derains & Gharavi, Paris; Honorary Chairman of the ICC Institute of World Business Law; former Chairman of the Comité Français de l'Arbitrage and Co-Chairman of the ICC Working Group on the reduction of costs and time in international Arbitration; Past Secretary General, International Court of Arbitration of the International Chamber of Commerce (ICC); and Member of the Paris Bar. He has acted as counsel or arbitrator in more than two hundred international proceedings throughout the world. He is the author of many publications on international arbitration.

HON. L. YVES FORTIER, PC, CC, OQ, KC (Montréal, Canada)

Hon. L. Yves Fortier is currently judge ad hoc of the International Court of Justice in the Hague. He was Chairman Emeritus and Senior Partner of Norton, Rose, Fulbright until 2012. In 2013, he became the Founding Partner of the Cabinet Yves Fortier in Montreal. Since 1992, he has acted as arbitrator and mediator in many major international arbitrations under the auspices of the ICC, LCIA, AAA, ICSID, CAS and others. From 1988 to 1992, he was Canada's Ambassador and Permanent representative to the United Nations in New York. In 1989, he was President of the Security Council. From 1998 to 2001, he was President of the LCIA. From 2013 to 2017, he was Chairman of the Sanctions Board of the World Bank, and he presently serves as Chairman of the Enforcement Committee of the EBRD. Mr Fortier is a Companion of the Order of Canada (C.C.) and an officer of the Ordre du Québec (O.Q.).

PROF. DR BERNARD HANOTIAU (Brussels, Belgium)

Prof. Dr Bernard Hanotiau is a member of the Brussels and Paris Bars. He is a founding partner of Hanotiau & van den Berg. Since 1978, he has been actively involved in more than six hundred international arbitration cases as party-appointed arbitrator, chairman, sole arbitrator, counsel and expert in all parts of the world. He is professor emeritus of the law school of Louvain University (Belgium). He is a member of the Council of the ICC Institute. He is also a former vice-president of the Institute of Transnational Arbitration (Dallas) and a former vice-president of the LCIA Court. He is a member of the Court of Arbitration of SIAC, of the Consultative board of HKIAC and a former Vice-President of the Governing Board of DIAC (Dubai).

HON. DOMINIQUE T. HASCHER (Paris, France)

Judge Dominique Hascher is an International Judge at the Supreme Court of Singapore. Previously, he was a Judge at the Supreme Judicial Court of France and served as General Counsel and Deputy Secretary General at the International Court of Arbitration of the International Chamber of Commerce, Hon. Bencher of Gray's Inn in London.

MS JEAN KALICKI (New York, USA)

Jean Kalicki is an independent arbitrator associated with Arbitration Chambers, specialising in investment disputes and complex international cases; until 2016, she was a Partner at Arnold & Porter LLP. She is a member of the ICCA Advisory Board and formerly was a Vice-President of the LCIA and a member of the ICC Commission and the AAA Board and Council. She is regularly ranked in Chambers' Band 1 ('Most In-Demand' Arbitrators) for both Global Arbitration and Public International Law, and was its only 'Star Arbitrator' (above Band 1) in the USA for 2019-2020. Best Lawyers in America has named her 'Lawyer of the

Year' five times in her jurisdiction and practice; Who's Who Legal annually lists her as a 'Thought Leaders: Global Elite'; and Global Arbitration Review named her the 'Best Prepared/Most Responsive Arbitrator' worldwide in 2017.

MR NEIL KAPLAN CBE, KC, SBS (Melbourne, Australia)

Mr Neil Kaplan is an arbitrator with Arbitration Chambers in both England and Hong Kong. Mr Kaplan was the Chairman of Hong Kong's WTO Review Body on Bid Challenges from 2000-2004 and was formerly Chairman of Hong Kong's Telecommunications (Competition Provision) Appeal Board. He is a Fellow of the Chartered Institute of Arbitrators and is a Chartered Arbitrator. He is also a Fellow of the Hong Kong Institute of Arbitrators as well as a panellist of CIETAC. In June 2001, he was awarded a CBE for services to international arbitration. In 2007, he was awarded the Silver Bauhinia Star by the Chief Executive of the Hong Kong SAR.

DR FATHI KEMICHA (Tunis, Tunisia)

Dr Fathi Kemicha is the founder of Kemicha Legal Consulting K.L.C. He has acted as arbitrator and counsel in numerous institutional and ad hoc commercial arbitrations. He is a former member of the United Nations International Law Commission (ILC) and the World Bank Group Sanctions Board. He served as Vice Chairman of the Commission on Arbitration at the International Chamber of Commerce (ICC) and was also a member of the Dubai International Arbitration Centre (DIAC) Board of Trustees. He was made Knight of the French Legion of Honor by President Jacques Chirac, President of the French Republic, and awarded by His Majesty King Hamad Bin Isa Al Khalifa, the King of the Kingdom of Bahrain, 'The Order of Bahrain' (First Class).

MR VLADIMIR KHVALEI (Moscow, Russian Federation)

Mr Vladimir Khvalei is a senior partner at Mansors Law Firm. Mr Khvalei has significant experience participating in litigation both in Russia and abroad and representing Russian and foreign companies operating in various industries, including oil and gas, construction, banking and others in complex international disputes. Mr Khvalei has also acted as counsel and arbitrator in international cases under a wide range of arbitration Rules including those of UNCITRAL, ICC, LCIA, SCC, MKAS, HKIAC, ICAC, CRCICA, ICSID and other arbitration institutions. Mr Khvalei is included in the lists of various arbitral institutions in Russia, Austria, Azerbaijan, Republic of Belarus, Kazakhstan, Kyrgyzstan, UAE, China, Hong Kong, South Korea, Malaysia, Singapore, Vietnam, US and Israel.

MR KAP-YOU (KEVIN) KIM (Seoul, Republic of Korea)

Kap-You (Kevin) is a senior founding partner at Peter & Kim in Seoul, a dispute resolution practice with offices in Korea, Switzerland, Australia and Singapore. Over the past thirty-five years, he has acted as counsel, presiding arbitrator, co-arbitrator and sole arbitrator in more than three hundred cases of international arbitration under various arbitration rules.

MS MEG KINNEAR (Washington, DC, USA)

Ms Meg Kinnear is a founding member of LKDR LLC, a boutique firm dedicated to acting as neutrals in international dispute settlement. She was the Secretary General of the International Centre for Settlement of Investment Disputes (ICSID) and a vice-president of the World Bank (2009-2024). She was formerly the Senior General Counsel and Director General of the Trade Law Bureau of Canada, where she was responsible for the conduct of all international investment and trade litigation involving Canada. Prior to this, she was Executive Assistant to the Deputy Minister of Justice of Canada and Counsel at the Civil Litigation Section of the Canadian Department of Justice.

PROF. ALEXANDER SERGEEVICH KOMAROV (Moscow, Russian Federation)

Prof. Alexander Komarov is currently Professor of International Private Law Chair at the Russian Academy of Foreign Trade and a Member of the Consultative Council at the Supreme Court of the Russian Federation. He is a CIArb Fellow and Chartered Arbitrator. He is also a member of the Presidium of the International Commercial Arbitration Court at the Chamber of Commerce and Industry of the Russian Federation. He was a Vice-President of the International Federation of Commercial Arbitration Institutions, an LCIA Member, and a Member of the Board of the Arbitration Institute of the Stockholm Chamber of Commerce.

MS CAROLYN BETH LAMM (Washington, DC, USA)

Ms Carolyn Lamm is a Partner at White & Case LLP and Distinguished Faculty Chair of the LLM Program in International Arbitration and Visiting Professor at the University of Miami. She is also the Chair of International Arbitration Americas and of the American-Uzbekistan Chamber of Commerce. She is a Member of the Board of the American-Turkish Council and American Indonesian Chamber of Commerce. She is a Member of the ICSID Panel of Arbitrators, a member of the ICDR International List, the American Law Institute's Council and its Advisory Committee on Restatement on International Arbitration and the US member of the NAFTA 2022 Committee.

MS MICHELLE AMANDA MACPHEE (London, United Kingdom)

Ms Michelle MacPhee has over twenty-five years of experience in international commercial arbitration and dispute resolution. She is currently the Managing Counsel of BP Legal's London based Dispute Resolution Team and also heads BP Legal's International Arbitration Centre of Expertise. Prior to joining BP in 2010, she was Of Counsel in Freshfields Bruckhaus Deringer's London International Arbitration Group. Her current responsibilities at BP include identifying, evaluating and managing legal, financial, business operation and reputational risks relating to all manner of major commercial disputes and potential disputes arising from BP's global businesses and group level activities.

CHIEF JUSTICE SUNDARESH MENON (Singapore)

Chief Justice of the Supreme Court of Singapore, Sundaresh Menon previously held office as Judge of Appeal and as Attorney-General of Singapore. He is a former Judicial Commissioner of the Supreme Court of Singapore. He previously served as Dy Chairman of the Singapore International Arbitration Centre and worked as Managing Partner at Rajah & Tann LLP and Partner at Jones Day and Head of International Litigation and Arbitration for Asia.

MS ZIA JAYDEV MODY (Mumbai, India)

Ms Zia Mody is the Founder and Senior Partner of AZB & Partners. She was the former Deputy Chairman and a Non-Executive Director, HSBC Asia Pacific Board, a former Member of the World Bank Administrative Tribunal and former Vice-President and member of the LCIA. She was also a member of the Committee on Corporate Governance formed by SEBI, the Godrej Committee on Corporate Governance and of the Reserve Bank of India Committee on Comprehensive Financial Services for Small Businesses and Low-Income Households.

DR MICHAEL JOSEPH MOSER (Hong Kong SAR)

Dr Michael Moser practices as an international arbitrator with 20 Essex Street Chambers and is a Chartered arbitrator and Fellow of the Chartered Institute of Arbitrators. He is a current board member of the Singapore International Arbitration Centre (SIAC) and the Vienna International Arbitral Centre (VIAC) and a Commission Member of CIETAC. He is an Honorary Past Chairman of the Hong Kong International Arbitration Centre and a past member of the LCIA Court and of the Stockholm SCC Arbitration Institute Board. He is the author of many books and articles, co-editor of *The Asia Arbitration Handbook* (Oxford Univ. Press, 2011) and former General Editor of the *Journal of International Arbitration*.

MS ELLEN GRACIE NORTHFLEET (Rio de Janeiro, Brazil)

Justice Ellen Gracie Northfleet is an attorney in private practice and arbitrator in Rio de Janeiro. She is the Former Chief Justice of the Brazilian Supreme Court. She currently acts as Vice-President of the Arbitration Chamber of the Federation of Industries of São Paulo – FIESP. She serves on the Board of the Brazilian Committee of Arbitration (CBAr) and on the Board of Directors of the World Justice Project. Gracie has acted as a member of the World Bank's Sanctions Board from 22 April 2013 until the end of her second term on 21 April 2019. She is also a member of the International Council of Arbitration for Sport (ICAS) and of the Inter-American Dialogue.

PROF. WILLIAM W. PARK (Cohasset, USA)

Prof. William W. (Rusty) Park is Professor of Law Emeritus at Boston University, where he lectures on tax, banking and international business transactions. He is a former General Editor of *Arbitration International*. He has served on the Appeals Tribunal for the International Commission on Holocaust Era Insurance Claims and as Arbitrator on the Claims Resolution Tribunal for Dormant Accounts in Switzerland. Prof. Park is also past President of the London Court of International Arbitration and past Chair of the ABA Committee on International Commercial Dispute Resolution.

PROF. DR MICHAEL PRYLES (Toorak, Australia)

Prof. Dr Michael Pryles was the Founder President of the SIAC Court of Arbitration and Chairman of the Board of SIAC. Prior to that, he was President of the Australian Centre for International Commercial Arbitration and the founding President of the Asia Pacific Regional Arbitration Group. He also served as a Commissioner of the United Nations Compensation Commission and a Court member of the London International Court of Arbitration. For his services to international arbitration, he was appointed an Officer in the Order of Australia. For several years, he was also a member of the Australian Government delegation to the Hague Conference on Private International Law.

PROF. DR KLAUS SACHS (Munich, Germany)

Prof. Dr Klaus Sachs is a senior partner at CMS Hasche Sigle and an honorary professor on international arbitration law at the Ludwig-Maximilian-University of Munich. He has more than twenty-five years of experience as chairman, sole arbitrator, co-arbitrator and counsel in more than 250 national and international arbitrations concerning commercial and investment disputes. He is a member of the Council of the German Arbitration Institute (DIS). He is a former Vice-President of the ICC International Court of Arbitration, a former Vice-President of the London Court of International Arbitration and a former member of the Board of ICCA. He is a co-editor of the *German Arbitration Journal.*

DR ANKE SESSLER (Frankfurt am Main, Germany)

Dr Sessler is a Partner in the Frankfurt office of Skadden, Arps, Slate, Meagher & Flom LLP. She is widely recognised as one of Germany's leading disputes lawyers, with extensive experience in international and domestic arbitration and complex litigation proceedings. She represents industrial corporations and financial service providers in disputes relating to, *inter alia*, M&A and supply contracts, joint ventures and other commercial agreements, as well as in shareholder litigation and disputes to corporate boards. She also represents states and investors in treaty arbitration proceedings. Dr Sessler holds positions in various arbitration institutions, including the ICC Court of Arbitration, the ICC Commission on Arbitration and the AAA board.

MR EDUARDO SIQUEIROS (Mexico City, Mexico)

Mr Eduardo Siqueiros is an independent arbitrator and a part-time professor and lecturer in Mexican law schools. He has authored articles on the subject of arbitration, corporate law, trade and investment. He has been included in Band 1 in Chambers and Partners Global and Latin America (2010-2015), and Legal 500 Latin America (2013-2015). He is also a member of the Mexican Arbitration

Institute (IMA), the Mexican Arbitration Committee (ICC) and is on the Panel of Arbitrators, ICSID.

PROF. YASUHEI TANIGUCHI (Tokyo, Japan)

Prof. Yasuhei Taniguchi is Professor Emeritus at Kyoto University in Japan. He is Judge of the Singapore International Commercial Court and Counsel at Matsuo & Kosugi. He is a former member of the Appellate Body of the World Trade Organization Dispute Settlement Body; Special Advisor of the Japan Commercial Arbitration Association; and Former President, Japan Association of Arbitrators and Civil Procedure Association. He is internationally recognised for his expertise in comparative and transnational legal studies. He is a leading scholar in several areas of law, including Civil Procedure, Alternative Dispute Resolution, Insolvency Law, and International Trade Law.

PROF. DR GUIDO SANTIAGO TAWIL (Punta del Este, Uruguay)

Prof. Dr Guido Tawil is an Independent Arbitrator, former Chair Professor of Administrative Law at the University of Buenos Aires School of Law and Senior Partner at M. & M. Bomchil in Buenos Aires, where he headed the International Arbitration, Administrative Law and Regulatory Matters practices for over twenty-five years. He is Honorary President, Founding Member and Past Chair of the Latin American Arbitration Association (ALARB), Past Co-Chair of the IBA's Arbitration Committee and Latin American Fora; Past Council member of the IBA's Legal Practice Division, Past Court Member of the LCIA, of the Institute for Transnational Arbitration (ITA) Academic Council, of the ICC Latin American Arbitration Group, and of the ICC Institute of World Business Law, current member of the SIAC's Court of Arbitration, among other positions.

PROF. DR PIERRE TERCIER (Fribourg, Switzerland)

Prof. Pierre Tercier is Professor Emeritus at the University of Fribourg, Switzerland and was Chairman of the International Court of Arbitration of the International Chamber of Commerce. He has an extensive international arbitration and dispute resolution experience, having served on numerous occasions in ICC, ICSID and other cases. He is highly respected in the international legal and business community as an arbitrator, lecturer and author. Prof. Tercier is Visiting Professor of Law at numerous universities, including Geneva and Paris. He is also affiliated with the law firm Peter & Kim, in Geneva, as Senior Counsel.

MS VERA VAN HOUTTE (Leuven, Belgium)

Ms Vera Van Houtte is a Belgian lawyer (Dr Juris of the University of Leuven and LLM of Harvard Law School). Till the end of 2012, she was a partner at the Benelux firm Stibbe in Brussels, heading the construction and energy law department. She has been active in international arbitration since more than thirty-five years, first as counsel, later as arbitrator, sitting in both commercial and investment arbitrations. Since 2013, she acts exclusively as an arbitrator. She is a listed ICSID Panel arbitrator and has handled cases under a variety of arbitration rules (ICC, ICSID, LCIA, DIAC, UNCITRAL, Arbitration Institute of the Finnish and of the Hungarian Chambers of Commerce, CEPANI) and ad hoc arbitrations.

HON. S. AMOS WAKO FCIARB, SC (Nairobi, Kenya)

The Hon. S. Amos Wako is a Fellow of the Chartered Institute of Arbitrators and was elected a member of the International Law Commission at the 61st Session of the United Nations General Assembly. He is a chairman of the Association of Professional Societies in East Africa and (founding) chairman of the Public Law Institute. His appointments have included: representative to the Board of Trustees of the United Nations Voluntary Fund for Victims of Torture, special Rapporteur of the U.N. Commission on Human Rights on the Question of Summary or Arbitrary Executions and special Envoy of the Secretary General to East Timor to investigate the 12th November 1991 incident in DILI.

DR SHENGCHANG WANG (Beijing, the People's Republic of China)

Dr Shengchang Wang is the Former Vice Chairman and Former Secretary General, China International Economic and Trade Arbitration Commission (CIETAC); Former Vice Chairman, China Maritime Arbitration Commission (CMAC); Former Member, London Court of International Arbitration (LCIA) and the Arbitration Institute of the Stockholm Chamber of Commerce (SCC), former member of Governing Board of the International Council for Commercial Arbitration (ICCA). He is currently the senior consultant of Beijing Hui Zhong Law Firm and the Director of Proarb LLC. As an arbitrator, he has handled more than two hundred international arbitration cases in various arbitration centres. As a counsel, he advises the clients on commercial and maritime arbitration, investment treaty arbitration and sports arbitration.

SIR DAVID WILLIAMS KNZM, KC (Auckland, New Zealand)

Prof. David Williams currently practises as a Barrister with Bankside Chambers in Auckland, New Zealand. For some years, he taught International Arbitration at the University of Auckland Law School. He was a member of the IBA Working Group which produced the IBA Guidelines on Conflicts of Interest in International Arbitration 2004; a member of the International Law Association, Committee on International Arbitration and an Honorary Professor of Law, University of Auckland 2010.

MS ARIEL YE (Nanshan District, Shenzhen, the People's Republic of China)

Ms Ariel Ye is a seasoned arbitration practitioner and arbitrator. She is a senior partner of King & Wood Malleson's Cross-Border Dispute Resolution Practice and a recognised expert on PRC-related dispute resolution in the Asia Pacific region. She frequently handles arbitration cases before CIETAC, HKIAC, ICC, and other international arbitration institutions. Ms Ye is a panel arbitrator of CIETAC, HKIAC, SIAC and the Shenzhen Court of International Arbitration. She is also an SIAC Board Member.

DR JIANLONG YU (Beijing, the People's Republic of China)

Dr Jianlong Yu is the Vice Chairman of the China Council for the Promotion of International Trade (CCPIT) and Executive Vice Chairman of the China Chamber of International Commerce (CCOIC); Vice Chairman of the World Chambers Federation. He is former Vice Chairman of the China International Economic and Trade Arbitration Commission (CIETAC); Vice Chairman of the China Maritime Arbitration Commission (CMAC). He is also a Former President of the Asia Pacific Arbitration Group (APRAG) and Former Vice Chairman of the China Academy of Arbitration Law (CAAL).

JUDGE ABDULQAWI AHMED YUSUF (The Hague, The Netherlands)

Judge Abdulqawi A. Yusuf is Judge at the International Court of Justice, The Hague, the Netherlands. He was elected as Judge to the Court in November 2008 and re-elected in November 2017. He was President of the Court from 6 February 2018 to 6 February 2021, Vice-President of the Court from 6 February 2015 to 6 February 2018. He is a member of the Institut de Droit International, and a former chief legal counsel to various intergovernmental organisations, including UNESCO and UNIDO. He is the founder of the African Institute of International Law (AIIL), Arusha, Tanzania and of the African Yearbook of International Law. He is the author of numerous publications on various aspects of international law. He holds a PhD in International Law from the IUHEI, Geneva.

PROF. EDUARDO ZULETA (New York, United States)

Prof. Eduardo Zuleta is an independent arbitrator. He has acted as chair and co-arbitrator in a vast number of commercial and investment cases under, *inter alia*, ICC, ICDR, ICSID, UNCITRAL, LCIA, OIC and IACAC as well as in ICSID annulment committees. Disputes in which Prof. Zuleta has acted include infrastructure, M&A, energy, financial products and distribution and involve parties, including state parties from Latam, Europe, Asia and the Middle East. Prof. Zuleta is a member of the Sanctions Board of the World Bank and Adjunct Professor at Georgetown Law.

www.ingramcontent.com/pod-product-compliance
Lightning Source LLC
LaVergne TN
LVHW020650300926
849161LV00004B/874
* 9 7 8 9 4 0 3 5 3 2 0 9 7 *